Lecture Notes in Artificial Intelligence 12876

Subseries of Lecture Notes in Computer Science

Series Editors

Randy Goebel
University of Alberta, Edmonton, Canada

Yuzuru Tanaka
Hokkaido University, Sapporo, Japan

Wolfgang Wahlster
DFKI and Saarland University, Saarbrücken, Germany

Founding Editor

Jörg Siekmann
DFKI and Saarland University, Saarbrücken, Germany

More information about this subseries at http://www.springer.com/series/1244

Ngoc Thanh Nguyen · Lazaros Iliadis ·
Ilias Maglogiannis · Bogdan Trawiński (Eds.)

Computational Collective Intelligence

13th International Conference, ICCCI 2021
Rhodes, Greece, September 29 – October 1, 2021
Proceedings

 Springer

Editors
Ngoc Thanh Nguyen 🆔
Wrocław University of Science
and Technology
Wrocław, Poland

Nguyen Tat Thanh University
Ho Chi Minh city, Vietnam

Ilias Maglogiannis 🆔
University of Piraeus
Piraeus, Greece

Lazaros Iliadis 🆔
Democritus University of Thrace
Kimmeria, Xanthi, Greece

Bogdan Trawiński 🆔
Wrocław University of Science
and Technology
Wrocław, Poland

ISSN 0302-9743   ISSN 1611-3349 (electronic)
Lecture Notes in Artificial Intelligence
ISBN 978-3-030-88080-4   ISBN 978-3-030-88081-1 (eBook)
https://doi.org/10.1007/978-3-030-88081-1

LNCS Sublibrary: SL7 – Artificial Intelligence

This Springer imprint is published by the registered company Springer Nature Switzerland AG
The registered company address is: Gewerbestrasse 11, 6330 Cham, Switzerland

Preface

This volume contains the proceedings of the 13th International Conference on Computational Collective Intelligence (ICCCI 2021), held in Rhodes, Greece, during September 29 – October 1, 2021. Due to the COVID-19 pandemic the conference was organized in a hybrid mode which allowed for both on-site and online paper presentations. The conference was hosted by the Democritus University of Thrace, Greece, and jointly organized by Wrocław University of Science and Technology, Poland, in cooperation with the IEEE SMC Technical Committee on Computational Collective Intelligence, the European Research Center for Information Systems (ERCIS), the University of Piraeus, Greece, and the International University-VNU-HCM, Vietnam.

Following the successes of the first ICCCI (2009) in Wrocław, Poland, the second ICCCI (2010) in Kaohsiung, Taiwan, the Third ICCCI (2011) in Gdynia, Poland, the 4th ICCCI (2012) in Ho Chi Minh City, Vietnam, the 5th ICCCI (2013) in Craiova, Romania, the 6th ICCCI (2014) in Seoul, South Korea, the 7th ICCCI (2015) in Madrid, Spain, the 8th ICCCI (2016) in Halkidiki, Greece, the 9th ICCCI (2017) in Nicosia, Cyprus, the 10th ICCCI (2018) in Bristol, UK, the 11th ICCCI (2019) in Hendaye, France, and the 12th ICCCI (2020) in Da Nang, Vietnam, this conference continued to provide an internationally respected forum for scientific research in the computer-based methods of collective intelligence and their applications.

Computational collective intelligence (CCI) is most often understood as a subfield of artificial intelligence (AI) dealing with soft computing methods that facilitate group decisions or processing knowledge among autonomous units acting in distributed environments. Methodological, theoretical, and practical aspects of CCI are considered as the form of intelligence that emerges from the collaboration and competition of many individuals (artificial and/or natural). The application of multiple computational intelligence technologies such as fuzzy systems, evolutionary computation, neural systems, consensus theory, etc., can support human and other collective intelligence, and create new forms of CCI in natural and/or artificial systems. Three subfields of the application of computational intelligence technologies to support various forms of collective intelligence are of special interest but are not exclusive: the Semantic Web (as an advanced tool for increasing collective intelligence), social network analysis (as the field targeted at the emergence of new forms of CCI), and multi-agent systems (as a computational and modeling paradigm especially tailored to capture the nature of CCI emergence in populations of autonomous individuals).

The ICCCI 2021 conference featured a number of keynote talks and oral presentations, closely aligned to the theme of the conference. The conference attracted a substantial number of researchers and practitioners from all over the world, who submitted their papers for the main track and nine special sessions.

The main track, covering the methodology and applications of CCI, included knowledge engineering and Semantic Web, social networks and recommender systems, collective decision-making, data mining and machine learning, computer vision techniques, and natural language processing, as well as the Internet of Things: technologies and

applications. The special sessions, covering some specific topics of particular interest, included cooperative strategies for decision making and optimization, IoT and
computational technologies for collective intelligence, smart industry and management
systems, machine learning in real-world data, knowledge-intensive smart services and
their applications, swarms of UAVs, low resource languages processing, computational
collective intelligence and natural language processing, and computational intelligence
for multimedia understanding.

We received over 230 papers submitted by authors coming from 45 countries around
the world. Each paper was reviewed by at least three members of the international
Program Committee (PC) of either the main track or one of the special sessions. Finally,
we selected 60 best papers for oral presentation and publication in one volume of the
Lecture Notes in Artificial Intelligence series and 58 papers for oral presentation and
publication in one volume of the Communications in Computer and Information Science
series.

We would like to express our thanks to the keynote speakers: Plamen Angelov from
Lancaster University, UK, Yannis Manolopoulos from the Open University of Cyprus,
Cyprus, Daniele Nardi from Sapienza Università di Roma, Italy, and Andrzej Skowron
from the Systems Research Institute of Polish Academy of Sciences, Poland, for their
world-class plenary speeches.

Many people contributed toward the success of the conference. First, we would like
to recognize the work of the PC co-chairs and special sessions organizers for taking good
care of the organization of the reviewing process, an essential stage in ensuring the high
quality of the accepted papers. The workshop and special session chairs deserve a special
mention for the evaluation of the proposals and the organization and coordination of the
nine special sessions. In addition, we would like to thank the PC members, of the main
track and of the special sessions, for performing their reviewing work with diligence. We
thank the Local Organizing Committee chairs, publicity chair, Web chair, and technical
support chair for their fantastic work before and during the conference. Finally, we
cordially thank all the authors, presenters, and delegates for their valuable contribution
to this successful event. The conference would not have been possible without their
support.

Our special thanks are also due to Springer for publishing the proceedings and to all
the other sponsors for their kind support.

It is our pleasure to announce that the ICCCI conference series continues to have a
close cooperation with the Springer journal Transactions on Computational Collective
Intelligence, and the IEEE SMC Technical Committee on Transactions on Computational
Collective Intelligence.

Finally, we hope that ICCCI 2021 contributed significantly to the academic excellence of the field and will lead to the even greater success of ICCCI events in the
future.

September 2021

Ngoc Thanh Nguyen
Lazaros Iliadis
Ilias Maglogiannis
Bogdan Trawiński

Organization

Organizing Committee

Honorary Chairs

Arkadiusz Wójs	Wrocław University of Science and Technology, Poland
Fotios Maris	Democritus University of Thrace, Greece

General Chairs

Ngoc Thanh Nguyen	Wrocław University of Science and Technology, Poland
Lazaros Iliadis	Democritus University of Thrace, Greece

Program Chairs

Costin Bădică	University of Craiova, Romania
Ilias Maglogiannis	University of Piraeus, Greece
Gottfried Vossen	University of Münster, Germany

Steering Committee

Ngoc Thanh Nguyen	Wrocław University of Science and Technology, Poland
Shyi-Ming Chen	National Taiwan University of Science and Technology, Taiwan
Dosam Hwang	Yeungnam University, South Korea
Lakhmi C. Jain	University of South Australia, Australia
Piotr Jędrzejowicz	Gdynia Maritime University, Poland
Geun-Sik Jo	Inha University, South Korea
Janusz Kacprzyk	Polish Academy of Sciences, Poland
Ryszard Kowalczyk	Swinburne University of Technology, Australia
Toyoaki Nishida	Kyoto University, Japan
Manuel Núñez	Universidad Complutense de Madrid, Spain
Klaus Solberg Söilen	Halmstad University, Sweden
Khoa Tien Tran	International University-VNUHCM, Vietnam

Special Session Chairs

Bogdan Trawiński	Wrocław University of Science and Technology, Poland
Elias Pimenidis	University of the West of England, UK

Doctoral Track Chairs

Marek Krótkiewicz   Wrocław University of Science and Technology,
                           Poland
Christos Makris   University of Patras, Greece

Organizing Chairs

Antonis Papaleonidas   Democritus University of Thrace, Greece
Krystian Wojtkiewicz   Wrocław University of Science and Technology,
                           Poland
Adrianna Kozierkiewicz   Wrocław University of Science and Technology,
                           Poland

Publicity Chairs

Antonios Papaleonidas   Democritus University of Thrace, Greece
Marcin Maleszka   Wrocław University of Science and Technology,
                           Poland

Webmaster

Marek Kopel   Wrocław University of Science and Technology,
                           Poland

Local Organizing Committee

Anastasios-Panagiotis Psathas   Democritus University of Thrace, Greece
Dimitris Boudas   Democritus University of Thrace, Greece
Vasilis Kokkinos   Democritus University of Thrace, Greece
Marcin Jodłowiec   Wrocław University of Science and Technology,
                           Poland
Rafal Palak   Wrocław University of Science and Technology,
                           Poland
Marcin Pietranik   Wrocław University of Science and Technology,
                           Poland

Keynote Speakers

Plamen Angelov   Lancaster University, UK
Yannis Manolopoulos   Open University of Cyprus, Cyprus
Daniele Nardi   Sapienza Università di Roma, Italy
Andrzej Skowron   Systems Research Institute, Polish Academy of
                           Sciences, Poland

Special Session Organizers

CCINLP 2021: Special Session on Computational Collective Intelligence and Natural Language Processing

Ismaïl Biskri	University of Québec à Trois-Rivières, Canada
Nadia Ghazzali	University of Québec à Trois-Rivières, Canada

CSDMO 2021: Special Session on Cooperative Strategies for Decision Making and Optimization

Piotr Jędrzejowicz	Gdynia Maritime University, Poland
Dariusz Barbucha	Gdynia Maritime University, Poland
Ireneusz Czarnowski	Gdynia Maritime University, Poland

IOTCTCI 2021: Special Session on Internet of Things and Computational Technologies for Collective Intelligence

Octavian Postolache	Instituto de Telecomunicações, ISCTE-IUL, Portugal
Madina Mansurova	Al-Farabi Kazakh National University, Kazakhstan

IWCIM 2021: International Workshop on Computational Intelligence for Multimedia Understanding

Davide Moroni	National Research Council of Italy (CNR), Pisa, Italy
Maria Trocan	Institut Supérieur d'Électronique de Paris, Paris, France
Behçet Uğur Töreyin	Istanbul Technical University, Istanbul, Turkey

KISSTA 2021: Special Session on Knowledge-Intensive Smart Services and Their Applications

Thang Le Dinh	University of Québec à Trois-Rivières, Canada
Thanh Thoa Pham Thi	Technological University Dublin, Ireland
Nguyen Cuong Pham	University of Science, Ho Chi Ninh City, Vietnam

LRLP 2021: Special Session on Low Resource Languages Processing

Ualsher Tukeyev	Al-Farabi Kazakh National University, Kazakhstan
Madina Mansurova	Al-Farabi Kazakh National University, Kazakhstan

MLRWD 2021: Special Session on Machine Learning in Real-World Data

Jan Kozak	University of Economics in Katowice, Poland
Krzysztof Kania	University of Economics in Katowice, Poland
Przemysław Juszczuk	University of Economics in Katowice, Poland
Barbara Probierz	University of Economics in Katowice, Poland

SIMS 2021: Special Session on Smart Industry and Management Systems

Marcin Fojcik	Western Norway University of Applied Sciences, Norway
Adam Ziębiński	Silesian University of Technology, Poland
Rafał Cupek	Silesian University of Technology, Poland
Dariusz Mrozek	Silesian University of Technology, Poland
Marcin Hernes	Wroclaw University of Economics and Business, Poland

SUAV 2021: Special Session on Swarms of UAVs

Frédéric V. G. Guinand	Normandy University – UNIHAVRE, France
François Guérin	Normandy University – UNIHAVRE, France
Grégoire Danoy	University of Luxembourg, Luxembourg
Serge Chaumette	University of Bordeaux, France

Senior Program Committee

Plamen Angelov	Lancaster University, UK
Costin Bădică	University of Craiova, Romania
Nick Bassiliades	Aristotle University of Thessaloniki, Greece
Mária Bieliková	Slovak University of Technology in Bratislava, Slovakia
Abdelhamid Bouchachia	Bournemouth University, UK
David Camacho	Universidad Autonoma de Madrid, Spain
Richard Chbeir	University of Pau and Pays de l'Adour, France
Shyi-Ming Chen	National Taiwan University of Science and Technology, Taiwan
Paul Davidsson	Malmo University, Sweden
Mohamed Gaber	Birmingham City University, UK
Daniela Godoy	ISISTAN Research Institute, Argentina
Manuel Grana	University of the Basque Country, Spain
William Grosky	University of Michigan, USA
Francisco Herrera	University of Granada, Spain
Tzung-Pei Hong	National University of Kaohsiung, Taiwan
Dosam Hwang	Yeungnam University, South Korea
Lazaros Iliadis	Democritus University of Thrace, Greece
Mirjana Ivanović	University of Novi Sad, Serbia

Piotr Jędrzejowicz	Gdynia Maritime University, Poland
Geun-Sik Jo	Inha University, South Korea
Kang-Hyun Jo	University of Ulsan, South Korea
Janusz Kacprzyk	Systems Research Institute, Polish Academy of Sciences, Poland
Ryszard Kowalczyk	Swinburne University of Technology, Australia
Ondrej Krejcar	University of Hradec Kralove, Czech Republic
Hoai An Le Thi	University of Lorraine, France
Edwin Lughofer	Johannes Kepler University Linz, Austria
Yannis Manolopoulos	Aristotle University of Thessaloniki, Greece
Grzegorz J. Nalepa	AGH University of Science and Technology, Poland
Toyoaki Nishida	Kyoto University, Japan
Manuel Núñez	Universidad Complutense de Madrid, Spain
George A. Papadopoulos	University of Cyprus, Cyprus
Radu-Emil Precup	Politehnica University of Timisoara, Romania
Leszek Rutkowski	Częstochowa University of Technology, Poland
Tomasz M. Rutkowski	University of Tokyo, Japan
Ali Selamat	Universiti Teknologi Malaysia, Malaysia
Edward Szczerbicki	University of Newcastle, Australia
Ryszard Tadeusiewicz	AGH University of Science and Technology, Poland
Muhammad Atif Tahir	National University of Computer and Emerging Sciences, Pakistan
Jan Treur	Vrije Universiteit Amsterdam, The Netherlands
Bay Vo	Ho Chi Minh City University of Technology, Vietnam
Gottfried Vossen	University of Munster, Germany
Lipo Wang	Nanyang Technological University, Singapore
Michał Woźniak	Wrocław University of Science and Technology, Poland
Farouk Yalaoui	University of Technology of Troyes, France
Slawomir Zadrozny	Systems Research Institute, Polish Academy of Sciences, Poland

Program Committee

Muhammad Abulaish	South Asian University, India
Sharat Akhoury	University of Cape Town, South Africa
Ana Almeida	GECAD-ISEP-IPP, Portugal
Bashar Al-Shboul	University of Jordan, Jordan
Adel Alti	University of Setif, Algeria
Taha Arbaoui	University of Technology of Troyes, France
Thierry Badard	Laval University, Canada
Amelia Bădică	University of Craiova, Romania
Hassan Badir	Ecole Nationale des Sciences Appliquees de Tanger, Morocco

Dariusz Barbucha	Gdynia Maritime University, Poland
Paulo Batista	Universidade de Evora, Portugal
Khalid Benali	University of Lorraine, France
Leon Bobrowski	Białystok University of Technology, Poland
Peter Brida	University of Žilina, Slovakia
Ivana Bridova	University of Žilina, Slovakia
Krisztian Buza	Budapest University of Technology and Economics, Hungary
Aleksander Byrski	AGH University of Science and Technology, Poland
Frantisek Capkovic	Institute of Informatics, Slovak Academy of Sciences, Slovakia
Kennedy Chengeta	University of KwaZulu Natal, South Africa
Raja Chiky	Institut Supérieur d'Electronique de Paris, France
Amine Chohra	Paris-East Créteil University, France
Kazimierz Choroś	Wrocław University of Science and Technology, Poland
Mihaela Colhon	University of Craiova, Romania
Jose Alfredo Ferreira Costa	Universidade Federal do Rio Grande do Norte, Brazil
Rafał Cupek	Silesian University of Technology, Poland
Ireneusz Czarnowski	Gdynia Maritime University, Poland
Camelia Delcea	Bucharest University of Economic Studies, Romania
Tien V. Do	Budapest University of Technology and Economics, Hungary
Rim Faiz	University of Carthage, Tunisia
Marcin Fojcik	Western Norway University of Applied Sciences, Norway
Anna Formica	IASI-CNR, Italy
Faiez Gargouri	University of Sfax, Tunisia
Mauro Gaspari	University of Bologna, Italy
K. M. George	Oklahoma State University, USA
Janusz Getta	University of Wollongong, Australia
Daniela Gifu	University "Alexandru Ioan Cuza" of Iasi, Romania
Antonio Gonzalez-Pardo	Universidad Autonoma de Madrid, Spain
Foteini Grivokostopoulou	University of Patras, Greece
Kenji Hatano	Doshisha University, Japan
Marcin Hernes	Wrocław University of Economics, Poland
Huu Hanh Hoang	Hue University, Vietnam
Frédéric Hubert	Laval University, Canada
Maciej Huk	Wrocław University of Science and Technology, Poland
Agnieszka Indyka-Piasecka	Wrocław University of Science and Technology, Poland
Joanna Jędrzejowicz	University of Gdańsk, Poland
Gordan Ježić	University of Zagreb, Croatia

Przemysław Juszczuk	University of Economics in Katowice, Poland
Petros Kefalas	University of Sheffield, Greece
Rafał Kern	Wrocław University of Science and Technology, Poland
Zaheer Khan	University of the West of England, UK
Marek Kisiel-Dorohinicki	AGH University of Science and Technology, Poland
Attila Kiss	Eotvos Lorand University, Hungary
Marek Kopel	Wrocław University of Science and Technology, Poland
Leszek Kotulski	AGH University of Science and Technology, Poland
Ivan Koychev	University of Sofia "St. Kliment Ohridski", Bulgaria
Jan Kozak	University of Economics in Katowice, Poland
Adrianna Kozierkiewicz	Wrocław University of Science and Technology, Poland
Dalia Kriksciuniene	Vilnius University, Lithuania
Dariusz Król	Wrocław University of Science and Technology, Poland
Marek Krótkiewicz	Wrocław University of Science and Technology, Poland
Jan Kubicek	VSB-Technical University of Ostrava, Czech Republic
Elżbieta Kukla	Wrocław University of Science and Technology, Poland
Julita Kulbacka	Wrocław Medical University, Poland
Marek Kulbacki	Polish-Japanese Academy of Information Technology, Poland
Kazuhiro Kuwabara	Ritsumeikan University, Japan
Halina Kwaśnicka	Wrocław University of Science and Technology, Poland
Philippe Lemoisson	French Agricultural Research Centre for International Development (CIRAD), France
Florin Leon	"Gheorghe Asachi" Technical University of Iasi, Romania
Mikołaj Leszczuk	AGH University of Science and Technology, Poland
Doina Logofatu	Frankfurt University of Applied Sciences, Germany
Juraj Machaj	University of Žilina, Slovakia
Bernadetta Maleszka	Wrocław University of Science and Technology, Poland
Marcin Maleszka	Wrocław University of Science and Technology, Poland
Urszula Markowska-Kaczmar	Wrocław University of Science and Technology, Poland
Adam Meissner	Poznań University of Technology, Poland
Héctor Menéndez	University College London, UK
Mercedes Merayo	Universidad Complutense de Madrid, Spain
Jacek Mercik	WSB University in Wrocław, Poland

Radosław Michalski	Wrocław University of Science and Technology, Poland
Peter Mikulecky	University of Hradec Kralove, Czech Republic
Miroslava Mikušová	University of Žilina, Slovakia
Javier Montero	Universidad Complutense de Madrid, Spain
Dariusz Mrozek	Silesian University of Technology, Poland
Manuel Munier	University of Pau and Pays de l'Adour, France
Laurent Nana	University of Brest, France
Anand Nayyar	Duy Tan University, Vietnam
Filippo Neri	University of Napoli Federico II, Italy
Linh Anh Nguyen	University of Warsaw, Poland
Loan T. T. Nguyen	International University-VNUHCM, Vietnam
Sinh Van Nguyen	International University-VNUHCM, Vietnam
Thi Thanh Sang Nguyen	International University-VNUHCM, Vietnam
Adam Niewiadomski	Lodz University of Technology, Poland
Adel Noureddine	University of Pau and Pays de l'Adour, France
Agnieszka Nowak-Brzezińska	University of Silesia, Poland
Alberto Núñez	Universidad Complutense de Madrid, Spain
Tarkko Oksala	Aalto University, Finland
Mieczysław Owoc	Wrocław University of Economics, Poland
Marcin Paprzycki	Systems Research Institute, Polish Academy of Sciences, Poland
Isidoros Perikos	University of Patras, Greece
Marcin Pietranik	Wrocław University of Science and Technology, Poland
Elias Pimenidis	University of the West of England, UK
Nikolaos Polatidis	University of Brighton, UK
Piotr Porwik	University of Silesia, Poland
Ales Prochazka	University of Chemistry and Technology, Czech Republic
Paulo Quaresma	Universidade de Evora, Portugal
Mohammad Rashedur Rahman	North South University, Bangladesh
Ewa Ratajczak-Ropel	Gdynia Maritime University, Poland
Virgilijus Sakalauskas	Vilnius University, Lithuania
Khouloud Salameh	University of Pau and Pays de l'Adour, France
Imad Saleh	Université Paris 8, France
Andrzej Siemiński	Wrocław University of Science and Technology, Poland
Paweł Sitek	Kielce University of Technology, Poland
Vladimír Soběslav	University of Hradec Kralove, Czech Republic
Klaus Söilen	Halmstad University, Sweden
Stanimir Stoyanov	University of Plovdiv "Paisii Hilendarski", Bulgaria
Libuše Svobodová	University of Hradec Kralove, Czech Republic
Martin Tabakov	Wrocław University of Science and Technology, Poland
Yasufumi Takama	Tokyo Metropolitan University, Japan

Zbigniew Telec	Wrocław University of Science and Technology, Poland
Trong Hieu Tran	VNU-University of Engineering and Technology, Vietnam
Bogdan Trawiński	Wrocław University of Science and Technology, Poland
Maria Trocan	Institut Superieur d'Electronique de Paris, France
Krzysztof Trojanowski	Cardinal Stefan Wyszyński University in Warsaw, Poland
Chrisa Tsinaraki	European Commission - Joint Research Center, Italy
Ualsher Tukeyev	Al-Farabi Kazakh National University, Kazakhstan
Olgierd Unold	Wrocław University of Science and Technology, Poland
Thi Luu Phuong Vo	International University-VNUHCM, Vietnam
Roger M. Whitaker	Cardiff University, UK
Izabela Wierzbowska	Gdynia Maritime University, Poland
Adam Wojciechowski	Łódź University of Technology, Poland
Krystian Wojtkiewicz	Wrocław University of Science and Technology, Poland
Drago Zagar	University of Osijek, Croatia
Danuta Zakrzewska	Łódź University of Technology, Poland
Constantin-Bala Zamfirescu	"Lucian Blaga" University of Sibiu, Romania
Katerina Zdravkova	University St Cyril and Methodius, Macedonia
Aleksander Zgrzywa	Wrocław University of Science and Technology, Poland
Haoxi Zhang	Chengdu University of Information Technology, China
Jianlei Zhang	Nankai University, China
Adam Ziębiński	Silesian University of Technology, Poland

Special Session Program Committees

CCINLP 2021: Special Session on Computational Collective Intelligence and Natural Language Processing

Ismaïl Biskri	Université du Québec à Trois-Rivières, Canada
Mounir Zrigui	Université de Monastir, Tunisia
Anca Pascu	Université de Bretagne Occidentale, France
Éric Poirier	Université du Québec à Trois-Rivières, Canad
Fatiha Sadat	Université du Québec à Montréal, Canada
Adel Jebali	Concordia University, Canada
Eva Hajiova	Charles University in Prague, Czech Republic
Khaled Shaalan	British University, Dubai, United Arab Emirates
Vladislav Kubon	Charles University in Prague, Czech Republic
Louis Rompré	Cascades, Canada
Rim Faiz	IHEC Carthage, Tunisia
Thang Le Dinh	Université du Québec à Trois-Rivières, Canada
Usef Faghihi	Université du Québec à Trois-Rivières, Canada
Amel Zouaq	Polytechnique Montréal, Canada

CSDMO 2021: Special Session on Cooperative Strategies for Decision Making and Optimization

Dariusz Barbucha	Gdynia Maritime University, Poland
Amine Chohra	Paris-East Créteil University, France
Ireneusz Czarnowski	Gdynia Maritime University, Poland
Joanna Jędrzejowicz	Gdansk University, Poland
Piotr Jędrzejowicz	Gdynia Maritime University, Poland
Edyta Kucharska	AGH University of Science and Technology, Poland
Antonio D. Masegosa	University of Deusto, Spain
Jacek Mercik	WSB University in Wrocław, Poland
Javier Montero	Complutense University of Madrid, Spain
Ewa Ratajczak-Ropel	Gdynia Maritime University, Poland
Iza Wierzbowska	Gdynia Maritime University, Poland
Mahdi Zargayouna	IFSTTAR, France

IOTCTCI 2021: Special Session on Internet of Things and Computational Technologies for Collective Intelligence

Octavian Postolache	Instituto de Telecomunicações, ISCTE-IUL, Portugal
Vítor Viegas	Portuguese Naval Academy, Portugal
Wolfram Hardt	Chemnitz University of Technology, Germany
Uyanga Sambuu	National University of Mongolia, Mongolia
Yadmaa Narantsetseg	Mongolian University of Science and Technology, Mongolia
Madina Mansurova	Al-Farabi Kazakh National University, Kazakhstan
Olga Dolinina	Yuri Gagarin State Technical University of Saratov, Russia
Vadim Zhmud	Novosibirsk State Technical University, Russia
Nadezhda Kunicina	Riga Technical University, Latvia
Jelena Caiko	Riga Technical University, Latvia
Mikhail Grif	Novosibirsk State Technical University, Russia
Baurzhan Belgibayev	Al-Farabi Kazakh National University, Kazakhstan
Sholpan Jomartova	Al-Farabi Kazakh National University, Kazakhstan
Assel Akzhalova	Kazakh-British Technical University, Kazakhstan
Aliya Nugumanova	S. Amanzholov East Kazakhstan State University, Kazakhstan

IWCIM 2021: International Workshop on Computational Intelligence for Multimedia Understanding

Enis Cetin	University of Illinois at Chicago, USA
Michal Haindl	Institute of Information Theory and Automation of the CAS, Czech Republic

Andras L. Majdik	MTA SZTAKI - Institute for Computer Science and Control, Hungarian Academy of Sciences, Hungary
Cristina Ribeiro	University of Porto, Porto, Portugal
Emanuele Salerno	National Research Council of Italy (CNR), Italy
Ales Prochazka	University of Chemistry and Technology, Czech Republic
Anna Tonazzini	National Research Council of Italy (CNR), Italy
Gabriele Pieri	National Research Council of Italy (CNR), Italy
Gerasimos Potamianos	University of Thessaly, Greece
Gorkem Saygili	Tilburg University, The Netherlands
Josiane Zerubia	Inria, France
Maria Antonietta Pascali	National Research Council of Italy (CNR), Italy
Marie-Colette van Lieshout	CWI Amsterdam, Netherlands
Marco Reggiannini	National Research Council of Italy (CNR), Italy
Nahum Kiryati	Tel Aviv University, Israel
Rozenn Dahyot	Trinity College Dublin, Ireland
Sara Colantonio	National Research Council of Italy (CNR), Italy
Massimo Martinelli	National Research Council of Italy (CNR), Italy
Shohreh Ahvar	Institut Supérieur d'Électronique de Paris, France
Tamás Szirányi	MTA SZTAKI - Institute for Computer Science and Control, Hungarian Academy of Sciences, Hungary

KISSTA 2021: Special Session on Knowledge-Intensive Smart Services and Their Applications

William Menvielle	Université du Québec à Trois-Rivières, Canada
Manh Chien Vu	Université du Québec à Trois-Rivières, Canada
Diarmuid O'Donoghue	Maynooth University, Ireland
Markus Helfert	Maynooth University, Ireland
Nhien-An Le-Khac	University College Dublin, Ireland
Joseph Timoney	Maynooth University, Ireland
Thuong Cang Phan	University of Cantho, Vietnam
Thanh Lam Hoang	IBM research, Dublin, Ireland
Thi My Hang Vu	University of Science, Ho Chi Minh City, Vietnam
Nam Le Nguyen Hoai	University of Science, Ho Chi Minh City, Vietnam
Nizar Bouguila	Concordia University, Canada
Jolita Ralyté	University of Geneva, Switzerland
Trung Bui	Adobe Research, USA
Elaine Mosconi	Université de Sherbrooke, Canada
Abdelaziz Khadraoui	University of Geneva, Switzerland

LRLP 2021: Special Session on Low Resource Languages Processing

Miguel A. Alonso	Universidade da Coruna, Spain
Pablo Gamallo	University of Santiago de Compostela, Spain
Nella Israilova	Kyrgyz State Technical University, Kyrgyzstan
Marek Kubis	Adam Mickiewicz University, Poland
Belinda Maia	University of Porto, Portugal
Madina Mansurova	Al-Farabi Kazakh National University, Kazakhstan
Gayrat Matlatipov	Urgench State University, Uzbekista
Marek Miłosz	Lublin University of Technology, Poland
Diana Rakhimova	Al-Farabi Kazakh National University, Kazakhstan
Altynbek Sharipbay	L. N. Gumilyov Eurasian National University, Kazakhstan
Ualsher Tukeyev	Al-Farabi Kazakh National University, Kazakhstan

MLRWD 2021: Special Session on Machine Learning in Real-World Data

Rafał Skinderowicz	University of Silesia, Poland
Grzegorz Dziczkowski	University of Economics in Katowice, Poland
Marcin Grzegorek	University of Lübeck, Germany
Ignacy Kaliszewski	Systems Research Institute, Polish Academy of Sciences, Poland
Krzysztof Kania	University of Economics in Katowice, Poland
Jan Kozak	University of Economics in Katowice, Poland
Przemysław Juszczuk	University of Economics in Katowice, Poland
Janusz Miroforidis	Systems Research Institute, Polish Academy of Sciences, Poland
Agnieszka Nowak-Brzezińska	University of Silesia, Poland
Dmitry Podkopaev	Systems Research Institute, Polish Academy of Sciences, Poland
Tomasz Jach	University of Economics in Katowice, Poland
Tomasz Staś	University of Economics in Katowice, Poland
Magdalena Tkacz	University of Silesia, Poland
Barbara Probierz	University of Economics in Katowice, Poland
Wojciech Wieczorek	University of Bielsko-Biała, Poland

SIMS 2021: Special Session on Smart Industry and Management Systems

Adam Ziębiński	Silesian University of Technology, Poland
Anne-Lena Kampen	Western Norway University of Applied Sciences, Norway
Artur Rot	Wrocław University of Economics and Business, Poland
Bogdan Franczyk	University of Leipzig, Germany
Damian Grzechca	Silesian University of Technology, Poland
Dariusz Frejlichowski	West Pomeranian University of Technology, Poland

Dariusz Mrozek	Silesian University of Technology, Poland
Helena Dudycz	Wrocław University of Economics and Business, Poland
Jarosław Wątróbski	University of Szczecin, Poland
Jerry Chun-Wei Lin	Western Norway University of Applied Sciences, Norway
Knut Øvsthus	Western Norway University of Applied Sciences, Norway
Marcin Fojcik	Western Norway University of Applied Sciences, Norway
Marcin Hernes	Wrocław University of Economics and Business, Poland
Mieczysław Owoc	Wrocław University of Economics and Business, Poland
Mykola Dyvak	Ternopil National Economic University, Ukraine
Paweł Weichbroth	Gdańsk University of Technology, Poland
Piotr Gaj	Silesian University of Technology, Poland
Rafał Cupek	Silesian University of Technology, Poland
Krzysztof Hauke	Wrocław University of Economics and Business, Poland
Łukasz Łysik	Wrocław University of Economics and Business, Poland
Piotr Tutak	Wrocław University of Economics and Business, Poland
Maciej Huk	Wrocław University of Science and Technology, Poland
Piotr Biernacki	Silesian University of Technology, Poland
Ewa Walaszczyk	Wrocław University of Economics and Business, Poland
Krzysztof Lutosławski	Wrocław University of Economics and Business, Poland
Krzysztof Tokarz	Silesian University of Technology, Poland

SUAV 2021: Special Session on Swarms of UAVs

Pierre Avanzini	Squadrone System, France
Pascal Bouvry	University of Luxembourg, Luxembourg
Serge Chaumette	University of Bordeaux, France
Grégoire Danoy	University of Luxembourg, Luxembourg
Simon G. Fabri	University of Malta, Malta
Isabelle Fantoni	CNRS, Nantes, France
Paola Flocchini	University of Ottawa, Canada
Antonio Franchi	University of Twente, The Netherlands
François Guérin	Normandy University, France
Frédéric V. G. Guinand	Normandy University, France
Chouaib El Houssein Harik	NIBIO, Norway

Samira Hayat   University of Klagenfurt, Austria
Sanaz Mostaghim   Otto-von-Guericke University, Germany
Giuseppe Prencipe   University of Pisa, Italy

Contents

Collective Decision-Making

Cooperative Strategies for Decision Making and Optimization

Data Mining and Machine Learning

Computer Vision Techniques

Internet of Things and Computational Technologies for Collective Intelligence

Computational Intelligence for Multimedia Understanding

Knowledge Engineering and Semantic Web

Negative Sampling for Knowledge Graph Completion Based on Generative Adversarial Network

Thanh Le[1,2](✉)[iD], Trinh Pham[1,2][iD], and Bac Le[1,2][iD]

[1] Faculty of Information Technology, University of Science,
Ho Chi Minh City, Vietnam
{lnthanh,lhbac}@fit.hcmus.edu.vn
[2] Vietnam National University, Ho Chi Minh City, Vietnam

Abstract. Knowledge graph, a semantic network, to organize and store data is increasingly interested in the research community and businesses such as Google, Facebook, Amazon. For the machine learning models to work well in this data, we need to prepare good quality negative samples. Generating these negative examples is challenging in the knowledge graph because it is pretty hard to determine whether a link that does not appear in the graph is a negative or positive sample. In this paper, we apply the generative adversarial network to the ConvKB method to generate negative samples, thereby producing a better graph embedding. Experiments show that our approach has quality improvement compared to the original method on well-known datasets.

Keywords: Knowledge graph · Link prediction · Negative sampling

1 Introduction

Efficient mining of knowledge graphs helps researchers understand what is behind the data and thereby benefit product users more conveniently and quickly. However, daily the data used to create it is also generated in large amounts and often challenging to control errors and inadequacies. This reason raises knowledge graph completion or link prediction. Currently, there are two main approaches to solving the link prediction problem. The first approach is to optimize the target function, or in other words, make a prediction based on the least error. Typically in this method there are RuDiK [17], AMIE [6], RuleN [12]. It is also widely used in entity classification and link classification. The other way is to produce a list of k candidates with scores representing diminishing confidence. The algorithms TransE [1], ConvKB [23] are typical examples.

With each of the above approaches, it was also divided into two smaller research branches. A rule-based branch likes RUGE [7], AnyBURL [13]; the other branch is based on graph embedding as shown in ConvE [5], TransE [1], ComplEx [21]. The graph embedding includes some approaches such as matrix

© Springer Nature Switzerland AG 2021
N. T. Nguyen et al. (Eds.): ICCCI 2021, LNAI 12876, pp. 3–15, 2021.
https://doi.org/10.1007/978-3-030-88081-1_1

factorization, geometry and deep learning [3]. Especially, the deep learning models achieve promising results compared to other methods and are suitable for graph embedding because they can learn complex representations from complex graph structures. Besides, with the strong development of hardware systems, deep learning models are increasingly popular due to their high accuracy. However, for the deep learning model to achieve good results, the graph embedding must ensure that a lot of information from the original graph is retained but with a low number of dimensions. Another aspect that also affects the quality of the deep learning paradigm is input data. The input samples extracted from the graph are usually classified as positive samples. Negative samples are almost a challenging problem. We can not consider unhappened links in the graph as true negative samples because they may appear in the future or due to data loss. Hence the negative samples generating will greatly impact the quality of the learning model.

Currently, there are many ways to generate negative samples such as random sampling, corrupting positive instance [20], typed sampling [11], relational sampling [11], Nearest Neighbor sampling [16]. Each method has strengths and weaknesses and depends on the nature of the data. In the following section, we will present these methods in detail. Since aiming to improve the negative sample generation, we tried to implement a GAN based model. A link prediction model, the convKB model, test their effectiveness. We choose the ConvKB model due to the high relevance and high results on knowledge graph completion. The experiments show that the ConvKB model has improved predictive results after being fed by these samples.

To interpret our contributions, we organize the article into six sections. The first section gives an overview of link prediction and the aspects we are interested in. The second part presents studies on current negative sampling and each method's strengths and weaknesses. In the next section, we offer the ConvKB and NoiGAN models on which we develop our model. Model improvement through applying NoiGAN to ConvKB model to generate negative patterns is shown in Sect. 4. Section 5 is experimental to point out the proposed model has improved the link prediction's quality. The last section summarizes what we have done and some ideas to implement soon.

2   Related Work

Good sampling will help the learning model create better separators, thereby increasing the predictive model results. For this reason, in this paper, we only focus on exploring negative sampling. An excellent negative sample is a relationship between two entities in the graph that is not allowed to exist or incorrect fact. Another criterion to evaluate the goodness of the negative samples is that they help the models learn how to separate well between the two types. Trivial negative triples like *(professor, teach, house)* often do not help the learning process. Hence, negative sample generation becomes an exciting challenge.

In general, the most straightforward negative sampling technique is random sampling. This method calls the triples (s, r, t) appearing in the graph as positive samples. Randomly generated instances that are not positive are considered negative. However, this method's disadvantage is that it makes many negative samples because the total number of possible triples is $|V|^2$, where V is the set of entities in the graph. Furthermore, we are unsure whether it is the correct negative sample because its randomness can produce accurate facts. And it can create trivial negative samples too.

Another way to create negative samples is to damage the positive instances. This technique is described in [20]. For each relationship (s, r, t) (positive triple) is in the graph, we replace either the source or the target entity to produce negative samples. This technique produces negative instances closer to positive instances compare with random sampling. However, if the graph has entities with too many relationships, we may not have enough target (source) entities to damage positive samples. The trivial negative triples are still encountered in this method. According to the analysis, the FreeBase and NELL datasets have a very close relationship between the entities. For example, the relationship *born_in* associates the entity types as *Person* and *City*. Therefore, the target entities used to create negative samples are selected to be compatible with the source entity. These negative triples are more explainable and are closer to the positive ones. If relations in the knowledge graph have characteristics that each entity join only one relationship, creating quality negative samples is quite simple. Just change the relationship between source and target or change one of the source and target entities that come with the new relation.

A different method of generating negative samples is to choose the nearest neighbour. After entities are encoded in an embedding space through a pre-train model, the process finds entities closest to the target entity so that they are not positive samples. Through that, the method generates negative instances that carry more certainty than other ways.

Recently, learning negative samples is a new approach. DNS [25], AutoML [10], KGPolicy [24] showed the effectiveness of this method. However, they still face some difficulties due to a lack of information to update the model. One of the powerful algorithms in image processing is the Generative Adversarial Network (GAN). Ian GoodFellow introduced the GAN architecture in 2014. GAN's applications include creating human faces, changing the age of faces, creating objects, simulating seasonal weather, and recognize text in an image. Therefore, we have strived to use a GAN network to create negative samples for the link prediction problem.

For the link prediction model, we specifically focus on the link prediction method based on graph embedding. Matrix factorization, edge reconstruction, graph kernel, generative model, and deep learning [3] are the main approaches in this way. Deep learning techniques are commonly used to embed graphs for link prediction because of their prompt and efficient collection of features. Some deep learning branches include convolutional neural networks, recurrent neural networks, capsule neural networks, and graph attention networks.

Convolutional neural networks use multiple layers, with each layer performing convolution on the input data with a low-dimensional filter. The result is a feature map, which then continues through a fully connected layer to compute the probability value. ConvE [5], ConvKB [15] are typical algorithms in this approach. Recurrent Neural Networks use one or more recurrent layer to analyze the entire path (a sequence of events/triples) retrieved from the training set, rather than just handling triples separately. Some algorithms such as RSN [8], G-DRNN [9] are implemented according to this method. Capsule Neural Networks group a bunch of neurons called capsules, each of which encodes special features of the input. The capsule network's advantage is that it helps to recognize features without losing spatial information compared to conventional convolutional computation. Typical algorithms are CapsE [19], CDC [18]. Graph Attention Networks use an attention mechanism to improve models in natural language processing. With each embedded vector, entities are aggregated information from neighbouring entities. After that, the attention information is superimposed and passed through a fully connected layer to turn to the final embedded vectors. GAT [22], KBGAT [14] are well-known in this group.

The graph embedding methods have their advantages and disadvantages, synthesized and evaluated by Cai in [3]. Among models having good results at present, we choose ConvKB method [15]. This model is based on deep learning and has quite impressive results. One model problem is that it depends on another model, TransE, to initialize the input embedding vector. We discover this model can be improved if provided with good negative samples. Therefore, we attempt to apply a GAN network model, particularly the NoiGAN [4], in the input vector initialization for the ConvKB algorithm. Through experiments, we found that this idea helped ConvKB model improve the quality of predictive links more.

3   Baseline Models

Before presenting the proposed model, we review some important points of the two original models on which we developed.

3.1   NoiGAN

Cheng et al. developed NoiGan for KG completion through the Generative Adversarial Networks framework. NoiGAN's task is to filter noise in the knowledge graph and select the best quality samples in negative instances. The NoiGAN model consists of two components. The first part is a graph embedding model representing entities and relations. The second part is a GAN model for calculating reliability for triples and select quality negative samples.

Given the graph $\mathcal{G} = \{E, R, \mathcal{T}\}$ where E is the set of entities, R is the set of relationships and $\mathcal{T} = \{(h, r, t) | h, t \in E, r \in R\}$ is the set of observed tuples. Firstly, the NoiGAN model uses an embedding model to create a vector space representing the graph. These embedded triplets often have errors. Through the NoiGAN model, it helps to remove noises from the embedding vectors. Let the confidence score of the triplets be $\{C(h, r, t) | \forall (h, r, t) \in \mathcal{T}\}$. In the experimental

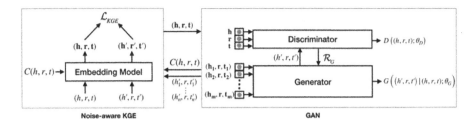

Fig. 1. NoiGAN framework [4]

process, the confidence score C(h, r, t) is calculated by the discriminator in GAN. The objective function follows Eq. 1.

$$\mathcal{L}_{KGE} = \sum_{(h,r,t)\in\mathcal{T}} [(-\log\sigma(\gamma - f_r(h,t))$$

$$+ \sum_{(h',r',t')\in\mathcal{N}(h,r,t)} \frac{1}{|\mathcal{N}(h,r,t)|} \log\sigma(\gamma - f_r(h',t')))] \tag{1}$$

Figure 1 describes the principle of operation of the NoiGAN model. Unlike traditional GAN models that focus on training for the best generator, the NoiGAN model focuses on training the discriminator to distinguish noisy triples from the correct ones better.

Discriminator and generator are two core components of the NoiGAN model. The purpose of the discriminator is to distinguish between true and noise instances. The positive and negative samples both participate in the training of the generator. Because the graph is noisy, the model only takes $k\%$ samples for each training batch. The $k\%$ samples have the nearest $f_r(h,t)$. Equation 2 is the objective function of the discriminator model.

$$\mathcal{L}_D = - \sum_{(h,r,t)\in\mathcal{T}_C} \log f_D(h,r,t)$$

$$- \sum_{(h',r,t')\in G(.|(h,r,t);\theta_G)} \log(1 - f_D(h',r,t')) \tag{2}$$

where $f_D(h,r,t) = \sigma(MLP(h,r,t))$. MLP is a two-layer neural network with the activation function ReLU, and $\sigma(x) = 1/(1 + e^x)$.

The generator's primary goal is to select high-quality negative instances from the negative samples candidate set. The generator is formed from two MLP layers. The first layer uses the ReLU function as the activation function. The second layer uses the softmax function to calculate the probability of whether the triple is the most likely noisy sample. The generator receives the reward from the discriminator. To deceive the discriminator, the generator is expected to maximize the reward from it. Equation 3 shows this reward.

$$\mathcal{R}_G = \sum_{h,r,t} \mathbb{E}_{(h',r,t')\sim G(.|(h,r,t);\theta_G)} [\log f_D(h',r,t')] \tag{3}$$

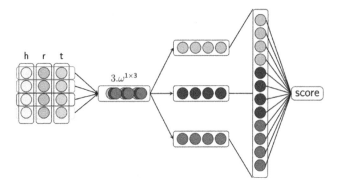

Fig. 2. Illustration of decoding layers of the ConvKB model with three filters

3.2   ConvKB

After representing the entities and relations in low-dimensional space, we use ConvKB to analyze the global features of triples on each dimension and generalize the model's features with convolutional layers. The score function of ConvKB is defined as Eq. 4.

$$f(t_{ij}^k) = \left(\|_{m=1}^{\omega} \mathrm{ReLU}([\overrightarrow{e_i}, \overrightarrow{r_k}, \overrightarrow{h_j}] * \omega^m) \right).\mathbf{W} \tag{4}$$

where t_{ij}^k contains either the negative or positive samples. e_i, r_k and h_j denote the k-dimensional embedding vectors, $\omega^m \in \mathbb{R}^{1 \times 3}$ represents the m_{th} convolutional filter. ConvKB have a lot of filters. Let Ω and τ note the set of filters and the number of filters, respectively. And $\tau = |\Omega|$, resulting in τ feature maps. $*$ is the operation that performs convolution.

The expression $(\|_{m=1}^{\omega} \mathrm{ReLU}([\overrightarrow{e_i}, \overrightarrow{r_k}, \overrightarrow{h_j}] * \omega^m))$ means the ConvKB executes the convolutional operation between embedding vectors and filters, then concatenates them together into the single vector $\in \mathbb{R}^{\tau k \times 1}$. And $\mathbf{W} \in \mathbb{R}^{\tau k \times 1}$ denotes the linear transformation matrix used to compute the final result triples. Figure 2 illustrates layers of the ConvKB model with three filters.

The model is trained with soft-margin as Eq. 5. The final output of the ConvKB model is the respective rating score of each prediction.

$$\mathcal{L} = \sum_{t_{ij}^k \in \{S \cup S'\}} \log(1 + exp(l_{t_{ij}^k} . f(t_{ij}^k))) + \frac{\lambda}{2} \parallel \mathbf{W} \parallel_2^2 \tag{5}$$

where $l_{t_{ij}^k} = \begin{cases} 1 & \text{for } t_{ij}^k \in S \text{ (postive samples)} \\ -1 & \text{for } t_{ij}^k \in S' \text{ (negative samples)} \end{cases}$

Convolutional neural networks are an excellent model to extract features from data. We believe that, with a relatively clean space, i.e. very little noise and a good representation of triples, the ConvKB model will achieve higher accuracy.

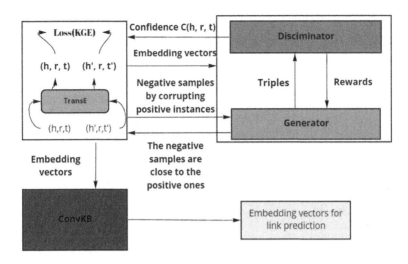

Fig. 3. Illustration of the NAGAN-ConvKB algorithm

4 NAGAN-ConvKB Model

We propose that the NAGAN-ConvKB model is a combination of two NoiGAN models and a ConvKB model. Instead of the ConvKB model, which takes the TransE model as the initialization embedding, we use the NoiGAN model to generate better embedding vectors. Figure 3 illustrates in detail the steps of the NAGAN-ConvKB model.

In addition, we replace the objective function in Eq. 1 with Eq. 6.

$$\mathcal{L} = \sum_{(h,r,t)\in S} \sum_{(h',r,t')\in S'_{(h,r,t)}} C(h,r,t)[d - d' + \gamma]_+ \tag{6}$$

We have this change because Eqs. 1 and 6 are both loss functions that serve the purpose of optimizing embedding vectors in the graph. Second, the ConvKB model takes vectors with the same number of dimensions for relationships and entities, so we choose the loss function in TransE model for ease of computation and acceleration. Besides, we add confidence scores from the NoiGAN model to this loss function to show that the input triples' quality is also still utilized in the following phases.

Specifically, our model is a combination of three main components. The first component is the vector embedding model TransE. This model is responsible for creating embedding vectors representing the graph with the objective function as in Eq. 7.

$$\mathcal{L} = \sum_{(h,r,t)\in S} \sum_{(h',r,t')\in S'_{(h,r,t)}} [d - d' + \gamma]_+ \tag{7}$$

where d and d' are calculated by $||h + r - t||_1$ and $||h' + r - t'||_1$, respectively; γ is the margin that helps the model accept some negative samples close to the positive to avoid overfitting.

The second component is the GAN algorithm model, which is responsible for selecting negative samples close to positive samples and calculating confidence scores. The input of the GAN is the $k\%$ embedding vectors that matches with the model, i.e. $k\%$ $||h + r - t||_1$ minimum with $\mathcal{N}(h, r, t)$ is a set of negative triples. After training the GAN model, the discriminator calculates the confidence of the true positive samples' vectors. This confidence can be a binary value or within the range $[0,1]$. Besides, the generator evaluates the proximity of the negative samples to the positive sample. Based on that, select **k** negative samples to train the TransE model. As a final component, we take the trained embedding vectors from the previous phase as input to the ConvKB model for link prediction.

Algorithm 1. NAGAN-ConvKB Algorithm

Require: Training set $S = (h, r, t)$, entities E, relations R
Input: Geneartor G and discriminator D and score functions $f_G(h, r, t)$ and $f_D(h, r, t)$, the embedding vectors of TransE
Output: The embedded vectors adapt sample selection and noise filtering.
for n in 1:N **do**
    take k% in the vector space that matches the most embedded graph. It means k% minimum $f_r(h, t)$
    $b \leftarrow 0$: variables used to reduce parameters during training
    repeat
        Create training batches $\mathcal{T}_{bacth}$ from set of triples
        $G_D \leftarrow 0$, $G_G \leftarrow 0$: assign gradient values to G_D and G_G
        $r_{sum} \leftarrow 0$
        for $(h, r, t) \in \mathcal{T}_{batch}$ **do**
            Create $Neg(h, r, t)$ negative random samples in a way that corrupts positive samples: $Neg(h, r, t) = \{(h'_i, r, t'_i)\}_{i=1,2,3,...N_s}$
            $p_i = softmax(f_G(Neg(h, r, t))); i \in \{1, 2, 3, ...N_s\}$
            Select a sample $\{(h'_s, r, t'_s)\}$ from set of negative samples $Neg(h, r, t)$ with the probability p_s
            $G_D \leftarrow G_D - \Delta_{\theta_D} \log f_D(h, r, t) - \sum_{(h',r,t') \in G(.|(h,r,t);\theta_G} \log(1 - f_D(h', r, t'))$
            $r \leftarrow -f_D(h'_s, r, t'_s)$, $r_{sum} \leftarrow r_{sum} + r$
            $G_G \leftarrow G_G + (r - b)\Delta_{\theta_G} \log p_s$
        end forend
        $\theta_G \leftarrow \theta_G + \mu_G G_G$, $\theta_D \leftarrow \theta_D - \mu_D G_D$
        $b \leftarrow r_{sum}/\mathcal{T}_{batch}$
    until converging
    Use the generator to select the negative samples closest to the positive samples and the discriminator to calculate the positive sample's noise.
    Train the TransE with the function:
    $\mathcal{L} = \sum_{(h,r,t) \in S} \sum_{(h',r,t') \in S'_{(h,r,t)}} C(h, r, t)[d - d' + \gamma]_+$
end forend
ConvKB: Feed samples to ConvKB.

In the NoiGAN model, the author does not publish the training source code of the GAN model. However, the KBGAN model [2] is developed on the GAN and has source code. Hence we reuse a portion of KBGAN's code related to the GAN to complete the NoiGAN algorithm. Specifically, we reuse KBGAN algorithm and replace the discriminator model with the one in NoiGAN model. Details of NAGAN-ConvKB model are presented in Algorithm 1. In this algorithm, we apply Eq. 6 to calculate the distance between the vectors.

5 Experiments

5.1 Datasets

Our experiment performed on two popular datasets, FB15k-237 [26] and WN18RR [27]. Each dataset includes three subsets: training set, validation set and testing set. Table 1 show details of these dataset configurations. FB15k [29], WN18 [28] are datasets extracted from the original FreeBase and WordNet. By eliminating inverse relations, datasets FB15k-237 [26] and WN18RR [27] represent suitable data in study the link prediction.

Table 1. The characteristics of datasets

Dataset	Entities	Relations	Triple		
			Train	Valid	Test
FB15K	14951	1345	483142	50000	59071
FB15K-237	14541	237	272115	17535	20466
WN18	40943	18	141442	5000	5000
WN18RR	40559	11	86835	3034	3134

5.2 Metrics

We use standard measures in link prediction on the knowledge graph. Specifically, the metrics include mean rank (MR), mean reciprocal rank (MRR), and hit@K. Mean rank (MR) is the average value of the ranks obtained for an accurate prediction (Eq. 8). MRR is the average relative rating, which is the inverse of the mean rank (Eq. 9). Hit@K (H@K) is the percentage of correct predictions whose rank is less than or equal to the threshold K (Eq. 10).

$$MR = \frac{1}{|Q|} \sum_{q \in Q} rank(q) \tag{8}$$

$$MRR = \frac{1}{|Q|} \sum_{q \in Q} \frac{1}{rank(q)} \tag{9}$$

$$H@K = \frac{|q \in Q : rank(q) \leq K|}{|Q|} \tag{10}$$

Table 2. Parameters in experiments

Dataset	μ	Epochs	dim	Margin γ
FB15K-237	1e$-$3	80000	100	24
WN18RR	5e$-$4	80000	50	6

5.3 Parameters and Training Process

First, we initialize the embedded vectors using the TransE model. To produce invalid initialization triples, we choose the corrupting positive instances method. Specifically, we replace the tail entities by taking some of the entities in the source set such that those tail entities do not form existed triples. The same goes for corrupting the head entity. We then proceed with two training phases. The first phase, known as an encoder, converts the initialization embedding vectors into new embedding vectors through the NoiAwareGAN model. The NoiAwareGAN's outputs are embedded vectors with the same number of dimensions as the original dimension in the TransE model. The second phase is, seen as the decoder, perform the task of prediction with the ConvKB model. It extracts features from the new embedding space and makes predictions. We use the Adam optimization function with a learning rate of $mu = 0.001$. The final dimension of the entity and the relation is equal to 100. The optimal hyperparameters are examined by the grid search algorithm (Table 2).

5.4 Results

We run experiments on Google Colab Tesla V100. The executable is written in Python version 3.8.2, uses Python built-in support functions and doesn't use any third-party libraries. The results are shown in detail in Table 3.

Table 3. Experimental results on FB15k-237 [26] and WN18RR [27]

	FB15k-237				WN18RR			
	H@1	H@10	MR	MRR	H@1	H@10	MR	MRR
TransE	0.145	0.368	529.4	0.22	0.0075	0.405	7821.6	0.175
ConvKB	**0.21**	**0.48**	**198.3**	**0.301**	0.048	0.51	2088	**0.244**
NAGAN-ConvKB	0.19	0.41	227	0.25	**0.048**	**0.51**	**2080.2**	**0.244**

In the WN18RR [27] data set, our model achieves a Hist@10 measure equal to that in the highest ConvKB model. For the MR metric, our model has the effective gain of 2080.2. Our results compared with the original results in the ConvKB model we tested completely on the machine we mentioned. Our model is 8 units higher in the measure MR, equal to the measures MRR, H@10 and H@1.

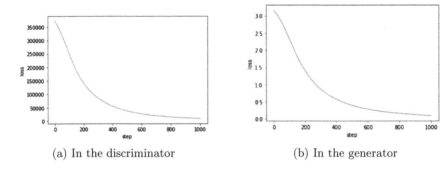

(a) In the discriminator   (b) In the generator

Fig. 4. Convergence of the loss function

For data set FB15k-237 [26], our model has a lower performance than the ConvKB model. Specifically, our model reached 0.19 at the H1 less than 0.02, getting 0.41 at H10 less than 0.07, going 227 at MR less than 28.7 and touching 0.25 at MRR less than 0.06 compared to the ConvKB model. The results showed that our model did not achieve high efficiency on the FB15k-237 [26] data set. The reason is that this data set is multidisciplinary. Finding an entity of the same type as the entity in the triples is difficult.

A necessary problem when using the GAN model is the proof of convergence. To demonstrate the GAN model's convergence in NAGAN-ConvKB, we use one epoch for the whole model and 1000 steps for GAN model training. Thereby, it shows that the model we propose tends to converge. Figure 4 illustrates the convergence of our GAN model.

6 Conclusion

Providing good negative samples will help models predict more effectively links in the knowledge graph, especially models based on deep learning. This paper applies the NoiGAN model to generate embedding samples for the link prediction model, namely ConvKB model. Through experiment, the proposed model has proven that good negative sampling has increased the model's accuracy. Although the initial results are modest, we expect further improvements in the negative sampling phase. It will be an essential prerequisite for a quality increase in the link prediction problem. The graph embedding helps to represent the entities and the relations of the knowledge graph into low-dimensional vectors. However, in reality, knowledge defined by entities and relationships may be independent of each other. Therefore, it is necessary to represent them into vectors of different dimensions. Besides, the ratio of dimensions is also an important issue that we need to research next time.

Acknowledgements. This research is funded by the Faculty of Information Technology, University of Science, VNU-HCM, Vietnam, Grant number CNTT 2021-03 and Advanced Program in Computer Science.

References

1. Bordes, A., Usunier, N., Garcia-Duran, A., Weston, J., Yakhnenko, O.: Translating embeddings for modeling multi-relational data. In: Neural Information Processing Systems (NIPS), pp. 1–9 (2013)
2. Cai, L. and Wang, W.Y: KBGAN: adversarial learning for knowledge graph embeddings. arXiv preprint arXiv:1711.04071 (2017)
3. Cai, H., Zheng, V.W., Chang, K.C.C.: A comprehensive survey of graph embedding: Problems, techniques, and applications. IEEE Trans. Knowl. Data Eng. **30**(9), 1616–1637 (2018)
4. Cheng, K., Zhu, Y., Zhang, M. and Sun, Y.: NoiGAN: noise aware knowledge graph embedding with adversarial learning (2019)
5. Dettmers, T., Minervini, P., Stenetorp, P., Riedel, S.: Convolutional 2D knowledge graph embeddings. In: Proceedings of the AAAI Conference on Artificial Intelligence, vol. 32, no. 1 (2018)
6. Galárraga, L., Teflioudi, C., Hose, K., Suchanek, F.M.: Fast rule mining in ontological knowledge bases with AMIE. VLDB J. **24**(6), 707–730 (2015)
7. Guo, S., Wang, Q., Wang, L., Wang, B., Guo, L.: Knowledge graph embedding with iterative guidance from soft rules. In: Proceedings of the AAAI Conference on Artificial Intelligence, vol. 32, no. 1 (2018)
8. Guo, L., Sun, Z., Hu, W.: Learning to exploit long-term relational dependencies in knowledge graphs. In: International Conference on Machine Learning, pp. 2505–2514. PMLR (2019)
9. Han, X., Zhang, C., Ji, Y., Hu, Z.: A dilated recurrent neural network-based model for graph embedding. IEEE Access **7**, 32085–32092 (2019)
10. Hutter, F., Kotthoff, L., Vanschoren, J.: Automated Machine Learning: Methods, Systems, Challenges, pp. 219. Springer, Heidelberg (2019). https://doi.org/10.1007/978-3-030-05318-5
11. Kotnis, B., Nastase, V.: Analysis of the impact of negative sampling on link prediction in knowledge graphs. arXiv preprint arXiv:1708.06816 (2017)
12. Meilicke, C., Fink, M., Wang, Y., Ruffinelli, D., Gemulla, R., Stuckenschmidt, H.: Fine-grained evaluation of rule-and embedding-based systems for knowledge graph completion. In: Vrandečić, D., et al. (eds.) ISWC 2018. LNCS, vol. 11136, pp. 3–20. Springer, Cham (2018). https://doi.org/10.1007/978-3-030-00671-6_1
13. Meilicke, C., Chekol, M.W., Ruffinelli, D., Stuckenschmidt, H.: Anytime bottom-up rule learning for knowledge graph completion. In: IJCAI, pp. 3137–3143 (2019)
14. Nathani, D., Chauhan, J., Sharma, C., Kaul, M.: Learning attention-based embeddings for relation prediction in knowledge graphs. In: Proceedings of the 57th Annual Meeting of the Association for Computational Linguistics (2019)
15. Nguyen, D.Q., Nguyen, T.D., Nguyen, D.Q., Phung, D.: A novel embedding model for knowledge base completion based on convolutional neural network. In: Proceedings of NAACL-HLT (2017)
16. Nickel, M., Murphy, K., Tresp, V., Gabrilovich, E.: A review of relational machine learning for knowledge graphs. Proc. IEEE **104**(1), pp. 11–33 (2015)
17. Ortona, S., Meduri, V.V., Papotti, P.: Robust discovery of positive and negative rules in knowledge bases. In: IEEE 34th International Conference on Data Engineering (ICDE), pp. 1168–1179 (2018)
18. Peng, B., Min, R., Ning, X.: CNN-based dual-chain models for knowledge graph learning. arXiv preprint arXiv:1911.06910 (2019)

19. Sabour, S., Frosst, N., Hinton, G.E.: Dynamic routing between capsules. In: Proceedings of the 31st International Conference on Neural Information Processing Systems (NIPS 2017) (2017)
20. Socher, R., Chen, D., Manning, C.D., Ng, A.: Reasoning with neural tensor networks for knowledge base completion. In: Advances in Neural Information Processing Systems, pp. 926–934 (2013)
21. Trouillon, T., Welbl, J., Riedel, S., Gaussier, É, Bouchard, G.: Complex embeddings for simple link prediction. In: International Conference on Machine Learning, pp. 2071–2080, PMLR (2016)
22. Veličković, P., Cucurull, G., Casanova, A., Romero, A., Lio, P., Bengio, Y.: Graph attention networks. arXiv preprint arXiv:1710.10903 (2017)
23. Vu, T., Nguyen, T.D., Nguyen, D.Q., Phung, D.: A capsule network-based embedding model for knowledge graph completion and search personalization. In: Proceedings of the 2019 Conference of the North American Chapter of the Association for Computational Linguistics: Human Language Technologies, vol. 1 (Long and Short Papers), pp. 2180–2189 (2019)
24. Wang, X., Xu, Y., He, X., Cao, Y., Wang, M. and Chua, T.S.: Reinforced negative sampling over knowledge graph for recommendation. In: Proceedings of The Web Conference 2020, pp. 99–109 (2020)
25. Zhang, W., Chen, T., Wang, J., Yu, Y.: Optimizing Top-N collaborative filtering via dynamic negative item sampling. In: Proceedings of the 36th International ACM SIGIR Conference on Research and Development in Information Retrieval, pp. 785–788 (2013)
26. Toutanova, K., Chen, D.: Observed versus latent features for knowledge base and text inference. In: Proceedings of the 3rd Workshop on Continuous Vector Space Models and their Compositionality, pp. 57–66 (2015)
27. Dettmers, T., Minervini, P., Stenetorp, P., Riedel, S.: Convolutional 2D knowledge graph embeddings. In Proceedings of the 32nd AAAI Conference on Artificial Intelligence (2018, page to appear)
28. Toutanova, K., Chen, D.: Observed versus latent features for knowledge base and text inference. In: Workshop on CVSMC, pp. 57–66 (2015)
29. Wang, Y., Ruffinelli, D., Broscheit, S., Gemulla, R.: On evaluating embedding models for knowledge base completion. Technical report. arXiv:1812.06410 (2018)

Learning Embedding for Knowledge Graph Completion with Hypernetwork

Thanh Le[1,2(✉)] , Duy Nguyen[1,2] , and Bac Le[1,2]

[1] Faculty of Information Technology, University of Science,
Ho Chi Minh City, Vietnam
{lnthanh,lhbac}@fit.hcmus.edu.vn
[2] Vietnam National University, Ho Chi Minh City, Vietnam

Abstract. Link prediction in Knowledge Graph, also called knowledge completion, is a significant problem in graph mining and has many applications for large companies. The more accurate the link prediction results will bring satisfaction, reduce and avoid risks, and commercial benefits. Almost all state-of-the-art models focus on the deep learning approach, especially using convolutional neural networks (CNN). By analysing the strengths and weaknesses of the CNN based models, we proposed a better model to improve the performance of the link prediction task. Specifically, we apply a CNN with specific filters generated through the Hypernetwork architecture. Moreover, we increase the depth of the model more than baseline models to help learn more helpful information. Experimental results show that the proposed model gets better results when compared to CNN-base models.

Keywords: Link prediction · Knowledge graph embedding · Convolutional neural network

1 Introduction

A knowledge graph is a form of knowledge representation that is of great interest to research communities, business and government because of its applicability. In social networks, we can consider vertices as users and edges describing relationships between them. We analyze this graph to make friend suggestions. In the context of the Covid epidemic, place and people are vertices, and edges can be the time and method of movement. We analyze the graph to trace who are at risk of infection. In criminal investigations, it is possible to determine or predict the action association of them. In a nutshell, knowledge representation as graphs along with the methods of analysis will yield valuable applications.

Link prediction is a task that based on observed information of the graph to infer the connections between vertices. In a static graph, the link prediction finds out the missing relations and generally referred to as the graph completion. Meanwhile, in a dynamic graph, link prediction identifies relationships that will appear the next time. In this paper, we only focus on predicting the missing

© Springer Nature Switzerland AG 2021
N. T. Nguyen et al. (Eds.): ICCCI 2021, LNAI 12876, pp. 16–28, 2021.
https://doi.org/10.1007/978-3-030-88081-1_2

links on a static graph. Approaches to solving this problem are divided into two main groups: supervised learning methods and unsupervised learning methods. Mining rules or calculating the similarity between vertices are algorithms that belong to the unsupervised learning group. Their advantages lie in simplicity and low training time. However, they are not universal on many types of graphs or many kinds of relationships, or governed by subjectivity when making measures. A supervised learning branch usually begins by embedding the graph in latent space with low-dimensional vectors, in which associated vertices tend to lie close together. The strength of the methods is that the feature is automatically learned. Consequently, the results are usually better. The trade-off, nevertheless, is the complexity of the learning model.

Today, deep learning is applied to many different problems such as image processing, natural language processing. Link prediction is also not out of this scope. Although more complex, it easily gets higher results compared to other approaches. With its own weights, the deep learning model can easily remember the information it learned and reflect the hidden distribution of data to predict more relationships that are not trained yet. Thanks to that advantage, we decided to research and improve the link prediction problem based on this field.

In this paper, we:

– Propose HyperConvKB model based on the Convolutional Neural Network to learn entity and relation embeddings for knowledge graph completion. Our model uses a specific relation-dependent filter to generate the feature map.
– Evaluate our model's effectiveness on two benchmark datasets, WN18RR and FB15k-237, in standard metrics such as MR, MRR, Hit@k and compare it to state-of-the-art models. The experiments show that our approach achieves promising results in dataset WN18RR.

2   Related Work

Firstly, we introduce notations used in this paper. Let $\mathcal{E}$ be a set of entities, $\mathcal{R}$ be a set of relations. Knowledge graph $\mathcal{G} \subseteq \mathcal{E} \times \mathcal{R} \times \mathcal{E}$. A triple $(s, r, t) \in \mathcal{G}$ where s, r, t denotes to source entity, relation, target entity, respectively. The scoring function $\phi_r(s, t)$ is a measure of the correctness of a triple in the embedding space.

The models to solve the link prediction can be divided into three branches: geometric model, matrix factorization and deep learning model [11]. The geometric-based approaches interpret relation as geometric transformations. Some well-known models in this area are TransE [2] with translation transformation, RotatE [14] with rotation transformation. TransE mines the transitional characteristic, which is the useful intuition on the knowledge graph. This model represents entities and relations into a low-dimensional vector space and assumes that the source entity in this embedding space will be translated by relation vector r. The result of the translation is a new point expected roughly equal to embedded target entity t. However, TransE does not carry one-to-many, many-to-one, many-to-many relations. To solve these problems, there are many models

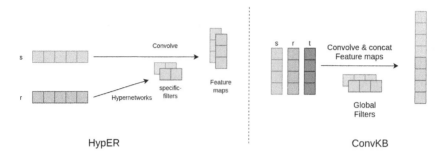

HypER   ConvKB

Fig. 1. The architecture of HypER and ConvKB to generate the feature maps. The HypER model uses specific filters generated by Hypernetwork to apply the CNN with these filters. The ConvKB model concatenates the embedding of source, relation and target as a matrix $A \in \mathcal{R}^{d \times 3}$ and apply CNN on this matrix. If the convolutional layer only uses one filter $[1, 1, -1]$, ConvKB will become TransE. Then, ConvKB can keep the idea of TransE and go further.

developed such as TransH [17], TransR [7], StransE [9]. These models still use the translation assumption but in a different way. For instance, TransH considers a relation as a hyperplane. After that, a transition operator on its source and target are projected on this hyperplane and expect a transitional vector to connect two projected vectors. Another idea of the geometric model is embedding graphs into more complex spaces such as QuatE [12]. Specifically, QuatE uses quaternion embedding to represent the knowledge graph.

Meanwhile, matrix factorization optimizes the scoring function using bilinear or non-bilinear product between the vectors of source and target entity and relation. DistMult [18], Complex [16] are the models in this branch using a bilinear product. The scoring of these model has the form:

$$\phi_r(s, t) = s \times r \times t \tag{1}$$

where $\times$ denotes to matrix product.

However, these models usually suffer from overfitting. Regularization is one of the solutions to solve this problem. Rescal-DURA [19] is one of the models developed from Rescal by using a new regularizer called DUality-induced RegulArizer (DURA) to improve the performance.

Both geometric and matrix factorization models are often designed with low parameters or insufficient depth to learn more information in the graph. Recently, many researchers have tried to implement the deep neural network for the link prediction problem. A deep neural network has many layers, and every layer can be designed to learn different information. Therefore, it can easily capture the hidden link that does not appear in the graph. Many models in this category, such as ConvKB [10], ConvE [4], HypER [1], utilized Convolutional Neural Network (CNN), one of the networks successfully applied in computer vision. D.Q. Nguyen proposes ConvKB model, which is only interactive in the same dimension of the embedding vector. In ConvKB (illustrated in Fig. 1), source, relation and target

(s, r, t) are concatenated without using reshape operator. Accordingly, ConvKB limits the reconstruction 2D structure of the embedding vector. With the input matrix, ConvKB uses 1×3 filters for the convolutional layer to create a feature map. In this way, it can keep the transitional characteristic of embedding space. HypER model (shown in Fig. 1) used a specific architecture called Hypernetwork [6] which includes two networks. A network is the main network that behaves like any other typical network. Its task is to learn to map the source to the target. Another network smaller than the primary network, also called Hypernetwork, takes every information about the structure of weights and generates the weights for the primary network. Generally, these models are not deep enough. They only do one layer convolution and one fully connected to calculate the ranking score. In a complex graph, these approaches may not be good because they can not capture enough information.

Based on the synthesis of the strengths and the weaknesses of the previous models in the convolution field, we propose some improvements. Specifically, we update the ConvE by avoiding using the reshape operator because this operator destroys the 2D structure of the embedding vector. Furthermore, we found that the transitional characteristic from ConvKB is good intuition when doing the link prediction task. Hence, we include this characteristic in our model. Primarily, our model uses the Hypernetwork architecture to generate specific filters instead of using global filters. The reason is that the specific filters can capture specific relationships better than global filters.

3   Proposed HyperConvKB Model

This section will introduce our model architecture in detail. Generally, the model is divided into two phases. The first phase is the feature extraction, and the ranking score calculation for triples is the second phase. To do that, we assume two principles: (i) the relationship of a pair of vertices in triple that represents the characteristic of that triple and (ii) the pair of similar vertices can share the information for each other. We also offer the loss function to optimize the model parameters.

Feature Extraction

In deep learning models, the feature extraction process is fundamental, which impacts on the model performance. We realize that the transitional characteristic is still one of the essential ideas to serve the problem. However, as we know, these ideas are not strong enough to solve the relationships in the knowledge graph because they do not handle the one-to-many, many-to-one and many-to-many relationships well. Therefore, we try to extract the characteristic that the transitional characteristic has not solved. We suppose that the information of the relations represents the characteristic of a pair of vertices. That means there is a function to transform $Feat(s, r, t) = F_r(s, t)$, where $Feat(s, r, t)$ is a feature of triple (s, r, t) and F_r is a function to extract the characteristic of a pair of vertices based on their relations. We use the convolutional neural network to

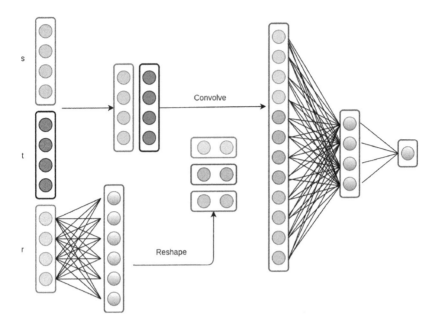

Fig. 2. Our model architecture. In this example, the embedding size d is 4, the number of relations is 4, and the number of filters k is 3. The relation after using a fully connected layer will reshape as a set of filters and apply the convolutional operator over the row of the input matrix. In this example, we do not concatenate the embedding of relation.

extract the feature of every dimension of the data point. Hence, it helps to avoid the interaction of different dimensions and keep the transitional characteristic. For the convolutional layer, F_r is the filter's weight, and input is the concatenated vector of source and target entity embeddings. Relation r can be concatenated to capture the transitional characteristic better.

We represent the model's input as a matrix $X \in \mathbb{R}^{d \times n_{col}}$ by concatenating row by row the embeddings of triple, where d is the dimensionality of the embedding vector, n_row is the number of rows of the input matrix. A set of filters with a fixed size, $1 \times n_{col}$, will apply the convolution operator over the row of the input matrix to generate the feature vector. A non-linear transformation, Hypernetwork, generates the weights of the convolution layer. The Hypernetwork uses the information from relations of triples as input and applies a fully connected layer with the activation function to create a vector with $k \times n_{col}$ dimensions, where k is the number of filters in the convolutional layer. This vector will reshape as a $k \times 1 \times n_{col}$ matrix which is a set of k matrices with a size of $1 \times n_{col}$. In which every matrix represents a filter of the convolutional layer.

Ranking Score Calculation

After the first step, we have a feature vector that represents the information of triples. This vector is used to calculate the ranking score for the confidence of this triple. The smaller the triple's ranking score, the better the confidence. In the knowledge graph, the positive triples are the facts, while negative triples do not exist. Therefore, the positive triples should have small scores and vice versa for the negative triples.

We use the second principle to calculate the ranking score. The main idea is based on the similarity of pairs to infer the missing relationship. We assume that if two pairs of vertices have a similarity, they will share the relationship for each. For example, let a pair of vertices (A, B) have relations (1, 2, 3) and (C, D) have relations (1, 2) as shown in Fig. 3. By somehow, if (A, B) is similar to (C, D), (C, D) will be suggested a relation (3) in future. To learn this rule, the feature vector from the first step is reduced in dimension to the number of relations. Therefore, we represent the feature vector at every dimensional as one information of relation. This process allows two different pairs of vertices to have the same feature vector. We use a fully connected layer with the number of units equal to the number of relations in the graph to extract this information. If this representation vector is a one-hot vector, each dimension of the vector represents the relation that the triple represents. Hence, if there are two different triplets with the same feature vector and one of them already exists in the graph, we will most likely accept the other triples as a missing link in the graph.

The feature vector of this step is used to calculate the ranking score of triples. Although there are many pairs with the same similarity, we only choose the pair with the best ranking score. Formally, the score function follows as Eq. 2.

$$\phi_r(s, t) = f(g(concat(s, \{r\}, t) * \omega_r)W_1)W_2 \tag{2}$$

where $\omega_r = reshape(tanh(Wr + b))$ is a Hypernetwork to generate weights for the convolutional layer; f and g is non-linear activation. We choose both f and g as rectified linear unit (ReLU) in our model.

To learn the parameters, we design the loss function to satisfy the problem requirements. Suppose that the input consists of two sets: one includes triples that have a link (positive triples) and the other consists of triples that do not have the link (negative triples). Our model will learn to calculate the ranking score so that the positive triples always get a better ranking score than negative triples. In other words, the positive triples will get a ranking score smaller than negative triples. We choose 0 as the boundary of positive triple and negative triple. If positive triples have label 1 and negative triples have label -1, $score \times label \leq 0$. It means that the model calculates a true ranking score. Otherwise, we have an amount of penalty view as the loss of wrong calculation. We propose use the loss function follow as Eq. 3 and Eq. 4

$$\mathcal{L}(x) = max(0, x)^b \tag{3}$$

or

$$\mathcal{L}(x) = log(1 + e^x) \tag{4}$$

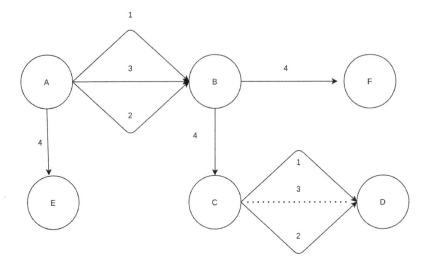

Fig. 3. The subgraph illustrates the second principle, where the arrow denotes the relations between a pair of vertices, and the dotted line denotes the recommended relationships for two vertices.

where $x = score \times label$ and $b \geq 1$. Both loss functions satisfy the condition. Figure 2 shows the end-to-end architecture of our model.

4   Experiments

To evaluate effectiveness, we compare our model with state-of-the-art models on two standard datasets, WN18RR and FB15k-237. We also evaluate the model based on common metrics such as MR, MRR, H@K.

4.1   Datasets

Normally, there are five common datasets used in the link prediction evaluation. They are WN18 [2], WN18RR[4], FB15k [2], FB15k-237 [15] and YAGO [13]. However, we only pay attention to two datasets: WN18RR and FB15k-237. WN18RR and FB15k-237 are correspondingly subsets of WN18 and FB15k. Both WN18 and FB15k have reversible relations that are easy to predict the missing link. We can easily infer the missing link by reverse the source and target when knowing the train triples. It makes the model overestimate and can not evaluate the model performance precisely. Therefore, WN18RR and FB15k-237 was created to solve this problem by removing the inverse relations. WN18RR contains 40943 entities and 11 relations, while FB15k-237 contains 14541 entities and 237 relations. Table 1 summarises the characteristics of these datasets.

Table 1. The characteristics of datasets used for experiments

Dataset	Entities	Relations	Triple		
			Train	Valid	Test
FB15K-237	14541	237	272115	17535	20466
WN18RR	40943	11	86835	3034	3134

4.2   Metrics

Link prediction is a task that finds the missing relation. Given a source entity and a relation, (s, r), we infer t. It is called head prediction. Similarly, a relation and a target entity, (r, t), infer s is called tail prediction. For predicting the relations, the source entity s is replaced by other entities in the graph if it is a head prediction or the target entity t if a tail prediction. After that, the model calculates the ranking score for triples. The smaller the rating score, the better the result. We use "filtered" setting protocol [2] to eliminate its misleading effect. This option does not take any triple that appears in the training set for the validation or test phase. The reason is that, in the training phase, the model has learned these triples. If they happen again in the test set, they donate other triples. It means that they often have a good score. The rank of triple in tail prediction was calculated by the Eq. 5 and rank for head prediction can be computed analogously:

$$r_t = |e \in \mathcal{E} \backslash \{t\} : \phi(s, r, e) > \phi(s, r, t) \wedge (s, r, e) \notin \mathcal{G}| + 1 \qquad (5)$$

where $\mathcal{E}$ is the set of entities and $\mathcal{G}$ is training graph.

We evaluated the model in metrics including mean rank (MR), mean reciprocal (MRR) and Hit at K (H@K). The formula of these metrics gives in Eq. 6, Eq. 7 and Eq. 8. Let Q is a set of rank of correct triples which we want to predict.

$$MR = \frac{1}{|Q|} \sum_{q \in Q} q \qquad (6)$$

Mean rank computes the average rank of a correct triple: the smaller MR, the better result.

$$MRR = \frac{1}{|Q|} \sum_{q \in Q} \frac{1}{q} \qquad (7)$$

It is the average of the inverse of the obtained ranks of the correct triple: the higher MRR, the better result.

$$H@K = \frac{|\{q \in Q | q \leq K\}|}{|Q|} \qquad (8)$$

It is the ratio of predictions for which the rank is equal or smaller than k.

When $score(s, r, t) = score(s, r, e)$, some policy will apply to calculate the rank of the correct triple. In this paper, we use the min policy and ordinal policy to evaluate the model. The min policy accepts the different triples to have the same rank if it has the same ranking score. Meanwhile, the ordinal policy ranks triples by their ordinal and does not accept other triples with the same rank.

4.3   Experiment Setup

We implement our model based on source code ConvKB in PyTorch version [10] which implemented on OpenKE framework [21]. The computer includes CPU intel core i7 9700K and GPU RTX 2080Ti running Ubuntu 16.04 LTS. We reuse some results of the authors [3,10], such as hyperparameter, embedding vectors pre-trained from TransE [3,10]. In the dataset WN18RR, the embedding dimension of entity and relation is 50, 100, and in FB15K-237, the embedding dimension is 100. We set the dropout ratio as 0 and 0.5. Convolution layer with a filter size of 1×2 and 1×3, respectively, if the relation was concatenated. The number of filters in the convolutional layer is default 64 with convolution $stride = 1$. The number of negative sampling is chosen from $\{1, 2, 5, 10\}$.

As we mentioned earlier, our model takes input consisting of 2 sets: positive triples and negative triples. However, the training datasets only have positive triples. Hence, we had to generate negative triples manually. We use the Bernoulli trick introduced by [7,17]. Besides, the Adagrad [5] optimizer is applied with a learning rate equal to 0.01 and Adam [20] with learning rate equal to 0.0001. Regularization is not applied. We train the model up to 300 epochs. After that, we use the best results of H@10 on the validation set to the testing model. Table 2 summaries the hyperparameters used in our model.

Evaluation protocol: Our implementation is based on OpenKE framework [21] and uses two policies (min, ordinal) when evaluating the model.

4.4   Result and Analysis

Table 3 showed the performance of models in the link prediction task. The results use the min policy show that in the WN18RR dataset, our model gets a better result than others at metrics MRR, H@1, H@3, H@10. Specifically, we increase 12% MRR when compared to RotH. Our model also increases H@1 above 10% when compared to Rescal-DURA which is the best model at H@1 in our comparison table. However, we found that the results on FB15k-237 are not good.

Table 2. Some hyperparameters used in our model.

Parameter	Value
Learning rate	0.01
Number of filter	64
Filter size	1×2
Number of negative sampling	$\{1, 2, 5, 10\}$
Exponent of loss function	$\{1, 2, 3\}$

Table 3. The experiment result of models on WN18RR and FB15K-237 test datasets. The results of stranse were obtained from the survey of Rossi et al. [22]. **HyperconvKB** is the model evaluated on ordinal policy and **HyperConvKB*** is the model evaluated on min policy.

	WN18RR					FB15K-237				
	MR	MRR	H@1	H@3	H@10	MR	MRR	H@1	H@3	H@10
StransE	5172	0.226	0.101	-	0.422	357	0.315	0.225	-	0.496
ConvE [4]	4187	0.43	0.40	0.44	0.53	244	0.325	0.237	0.356	0.501
ConvKB [10]	2554	0.248	-	-	0.525	257	0.396	-	-	0.517
HypER [1]	5798	0.465	0.436	0.477	0.522	250	0.341	0.252	0.376	0.520
KBGAT [8]	1940	0.440	0.361	0.483	0.581	210	**0.518**	**0.46**	**0.54**	**0.626**
QuatE [12]	2314	0.488	0.438	0.508	0.582	**87**	0.348	0.248	0.382	0.550
Rescal-DURA [19]	-	0.498	0.455	-	0.577	-	0.368	0.276	-	0.550
RotatE [14]	3340	0.476	0.428	0.492	0.571	177	0.338	0.241	0.375	0.533
Ours HyperConvKB	**1304**	0.410	0.331	0.458	0.549	318	0.269	0.183	0.296	0.442
Ours HyperConvKB*	3080	**0.624**	**0.558**	**0.684**	**0.719**	440	0.296	0.193	0.340	0.500

The FB15k-237 is large and contains data from multiple fields, while our model is not deep enough to capture the relations. As shown in the comparison table, the KBGAT model is still good when doing the link prediction task in FB15k-237. Using the Graph Attention network to capture the graph structure, KBGAT gives better prediction for the multiple domain dataset such as FB15k-237. When using the ordinal policy, although performance has changed and is no longer the best, our model still better than some model also use the Convolution neural network such as ConvE, ConvKB.

Table 4. Performance on head prediction and tail prediction of our model. '*' donotes to model evaluate with ordinal policy.

	Head prediction			Tail prediction		
	MR	MRR	H@10	MR	MRR	H@10
WN18RR	3789	0.631	0.725	2370	0.617	0.712
FB15k-237	643	0.225	0.393	237	0.367	0.607
WN18RR*	1677	0.380	0.500	930	0.440	0.598
FB15k-237*	499	0.178	0.330	318	0.360	0.553

Moreover, we also evaluate our model in two other aspects, head prediction and tail prediction. The detailed results are shown in Table 4. In FB15k-237 dataset, there is a quite difference between head and tail prediction. The tail prediction gets better results than the head prediction. That is the reason that reducing the overall performance of our model in this dataset. In contrast, our model achieves a stable result on WN18RR in both head and tail prediction. Therefore, depending on the type of dataset, we should choose a suitable prediction protocol to achieve the best performance.

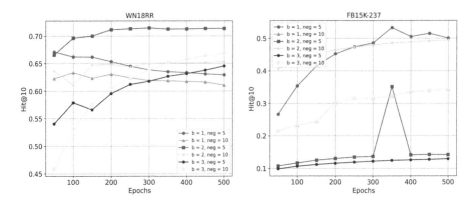

Fig. 4. The effectiveness of hyperparameters in our model. The figure on the left is for the WN18RR dataset, and the figure on the right is for the FB15k-237 dataset. In the WN18RR dataset, we easily find hyperparameters to get a better result. With different hyperparameters, the model nearly achieves the same result and gets the best result when b = 2 and negative sampling = 5. Otherwise, in the FB15k-237 dataset, we must choose suitable hyperparameters. If not, the result is awful.

We also evaluate the influence of hyperparameters to the model's performance. Because our model has developed from ConvKB, so we suppose that the hyperparameters of our model will be the same as ConvKB. The two main parameters of the model are the exponential factor of the loss function and the number of negative sampling. Result show in Fig. 4. We found that the performance in the FB15k-237 is not stable, it just gets better results when choosing right parameters and it often gets bad results on almost all cases of hyperparameters. While the dataset WN18RR is completely opposite, it easily gets a good result. As we show in Fig. 4, for WN18RR the best hyperparameter is b = 2 (3), number of negative sampling is 5 and b = 1, number of negative sampling is 5 for FB15k-237.

Furthermore, we evaluate the influence of hyperparameters to the model's performance. Because our model has developed from ConvKB, we apply the hyperparameters similar to ConvKB. The two other parameters are the exponential factor of the loss function and the number of negative sampling. The results are shown in Fig. 4. We found that the performance in the FB15k-237 dataset is not stable. It gets better results when choosing the correct parameters. However, in general, it often gets terrible results in every case of hyperparameters. Oppositely, for the WN18RR dataset, it gets a good result overall.

5   Conclusion

This paper proposed a model for link prediction task using Hypernetwork to generate parameters and applying two helpful principles to design model architecture. The experiments show that our proposed model gets better results in the WN18RR dataset. Specifically, we achieve approximately 10% higher than the state-of-the-art models on the MRR, H@K metrics, except MR. For the FB15k-237 dataset, the performance of the model is not expected. Because of inconsistency, the FB15k-237 dataset causes the learning model could not capture many cases well. It is proved through evaluating the head prediction and tail prediction and the effects of the metadata on the model. In the future, we intend to increase the number of parameters and the depth of the model to help it learn much hidden information.

Acknowledgements. This research is funded by the Faculty of Information Technology, University of Science, VNU-HCM, Vietnam, Grant number CNTT 2021-03 and Advanced Program in Computer Science.

References

1. Balažević, I., Allen, C., Hospedales, T.M.: Hypernetwork knowledge graph embeddings. In: Tetko, I., Kurková, V., Karpov, P., Theis, F. (eds.) International Conference on Artificial Neural Networks. LNCS, vol. 11731, pp. 553–565, Springer, Cham (2019). https://doi.org/10.1007/978-3-030-30493-5_52
2. Bordes, A., Usunier, N., Garcia-Duran, A., Weston, J., Yakhnenko, O.: Translating embeddings for modeling multi-relational data. In: Neural Information Processing Systems (NIPS), pp. 1–9 (2013)
3. Nguyen, D.Q., Vu, T., Nguyen, T.D., Nguyen, D.Q., Phung, D.: A capsule network based embedding model for knowledge graph completion and search personalization. In: NAACL-HLT, pp. 2180–2189 (2019b)
4. Dettmers, T., Minervini, P., Stenetorp, P., Riedel, S.: Convolutional 2D knowledge graph embeddings. In: Proceedings of the AAAI Conference on Artificial Intelligence, vol. 32, no. 1 (2018)
5. Duchi, J., Hazan, E., Singer, Y.: Adaptive subgradient methods for online learning and stochastic optimization. J. Mach. Learn. Res. **12**(7) (2011)
6. Ha, D., Dai, A., Le, Q.V.: Hypernetworks. In: International Conference on Learning Representations (2016)
7. Lin, Y., Liu, Z., Sun, M., Liu, Y., Zhu, X.: Learning entity and relation embeddings for knowledge graph completion. In: Proceedings of the AAAI Conference on Artificial Intelligence, vol. 29, no. 1 (2015)
8. Nathani, D., Chauhan, J., Sharma, C., Kaul, M.: Learning attention based embeddings for relation prediction in knowledge graphs. In: ACL, pp. 4710–4723 (2019)
9. Nguyen, D.Q., Sirts, K., Qu, L., Johnson, M.: STransE: a novel embedding model of entities and relationships in knowledge bases. In: Proceedings of the 16th Annual Conference of the North American Chapter of the Association for Computational Linguistics: Human Language Technologies (NAACL-HLT), pp. 327–333 (2016)
10. Nguyen, D.Q., Nguyen, T.D., Nguyen, D.Q., Phung, D.: A novel embedding model for knowledge base completion based on convolutional neural network. In: Proceedings of the 16th Annual Conference of the North American Chapter of the Association for Computational Linguistics: Human Language Technologies (NAACL-HLT), pp. 327–333 (2017)
11. Rossi, A., Barbosa, D., Firmani, D., Matinata, A., Merialdo, P.: Knowledge graph embedding for link prediction: a comparative analysis. ACM Trans. Knowl. Discov. Data (TKDD) **15**(2), 1–49 (2021)

12. Zhang, S., Tay, Y., Yao, L., Liu, Q.: Quaternion knowledge graph embeddings. Adv. Neural Inf. Process. Syst. **32**, 2735–2745 (2019)
13. Suchanek, F.M., Kasneci, G., Weikum, G.: Yago: a core of semantic knowledge. In: Proceedings of the 16th International Conference on World Wide Web, pp. 697–706 (2007)
14. Sun, Z., Deng, Z.H., Nie, J.Y. and Tang, J.: Rotate: knowledge graph embedding by relational rotation in complex space. In: Seventh International Conference on Learning Representations, pp. 1–18 (2019)
15. Toutanova, K., Chen, D.: Observed versus latent features for knowledge base and text inference. In Proceedings of the 3rd Workshop on Continuous Vector Space Models and Their Compositionality, pp. 57–66 (2015)
16. Trouillon, T., Welbl, J., Riedel, S., Gaussier, É., Bouchard, G.: Complex embeddings for simple link prediction. In: International Conference on Machine Learning, pp. 2071–2080. PMLR (2016)
17. Wang, Z., Zhang, J., Feng, J., Chen, Z.: Knowledge graph embedding by translating on hyperplanes. In: Proceedings of the AAAI Conference on Artificial Intelligence, vol. 28, no. 1 (2014)
18. Yang, B., Yih, W.T., He, X., Gao, J., Deng, L.: Embedding entities and relations for learning and inference in knowledge bases. arXiv preprint arXiv:1412.6575 (2014)
19. Zhang, Z., Cai, J., Wang, J.: Duality-induced regularizer for tensor factorization based knowledge graph completion. In: Advances in Neural Information Processing Systems, vol. 33 (2020)
20. Kingma, D., Ba, J.: Adam: a method for stochastic optimization. arXiv preprint arXiv:1412.6980 (2014)
21. Han, X., et al.: OpenKE: an open toolkit for knowledge embedding. In: Proceedings of EMNLP (2018)
22. Rossi, A., Firmani, D., Matinata, A., Merialdo, P., Barbosa, D.: Knowledge graph embedding for link prediction: a comparative analysis. **1**(1), 43, Article no. 1 (2016)

RotatHS: Rotation Embedding on the Hyperplane with Soft Constraints for Link Prediction on Knowledge Graph

Thanh Le[1,2]([envelope]) [iD], Ngoc Huynh[1,2] [iD], and Bac Le[1,2] [iD]

[1] Faculty of Information Technology, University of Science, Ho Chi Minh City, Vietnam
{lnthanh,lhbac}@fit.hcmus.edu.vn
[2] Vietnam National University, Ho Chi Minh City, Vietnam

Abstract. Embedding vertices and relations is the main direction and poses many challenges for the research community in link prediction on the knowledge graph. Among the state-of-the-art approaches, the approach based on the geometric transformations has the strong point of good intuition representation. Besides, the relations in the knowledge graph is diverse, so the embedding needs to be flexible. For that reason, we focus on analyzing the characteristics of the relations and the suitability for each transformation. As a result, we proposed a new method of embedding to capture better symmetric and composed relations. Furthermore, the self-adversarial sampling scheme is applied to reduce the influence of negative samples that do not carry meaningful information to the learning process. In addition, we also optimized the loss function by using the unlimited loss function. Experiments reflect the suggestions increasing the accuracy of the original model on the standard datasets.

Keywords: Link prediction · Knowledge graph · Rotation embedding · Hyperplane

1 Introduction

Although the concept of knowledge graph (KG) was born a long time ago, it was not until 2012 that this term became popular after Google released a dataset based on FreeBase, which raised the quality of search engine results. Next, a series of companies such as Facebook, Apple, and LinkedIn also embarked on building and exploiting graph data. Among the problems on the KG, we pay much attention to the link prediction (LP) which aims to find a triplet that does not exist in the data. LP is being widely used in all aspects of life, especially in the field of e-commerce. For example, Facebook used the LP for proposing friendships. In the scientific field, LP is used to analyze protein interactions. In the area of investigation, we predict the relationships between individuals and criminal organizations through linkage analysis.

© Springer Nature Switzerland AG 2021
N. T. Nguyen et al. (Eds.): ICCCI 2021, LNAI 12876, pp. 29–41, 2021.
https://doi.org/10.1007/978-3-030-88081-1_3

The challenges of the LP are that each relation has a different connection pattern, quality negative samples are often difficult to generate, data is large and heterogeneity [3]. These issues all affect the accuracy and timing of the prediction system. In order to solve the problems, the researchers proposed different solutions and divided them into three main groups: matrix factorization (MF), deep learning (DL), and geometric [3]. The MF is the method of viewing the KG as a 3-dimensional tensor which is decomposed into lower-dimensional vector, then the vectors are used to embed entities and relations. This method is also divided into two smaller research branches: bilinear model and non-bilinear. A bilinear model has a linear score function $\phi(h, r, t) = hrt$ in each argument. For the first entity h_{Rd} and the tail entity t_{Rd}, the model will represent the relation as a square matrix r_{Rdd}. The popular models under the bilinear model are DistMult [14], SimplE [6]. Similarly, the non-bilinear model combines the embedding of the head entity, relation, and tail entity together. However, it uses another score function, for example, circular correlation. Some well-known models are HolE [10], TuckER [1]. The advantage of MF is that it has little or no parameter sharing, so it is lightweight and easy to train.

The DL method uses deep neural networks to demonstrate the task of the LP problem. Neural networks learn parameters such as weights or deviations and combine them with input data to extract features or identify important patterns. Because of sharing the same parameters, the DL network model becomes more flexible. However, it is harder to train, heavier and more susceptible to overfitting. Models such as ConvE [4], ConvKB [9] belong to convolution neural networks, CapsE [11] belongs to capsulation neural networks.

Geometry method represents entities and relations as one-dimensional vectors and consider relation as a geometry transformation. The main idea of this approach is to synthesize the head entity and relation vectors to get a new vector and expect to be as close to the tail entity embedding vector as possible. TransE [2], TransH [13] and RotatE [12] are classic algorithms in this group. The most obvious and striking merit is the visualization of the model, explaining the cause of the connection. However, training costs are high because of many parameters, generalization is difficult because of large graph and complicated connection. Recently, many works have sought to transform geometry such as projecting relations on different spaces which improved the quality of models. This is also suitable for KGs when the properties of different relationships need a corresponding representation dimension. From that, we have analyzed and experimented with many different ideas to improve the accuracy of the model.

The remaining content of this paper is organized into 5 sections. State-of-the-art approaches in geometry-based orientation will be summarized in the next section. The second section presents the fundamental methods which led to our improvement. The proposed model is mentioned in the third section. This method is based on projection and rotation. Next, we experimented and evaluated our method to compare with state-of-the-art methods on standard datasets. Finally, we conclude what we have done and the direction to develop in the future.

2   Related Work

Except for the branch that extracts the rules directly from the graph, most LP methods start with embedding the graph into another space. A good representation retains structure and semantic information in the graph. Then depending on the model, there are a host of different ways of calculating the score. As regards the geometric approaches, the scoring function depends on vector operations to perform the moves of the head or tail entity through the relation. Besides, through the process of examining relations in the KG, it is found that the relations can be divided into four groups: one-to-one, one-to-many, many-to-one and many-to-many relations. Another classification is a relationship that is symmetry, antisymmetry, inversion and composition. Each group has different geometrical transformations and needs suitable methods. TransE [2] can be seen as one of the classics that appeared initially in this branch. TransE models each relation as a translation in the embedding space. This model has some pros and cons, which are mentioned later.

To improve the disadvantages of TransE, a series of ideas are proposed such as translating with additional embedding, combining multiple embeds with graph entities and relations. These methods not only improve the quality of the prediction but also reduces the learning costs. Two popular methods in this group are STransE [8] and CrossE [15]. The main idea of the STransE model is combining two models Structured Embeddings and TransE [2], which reduces affect of relation problems but the complexity is higher than TransE. Meanwhile, CrossE performs additional relation-specific embedding. The interactive embedding represents the entity and the relation from the cross interactions. CrossE has low complexity, rich representation and generalization, and fewer additional parameters. Another approach to improving prediction is TransH [13]. Entities have many different representations when involved in many types of relationships.

The recent approach that uses rotational transformations or combining rotation with translation instead of using pure translation. The term roto-translational is used to describe the algorithms in this group. Two methods with good results are TorusE [5] and RotatE [12]. As regards TorusE, this method embeds entities and relations in torus space. Thereby, it converts the embedded space and the n-dimensional real vector into a more compact space to avoid the problems of normalization and the embedded space is not infinitely diverging. The merit of TorusE is that it is easy to scale with large KGs, low algorithm complexity compared to other methods. Meanwhile, RotatE which models each relation as a rotation in the embedding space will be discussed in detail later.

From the significant advantages of roto-translational approach, we propose a new way of embedding for entities and relations to better predict relation types. In addition, the self-adversarial sampling scheme is applied to reduce the influence of negative samples that do not bring meaningful information to the learning process. We also optimized the loss function by switching to the unlimited loss function. Details are presented in the following sections (Fig. 1).

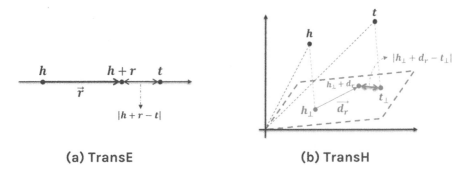

(a) TransE   (b) TransH

Fig. 1. Embedding by translating in (a) TransE, (b) TransH

3 Baseline

To begin with, we describe some symbols used in this paper. E and R is the set of entities and relations in the dataset. h, r, t represents the head entities, relations and tail entities. Bold symbols $\mathbf{h}, \mathbf{r}, \mathbf{t}$ represent the corresponding embedded vector of them. Δ represents the set of positive triplets which included in the dataset. Δ' in Eq. 1 represents the set of negative triplets, those that are randomly generated that are not in the dataset.

$$\Delta'_{(h,r,t)} = \{(h',r,t)|h' \in E, (h',r,t) \notin \Delta\} \cup \{(h,r,t')|t' \in E, (h,r,t') \notin \Delta\} \quad (1)$$

3.1 TransE

Introduced in 2013, TransE model [2] represents entities and relations as one-dimensional vectors of the same length, each relation as a translational in embedded space such that the sum of the vector embeds head and relation is expected to be as close to the tail embedding vector as possible. Given the triplet, the head or tail entity is split and put in another entity so that the newly created triplet is not in the dataset, then the distance function is applied. If the distance is within a given threshold, the newly created triplet will be treated as a valid triplet. The score function has the form:

$$\|\mathbf{h} + \mathbf{r} - \mathbf{t}\| \quad (2)$$

To optimize the embedding of entities and relations, the loss function in Eq. 3 is used.

$$L = \sum_{(h,r,t)\in\Delta} \sum_{(h',r,t')\in\Delta'_{(h,r,t)}} [\gamma + d(\mathbf{h} + \mathbf{r}, \mathbf{t}) - d(\mathbf{h}' + \mathbf{r}, \mathbf{t}')]_+ \quad (3)$$

where $\mathbf{h}, \mathbf{r}, \mathbf{t} \in \mathbb{R}^k$, $[x]_+$ is ReLU function, $\gamma > 0$ is fixed margin.

Some of the good points of TransE are that it is easy to learn, the model has low complexity and high extensibility, each relation is like a bijection between the head and tail entities, so it can model the permutation relationship.

However, TransE has some drawbacks that need to be mentioned, such as not properly handling 1-to-n, n-to-1, n-to-n relations that are symmetric and composed. Embedded entities must be on the same super hyperplane makes the ability to meet the translational constraint be limited. The learning costs are high for a model with a large number of parameters.

TransE does not handle the above categories of relations well because this model represents the same embeddings of entities which join many different relations. With a triplet (h, r, t), TransE tries to embed such that $\mathbf{h} + \mathbf{r} - \mathbf{t} = 0$. From there, there are a number of cases that could happen:

- If $(h, r, t) \in \Delta$ and $(t, r, h) \in \Delta$, r is symmetric relation, then $\mathbf{r} = 0$ and $\mathbf{h} = \mathbf{t}$.
- If $\forall i \in 0, ..., m, (h_i, r, t) \in \Delta$, r is n-to-1 relation, then $\mathbf{h}_0 = ... = \mathbf{h}_m$.
- If $\forall i \in 0, ..., n, (h, r, t_i) \in \Delta$, r is 1-to-n relation, then $\mathbf{t}_0 = ... = \mathbf{t}_n$.

The basic idea for the our proposed method starts with two models RotatE and TransH because both models have better prediction on properties of the relation than TransE.

3.2   TransH

To improve TransE's disadvantages in its ability to model the relations analyzed above, TransH [13] represents an entity in a variety of ways when it joins different relations by modelling each relation as a hyperplane $\mathbf{w}_r$ with a translational $\mathbf{d}_r$ on it. The distance function for the head and tail entities is calculated by Eq. 4.

$$f_r(\mathbf{h}, \mathbf{t}) = \|(\mathbf{h} - \mathbf{w}_r^T \mathbf{h} \mathbf{w}_r) + \mathbf{d}_r - (\mathbf{t} - \mathbf{w}_r^T \mathbf{t} \mathbf{w}_r)\|_2^2 \qquad (4)$$

where $\mathbf{w}_r, \mathbf{d}_r \in \mathbb{R}^k$, $\mathbf{h} - \mathbf{w}_r^T \mathbf{h} \mathbf{w}_r$ is the coordinate of point $\mathbf{h}$ on the hyperplane $\mathbf{w}_r$, similar to $\mathbf{t}$.

Specifically, the head entity ($\mathbf{h}$), after being projected onto the hyperplane ($\mathbf{h}_\perp$) and translating to $\mathbf{d}_r$, is expected to be close to the tail entity on the hyperplane ($\mathbf{t}$). The simple scoring function is considered as:

$$\|\mathbf{h}_\perp + \mathbf{d}_r - \mathbf{t}_\perp\|_2^2 \qquad (5)$$

and is expected to be within the threshold γ, long-distance triplets will be treated as invalid triplets. To distinguish between the positive triplets and the negative triplets, the loss function based on the margin-based ranking loss is used:

$$L = \sum_{(h,r,t) \in \Delta} \sum_{(h',r',t') \in \Delta'_{(h,r,t)}} [f_r(\mathbf{h}, \mathbf{t}) + \gamma - f_{r'}(\mathbf{h}', \mathbf{t}')]_+ \qquad (6)$$

The most striking and obvious advantage of these models is well predictions of symmetric, antisymmetric, inverse and composed relations (Fig. 2).

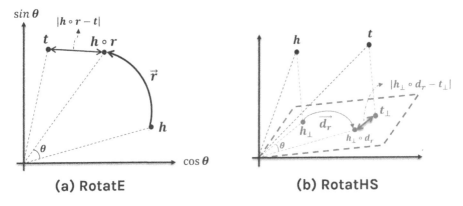

Fig. 2. Embedding by rotation embeddings in (a) RotatE, (b) RotatHS

3.3   RotatE

The idea of the RotatE model [12] starts from the Euler equation: $e^{i\theta} = \cos\theta + i\sin\theta$, the complex number i is seen as a rotation in the complex space. The RotatE treats each relation as a rotation in an embedded space. Specifically, the head entity $\mathbf{h}$ after rotating an angle θ ($\theta \in [0, 2\pi]$) corresponding to each relationship is expected to be close to the tail entity $\mathbf{t}$ according to the L1 standard. The distance function:

$$\|\mathbf{h} \circ \mathbf{r} - \mathbf{t}\| \tag{7}$$

where $\mathbf{h}, \mathbf{r}, \mathbf{t} \in \mathbb{C}^k, r_i = \pm 1$ is expected within the given threshold γ.

For each dimension i in complex space then $\mathbf{t}_i = \mathbf{h}_i r_i$ where $|r_i| = 1$. Loss function is used to optimize the model based on distance:

$$L = -\log\sigma(\gamma - d_r(\mathbf{h}, \mathbf{t})) - \sum_{i=1}^{n} \frac{1}{k}\log\sigma(d_r(\mathbf{h}'_i, \mathbf{t}'_i) - \gamma) \tag{8}$$

where γ is the fixed margin, σ is the sigmoid function and (h'_i, r, t'_i) is the i-th negative triplet.

In addition, self-adversarial negative sampling is used to reduce the influence of negative samples that do not bring meaningful information to the learning process, the loss function now becomes:

$$L = -\log\sigma(\gamma - d_r(\mathbf{h}, \mathbf{t})) - \sum_{i=1}^{n} p(h'_i, r, t'_i)\log\sigma(d_r(\mathbf{h}'_i, \mathbf{t}'_i) - \gamma) \tag{9}$$

Some merits of the RotatE model can be mentioned such as the linear complexity of space and time making the model easy to expand with large graphs, good predictions with many relations such as symmetry, antisymmetry, inversion and composition.

4   Our Proposed Model

On the other hand, the two algorithms mentioned above still have some demerits that we need to consider. Regarding RotatE, this model only represents the same embeddings for head and tail entities with different kinds of relations. Besides, our experimental results show that TransH does not work well with 1-to-n and n-to-1 relations. To improve the embedding results of these models, the RotatHS model is given to be able to help entities have many different representations depending on their relations and improve predictive results across categories of relations between each other.

4.1   Rotation Matrix

For each relation r provides a rotation matrix R which is the transformation matrix used to represent a rotation in Euclidean space. Matrix:

$$R = \begin{bmatrix} \cos\theta & -\sin\theta \\ \cos\theta & \sin\theta \end{bmatrix} \tag{10}$$

where $\theta \in [0, 2\pi]$, rotates the points on the xy-plane counterclockwise by an angle θ to the Ox axis in the Oxy coordinate system.

To find the coordinate of point h' after rotating the point $h(x, y)$ with an angle θ, we have:

$$h_r = R\mathbf{h} = \begin{bmatrix} \cos\theta & -\sin\theta \\ \cos\theta & \sin\theta \end{bmatrix} \begin{bmatrix} x \\ y \end{bmatrix} = \begin{bmatrix} x\cos\theta - y\sin\theta \\ x\sin\theta + y\cos\theta \end{bmatrix} \tag{11}$$

where x is regarded as the dimension of real number and y is the dimension of imaginary number. The point h' after the rotation has coordinates $(x\cos\theta - y\sin\theta, x\sin\theta + y\cos\theta)$.

4.2   Projection on Hyperplane

For each relation r, vector $\mathbf{w}_r = [x_0, x_1, ..., x_k]$ is created where k is the number of dimensions of the embedding space representing the relation-specific hyperplane.

Let $a \in \mathbb{R}$ be the ratio of the distance from point $\mathbf{h}$ to the hyperplane corresponding to vector $\mathbf{w}_r$:

$$\mathbf{h} - \mathbf{h}_\perp = a\mathbf{w}_r \tag{12}$$

Let the distance from point $\mathbf{h}$ to the hyperplane be $d_{\mathbf{h}, \mathbf{w}_r}$, we have:

$$d_{\mathbf{h}, \mathbf{w}_r} = \frac{\mathbf{w}_r^T \mathbf{h}}{\|\mathbf{w}_r\|_2} = a \Rightarrow \mathbf{h} - \mathbf{h}_\perp = \frac{\mathbf{w}_r^T \mathbf{h}}{\|\mathbf{w}_r\|_2} \mathbf{w}_r \tag{13}$$

Restricting $\|\mathbf{w}_r\|_2 = 1$, the coordinate of point $\mathbf{h}$ on the embedded space is calculated by following the formula:

$$\mathbf{h}_\perp = \mathbf{w}_r^T \mathbf{h} \mathbf{w}_r \tag{14}$$

4.3 RotatHS Model

Combining two models TransH and RotatE, RotatHS considers each relation as a hyperplane, projects the head and tail entities on the plane corresponding to the relations that they join, then rotates the head entity which is on the hyperplane with the relation-specific angle. After rotation, the point is expected to close to the tail entity on the hyperplane. To be more precise, the concept of this model is divided into 3 steps:

- **Step 1:** Vectors $\mathbf{w}_r$ are created corresponding to relation r, head and tail entities are projected onto the hyperplane, we have:

$$\mathbf{h}_\perp = \mathbf{h} - \mathbf{w}_r^T \mathbf{h} \mathbf{w}_r \text{ and } \mathbf{t}_\perp = \mathbf{t} - \mathbf{w}_r^T \mathbf{t} \mathbf{w}_r \qquad (15)$$

  where $\mathbf{h}_\perp$ and $\mathbf{t}_\perp$ are the coordinates of $\mathbf{h}$ and $\mathbf{t}$ projected on the hyperplane $\mathbf{w}_r$, and $\mathbf{h}, \mathbf{w}_r, \mathbf{t} \in \mathbb{C}^k$.
- **Step 2:** Rotating point $\mathbf{h}$ by angle θ_r corresponding to the relation:

$$\mathbf{h}_r = \mathbf{h}_\perp \circ \mathbf{d}_\perp \qquad (16)$$

  where $\mathbf{h}_r$ is the coordinate of $\mathbf{h}_\perp$ after rotation, and $\mathbf{d}_\perp$ is calculated based on the Eq. 10, $\mathbf{h}_r$ is expected to be distance from $\mathbf{t}_\perp$ within the threshold γ.
- **Step 3:** Calculating the distance between 2 points $\mathbf{h}_r$ and $\mathbf{t}_\perp$:

$$f(h, r, t) = \|\mathbf{h}_r - \mathbf{t}_\perp\|_2^2 \qquad (17)$$

By doing these steps, the overall score function is used in RotatHS model:

$$f_r(\mathbf{h}, \mathbf{t}) = \|(\mathbf{h} - \mathbf{w}_r^T \mathbf{h} \mathbf{w}_r) \circ \mathbf{d}_r - (\mathbf{t} - \mathbf{w}_r^T \mathbf{t} \mathbf{w}_r)\|_2^2 \qquad (18)$$

To optimize the model after each step, the loss function is used:

$$L = -\log \sigma(\gamma - f_r(\mathbf{h}, \mathbf{t})) - \sum_{i=1}^{n} \frac{1}{k} \log \sigma(f_r(\mathbf{h}_i', \mathbf{t}_i') - \gamma) \qquad (19)$$

where σ is the sigmoid function, $f_r(\mathbf{h}, \mathbf{t})$ is the above scoring function.

This is a loss function similar to that for negative sampling [7], which is often ineffective because it is considered that the probabilities of the negative triplets are the same while some of the negative samples remain completely insignificant during training process. Therefore, self-adversarial negative sampling is used to create negative triplets based on the embedding model, negative triplets is taken according to distribution:

$$p(h_j', r, t_j' | \{(h_i, r_i, t_i)\}) = \frac{\exp \alpha f_r(\mathbf{h}_j', \mathbf{t}_j')}{\sum_i \exp \alpha f_r(\mathbf{h}_i', \mathbf{t}_i')} \qquad (20)$$

where α is the temperature of sampling. The loss function becomes:

$$L = -\log \sigma(\gamma - f_r(\mathbf{h}, \mathbf{t})) - \sum_{i=1}^{n} p(h_i', r, t_i') \log \sigma(f_r(\mathbf{h}_i', \mathbf{t}_i') - \gamma) \qquad (21)$$

In addition, there are three restrictions on offer to minimize the loss function.

$$\forall e \in E, \|e\|_2 \leq 1$$

$$\forall r \in R, \frac{|\mathbf{w}_r^T \mathbf{d}_r|}{\|\mathbf{d}_r\|_2} \leq \epsilon$$

$$\forall r \in R, \|\mathbf{w}_r\|_2 = 1 \tag{22}$$

Instead of optimizing the loss function directly with constraints, soft constraints are more flexible by switching to the unlimited loss function:

$$L = -\log \sigma(\gamma - f_r(\mathbf{h}, \mathbf{t})) - \sum_{i=1}^{n} p(h_i', r, t_i') \log \sigma(f_r(\mathbf{h}_i', \mathbf{t}_i') - \gamma)$$

$$+ C\left\{ \sum_{e \in E} [\|e\|_2^2 - 1]_+ + \sum_{r \in R} [\frac{(\mathbf{w}_r^T \mathbf{d}_r)^2}{\|\mathbf{d}_r\|_2^2} - \epsilon^2]_+ \right\} \tag{23}$$

where C is the regularization parameter that evaluates the influence of soft constraints. Adam optimizer is used to reduce loss after each training epoch. Adam optimizer is an optimization algorithm that can be used instead of SGD to repeatedly update network weights based on training data.

5   Experiments

5.1   Datasets

We used five benchmarks datasets to evaluate the proposed model. Specifically, these are FB15k [2], FB15k-237 [3], WN18 [2], and WN18RR [4].

FB15k and FB15k-237 is the subset of the Freebase dataset, which is multiple domains about movies, sports, awards, actors, sport clubs. The FB15k dataset consists of 14951 entities and 1345 relations. The FB15k dataset has test leakage properties while the FB15k-237 removes the test leakage relations in the FB15k dataset. FB15k-237 consists of 14541 entities and 237 relations.

WN18 and WN18RR is the subset of the WordNet dataset, which is a dataset of the English vocabulary. The WN18 dataset consists of 40943 entities and 18 relations. The WN18 dataset has test leakage properties while the WN18RR removes 7 test leakage relations in the WN18RR dataset. WN18RR consists of 40943 entities and 11 relations.

5.2   Parameters and Metrics

We rerun the base models with the settings based on the original articles. It was then adjusted to suit the experimental hardware as well as the results. To be more precise, we set $k = 1000, batch\_size = 1024, negative\_size = 256, adver = 1.0$ for FreeBase dataset while the WordNet datasets are implemented with $k = 500, batch\_size = 512, negative\_size = 1024, adver = 0.5$.

To evaluate the models, we use common metrics including Mean Rank (MR), Mean Reciprocal Rank (MRR), Hits@K [3].

5.3   Environment

The experiment was conducted on a machine with Ubuntu 18.04 operating system, Intel (X) Xeon (R) CPU E5-2698 v4 @ 2.20 Ghz, 26 GB RAM and 32 GB NVIDIA Tesla V100-DGXS GPU. The source code is programmed in Python language with the support of the Pytorch library.

5.4   Results

We inherit and develop the source code from the publicly available RotatE [12]. RotatE and TransH models are run with the same parameters as the original articles published to draw the chart below. Our RotatHS model is implemented with the parameters mentioned in the previous section. The remaining classical algorithms we extracted from the available publications illustrate the improvement of the proposed model. Detailed results are shown in Table 1 and Table 2.

Table 1. Results of models with test leakage datasets

	FB15k					WN18				
	MRR	MR	Hits@1	Hits@3	Hits@10	MRR	MR	Hits@1	Hits@3	Hits@10
DistMult	0.784	173	0.736	–	0.863	0.824	675	0.726	–	0.946
SimplE	0.726	138	0.661	–	0.836	0.938	759	0.933	–	0.946
TransE	0.628	45	0.494	–	0.847	0.646	279	0.406	–	0.949
STransE	0.543	69	0.398	–	0.796	0.656	208	0.431	–	0.935
CrossE	0.702	136	0.601	–	0.862	0.934	441	0.733	–	0.950
TorusE	0.746	143	0.689	–	0.840	0.947	525	0.943	–	0.954
ConvE	0.688	51	0.595	–	0.849	0.945	413	0.939	–	0.957
ConvKB	0.211	324	0.114	–	0.408	0.709	202	0.529	–	0.949
TransH	0.748	32	0.661	0.813	0.884	0.823	452	0.721	0.929	0.954
RotatE	0.797	40	0.746	0.830	0.884	0.949	309	0.944	0.952	0.959
RotatHS	0.789	43	0.736	0.824	0.880	0.948	326	0.941	0.951	0.959

A quick glance at Table 1, we can see that our RotatHS model predicts quite well on the FB15k and WN18 datasets. The MRR and Hits@K results have the second best compared other methods and just slightly lower than RotatE results, except Hits@10 values on the WN18 dataset. As can be seen from Table 2, the RotatHS model predicts quite well on the measures using different benchmark datasets compared to other models. Despite not good result on the MR metric, the results on the remaining 4 measures are superior to the 2 baseline models (RotatE and TransH) and the given state-of-the-art models.

In addition, we examine the performance of RotatHS on a variety of categories of relation: 1-to-1, 1-to-n, n-to-1, n-to-n. Results of the RotatHS model on different relation types using different datasets are summarized in Table 3 and Table 4. The prediction head is computed by taking each of the positive triplets, removing the head entity, keeping the relation and tail entity. After that, we choose a number of entities to replace and predict if the newly created triplets

Table 2. Results of models with no test leakage datasets

	FB15k-237					WN18RR				
	MRR	MR	Hits@1	Hits@3	Hits@10	MRR	MR	Hits@1	Hits@3	Hits@10
DistMult	0.313	199	0.224	–	0.490	0.433	5913	0.397	–	0.502
SimplE	0.179	651	0.100	–	0.344	0.398	8764	0.383	–	0.427
TransE	0.310	209	0.217	–	0.496	0.206	3936	0.028	–	0.495
STransE	0.315	357	0.225	–	0.496	0.226	5172	0.101	–	0.422
CrossE	0.298	227	0.212	–	0.405	0.405	5212	0.381	–	0.450
TorusE	0.281	211	0.196	–	0.447	<u>0.463</u>	4873	0.427	–	0.534
ConvE	0.305	281	0.219	–	0.476	0.427	4944	0.390	–	0.508
ConvKB	0.230	309	0.140	–	0.415	0.249	<u>3429</u>	0.056	–	0.525
TransH	<u>0.339</u>	**168**	<u>0.243</u>	<u>0.375</u>	0.531	0.233	4345	0.044	0.395	0.524
RotatE	0.337	<u>177</u>	0.241	<u>0.375</u>	<u>0.533</u>	**0.477**	**3340**	<u>0.428</u>	0.492	**0.571**
RotatHS	**0.342**	181	**0.245**	**0.381**	**0.537**	**0.477**	4525	**0.436**	**0.493**	<u>0.557</u>

Table 3. Prediction head results of RotatHS on datasets

RotatHS	FB15k				WN18			
	1-to-1	1-to-n	n-to-1	n-to-n	1-to-1	1-to-n	n-to-1	n-to-n
MRR	0.879	0.939	0.474	0.797	0.976	0.959	0.943	0.939
MR	147	16	177	27	798	106	485	414
Hits@1	0.848	0.919	0.408	0.741	0.976	0.953	0.936	0.931
Hits@3	0.910	0.953	0.498	0.835	0.976	0.960	0.949	0.943
Hits@10	0.924	0.971	0.606	0.893	0.976	0.968	0.953	0.954

are valid or not. It means we need to predict $(?, r, t)$. Similarly, we need to predict $(h, r, ?)$ with prediction tail.

From Table 3, we can see that the model works well on the three relation categories: 1-1, 1-n, and n-n when predicting head in FB15k dataset. The main reason is that these three datasets contain information about multiple domains. As regards WN18 dataset which is constructed by a strict structure, the results in different types of relations are almost similar.

From Table 4, we can see that RotatHS is good on three relation types: 1-1, n-1 and n-n when predicting the tail entity in FB15k dataset. The results on the WN18 dataset are quite uniform across all relation types.

Figure 3a shows the values of loss gradually decreasing through epochs, which proves the effectiveness of our model. Two datasets, WN18 and WN18RR, are converging quite early, ranging from epochs 40,000 while two remaining datasets, FB15k and FB15k237, converge at epoch 80,000 and 60,000 corresponding. As can be seen from Fig. 3b, RotatHS model is significantly superior to RotatE and TransH on the FB15k-237 dataset.

Table 4. Prediction tail results of RotatHS on datasets

RotatHS	FB15k				WN18			
	1-to-1	1-to-n	n-to-1	n-to-n	1-to-1	1-to-n	n-to-1	n-to-n
MRR	0.882	0.611	0.913	0.823	0.976	0.939	0.960	0.936
MR	110	169	18	19	33	482	110	433
Hits@1	0.850	0.567	0.881	0.764	0.976	0.932	0.954	0.930
Hits@3	0.908	0.629	0.937	0.864	0.976	0.942	0.963	0.939
Hits@10	0.924	0.698	0.964	0.919	0.976	0.949	0.973	0.948

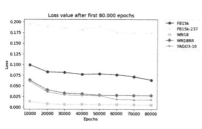

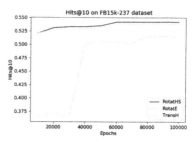

(a) Loss value after first 80,000 epochs in RotatHS training

(b) Hits@10 values on validation set per epoch

Fig. 3. Experiment of lost value and Hits@10

6   Conclusion

In this paper, we base on the geometry approach to train the model for the problem of LP in KG. Start with the analysis and assessment of pros and cons of two models having good results, the RotatE and the TransH model. Then, a new vertex and relation embedding method is proposed to represent the embedding more suitable for the problem. Specifically, the head and tail entity is initially projected onto the hyperplane corresponding to each relation. Next, the head entity is rotated at a relation-specific angle so that after rotation, the point is the closest distance to the projected point of the tail entity. To reduce the effect of negative samples containing little meaningful information for the learning process, we adopt the self-adversarial sampling scheme. The loss function of the model is updated to an unlimited loss function. Experimental results evaluated on the standard data sets show that the changes bring about significant improvements. In the future, we will consider each relation in detail and justify the suitable transformation for them.

Acknowledgements. This research is funded by the Faculty of Information Technology, University of Science, VNU-HCM, Vietnam, Grant number CNTT 2021-03 and Advanced Program in Computer Science.

References

1. Balaževič, I., Allen, C. and Hospedales, T.M.: TuckER: tensor factorization for knowledge graph completion. In: Proceedings of the 2019 Conference on Empirical Methods in Natural Language Processing and the 9th International Joint Conference on Natural Language Processing (EMNLP-IJCNLP) (2019)
2. Bordes, A., Usunier, N., Garcia-Duran, A., Weston, J., Yakhnenko, O.: Translating embeddings for modeling multi-relational data. In: Neural Information Processing Systems (NIPS), pp. 1–9 (2013)
3. Cai, H., Zheng, V.W., Chang, K.C.C.: A comprehensive survey of graph embedding: problems, techniques, and applications. IEEE Trans. Knowl. Data Eng. **30**(9), 1616–1637 (2018)
4. Dettmers, T., Minervini, P., Stenetorp, P., Riedel, S.: Convolutional 2D knowledge graph embeddings. In: Proceedings of the AAAI Conference on Artificial Intelligence, vol. 32, no. 1 (2018)
5. Ebisu, T., Ichise, R.: TorusE: knowledge graph embedding on a lie group. In: Proceedings of the AAAI Conference on Artificial Intelligence, vol. 32, no. 1 (2018)
6. Kazemi, S.M., Poole, D.: Simple embedding for link prediction in knowledge graphs. In: NeurIPS (2018)
7. Mikolov, T., Sutskever, I., Chen, K., Corrado, G., Dean, J.: Distributed representations of words and phrases and their compositionality. In: Proceedings of the 26th International Conference on Neural Information Processing Systems, Volume 2 (NIPS 2013) (2013)
8. Nguyen, D.Q., Sirts, K., Qu, L., Johnson, M.: STransE: a novel embedding model of entities and relationships in knowledge bases. In: Proceedings of the 2016 Conference of the North American Chapter of the Association for Computational Linguistics: Human Language Technologies, pp. 460–466 (2016)
9. Nguyen, D.Q., Nguyen, T.D., Nguyen, D.Q., Phung, D.: A novel embedding model for knowledge base completion based on convolutional neural network. In: Proceedings of the 2018 Conference of the North American Chapter of the Association for Computational Linguistics: Human Language Technologies, Volume 2 (Short Papers), pp. 327–333 (2018)
10. Rocktäschel, T., Riedel, S.: End-to-end differentiable proving. In: NIPS, pp. 3791–3803 (2017)
11. Sabour, S., Frosst, N., Hinton, G.E.: Dynamic routing between capsules. In: 31st Conference on Neural Information Processing Systems (NIPS 2017) (2017)
12. Sun, Z., Deng, Z.H., Nie, J.Y., Tang, J.: Rotate: knowledge graph embedding by relational rotation in complex space. In: Seventh International Conference on Learning Representations (2019)
13. Wang, Z., Zhang, J., Feng, J., Chen, Z.: Knowledge graph embedding by translating on hyperplanes. In: Proceedings of the AAAI Conference on Artificial Intelligence, vol. 28, no. 1 (2014)
14. Yang, B., Yih, W.T., He, X., Gao, J., Deng, L.: Embedding entities and relations for learning and inference in knowledge bases. In: Proceedings of the International Conference on Learning Representations (ICLR) (2015)
15. Zhang, W., Paudel, B., Zhang, W., Bernstein, A., Chen, H.: Interaction embeddings for prediction and explanation in knowledge graphs. In: Proceedings of the Twelfth ACM International Conference on Web Search and Data Mining, pp. 96–104 (2019)

Assessing Ontology Alignments on the Level of Instances

Bogumiła Hnatkowska[1] , Adrianna Kozierkiewicz[1] , Marcin Pietranik[1]([⊠]) ,
and Hai Bang Truong[2]

[1] Faculty of Computer Science and Management, Wroclaw University of Science
and Technology, Wybrzeze Wyspianskiego 27, 50-370 Wroclaw, Poland
{bogumila.hnatkowska,adrianna.kozierkiewicz,marcin.pietranik}@pwr.edu.pl
[2] Faculty of Information Technology, Nguyen Tat Thanh University,
Ho Chi Minh City, Vietnam
thbang@ntt.edu.vn

Abstract. Metrics, such as Precision and Recall, are used to evaluate
ontologies at both the design and application stages. The aim of the
paper is to introduce two metrics that assess ontology alignments at
the instance level, which can be used by people interested in ontology
integration. These metrics allow to select the best mapping from existing
ones. The usefulness of the metrics has been confirmed by their practical
and experimental validation.

1 Introduction

Ontologies, due to their semantic expressivity, are a common tool of knowledge
representations. At their core, they contain a set of concepts (which represent
classes of objects from some universe of discourse) and relations defined between
them. Those concepts are also described with instances that can be understood as
specific materializations of the concepts. Such approach asserts great flexibility
in modeling of some assumed universe of discourse.

However, the aforementioned flexibility is a source of the biggest obstacle if
the communication of two independent information systems that utilize ontologies is expected. The common solution for this problem is called ontology alignment and it can be treated as a method of providing a bridge between two
ontologies. Formally, it is a set of corresponding elements taken from aligned
ontologies. In the literature, it is easy to find a plethora of methods for providing ontology alignments.

The most common way of evaluating the quality of the alignment method
is using benchmark data provided by Ontology Alignment Evaluation Initiative
(OAEI). These benchmarks contain a set of ontologies and their validated alignments. Such alignment can be therefore treated as a reference alignment with
which the outcomes of different ontology alignments methods can be confronted.

In practical scenarios (for example, when the of interoperability of Internet
of Things platforms is required [4]), no one can expect that any kind of reference

© Springer Nature Switzerland AG 2021
N. T. Nguyen et al. (Eds.): ICCCI 2021, LNAI 12876, pp. 42–52, 2021.
https://doi.org/10.1007/978-3-030-88081-1_4

alignment exists. However, the need of assessing two competing alignments still remains. Therefore, we developed two novel approaches to assessing ontology alignments that do not require such a reference mapping. The first one is built on top of the criterion based on the depth of concepts in their hierarchy, while the second is based on a criterion of continuity of mappings. Both can be used to assess mappings of concepts and instances. In our earlier publication [10] we presented the experimental evaluation of those methods used on the level of concepts. In this paper, we present the experimental results gathered on the level of instances.

The remainder of the article is structured as follows. In Sect. 2 an overview of related research is provided. In Sect. 3 we provide basic mathematical notions that are used throughout the paper. The main contribution of the article can be found in Sects. 4 and 5 which respectively contain the developed algorithms and results obtained from their experimental evaluation. The final conclusion and a brief description of our upcoming research plans can be found in the last section.

2   Related Works

The number of systems for ontology alignment determination increases each year. However, the results of developed systems have different quality. This problem has been noticed by OAEI (Ontology Alignment Evaluation Initiative). Since 2004, OAEI organizes annual campaigns aiming at evaluating ontology matching technologies. OAEI provides the benchmark datasets which contain a set of ontologies and reference alignment which plays the role of the "gold standard". The mappings determined by competing systems are compared with this reference alignment. The assessment criteria are execution time, the number of correspondences, precision, recall, recall+, F-measure, and consistency [2]. Precision and recall are the most widely used, however, they are not ideal in the context of assessing ontology mappings.

The main problem of the method described above is their binary characteristic [3]. They compare only two sets of correspondences without considering if these correspondences are semantically equivalent. Considering values of recall and precision separately also entails many problems. Considering only precision it is easy to create an empty set of mappings and obtain the highest precision. On the other hand, an alignment containing all possible correspondences would have a 100% recall.

The F-measure is a harmonic mean of the precision and recall values free from aforementioned drawbacks. In the literature there exist some modification of the mentioned measures like a semantic version of recall and precision [3], recall+ [1] or conservativity and consistency principles violations [13,14], however, all mentioned methods for ontology mappings assessment requires reference alignments. Creating benchmark alignments is cost- and time-consuming. In a real situation, assessing a mapping by comparing it with the gold standard is actually impossible. Thus, the easiest method for mappings assessment is based on involving domain expert [6], however, such a solution may be error-prone when ontologies and their alignments are relatively large.

It is completely impractical and impossible to create reference mappings during the development of ontology-based systems. In [5] authors proposed an alternative evaluation method based on estimating the number of the most frequently used correspondences. The authors assumed that evaluation of a random sample of all correspondences can be generalized to the results to get an estimate of the quality of the alignment as a whole. However, this evaluation method requires end-user support (which filled a prepared query scenario) and is not fully automatic

In [7] authors introduced quality measures that are based on the notion of mapping incoherence. Such a solution was motivated by the idea that the incoherence of mapping will hinder its sensible use even though it might contain a significant amount of correct correspondences. The main problem of the proposed measure is the lack of experimental verification or application in a real system.

Different approaches have been proposed in [15] where some quality metrics to assess the logical soundness of the alignment was defined. Authors additionally developed an approach to detect and minimize the violations of the so-called conservativity principle where novel subsumption entailments between named concepts in one of the input ontologies are considered unwanted.

To the best of our knowledge, the problem of the evaluation of the quality of alignment has not been widely investigated. Our thesis is also confirmed in [16] where authors pointed out that there is significant room for future work on the challenges relevant to these metrics. Existing work primarily consists of manually intensive evaluation strategies that were uniquely developed for particular cases. This paper is an extension of our previous paper [10] where the proposed measures has been defined, but not experimentally verified.

3   Basic Notions

The further parts of the paper are based on the base definition of ontologies which is a tuple:

$$O = (C, H, R^C, I, R^I) \tag{1}$$

where C represents the set of concepts; H denotes concepts' hierarchy; R^C is a set of concept relations such that $R^C = \{r_1^C, r_2^C, ..., r_n^C\}$, $n \in N$ and $\forall_{r_i^C \in R^C} r_i^C \subset C \times C$. I represents a set of instances, while $R^I = \{r_1^I, r_2^I, ..., r_n^I\}$ is a set of instance relations.

For clarity, we define a number of auxiliary functions. $Type(O, i)$ is a function which for given instance i returns a set of concepts from C to which it is assigned. On the other hand, by $Ins(O, c)$ we denote a function which for a given concept c returns a set of all of its instances. The taxonomy denoted in the Eq. 1 as H, allows to track hierarchical relations between concepts. Its root is an abstract concept *Thing*, from which all other concepts inherit. In consequence it is possible to define a number of related properties.

Definition 1. *For a given ontology O the depth of its hierarchy H (denoted as $Depth(O)$) is the number of sub-consumption relationships that exist between the concept Thing and the most distant inheritance hierarchy of the concepts from that ontology.*

Definition 2. *For a given ontology O and one of its concepts c, the depth of this concept (denoted as $Depth(O, c)$) is the highest number of subsumption relationships in H between the considered concept and the concept Thing.*

Designating a mapping between two ontologies can be described as finding their common parts. The result of such process is a set of correspondences between elements from two compared ontologies, connected by some kind of relationship (equivalence, refinement, generalization) and its confidence level.

Definition 3. *For two ontologies O^1 and O^2, an alignment A between them can be defined as a set of tuples $\langle e^1, e^2, r, n \rangle$ (referred to as correspondences). e^1, e^2 are elements from O^1 and O^2 respectively (either concepts or instances). A relationship $r \in \{=, <, >\}$ is a connection describing a type of correspondence (equivalence, refinement, generalization) and $n \in [0,1]$ is a real number representing a confidence level of a correspondence. Note that both e^1 and e^2 must be elements from the same level.*

The formal definition from Eq. 1 entails that there are three distinguished levels of ontology mappings: concepts, instances and relations. However, the aforementioned OAEI organization and the majority of ontology mapping tools address only the levels of concepts and instances. In our previous publication [10] we focused on the level of concepts. For this reason, in this paper we focused only on the ontology alignment on the level of instances.

4   Methods of Ontology Alignment Assessment

4.1   Criterion Based on the Depth of the Mapped Classes

In our research, we claim that aligning concepts that are located deeper in their hierarchy are more important than alignments of general concepts placed shallow in the taxonomy. Starting with the most general concepts which categorise elements of the universe of discourse at a high level of abstraction, more and more complications may appear as concepts go deeper into ontology. The deeper the concepts are in the hierarchy, the more detailed knowledge they expresses, and, therefore, providing alignments of such concepts may be more difficult. In consequence, alignments of instances of such "deep" concepts are also more valuable.

These remarks are a backbone of the criterion, calculated as a function ψ_D, based on the depth of the mapped classes. It is based on the analysis of the concepts the instances belong to. If the concepts of mapped instances are disjoint, then the value of ψ_D is equal to 0. Otherwise, ψ_D is designated based on the depth of the concepts in the ontology. Since instances may belong to multiple concepts we introduce an auxiliary function ψ_D^C which can be used to evaluate instance mapping for two particular concepts. Formally it can be defined as:

$$\psi_D^C(O^1, O^2, c, c') = \begin{cases} \frac{1}{Depth(O^1) - Depth(O^1, c)) + 1} + \frac{1}{Depth(O^2) - Depth(O^2, c') + 1} & \text{if } c \equiv c' \\ 0 & \text{if } c \not\equiv c' \end{cases} \quad (2)$$

Formally, the overall evaluation function ψ_D for correspondence $corr_{ii'} = \langle i, i', =, n \rangle$ (one of the elements of the alignment A from Definition 3) of two instances from ontologies O^1 and O^2 is defined as:

$$\psi_D(O^1, O^2, A, corr_{ii'}) = \max_{(c,c') \in Type(O^1,i) \times Type(O^2,i')} \psi_D^C(O^1, O^2, c, c') \quad (3)$$

The evaluation function of ontology alignments $\sigma_D : \tilde{O} \times \tilde{O} \times \tilde{A} \to \mathbb{R}^+$, based on the depth of the classes of mapped instances, accepts two ontologies and their alignment as an input and returns sum of ψ_D calculated for all instance correspondences'. $\tilde{O}$ denotes a set of all possible ontologies and $\tilde{A}$ a set of all possible alignments. Formally, σ_D is defined as:

$$\sigma_D(O^1, O^2, A) = \sum_{corr_{ii'} \in A} \psi_D(O^1, O^2, A, corr_{ii'}), \quad (4)$$

When a mapping consists of instances classified into detailed concepts placed deeper in the taxonomical hierarchy is more expressive, it carries more meaning about the interoperability of ontologies. In other words - it describes in more detail how two ontologies cover some topic.

For example, when two medical systems, which utilize different ontologies (e.g. SNOMED-CT or ICD10), need to communicate it is necessary to find which parts of their knowledge bases refer to the same concepts in the real world [11]. In this context, we can claim that exchanging specific messages, which contain knowledge of certain medical conditions, is more useful than communicating through messages containing only generic, high-level concepts. Therefore, the practical assessment of the proposed measure is very high, entailing its usefulness for ontology engineers who require to evaluate ontology alignments.

4.2   Criterion Based on the Continuity of Mapped Classes

In this section, we present the second ontology alignment evaluation function, based on the continuity of mapped classes. It favors alignments of instances of concepts that are less dispersed and cover certain parts of the domain in more detail. Differences of this type may appear if one of the compared tools of ontology alignment incorporates some general knowledge and basic methods of finding correspondences, while the other mapping approaches can find less obvious connections. The final ontology alignment provided by the latter approach is far more valuable, even if its size is relatively small. Only advanced ontology mapping methods can produce mapping more focused on certain ontology fragments, providing more detailed outcomes.

For this criterion, an auxiliary measure ψ_C that gets a set of instances s was defined:

$$\psi_C(s) = |s_A|^2, \tag{5}$$

where $|s_A|$ is the number of instances mapped by alignment A.

The function $\sigma_C : \tilde{O} \times \tilde{O} \times \tilde{A} \to \mathbb{N}$, which is an ontology alignment evaluation method based on the continuity of the mapped instances, accepts two ontologies and their alignment as in input, and returns sum of all ψ_C of mapped instances sets. $\tilde{O}$ is a set of all possible ontologies, and $\tilde{A}$ denotes a set of all ontology alignments. The function is formally defined below:

$$\sigma_C(O^1, O^2, A) = \sum_{c \in C^1} \psi_C(Ins(O^1, c)) + \sum_{c \in C^2} \psi_C(Ins(O^2, c)), \tag{6}$$

where $Ins(O^1, c)$ and $Ins(O^2, c)$ are the sets of instances of the given classes.

Algorithm 1. Evaluation based on the continuity of mapped instances

---

Require: O^1, O^2, A
Ensure: σ_C
1: $\sigma_C^{O^1} \leftarrow$ GETINSTANCECONSISTENCYSCORE (A, O^1)
2: $\sigma_C^{O^2} \leftarrow$ GETINSTANCECONSISTENCYSCORE (A, O^2)
3: $\sigma_C \leftarrow \sigma_C^{O^1} + \sigma_C^{O^2}$
4: **return** σ_C
5: **procedure** GETINSTANCECONSISTENCYSCORE(A, O)
6:       $\sigma_C^O \leftarrow 0$
7:       **for all** $c \in C$ **do**
8:             $s \leftarrow Ins(O, c)$
9:             $s_A \leftarrow$ empty collection
10:            **for all** $ins \in s$ **do**
11:                  **if** $\exists_{corr_{ii'} \in A}(ins = i \vee ins = i')$ **then**
12:                        add ins to s_A
13:                  **end if**
14:            **end for**
15:            $\psi_C = size(s_A)^2$
16:            $\sigma_C^O \leftarrow \sigma_C^O + \psi_C$
17:      **end for**
18:      **return** σ_C^O
19: **end procedure**

The method of calculating values of σ_C function is presented on Algorithm 1. Within in, an auxiliary function *getInstanceConsistencyScore* is defined (line 5), which eventually used for both ontologies (lines 1–2). It iterates through concepts from the given ontology (line 7) and for each of them generates a set of its instances (line 12) which are present in the given alignment (line 11). Such each of such sets the value of ψ_C is calculated which increases the overall evaluation rating σ_C^O (lines 15–16). The procedure returns its outcome (line 18) and the final value of the algorithm is calculated as the sum of the scores of both ontologies (line 3).

The usefulness of the presented method is straightforward. It gives a different perspective on ontology alignment but is similarly useful to the ontology alignment evaluation function presented in Sect. 4.1. It follows a common sense approach to ontology development - for two competing ontology mappings, the one which contains mappings of instances of concepts that are closely related (therefore, more focused on a single topic of interest) should be treated as better (for example, due to its expressivity).

Given the context of two communicating medical systems from the end of Sect. 4.1, a detailed message exchange about a selected topic is more valuable than a sketchy communication addressing multiple different topics. Therefore, the ontology alignment assessment method based on the continuity of mapped classes can be very useful for ontology developers whose applications require the practical evaluation of ontology alignments.

5   Experimental Verification

Metrics, to be used effectively, require validation, which can be done practically, theoretically, and/or empirically [8,12]. The practical evaluation of the metric proves its practical utility (see Sect. 4). Theoretical validation confirms that the measure works as intended (it checks the construct validity of the measure). Typically one checks expected measure properties, e.g. association, consistency, discrimination, power tracking, predictability, and repeatability (Schneidewind's criteria). This set can be extended and include e.g. measure simplicity, language independence, etc. Experimental validation brings empirical evidence of the usefulness of the metric. This type of validation can be preliminary (applying the metrics to different test cases and examples) or advanced (tested by using real projects from the industry). This chapter presents the result of the empirical metric's evaluation.

5.1   Experimental Methodology

The experiment tries to answer the question if the metrics defined in Sect. 4 can be used as useful alignment comparison mechanisms (at instance level) from the integrators' points of view. In our experiment we try to verify our innovative methods of evaluating ontology alignments which allows assessing their quality without the aforementioned reference alignment.

The metrics do not have a normalized scale. They serve for comparison of two (or more) instance mappings for ontologies integration. Better measures results mean better alignment. For our purposes, an alignment is given in RDF format and ontologies, consisting of many elements with a multilevel taxonomic hierarchy, are in OWL format. We used the widely known benchmark datasets provided by the OAEI organization. The IIMB (ISLab Instance Matching Benchmark), ontology test suit was used as input for the experiment [17]. The suit contains 80 test cases, where each scenario has been created by systematically applying a set of transformations to the reference ontology. The following pool of transformations on the ontology instances have been made: data value transformations, data structure transformations, data semantics transformations, and mixed transformations (value, structure, and semantics). Each test case defines two ontologies (source and target) with a reference (defined by experts) mapping between instances. The other input is a set of alignments generated by authors with the LogMap [18] tool for all test cases.

To process test cases, a Java program was implemented. The program reads each test case (source and target ontology) and calculates σ_D and σ_C measures. The program additionally reads two alignments – generated by LogMap (predicted classes) and the referenced one (actual classes), and calculates performance measures (accuracy, precision, recall, and F1 score). Thus, we obtain six samples: σ_D, σ_C calculated according to equation (4) and (6), respectively, and accuracy, precision, recall, and F1 measure calculated by comparing the determined with the reference alignment.

5.2 Data Analysis

In our experiment, we wanted to verify a hypothesis that there exists a statistical dependency between metrics σ_D and σ_C, and performance measures. The whole analysis was made with a significance level $\alpha = 0.05$. Before selecting a proper test we had analyzed the distribution of all samples using the Shapiro-Wilk test. None of the samples has come from normal distribution thus for further analysis we have selected Spearman's rank-order correlation coefficient.

The results of the analysis are presented in Tables 1 and 2. The correlation between the developed measure and performance measures are quite low. Only Recall an F1 score demonstrated a moderate, statistically significant convergence with σ_D.

Table 1. The result of Spearman's monotonic correlation r for σ_D

σ_D	Accuracy	Precision	Recall	F1
r	−0.032	−0.064	0.098	0.192
std. err. for r	0.113	0.113	0.112	0.111
t-statistic for r	−0.282	−0,564	0.871	1.729
$p - value$	0.779	0.574	0.386	0.088

Table 2. The result of Spearman's monotonic correlation r for σ_C

σ_C	Accuracy	Precision	Recall	F1
r	−0.013	0.124	0.469	0.575
std. err. for r	0.113	0.112	0.099	0.093
t-statistic for r	-0.117	1.109	4.691	6.22
$p - value$	0.907	0.271	0.000011	<0.000001

Table 3. The result of Spearman's monotonic correlation r for σ_D

σ_D	Accuracy	Precision	Recall	**F1**
r	−0,344	0.039	0.511	0.492
std. err. for r	0.143	0.152	0.131	0.132
t-statistic for r	−2.403	0.257	3.903	3.701
$p - value$	0.02066	0.798	0.00033	0.000606

Table 4. The result of Spearman's monotonic correlation r for σ_C

σ_C	Accuracy	Precision	Recall	F1
r	0.099	0.555	0.899	0.893
std. err. for r	0.151	0.127	0.066	0.068
t-statistic for r	0.658	4.369	13.468	13.038
$p - value$	0.514	0.000077	<0.000	<0.000001

However, a careful analysis of the collected data indicated that in many cases instances in the ontologies are not assigned to any concept, thus rendering the proposed measures was unsuitable. In real applications, such data would not appear, because instances without concepts have no practical value. To support our statement, we follow a procedure taken from [9], where one of the steps creating individual instances relies on choosing a class and creating an individual instance of that class. Therefore, for the second part of the analysis, we have chosen only test cases where instances have assigned types. The results of the analysis of the limited dataset (for 45 test cases) are presented in Tables 3 and 4.

The obtained results prove the utility of our methods of ontology alignment assessment. The conducted analysis showed us the moderate correlation of Recall and F1 scores values with σ_D, and Precision with σ_C. However, there exist strong monotonic relations between Recall, F1, and σ_C. Those dependencies are directly proportional. If the alignment determined by LogMap were highly rated in terms of Recall and F1 measure it also reached the higher values of the developed σ_D and σ_C measures. It allows us to claim, that the methods proposed in this paper can be used to reliably evaluate the quality of mappings at the instance level without any kind of pre-prepared reference alignment. Both measures can be used in real-world ontology alignment comparison tasks without an available "gold standard".

6   Summary and Future Works

Ontology alignment is one of the most frequently researched topics - it addresses a seemingly simple issue of finding which parts of two ontologies describe the same part of reality. In the literature, a plethora of different approaches can be found, and therefore a reliable way of evaluating their outcomes is highly desired.

The most common way of evaluating the quality of the different mappings of two ontologies is by comparing them with the alignments considered as correct, based on calculating values of Precision and Recall. These correct mappings can be found in benchmark datasets provided by Ontology Alignment Evaluation Initiative (OAEI).

However, in practical scenarios, the existence of a correct, reference alignment cannot be expected. In consequence, there is no way to assess the quality of the alignment designated some ontology alignment method.

Therefore, the goal of the paper was to introduce two new metrics for ontology integrators to help them decide which alignment at the instance level is better. The first one is built on top of the criterion based on the depth of concepts in their hierarchy, while the second is based on a criterion of continuity of mappings. Both can be used to assess mappings of concepts and instances.

The usefulness of metrics has been proven on practical and empirical levels. The conducted experiment showed a correlation between σ_D and σ_C and performance values in relation to the reference alignments. Their biggest flaw is the fact that their values are not normalized (e.g. to the range $[0–1]$).

In the nearest future, we plan to extend experimental procedures for larger ontologies and ontology alignment. We intend to use biomedical ontologies and check how the developed measures perform in such an environment. We also intend to evaluate the metrics on the theoretical level and normalize their values.

References

1. Cruz, I.F., Antonelli, F.P., Stroe, C., Keles, U.C., Maduko, A.: Using Agreement-Maker to align ontologies for OAEI 2009: overview, results, and outlook. In: Proceedings of the 4th International Workshop Ontology Matching OM Collocated 8th International Semantic Web Conference ISWC, pp. 135–146 (2009)
2. Euzenat, J., Stuckenschmidt, M., Ch, H., Shvaiko, P., Trojahn, C.: Ontology alignment evaluation initiative: six years of experience. J. Data Semant. **15**, 158–192 (2011)
3. Euzenat, J.: Semantic precision and recall for ontology alignment evaluation. In: Proceedings of the 20th International Joint Conference on Artificial Intelligence, IJCAI, Hyderabad, India, pp. 348–353 (2007)
4. Ganzha, M., Paprzycki, M., Pawłowski, W., Szmeja, P., Wasielewska, K.: Towards common vocabulary for IoT ecosystems—preliminary considerations. In: Nguyen, N.T., Tojo, S., Nguyen, L.M., Trawiński, B. (eds.) ACIIDS 2017. LNCS (LNAI), vol. 10191, pp. 35–45. Springer, Cham (2017). https://doi.org/10.1007/978-3-319-54472-4_4

5. Hollink, L., van Assem, M., Wang, S., Isaac, A., Schreiber, G.: Two variations on ontology alignment evaluation: methodological issues. In: Bechhofer, S., Hauswirth, M., Hoffmann, J., Koubarakis, M. (eds.) ESWC 2008. LNCS, vol. 5021, pp. 388–401. Springer, Heidelberg (2008). https://doi.org/10.1007/978-3-540-68234-9_30
6. Li, H., Dragisic, Z., Faria, D., Ivanova, V., Jiménez-Ruiz, E., Lambrix, P., Pesquita, C.: User validation in ontology alignment: functional assessment and impact. Knowl. Eng. Rev. **34**, E15 (2019). https://doi.org/0.1017/S0269888919000080
7. Meilicke, C., Stuckenschmidt, H.: Incoherence as a basis for measuring the quality of ontology mappings. In: Proceedings of the 3rd International Workshop Ontology Matching (OM) Collocated, ISWC, pp. 1–12 (2008)
8. Misra, S., Akman, I., Colomo-Palacios, R.: A Framework for evaluation and validation of software complexity measures. IET Softw. **6**(4), 323–334 (2012)
9. Noy, N., Mcguinness, D.: Ontology development 101: a guide to creating your first ontology. Knowl. Syst. Lab. **32** (2001)
10. Pietranik, M., Kozierkiewicz, A., Wesołowski, M.: Assessing ontology mappings on a level of concepts and instances. IEEE Access **8**, 174845–174859 (2020). https://doi.org/10.1109/ACCESS.2020.3026397
11. Rodrigues, J.M., et al.: Sharing ontology between ICD 11 and SNOMED CT will enable seamless re-use and semantic interoperability. In: MedInfo, pp. 343–346. (2013)
12. Srinivasan, K.P., Devi, T.: Software metrics validation methodologies in software engineering. Int. J. Softw. Eng. Appl. (IJSEA), **5**(6), 87 (2014)
13. Solimando, A., Jiménez-Ruiz, E., Guerrini, G.: Detecting and correcting conservativity principle violations in ontology-to-ontology mappings. In: Mika, P., et al. (eds.) ISWC 2014. LNCS, vol. 8797, pp. 1–16. Springer, Cham (2014). https://doi.org/10.1007/978-3-319-11915-1_1
14. Solimando, A., Jiménez-Ruiz, E., Guerrini, G.: A multi-strategy approach for detecting and correcting conservativity principle violations in ontology alignments. In: Proceedings of the OWL Experiences and Directions Workshop OWLED, pp. 13–24 (2014)
15. Solimando, A., Jimenez-Ruiz, E., Guerrini, G.: Minimizing conservativity violations in ontology alignments: algorithms and evaluation. Knowl. Inf. Syst.**51**(3), 775–819 (2017)
16. Zhou, L., et al.: Towards evaluating complex ontology alignments. Knowl. Eng. Rev. **35**, E21 (2020). https://doi.org/10.1017/S0269888920000168
17. http://islab.di.unimi.it/content/im_oaei/2018/
18. LogMap matcher. https://github.com/ernestojimenezruiz/logmap-matcher

Describing Semantics of Data Metamodels: A Case Study of Association-Oriented Metamodel

Marcin Jodłowiec[(✉)] and Marek Krótkiewicz

Department of Applied Informatics, Wrocław University of Science and Technology,
Wybrzeże Stanisława Wyspiańskiego 27, 50-370 Wrocław, Poland
{marcin.jodlowiec,marek.krotkiewicz}@pwr.edu.pl

Abstract. In this paper, we describe the method for expressing the semantics of data metamodels using a concept system. The method abstract from metamodels' syntax and deems to enable the modeler to compare different data metamodels, and express semantics-aware translations between different metamodels. The method is based on the Semantics Of Business Vocabulary And Rules standard. Moreover, the paper describes the Association-Oriented Metamodel as a case study for the method.

Keywords: Conceptualization · Association-Oriented Metamodel · Data metamodel · Data modeling · Metamodeling · SBVR

1 Introduction

The area of this paper is the issue of data metamodeling. Each metamodel has its unique semantics. By metamodel semantics, we mean the ability to express thought concepts within the metamodel itself. An essential issue in this context is the definition of this semantics, which is understood as the semantics of individual categories of the metamodel and expressions built upon the syntax of the metamodel.

The semantics of a metamodel can be defined in many ways, as there is no single universal metamodel for this purpose. For this reason, some metamodels are formally defined, e.g., in the language of mathematics, including logic. Some of them use semi-formal methods, including natural language. In this article, we present a solution based on a concept system defined using Semantics of Business Vocabulary and Rules (SBVR) [12]. The Common Layer of Metamodels (CLoM) [5] developed for this purpose is general, i.e., not related to any specific area of reality.

This work aims to present a method of describing the semantics of data metamodels on the example of Association-Oriented Metamodel (AOM) [9]. The essential features of the proposed approach include semantic atomization and the extraction of semantics in such a way that it becomes, in a sense, independent of

© Springer Nature Switzerland AG 2021
N. T. Nguyen et al. (Eds.): ICCCI 2021, LNAI 12876, pp. 53–65, 2021.
https://doi.org/10.1007/978-3-030-88081-1_5

syntactic constraints. Semantic atomization is the breakdown of semantics into the smallest (indivisible) semantic elements possible. These atoms can be used to build more complex semantic structures (molecules). The critical component for extracting semantics in isolation from the grammatical constraints of the metamodel is the [5] concept system CLoM. It was defined using SBVR, which provides, on the one hand, a certain level of formalism, and on the other hand, high comprehensibility.

The issues raised are important from the point of view of the possibility of comparing metamodels, e.g., in the context of semantic capacity and expressive power, as well as semantic interoperability [10], being indirectly applied in the process of data and knowledge integration [8]. Moreover, a fundamental issue from the theoretical and practical point of view is translation. This operation consists of transforming expressions written in one metamodel into expressions written in another metamodel. Many vital issues related to, for example, the change in semantics that occur during this type of translation are challenging to grasp when these meta-models were defined using various formal or semi-formal methods. For this reason, a common conceptual layer is a basis for many considerations in the area of meta-modeling.

The paper is structured as follows. In the Sect. 2 the overview of the CLoM concept system has been presented. The next section contains the idea of the semantics extraction method. This idea has been exemplified in Sect. 5 using AOM, which has been introduced in Sect. 4. The related works are mentioned in Sect. 6. The last one contains conclusions and a summary.

2   Description of Conceptual Layer of Metamodels

CLoM is a concept system with a semi-formal ontology based on SBVR as a way of expression. This system includes its approach to metamodeling and a superset of concepts that perform essential functions in the field of data modeling, their characteristics, and determines the possibilities of their binding. The semantics of CLoM concepts is based on the definitions of both concepts with related terms, as well as verbal concepts with verbalizations and necessities. Within the system, both the concepts of an intensional character (with modeling concepts defining schemata, data types) and extensional (instance) character have been distinguished. The system can be divided into a group of concepts (Fig. 1): *core, classifiers, entities, relationships, categorization, features, collections.*

CLoM is based on a taxonomy of potential characteristics (constraints) inherent in the relevant modeling concepts. It allows us to capture the semantic richness of many metamodels, often mutually exclusive. The characteristics may or may not be associated with additional concepts that increase the precision in determining the properties of a given characteristic. Moreover, the system has not been defined for any particular modeling layer (e.g., *metamodel - model*), but its use presupposes a particular reference point in this respect. In this article, the system was used to describe the semantics of a metamodel so that the intensional concepts will be assigned to metamodel categories. Sample dictionary entries CLoM containing definitions of terms are presented below.

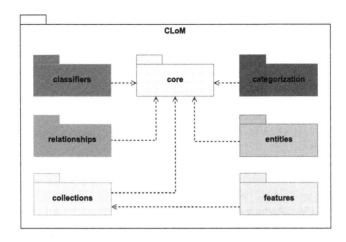

Fig. 1. Package diagram representing CLoM concept groups

entity

> Definition: instance that can *store* values and can *be classified by* entiy type
> General concept: instance

entity type

> Definition: classifier that can *have* attribute and *classifies* entity
> General concept: classifier

entity type *classifies* entity

> Synonymous form: entity *is classified by* entity type

3   The Concept of Semantics Extraction

The semantics extraction is an activity that results in a description of the metamodel's semantics. The semantics is formed as a set of semantic atoms of that metamodel. In general, the semantics of the metamodels are implicit, i.e., written in natural language, formal expressions, etc. The idea of extracting semantics is to capture it explicitly, consistent with the concept system. To extract the semantics of a metamodel, the analyst must conceptualize its grammatical categories, i.e., to·map these categories into the concept system. Next, the individual characteristics of these categories and the links between the categories (elementary constructions) should be identified and expressed in the concept system in the form of semantic atoms operating on the concepts representing the metamodel categories.

The extraction of the metamodel $\mathcal{M}$ can be depicted in three transformations:

– The definition of concepts (*ConceptDefinition*, Eq. 1) – a transformation to extract from $\mathcal{M}$ the concepts representing the categories of this metamodel. It transforms the set of semantic categories $\mathcal{M}$ into a set of unit concepts representing these categories.

$$\{k_1, k_2, \ldots, k_{kn} | k_i \in K_\mathcal{M}\} \xmapsto{Concept\,Definition} \{c_1, c_2, \ldots, c_{kn} | c_j \in \mathcal{C}_\mathcal{M}\}, \quad (1)$$

where:

$\mathcal{M}$ – the metamodel,

$K_\mathcal{M}$ – the set of metamodel $\mathcal{M}$ categories,

$\mathcal{C}_\mathcal{M}$ – the set of individual concepts expressed within CLoM representing categories of $\mathcal{M}$.

– The extraction of monadic semantic atoms (*MonadicSemanticAtomExtraction*, Eq. 2) – a transformation to capture from the $\mathcal{M}$ metamodel its essential characteristics, i.e., the properties and constraints relating to one concept representing the category of the metamodel. It converts a tuple consisting of a set of concepts representing the $\mathcal{M}$ category and $\mathcal{M}$ itself into a set of semantic atoms. The metamodel itself participates in this transformation because it holds the semantics that this transformation extracts.

$$(\{c_1, c_2, \ldots, c_{kn} | c_i \in \mathcal{C}_\mathcal{M}\}, \mathcal{M}) \xmapsto{Monadic\,Semantic\,Atom\,Extraction} \left\{a_1, a_2, \ldots, a_{an} | a_j \in \mathcal{A}_\mathcal{M}^{(1)}\right\}, \quad (2)$$

where:

$\mathcal{M}$ – the metamodel,

$\mathcal{C}_\mathcal{M}$ – the set of individual concepts expressed within CLoM representing categories of $\mathcal{M}$,

$\mathcal{A}_\mathcal{M}^{(1)}$ – the set of monadic semantic atoms[1] of $\mathcal{M}$,

– The extraction of polyadic semantic atoms (*PolyadicSemanticAtomExtraction*, Eq. 3) – a transformation aimed at capturing from the $\mathcal{M}$ metamodel the relationships between the concepts representing its categories. The transformation method is analogous to the extraction of monadic semantic atoms.

$$(\{c_1, c_2, \ldots, c_{kn} | c_i \in \mathcal{C}_\mathcal{M}\}, \mathcal{M}) \xmapsto{Polyadic\,Semantic\,Atom\,Extraction} \left\{a_1, a_2, \ldots, a_{an} | a_j \in \mathcal{A}_\mathcal{M}^{(+)}\right\}, \quad (3)$$

where:

$\mathcal{A}_\mathcal{M}^{(+)}$ – the set of polyadic semantic atoms[2] of $\mathcal{M}$.

The metamodel's semantic thus can be depicted as the set of concepts and set of semantic atoms, which is the union of monadic and polyadic semantic atoms.

---

[1] A *monadic semantic atom* is a semantic atom that only references one concept corresponding to a metamodel category. For example: aom: BaseNode *is abstract*. Monadic semantic atoms are used to represent properties or characteristics of concepts.

[2] A *polyadic semantic atom* is a semantic atom that references two or more concepts. For example: aom:Assoc *has* aom:Role. Note that in this method the term *polyadic* also applies to dyadic atoms.

$$\mathcal{S}_{\mathcal{M}} = \left(\mathcal{C}_{\mathcal{M}}, \left\{ \mathcal{A}_{\mathcal{M}}^{(1)} \cup \mathcal{A}_{\mathcal{M}}^{(+)} \right\} \right) \tag{4}$$

The extraction process has been depictedin the Fig. 2. The figure shows all three transformations (*ConceptDefinition*, *MonadicSemanticAtomExtraction*, *PolyadicSemanticAtomExtraction*) described above in a simplified manner. These transformations are done using CLoM, which has been defined in the SBVR framework, and allow to extract concepts and semantic atoms from the metamodel.

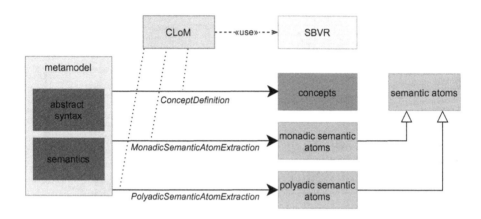

Fig. 2. The conceptual schema of semantics extraction process

4   Association-Oriented Metamodel

AOM is a novel data modeling solution designed to model complex systems, e.g., knowledge representation systems [6]. Its pivotal features have been contained within the **I USE** concept:

- **I**mplementivity: Possibility to create native, physical data sets without translation to other metamodels, without any simplifications and maintaining all properties and mechanisms occurring both at the conceptual and logical level.
- **U**nambiguity: The minimization of ways of interpreting the metamodel category and individual elements of grammatical constructions.
- **S**emantic capacity: The maximization of the set of mental concepts that can be represented by the notions and grammatical structures of a metamodel.
- **E**xpressiveness: The maximization of the degree of complexity of the modeled mental structures in relation to the degree of complexity of the syntactic structures of the metamodel representing them.

Figure 3 depicts the AOM's metastructure presented using Unified Modeling Language (UML) class diagram. Both abstract and concrete syntax as well as its semantics has been thoroughly described in [9].

58 M. Jodłowiec and M. Krótkiewicz

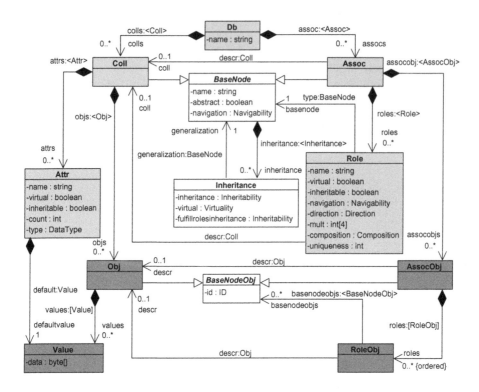

Fig. 3. Association-Oriented Metamodel metastucture

5 Definition of Association-Oriented Metamodel's Semantics

In order to exemplify the adopted approach to semantics extraction, this article presents the semantics of the AOM in the form of a set of concepts and semantic atoms. This metamodel is characterized by a high level of semantic capacity, and at the same time does not have an extensive system of semantic categories. One reason for this is that aom:Role is a concept that participates in a large number of semantic atoms. Another reason is that the individual semantic categories AOM are relatively clearly separable in terms of their functions in the metamodel. From the point of view of the description of semantics, this manifests itself in a relatively flat taxonomic structure in the light of the categorization of general concepts CLoM and unit concepts representing the categories of the metamodel AOM.

5.1   Concepts

The separate unit concepts representing the categories of the AOM are presented below. Within each of the concepts, a reference to the general concept from the CLoM system was provided, referring to the function that the concept performs in the context of metamodeling and modeling.

aom:BaseNode

General concept: classifier

aom:Coll

General concept: entity type

aom:Assoc

General concept: association

aom:Attr

General concept: attribute

aom:Role

General concept: role
General concept: association

aom:Inheritance

General concept: categorization

The entries below depict concepts representing auxiliary semantic categories.

aom:Composition

General concept: atomic type
Definition: aom:inOwner or aom:inDest or aom:inBoth or aom:none

aom:DataType

General concept: atomic type
General concept: domain
Definition: aom:int8 or aom:int16 or aom:int32 or aom:int64 or aom:float or aom:double or aom:bool or aom:ascii or aom:unicode or aom:date or aom:time or aom:date or aom:time or aom:object or aom:reference or aom:byte or aom:ascii-string or aom:unicode-string or aom:byte-array

aom:Direction

General concept: atomic type
Definition: aom:toOwner or aom:toDest or aom:biDir

aom:Inheritability

General concept: atomic type
Definition: aom:none or aom:disable or aom:nochange

aom:Navigability

General concept: atomic type
Definition: aom:uniNav or aom:biNav

aom:Virtuality

General concept: atomic type
Definition: aom:natural or aom:virtual or aom:real

5.2   Semantic Atoms

In this section, the semantic atoms in the form of the expressions SBVR. These expressions define the properties of each AOM concept – this applies to monadic atoms. In the case of polyadic atoms, they represent relationships between two or more concepts. Individual atoms are represented by the ⚛ symbol and a successive natural number. The ◊ symbol denotes possible atoms, i.e., atoms that are optional. The description of atoms includes definitions related to the semantics of a given atom on the basis of CLoM, as well as the necessities and possibilities resulting from the metamodel.

5.2.1   Monadic Semantic Atoms

aom:BaseNode can *be abstract*   ⚛$\Diamond$[1] AOM

Definition: if **aom:BaseNode** is abstract then **aom:BaseNode** is feature by non-instantiability

aom:BaseNode can *be uninavigable*⚛$\Diamond$[2] AOM

Definition: if **aom:BaseNode** is uninavigable then destination of each role that fulfills a given **aom:BaseNode** in association, is non-navigable

aom:Attr can *be inheritable*   ⚛$\Diamond$[3] AOM

Definition: if **aom:Attr** is inheritable then **aom:Attr** is featured by inheritability

aom:Attr can *be virtual*   ⚛$\Diamond$[4] AOM

Definition: if a given **aom:Attr** is virtual then each **aom:Attr** in acquired features that is featured by equal name is the given **aom:Attr**

aom:Role can *be virtual*   ⚛$\Diamond$[5] AOM

Definition: if a given **aom:Role** is virtual then each **aom:Role** in acquired features that is featured by equal name is the given **aom:Role**

aom:Role can *be inheritable*   ⚛$\Diamond$[6] AOM

Definition: if **aom:Role** is inheritable then **aom:Role** is featured by inheritability

aom:Role can *be uninavigable*   ⚛$\Diamond$[7] AOM

Definition: if **aom:Role** is uninavigable then destination of **aom:Role** is non-navigable

aom:Role can *be directed to owner*⚛$\Diamond$[8] AOM

Definition: if **aom:Role** is directed to owner then **aom:Role** is featured by semantic direction equal destination→source

aom:Role can *be directed to destination* ⚛$\Diamond$[9] AOM

Definition: if **aom:Role** is directed to destination then **aom:Role** is featured by semantic direction equal destination→source

aom:Role can *be bidirectional*   ⚛$\Diamond$[10] AOM

Definition: if **aom:Role** is bidirectional then **aom:Role** is featured by semantic direction equal bidirectional

aom:Role can *have composition in owner* ⚛$\Diamond$[11] AOM

Definition: if **aom:Role** has composition in owner then source of **aom:role** is featured by lifetime dependency

aom:Role can *have composition in destination* ⚛$\Diamond$[12] AOM

Definition: if **aom:Role** has composition in destination then destination of **aom:role** is featured by lifetime dependency

5.2.2   Polyadic Semantic Atoms

aom:BaseNode₁ can *inherit from* **aom:BaseNode₂**   ⚛$\Diamond$[13] AOM

Definition: if **aom:BaseNode₁** inherits from **aom:BaseNode₂** then **aom:BaseNode₂** categorizes **aom:BaseNode₁**
Definition: **aom:Inheritance**

aom:Inheritance *is of type* **aom:Inheritability** *in the aspect of member inheritance*   ⚛[14] AOM

Possibility: if aom:Inheritability equals **aom:none** then **aom:Inheritance** does not contain inheritance
Possibility: if **aom:Inheritability** equals **aom:disable** then acquired features are featured by noninheritability

Possibility: if **aom:Inheritability** equals **aom:nochange** then **aom:Inheritance** contains inheritance

aom:Inheritance *is of type* **aom:Inheritability** *in the aspect of role fulfillment inheritance*   ⚛[15] AOM

Possibility: if **aom:Inheritability** equals **aom:none** then **aom:Inheritance** does not contain polymorphism
Possibility: if **aom:Inheritability** equals **aom:disable** then classifiers categorized by specialization can not be substituted for generalization
Possibility: if **aom:Inheritability** equals **aom:nochange** then **aom:Inheritance** contains polymorphism

aom:Inheritance *is of type* **aom:Virtuality** *in terms of virtuality*   ✳[16]_{AOM}

Possibility: if **aom:Virtuality** *equals* **aom:virtual** then each acquired feature *becomes virtual*
Possibility: if **aom:Virtuality** *equals* **aom:real** then each acquired feature *that is virtual ceased being virtual*

aom:Coll *can have* **aom:Attr**   ✳[17]_{AOM}

Necessity: each **aom:Attr** must *be possessed by* exactly one **aom:Coll**

aom:Attr *has cardinality of* positive integer ✳[18]_{AOM}

Possibility: if positive integer *is greater than* 1 then **aom:Attr** *is featured by* multivalency

aom:Attr *is of type* **aom:DataType** ✳[19]_{AOM}

Definition: **aom:Attr** *is featured by* domain that *equals* **aom:DataType**

aom:Attr *has default value* **aom:Value** ✳[20]_{AOM}

Definition: **aom:Attr** *is featured by* default value that *equals* **aom:Value**

aom:Assoc *can have* **aom:Role**   ✳◇[21]_{AOM}

Necessity: each **aom:Role** must *be possessed by* exactly one **aom:Assoc**

aom:Assoc *can be described by* **aom:Coll** ✳◇[22]_{AOM}

Definition: **aom:Coll** *fulfills role of* description in **aom:Assoc**
Necessity: destination of description *is featured by* multiplicity that *has* upper bound *equal* 1
Necessity: destination of description *is non-navigable*

aom:BaseNode *can fulfill* **aom:Role**✳◇[23]_{AOM}

Definition: if **aom:BaseNode** *fulfills* **aom:Role** then **aom:BaseNode** *fulfills role of* **aom:Role** in **aom:Assoc**that *has* given **aom:Role**

aom:Role *can have uniqueness equal positive integer*   ✳◇[24]_{AOM}

Definition: if **aom:Role** *has uniqueness equal* positive integer then **aom:Role** *is featured by* repeatability that *is specified by* this positive integer

multiplicity of **aom:Role** *has upper bound equal* unlimited positive integer *in owner* ✳[25]_{AOM}

Definition: if unlimited positive integer *is integer* then source of **aom:Role** *is featured by* multiplicity that *has* upper bound *equal* this unlimited positive integer

multiplicity of **aom:Role** *has lower bound equal* non-negative integer *in owner* ✳[26]_{AOM}

Definition: source of **aom:Role** *is featured by* multiplicity that *has* lower bound *equal* 1

multiplicity of **aom:Role** *has upper bound equal* unlimited positive integer *in destination* ✳[27]_{AOM}

Definition: if unlimited positive integer *is integer* then destination of **aom:Role** *is featured by* multiplicity that *has* upper bound *equal* this unlimited positive integer

multiplicity of **aom:Role** *has lower bound equal* non-negative integer *in destination* ✳[28]_{AOM}

Definition: if non-negative integer *is natural number* then destination of **aom:Role** *is featured by* multiplicity that *has* lower bound *equal* this non-negative integer

aom:Role *can be described by* **aom:Coll** ✳◇[29]_{AOM}

Definition: **aom:Coll** *fulfills role of* role description in **aom:Role**
Necessity: destination of role description *is featured by* multiplicity that *has* upper bound *equal* 1

5.3 Evaluation

The following evaluation criteria were proposed, divided into three groups:

– *metamodel* – describes the characteristics of the semantics of the metamodel as a whole,

- *CLoM meta-concepts* – describes the characteristics of the semantics of a metamodel in terms of the concept system (CLoM), taking into account the basic groups of concepts *classifiers, relationships, features, categorization entities, collections,*
- *concepts* – describes the semantics characteristics of each metamodel concept.

The following criteria were adopted for the *metamodel*:

- **TC^{AOM}** – number of extracted core concepts from AOM metamodel,
- **TCA^{AOM}** – number of extracted auxiliary concepts from AOM metamodel,
- **TSA^{AOM}** – AOM semantic atoms count,
  - **TMSA^{AOM}** – AOM monadic semantic atoms count,
  - **TPSA^{AOM}** – AOM polyadic semantic atoms count.

Table 1. Evaluation of AOM semantics extraction – *metamodel* criteria

	TC^{AOM}	TCA^{AOM}	TSA^{AOM}	TMSA^{AOM}	TPSA^{AOM}
AOM	6	6	29	12	17

In the Table 1 the concepts and AOM semantic atoms have been counted. The number of AOM concepts is small because the metamodel is relatively simple. The metamodel is balanced in terms of its ability to express semantics about the characteristics of individual concepts and the semantics of relating concepts together, with the latter slightly dominating. The total number of atoms (**TMSA^{AOM}**) expresses the semantic complexity of the metamodel, it is a certain premise that translates into semantic capacity.

The evaluation criteria for *AOM meta-concepts* group apply to the semantic atoms relating to meta-concept semantics (*classifiers, relationships, features & collections, categorization entities*):

- **TSA$^{AOM}_{<meta-concept>}$** – total number of AOM semantic atoms connected with a given meta-concept,
  - **TMSA$^{AOM}_{<meta-concept>}$** – number of AOM monadic semantic atoms connected with a given meta-concept,
  - **TPSA$^{AOM}_{<meta-concept>}$** – number of AOM polyadic semantic atoms connected with a given meta-concept.

The Table 2 shows the count of semantic atoms, taking into account monadic and polyadic atoms, in terms of grouping the notions appearing in them into *meta-concepts* relating to individual branches of *CLoM*. In this approach, most of the AOM semantics concerns *relationships*. This is because at the center of AOM are the concepts of association and role representing relationship modeling. The least number of semantic atoms concerns *classifiers* and *entities*, as it is a group of concepts at a relatively high level of generality.

For *concepts* the following criteria have been adopted:

Table 2. Evaluation of AOM semantics extraction – CLoM meta-concepts criteria

	Meta-concepts				
	Classifiers	*Relationships*	*Features & collections*	*Categorization*	*Entities*
$\mathrm{TSA}^{\mathrm{AOM}}_{<\mathrm{meta\text{-}concept}>}$	2	15	5	4	3
$\mathrm{TMSA}^{\mathrm{AOM}}_{<\mathrm{meta\text{-}concept}>}$	2	6	4	0	0
$\mathrm{TPSA}^{\mathrm{AOM}}_{<\mathrm{meta\text{-}concept}>}$	0	9	1	4	3

- **$\mathrm{TMSA}^{\mathrm{AOM}}_{<\mathrm{concept}>}$** – number of monadic atoms concerning a given AOM *concept*,
- **$\mathrm{TPSA}^{\mathrm{AOM}}_{<\mathrm{concept}>}$** – number of polyadic atoms concerning a given AOM *concept*.

Table 3. Evaluation of AOM semantics extraction – *concepts* criteria

	concepts					
	aom:BaseNode	aom:Coll	aom:Assoc	aom:Attr	aom:Role	aom:Inheritance
$\mathrm{TSA}^{\mathrm{AOM}}_{<\mathrm{concept}>}$	4	3	2	6	16	4
$\mathrm{TMSA}^{\mathrm{AOM}}_{<\mathrm{concept}>}$	2	0	0	2	8	0
$\mathrm{TPSA}^{\mathrm{AOM}}_{<\mathrm{concept}>}$	2	3	2	4	8	4

The Table 3 aggregates the semantic atoms into the concepts that contribute to those atoms. The concept representing the category that participates in the greatest number of semantic atoms is <u>aom:Role</u>. The least semantics can be expressed about <u>aom:Assoc</u>, which plays the role of a set of roles, while having the character of a first-class entity.

6   Related Works

There are a number of approaches to conceptualizing metamodels. Many of them assume that they are based on the Bunge-Wand-Weber (BWW) [14] metamodel based on the Bunge [2] ontology. It should be noted, however, that Bunge developed his ontology for material things, and not for the conceptualization of virtual things, such as meta-models. An interesting attempt to create a master layer unifying data meta-models such as UML, the Entity Relationship Approach and Object-Role Modeling was proposed in [7]. The development of unification approaches is important in the field of *semantic interoperability* of data, applicable, i.a. in the processes of translation and transformation of schemata and models [1]. An important approach in this respect is the ontology-driven conceptual modeling proposed by Guizzardi, which is, in a sense, an extension to BWW, outlining the relationship between ontology, language and [4].

The SBVR constitutes a standard that is also under active research. The recent works and novel applications of SBVR involve its usage in expressing integrity constraints in database conceptual models [13], automated translation of constraints [11], extracting business vocabularies and rules from data models [3].

7 Conclusions

The article proposes a solution for describing semantic of data metamodels in a concept system. As a case study, AOM metamodel has been chosen, what has been justified in the Sect. 5. The problem of the description of semantics is an important research problem concerning the study of issues related to the concept of the semantic capacity of a data metamodel. Solving this problem may support the process of qualitative and quantitative comparison of metamodels, e.g., in order to select the optimal solution, but it may also assist in the translation of data schemata expressed as models compatible with different data metamodels.

The most important features of the solution are listed below:

– semi-formalization of the concept system based on SBVR, easily comprehensible by the analyst,
– capturing semantics in an atomic way, taking into account the characteristics of the concepts corresponding to the categories of metamodels (monadic atoms) and the relationships between the concepts (polyadic atoms).

Future work will focus on defining the semantics of other metamodels such as Enhanced Entity-Relationship Model (EER), UML, Object-Role Modeling (ORM) under CLoM and developing a method to use extracted semantics to describe the mapping patterns between these metamodels.

References

1. Atzeni, P., Cappellari, P., Torlone, R., Bernstein, P.A., Gianforme, G.: Model-independent schema translation. VLDB J. **17**(6), 1347–1370 (2008)
2. Bunge, M.: Treatise on Basic Philosophy: Ontology I: The Furniture of the World, vol. 3. Springer, Heidelberg (1977). https://doi.org/10.1007/978-94-010-9924-0
3. Danenas, P., Skersys, T., Butleris, R.: Enhancing the extraction of SBVR business vocabularies and business rules from UML use case diagrams with natural language processing. In: Proceedings of the 23rd Pan-Hellenic Conference on Informatics, PCI 2019, pp. 1–8. Association for Computing Machinery, New York (2019)
4. Guizzardi, G.: On ontology, ontologies, conceptualizations, modeling languages, and (meta) models. Front. Artif. Intell. Appl. **155**, 18 (2007)
5. Jodłowiec, M., Krótkiewicz, M.: An approach to expressing metamodels' semantics in a concept system. In: Fujita, H., Selamat, A., Lin, J.C.-W., Ali, M. (eds.) IEA/AIE 2021. LNCS (LNAI), vol. 12798, pp. 274–282. Springer, Cham (2021). https://doi.org/10.1007/978-3-030-79457-6_24

6. Jodlowiec, M., Krótkiewicz, M., Wojtkiewicz, K.: Defining semantic networks using association-oriented metamodel. J. Intell. Fuzzy Syst. **37**(6), 7453–7464 (2019)

7. Keet, C.M., Fillottrani, P.R.: An ontology-driven unifying metamodel of UML class diagrams, EER, and ORM2. Data Knowl. Eng. **98**(1C), 30–53 (2015)

8. Kozierkiewicz-Hetmańska, A., Pietranik, M., Hnatkowska, B.: The knowledge increase estimation framework for ontology integration on the instance level. In: Nguyen, N.T., Tojo, S., Nguyen, L.M., Trawiński, B. (eds.) ACIIDS 2017. LNCS (LNAI), vol. 10191, pp. 3–12. Springer, Cham (2017). https://doi.org/10.1007/978-3-319-54472-4_1

9. Krótkiewicz, M.: Formal definition and modeling language of association-oriented database metamodel (AssoBase). Vietnam J. Comput. Sci. **06**(02), 91–145 (2019)

10. Lombello, L.O., de Cassia Catini, R., Bonacin, R., dos Reis, J.C.: A metamodel for bridging heterogeneous ontologies. SN Comput. Sci. **2**(1), 1–17 (2021)

11. Mohanan, M.: Automated transformation of NL to OCL constraints via SBVR. Int. J. Adv. Intell. Paradigms **16**(3–4), 229–240 (2020)

12. OMG: Object Management Group, Semantics Of Business Vocabulary And Rules 1.5 (2019). http://www.omg.org/spec/SBVR/1.5/

13. Pereira Toledo, A., Rodriguez Morffi, A., Pérez Alonso, A., Morfa Hernández, A., Gonzalez Gonzalez, L.M.: A method for expressing integrity constraints in database conceptual modeling. Computación y Sistemas **24**(1), 75–95 (2020). https://doi.org/10.13053/CyS-24-1-3217

14. Wand, Y., Weber, R.: An ontological model of an information system. IEEE Trans. Softw. Eng. **16**(11), 1282–1292 (1990)

A Knowledge Graph Embedding Based Approach for Learning Path Recommendation for Career Goals

Thu Tran Minh Nguyen[1,2(✉)] and Thinh Pham Quoc Tran[1,2(✉)]

[1] Faculty of Information Technology, University of Science, Ho Chi Minh City, Vietnam
ntmthu@fit.hcmus.edu.vn, 1612659@student.hcmus.edu.vn
[2] Viet Nam National University, Ho Chi Minh City, Vietnam

Abstract. Nowadays, many online courses in the Information Technology (IT) field provided by different organizations make it difficult for learners to screen the courses that are best suitable for their career development. Many approaches have been raised to suggest a personalized learning path based on the learner's career goals; however, most of them use traditional techniques and face the problems of sparse data, cold start, and lack of advisory results' interpretation. In this paper, we address these problems by using Knowledge Graph Embedding (KGE) which is known as one of approaches of Graph-based models. This approach has emerged as a phenomenon and has not been widely applied in the field of learning path recommendation. We propose a new knowledge graph (KG) architecture for representing entities and their semantic relationships. The main entities identified in the KG are courses, occupations, the units of knowledge, and the relationships are the semantic connections between these entities. In existing KG architectures only exploit the hierarchy of intermediate knowledge units. Whereas, our KG architecture provides a specific classification of these learning objects, and this helps the semantic relationship of the subjects become more unambiguous and connected. Then, we explore and build experiments for our proposed KG architecture by using KGE techniques to prove the effectiveness. The experimental results show that our solution is worth considering and promises to bring a high degree of efficiency in the learning path recommendation system.

Keywords: Knowledge graph embedding · Knowledge graph structure · Learning path recommendation for career goals · Graph database

1 Introduction

Recommender System (RS) is one of the major techniques to overcome the problem of information explosion and overload as well as enhance user experience in various online application domains. RS has emerged as an important research that aims to suggest users with appropriate and relevant items. Nowadays, RS are widely applied in many different application areas such as music, movies, products, courses, etc. Although RS are increasingly making efforts to achieve the users' explicitly mentioned preferences and

© Springer Nature Switzerland AG 2021
N. T. Nguyen et al. (Eds.): ICCCI 2021, LNAI 12876, pp. 66–78, 2021.
https://doi.org/10.1007/978-3-030-88081-1_6

objective behaviors. RS still faces several issues and challenges, such as data sparsity problem, cold start problem means that when a new user enters the system or a new product is added to the catalogue, and as well as the explanation for the recommended results [1–5].

In recent years, the use of KG in the RS field has attracted many researchers. A KG is a multi-relational graph composed of entities (nodes) and relations (different types of edges). Each edge is represented as a triple of the form (head entity, relation, tail entity), also called a fact, indicating that two entities are connected by a specific relation [6]. For example, with the fact *Spratly Islands - belong to - Vietnam*, *"Spratly Islands"* is head entity, *"Vietnam"* is tail entity, and *"belong to"* specify the relation of head and tail entities. Such a graph has a strong semantic representation capacity because many high-level properties and relationships of entities can be explored through the links in the graph. Based on a powerful representation capacity, KG-based recommendation approach can solve the above-mentioned problems as well as providing explanation for good suggestion results [4, 5, 7]. KGE technique aims to embed entities and relations in a KG into a low-dimensional continuous vector space, so as to simplify computations on the KG. And this is the reason why KGE is known as one of the important approaches that are often applied to KG based RS in many different fields.

In recent years, the online learning platform such as Edx, Udemy, Cousera, etc., is being developed very strongly, the number of courses and participants are increasing each day, which leads to the learners easily being overwhelmed to decide to choose the right and useful course for a particular career goal in their future. Learners attend many different courses, but often do not know if these courses will be helpful for their desired job and the pathway to learn how to gain the skills needed to become a brilliant candidate for the job position [8]. After researching the previous course recommendation approaches, we found that there are very few solutions which consider a learner's future career goals. Instead, they offer courses from a community perspective, such as previous learners' responses to the course, the connected learners' preferences with ratings given to learning content by similar users, the courses learners had taken in previous semesters, etc. In the scope of this research, we proposed a model that suggests a learning path (series of courses) based on the career goals of the learner in the IT field by using KG based approach. We also realized that many important features such as the nature of the course, the learner's background, the time to complete the course, technical skills of course (hard skills), etc. have been used to create appropriate learning paths in the suggestion process [9]. However, our solution focuses on hard skills that help learners discover relevant technical skills and courses based on their particular career interests. In addition, the term Learning Objects (LOs) are mentioned as the small units of learning content or "knowledge units", which help build certain learning goals [9–11]. Accordingly, LOs are the knowledge units related to IT technical skills used in our solution.

Our main contribution is to construct a new heterogeneous KG framework which represents entities and the semantic relationship between them. Our next contribution is to build a learning path RS for career goals based on exploiting the already built graph architecture. The KGE approach was also used in our solution to embed the graph architecture into a low dimensional vector space to speed up the processing of informa-tion mining. We also collected a dataset in this application domain for experimenting and evaluating for our solution. Experimental results show that our proposed solution is worth considering and promises to bring a high degree of efficiency in learning path recommendation.

The rest of this paper is organized as follows: The introduction of paper is in Sect. 1; Sect. 2 presents the state of the art in the research field; Our proposed KG architecture is presented in Sect. 3; We describe the processing steps for our learning path RS in Sect. 4; Sect. 5 present the way to collect data set and build experiments as well the experimental results and comments; Conclusion and future work is in Sect. 6.

2 Related Work

Based on Qingyu Guo's work [4], KG-based recommender techniques are grouped in three categories: embedding-based methods, path-based methods, and unified methods. Compared to embedding-based methods, path-based methods often need a large number of relationships between entities to make a prediction, while unified methods have a system that is too complex and slow in analyzing. The authors [12] proposed the Collaborative Knowledge Embedding model to make recommendations in the film field. Besides exploiting information from KG, the authors' model also uses other types of information to analyze the recommendation results, such as textual descriptive information on product content, image information about product cover, etc. Diversity of information helps achieve the recommendation with high accuracy, but on the contrary, it comes with a trade-off in terms of speed up processing time and complexity in the data creation process.

In work [13], the authors use the Deep Knowledge Network model to suggest new news to users. Combination of the KGE architecture and Neural network model has given fairly effective predictive results. However, experimental results showed many limitations of this approach, such as the problem of multivalued tails that mean the same head has many different values of tail in a relation triple, and this makes the prediction of the tail values confused.

The Collaborative Filtering Knowledge Graph architecture is used to exploit the information of both products and users in [14]. The model made good use of the entity diversity and flexibility in this graph but would be limited to products that lack or less descriptive and user interaction information with them. In general, KGE used in the above works shows the effectiveness of consultancy. For example, the work [12] shows that the effectiveness of Collaborative Knowledge Base Embedding is better than traditional approaches for both movie and book recommendation scenarios. Or on a real online news platform, Deep Knowledge-aware Network in [13] reaching a higher score in comparison with some others recommendation models. However, these works have not mentioned the KG architecture in more detail and still have many limitations.

Currently, KGE has not been exploited much in the learning path RS in the field of online education. Most of the consulting results of general RS are to offer a related product, the recommendation results of the learning path must show a set of courses. In addition, these courses need to link or connect with each other in order through certain rules to create a learning path. We found that many recent existing works recommend learning paths based on Data Mining techniques such as K-means algorithm [15], the ant colony optimization method [16], Item Response Theory (IRT) [17], Bayes theorem [18], etc. By contrast, there are very few works that approach using KG as well as KGE. By this approach, the authors in [10, 19] had done experiments by using graph theory in representing the dependency relationships of LOs to make recommendations. Shi et al. [20] has built a Multidimensional Knowledge Graph framework to organize and separately store LOs in different layers. Or recently, Son et al. [21] used a metaheuristic algorithm to analyze a user's career goals to suggest learning paths. However, the mentioned works have not experimented with their recommendation solution using the embedding-based method [20], there is still no typical graph architecture for Learning Path [10, 19], or both [21].

Through analyzing the current state of the studies, we have a full range of scientific bases to give a solution to recommend an effective Learning Path (LP) for Career Goals (CG)s based on KGE techniques. Our major contributions are also mentioned in Sect. 1.

3   Description of Proposed Knowledge Graph Architecture

In the field of LP recommendation, a knowledge topic is usually divided into a large amount of smaller LOs. For example, the work [22] would divide a knowledge topic into Raw Elements, Information Objects, LOs, Aggregate Assemblies or Nabizadeh et al. [23] break it into Course, Lesson, Topic, LOs. The one-dimensional KG architecture of these works makes RS easy to identify LOs on the same topic. However, they are often due with information duplication and there are weak semantic links among the content of topics.

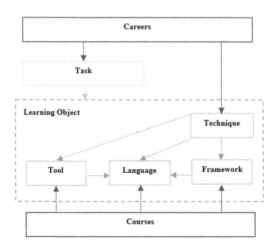

Fig. 1. The proposed knowledge graph architecture.

In the work [19], the multiple classes graph was proposed by Shi et al. for defining and organizing LOs. This architecture classifies the entities based on their own semantic fields. And between classes, there are links to connect with each other. Shi's architecture is more optimal in exploiting semantics of the graph than one-dimensional one's.

However, the LOs in each class have not been classified clearly into each specific type of object. This easily leads to recommender results often containing redundant LOs and not focusing on a specific topic.

Existing work underpins and promotes our research which we have developed and built up a new KG architecture. Inheriting and promoting the strengths of existing architectures, our proposed KG architecture is a multiple classes graph which classified entities into their roles. Besides, our KG architecture has an improvement to divide LOs related to entities into multiple entity types according to their meaning. This approach helps the proposed LP could cover all the basic content and skills of a career. Thereby, users can easily develop higher skills in accordance with their next career orientations. The proposed KG architecture is shown in Fig. 1 and an illustrative representation of the architecture is shown in Fig. 2.

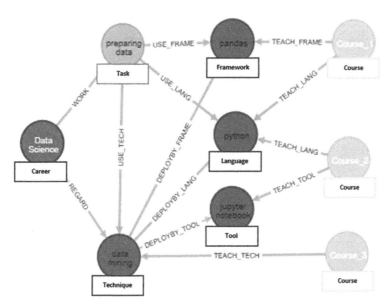

Fig. 2. An instance of the knowledge graph architecture.

There are 4 main classes in proposed KG architecture: Career (CR), Task (TA), Learning Object (LO) and Course (CS). LO is a collection of many other types of entities representing different domains of knowledge. The entities in KG are explained in more detail as follows:

- **Career (CR)** represents the user's occupation entities.
- **Task (TA)** is an instance of a specific task (e.g., works, assignments, …) that are required to perform for a CR.
- **Learning Object (LO)** is the knowledge unit related to CR and CS in the IT field. In the context of the link between LO and CS, LO is considered the knowledge unit that CS provides to learners, and LO is considered as technical skills used to implement a TA in the context of the relation between LO and CR. Normally a CS will provide

several LOs related to the LOs that a CR needs, and there also are some other LOs that CR does not need. These are called primary LOs and secondary LOs in which primary LOs are required LOs and primary LOs are not required LOs for a particular Career. LOs are classified into four major categories that apply to (CS)s and (CR)s in the IT field as follows:

+ **Technique (TE)** represents a technology topic, a programming technique, or a problem-solving method.
+ **Language (LA)** is understood as a programming language.
+ **Framework (FR)** is known as frameworks, or libraries that support programming and coding in the IT field.
+ **Tool (TO)** represents software tools used to execute and support for some tasks.

– **Course (CS)** represents course entities. Collection of courses linked in the order is a LP.

In addition, the entities in our KG architecture are linked to each other by 15 types of relationships, shown in Table 1. Details of these relationships are explained as follows:

1. **WORK** is the relationship between the CR and the TA(s), indicating that a CR will have to perform these (TA)s.
2. **REGARD** is the relationship between CR and TE(s), indicating that a CR is related to certain (TE)s.
3. **USE_FRAME** is the relationship between TA and FR, indicating that a TA needs to use FR(s) in processing.
4. **USE_TOOL** is the relationship between TA and TO, indicating that a TA needs to use (TO)s in processing.
5. **USE_LANG** is the relationship between TA and LA, indicating that a TA needs to use (LA)s in processing.
6. **USE_TECH** is the relationship between TA and TE, indicating that a TA needs to use (TE)s in processing.
7. **DEPLOYBY_FRAME** is the relationship between TE and FR, indicating that a TE can be deployed against (FR)s.
8. **DEPLOYBY_TOOL** is the relationship between TE and TO, indicating that a TE can be operated using (TO)s.
9. **DEPLOYBY_LANG** is the relationship between TE and LA, indicating that a TE can be deployed using (LA)s.
10. **INTERACT_WITH** is the relationship between TO and LA, indicating that a TO can use a type of LA.
11. **BUILD_ON** is the relationship between FR and LA, indicating that a FR is built from a LA.
12. **TEACH_FRAME** is the relationship between CS and FR, indicating that a CS will teach the knowledge related to FR(s).
13. **TEACH_TOOL** is the relationship between Cs and TO, indicating that a CS will teach the knowledge related to (TO)s.

14. **TEACH_LANG** is the relationship between CS and LA, indicating that a CS will teach the knowledge related to (LA)s.
15. **TEACH_TECH** is the relationship between CS and TE, indicating that a CS will teach the knowledge related to the (TE)s.

Table 1. Relationships between entities in the KG architecture.

Head object		Tail object				
		TA	LO			
			TE	TO	FR	LA
CR		WORK	REGARD	–	–	–
TA		–	USE_TECH	USE_TOOL	USE_FRAME	USE_LANG
LO	TE	–	–	DEPLOYBY_TOOL	DEPLOYBY_FRAME	DEPLOYBY_LANG
	TO	–	–	–	–	INTERACT_WITH
	FR	–	–	–	–	BUILD_ON
CS		–	TEACH_TECH	TEACH_TOOL	TEACH_FRAME	TEACH_LANG

4 Recommendation System Based on Knowledge Graph Embedding

In this section, we describe our proposed RS model based on the KG approach. Our solution to deploy the model is to use KGE technique and some important algorithms are built to find a (LP)s that matches (CG)s. Our proposed architecture and processing steps are shown in Fig. 3. The following is the details of each processing steps:

- **Step 1:** We use Embedding-based techniques to embed the KG architecture into a low-dimensional vector space. The triplet such as (Courses, relation, LOs), (Career, relation, LOs), etc. would be taken out for embedding. To process this step, we have studied and applied in testing five KGE methods, including: TransE [24], DistMult [25], ComplEx [26], HolE [27], and ConvE [28] for KGE to test the semantic cohesion level of the proposed KG architecture. Details of the experimental and analytical results shown in Sect. 5. Based on the accuracy measurement results of each model on our dataset, we decided to use HolE for processing the following next steps. The output of this process will generate an ***Embedding map (EM)***, which is stored and used for the 4th step of this workflow.
- **Step 2:** When a specific CG is put into the system, CR-related LOs will be filtered out by mining KG architecture. At the end of **Step 2** we obtained the ***Career_LO*** list, which includes all LOs related to CG.
- **Step 3:** At this step, we would filter out all (CS)s which have LOs related to LOs of (CR)s in ***Career_LO***. The result of this step is the ***Career_all_CS list*** which is a list of courses meeting the mentioned requirements.

- **Step 4:** This step we calculate the similarity of each CS in **Career_all_CS** with the input CG. The similarity of CS and CR is considered based on the number of LOs related between them. The similar calculation is happening on EM that was built in **Step 1**. Euclidean Distance and Cosine similarity [29] were chosen for measuring pairs of vectors, which represents the pairs of entities CS and CR. These two measures are selected because they have shown their effectiveness in exploiting the relationship of number vectors, especially numerical vectors of embedding values [30–32]. The result of this step is the **all_CS_Sort** set, which contains the (CS)s sorted by their decreasing similarity to the CG.
- **Step 5:** We built an algorithm to filter out a set of courses in **all_CS_sort** so that their set of LOs covers the LOs required by CG. This is a group of the highest similarity score courses, and there are at least one different LOs in each course. These course lists are called **Candidate_Course** sets, and we use all these courses to create a CP for CG.
- **Step 6:** In this step, we build an algorithm to rearrange the CS in the **Candidate_Course** set to create a LP suitable for learners' different CG.

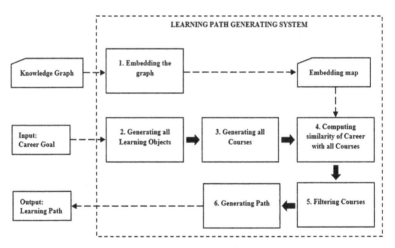

Fig. 3. The architecture of learning path generate system

5 Experimental and Evaluation

Based on our proposed KG architecture, we do the data collection tasks to create our dataset for experimentation. Regarding CR related data, we select some popular careers in IT and synthesize descriptive information from Wikipedia [33]. CS related data is obtained from the Udemy online courses page [34]. We have collected 20 occupations, 124 tasks, 727 learning objects, and 1121 courses. In experimenting with our LP recommendation system, we extract a subset which includes 5 careers, 24 tasks, 143 learning objects and 113 courses for testing and measuring results. These entities in subsets are linked through 520 relations, with the 15 main types of relationships mentioned in Sect. 3.

Table 2. Experimental accuracy results of embedding models on our dataset.

Model	MRR	Hits@1	Hits@3	Hits@10
ConvE	0.20	0.15	0.15	0.37
TransE	0.48	0.32	0.58	0.72
DistMult	0.58	0.52	0.58	0.73
ComplEx	0.65	**0.57**	**0.68**	0.92
HolE	**0.66**	**0.57**	**0.68**	**0.95**

Table 3. Measurement values of two KGE models on Our WN18, FB15k, and our dataset.

Dataset	Model	MRR	Hits@1	Hits@3	Hits@10
WN18	ComplEx	0.941	0.936	0.945	0.947
	HolE	0.938	0.93	0.945	0.949
FB15K	ComplEx	0.692	0.599	0.759	0.840
	HolE	0.524	0.402	0.613	0.739
Our Dataset	ComplEx	0.65	0.57	0.68	0.92
	HolE	0.66	0.57	0.68	0.95

Table 2 shows that two models, ComplEx and HolE give more accurate results than the other models. To test the stability of these two models before using them, we also compare the score of them on our dataset with two previously published datasets including WN18 [35] and FB15K [36]. The results are shown in Table 3, and it also shows that the measurement values of these models on the two standard datasets and on our dataset are not significantly different. Those asymptotic measurement scores between proposed graphs and other standard graphs are the premise for applying our graph architecture to solve the LP recommending problem.

In the process of creating a LP, we used KGE technique to exploit information on graphs. The Embedding-based technique compresses the KG on a low-dimensional and simpler space than the original architecture. From there, calculations and information extraction will be easier, more convenient, and quicker. However, each KGE model has its own characteristics that are suitable for different types of KG architectures. To choose a KGE model that fits our proposed KG architecture, we did experiments for five models TransE, DistMult, ComplEx, HolE, and ConvE on our dataset. Mean Reciprocal Rank (MRR) [37] and Hits @ k (k = 1, 3, 10) (mentioned in [24]) measures are used to measure the accuracy of representations of triplet in the new embedding space. In which, MRR

Table 4. Statistic values of learning paths from proposed system.

Evaluation criteria	Data science	Data administrator	Front-end developer	Back-end developer	Software architect
Number of skills required	23	25	19	23	26
Number of courses related	20	30	16	28	35
Number of courses in path	Euclide 14	Euclide 14	Euclide 11	Euclide 12	Euclide 19
	Cosine 10	Cosine 12	Cosine 12	Cosine 13	Cosine 18
Number of LOs in the path	Euclide 32	Euclide 42	Euclide 22	Euclide 33	Euclide 39
	Cosine 33	Cosine 37	Cosine 24	Cosine 35	Cosine 50
The percentage of coverage of LOs in career	Euclide 100%	Euclide 100%	Euclide 100%	Euclide 100%	Euclide 100%
	Cosine 100%	Cosine 100%	Cosine 100%	Cosine 100%	Cosine 100%
The percentage of sub LOs in path	Euclide 28%	Euclide 25%	Euclide 13%	Euclide 18%	Euclide 35%
	Cosine 30%	Cosine 27%	Cosine 20%	Cosine 15%	Cosine 48%

is the average inverse rank for all test triples. And Hits @ k is the percentage of ranks lower than or equal to k. For both measurements, the higher the value is obtained, the better the accuracy of the model. The experimental results are shown in Table 2.

According to the experimental results in Table 2, we chose HolE model to create the EM of KG architecture. And then, we do all the next following steps to build our completeness RS. After all, our RS can suggest the LPs for each specific CG. To check the effectiveness of our proposed RS, we conduct testing recommending five careers including: Data Science, Data Administrator, Front-end developer, Back-end Developer, Software Architecture. In Table 4, we evaluate the LP result through some statistical values, including: total number of courses involved, total number of courses included in the LP, coverage (%) of primary LOs and secondary LOs in the itinerary.

Statistical results presented in Table 4 show that all proposed LPs are quite effective when it could cover all LO that a CG required. In addition to the primary LOs, a limited number of secondary LOs are included. By using the Euclidean distance similarity measure, almost the number of the courses in the recommended LP are much more than Cosine's. However, the number of secondary LOs in the Euclidean' LP is less than Cosine ones. This helps learners of the Euclidean based LP do not have to learn many unnecessary skills. On the contrary, the Cosine based LP would make a faster completion of the path.

6   Conclusion and Future Work

In this work, we have built an effective solution for the RS that suggests a LP according to (CG)s in the IT field. Our contribution is to build a new KG architecture to apply to the online education recommendation field. To exploit KG effectively, we also use Embedding-based to bring the proposed architecture into a low-dimensional vector space to increase processing speed. Besides, we have also built a unified Learning Path Recommender System. The experimental results show that our RS solution is very potential, the LP ensures that all the necessary LOs of a CR are proposed with the least possible set of courses. This also proves that our proposed architecture is suitable and can be applied to recommend LP for CG in real applications. However, our proposed solution still includes several unrelated LOs as well as has not yet dealt with the different needs of learners such as Background Knowledge, Learning Style, etc.

In the future, we will expand the scope of KG's architecture as well as expand the empirical dataset that can address many other goals in the fields of education and career guidance. In addition, we will also consider applying the weighted graph to show the importance of relationships between entities, helping to build and propose a more optimal LP.

Acknowledgments. This research is partially supported by the research funding from the Faculty of Information Technology, University of Science, Ho Chi Minh city, Vietnam.

This research is funded by the Faculty of Information Technology, University of Science, VNU-HCM, Vietnam, Grant number CNTT2020-10.

References

1. Sridevi, M., Rajeshwara Rao, R., Varaprasad Rao, M.: A survey on the recommender system. Int. J. Comput. Sci. Inf. Secur. **14**(5), 265 (2016)
2. Bobadilla, J., et al.: Recommender systems survey. Knowl. Based Syst. **46**, 109–132 (2013)
3. Lu, J., et al.: Recommender system application developments: a survey. Decis. Support Syst. **74**, 12–32 (2015)
4. Guo, Q., et al.: A survey on knowledge graph-based recommender systems. IEEE Trans. Knowl. Data Eng. (2020)
5. László, G.-G., Filzmoser, P., Werthner, H.: Recommendations on a knowledge graph. In: 1st International Workshop on Machine Learning Methods for Recommender Systems, MLRec (2015)
6. Quan, W., et al.: Knowledge graph embedding: a survey of approaches and applications. IEEE Trans. Knowl. Data Eng. **29**(12), 2724–2743 (2017)
7. Chan, L., et al.: A survey of recommendation algorithms based on knowledge graph embedding. In: 2019 IEEE International Conference on Computer Science and Educational Informatization (CSEI), IEEE (2019)
8. Majidi, N.: A Personalized Course Recommendation System Based on Career Goals. Memorial University of Newfoundland, Diss (2018)
9. Nabizadeh, A.H., et al.: Learning path personalization and recommendation methods: a survey of the state-of-the-art. Expert Syst. Appl. 113596 (2020)
10. Belacel, N., Durand, G., Laplante, F.: A binary integer programming model for global optimization of learning path discovery. In: EDM (Workshops) (2014)

11. Dharani, B., Geetha, T.V.: Adaptive learning path generation using colored Petri nets based on behavioral aspects. In: 2013 International Conference on Recent Trends in Information Technology (ICRTIT), IEEE (2013)
12. Zhang, F., et al.: Collaborative knowledge base embedding for recommender systems. In: Proceedings of the 22nd ACM SIGKDD International Conference on Knowledge Discovery and Data Mining (2016)
13. Wang, H., et al.: DKN: deep knowledge-aware network for news recommendation. In: Proceedings of the 2018 World Wide Web Conference (2018)
14. Zhang, Y., et al.: Learning over knowledge-base embeddings for recommendation. arXiv preprint arXiv:1803.06540 (2018)
15. Jain, A.K.: Data clustering: 50 years beyond K-means. Pattern Recogn. Lett. **31**(8), 651–666 (2010)
16. Dorigo, M., Stützle, T.: Ant colony optimization: overview and recent advances. In: Handbook of Metaheuristics, pp. 311–351 (2019)
17. Maryam, Y., Jahankhani, H., Tawil, A.: A personalized adaptive e-learning approach based on semantic web technology. Webology **10**(2), Art-110 (2013)
18. Xu, D., et al.: Personalized learning path recommender based on user profile using social tags. In: 2012 Fifth International Symposium on Computational Intelligence and Design, vol. 1, IEEE (2012)
19. Li, Z., Papaemmanouil, O., Koutrika, G.: Course Navigator: interactive learning path exploration. In: Proceedings of the Third International Workshop on Exploratory Search in Databases and the Web (2016)
20. Shi, D., et al.: A learning path recommendation model based on a multidimensional knowledge graph framework for e-learning. Knowl.-Based Syst. **195**, 105618 (2020)
21. Son, N.T., et al.: Meta-heuristic algorithms for learning path recommender at MOOC. IEEE Access (2021)
22. Duval, E., Hodgins, W.: A LOM Research Agenda. WWW (Alternate Paper Tracks) (2003)
23. Nabizadeh, A.H., Jorge, A.M., Leal, J.P.: Rutico: recommending successful learning paths under time constraints. In: Adjunct Publication of the 25th Conference on User Modeling, Adaptation and Personalization (2017)
24. Bordes, A., et al.: Translating embeddings for modeling multi-relational data. In: Neural Information Processing Systems (NIPS) (2013).
25. Yang, B., et al.: Embedding entities and relations for learning and inference in knowledge bases. arXiv preprint arXiv:1412.6575 (2014)
26. Trouillon, T., et al.: Complex embeddings for simple link prediction. In: International Conference on Machine Learning. PMLR (2016)
27. Nickel, M., Rosasco, L., Poggio, T.: Holographic embeddings of knowledge graphs. In: Proceedings of the AAAI Conference on Artificial Intelligence, vol. 30, no. 1 (2016)
28. Dettmers, T., et al.: Convolutional 2d knowledge graph embeddings. In: Proceedings of the AAAI Conference on Artificial Intelligence, vol. 32. no. 1 (2018)
29. Rajaraman, A., Ullman, J.D.: Mining of Massive Datasets. Cambridge University Press (2011)
30. Lee, Y.-Y., et al.: Combining and learning word embedding with WordNet for semantic relatedness and similarity measurement. J. Assoc. Inf. Sci. Technol. **71**(6), 657–670 (2020)
31. Huang, C., Loy, C.C., Tang, X.: Local similarity-aware deep feature embedding. arXiv preprint arXiv:1610.08904 (2016)
32. Wu, L., et al.: Deep adaptive feature embedding with local sample distributions for person re-identification. Pattern Recognit. **73**, 275–288 (2018)
33. Wikipedia. https://en.wikipedia.org/wiki/Wikipedia (2021). Accessed 30 Apr 2021
34. Online Courses – Learn Anything On Your Schedule. https://www.udemy.com/ (2021). Accessed 30 Apr 2021

35. Fellbaum, C.: WordNet: An Electronic Lexical Database. Bradford Books (1998)
36. Bollacker, K., et al.: Freebase: a collaboratively created graph database for structuring human knowledge. In: Proceedings of the 2008 ACM SIGMOD International Conference on Management of Data (2008)
37. Craswell, N.: Mean Reciprocal Rank. In: Liu, L., Özsu, M.T. (eds.) Encyclopedia of Database Systems, pp. 1703–1703. Springer US, Boston, MA (2009). https://doi.org/10.1007/978-0-387-39940-9_488

Social Networks and Recommender Systems

Collective Consciousness Supported by the Web: Healthy or Toxic?

Shima Beigi⬤ and Francis Heylighen⁽⊠⁾⬤

Vrije Universiteit Brussel, Brussels, Belgium
sbeigi@vub.be, fheyligh@vub.ac.be

Abstract. We define the noosphere as the conscious level of the web, where global conversations are being held about collective challenges. To understand its dynamics, we review three neuroscientific theories of consciousness: information integration, adaptive resonance, and global workspace. These suggest that conscious thoughts are characterized by a "resonant", self-maintaining pattern of circulating information. This pattern should be sufficiently stable to be examined and dependably stored, yet sufficiently plastic to adapt to new input. The self-organizing dynamics of ideas circulating on the web, however, may settle in an attractor that is too resistant to accommodate new information. This results in a closed, toxic form of collective consciousness exemplified by conspiracy theories. We review the global discussion of the COVID-19 pandemic to illustrate healthy and unhealthy forms of noospheric consciousness. We then argue for the need to promote the healthy form via the modelling of the dynamics of idea propagation and the dissemination of narratives promoting open conversation.

Keywords: Noosphere · Collective intelligence · Consciousness · Neuroscience · Global brain · COVID-19 · Conspiracy theories

1 Introduction

Collective intelligence is the ability of a group of agents to solve problems together that the same agents working individually cannot solve [1]. Computational collective intelligence [2] further enhances that ability by harnessing the power of computers, networks and algorithms to support the sharing of information between the different agents in the group. An impressive application of such collective intelligence is Wikipedia, the global encyclopedia that covers nearly the whole of human knowledge. Such a vast network of structured knowledge could never have been assembled without the technology of the World-Wide Web, which allowed millions of users worldwide to collaborate easily and effectively, by adding, linking, and editing pieces of knowledge made available on a shared platform.

The basic mechanisms underlying such distributed cognition are the propagation of information between agents, the integration and processing of that information so as to extract coherent patterns, the filtering out of errors, and the consolidation of the resulting insights in a shared memory (such as Wikipedia), so that they remain available for later

© Springer Nature Switzerland AG 2021
N. T. Nguyen et al. (Eds.): ICCCI 2021, LNAI 12876, pp. 81–93, 2021.
https://doi.org/10.1007/978-3-030-88081-1_7

use. An important role here is played by the algorithms that control the routing, selection and processing of information. Inadequate algorithms may lead to valuable information being ignored, or poor-quality data being inappropriately relied on.

Yet, next to algorithms, the outcome of the process also depends on social interactions: who communicates what with whom? When people propagate information, e.g., by distributing an email, posting a message on social media, or making an edit in Wikipedia, they rely on their own judgment about what is appropriate to communicate. That judgment will depend on subjective factors, such as their feelings, personal beliefs, norms about public behavior, and relationships with others. These social and psychological variables affect the quality of the information being propagated, processed and stored, and therefore the collective intelligence of the overall human-computer network. To enhance the quality of the solutions produced, we need to better understand the dynamics of this immensely complex network of interacting agents.

The problem is that the number and diversity of all the human and computational variables involved is so large that it seems impossible to model this process in any detail. In previous research, we have therefore proposed to view this world-wide collective intelligence as a *global brain* [3, 4]. The idea is that we may better understand this network through its similarity with another extremely complex, self-organizing network, the human brain. In this analogy, individual agents (people, computers, websites, applications…) play the role of neurons in the brain. Messages being communicated between these agents are similar to electrical impulses or "activation" being transmitted between neurons via their connecting synapses. The links between agents—such as "friend" or "follower" links on social media, routing directions between computers or hyperlinks between web pages—play the role of these synapses. This "neural network" learns new knowledge when consolidated information is registered in a shared database or linking pattern.

In earlier work, we have investigated this model of the world-wide web as a global brain mostly at the level of algorithms that would create and exploit link structures to guide the propagation of information [1, 4]. This implements the brain mechanism of activation spreading in parallel along the strongest links. The idea is to support collective intelligence by connecting people or problems with the for them most appropriate solutions. Here, we wish to address the more complex issue of how new solutions, or more generally *new insights*, can be collectively generated through the synthesis of information from a variety of sources. This requires the more advanced brain mechanism of *conscious reflection*, in which different ideas and observations are critically examined, selectively accepted or rejected, improved and finally integrated into an overall interpretation that can guide further action.

We will illustrate this with the example of the ongoing global discussion about the causes of the COVID-19 pandemic and the best strategies to deal with them. To better understand how such a process takes place, we will introduce the concept of the *noosphere*, as the medium in which such discussions take place. We will briefly review contemporary theories of consciousness in the human brain, and suggest how they may be extended to the noosphere. This will provide us with a preliminary model for the self-organizing dynamics that characterizes the emergence of collective understanding. We will in particular distinguish healthy from unhealthy forms of collective consciousness, and suggest strategies to promote the former and prevent the latter.

2 Noospheric Consciousness

The great majority of cognitive processes in the human brain are *subconscious*: they take place immediately and automatically in the background, leaving no occasion for the mind to examine precisely how or why the process came to a certain conclusion [5, 6]. For example, we know from neural network simulations that processing perceived sound into meaningful sentences is an extremely complex process, which involves thousands of variables, and which must pass through several stages or layers of abstraction. Yet, our brain does it effortlessly—although we have no idea how that happens, and we would not be able to prevent it from happening, even if the final interpretation turns out to be incorrect. The process also does not leave any trace in our memory: we may remember the final interpretation, but the intermediate stages in coming to that conclusion are not retrievable.

Another example of a subconscious process is the control of walking: we may consciously intend to go in a particular direction, but we are not aware of how our nervous system generates the precise muscular contractions that make our legs perform the right movements without losing our balance or swerving from the path. It is only when the situation deviates from our expectations—for example when we stumble on an obstacle we had not noticed—that we become conscious of the positioning of our body. That conscious focus is necessary to make sense of the novel challenge and to consider possible ways to deal with it. As long as the incoming information confirms our subconscious expectations, the brain assumes that it can trust those automatic processes, and that therefore there is no need for conscious reflection [5].

Computer-supported systems for distributed cognition, such as the World-Wide Web, follow this logic of automatic processes that are implicitly trusted to produce the right result. For example, when you send an email, you assume by default that it will reach the right address, and when you search for information on a well-known subject, such as tuberculosis, you assume that the page (e.g. in Wikipedia) you find will provide correct information. However, when a novel, unexpected challenge appears, such as the COVID-19 pandemic, there are no established routines or knowledge bases available that specify how to deal with it. Such a situation requires conscious reflection. But because the challenge is much too large and complex for any individual to solve, that reflection must be collective, distributed and global, i.e. it must take into account the widest possible range of people, observations and hypotheses. That requires an on-going global exchange of ideas, opinions and data, a critical examination of those ideas, and a mechanism to integrate these ideas into an overall understanding and strategy.

Nearly a century ago, the visionary scientist and philosopher Teilhard de Chardin proposed the concept of the *noosphere* ("mind sphere"), which he conceived as a layer of thought that envelops the Earth, or as a collective brain constituted out of billions of individual brains communicating via a network of links [7, 8]. While this concept to some degree anticipated the World-Wide Web, it adds that this network would support a global reflection that would allow humanity to resolve its problems, and thus converge to a coherent understanding. Therefore, we can interpret the noosphere as the conscious level of the global brain, with the web as the infrastructure that supports the required propagation of information. To better understand the dynamics of the noosphere, we can draw inspiration from contemporary neuroscientific theories of consciousness in the brain.

3   Neuroscientific Theories of Consciousness

Attempts to define consciousness are copious. Yet, consciousness remains an open scientific challenge, subject to much debate and controversy. Historically, consciousness studies have been mostly centered on the study of subjective experiences, aka 'qualia'. The complexity of these experiences has stimulated the scientific study of the underlying neural mechanisms of consciousness, with Crick and Koch among the pioneers [9]. Given that there is no obvious equivalent of subjective experience in the noosphere, we will here focus on a more concrete aspect of consciousness that has been called "access consciousness" [10]. This refers to the ability to monitor, examine, register and, if necessary, redirect mental processes [5]. As we noted, the ability to access mental functioning is precisely what distinguishes a conscious process from a subconscious one, whose automatism prevents it from being examined, corrected or redirected.

The more recent neuroscientific theories of consciousness have been able to capture some of the complexity of consciousness without compromising on the need for scientific evidence or *a priori* alienating philosophical, mystical and spiritual views of consciousness. These theories include, but are not limited to, Information Integration, Global Workspace, and Adaptive Resonance. These theories, although different in their perspective, share the basic idea that the flow of information in the brain is key to understanding consciousness. In the following sections we expand on each theory.

3.1   Information Integration Theory (IIT)

IIT was developed by Giulio Tononi in order to address two of the most difficult challenges in investigating the generation of consciousness within/among brain regions. The first challenge is to specify the conditions that determine a brain area's role in generating conscious experiences. The second challenge is to determine the relative significance of certain regions of the brain, for example thalamocortical region in comparison to cerebellum [11]. Considering these two challenges, Tononi defines consciousness as "the capacity of a system to integrate information." This capacity is determined by the coherency of the underlying neural processes. Coherency measures the extent to which integration has reduced relative uncertainty (in the information theoretic sense [12]) between activities in different parts of the network.

IIT has become one of the key models for the underlying role of neurobiological factors in shaping subjective experiences. Moreover, because the mathematical measure Φ for information integration can in principle be applied to systems of any kind, it has initiated a discussion about the degree to which consciousness can be found in non-biological systems such as countries, networks of logic gates, or the Internet. On the other hand, the theory has been criticized for being too abstract and general, overlooking concrete neural conditions prerequisite for conscious experience, such as the binding together of sensory, motor and emotional activation patterns in the brain in the form of "semantic pointers" [13].

As research on consciousness progresses, it becomes increasingly evident that the subjectivity of conscious experience should no longer be seen as a purely mystical phenomenon [14]. It can rather be formulated as a synthetic phenomenon partly generated/influenced by neurophysiological factors and partly by individual differences in perception, learning styles, mental models and cultural backgrounds. This synthetic perspective has been framed as an opportunity to move towards a more systemic take on the study of consciousness [15].

3.2 Adaptive Resonance Theory

One of the criticisms of IIT is that it reduces consciousness to a static information measure, thus neglecting the complex dynamics of experience. In the Adaptive Resonance Theory (ART) developed by Stephen Grossberg, the emphasis is not initially on consciousness. Instead, ART positions itself as a cognitive neural theory that models the dynamics of the concrete processes within the brain, including categorization of information, learning, expectation, attention, synchronization, memory and search. These in turn support perception, cognition, and finally consciousness [16].

Attention regulates whether some new information is learned or ignored. Therefore it plays a key role in the ART approach. Learning takes place above a certain threshold determined by a vigilance parameter that controls the relative importance of bottom-up (incoming data) and top-down processes (expected patterns). One of the key issues addressed by ART is the *stability-plasticity dilemma*, which is well-known within both artificial and biological systems [17]. It refers to the need for a system to be sufficiently plastic so that it can integrate new knowledge, yet sufficiently stable to prevent the loss of previously learned knowledge. ART investigates the delicate balance between stability and plasticity so as to prevent the problem of catastrophic forgetting in artificial neural networks [18].

ART proposes that conscious states in the brain are characterized by activation circulating back and forth between different neural regions, and in particular between perceptual layers (incoming data) and higher-level concepts that explain the perceptions (interpretations, expectations). This self-reinforcing "resonance" between zones in the brain's neural network produces a pattern of activation that is sufficiently intense and persistent to create a clear focus of attention and to become registered into long-term memory, while remaining sufficiently fluid to adapt to novel input.

The stability-plasticity dilemma has direct applications to hybrid human-technological systems. The flexible coupling and decoupling of biological as well as artificial agents with their surrounding environment has become a key area of investigation in designing systems that that need to adapt to changing environments. However, the balance between being sufficiently adaptive to acquire novel information (plasticity), while dependably retaining older information (stability) remains elusive.

Achieving it is especially difficult when it comes to intervention strategies in times when regular patterns break down, like during disasters and systemic shocks [19]. The resulting confusion can result in pathological forms of adaptation. Too strong tendencies towards either stability or plasticity can lead to the formation of maladaptive patterns of understanding, such as the conspiracy theories that we will discuss further. In such a situation, constructive intervention becomes extremely difficult because the system tends to get locked into a polarized, black-and-white, view of reality, lacking the fluidity to deal with conflicting information. While the underlying mechanisms that primate brains use to deal with the Stability-Plasticity dilemma remain unclear, ART and the model of noospheric consciousness discussed in this paper both endeavor to find ways to offset the loss of valuable knowledge from the system, while increasing its resilience against perturbations.

3.3   Global Workspace

The last neuroscientific theory of consciousness we wish to review, the Global (Neuronal) Workspace, was proposed by Bernard Baars [20] and elaborated in particular by Stanislas Dehaene [6]. Its main idea is that neural activity becomes conscious when it is "broadcasted" across the *global workspace*, which is a central crossroads of neural connections in the brain. As such, this activity can be examined by different more specialized brain modules that otherwise have few connections. The global workspace functions like a public forum or shared medium where these modules, playing the role of the agents that constitute the "society of mind", can enter in a conversation so as to come to a consensus on what to do. This is analogous to the noosphere where the web functions as a medium for global conversation between all cognitive agents.

Broadcasting in the brain requires widespread and intense activation that "reverberates" or circulates across the workspace network. For a subconscious stimulus to become conscious, the initial activation must be non-linearly amplified until it crosses the threshold for "ignition" [6], when the circulating activity is strong enough to become self-sustaining and reach all parts of the workspace. That allows it to be maintained for a while in working memory, where it can now be consciously examined and processed by more specialized brain circuits. This theory confirms that conscious activity is characterized by widespread, coherent circulation, but adds that this allows it to be scrutinized and if necessary redirected, thus supporting the access perspective.

Table 1 summarizes IIT, ART and Global Workspace commonalities and offers possible avenues of application at the noospheric level.

Table 1. Implementing neuroscientific theories of consciousness at noospheric levels

Neuroscientific theories	Commonalities	Noospheric level implementation
Information integration theory	Coherence of process	Communication patterns
Adaptive resonance theory	Making sense of information	Remaining open/learning
Global workspace theory	Collective interactions	Planetary conversation

4   Self-organization of Dynamic Patterns

The recurrent theme in the different neuroscientific theories we reviewed is that consciousness arises from activation circulating back and forth between different parts of the brain, thus making the activity across these regions coherent or integrated. Such "resonance" moreover stabilizes the pattern of activity long enough for it to be kept in a working memory or global workspace, where it can be examined by various more specialized "agents" that may selectively reinforce, add or subtract elements of the pattern. A sufficiently stable pattern will be transferred to long-term memory, where it remains stored indefinitely and can be recalled when needed. On the other hand, while circulating, the pattern should remain sufficiently plastic to quickly adapt to new inputs from perception, thought or memory.

The emergence of such a coherent, dynamic pattern can be modelled as a process of *self-organization*, i.e. the appearance of a global order out of local interactions [21]. For the brain, this process is typically modelled with neural network simulations, where the stable pattern can be seen as an attractor of the dynamics of activation propagating between neurons via the connecting synapses. However, such a model seems less appropriate for the noosphere, where what is circulating is not one-dimensional "activation", but a variety of ideas that belong to different categories or species.

A perhaps more accurate modelling language is *reaction networks*, a formalism inspired by chemical reactions [4, 22]. A reaction network consists of a set of "species": $S = \{a, b, c, ...\}$ and a set of reactions $R = \{r_1, r_2, r_3, ...\}$. A reaction transforms a combination of species (its input or "reactants"), which are necessary for the reaction to take place, into another combination (its output or "products") that are generated by the reaction. Here is an example of a simple reaction network:

$$r_1 : a + b \rightarrow c; \quad r_2 : c \rightarrow c + a + d; \quad r_3 : d \rightarrow b \tag{1}$$

A reaction has a rate, which specifies how quickly it consumes reactants and generates products. This rate parameter plays a role similar to the weight of a connection in a neural network. As a reaction runs, the amount of its products increases, while the one of its reactants decreases. Dittrich [23] has shown that a sufficiently rich reaction network tends to settle into a particular subset of the participating species and reactions, which he called a "chemical organization". Such an organization is "closed", in the sense that no new species are added by reactions acting on the set. It is also "self-maintaining", in the sense that any species consumed by reactions will be produced by other reactions at least as much as it is consumed. That means that while the reactions consume and produce individual species, the organization as a whole remains stable, because any species removed is eventually reconstituted (as exemplified by network (1)). Such on-going self-(re)production is called *autopoiesis*.

An organization is an *attractor* of the dynamics imposed by the reactions: once the system gets into this regime, it will stay there. Still, an organization may be perturbed by the external addition or removal of species or reactions. This will generally result in a new organization, consisting of a different mixture of species and reactions. Yet, some organizations may exhibit strong resistance to change, in the sense that their reactions are able to neutralize such perturbations. They thus exhibit a form of persistent goal-directedness, returning again and again to their preferred state of autopoiesis [22].

An organization in this sense resembles an adaptive resonance in which self-reinforcing processes circulate between multiple components, while maintaining a stable pattern of activity. Resistant organizations are particularly stable. However, this means they may lack the plasticity necessary to adapt to new input. This may lead to a common pathology of the noosphere, in which ideas circulating through the socio-technological network form a self-reinforcing pattern that a priori rejects contradictory evidence. We will now illustrate such dynamics by examining how different interpretations of the COVID-19 pandemic have reverberated through the noosphere.

5   The Impact of COVID-19 on Noospheric Consciousness

COVID-19, a disease caused by the SARS-CoV-2 virus, was first observed on 12 December 2019 in Wuhan, China. Shortly after, the city of Wuhan became the first epicenter of COVID-19 [24]. On 11 March 2020, the World Health Organization triggered the global health pandemic protocol, and issued a set of public health guidelines in the majority of affected areas. The resulting lockdown measures resulted in catastrophic losses of jobs, sources of income and last but not least increased systemic unemployment [25]. Stressors such as pandemics are often categorized as *systemic shocks*, since they drastically perturb the dynamics of the societal system. Such shocks trigger multi-level change and adaptive responses [26], but may offer the possibility of renewal, transformation and learning.

The noosphere as we defined it is the realm of collective reflection. Dysfunctional thought patterns and maladaptive strategies circulating in this space can result in a systemic loss of trust and the spread of dangerously false information. In this age of global interconnectivity, it is critical to be aware of the impact of thinking patterns and adaptive strategies on the propagation of information. In spite of the manifest economic and psychological impact of COVID-19 health measures on the social fabric, to our knowledge their influence on the noosphere has not been studied in any detail yet. Loss of loved ones, social isolation, stress and confusing information are just a few of the direct effects, with possibly a myriad of future impacts yet to be realized. These may radically shift the current dynamics of the noosphere towards either health or toxicity.

As the pandemic unfolded and measures taken triggered strong reactions from the population, different thought-sharing practices began to emerge. On the one hand, we saw a surge in scientific research, resulting in an unprecedented number of publications on COVID-19 being exchanged. This led to the formation of a new thought-sphere or noosphere discussing the various aspects of the virus, its propagation rate, its ability to evolve to more contagious variants, and last but not least the effectiveness of treatments [27]. On the other hand, the public began its own noospheric process of making sense of the situation. The great uncertainty along with the consequent fears for an unpredictable future, the need to belong to a community, the need for security, reduced trust in institutions, and global confusion led to a bottom-up surge of conspiracy thinking [28]. Let us examine these divergent noospheric dynamics in more detail.

At the onset of the pandemic, global society was worried and wanted to understand as quickly as possible the cause and remedies of this disease. Since the available information was highly scattered, fragmentary and ever-changing, the only way to make sense of it had to be distributed: harnessing the collective intelligence of millions of individuals, databases and processing algorithms connected by the Internet to achieve a coherent understanding. This triggered perhaps the largest noospheric process of global reflection yet. At present (summer 2021), a broad consensus seems to have emerged among scientists and international organizations about the strategy to follow: slowing down the spread of the virus through measures such as face masks, social distancing, and travel limitations, while preventing infection by inoculating as many people as possible with an array of vaccines that have proven their efficacy. These recommendations have been recorded in shared memory, e.g. on Wikipedia and governmental websites. Note that these recommendations have changed over the months as new observations were integrated. For example, the emerging insight that virus particles are spread primarily through the air emphasized the need for aeration, open-air meetings and face masks, while reducing the initial focus on disinfection and hand washing.

This global scientific discussion exemplifies a healthy balance between plasticity (incorporating new insights) and stability (repeatedly confirming and dependably recording the acquired insights). However, in parallel, a number of alternative narratives were circulating across the noosphere that were much less healthy. As an illustration, we will reconstruct one of these, a conspiracy theory centered on billionaire philanthropist and former Microsoft chairman Bill Gates [29].

The origins of this narrative lie in facts known before the pandemic: Bill Gates through his foundation promoted vaccination, warned a few years ago about the danger of a pandemic, directed a company that was collecting data, and funded pharmaceutical research. A more dubious idea that circulated is that vaccines are inherently dangerous. When the pandemic seemed to appear out of nowhere, while vaccines were being touted as the only long-term solution, many people felt a need to explain why this happened, while justifying their fear of vaccines. It was sufficient for some to suggest that Gates would have an interest in everybody getting vaccinated to see a coherent interpretation emerge: Bill Gates funded research to engineer the virus that caused the pandemic in order to convince otherwise reluctant people to get a vaccine that would collect data on them via an injected microchip. The different ideas supporting this theory mutually reinforce each other. The creation of the virus by Gates explains why he was able to predict the pandemic in advance, his involvement in Microsoft why he wants to collect data, his investment in pharmaceutical companies why he was able to get the virus and vaccine produced, the microchip why vaccines are dangerous [29].

In future research, we hope to model such mutual reinforcement with the help of a reaction network formalism. In this model, the "species" would denote circulating ideas, their concentration the number of people entertaining these ideas, and the reactions the dynamics by which people entertaining ideas on the input side of the reaction tend to convince themselves and others of the ideas on the output side—e.g. by posting messages affirming these ideas on social media. Below are some examples of conceivable reactions, where $x \to y$ can be read as "idea x explains, confirms, or makes plausible idea y". (Note that in proper reaction network language, this should be written as $x \to y + x$, because species x remains present after the reaction: it is not "consumed". But to simplify notation we have left out the repeated occurrence of *x*.)

> *desire to collect data* → *need for microchip implantation*
> *need for microchip implantation* → *desire to get people vaccinated*
> *desire to get people vaccinated* → *intent to create virus* + *vaccination promotion*
> *intent to create virus* → *prediction of pandemic*
> *intent to create virus* + *pharmaceutical research* → *creation of virus* → *pandemic*
> *pandemic* + *vaccination promotion* → *people getting vaccinated*
> *people getting vaccinated* → *collection of data* → *desire to collect data*

Such a rudimentary model will further need to include the rate with which a reaction convinces people. If these rates are high enough, the system of ideas making up the conspiracy theory would become self-maintaining, i.e. being produced in sufficient amounts to keep the theory alive, in spite of forgetting, competition with rival systems of propagating ideas, and "perturbing" counterarguments that reduce belief in certain component ideas (i.e. that "consume" the species corresponding to these ideas). Using the software simulation developed in our research group [22], we may then try to determine the precise conditions under which this idea system would survive and grow.

A characteristic of conspiracy theories is that they are highly resistant to perturbations, because lack of confirming evidence, or even counterevidence, is interpreted merely as a confirmation that the conspirators (here, Bill Gates and confederates) are powerful enough to effectively disguise their activities. Another reason for the success of such a theory is that it is simple, unambiguous and concrete. For people who were not able to follow the much more complex scientific discussion, this narrative suddenly explains everything they had difficulty understanding, while providing them with a clear guideline: do not get vaccinated! Such a theory is not only incorrect, it is plain dangerous, because it allows the virus to continue infecting and killing people that refused the vaccination. Yet, conspiracy theories such as this continue circulating among millions of people on social media all across the world [28].

6   Promoting a Healthy Noospheric Consciousness

"Resistant" ideas such as conspiracy theories shift the dynamics of noospheric consciousness towards maladaptive behavior and loss of resilience (i.e. ability to recover from a systemic shock). Addressing the impact of complex challenges such as the COVID-19 pandemic on global society requires a systemic level of collective intelligence—one that is aware of complex trade-offs such as the stability-plasticity dilemma, and in particular the danger of self-reinforcing toxic thought patterns.

More generally, we can define the health of the noosphere as its ability to make sense of the global situation, by integrating a wide range of observations, coming from diverse human and computational agents, and thus developing a coherent strategy to solve problems in a sustainable manner. This requires being sufficiently plastic (open to new information) to adapt quickly to changes, while providing guidelines that are sufficiently stable and clear to concretely depend on. We believe that a healthy noosphere requires the following critical abilities.

First, it should be capable of harnessing the bottom-up intelligence emerging from millions of individual agents while steering it towards collective understanding, knowledge, wisdom, mindfulness, and resilience. As such, it would reduce confusion, conflict and uncertainty, while contributing to the overall well-being of the world population. A variety of apps and web communities have appeared over the past years that provide people with emotional and social support while relieving their stress and anxiety by proposing advice and supporting practices, such as meditation, healthy lifestyles, and mutual help. Such creative noospheric initiatives were motivated by human compassion combined with technologies to heal noospheric sufferings and pains [30].

Second, a healthy noosphere should be capable of recognizing toxic thought patterns and preventing their spread before they contaminate collective consciousness. These thought patterns include conspiracy theories and related denials of plain evidence, e.g. of climate change. Most dangerous are closed worldviews that a priori reject non-conforming ideas while demonizing opponents and thus inciting potentially violent conflict, as exemplified by the ideology of the Islamic State terrorist group, and certain forms of populism, nationalism and fundamentalism. Developing strategies to prevent their spread requires further research on the psychological and social factors that promote such thinking [31]. It also requires an investigation into the algorithms that social media use to selectively propagate information to individuals depending on what they are most interested in. These algorithms tend to create "echo chambers" and "filter bubbles" in which people only see news that reinforces their existing opinions [32], thus closing them off from divergent ideas, while creating a strongly "resonant", autopoietic dynamics. Simulations of how resistant "organizations" [22, 23] of mutually reinforcing ideas self-organize and grow may help us to understand and regulate such dynamics.

Teilhard's conceived unification of thought in the Noosphere does not imply homogeneity nor reducing the uniqueness of individuals [8]; it rather means cultivating an unlimited dialogue and welcoming a diversity of perspectives, because different ideas can complement each other, thus accelerating collective learning and evolution. Our proposal for a healthy noosphere is one that cultivates planetary interconnectivity, an interlinked network of consciousness and information, and last but not least a convergence of individual actions towards the wellbeing of the common good.

This further requires the development and dissemination of worldviews and narratives that promote an open-minded, cooperative and sustainable society and that make people aware of the importance of interdependence and global conversation. A well-thought out example of such an approach is the noopolitik for the noosphere strategy proposed by Ronfeldt and Arquilla [33]. Another example is the recently founded *Human Energy Project* (HEP, https://humanenergy.io/). Inspired by the work of Teilhard de Chardin and the concept of noosphere, the HEP is an initiative to develop a new planetary narrative called "the Third Story", which goes beyond traditional religious and reductionist worldviews to focus on the long-term evolution of life, mind and society. It in particular tries to reach young people, presenting them with an optimistic view of the future and a sense of meaning and direction that is consistent with science without being inconsistent with more spiritual beliefs. The project aims at fostering such awareness by clarifying what the noosphere is and how it functions, formulating strategies for its development towards an open, self-aware consciousness, while disseminating such insights towards the general public via publications, videos, the web and social media. The present paper can be seen as a contribution to these objectives.

Acknowledgments. This research was supported by the Kacyra Family Foundation as part of its Human Energy Project and by the John Templeton Foundation through its grant ID61733 "The Origins of Goal-Directedness".

References

1. Heylighen, F.: Collective Intelligence and its Implementation on the web: algorithms to develop a collective mental map. Comput. Math. Organ. Theory. **5**, 253–280 (1999). https://doi.org/10.1023/A:1009690407292
2. Nguyen, N.T., Hwang, D., Szczerbicki, E.: Computational collective intelligence for enterprise information systems. Enterp. Inf. Syst. **13**, 933–934 (2019). https://doi.org/10.1080/17517575.2019.1640394
3. Heylighen, F.: From human computation to the global brain: the self-organization of distributed intelligence. In: Michelucci, P. (ed.) Handbook of Human Computation, pp. 897–909. Springer, New York (2013). https://doi.org/10.1007/978-1-4614-8806-4_73
4. Heylighen, F.: The offer network protocol: mathematical foundations and a roadmap for the development of a global brain. Eur. Phys. J. Special Top. **226**(2), 283–312 (2016). https://doi.org/10.1140/epjst/e2016-60241-5
5. Heylighen, F.: Mind, Brain and Body. An Evolutionary Perspective on the Human Condition. Vrije Universiteit Brussel, Belgium (2020)
6. Dehaene, S.: Consciousness and the Brain: Deciphering How the Brain Codes Our Thoughts. Penguin (2014)
7. Shoshitaishvili, B.: From anthropocene to noosphere: the great acceleration. Earth's Future (2021). https://doi.org/10.1029/2020EF001917
8. Teilhard de Chardin, P.: The formation of the noosphere. In: The Future of Man, p. 165. Image Books Doubleday, New York (1959)
9. Crick, F., Koch, C.: The problem of consciousness. Sci. Am. **267**, 152–159 (1992)
10. Block, N.: On a confusion about a function of consciousness. Behav. Brain Sci. **18**, 227–287 (1995)
11. Tononi, G.: An information integration theory of consciousness. BMC Neurosci. **5**, 42 (2004). https://doi.org/10.1186/1471-2202-5-42
12. Shannon, C.E.: A mathematical theory of communication. Bell Syst. Tech. J. **27**, 379–423 (1948). https://doi.org/10.1002/j.1538-7305.1948.tb01338.x
13. Thagard, P., Stewart, T.C.: Two theories of consciousness: semantic pointer competition vs. information integration. Conscious. Cogn. **30**, 73–90 (2014). https://doi.org/10.1016/j.concog.2014.07.001
14. Lindhard, T.: Consciousness from the outside-in and inside-out perspective. J. Conscious. Explor. Res. **10** (2019)
15. Aru, J., Suzuki, M., Larkum, M.E.: Cellular mechanisms of conscious processing. Trends Cogn. Sci. **24**, 814–825 (2020). https://doi.org/10.1016/j.tics.2020.07.006
16. Grossberg, S.: Adaptive resonance theory. In: Encyclopedia of Cognitive Science. American Cancer Society (2006). https://doi.org/10.1002/0470018860.s00067
17. Grossberg, S.: The attentive brain. Am. Sci. **83**, 438–449 (1995)
18. Mermillod, M., Bugaiska, A., Bonin, P.: The stability-plasticity dilemma: investigating the continuum from catastrophic forgetting to age-limited learning effects. Front. Psychol. (2013). https://doi.org/10.3389/fpsyg.2013.00504

19. Verbeke, P., Verguts, T.: Learning to synchronize: how biological agents can couple neural task modules for dealing with the stability-plasticity dilemma. PLOS Comput. Biol. **15**, e1006604 (2019). https://doi.org/10.1371/journal.pcbi.1006604
20. Baars, B.J.: Global workspace theory of consciousness: toward a cognitive neuroscience of human experience. In: The Boundaries of Consciousness: Neurobiology and Neuropathology, pp. 45–53. Elsevier (2005). https://doi.org/10.1016/S0079-6123(05)50004-9
21. Heylighen, F.: The science of self-organization and adaptivity. In: The Encyclopedia of Life Support Systems. pp. 253–280. EOLSS Publishers Co Ltd. (2001)
22. Veloz, T., et al.: An analytic framework for systems resilience based on reaction networks. Complexity (2021)
23. Dittrich, P., di Fenizio, P.S.: Chemical organisation theory. Bull. Math. Biol. **69**, 1199–1231 (2007). https://doi.org/10.1007/s11538-006-9130-8
24. Surveillances, V.: The epidemiological characteristics of an outbreak of 2019 novel coronavirus diseases (COVID-19)—China, 2020. China CDC Wkly **2**, 113–122 (2020)
25. Beigi, S.: How do the Covid-19 Prevention Measures Interact with Sustainable Development Goals? ArXiv201102290 Phys. Q-Fin (2020). https://doi.org/10.20944/preprints202010.0279.v1
26. Beigi, S.: The COVID-19 Pandemic: A Wakeup Call to Enhance Systemic Resilience Globally. Wiley J (2021)
27. Le Thanh, T., et al.: The COVID-19 vaccine development landscape. Nat. Rev. Drug Discov. **19**, 305–306 (2020). https://doi.org/10.1038/d41573-020-00073-5
28. Douglas, K.M.: COVID-19 conspiracy theories. Group Process. Intergroup Relat. **24**, 270–275 (2021). https://doi.org/10.1177/1368430220982068
29. Thomas, E., Zhang, A.: ID2020, Bill Gates and the Mark of the Beast: How COVID-19 Catalyses Existing Online Conspiracy Movements. Australian Strategic Policy Institute (2020)
30. Edwards, S.D.: AI in the noosphere: an alignment of scientific and wisdom traditions. AI Soc. **36**(1), 397–399 (2020). https://doi.org/10.1007/s00146-020-00999-9
31. Uscinski, J.E., et al.: Why do people believe COVID-19 conspiracy theories? Harv. Kennedy Sch. Misinformation Rev. 1 (2020). https://doi.org/10.37016/mr-2020-015
32. Terren, L., Borge-Bravo, R.: Echo chambers on social media: a systematic review of the literature. Rev. Commun. Res. **9**, 99–118 (2021)
33. Ronfeldt, D., Arquilla, J.: The Continuing Promise of the Noösphere and Noöpolitik: Twenty Years After. Social Science Research Network, Rochester, NY (2018). https://doi.org/10.2139/ssrn.3259425

Equilibrium Analysis for Within-Network Dynamics: From Linear to Nonlinear Aggregation

Jan Treur[(⊠)]

Social AI Group, Vrije Universiteit Amsterdam, Amsterdam, Netherlands
j.treur@vu.nl

Abstract. In this paper, it is shown how, in contrast to often held beliefs, certain classes of nonlinear functions used for aggregation in network models enable analysis of the emerging within-network dynamics like linear functions do. In addition, two specific classes of nonlinear functions for aggregation in networks (weighted euclidean functions and weighted geometric functions) are introduced. Focusing on them in particular, it is illustrated in detail how methods for equilibrium analysis (based on a symbolic linear equation solver), can be applied to predict the state values in equilibria for such nonlinear cases as well.

1 Introduction

Social dynamics described by dynamics of node states (for example, for the individuals' opinions, intentions, emotions, beliefs,...) in social network models depend on a number of network characteristics for the connectivity and the aggregation of impacts from different nodes. While for networks usually there is much attention for the connectivity, the role of the aggregation characteristics is not often analysed. Nevertheless, these aggregation characteristics also play an important role in the dynamics within a network; for example, whether or not within a well-connected group in the end a common opinion, intention, emotion or belief is reached (a common value for all node states) also depends on them. Often, the tradition is that silent asumptions are made about these aggregation characteristics. For social network models usually linear forms of aggregation are applied. Then theorems exist specifying conditions under which all node states converge to the same value, in particular when the network is strongly connected: from every node there is a path to every other node. In contrast, for neural network models traditionally often some type of logistic sum format is applied and for such functions analysis is indeed much harder than for linear functions.

The often occurring use of linear functions for aggregation for social network models may be based on a more general belief that dynamical system models can be analysed better for linear functions than for nonlinear functions. Although there may be some truth in this if specifically logistic nonlinear functions are compared to linear functions, in the current paper it is shown that such a belief is not correct in general. It is shown that also classes of nonlinear functions exist that enable good analysis possibilities when it comes to the emerging dynamics within a network model. Such classes and the dynamics

© Springer Nature Switzerland AG 2021
N. T. Nguyen et al. (Eds.): ICCCI 2021, LNAI 12876, pp. 94–110, 2021.
https://doi.org/10.1007/978-3-030-88081-1_8

they entail are analysed here in some depth, thereby also not using any conditions on the connectivity but instead exploiting for any network its structure of strongly connected components. Among others, following [7] in the current paper theorems are discussed specifying conditions under which all node states converge to the same value (for example, achieving a common decision or belief within a group). These theorems do not impose any conditions on connectivity and for aggregation apply to classes of nonlinear functions as well as they apply to linear functions. Moreover, for some (but not all) of these classes of 'well-behaving' nonlinear functions it is found out that they can be (indirectly) related to linear functions by some form of function transformation, which then enables application of linear analysis methods such as symbolically solving sets of linear equations including parameters.

2 Modeling and Analysis of Dynamics Within Networks

In this section, the underlying network-oriented modelling approach used is briefly discussed. Following [8], a temporal-causal network model is specified by the following types of network characteristics (here X and Y denote nodes of the network, also called states, which have state values $X(t)$ and $Y(t)$ over time t):

- **Connectivity characteristics.** Connections from a state X to a state Y and *weights* $\omega_{X,Y}$
- **Aggregation characteristics.** For any state Y, some *combination function* $c_Y(V_1, ..., V_k)$ defines the aggregation that is applied to the *single impacts* $V_i = \omega_{X_i,Y}X_i(t)$ on Y from its incoming connections from states $X_1, ..., X_k$.
- **Timing characteristics.** Each state Y has a *speed factor* η_Y defining how fast it changes.

The following generic difference equation used for simulation and analysis purposes incorporates these network characteristics $\omega_{X,Y}$, c_Y, η_Y in a numerical format:

$$Y(t + \Delta t) = Y(t) + \eta_Y[\mathbf{aggimpact}_Y(t) - Y(t)]\Delta t \qquad (1)$$

where $\mathbf{aggimpact}_Y(t) = c_Y(\omega_{X_1,Y}X_1(t), ..., \omega_{X_k,Y}X_k(t))$ for any state Y and X_1 to X_k are the states from which Y gets its incoming connections.

This expresses the general principle that within-network dynamics is implied (or entailed) by the network's structure characteristics; see also Fig. 1.

Fig. 1. The general principle that a network's structure implies the within-network dynamics

The timing characteristics specified by speed factors η_Y enable to model more realistic processes for which not all states change in a synchronous manner. Network models that do not possess this option are less flexible as they silently impose synchronous processing as an artefact. The aggregation characteristics specified by the choice of combination functions c_Y and their parameters provide another form of flexibility to fit better to specific realistic applications. Also in this case, network models that do not possess such an option are less flexible and also silently impose artefacts that may make them fit less to specific applications. For example, for aggregation in social networks often linear functions are used for aggregation.

The following types of properties are often considered to analyse the behaviour of dynamical systems in general.

Definition (stationary point, increasing, decreasing, equilibrium)
Let Y be a network state.

- Y has a *stationary point* at t if $dY(t)/dt = 0$
- Y is *increasing* at t if $dY(t)/dt > 0$
- Y is *decreasing* at t if $dY(t)/dt < 0$
- The network model is in *equilibrium* at t if every state Y of the model has a stationary point at t.

For network models, the following criteria in terms of the network characteristics $\omega_{X,Y}$, c_Y, η_Y can be derived from the generic difference Eq. (1); see also [5, 6]:

Criteria for network model dynamics
Let Y be a state and $X_1,..., X_k$ the states connected toward Y. For nonzero speed factors η_Y the following criteria apply; here $\mathbf{aggimpact}_Y(t) = c_Y(\omega_{X_1,Y}X_1(t), \ldots, \omega_{X_k,Y}X_k(t))$:

- Y has a stationary point at t $\Leftrightarrow$ $\mathbf{aggimpact}_Y(t) = Y(t)$
- Y is increasing at t $\Leftrightarrow$ $\mathbf{aggimpact}_Y(t) > Y(t)$
- Y is decreasing at t $\Leftrightarrow$ $\mathbf{aggimpact}_Y(t) < Y(t)$
- The network model is in equilibrium a t $\Leftrightarrow$ $\mathbf{aggimpact}_Y(t) = Y(t)$ for every state Y

As can be noted, the above criterion for a network being in an equilibrium strongly depends on the combination function c_Y used for aggregation. In this paper, it will be analysed how such a criterion depends on certain properties of the chosen combination functions (properties such as strict monotonicity and being scalar-free, as will be introduced in Sect. 4) and these properties will not only apply to linear functions but also to a wider class of functions extending the class of linear functions beyond the border with the class of nonlinear functions. Exploring nonlinear functions in this class and how some of them still may relate to linear functions is the main aim of this paper.

3 Preliminaries

In this section a few basic types of functions needed in Sects. 4 and further are briefly reviewed. Proofs can be found at URL [10].

Below, the subset $R \subseteq \mathbb{R}$ used as domain for the considered functions v in principle will be $\mathbb{R}$ or an interval within $\mathbb{R}$ of the form $\mathbb{R}_{>0} = (0, \infty)$, although in some cases also other intervals may be considered. Note that the symbol o is used to denote function composition ($g \circ f$ is read for functions f and g as 'g over f' or 'g on f'). Sometimes it is left out: gf means $g \circ f$. The domain of a function f is denoted by Dom(f) and the range f(Dom(f)) by Range(f).

Definition (additive, multiplicative, log-like, exp-like)

a) A function $\theta: R \to \mathbb{R}$ is called *additive* if $\theta(\alpha + \beta) = \theta(\alpha) + \theta(\beta)$ for all $\alpha, \beta \in R$.
b) A function $\theta: R \to \mathbb{R}$ is called *multiplicative* if $\theta(\alpha\beta) = \theta(\alpha)\theta(\beta)$ for all $\alpha, \beta \in R$.
c) A function $\theta: R \to \mathbb{R}$ is called *log-like* if $\theta(\alpha\beta) = \theta(\alpha) + \theta(\beta)$ for all $\alpha, \beta \in R$.
d) A function $\theta: R \to \mathbb{R}$ is called *exp-like* if $\theta(\alpha + \beta) = \theta(\alpha)\theta(\beta)$ for all $\alpha, \beta \in R$.
e) The standard (natural, based on the number e) exponential and logarithmic functions will be denoted by exp and log, respectively.

Note that multiplicative and log-like functions are typically used for domains R that are closed under multiplication and division such as $R = \mathbb{R}_{>0}$, whereas additive and exp-like functions are typically used for domains R that are closed under addition and subtraction such as $R = \mathbb{R}$.

Proposition 1 (relating additive, multiplicative, log-like, and exp-like functions)
Let $\theta: R \to S$ be any function for a finite or infinite interval R in $\mathbb{R}$, then it holds:

a) If θ is multiplicative and $S \subseteq \mathbb{R}_{>0}$, then $\log \circ \theta$ is log-like.
b) If $R \subseteq \mathbb{R}_{>0}$ and θ is log-like, then $\theta \circ \exp$ is additive.
c) If θ is exp-like, then $\log \circ \theta$ is additive.
d) If θ is multiplicative and $S \subseteq \mathbb{R}_{>0}$, then $\log \circ \theta \circ \exp$ is additive.
e) For any multiplicative function such that $\theta(\alpha) = 0$ for some $\alpha \neq 0$, it holds that $\theta(\alpha) = 0$ for all α. For any nonzero multiplicative function θ it holds $\theta(1) = 1$ and $\theta(\alpha^{-1}) = \theta(\alpha)^{-1}$ for all α.
f) If a multiplicative θ is injective on Dom(θ), then it has an inverse θ^{-1} with Dom(θ^{-1}) = Range(θ) and Range(θ^{-1}) = Dom(θ); this inverse θ^{-1} is also multiplicative.

The following theorem provides characterisations of these different types of functions.

Theorem 1 (characterisation of additive, multiplicative, log-like and exp-like)
Let $v: R \to \mathbb{R}$ be continuous. Then the following hold.
a) Assume $R \subseteq \mathbb{R}$ is closed under addition and subtraction with $1 \in R$, then it holds
  θ is additive $\Leftrightarrow$ for some c $\in \mathbb{R}$ for all X it holds $\theta(X) = c\,X$
b) Assume $R \subseteq \mathbb{R}_{>0}$ is closed under multiplication and division with e $\in R$, then it holds
  θ is multiplicative $\Leftrightarrow$ for some c $\in \mathbb{R}$ for all X it holds $\theta(X) = X^c$.
c) Assume $R \subseteq \mathbb{R}_{>0}$ is closed under multiplication and division with e $\in R$, then it holds
  θ is log-like $\Leftrightarrow$ for some c $\in \mathbb{R}$ for all X it holds $\theta(X) = c\,\log(X)$.
d) Assume $R = \mathbb{R}$ is closed under addition and subtraction with $1 \in R$, then it holds
  θ is exp-like $\Leftrightarrow$ for some c $\in \mathbb{R}$ for all X it holds $\theta(X) = \exp(cX)$.

4   Weakly Scalar-Free and Scalar-Free Functions

It is sometimes believed that for dynamical models the borderline between linear and nonlinear functions is also the borderline between well-analyzable behavior and less well-analyzable behavior. In contrast to this, for contagion in social networks it has been found that this borderline between well-analyzable behavior and less well-analyzable behavior lies somewhere within the domain of nonlinear functions: between one class (called monotonic scalar-free functions) covering both linear and nonlinear functions and another subclass of the class of nonlinear functions not satisfying these.

More specifically, whether or not combination functions are scalar-free is an important factor determining whether or not by social contagion all members of a well-connected social network converge to the same level of emotion, opinion, information, belief, intention, or any other mental or physical state; e.g., [7] and [8], Ch 11 and 12. The class of scalar-free functions includes all linear functions but also includes a number of types of nonlinear functions, such as the weighted euclidean functions and weighted geometric functions (as will be defined in Sect. 5 below). To get some more insight in this, in this section some further analysis is made of scalar-free functions, thereby also using a weakened variant of them called weakly scalar-free functions. The definitions are as follows.

Definition (weakly scalar-free and scalar-free functions)
Consider functions $f: R^k \to \mathbb{R}$ and $\theta: R \to \mathbb{R}$ for some subset $R \subseteq \mathbb{R}$ which is $\mathbb{R}$ or $\mathbb{R}_{>0}$.
a) A function $f: R^k \to \mathbb{R}$ is called *weakly scalar-free* for function θ if for all
    $V_1, ..., V_k \in R$ and all $\alpha \in R$ it holds $f(\alpha V_1, ..., \alpha V_k) = \theta(\alpha) f(V_1, ..., V_k)$
b) A function $f: R^k \to \mathbb{R}$ is called *scalar-free* if for all $V_1, ..., V_k \in R$ and all $\alpha \in R$ it
    holds $f(\alpha V_1, ..., \alpha V_k) = \alpha \, f(V_1, ..., V_k)$
c) A function $f: R^k \to \mathbb{R}$ is called *strictly (monotonically) increasing* if for all $U_1, ...,$
    $U_k, V_1, ..., V_k \in R$ such that $U_i \leq V_i$ for all i and $U_j < V_j$ for at least one j it holds

$$f(U_1, \ldots, U_k) < f(V_1, \ldots, V_k)$$

d) A function $f: R^k \to \mathbb{R}$ is called *normalised* if $f(1, ..., 1) = 1$.

The following basic properties can easily be verified.

Proposition 2 (scalar-free and strictly increasing functions)
a) Any function composition of scalar-free functions is scalar-free
b) Any function composition of strictly increasing functions is strictly increasing
c) All linear functions with positive coefficients are scalar-free and strictly increasing
d) Any scalar-free function f is weakly scalar-free for $\theta = $ id, the identity function.

Examples (weakly scalar-free functions)
There are many examples of weakly scalar-free functions. For example, the following functions $f(V) = V^k$ and $f(V_1, ..., V_k) = V_1 * ... * V_k$ on proper domains are weakly

scalar-free with function $\theta(\alpha) = \alpha^k$. The example $f(V_1, V_2, V_3) = w_1 V_1V_2 + w_2 V_2V_3 + w_3 V_3V_1$ is weakly scalar-free with function $\theta(\alpha) = \alpha^2$.

Definition (Cartesian Product Function)
For functions $\theta_1,.., \theta_k: R \to R$ their *cartesian product function* $X_{i=1}^k\theta_i: R^k \to R^k$ is defined by $X_{i=1}^k\theta_i(V_1, ..., V_k) = (\theta_1(V_1), ..., \theta_k(V_k))$.

When all θ_i are equal to one θ, this cartesian product function $X_{i=1}^k\theta_i$ is also denoted by $X^k\theta$, and then is also called a *cartesian power function* of θ.

The following theorem describes some properties of scalar-free and weakly scalar-free functions. Again, proofs can be found in the Appendix at URL [10].

Theorem 2 (relating weakly scalar-free and scalar-free functions)
Consider functions $f: R^k \to \mathbb{R}$ and $\theta: R \to \mathbb{R}$ for some subset $R \subseteq \mathbb{R}$ which is $\mathbb{R}$ or $\mathbb{R}_{>0}$.
a) If a nonzero function f is weakly scalar-free for function θ, then θ is multiplicative.

If, moreover, f is (strictly) monotonically increasing and has at least one positive value, then θ is also (strictly) monotonically increasing.

Therefore for the strict monotonically increasing case, θ is injective and has an inverse θ^{-1} on Range(θ), which is also multiplicative.
b) Any nonzero multiplicative function θ is weakly scalar-free for itself.
c) For any weakly scalar-free function f for θ the following are equivalent:
    (i) Range(f) $\subseteq$ Range(θ)
    (ii) For all $V_1, ..., V_k$ an $\alpha \in R$ exists such that $f(\alpha V_1, ..., \alpha V_k) = 1$
d) For each weakly scalar-free function $f: R^k \to \mathbb{R}$ for any injective θ, the function g: Range(θ)$^k \to \mathbb{R}$ defined by $g = f \; X^k\theta^{-1}$ is scalar-free. If, moreover, Range(f) $\subseteq$ Range(θ), then also the function $h: R^k \to \mathbb{R}$ defined by $h = \theta^{-1}f$ is scalar-free. For strictly increasing f and v, these functions g, h are strictly increasing too.
e) For each set of strictly increasing and weakly scalar-free functions $f_i: R^k \to \mathbb{R}_{\geq 0}$ for the same strictly increasing θ, for any linear combination f of the f_i with positive coefficients, the function $g: R^k \to \mathbb{R}$ defined by $g = f \; X^k\theta^{-1}$ is strictly increasing and scalar-free. If, moreover, Range(f) $\subseteq$ Range(θ), then also the function $h: R^k \to \mathbb{R}$ defined by $h = \theta^{-1}f$ is strictly increasing and scalar-free.
f) If $f: R^k \to \mathbb{R}$ is scalar-free, $\theta: R \to R$ is multiplicative and $g = f \circ X^k\theta: R^k \to \mathbb{R}$, then g is weakly scalar-free for θ. This holds in particular if f is linear.

Examples (from weakly scalar-free to scalar-free functions)
From Theorem (2d) it follows that the function.
$$g(V_1, V_2, V_3) = v^{-1}f(V_1, V_2, V_3) = \sqrt{(w_1V_1 * V_2 + w_2V_2 * V_3 + w_3V_3 * V_1)}$$ is scalar-free. Also, by Theorem 2e)
$$h(V_1, V_2, V_3) = \left[V_1 + V_2 + V_3 + \sqrt{(w_1V_1 * V_2 + w_2V_2 * V_3 + w_3V_3 * V_1)}\right]/\lambda$$ is scalar-free

5 Scalar-Free Functions Based on Function Conjugates

In this section it is analysed how from given scalar-free functions other scalar-free functions can be obtained by applying some transformation. The type of transformation applied can be interpreted as a form of scale transformation or coordinate transformation. It is done by generating conjugates of scalar-free functions defined as follows.

Definition (function conjugates)
Let subsets $R, S \subseteq \mathbb{R}$ be given. The function $g: S^k \to S$ is a *(function) conjugate* of f: $R^k \to R$ by θ if $\theta: S \to R$ is a bijective function and $g = \theta^{-1} \circ f \circ X^k \theta$.

Proposition 3 (function conjugate operator)
Let subsets $R, S \subseteq \mathbb{R}$ be given, and functions $g: S^k \to S$, $f: R^k \to R$, and bijective $\theta: S \to R$. Then the following hold:

a) Then the following are equivalent:
   (i) g is a function conjugate of f by θ
   (ii) The following commutation rules hold: $\theta\, g = f\, X^k \theta$ and $\theta^{-1} f = g\, X^k \theta^{-1}$

b) If a)(i) and (ii) hold, then for any g such an f is unique and can be denoted by $f = S_\theta(g)$ for a *function conjugate operator* S_θ; similarly, $g = S_{\theta-1}(f)$ for function conjugate operator $S_{\theta-1}$, so it holds: $\theta g = S_\theta(g)\, X^k \theta$ and $\theta^{-1} f = S_{\theta-1}(f)\, X^k \theta^{-1}$

   These operators S_θ and $S_{\theta-1}$ are each other's inverse and they preserve function addition and composition: for all f, g, f_1, f_2, g_1 and g_2 of proper types it holds

$$S_{\theta-1} S_\theta(g) = g$$

$$S_\theta S_{\theta-1}(f) = f$$

$$S_\theta(g_1 + g_2) = S_\theta(g_1) + S_\theta(g_2)$$

$$S_\theta(g_1 \circ g_2) = S_\theta(g_1) \circ S_\theta(g_2)$$

$$S_{\theta-1}(f_1 + f_2) = S_{\theta-1}(f_1) + S_{\theta-1}(f_2)$$

$$S_{\theta-1}(f_1 \circ f_2) = S_{\theta-1}(f_1) \circ S_{\theta-1}(f_2)$$

Moreover, when conjugate operators S_{θ_1} and S_{θ_2} and θ_2 are applied in turn, it holds

$$S_{\theta_1\theta_2}(g) = S_{\theta_1} S_{\theta_2}(g) S_{\theta_1}(X^k \theta_2) X^k \theta_1 X^k \theta_2^{-1} X^k \theta_1^{-1} \text{ for all } g$$

If in addition, $\theta_1\theta_2 = \theta_2\theta_1$ then $S_{\theta_1} S_{\theta_2} = S_{\theta_1\theta_2}$:

$$S_{\theta_1} S_{\theta_2}(g) = S_{\theta_1\theta_2}(g) \text{ for all } g$$

Definition (weighted euclidean and geometric functions)

a) A function g is a *weighted euclidean function* of order n if

$$g(V_1, \ldots, V_k) = \sqrt[n]{w_1 V_1^n + \ldots + w_k V_k^n}$$

for some weights $w_1, \ldots, w_k$. A weighted euclidean function is *normalised* if $g(V, \ldots, V) = V$ for all V, i.e., if the sum of its weights is 1, in which case it is called a *weighted euclidean average function*. A weighted euclidean function of order $n = 1$ is called a *linear function*.

b) A function g is a *weighted geometric function* if

$$g(V_1, \ldots, V_k) = V_1^{w_1} \cdot \ldots \cdot V_k^{w_k}$$

for some weights $w_1, \ldots, w_k$. A weighted geometric function is *normalised* if $g(V, \ldots, V) = V$ for all V, i.e., if the sum of its weights is 1, in which case it is called a *weighted geometric mean function*.

c) The *scaled euclidean function* $\mathbf{eucl}_{n,\lambda}$ of order n is defined by

$$\mathbf{eucl}_{n\lambda}(V_1, \ldots, V_k) = \sqrt[n]{\frac{V_1^n + \ldots + V_k^n}{\lambda}}$$

and the *scaled geometric mean function* $\mathbf{sgeomean}_\lambda$ is defined by

$$\mathbf{sgeomean}_\lambda(V_1, \ldots, V_k) = \sqrt[k]{\frac{V_1 * \ldots * V_k}{\lambda}}$$

In this section, it is established that the above-defined nonlinear functions are scalar-free. First, in a more general setting in Theorem 3 this will be addressed for weighted euclidean functions. Moreover, it is analysed how weighted euclidean functions can be related to linear functions: it turns out that they can be interpreted as conjugates of linear functions via some multiplicative function θ. This is explained by the following:

Theorem 3 (from scalar-free functions to scalar-free conjugates by multiplicative v)

a) For any scalar-free function $f: R^k \to R$ with $R = \mathbb{R}_{\geq 0}$, all of its conjugates $\theta^{-1} \circ f \circ X^k \theta$ by a multiplicative $\theta: R \to R$ are also scalar-free.

b) More specifically, for any scalar-free function f, for any positive real number n the function g defined by

$$g(V_1, \ldots, V_k) = \sqrt[n]{f(V_1^n, \ldots, V_k^n)}$$

is a conjugate $\theta^{-1} \circ f \circ X^k \theta$ of f by the multiplicative function $\theta: X \to X^n$ and therefore is also scalar-free.

c) All weighted euclidean functions are conjugates of linear functions by a multiplicative function θ and therefore are scalar-free. In particular, this holds for all functions $\mathbf{eucl}_{n,\lambda}$.

Next, in a more general setting in Theorem 4 it is established that weighted geometric functions are scalar-free and how they can be related to linear functions. Again, it turns out that they can be considered conjugates of linear functions, this time not via a multiplicative function but via a log-like function θ. This is explained by the following:

Theorem 4 (from linear to scalar-free conjugates by log-like θ)

a) For any normalised linear function all of its conjugates $\theta^{-1} \circ f \circ X^k \theta$ by a log-like θ are scalar-free.
b) More specifically, for any normalised linear function f, the function g defined by

$$g(V_1, \ldots, V_k) = \exp(f(\log(V_1), ..., \log(V_k)))$$

is a conjugate $\theta^{-1} \circ f \circ X^k \theta$ of a linear function by the standard log-like function $\theta = \log$ and therefore is scalar-free.
c) All weighted geometric functions are conjugates of a normalised linear function by a log-like function θ and therefore are scalar-free. In particular, this also holds for all functions $\mathbf{sgeomean}_\lambda$.

Note that in Theorem 4c) the scaled geometric mean function $\mathbf{sgeomean}_1$ is scalar-free as it is a special case of a weighted geometric function with all weights 1 and therefore $\mathbf{sgeomean}_1 = \theta^{-1} \circ f \circ X^k \theta$ with f linear and normalised, whereas $\mathbf{sgeomean}_\lambda$ for $\lambda \neq 1$ is not a weighted geometric function and conjugate itself but it is a constant factor $c = 1/\sqrt[k]{\lambda}$ times the weighted geometric function, so $\mathbf{sgeomean}_\lambda = c \; \theta^{-1} \circ f \circ X^k \theta$; therefore $\mathbf{sgeomean}_\lambda$ is scalar-free too.

6 General Equilibrium Analysis for Nonlinear Functions

In this section the analysis is addressed not at the level of specific network structures and implied within-network dynamics but at a more abstract level of properties of network structures and properties of within-network dynamics implied by them; see Fig. 2. As an illustration, consider the example of a mental network model with connectivity depicted in Fig. 3. This is a mental network model for how a person is sensing (sensor state ss_s) a stimulus s in the world (word state ws_s), represents this (representation state srs_s), and is triggered to prepare (preparation state ps_a) and perform (execution state es_a) action a, after evaluation of the predicted (predicted effect representation state srs_e) effect e of this action.

In simulations it can be seen that as a result of a constant value a of stimulus ws_s all state values are increasing until they reach an equilibrium value a as well. The question then is whether these observations based on one or more simulation experiments are in agreement with a mathematical analysis. This will be addressed in two ways.

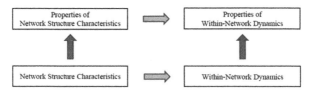

Fig. 2. Relating properties of within-network dynamics to properties of network structure

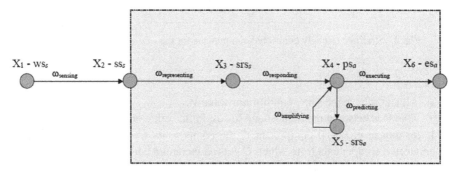

Fig. 3. Connectivity of the example network model

First, in the current section a general perspective is followed and theorems are discussed that have been found based on the network's strongly connected components [7]. Next, in Sects. 7 and 8 a more specific approach is followed that for specific combination functions chosen obtains detailed formulae for the predicted equilibrium values in terms of the network characteristics.

The perspective in the current section is based on the notion of *(strongly connected) component* of a network; this is a maximal subnetwork C such that every node within C can be reached from every other node via a path following the direction of the connections; e.g., [1, 3, 4, 9]. These components form a partition of the set of nodes. In Fig. 4 these components are shown for the example network: C_1 to C_5. In [7] the notion of *stratification* was introduced for such a partition of a network so that each component gets a level (or stratum) assigned. In this case the levels are 0 to 4 as indicated in Fig. 4. Based on the levels defined by this notion of stratification, a number of general theorems and corollaria have been found and proven and presented in [7]; see also [8], Ch 12 and 15. For aggregation these are not limited to linear functions and for connectivity no condition at all is demanded; some of them are the following:

Theorem 5 (equilibrium values related to strongly connected components)
If the following aggregation conditions are fulfilled.

• The combination functions are normalised, scalar-free and strictly increasing

then in an achieved equilibrium:

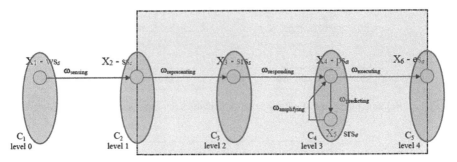

Fig. 4. Stratified strongly connected components for the example network model

a) In any level 0 component C
  - All states have the same equilibrium value V
  - This V is between the highest and lowest initial value of states within C
b) If for any level $i > 0$ component C the components $C_1,.., C_k$ are the strongly connected components from which C gets an incoming connection, then
  - If all states in $C_1,.., C_k$ have the same equilibrium value V, then also all states in C have this same equilibrium value V
  - The equilibrium values of the states in C are between the highest and lowest equilibrium values of the states in $C_1,.., C_k$

Corollary 1 (dependence of all equilibrium values on the values in level 0 components)
If the following aggregation conditions are fulfilled
  - The combination functions are normalised, scalar-free and strictly increasing

then in an achieved equilibrium:
a) If all states in all level 0 components C have the same equilibrium value V, then all states of the whole network have that same equilibrium value V
b) The equilibrium values of all states in the network
  - are between the highest and lowest equilibrium values of the states in the level 0 components
  - are between the highest and lowest initial values of the states in the level 0 components

For the special case of a strongly connected network (consisting of one component), this implies:

Corollary 2 (strongly connected networks)
If the following connectivity and aggregation conditions are fulfilled
  - The network is strongly connected
  - The combination functions are normalised, scalar-free and strictly increasing

then in an achieved equilibrium:

- All states have the same equilibrium value V
- This equilibrium value V is between the highest and lowest initial values of the states

Given that in the example network model there is only one level 0 component with constant value a, by Theorem 5 or Corollary 1 above it can be concluded that all states will have equilibrium value a, as long as the aggregation conditions are fulfilled.

7 Solving Nonlinear Equations for Euclidean Functions

In Sect. 5 it was found that two specific types of scalar-free functions are conjugates of linear functions. This is not only a theoretical result but can also be used in practice to solve equilibrium equations for them. The idea is to apply the conjugate to transform the equations into linear equations, solve these linear equations by a symbolic solver and transform the found solutions back. This will be illustrated for two examples, for a euclidean function $\mathbf{eucl}_{n,\lambda}$ in the current section and for a geometric function in Sect. 7. The euclidean combination function is defined by. In terms of Sect. 5, this function can be written as a conjugate relation.

$$\mathbf{eucl}_{n,\lambda} = \theta^{-1} o f \, o \, X^k \theta$$
$$\text{where } \theta(X) = X^n \text{ and } f(V_1, \ldots, V_k)$$
$$= (V_1 + \ldots + V_k)/\lambda$$

An equilibrium equation involving this combination function for a state $Y = X_j$ typically is of the form.

$$X_j = \sqrt[n]{\frac{V_1^n + \ldots + V_k^n}{\lambda}} \qquad \text{where } V_i = \omega_{X_i, X_j} X_i(t) \text{ are single impacts}$$

This can be rewritten into

$$X_j^n = (\omega_{X_1, X_j^n} X_1^n + \ldots + \omega_{X_k, X_j^n} X_k^n)/\lambda$$

Now take $Y_i = \theta(X_i) = X_i^n$ (with inverse relation $X_i = \theta^{-1}(Y_i) = \sqrt[n]{Y_i}$) and rewrite the above equation into a linear equation in Y_i; this obtains

$$Y_j = (\omega_{X_1, X_j^n} Y_1 + \ldots + \omega_{X_k, X_j^n} Y_k)/\lambda$$

$$\lambda Y_j = (\omega_{X_1, X_j^n} Y_1 + \ldots + \omega_{X_k, X_j^n} Y_k)/\lambda$$

According to the criterion in Sect. 2, for the linear case of a sum function the equation expressing that state ps_a is stationary at time t is

$$\omega_{\text{responding}} X_3(t) + \omega_{\text{amplifying}} X_5(t) = X_4(t)$$

which in a simplified notation is the following equation for the state values X_3, X_4, X_5 for the three states:

$$\omega_{\text{responding}} X_3(t) + \omega_{\text{amplifying}} X_5(t) = X_4$$

Now, consider that for ps_a (which is X_4) a weighted Euclidean combination function $\mathbf{eucl}_{2,\lambda}(V_1, V_2)$ of order 2 is used. Remember from Sect. 5 that these scaled Euclidean functions are conjugates of linear functions f by a multiplicative θ:

$$\mathbf{eucl}_{2,\lambda} = \theta^{-1} \circ f \circ X^k \theta \text{ where } \theta(X) = X^2 \text{ and } f(V_1, V_2) = (V_1 + V_2)/\lambda$$

Note that

$$V_1 = \omega_{\text{responding}} X_3 \qquad V_2 = \omega_{\text{amplifying}} X_5$$

According to this, putting $Y_i = \theta(V_i) = V_i^2$, the above equation for X_4 becomes

$$\sqrt{((\omega_{\text{responding}} X_3)^2 + (\omega_{\text{amplifying}} X_5)^2)/\lambda} = X_4$$

$$((\omega_{\text{responding}} X_3)^2 + (\omega_{\text{amplifying}} X_5)^2)/\lambda = X_4^2$$

$$(\omega_{\text{responding}}^2 Y_3 + \omega_{\text{amplifying}}^2 Y_5)/\lambda = Y_4$$

Using $Y_i = \theta(V_i) = V_i^2$, for the general case all equations become

$$Y_1 \quad \text{ws}_s \qquad Y_1 = Y_1$$
$$Y_2 \quad \text{ss}_s \qquad \omega_{\text{sensing}}^2 Y_1 = Y_2$$
$$Y_3 \quad \text{srs}_s \qquad \omega_{\text{representing}}^2 Y_2 = Y_3$$
$$Y_4 \quad \text{ps}_a \qquad \omega_{\text{responding}}^2 Y_3 + \omega_{\text{amplifying}}^2 Y_5 = \lambda Y_4$$
$$Y_5 \quad \text{srs}_e \qquad \omega_{\text{predicting}}^2 Y_4 = Y_5$$
$$Y_6 \quad \text{es}_a \qquad \omega_{\text{executing}}^2 Y_5 = Y_6$$

This transforms the quadratic equations in the X_i into linear equations in Y_i. These linear equations can be solved symbolically in an automated manner by a Linear Solver, such as the WIMS solver available online at URL.

https://wims.univ-cotedazur.fr/wims/en_tool~linear~linsolver.en.html.

In Fig. 5 it is shown how this set of equations was entered in this Linear Solver and (in the shaded lower area) what solutions are found. These solutions are (note that a is used as a parameter for an assumed stimulus level represented by X_1) translated back from the Y_i to the solutions in terms of the X_i as follows:

$$X_1^2 = a^2 \qquad X_2^2 = \omega_{\text{sensing}}^2 a^2 \qquad X_3^2 = \omega_{\text{representing}}^2 \omega_{\text{sensing}}^2 a^2$$
$$X_4^2 = \omega_{\text{responding}}^2 \omega_{\text{representing}}^2 \omega_{\text{sensing}}^2 a^2 /(\lambda - \omega_{\text{amplifying}}^2 \omega_{\text{predicting}}^2)$$

$$X_5^2 = \omega_{\text{predicting}}^2 \omega_{\text{responding}}^2 \omega_{\text{representing}}^2 \omega_{\text{sensing}}^2 a^2 /(\lambda - \omega_{\text{amplifying}}^2 \omega_{\text{predicting}}^2)$$

$$X_6^2 = \omega_{\text{executing}}^2 \omega_{\text{predicting}}^2 \omega_{\text{responding}}^2 \omega_{\text{representing}}^2 \omega_{\text{sensing}}^2 a^2 /(\lambda - \omega_{\text{amplifying}}^2 \omega_{\text{predicting}}^2)$$

Therefore, the solutions are:

$$X_1 = a \qquad X_2 = \omega_{\text{sensing}} a \qquad X_3 = \omega_{\text{representing}} \omega_{\text{sensing}} a$$

$$X_4 = \omega_{\text{responding}} \omega_{\text{representing}} \omega_{\text{sensing}} a / \sqrt{(\lambda - \omega_{\text{amplifying}}^2 \omega_{\text{predicting}}^2)}$$

$$X_5 = \omega_{\text{predicting}} \omega_{\text{responding}} \omega_{\text{representing}} \omega_{\text{sensing}} a / \sqrt{(\lambda - \omega_{\text{amplifying}}^2 \omega_{\text{predicting}}^2)}$$

$$X_6 = \omega_{\text{executing}} \omega_{\text{predicting}} \omega_{\text{responding}} \omega_{\text{representing}} \omega_{\text{sensing}} a / \sqrt{(\lambda - \omega_{\text{amplifying}}^2 \omega_{\text{predicting}}^2)}$$

This provides explicit predictions for the equilibrium values that are reached. In particular, for all connection weights 1 except $\omega_{\text{responding}}$ and $\omega_{\text{amplifying}}$ which are 0.5 and $\lambda = 0.5$ (which guarantees normalisation), the predicted values are $X_i = a$ for all i, which is confirmed from a practical perspective by the example simulations performed and from a theoretical perspective by the general theorems in Sect. 6.

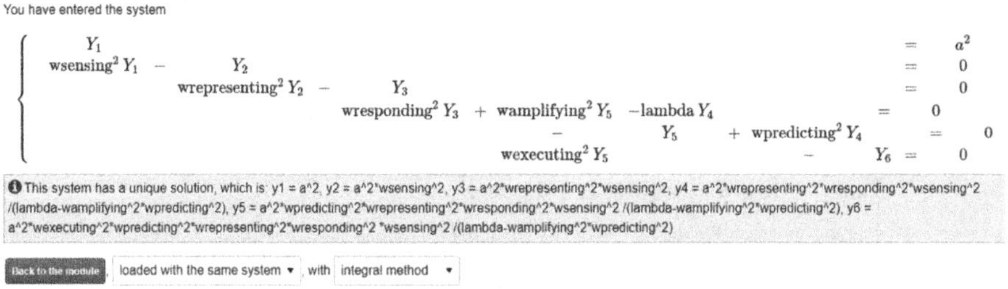

You have entered the system

$$
\begin{cases}
Y_1 & = & a^2 \\
\text{wsensing}^2\, Y_1 \quad - \qquad\quad Y_2 & = & 0 \\
\qquad\qquad \text{wrepresenting}^2\, Y_2 \quad - \qquad\quad Y_3 & = & 0 \\
\qquad\qquad\qquad\qquad \text{wresponding}^2\, Y_3 \;+\; \text{wamplifying}^2\, Y_5 \;-\text{lambda}\, Y_4 & = & 0 \\
\qquad\qquad\qquad\qquad\qquad\qquad\qquad - \qquad\qquad Y_5 \;+\; \text{wpredicting}^2\, Y_4 & = & 0 \\
\qquad\qquad\qquad\qquad\qquad\qquad\qquad\qquad \text{wexecuting}^2\, Y_5 \quad - \qquad Y_6 & = & 0
\end{cases}
$$

ⓘ This system has a unique solution, which is: y1 = a^2, y2 = a^2*wsensing^2, y3 = a^2*wrepresenting^2*wsensing^2, y4 = a^2*wrepresenting^2*wresponding^2*wsensing^2 /(lambda-wamplifying^2*wpredicting^2), y5 = a^2*wpredicting^2*wrepresenting^2*wresponding^2 *wsensing^2 /(lambda-wamplifying^2*wpredicting^2), y6 = a^2*wexecuting^2*wpredicting^2*wrepresenting^2*wresponding^2 *wsensing^2 /(lambda-wamplifying^2*wpredicting^2)

Back to the module   loaded with the same system ▾ , with integral method ▾

Fig. 5. Using the WIMS Linear Solver to solve the nonlinear equilibrium equations for weighted Euclidean functions used for aggregation within the example network

8 Solving Nonlinear Equations for Geometric Functions

In this section the scaled geometric mean combination function **sgeomean**$_\lambda$ is addressed. As found in Sect. 5 the conjugate relation.
sgeomean$_\lambda = c\, \theta^{-1} \circ f \circ X^k \theta$ where $c = 1/\sqrt[k]{\lambda}$ holds for $\theta = \log$ and

$$f(V_1, ..., V_k) = (V_1 + \cdots + V_k)/k$$

An equilibrium equation involving this combination function for state $Y = X_j$ typically is of the form.

$$X_j = \sqrt[k]{\frac{V_1 ... V_k}{\lambda}} \qquad \text{where } V_i = \omega_{X_i, X_j} X_i(t) \text{ are single impacts}$$

This can be rewritten into

$$X_j = (\omega_{X_1, X_j} X_1 \cdots \omega_{X_k, X_j} X_k)/\lambda$$

$$\lambda X_j^k = \omega_{X_1, X_j} X_1 ... \omega_{X_k, X_j} X_k$$

$$\log(\lambda X_j^k) = \log \omega_{X_1, X_j} X_1 ... \omega_{X_k, X_j} X_k$$

$\log(\lambda) + k \log(X_j) = \log(\omega_{X_1, X_j}) + \log(X_1) + ... + \log(\omega_{X_k, X_j}) + \log(X_k)$
Take $Y_i = \log(X_i)$ (with inverse relation $X_j = \exp(Y_j)$) and rewrite into a linear equation in Y_i

$$\log(\lambda) + k\, Y_j = \log(\omega_{X_1, X_j}) + Y_1 + \cdots + \log(\omega_{X_k, X_j}) + Y_k$$

$$Y_1 + \ldots + Y_k - k\,Y_j = \log(\boldsymbol{\lambda}) - (\log(\omega_{X_1,X_j}) + \ldots + \log(\omega_{X_k,X_j}))$$

$$Y_1 + \cdots + Y_k - k\,Y_j = \log(\boldsymbol{\lambda}/(\omega_{X_1,X_j} \cdots \omega_{X_k,X_j}))$$

As an illustration, assume in the example of Sect. 7 for ps_a (which is X_4) the combination function **sgeomean**$_\lambda$ is used, with $k = 2$ and $\lambda = 0.5$ and for the other states X_2, X_3, X_5, X_6 the function **sgeomean**$_\lambda(V_1)$ is used, with $\lambda = 1$, which is the identity function. Then the equation for X_4 becomes

$$Y_3 + Y_5 \ - \ 2Y_4 \ \log(\lambda/(\omega_{\text{responding}}\omega_{\text{amplifying}}))$$

Using $Y_i = \log(X_i)$ for all states all equations are transformed into the following set of linear equations:

$Y_1\text{ws}_s \quad Y_1 = Y_1$

$Y_2\text{ss}_s \quad \log(\omega_{\text{sensing}}) + Y_1 = Y_2$

$Y_3\text{srs}_s \quad \log(\omega_{\text{representing}}) + Y_2 = Y_3$

$Y_4\text{ps}_a \qquad Y_3 + Y_5 \ - \ 2Y_4 = \log(\lambda/(\omega_{\text{responding}}\ \omega_{\text{amplifying}}))$

$Y_5\text{srs}_e \quad \log(\omega_{\text{predicting}}) + Y_4 = Y_5$

$Y_6\text{es}_a \qquad \log(\omega_{\text{executing}}) + Y_5 = Y_6$

Again applying the Linear Solver to them, as shown in Fig. 6, provides the following solutions:

$b = \ \log(\lambda/(\omega_{responding} * \omega_{amplifying}))$

$\log(X_1) = \ \log(a)$

$\log(X_2) = \ \log(\omega_{\text{sensing}}) + \log(a)$

$\log(X_3) = \log(\omega_{\text{representing}}) + \log(\omega_{\text{sensing}}) + \ \log(a)$

$\log(X_4) = \ \log(\omega_{\text{responding}}) + \ \log(\omega_{\text{representing}}) + \log(\omega_{\text{sensing}}) + \ \log(a) - b$

$\log(X_5) = \ 2\log(\omega_{\text{predicting}}) + \ \log(\omega_{\text{representing}}) + \log(\omega_{\text{sensing}}) + \ \log(a) - b$

$\log(X_6) = \ \log(\omega_{\text{executing}}) + 2\log(\omega_{\text{predicting}}) + \log(\omega_{\text{representing}}) + \log(\omega_{\text{sensing}}) + \ \log(a) - b$

Therefore, the solutions are:

$$X_1 = a \quad X_2 = \omega_{\text{sensing}}a \quad X_3 = \omega_{\text{representing}}\omega_{\text{sensing}}a$$

$$X_4 = \omega_{\text{responding}}\omega_{\text{representing}}\omega_{\text{sensing}}a/b$$

$$= \omega_{\text{responding}}\omega_{\text{representing}}\omega_{\text{sensing}}\omega_{\text{responding}}\omega_{\text{amplifying}}a/\lambda$$

$$X_5 = \omega^2_{\text{predicting}}\omega_{\text{representing}}\omega_{\text{sensing}}a/b$$

$$= \omega^2_{\text{predicting}}\omega_{\text{representing}}\omega_{\text{sensing}}\omega_{\text{responding}}\omega_{\text{amplifying}}a/\lambda$$

Substituting 0.5 for $\omega_{\text{responding}}$, $\omega_{\text{amplifying}}$, and λ, again provides $X_i = a$ for all i, which again is confirmed from a practical perspective by example simulations and from a theoretical perspective by the general Theorem 5 and Corollary 1 in Sect. 6.

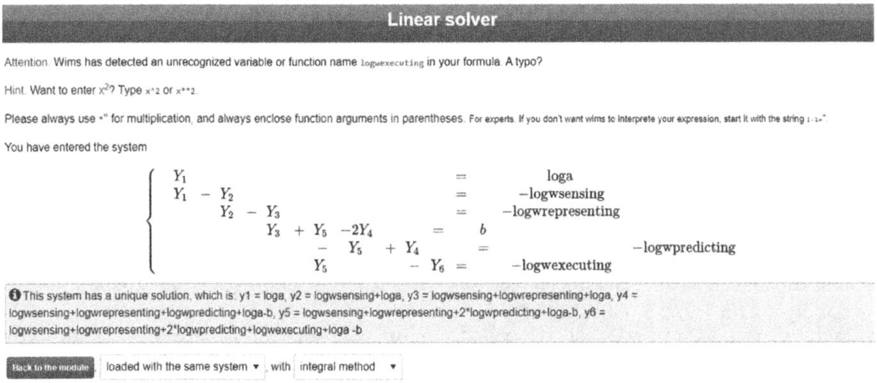

Fig. 6. Using the WIMS Linear Solver to solve the nonlinear equilibrium equations for weighted geometric functions used for aggregation within the example network

9 Discussion

In this paper, it was shown how, in contrast to often held beliefs, certain classes of nonlinear functions used for aggregation in network models enable analysis of the emerging within-network dynamics like linear functions do. The presented work adopts elements from [7], but also includes a number of new concepts and methods introduced here especially for this type of network analysis, such as weakly scalar-free function, conjugate functions and the use of a linear solver to solve nonlinear equations. These new concepts and methods enable to get more insight in some of the types of nonlinear functions for which analysis is well-feasible.

Nevertheless, still more work is needed, as no complete classification of all possible types of nonlinear functions that are scalar-free has been obtained yet; this still stands as a remaining challenge. Note that from scalar-free functions in a combinatorial manner new scalar-free functions can be generated easily, using (1) linear combinations of them, (2) function compositions of them, and (3) conjugates of them. By iteratively combining these three methods, scalar-free functions can be built of arbitrarily high complexity. This shows that there is a very large space of such nonlinear functions, which all still are well-suitable for analysis.

References

1. Bloem, R., Gabow, H.N., Somenzi, F.: An algorithm for strongly connected component analysis in n log n symbolic steps. Form. Methods Syst. Des. **28**, 37–56 (2006)
2. Fleischer, L.K., Hendrickson, B., Pınar, A.: On identifying strongly connected components in parallel. In: Rolim, J. (ed.) IPDPS 2000. LNCS, vol. 1800, pp. 505–511. Springer, Heidelberg (2000). https://doi.org/10.1007/3-540-45591-4_68
3. Harary, F., Norman, R.Z., Cartwright, D.: Structural Models: an Introduction to the Theory of Directed Graphs. Wiley, New York (1965)
4. Łacki, J.:Improved deterministic algorithms for decremental reachability and strongly connected components. ACM Trans. Algorithms **9**(3), Article 27 (2013)

5. Treur, J.: Verification of temporal-causal network models by mathematical analysis. Vietnam J. Comput. Sci. **3**, 207-221 (2016)
6. Treur, J.: Relating Emerging Network Behaviour to Network Structure. In: Network-Oriented Modeling for Adaptive Networks: Designing Higher-Order Adaptive Biological, Mental and Social Network Models. SSDC, vol. 251, pp. 251–280. Springer, Cham (2020). https://doi.org/10.1007/978-3-030-31445-3_11
7. Treur, J.: Analysis of a network's asymptotic behaviour via its structure involving its strongly connected components. Netw. Sci. **8**(S1), S82-S109 (2020a)
8. Treur, J.: Network-oriented Modeling for Adaptive Networks: Designing Higher-order Adaptive Biological, Mental and Social Network Models. Springer, Switzerland (2020b). https://doi.org/10.1007/978-3-030-31445-3
9. Wijs, A., Katoen, J.P., Bošnacki, D.: Efficient GPU algorithms for parallel decomposition of graphs into strongly connected and maximal end components. Form. Methods Syst. Des. **48**, 274–300 (2016)
10. Appendix as Linked Data at URL https://www.researchgate.net/publication/350693687 (2021)

The Effect of Emergent Team Roles on Team Performance: A Computational Network Model

Shairoz A. Evegroen[1], Yagel Schoonderbeek[2], and Jan Treur[3]($\boxtimes$)

[1] Athena Institute, Vrije Universiteit Amsterdam, Amsterdam, Netherlands
[2] Computational Science, University of Amsterdam, Amsterdam, Netherlands
[3] Social AI Group, Department of Computer Science, Vrije Universiteit Amsterdam, Amsterdam, Netherlands
j.treur@vu.nl

Abstract. Much research has been done into the role of different team members through team problem-solving processes, though less research has been done into an optimal combination of members and the influence of their dominance on the team's performance. Therefore, in this paper it is addressed what is the most effective combination of team members and whether dominance can increase team performance. For this purpose, an adaptive computational network model has been designed for a team problem-solving process. Different scenarios were simulated including a respectively homogeneous team and the representation of different dominant roles carried out by several team members. From these simulations, it can be concluded that heterogeneous teams perform better than homogeneous teams. Additionally, this study's results showed that dominance can have both negative and positive effects on team performance.

1 Introduction

Teamwork and projects are key in the organization of firms [16]. One of the reasons for teams being so popular in organizations is the need for faster and better problem solving [5]. For a team to perform well, Belbin's [6, 7] classic team role theories are evaluated in terms of the claim that high team performance is associated with balanced teams in which different team roles are represented amongst team members. However, assessing team performance is a difficult task as many tangible but also intangible factors play a role in team dynamics [36]. These intangible factors are harder to identify than tangible factors. For instance, group cohesion tends to impact team performance [11, 19]. In addition, individuals in a team will not only bring the characteristics of their functional roles as members of teams, but they will also, naturally, take up one or more team roles [32]. In team meetings, many different people with different roles and skills are being present [2]. Therefore, it is interesting to see how these individual roles develop in teams and how they contribute to the team performance.

Next to the balance of team roles and how they interact, the number of team members is also highly investigated [25]. Research shows that the ideal team size is between five to seven people. A smaller or bigger team than five or seven can negatively influence

© Springer Nature Switzerland AG 2021
N. T. Nguyen et al. (Eds.): ICCCI 2021, LNAI 12876, pp. 111–125, 2021.
https://doi.org/10.1007/978-3-030-88081-1_9

the team performance and processes [28, 30]. In addition, team processes can be distinguished into many different phases or states [8, 12, 27]. Even though numerous research into problem solving has been done on an individual level, little attention has been paid to team level problem solving [37].

For these reasons, the aim of this study is to investigate the impact of combinations of team roles and dominance within a group in a problem solving process, specifically in team meetings. This is addressed by computational modeling and simulation. The research question aligned with this aim is: What is the most effective combination of team members and can dominance increase the team performance?

2   Background Knowledge

In this section, background information about this study's topic will be elaborated on. First, team roles and team performance will be highlighted after which the phases in problem solving will be discussed. After this, individual roles in team, ideal team sizes and group homogeneity will be pointed out. Finally, dominance, team effectiveness and social networks and network modelling will be discussed.

Team Roles and Team Performance. Both effectively working teams and team performance are key in organizations [2]. Hereby, a lot of research has been carried out into the impact of several factors to this team performance. As in the organizational context we are dealing with many different types of people [2], many scientists have researched the effectiveness of teams as this varies greatly among organizations [31]. For instance, team diversity is one of these influencing factors [2]. Research suggests that teams can operate most effectively if the right combinations of these different and heterogenous roles are present [31]. One commonly used model that was created from this philosophy to investigate team roles is the Belbin role theory [2]. This model does not only focus on dividing preoccupied roles, but also on the ways in which the roles develop, change and interact with other patterns of behavior over time. Although more theories exist that emphasize team roles and contributions in team performance [2], the Belbin model is most widely used. Furthermore, within these different models, two types of contributions can be distinguished; 'Socio-emotional roles' and 'task roles'. On the one hand, the task centered roles are more focused on problem solving activities and the coordination of the group. While on the other hand, socio-emotional roles are more concerned with promoting group-centered behavior. Interestingly, both roles appear to be important to the task performance [2]. In addition, team roles and performances are influenced on different levels in an organization; individual level, team member level and organizational level. On individual and team member level behavior contributes to the team effectiveness [17]. Relating to team performance, the individual contribution of a person in a team affects the team performance. Subsequently, shifting to team level we can look into how the characteristics of role holders impact team performance as a whole [22]. To create an effective team and well team performance, individuals in a team need to be able to adapt to or cope with changes to their work roles and their environment [17]. Also, it is found that the extent to which team members adapt their roles in order to align with their external environment positively influences the team performance [29].

Phases in Problem Solving. Many ways exist to describe and distinct a problem-solving process [8, 12, 27]. Some scientists assume the problem-solving process to be a linear process in which one phase follows up the next [10]. Others see problem solving as a dynamic process in which different processes occur at various times [15]. Problem-solving phases are defined as 'qualitatively different sub periods within a total continuous period of interaction in which a group proceeds from initiation to completion of… problem solving' ([3], p. 485). In most research it emerges that a form of problem identification or problem recognizing is the beginning of a problem solving process. After that most processes are focused on finding the problem, after which a concluding phase occurs in which also a form of reflection on the preceding process takes place [8, 12, 27].

Individual Roles in Teams. During team meetings employees interact, exchange information, build common ground, create new ideas and manage relationships [27]. In particular, Lehmann-Willenbrock et al. [24] put communication at the center of team functioning. They also confirm that team roles in group processes are emergent [24]. This research also shows that not all team roles equally contribute to team success. In Table 1 an overview of the found results are shown distinguished in several clusters of different team roles [24]. In this table a five cluster solution of team composition is shown (cluster 1: the complainer, cluster 2: the solution seeker, cluster 3: the problem analyst, cluster 4: the indifferent, cluster 5: the procedural facilitator).

Table 1. Means, standard deviations, and distribution of communication aspects (in %) for the five-cluster-solution.

	M	SD	Cluster 1	Cluster 2	Cluster 3	Cluster 4	Cluster 5
Differentiating a problem	8.16	5.22	6.52	8.25	**14.19**	6.11	5.40
Cross-linking a problem	4.33	3.39	3.77	4.30	**7.23**	1.87	5.42
Differentiating a solution	4.80	3.70	3.58	**9.13**	4.22	2.71	4.79
Cross-linking a solution	3.21	2.95	1.92	**6.55**	3.28	1.97	2.75
Statements about the organization	9.89	6.54	11.41	10.43	11.67	5.28	7.31
Knowledge management	3.93	3.52	3.94	5.07	3.45	1.52	**7.32**
Positive procedural statements	5.63	8.28	2.53	5.96	5.83	2.02	**26.18**
Negative procedural statements	3.67	4.43	**6.21**	1.73	3.17	2.70	0.66
Positive socio-emotional statements	18.05	8.55	20.97	18.97	20.01	9.42	16.51
Negative socio-emotional statements	31.10	18.48	27.02	24.19	22.45	**61.87**	21.51
Proactive statements	1.22	1.72	1.12	**2.28**	0.88	0.68	0.84
Counteractive statements	6.01	5.90	**11.01**	3.15	3.63	3.84	1.32

Note. $N = 357$ individuals. All behaviors per 60-minute period. Values printed in bold stand out in comparison with the other clusters, respectively. For example, 14.19% of statements coded as "differentiating a problem" belonged to Cluster 3.

Ideal Team Size. Team size influences a team's performance [25]. It is even shown that increasing team size can hurt a team's productivity in several ways. For instance, it can increase the temptation of free riding on the efforts of others. In specific crisis circumstances for example a big team can even be counterproductive due to over-coordination [25]. Studies show that an optimal group size is between five to seven members [28, 30].

Homogeneity in Groups. Research shows a variety of results about whether a homogeneous group or heterogenous group is positively impacting team performance [33]. On the one hand, studies show that homogeneity in groups is positively related to group performance and well-being. Shared mental model research shows that if team members share similar mental models of the abilities, skills, and processes of the group, they will be able to perform better [26]. On the other hand, it seems that other research suggests different conclusions. In particular, it is found that interpersonal heterogeneity actually leads to creative problem solving and enhanced team performance [4, 18, 20]. Simultaneously, it has been shown that interpersonal heterogeneity could even be more important than individual ability [21].

Dominance and Team Effectiveness. The degree of hierarchy in groups can negatively and positively affect team performance [34]. Despite the fact that leadership and power is also positively related to team effectiveness, research shows that the effects of leadership and power are not always positively influencing team effectiveness. A recent study shows that a lower level of power positively influences the team performance [34]. Also, team effectiveness in problem solving can be influenced by different types of leadership [38] and how a leader responds to developments in teams can influence this process as well [24]. For instance, power differences can negatively influence team learning [34].

Social Networks and Network Modelling. One of the unique aspects of humans compared to other animals is their social engagement. Mankind has been able to organise itself in complex structures that form our society. These structures are called social networks, a widely researched subject within sociology [23]. In principle, a social network is a social structure of individuals within a certain setting and the interactions between these persons within this setting. Examples are hierarchy structures within companies or friendships within a high school. With the rise of social media, the possibilities for this research have grown immensely. It has been shown that the structure of online social networks also mirror those in the offline world, which allows for research to be based on these online social networks. Ever since, social networks and their complexity are studied intensively [9, 14]. Unsurprisingly, network modelling has proven itself to be a very powerful tool for researching social networks; this will be addressed in next section.

3 The Modeling Approach Used

In the Network-Oriented Modeling approach based on temporal-causal networks described in [35], a network structure is defined by *network characteristics* for connectivity (connection weights ω for the strengths of the connections), aggregation (combination functions c and their parameters for how different effects aggregate) and timing (speed factors η for how fast an effect occurs), respectively. Network nodes have activation values that change over time: they serve as state variables and are also called (mental) states. Such states are depicted by the small ovals and the causal relations between them (connections in the causal network) by arrows. The processing over time takes place according to the following standard equation:

$$Y(t + \Delta t) = Y(t) + \eta_Y \big[\mathbf{c}_Y \big(\omega_{X_1, Y} X_1(t), \dots, \omega_{X_k, Y} X_k(t) \big) - Y(t) \big] \Delta t \qquad (1)$$

For the learning and the control of the learning, the approach is inspired by the more general idea of self-referencing or 'Mise en abyme', sometimes also called 'the Droste-effect' after the famous Dutch chocolate brand who uses this effect in packaging and advertising of their products already since 1904. This idea is applied to model adaptation for a network by adding *self-models* to it as introduced in [35]. This leads to *self-modeling networks*, also called reified networks. These are networks that represent some of the network structure characteristics by self-model network states. For example, the weight $\omega_{X,Y}$ of a connection from state X to Y can be represented by a (first-order) self-model state $\mathbf{W}_{X,Y}$, or simply indicated by $\mathbf{W}$. Such a first-order self-model state is depicted in a 3D format in a separate (blue) plane above the (pink) plane for the base network. As like any other state, such a self-model state $\mathbf{W}$ has an activation value that changes over time. The (pink) downward arrow from $\mathbf{W}$ to the related base state makes that for the base network the value of $\mathbf{W}$ is actually used for that base state as the represented connection weight of the incoming connection to it.

4 Social Network Model

In this section, the precise layout of the model will be explained and visualized. In [1], the precise values used in the simulations can be found. As stated above, current research generally finds the ideal size of a team to be five to seven members. Due to limitations in time and resources for this study, the model takes four members into account. Based on the research by [13, 24], this study's model includes: a problem specialist, a solution specialist, a procedural specialist and a complainer, respectively called *person J, person S, person Y and person N.*

Phases Used in the Model. In Sect. 2 it was described that many different distinctions between problem solving phases in team meetings are made over the years [8, 12, 27]. Therefore, based on previous research, this study created four phases to go through in order to identify a problem, finding a solution and deciding on which solution the team will focus on and to conclude results, which also includes evaluating the process (Fig. 1).

Fig. 1. Phases in problem solving in team meetings included in this study.

State Variables Used in the Model. The mental model of each individual was categorized into 5 variables, based again on the research done by Lehmann-Willenbrock et al. [24]: *problem state, solution state, socioemotional state, active state and procedural state.* These states represent the activity of an individual making statements related to that specific category. Socioemotional statements address the atmosphere and appreciation, active statements show interest or responsibility in the subject and procedural statements go into the procedure of the debate and execution of ideas. Problem and solution statements are self-explanatory. Note that states can be negative, which models negative contributions within a specific category. In addition to mental models per individual, a shared mental model was used to simulate the team progress of the process. As often used in similar research, four phases were distinguished for the team: *problem identification, solution finding, solution decision and concluding the results* (Fig. 1). In order to model the time development of these phases, a first-order adaptivity was added to the model in the form of control states for each of these phases. These control states $W_{id\ problem}$, $W_{find\ sol}$, $W_{dec\ sol}$, and W_{concl} represent the connection weight of individual characteristics to the shared variables. This can be found in Fig. 2. Lastly, a world problem state was used to model input of a problem. This world problem state was set to decrease over time, in order to prevent re-initiation of the model.

Connections and Connection Weights. The connections can be categorized into four types: the phases of the team meeting (Fig. 2), the influence of individuals on the team process (Fig. 4), the connections between individuals (Fig. 5) and the connections within individuals (Fig. 6). Firstly, this study uses a first order adaptivity to model time development of phases, as mentioned earlier. Furthermore, after the completion of a phase, a phase state is stimulated, which in turn stimulates the states related to the next phase and damps the states related to the previous phase (Fig. 2). For the second type, it was chosen that the socioemotional, active and procedural statements influenced all phases of the process. In the last phase, an extra activation of procedural statements was included in the model to make those statements contribute more. Problem statements were linked to the problem phase and solution statements to the two solution phases (Fig. 3).

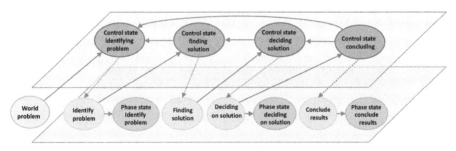

Fig. 2. Phases included in this study's model.

Furthermore, it was chosen that individuals had a small stimulus on each other for the same statements. An example of this is: if person J becomes active in problem statements, the other individuals get a small stimulus of being active as well in problem statements. Lastly, all variables within an individual have a small negative connection, as becoming active in making one specific statement has the consequence that that individual is less active in other statements. The precise values can be found in [1], which were based on the research of Lehmann-Willenbrock et al. [24] in combination with some trial and error experimentation.

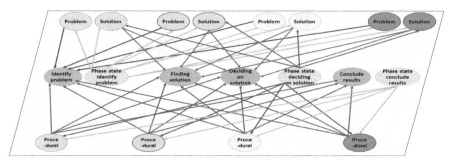

Fig. 3. Links between problem-, solution-, and procedural states to phases.

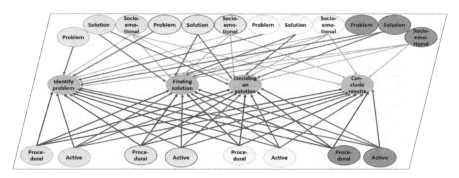

Fig. 4. State influences on phases in the team process.

Initial Values, Speed Factors and Combination Function Parameters. The initial values of all the shared team states were set at 0 at the beginning of each simulation. The same was done for the control states and the phase states. The initial values for the individual were based on [24]; see also [1].

For the speed factors, all individuals were set at the same speed. The speed was set relatively high compared to the speed of the shared states, as statements dynamics develop quicker than team processes. An exception to this was both the socioemotional states and the active states, which were set to develop little during a team process. The control states and phase states were chosen at the highest speeds, as these needed to function as gates. All states were modelled by the advanced logistic function. The steepness and threshold for the individual states were set low in order for them to develop quickly and to be sensitive to the situation. The steepness for the shared states was set slightly higher, as these are expected to develop less quickly, as stated before. Their threshold was set high due to the many incoming connections. The control states and phase states were given both high steepness and thresholds as again these variables function as gates.

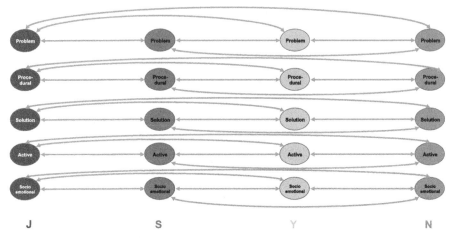

Fig. 5. Connections between individuals.

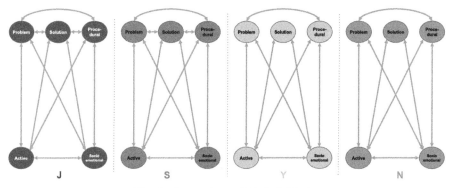

Fig. 6. Connections within individuals.

5 Simulation

In this section, the simulations performed in this study will be shown. First, the base scenario will be described. Second, a homogeneous scenario will be outlined. Third, a dominance scenario of all individuals included in the model will be shown.

Base Scenario. For the model described above, the results as shown in Fig. 7 were found. As can be seen, the phases nicely follow each other up in time. The problem and solution statements are mostly active during the relevant phases. Similarly, the procedural statements become extra stimulated in the final process (concluding results). Person N, the complainer, mostly has negative values, which also contributes negatively to the shared states. However, the team is still able to complete all required phases in order to successfully complete the problem solving meeting. The x-axis can be interpreted as time in minutes, though this could also be scalable to other time-sizes. As stated earlier, the socioemotional- and active statements vary little over time. However, due to successes in the process, they grow over time, except for the states of the complainer, person N.

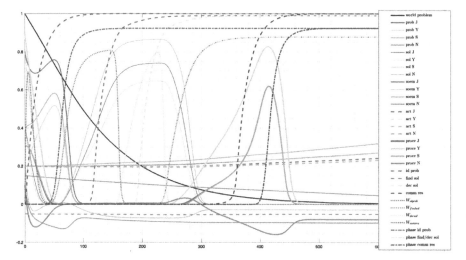

Fig. 7. All the variables of the base scenario.

Homogeneous Scenario. Furthermore, a more homogenous group was simulated, i.e. the initial values and connection weights of the different types of statements for the individuals were brought closer to the average. Therefore, the overall sensitivity of the group to make certain statements would be the same, but the group would have less specialized individuals. In Fig. 8, the whole problem-solving process is shown. Identifying the problem is done by roughly the same speed.

However, the solution phase takes more time for the homogeneous group compared to the base scenario (Fig. 7), namely *300 (seconds) instead of 240 (seconds)*. Moreover, concluding the process is an even bigger challenge for this group, which is only finished at *540 (seconds) instead of 400 (seconds)*. Interestingly, the states of person N have become only slightly less negative, whilst other individual variables, e.g. the solution state of person S, have become significantly less strong.

Dominance Scenario. In addition to the homogeneous group, simulations were performed in which each individual was made dominant within the group, by increasing

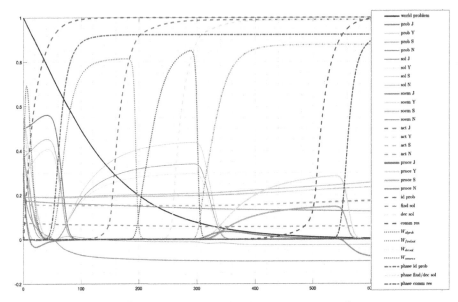

Fig. 8. All the variables of the homogeneous scenario.

their connection weight with other individuals as well as the shared states. The connection weights of the other individuals were decreased such that the average connectivity remained at the same value. In Figs. 9 & 10, the results of the dominance of the problem analyst (person J) and the solution seeker (person S) are depicted. The resulting dynamics of the two scenarios are very similar, as activity in problem- and solution statements are strongly correlated, as found by Lehmann-Willenbrock et al. [24]. In both scenarios the first three phases are completed in very similar times. The group again is relatively inefficient in concluding the process as this is only finished *after 500 (seconds)* by dominance of person J and *after 540 (seconds)* by dominance of person S compared to *400 (seconds)* in the base scenario (Fig. 7). Subsequently, person Y (the procedural facilitator) was made dominant by the same method.

In Fig. 11, the resulting dynamics are shown. In this scenario, the group performs the best as all phases are finished quicker than the base scenario (Fig. 7). Concluding the results is finished *around 280 (seconds)* compared to the base value of *400 (seconds)*, which is a significant speed up. It must be noted that this result is caused by a specific modelling choice. Namely, the procedural statements have an influence on all parts of the process. Dominance of person Y causes the groups procedural behavior to be amplified, which results in the fastest development in the whole process.

Lastly, dominance of the complainer (person N) was simulated, depicted in Fig. 12. The group dynamics were catastrophically influenced by person N. Only the first phase was rounded off in a similar manner as before. Subsequently, the dominance of the complainer prevented the group of moving through the other phases of the problem-solving process.

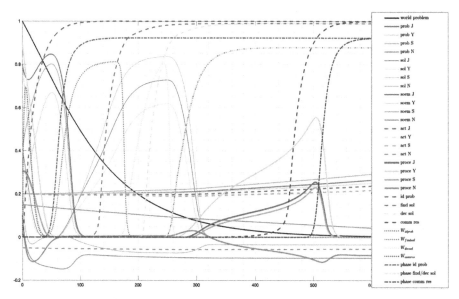

Fig. 9. All the variables of the dominance J scenario.

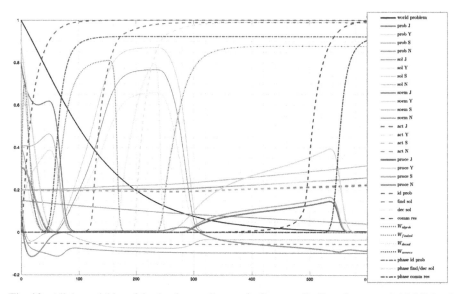

Fig. 10. All the variables of the dominance S scenario. In appendix C, each process is highlighted and shown more clearly.

6 Discussion

The aim of this study was to investigate the impact of combinations of team roles and dominance within a group on a problem solving process, specifically in team meetings. Hereby, the research question aligned with this aim was: What is the most effective combination of team members and can dominance increase the team performance? First, it can be concluded that the hypothesis of heterogeneous teams performing better than homogeneous teams is confirmed in this study's model. It was seen that the phase of identifying the problem developed similar in both scenarios. However, finding solutions & deciding on a solution took the homogeneous team significantly more time. This difference became more visible in concluding the process, which is the last phase of the team meeting. According to Hong and Page [21], diversity of a population in a group or team improves collective understanding and collective problem solving. In our research it is yet hard to tell whether diversity improves collective understanding, though it can be stated that diversity in teams as simulated in this study, improves the problem solving process.

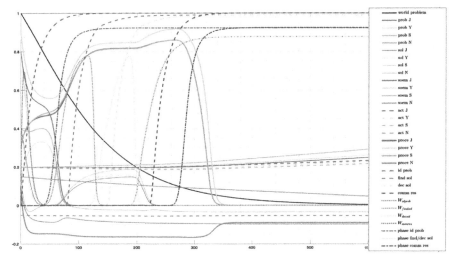

Fig. 11. All the variables of the dominance Y scenario.

Second, this study's model seems to agree with the literature that dominance can have both negative and positive effects on team performance. Moreover, the results suggest that in particular, only dominance by the procedural facilitator-role delivers these positive effects. Interestingly, Lehmann-Willenbrock et al. [24] found as well that the participation of the procedural facilitator (Person Y in this study), led to higher Meeting Process Satisfaction for Teams. Therefore, in further research it could be interesting to investigate the impact of this team satisfaction in relation to the positive effects on team performance in this study as this study did not focus on the impact for the Meeting Process Satisfaction in relation to the team performance.

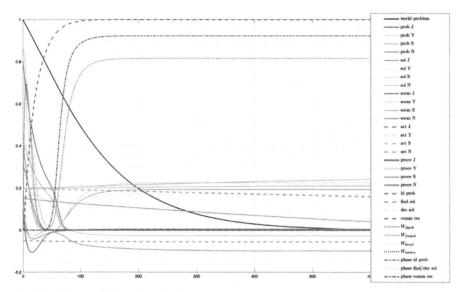

Fig. 12. All the variables of the dominance N scenario. In appendix C, each process is highlighted and shown more clearly.

Nevertheless, one must take certain choices made for this study's model into consideration. For example, the connection weights of all types of statements were set to the same value. This could be researched and specified further in order to bring the model closer to reality. In addition, the first phase, identification of the problem, was set rather shortly and the observed dynamics for different scenarios were indifferent. By variation of the lengths of the phases, different dynamics might be found, which could tell us more about the possible developments in team meetings. Lastly, for this model, procedural statements were made influencing, as those were connected to all phases and some individual procedural variables had high values. Whether this is a correct manner of modelling has to be studied further.

Furthermore, additional research is recommended on this model in order to relate it better to real-life scenarios. A first step in this should be validation of the model on real-life data of team meetings. By this validation, the model could be used for exploration of new settings and its explanatory value would improve. Next, the individual mental models could be extended such that the perception of statements in a team meeting is taken into account. This would drastically increase the required computational power, but such a detailed model allows for precise clarification of the group dynamics at play. Lastly, it should be noted that the combination function for the variables in this model should be studied and varied. It was not solidly argued for this model why the advanced logistic function was used. It could very well be that the simple homophily function, where attraction and repulsion takes place depending on the closeness of two variables, provides a more realistic depiction.

References

1. Appendix Linked Data at ResearchGate URL: https://www.researchgate.net/publication/348 415599 (2021)
2. Aritzeta, A., Swailes, S., Senior, B.: Belbin's team role model: development, validity and applications for team building. J. Manage. Stud. **44**(1), 96–118 (2007)
3. Bales, R.F., Strodtbeck, F.L.: Phases in group problem-solving. Psychol. Sci. Public Interest **46**(4), 485 (1951)
4. Bantel, K.A., Jackson, S.E.: Top management and innovations in banking: does the composition of the top team make a difference? Strategic Manag. J. **10**(S1), 107–124 (1989)
5. Basadur, M., Head, M.: Team performance and satisfaction: a link to cognitive style within a process framework. J. Creative Behav. **35**(4), 227–248 (2001)
6. Belbin, R.M.: Management Teams: Why They Succeed or Fail. Heinemann, London (1981)
7. Belbin, R.M.: Team Roles at Work. Buccerworth-Heineman, Oxford (1993)
8. Bell, M.A.: Phases in group problem-solving. Small Group Behav. **13**(4), 475–495 (1982)
9. Boase, J., Wellman, B.: Personal relationships: on and off the Internet. Cambridge Handb. Personal Relation. **8**, 709–723 (2006)
10. Carlson, M.P., Bloom, I.: The cyclic nature of problem solving: an emergent multidimensional problem-solving framework. Educ. Stud. Math. **58**(1), 45–75 (2005)
11. Carron, A.V., Colman, M.M., Wheeler, J., Stevens, D.: Cohesion and performance in sport: a meta-analysis. J. Sport Exerc. Psychol. **24**, 168–188 (2002)
12. Delbecq, A.L., Van de Ven, A.H.: A group process model for problem identification and program planning. J. Appl. Behav. Sci. **7**(4), 466–492 (1971)
13. Dowell, N.M., Lin, Y., Godfrey, A., Brooks, C.: Exploring the relationship between emergent sociocognitive roles, collaborative problem-solving skills, and outcomes: a group communication analysis. J. Learn. Anal. **7**(1), 38–57 (2020)
14. Dunbar, R.I.M., Arnaboldi, V., Conti, M., Passarella, A.: The structure of online social networks mirrors those in the offline world. Soc. Netw. **43**(2015), 39–47 (2015)
15. Fiore, S.M., Smith-Jentsch, K.A., Salas, E., Warner, N., Letsky, M.: Towards an understanding of macrocognition in teams: developing and defining complex collaborative processes and products. Theor. Issues Ergon. Sci. **11**(4), 250–271 (2010)
16. Georgiadis, G.: Projects and team dynamics. Rev. Econ. Stud. **82**(1), 187–218 (2015)
17. Griffin, M.A., Neal, A., Parker, S.K.: A new model of work role performance: positive behavior in uncertain and interdependent contexts. Acad. Manag. J. **50**(2), 327–347 (2007)
18. Hambrick, D.C., Cho, T.S., Chen, M.J.: The influence of top management team heterogeneity on firms' competitive moves. Admin. Sci. Quart. **41**(4), 659–684 (1996)
19. Heuzé, J.P., Sarrazin, P., Masiero, M., Raimbault, N., Thomas, J.P.: The relationships of perceived motivational climate to cohesion and collective efficacy in elite female teams. J. Appl. Sport Psychol. **18**, 201–218 (2006)
20. Hoffman, L.R., Maier, N.R.F.: Quality and acceptance of problem solutions by members of homogeneous and heterogeneous groups. J. Abnormal Soc. Psych. **62**(2), 401–407 (1961)
21. Hong, L., Page, S.E.: Groups of diverse problem solvers can outperform groups of high-ability problem solvers. Proc. Natl. Acad. Sci. USA **101**(46), 16385–16389 (2004)
22. Humphrey, S.E., Morgeson, F.P., Mannor, M.J.: Developing a theory of the strategic core of teams: a role composition model of team performance. J. Appl. Psychol. **94**(1), 48 (2009)
23. Kadushin, C.: Understanding Social Networks: Theories, Concepts, and Findings. Oup USA (2012)
24. Lehmann-Willenbrock, N., Beck, S.J., Kauffeld, S.: Emergent team roles in organizational meetings: identifying communication patterns via cluster analysis. Commun. Stud. **67**, 37–57 (2016)

25. Mao, A., Mason, W., Suri, S., Watts, D.J.: An experimental study of team size and performance on a complex task. PLoS ONE **11**(4), e0153048 (2016)
26. Mason, C.M.: Exploring the processes underlying within-group homogeneity. Small Group Res. **37**(3), 233–270 (2006)
27. Meinecke, A.L., Lehmann-Willenbrock, N.: Social dynamics at work: Meetings as gateway. The Cambridge Handbook of Meeting Science, vol. 325, no. 356, p. 15. Cambridge University Press, New York, NY (2015)
28. Michaelsen, L.K., Sweet, M., Parmelee, D.X. (Eds.): Team-Based Learning: Small Group Learning's Next Big Step: New Directions for Teaching and Learning, Number 116, vol. 103. John Wiley & Sons (2011)
29. Moon, H., et al.: Asymmetric adaptability: dynamic team structures as one-way streets. Acad. Manag. J. **47**, 681–695 (2004)
30. Plsek, P.: Institute of Medicine. Crossing the Quality Chasm: A New Health System for the Century. National Academies Pr, Washington, DC (2001)
31. Prichard, J., Stanton, N.: Testing Belbin's team role theory of effective groups. J. Manag. Dev. **18**(8), 652–665 (1999). https://doi.org/10.1108/02621719910371164
32. Senior, B.: Team roles and team performance: is there 'really' a link? J. Occup. Organ. Psychol. **70**(3), 241–258 (1997)
33. Smith, E.B., Hou, Y.: Redundant heterogeneity and group performance. Organ. Sci. **26**(1), 37–51 (2015)
34. Tost, L.P., Gino, F., Larrick, R.P.: When power makes others speechless: the negative impact of leader power on team performance. Acad. Manag. J. **56**(5), 1465–1486 (2013)
35. Treur, J.: Network-Oriented Modeling for Adaptive Networks: Designing Higher-Order Biological, Mental and Social Network Models. Springer Nature, Cham (2020)
36. Warner, S., Bowers, M.T., Dixon, M.A.: Team dynamics: a social network perspective. J. Sport Manag. **26**(1), 53–66 (2012)
37. Wiltshire, T.J., Butner, J.E., Fiore, S.M.: Problem-solving phase transitions during team collaboration. Cogn. Sci. **42**(1), 129–167 (2018)
38. Zaccaro, S.J., Rittman, A.L., Marks, M.A.: Team leadership. Leader. Q. **12**(4), 451–483 (2001)

A Second-Order Adaptive Network Model for Shared Mental Models in Hospital Teamwork

Laila van Ments[1], Jan Treur[2,3(✉)], Jan Klein[3], and Peter Roelofsma[3]

[1] AutoLeadStar, Jerusalem, Israel
laila@autoleadstar.com
[2] Social AI Group, Vrije Universiteit Amsterdam, Amsterdam, The Netherlands
j.treur@vu.nl
[3] Delft University of Technology, Center for Safety in Healthcare, Delft, The Netherlands
{j.klein,p.h.m.p.roelofsma}@tudelft.nl

Abstract. This paper describes a second-order adaptive network model for mental processes making use of shared mental models for team performance. The paper illustrates the value of adequate shared mental models for safe and efficient team performance and in cases of imperfections of such shared team models how this complicates the team performance. It is illustrated for a context of a medical team performing a tracheal intubation. Simulations illustrate how the adaptive network model is able to address the type of complications that can occur in realistic scenarios.

Keywords: Shared mental model · Second-order network model · Hospital · Team performance · Healthcare safety

1 Introduction

The concept of a shared mental model (SMM) has recently received increased attention in medical team performance literature as well as in other domains. SMM's are often brought in relation to the quality of team performance and safety [4, 5, 12, 17, 18, 23]. A team has a shared mental model when relevant knowledge structures concerning how reality works or should work are held by all team members and when there is sufficient alignment in the internal representations of these knowledge structures [9, 13, 14]. Like mental models in general, shared mental models are used in mental processes for internal mental simulation and decision making based on their outcomes; e.g., [6]. Moreover, they often are adaptive in the sense that they can be learnt or forgotten, and for such adaptation usually a form of control is applied. These aspects of shared mental models are all addressed in the current paper. It is illustrated in particular for the mental processes of members of a medical team. The real-world challenge addressed here is to cover (1) the errors and other imperfections that are daily practice in such teams and (2) the way in which such teams handle them.

In Sect. 2, a general introduction and background is described. This section also describes the domain specifics of the example scenario addressing a tracheal intubation

© Springer Nature Switzerland AG 2021
N. T. Nguyen et al. (Eds.): ICCCI 2021, LNAI 12876, pp. 126–140, 2021.
https://doi.org/10.1007/978-3-030-88081-1_10

performed by a medical team consisting of a specialist and a nurse. In Sect. 3 the design of the adaptive network model for this type of shared mental model is presented. Section 4, then, describes the illustrative simulation example. Section 5 provides a discussion of the adaptive network model to support healthcare safety.

2 Background

The second-order adaptive network model introduced here integrates knowledge of mental models from psychology, team mental models from social sciences, hospital protocols from medical- and safety sciences, and the AI-domain of network modeling.

Mental Models. In his book Craik [6], describes a mental model as a *small-scale model* that is carried by an organism within its head as follows; see also [22]:

'If the organism carries a "small-scale model" of external reality and of its own possible actions within its head, it is able to try out various alternatives, conclude which is the best of them, react to future situations before they arise, utilize the knowledge of past events in dealing with the present and future, and in every way to react in a much fuller, safer, and more competent manner to the emergencies which face it.' ([6], p. 61)

Note that this quote covers both the usage of a mental model based on so-called internal mental simulation ('try out various alternatives') and the learning of it ('utilize the knowledge of past events'). For more on mental models, see, e.g., [2, 3, 7, 20].

Shared Mental Models. Team errors have often been linked to inadequacies of the shared mental model and the lack of adaptivity of it [4, 5, 12, 17, 18, 23]. This has major implications for health care and patent safety in the operation room, e.g., concerning open heart operation and tracheal intubation [12, 17].

Case Description. The general setting of the addressed case is an emergency department where an emergency team is coming together for preparing to intubate a critically ill patient with deteriorating conscious state. The airway has been assessed as being normal and there is no expectation that there are going to be any difficulties with intubation. A doctor (D) is called in to perform a tracheal intubation in collaboration with a nurse (N). In general, a tracheal intubation induces stress for D and A. The call of the doctor triggers the activation of the initial state of a shared mental model with separate roles and activities for the tracheal intubation for the D and N. The roles and activities are unique for D and N. The roles for the doctor are: team leader, prepare team, prepare for difficulties and the role of intubator. The roles for the nurse are: intubator's assistant, prepare patient, prepare equipment, prepare drugs, give drugs, monitoring the patient, cricoid force, and the role of runner for help and/or additional equipment. In addition to the allocation of roles, the shared mental model contains the corresponding (temporal) sequence of activities for D and N. For the chosen example scenario based on an imperfect shared mental model considered here, this consists of the following sequence. The nurse prepares the patient. According to the protocol she should then have performed the preparation of the equipment; but she forgets this and goes on to perform the preparation of the drugs. The doctor executes pre oxygenation and starts with the preparation of the team and the preparation for difficulties. The nurse listens and observes to the doctor's team preparation. The nurse gives drugs to the patient and applies cricoid pressure to the patient. Then the doctor initiates the executing of plan A Larynscopy and starts the first intubation attempt. The nurse assists the doctor in the intubation attempt. The nurse monitors the patient. When the first attempt is finished, the nurse seeks confirmation of its success by monitoring the capnograph. Then N realizes the earlier omission and sees that the capnograph is not active N verbalizes this to the doctor who then verbalizes the failed attempt.The intubation attempt is repeated with the exclusion of the preparation and the giving of the drugs to the patient by N. Also the preparation of the team for the intubation and for difficulties are not performed by D. All other tasks are repeated in a second round and when this is not successful also in a third attempt. According to the protocol the doctor should have asked for help when the third attempt is not successful. But she does not do this.

Network-oriented Modeling. The Network-Oriented Modelling approach from [19] is a suitable modeling approach to represent causal relations and the way they can be processed to generate mental processes, as needed for the use of shared mental models as described above. In particular, in [19] it is described how adaptive networks of different orders can be modelled relatively easily. Therefore, following the cognitive architecture for mental models described in [20], this approach was used to design a second-order adaptive network model for using shared mental models in team members' mental processing and acting.

Network nodes X have state values indicated by real numbers $X(t)$ that vary over time t; nodes are also called states. The characteristics defining a network model are *connection weights* $\omega_{X,Y}$ for connectivity, *combination functions* c_Y for aggregation of impact, and *speed factors* η_Y specifying timing of states. The numerical representation created by the available dedicated software environment is based on the following equations based (where $X_1, \ldots, X_k$ are the states from which state Y gets incoming connections):

$$\textbf{impact}_{X,Y}(t) = \omega_{X,Y}X(t) \tag{1}$$

$$\textbf{aggimpact}_Y(t) = \mathbf{c}_Y(\textbf{impact}_{X_1,Y}(t), \ldots, \textbf{impact}_{X_k,Y}(t)) = \mathbf{c}_Y(\omega_{X_1,Y}X_1(t), \ldots, \omega_{X_k,Y}X_k(t)) \tag{2}$$

$$\begin{aligned} Y(t + \Delta t) &= Y(t) + \eta_Y\big[\textbf{aggimpact}_Y(t) - Y(t)\big]\Delta t \\ &= Y(t) + \eta_Y[\mathbf{c}_Y(\omega_{X_1,Y}X_1(t), \ldots, \omega_{X_k,Y}X_k(t)) - Y(t)]\Delta t \end{aligned} \tag{3}$$

A computational network engine developed within this software environment based on the generic Eqs. (3) takes care for the processing of all network states thereby using their connections and other network characteristics.

Self-modeling Networks to Model Adaptivity and Control. First-order adaptation (also called *plasticity*) is applied here to the relations (connections) within a mental model using Hebbian learning [11]. Second-order adaptation is applied to model *metaplasticity* [1, 10], for a control effect of the contextual stress on the first-order adaptation process of learning and forgetting. These are modeled using *self-models* in the network: for some of the network characteristics ω, $\mathbf{c}$, η as mentioned above, network states are added to the network that represent their value. For some connection weights $\omega_{X,Y}$ an additional state $\mathbf{W}_{X,Y}$ (called *self-model state*) is added to the network that represents this weight and is used for that weight in the processing. Next, for the combination function of such a self-model state $\mathbf{W}_{X,Y}$, a persistence parameter $\mu_{\mathbf{W}_{X,Y}}$ is used that is represented by another self-model state $\mathbf{M}_{\mathbf{W}_{X,Y}}$. The latter network state is a *second-order self-model state* as it represents a network characteristic related to (first-order) self-model state $\mathbf{W}_{X,Y}$.

3   The Adaptive Network Model Using a Shared Mental Model

The second-order adaptive network model introduced here follows the generic three-level cognitive architecture for mental models described in [20]. It has connectivity as depicted in Fig. 1; for an explanation of the states, see Tables 1, 2 and 3. The scenario concerns a sequence of actions with actors assigned performing them and their temporal order, according to the realistic case described in Sect. 2.

Base Level: Overview. Within the base plane, the world states indicating the actual steps in the world for this scenario are depicted in Fig. 1 by the blue nodes with their connections in the middle area of the base plane. A contextual stress factor is represented by the green node on the left. The actor is indicated within a world state name by D for doctor or N for nurse. The shared mental model consists of two individual mental models for D and N. These mental models are shown in the base level plane and reflect

Table 1. Overview of the world states (WS) and the mental model states for the doctor (DS) and nurse (NS) reflecting these world states

	World, Doctor and Nurse			Explanation
WS0			Context	Contextual stress factor
WS1	DS1	NS1	Call_intub	External call for intubation
WS2	DS2	NS2	Prep_p_N	Preparation of the patient by the nurse
WS3	DS3	NS3	Prep_eq_N	Preparation of the intubation equipment by the nurse
WS4	DS4	NS4	Prep_dr_N	Nurse prepares drugs for the patient
WS5	DS5	NS5	Pre_oxy_D	Doctor executes pre oxygenation
WS6	DS6	NS6	Prep_team_D	Doctor prepares the team for intubation
WS7	DS7	NS7	Prep_dif_D	Doctor prepares the team for difficulties
WS8	DS8	NS8	Give_dr_N	Nurse gives the patient drugs
WS9	DS9	NS9	Give_cr_N	Nurse applies cricoid to the patient
WS10	DS10	NS10	E_A_D	Doctor executes plan A Laryngoscopy
WS11	DS11	NS11	E_intub_D	Doctor intubates the patient
WS12	DS12	NS12	Mon_p_N	Nurse monitors patient
WS13	DS13	NS13	Obs_c_N	Nurse observes capnograph
WS14		NS14	Verb_fail_N	Nurse verbalizes failure of intubation
WS15		NS15	Verb_succ_N	Nurse verbalizes success of intubation
WS16	DS16		Verb_fail_D	Doctor verbalizes failure of intubation
WS17	DS17		Verb_succ_D	Doctor verbalizes success of intubation
WS18	DS18	NS18	Call_help_D	Doctor calls for help

the ordered structure specified in the addressed use case. They are depicted by the red nodes (in the long light-red oval) and yellow nodes (in the yellow-green oval) in the base plane and their connections, respectively.

The states within the mental models refer to the world states they model and like these world states they also specify an actor, indicated by D for doctor or N for nurse. The two individual mental models are two instances of an overall team mental model incorporating both the course of actions and the roles of the different team members for these actions. These individual instances of the team mental model can have differences, as in general not all team members will possess a perfect team mental model.

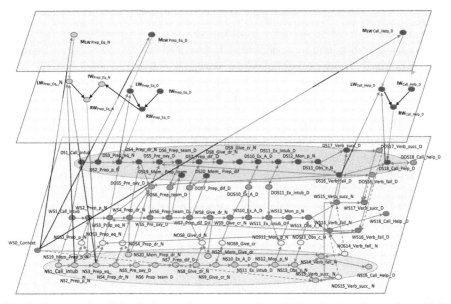

Fig. 1. Connectivity of the designed adaptive network model for the shared mental model. It includes the two mental models of the nurse (long yellow oval) and of the doctor (long red oval) and the self-models for the first-order (the pink plane) and second-order (the purple plane) adaptation. Dashed connections indicate connections with negative weights. (Color figure online)

Base Level: Memory States in the Mental Models. Within the mental models some specific states enable to take into account what has occurred in the past; these mental model states are called *memory states*. These are particularly useful if parts of the processes have to be repeated because of failures. Usually then only some of the actions have to be redone, while other actions can be skipped, as is illustrated in the addressed scenario. For example, preparation of the patient does not need to be redone, but preparation of the equipment has to be redone when the process has to be repeated. The memory states within the mental models are a crucial element to obtain this form of flexibility as they enable to model such issues in a context-sensitive manner taking into account the history of the process.

Base Level: Action Ownership States. By each of the two team members, their own mental model is used to determine their actions in the world. This goes through the member's action ownership states (indicated in light red for the doctor and in light yellow for the nurse). These ownership states are not considered to be part of the mental models. Instead, they use input from the mental models and realise a form mediation from mental model to the real world by initiating the execution of the indicated actions, which leads to affecting the related world states. In this way, the mental models affect the decisions for actions activating the world states. Conversely, connections from world states to corresponding mental model states are (at some points) used to feed information about the world into the mental models.

Middle Level: Adaptation of the Mental Models (Plasticity). The middle (blue) plane addresses the mental processes for learning and forgetting of the mental models. In particular, this addresses the connection within the nurse's mental model from the mental model state for preparation of the patient to the mental model state for preparation of the equipment. Inspired by [2, 3], where it was shown how instructional learning and observational learning of mental models can be integrated, in a similar manner two types of learning are covered here:

Table 2. Overview of the memory states and ownership states for the doctor and nurse

	Name	Explanation
DS19	Mem for Prep team D	Memory state of Doctor for the action of preparing the team
DS20	Mem for Prep dif D	Memory state of Doctor for the action of preparing the team for difficulties
DOS5	DOS for Pre_oxy_D	Ownership state for the action of preoxygenation
DOS6	DOS for Prep_team_D	Ownership state for the action of preparing the team
DOS7	DOS for Prep_dif_D	Ownership state for the action of preparing the team for difficulties
DOS10	DOS for E_A_D	Ownership state for the action of plan A Laryngoscopy by doctor
DOS11	DOS for E_intub_D	Ownership state for the action of intubating first attempt by doctor
DOS16	DOS for Verb_fail_D	Ownership state for the action of verbalizing that attempt has failed by doctor
DOS17	DOS for Verb_succ_D	Ownership state for the action of verbalizing that attempt has succeeded by doctor
DOS18	DOS for Call_help_D	Ownership state for the action of call for help, by doctor
NS19	Mem for Prep_p N	Memory state of Nurse for the action of preparing the patient
NS20	Mem for Prep_dr N	Memory state of Nurse for the action of preparing the drugs
NS21	Mem for Give_dr N	Memory state of Nurse for the action of giving the drugs
NOS2	NOS for Prep_N	Nurse Ownership State for Preparation patient
NOS3	NOS for Prep_eq_N	Nurse Ownership State for Preparation equipment
NOS4	NOS for Prep_dr_N	Nurse Ownership State for preparing drugs
NOS8	NOS for Give_d_N	Nurse Ownership State for Nurse gives drugs
NOS9	NOS for Give_cr_N	Nurse Ownership State for Nurse gives cricoid
NOS12	NOS for Mon_p_N	Nurse Ownership State for Nurse monitors patient
NOS13	NOS for Obs_c_N	Nurse Ownership State for observing capnograph
NOS14	NOS for Verb_fail_N	Nurse Ownership State for verbalizing that attempt has failed
NOS15	NOS for Verb_succ_N	Nurse Ownership State for verbalizing that attempt has succeeded

- Learning by instruction from the Doctor (modelled by the Nurse's **IW**-state and its incoming connection from the Doctor's **RW**-state)
- Hebbian learning [11] based on internal simulation, among others triggered by observation (modelled by the Nurse's **LW**-state with its incoming connections from the two relevant Nurse's mental model states)

The values of these two states are integrated in the **RW**-state, which represents the overall value that is actually used as connection weight in the internal simulation at the base level. The Hebbian learning applied for the **LW**-state includes a persistence factor μ that represents the fraction (of the learnt value) that persists per time unit. For example, if μ is 0.9, then every time unit 10% of the learnt value is lost (forgotten).

Table 3. Overview of the first-and second-order self-model states

	Name	Explanation
W1	**LW**_{Prep p Nurse → Prep eq Nurse}	First-order self-model state for the Nurse's weight of the connection from the preparing the patient mental model state to the preparing the equipment mental model state as learnt by Hebbian learning
W2	**IW**_{Prep p Nurse → Prep eq Nurse}	First-order self-model state for the Nurse's weight of the connection from preparing the patient mental model state to preparing the equipment mental model state as learnt from instruction by the doctor
W3	**RW**_{Prep p Nurse → Prep eq Nurse}	First-order self-model state for the Nurse's overall weight of the connection from preparing the patient mental model state to preparing the equipment mental model state
W4	**LW**_{Prep p N D → Prep eq N D}	First-order self-model state for the Doctor's weight of the connection from preparing the patient by the Nurse mental model state to preparing the equipment by the Nurse mental model state as learnt by Hebbian learning
W5	**IW**_{Prep p N D → Prep eq N D}	First-order self-model state for the Doctor's weight of the connection from preparing the patient by the Nurse mental model state to preparing the equipment by the Nurse mental model state as known to the Doctor
W6	**RW**_{Prep p N D → Prep eq N D}	First-order self-model state for the Doctor's overall weight of the connection from preparing the patient by the Nurse mental model state to preparing the equipment by the Nurse mental model state
W7	**LW**_{Verb fail D → Call help D}	First-order self-model state for the Doctor's weight of the connection from verbalisation of failure mental model state to call for help mental model state as learnt by Hebbian learning
W8	**IW**_{Verb fail D → Call help D}	First-order self-model state for the Doctor's weight of the connection from verbalisation of failure mental model state to call for help mental model state as known to the Doctor
W9	**RW**_{Verb fail D → Call help D}	First-order self-model state for the Doctor's overall weight of the connection from verbalisation of failure mental model state to call for help mental model state
M1	**M**_{LW Prep p Nurse → Prep eq Nurse}	Second-order self-model state for the persistence factor of the Nurse's weight of the connection from preparing the patient mental model state to preparing the equipment mental model state as learnt by Hebbian learning
M2	**M**_{LW Prep p N D → Prep eq N D}	Second-order self-model state for the persistence factor of the Doctor's weight of the connection from preparing the patient by the Nurse mental model state to preparing the equipment by the Nurse mental model state as learnt by Hebbian learning
M3	**M**_{LW Verb fail D → Call help D}	Second-order self-model state for the persistence factor of the Doctor's weight of the connection from preparing the patient by the Nurse mental model state to preparing the equipment by the Nurse mental model state as learnt by Hebbian learning

Upper Level: Control of the Adaptation of Mental Models (Metaplasticity). Within the adaptive network model, the persistence factor μ depends on circumstances: μ is made adaptive by including a second-order self-model M-state within the upper-level plane that represents it (metaplasticity, e.g., [1, 10]). For the considered scenario, it is assumed that in particular a high stress level leads to a decreased value of the M-state; in this way forgetting due to stressful circumstances is modelled, in line with [10]. This is specified by the (suppressing) upward connections from the stressful context state in the base level to the M-states.

The combination functions from the combination function library available within the software environment used here are shown in Table 4.

Table 4. Combination functions from the library used in the introduced network model

	Notation	Formula	Parameters
Steponce	**steponce**(V)	1 if $\alpha \le t \le \beta$, else 0	α start, β end time
Scalemap	**scalemap**$_{\lambda,\upsilon}(V)$	$\lambda + (\upsilon - \lambda)\,V$	Lower bound λ; Upper bound υ
Advanced logistic sum	**alogistic**$_{\sigma,\tau}(V_1, ...,V_k)$	$\left[\dfrac{1}{1+e^{-\sigma(V_1+...+V_k-\tau)}} - \dfrac{1}{1+e^{\sigma\tau}} \right](1 + e^{-\sigma\tau})$	Steepness $\sigma > 0$ Excitability threshold τ
Hebbian learning	**hebb**$_{\mu}(V_1, V_1, W)$	$V_1 V_2\,(1\text{-}W) + \mu\,W$	V_1,V_2 activation levels of the connected states; W activation level of the self-model state for the connection weight μ persistence factor

4   Simulation for the Example Scenario

Recall from the introduction that the main real-world challenge addressed for the designed adaptive network model is that it is able to cover (1) the errors and other imperfections that are daily practice in medical teams and (2) the way in which such teams handle them. This can be considered a performance indicator against which the model can be validated. In this section, it will be shown by the realistic example simulation scenario from Sect. 2 how the model indeed satisfies this performance indicator. In this simulation, a repeatedly unsuccessful intubation process is shown.

The network characteristics defining the network model introduced above have been specified in a standard table format (called role matrices) that can be used as input for the available dedicated software environment; see also the Appendix as Linked Data at URL https://www.researchgate.net/publication/351282051. The example simulation discussed here was run over a time interval of 0 to 180 with step size $\Delta t = 0.5$. This provides graphs of state activations based on the values chosen for the network characteristics. The contextual stress level has been set relatively high (0.5). For reasons of clarity, the figures have split the world states (Fig. 2), the doctor's states (Fig. 3), the nurse's states (Fig. 4), and the adaptivity states (Fig. 5), but they all happen in the same simulation at the indicated time points.

The World States. Figure 2 shows the simulation output for how the actual process in the world proceeds. In time period $t = 10$–30 a call for intubation takes place, which sets in motion the intubation sequence for the scenario. After this call, the Nurse starts preparing the patient (the light green line). In this scenario, the purple line indicating the preparation of the equipment starting at time $t = 15$ does not reach an adequate level of activation, only around 0.375, meaning that this preparation of equipment is not (sufficiently) executed in the world. However, the next step in the scenario of preparing the drugs becomes active around $t = 33$ and does get activated enough. Subsequently, also the rest of the steps in the scenario continue as prescribed by the shared mental model. Between $t = 40$ and $t = 45$, the doctor's first actions become activated: the pre-oxygenation of the patient, the preparation of the team and the preparation for difficulties. After this, the nurse continues with giving the drugs to the patient (dark green around $t = 47$), and applies the cricoid force right after. Now, the execution of the attempt laryngoscopy A, and the intubation action itself both become activated between $t = 47$ and $t = 50$. This also activates the nurse's actions to monitor the patient, around $t = 55$, and to observe the capnograph equipment around $t = 60$. Around this time, the nurse will realize she did not prepare the equipment (remember the non-activated prepare equipment state), and verbalize the failed intubation attempt as a result, around $t = 67$. Soon after, around $t = 69$, the doctor confirms this by also verbalizing the failed intubation attempt.

After this verbalization of failure, the doctor and nurse will start their second attempt. This time, it starts with the nurse preparing the equipment: the light purple prepare equipment line now does reach activation around $t = 77$. This time, the preparation of the patient and drugs are skipped by the nurse because they do not need to happen more than once. There is a slight gap, until the pre-oxygenation gets activated around $t = 93$: the orange line. After this, the doctor skips the preparation of the team and for difficulties, because these steps already happened and do not need to be repeated. Around $t = 100$, the nurse gives cricoid force, and the doctor starts the second intubation attempt. Again, the nurse monitors the patient, and the capnograph, but unfortunately also this intubation attempt fails. The nurse verbalizes this failed attempt around $t = 120$, and the doctor verbalizes the failure around $t = 125$. The team now continues with a third intubation attempt, see the activation of the preparation of the equipment at $t = 133$. The third pre-oxygenation becomes activated around $t = 145$, and the nurse applies the cricoid around $t = 155$. This activates the third intubation attempt and intubation action, and the monitoring of the patient and the capnograph by the nurse. Note that also in this attempt the same actions are skipped as in the second attempt, because they do

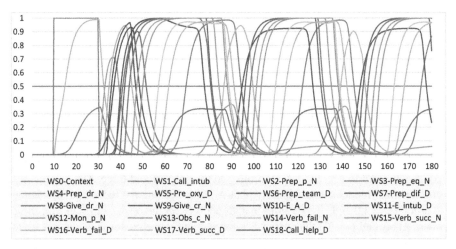

Fig. 2. World states of a repeated failing intubation process (Color figure online)

not need to happen again. This attempt fails too and this is verbalized by the nurse at t = 170, and right after by the doctor as well. In the simulation the same pattern keeps on repeating after this time point. Note that after the failure verbalisations the 'call for help' state (the dark blue line) gets a low level of activation, up to around 0.35, but this is not enough to actually happen, so no help is called in this simulation scenario. Figures 3 and 4 show for the addressed scenario, what precedes the world state activations described above: the internal simulations by the doctor and nurse of their own mental model and activating their ownership states for the actions accordingly.

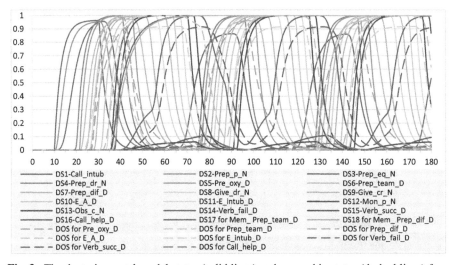

Fig. 3. The doctor's mental model states (solid lines) and ownership states (dashed lines) for a repeated failing process (Color figure online)

The Doctor's Mental Processes Based on her Mental Model. Figure 3 shows the doctor's mental model states and the doctor's ownership states simulated over time. After the call for intubation at $t = 10$, the doctor's mental model for the nurse preparing the patient, equipment and drugs gets activated at $t = 15$ (note that at this point this action only happens in the doctor's mental model, but not in the real world). Then the mental model states for the doctors first own actions get activated: to pre oxygenate the patient, prepare the team and prepare for difficulties, around $t = 20$. Now, the doctor's ownership states for the doctor's actions (pre oxygenate, preparing the team and for difficulties) get activated at $t = 30$, which will ultimately lead to the corresponding real-world actions. Around $t = 32$ some mental model states of actions the nurse have to do, become activated: to give the patient drugs and to apply cricoid force. This triggers the doctor's mental model state of starting plan A of intubation, and the actual intubation, also around $t = 32$, and slightly after that around $t = 35$ the ownership states for these actions. At around $t = 37$, the nurse's actions activate in the doctor's mental model: to monitor the patient and to observe the capnograph. This leads to the doctor to verbalize failure in her mental model around $t = 50$, and to develop activation of ownership of this verbalisation action after that. The call for help does not get proper activation. This round ends around $t = 75$, after which the next round starts as an emergent process.

The Nurse's Mental Processes Based on her Mental Model. Figure 4 shows the nurse's mental model states and the nurse's ownership states over time. Right after the call for intubation at $t = 10$, the nurse's mental model for herself preparing the patient gets activated at $t = 15$, and right after also the ownership state for the first action gets activated, meaning the nurse executes the preparation of the patient.

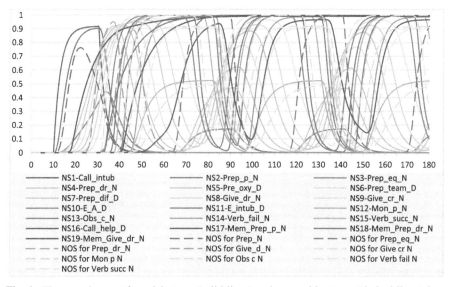

Fig. 4. The nurse's mental model states (solid lines) and ownership states (dashed lines) for a repeated failing intubation process

At around $t = 25$, the memory state of the nurse for preparing the patient reaches activation, meaning that the nurse can remember that she did this and does not have to repeat this action. Around this time, the prepare equipment mental state reaches partial activation, but not enough to activate the ownership state for this action. From $t = 24$ until around $t = 37$, the mental model states for the preparation and execution actions of the intubation get activated, with the mental model state for the intubation reaching activation around $t = 39$. Also, the ownership states for most actions become activated in this time period, although the ownership state for 'prepare equipment' does not become activated, indicating that the nurse does not execute this action. At $t = 40$, the mental model state for monitoring the patient, and around $t = 44$ the mental model state for observing the capnograph become activated. At $t = 49$ the nurse's mental model state for verbalizing failure gets activation, and interestingly at $t = 69$, the nurse's mental model state for calling for help gets activated, even though this does not get executed by the doctor in the real world.

Note how also the memory states for preparing the patient, preparing the drugs and giving the drugs become activated at respectively $t = 25$, $t = 45$ and $t = 54$, after the ownership states for the same actions, causing the nurse to remember and not execute these actions in following rounds. At $t = 70$, the ownership state for preparing the equipment becomes activated, indicating the start of the second attempt at intubation. Note that the mental model state for the equipment preparation does not reach activation, showing that the nurse gets this input from an external source (the verbalization of failure of the intubation, by the doctor).

The Learning and Forgetting States. Figure 5 shows the activation levels of the states involved in adaptation (learning and forgetting) of the mental models, as shown in the first- and second-order self-model levels in Fig. 1.

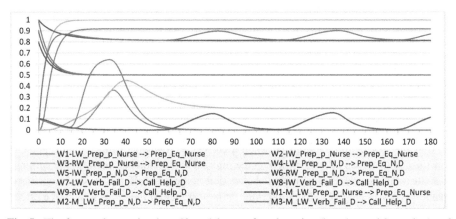

Fig. 5. The first- and second-order self-model states for adaptation (learning and forgetting) and control of it (stress leading to forgetting)

For the sake of simplicity there are only three places in the model where learning and forgetting have been incorporated: in the nurse's mental model between the 'prepare equipment' state and the 'prepare drugs' state, in the doctor's mental model between the 'prepare equipment' state and the 'prepare drugs' state, and finally in the doctor's mental model between the 'verbalization of failure' state and the 'call for help' state. In each of these cases, the applied adaptation mechanism was built upon three sub-mechanisms:

- **LW**-states, representing the Hebbian learning. This means that the person learns by activation of connected states of the mental model, for example, by using the mental model for internal simulation or triggered by observing the corresponding states in the real world. In the model, an **LW**-state is activated from the source and destination mental model states of the learnt connection. The persistence involved in the adaptation represented by an **LW**-state is controlled by an **M**-state in the second-order adaptation level (which represents the persistence factor μ).
- **IW**-states, representing instructional learning. This means that the nurse learns by getting information from the doctor, either during the process or before. The doctor applies previously acquired knowledge for this.
- **RW**-states, which models just a combination of the above two states.

In Fig. 5, the above three mechanisms are shown in a simulation graph. All three **M**-states start at a high level (0.8, 0.9 or 1) and due to the high stress level drop to 0.5 around $t = 10$. There are a few states that get activated around $t = 15$: **RW** for preparing the equipment in the doctor's mental model (W6), **RW** for the verbalization of failure by the doctor (W9) and **IW** for calling for help by the doctor (W8). Besides that, none of the learning states really reach proper activation. Therefore, while the learning mechanisms in principle are working as can be seen from the changing activation levels, they only have an overall negative impact, due to the forgetting that is induced by the high stress level [10], making the persistence factor representations **M** low. This negative effect contributes to the omission of the preparation of the equipment by the nurse in the first round and also to not calling for help after each failed round.

5   Discussion

In this paper, a quite flexible second-order adaptive computational network model was introduced enabling simulation of mental processes involving a shared mental model for teams, illustrated for a doctor and a nurse performing tracheal intubation of a patient. The model allows for the representation and processing of the actions in the world, the preceding internal simulation of the two mental models of the nurse and doctor and the dynamics of the interactions between them via the ownership states that represent how the actors actually decide based on the internal simulation and perform the actions. A contextual stress factor is included that determines the effects of stress on these mental processes, in particular forgetting parts of a mental model as a negative effect of metaplasticity [1] as described in more detail in [10]. Accordingly, in simulation experiments it was shown how learning and forgetting of shared mental models can happen and how failing team processes and redoing them can be modelled in a context-sensitive and flexible manner.

The computational model was developed based on the network-oriented modeling approach described in [19] and its dedicated software environment described in [19],

Ch 9. Other computational approaches such as described in [8, 15, 16], use agent-based models (which usually brings more added complexity), dynamical system models or program code. This lacks a well-defined description at a modelling level and makes it hard if not impossible to incorporate second-order adaptation in a transparent manner in the model, as needed here. Otherwise it is hard to cover the positive and negative effects of metaplasticity as described in [10]. In contrast, the current paper describes at a modelling level a very flexible second-order adaptive network model. It addressing shared mental models for teamwork and illustrates this by a hospital teamwork scenario.

A less flexible precursor of the second-order adaptive network model introduced in the current paper was described in [21]. The latter network model only addressed parts (not including memory states) of the base level. Therefore, it was nonadaptive and also did not cover errors and other imperfections of the team members occurring in their daily practice. It was shown that the adaptive network model introduced here is able to model forgetting part of a shared mental model as illustrated in the simulated scenario, failure of the action and redoing the process in a context-sensitive manner after it has turned out to fail. In this way, the current model has been shown to be much closer to real-world team processes.

To achieve this, the two levels of self-models for first-order and second-order adaptation are new in the current model; this enabled modelling the positive and negative effects of metaplasticity as described in [10] in the form of learning and forgetting parts of a mental model. In addition, also the use of memory states to be able to redo a failed attempt in a history-context-sensitive manner is new, providing a mechanism for only redoing the actions that are needed and skipping the ones that are not needed again as can be observed naturally in practice; the precursor model from [21] is much more rigid and lacks also this type of flexibility.

A next step will be to model the occurrence of a wider variety of errors and incidents – and their solutions – that are specific for team and group performance. Examples are: false consensus, group think, escalation of commitment and group polarization [13]. Another relevant issue would be to examine the effect of group dynamics as a function of the team size. Often it is suggested that increasing the team would lead to more safety and efficiency [12], but increasing group size also leads to new group dynamics with corresponding potential problems. As mentioned, shared mental models are used in a variety of safety-related situations such as aviation, firefighting teams, dealing rooms, shipping control, etc. An important line for future research is to examine the descriptive validity of our model and further extensions of it for such domains.

References

1. Abraham, W.C., Bear, M.F.: Metaplasticity: the plasticity of synaptic plasticity. Trends Neurosci. **19**(4), 126–130 (1996)
2. Bhalwankar, R., Treur, J.: Modeling the development of internal mental models by an adaptive network model. In: Proc. of the 11th Annual International Conference on Brain-Inspired Cognitive Architectures for AI, BICA*AI 2020. Procedia Computer Science, Elsevier (2021)
3. Bhalwankar, R., Treur, J.: A Second-Order Adaptive Network Model for Learner-Controlled Mental Model Learning Processes. In: Benito, R.M., Cherifi, C., Cherifi, H., Moro, E., Rocha, L.M., Sales-Pardo, M. (eds.) COMPLEX NETWORKS 2020 2020. SCI, vol. 944, pp. 245–259. Springer, Cham (2021). https://doi.org/10.1007/978-3-030-65351-4_20

4. Burtscher, M.J., Kolbe, M., Wacker, J.: Interaction of team mental models and monitoring behaviors predict team performance in simulated anesthesia inductions. J. Exp. Psychol. Appl. **17**(3), 257–269 (2011)
5. Burtscher, M., Manser, T.: Team mental models and their potential to improve teamwork and safety: a review and implications for future research in healthcare. Saf. Sci. **50**(5), 1344–1354 (2012). https://doi.org/10.1016/j.ssci.2011.12.033
6. Craik, K.J.W.: The Nature of Explanation. University Press, Cambridge, MA (1943)
7. De Kleer, J., Brown, J.: Assumptions and ambiguities in mechanistic mental models. In: Gentner, D., Stevens, A. (eds.), Mental Models, pp. 155–190. Lawrence Erlbaum Associates, Hillsdale, NJ (1983)
8. Dionne, S.D., Sayama, H., Hao, C., Bush, B.J.: The role of leadership in shared mental model convergence and team performance improvement: an agent-based computational model. Leadersh. Q. **21**(2010), 1035–1049 (2010)
9. Fischhof, B., Johnson, S.: Organisational Decision Making. Cambridge University Press, Cambridge (1997)
10. Garcia, R.: Stress, metaplasticity, and antidepressants. Curr. Mol. Med. **2**, 629–638 (2002)
11. Hebb, D.O.: The Organization of Behavior: A Neuropsychological Theory. John Wiley and Sons, New York (1949)
12. Higgs, A., et al.: Guidelines for the management of tracheal intubation of critically ill adults. Br. J. Anaesth. **120**(2), 323–352 (2018)
13. Jones, P.E., Roelofsma, P.H.M.P.: The potential for social contextual and group biases in team decision making: biases, conditions and psychological mechanisms. Ergonomics **43**(8), 1129–1152 (2000)
14. Mathieu, J.E., Hefner, T.S., Goodwin, G.F., Salas, E., Cannon-Bowers, J.A.: The influence of shared mental models on team process and performance. J. Appl. Psychol. **85**(2), 273–283 (2000)
15. Outland, N.B.: A computational cognitive architecture for exploring team mental models, p. 289. College of Science and Health Theses and Dissertations. https://via.library.depaul.edu/csh_etd/289 (2019)
16. Scheutz, M.: Computational Mechanisms for Mental Models in Human-Robot Interaction. In: Shumaker, R. (ed.) VAMR 2013. LNCS, vol. 8021, pp. 304–312. Springer, Heidelberg (2013). https://doi.org/10.1007/978-3-642-39405-8_34
17. Seo, S., Kennedy-Metz, L.R., Zenati, M.A., Shah, J.A., Dias, R.D., Unhelkar, V.V.: Towards an AI Coach to Infer Team Mental Model Alignment in Healthcare. Department of Computer Science, Rice University, Houston, TX, USA (2021)
18. Todd, J.: Audit of compliance with WHO surgical safety checklist and building a shared mental model in the operating theatre. BJM Leader **2**(1), 32–135 (2018)
19. Treur, J.: Network-Oriented Modeling for Adaptive Networks: Designing Higher-Order Adaptive Biological, Mental and Social Network Models. Springer Nature, Cham (2020)
20. Van Ments, L., Treur, J.: Reflections on dynamics, adaptation and control: a cognitive architecture for mental models. Cognitive Syst. Res. **70**, 1–9 (2021)
21. van Ments, L., Treur, J., Klein, J., Roelofsma, P.: A computational network model for shared mental models in hospital operation rooms. In: Mahmud, M., Kaiser, M.S., Vassanelli, S., Dai, Q., Zhong, N. (eds.) Brain Informatics. BI 2021. LNCS, vol 12960. pp. 67–78. Springer, Cham. https://doi.org/10.1007/978-3-030-86993-9_7
22. Williams, D.: The mind as a predictive modelling engine: generative models, structural similarity, and mental representation. Ph.D. Thesis. University of Cambridge, UK (2018)
23. Wilson, A.: Creating and applying shared mental models in the operating room. J. Perioper. Nurs. **32**(3), 33–36 (2019)

Modeling an Epidemic - Multiagent Approach Based on an Extended SIR Model

Mihailo Ilić[(⊠)] and Mirjana Ivanović

Faculty of Sciences, University of Novi Sad, Novi Sad, Serbia
{milic,mira}@dmi.uns.ac.rs
https://www.pmf.uns.ac.rs/

Abstract. This paper highlights the use of software agents in simulating real world phenomena. A brief overview of different approaches and tools for developing software agents and simulating real world phenomena are given. One of the more recent tools was utilized in this paper to develop a model of disease spread in a population of agents. Multiple factors affect the longevity of a pathogen in a given population, one of which is the deadliness of the disease whose impact is shown in this paper.

Keywords: Software agents · Agent systems · Modeling and simulation · Epidemics

1 Introduction

Software Agents, in the broadest sense, are programs which act on behalf of someone else. These agents are defined by their behaviour and their ability to act with a degree of autonomy. The first mention of an idea resembling today's understanding of software agents dates back to the seventies, when Hewitt described his *actor model* [14]. These actors communicate through messages, and can modify only their own private state. If they intend to modify the states of other actors, they must do that by sending messages, to which the target actor reacts to.

The majority of authors agree on some *universal* definitions [10], such as they are based on the actor model, and that all software agents share common properties [20,21] which include: *Autonomy* - they act on their own; *Social ability* - agents usually interact with other agents; *Reactivity* - they are able to react when prompted by other agents or when changes in the environment occur; *Proactiveness* - agents are not only reactive, but they actively take action which in most cases is goal-oriented, meaning they wish to achieve a specific goal.

Agents are capable of acting and reacting when confronted with other agents and the environment they're in. During the history of developing and using software agents various programming languages and frameworks have been developed.

N. T. Nguyen et al. (Eds.): ICCCI 2021, LNAI 12876, pp. 141–153, 2021.
https://doi.org/10.1007/978-3-030-88081-1_11

Programming Languages for Agent Development - Commonly used programming languages like Java, C, C++ and others all have their own tools and frameworks for handling agents and multi-agent systems. On the other hand, there exist various prototype languages which provide useful abstractions when constructing agents and agent based systems. According to [10], these languages can be classified into multiple groups based on their most relevant aspects regarding agent modeling: *Agent oriented programming (AOP) languages*, *Belief-desire-intention languages (BDI)* and *Hybrid languages*.

Agent Platforms - Various tools and platforms for developing agent systems and agent modeling have been developed over the years. A large number of both open source and commercial tools are available today, since agent based modeling is a powerful tool researchers can benefit from. The authors in [16] split modern agent frameworks into 2 main categories:

1. ***General purpose***: open source; commercial
2. ***Special purpose***: Cognitive, social and affective agents; Artificial intelligence research; Modeling and simulation; Transport-related simulations

The advantage of *general purpose platforms* is their lack of domain focus, which makes them flexible and allows for a wide range of uses. Because of this, various widely used programming languages are used to implement them, while some even have *graphical user interfaces*. Open source variants, such as AgentScript [1], JADE [5,11], Mesa [15] and Repast [7] use general purpose programming languages such as *Java, C#, JavaScript and Python*, while other like JaCaMo [4] rely on specialized languages for agent modeling like *AgentSpeak* [19] which is a BDI language. Commercial tools like AnyLogic [2] and Wolfram SystemModeler [8] provide a large number of features and supporting software, along with industrial strength simulations.

Special purpose platforms are designed to effectively handle specific problems. By sacrificing flexibility, they provide tools and mechanisms designed for solving specific problems. For modeling human behaviour the ACT-R [17] platform is used while for modeling relationships between societies and their environments, Cormas [3] is used. In artificial intelligence research, tools like MAgent [22] allow for multiagent reinforcement learning while MADP [6] is used in research of decision planing and learning in agent systems.

The goal of this paper is to illustrate how software agents can be applied in modeling real-world systems, such as the spread of disease. Multiple factors influence the longevity of a pathogen in a given population, which is shown in experiments conducted during this research.

The rest of the paper is organised as follows. The second section covers work done in the field of epidemic modeling. In the third section, a brief overview of the Mesa agent modeling framework is given, along with the explanation of the disease model constructed for the purpose of this experiment. Results of the simulations are shown in Sect. 4. Concluding remarks are given in the last section.

2   Related Work

Agent systems give the power to model behaviour of entities capable of making decisions when interacting with their environment. It is possible to simulate complex systems which include hundreds or thousands of agents. These models can be simple or complex, depending on the domains and problems that are planned to be solved by agent system. This is the reason that they find use in both academic research and industry. Intensive use of agents can be found in numerous domains like video games, transportation and logistics, power grids, medicine and many other.

The authors in [12] acknowledge the use of agent systems in urban planning, specifically in the field of road network planning. Existing systems model the behaviour of drivers in normal conditions, with the goal to optimise traffic light sequences among other things. However, these models fail to provide support for modeling traffic in uncommon conditions, which can be caused by a wide variety of events, such as natural disasters. The authors propose a new model, which takes into account finer details of entities involved in traffic [12]. These properties include car length and maximum speed, personality of drivers along with road infrastructure. The decision of a single driver to leave his/her car during a crisis event can have a huge impact on the entire system, blocking hundreds of other cars. The authors propose a new model called MOSAIIC, which takes into account these finer details while modeling traffic. The idea of simulating and handling such complex systems in unpredictable situations can be transferred to studying and simulating epidemiological outbreaks.

Agent systems also find their use in the field of medicine as well, more specifically - epidemiology. The authors in [9] recognize the potential of applying agent systems in helping to understand the dynamics of an epidemiological outbreak. By using the *GAMA* simulation development environment, a standard SIR (*Susceptible-Infected-Recovered*) model where each agent can be either Susceptible, Infected or Recovered has been constructed. The agents are placed in a continuous space, where each agent is a point in 2D space capable of moving through the environment with traits as speed and direction defined.

The authors in [18] give a general overview of agent based systems, including an explanation of their computational construction. They emphasize that it is not imperative to include every single detail in modeling complex systems, as technical limitations don't allow this. However, it is suggested that adding as much traits of the system as possible helps in recreating the real world system which allows researchers to create precise models. The agent model depicted in [18] is also focused on disease spread, relying on the standard SIR model which is also used in [9]. The opposite to the approach shown in paper [9], in our approach agents are placed in a grid space, where each cell in the grid represents a "room" which multiple agents can share. This way, the disease can only spread between agents located in the same cell. The simulation in [18] is conducted on a 20×20 grid, with each agent at a fixed position and the disease can only spread between agents in adjacent cells of the grid. Our approach presented in the paper builds upon the idea presented in [18] by allowing multiple agents to be located in the same cell, and also allowing agents to migrate to adjacent cells at each step of the simulation.

As stated in [13], *human mobility* is one of the main factors which impact how fast a disease can spread through a population. The authors mention recent outbreaks such as SARS in 2003 and H1N1 in 2009. We are now experiencing a similar situation with the current COVID-19 pandemic. Given enough data, researcher can model the spread of disease on different levels (for example city wide or even world wide). In [13], a demonstration was conducted by modeling the metropolitan area of Zurich, Switzerland. Since the population size is roughly 1.5 million people, only 1% of the population (15 286 agents) was used to model the spread of seasonal flu. The authors propose linking transport and epidemiological modeling in order to simulate outbreaks of infectious diseases more precisely. They also mention the fact that the results of the simulation can vary depending on the number of parameters taken into account. Simpler models only account for healthy, infected and recovered individuals, while other parameters such as vaccination, immunity, gender, age etc. could help in giving more accurate results.

In this paper a simulation of an epidemic is conducted. Agents are placed on a grid, and are able to move between cells. Cells represent some shared space (e.g. a room or building), and on this level infected agents have a chance of spreading the disease to healthy agents. This chance increases if the healthy agent is exposed to multiple infected agents occupying the same cell. Our simulation extends the standard SIR model by including a new *deceased* state, which represents agents who have succumbed to the disease.

3   Modeling the Spread of Disease

One of the main goals of this paper is to present how one could model a real world problem using software agents. The topic of infectious diseases, more precisely viruses, and how they spread is catching more attention with the spread of *COVID-19*. The ongoing pandemic was also an inspiration for our model and simulations. By understanding how viruses affect the human body and how they spread, we can reduce their negative effect. The latter can be modeled using software agents, as shown in [13].

As we briefly presented in previous parts of the paper there are still some flexible, widely used programming languages, which support adequate utilization of software agents in solving specific problems. In our experiments we will use the Python-based Mesa framework.

Mesa Overview - *Mesa* is a recent open-source framework written in Python, which gives users the ability to quickly construct agent models. These models can then be easily visualized and analyzed using various other Python frameworks and libraries. One useful tool which this framework has built in [15] is the data collector which will be showcased in this paper.

The main concepts this framework revolves around are the *Model* and the *Agent*. These core classes serve as the building blocks of any agent model. Mesa is highly modular [15], which means it doesn't make any assumptions in the way of how a model should operate and also provides multiple different *schedulers* which are in charge of handling the activation of agents.

The agent is the main actor in a Mesa model. A class which extends the *mesa.Agent* class needs to override it's *step* method. A Mesa model defines the passage of time as a series of *steps*, and by overriding this method in the Agent class, we can define the behavior of an agent at each step of the simulation.

The model class models the entire system, which includes the agents and their environment. The class which inherits the *mesa.Model* class serves as a container for all other elements and global parameters which are used to run the simulation.

The space component represents the space which is populated by agents (Fig. 1). Multiple components are located in the *mesa.space* module, some of which are:

– *Continuous space* - Agents are treated as points and they can have an arbitrary position.
– *Grid* - This is the base class for a square grid. Multiple other classes extend the functionality of this one, like a grid realized as a torus.
– *HexGrid* - Represents a hexagonal grid.

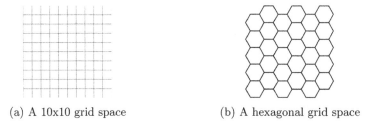

(a) A 10x10 grid space   (b) A hexagonal grid space

Fig. 1. Examples of different *Grid* space components

Each space component provides functionality for selecting agents at specific coordinates, along with iterating through neighbouring cells or finding neighbouring agents within a certain radius. A type of grid space will be used in our simulation.

Another core component is the *scheduler*, located in the *mesa.time* module. Schedulers are components that we will use in our simulations, which control when agents are to be activated and run their step methods. The activation order can be crucial for the outcome of the entire system, so it is important to choose the right one. Some of the predefined schedulers are:

– *Base scheduler* - Calls each agent's step function in the order they were added.
– *Random activation* - Activates agents in a random order.
– *Simultaneous activation* - It simulates simultaneous activation of every agent.

Data collectors are a built in tool which enable users to collect multiple types of data such as model/agent level data, along with tables.

3.1   Definition of the Disease Model

In order to run a simulation and collect data, all of the components mentioned in the previous section need to be put in use. The goal of our experiment is to model disease spread among a population of agents. As stated in [13], one of the main factors of disease spread is agent mobility. Hence, we need to define a space which the agents can traverse in this model. For this purpose, a *MultiGrid* from the *mesa.space* module will be used. In this paper, cells in the grid will be analogous to rooms in a building, with agents being able to move between adjacent rooms (cells). Agents in this case represent people moving around inside a building. The reason behind using a MultiGrid is the possibility of having multiple agents occupy a cell. Unlike the standard SIR model used in [9,18] where each agent can either be susceptible, infected or recovered, we considered an additional state - "deceased", for agents which do not survive the infection. Accordingly, each agent can be in one of four states:

1. *Healthy* - Healthy agents which are not carriers of said disease.
2. *Infected* - Infected agents are carriers of the disease.
3. *Deceased* - Such agents have succumbed to the disease which is being modeled and no longer have the ability to move between cells and cannot infect further agents.
4. *Immune* - Agents which have survived the initial infection, and are now immune to the pathogen.

If an agent is infected, it has a chance of recovery or death. Once an agent recovers, it becomes immune and can no longer be infected. These values are defined globally, which means all agents are the same in terms of age, sex, immunity etc. In order to obtain more accurate models, one could implement these agent-level properties, but for this paper these factors haven't been taken into account. Infected agents also have the possibility of spreading the disease to another healthy agent occupying the same cell. If a healthy agent is located at a cell which is also occupied by infected agents, the chance of the infection spreading to the new agent is calculated as in [18].

$$P_{infection}[state_{a,s+1} = Infected | state_{a,s} = Healthy] = 1 - (1 - c)^k \quad (1)$$

The chance of an agent a to transition from a healthy state to an infected state between steps s and $s+1$ of the simulation depends on the number of infected agent k occupying the same cell. In this equation, c represent the initial chance of infection, which is a global parameter of the model.

At the end of each step, an agent also has the ability to migrate to a different cell. The chance of this occurring is also configured globally. Each agent can perform the following actions: *transmit the disease; migrate to another cell.* They also have predefined global chances to: *recover from the disease; pass away* - if this happens to an agent, it becomes inactive and performs no more actions during the simulation.

We used a random scheduler during modeling. To ensure the same results each time the simulation is run, it is imperative to set the seed of the random number generator to a fixed value.

A data collector was also used in order to collect data after each step in the simulation. The following values were computed after each step:

1. The number of healthy agents in the entire grid. Immune agents will also be included, since they have recovered from the disease.
2. The number of infected agents in the grid.
3. The number of deceased agents in the entire grid.
4. Multiple matrices containing the number of each type of agent according to their health status per cell.

Finally, all of these components are aggregated in the *DiseaseModel* class which extends the *mesa.Model* class. This class takes in multiple parameters for defining the simulation:

- N - The number of agents in the system.
- *Width* - The width of the grid.
- *Height* - The height of the grid.
- *Chance of death* - The possibility of one succumbing to the disease.
- *Chance of spread* - The chance of the disease spreading from one infected agent to a healthy one.
- *Chance of the illness ending* - The chance for an agent to reach the end of the illness, either by recovering and becoming immune or by succumbing to the disease.
- *Chance of migration* - The chance of an agent moving to an adjacent cell.
- *Infected on start ratio* - Defines the ratio of the entire population which will be disease carriers at the start of the simulation.

4   Experimental Results

By utilising the model described in Sect. 3.1, one could model the impact of a disease with different starting parameters. One key parameter is the chance of death of the disease. Pathogens rely on the bodies of hosts they inhabit, where they live and replicate at the expense of their victim. As all living things, their goal is to live long enough to replicate their genetic material. By doing too much harm to the bodies of their hosts and killing them off too soon, the pathogens lower the chance they have to effectively replicate and spread themselves to other hosts. As a result of them being to deadly (too harmful to their hosts), they have a negative effect on themselves.

It is possible to simulate this using the model mentioned in Sect. 3.1. Two different simulations will be run, with common parameter setting being: number of agents - 500, grid dimensions - 10×10, number of simulation steps - 100, chance of spread - 4.7%, chance of the illness ending - 16.67%, chance of migration - 50%, ratio of infected agents at the start of the simulation - 1%.

The authors in [18] concluded in their simulations that the chance of spread of 4.7% would yield a result of one infected agent infecting 1.6 healthy agents on average. Hence, we will use this value in our simulations as well. Furthermore, in [18] an agent carries the infection 3 to 6 steps in total. Similarly, with the chance of the illness ending set to 16.67%, an agent in our simulation will stop carrying the disease after 6 steps on average.

To see the effect the chance of death has on the population and on the spread of the pathogen, two different simulations will be run with different values for this parameter.

Lower Chance of Death - The first test conducted was with a lower chance of death in comparison to the second test discussed in the rest of the section. According to the World Health Organisation, as of April 2021 around ***2.1%***[1] of confirmed COVID-19 cases ended in death. With a chance of death set to this value, and 5 agents infected at start (1% of the entire population), the progress of the disease can be seen in Fig. 2.

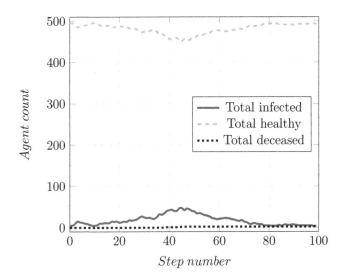

Fig. 2. The timeline of the disease during the 100 simulated steps with a morality rate of 2.1%

A slow but steady increase in the number of infected agents can be seen in the first half of the simulation. The peak is measured at step 44, with 47 infected agents at that time.

In Table 1, the agent count for each state is shown at some key steps. The pathogen persisted for the entirety of the simulation which lasted for 100 steps. Key steps include step 39 which marked the first death from the disease, and step 44 where the peak was reached.

---

[1] https://covid19.who.int/ - Official WHO worldwide COVID-19 statistics.

Table 1. Agent count by their status at various steps

Step #	Infected #	Healthy #	Deceased #
0	5	495	0
5	12	488	0
10	5	495	0
15	11	489	0
20	12	488	0
30	25	475	0
39	**40**	**459**	1
40	42	457	1
44	**47**	**452**	1
50	39	459	2
99	4	493	3

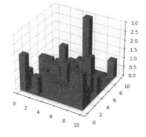
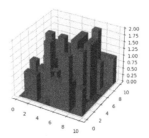

(a) Step 39 - First death occurred.   (b) Step 44 - The peak of infections.

Fig. 3. Infected agents at key steps

Figures 3a and 3b visualise the number of infected agents on the entire grid at key steps.

Higher Chance of Death - This second simulation had a chance of death of 7%, which is more than 3 times greater than in the previous experiment.

When comparing Fig. 4 to Fig. 2, it is possible to see that the peak of infections happens earlier, and is much lower than in the first experiment. The pathogen acts too aggressively to it's host, with a 7% chance of killing the carrier, while only having a 4.7% chance of spreading. This makes it harder for the disease to make it to another host, and thus prolong the existence of the pathogen in the population. As noted in Table 2, the first death occurred earlier, at step 14, and the peak of infections is at step 23. As a result of this higher chance of death, the pathogen died out by step 50, with no more infected agents present at that time.

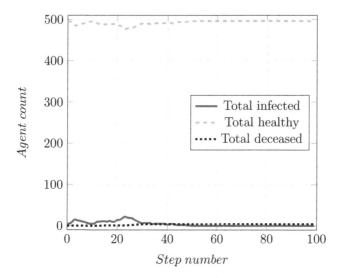

Fig. 4. The timeline of the disease during the 100 simulated steps with a mortality rate of 7%

Figures 5a and 5b visualise the number of infected agents on the entire grid at key steps of the simulation with a chance of death set to 7%.

By looking at Figs. 6a and 6b, we can see what difference the change in the chance of death made on the overall impact on the pathogen and population of agents. The disease which had a lower chance of death managed to reach far more agents in the population than it's counterpart with the higher mortality rate. At the end of the first experiment, 54.4% of agents are immune, but the pathogen

Table 2. Agent count by their status at various steps

Step #	Infected #	Healthy #	Deceased #
0	5	495	0
5	12	488	0
10	5	495	0
14	**11**	**488**	1
15	11	488	1
20	14	485	1
23	**22**	**477**	1
30	6	490	4
40	3	493	4
50	**0**	**496**	**4**

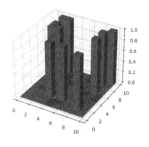 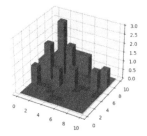

(a) Step 14 - First death occurred.   (b) Step 23 - Peak of infections.

Fig. 5. Infected agents at key steps.

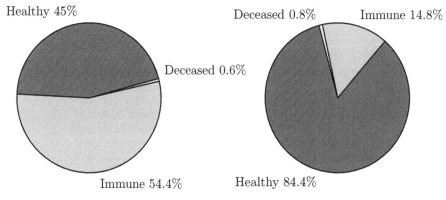

(a) State distribution for experiment 1.   (b) State distribution for experiment 2.

Fig. 6. The distribution of healthy, immune and deceased agents at the end of both simulations.

is still present in the population, while in the second experiment, only 14.8% of all agents have become immune. Furthermore, the second pathogen failed to survive the entirety of the simulation. It was eliminated from the population at step 50.

5   Conclusion

Software agents are a powerful mechanism for simulating different processes in a wide range of domains. Given enough information of some real-world system, it is possible to simulate how it can evolve through time and how it will react to different starting conditions and different events which could unfold. Even subtle changes in starting parameters could give wildly different results. Systems such as proposed in [13] which take into account the fine details can help researchers get a better sense of the problems they face.

The value and versatility of software agents is further bolstered by the number of existing programming languages and tools which assist in working with them. These tools can cover a wide variety of use, with some being general purpose and others being more suited for specific fields of research.

In this paper a newer general purpose agent framework was utilised [15] in modeling the spread of disease through a population of agents. Even with a fairly simple model, it is possible to obtain interesting results. Further research of this topic would include adding finer parameters to the agents, making each one of them distinct in their behaviour, and looking into how their decision making impacts the overall spread of a pathogen.

Acknowledgements. The authors acknowledge financial support of the Ministry of Education, Science and Technological Development of the Republic of Serbia (Grant No. 620 451-03-68/2020-14/200125).

References

1. Agentscript project page. https://github.com/backspaces/agentscript/. Accessed 15 Apr 2021
2. Anylogic. https://www.anylogic.com/features/. Accessed 15 Apr 2021
3. Cormas. http://cormas.cirad.fr/indexeng.htm. Accessed 15 Apr 2021
4. Jacamo project. http://jacamo.sourceforge.net/. Accessed 15 Apr 2021
5. Java agent development framework. https://jade.tilab.com. Accessed 15 Apr 2021
6. Madp project. https://github.com/MADPToolbox/MADP. Accessed 15 Apr 2021
7. Repast. https://repast.github.io/. Accessed 15 Apr 2021
8. Wolfram systemmodeler. https://www.wolfram.com/system-modeler/. Accessed 15 Apr 2021
9. Bădică, A., Bădică, C., Ganzha, M., Ivanović, M., Paprzycki, M.: Multi-agent simulation of core spatial sir models for epidemics spread in a population. In: 2020 5th IEEE International Conference on Recent Advances and Innovations in Engineering (ICRAIE), pp. 1–7. IEEE (2020)
10. Bădică, C., Budimac, Z., Burkhard, H.-D., Ivanovic, M.: Software agents: languages, tools, platforms. Comput. Sci. Inf. Syst. **8**(2), 255–298 (2011)
11. Bellifemine, F.L., Caire, G., Greenwood, D.: Developing Multi-agent Systems with JADE, vol. 7. Wiley, New York (2007)
12. Czura, G., Taillandier, P., Tranouez, P., Daudé, É.: MOSAIIC: city-level agent-based traffic simulation adapted to emergency situations. In: Takayasu, H., Ito, N., Noda, I., Takayasu, M. (eds.) Proceedings of the International Conference on Social Modeling and Simulation, plus Econophysics Colloquium 2014. SPC, pp. 265–274. Springer, Cham (2015). https://doi.org/10.1007/978-3-319-20591-5_24
13. Hackl, J., Dubernet, T.: Epidemic spreading in urban areas using agent-based transportation models. Future Internet **11**(4), 92 (2019)
14. Hewitt, C., Bishop, P., Steiger, R.: A universal modular actor formalism for artificial intelligence, IJCAI3. In: Proceedings of the 3rd International Joint Conference on Artificial Intelligence, pp. 235–245 (1973)
15. Masad, D., Kazil, J.: Mesa: an agent-based modeling framework. In: 14th PYTHON in Science Conference, pp. 53–60. Citeseer (2015)
16. Pal, C.-V., Leon, F., Paprzycki, M., Ganzha, M.: A review of platforms for the development of agent systems. arXiv preprint arXiv:2007.08961 (2020)

17. Ritter, F.E., Tehranchi, F., Oury, J.D.: Act-R: a cognitive architecture for modeling cognition. Wiley Interdiscip. Rev. Cognit. Sci. **10**(3), e1488 (2019)
18. Shoukat, A., Moghadas, S.M.: Agent-based modelling: an overview with application to disease dynamics (2020)
19. Weerasooriya, D., Rao, A., Ramamohanarao, K.: Design of a concurrent agent-oriented language. In: Wooldridge, M.J., Jennings, N.R. (eds.) ATAL 1994. LNCS, vol. 890, pp. 386–401. Springer, Heidelberg (1995). https://doi.org/10.1007/3-540-58855-8_25
20. Wooldridge, M., Jennings, N.R.: Agent theories, architectures, and languages: a survey. In: Wooldridge, M.J., Jennings, N.R. (eds.) ATAL 1994. LNCS, vol. 890, pp. 1–39. Springer, Heidelberg (1995). https://doi.org/10.1007/3-540-58855-8_1
21. Wooldridge, M.J., Jennings, N.R.: Intelligent agents: theory and practice. Knowl. Eng. Rev. **10**(2), 115–152 (1995)
22. Zheng, L., et al.: Magent: a many-agent reinforcement learning platform for artificial collective intelligence. In: Proceedings of the AAAI Conference on Artificial Intelligence, vol. 32 (2018)

News Recommendations by Combining Intra-session with Inter-session and Content-Based Probabilistic Modelling

Panagiotis Symeonidis[1]([✉]) [iD], Dmitry Chaltsev[2] [iD], Markus Zanker[2,4] [iD],
and Yannis Manolopoulos[3] [iD]

[1] University of the Aegean, Samos, Greece
psymeon@aegean.gr
[2] Free University of Bolzano, Bolzano, Italy
markus.zanker@unibz.it
[3] Open University of Cyprus, Nicosia, Cyprus
manolopo@csd.auth.gr, yannis.manolopoulos@ouc.ac.cy
[4] University Klagenfurt, Klagenfurt, Austria

Abstract. Recommender systems in news industry use the time dimension to reveal users' preferences over time, but they miss to exploit adequately the information encapsulated inside user sessions. Here, we combine intra- with inter-session item transition probabilities to reveal the short- and long-term intentions of individuals along with the public preference over news topic categories. Thus, we are able to better capture the similarities among items that are co-selected inside a session but also within any two consecutive sessions. We have evaluated experimentally our method and compare it against state-of-the-art algorithms on two real-life datasets. We show the superiority of our method over its competitors.

Keywords: News recommendation · Evolving user preferences · Session-based recommendations

1 Introduction

Previous work in news articles recommendation has addressed the fact that user preferences evolve over time [3,10]. However, they missed to adequately exploit user sessions, which are short-time interactions of users with a system, and can reveal their very last and concrete intentions.

In this paper, we provide session-based news recommendations, by distinguishing the short-term preferences of the users over news topic categories from their very last intentions over single items. First, to reveal the very last user's intention, we analyze the item interactions inside his latest sessions separately (i.e., **intra-session item similarity**). Next, to deal with the problem that in the

---

Y. Manolopoulos—Professor Emeritus, Aristotle University of Thessaloniki.

N. T. Nguyen et al. (Eds.): ICCCI 2021, LNAI 12876, pp. 154–166, 2021.
https://doi.org/10.1007/978-3-030-88081-1_12

beginning of each session, there is not enough information to learn much about user's concrete intention, we also use the information that comes from other recent sessions (**i.e., inter-session item similarity**). Our model also takes under consideration the main categories of news articles that a user/community is interested in (e.g., politics, sports, etc.) and tracks the evolution of these preferences by using a sliding time window to disregard articles/categories that are outdated. Thus, our model continuously is updated with every new users' clicks, which makes it sensitive to adapt to the changes of their preferences.

The rest of the paper is organized as follows. Section 2 summarizes the related work. Section 3 provides the problem formulation, whereas Sect. 4 presents our proposed methodology. Experimental results are given in Sect. 5. Finally, Sect. 6 concludes the paper.

2   Related Work

Session-based recommendation usually refers to the case scenario, where we have only anonymous sessions and we are not able to build a user's profile. Recently, session-based recommendations have been modeled with Recurrent Neural Networks (RNNs). Hidasi et al. [5] presented a recommender system based on Gated Recurrent Unit (GRU), which learns when and how much to update the hidden state of the GRU model. However, a more recent study has shown that a simple k-nearest neighbor (session-kNN) scheme adapted for session-based recommendations often outperforms the GRU model [7]. The authors claim that best results are achieved when a session-based kNN model is combined with GRU model in a weighted hybrid approach. Nevertheless, several new adjustments were proposed during last years that improve the performances of the initial RNN model [4,6,14–16].

For the news recommendation task, in [9] it has been shown that a way to increase accuracy is to consider the context of the user (i.e., time, location, mood, etc.). For example, Das et al. [2] generated recommendations based on collaborative filtering that takes under consideration the co-visitation count of articles, which is the number of times a news story was co-visited with another news stories in the user's click-history. Liu et al. [10] combined the content-based method with the collaborative filtering method previously developed for Google News [2] to generate personalised news recommendations. The hybrid method develops a Bayesian framework for predicting users' current news interests based on profiles learned from: (i) the target user's activity and (ii) the news trends demonstrated in the activity of all users. Ludmann's recommender system [12], denoted as Ody4, won the CLEF NewsREEL 2017 contest, which was about recommending effectively and efficiently news articles. Ody4 is a stream-based recommender system, which relies on the open source data stream management system Odysseus. Ody4 continuously calculated the most-read articles based on a stream of impression events (i.e., most clicked articles of a 12-hour sliding time window). That is, by analyzing impression events of users, he calculated a set of recommendations based on the item popularity in a given time window.

3 Problem Formulation

Let $\mathcal{U}$ denotes the set of users that visit the online news web site, and $\mathcal{I}$ be the increasing set of incoming articles. We keep track of the users' actions over items in the website. In particular, whenever a user reads one or more articles in a short time period (i.e., 30 min.), we store these interactions in the database as a user's session. These interactions with items have a sequence. That is, we know for every item that belongs in a session, if it is selected first, second or last, the time that it is selected by the user, and how much time he interacted with it inside the session. For example, session $S_1(user = u_1, TimeStarted = t_1 | \{i_1, 20sec\}, \{i_2, 145sec\})$ indicates that within session S_1 that started at timepoint t_1 from user u_1, item i_1 was selected first and it was read for 20 s and i_2 was selected second and it was read for 145 s.

Each news article belongs proportionally to different categories, based on the words it contains. This probability distribution is represented in the form of a vector $\boldsymbol{a_i} = (a_{i,c_1}, a_{i,c_2}, \ldots, a_{i,c_n})$ and its dimensionality is n, which is equal to the number of news categories. This vector is normalised, i.e., elements' sum of this vector is equal to 1:

$$\sum_{k=1}^{n} a_{i,c_k} = 1 \tag{1}$$

To better explain our approach, we will use as our running example the following graphical representation, which is shown in Fig. 1. In our running example, we have 3 users and we want to predict the news story that user 2 will click next in his unfinished session (i.e. session S_7). For computing the similarities between the target user 2 with the other two users, please notice that sessions S_1 and S_2 cannot be considered, because they are outside of the sliding time window w valid interval that we have set $(t - w, t]$. This sliding time window captures the notion of recency of news stories. When two or more items are selected within one session, these items can be considered as more similar compared to items that were selected in different sessions from the same user. For example, by taking into account actions of user 1 (i.e., U_1) we can infer that item i_4 is more

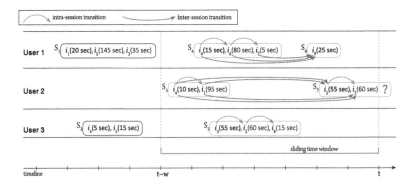

Fig. 1. A visual representation of our toy example (User-Items-Sessions)

similar to item i_6 and i_7 rather than item i_9, since they were selected inside the same session S_4 with the item i_4.

In our running example, as depicted in Fig. 1, session S_7 is still open and it is running for user U_2. Thus, items i_2 and i_3 of session S_7 can be matched to make item recommendations to user U_2. As shown, user U_3 has also selected the same items (inside the valid window time interval) with U_2. He has also selected i_8, which could be a nice recommendation for U_2.

4 Our Proposed Method

Our method tries to capture the user behavior by taking under consideration 4 different prediction models: (i) the short term user preferences combined with his very last intention (ii) the long term user preferences over topic categories, (iii) the short term public preference interests in $t_p = [t - w, t)$ over categories, and (iv) the long term public preference interests over categories.

4.1 Individual Preferences and Latest Intentions

Short-Term Individual Preferences and the very Last Intention

Based on the Bayesian inference that considers independence among evidences, we can predict the items that will be included in a last session S_N of a user u based on the items that are already included in S_N. In particular, we can use the following formula to build the **intra-session** transition probabilities between any two subsequent items in each distinct session in time window t_p as follows:

$$p\big(j \in S_N | i_{1:m} \in S_N)\big) \propto \prod_{\substack{i_k \in S_N \ k=1..m}} p(j \in S_N | i_k \in S_N) \tag{2}$$

where i_k is the set of items that user u already has clicked in current session S_N, and j is the item to be predicted as next recommended item in S_N. However, to deal with the problem that at the start of the session there is not much information about the user's current interests, we can also learn from other recent sessions (**inter-session**) item transition similarities, and predict the user's interest in the current session. We can extend the above formula by taking into account also the **inter-session** transition probabilities among items of any two subsequent sessions:

$$p\big(j \in S_N | i_{1:m} \in S_N \wedge (S_{n+1}, S_n)\big) \propto$$
$$\prod_{\substack{i_k \in S_N \\ k=1..m}} p(j \in S_N | i_k \in S_N) \prod_{\substack{i_k \in S_N \\ S_n \in S}} \frac{p(j \in S_{n+1} \wedge i_k \in S_n)}{p(i_k \in S_n)} \tag{3}$$

That is, to capture user's behavior when he interacts with the system, a transition probability matrix T that expresses the transition from one item that belongs to an old session S_n to another item that belongs to the next session S_{n+1} is constructed as follows:

$$T_{i_1,i_2} = p(i_2 \in S_{n+1} \mid i_1 \in S_n), \tag{4}$$

where i_1 and i_2 are items that belong to S_n and S_{n+1}, respectively. The probability that a user will be interested in a news article j given the previous items of session S_N can be defined as the mean over all transition probabilities from the previous items of this session to this article:

$$p(j|i_{1:m} \in S_N) = \frac{1}{m} \cdot \sum_{i_k \in S_N \, k=1..m} p(j \in S_{N+1} \mid i_k \in S_N) \tag{5}$$

where m is the number of items in the current session. Next, using the maximum likelihood estimator we can compute the transition probability between any two articles $\boldsymbol{T}_{i_1,i_2}$ that belong in subsequent sessions as follows:

$$p(i_2 \in S_{n+1} \mid i_1 \in S_n) = \frac{|\{(S_{n+1}, S_n) : \ i_2 \in S_{n+1} \wedge i_1 \in S_n\}|}{|\{(S_{n+1}, S_n) : i_1 \in S_n\}|} \tag{6}$$

where the numerator expresses the number of times item i_1 was included in S_n and i_2 in S_{n+1}. The denominator expresses the number of times that a session contains item i_1 in time period t_p.

Based on Eq. 6, in our running example, the transition probability from item i_4 to item i_2 is equal to $\frac{1}{2}$, where the numerator is equal to one, since there is only one instance of the two consecutive sessions where i_4 belongs to the first session (S_3) of the two sessions and i_2 belongs to the second session (S_7) of the two sessions; and the denominator is equal to two since there are two sessions with i_4 (sessions S_3 and S_4). The inter-session transition probability matrix is presented in Table 1 (rows and columns with zeros are not shown).

Table 1. Inter-session transition probability matrix of our running example.

Inter-session TPM	i_2	i_3	i_9
i_1	1	1	0
i_4	0.5	0.5	0.5
i_6	0	0	1
i_7	0	0	1

As far as the **intra-session** item transition probability is concerned, by using a first-order Markov Chain, we can describe the transition probability between two subsequent events in a session. That is, we can simply count how often users viewed item i_b immediately after viewing item i_a.

Let a session S_n be a chronologically ordered set of item click events $S_n = (i_1, i_2, \ldots, i_m)$ and S be a set of all sessions $S = \{S_1, S_2, \ldots, S_N\}$. Given a user's current session S_N with i_m being the last item in S_N, we can define the score for a recommendable item j as follows:

$$p(j \in S_N | i_m \in S_N) = score(j, i_m) = \frac{1}{\sum\limits_{\substack{S_n \in S \\ n=1..N}} \sum\limits_{\substack{i_k \in S_n \\ k=1..m-1}} isSame(i_m, i_k)} \cdot$$

$$\cdot \sum\limits_{\substack{S_n \in S \\ n=1..N}} \sum\limits_{\substack{i_k \in S_n \\ k=1..m-1}} isSame(i_m, i_k) \cdot isSame(j, i_{k+1}) \qquad (7)$$

where the function $isSame(i_a, i_b)$ indicates where i_a and i_b refer to the same item as follows:

$$isSame(i_a, i_b) = \begin{cases} 1, & \text{if } i_a = i_b; \\ 0, & \text{if } i_a \neq i_b. \end{cases}$$

Based on Eq. 7, in our running example of Fig. 1, transition probability from item i_4 to item i_6 is equal to $\frac{1}{2}$, and it is so since in all the sessions of time window t_p there is only one case where i_4 is followed by i_6 (session S_4); and the denominator is equal to two, since there are two sessions where i_4 is followed by any other item (sessions S_3 and S_4). The intra-session transition probability matrix is presented in Table 2 (rows and columns with zeros are not shown).

Table 2. Intra-session transition probability matrix of our running example.

Intra-session TPM	i_1	i_2	i_3	i_6	i_7	i_8
i_2	0	0	0.5	0	0	0.5
i_3	0	1	0	0	0	0
i_4	0.5	0	0	0.5	0	0
i_6	0	0	0	0	1	0

To summarize, intra-session TPM infers similarity among items inside each session independently from other sessions, whereas inter-session similarity captures the notion of similarity between any two consecutive sessions. As will be shown experimentally, the inter-session similarity is more effective, when we increase the size of the sliding time windows, which means that it can better capture the long-term user preferences, whereas the intra-session similarity is more effective with smaller window sizes, which makes it more suitable to capture the short term preferences.

Long-Term Individual Preferences over Categories
To capture individual's long-term preferences over categories, we adopt Google's content-based algorithm [10]. The idea is that the long term interest of a user u for a topic category c_k^{ul} (where u in abbreviation stands for user interest and l stands for long-term period) can be considered as the probability of clicking on an article about c_k, as shown by Eq. 8.

$$p(click \mid category = c_k) = \frac{p(category = c_k \mid click) \ p(click)}{p(category = c_k)} \qquad (8)$$

where $p(click \mid category = c_k)$ is the probability of the user clicking on an article from category c_k and $p(category = c_k \mid click)$ is the probability that user's clicks being in category c_k. Thus, the long-term interest for topic categories of news articles of an individual is captured by the following equation:

$$c_k^{ul} = interest\ (category = c_k^{ul}) = \frac{p(click) \times \sum_t \left(N_t \times \frac{p_t(category=c_k^{ul}\ \mid\ click)}{p_t(category=c_k^{ul})} \right)}{\sum_t N_t} \quad (9)$$

where N_t is the total number of clicks made by a user in all the past till present time t_p, and $p(click)$ is the prior probability of the user clicking on any news article, regardless of the article category. Please notice that the created transition probability matrix refers to topic categories, whereas in the previous section we have built a transition probability matrix over items and thus we have to transform it for items, as will be shown in Sect. 4.3.

4.2 Public Preferences

Short-Term Public Preference Over Categories
For each category c_k general public interest is estimated as the sum of values representing a topic category for each news article that was selected by users during period of sliding time window $t_p = [t - w, t)$ and multiplied by the number of clicks that this particular news article received, as follows:

$$c_k^{ps} = p(c_k \mid i \in S^{t_p}) = \sum_{i \in S^{t_p}} a_{i,c_k} \cdot m_i \quad (10)$$

S^{t_p} in the above equation is a set of all sessions made by the general public during t_p, and m_i is the number of clicks that a news article i received during t_p. The output of this algorithm is a vector $\mathbf{V}^{ps} = (c_1^{ps}, c_2^{ps}, \ldots, c_n^{ps})$, that represents short-term public interest (we use letters p and s for words public and short, respectively). Please notice that these values are normalized over all categories to make it comparable with the results of predictions from other prediction models.

Long-Term Public Preferences Over Categories
This method is quite similar to the previous one. The difference here is the longer period that we consider for the sliding time window. The goal is to capture long term preferences of the general public. All sessions of all users are considered over the period of one year $t_y = [t - year, t)$ as follows:

$$c_k^{pl} = p(c_k \mid i \in S^{t_y}) = \sum_{i \in S^{t_y}} a_{i,c_k} \cdot m_i \quad (11)$$

Again, the resulting vector $\mathbf{V}^{pl} = (c_1^{pl}, c_2^{pl}, \ldots, c_n^{pl})$ is normalized over all categories.

4.3   Recommendation List Creation

Here, we describe the linear combination of our different models to predict the next item to be clicked in a user session. As discussed, news topic categories can reveal the long-term preferences of users. However, we are not interested in predicting the next topic category to be clicked. Thus, to make item predictions, instead of category predictions, from all three aforementioned types of news topic category predictions (i.e., long-term individual, short- and long-term public), and for each topic category c_k^{ul}, c_k^{ps}, c_k^{pl} a subset of articles is selected from the set of articles that users have interacted with during time window t_p as follows:

$$\{i \in I_{c_k} | a_{i,c_k} > a_{j,c_k}, j \notin I_{c_k}\} \tag{12}$$

Please notice that the subsets of articles for each different topic category, include also the articles that were recently added to the system as fresh news stories. The score of each article i depends on both the probability distribution of this article a_{i,c_k} and the score of each category c_k^*, where $*$ could be any of ul, ps, pl. As an example let us consider how we can compute the score of an article i, when we use only the long-term public interest:

$$score(i, pl) = a_{i,c_k} \cdot c_k^{pl} \tag{13}$$

Next, if a given article is present in all resulted subsets or articles, its final score is the sum of scores within each subset as follows:

$$score(i, final) = \alpha \cdot score(i, us) + \beta \cdot score(i, ul) + \gamma \cdot score(i, ps) + \delta \cdot score(i, pl) \tag{14}$$

The final list of recommended articles contains those articles with the highest final score. Coefficients α, β, γ, and δ give us flexibility to boost one prediction model over another. In the default mode all these coefficients are equal to 0.25 and sum up at 1.

5   Experimental Evaluation

5.1   Log Analysis of Data Sets

Italian News Provider Data Set: For the Italian news provider, the data set accommodates 14367 interactions/ events on 2081 articles of 10421 unique users in one year (i.e. from 1st April 2016 to 30th March 2017). The interactions of each session are logged with the following information: the user session's identifier, the interaction's time stamp and duration, the article's textual content. User sessions have an average number of interactions equal to 2.78 after removing sessions that had only one item. Based on the articles' text, we trained a Latent Dirichlet Allocation (LDA) [1] model and found five topic categories in which an article may belong to. Thus, we have classified news articles into five topic categories, $C = \{c_1, c_2, \ldots, c_n\}$, including , "Politics", "Chronicles", "Culture/Education", "Justice", and "Sports". In addition, Fig. 2a shows how evolves the crowd's interest over the 5 topic categories during a year. As shown, some news categories (e.g., Chronicles, Culture/Education and Politics) have greater variation than others (e.g. Sports and Justice). Please notice that the Italian-speaking population is very interested in news stories about Culture/Education, which is the third topic category that interests the public on average during the whole year.

German News Provider Data Set: For the German news provider, the data set accommodates 5536 interactions on 468 articles of 3626 unique users in one year. User sessions have an average number of interactions equal to 3.07. We have also classified news articles into five topic categories, including "Politics and Local News", "Tourism", "Economic News", "Chronicles", and "Sport", as it is shown in Fig. 2b. Three out of five topic categories are the same with those shown for the Italian news provider. However, for the German-speaking population there is also more public interest for Economic News and Tourism. The German speaking population is very interested in Economic news, in contrast to the Italian-speaking population who is interested more in Culture and Education, as discussed previously. This is a clear indication that different cultural communities have different interests over news, which can be taken under consideration for providing news recommendations. This is something that has not been explored previously, since related work has explored topic categories only in the level of countries [3,10].

5.2   Prequential Evaluation Protocol

In this section, we present our evaluation protocol, which is in the same direction, with the one introduced by Dietmar et al. [7,11] for predicting the next item

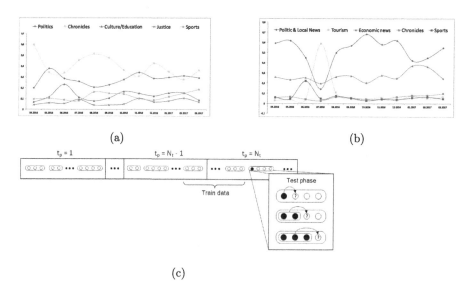

(a)   (b)

(c)

Fig. 2. A visual representation showing the public interest for 5 topics over the last 12 months in the area of Alto Adige in Italy for the (a) Italian language and (b) German language news providers. (c) Prequential Evaluation Protocol.

inside a session, known also as prequential evaluation in stream mining [13,17]. As shown in Fig. 2c, in prequential evaluation, future articles are first predicted by the model, so that the quality of the model is evaluated; then articles with their true labels are used for model learning, which means that approaches adapt to the user's every next click. As also shown in Fig. 2c, results are obtained when applying a sliding-window protocol, where we split the data into several slices of equal size. An important parameter of this protocol is the sliding time window size of the training data. If this sliding time window is too large the system is not sensitive to changes (concept drifts). if it is too small there is not enough data to build a model predicting the next items in a session. Finally, we evaluate the precision (i.e., the number of hits divided by the number of recommended items) we get when we recommend top-5 articles for each next item prediction inside a session. We split time in N_t time periods, so that we can aggregate the precision results for each different time period t_p.

5.3 Sensitivity Analysis of the Proposed Method

In this section, we study the accuracy performance of our (i) intra-session-TPM (intra-TPM), (ii) inter-session-TPM (inter-TPM), (iii) intra- with inter-TPM, and (iv) their combination with news category-based TPM (Cat-TPM) [10], where TPM stands for transition probability matrix. We will explore, how the precision accuracy of the aforementioned methods changes as we vary different parameters such as (i) different time period splits: $N_t = 183, 365, 730$ (ii) various time window sizes: $w = 1, 2, 4$ and (iii) their linear combination in a hybrid weighted model where all three methods have equal weight (0.33).

For the Italian news provider data set, in Figs. 3a, 3b, and 3c, we set the sliding time window $w = 1$ and change the number of time period splits $N_t = 183, 365, 730$, which consider a time slot t_p equal to 2 days, 1 day, and 12 h, respectively. Please notice that for all N_t values we aggregate the results in the level of months and show their average precision score also over a month. The reason is two-fold: (i) we present results that are statistical significant and (ii) we show more meaningful aggregated visual analytics. All presented measurements (i.e., the average of the reported values between the runs over a month), based on two-tailed t-test, are statistically significant at the 0.05 level.

As shown in Figs. 3, the combination of "intra-, inter-TPM, with cat-TPM" achieves better results than "intra- with inter-TPM", for almost all time points. In particular, as it is shown also in Table 3, the combination of "inter- with intra- and cat-TPM" attains the best average precision over the whole year equal to 3.82%, when we set $N_t = 365$ and $w = 1$. That is, by forgetting faster older news is better. In other words, when we consider for our prediction model only the articles of the previous day before the target session for which we want to make article predictions, then we get the best precision. This is as expected, since the life span of articles is short and news stories become the focus of interest quickly and disappear just as quickly. Please notice that when we run experiments with $N_t = 730$ and $w = 1$, precision is again decreased, which means that when we predict recommendations based on half day (12 h) is more effective than making recommendations based on just 6 h.

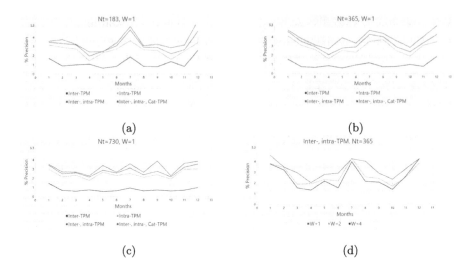

Fig. 3. For the Italian news provider, precision comparison of intra-TPM, inter-TPM, "intra- with inter-TPM", and "intra- with inter- and cat-TPM" for (a) window size $w = 1$ and $N_t = 365$ time points, (b) $w = 1$ and $N_t = 730$, (c) $w = 1$ and $N_t = 1460$. (d) Precision of "intra- with inter- and cat-TPM" vs. different sliding time window sizes $w = 1, 5,$ and 10 for $N_t = 730$ time slots.

For the German news provider, results are similar with those shown in Fig. 3. However, due to space limitation we will present only single-value precision results over the year, which will be discussed in the next section (see Table 3).

Next, measure the performance of the combined method "intra-, inter- and cat-TPM" as we use different time window sizes: $w = 1, 2, 4$, for time slots $N_t = 365$. As shown in Fig. 3d the windows size $w = 1$ attains the best average precision over the year equal to 3.82% and as we increase w precision drops. For further experiments, we fix our method for $N_t = 365$ and $w = 1$.

5.4   Comparison with Other Methods

In this Section, we compare our method with the following algorithms: (i) Most Popular Recent Items (Recently POP), (ii) Item-based Collaborative Filtering (IBCF) [2], (iii) News Category-based Transition Probability Matrix (Cat-TPM)[10], (iv) the k nearest sessions (Session-knn) [8], and the (v) neural-network (GRU4REC) [5].

Table 3 reports the average precision of the under comparison algorithms for $N_t = 65$ and $w = 1$ for the Italian and the German news provider, since this number of time slots (i.e., 1 day) attains the best precision. As shown in the last row of the table, our proposed approach has the best average precision over the year. The reason is that when we combine all three models together (i.e., inter-, intra-, and cat-TPM), we are able to capture the short and long preferences of both individuals and the public. In our combined approach, Cat-TPM incorporates 3 different transition probabilities matrices to capture the individual's long and the public short and long term preferences over categories (see Eq. 14). This is a proof that the news topic categories should be incorporated into prediction models because they provide information about the long term user preferences.

Table 3. For the Italian and the German News Providers, average precision results (%) for $N_t = 365$ with window size $W = 1$.

Methods	Italian News Portal Precision (%)	German News Portal Precision (%)
Recently POP	2.95	5.82
IBCF [2]	1.65	2.20
Cat-TPM [10]	0.76	2.28
Session-knn [8]	0.68	2.14
GRU4REC [5]	0.57	2.08
Inter-TPM	0.93	2.36
Intra-TPM	2.82	4.61
Inter-, intra-TPM	3.29	5.75
Inter-, intra-, Cat-TPM	**3.82**	**6.21**

Notice that the Italian and the German News data sets have avg. number of items per session 2.78, and 3.07 respectively, which means that there is a severe data sparsity. However, the performance of all methods for German news provider is 2 times better than their performance for the Italian news provider in all measurements. The reason is that news articles in German news providers web site are viewed almost twice as much comparing to the news articles on the Italian news provider web site. In particular, the average views per article for the german news provider data set is 11.8 and 6.9 for the Italian news provider.

6   Conclusion

In this paper, we combined intra- and inter-session TPM together with category-based TPM to reveal the short- and long-term intentions of individuals along with the public preference over news topic categories. We evaluated experimentally our method and compare it against state-of-the-art algorithms on two real-life datasets. We have shown the superiority of our method over its competitors. As future work, we will run more experiments with different sliding window sizes between the intra-, inter-session and cat-TPM methods, to better model the fact that items' life span is also depended on the news topic category they belong to.

166 P. Symeonidis et al.

References

1. Blei, D.M.: Probabilistic topic models. Commun. ACM **55**(4), 77–84 (2012)
2. Das, A.S., Datar, M., Garg, A., Rajaram, S.: Google news personalization: scalable online collaborative filtering. In: Proceedings 16th International Conference on World Wide Web (WWW), pp. 271–280, Banff, Canada (2007)
3. Epure, E.V., Kille, B., Ingvaldsen, J.E., Deneckere, R., Salinesi, C., Albayrak, S.: Recommending personalized news in short user sessions. In: Proceedings 11th ACM Conference on Recommender Systems (RecSys), pp. 121–129, Como, Italy (2017)
4. Hidasi, B., Karatzoglou, A.: Recurrent neural networks with top-k gains for session-based recommendations. In: Proceeding 27th ACM International Conference on Information & Knowledge Management (CIKM), pp. 843–852, Torino (2018)
5. Hidasi, B., Karatzoglou, A., Baltrunas, L., Tikk, D.: Session-based recommendations with recurrent neural networks. In: Track Proceedings 4th International Conference on Learning Representations (ICLR), San Juan, Puerto Rico (2016)
6. Hidasi, B., Quadrana, M., Karatzoglou, A., Tikk, D.: Parallel recurrent neural network architectures for feature-rich session-based recommendations. In: Proceedings 10th ACM Conference on Recommender Systems (RecSys), pp. 241–248, Boston, MA (2016)
7. Jannach, D., Lerche, L., Jugovac, M.: Adaptation and evaluation of recommendations for short-term shopping goals. In: Proceedings 9th ACM Conference on Recommender Systems (RecSys), pp. 211–218, Vienna, Austria (2017)
8. Jannach, D., Ludewig, M.: When recurrent neural networks meet the neighborhood for session-based recommendation. In: Proceedings 11th ACM Conference on Recommender Systems (RecSys), pp. 306–310, Como, Italy (2017)
9. Li, L., Zheng, L., Yang, F., Li, T.: Modeling and broadening temporal user interest in personalized news recommendation. Expert Syst. Appl. **41**(7), 3168–3177 (2014)
10. Liu, J., Dolan, P., Pedersen, E.R.: Personalized news recommendation based on click behavior. In: Proceedings 15th International Conference on Intelligent User Interfaces (IUI), pp. 31–40, Hong Kong, China (2010)
11. Ludewig, M., Jannach, D.: Evaluation of session-based recommendation algorithms. In: User Modeling and User-Adapted Interaction, pp. 331–390 (2018). https://doi.org/10.1007/s11257-018-9209-6
12. Ludmann, C.A.: Recommending news articles in the CLEF news recommendation evaluation lab with the data stream management system Odysseus. In: Working Notes, Conference & Labs of the Evaluation Forum (CLEF), Dublin, Ireland (2017)
13. Quadrana, M., Cremonesi, P., Jannach, D.: Sequence-aware recommender systems. ACM Comput. Surv. **51**(4), 66:1–66:36 (2018)
14. Quadrana, M., Karatzoglou, A., Hidasi, B., Cremonesi, P.: Personalizing session-based recommendations with hierarchical recurrent neural networks. In: Proceedings 11th ACM Conference on Recommender Systems (RecSys), pp. 130–137 (2017)
15. Smirnova, E., Vasile, F.: Contextual sequence modeling for recommendation with recurrent neural networks. In: Proceedings 2nd RecSys Workshop on Deep Learning for Recommender Systems (DLRS), pp. 2–9, Como, Italy (2017)
16. Tan, Y.K., Xu, X., Liu, Y.: Improved recurrent neural networks for session-based recommendations. In: Proceedings 1st Workshop on Deep Learning for Recommender Systems (DLRS), pp. 17–22, Boston, MA (2016)
17. Vinagre, J., Jorge, A., Gama, J.: Evaluation of recommender systems in streaming environments. In: Proceedings RecSys Workshop on Recommender Systems Evaluation: Dimensions and Design (REDD), Silicon Valley, CA (2014)

Deep Matrix Factorization for Learning Resources Recommendation

Tran Thanh Dien(ID), Nguyen Thanh-Hai(ID), and Nguyen Thai Nghe$^{(\boxtimes)}$(ID)

College of Information and Communication Technology, Can Tho University,
Can Tho, Vietnam
{thanhdien,nthai.cit}@ctu.edu.vn
ntnghe@cit.ctu.edu.vn

Abstract. Learning should last all through people's lives. With traditional learning, learners can meet face-to-face with their teachers or tutors. However, in some circumstances, learners cannot interact with their teachers. Learning resources (e.g., books, journals, slides, etc.) would be helpful for learners to get knowledge. With a large number of learning resources, how to select appropriate learning resources to learn is very important. In this work, a deep matrix factorization model extended from the standard matrix factorization is proposed for learning resources recommendation. We validate the proposed model on five published learning resources datasets and compare it with other well-known methods in recommender systems. The experimental results show that the proposed deep matrix factorization model works well, especially it can be a good choice for large-scale datasets.

Keywords: Learning resources recommendation · Deep learning · Knowledge search · Book recommendation · Matrix factorization · Deep matrix factorization

1 Introduction

Learning resources and materials are an important part of education. Learners and educators can be benefited from using them. Firstly, learning resources provide various digital learning environments such as open textbooks, open visual materials, open courses, and self-assessment tools. Then, numerous high-quality learning resources are possible to be updated and edited frequently. Another advantage of learning resources is that self-study, testing, or group learning are supported. With the development of information technology, it tends to move from traditional to online reading. Nowadays, information can be searched or exploited from e-libraries or on the Internet. Students and educators tend to search for their preferred learning materials on online resource systems. Universities have also provided open educational resources. They may consider an investment in open resources a sustainable human development. Open learning resources increase access to high-quality education and lower the cost of education worldwide. People around the world can share, contribute and access

N. T. Nguyen et al. (Eds.): ICCCI 2021, LNAI 12876, pp. 167–179, 2021.
https://doi.org/10.1007/978-3-030-88081-1_13

knowledge. These resources refer to all aspects of social life, helping readers to exploit aspects and information about the problem they need to research. However, various educational resource and material systems may cause difficulties for users to select appropriate learning resources. With the explosion of e-library websites, volumes of data have been increasing. Today, most resources and materials system websites allow their users to write comments or/and reviews on the materials to express their feelings in a more precise and more detailed way about the materials they had read. This information enables us to conduct studies based on users' ratings for providing valuable suggestions.

In this study, a method based on deep learning and the state-of-the-art matrix factorization models is proposed to provide recommendations on learning resources. The work includes multi-fold contributions as follows:

- Propose a deep matrix factorization model with detailed architecture and parameters for learning resources recommendation.
- Compare the proposed model with other well-known methods in recommender systems to validate the results.
- Test on five learning resource datasets and compare the results of original data with pre-filtered data.
- Show that the deep matrix factorization model, a dimensional reduction approach, could be a good choice for large-scale datasets.

Section 2 presents some state-of-the-arts related to book recommendation systems. In Sect. 3, we present our proposed methods for this work. The experimental results of our proposed methods obtained are discussed concerning different parameters in Sect. 4. This section is followed by Sect. 5 containing the paper's conclusion.

2   Related Work

Numerous studies have been proposed to design automatic book recommendation systems using various methods, including classic machine learning, deep learning techniques, and hybrid methods on vast datasets that can range from a few features or even hundreds of attributes.

[1] stated that existing recommendation systems skipped the characteristics of readers' personalized information. Hence, their work proposed a library recommendation system based on a restricted Boltzmann machine and collaborative filtering algorithm to improve the performance to provide a good application effect. The work of [2] provided a system for exploring the data concerning to reading, including three categories.

There are numerous proposed methods and models, including user/item collaborative filtering, filtering based on content, association rule mining, hybrid recommender system, as well as recommendations. Though such techniques have exposed interesting characteristics, those can be inefficient in generating appropriate recommendations in some particular cases. Therefore, numerous hybrid approaches have been investigated to integrate various methods to perform better recommendations [3]. A hybrid-based method presented in [4] has integrated to use both attribute and personality of users for book recommendation systems. Another hybrid-based method was introduced by [5] to consider customer's demographic information such as sex, age, geographical location, and book information such as title and ISBN for the rating of book prediction with values ranging from 1 to 5 classified with Multilayer Perceptrons models. A model learned from learner profile, and the learning content was proposed by [6] using two ontologies.

[7] considered that contextual information including location and emotion could enhance greatly product or service recommendations to be included in the recommender system. The authors determined several user characteristics and product features. In some studies, students' scores or courses are used as learning resources for the recommendation using deep learning techniques. [8] leveraged some techniques such as Quantile Transformation, MinMax Scaler to perform the prediction tasks. Another research of [9] proposed to use MultiLayer Perceptron and pre-processing methods on four million mark records of a university to give appropriate recommendations on course selection.

Based on the previous works as mentioned above, in this study, we proposes an approach based on deep learning and the state-of-the-art matrix factorization models to provide good recommendations on learning resources (e.g., books, journals, etc.). We also compare the proposed model with other well-known recommender systems to prove state-of-the-arts of the proposed model.

3   Proposed Method

3.1   Problem Formulation

Let denote u as the user/learner, i as the learning resource (e.g., book, journal, paper, etc.), and r is the feedback from user u on learning resource i (rating). In general, the learning resources recommendation can be mapped to rating prediction problem in recommender systems as follows:

Learner, reader, or student $\mapsto$ User

Learning resource (book, journal, or paper, etc.) $\mapsto$ Item

Feedback (rating, number of views or clicks, etc.) $\mapsto$ Rating

- **Prediction phase:** Given a dataset $\mathcal{D}$ with available (u, i, r) We want to build the model to predict the rating (score) of the learning resources which have not been seen/read by the user (the empty values in this matrix).
- **Recommendation phase:** After having the prediction results, we sort the rating scores by ascending and selecting top N learning resources with the highest scores for recommendation (N could be 3, 5, or other value depending on the system interface).

3.2 Deep Matrix Factorization for Learning Resource Recommendation

Based on previous works [10,11], in this study, we proposed the prediction model using Deep Matrix Factorization (DMF) that is described in detail in Fig. 1.

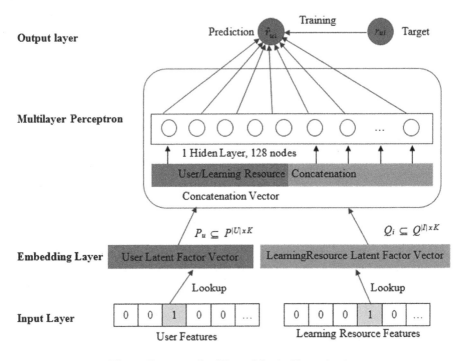

Fig. 1. Framework of Deep Matrix Factorization

The proposed model has four layers. An input layer represents the current user/learning resource; an embedding layer for embedding user and learning resource features. These embedding features are concatenated as the input for the Multilayer Perceptron (MLP) layer. Finally, an output layer for the prediction score. The MLP has 128 nodes (neurons). However, we can set up different numbers of hidden layers (e.g., adding more layers) and the different number of neurons dependent on different datasets/domains. In this study, the number of nodes is selected using hyper-parameter search, which will be carefully presented in the experimental results section (Sect. 4.4). The network uses Adam optimizer function, using a batch size of 256 while the learning rate is 0.001. Moreover, to explore the difference between the proposed DMF model and the standard Matrix Factorization (MF), we present the MF in Fig. 2. Instead of using an MLP as the DMF, the standard MF only does a DOT product between two users and learning resource feature vectors.

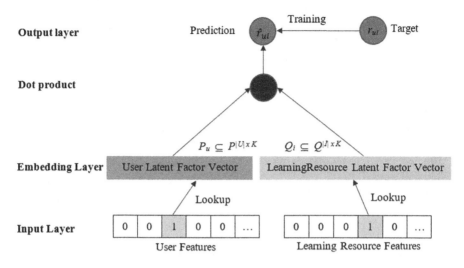

Fig. 2. Framework of Matrix Factorization

Table 1. Descriptions of five considered full datasets

No.	Dataset	#user	#item	#ratings
1	Ratings	53,424	10,000	981,756
2	LibraryThings	70,618	385,251	1,387,125
3	BX-Book-ratings	105,283	340,556	1,149,780
4	Related-Article Recommendation	2,663,825	7,224,279	48,879,167
5	Ratings-Books	8,026,324	2,330,066	22,507,155

Table 2. Descriptions of five considered datasets for at least 5 ratings per User/Learning Resource

No.	Dataset	#user	#item	#ratings
1	Ratings	32,492	10,000	916,880
2	LibraryThings	25,930	41,900	802,957
3	BX-Book-ratings	19,109	34,751	573,305
4	Related-Article Recommendation	2,368,923	2,225,631	37,145,643
5	Ratings_Books	622,558	596,401	9,389,719

4   Experimental Results

4.1   Data Description

1. **Ratings** dataset[1] contains all users' ratings of the books (a total of 980,000 ratings, for 10,000 books, from 53,424 users). It introduces and demonstrates collaborative filtering; allows us to take a deeper look at data-driven book recommendations.
2. **BX-Book-ratings** dataset[2] contains a collection of book ratings including 105,283 users providing 1,149,780 ratings (explicit and implicit) of about 340,556 books.
3. **Ratings-Books** dataset[3] contains product ratings from Amazon, updated in 2018, including user, item, rating, and timestamp tuples.
4. **Related-Article Recommendation** dataset[4] is based on data from a recommender system in the digital library and reference management software domain. The datasets are from the books. It contains 2,663,825 users, 7,224,279 books and 48,879,167 ratings.
5. **LibraryThings** dataset[5] contains ratings and social relationships of users. It contains 70,618 users, offering 1,387,125 ratings of 385,251 books. In the dataset, the combination of social relations and rating similarity achieved the best results.

The number of users, learning resources, and ratings of these datasets are described in Table 1.

These datasets are very sparse, which means that the users or learning resources may have a few ratings. This problem is a challenge for every machine learning method. For comparison purposes, we present other versions of these datasets by keeping those users/learning resources with at least five ratings. The new version of these datasets is presented in Table 2.

4.2   Baselines for Comparison

In order to evaluate the effectiveness of the proposed DMF model, we compare it with other popular baselines for recommendation systems including User KNN, Item KNN, Co-Clustering, Global Average, User Average, Item Average, and Matrix Factorization.

Let denote u as the user/learner, i as the learning resource (e.g., book, journal, paper, etc.), and r is the feedback from user u on learning resource i (rating). These baselines can summarize as follows:

---

[1] https://www.kaggle.com/philippsp/book-recommender-collaborative-filtering-shiny.
[2] https://www.kaggle.com/ruchi798/bookcrossing-dataset.
[3] https://jmcauley.ucsd.edu/data/amazon/.
[4] https://doi.org/10.7910/DVN/AT4MNE.
[5] https://cseweb.ucsd.edu/~jmcauley/datasets.html.

The Global Average method generates rating prediction ($\hat{r}_{ui}$) for user u on learning resource i by averaging the ratings in training dataset using Eq. 1 [12, 13].

$$\hat{r}_{ui} = \frac{\sum_{r \in \mathcal{D}^{train}} r}{|\mathcal{D}^{train}|} \tag{1}$$

The User Average method generates rating prediction ($\hat{r}_{ui}$) for user u on learning resource i by using Eq. 2 [12,13].

$$\hat{r}_{ui} = \frac{\sum_{(u',i,r) \in \mathcal{D}^{train}|u'=u} r}{|\{(u',i,r) \in \mathcal{D}^{train}|u'=u\}|} \tag{2}$$

The Item Average is Learning Resource Average performing the predictions of the rating for the user u on learning resource i by using Eq. 3 [12,13].

$$\hat{r}_{ui} = \frac{\sum_{(u,i',r) \in \mathcal{D}^{train}|i'=i} r}{|\{(u,i',r) \in \mathcal{D}^{train}|i'=i\}|} \tag{3}$$

The User KNN generates the rating prediction by using Eq. 4 [12,13].

$$\hat{r}_{ui} = \bar{r}_u + \frac{\sum_{u' \in K_u} sim(u,u') \cdot (r_{u'i} - \bar{r}_{u'})}{\sum_{u' \in K_u} |sim(u,u')|} \tag{4}$$

where K_u is the k-nearest neighbors of user u and $sim(u,u')$ is the Cosine similarity between two users [12,13], which is calculated by

$$sim_{cosine}(u,u') = \frac{\sum_{i \in I_{uu'}} r_{ui} \cdot r_{u'i}}{\sqrt{\sum_{i \in I_{uu'}} r_{ui}^2} \cdot \sqrt{\sum_{i \in I_{uu'}} r_{u'i}^2}} \tag{5}$$

where $I_{uu'}$ is a set of learning resources which have rated by both user u and u'.

The Item KNN (Learning Resource KNN) generates the rating prediction by using Eq. 6 [12,13].

$$\hat{r}_{ui} = \bar{r}_i + \frac{\sum_{i' \in K_i} sim(i,i') \cdot (r_{ui'} - \bar{r}_{i'})}{\sum_{i' \in K_i} |sim(i,i')|} \tag{6}$$

where K_i is the k-nearest neighbors of learning resource i and $sim(i,i')$ is the Cosine similarity between two learning resources, which is calculated by

$$sim_{cosine}(i,i') = \frac{\sum_{u \in U_{ii'}} r_{ui} r_{ui'}}{\sqrt{\sum_{u \in U_{ii'}} r_{ui}^2} \cdot \sqrt{\sum_{u \in U_{ii'}} r_{ui'}^2}} \tag{7}$$

where $U_{ii'}$ is a set of users who studied/rated both learning resource i and i'

The Co-Clustering method generates the rating prediction by using Eq. 8 [14].

$$\hat{r}_{ui} = \bar{C}_{ui} + (\mu_u - \bar{C}_u) + (\mu_i - \bar{C}_i) \tag{8}$$

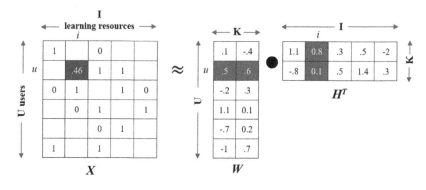

Fig. 3. Diagram of matrix factorization decomposition

where $\bar{C}_{ui}$ is the average rating of co-cluster C_{ui}, $\bar{C}_u$ is the average rating of u's cluster, and $\bar{C}_i$ is the average rating of i's cluster. If the user is unknown, the prediction is $\hat{r}_{ui} = \mu_i$. If the learning resource is unknown, the prediction is $\hat{r}_{ui} = \mu_u$. If both the user and the learning resource are unknown, the prediction is $\hat{r}_{ui} = \mu$.

Matrix Factorization has been used widely in a vast of studies [12,13,15]. A matrix X is decomposed to two sub-matrices W and H as exhibited in Eq. 9:

$$X \approx WH^T \tag{9}$$

where $W \in \mathbb{R}^{|U| \times K}$ while $H \in \mathbb{R}^{|I| \times K}$ and K is latent factors, $K << |U|, K << |I|$. The Eq. 9 demonstrated as Fig. 3.

4.3   Evaluation Metrics

To compare the perform, the root mean squared error (RMSE) is used to evaluate the models. It calculated by Eq. 10 below:

$$\sqrt{\frac{1}{n} \sum_{i=1}^{n}(y_i - \hat{y}_i)^2} \tag{10}$$

where y_i is the true value, and $\hat{y}_i$ is the predicted value.

4.4   Evaluation Results

The experimental results include an investigation on the impacts of the number of neurons (Fig. 4), the number of latent factors on the recommendation performance (Fig. 5), the performance of phases of training and testing during the learning (Fig. 6). Moreover, the results of various methods on the five considered datasets are exhibited in Figures of 7, 8, 9, 10, and 11.

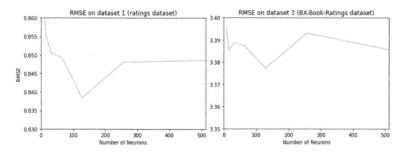

Fig. 4. The chart shows relationship between Number of Neurons for DMF models and RMSE performance

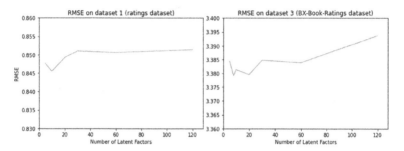

Fig. 5. The chart shows relationship between Number of Latent Factors (Features) for DMF models and RMSE performance.

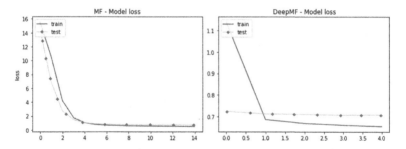

Fig. 6. Comparison of train loss and validation loss of the MF and DMF on Ratings dataset

In this study, the five published datasets are used for the experiments as follows.

The relationship between the error rate and the number of neurons for DMF models is exhibited in Fig. 4 while the effect of the Number of Latent Factors (Features) for DMF models on the error rate prediction is shown in Fig. 5. Two charts in Fig. 4 exhibit similar patterns in the performance. The number of neurons can increase the performance to a peak, then the loss goes up and tends

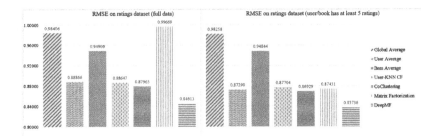

Fig. 7. RMSE comparison on dataset 1

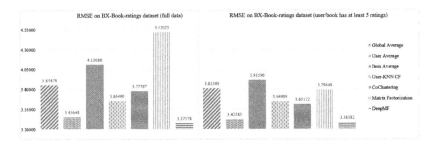

Fig. 8. RMSE comparison on dataset 2

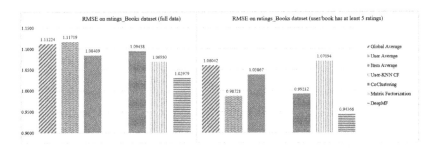

Fig. 9. RMSE comparison on dataset 3

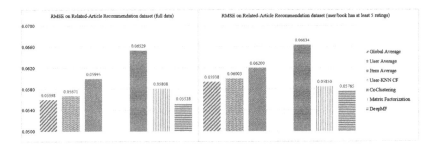

Fig. 10. RMSE comparison on dataset 4

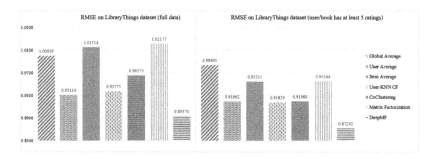

Fig. 11. RMSE comparison on dataset 5

to be saturated. On dataset 1, the lowest RMSE is achieved with around 100 neurons. A similar result is also obtained on dataset 3.

Figure 6 evaluates the overfitting of approaches during the learning. As shown in the figure, the training error and testing error of MF tends to converge after four epochs while DeepMF remains stable, the error rate only after two epochs. Moreover, MF suffers less overfitting than DeepMF when the learning progresses further.

Also, we compare DeepMF to a variety of methods including Item Average, User-KNN CF, Global Average, User Average, CoClustering, and Matrix Factorization in RMSE metric shown in Fig. 7 on dataset 1, Fig. 8 on dataset 2, and Fig. 9 on dataset 3, Fig. 10 on dataset 4, and Fig. 11 on dataset 5. For the datasets of 2 and 3, although we have deployed the experiments on the server with 320 GB in RAM, the learning of User-KNN CF cannot be done on two datasets of 3 and 4 due to the limitation of memory resources. In general, DeepMF outperforms most of the previous state-of-the-arts. Some better results can be obtained when we only consider the users/books with at least five ratings. Matrix Factorization seems to be the worst among the considered methods with the highest error rates on full datasets 1 and 5 and on dataset 3, including books/users with at least five ratings. The performance of User Average is almost near to DeepMF, but it only gets a better result on full dataset four and is defeated on other cases. From the prediction results, online learning resource systems can sort the resources/materials based on the rating scores corresponding to each user and then provide appropriate resources/materials suggestions to him or her as mentioned in the work of [9]. If a user logs into the system, it can extract the top five or top ten resources and materials with the highest predicted rating for that user. In the case the user does not log in, the systems can provide the top five or ten resources and materials which obtain the highest average predicted rating for all users.

5   Conclusion

In this work, we have proposed a DMF model extended from the standard matrix factorization for learning resources recommendations. We validate the proposed model on five public published learning resources datasets and also compare it with other well-known baselines of recommender systems. The experiments show that the proposed model can obtain well results on various datasets. Primarily, it can be a good choice for large-scale datasets. However, in this work, some methods can not be done due to requiring a large amount of memory for running, e.g., User-KNN CF as revealed in the experiments. In future work, adding more information to the deep learning model (e.g., time, sequence, multi-relational effects) could be exciting for improving the model's performance.

Availability of Data, Codes, and Materials

The experimental scripts and a data sample of this study are published at **learning-resources-rs**: https://github.com/thnguyencit/learning-resources-rs.

References

1. Wang, X., Huang, H.: Research on library personalized recommendation system based on restricted Boltzmann machine. In: 2020 5th International Conference on Education and Social Development (ICESD 2020), pp. 293–297 (2020). https://doi.org/10.12783/dtssehs/icesd2020/34428
2. Xu, H., Ren, S., Yan, J., Li, Z.: Research and design of recommendation in book circle system. J. Phys. Conf. Ser. **1629**(1), 012063 (2020). https://doi.org/10.1088/1742-6596/1629/1/012063
3. Passi, R., Jain, S., Singh, P.K.: Hybrid approach for recommendation system. Adv. Intell. Syst. Comput. **828**, 117–128 (2019). https://doi.org/10.1007/978-981-13-1610-4_12
4. Hariadi, A.I., Nurjanah, D.: Hybrid attribute and personality based recommender system for book recommendation. In: 2017 International Conference on Data and Software Engineering (ICoDSE), pp. 1–5. IEEE (2017). https://doi.org/10.1109/ICODSE.2017.8285874
5. Nirwan, H., Verma, O.P., Kanojia, A.: Personalized hybrid book recommender system using neural network. In: 2016 3rd International Conference on Computing for Sustainable Global Development (INDIACom), pp. 1281–1288 (2016)
6. Aissaoui, O.E., Oughdir, L.: A learning style-based Ontology Matching to enhance learning resources recommendation. In: 2020 1st International Conference on Innovative Research in Applied Science, Engineering and Technology (IRASET), pp. 1–7 (2020). https://doi.org/10.1109/IRASET48871.2020.9092142
7. Arabi, H., Balakrishnan, V., Mohd Shuib, N.L.: A context-aware personalized hybrid book recommender system. J. Web Eng. **19** (2020). https://doi.org/10.13052/jwe1540-9589.19343
8. Dien, T.T., Luu, S.H., Thanh-Hai, N., Thai-Nghe, N.: Deep learning with data transformation and factor analysis for student performance prediction. Int. J. Adv. Comput. Sci. Appl. **11**(8), 711–721 (2020). https://doi.org/10.14569/IJACSA.2020.0110886
9. Dien, T.T., Hoai-Sang, L., Thanh-Hai, N., Thai-Nghe, N.: Course recommendation with deep learning approach. In: Dang, T.K., Küng, J., Takizawa, M., Chung, T.M. (eds.) FDSE 2020. CCIS, vol. 1306, pp. 63–77. Springer, Singapore (2020). https://doi.org/10.1007/978-981-33-4370-2_5

10. Zhang, F., Song, J., Peng, S.: Deep Matrix Factorization for Recommender Systems with Missing Data not at Random. Journal of Physics: Conference Series 1060, 012001 (2018). https://doi.org/10.1088/1742-6596/1060/1/012001
11. Guo, H., Tang, R., Ye, Y., Li, Z., He, X.: Deepfm: a factorization-machine based neural network for CTR prediction. In: Proceedings of the 26th International Joint Conference on Artificial Intelligence, IJCAI 2017, pp. 1725–1731. AAAI Press (2017). https://doi.org/10.24963/ijcai.2017/239
12. Khanal, S.S., Prasad, P.W.C., Alsadoon, A., Maag, A.: A systematic review: machine learning based recommendation systems for e-learning. Edu. Inf. Technol. **25**(4), 2635–2664 (2019). https://doi.org/10.1007/s10639-019-10063-9
13. Gomez-Uribe, C.A., Hunt, N.: The netflix recommender system: algorithms, business value, and innovation. ACM Trans. Manage. Inf. Syst. **6**(4) (2015). https://doi.org/10.1145/2843948
14. George, T., Merugu, S.: A scalable collaborative filtering framework based on co-clustering. In: Fifth IEEE International Conference on Data Mining (ICDM 2005), p. 4 (2005)
15. Koren, Y., Bell, R., Volinsky, C.: Matrix factorization techniques for recommender systems. Computer **42**(8), 30–37 (2009). https://doi.org/10.1109/MC.2009.263

Impact of the Stroop Effect on Cognitive Load Using Subjective and Psychophysiological Measures

Patient Zihisire Muke⬥, Mateusz Piwowarczyk⬥, Zbigniew Telec⬥,
Bogdan Trawiński^(✉)⬥, Putri Ayu Maharani, and Patryk Bresso

Department of Applied Informatics, Wrocław University of Science and Technology, Wrocław,
Poland
{patient.zihisire,mateusz.piwowarczyk,zbigniew.telec,
bogdan.trawinski}@pwr.edu.pl

Abstract. The Stroop effect is a delay in human response between congruent and incongruent stimuli, in which color names interfere with the ability to determine the color of the ink used to print those names. The results of the Stroop test used in our experiment were analyzed from the point of view of human cognitive load. 62 volunteers took part in a study conducted on the iMotions biometric platform in laboratory conditions. Data were collected using observations, Single Ease Question (SEQ) and NASA Task Load Index (NASA-TLX) self-report questionnaires, and galvanic skin response (GSR) biosensor. In total, based on the collected data, 18 performance, subjective and psychophysiological metrics were calculated to measure cognitive load based on Stroop test. Non-parametric tests of statistical significance of differences between individual metrics were performed for the Stroop tasks for the easy and hard level of difficulty. The Spearman's rank correlation between individual metrics was also analysed. The conducted research allowed to make many interesting observations and showed the usefulness of most measures in the analysis of the cognitive load associated with the Stroop effect.

Keywords: Stroop effect · Cognitive load · Galvanic skin response · NASA-TLX questionnaire

1 Introduction

The Stroop test requires the participant in the experiment to read a list of words denoting different colors, but the words are printed in a color different from the meaning of the words themselves. For example, the word "blue" would appear in the text but printed in red. As regular readers, we encounter and understand words often enough that reading is almost effortless, but color declaration requires additional cognitive effort. The cognitive load will increase as soon as there is a dissonance between the two sources of information, so our brain will have to work harder to correct the difference that occurs. Processing the color of words and resolving information dissonance increases the time needed to complete a task and slows down our reactions [1].

© Springer Nature Switzerland AG 2021
N. T. Nguyen et al. (Eds.): ICCCI 2021, LNAI 12876, pp. 180–196, 2021.
https://doi.org/10.1007/978-3-030-88081-1_14

Due to the limited capacity of human working memory, a number of studies have been undertaken in the field of cognitive load to provide solutions for optimal use of working memory, especially in the learning process. In turn, in the field of computer science, the concept of cognitive load has become an important parameter in the design of user interfaces and user experience. Several methods for measuring cognitive load have been developed, namely performance, subjective, and psychophysiological methods. Psychophysiological methods are beginning to gain interest because of their ability to measure cognitive load by using data from biosensors when performing a given cognitive task. A wide variety of biosensory devices and biometric techniques such as electroencephalography (EEG), eye tracking, facial expression analysis, galvanic skin response (GSR), electrocardiography (ECG) and electromyography (EMG) [2] allow researchers to conduct comparative analysis that can determine the level of cognitive load.

The aim of the study was to measure the cognitive load when performing Stroop tasks on a stand-alone computer application using galvanic skin response (GSR) as a psychophysiological technique. The second goal was to conduct a comparative analysis of the performance, subjective, and psychophysiological measures of cognitive load in the same context.

The experiment was conducted using the integrated iMotions platform with 62 participants. The stimulus design was based on standardized tests that have been validated to measure cognitive load. In this study, the Stroop test was applied as the main stimulus, which consisted of two levels of difficulty (easy and hard). Participants from among young people with higher education were recruited to take part in the experiment. The analysis of the collected data was performed using non-parametric tests of statistical significance of differences between individual metrics. The correlation between individual metrics was also examined employing the Spearman's correlation test.

2   Background and Related Works

2.1   Cognitive Load

The cognitive load concept emerges from early work in the area of teaching and education and was expressed in cognitive load theory (CLT) [3–6]. The theory of cognitive load from the point of view of cognitive science is based on the multidimensional model of human memory, and connected with sensory, long term and working memory. Sensory memory holds information which has been presented briefly (i.e. <0.25 s). It makes up your ability to process and recall what you see. Working memory, for a short time, retains more processed input material (i.e. <30 s), only able to process certain pieces of information. Lastly, long-term memory is the storehouse for a learner's whole knowledge for a long period time.

In terms of physiological responses to cognitive load, when people experienced a psychophysiological load, meaning, in the nature of a demanding task, the activation of the sympathetic nervous system increases. The increased activation speeds up certain processes in the body ("fight or flight" response). It increases blood pressure, breathing rate, sweat rate, and heart rate; the equidistance of the heartbeats is experimented; reduces the flow of saliva; dilate the pupils, blood flow is restricted from the extremities and is reoriented to vital organs. After the loading of the memory, the sympathetic nervous system response decelerates, the pathological nervous system reverses physiological changes and launches the repair and relaxation processes [7].

At the same time, the cognitive load of a task based on the time-based resource sharing (TBRS) model [8] is the proportion of time during which this task attracts attention and hinders maintenance activities. Alternatively, in other words cognitive load is the duration of attentional capture divided by the total time permitted to carry out the task. When the cognitive load is too high, that become challenging for the memory to process the required information and can even cause the learning process to stop. Nevertheless, it has been shown that humans can increase cognitive effort in order to match the demands of a task, which can as well increase the limit of their mental capacity. However, if the cognitive load exceeds its capacity due to increased task demands, the effect can contribute to decreased performance and an increase in errors and contextual variables such as stress. Additional factors that can affect performance are individual abilities, skills, and capacities, as well as other secondary effects such as motivation, pressure, and environmental influences generally [9].

Cognitive load may change from time to time or be very dynamic during the performance of a given task. Different levels of cognitive load in different people can be simulated when performing a task or learning a new skill. Age, knowledge of a task, level of prior experience or knowledge, nationality, mental or physical barriers may cause differences in levels of stress when performing cognitive tasks. Consequently, a given task may present a high cognitive load for one person but require a low cognitive load for others due to the varying levels of experience in the same task.

Cognitive load on its own is defined as the total working memory resource needed to carry out a learning task [10]. This theory is related to instructional design, which aims to reduce the complexity of unnecessary information on the working memory while processing new knowledge, thus, lowering the level of cognitive load [11].

This theory refers as well to the two categories of knowledge suggested by Geary [12–14] and Geary & Berch [15], namely primary biological knowledge and secondary biological knowledge. The primary biological knowledge is the basic knowledge that can be acquired naturally and effortlessly by living things as a result of evolution over many generations [16]. Abilities such as problem solving, face recognition, planning, communicating with each other, social relationships, and other generic cognitive abilities, which are most likely the result of evolution over different periods, are biologically primary knowledge [17]. In contrast to that, biologically secondary knowledge is knowledge obtained by using mental effort and require to be learned with explicit instructions [18, 19].

Learning to speak a native language or listening is an example of obtaining primary biological knowledge, whereas learning any another language as an adult or learning to write and to read in any language are examples of obtaining secondary knowledge [20, 21]. As secondary knowledge cannot be obtained automatically or unconsciously, it is necessary to consider the best way to provide information. This is what the cognitive load theory focuses on, and it also has implications for the success of all forms of computer instruction.

2.2   Stroop Effect

By employing the Stroop test, we are able to evaluate a person's cognitive processing speed, attention span, and the magnitude of cognitive control (also called executive function). These capabilities and characteristics are reflected in many ways in which we interact with the world, pointing out that this test provides a brief – but exciting – overview of human thinking and behavior [1].

The Stroop test is usually employed to examine the psychophysiological response of humans to cognitive load. By itself, the Stroop test is a presentation of interference in the response of a task. In agreement with Renaud and Blonden, this mechanism is extensively employed in a variety of cognitive-perceptual processes [22, 23]. In accordance with Williams et.al, this is a color-naming type of tasks as well as a classic standard in the neurophysiological evaluation of mental aptness [23, 24]. The Stroop pattern consists of three groups: congruent, incongruent and neutral. In the Stroop test, the stimulus word is shown to the participant during the test in a color similar or different from the word to which it refers. Neutral stimuli are stimuli of the same color or text that is presented to the participant during the test. In a congruent stimulus, the color and the name of the color are identical [23].

2.3   Galvanic Skin Response

The galvanic skin response (GSR) is a part of electrodermal activity (EDA) measurement, which keeps track of sweat glands' activity. Through connected electrodes to the skin, the GSR device sends constant and imperceptible electric currents. After obtaining the data about voltage and current flow, it is possible to measure the skin's conductance, which changes when a particular person starts sweating. Sweat conduct electricity, with an increase of sweat amount, skin conductivity increases as well. Skin conductance is expressed in micro Siemens units [25]. GSR measures can be divided actually into two groups: tonic and phasic ones. Tonic measures slowly adapt to stimulus and produce responses over the whole time of the ongoing stimulus. On the other hand, phasic changes occur rapidly and likewise stop very quickly [26].

As the level of stress increases, GSR increases significantly. Previous researches show a relation between stress and cognitive load. An increase in the difficulty level of the task intensifies cognitive load. This causes a stressful situation for the participant of the experiment [27–29].

2.4   Subjective Cognitive Load Measurement

According to the literature, traditionally, the subjective cognitive load measurement approach provides the most reliable results [30]. In this measurement method, a detailed explanation is demanded from users, and through direct interviews; they are also asked to reflect each other's perceptions about cognitive load. Through this approach, users are asked to do their evaluation of their psychological requests by fulfilling a series of evaluation questions, which are generally in the form of questionnaires, instantly after the research scenario is carried out. There are two categories of subjective rating scales: the unidimensional scale measures the total cognitive load, such as the subjective cognitive load measurement scale [9]; multidimensional scales, which focus on various load components [9].

The most commonly used questionnaire based on a multidimensional scale is the NASA Task Load Index (*NASA-TLX*). It consists of six subscales that represent independent dimensions: Mental, Physical, and Temporal Demands, Frustration, Effort, and Performance. This combination of dimensions is supposed to represent the "workload" experienced by most people performing most tasks [31, 32].

Another subjective rating scale measure used by researchers, especially in usability and user experience testing, is the Single Ease Question (*SEQ*). It is a 7-point rating scale to evaluate how difficult participants find a task [33].

3 Experimental Setup

The experiment was conducted with 62 volunteers on the iMotions biometric platform using various stimuli and biometric techniques. In this paper, due to the limited space, we present only small part of the results that relate to the study of the impact of the Stroop effect on human cognitive load using only one biosensor technique, namely galvanic skin response (GSR). The experiment was carried out during the COVID-19 pandemic, and both researchers and participants had to follow strict sanitation rules in the lab during the experiment sessions to reduce the likelihood of spreading the virus. The research was approved by the Committee for Ethics of Scientific Research in the discipline of Information and Communication Technology at the Wroclaw University of Science and Technology.

3.1 Participants

We recruited sixty-two participants ranging in age from 19 to 38 years (48 males and 14 females), with an average age of 25.7 years. 39 participants were university students, plus 1 high school student, 6 doctoral students, 9 computer scientists, 1 researcher, and 6 other professions. Most participants were right-handed: 53 right-handed, 6 left-handed, and 3 have no dominant hand. 42 participants had good eyesight, 12 had visual impairment and wore glasses, 5 had visual impairment and wore contact lenses, and 3 had to use reading glasses. The participants came from different countries: 26 from Poland, 24 from India, 10 from Indonesia, 1 from another country in Asia, and 1 from a country in Africa. The participants had good knowledge of mathematics, logical reasoning, and word processing skills. Prior to the experiment, participants signed a consent form to participate in the study. They were rewarded with a gift of small value for participating in the experiment.

3.2 Stroop Test

The Stroop test applied in our experiment test consisted of five tasks with an easy level of difficulty and five tasks with a hard level of difficulty. In each task we used words that were color names both in the question and in the choice of answers. The participants were asked to select the name of the ink color in which the word in the question was written, regardless of the meaning of the word. The level of difficulty was determined by words constituting a set of answers. In easy-level tasks, the name of the color matched the color of the ink in which it was written, i.e. the words were written in congruent colors. However, in tasks on the difficult level, the name of the color did not match the color of the ink, i.e. the words were written in incongruent colors. On the other hand, in both types of tasks, color names in the question were incongruent, they did not match the color of the ink. The examples of tasks used in the experiment are presented in Fig. 1.

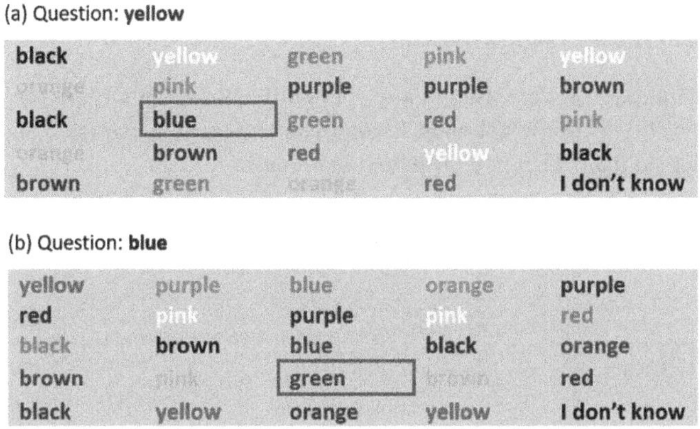

(a) Question: **yellow**

black	yellow	green	pink	yellow
orange	pink	purple	purple	brown
black	blue	green	red	pink
orange	brown	red	yellow	black
brown	green	orange	red	I don't know

(b) Question: **blue**

yellow	purple	blue	orange	purple
red	pink	purple	pink	red
black	brown	blue	black	orange
brown	pink	green	brown	red
black	yellow	orange	yellow	I don't know

Fig. 1. Examples of tasks in the Stroop test carried out during the experiment with the correct answers marked: (a) – easy level – *StrE*, (b) – hard level – *StrH*. (Color figure online)

We used the same set of nine colors for the color names and ink colors, i.e. red, blue, green, brown, purple, yellow, orange, pink and black, because these colors were clearly visible and distinguishable on the laptop screen. The number of options to select from in the answer set was 24. In the easy-level task, if the word "*yellow*" was written in blue, the expected answer was the word "*blue*", which was written in blue ink. In a hard-level task, if the word "*blue*" was written in green, the participant was expected to choose the word "green", even if that word was written in purple. Difficulty levels are labeled as *StrE* for low level and *StrH* for hard level in the rest of the paper.

3.3   Self-report Questionnaires Used

For the subjective measurement, we used two types of self-report questionnaires administered after each group of tasks. The modified version of the NASA Task Load Index questionnaire was applied in this study because we did not use the weighting scheme in calculating the overall score. This simplified version is sometimes named Raw TLX (*RTLX*). Moreover, instead of the original scale we used the 7-point Likert scale to rate each question. We assumed that this scale could easy the participants for providing more reliable assessments in a shorter time. The other questionnaire was the Single Ease Question (*SEQ*). *SEQ* is a 7-point rating scale that used to obtain the participants' perception about the difficulty level of the tasks. All 7-point scales ranged from extremely low, very low, moderately low, neither low nor high, moderately high, very high to extremely high.

3.4 Biometric Techniques and Biosensors Used

The Shimmer 3 GSR+ device was used to measure the electrodermal activities. This biosensor collected data while participants solved tasks during the experiment and automatically saved them on the iMotions platform. We placed the GSR on the wrist of their non-dominant hand and the electrodes were placed on the index and middle fingers. The reason for placing the GSR on a non-dominant hand was that participants had to use their dominant hand to operate the mouse during the experiment.

3.5 Metrics to Assess Cognitive Load

Three types of measures were used to assess cognitive load, namely performance, subjective, and psychophysiological ones. In total 18 metrics were extracted and computed based on collected data. They are presented in Table 1.

Table 1. Metrics used to assess cognitive load

Type	Metrics	Denotation
Performance metrics	Task completion rate	Per01
	Task completion time	Per02
Subjective metrics	Task difficulty (SEQ)	Sub01
	NASA-TLX – Overall	Sub02
	NASA-TLX – Complexity	Sub03
	NASA-TLX – Physical demand	Sub04
	NASA-TLX – Time pressure	Sub05
	NASA-TLX – Performance satisfaction	Sub06
	NASA-TLX – Mental effort	Sub07
	NASA-TLX – Frustration	Sub08
Psychophysiological metrics	GSR peak count	Psy01
	GSR peaks per minute	Psy02
	GSR mean value	Psy03
	GSR mean value (normalized)	Psy04
	GSR Max value	Psy05
	GSR Max value (normalized)	Psy06
	GSR accumulative value	Psy07
	GSR accumulative value (normalized)	Psy08

Due to erroneous GSR measurements, we had to discard the results of 3 respondents. As a result, all metrics were calculated based on data collected for 59 participants. Moreover, considering the fact that the participants performed five easy-level and five hard-level tasks, each measure for *StrE* and *StrH* is the mean value of the measurements of the five tasks.

We used two performance measures, namely task completion rate and task completion time. The former was calculated as the percentage of successfully completed tasks and the latter as the average task completion time.

Subjective metrics were calculated on the basis of the results of SEQ and NSA-TLX questionnaires administered to the participants after completing a group of 5 tasks of a given type. The score values for each question ranged from 1 to 7. The overall NASA-TLX was calculated as the average score of the six questions in the survey.

Psychophysiological metrics were computed for data collected from GSR biosensors using two iMotions post-processing algorithms, namely (1) GSR Peak Detection [34, 35] and (2) GSR Epoching Pre-processing [36, 37]. The first algorithm gives the number of peaks (*Psy01*) and peaks per minute (*Psy02*) for each task-participant pair. Fluctuations in the phase component of the GSR signal are treated as GSR peaks. This phasic response is sensitive to emotional stimuli and can be taken as an indicator of the participant's arousal while performing a specific task. In turn, the second algorithm prepare the original raw signal for dimensionality reduction, called epoching, by applying some preprocessing steps which include a low-pas zero phase filter, a gap interpolation, and an optional median filter. The epochs can be determined by a fixed time window; in our case 1000 ms per epoch for each task-participant pair. The output of this algorithm includes mean, median, maximum and minimum values, and standard deviation of the GSR signal in each epoch. To calculate the *Psy03 – Psy08* metrics we employed the mean values (denoted as $GSR_{Mean(e)}$) and maximum values (denoted as $GSR_{Max(e)}$) of the GSR signal in individual epochs. Formulas 1 through 7 show how to calculate the measures: GSR mean value, GSR max value, and GSR accumulative value for each participant i and for each task t and for each epoch e. E_{it} stands for the number of epochs for a task-participant pair. In order to compensate for the subjective impact of the GSR values of individual participants, the baseline value was calculated for each participant based on the data collected during the completion of the personal questionnaire q. It is given by Formula 2, where E_{iq} stands for the number of epochs during the time period the participant completed the personal survey.

$$Psy03(i, t) = MEAN_{e=1}^{E_{it}} \left(GSR_{Mean(e)}(i, t, e) \right) \tag{1}$$

$$BaselineGSR(i) = MEAN_{e=1}^{E_{iq}} \left(GSR_{Mean(e)}(i, q, e) \right) \tag{2}$$

$$Psy04(i, t) = Psy03(i, t)/BaselineGSR(i) \tag{3}$$

$$Psy05(i, t) = MAX_{e=1}^{E_{it}} \left(GSR_{Max(e)}(i, t, e) \right) \tag{4}$$

$$Psy06(i, t) = Psy05(i, t)/BaselineGSR(i) \tag{5}$$

$$Psy07(i, t) = SUM_{e=1}^{E_{it}} \left(GSR_{Mean(e)}(i, t, e) \right) \tag{6}$$

$$Psy08(i, t) = PsyY07(i, t)/BaselineGSR(i) \tag{7}$$

4 Analysis of Experimental Results

The aggregated results of performance, subjective, and psychophysiological measures are visualized in Figs. 2, 3 and 4, respectively. They contain the mean and median values of the individual metrics for 59 participants. Moreover, tests of statistical significance of the differences between individual metrics for *StrE* and *StrH* were conducted.

The Shapiro-Wilk tests revealed that vast majority of results provided by performance, subjective, and psychophysiological metrics were not distributed normally. Therefore, non-parametric Wilcoxon matched pairs tests was applied. The null hypotheses assumed that there were not significant differences in individual metrics values between *StrE* and *StrH* tasks. The results of the Wilcoxon test for individual metrics are placed in Table 2, where the $+$ sign indicates that the value of the metric is statistically significantly greater for the *StrH* task compared to the *StrE* task. Sign $-$ means the opposite situation that the value of the metric is statistically significantly lower for the *StrH* task compared to the *StrE* task. In turn, the sign $\approx$ means that there was not sufficient evidence to reject the null hypothesis. The significance level for rejecting the null hypothesis was set to 0.05.

In terms of performance measures, both the mean and median of task completion rates (*Per01*) were higher for *StrE* compared to *StrH*. However, the differences were not statistically significant. In turn, the means and medians of task completion times (*Per02*) were lower for *StrE* compared to *StrH*, and the differences were statistically significant.

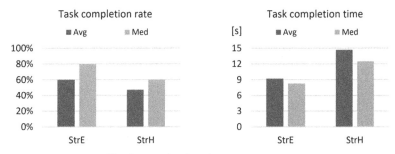

Fig. 2. Results of performance measures

For subjective measures, the results for seven of the eight measures were similar. Perceived task difficulty (*Sub01*), task complexity (*Sub03*), physical demand (*Sub04*), time pressure (*Sub05*), mental effort (*Sub07*), frustration (*Sub08*) as well as the overall NASA-TLX score (*Sub02*) were significantly greater for *StrH* compared to *StrE*. Only in the case of performance satisfaction (*Sub06*) the average scores were almost equal for *StrE* and *StrH* and differences were statistically insignificant.

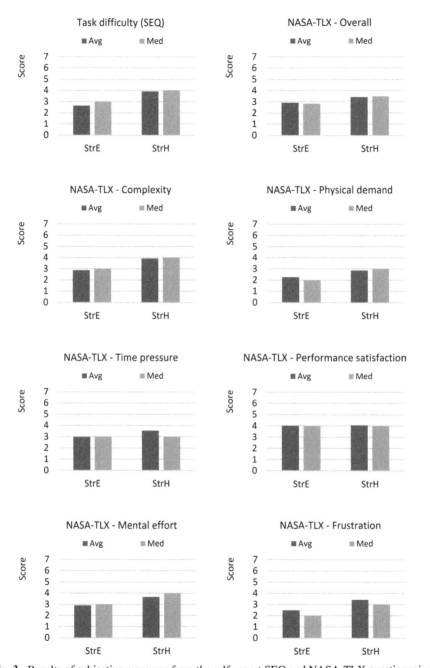

Fig. 3. Results of subjective measures from the self-report SEQ and NASA-TLX questionnaires

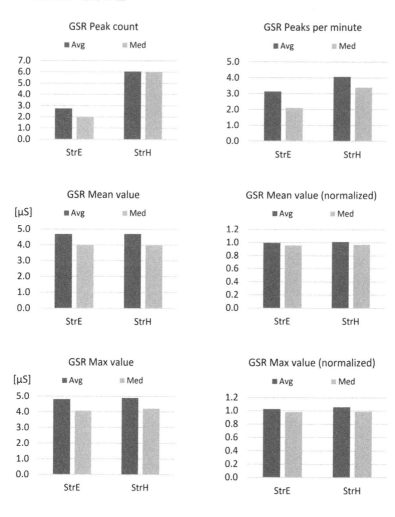

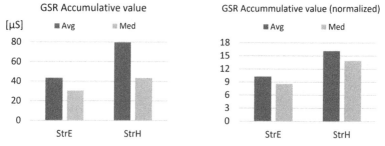

Fig. 4. Results of psychophysiological measures from the GSR sensor

Table 2. Wilcoxon test results for metrics comparison on StrE and StrH tasks.

Metrics	StrE vs StrH	Metrics	StrE vs StrH
Per01	≈	Per02	+
Sub01	+	Psy01	+
Sub02	+	Psy02	+
Sub03	+	Psy03	≈
Sub04	+	Psy04	≈
Sub05	+	Psy05	≈
Sub06	≈	Psy06	≈
Sub07	+	Psy07	+
Sub08	+	Psy08	+

Within psychophysiological measures, the means and medians of four measures, namely GSR Peak count (*Psy01*), GSR Peaks per minute (*Psy02*), GSR Accumulative value (*Psy07*), and GSR Accummulative value normalized (*Psy08*) turned out to be higher for *StrH* compared to *StrE* and the differences were statistically significant. However, the differences between means and medians of the other four measures: GSR Mean value (*Psy03*), GSR Mean value normalized (*Psy04*), GSR Max value (*Psy05*), GSR Max value normalized (*Psy06*) were slight and statistically insignificant.

We performed also tests of correlations between different metrics for *StrE* and *StrH*. We applied the Spearman rank order correlation because most the values of metrics were not distributed normally. Due to the limited space in this paper and the fact that *StrH* was stronger stimuli than *StrE* we present selected correlation results for only *StrH*. The correlation coefficient between performance metrics *Per01* and *Per02* was 0.16 and was insignificant. Correlation coefficients between the majority of subjective metrics ranged from 0.33 to 0.85 and were statistically significant. Only performance satisfaction (*Sub06*) provided the lowest values of Spearman's rank correlation coefficient and was not significantly correlated with *Sub04*, *Sub05*, and *Sub08*.

Spearman's rank correlation coefficients between psychophysiological metrics for StrH tasks are presented in Table 3. The correlation between most of these metrics is statistically significant. GSR Peak count (*Psy01*), GSR Peaks per minute (*Psy02*), and GSR Accumulative value (*Psy07*) correlate significantly with all metrics. In turn, Mean value (*Psy03*) and GSR Max value (*Psy05*) are not significantly correlated with the normalized measures *Psy04*, *Psy06* and *Psy08*.

Table 3. Spearman's rank correlation coefficients between psychophysiological metrics for *StrH* tasks (significant correlations are in bold)

	Psy01	Psy02	Psy03	Psy04	Psy05	Psy06	Psy07	Psy08
Psy01		**0.89**	**0.59**	**0.48**	**0.60**	**0.55**	**0.72**	**0.57**
Psy02	**0.89**		**0.55**	**0.38**	**0.56**	**0.44**	0.58	0.31
Psy03	**0.59**	**0.55**		0.20	**0.99**	0.20	**0.90**	0.18
Psy04	**0.48**	**0.38**	0.20		0.21	**0.98**	0.28	**0.65**
Psy05	**0.60**	**0.56**	**0.99**	0.21		0.22	**0.91**	0.20
Psy06	**0.55**	**0.44**	0.20	**0.98**	0.22		**0.31**	**0.68**
Psy07	**0.72**	**0.58**	**0.90**	0.28	**0.91**	**0.31**		**0.50**
Psy08	**0.57**	**0.31**	0.18	**0.65**	0.20	**0.68**	**0.50**	

Table 4 shows the Spearman's rank correlation coefficients between subjective and psychophysiological metrics for *StrH* tasks. *Psy04* correlates significantly with most subjective measures except *Sub04* and *Sub08*. *Psy06* correlates significantly with most subjective measures except *Sub04*, *Sub06* and *Sub08*. In turn, the *Sub04* and *Sub08* measures are not significantly correlated with any psychophysiological metrics, and *Sub06* is significantly correlated with only one *Psy04* measure.

Table 4. Spearman's rank correlation coefficients between subjective and psychophysiological metrics for *StrH* tasks (insignificant correlations are in bold)

	Sub01	Sub02	Sub03	Sub04	Sub05	Sub06	Sub07	Sub08
Psy01	0.22	0.18	0.25	0.13	0.12	0.18	**0.34**	0.06
Psy02	0.15	0.18	0.24	0.20	0.07	0.21	**0.30**	0.03
Psy03	0.15	0.12	0.18	0.20	0.02	0.01	0.23	0.03
Psy04	**0.33**	**0.29**	**0.42**	0.09	**0.32**	**0.29**	**0.31**	0.20
Psy05	0.15	0.12	0.18	0.19	0.02	0.01	0.23	0.02
Psy06	**0.30**	**0.26**	**0.40**	0.07	**0.31**	0.26	**0.29**	0.17
Psy07	**0.28**	0.16	0.25	0.15	0.11	0.03	**0.30**	0.10
Psy08	**0.42**	0.20	**0.31**	0.02	**0.28**	0.11	**0.27**	0.24

5 Conclusions

In this paper, cognitive load while performing Stroop tasks on a standalone computer application using galvanic skin response (GSR) and self-report questionnaires was analyzed. 62 participants ranging from the age of 19 to 38 years including 48 males and 14 females were involved in the experiment. Data were collected using the iMotions integrated biometric platform. In total, based on the collected data, 18 psychophysiological, subjective and performance metrics of cognitive load were calculated and then compared. The stimulus was the Stroop test, which consisted of five tasks with an easy level of difficulty and five tasks with a hard level of difficulty. The analysis of GSR measures was carried out in order to assess the suitability of individual metrics for the measurement of cognitive load. Non-parametric tests of statistical significance of differences between individual metrics for Stroop tasks with easy and hard difficulty level were carried out, and the Spearman's rank correlation between individual metrics was also analyzed.

This study examined eight GSR metrics that can provide further insights into the experienced level of cognitive load. The results showed that the $Psy01$, $Psy02$, $Psy07$ and $Psy08$ were lower in the event of $StrE$ and higher in the event of $StrH$. The reason for this is that in the case of $StrE$, participants were more confident, less frustrated and less stressed with the tasks, while the values of GSR measures were larger in the case of $StrH$, where there was more frustration due to the higher level of difficulty. In contrast, $Psy03$, $Psy04$, $Psy05$ and $Psy06$ across participants remained at similar levels for both $StrE$ and $StrH$ conditions of cognitive load level. In summary, we concluded that $Psy01$, $Psy02$, $Psy07$, and $Psy08$ measures better reflect the total amount of cognitive load experienced by the participants.

To show to what extent the Stroop test is an appropriate stimulus to measure cognitive load, psychophysiological, subjective and performance measures were compared. The results of non-parametric tests of statistical significance of differences and Spearman's rank correlation between individual metrics revealed the following. In terms of task performance measures, the differences in the task completion rates ($Per01$) for $StrE$ and $StrH$ were not statistically significant. However, for the task completion time ($Per02$) the differences for $StrE$ and $StrH$ turned out to be statistically significant. Moreover, for subjective measures, seven of eight measures were significantly larger for $StrH$ compared to $StrE$. Only in the case of satisfaction with task completion ($Sub06$) the mean results were almost equal for $StrE$ and $StrH$, and the differences were statistically insignificant. Moreover, the four psychophysiological measures, $Psy01$, $Psy02$, $Psy07$, and $Psy08$, were statistically significantly larger for $StrH$ compared to $StrE$. However, no significant differences were observed for $Psy03$, $Psy04$, $Psy05$, and $Psy06$.

Lastly, almost all Spearman's rank correlation coefficients between psychophysiological metrics for StrH tasks were statistically significant. Only $Psy03$ and $Psy05$ were not significantly correlated with the normalized measures $Psy04$, $Psy06$ and $Psy08$. In turn, almost all the Spearman's rank correlation coefficients between subjective and psychophysiological metrics for $StrH$ tasks are statistically significant, only $Sub04$ and $Sub08$ are not significantly correlated with any psychophysiological metrics, and $Sub06$ is significantly correlated with only one which is $Psy04$.

In conclusion, our study showed that the following measures are most useful for measuring and analyzing the cognitive load associated with the Stroop effect: task completion time (*Per02*), perceived task difficulty (*Sub01*), overall NASA-TLX score (*Sub02*), GSR Peak count (*Psy01*), GSR Peaks per minute (*Psy02*), GSR Accumulative value (*Psy07*), and GSR Accummulative value normalized (*Psy08*). It should also be noted that similar and significantly correlated results were provided by two self-report questionnaires the NASA Task Load Index and Single Ease Question.

Work in progress will focus on comparing the effects of other stimuli besides the Stroop test on cognitive load. In the same perspective of cognitive load measurement, future work will also aim to combine different stimuli and different biometric techniques with multiple machine learning algorithms to predict the level of human cognitive load from the human-computer interaction point of view.

References

1. Farnsworth, B.: The Stroop effect – how it works and why. https://imotions.com/blog/the-stroop-effect/ (2019)
2. Young, M.S., Brookhuis, K.A., Wickens, C.D., Hancock, P.A.: State of science: mental workload in ergonomics. Ergonomics **58**(1), 1–17 (2015)
3. Sweller, J.: Cognitive load during problem solving: effects on learning. Cogn. Sci. **12**(1), 257–285 (1988). https://doi.org/10.1016/0364-0213(88)90023-7
4. Sweller, J.: Cognitive load theory, learning difficulty, and instructional design. Learn. Instr. **4**(4), 295–312 (1994). https://doi.org/10.1016/0959-4752(94)90003-5
5. Sweller, J., Van Merrienboer, J.J.G., Paas, F.G.W.C.: Cognitive architecture and instructional design. Educ. Psychol. Rev. **10**(3), 251–296 (1998). https://doi.org/10.1023/A:1022193728205
6. Sweller, J.: Cognitive load theory. Psychology of Learning and Motivation – Advances in Research and Theory, vol. 55. Elsevier Inc. (2011). https://doi.org/10.1016/B978-0-12-387691-1.00002-8
7. Pejović, V., Gjoreski, M., Anderson, C., David, K., Luštrek, M.: Toward cognitive load inference for attention management in ubiquitous systems. IEEE Pervasive Comput. **19**(2), 35–45 (2020). https://doi.org/10.1109/MPRV.2020.2968909
8. Barrouillet, P., Camos, V.: Working Memory: Loss and Reconstruction. Psychology Press (2014). https://doi.org/10.4324/9781315755854
9. Chen, F., Zhou, J. (eds.): Robust Multimodal Cognitive Load Measurement. HIS, Springer, Cham (2016). https://doi.org/10.1007/978-3-319-31700-7
10. Sweller, J.: Cognitive load during problem solving: effects on learning. Cogn. Sci. **12**(2), 257–285 (1988)
11. Sweller, J., Merriënboer, J., Paas, F.: Cognitive architecture and instructional design: 20 years later. Educ. Psychol. Rev. **31**(2), 261–292 (2019). https://doi.org/10.1007/s10648-019-09465-5
12. Geary, D.C.: Educating the evolved mind: conceptual foundations for an evolutionary educational psychology. In: Carlson, J.S., Levin, J.R. (eds.) Educating the Evolved Mind: Conceptual Foundations for an Evolutionary Educational Psychology Information Age Charlotte. *NC, 1*, p. 99 (2007)
13. Geary, D.C.: An evolutionarily informed education science. Educ. Psychol. **43**(4), 179–195 (2008)

14. Geary, D.C.: Evolutionary educational psychology. APA Educational Psychology Handbook, vol. 1: Theories, Constructs, and Critical Issues, pp. 597–621. American Psychological Association (2012)

15. Geary, D., Berch, D.: Evolution and children's cognitive and academic development. In: Geary, D.C., Berch, D.B. (eds.) Evolutionary perspectives on child development and education. EP, pp. 217–249. Springer, Cham (2016). https://doi.org/10.1007/978-3-319-29986-0_9

16. Kirschner, P.A., Sweller, J., Kirschner, F., Zambrano, J.: From cognitive load theory to collaborative cognitive load theory. Int. J. Comput. Support. Collab. Learn. **13**(2), 213–233 (2018)

17. Tricot, A., Sweller, J.: Domain-specific knowledge and why teaching generic skills does not work. Educ. Psychol. Rev. **26**(2), 265–283 (2014)

18. Kirschner, P.A., Sweller, J., Clark, R.E.: Why minimal guidance during instruction does not work: an analysis of the failure of constructivist, discovery, problembased, experiential, and inquiry-based teaching. Educ. Psychol. **41**(2), 75–86 (2006)

19. Sweller, J., Kirschner, P.A., Clark, R.E.: Why minimally guided teaching techniques do not work: a reply to commentaries. Educ. Psychol. **42**(2), 115–121 (2007)

20. Jia, L., Kalyuga, S., Sweller, J.: Altering element Interactivity and variability in example-practice sequences to enhance learning to write Chinese characters. Appl. Cogn. Psychol. **34**(4), 837–843 (2020). https://doi.org/10.1002/acp.3668

21. Roussel, S., Joulia, D., Tricot, A., Sweller, J.: Learning subject content through a foreign language should not ignore human cognitive architecture: a cognitive load theory approach. Learn. Instr. **52**, 69–79 (2017)

22. Renaud, P., Blondin, J.P.: The stress of Stroop performance: physiological and emotional responses to color-word interference, task pacing, and pacing speed. Int. J. Psychophysiol. **27**(2), 87–97 (1997)

23. Petkar, H.C: Effects of working memory demand on performance and mental stress during the Stroop task. Masters Thesis, Concordia University (2011)

24. Williams, J.M.G., Mathews, A., MacLeod, C.: The emotional Stroop task and psychopathology. Psychol. Bull. **120**(1), 3–24 (1996)

25. Wagner, P., Wagner, T.: The Galvanic Skin Response GSR Investigation Cheating. http://www.rsu.edu/wpcontent/uploads/2015/06/TheGalvanicSkinResponseGSRInvestigationCheating.pdf (2013). Retrieved 8 Dec 2020

26. Braithwaite, J., Watson, D., Jones, R., Rowe, M.: A Guide for Analysing Electrodermal Activity (EDA) Skin Conductance Responses (SCRs) for Psychological Experiments. Technical Report, 2nd version. University of Birmingham, UK (2015)

27. Nourbakhsh, N., Wang, Y., Chen, F., Calvo, R.A.: Using galvanic skin response for cognitive load measurement in arithmetic and reading tasks. In: Proceedings of the 24th Australian Computer-Human Interaction Conference, OzCHI 2012, pp. 420–423 (2012). https://doi.org/10.1145/2414536.2414602

28. Shi, Y., Ruiz, N., Taib, R., Choi, E., Chen, F.: Galvanic skin response (GSR) as an index of cognitive load. In: CHI 2007 Extended Abstracts on Human Factors in Computing Systems, pp. 2651–2656 (2007)

29. Yoshihiro, S., Takumi, Y., Koji, S., Akinori, H., Koichi, I., Tetsuo, K.: Use of frequency domain analysis of skin conductance for evaluation of mental workload. J. Physiol. Anthropol. **27**(4), 173–177 (2008)

30. O'Donnell, R.D., Eggemeier, F.T.: Workload assessment methodology. Handbook of Perception and Human Performance. Vol. 2. Cognitive Processes and Performance. K.R. Boff, L. Kaufman and J.P. Thomas (1986)

31. Hart, S.G., Staveland, L.E.: Development of NASA-TLX (task load index): results of empirical and theoretical research. Adv. Psychol. **52**(3), 139–183 (1988)

32. Hart, S.G.: NASA-task load index (NASA-TLX); 20 years later. In: Proceedings of the 50th Annual Meeting on Human Factors and Ergonomics Society, pp. 904–908 (2006)
33. Gibson, A., et al.: Assessing usability testing for people living with dementia. In: ACM International Conference Proceeding Series, October, 25–31 (2016). https://doi.org/10.1145/3051488.3051492
34. GSR R-Notebooks: Processing in iMotions and algorithms used (Latest Version). https://help.imotions.com/hc/en-us/articles/360010312220-GSR-R-Notebooks-Processing-in-iMotions-and-algorithms-used-Latest-Version (2021). Last accessed 6 Jan 2021
35. Benedek, M., Kaernbach, C.: A continuous measure of phasic electrodermal activity. J. Neurosci. Methods **190**(1), 80–91 (2010). https://doi.org/10.1016/j.jneumeth.2010.04.028
36. R Notebooks (EDA): GSR Epoching, https://help.imotions.com/hc/en-us/articles/360013685940-R-Notebooks-EDA-GSR-Epoching (2021). Last accessed 6 Jan 2021
37. Gautam, A., Simoes-Capela, N., Schiavone, G., Acharyya, A., de Raedt, W., Van Hoof, C.: A data driven empirical iterative algorithm for GSR signal pre-processing. In: 26th European Signal Processing Conference (EUSIPCO), pp. 1162–1166 (2018). https://doi.org/10.23919/eusipco.2018.8553191

Collective Decision-Making

Toward a Computing Model Dealing with Complex Phenomena: Interactive Granular Computing

Soma Dutta[1] and Andrzej Skowron[2,3]

[1] University of Warmia and Mazury in Olsztyn, Słoneczna 54, 10-710 Olsztyn, Poland
[2] Systems Research Institute, Polish Academy of Sciences,
Newelska 6, 01-447 Warsaw, Poland
skowron@mimuw.edu.pl
[3] Digital Science and Technology Centre, UKSW, Dewajtis 5, 01-815 Warsaw, Poland

Abstract. This paper is a continuation of our earlier works in establishing the need for introducing Interactive Granular Computing (IGrC) in developing Intelligent Systems (IS's) and/or Decision Support Systems (DSS's) dealing with complex phenomena. Among several crucial points, this paper argues in favour of the necessity to provide tools for learning models of complex vague concepts based on the perceived situations, where perception about the situation itself should be relativized based on the particular spatio-temporal windows of the physical world and real physical interactions among objects lying in the scope of those windows. The main idea is to develop a computing model which can link the abstract theory with its physical semantics in a way where the information about the world is grounded in the physical process of obtaining it and learning that information requires a proper implementation of interactions among real physical objects. The basic objects in IGrC are known as the complex granules (c-granules, for short). They make it possible to link the abstract and physical worlds, and help to realize the paths of judgments starting from generating a plan for obtaining sensory measurement or perception about a particular fragment of the physical world, to translating the plan to real physical interactions and verifying the properties obtained thereby with available knowledge. The c-granules, which are extended by information layers, are called informational c-granules (ic-granules, for short), and they can create the basis for modeling a notion of control conducting the whole process of computation over the c-granules. In this process an important role is played by so called implementational ic-granules responsible for the real physical realisation of the formal specification available in the information layer. Moreover, the networks of c-granules with distributed control are introduced and their role in IS's dealing with complex phenomena is discussed.

Keywords: Complex granule (c-granule) · Informational c-granule (ic-granule) · Implementational ic-granule · Control of c-granule · Perception of situation · Interactive granular computing (IGrC)

© Springer Nature Switzerland AG 2021
N. T. Nguyen et al. (Eds.): ICCCI 2021, LNAI 12876, pp. 199–214, 2021.
https://doi.org/10.1007/978-3-030-88081-1_15

1   Introduction

> *Tomorrow, I believe, we will use DECISION SUPPORT SYSTEMS or INTELLIGENT SYSTEMS to support our decisions in defining our research strategy and specific aims, in managing our experiments, in collecting our results, interpreting our data, in incorporating the findings of others, in disseminating our observations, in extending (generalizing) our experimental observations – through exploratory discovery and modeling – in directions completely unanticipated.*

This is how the present needs of Artificial Intelligence in designing intelligent systems or decision support systems, dealing with complex phenomena, are characterised in [3]. The question arises, whether the existing methods of modeling are satisfactory for designing decision support systems or intelligent systems dealing with complex phenomena. An answer can be found in the following opinion of Frederick Brooks, one of the Turing award winners [5].

> *Mathematics and the physical sciences made great strides for three centuries by constructing simplified models of complex phenomena, deriving properties from the models, and verifying those properties experimentally. This worked because the complexities ignored in the models were not the essential properties of the phenomena. It does not work when the complexities are the essence.*

The necessity of linking abstract and physical worlds in the *Interactive Granular Computing* (IGrC) model follows from the requirement that we would like to use this model in designing Intelligent Systems (IS's) or Decision Support Systems (DSS's) dealing with complex phenomena. The problem of linking abstract model with the physical world is a widely discussed issue in connection to the grounding symbol problem (see, *e.g.*, [14,19,29,30,35,38]). According to Pierce [38] the meaning of a symbol arises from the process of semiosis, which is the interaction between form, meaning and referent.

It is worth to be noted what Franz Brentano [4] says in [23].

> *[...] it would be possible for us to characterize physical phenomena easily and exactly in contrast to mental phenomena by saying that they are those phenomena which appear extended and localized in space.*

So, if our target is to make a model behaving like an intelligent agent working in a real physical environment, apart from the general physical laws, we also need to specify the spatio-temporal windows describing agent's location as well as where the agent's action is supposed to be localized. This is what, on which we emphasize, in designing IGrC. Moreover, the model should have the ability to perceive the real physical world through continuous interactions, and discover an abstract model that fits well to the physical reality, localized in a given time and space, and be able to adaptively change its rules of computation based on the changes of spatio-temporal windows as well as needs of the computation.

Here we need to first understand what does a complex phenomenon or a complex system mean, and then comes the point of understanding how a model can be built so that it remains grounded in the physical reality. As mentioned in [13], the complex systems can be described as follows.

> *Complex system: the elements are difficult to separate. This difficulty arises from the interactions between elements. Without interactions, elements can be separated. But when interactions are relevant, elements co-determine their future states. Thus, the future state of an element cannot be determined in isolation, as it co-depends on the states of other elements, precisely of those interacting with it.*

Hence, to understand and reason about a complex system or phenomenon we need a computing model which can (i) continuously monitor the relevant properties of the respective spatio-temporal fragments of the real physical world, (ii) learn and predict properties or rules for the seen and possibly unseen cases based on already stored knowledge and observations, (iii) control the interaction process, as a part of a physical procedure, to reach a desired goal, and (iv) update new information in the knowledge base. According to the authors of [37].

> *The theory of complex systems is the theory of generalized time-varying interactions between elements that are characterized by states. Interactions typically take place on networks that connect those elements.*

Here, the additional concern is that we can only partially perceive these elements and their dynamics; as a result we have only partial description of the states representing these elements and the transition relation representing their dynamics. So, for a new model of computation apart from a given family of sets $\{X_i\}_{i \in I}$ and a transition relation $tr_i \subseteq X_i \times X_i$, we need to incorporate the components which can specify (i) how elements of X_i are perceived in the real physical environment, and (ii) how the transition relation tr_i is implemented in the real physical world and how the transition from one state to another is observed through the reflection of the changes in the perception of the real physical world.

Perception about the real physical world and interactions with the real physical world are two important factors that, we think, need an utmost attention in order to bring in a proper coordination between abstract modeling and its real physical semantics. In [12], while describing the process of thinking by a smart machine author mentioned:

> *I'll outline some of the key ideas that enable intelligent machines to perceive and interact with the world.*

In [9] we already explained how the existing approaches to soft computing, such as rough sets [26], fuzzy sets [41], and other tools used in machine learning lack in considering the above mentioned two components. Representing a complex physical phenomena by a fixed, a priori set of attributes or a fixed function refers back to the problem mentioned in Frederick Brooks' comment.

One more point to be emphasized here is about the relationship between cognition about a computation and its implementation. Let us quote the following lines from [22].

> [...] *The computational method of describing the ways information is processed is usually abstract - but cognition is possible only when computation is realized physically, and the physical realization is not the same thing as its description. The mechanistic construal of computation allows me to show that no purely computational explanation of a physical process will ever be complete. This is because we also need to account for how the computation is physically implemented, and in explaining this, we cannot simply appeal to computation itself. In addition, we need to know how the computational mechanism is embedded in the environment, which, again, is not a purely computational matter.*

Following the above needs, it is to be emphasized that incorporating perceptions, interactions, and the issues connecting information specification with the process of implementation are a few most prominent factors that we endorse in *Interactive Granular Computing. Interactive* symbolizes *interaction between the abstract world and the real physical world*, and *Granular Computing* symbolizes *computation over imperfect, partial, granulated information perceived from the real physical world* [8,10,18,19,32–34].

In IGrC computations are performed on complex granules (c-granules, for short) which are networks of more basic c-granules associated with an information layer (called ic-granules, for short), grounded in the physical reality. In the sequel below we attempt to present a brief description of c-granules and interactive computations based on c-granules.

This paper is a continuation and a substantial extension of [9] and the keynote by the second author at ICIS 2020[1] In particular, in Sect. 2, we make a brief introduction of c-granule and ic-granule. In the following subsections of the same section a few important characteristics, such as real physical semantics of a spatio-temporal window and the roles of a control in connecting and accessing information respective to such an abstract specification of the spatio-temporal window, are discussed. Section 3 presents a brief outline of how a complex phenomenon can be modelled as a complex game in a network of c-granules.

2   General Idea of IGrC

As mentioned in [9], rough sets play a crucial role in the development of Granular Computing (GrC) [27,28,42]. But IGrC [18,32,33][2]) requires a more generalization of the basic concepts of rough sets and GrC. IGrC takes into account the granularity of information from GrC paradigm, and add to that the component

---

[1] http://www.intsci.ac.cn/icis2020/speaker.jsp.
[2] See also publications about IGrC listed at https://dblp.uni-trier.de/pers/hd/s/Skowron:Andrzej.

of real physical interactions through which perception and information about the world are obtained.

In [9] we already discussed about the basic structure of a c-granule and different kinds of informational c-granules (ic-granules), that are responsible for different subtasks of a computation process; performing different subtasks such as perceiving the environment, generating the plan of actions, translating the plan into a lower level language, implementing the plan through real physical actuators, and recording and matching the newly perceived information with the expected information, is also discussed with example in a step-by-step manner. That was a general brief overview of the overall idea of computation in IGrC. In this paper, we would try to concentrate on explaining in more detail the process of connecting the specification of a spatio-temporal window, available in the information layer of an ic-granule, with the respective real physical fragment. This will clarify two aspects, viz., where and how to make an interaction with the real physical world in the process of perceiving properties. In this regard, let us first start with once again re-emphasizing the notion of c-granules and ic-granules.

2.1   Complex Granules (c-granules)

As mentioned in [9], c-granules are composed of three parts, namely soft_suit, link_suit, and hard_suit. In general each c-granule is localized to a space-time window and hence each c-granule has its relevant scope which determines the part of the physical reality to which that particular c-granule corresponds. The soft_suit represents those objects in the physical reality which are directly accessible and/or about which already some information is gathered (by sensors or actuators). The hard_suit corresponds to those objects which are in the scope of the c-granule but not yet accessed or are not in the direct reach at that point of time of the c-granule. The link_suit represents a communication channel, that is a chain of objects in the passage between soft_suit and hard_suit. That is, the objects in the link_suit create, in a sense, a physical pointer that links objects from the soft_suit to the hard_suit; this in turn makes it possible to propagate interactions among physical objects, in particular among objects of hard_suit and soft_suit. A c-granule with an information layer is called as informational c-granule, in short ic-granule. The information layer of an ic-granule may contain specifications of different kinds of information starting from properties of already perceived objects from the soft_suit, specification of the spatio-temporal window where a particular action plan needs to be embedded, to specification of a plan of actions.

Information in the informational layer of a c-granule is, in a sense, distributed among different formal specifications of spatio-temporal widows. Any such formal specification of spatio-temporal window is labeled by the information that is perceived using that window. So, the whole information layer is clustered based on the information relevant to different sub-scopes of the whole scope of the c-granule. Each of these spatio-temporal windows, labeled with relevant information, can be considered as the informational layers of different ic-granules,

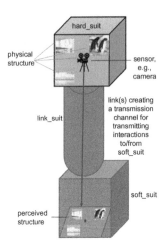

Fig. 1. Basic structure of c-granule

which are basically the sub-granlues of the concerned c-granule. The informational layers of some ic-granules of the c-granule may be complex in nature; for example, in the case of ic-granules representating the domain knowledge there can be different sub-clusters in the informational layer corresponding to different aspects of the domain knowledge. So, an ic-granule may contain several other ic-granules inside its scope. The robustness of ic-granule to interactions from outside of its scope is related to the concept of niche introduced by Holland [17]. The picture presented in Fig. 1 may help the readers to visualise the notion of c-granule.

By directly accessible we mean that some features (or attribute values) of such objects can be directly measurable, or changes of some features (or attribute values) of such objects in the successive moments of local time of the c-granule (or in a given period of time) can be directly measurable, or some features (or attribute values) of such objects can be directly changed by a central notion of c-granule like control mechanism.

In [9], we already introduced the notion of the control of a c-granule. It is the control of a c-granule which is responsible for aggregating, deleting, or generalising the information from the existing clustered of information layers and thus is able to generate new information layers. These changes, happening with time, induce new ic-granules, and thus IGrC incorporates the process of hierarchical learning toward discovering relevant building blocks for cognition[3].

In our previous works, we introduced the concept of c-granule without explicitly distinguishing the informational layer and the control. For modeling computations of Intelligent Systems (IS's) or Decision Support Systems (DSS's) addition of these new components seems to be important. This allows us to model processes of perception of physical objects as well as interactions among physical objects, and thus leads an IS or a DSS to perceive the current situation and

---

[3] see http://people.seas.harvard.edu/~valiant/researchinterests.htm.

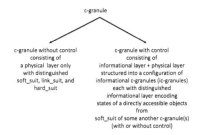

Fig. 2. Two basic kinds of c-granules

select the relevant decisions. The c-granules without control (or empty control) consist of physical objects distributed over three parts called soft_suit, link_suit and hard_suit (see Fig. 2). In the next subsection we will throw some light on the role of control. In general, we consider two basic kinds of c-granules, namely c-granules with and without control (see Fig. 2).

2.2   Control of a c-granule

C-granules are dynamic in nature and change with their (local) time. We already mentioned that each c-granule has its scope and within its scope at some point of time some objects are directly perceivable and some are not. Over the time previously unaccessible objects of a c-granule may become perceivable and hence the soft_suit, link_suit and hard_suit of the same c-granule may change over time. Now as a complex phenomenon may be modeled by a network of c-granules, the question arises how the behaviour of one c-granule is perceived by another c-granule. Intuitively, we may consider this question as follows. Suppose a complex phenomenon is represented by a network of c-granules, some of which may change with time based on their own plan of actions and respective implementations. Now changes happening to a particular c-granule in the network, can be considered as a remote event to another c-granule from the same network. We can consider the other c-granule as an observer. So, as an observer to notice changes happening in a c-granule, the other c-granule must be endowed with such mechanisms that allow it to perceive objects out of its current scope. Overall such mechanisms can be realised by the notion of control of a c-granule.

The behaviour of the control depends on the information stored in the informational layer of the c-granule. The information is treated as an abstract object which can be (i) encoded[4] on the basis of measurements made on the directly accessible parts of the (objects from) soft_suit or (ii) induced from already perceived information. In the latter case, based on the domain knowledge as well as physical laws the control is entitled to use a reasoning process to induce information about the objects that are not directly accessible. In Fig. 3 a basic role of the control of a c-granule, determined by its ic-granules, is illustrated.

---

[4] The above mentioned encoding can be modeled using a notion of infomorphism from the theory of information flow [2,10].

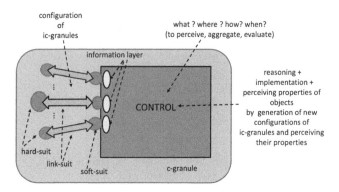

Fig. 3. A basic role of control of c-granule

Informally speaking the control of a c-granule contains all the information layers of the ic-granules within its scope as well as some relations over them representing different kinds of reasoning mechanisms and transitions among different pieces of information.

(i) Specifically, the control contains a family of generic ic-granules together with a family of formal specifications describing the transformations of some sets of ic-granules into new one. These generic ic-granules have different roles, such as representing domain knowledge, generating plan of actions, translating the plan of actions to an implementational level language, embedding the plan of actions on the real physical environment by realisation of actions, perceiving the properties of the changed environment and updating the information to the information layer.

(ii) Among these ic-granules the implementational ic-granules [9] are of special interest as they are responsible for embedding the abstract specifications of the action plans on the relevant fragment of the environment, which may contain some other ic-granules. Thus, implementational ic-granules create a connection between the abstract description of a process and its real physical realisation. Here comes the dynamic aspect of the proposal. The implementational ic-granules can be like compiler of a program which generates the real physical output from a specification of the desired actions presented in a coded language.

(iii) The relations among the pieces of information can be treated as the rules using which the control can decide what changes are needed in the computation process in order to match to the goal specification of the c-granule. In the information layer of the ic-granule related to the domain knowledge already some forms of relations, in the form of rules, are stored. With the help of the already perceived information available at the information layer of the perception related ic-granule, and based on the forms of the rules the formal specification for the required configuration of the expected ic-granule(s) is derived. At a given time point, the control selects rules by matching the perception specification of the current state of the ic-granule with the patterns on the left hand sides of the rules; on matching to a satisfactory degree with a particular rule, the control proceeds to the implementation related ic-granules (called implementational ic-granules) in order to generate the ic-granule, specified in the right hand sides of such rules.

So, more formally the informational structure of the control of a c-granule consists, in particular of the following components:

- F_{gen} – a family information layers respective to a family of generic ic-granules, in particular

  - $Inf_{g_{KB}}$, $R(KB\_str)$ – the informational layer of the ic-granule g_{KB} for domain knowledge and its relational structure respectively;
  - $Inf_{g_{curr}}$ – the information layer of the ic-granule g_{curr} representing the perception about the current situation;

- $R(BP_{par})$ – the information related to the relational structure representing a family of parameterized behavioral patterns BP_{par} (formal specifications of spatio-temporal windows are examples of such parameters of the expected properties of the real physical fragments of the world corresponding to those spatio-temporal windows);
- $Inf_{g_{FS-PICG}}$, $R(FS - PICG\_str)$ – the information layers of a family of parameterised formal specifications of implementational ic-granules $g_{FS-PICG}$ and the parameterised formal specifications of transformations of tuples of ic-granules from $g_{FS-PICG}$ into new ic-granules with the expected behavioural properties, specified as relational constraints.

We can see that the control is not only responsible for storing, representing and manipulating information; it is also responsible for touching and connecting with the real physical fragment corresponding to the information specifications, that are already available or derived. Analogous to the notion of *zoom structure* [11], the formal specifications of relational structures over the information layers of the control of a c-granule at a particular time point can be presented as a tuple $(D, E, \Gamma, \Delta, \{D_i\}_{i \in \Gamma}, \{E_j\}_{j \in \Delta})$ where $D = Inf_{g_{KB}} \cup Inf_{g_{curr}} \cup Inf_{g_{FS-PICG}}$, E is the set of edges generated from $R(KB\_str) \cup R(BP_{par}) \cup R(FS - PICG\_str)$, and Γ and Δ respectively determine which sub-family of D (information layers) and which sub-family of E (relations over them) are active at that time point.

2.3 Real Physical Semantics of Spatio-Temporal Windows and Time Clock

It is worthwhile to refer to [15], where the physical objects are viewed as four-dimensional hunks of matter containing the factors like space, time. However, in our approach, four-dimensional hunks of matter are relative to a given c-granule and are localised by means of formal spatio-temporal windows specified in the informational layer of the c-granule; this corresponds to the parts of the physical space in which hunks of matter are embedded.

According to IGrC, physical objects are pointed based on the specification of the spatio-temporal windows and then their properties are perceived by the control. In general the process looks as follows.

- The formal specifications of the spatio-temporal windows, say w, are encoded in the information layer of the ic-granule, in the scope of which the physical object lies.
- Now in order to touch that fragment of the reality the relevant implementational ic-granules need to generate the physical pointer between the soft_suit of the concerned ic-granule and its hard_suit; this physical pointer creates a communication channel through the objects in the link_suit. Here to be noted, that these implementational ic-granules may be counted as the sub-ic-granules of the main ic-granule, and are related to more decomposed, finer spatio-temporal windows pointing to the concerned fragment of the physical world or to the process of reaching it.
- After establishing a physical connection with the real physical fragment corresponding to the concerned formal specifications of the spatio-temporal windows w, it is the turn of the reasoning mechanisms, available at the information layer of the control of the ic-granule, to justify whether the proper physical objects are pointed out. That is, the properties of the newly touched fragment of the physical world are perceived and verified with the expected behavioural pattern available at BP_{par} or derived from $R(BP_{par})$ for that parametrized window w.

So, formally for any formal specification w of spatio-temporal window its (intended) semantics can be defined as a function $time_w$ of the form $time_w : T \longrightarrow \mathcal{P}(\Re^3)$, where T is the set of discrete or continuous time points and $\Re$ is the set of reals. The set T is defined relative to a given c-granule. Hence, the time is locally defined for c-granules. In this paper, we assume T to be a discrete linear set of time points of a c-granule. The time clock of a c-granule is defined by a special sub-ic-granule, called the time clock of the c-granule; whereas the real physical implementation of w is defined by a relevant implementational ic-granule of the main c-granule.

Example 1. An example of spatio-temporal function.
In this example, $T = \{1, \ldots, N\}$, where N is the maximal time point and each $time(i)$ is a ball in $\Re^3$ with a center c_i and radius r_i (for $i \in \{1, \ldots, N\}$). This kind of functions representing time-windows is typical in problems of video tracking (see, *e.g.*, [21] and Fig. 4).

Any c-granule can have its local time clock represented by an ic-granule. Let us consider a simple example of such an ic-granule. It has in its soft_suit a local memory (buffer). From this buffer binary information about the value of the attribute representing the current state of the buffer and its previous state is decoded and stored in the information layer. In another register of the soft_suit is stored a decimal representation of natural numbers which is increased by one each time when the value of the attribute changes from 0 to 1 in the buffer, *i.e.*,

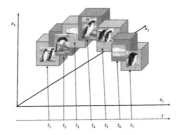

Fig. 4. Links to a spatio-temporal hunks of matter specified by the time functions relative to the specified windows, pointing to different fragments (portions of matter) of the 3 dimensional physical world in different moments $t_1, \ldots, t_7$ of the local time of the c-granule

the contents of this buffer is 01. The contents of the buffer is changing on the basis of the signal from hard_suit transmitted by the link_suit. The hard suit is created by a quartz generator producing a stable wave signal (see Fig. 5). Using, the information stored in the information layer of the c-granule, the physical laws and the properties provided by the physical structure of the described ic-granule, the c-granule judges that the ic-granule behaves according to the required properties of clock. It should be noted that the rules of judgment not always return the true facts because, *e.g.*, interaction of the clock with the environment may cause some disturbances in its behaviour. The above mentioned special encoding of the properties of the physical objects in the soft_suit (e.g., buffers, registers) to information (in the information layer) next can be stored in the local memory by the relevant actions of the control of the c-granule assuming that these physical objects are directly accessible by the control. In our example, the register and the buffer are the physical objects located in the soft_suit of the corresponding ic-granule which are directly accessible by the control of the c-granule. Due to this, the state of such objects can be encoded and stored in the information layer. Such an information may be stored in a local memory (using another ic-granule related to this memory). The formal properties of encoding may be explained using the notion of infomorphism used in the information flow approach [2,10].

3 Networks of c-granules and Distributed Control in Such Networks

In the section above we discussed about c-granules representing complex computations localized to a spatio-temporal fragment of the real physical world. So, the discussion concerns about how the process of computation may look like from the perspective of a single c-granule. In this section, we outline the issues related to networks of c-granules because any complex phenomenon can be considered as a network of c-granules. So, here the issues of concern are the methods of generation of such networks, their dynamics, distributed control, self-organization, autonomy, locality, or asynchrony. These issues are fundamental for distributed

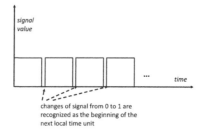

Fig. 5. Signal generated by hard_suit of an ic-granule representing the local clock of c-granule

systems (see, *e.g.*, [1, 2, 6, 7, 16, 20, 24, 31, 36, 39, 40, 43]). In this context, we present here only initial comments emphasising on the role of IGrC.

In IGrC, a network of c-granules is also treated as a c-granule. It can be obtained, *e.g.*, by aggregation of 'societies' of c-granules which can cooperate or compete to achieve their goals to some satisfactory degrees as well as to assure that the goal of the whole aggregated network may be achieved. Constructing distributed controls for such very complex networks is one of the greatest challenges for science and applications.

Informally, the communication of c-granules with other ones can be described as follows. The control of each c-granule consists of special rules which can be generic, *i.e.*, embedded by the designer or learned by the control from acquired data. Any such rule has the form $\alpha \Rightarrow \beta$, where

- α is a formula expressing property of the pattern perceived by the c-granule;[5]
- β is a formal specification of new ic-granule(s) which the control of the c-granule should generate (or modify) when the condition α is satisfied.

The formula α may represent a static pattern related to some part of the already perceived physical space corresponding to a given formal specification of window. Any dynamic pattern of changes of physical objects, perceived by the c-granules, can be represented by some spatio-temporal patterns of behaviour. These objects are localised in parts of the physical space corresponding to some given formal specifications of spatio-temporal windows. In the case of a 'society' of c-granules such patterns may need to be represented in a specific language used by this network corresponding to this whole 'society' of the c-granules, and this language should be understandable by the controls of all the c-granules present in the considered 'society'. It should be noted that the aggregated information about such patterns may also be an outcome of the aggregation of some parts of the controls of different c-granules in the network satisfying some required behaviour. This is one of the challenging problem in swarm intelligence.

The formula β may even represent a formal specification of the operation for generating the desired ic-granule. Here, one can consider two possibilities. One

---

[5] In real-life applications these patterns are often approximations of complex vague concepts which are adapted according to the changes perceived in the gathered data.

possibility is that the control of the c-granule through a special implementational ic-granule realise this operation. In the second case, the control, through a decomposition may search for synthesizing such operation from existing implementational ic-granules.

It is worthwhile to recall here again the concept of niche introduced by Holland [17]. The patterns learned in the scope of the c-granule representing the network of c-granules should be robust to a satisfactory degree with respect to the interactions from outside of this scope. This can make the process of generating new ic-granules more resistant to interactions with the environment on the basis of satisfiability of patterns.

The above mentioned case of the rules is the simplest one. More general cases are those where after identifying a given property α, observed in the behaviour of some physical objects, the control of the c-granule needs to initiate a dialogue with some members of the network in order to fix the relevant scheme for construction of the new ic-granules. The implementation of this new scheme may lead to generation, *e.g.,* of new ic-granules realising a modified version of the initially required properties which were required before the dialogue was initiated.

The aim of the distributed control, as outlined above, is to synthesise complex networks of c-granules based on the requirements of the distributed control. These requirements, that is the task specifications, are formulated from the bahaviour of the whole population of the information layers and the physical objects involved in the interactions within the network. The relevant distributed control may by synthesised using mechanisms of cooperation, competition or dialogue between different societies of c-granules present in the network.

4   Concluding Remarks

In the introduction we mentioned about a few most important features of IGrC paradigm which allow it to bridge a connection between the abstract modeling and its real physical semantics. Among those features, one is the ability to perceive information about the real physical world by initiating real physical interactions among the objects lying there. This needs, first, to touch the relevant fragment of the physical world based on its abstract specification of the spatio-temporal window, and then transfer the abstract description of a method to the real physical actuators, which help in implementing the method of measuring/perceiving properties of the objects belonging to that fragment.

In this regard, we discussed about the real physical semantics of the spatio-temporal windows and the role of the control in conducting the whole computation starting from deriving plan of actions to implementing them through sensors/actuators. We also discussed about the interactions among different c-granules involved in a network of c-granules as a part of a complex (cooperative/competitive) game representing complex phenomenon.

Our main target in this paper has been to convince the readers about the role of perception and interaction in IS's dealing with complex real physical phenomena. The quotations cited in the Introduction are motivating enough to realize the need. An overview of how such an endeavour can be taken is presented in Sects. 2 and 3.

Keeping the page limitation in mind, we have not much entered into the technical process of perception based learning of a c-granule. So, as a concluding remark let us cite an example, very aptly formulated in [25], to explain how should perception be counted in a computation process.

> *...perceiving is a way of acting.... Think of a blind person tap-tapping his or her way around a cluttered space, perceiving that space by touch, not all at once, but through time, by skillful probing and movement. This is or ought to be, our paradigm of what perceiving is.*

This seems quite appropriate for our vision of IGrC. Here, the control of the c-granule, in the scope of which the blind person belongs, performs reasoning (called judgment) based on domain knowledge, and already perceived objects from its soft_suit. This gradually leads to the perception (understanding) of the of previously unknown objects from its hard_suit. Most importantly the point to note is that this reasoning process is not only performed based on mere matching of some rules; rather the reasoning process is realised over time by implementing interactions through the objects in the link_suit, such as the stick of the blind person, to access information about the further objects.

Acknowledgement. Andrzej Skowron was partially supported by the ProME (Prognostic Modeling of the COVID-19 Epidemic) grant.

References

1. Ahn, H.-S.: Formation Control Approaches for Distributed Agents. Studies in Systems, Decision and Control, vol. 205. Springer, Cham (2020). https://doi.org/10.1007/978-3-030-15187-4
2. Barwise, J., Seligman, J.: Information Flow. The Logic of Distributed Systems. Cambridge University Press, Cambridge, NY (1997). https://doi.org/10.1017/CBO9780511895968
3. Bower, J.M., Bolouri, H. (eds.): Computational Modeling of Genetic and Biochemical Networks. MIT Press, Cambridge, MA (2001)
4. Brentano, F.: Psychologie vom empirischen Standpunkte. Dunker & Humboldt, Leipzig (1874). https://archive.org/details/psychologievome02brengoog/page/n4/mode/2up
5. Brooks, F.P.: The Mythical Man-Month: Essays on Software Engineering. Addison-Wesley, Boston (1975). (Extended Anniversary Edition in 1995)
6. Díaz-Muñoz, S.L., Sanjuán, R., West, S.: Sociovirology: conflict, cooperation, and communication among viruses. Cell Host Microbe **22** 437–441 (2017). https://doi.org/10.1016/j.chom.2017.09.012
7. Dolgin, E.: The secret social lives of viruses. Nature **570** 290–292 (2019). https://doi.org/10.1038/d41586-019-01880-6
8. Dutta, S., Jankowski, A., Rozenberg, G., Skowron, A.: Linking reaction systems with rough sets. Fundamenta Informaticae **165**, 283–302 (2019). https://doi.org/10.3233/FI-2019-1786

9. Dutta, S., Skowron, A.: Interactive granular computing model for intelligent systems. In: Shi, Z., Chakraborty, M., Kar, S. (eds): Intelligence Science III. 4th IFIP TC 12 International Conference, ICIS 2020, Durgapur, India, 24–27 February 2021, Revised Selected Papers. IFIP Advances in Information and Communication Technology (IFIPAICT) Book Series, vol. 623, pp. 37–48. Springer, Cham (2021). https://doi.org/10.1007/978-3-030-74826-5_4

10. Dutta, S., Skowron, A., Chakraborty, M.K.: Information flow in logic for distributed systems: extending graded consequence. Inform. Sci. **491**, 232–250 (2019). https://doi.org/10.1016/j.ins.2019.03.057

11. Ehrenfeucht, A., Rozenberg, G.: Zoom structures and reaction systems yield exploration systems. Int. J. Found. Comput. Sci. **25**(3), 275–305 (2014). https://doi.org/10.1142/S0129054114500142

12. Gerrish, S.: How Smart Machines Think. MIT Press, Cambridge, MA (2018)

13. Gershenson, C., Heylighen, F.: How can we think the complex? In: Richardson, K. (Ed.): Managing Organizational Complexity: Philosophy, Theory and Application, pp. 47–61. Information Age Publishing (2005)

14. Harnad, S.: The symbol grounding problem. Physica **D42**, 335–346 (1990). https://doi.org/10.1016/0167-2789(90)90087-6

15. Heller, M.: The Ontology of Physical Objects. Four Dimensional Hunks of Matter. Cambridge Studies in Philosophy. Cambridge University Press, Cambridge, UK (1990)

16. Hoare, C.A.R.: Communicating sequential processes. Commun. ACM **21**(8), 666–677 (1978). https://doi.org/10.1145/359576.359585

17. Holland, J.: Signals and Boundaries: Building Blocks for Complex Adaptive Systems. The MIT Press, Cambridge, MA (2014)

18. Jankowski, A.: Interactive Granular Computations in Networks and Systems Engineering: A Practical Perspective. LNNS. Springer, Heidelberg (2017). https://doi.org/10.1007/978-3-319-57627-5

19. Jankowski, A., Skowron, A.: A Wistech paradigm for intelligent systems. Trans. Rough Sets J. Subline **6**, 94–132 (2007). https://doi.org/10.1007/978-3-540-71200-8_7. (LNCS 4374; Springer, Heidelberg)

20. Jia, W., Zhou, W.: Distributed Network Systems. From Concepts to Implementations. Network Theory and Application, vol. 15. Springer, Boston (2005). https://doi.org/10.1007/b102545

21. Maggio, E., Cavallaro, A.: Video Tracking-Theory and Practice. Wiley, West Sussex, UK (2010)

22. Miłkowski, M.: Explaining the Computational Mind. The MIT Press, Cambridge MA (2013)

23. Moran, D., Mooney, T. (eds.): The Phenomenology Reader. Rutledge, New Your, NY (2002)

24. Nakano, T., Eckford, A.W., Haraguchi, T.: Molecular Communication. Cambridge University Press, New York (2013). https://doi.org/10.1017/CBO9781139149693

25. Nöe, A.: Action in Perception. MIT Press, Cambridge, MA (2004)

26. Pawlak, Z.: Rough sets. Int. J. Comput. Inf. Sci. **11**, 341–356 (1982)

27. Pedrycz, W., Skowron, S., Kreinovich, V. (eds.): Handbook of Granular Computing. Wiley, Hoboken, NJ (2008)

28. Pedrycz, W.: Granular computing for data analytics: a manifesto of human - centric computing. IEEE/CAA J. Automatica Sinica **5**, 1025–1034 (2018). https://doi.org/10.1109/JAS.2018.7511213

29. Peirce, Ch.S.: The Philosophy of Peirce: Selected Writings. AMS Press, New York (1978)

30. Pietarinen, A.V.: Signs of Logic Peircean Themes on The Philosophy of Language, Games, and Communication. Springer, Heidelberg (2006). https://doi.org/10.1007/1-4020-3729-5

31. Russell, S., Norvig, P. (eds.): Artificial Intelligence. A Modern Approach, 4th Edn. Pearson Education, Hoboken, NJ (2021)

32. Skowron, A., Jankowski, A., Dutta, S.: Interactive granular computing. Granul. Comput. **1**(2), 95–113 (2016). https://doi.org/10.1007/s41066-015-0002-1

33. Skowron, A., Jankowski, A.: Rough sets and interactive granular computing. Fundamenta Informaticae **147**, 371–385 (2016). https://doi.org/10.3233/FI-2016-1413

34. Skowron, A., Jankowski, A.: Interactive computations: toward risk management in interactive intelligent systems. Nat. Comput. **15**(3), 465 – 476 (2016). https://doi.org/10.1007/s11047-015-9486-5

35. Steiner, P.: C.S. Peirce and artificial intelligence: historical heritage and (new) theoretical stakes. In: Müller, V. (ed.), Philosophy and Theory of Artificial Intelligence. Studies in Applied Philosophy, Epistemology and Rational Ethics, vol. 5, pp. 265–276. Springer, Heidelberg (2013). https://doi.org/10.1007/978-3-642-31674-6_20

36. Tanenbaum, A.,S., van Steen, M.: Distributed Systems. Principles and Paradigms. Pearson, Prentice Hall, Upper Saddle River, NJ (2006)

37. Thurner, S., Hanel, R., Klimek, P.: Introduction to the Theory of Complex Systems. Oxford University Press, Oxford (2018)

38. Vogt, P.: Language evolution and robotics: issues on symbol grounding and language acquisition. In: Loula, A., Gudwin, R., Queiroz, J. (eds.) Artificial Cognition Systems, pp. 176–209. Idea Group, Hershey, PA (2006)

39. Yu, W., Wen, G., Chen, G., Cao, J.: Distributed Cooperative Control of Multi-Agent Systems. Higher Education Press. Wiley, Singapore (2016)

40. Witzany, G. (ed.): Biocommunication of Phages. Springer, Cham (2020). https://doi.org/10.1007/978-3-030-45885-0

41. Zadeh, L.A.: Fuzzy sets, information and control **8**(3), 338–353 (1965). https://doi.org/10.1016/S0019-9958(65)90241-X

42. Zadeh, L.: Toward a theory of fuzzy information granulation and its centrality in human reasoning and fuzzy logic. Fuzzy Sets Syst. **90**, 111–127 (1997). https://doi.org/10.1016/S0165-0114(97)00077-8

43. Zhang, H., Lee, J., Quek, T.Q.S., Chih-Lin, I. (eds.): Ultra-Dense Networks. Principles and Applications. Cambridge University Press, Cambridge, UK (2020). https://doi.org/10.1017/9781108671323

Coordination and Cooperation in Robot Soccer

Vincenzo Suriani$^{(\boxtimes)}$, Emanuele Antonioni , Francesco Riccio ,
and Daniele Nardi

Department of Computer, Control, and Management Engineering,
Sapienza University of Rome, Rome, Italy
{suriani,antonioni,riccio,nardi}@diag.uniroma1.it

Abstract. Aiming at improving our physical strength and expanding
our knowledge, tournaments and competitions have always contributed
to our personal growth. Robotics and AI are no exception, and since
beginning, competitions have been exploited to improve our understanding of such research areas (e.g. Chess, VideoGames, DARPA). In fact,
the research community has launched (and it is involved) in several
robotics competitions that provide a two-fold benefit of (i) promoting novel approaches and (ii) valuate proposed solutions systematically
and quantitatively. In this paper, we focus on a particular research
area of Robotics and AI: we analyze multi-robot systems deployed in
a cooperative-adversarial environment being tasked to collaborate to
achieve a common goal, while competing against an opposing team.
To this end, RoboCup provide the best benchmarking environment by
implementing such a challenging problem in the game of soccer. Sports,
in fact, represent extremely complex challenge that require a team of
robots to show dexterous and fluid movements and to feature high-level
cognitive capabilities. Here, we analyse methodologies and approaches
to address the problem of coordination and cooperation and we discuss
state-of-the-art solutions that achieve effective decision-making processes
for multi-robot adversarial scenarios.

Keywords: Strategies in robotic games · Robotic competition · Soccer
robots RoboCup SPL

1 Introduction

Games and sport competitions offer a suitable application where both teammates
cooperation and opponents management play a key role. Hence, being able to
deploy a artificial agent capable of showing human (or even super-human) performance in these contexts, is one of the most difficult and fascinating goal that
lies at the intersection of robotics and artificial intelligence. Several milestones
have already been reached in this race for progress and technological advancement.

V. Suriani and E. Antonioni—Contributed equally.

© Springer Nature Switzerland AG 2021
N. T. Nguyen et al. (Eds.): ICCCI 2021, LNAI 12876, pp. 215–227, 2021.
https://doi.org/10.1007/978-3-030-88081-1_16

One of the first steps, most known to the mass, is undoubtedly the chess playing AI that beat the human world-champion for the first time, DeepBlue. More recently, but still in the context of board-games, we acknowledge AlphaGo [23] that, similarly to its predecessor, beat the world-champion in the most complex board-game in history, the game of GO. Moreover, the techniques investigated in recent years show promising results being generalizable to different scenarios and agnostic to the state representation. In fact, more related to the work we address in this survey, we also want to report the breakthrough achieved in [17] where the authors successfully beat a team of humans in an highly-interactive, partially observable, multi-agent scenarios in a continuous state-space world.

Assuming a different perspective in the wide spectrum of multi-agent approaches, here, we investigate how the research community tackles the problem of deploying such techniques on real robots playing soccer. In particular, we explore: (i) individual strategies in multi-agent scenario; (ii) cooperative and strategic decision-making; and (iii) opponent behavior analysis in adversarial settings. Operating in the real world adds new challenges and complexity to problems to solve. In fact, in this context, proposed techniques have to necessarily take into account system failures, noisy perceptions, unpredictable and non-stationary environments, and numerous unknown events ranging from faulty physical components to opponents high-level strategies. Hence, in order to highlight the most promising techniques and determine next research directions, we believe that categorizing the main contributions implemented within the RoboCup competitions is key to provide a solid basis in the deployment of state-of-the-art approaches to coordination and cooperation on physical robot.

It is very difficult to develop and deploy an autonomous agent able to understand and act in the physical world. In fact, when operating in uncontrolled scenarios, robots must show robust and effective skills to support perception, reasoning and coordinated behaviors with people and of course, other agents. To this end, the research community is constantly promoting robotic competitions in order to solve particular tasks and to develop and deploy operating agents in the real world. In this context, RoboCup is one of the leadership organization that challenges participants world-side in the game of soccer [4] with the aim to develop and end-to-end robotic system capable of perceiving the environment, high-level reasoning and performing agile and smooth motions.

In this context, perception and reasoning are enabling factors to enter the soccer field, but coordinated effective robot behaviors are the key factor for winning.

Each RoboCup league is designed to address a particular challenge in developing and deploying a fully autonomous robot soccer player (see Fig. 1). In fact, tackling sports at once is extremely difficult and attempting to tackle all the research questions at the same time leads to unpractical and under-performing systems. Hence, each of the RoboCup leagues is carefully defined to operate in a particular research area – even though a certain amount of overlap is guaranteed. Such an organization allows to divide the soccer game in sub-problems and to better formalize solutions for each of them. Usually, we can categorize

Fig. 1. RoboCup soccer leagues.

proposed approaches in accordance with the sense-plan-act paradigm, and intuitively, each league mainly targets one of these macro areas. In this paper, we categorize the contributions made in the context of RoboCup with a particular focus on coordination and collective behavior across different leagues. Our goal is to understand the most competitive methodologies currently used, and to highlight the most promising trends of research that will guide us to implement a fully autonomous team of robots. Our focus is to survey proposed solutions that contribute in enabling a team of robots to collectively perceive the world, asynchronously reason on current state of the environment and optimally coordinate their action to achieve a common goal while competing with other robots.

2   RoboCup Leagues and Organization

RoboCup competitions are organized in several leagues each of which aims at tackling a particular research challenge. In this paper we focus on coordination and cooperation approaches which are a characterizing aspect of RoboCup soccer leagues. Our goal is to analyze proposed techniques in order to highlight research trends and understand their enabling factor. Such leagues are particularly suitable to advance in our understanding of multi-agent systems. In fact, the sport of soccer forces the team of robots to demonstrate robust individual and collective behaviors while competing against another teams in an adversarial setting.

However, solving the game of soccer at once is not an easy task and the organization split the problem in different research areas, each of which is assigned to a particular league. Hence, such leagues features their own challenges being designed with different environmental and structural assumptions. One of the most sharp categorization that affects the methodologies proposed in the competitions is determined by the physical implementation of the agents, i.e. the platform hardware. Leagues, in fact, range from simulated agents to heavy-hardware platforms. *Simulation2D* (Sim2D) and *Simulation3D* (Sim3D) are the less hardware-demanding leagues which makes them the most suitable scenario to promote research in designing complex collective behavior at scale. The

Small Size (SSL) and the *Middle Size* (MSL) represent the first gate to physical agents. These leagues employ wheeled robots which alleviate locomotion constraints and are capable of performing dexterous maneuvers at high speed. Then, the *Standard Platform League* (SPL) forces all participants to use the same robotic platform, that currently is the Aldebaran humanoid NAO robot. Such a setting allows researchers to focus more on the behavior of the different agent rather than their hardware components. However, it includes in the challenge noisy perception, partial observability and bipedal locomotion. Finally, *Humanoid* Leagues (HL) represent the most hardware-demanding configuration. In this leagues robot can be 1.6 m tall, teams are completely in charge of the hardware components and engineering smooth and agile movements. Intuitively, however, the decision-making and cognitive behaviors are less demanding and games features a maximum of 2 vs. 2 robots.

3 Cooperation Strategies

Robots involved in the RoboCup competitions are designed to understand the external world and to exhibit robust and effective behaviors. In soccer, to this end, an agent has to show individual decision-making skills to (i) promptly react local situations [13]; (ii) reason at the collective level with other teammates in order to efficiently achieve a common goal [8]; and (iii) acknowledge opposing agents in the environment that act against [5]. Accordingly, we structure our discussion in three subsections – each of them describing specific problems to be solve in these areas and relating exiting work.

3.1 From Individual to Collective Strategies

An effective behavior for an autonomous multi-agent system is strictly related to the single agents capabilities. In fact, one of the requirements to build an effective multi-agent behavior, is a stable single player behavior. If we take a closer look to the single-agents, we can classifying their behaviors into two set of categories based on their abstraction level: skills and behaviors. Skills execute primitive actions that are usually related to the core motions of the agent, while behaviors determine how to select those primitive actions to achieve a specific goal.

In multi-agent adversarial settings, *Individual strategies* are a key factor for achieving success. To feature competitive behaviors, a robot must reconstruct a model of the world by relying on its local perceptions. Then it has to feature a robust decision-making system to determine the next set of actions to perform in order to reach a given goal. To this end, a single robot has to be capable of performing dexterous low-level motions while executing sophisticated high-level behaviors.

A low-level skill is usually defined as a predefined command for robot actuators to implement action primitive. In the soccer context these are represented by the routines for kicking, passing, dribbling, diving and getting-up. Individual behaviors are generated by composing skills and/or recursively including individual behaviors [31]. Behavior design, however, has to take into account different aspects characterizing the physical robot platforms, environmental constraints and task specifics. In RoboCup, researchers investigate a large amount of approaches and technologies in order to always show more sophisticated robot capabilities. The most common approaches are based on *state machines* [21], *planners* [9] and various learning techniques, as *Evolutionary Learning* [30], *Statistical Learning, Deep Learning* [12,18].

A state-machine approach, for example, can be deployed to easily model the defender behavior of the agent that have to stop the ball to avoid the goal. On the other hand, some game situations can benefit from the use of deep reinforcement learning approaches more than a model ones. For example, during penalty-kicks or in corner-kick situations. In this kind of contexts, learning-based approaches have started to be used and have been deployed even in place of the modeled approaches, as in [3,15], where two different statistical learning methods are adopted for solving behavioral problems. In the first one, the state evaluation of a decision-making process has been carried out by means of a Learning to Rank Algorithm. In the latter, the position of the goalkeeper agent in a MSL game has been determined with a linear regression approach. Behavior modeling has been also tackled with Reinforcement Learning approaches. In fact, in [27] within the context of the Simulation 3D, an agent has been trained to score goals without previous knowledge. This result has been achieved by means of a transfer learning system instead of the classical reward shaping approach. Within the context of the SPL, in [20] the authors addressed the problem of shaping the strategy of a defender robot adapting it to the strategy of the opponents. The method used is a combination of Monte Carlo search and data aggregation (MCSDA) that allowed to adapt the discrete-action soccer policies of the defender player. Finally, for solving the static free-kick task, a classical bandit approach has been exploited in [16].

3.2 Collective Strategies

RoboCup soccer leagues forces researchers to program robots to show to show effective individual and local behaviors, but also to demonstrate robust teamwork and cooperative behaviors. Suggestively, developing multi-robot decision making system is a much more complex challenge due to several factors: multiple environment perception streams, distributed world representations, dynamic role-assignment and asynchronous decision-making. Moreover, in RoboCup teammates are connected via Wi-Fi which, during games, is noisy and too prone to faulty behaviors.

Hence, in order to trade-off robustness and efficiency, and to guarantee competitive collective behaviors, researchers not only rely on the current data stream but they also provide robots with a model of the environment that can be used as a surrogate representation to embed the state of the external world [19]. Among the proposed approaches to multi-robot cooperation and collaboration, we highlight two major classes: positioning approaches and role-assignment approaches.

As the name suggests, the former category of approaches has the goal of finding the best team positioning within the field. Such a positioning can be an extremely difficult task which grows exponentially with the number of players and that is subjects to numerous factors. For example, the authors in [14] assess that the contexts in which the game is currently evolving is key to re-position teammates. For instance, team formation can be adjusted depending on whether the players are in an defensive or attacking context, or equivalently depending on the current score, players can be more aggressive or more cautious if they have to manage the opponents.

Conversely, dynamic-role assignment attempts to find the optimal mapping between a set of robots and a set of active task. For example, the authors in [6,19] use utility functions to estimate how good a robot can perform a certain task at a given time. Utility functions are particularly suitable to evaluate and coordinate teams of heterogeneous robots acting collectively. Equivalently, the authors in [24] exploit MDP to formalize individual behavioral models and determine affinity with a set of given tasks. Differently, Catacora et al. [7] use a learning-based approach to coordinate a team of robots. Their approach shows promising results and successfully coordinates two robots in particular in-game situations (e.g. penalty-kicks). However, the computational demand of such a methodology limits its application and, at the moment, they cannot run the learned policy on large teams of robots.

3.3   Opponent Analysis for Cooperation

In adversarial multi-robot environments, having an understanding of the opponents behaviors represents a remarkable advantage. In fact in such a context, if a team of robots is able to counter opponents movements, both analyzing individual behaviors and forecasting team strategies, then it can react more precisely to the situation at hand – and thus improve the team performance. In RoboCup, we report that the majority of contributions in opponent analysis comes from leagues where perception is more reliable [26] (e.g. Sim2D, Sim3D, SSL and MSL). In such leagues we notice that opponents analysis approaches can be coarsely categorized in two classes: action sequence analysis and behavior forecasting.

The former group attempts to find patterns in the action sequences of the opponents teams in order to recognize recurring strategies. For example, in [10], the authors proposed an offline opponent action analysis approaches that processes game logs in order to extrapolate action primitives. Such primitives are then coupled with in-game states and organized in an opponents behavior tree. Yasui et al. [29], instead, formalize a dissimilarity function among state-action pairs which is then used for clustering and classification. The authors extend their work to improve computational efficiency [1] and propose an clustering algorithm to analyze the agents behaviors online and promptly react by position in order to prevent the opponents to score [2].

The latter group aims at solving a forecasting task. In other words, given the current state of teammates and sequence of opponent actions, the goal is to predict the intentions of other agents and the next state of the environment. Such a capability is key to anticipate opponents' intentions and gain a substantial advantage on them. In this setting, Li et al. [11] proposes a fuzzy inference system to classify particular in-game situation (e.g. corner-kick, passing); predict opponent trajectories; and re-position the team formation accordingly. They show that by inferring opponents intentions it is possible to double the number of won games. Similarly, the authors in [25] introduce FOSSE, a deep model-free approach that given state representation attempts to learn a transition model, forecast future states of the environment and (as in the previous case) adjusts the team formation. Finally, in [22] the authors achieve an important milestone by rolling out a learning approach on a humanoid robot in the SPL. The authors introduce SAFEL, a real-time learning-based algorithm that is capable of generating an opponent behavioral model of an agent, and counter-react strategically.

4 Analysis and Classification of the Proposed Approaches

In this paper, we survey the implementation of the different approaches to decision-making, both at the individual and collective level. In particular, we analyzed how single agent skills, coordinated team actions and opponent analysis can contribute to implement effective multi-robot systems in cooperative-adversarial scenario characterized by different specific challenges (e.g. used platform, low communication, scalable behaviors).

However, there are different considerations that can be done in order to better classify the proposed approaches in this particularly challenging context. Such categorizations provide a thorough comparison and slice the state-of-the-art along different perspectives:

Centralized vs. Distributed. Existing solutions to multi-robot coordination include a staggering amount of different techniques, each of which comes with its own advantages and disadvantage. Most contributions to the field of multi-robot coordination depend on the environmental configuration. For example, in low-bandwidth and noisy communication scenarios, a fully distributed approach is typically to be preferred in order to allow robots to act individually even though the information about teammates is outdated – or simply not coming in. Conversely, if the overall setup is characterized by a reliable communication, a centralized approach is implemented to guarantee robustness and optimally coordinated robots (e.g. Kiva system [28]).

In RoboCup, the technical committee enforces noisy and non-constant communication environments in most of the leagues, thus imposing a bias in the type of coordination architecture that can be deployed. Moreover, in the SPL data among teammates can be exchanged only once every second. There is, however, one league that hosts only centralized approaches. The SSL, in fact, has a single computer that receives sensory data streams; performs the computation; and deliberates collective and individual robot actions.

In the SSL we can observe the benefits of featuring a centralized coordination system where robots do not compete for shared resources; do not clash in ambiguous situations; and in general do not show the artifacts of a distributed approach where optimality in positioning and role-assignment is compromised to favor reactivity and individual behavior of a single player. Finally, we notice that in RoboCup, but also in other applications, centralized coordination architectures are deployed when robots can assume that the world is stationary and fully observable. Otherwise, it would be impossible to guarantee optimal behaviors even with a centralized strategy.

When considering extreme and dynamic environments, distributed architecture, are in general more robust to faulty communication; partial observability and non-stationary environments. The SPL, and in general all the humanoid leagues, are a clear example of such environments. Here, distributed coordination approaches are the most effective solution that researcher can resort to. Usually, a distributed coordination is achieved only exchanging local information among the teammates in order to reconstruct of global representation of the world state. Such information can have different format and might represent different concepts. The majority of distributed coordination systems exchanges either utility vectors or bid in auction-based methods in order to address dynamic-role assignment. Conversely, few approaches attempt to reconstruct a more sophisticated global world model by exchanging events that robots perceive locally and embedding them in a global (approximated) representation – which is updated iteratively. Finally, we notice that a common denominator of such techniques is that, distributed coordination systems are ready to recover from situation where a single unit might act individually and still trying to solve the task assigned to the team. With that firm in mind, existing approaches usually set a priority of the tasks to be complete. Then, the coordination system allocates roles in order to guarantee that the most important tasks are always active.

Cooperative vs. Adversarial. RoboCup is challenging from different points-of-views. In particular, given the structure of the problem and the environment, researchers are forced to investigate and find a solution to different problems at once. In this setting, for example, it is not possible to address separately multi-robot coordination and adversarial analysis.

Due to the individual leagues rules, an effective coordination is achieved differently across RoboCup competitions. Typically, coordination is achieved by balancing a strategic positioning of the different players within the field and dynamic role-assignment. In leagues where perception and hardware is not a limiting factor, coordination and cooperation also involves strategic setups, in-game schemes and multi-agent plays such as give-and-go. As observed in the previous sections, this is the case of simulated leagues and the SSL where perception is guaranteed to each agent; and specific to the latter scenario, computation is centralized.

Instead, we observe that dynamic role-assignment is constant in all leagues – where participants intuitively exploit the possibility to replace units without complications. Such a problem can be formalized as set of agents and a set of tasks, and the aim is to dynamically assign optimally each task to a particular agent. In the SPL, for example, role-assignment is achieved in a distributed fashion where each player takes individual actions but attempting to satisfy a team goal attempts to achieve a team. In this setting, approaches usually employ auction-based or utility-based solutions in order to trade-off robustness and reactiveness of the dynamic constraints of the environment. In the SSL, there are few approaches that implicitly assign all tasks/roles at once by means of a learning algorithm. They achieve good in-game performance but, such approaches are usually computationally inefficient and assume a reliable perception and localization. In fact, we notice that, the less these two assumptions hold, the simpler is the coordination strategy – which in extreme cases forces teams to implement static coordination approaches.

The adversarial nature of sports makes RoboCup an excellent testbed to promote research in the area of Adversarial MRS. However, there is only a subset of leagues that explicitly takes into account actions of the opponent teams, such as simulation leagues, SSL. But, there is an emergent trend in one of the humanoid leagues, i.e. SPL, that started to investigate how to react to opponent actions. In general, existing methodologies are coarsely categorized in behavior (and formation) classification and episodic reactive strategies. While the former involves long term strategies and re-positioning the robots in the field, as in the SSL, the latter shows more basic behavior that are reactions to movements of other players. Such strategies influence decisions of the robots and trigger local routines depending on the particular joint state of the players (both teammates and opponents). Also in this case, as for the coordination methodologies noisy-perceptions and hardware might become an obstacle that leads to techniques that promote robustness and compromise scalability.

Simulation vs. Hardware. We attempt to highlight which are the major factors that impact and influence the realization of effective multi-robot behaviors for physical agents in robotic soccer. The research conducted in simulated leagues supports the design and implementation of the most sophisticated coordination behaviors and collective strategies. In fact, given reliable perception and guaranteed computation power, simulated leagues have the privilege to only focus on behavior generation. From a different point-of-view, hardware oriented leagues like the Humanoid, historically focused their effort on behavior modeling for individual agents, limiting the environment to a pure adversarial setting. Recently, however, more robots have been added to the game, forcing teams to implement coordinated actions also for such platforms. Due to the constraints and size of such robots, current solutions to coordinated behaviors are basic and carefully handcrafted. But, the evolution of cooperative and collective behavior can only move forward, and as it happened for other leagues, researchers are experimenting with planning and machine learning approaches, moving away from ad-hoc modeling. We can conclude, that hardware is definitely one of the most critical factors in the development of coordination approaches. In fact to-date, heavy-platforms limit the research in collective behaviors and their deployment on the field.

Model-Based vs. Learning-Based. At the current stage, model-based approaches represent the most effective in-game choice for behavior generation and coordination due to their fast deployment and intelligibility. Learning-based methods, however, show the most promising results achieving more accurate and efficient solutions even if they suffer from high-computational demand, sample inefficient and they may result in brittle solutions. For these reasons, the use of pure learning-based approaches is limited and researchers tend to combine both paradigms to alleviate some of these issues. However, it is worth noticing that in leagues where high-computational support is guaranteed, and less complex platforms are used, learning approaches are more often deployed and have the chance to showcase their benefits. Examples of such environments are the Simulated Leagues and the Small-Size League. As a consequence, results shown by DL methods motivates teams to investigate learning-based approaches across all RoboCup leagues. In fact, during this survey, we encountered several learning methodologies which have been proposed to address and optimize particular in-game situations even in more complex and hardware-demanding leagues. But, to-date, such methodologies are deployed in an end-to-end fashion, and they are rather used to support planning-based solutions.

5   Conclusions

RoboCup competitions represent a exciting environment to foster novel research and excellent testbed to deploy and validate novel methodologies on physical agents. The research conducted within this context is fundamental develop autonomous end-to-end agents and already contributed to numerous applications outside the soccer field. We report that in recent years more sophisticated approaches have been proposed to optimize coordination and collective behavior at the decision-making level. However, it is worth noticing that not all the proposed approaches find a direct implementation in the actual competition. In fact, researcher tend to prefer planning-based approaches for in-game situations while learning-based methods seem to remain at a research phase. However, even if the solutions within the latter category are sample inefficient, not intelligible and may feature brittle behaviors, learning-based techniques show the most promising results improving performance in particular settings and generalizing to unknown scenarios.

Finally, we can summarize that the research conducted in robotics competitions is key for advancing and building effective teams of robotic agents. Competitions, in fact, represent a good balance between research and engineering of novel solutions that force the research community to develop techniques that can actually be implemented and can interact with the real world.

References

1. Adachi, Y., Ito, M., Naruse, T.: Classifying the strategies of an opponent team based on a sequence of actions in the RoboCup SSL. In: Behnke, S., Sheh, R., Sariel, S., Lee, D.D. (eds.) RoboCup 2016: Robot World Cup XX. LNCS, vol. 9776, pp. 109–120. Springer, Cham (2017). https://doi.org/10.1007/978-3-319-68792-6_9
2. Adachi, Y., Ito, M., Naruse, T.: Online strategy clustering based on action sequences in RoboCupSoccer small size league. Robotics 8(3), 58 (2019)
3. Akiyama, H., Tsuji, M., Aramaki, S.: Learning evaluation function for decision making of soccer agents using learning to rank. In: 2016 Joint 8th International Conference on Soft Computing and Intelligent Systems (SCIS) and 17th International Symposium on Advanced Intelligent Systems (ISIS), pp. 239–242 (2016). https://doi.org/10.1109/SCIS-ISIS.2016.0059
4. Antonioni, E., Suriani, V., Riccio, F., Nardi, D.: Game strategies for physical robot soccer players: a survey. IEEE Trans. Games 1 (2021). https://doi.org/10.1109/TG.2021.3075065
5. Bakkes, S.C., Spronck, P.H., Van Den Herik, H.J.: Opponent modelling for case-based adaptive game AI. Entertain. Comput. 1(1), 27–37 (2009)
6. Castelpietra, C., Iocchi, L., Nardi, D., Piaggio, M., Scalzo, A., Sgorbissa, A.: Communication and coordination among heterogeneous mid-size players: Art99. In: Stone, P., Balch, T., Kraetzschmar, G. (eds.) Robot Soccer World Cup. LNCS, vol. 2019, pp. 86–95. Springer, Heidelberg (2000). https://doi.org/10.1007/3-540-45324-5_7
7. Catacora Ocana, J.M., Riccio, F., Capobianco, R., Nardi, D.: Cooperative multi-agent deep reinforcement learning in a 2 versus 2 free-kick task. In: Chalup, S., Niemueller, T., Suthakorn, J., Williams, M.A. (eds.) RoboCup 2019: Robot World Cup XXIII. LNCS, vol. 11531, pp. 44–57. Springer, Cham (2019). https://doi.org/10.1007/978-3-030-35699-6_4
8. Dorri, A., Kanhere, S.S., Jurdak, R.: Multi-agent systems: a survey. IEEE Access 6, 28573–28593 (2018). https://doi.org/10.1109/ACCESS.2018.2831228
9. Ghallab, M., Nau, D., Traverso, P.: Automated Planning and Acting. Cambridge University Press, Cambridge (2016)
10. Iglesias, J.A., Ledezma, A., Sanchis, A.: Opponent modeling in RoboCup Soccer simulation. In: Fuentetaja Pizán, R., García Olaya, Á., Sesmero Lorente, M.P., Iglesias Martínez, J.A., Ledezma Espino, A. (eds.) Advances in Physical Agents, vol. 855, pp. 303–316. Springer, Cham (2019). https://doi.org/10.1007/978-3-319-99885-5_21
11. Li, X., Chen, X.: Fuzzy inference based forecasting in soccer simulation 2D, the RoboCup 2015 soccer simulation 2D league champion team. In: Almeida, L., Ji, J., Steinbauer, G., Luke, S. (eds.) RoboCup 2015: Robot World Cup XIX. LNCS, vol. 9513, pp. 144–152. Springer, Cham (2015). https://doi.org/10.1007/978-3-319-29339-4_12
12. Lillicrap, T.P., et al.: Continuous control with deep reinforcement learning. arXiv preprint arXiv:1509.02971 (2015)
13. Luger, G.F.: Artificial Intelligence: Structures and Strategies for Complex Problem Solving. Pearson Education, London (2005)
14. MacAlpine, P., Barrera, F., Stone, P.: Positioning to win: a dynamic role assignment and formation positioning system. In: Workshops at the Twenty-Sixth AAAI Conference on Artificial Intelligence (2012)

15. Masterjohn, J.G., Polceanu, M., Jarrett, J., Seekircher, A., Buche, C., Visser, U.: Regression and mental models for decision making on robotic biped goalkeepers. In: Almeida, L., Ji, J., Steinbauer, G., Luke, S. (eds.) RoboCup 2015: Robot World Cup XIX. LNCS, vol. 9513, pp. 177–189. Springer, Cham (2015). https://doi.org/10.1007/978-3-319-29339-4_15

16. Mendoza, J.P., Simmons, R., Veloso, M.: Online learning of robot soccer free kick plans using a bandit approach. In: Twenty-Sixth International Conference on Automated Planning and Scheduling (2016)

17. OpenAI: OpenAI five. https://blog.openai.com/openai-five/ (2018)

18. Pierson, H.A., Gashler, M.S.: Deep learning in robotics: a review of recent research. Adv. Robot. **31**(16), 821–835 (2017)

19. Riccio, F., Borzi, E., Gemignani, G., Nardi, D.: Context-based coordination for a multi-robot soccer team. In: Almeida, L., Ji, J., Steinbauer, G., Luke, S. (eds.) RoboCup 2015: Robot World Cup XIX. LNCS, vol. 9513, pp. 276–289. Springer, Cham (2015). https://doi.org/10.1007/978-3-319-29339-4_23

20. Riccio, F., Capobianco, R., Nardi, D.: Using Monte Carlo search with data aggregation to improve robot soccer policies. In: Behnke, S., Sheh, R., Sarıel, S., Lee, D.D. (eds.) RoboCup 2016: Robot World Cup XX. LNCS, vol. 9776, pp. 256–267. Springer, Cham (2017). https://doi.org/10.1007/978-3-319-68792-6_21

21. Risler, M., von Stryk, O.: Formal behavior specification of multi-robot systems using hierarchical state machines in XABSL. In: AAMAS08-Workshop on Formal Models and Methods for Multi-robot Systems, pp. 12–16. Citeseer (2008)

22. Rizzi, C., Johnson, C.G., Vargas, P.A.: Fear learning for flexible decision making in RoboCup: a discussion. In: Akiyama, H., Obst, O., Sammut, C., Tonidandel, F. (eds.) RoboCup 2017: Robot World Cup XXI. LNCS, vol. 1117, pp. 59–70. Springer, Cham (2018). https://doi.org/10.1007/978-3-030-00308-1_5

23. Silver, D., et al.: Mastering the game of go with deep neural networks and tree search. Nature **529**, 484–503 (2016)

24. Spaan, M.T., Vlassis, N., Groen, F.C., et al.: High level coordination of agents based on multiagent Markov decision processes with roles. In: IROS, vol. 2, pp. 66–73 (2002)

25. Suzuki, Y., Nakashima, T.: On the use of simulated future information for evaluating game situations. In: Chalup, S., Niemueller, T., Suthakorn, J., Williams, M.A. (eds.) RoboCup 2019: Robot World Cup XXIII. LNCS, vol. 11531, pp. 294–308. Springer, Cham (2019). https://doi.org/10.1007/978-3-030-35699-6_23

26. Trevizan, F.W., Veloso, M.M.: Learning opponent's strategies in the RoboCup small size league. In: Proceedings of the AAMAS, vol. 10. Citeseer (2010)

27. Watkinson, W.B., Camp, T.: Training a RoboCup striker agent via transferred reinforcement learning. In: Holz, D., Genter, K., Saad, M., von Stryk, O. (eds.) RoboCup 2018: Robot World Cup XXII. LNCS, vol. 11374, pp. 109–121. Springer, Cham (2019). https://doi.org/10.1007/978-3-030-27544-0_9

28. Wurman, P.R., D'Andrea, R., Mountz, M.: Coordinating hundreds of cooperative, autonomous vehicles in warehouses. AI Mag. **29**(1), 9 (2008). https://doi.org/10.1609/aimag.v29i1.2082. https://ojs.aaai.org/index.php/aimagazine/article/view/2082

29. Yasui, K., Kobayashi, K., Murakami, K., Naruse, T.: Analyzing and learning an opponent's strategies in the RoboCup small size league. In: Behnke, S., Veloso, M., Visser, A., Xiong, R. (eds.) RoboCup 2013: Robot World Cup XVII. LNCS, vol. 8371, pp. 159–170. Springer, Heidelberg (2014). https://doi.org/10.1007/978-3-662-44468-9_15

30. Zhou, Z.H., Yu, Y., Qian, C.: Evolutionary Learning: Advances in Theories and Algorithms. Springer, Singapore (2019). https://doi.org/10.1007/978-981-13-5956-9
31. Ziparo, V.A., Iocchi, L., Nardi, D., Palamara, P.F., Costelha, H.: Petri net plans: a formal model for representation and execution of multi-robot plans. In: Proceedings of the 7th International Joint Conference on Autonomous Agents and Multiagent Systems-Volume 1, pp. 79–86. International Foundation for Autonomous Agents and Multiagent Systems (2008)

Improving Pheromone Communication for UAV Swarm Mobility Management

Daniel H. Stolfi[1]([✉])(ID), Matthias R. Brust[1](ID), Grégoire Danoy[1,2](ID), and Pascal Bouvry[1,2](ID)

[1] Interdisciplinary Centre for Security, Reliability and Trust (SnT), University of Luxembourg, Esch-Sur-Alzette, Luxembourg
{daniel.stolfi,matthias.brust,gregoire.danoy,pascal.bouvry}@uni.lu
[2] FSTM/DCS, University of Luxembourg, Esch-Sur-Alzette, Luxembourg

Abstract. In this article we address the optimisation of pheromone communication used for the mobility management of a swarm of Unmanned Aerial Vehicles (UAVs) for surveillance applications. A genetic algorithm is proposed to optimise the exchange of pheromone maps used in the CACOC (Chaotic Ant Colony Optimisation for Coverage) mobility model which improves the vehicles' routes in order to achieve unpredictable trajectories as well as maximise area coverage. Experiments are conducted using realistic simulations, which additionally permit to assess the impact of packet loss ratios on the performance of the surveillance system, in terms of reliability and area coverage.

Keywords: Unmanned aerial vehicle · Pheromones · Evolutionary algorithm · Surveillance system · Swarm robotics · Mobility model

1 Introduction

Unmanned Aerial Vehicles (UAVs) initially developed for military applications are nowadays paving their way into multiple civilian domains [10]. These include cargo delivery, road traffic surveillance, fire fighting, environmental monitoring, architecture surveillance, and farming. Considering surveillance applications [19], UAVs allow to provide a mobile and controllable bird's-eye view for a fraction of the cost existing solutions (e.g. helicopters). However, UAVs are typically small to medium size battery powered devices which therefore feature limited flight time and payload capacity. One promising approach to overcome those limitations is to use multiple autonomous UAVs simultaneously, also referred to as a swarm, where collaborations with other types of vehicles [18] are possible.

Unpredictability of vehicle trajectories [5] in surveillance scenarios is a desired characteristic to prevent the use of possible detection strategies, especially in military applications where an attacker is present. Some mobility models, like CROMM (Chaotic Rössler Mobility Model) [13], use chaotic trajectories to avoid route prediction but UAVs tend to visit the same locations frequently. CACOC (Chaotic Ant Colony Optimisation for Coverage) [13] is another chaos based

© Springer Nature Switzerland AG 2021
N. T. Nguyen et al. (Eds.): ICCCI 2021, LNAI 12876, pp. 228–240, 2021.
https://doi.org/10.1007/978-3-030-88081-1_17

mobility model conceived to address that issue by using virtual pheromones, shared between UAVs to improve area coverage. These pheromones must be efficiently exchanged between UAVs to ensure a good global performance of the swarm. However, communications in such highly dynamic *ad hoc* networks are very challenging [8].

This article proposes to evaluate and optimise the communications between autonomous UAVs as members of a swarm performing surveillance tasks. More precisely, the parameters of CACOC+ (a parameterised version of CACOC) are optimised using a genetic algorithm in order to maximise area coverage, even when communications are restricted in packet size, and UAVs have to base their mobility decisions on their own local data, e.g. their virtual pheromone map. Experiments using realistic simulations permit to consider limited communication range, transmissions consuming energy, and radio packets that might be lost before reaching destination due to interferences.

The remainder of this paper is organised as follows. In the next section, we review the state of the art related to our proposal. In Sect. 3 our approach is presented. The optimisation algorithm is described in Sect. 4. Our case studies and experimental results are presented and analysed in Sect. 5. Finally, Sect. 6 brings discussion and future work.

2   Related Work

UAV communications has been addressed by several authors. In [1] a concept-level proposal and literature review for the use of cellular networks as the communication infrastructure for UAV swarms is presented. The authors highlight the practically unlimited range of communications using cellular data coverage (3G in the United States) and the reliability of its base stations. This proposal is tested in the real world using custom built quadcopters and the MAVLink communication protocol [3]. In [11] the authors address the problem of UAV swarm formation in areas covered by 3G/4G mobile networks and present an algorithm for multi-robot coordination which is also bandwidth-efficient. The proposed protocol for UAV coordination uses the group-cast and group management facilities of the authors' mobile communication middleware. Several test were done in a swarm of ten simulated UAVs.

In [4] a study about communication performance between UAVs in the 2.4 GHz band is presented. It takes into account how existing interferences and packet loss ratio affect a stable communication link. Their findings include that the degree of vibration generated by propellers interferes with the link signal, although the larger interferences come from the remote controllers, since they work in the same frequency band. Delay in the wireless network and its stability are analysed in [21]. A swarm of three cellular-connected UAVs, positioned in a triangle formation, is proposed to be optimised. The maximum allowable delay required to prevent the instability of the swarm is also analysed. Path planning for multiple robots for persistent surveillance with connectivity constraints is studied in [15]. Greedy and cooperative strategies are proposed for the robots to reach all sensing locations, being the performance of the former higher when the number of robots or the communication range is large enough.

In this article we focus on the optimisation of the communications between UAVs by controlling the amount of data shared by drones during their interactions. The use of *ad hoc* communications allows to work in a private network with an increment in the security of the radio links. Although reliable communications are assumed, we investigate the consequences of packet loss. To the best of our knowledge, this study involving the optimisation of the parameters of CACOC+, to deal with communication constraints and pheromone maps, has not been done before. In the following section we describe CACOC+, followed by the bio-inspired algorithm proposed for optimising its parameters.

3   Pheromone Based Swarm Mobility

In a previous article [16] the optimisation of the CACOC mobility model to maximise area coverage was proposed. CACOC is a mobility model for UAV swarms that uses chaotic dynamics and pheromone methods for improving area coverage using unpredictable trajectories. When using CACOC, UAVs leave pheromones as they move in the environment to indicate recently covered areas. Pheromones have a repulsive effect and thus, aim to better spread UAVs in the area avoiding visiting the same spots too frequently. As pheromone trails evaporate, a UAV will eventually visit again the same region of the map.

The diagram of CACOC is shown in Fig. 1. The next moving direction is calculated using chaotic dynamics when there are no pheromones in the UAV's neighbourhood. Values from the first return map (ρ) from a chaotic attractor, obtained by solving a Rössler ordinary differential equation system [14], are used to replace the random part of the mobility model, as proposed in [13]. On the other hand, when virtual pheromones are detected, they work as repellers, stochastically modifying the UAV's next moving direction. The amount of pheromones detected in each scanned direction is used to calculate the probabilities $P_L = \frac{phe\_total-phe\_left}{2 \times phe\_total}$, $P_R = \frac{phe\_total-phe\_right}{2 \times phe\_total}$, for the next move.

In [16], three parameters for CACOC were proposed to adapt this model to different scenarios and improve area coverage (it will be referred to as CACOC+ hereafter). These parameters are depicted in Fig. 2, and are described as: the optimised amount of pheromones left by each vehicle (τ_a), the pheromone radius (τ_r) and maximum detection distance (τ_d). The pheromone decay rate used is the same value as in CACOC, i.e. one unit per second.

3.1   Pheromone Communication

In previous works, CACOC and CACOC+ assumed perfect communications, where vehicles were always in their respective communication range, and there was no packet loss. This article considers a more realistic scenario featuring limited communication ranges and interferences by using the well-known ARGoS simulator [12] and its communication model between robots. Additionally, in this

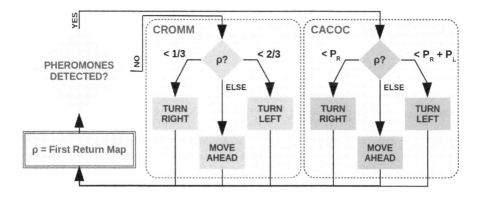

Fig. 1. Diagram of the CACOC (and CACOC+) mobility models.

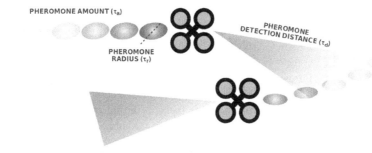

Fig. 2. Three parameters proposed for CACOC+.

study we address the validation of CACOC+ in a different simulator as it was previously tested only in the HUNTED Sim [17].

As part of a swarm of autonomous vehicles, each member has to take local decisions to achieve a common global goal, e.g. maximising area coverage. In CACOC+ each vehicle has its own local pheromone map composed by its own pheromone trails and portions of pheromone maps received from the other vehicles in the scenario (Fig. 3(b) and (c)). They are shared by using *ad hoc* communications which are subject to disruptions and interferences. The complete pheromone map is represented in Fig. 3(a).

Moreover, larger data packets imply more energy consumption and a higher probability of data loss. Consequently, we propose the optimisation of the CACOC+ parameters where UAVs share different amount of data, and an analysis of how it affects the system performance when each swarm member only knows partially the pheromone map. Therefore, our problem representation is the vector $x = \{\tau_{a_1}, \tau_{r_1}, \tau_{d_1}, \ldots, \tau_{a_N}, \tau_{r_N}, \tau_{d_N}\}$ where N is the number of UAVs in the swarm. Thus, vector x defines the configuration of the surveillance system which comprises the parameters of each UAV in the swarm represented by integer values. Note that the amount of shared pheromones is not included in the problem representation since it is part of the characteristics of each case study.

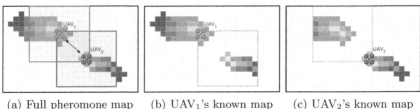

(a) Full pheromone map   (b) UAV$_1$'s known map   (c) UAV$_2$'s known map

Fig. 3. Pheromone map shared between UAVs according to their communication range. Each UAV knows its own map and the map portions received from the others (dashed squares in (b) and (c)).

3.2 Collision Avoidance

The implemented collision avoidance algorithm relies on repelling forces between UAVs. Given $u \in UAVs$, the distances between u and the rest of vehicles in $UAVs$ are calculated. Those UAVs closer than a minimum distance δ_{min} (a fixed parameter, e.g. 6 m) modify the vector r_u, which will contain the resultant repelling force for u, to be used to modify its trajectory.

We have implemented this straightforward algorithm as UAVs following their mobility model decisions will eventually divert to no colliding trajectories avoiding any possible deadlock. As a consequence of the implemented algorithm, which requires to know the position of the other UAVs in the neighbourhood, communications between vehicles also include the coordinates of the transmitting UAV.

4 Optimisation Algorithm

We have designed a Genetic Algorithm (GA) which uses operators for continuous optimisation, in order find the parameterisation of CACOC+ which maximises the area coverage for different pheromone block sizes shared between UAVs. The proposed GA is based on an Evolutionary Algorithm (EA) [6,9] which is an efficient method for solving combinatorial optimisation problems. EAs simulate processes present in evolution such as natural selection, gene recombination after reproduction, gene mutation, and the dominance of the fittest individuals over the weaker ones. This is a generational GA where an offspring of λ individuals is obtained from the population μ, so that the auxiliary population Q contains the same number of individuals as the population Pop. The number of individuals was set to 16 since their evaluations require expensive simulations.

Algorithm 1 shows the pseudocode of the GA. After initializing t and $Q(0)$, $Pop(0)$ is generated by using the *Initialization* function. Then, the main loop is executed while the *TerminationCondition* is not fulfilled (in our case we stop after 1,000 evaluations). Into the main loop, the *Selection* operator is applied to populate $Q(t)$ using Binary Tournament [7]. Next, the *Crossover* operator is applied and after that, the *Mutation* operator slightly modifies the new offspring. Finally, after the *Evaluation* of $Q(t)$, the new population $Pop(t+1)$ is obtained

Algorithm 1. Pseudocode of the Genetic Algorithm (GA).

---

procedure GA(N_i, P_c, P_m)
    $t \leftarrow \emptyset$
    $Q(0) \leftarrow \emptyset$ ▷ Q = auxiliary population
    $Pop(0) \leftarrow Initialization(N_i)$ ▷ Pop = population
    while *not TerminationCondition()* **do**
        $Q(t) \leftarrow Selection(Pop(t))$
        $Q(t) \leftarrow Crossover(Q(t), P_c)$
        $Q(t) \leftarrow Mutation(Q(t), P_m)$
        $Evaluation(Q(t))$
        $Pop(t+1) \leftarrow Replacement(Q(t), Pop(t))$
        $t \leftarrow t + 1$

---

by applying the *Replacement* operator. It consists in selecting the best individual in $Q(t)$ to replace the worst one in $Pop(t)$ if it is best valued [2]. This contributes to avoid population stagnation and preserves its diversity.

4.1 Crossover Operator

The crossover operator implements the one-point crossover [9] using vehicle configuration blocks. Two individuals x and y are taken from the population Q and the recombination operator is applied to them if a generated random number is less than the crossover probability $P_c = 0.9$. The crossing point is then calculated using a uniformly distributed, random integer value cp. The crossover is made at UAV level: as there are three parameters per UAV, possible values of cp are 3, 6, 9, etc. The UAVs' configurations in x and y after the cp-th position are swapped and added to the destination population $Q\prime$. This process is repeated for the rest of the individuals in Q (taken in groups of two) to complete the new population $Q\prime$, to be subject to mutation.

4.2 Mutation Operator

The mutation operator (Algorithm 2) is based on the one proposed in [2], and adapted to our problem characteristics. First, each position of the individual x in Q is subject to mutation according to the mutation probability $P_m = \frac{1}{L}$, where L is the length of the solution vector. If a component of x is selected for mutation, a new M value is randomly calculated according to a uniform probability distribution. Then, the value of Δ is obtained taking into account the bounds of the parameter associated to each component of x, and k (Eq. 1). The value of k begins in 1 and exponentially decreases during the execution of the algorithm to increase the exploration in the early stages and focus on the exploitation of the solutions found, in the last generations of the GA.

$$\Delta(i, M, k) = k \times \frac{UpBd(x[i]) - LowBd(x[i])}{M} \tag{1}$$

Algorithm 2. Pseudocode of the Mutation Operator.

---

function MUTATION(Q, P_m, k)
    $Q\prime \leftarrow \emptyset$
    for $\{x\} \in Q$ **do**
        $x\prime \leftarrow x$
        for $i \leftarrow 1, L$ **do** $\triangleright \; L = length(x)$
            if $rnd() < P_m$ **then** $\triangleright$ mutation probability
                $M \leftarrow randInt(1, 10)$
                if $rnd() < 0.5$ **then** $\triangleright$ increment/decrement
                    $x\prime[i] \leftarrow \min(x[i] + \Delta(i, M, k), UpBd(x[i]))$
                else
                    $x\prime[i] \leftarrow \max(x[i] - \Delta(i, M, k), LowBd(x[i]))$
        $Q\prime \leftarrow Q\prime \cup \{x\prime\}$
    return $Q\prime$

The current value of the parameter in the solution vector is either increased or decreased (equally probable) taking into account the parameters' bounds, and finally, the new individual $x\prime$ is added to the new population $Q\prime$.

4.3 Fitness Function

Our objective is maximising the covered area to improve the surveillance performed by the UAV swarm under different communication restrictions. Therefore, the evaluation of each system configuration is achieved taking into account the percentage of area visited during the simulation time (600 s). Each scenario is mapped as a lattice of 100×100 cells for evaluation purpose. We assumed that a UAV explores an area of 3×3 cells at each simulation tick (note that they are still moving in the continuous coordinated space provided by ARGoS). Consequently, the fitness value of a given configuration is calculated as shown in Eq. 2. As we are maximising the explored area, the higher the value of $F(x)$, the better.

$$F(x) = \frac{\# \; of \; explored \; cells}{\# \; of \; cells \; in \; the \; scenario} \tag{2}$$

5 Experiments

In this section we describe our case studies, perform the optimisation of CACOC+, compare its performance against CROMM and CACOC, and analyse the effects of packet loss. Our experiments were conducted in parallel on computing nodes equipped with Intel Xeon Gold 6132 @ 2.6 GHz and 128 GB of RAM. The total optimisation time was equivalent to 12 days.

5.1 Case Studies

We propose three case studies consisting in four scenarios each, where different amount of pheromones are shared. Swarms of two, four and six UAVs are analysed in each case study respectively, which begin their surveillance tasks in the centre of the map. The four possible scenarios are: (i) CACOC+ where the entire pheromone map is shared between UAVs in communication range, (ii) CACOC+.10 where a square of 21×21 cells is shared, (iii) CACOC+.05 where a square of 11×11 cells is shared, and (iv) CACOC+.00 where no pheromone map is shared between UAVs.

The communication range is set to 10 m where the collision avoidance algorithm also takes place. Consequently, the communication packet also includes the UAV's identifier (8 bits) and its 2-D coordinates (2×32 bits) as every UAVs is assumed to fly at the same altitude. All in all, packet length is 10,009 bytes in CACOC+, 450 bytes in CACOC+.10, 130 bytes in CACOC+.05, and 9 bytes in CACOC+.00. Note that this is actually the payload of the communication packet as we are not considering protocol specific data in our study. The communication layer used was "range and bearing" as provided by ARGoS.

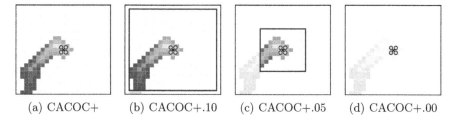

(a) CACOC+   (b) CACOC+.10   (c) CACOC+.05   (d) CACOC+.00

Fig. 4. Pheromone transmission scenarios. In CACOC+ each UAV shares all its pheromone map (10,000 cells). UAVs share 441 cells in CACOC+.10, 121 cells in CACOC+.05, and none in CACOC+.00.

Figure 4 shows an example of the pheromone map shared by a UAV via *ad hoc* wireless communications corresponding to each scenario analysed in our approach. It is worth mentioning that each UAV has access to its own pheromone map at any time. What a UAV receives is the portion of the global pheromone map transmitted (known) by the other (neighbouring) UAVs. We assumed that at the flying altitude there are no obstacles in the scenario.

5.2 CACOC+ Optimisation

We have performed 30 independent runs of the proposed GA on each case study and scenario, i.e. 360 runs in total. GA was configured to stop after 1,000 evaluations, a population of 16 individuals ($\lambda = \mu = 16$), 0.9 as crossover probability (P_c), and $\frac{1}{L}$ as mutation probability (P_m). The results obtained during the optimisation process are shown in Table 1.

Table 1. Optimisation results: fitness values (average, standard deviation, and maximum) of each optimisation run for each case study and scenario.

Case study	Scenario	Fitness			Friedman rank	Wilcoxon p-value
		Avg.	SD.	Max.		
2 UAVs	CACOC+	0.524	0.005	0.538	2.50	0.365
	CACOC+.10	0.523	0.006	0.535	2.10	0.325
	CACOC+.05	0.525	0.006	0.535	2.68	0.802
	CACOC+.00	**0.526**	0.007	**0.539**	**2.72**	—
4 UAVs	CACOC+	0.769	0.006	0.780	2.28	0.087
	CACOC+.10	0.771	0.007	**0.788**	2.70	0.640
	CACOC+.05	0.769	0.005	0.782	2.22	0.120
	CACOC+.00	**0.772**	0.006	0.786	**2.80**	—
6 UAVs	CACOC+	0.885	0.005	0.895	2.48	0.246
	CACOC+.10	**0.887**	0.004	**0.897**	**2.70**	—
	CACOC+.05	0.885	0.004	0.893	2.52	0.133
	CACOC+.00	0.884	0.006	0.896	2.30	0.058

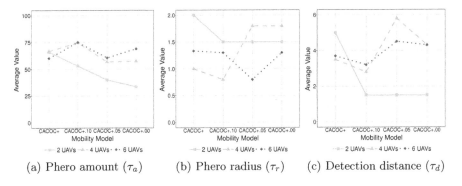

(a) Phero amount (τ_a)   (b) Phero radius (τ_r)   (c) Detection distance (τ_d)

Fig. 5. Average values of the CACOC+'s optimised parameters for each UAV.

It can be seen that CACOC+ achieves very similar results for all the scenarios of each case study. Best average fitness values of CACOC+ for 2 UAVs are 0.526, 0.772 for 4 UAVs, and 0.887 for 6 UAVs. Statistical tests (Friedman Rank and Wilcoxon p-value) show that the differences between the results of each case study are not statistically significant (p-value always greater than 0.01). This means that CACOC+ has compensated the lack of information about the global pheromone map by adapting their operational parameters to keep competitive fitness values, as shown in Fig. 5. Two UAVs show a clear parameter decreasing pattern when less data are shared, although the others case studies do not present such a pattern. We believe that it is due to the fact that there are more UAVs in the scenarios and the number of iterations (including collision avoidance) are higher as well as the complexity of the problem.

5.3   Experimental Results

The next experiment consisted in comparing the CACOC+ results against CACOC and CROMM. Table 2 shows the area coverage values of those mobility models. It can be seen that the values achieved by CACOC+ are consistent with the fitness values previously reported. UAVs using CACOC cover less area than CACOC+ as expected. When the UAVs controlled by CACOC were subject to the same communication restrictions as CACOC+, their coverage values showed bigger variability, being notably affected by the amount of pheromones shared between them, especially when there are more pheromones in the scenario (more UAVs). Note that each UAV still has access to its own pheromone map even if there is no communication with its counterparts.

The lowest CROMM coverage values confirm the need of virtual pheromones as a complement of chaotic mobility to improve the area coverage of the surveillance system. All in all, CACOC+ covered up to 53.9% of the surveillance area when using 2 UAVs, up to 78.8% when using 4 UAVs, and up to 89.7% when using 6 UAVs. That represents a maximum increment of around 7% with respect to CACOC and of around 41% with respect to CROMM. When there are communication restrictions, CACOC+ shown increments up to 15% in area coverage. Note that unpredictable chaotic trajectories perform unexpected turns and usually visit the same spot (despite pheromones). This is a desired feature in a surveillance system which, in turn, reduces the total area explored by UAVs compared with a highly predictable lawnmower model.

Table 2. Area coverage achieved by each scenario of CACOC+. CROMM and CACOC with the same communication restrictions are also included for comparison.

Case study	2 UAV	4 UAV	6 UAV
CROMM	13.3%	43.5%	52.2%
CACOC	46.5%	71.0%	85.8%
CACOC.10	46.5%	68.7%	85.8%
CACOC.05	46.5%	71.6%	84.2%
CACOC.00	38.8%	70.2%	80.0%
CACOC+	53.8%	78.0%	89.5%
CACOC+.10	53.5%	**78.8%**	**89.7%**
CACOC+.05	53.5%	78.2%	89.3%
CACOC+.00	**53.9%**	78.6%	89.6%

5.4   Interferences and Packet Loss

The last study comprises an analysis about the resilience of CACOC+ when it is subject to interferences, e.g. packet loss. Figure 6 shows the area coverage achieved by CACOC+ subject to different packet loss probabilities. Since the collision avoidance algorithm also uses radio communications to detect and avoid other UAVs, the vehicle trajectories were also affected by these new late detections as seen in CACOC+.00. Moreover, we were unable to complete our tests up to 100% packet loss for 4 and 6 UAVs since some vehicles were closer than the safety threshold (2 m) and the simulation was stopped. The amount of area covered decreased when the communication link failed, as expected. However, in most of the analysed scenarios, before reaching very low coverage values, the rest of the system features were degraded, e.g. the collision avoidance algorithm, especially when the number of UAVs was higher and the collisions were more probable. It can be seen a small increment in the area coverage for some case studies at higher packet loss probabilities. Even if the maximum coverage (at zero packet loss) is never reached, this counter-intuitive behaviour has to be further analysed in a future work.

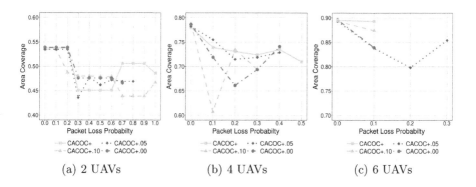

(a) 2 UAVs   (b) 4 UAVs   (c) 6 UAVs

Fig. 6. Area coverage achieved using CACOC+ vs. packet loss probability.

6   Conclusions and Future Work

In this article we have proposed a more realistic approach to a swarm of UAVs using the CACOC mobility model by modelling real communication links. We have optimised its parameterised version, CACOC+, initially proposed to improve area coverage, with the aim of keeping good performance values even when each UAV knows only its own local pheromone map. The well-known simulator ARGoS was used in our experimentation to implement the mobility models and the data transmission layer.

Our results show that CACOC+ still improves CACOC under these new conditions and that the versatility of the UAV parameterisation has compensated the reduced knowledge of the pheromone neighbourhood. Furthermore, the UAVs trajectories, now adapted to the new environmental conditions, keep obtaining good coverage values until the defective communications affect other aspects of the system, such as the collision avoidance algorithm.

As larger data packets increase the probability of transmission errors, CACOC+ showed to be more resilient to communications failures as the amount of transmitted data can easily be reduced from 10,009 to 9 bytes (99.9% shorter) without experiencing a reduction of the area explored by UAVs. The energy consumed by vehicles was not analysed but it is assumed to be lower as their onboard radio has a reduced duty cycle.

As a matter of future work we would like to test our approach on larger scenarios, including more UAVs, and improve the system precision by using a specific parameter for each UAV, to define the portion of its pheromone map to be shared with the others. The analysis of the influence of each parameters on the results is another interesting future work. An alternative collision avoidance algorithm is to be tested using, for example, a different approach based on onboard sensors. Finally, we intend to validate our trajectories using real drones and also extend our analysis taking into account power consumption.

Acknowledgments. This work relates to Department of Navy award N62909-18-1-2176 issued by the Office of Naval Research. The United States Government has a royalty-free license throughout the world in all copyrightable material contained herein. This work is partially funded by the joint research programme UL/SnT-ILNAS on Digital Trust for Smart-ICT. The experiments presented in this paper were carried out using the HPC facilities of the University of Luxembourg [20] – see https://hpc.uni.lu.

References

1. Campion, M., Ranganathan, P., Faruque, S.: UAV swarm communication and control architectures: a review. J. Unmanned Veh. Syst. **7**(2), 93–106 (2019). https://doi.org/10.1139/juvs-2018-0009
2. Chelouah, R., Siarry, P.: Continuous genetic algorithm designed for the global optimization of multimodal functions. J. Heuristics **6**(2), 191–213 (2000). https://doi.org/10.1023/A:1009626110229
3. Dronecode Project: MAVLink: Micro Air Vehicle Communication Protocol (2021). https://mavlink.io/en/
4. Fabra, F., Calafate, C.T., Cano, J.C., Manzoni, P.: On the impact of inter-UAV communications interference in the 2.4 GHz band. In: 2017 13th International Wireless Communications and Mobile Computing Conference (IWCMC), pp. 945–950. IEEE (2017). https://doi.org/10.1109/IWCMC.2017.7986413
5. Galceran, E., Carreras, M.: A survey on coverage path planning for robotics. Robot. Auton. Syst. **61**(12), 1258–1276 (2013). https://doi.org/10.1016/j.robot.2013.09.004
6. Goldberg, D.E.: Genetic Algorithms in Search, Optimization and Machine Learning, 1st edn. Addison-Wesley Longman Publishing Co. Inc., Boston, MA, USA (1989)
7. Goldberg, D.E., Deb, K.: A comparative analysis of selection schemes used in genetic algorithms. Found. Genet. Algorithms **1**, 69–93 (1991). https://doi.org/10.1016/B978-0-08-050684-5.50008-2
8. Gupta, L., Jain, R., Vaszkun, G.: Survey of important issues in UAV communication networks. IEEE Commun. Surv. Tutor. **18**(2), 1123–1152 (2016). https://doi.org/10.1109/COMST.2015.2495297

9. Holland, J.H.: Adaptation in Natural and Artificial Systems. The MIT Press (1992). https://doi.org/10.7551/mitpress/1090.001.0001
10. McNeal, G.S.: Drones and the future of aerial surveillance. George Wash. Law Rev. Arguendo **84**(2), 354–416 (2016)
11. Olivieri de Souza, B.J., Endler, M.: Coordinating movement within swarms of UAVs through mobile networks. In: 2015 IEEE International Conference on Pervasive Computing and Communication Workshops (PerCom Workshops), pp. 154–159. IEEE (2015). https://doi.org/10.1109/PERCOMW.2015.7134011
12. Pinciroli, C., et al.: ARGoS: a modular, parallel, multi-engine simulator for multi-robot systems. Swarm Intell. **6**(4), 271–295 (2012). https://doi.org/10.1007/s11721-012-0072-5
13. Rosalie, M., Danoy, G., Chaumette, S., Bouvry, P.: Chaos-enhanced mobility models for multilevel swarms of UAVs. Swarm Evol. Comput. **41**, 36–48 (2018). https://doi.org/10.1016/j.swevo.2018.01.002
14. Rosalie, M., Letellier, C.: Systematic template extraction from chaotic attractors: II. Genus-one attractors with multiple unimodal folding mechanisms. J. Phys. A: Math. Theor. **48**(23), 235101 (2015). https://doi.org/10.1088/1751-8113/48/23/235101
15. Scherer, J., Rinner, B.: Multi-robot persistent surveillance with connectivity constraints. IEEE Access **8**, 15093–15109 (2020). https://doi.org/10.1109/ACCESS.2020.2967650
16. Stolfi, D.H., Brust, M.R., Danoy, G., Bouvry, P.: A cooperative coevolutionary approach to maximise surveillance coverage of UAV swarms. In: 2020 IEEE 17th Annual Consumer Communications and Networking Conference. CCNC 2020, pp. 1–6. IEEE (2020). https://doi.org/10.1109/CCNC46108.2020.9045643
17. Stolfi, D.H., Brust, M.R., Danoy, G., Bouvry, P.: Competitive evolution of a UAV swarm for improving intruder detection rates. In: 2020 IEEE International Parallel and Distributed Processing Symposium Workshops (IPDPSW), pp. 528–535. IEEE (2020). https://doi.org/10.1109/IPDPSW50202.2020.00094
18. Stolfi, D.H., Brust, M.R., Danoy, G., Bouvry, P.: Emerging inter-swarm collaboration for surveillance using pheromones and evolutionary techniques. Sensors **20**(9) (2020). https://doi.org/10.3390/s20092566
19. Stolfi, D.H., Brust, M.R., Danoy, G., Bouvry, P.: UAV-UGV-UMV multi-swarms for cooperative surveillance. Front. Robot. AI **8** (2021). https://doi.org/10.3389/frobt.2021.616950
20. Varrette, S., Bouvry, P., Cartiaux, H., Georgatos, F.: Management of an academic HPC cluster: the UL experience. In: 2014 International Conference on High Performance Computing & Simulation (HPCS), pp. 959–967. IEEE, Bologna, Italy (2014). https://doi.org/10.1109/HPCSim.2014.6903792
21. Zeng, T., Mozaffari, M., Semiari, O., Saad, W., Bennis, M., Debbah, M.: Wireless communications and control for swarms of cellular-connected UAVs. In: 2018 52nd Asilomar Conference on Signals, Systems, and Computers, pp. 719–723. IEEE (2018). https://doi.org/10.1109/ACSSC.2018.8645472

UAV-UGV Multi-robot System for Warehouse Inventory: Scheduling Issues

Frédéric Guinand[1,2]($\boxtimes$) (ID), François Guérin[3] (ID), and Etienne Petitprez[1,4] (ID)

[1] Normandie Univ, UNIHAVRE, LITIS, Le Havre, France
`frederic.guinand@univ-lehavre.fr`
[2] Cardinal Stefan Wyszynski University in Warsaw, Warsaw, Poland
[3] Normandie Univ, UNIHAVRE, GREAH, Le Havre, France
`francois.guerin@univ-lehavre.fr`
[4] Squadrone System, Grenoble, France
`etienne.petitprez@squadrone-system.com`

Abstract. Warehouse inventory is a tricky, costly and time-consuming operation. The advent of low cost off-the-shelf UAVs enables companies to envision, at short term, the deployment of fully automated solutions. The present work proposes a solution that sets up UAVs and UGVs for performing such tasks. Task allocation between UAVs and UGVs is driven by efficiency and security criteria. UAVs' role consists in performing the inventory (limited in our study to the task of reading bar codes on pallets located on racks). UGVs's role is to bring-and-drop UAVs at the extremities of aisles and to collect them after the completion of their inventory tasks. UAVs localization, within each aisle, is obtained by UWB-equipped plots installed by UGVs at each extremity of aisles. Resolution of the choreography of the whole, UGVs and UAVs, expressed as an optimization problem, constitutes the core of this work.

Keywords: Multi-robot system · Warehouse inventory · UAV-UGV cooperation · Optimization

1 Introduction

Inventory in large logistics warehouses is an unavoidable task incurring costs in time and money. In addition, performing inventory of goods gathered into pallets on racks, requires people to go up to 10 or even 15 meters high in the warehouse. For coping with these situations, that might be dangerous, the warehouse and the conditions in which the inventory can be done have to be carefully and long prepared. Using robots offers an alternative solution that could enable companies to save time and money and that would also reduce the risk of injuries for people working in the warehouse. Because of the height any robotic-based inventory solution requires the use of devices able to reach the top of racks. This could be done using a robot moving on the ground equipped with a vertical mast or

© Springer Nature Switzerland AG 2021
N. T. Nguyen et al. (Eds.): ICCCI 2021, LNAI 12876, pp. 241–254, 2021.
https://doi.org/10.1007/978-3-030-88081-1_18

using UAVs (unmanned aerial vehicles). The first solution implies the presence of reading devices all along the mast since labels (bar codes for instance) are usually not regularly positioned on the pallets. The size of the mast has to suit exactly the height of the racks, it can be telescopic and one difficulty is its stabilization while the ground robot is moving. Geodis and Delta Drone proposed a solution by using a drone for this stabilization [1]. The second solution offers more flexibility since UAV can reach pallets located at whatever height, and several big companies have already investigated the problem of using UAVs for inventory but very few information about technical details or architecture design have been published. The problem can be addressed at different level, from theoretical approaches to functional prototypes development.

In [4], the authors proposed a prototype composed of one UGV and one UAV. Using IR camera and diodes, the UGV plays the role of a beacon enabling the UAV to localize itself in the aisle of the warehouse and to realize the reading of bar codes thanks to an embedded smartphone [2]. When multiple UAVs are considered, Ong and his colleagues [6] proposed in 2007 one of the first works dedicated to this problem. They consider a set of six UAVs equipped with RFID readers. The movements of UAVs is described as a "vertical zigzag motion" and they randomly change when an obstacle is detected. In their work UAVs are not collaborating, and thus can read the same RFID tags at different moment of time, but, despite this absence of coordination, simulation results suggest that the time needed to complete the inventory decreases linearly with the number of deployed machines. Computing trajectories for several UAVs is also investigated in the work of Choi and his colleagues [3]. The issue is expressed as an optimization problem with the objective of minimizing the inventory time and to guarantee collision-free trajectories. The solution is computed in two phases. For the first phase, the warehouse is modeled as a graph and the initial and final depots are two nodes. The resulting problem is formulated as an arc-based routing problem coming with a set of constraints. Arcs represent routes that can be used by UAVs for moving with the warehouse but also represent inventory tasks for the shelves, in which case they have to be scanned. Once the vehicle routing problem has a solution, the second phase determines collision-free trajectories. With respect to our present work, the inventory of shelves located on one side of each aisle is performed by only one UAV, preventing any collision risk.

Recently, in [5], the authors address the inventory problem by an autonomous system composed of both UGVs (TIAGo Base) and UAVs (PX4-based). Experiments were conducted in a virtual environment modeled using the Gazebo software. Close to the idea developed in our work, UGVs are used for carrying UAVs, such that drones are flying only when they are located within aisles. Like in [4], UGVs positions are references for UAVs to perform tags reading but, unlike in our model, UAVs are only flying vertically, no horizontal move is allowed, and between two vertical movements at different horizontal positions, UAVs land on and then takeoff from the UGVs.

In this paper, we address the warehouse inventory problem and for solving it, we propose a system based on the cooperation between Unmanned Ground Vehicles (UGV) and Unmanned Aerial Vehicles (UAV) to cover large scale facilities. To avoid pre-installation of indoor localisation systems and to enable UGVs to move away from UAVs, Ultra Wide Band plots (UWB) are settled at the extremities of aisles. Plots are placed by UGVs at the ends of aisles and UAVs can start their inventory task for one aisle only when one plot is present at each extremity of the aisle. When a UAV has completed its task in one aisle, it waits for a UGV to collect it. We first model the problem and show that a relaxed version of it remains NP-Hard. The problem is formulated as an optimization problem. We show that UAVs have not to be considered explicitly for solving the problem. We then propose two methods, a greedy one and an iterative one for scheduling UGV tasks.

In Sect. 2 the problem is modeled, and the optimization problem corresponding to the warehouse inventory is analysed and a lower bound is determined. Two methods, a greedy one based on a priority list, and an iterative one are described in Sect. 3 and their results are compared with each other and with the lower bound in Sect. 4.

2   Models and Problem Analysis

2.1   Problem Description

In the context of our study, the inventory task consists in reading barcodes on pallets using ground robots (UGVs) and aerial drones (UAVs). For localization purpose, drones can perform their tasks within one aisle only when two plots are positioned on both extremities of it. Plots and UAVs are carried by UGVs. UAVs can only fly within aisles but not between two different aisles. Moving UAVs and plots from one part of the warehouse to another part is done by UGVs. In the current problem we consider that each aisle is processed by two UAVs, one for each side of the aisle.

UGVs thus perform four different tasks: drop a plot, drop a drone, collect a plot and collect a drone. These tasks are respectively denoted by $T_{dp}, T_{dd}, T_{cp}, T_{cd}$. UGVs are also moving within the warehouse, following predefined and constrained paths.

UAVs perform four different tasks: takeoff from the UGV and move to the starting point, make inventory (work), fly to the collect point, land on the UGV. These tasks are respectively denoted by $T_{fs}, T_w, T_{fc}, T_{fu}$.

The problem under study consists in determining the best scheduling of UGV tasks such as to minimize the time needed for completing the inventory of the whole warehouse. Using scheduling terminology, the objective is to minimize the makespan denoted as C_{max}.

2.2   Optimization Problem Analysis

In order to have an idea of the complexity of the problem we relax the problem in four steps. For simplifying the problem we gather tasks T_{dp} and T_{dd} into only one task T_{drop}. Thus, when UGV is positioned at one extremity of an aisle, it drops simultaneously one plot and one drone. Symmetrically, collection of a plot and a drone is considered as only one task: $T_{collect}$.

Tasks performed by drones form a precedence chain: $T_{fs} \prec T_w \prec T_{fc} \prec T_{fu}$, where $a \prec b$ means a precedes b. Then, as there is no freedom for the execution order of the tasks by a drone, we gather all the tasks into only one: T_{inv}

UGVs are not directly concerned by UAVs tasks. If we consider that each task T_{drop} and $T_{collect}$ are one unit execution time tasks and that T_{inv} are k units execution time tasks, the precedence task graph that should be performed by UGVs can be represented as illustrated by Fig. 1. This relaxation enables UAVs to be removed from the problem formulation.

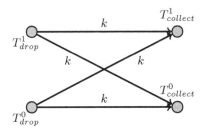

Fig. 1. Precedence tasks graph for UGVs's tasks for one aisle.

From a relaxation point of view, we may consider either that each robot can carry as many UAVs and plots as needed or that it can only carry two UAVs and two plots. Considering number of UGVs, we can consider an unlimited number of UGVs or only one.

Let now consider the following problem formulation which constitutes a simplification of the original one.

- the system is composed on one UGV that carries two UAVs and two plots,
- the robot can only process one aisle at a time since two plots are required for a UAV to make the inventory,

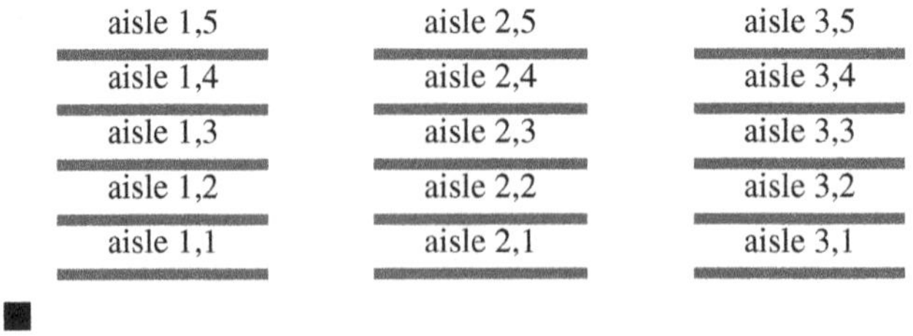

aisle 1,5	aisle 2,5	aisle 3,5
aisle 1,4	aisle 2,4	aisle 3,4
aisle 1,3	aisle 2,3	aisle 3,3
aisle 1,2	aisle 2,2	aisle 3,2
aisle 1,1	aisle 2,1	aisle 3,1

Fig. 2. Simplified version of a warehouse. Red lines represent aisles. The warehouse is composed of 3 zones of 5 aisles. (Color figure online)

- we also suppose that the inventory task is non preemptable (cannot be interrupted),
- when the inventory of one aisle is done, the UGV chooses another one for processing it,
- when all aisles are done, UGV turn back to its initial position.

From these elements, the processing of aisle A_i can be considered as a task T_i gathering all UGV's and UAV's tasks. If we consider a warehouse as the one illustrated by Fig. 2, in the initial configuration of the problem, the UGV (black rectangle) has to go through all aisles before turning back to its initial position. Between two tasks, UGV has to move, but the time needed for moving from one aisle to another one depends on the current position of the robot (to the left or to the right of the processed aisle), in order to simplify the problem, we consider only the minimum distance between two aisles.

This problem can be represented as a full-connected task graph. Each vertex T_i of the graph represents the homonym task (T_i gathers all UGV's and UAVs tasks performed on aisle A_i) and an edge between two vertices represent the minimum distance/time needed for the UGV to move from one aisle to the other one, as represented by Fig. 3). The goal of the UGV is to visit all vertices while minimizing the total traveled distance. This problem corresponds to the well known traveling salesman problem (TSP), known to be NP-hard. As a consequence, without additional information about distances between aisles, the original problem under study in this work is also NP-hard which leads us to propose heuristic methods for computing schedules.

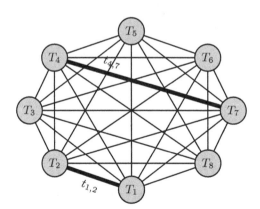

Fig. 3. Representation of the problem as a full-connected tasks graph. Each task gathers all the tasks needed to make the inventory of one aisle. Edges between Vertices are valuated by the time $t_{i,j}$ (or distance if we consider a constant speed) required by the UGV to move from aisle A_i to aisle A_j or from aisle A_j to A_i.

2.3   A Simple Lower Bound

However, in order to be able to compare algorithms performances, we propose to compute a simple lower bound on the time needed for performing the warehouse inventory. If we denote by T_{inv} the time needed for a drone to process one side on an aisle, and if the warehouse is composed of n aisles, the total amount of inventory time is $2n \times T_{inv}$, and if our system is composed of k drones then,

$$C_{max}^* \geq L_{min} = \frac{2n \times T_{inv}}{k}$$

3   Methods and Algorithms

From the conclusion of the previous section, we propose two different approaches. The first one, a list-scheduling algorithm, aims at computing quickly a schedule for UGVs. This is a greedy algorithm, once a task has been allocated to an UGV, this choice cannot be changed. The second approach, a probabilistic iterative method, builds a solution based on choosing actions according to the probability of each available action and the previous ones. For each iteration, it runs the same process but ends probably to another solution. In the end, the algorithm selects the best solution discovered.

The warehouse is modeled as a graph whose vertices correspond to positions where UGVs perform their drop and collect tasks and have thus a precise localization in the warehouse. We denote by $E_{i,j}$ (reps. $W_{i,j}$) the nodes of the East (resp. West) extremity of the jth aisle of the ith zone. One more vertex, denoted by G (standing for garage), is added to the graph for modeling the place where UGVs are initially positioned before starting the inventory. Edges are routes on which UGVs move to travel from one point to another (see Fig. 4). The mobility of UGVs follows the Manhattan-like mobility model, allowing only horizontal and vertical moves. If L denotes the length of an aisle, l_z the distance between two neighbor zones and l_a the distance between two contiguous aisles, the distance between $E_{i,j}$ and $W_{i',j'}$ is:

– if $i' > i$,

$$d(E_{i,j}, W_{i',j'}) = (i' - i)l_z + vabs(j' - j)l_a + 2L$$

– if $i' < i$

$$d(E_{i,j}, W_{i',j'}) = (i - i')l_z + vabs(j' - j)l_a$$

– if $i = i'$

$$d(E_{i,j}, W_{i,j'}) = vabs(j' - j)l_a + L$$

Collisions between UGVs are not taken into account.

The task model considered for UGVs is different in the two proposed approaches. In the list-scheduling algorithm, each UGV performs only two types of tasks: drop and collect of both plots and drones, while in the iterative method, each UGV performs four different tasks, the ones originally described in the introduction: T_{dp}, T_{dd}, T_{cp} and T_{cd}. However, in both cases, UAVs can start inventory of one aisle only when each extremity has a plot positioned.

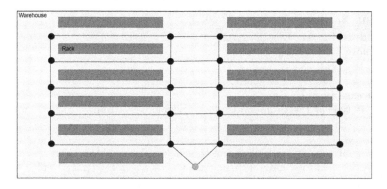

Fig. 4. Warehouse model. Two zones, each of 5 aisles. Black vertices are locations were plots and UAVs are dropped and collected. Edges, black and red, are paths UGVs can use for moving from one place to another one

3.1   List-Scheduling Algorithm

The first proposed method is a list-scheduling algorithm based on a priority computed from estimated tasks completion times. All tasks, executed by UAVs and UGVs, and their duration are assumed to be known offline. Each drop (resp. collect) task is denoted E^d_{place} or W^d_{place} (resp. E^c_{place} or W^c_{place}), where *place* corresponds to the position (zone number, aisle number) in the warehouse at which the task should be done. A task is said available if all tasks that precede it have been completed. For each available task its release date is computed. At start, all drop tasks are available and no collect task is available. Initially drop tasks release dates are equal to 0, but their completion time differs since the date at which plots and drones can be dropped depends on to task position in the warehouse.

At start, all UGVs are located in G thus, if we denote $c(T)$ the completion time of task T, T_{pos} its position and $e(T)$ its execution time (described in Algorithm 1): $c(T) = t_{move}(G, T_{pos}) + e(T)$ where $t_{move}(G, T_{pos})$ denotes the time needed for an UGV to move from G to the position of task T.

Algorithm 1. Initialization of the priority List

1: **procedure** Init(L_{prio})
2:     **for** $i \leftarrow 1$ to z **do**
3:         **for** $j \leftarrow 1$ to m **do**
4:             $c(E^d_{i,j}) \leftarrow t_{move}(G, E_{i,j})$
5:             insert $\{(E^d_{i,j}, c(E^d_{i,j}), U_0)\}$ in L_{prio}

More generally, if U_k denotes a UGV and P_k its current position, the completion time of a drop task T, on U_k, is greater or equal to its release date, $r(T)$, plus the time needed for U_k to move from its current position to

---

Algorithm 2. Update Priority of task T

1: **procedure** UPDATETASK(T, L_{prio})
2:     remove T from L_{prio}
3:     $c(T) \leftarrow \infty$
4:     $U_{chosen} \leftarrow \emptyset$
5:     **for** each UGV U_k **do**
6:         **if** type of T is drop and U_k has available UAV **then**
7:             $c'(T) \leftarrow t_{available}(U_k) + t_{move}P(P_k, T_{pos}) + e(T)$
8:         **else**
9:             **if** type of T is collect and U_k has less than r UAVs **then**
10:                $c'(T) = max(r(T), t_{available}(U_k) + t_{move}(P_k, T_{pos})) + e(T)$
11:        **if** $c'(T) < c(T)$ **then**
12:            $c(T) \leftarrow c'(T)$
13:            $U_{chosen} \leftarrow U_k$
        insert $\{(T, c(T), U_{chosen})\}$ in L_{prio}

---

the task position, $(t_{move}(P_k, T_{pos}))$, plus its execution time, $e(T)$: $c(T, U_k) = r(T) + t_{move}(P_k, T_{pos}) + e(T)$ For each such task T, the minimum completion time over all UGV is computed (as described by Algorithm 2):

$$(c_{min}(T), U_{min}) = \min_{U_k \in \{UGVs\}} (r(T) + t_{move}(P_k, T_{pos}) + e(T))$$

and the triplet $(T, c_{min}(T), U_{min})$ is added to the priority list L_{prio}: $L_{prio} = L_{prio} \cup \{(T, c_{min}(T), U_{min})\}$

When all available tasks have been added to the list, the one with the highest priority is allocated to the corresponding UGV and UGV characteristics are updated (described in Algorithm 3). During the scheduling, if, for one specific aisle, one drop task has been scheduled (for instance task $E_{i,j}^d$ has been scheduled), then the second drop task ($W_{i,j}^d$) is given a priority higher than the priority of other drop or collect tasks (Algorithm 2). When the two drop tasks of the same aisle, $E_{i,j}^d$ and $W_{i,j}^d$, have been scheduled, the corresponding collect tasks, $E_{i,j}^c$ and $W_{i,j}^c$, are considered as available, their release dates are equal to:

Algorithm 3. Update the schedule

1: **procedure** UPDATESCHEDULE(T, U_k, L_{prio})
2:     $t_{availability}(U_k) \leftarrow c(T)$
3:     update number of available UAVs (and plots) of U
4:     $P_k \leftarrow T_{pos}$
5:     **if** type of T is drop and sister(T) is scheduled **then**
6:         given E_{pos}^c and W_{pos}^c the corresponding collect tasks
7:         $r(E_{pos}^c) \leftarrow c(T) + T_{inv}$
8:         $r(W_{pos}^c) \leftarrow c(T) + T_{inv}$
9:         insert $\{(E_{pos}^c, \infty, U_k)\}$ in L_{prio}
10:        insert $\{(W_{pos}^c, \infty, U_k)\}$ in L_{prio}

Algorithm 4. List-Scheduling Algorithm
1: **procedure** SCHEDULE
2:     $k \leftarrow$ number of UGVs
3:     $r \leftarrow$ number of UAVs per UGV
4:     $z \leftarrow$ number of zones
5:     $m \leftarrow$ number of aisles per zone
6:     $L_{prio} \leftarrow \emptyset$
7:     **for** each UGV U_k **do**
8:         $P_k \leftarrow G$ // initial position of UGVs
9:         $d_{available}(U_k) \leftarrow 0$
10:    Init(L_{prio})
11:    **while** $L_{prio} \neq \emptyset$ **do**
12:        $(T, c(T), U) \leftarrow$ remove first element of L_{prio}
13:        UpdateSchedule(T,U,L_{prio})
14:        **for** each task $T \in L_{prio}$ **do**
15:            UpdateTask(T,L_{prio})

$$r(E_{i,j}^c) = r(W_{i,j}^c) = \max\left(c(E_{i,j}^d), c(W_{i,j}^d)\right) + T_{inv}$$

and their completion time depends on the chosen UGV. The completion time of $E_{i,j}^c$ on U_k is equal to $c(E_{i,j}^c) = \max\left(r(E_{i,j}^c), d_{available}(U_k) + t_{move}(P_k, E_{i,j}))\right) + e(E_{i,j}^c)$ where $d_{available}(U)$ denotes the date at which UGV U will complete its last scheduled task (Algorithm 3).

From what precedes, we propose algorithm 4 for computing the scheduling of UGVs's tasks.

3.2   An Iterative/Probabilistic Method

Unlike the previous algorithm, UGVs do not necessarily drop simultaneously plots and UAVs, but for a given aisle, a UGV can drop a UAV only if a plot is already positioned at one of its extremities.

Algorithm 5. Iterative Probabilistic Algorithm
1: **procedure** SCHEDULE
2:     **while** $\exists$ tasks to achieve **do**
3:         Selection of the next available UGV_k
4:         Update tasks available for UGV_k
5:         Selection of the next task T_i for UGV_k
6:         Update state variables of UGV_k (location, tasks, resources)
7:         Time of UGV_k increases by duration of realization of T_i
8:         **for** each aisle n **do**
9:             **if** $n \subset$ plots $== 2$ and UAVs ≥ 1 **then**
10:                Start inventory in aisle n
11:        Update tasks

The algorithm presented in this section constructs solution step by step according to the warehouse inventory progress. During the inventory process, when an UGV has completed its last task, it chooses a new one among the set of available tasks.

In order to assess the weight of a choice over others and compute its probability of selection, the algorithm firstly estimates their interests. The interest of a task T_i is defined as the product of decision-making factors to the power of their importance. Thus, we considered two factors for each task:

- The quality η which is only a function of the completion time of the UGV concerned since it depends on its current location;
- The priority χ which gives more or less weight to quality according to optimality criteria.

For a UGV at instant t, the probability of selection P_i of T_i is defined by:

$$P_i(t) = \frac{\eta_i^\alpha * \chi_i^\beta}{\sum_i^n \eta_i^\alpha * \chi_i^\beta} \tag{1}$$

To determine the factor χ, we stated three levels of priority: low, medium and high, respectively denoted by L_p, M_p and H_p. Each type of task matches a rule to determine its priority.

When a T_{cp} task (collect a plot) is available, this means that all UAVs on the aisle have been picked up and at least one UGV is nearby. Thus, the priority of T_{cp} is set to high to limit one UGV to come-back later on and favor the renewal of resources. A T_{dp} (drop a plot) task is defined as a medium priority except when the other one of the aisle is installed, then it is set to high. As a reminder, T_{dd} (drop UAV) task can be chosen once a plot is settled in the aisle. The priority is then defined as high but is lowered with the amount of UAVs and drops when the number of UAVs in the aisle has reached the number of inventorable sides. Therefore, we designed a criterion C_{dd} to express this. For k the number of UAVs in the aisle:

$$C_{dd} = \begin{cases} H_p \text{ if } \lceil \frac{2}{k} \rceil > 1 \\ L_p \text{ else} \end{cases} \tag{2}$$

Finally, the collect UAV task priority depends on aisle inventory time estimated plus the travel time to the pick up location. The closer an UGV is reaching the sum of these durations in its time frame, the more prioritized is the task up to a maximum threshold that no longer fluctuates until it is handled. We synthesized it as C_{cd}.

$$C_{cd} = H_p * max \left(\frac{t + T_{travel}}{T_{inv}}, 1 \right) \tag{3}$$

Thereby, we depict the decision-making factors as followed:

$$\eta_i = \frac{\sum_i^n T_{task} + T_{travel}}{T_{task} + T_{travel}} \qquad \chi_i = \begin{cases} H_p \text{ if } T_{cp} \\ M_p \text{ or } H_p \text{ if } T_{dp} \\ C_{cd} \text{ if } T_{cd} \\ C_{dd} \text{ if } T_{dd} \end{cases} \tag{4}$$

4   Simulations/Use Case/Experimental Results

The two previously presented algorithms have been tested on the same use case for their simulation. In order to compare them, results are calculated according to the distance in percentage to the lower bound L_{min} depicted previously.

4.1   Use Case

For standard simulations, the warehouse is made up of two groups of six aisles. These are separated by rows containing the bar codes that must be read by the UAVs. The starting point of the UGVs is considered as punctual and of coordinates (24.1,5.5) in the warehouse plan with the origin at the bottom left. The nodes of the graph are arranged at a distance of ± 1.5 m along the y axis and ± 1 m for the x axis from the aisles as shown in Fig. 5. Each side of aisles is supposed to be inventoried within $T_{inv} = 306$ seconds here.

Regarding resources, we set two UGVs each carrying two UAVs and two plots. Regardless their autonomy, UGVs are moving at an average speed of 1 m/s.

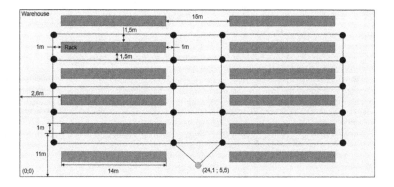

Fig. 5. Warehouse dimensions

4.2   Experimental Results

More than just comparing both methods, different scenarios were conducted to find relations between the warehouse composition (groups and number of aisles), the agents (UGVs and UAVs) and the time duration of the aisle inventory by one drone.

Therefore, we designed three following tests according to our forebodings.

– Scenario 1: for a constant total number of 8 UAVs, we varied the number of UGVs between 1 and 8.

- Scenario 2: we considered only one group of aisles, which number progressively increased, from 1 to 14.
- Scenario 3: we varied the value of T_{inv} (inventory time) from 82 to 658.

From the standard model of simulation, we varied one parameter and studied the completion time of the whole warehouse inventory.

For the iterative probabilistic algorithm, a hundred runs were conducted and each run corresponds to the best solution found over a hundred iterations. On the other side, the list-scheduling algorithm is a deterministic method which means that the result do not change with the same initial configuration.

In the table below, we gathered experimental results of each algorithm compared to the lower bound in percentage.

Scenario n°	Var.	Worst	Average	Best	List-Sch.
1 (# UGV)	1	259.43	238.78	209.86	98.04
	2	139.80	126.18	102.77	49.24
	4	75.87	67.40	53.64	29.09
	8	42.54	35.40	27.51	22.55
2 (# aisles)	1	64.89	64.89	64.89	159.48
	2	39.63	37.32	37.02	38.89
	3	40.37	37.31	32.52	69.28
	4	40.41	34.59	29.95	31.54
	5	40.82	35.87	27.75	51.24
	6	43.49	36.95	28.35	29.09
	7	45.50	38.19	23.84	43.51
	8	46.84	38.86	24.61	27.86
	9	46.21	39.90	31.90	39.22
	10	49.10	41.01	32.83	27.12
	11	49.69	42.50	34.18	36.48
	12	48.33	42.40	31.88	26.63
	13	49.03	42.80	33.20	34.59
	14	49.27	43.46	34.61	26.28
3 (T_{inv})	82	157.81	142.34	118.94	98.78
	218	68.40	59.59	47.03	37.16
	306	50.41	44.71	34.40	26.47
	438	40.16	32.10	23.38	18.49
	658	29.64	23.46	17.52	12.31

Simulation Results for Scenario 1. Variable number of UGVs and total number of UAVs: 8

Simulation Results for Scenario 2 (varying number of aisles)

Simulation Results for Scenario 3 (T_{inv} varying)

In the first experience, the warehouse inventory time shows small variations even if the number of UGVs fluctuates for the same amount of UAVs (except for one UGV). It can also be noted that the difference between the list-scheduling algorithm and the Iterative Probabilistic Algorithm (IPA) decreases when the number of UGVs increases.

In the second one, the quality of the schedules computed by IPA decreases when the number of aisles increases. This is due to the fact that number of iterations of IPA remains unchanged when the number of aisles increases. The results obtained by the list-scheduling algorithm depends on the parity of the number of aisle. If the number is even the obtained results are better than for odd numbers of aisles. This is due to the fact that only one UAV is allowed to perform the inventory on one side of every aisle, while IPA allows several UAVs to collaborate for one side inventory. The set of two UAVs per UGVs and two UGVs can carry on the inventory of two aisles at a time. For three UAVs, it would have been the same but every three aisles. It demonstrates the relation between the number of UAVs and the number of aisles.

In the last scenario, when the inventory time of a side of an aisle decreases, the ratio between C_{max} and L_{min} increases drastically. Indeed, when T_{inv} is large, the impact of UGVs's movement, which is not taken into account for computing L_{min}, is reduced. To which is added the fact that the movement for dropping the first UAV and plot and the last movement for collecting the last UAV and plot will never be overlapped by UAV's inventory tasks. On the overall set of experiences we made, the list-scheduling algorithm seems more efficient than the probabilistic one. However, the second scenario proves its robustness and adaptability to specific situations where the number of UGVs/UAVs is not well-suited with respect to the warehouse configuration.

5 Conclusion and Perspectives

In order to carry out efficiently a warehouse inventory, we proposed two methods using the cooperation of UGVs and UAVs. The list algorithm determines a schedule by gathering dropping tasks on one side and collecting tasks on the other. The probabilistic iterative algorithm constructs a sequence by selecting the next task at each step according to a weighted probability. As a consequence the search space considered by the probabilistic algorithm is much larger than the one considered by the list algorithm, this may explain that results obtained by the list algorithm are often better than the ones computed by the probabilistic algorithm. However, for specific cases, improvement can be expected for this second algorithm as illustrated by scenario 2. From the application point of view, it seems that for a given number of UAVs, increasing the number of UGVs improves the performances but a limit appears when the number of UAVs per UGV is equal to 2. Further experiments have to be carried to confirm this observation. From scenario 3 we can deduce that UGVs movements impact the performances as well as the relative time needed for dropping and collecting UAVs and plots. An in-depth analysis of produced schedules is required to draw relevant conclusions.

References

1. Geodis and delta drone countbot: an innovative warehouse-inventory solution. https://geodis.com/tr/en/press-release/geodis-and-delta-drone-launch-geodis-countbot-innovative-warehouse-inventory-solution. Accessed 30 Apr 2021
2. Drivelog project: UAV-UGV warehouse inventory prototype demonstration (2016). https://youtu.be/DzpY3pEbeYE. Accessed 30 Apr 2021

3. Choi, Y., Martel, M., Briceno, S.I., Mavris, D.N.: Multi-UAV trajectory optimization and deep learning-based imagery analysis for a UAS-based inventory tracking solution. In: AIAA Scitech 2019 Forum. American Institute of Aeronautics and Astronautics, January 2019
4. Harik, E.H.C., Guérin, F., Guinand, F., Brethé, J.F., Pelvillain, H.: Towards an autonomous warehouse inventory scheme. In: 2016 IEEE Symposium Series on Computational Intelligence (SSCI), pp. 1–8, December 2016
5. Khazetdinov, A., Aleksandrov, A., Zakiev, A., Magid, E., Hsia, K.-H.: RFID-based warehouse management system prototyping using a heterogeneous team of robots. In: Robots in Human Life. CLAWAR Association Ltd., August 2020
6. Ong, J.H., Sanchez, A., Williams, J.: Multi-UAV system for inventory automation. In: 2007 1st Annual RFID Eurasia. IEEE, September 2007

An Effective Correlation-Based Pair Trading Strategy Using Genetic Algorithms

Chun-Hao Chen[1] (iD), Wei-Hsun Lai[2] (iD), and Tzung-Pei Hong[2,3]([⊠]) (iD)

[1] Department of Information and Finance Management, National Taipei
University of Technology, Taipei 106, Taiwan
chchen@ntut.edu.tw
[2] Department of Computer Science and Engineering, National Sun Yat-Sen University,
Kaohsiung 804, Taiwan
m083040004@student.nsysu.edu.tw
[3] Department of Computer Science and Information Engineering, National
University of Kaohsiung, Kaohsiung 811, Taiwan
tphong@nuk.edu.tw

Abstract. In the stock market, trading strategies are commonly utilized to find trading signals to make a more profitable trading, and can be formed by various technical indicators. Based on the correlation of stocks, the pair trading strategy is then developed for trading. The process of a pair trading can be divided into two parts that are finding potential stock pairs and then deriving trading signals, including buying and selling signals. In the process, many parameters should be considered and it is not easy to obtain their appropriate setting. In this paper, we thus propose an approach for finding those parameters by the genetic algorithms. It first encodes the parameters of the correlation coefficient and Bollinger bands into a chromosome. The fitness value of every possible solution is evaluated by the return and number of trading. Experiments are also conducted on real datasets to show that the proposed method is better than the previous one in terms of return.

Keywords: Bollinger bands · Correlation coefficient · Genetic algorithms · Pair trading · Trading strategy

1 Introduction

Financial markets refer to activities and venues with a certain scale of financing, currency lending, and securities trading. In a modern and convenient society, transactions completed through electronic communications can also be regarded as part of the financial market. Participants in the financial market are not only the supply and demand of funds, but also individuals, enterprises, banks, brokers, securities companies, insurance companies, investment institutions and government agencies.

There are many investment tools in the financial market that can be used by investors, such as stock trading, foreign currency investment, passbook deposit, virtual currency trading, etc. The traditional and common trading method is to buy low and sell high.

© Springer Nature Switzerland AG 2021
N. T. Nguyen et al. (Eds.): ICCCI 2021, LNAI 12876, pp. 255–263, 2021.
https://doi.org/10.1007/978-3-030-88081-1_19

However, there are too many factors that affect the value of financial products. Investors cannot obtain all the information. Even if they obtain a large amount of information, they cannot accurately predict the trend. As a result, it is often different from the analysis. The direction of the market is often affected by events in the country and society, so investors are even more unable to predict these trends. Therefore, in addition to technical analysis, an investment must also take into account many factors and even speculate on future trends. This makes the investment strategy difficult and shows the importance of the investment strategy.

Pair trading is a widely used market-neutral strategy [1]. It is a common trading strategy that has nothing to do with market trends. It is also a statistical arbitrage method. The pairs trading allows investors to find two assets with related trends based on historical data. It predicts the future trend and obtains profit. Pair trading is not always profitable. When the portfolio of investment targets we hold has a trend that is not as expected, an appropriate stop loss is a necessary operation. Therefore, many studies focus on optimizing trading strategies have been proposed [2, 7–9].

In this research, based on the correlation coefficient and Bollinger bands, we propose a GA-based approach for finding parameters for pair trading. In chromosome representation, six parameters, including *cDay*, *cLimit*, *BBentryWidth*, *BBoutWidth*, *mDay*, and *oDay*, are encoded into a chromosome. The first two parameters are utilized to find the qualified stock pairs. The following four parameters are employed to find trading signals. Every chromosome is evaluated by the returns of all stock pairs and the number of trading. The genetic process is repeated until the termination conditions are reached. Experiments were also conducted on the real datasets to show the effectiveness of the proposed approach.

2 Literature Review

Pair trading is an essential statistical arbitrage technique used by hedge funds. In the 1980's, it was developed by the quantitative group under Nunzio Tartaglia at Morgan Stanley. The central concept of pair trading is to find two relevant investment targets through historical data analysis and predict their future trends. Another critical point of pair trading is the judgment of entering and exiting the market. Investors must set the judgment criteria so that the pair trading strategy can start and finish transactions.

Krauss et al. present an overview of pairs trading methods [1]. The research demonstrates five categories: (1) Distance methods. In this category, the baseline approach is proposed by Gatev et al. [3]. Their research is known as the GGR method. It is the first research based on the distance method that uses standardized historical prices to find potential pairs. In addition, Do et al. confirmed pair trading strategies performed well in profitability during long-term turbulence [4]. (2) Cointegration methods. Vidyamurthy provides the most cited work in this category [5]. The research develops a univariate cointegration approach to pair trading. (3) Time series methods. In this part, Elliott et al. described explicitly the spread with a mean-reverting Gaussian Markov chain observed in Gaussian noise is the well-known approach [6]. (4) Stochastic control methods, and (5) Other methods.

Besides, in recent years, Ronnachai et al. presented a method using the machine learning algorithm to learn the pair trading strategy in foreign exchange rates [2]. The results showed that the machine learning models can classify the profitable signal from price behavior but may lack consistency. Fil et al. presented the research of using pair trading in crypto-currency markets [7]. They applied the distance and cointegration methods, and the results showed that higher-frequency trading delivers significantly better performance. Shen et al. proposed a method that combines the cointegration concepts and pairs trading algorithms [8]. The results indicated that the trading algorithm they proposed can achieve outstanding performances. Huang et al. proposed the genetic Bollinger-band and correlation-coefficient based pairs trading algorithm [9]. In that algorithm, the genetic algorithms (GA) is utilized to find the three parameters that are (1) The correlation coefficient threshold, $cLimit$; (2) The parameter that affects the entry band of companies, $BBentryWidth$; (3) The parameter that affects the exit band of companies, $BBexitWidth$. Experiments showed that their algorithm is profitable. However, to find to a more profitable pair trading strategy, many factors should also be considered. In this paper, based on their approach, we attempted to design a more profitable algorithm for pair trading.

3 Proposed Approach

In this section, the proposed approach is stated. Firstly, the main components of the proposed approach are described, including chromosome representation, fitness function, and genetic operators. The pair trading process contains two phases: finding the stock pair and trading signals, and six parameters should be tuned. The chromosome representation is shown in Table 1.

Table 1. Chromosome representation.

cDay	cLimit	BBentryWidth	BBoutWidth	mDay	oDay

In Table 1, the first two parameters are used to find stock pairs. The first one means that $cDay$ days stock prices are used as a period to calculate the correlation coefficient. The second parameter $cLimit$ is a threshold, which is utilized to identify whether a stock pair is qualified. Because the Bollinger bands is used to find trading signals, it needs a predefined period to calculate the moving average value, $mDay$, a parameter to generate the up and down channels for finding buying signal, $BBentryWidth$, and a parameter to generate the up and down channels for finding selling signal, $BBoutWidth$. At last, the parameter $oDay$ is used to generate the range $[E_{T-oDay}, E_T]$, and then using the range to check whether the up or down channel value at time T is inside or outside the range to determine the selling or buying signals. The fitness value of a chromosome is calculated by the following formula:

$$Fitness(C_q) = \frac{\sum_{h=0}^{|entryList|} totalProfit_h(s_i, s_j)}{tradeCount}, \tag{1}$$

where $totalProfit_h(s_i, s_j)$ represents the total return of the h-th pair trading for the stock s_i and s_j, $entryList$ is a set that contains qualified stock pairs, and $tradeCount$ is the number of trading pairs. In other words, the fitness value of a chromosome is evaluated by the average return of all trading pairs.

As to the genetic operations, for the selection operation, it randomly compares two chromosomes and selects the better one to the next population until the number of chromosomes matches the population size. Then, the max-min arithmetical (*MMA*) crossover is used to generate new offspring. It first generates four offspring using the parent chromosomes, and then the best two out of the four chromosomes are kept. In the mutation process, the one-point mutation is employed to generate a new value randomly from a predefined range. The flowchart of the proposed approach is shown in Fig. 1.

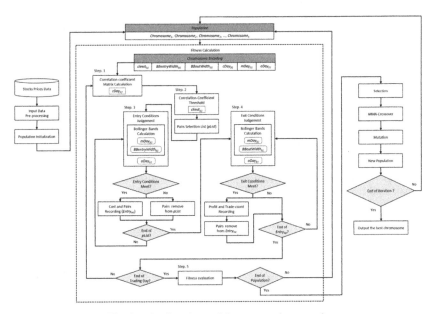

Fig. 1. The flowchart of the proposed approach.

Firstly, it collects the data and does pre-processing. Next, the population is initialized according to the encoding scheme and the population size randomly. For fitness calculation, in each trading day T, it calculates the correlation coefficient matrix of all companies (Step 1). The number of days for the calculation is the gene: *cDay*. After the matrix is produced, the gene: *cLimit* is used to check whether stock pairs are qualified (Step 2). Here, when the negative correlation of a stock pair large than *cLimit*, it is a qualified stock pair. The formula of the correlation coefficient is given as follows:

$$CC_{s_i s_j} \frac{\sum_{k=T-cDay_{ci}}^{T-1}\left(E_{ik} - \mu_{s_i}\right)\left(E_{jk} - \mu_{s_j}\right)}{\sqrt{\sum_{k=T-cDay_{ci}}^{T-1}\left(E_{ik} - \mu_{s_i}\right)^2\left(E_{jk} - \mu_{s_j}\right)^2}}. \tag{2}$$

Then, it generates the Bollinger-band channels for stock pairs (Step 3). The channels are calculated using the genes: *mDay* and *BBentryWidth*. *mDay* is used to calculate the moving average on date T. $BBentryWidth$ is used to calculate the upper and the lower channels. The formulas are given as follows:

$$UB_i(T) = MA_i(T) + BBentryWidth_{(c_i)} * \sqrt{\frac{\sum_{k=T-mDay_{ci}}^{T-1}(E_{ik} - \mu)^2}{mDay_{ci}}} \tag{3}$$

$$LB_i(T) = MA_i(T) - BBentryWidth_{(c_i)} * \sqrt{\frac{\sum_{k=T-mDay_{ci}}^{T-1}(E_{ik} - \mu)^2}{mDay_{ci}}} \tag{4}$$

$$MA_i(T) = \frac{\sum_{k=T-mDay_{ci}}^{T-1} E_{ik}}{mDay_{ci}} \tag{5}$$

Then, $oDay$ is used to check whether a qualified stock pair (s_i, s_j) is satisfied with the entry conditions that are (1) for stock s_i: $E_{i(T-oDay)} > UB_i(T) > E_{iT}$ and (2) for stock s_j: $E_{j(T-oDay)} < LB_j(T) < E_{jT}$, where $E_{h(T)}$ is the close price of stock s_h on date T. When both conditions are reached and $E_{iT} > E_{jT}$, the proposed approach will sell s_i and buy s_j, and the pair (s_i, s_j) will also be put into the set $enrtyList$. It then goes on the entry conditions judgment for the next pair until all pairs are processed.

Next, in Step 4, according to the $mDay$ and $BBoutWidth$, the Bollinger-band channels are generated again for the pair in the $enrtyList$. The channels are calculated using the following formulas:

$$US_i(T) = MA_i(T) + BBoutWidth_{(c_i)} * \sqrt{\frac{\sum_{k=T-mDay_{c_i}}^{T-1}(E_{ik} - \mu)^2}{mDay_{ci}}}, \tag{6}$$

$$LS_i(T) = MA_i(T) - BBoutWidth_{(c_i)} * \sqrt{\frac{\sum_{k=T-mDay_{ci}}^{T-1}(E_{ik} - \mu)^2}{mDay_{ci}}}. \tag{7}$$

When the pair meets the exiting conditions that are (1) for stock s_i: $E_{i(T-oDayci)} > LS_i(T) > E_{iT}$ and (2) for stock s_j: $E_{j(T-oDay)} < US_i(T) < E_{jT}$, the proposed approach will buy s_i and sell s_j. When a stock pair trading is done, it records the profit: $profit(s_i, s_j) = income(s_i, s_j)/cost(s_i, s_j)$, and the number of trading will plus one, $tradeCount$. After that, the trading pair (s_i, s_j) is removed from the $enrtyList$, and it goes to the exit conditions judgment for the next pair until all pairs are processed. Finally, the fitness value of a chromosome is set using formula (1), which is the profit of all trading pairs divided by the number of trading in Step 5. The genetic operators are executed to generate new offspring until the termination conditions are reached.

Based on the flowchart, the pseudocode of the proposed algorithm is stated in Table 2.

Table 2. Pseudocode of the proposed algorithm.

Proposed Pari Trading Optimization Algorithm:
Input:
Stocks $S = \{s_1, s_2, s_3, ..., s_n\}$, stock prices of a company $s_i = \{E_{i1}, E_{i2}, E_{i3}, ..., E_{iDayL}\}$.
Parameters:
Population P, population size $pSize$, number of iteration Itr, mutation rate r_m, crossover rate r_c, MMA value d, trading days Day_T, Last days Day_L.
Output:
The best chromosome.

1.	$S' \leftarrow$ DataPreprocessing(S);
2.	$P \leftarrow$ InitialPopulation ($pSize$);
3.	**WHILE** $i < Itr_{Max}$ **DO**
4.	**FOR** $q = 0$ to $pSize$ **DO**
5.	**FOR** $k = Day_T$ to Day_L **DO**
6.	$MT \leftarrow$ CCMatrixOperator(k, C_q, $cDay$, S');
7.	$pList \leftarrow$ CCThreshold(C_q, $cLimit$);
8.	$Entry_{list} \leftarrow$ EntryJudg(k, C_q, $mDay$, $BBentryWidth$, $oDay$, S');
9.	$gtsProfit$, $gtsCost$, $gtsTCount$
	$\leftarrow$ ExitJudg(k, C_q, $mDay$, $BBoutWidth$, $oDay$, $Entry_{list}$, S');
10.	**END** k **FOR LOOP**
11.	$P' \leftarrow$ FitnessCalculation(C_q, $gtsProfit$, $gtsCost$, $gtsTCount$);
12.	**END** q **FOR LOOP**
13.	$P' \leftarrow$ CrossoverOperator (P', R_c, d);
14.	$P''' \leftarrow$ MutationOperator (P'', R_m);
15.	$P \leftarrow$ SelectionOperator (P''', $pSize$);
16.	**END OF WHILE**
17.	**RETURN** OutputBestChromosome(P)

From Table 2, the data pre-processing is done, and the initial population P is randomly according to the predefined *pSize* (Lines 1 to 2). Then, the evolution process starts to find the solution (Lines 2 to 16). The fitness values of chromosomes are calculated based on the return and number of trading (Lines 4 to 12). For every chromosome, the correlation coefficient matrix is generated to find the qualified stock pairs, and they are put into *pList*. Then, the entry and exit conditions of every stock pair are discovered to get the return and number of trading (Lines 6 to 9). After that, the genetic operators are executed to generate offspring, including selection, crossover and mutation (Lines 13 to 15). Finally, if reaching the termination condition, the best chromosome is outputted (Lines 16 to 17).

4 Experimental Results

4.1 Dataset Description

The real-world datasets that contain 44 stocks selected from the Taiwan stock market are used in the experiments. The first dataset is collected from 2009 to 2013 for comparing the proposed approach with the previous approach [9]. The training period is four-years data (2009–2012), and the testing period is one-year data (2013). The second dataset is collected from 2016 to 2020, which is used to verify whether the proposed algorithm is profitable in recent years.

4.2 Comparison of the Proposed and Previous Approaches

In the experiments, the proposed approach is compared to the previous approach in terms of returns. The training period is from 2009 to 2012, and the testing period is 2013 for both approaches. The results are shown in Fig. 2.

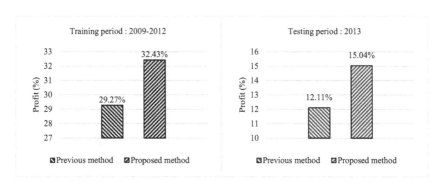

Fig. 2. Comparison between the previous and proposed approaches.

From Fig. 2, we can observe that the proposed approach is better than the previous approach in terms of returns, no matter in training or testing phases. The results show that the proposed approach is effective.

4.3   Results of the Second Dataset

In this subsection, experiments were then made to see whether the proposed approach is profitable in recent years. The periods of training and testing are from 2016 to 2019 and 2020, respectively. The returns of the proposed approach are shown in Fig. 3.

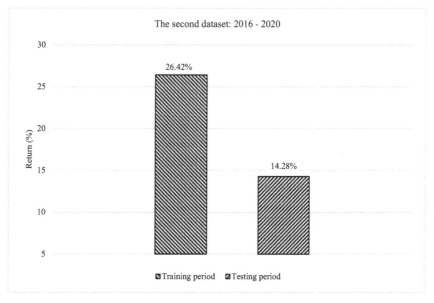

Fig. 3. Returns of the proposed approach on the second dataset.

From Fig. 3, we can see that the returns of the proposed approach in training and testing datasets are around 26% and 14%, which indicate that the proposed algorithm is profitable in recent years.

5   Conclusion and Future Work

In this paper, we have proposed an algorithm to optimize parameters for the correlation-based pair trading strategy. Because the correlation coefficient and Bollinger bands are used in the proposed approach, there are six parameters that should be tuned. Hence, the six parameters are encoded into a chromosome. Using the six parameters in a chromosome, the qualified stock pairs are generated and used to calculate the returns. Every chromosome is evaluated by the returns and number of trading. In the experiments, the results indicated that the proposed approach is better than the previous approach in terms of returns and profitability in the recent dataset. In the future, we will continue to enhance the proposed approach. For instance, different optimization algorithms, such as the particle swarm optimization, can be utilized to search solutions. We may also design a more efficient approach to speed up the evolution process, like using graphics processing units.

Acknowledgment. This research was supported by the Ministry of Science and Technology of the Republic of China under grants MOST 109-2221-E-390-015-MY3.

References

1. Krauss, C.: Statistical arbitrage pairs trading strategies: review and outlook. J. Econ. Surv. **31**, 513–545 (2017)
2. Ronnachai, J., Naragain, P.: Prediction of the profitability of pairs trading strategy using machine learning. In: IEEE International Conference on Industrial Engineering and Applications, pp. 1025–1030 (2020)
3. Gatev, E., Goetzmann, W.N., Rouwenhorst, K.G.: Pairs trading: performance of a relative-value arbitrage rule. Rev. Financ. Stud. **19**(3), 797–827 (2006)
4. Do, B., Faff, R.: Does simple pairs trading still work? Financ. Anal. J. **66**(4), 83–95 (2010)
5. Vidyamurthy, G.: Pairs trading: quantitative methods and analysis. John Wiley & Sons, Hoboken, NJ (2004)
6. Elliott, R.J., Van Der Hoek, J., Malcolm, W.P.: Pairs trading. Quantit. Financ. **5**(3), 271–276 (2005)
7. Fil, M., Kristoufek, L.: Pairs trading in cryptocurrency markets. IEEE Access **8**, 172644–172651 (2020)
8. Shen, L., Shen, K., Yi, C., Chen, Y.: An evaluation of pairs trading in commodity futures markets. In: IEEE International Conference on Big Data, pp. 5457–5462 (2020)
9. Huang, C.C.: Correlation-based Pair Trading Optimization Techniques. Department of Computer Science and Information Engineering, Tamkang University (2020)

Exploration Strategies for Model Checking with Ant Colony Optimization

Tsutomu Kumazawa[1]([✉]), Munehiro Takimoto[2], and Yasushi Kambayashi[3]

[1] Software Research Associates, Inc., 2-32-8 Minami-Ikebukuro, Toshima-ku, Tokyo 171-8513, Japan
kumazawa@sra.co.jp
[2] Tokyo University of Science, 2641 Yamazaki, Noda-shi, Chiba 278-8510, Japan
mune@rs.tus.ac.jp
[3] Nippon Institute of Technology, 4-1 Gakuendai, Miyashiro-machi, Minamisaitama-gun, Saitama 345-8501, Japan
yasushi@nit.ac.jp

Abstract. Model checking is a formal verification technique to show that a software system behaves in accordance with the given specification. Traditional model checking uses exhaustive search techniques for finding a violative behavior of the specification, and the techniques often do not work for huge systems. Because it demands a large amount of computational resources. In order to solve this problem, Search-Based Software Engineering is proposed and used. It is known that Search-Based Software Engineering is an effective approach for model checking. Its efficiency and qualities of solutions are balanced using swarm intelligence and metaheuristic methods. In this paper, we focus on the state-of-the-art model checking with Ant Colony Optimization, which is a multi-agent optimization algorithm, and attempt to extend it for efficiency. We propose two exploration strategies to enhance the performance of model checking based on Ant Colony Optimization. The proposed strategies introduce different kinds of randomized selection mechanisms to diversify solutions found by many agents. The strategies help the search algorithm extend the reachable regions effectively. Through numerical experiments, we confirmed that the proposed strategies require less computation time and memory as compared to the existing model checking with Ant Colony Optimization at the cost of finding slightly less qualified solutions.

Keywords: Agent · Multi-agent · Swarm Intelligence · Ant Colony Optimization · Model checking · State explosion problem · Search-Based Software Engineering

1 Introduction

Search-Based Software Engineering (SBSE) [13] is a research domain that aims to solve software engineering problems using search methodologies. The search methodologies contain Swarm Intelligence and metaheuristics, which are based on distributed, multi-agent and collectively intelligent approaches for finding better solutions. While SBSE is applied to many kinds of research topics, e.g., project management, software design and refactoring, one of the most promising domains is formal verification. Formal verification is a mathematical approach to prove or refute correctness of software systems. In this paper, we focus on *model checking*, which aims to verify software systems' behavioral aspects automatically [7,8]. Given a model describing a target system and its desired specification, model checking decides whether the model satisfies the specification or not. The problem can be reduced to the exhaustive search problem over the state space constructed from the model and the specification. A model checking tool outputs a violative behavior, i.e., a *counterexample*, if it concludes that the model does not satisfy the specification. There are two major research challenges of model checking: *State Explosion Problem* and the problem of *Generating Comprehensible and Short Counterexamples*. State spaces built from models and specifications tend to be huge. For example, the number of states in a concurrent and multiprocessing system often grows exponentially as the number of component processes increases linearly. The state explosion problem claims that huge state spaces make model checking infeasible in practice because the classical exhaustive algorithms deplete computational resources. On the other hand, the generation of comprehensible counterexamples is a usability problem. A counterexample provides diagnostic information that helps human users understand a specification's violation easily. Therefore, it is more favorable to obtain short counterexamples than to obtain lengthy ones.

In order to solve the problems above, researchers have actively developed non-exhaustive verification techniques using swarm intelligence and metaheuristics [15]. Alba *et al.* first proposed a verification method using Genetic Algorithm (GA) [3] and Yousefian *et al.* applied GA for model checking [28]. Ferreira *et al.* employed Particle Swarm Optimization (PSO) as a verification technique [11]. Chicano *et al.* applied Simulated Annealing (SA) to formal verification [6]. They reported that metaheuristic methods outperform classical deterministic methods through their comparative experiments. Other than the above, Ant Colony Optimization (ACO) [12,21], Estimation of Distribution Algorithm [24,25], Bayesian Optimization Algorithm [19] and Monte Carlo Tree Search [18,20] are employed in model checking. Several researches employed hybrid approaches, which combine more than one search method to make model checking more efficient. Rafe *et al.* combined the Gravitational Search and PSO [22], while Rezaee and Momeni hybridized Artificial Bee Colony algorithm and SA [23]. One of the important non-exhaustive search algorithms is *ACOhg* [1], a variant of ACO suitable for huge state spaces. ACO is a famous swarm intelligence method that solves the shortest path search problem effectively. ACOhg has been applied to model checking [2,4,14,16]. ACOhg-live [5] is a state-of-the-art model checking algorithm by running two phases of ACOhg as subroutines.

In this paper, we propose two exploration strategies with the aim of enhancing the performance of ACOhg-live. For the design of swarm intelligence, we must carefully consider the balance between exploration and exploitation. In general, many states should be explored to arrive goal states for large state spaces. Based on the idea, the proposed strategies adopt simply randomized approaches to realize the effective and efficient exploration of many states. By conducting comparative experiments, we confirmed that the proposed strategies outperform ACOhg-live with respect to running time and memory consumption at the expense of finding slightly long counterexamples.

The rest of this paper is organized as follows. Section 2 explains the outlines of model checking, namely ACOhg, and ACOhg-live. Section 3 proposes our exploration strategies. Section 4 reports the results of our comparative experiments between ACOhg-live and the proposed strategies. We conclude our discussion in Sect. 5.

2   Background

This section briefly introduces an automata-theoretic approach of model checking and a model checking method based on Ant Colony Optimization.

2.1   Automata-Theoretic Model Checking

Model checking is an automated approach to verify software systems in a formal fashion. It checks the behavior of the target software system and determines whether it conforms to the predefined specifications. In this paper, we focus on an automata-theoretic approach for model checking [27]. The automata-theoretic approaches assume that state spaces are represented as finite automata. The model checking problem is reduced to the emptiness checking of the automata. The automata that are used in model checking are called Büchi automata (BA). Just like a classical Nondeterministic Finite Automaton (NFA), a BA consists of a set of states and a set of transition edges, a set of accepting states, and at least one initial state. A BA can be represented as a directed graph. While a NFA accepts the finite words that reach some accepting state, a BA recognizes the words of infinite length that visit some accepting state infinitely many times. In other words, the BA accepts a word whose path, i.e., a sequence of states, has a cycle containing some accepting state.

Model checking is conducted in the following manner. First, we construct a BA that accepts the words conforming to the system model but contrary to the specification. Then, the emptiness of the BA is examined with graph search algorithms. Classical model checking adopts exhaustive search algorithms to find strongly connected components on directed graphs [26]. If the BA has an accepted word, the word is reported to the user as a counterexample. Otherwise, it concludes that the model does not violate the specification. A counterexample is comprised of a cycle having an accepting state and a path from an initial state to the accepting state (Fig. 1). In this paper, we indicate an initial state by an incoming edge without source state. A doubly concentric circle represents an accepting state. For example, consider a BA in Fig. 2. It has two states 0 and 1, where 0 is the initial state and 1 is the accepting state respectively. The BA accepts counterexamples passing state 1 infinitely many times, e.g., $0, 1, 1, 1, \ldots$.

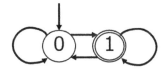

Fig. 1. Structure of a counterexample   **Fig. 2.** Example Büchi Automaton

2.2 Model Checking Based on Ant Colony Optimization

We introduce an automata-theoretic model checking technique using a variant of Ant Colony Optimization (ACO) [9], called ACOhg [1]. ACO is motivated by foraging behavior of worker ants. In ACO, many mobile agents (ants) search for paths over the given graph from an initial state (nest) to some goal state (food). They communicate with each other by means of pheromone deposited by the preceding agents. When each agent transits from a state to the adjacency, it prefers a state with more pheromone trails to the ones with less pheromone trails. After the exploration, it puts the pheromone trail on its path. ACO converges to the shortest path since the more pheromone trails a path has, the more likely it is selected by the succeeding agents. Pheromone trails evaporate as time elapses with the aim of avoiding local optima. ACO often suffers from state explosion for huge graphs because agents have to visit too many states. ACOhg is an extension of ACO specific to exploring huge graphs. In order to avoid depleting computational resources, ACOhg introduces the upper bound λ_{ant} to the length of the path that an agent traverses. Agents gradually go to distant states by updating their initial states to the ones that the preceding agents have reached on a regular basis. Algorithm 1 summarizes ACOhg (see [1,5] for details).

Algorithm 1. ACOhg [1,5]

1: Initialize pheromone;
2: **while** step count is less than or equal to $msteps$ **do**
3:    **for each** agent in $colsize$ agents **do**
4:       Explore the state space until either the length of its path reaches λ_{ant} or it arrives at some goal state;
5:       Select best paths;
6:    **end for**
7:    Update pheromone;
8:    Update initial states once every σ_s steps;
9: **end while**

After the initialization of pheromone trails to random degrees (line 1), the search process is repeated $msteps$ times (line 2). The number of agents, i.e., the colony size, is denoted by $colsize$ (line 3). At line 4, each agent in the colony starts an initial state and keeps on moving over the state space until either the length of its path reaches λ_{ant} or it encounters a goal state. The probability p_{ij}^k that agent k in state i selects the adjacent state j is computed as follows:

$$p_{ij}^k = \frac{[\tau_j]^\alpha [\eta_{ij}]^\beta}{\Sigma_{l \in N_i} [\tau_l]^\alpha [\eta_{il}]^\beta}, \quad j \in N_i, \tag{1}$$

where τ_j is the degree of pheromone deposited on state j, η_{ij} is an appropriate heuristics, N_i is a set of successors of state i, and α and β are the scaling parameters. The pheromone trails on the visited states are weakened at a constant rate ξ, i.e., $\tau_j = (1 - \xi)\tau_j$. After the traversal, the highly qualified paths are selected with the objective function f so that the shorter a path is, the better the value of f is (line 5). The value of f for a path π^k of agent k is defined as follows:

$$f(\pi^k) = \begin{cases} |\pi_{full}^k|, & \text{if } \pi_{-1}^k \text{ is a goal state,} \\ |\pi_{full}^k| + h(\pi_{-1}^k) + p_p + p_c \dfrac{\lambda_{ant} - |\pi^k|}{\lambda_{ant} - 1}, & \text{if } \pi_{-1}^k \text{ is not a goal state,} \end{cases} \tag{2}$$

where π_{-1}^k is the last state of π^k, π_{full}^k is a path from the initial state of ACOhg to π_{-1}^k, and h is a heuristic function. The parameters p_p and p_c are the scales of the penalties for paths that do not reach any goal states and paths having cycles respectively. Pheromone trails evaporate at a constant rate ρ, i.e., $\tau_i = (1 - \rho)\tau_i$ for each state i (line 7). The lower bound of the trails is controlled by the parameter a. The pheromone trails deposited on the best-so-far path are then intensified using the value of the objective function f. At line 8, the initial states are updated to the last states of the best paths selected at line 5. The number of the updated initial states is up to the value of parameter ι. ACOhg conducts the procedure of line 8 once every σ_s times, where σ_s is a parameter.

ACOhg-live [5] is a model checking algorithm that finds short counterexamples. It uses ACOhg at two phases: one for detecting a path from an initial state to some accepting state, and the other for detecting a cycle containing the accepting state. Algorithm 2 summarizes ACOhg-live. If ACOhg-live finds some accepting state at the first phase (line 2), it starts the second phase to search for the path from the state to itself (lines 3–5). Once the second phase finds such a path, ACOhg-live stops and outputs the counterexample. Otherwise, the first phase is conducted again until it fails to find any accepting states (line 6).

Algorithm 2. ACOhg-live [5]

1: **repeat**
2:    Find accepting states with ACOhg; {1st Phase}
3:    **for all** accepting states **do**
4:       Find a cycle with ACOhg;{2nd Phase}
5:    **end for**
6: **until** no accepting state is found

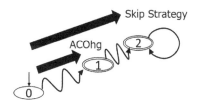

Fig. 3. Comparison between ACOhg and Skip Strategy

3   Proposed Exploration Strategies

This section proposes two novel strategies to enhance the exploration capability of ACOhg-live. Note that the proposed strategies have no additional parameters.

3.1   Skip Strategy

The first phase of ACOhg-live finds an accepting state in a BA. However, when the BA has several accepting states and some of them are aligned with a path, the first phase ACOhg can retard agents' exploring due to the intensive search within the small region. Since a BA has more than one accepting state in general, this problem deteriorates the performance of ACOhg-live strikingly. Consider applying ACOhg-live to a BA shown in Fig. 3. Although the first phase finds a path from the initial state 0 to an accepting state 1, the consecutive second phase fails because state 1 is not a part of a strongly connected component. Thus, the first phase has to start from state 0 again to find the other accepting state 2. If ACOhg arrived at state 2 by further exploration, ACOhg-live would succeed in finding a cycle without running the first phase repetitively.

We propose the skip strategy to address this problem. The idea of the skip strategy is that each agent keeps on moving until the length of its path reaches the upper bound λ_{ant} even when it encounters some goal state halfway. After it stops exploring, the strategy extracts one of the subpaths that ends at goal states randomly. Back to the example in Fig. 3, when $\lambda_{ant} > 2$, the idea of the skip strategy enables the first phase ACOhg to reach both state 1 and 2.

Algorithm 3 summarizes the modified ACOhg with the skip strategy. The major differences of Algorithm 3 from the original ACOhg are lines 2–5. At line 2, we add another termination condition such that the algorithm ends if there are one or more agents that arrive at one of the goal states. The modified condition is equivalent to the one adopted in [4] and is necessary for the efficiency of the skip strategy. At line 4, an agent repeatedly transits states up to visiting λ_{ant} states. If it comes across accepting states on its way, it ignores the states and keep on moving. After the agent builds a path, a random selection is conducted to extract one of its subpaths whose last state is a goal state (line 5). We expect to enumerate all of the nearby accepting states as candidates if the size of the colony is sufficiently large. When the agent cannot find any paths passing goal states and there is no subpath to be extracted, the full path is evaluated using Eq. (2) at line 6.

Algorithm 3. Skip Strategy

1: Initialize pheromone;
2: **while** step count is less than or equal to msteps and no agent reaches goal states
   do
3:    **for each** agent in *colsize* agents **do**
4:        Explores the state space until the length of its path reaches λ_{ant};
5:        Select a subpath that ends at some accepting states randomly;
6:        Select best paths;
7:    **end for**
8:    Update pheromone;
9:    Update initial states once every σ_s steps;
10: **end while**

3.2   Replacement Strategy

Agents in ACOhg need to extend their exploration and their paths to goal states when their preceding agents do not reach goal states. However, if the paths found by the preceding ants are evaluated well as compared to the ones found by the followers, it is likely that the already-known paths are selected many times at line 5 of Algorithm 1. This stagnation is unfavorable because the agents tend to explore some small region of the huge state space intensively and cannot extend their exploration.

In order to address the problem, we introduce the other exploration strategy called the replacement strategy. The idea of the replacement strategy is to jump into relatively inferior solutions stochastically in case of stagnation. When agents fail to find superior paths, the proposed strategy selects some of the superior paths randomly and replaces them with inferior ones. After the exploration step at lines 4–6 of Algorithm 1, we identify the stagnation by checking whether or not the selected paths at line 5 are the same as the one before the selection. The replacement strategy then removes each of the paths at probability 0.5. The highly ranked paths found at line 4 are added to the remaining best-so-far paths so that the number of the selected paths can be up to the parameter ι to conduct line 7 and its subsequent lines without modifying Algorithm 1.

4   Experiments

We conducted performance comparisons between the original ACOhg-live and the modified ACOhg-live with the proposed strategies using a benchmark system.

We implemented the prototype tool that runs ACOhg-live and the proposed strategies with Python 3.6.8. The inputs to the prototype are model descriptions, the specification to be checked, and the setting information. The models and the specifications are formatted by Labeled Transition Systems (LTSs) [17]. LTSs are suitable for describing state transition systems firing event sequences. The setting information contains the values of the parameters for ACOhg-live and the proposed strategies to be applied. The prototype runs ACOhg-live using

Table 1. Parameter settings

Parameter	1st Phase ACOhg	2nd Phase ACOhg
$msteps$	10	10
$colsize$	10	10
λ_{ant}	20	10
σ_s	2	2
ι	10	10
ξ	0.7	0.5
a	5	5
ρ	0.2	0.2
α	1.0	1.0
β	2.0	2.0
p_p	1000	1000
p_c	1000	1000

the configurations written in the setting information. The tool outputs either a counterexample as an event sequence if a violation is found, or None, i.e., a special value built in Python, otherwise. In order to make the prototype efficient, we implemented on-the-fly checking [8], which creates the state space as needed.

We described the models and the specifications used in the experiments based on a database ring system [17]. The database ring is a description of a distributed database that consists of several nodes organizing a ring-shaped network. Each node receives update information from one of its adjacent nodes, and changes its internally stored data. The node notifies the other adjacent node of the information to keep the consistency of the network. We prepared three specifications, called Spec. A, B and C, which are related to the requirements that the all nodes update their internal states successfully.

We set the following search conditions and ran the prototype 30 times for each specification and each experimental condition:

- **OR**: running the original ACOhg-live without our proposed strategies,
- **ORT**: running the original ACOhg-live by corresponding the terminal condition of its first phase to that of the skip strategy, with the aim of evaluating our strategies under the fair terminal condition,
- **SK**: applying the skip strategy to the first phase,
- **RE**: applying the replacement strategy to the second phase,
- **RET**: running the first stage of the original ACOhg-live by corresponding the terminal condition to that of the skip strategy and applying the replacement strategy to the second phase, and,
- **HY**: applying the skip strategy and the replacement strategy to the first and the second phase respectively.

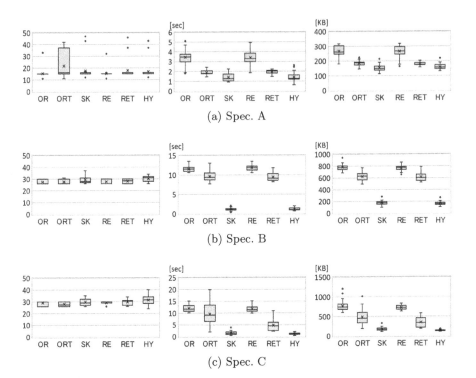

Fig. 4. Box Plots of Experimental Results. For each case (a), (b) and (c), the plots are placed in order of *Lengths of Counterexamples, Running Time [sec]* and *Memory Consumption [KB]* from left to right.

For each run of the prototype, we measured the length of the detected counterexample, the running time, and the memory consumption. We used the settings of the parameters shown in Table 1. We selected the configuration by tuning the one in [5] through the preliminary trials. ACOhg is assumed to combine heuristics that estimate the distances or steps needed to reach goal states as discussed in Sect. 2.2. In our experiments, we did not use any heuristics for the first phase since the accepting states are not known in advance. For the second phase, we employed a heuristics of estimating the distances between the current state and the accepting state to be searched. The heuristics is the hamming distance of binary representations of states discussed in [5]. We used HP ProDesk 600 G4 SFF with Intel Core i7-8700, CPU 3.20 GHz, RAM 16.0 GB, and Windows 10 Pro for the experiments. The garbage collection built in Python is turned off when running the prototype in order to avoid its influence on the performance.

We show the results of our experiments in Fig. 4 and Table 2. We first discuss the results of the skip strategy (SK). SK highly improved the running time and the memory consumption of the original ACOhg-live (OR) for each specification of the database ring. Compared to the cases of adopting only the termination condition of the skip strategy (ORT and RET), the running time and the memory

Table 2. Summary of experimental results

			OR	ORT	SK	RE	RET	HY
Spec. A	Length of counterexample	Mean	15.23	21.67	17.50	**15.17**	17.87	16.90
		Std. Dev.	3.48	10.44	7.42	**3.33**	7.51	6.33
		Median	**15**	16	16	**15**	**15**	16
	Running time [sec]	Mean	3.45	1.87	1.41	3.40	1.94	**1.40**
		Std. Dev.	0.70	0.24	0.39	0.68	**0.20**	0.47
		Median	3.49	1.81	**1.25**	3.29	2.02	1.26
	Memory consumption [KB]	Mean	267.35	184.18	**154.59**	266.97	176.98	158.70
		Std. Dev.	35.38	15.72	23.89	41.48	**11.96**	19.72
		Median	262.51	187.37	**148.71**	267.49	174.33	156.24
Spec. B	Length of counterexample	Mean	**27.47**	27.57	29.40	27.60	28.03	30.17
		Std. Dev.	**1.93**	1.94	2.74	1.96	1.97	2.31
		Median	**26**	**26**	28	**26**	28.5	31
	Running time [sec]	Mean	11.53	9.66	**1.16**	11.83	9.44	**1.16**
		Std. Dev.	0.68	1.18	0.37	0.73	1.07	**0.32**
		Median	11.53	9.40	1.09	11.84	9.15	**1.04**
	Memory consumption [KB]	Mean	785.81	622.97	175.72	765.14	615.33	**164.95**
		Std. Dev.	66.24	70.35	35.88	42.26	65.18	**28.88**
		Median	773.68	628.91	174.52	774.07	603.93	**160.18**
Spec. C	Length of counterexample	Mean	28.93	**28.00**	29.70	29.07	29.77	31.30
		Std. Dev.	1.77	1.83	2.84	**1.69**	2.33	3.62
		Median	30	**27.5**	29	30	30.5	31.5
	Running time [sec]	Mean	12.04	9.56	1.49	11.78	4.83	**1.12**
		Std. Dev.	1.35	4.36	0.74	1.35	2.34	**0.39**
		Median	11.71	9.16	1.41	11.42	4.55	**1.03**
	Memory consumption [KB]	Mean	770.61	483.03	176.92	726.17	349.29	**142.43**
		Std. Dev.	129.75	193.30	44.22	52.75	124.68	**19.11**
		Median	741.25	454.47	175.67	723.51	340.87	**139.15**

consumption of the skip strategy are also efficient. The results suggest that the skip strategy promotes effective state space exploration of ACOhg-live. SK tends to generate a bit longer counterexamples as compared to OR, ORT and RE on average for Spec. B and C. SK makes many agents extend on their exploration preferentially and weakens the feature of ACOhg-live to generate short counterexamples.

We discuss the effect of the replacement strategy (RE) next. According to our experimental results, RE does not present significant differences about the performance as compared to OR. The observation indicates that it is difficult to improve the performance of ACOhg-live with the replacement strategy alone.

We then discuss the effectiveness of combining both the skip and replacement strategies (HY). For the running time in Spec. A, the average and the median of HY are almost comparable to those of SK, and are small as compared to those of OR, ORT, RE and RET. According to the result in Spec. B, both the average, standard deviation and median of the memory consumption of HY are the smallest. HY is the most efficient with respect to both the running time and memory consumption for Spec. C. Except the result of the running time in Spec. A, we see that HY tends to decrease the standard deviations of the running time and memory consumption as compared to SK. Although the lengths of counterexamples found by HY deteriorates especially for Spec. B and C as compared to the other conditions, we believe that the performance improvement with the hybridization of our strategies compensates for the disadvantage of detecting long counterexamples. Our strategies is expected to provide ACOhg-live with the good balance between performance and comprehensibility of counterexamples.

Finally, we discuss generality of our experimental results. The benchmark that we used in our experiments is a typical distributed database system consisting of several concurrent processes. Since one of the most important features of model checking is verifying complicated and concurrent systems [8], we believe that our experiments are appropriate for evaluating the performance of the proposed strategies under a representative use case of model checking.

5   Conclusion

This paper tackles with two main challenges in model checking: the state explosion problem and the problem of finding short counterexamples. Our approach is involved with Search-Based Software Engineering, which tries to overcome the problems with non-exhaustive search algorithms based on swarm intelligence. We propose two novel exploration strategies for making an existing model checking technique based on Ant Colony Optimization, ACOhg-live, more efficient. Our experimental results lead us to the conclusion that ACOhg-live with the proposed strategies outperforms the original one with respect to runtime performance. Although our strategies detect longer counterexamples than the original ACOhg-live does, we believe that the drawback is subtle.

As future work, we plan to combine appropriate heuristics with our strategies. The choice of heuristics is a key issue in ACOhg-live because the heuristics have great influences on its performance. Several heuristics are investigated in the context of Directed Model Checking [10]. We also have to compare the proposed strategies with the search methods other than ACOhg-live. The candidates are classical search techniques, e.g., [26], and the methods discussed in Sect. 1.

References

1. Alba, E., Chicano, F.: ACOhg: dealing with huge graphs. In: Proceedings of the 9th Annual Conference on Genetic and Evolutionary Computation, pp. 10–17 (2007). https://doi.org/10.1145/1276958.1276961
2. Alba, E., Chicano, F.: Finding safety errors with ACO. In: Proceedings of the 9th Annual Conference on Genetic and Evolutionary Computation, pp. 1066–1073 (2007). https://doi.org/10.1145/1276958.1277171
3. Alba, E., Troya, J.M.: Genetic algorithms for protocol validation. In: Proceedings of the 4th International Conference on Parallel Problem Solving from Nature, pp. 870–879 (1996). https://doi.org/10.1007/3-540-61723-X_1050

4. Chicano, F., Alba, E.: Ant colony optimization with partial order reduction for discovering safety property violations in concurrent models. Inf. Process. Lett. **106**(6), 221–231 (2008). https://doi.org/10.1016/j.ipl.2007.11.015

5. Chicano, F., Alba, E.: Finding liveness errors with ACO. In: Proceedings of the IEEE Congress on Evolutionary Computation, pp. 2997–3004 (2008). https://doi.org/10.1109/CEC.2008.4631202

6. Chicano, F., Ferreira, M., Alba, E.: Comparing metaheuristic algorithms for error detection in Java programs. In: Proceedings of the Third International Conference on Search Based Software Engineering, pp. 82–96 (2011). https://doi.org/10.1007/978-3-642-23716-4_11

7. Clarke, E.M., Emerson, E.A.: Design and synthesis of synchronization skeletons using branching time temporal logic. In: Kozen, D. (ed.) Logic of Programs 1981. LNCS, vol. 131, pp. 52–71. Springer, Heidelberg (1982). https://doi.org/10.1007/BFb0025774

8. Clarke, E.M., Jr., Grumberg, O., Kroening, D., Peled, D., Veith, H.: Model Checking, 2nd edn. MIT Press, Cambridge (2018)

9. Dorigo, M., Stützle, T.: Ant Colony Optimization. MIT Press, Bradford Company (2004)

10. Edelkamp, S., Schuppan, V., Bošnački, D., Wijs, A., Fehnker, A., Aljazzar, H.: Survey on directed model checking. In: Peled, D.A., Wooldridge, M.J. (eds.) MoChArt 2008. LNCS (LNAI), vol. 5348, pp. 65–89. Springer, Heidelberg (2009). https://doi.org/10.1007/978-3-642-00431-5_5

11. Ferreira, M., Chicano, F., Alba, E., Gómez-Pulido, J.A.: Detecting protocol errors using particle swarm optimization with Java pathfinder. In: Proceedings of the High Performance Computing & Simulation Conference, pp. 319–325 (2008)

12. Francesca, G., Santone, A., Vaglini, G., Villani, M.L.: Ant colony optimization for deadlock detection in concurrent systems. In: Proceedings of IEEE 35th Annual Computer Software and Applications Conference, pp. 108–117. IEEE Computer Society (2011). https://doi.org/10.1109/COMPSAC.2011.22

13. Harman, M., Mansouri, S.A., Zhang, Y.: Search-based software engineering: trends, techniques and applications. ACM Comput. Surv. **45**(1), 111–1161 (2012). https://doi.org/10.1145/2379776.2379787

14. Kumazawa, T., Takada, K., Takimoto, M., Kambayashi, Y.: Ant colony optimization based model checking extended by smell-like pheromone with hop counts. Swarm Evol. Comput. **44**, 511–521 (2019). https://doi.org/10.1016/j.swevo.2018.06.002

15. Kumazawa, T., Takimoto, M., Kambayashi, Y.: A survey on the applications of swarm intelligence to software verification. In: Handbook of Research on Fireworks Algorithms and Swarm Intelligence, pp. 376–398 (2020). https://doi.org/10.4018/978-1-7998-1659-1.ch017

16. Kumazawa, T., Yokoyama, C., Takimoto, M., Kambayashi, Y.: Ant colony optimization based model checking extended by smell-like pheromone. EAI Endorsed Trans. Ind. Netw. Intell. Syst. **16**(7) (2016). https://doi.org/10.4108/eai.21-4-2016.151156

17. Magee, J., Kramer, J.: Concurrency: State Models & Java Programming, 2nd edn. Wiley, Hoboken (2006)

18. Milewicz, R.M., Poulding, S.: Scalable parallel model checking via Monte-Carlo tree search. ACM SIGSOFT Softw. Eng. Notes **42**(4), 1–5 (2018). https://doi.org/10.1145/3149485.3149495

19. Pira, E., Rafe, V., Nikanjam, A.: Deadlock detection in complex software systems specified through graph transformation using Bayesian optimization algorithm. J. Syst. Softw. **131**, 181–200 (2017). https://doi.org/10.1016/j.jss.2017.05.128
20. Poulding, S., Feldt, R.: Heuristic model checking using a Monte-Carlo tree search algorithm. In: Proceedings of the 2015 Annual Conference on Genetic and Evolutionary Computation, pp. 1359–1366 (2015). https://doi.org/10.1145/2739480.2754767
21. Rafe, V., Darghayedi, M., Pira, E.: MS-ACO: a multi-stage ant colony optimization to refute complex software systems specified through graph transformation. Soft Comput. **23**(12), 4531–4556 (2019). https://doi.org/10.1007/s00500-018-3444-y
22. Rafe, V., Moradi, M., Yousefian, R., Nikanjam, A.: A meta-heuristic solution for automated refutation of complex software systems specified through graph transformations. Appl. Soft Comput. **33**(C), 136–149 (2015). https://doi.org/10.1016/j.asoc.2015.04.032
23. Rezaee, N., Momeni, H.: A hybrid meta-heuristic approach to cope with state space explosion in model checking technique for deadlock freeness. J. AI Data Min. **8**(2), 189–199 (2020). https://doi.org/10.22044/jadm.2019.7564.1900
24. Staunton, J., Clark, J.A.: Searching for safety violations using estimation of distribution algorithms. In: Proceedings of the 2010 Third International Conference on Software Testing, Verification, and Validation Workshops, pp. 212–221 (2010). https://doi.org/10.1109/ICSTW.2010.24
25. Staunton, J., Clark, J.A.: Finding short counterexamples in promela models using estimation of distribution algorithms. In: Proceedings of the 13th Annual Conference on Genetic and Evolutionary Computation, pp. 1923–1930 (2011). https://doi.org/10.1145/2001576.2001834
26. Tarjan, R.: Depth first search and linear graph algorithms. SIAM J. Comput. **1**(2), 146–160 (1972)
27. Vardi, M.Y., Wolper, P.: An automata-theoretic approach to automatic program verification. In: Proceedings of the First Symposium on Logic in Computer Science, pp. 322–331 (1986)
28. Yousefian, R., Rafe, V., Rahmani, M.: A heuristic solution for model checking graph transformation systems. Appl. Soft Comput. **24**, 169–180 (2014). https://doi.org/10.1016/j.asoc.2014.06.055

Periodic Distributed Delivery Routes Planning Subject to Uncertainty of Travel Parameters

Katarzyna Rudnik[1], Grzegorz Bocewicz[2]([⊠]), Czesław Smutnicki[3], Jarosław Pempera[3], and Zbigniew Banaszczak[2]

[1] Faculty of Production Engineering and Logistics, Opole University of Technology, Opole, Poland
k.rudnik@po.edu.pl

[2] Faculty of Electronics and Computer Science, Koszalin University of Technology, Koszalin, Poland
{grzegorz.bocewicz,zbigniew.banaszak}@tu.koszalin.pl

[3] Department of Control Systems and Mechatronics, Faculty of Electronics, Wrocław University of Science and Technology, Wrocław, Poland
{czeslaw.smutnicki,jaroslaw.pempera}@pwr.edu.pl

Abstract. In the Periodic Vehicle Routing Problem (PVRP), in which scheduling of the fleet of vehicles is based on constituting the timetable for the passage of individual vehicles along the planned routes, the imprecise nature of transport/service operation times implies the need to take into account the fact that the accumulating uncertainty of previously performed operations results in increased uncertainty of timely execution of subsequent operations. In the article, the authors pose the question as to the method of avoiding additional uncertainty introduced during aggregating uncertain operation execution deadlines. Due to the above fact, an algebraic model for calculating fuzzy schedules for individual vehicles, and for planning time buffers enabling the adjustment of the currently calculated fuzzy schedules is developed. The model uses Ordered Fuzzy Numbers (OFNs) to conduct the uncertainty of times. The advantage of using the OFNs formalism for algebraic operations is non-expanding of fuzzy number support. However, the possibility of carrying out algebraic operations is limited to selected domains of computability of these supports. Due to this fact a constraint satisfaction problem framework has been adapted. The conducted research demonstrated that the proposed approach allows to develop conditions following the calculability of arithmetic operations of OFNs and guarantee interpretability of results obtained.

Keywords: Ordered Fuzzy Numbers · Periodic Vehicle Routing Problem · Ordered fuzzy constraint satisfaction problem

---

Supported by organization x.

N. T. Nguyen et al. (Eds.): ICCCI 2021, LNAI 12876, pp. 277–289, 2021.
https://doi.org/10.1007/978-3-030-88081-1_21

1   Introduction

In real-life settings of Out-Plant Operating Supply Networks (OPOSN), [10,13], apart from randomly occurring disturbances (changes in the execution of already planned requests/orders and the arrival of new ones, traffic jams, accidents, etc.), an important role is played by the imprecise nature of the parameters which determine the timeliness of the services/deliveries performed [19]. The imprecise nature of these parameters is caused by the operator's psychophysical disposition, disturbances in the flow of traffic, etc. Therefore, the time values of the operations performed vary and are uncertain.

The non-stationary nature of the uncertainty of the parameters mentioned, and the usually small set of available historical samples in practice limits the choice of a formal data model to a fuzzy numbers driven one. It means the uncertainty of OPOSN data connected with traffic disturbances as well as changes in service delivery dates requires the use of a model based on the formalism of fuzzy sets. However, it is worth noting that the specificity of the processes involved in the course of planning a services delivery schedule makes it necessary to determine the sequentially cumulative uncertainty of the performance of the operations involved in it. The question that arises concerns the method of avoiding additional uncertainty introduced in the combinations of aggregating uncertainties of cyclically executed operations in cyclic production [3] or distribution [2]. In this context, in contrast to standard fuzzy numbers, the support of a fuzzy number obtained by algebraic operations performed on the Ordered Fuzzy Numbers (OFNs) domain does not expand. However, the possibility of carrying out algebraic operations is limited to selected domains of computability of these supports.

Most Periodic Vehicle Routing Problems (PVRP) are aimed at searching for an optimal periodic distribution policy, i.e., a plan regarding whom to serve, how much to deliver, and what regularly repeated routes to travel by what fleet of vehicles [4,14]. Examples of such problems [7] include both simple ones, such as the Mix Fleet VRP, Multi-depot VRP, Split-up Delivery VRP, Pick-up and Delivery VRP, VRP with Time Windows, VRP with Backhauls, and more complex ones, such as a combination of variants of the VRP with multiple trips, VRP with a time window, and VRP with pick-up delivery. Regardless of problems that accentuate the dynamic or static character of vehicle routing [6,7,9,16,17,21] the goal is always to search for optimal solutions. In these studies, assumptions regarding congestion-free flow of concurrently executed transport processes and/or robustness of planned routings and schedules to assumed disturbances and/or uncertainty of variables are tacitly accepted [12,17,22]. An exhaustive review of VRP taxonomy-inspired problems can be found in [4,18].

The PVRPs developed so far have limited use due to the data uncertainty observed in practice. The values describing parameters such as transport time or loading/unloading times, depend on the human factor, which means they cannot be determined precisely. It is difficult to account for data uncertainty by using fuzzy variables due to the imperfections of the classical fuzzy numbers algebra [3,8]. Equations which describe the relationships between fuzzy variables (variables with fuzzy values) using algebraic operations (in particular, addition and multiplication) do not meet the conditions of the Ring. In addition, algebraic operations based on standard fuzzy numbers follow Zadeh's extension principle which means that the uncertainty of variables increases with successive cycles of the system operation (i.e., caused by the need of intermediate approximations), until the information about their value is no longer useful. Despite this the Fuzzy VRP assuming vagueness for fuzzy customer demands to be collected and fuzzy service- or travel times are the subject of a growing body of research [1,2,5,15,22]. Most of contributions however seem to lack any formal analytical approach enabling both qualitative and quantitative refinement of delivery routings. The current paper aims to fill this gap by introduction the OFN algebra framework. In other words, the objective is to develop an algebraic model aimed at rapid calculation of fuzzy schedules for individual vehicles as well as planning time buffers that permit to adjust currently calculated fuzzy schedules to baseline schedules assuming that operation times are deterministic values. Especially the paper focuses on the development of sufficient conditions implying the calculability of arithmetic operations that guarantee the interpretability of the results obtained. The main contributions to this study can be summarized as follows:

1. Provide decision support for the rationale behind vehicle fleet cyclic scheduling in the OPOSNs while taking into account the uncertainty of the deliveries operation times.
2. Analyze the impact of vehicle fleet size as well as time buffers size and allocation on the OPOSN design.
3. Provide a trade-off between the sizes of delivery cycles and the size of time buffers (laytimes), taking into account the uncertainty of the deliveries operation times and the data characterizing the OPOSN.

The sections below include formulation of the problem and a description of the methodology used to solve it. All this is supplemented by an illustrative example and recommendations for future work.

2 Problem Definition

Let us consider graph $G = (N, E)$ modeling the OPOSN. The set of nodes $N = \{N_1, \ldots, N_\lambda, \ldots, N_n\}$ includes one node representing distribution center N_1 and $N_2, \ldots, N_n$ nodes representing customers. The set of edges $E = \{(N_i, N_j) \mid i, j \in N, i \neq j\}$ determines the possible connections between nodes. Given is a fleet of vehicles $U = \{U_1, \ldots, U_k, \ldots, U_K\}$. The customers are cyclically serviced (with period T) by vehicles U_k traveling from node N_1. Variable Q_k denotes the payload capacity of vehicles U_k. Execution of the ordered delivery z_λ by the customer N_λ takes place in the period t_λ. The moment of starting the mission of vehicles U_k (on the distribution center N_1) is indicated by variable s^k. In turn the moment when the vehicle U_k starts delivery to the customer N_λ is indicated by variable y_λ^k. The deliveries ordered by the customer

N_λ are carried out in the period $\Delta_\lambda = [ld_\lambda; ud_\lambda]$ (delivery service deadline), i.e. $y_\lambda^k \geq ld_\lambda$ and $y_\lambda^k + t_\lambda \leq ud_\lambda$. It is assumed that the variable $d_{\beta,\lambda}$ determines traveling time between nodes N_β, N_λ, where: $(N_\beta, N_\lambda) \in E$. The routes of U_k are represented by sequences: $\pi_k = (N_{k_1}, \ldots, N_{k_i}, N_{k_{i+1}}, \ldots, N_{k_\mu})$, where: $k_i \in \{1,..,K\}$, $(N_{k_i}, N_{k_{i+1}}) \in E$. Moreover the following assumptions are met: Z denotes a set of required amounts of goods z_λ, $\lambda = 1 \ldots n$; Π denotes a set of routes π_k, $k = 1 \ldots K$; node N_1 representing distribution center occurs only once in each route of the set Π; node representing the customer N_λ ($\lambda > 1$) occurs only once in the route belonging to the set Π; the amount of goods transported by U_k cannot exceed payload capacity Q_k, deliveries are being made over a given periodically repeating time horizon T. The adopted assumptions allow to formulate the question: *Does there exist a set of routes Π of fleet U guaranteeing the timely delivery (according to given delivery service deadlines Δ_λ and in a time window T) of the required amount of goods Z, to the customers from the set N?*

For the purpose of illustration, let us consider network G shown in the Fig. 1, where 10 nodes (1 distribution center and 9 customers) are serviced by fleet $U = \{U_1, U_2, U_3\}$. The following routes: $\pi_1 = (N_1, N_3, N_9, N_2)$ (green line), $\pi_2 = (N_1, N_5, N_{10}, N_7)$ (red line), $\pi_3 = (N_1, N_6, N_8, N_4)$ (violet line) guarantee the delivery of the required amount of goods to all customers cyclically (within the period $T = 1800$).

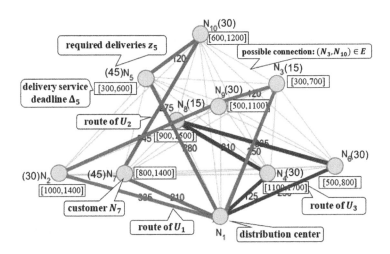

Fig. 1. Graph G modeling the considered OPOSN (Color figure online)

The solution was determined assuming that the vehicle payload capacity Q_k is equal to 120. The corresponding cyclic schedule is shown in the Fig. 2a). This solution assumes that both traveling times $d_{\beta,\lambda}$ (see CN rows in the Fig. 3) as well as times of node occupation t_λ (time of the service provided) are crisp ($t_\lambda = 120$, $\lambda = 1 \ldots 10$). The vehicles of the U fleet deliver services on the dates specified by delivery service deadline Δ_λ. The delivery cycle period T is equal to 1800. The vehicles complete their missions (return to node N_1) on times: $1710 + c \times T$, $1485 + c \times T$, $1790 + c \times T$, ($c \in \mathbb{N}$) respectively and are waiting at the distribution center for further deliveries to begin. Laytimes which are assumed to be represented by crisp values w_1^1, w_1^2, w_1^3 (where subscripts and superscripts of w_λ^k correspond to N_λ and U_k) spent in the so called distribution center are: 270, 435, 400, respectively (see CN rows in the Fig. 3).

In this context, the service point located in distribution center N_1 can be treated as a time buffer that allows for adjusting the schedule of implemented missions in situations of accumulating uncertainty, caused by delays following disruptions occurring in the course of the transport operations. It is worth noting that the issue concerning laytimes sizing and allocation guaranteeing the existence of schedules that meet the ordered delivery times in the OPOSN is still an open problem.

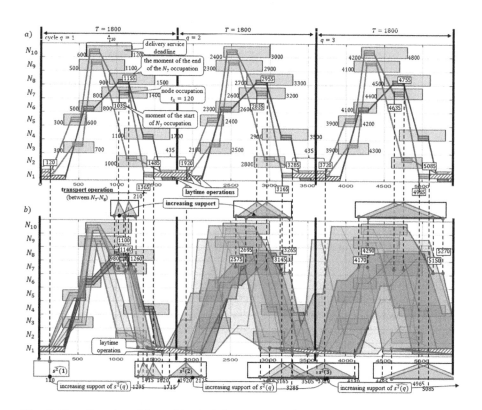

Fig. 2. Base line a) and fuzzy b) schedules corresponding to the routes from the Fig. 1. (Color figure online)

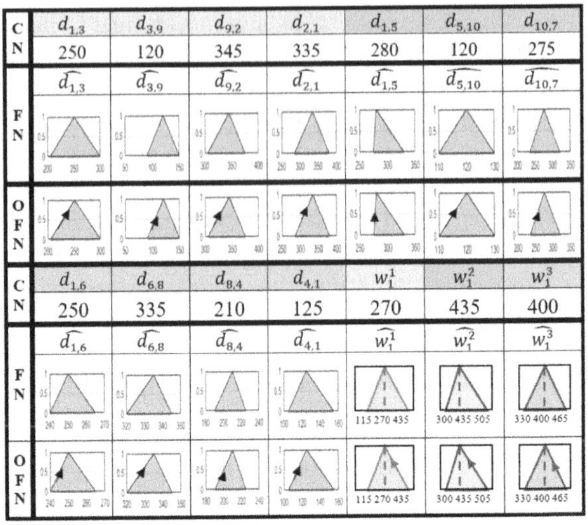

C N	$d_{1,3}$	$d_{3,9}$	$d_{9,2}$	$d_{2,1}$	$d_{1,5}$	$d_{5,10}$	$d_{10,7}$
	250	120	345	335	280	120	275
F N	$\widehat{d_{1,3}}$	$\widehat{d_{3,9}}$	$\widehat{d_{9,2}}$	$\widehat{d_{2,1}}$	$\widehat{d_{1,5}}$	$\widehat{d_{5,10}}$	$\widehat{d_{10,7}}$
O F N							

C N	$d_{1,6}$	$d_{6,8}$	$d_{8,4}$	$d_{4,1}$	w_1^1	w_1^2	w_1^3
	250	335	210	125	270	435	400
F N	$\widehat{d_{1,6}}$	$\widehat{d_{6,8}}$	$\widehat{d_{8,4}}$	$\widehat{d_{4,1}}$	$\widehat{w_1^1}$	$\widehat{w_1^2}$	$\widehat{w_1^3}$
O F N					115 270 435	300 435 505	330 400 465

CN – Crisp Number; FN–Fuzzy Number; OFN–Ordered Fuzzy Number

Fig. 3. Assumed travel time values. (Color figure online)

An example illustrating imperfections of the classic fuzzy numbers algebra [2,3] is shown in the Fig. 2b, where the level of uncertainty increases with successive cycles. Fuzzy values of variables (i.e. fuzzy travel times $\widehat{d_{\beta,\lambda}}$ and fuzzy laytimes $\widehat{w_1^1}$, $\widehat{w_1^2}$, $\widehat{w_1^3}$) used are collected in the Fig. 3 (see FN rows). Figure 2 distinguishes the fuzzy values of the start/end moments of service operations carried out on nodes N_7 and N_1 located along the route selected for U_2 (red line). The attainable values of these moments are characterized by an increasing fuzzy value supports in subsequent cycles (the level of uncertainty increases), as seen in the Fig. 2b.

In particular, this means that the moments of starting the mission $\widehat{s^k(q)}$ of U_k in subsequent q cycles assume fuzzy values with increasingly larger supports. Therefore, the degree of the cumulative uncertainty $\Sigma(q)$ of the fleet $U = \{U_1, \ldots, U_k, \ldots, U_K\}$ carried over to subsequent cycles of q can be expressed by the largest support of variables $\widehat{s^k(q)}$: $\Sigma(q) = \max_{k=1\ldots K} \left\{ supp_{s^k(q)} \right\}$, where $supp_X$ is the support of $\widehat{X}$. For example, Fig. 2b shows how the support of $\widehat{s^2(q)}$ for the vehicle U_2 increases in the following cycles, i.e. incrementing by a constant value of 270: 0, 270, 540, $\ldots$, respectively. Consequently, in the considered example (Fig. 2b) the degree of cumulative uncertainty $\Sigma(q)$ is respectively:

1. $\Sigma(1) = 0$ when $supp_{s^1(1)} = 0$; $supp_{s^2(1)} = 0$ (see Fig. 2b); $supp_{s^2(1)} = 0$;
2. $\Sigma(2) = 640$ when $supp_{s^1(1)} = 640$; $supp_{s^2(1)} = 410$ (see Fig. 2b); $supp_{s^2(1)} = 270$;
3. $\Sigma(3) = 1280$ when $supp_{s^1(1)} = 1280$; $supp_{s^2(1)} = 820$ (see Fig. 2b); $supp_{s^2(1)} = 540$.

It means that in the considered case the fuzzy variable carriers of the successive cycles q are increased by 640.

In this framework the nascent problem boils down to setting for the given ranges of uncertainty (e.g. concerning travel and service delivery operation times) the time buffers of size (laytimes) that allowing to reduce the cumulative uncertainty ($\Sigma(q) = 0$ for $q = 1 \ldots Q$) to such an extent that it does not transfer to the next cycles?

3   Ordered Fuzzy Numbers Algebra

In the case of classic fuzzy numbers $\widehat{a}$, $\widehat{b}$, $\widehat{c}$ (fuzzy numbers are marked with the symbol " $\frown$ "), the following implication $(\widehat{a} + \widehat{b} = \widehat{c}) \Rightarrow [(\widehat{c} - \widehat{b} = \widehat{a}) \wedge (\widehat{c} - \widehat{a} = \widehat{b})]$ does not hold. This makes it impossible to solve a simple equation $\widehat{A} + \widehat{X} = \widehat{C}$. This fact significantly hinders the application of approaches based on declarative models. Therefore we propose a declarative model based on OFN algebra in which it is possible to solve algebraic equations. OFNs can be defined [11] as a pair of continuous real functions (f_A – "up"; g_A- "down") i.e.:

$$\widehat{A} = (f_A, g_A), where : f_A, g_A : [0, 1] \rightarrow \mathbb{R}. \tag{1}$$

Assuming that f_A is increasing and g_A is decreasing as well as that $f_A \leq g_A$, the membership function μ_A of the OFN $\widehat{A}$ is as follows (see OFN in the Fig. 3):

$$\mu_A(x) = \begin{cases} f_A^{-1}(x) & when \ x \in UP_A \\ g_A^{-1}(x) & when \ x \in DOWN_A \\ 1 & when \ x \in CONST_A \\ 0 & \text{in the remaining cases} \end{cases} \tag{2}$$

where, $UP_A = (l_{A0}, l_{A1})$, $CONST_A = (l_{A1}, p_{A1})$ and $DOWN_A = (p_{A1}, p_{A0})$. OFNs have two types of orientations [11,20]: **positive**, when $\widehat{A} = (f_A, g_A)$; **negative**, when $\widehat{A} = (g_A, f_A)$. The definitions of algebraic operations used in the proposed model are as follows:

Definition 1. Let $\widehat{A} = (f_A, g_A)$, $\widehat{B} = (f_B, g_B)$, and $\widehat{C} = (f_C, g_C)$ be OFNs. $\widehat{A}$ is a number equal to $\widehat{B}$ ($\widehat{A} = \widehat{B}$), or ($\widehat{A} > \widehat{B}$; $\widehat{A} \geq \widehat{B}$), ($\widehat{A} < \widehat{B}$; $\widehat{A} \leq \widehat{B}$) if: $_{x \in [0,1]} f_A(x) * f_B(x) \wedge g_A(x) * g_B(x)$, where: "$*$" stands for: =, >, $\geq$, <, or $\leq$.

The operations of: $\widehat{C} = \widehat{A} + \widehat{B}$; $\widehat{C} = \widehat{A} - \widehat{B}$; $\widehat{C} = \widehat{A} \times \widehat{B}$; $\widehat{C} = \widehat{A}/\widehat{B}$ are defined as follows: $_{x \in [0,1]} f_C(x) = f_A(x) * f_B(x) \wedge g_C(x) = g_A(x) * g_B(x)$, where: "$*$" stands for +, $-$, $\times$, or $\div$.

The ordered fuzzy number $\widehat{A}$ is a proper OFN [20] when one of the following conditions is met: $f_A(0) \leq f_A(1) \leq g_A(1) \leq g_A(0)$ (for positive orientation) or $g_A(0) \leq g_A(1) \leq f_A(1) \leq f_A(0)$ (for negative orientation). They allow us to specify the conditions which guarantee that the result of algebraic operations is a proper OFN:

Theorem 1. *Let $\widehat{A}$ and $\widehat{B}$ be proper OFNs with different orientations: $\widehat{A}$ (positive orientation), $\widehat{B}$ (negative orientation). If one of the following conditions holds: $(|UP_A| - |UP_B| \geq 0) \wedge (|CONST_A| - |CONST_B| \geq 0) \wedge (|DOWN_A| - |DOWN_B| \geq 0)$, or $(|UP_B| - |UP_A| \geq 0) \wedge (|CONST_B| - |CONST_A| \geq 0) \wedge (|DOWN_B| - |DOWN_A| \geq 0)$, then the result of the operation $\widehat{A} + \widehat{B}$ is a proper OFN $\widehat{C}$.*

The above theorem allows the construction of models in which decision variables resulting from algebraic operations (in particular sums) take values which are proper OFNs (numbers which are easy to interpret). Moreover, the fulfillment of the conditions underlying the above theorem may lead to a reduction in the fuzziness of the sum of OFNs with different orientations.

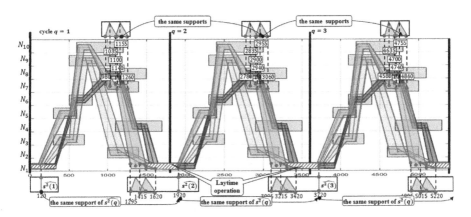

Fig. 4. Cyclic fuzzy schedules following Theorem 1 and corresponding to the routes from the Fig. 1 - a cycle period $T = 1800$

4   Ordered Fuzzy Constraint Satisfaction Problem

The problem being considered can be perceived as an Ordered Fuzzy Constraint Satisfaction (OFCS) Problem (3):

$$\widehat{FCS} = \left(\left(\widehat{V}, \widehat{D} \right), \widehat{C} \right), \tag{3}$$

where:

$\widehat{V}$ – a set of decision variables, including variables representing routes $(x_{\beta,\lambda}^k)$ and schedule $(c_\lambda^k, \widehat{s^k}, \widehat{y_\lambda^k}, \widehat{w_\lambda^k}, \Sigma)$:

$x_{\beta,\lambda}^k$: binary variable indicating the travel of U_k between nodes N_β, N_λ: $x_{\beta,\lambda}^k = 1$ if U_k travels from node N_β to node N_λ; $x_{\beta,\lambda}^k = 0$ otherwise,

c_λ^k: weight of goods delivered to N_λ by vehicle U_k,

$\widehat{y_\lambda^k}$: fuzzy time at which vehicle U_k arrives at node N_λ, (OFN representation),

$\widehat{w_\lambda^k}$: laytime at node N_λ for U_k (OFN representation),

$\widehat{s^k}$: take-off time of vehicle U_k (OFN representation),

Σ: cumulative uncertainty ($\Sigma = \Sigma(1)$, i.e. for $q = 1$),

$\widehat{D}$ – a finite set of decision variable domains: $\widehat{s^k}$, $\widehat{y_\lambda^k}$, $\widehat{w_\lambda^k} \in F$ (F is a set of OFNs (1)), $x_{\beta,\lambda}^k \in \{0,1\}$,

$\widehat{C}$ – a set of constraints specifying the relationships between decision variables, such as:

$$\widehat{s^k} \geq 0 \; ; k = 1 \ldots K, \tag{4}$$

$$\sum_{j=1}^{n} x_{1,j}^k = 1 \; ; k = 1 \ldots K, \tag{5}$$

$$\left(x_{1,j}^k = 1 \right) \Rightarrow \left(\widehat{y_j^k} = \widehat{s^k} + \widehat{d_{1,j}} \right) \; ; j = 1 \ldots n, \tag{6}$$

$$\left(x_{i,j}^k = 1 \right) \Rightarrow \left(\widehat{y_j^k} = \widehat{y_i^k} + \widehat{d_{i,j}} + \widehat{t_i} + \widehat{w_\lambda^k} \right), \tag{7}$$

$$\widehat{s^k} + T = \widehat{y_1^k} + \widehat{t_1} + \widehat{w_1^k}; \; k = 1 \ldots K, \tag{8}$$

$$\widehat{y_i^k} \geq 0; \; i = 1 \ldots n; \; k = 1 \ldots K, \tag{9}$$

$$\sum_{j=1}^{n} x_{i,j}^k = \sum_{j=1}^{n} x_{j,i}^k; \; i = 1 \ldots n; \; k = 1 \ldots K, \tag{10}$$

$$c_i^k \leq Q_k \times \sum_{j=1}^{n} x_{i,j}^k; \; i = 1 \ldots n; \; k = 1 \ldots K, \tag{11}$$

$$\left(x_{i,j}^k = 1 \right) \Rightarrow c_j^k \geq 1; \; k = 1 \ldots K; \; i = 1 \ldots n, \tag{12}$$

$$\sum_{k=1}^{K} c_i^k = z_i; \; i = 2 \ldots n, \tag{13}$$

$$\widehat{y_i^k} \leq T; \; i = 1 \ldots n; \; k = 1 \ldots K, \tag{14}$$

$$x_{i,i}^k = 0; \; i = 1 \ldots n; \; k = 1 \ldots K, \tag{15}$$

$$ld_\lambda + \widehat{t_i} \leq \widehat{y_i^k} + \widehat{t_i} + c \times T \leq ud_\lambda, i = 1 \ldots n \tag{16}$$

$$\Sigma = \max_{k=1 \ldots K} \{supp_{s^k}\} = 0 \, . \tag{17}$$

It is assumed that the arithmetic operations contained in the above constraints meet the conditions of Definition 1 and Theorem 1. To solve $\widehat{FCS}$ (3), the values of the decision variables from the adopted set of domains for which the given constraints are satisfied must be determined. In other words, routings

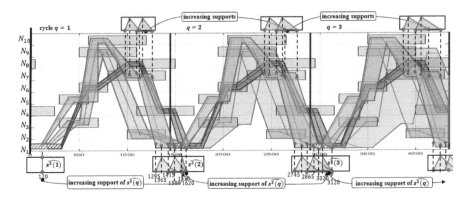

Fig. 5. Cyclic fuzzy schedules following Theorem 1 and corresponding to the routes from the Fig. 1 - a cycle period $T = 1450$

$(x_{\beta,\lambda}^k)$ and the corresponding schedule $(\widehat{s^k}, \widehat{y_\lambda^k}, \widehat{w_\lambda^k}, \Sigma)$ are sought that guarantee timely deliveries (according to given delivery service deadlines Δ_λ) despite travel times uncertainty $(\widehat{d_{\beta,\lambda}})$. Moreover, it is assumed that the feasible solution sought does not result in the accumulation of uncertainty in subsequent cycles (laytimes allow for uncertainty reduction $\Sigma = 0$). For fuzzy travel times $\widehat{d_{\beta,\lambda}}$ given in the form of OFN (see Fig. 3) solution (IBM ILOG CPLEX environment where OFN values are represented by discrete forms [3]) to the problem of the vehicle fleet scheduling in the OPOSN from the Fig. 1 is shown in the Fig. 4. It should be noted that the cumulative uncertainty value is reduced at the end of each cycle $(\Sigma(q) = 0)$. Fuzzy variables describing the waiting time of vehicles at node N_1 have a negative orientation (Fig. 3 – laytimes $\widehat{w_1^1}$, $\widehat{w_1^2}$ and $\widehat{w_1^3}$), which means that the results of the algebraic operations (e.g. $\widehat{y_1^1} + \widehat{t_1} + \widehat{w_1^1}$) using these variables lead to a decrease in uncertainty (support of $\widehat{s^1} = 1$). This means that, in contrast to the solution of the Fig. 2b), the supports of the all OFN decision variables $(\widehat{y_\lambda^k})$ do not increase in subsequent schedule cycles (Fig. 4).

For the case under consideration a series of experiments aimed at assessments of cumulative uncertainty $\Sigma(q)$ reduction depending on changes in the cycle period $(T = 1300-1850)$ and laytimes $(\widehat{w_\lambda^k} = \widehat{0}...\widehat{550})$. Figure 6 shows the space of solutions, among which only solutions with cycle period $T \geq 1685$ enable the reduction of uncertainty $(\Sigma(q) = 0)$. Proper example of such a solution is: $T = 1800; \widehat{w_\lambda^k} = \widehat{270}$ determining the schedule from the Fig. 4. On the other hand, assuming the value of $T = 1450$, makes it impossible to reduce the uncertainty, which is illustrated in Fig. 5.

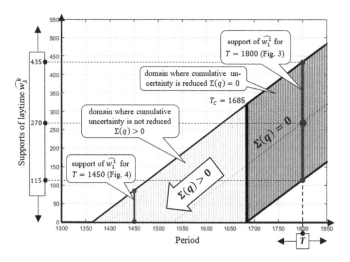

Fig. 6. Trade-off between the cycle period T and the laytime support $\widehat{w}_\lambda^k$

Table 1. Results of computational experiments

Number of nodes n	Number of vehicles K	Calculation time [s]
8	1	<1
8	2	3
8	3	7
10	1	11
10	2	24
10*	3	31
12	1	151
12	2	331
12	3	574
14	1	258
14	2	464
14	3	854
16	1	521
16	2	723
16	3	>900
18	1	>900
18	2	>900
18	3	>900

Therefore, the presented trade-off (see Fig. 6) allows to determine such part of the solution space (above the limit $T_C = 1685$) in which the cycle period T and the laytimes values $\widehat{w}_\lambda^k$ guarantee timely deliveries without the accumulation of uncertainty in subsequent cycles.

In addition to the above experiments, the effectiveness of the proposed approach was evaluated for distribution networks of different sizes (different numbers of customers and vehicles). The results are collected in the Table 1. The experiments were carried out for networks containing 6–18 nodes in which services were made by sets consisting of 1–3 vehicles. The problems considered can be solved in online mode (<900 s) when the size of service distribution network does not exceed 16 nodes. In the case of larger networks, the effect of combinatorial explosion limits the practical use of this method.

5   Conclusions

Conditions of the theorem proposed allow to construct models in which decision variables resulting from algebraic operations take values which are proper OFNs. Consequently, the arithmetic operations defined on OFNs enable to avoid some drawbacks of the classical approach while can be characterized by easy to interpret convex membership functions.

In addition to its capability to handle the fuzzy nature of variables through an algebraic approach, the proposed method can be used to rapidly prototype the sizing and allocation of time buffers. The related issue of vehicle mission planning subject to changing order uncertainty constraints will be the topic of our future studies.

References

1. Bansal, S., Goel, R., Katiyar, V.: A novel method to handle route failure in fuzzy vehicle routing problem with hard time windows and uncertain demand. Int. J. Adv. Oper. Manag. **9**(3), 169–187 (2017). https://doi.org/10.1504/IJAOM.2017. 088243
2. Bocewicz, G., Banaszak, Z., Rudnik, K., Witczak, M., Smutnicki, C., Wikarek, J.: Milk-run routing and scheduling subject to fuzzy pickup and delivery time constraints: an ordered fuzzy numbers approach (2020). https://doi.org/10.1109/ FUZZ48607.2020.9177733
3. Bocewicz, G., Nielsen, I., Banaszak, Z.: Production flows scheduling subject to fuzzy processing time constraints. Int. J. Comput. Integr. Manuf. **29**(10), 1105–1127 (2016). https://doi.org/10.1080/0951192X.2016.1145739
4. Braekers, K., Ramaekers, K., Van Nieuwenhuyse, I.: The vehicle routing problem: state of the art classification and review. Comput. Ind. Eng. **99**, 300–313 (2016). https://doi.org/10.1016/j.cie.2015.12.007
5. Ghannadpour, S., Simak, N., Reza, T., Keivan, G.: A multi-objective dynamic vehicle routing problem with fuzzy time windows: model, solution and application. Appl. Soft Comput. **14**, 504–527 (2014). https://doi.org/10.1016/j.asoc.2013.08. 015
6. Hanshar, F., Ombuki-Berman, B.: Dynamic vehicle routing using genetic algorithms. Appl. Intell. **27**(1), 89–99 (2009). https://doi.org/10.1007/s10489-006-0033-z
7. Holborn, P.: Heuristics for dynamic vehicle routing problems with pickups and deliveries and time windows. Cardiff University, School of Mathematics, School of Mathematics (2013)

8. Khairuddin, S., Hasan, M., Hashmani, A., Azam, M.: Generating clustering-based interval fuzzy type-2 triangular and trapezoidal membership functions: a structured literature review. Symmetry **13**(2) (2021). https://doi.org/10.3390/sym13020239

9. Khosiawan, Y., Scherer, S., Nielsen, I.: Toward delay-tolerant multiple-unmanned aerial vehicle scheduling system using multi-strategy coevolution algorithm. Adv. Mech. Eng. **10**(12) (2018). https://doi.org/10.1177/1687814018815235

10. Kilic, H., Durmusoglu, M., Baskak, M.: Classification and modeling for in-plant milk-run distribution systems. Int. J. Adv. Manuf. Technol. **62**(9), 1135–1146 (2012). https://doi.org/10.1007/s00170-011-3875-4

11. Kosinski, W., Prokopowicz, P., Slezak, D.: On algebraic operations on fuzzy numbers. In: Kłopotek, M.A., Wierzchoń, S.T., Trojanowski, K. (eds.) Intelligent Information Processing and Web Mining. Advances in Soft Computing, vol. 22. Springer, Heidelberg (2003). https://doi.org/10.1007/978-3-540-36562-4_37

12. Liu, C., Huang, F.: Hybrid heuristics for vehicle routing problem with fuzzy demands. In: Third International Joint Conference on Computational Sciences and Optimization (CSO 2010), Huangshan (2010)

13. Meyer, A.: Milk run design (definitions, concepts and solution approaches). Ph.D. thesis, Institute of Technology. Fakultät für Mas-chinenbau, KIT Scientific Publishing (2015)

14. Mor, A., Speranza, M.G.: Vehicle routing problems over time: a survey. 4OR **18**(1), 44–61 (2020). https://doi.org/10.1007/s10288-020-00433-2

15. Nucci, F.: Multi-shift single-vehicle routing problem under fuzzy uncertainty. In: Kahraman, C., Cevik Onar, S., Oztaysi, B., Sari, I.U., Cebi, S., Tolga, A.C. (eds.) INFUS 2020. AISC, vol. 1197, pp. 1620–1627. Springer, Cham (2021). https://doi.org/10.1007/978-3-030-51156-2_189

16. Okulewicz, M., Mańdziuk, J.: A metaheuristic approach to solve dynamic vehicle routing problem in continuous search space. Swarm Evol. Comput. **48**, 44–61 (2019). https://doi.org/10.1016/j.swevo.2019.03.008

17. Pavone, M., Bisnik, N., Frazzoli, E., Isler, V.: A stochastic and dynamic vehicle routing problem with time windows and customer impatience. Mobile Netw. Appl. **14**(3) (2008). https://doi.org/10.1007/s11036-008-0101-1

18. Pillac, V., Gendreau, M., Guéret, C., Medaglia, A.: A review of dynamic vehicle routing problems. Eur. J. Oper. Res. **225**(1), 1–11 (2013). https://doi.org/10.1016/j.ejor.2012.08.015

19. Polak-Sopinska, A.: Incorporating human factors in in-plant milk run system planning models. In: Ahram, T., Karwowski, W., Taiar, R. (eds.) IHSED 2018. AISC, vol. 876, pp. 160–166. Springer, Cham (2019). https://doi.org/10.1007/978-3-030-02053-8_26

20. Prokopowicz, P., Ślęzak, D.: Ordered fuzzy numbers: definitions and operations. In: Prokopowicz, P., Czerniak, J., Mikołajewski, D., Apiecionek, Ł, Ślęzak, D. (eds.) Theory and Applications of Ordered Fuzzy Numbers. SFSC, vol. 356, pp. 57–79. Springer, Cham (2017). https://doi.org/10.1007/978-3-319-59614-3_4

21. Sung, I., Nielsen, P.: Zoning a service area of unmanned aerial vehicles for package delivery services. J. Intell. Robot. Syst. **97**(3) (2020). https://doi.org/10.1007/s10846-019-01045-7

22. Sáez, D., Cortés, C., Núñez, A.: Hybrid adaptive predictive control for the multivehicle dynamic pick-up and delivery problem based on genetic algorithms and fuzzy clustering. Comput. Oper. Res. **35**(11), 3412–3438 (2008). https://doi.org/10.1016/j.cor.2007.01.025

Decision Support Model for the Configuration of Multidimensional Resources in Multi-project Management

Jarosław Wikarek[1] , Paweł Sitek[1(✉)] , and Zbigniew Banaszak[2]

[1] Kielce University of Technology, Kielce, Poland
{j.wikarek,sitek}@tu.kielce.pl
[2] Faculty of Electronics and Computer Science,
Koszalin University of Technology, Koszalin, Poland
banaszak@ie.tu.koszalin.pl

Abstract. In today's competitive knowledge-based economy, the introduction of new solutions, i.e. new products and services, new technologies, new organizational structures, etc., most often requires a project approach. Due to constrained resources, tight deadlines and, usually, a large number of implemented projects, the multi-project environment is used in practice. The key element in multi-project management is appropriate configuration and the use of constrained resources (e.g. machines, tools, software, employees, etc.). Modern resources are characterized not only by their availability and abundance, but also have many additional features that may affect the functionality and configurability of a given resource. Hence, before commencing the implementation of a project, and even more so for a set of projects, managers must answer a few key questions related to such resources, such as: *Do we have resources with proper features/functions to implement the set of projects on the given date and schedule? If not, what resources and features are missing?* etc. Obtaining answers to these types of questions may decide about the success of projects. The paper presents a decision support model for the configuration of multidimensional resources in a multi-project environment, which can be used in both a proactive and reactive approach. Many computational experiments were also carried out to verify the model itself and the methods of its implementation.

Keywords: Multi-project environment · Decision support · Resource allocation · Mathematical programming · Proactive and reactive approach

1 Introduction

The continuous development of companies is related to the implementation of new technological solutions in the IT area, modern organizational forms, new methods of communication and marketing, introducing new products and services to the market, etc. All this means that companies are forced to implement an increasing number of projects at the same time. This trend has resulted in a significant increase in the role of

© Springer Nature Switzerland AG 2021
N. T. Nguyen et al. (Eds.): ICCCI 2021, LNAI 12876, pp. 290–303, 2021.
https://doi.org/10.1007/978-3-030-88081-1_22

multi-project management [1, 2]. The effective implementation of simultaneous projects, very often from different areas of operation, enables the company to quickly develop [3]. Today, most companies manage multiple projects, although they are still looking for the best decision support tools in these complex environments.

Most modern IT tools supporting multi-project management [4] include scheduling, task prioritization, risk management [5], etc. Some also enable resource allocation [6]. Wherein the allocation of resources, if already included in such tools, is usually in the quantitative aspect. Contemporary resources can fulfill various functions. They can also be configurable, extended with new functionalities, etc. This completely changes the approach to the problem of resource allocation. In this case we can talk about multi-dimensional resources, each dimension of which is a specific function/features that the resource carries out. A good example of such a resource is a modern employee, and functions are his competencies. Another example is a computer/microprocessor and the functions are the corresponding software.

In this context it is extremely important to correctly allocate appropriately configured resources to individual project tasks. The problem can be formulated more generally than the allocation itself. *Do we have a sufficient amount of properly configured resources to implement a set of projects? Are any resource features missing?*

The main contribution of the paper is a resource configuration model that takes into account individual features/functions of resources and its implementation using the universal modeling language AMPL (A Mathematical Programming Language) [7]. The model enables decision support in multi-project management in the context of resource allocation and configuration. In particular, decisions regarding project feasibility in the context of available resources, defining missing resources or the need to reconfigure existing resources, etc.

2   Problem Statement and Illustrative Example

The problem of the configuration and allocation of multidimensional resources in multi-project management is discussed. The most basic definition of multi-project management (MPM) is managing an environment in which people are working on multiple projects simultaneously [8]. In such an environment, management has to deal with parallel projects of different dates and sizes, but with a common pool of resources. The very concept of multi-project management is quite new, so there is a lack of strategies, techniques and tools to deal with it effectively. Many project managers complain about a shared pool of resources, which often results in shuffling people and other resources that are used in their projects [9].

The problem of the configuration and allocation of resources in the multi-project environment is defined as follows:

- A set of projects to be performed is given (o – project index $o \in O$). The project consists of a set of tasks (k – task index $k \in K$). Failure to complete any task is tantamount to failure to complete the entire project.

- Each project is characterized by a specific/given schedule of performing tasks, which is known and unchanging. Note: So, the problem under consideration is not a scheduling problem, but a variation and development of the resource allocation problem. This has some practical justification, as in many cases the contracting authority imposes a project implementation schedule.
- Resources with certain features/functions (e – feature index $e \in E$) are needed for each task. The general idea of multidimensional resources is shown in Fig. 1. Table 1 shows sample resources and their features with values in parentheses.
- If several resource features/functions are required to perform a task, a resource with all the necessary features is allocated.
- Generally, resources can be configured, i.e. supplemented with new features (note: not every resource can be supplemented with every feature).
- A feature of a resource can be equated with its dimension. A resource can generally have many dimensions, or it can be supplemented with further dimensions. Therefore, this type of resource is called multidimensional resources.
- Resources may be temporarily unavailable.

Table 1. Resources and their features

Resource	Feature (values)
Employee	Employee competencies (programmer, analyst, welder, miller, etc.)
Computer	Software (SQL database, C #, Java, Phyton, Android, etc.)
CNC	Tools (drill bits, cutters, etc.)

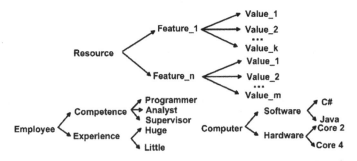

Fig. 1. Model of multidimensional resources/resource-feature-value of the feature

For such a problem, a few basic questions can be formulated (Table 2) which are crucial for the project management process in the context of resources.

Obtaining answers to the above questions is very important in multi-project management and may determine the success of a given set of projects. It also enables efficient management of resources and their rational use. It also facilitates the reaction if there is a lack of a resource or if the resource does not have the needed feature. The proposed questions concern both reactive decisions (Q1A, Q1B, Q2, Q3A, Q4A) and proactive decisions (Q1C, Q3B, Q4B). In order to present the defined problem of the configuration of multidimensional resources let us consider the illustrative example exam_01.

Table 2. Questions regarding resources in multi-project management

Question	Description
Q1A	Is your set of multidimensional resources sufficient to ensure that your set of projects is carried out on schedule?
Q1B	If not, what resources and how many features are missing?
Q1C	How and which resources should be modified and/or new ones acquired?
Q2	If a new project with a given structure and schedule is added to the set of implemented projects, will the available resources be sufficient to implement it without changes to the already implemented projects?
Q3A	Will the lack of a specific $i \in I$ resource enable the implementation of a set of projects?
Q3B	How should the configuration of resources be changed in order to complete the set of projects on schedule and on time when the resource $i \in I$ is unavailable?
Q4A	Will the lack of any $i \in I$ resource enable the implementation of a set of projects?
Q4B	How should the configuration of resources be changed in order to complete the set of projects on schedule and on time in the absence of any resource $i \in I$?

Illustrative Example exam_01. A set of five projects $o_1..o_5$ is given, which should be implemented in accordance with the schedule shown in Fig. 2. As part of the implementation of the above set of projects, tasks $k_1..k_{25}$ should be implemented. Appropriate features $e_1..e_{10}$ of resources are necessary for the implementation of each task. The list of the required features of the resources necessary for the implementation of individual tasks in the orders is presented in Table 3. Table 4 presents the list of resources and their features. A three-value coding was used for this: 1-means that a given resource has a given feature, 0-means that a given resource does not have a given feature but can acquire it, -1-means that a given resource does not have a given feature and cannot acquire it.

For illustrative example *exam_01*, questions Q1A and Q1B were formulated with the data instances as in the tables (Table 3, Table 4).

The answer to question Q1A required a lot of work by the operator who, by manually analyzing the data from Tables 2 and 3, the Gantt chart (Fig. 2), after many attempts stated that the resources with specific characteristics (Table 4) do not allow the implementation of projects $o_1..o_2$ according to the specified schedule (Fig. 2).The answer to question Q1B and the remaining questions, Q2..Q4, despite the small size of *exam_01*, was unsuccessful. It was not possible to answer this question by performing manual analysis with an acceptable amount of work and operator time, e.g. within an hour.

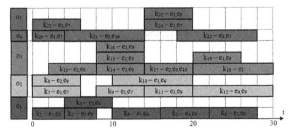

Fig. 2. Schedules for the implementation of project tasks with the required features

Table 3. Required resource characteristics for the implementation of individual project tasks

Project	Task	Time	Resources									
			e_1	e_2	e_3	e_4	e_5	e_6	e_7	e_8	e_9	e_{10}
o_1	k_1	4	+	−	−	−	−	−	−	+	−	−
	k_2	4	−	+	−	−	−	−	−	−	+	−
	k_3	6	−	−	+	−	−	+	−	−	−	−
	k_4	6	+	−	−	−	−	+	−	−	−	−
	k_5	6	−	−	−	+	−	−	−	−	+	−
	k_6	6	+	−	−	−	−	−	−	−	+	−
o_2	k_7	6	+	−	−	−	−	−	+	−	−	−
	k_8	6	−	+	−	−	−	−	−	−	+	−
	k_9	6	+	−	−	−	−	−	+	−	−	−
	k_{10}	10	+	−	−	−	−	+	−	−	−	−
	k_{11}	6	−	−	+	−	−	−	−	−	+	−
	k_{12}	10	−	−	−	+	−	−	−	−	+	−
o_3	k_{13}	6	−	+	−	−	−	−	−	−	+	−
	k_{14}	6	−	−	+	−	−	−	−	−	+	−
	k_{15}	6	+	−	+	−	−	−	−	−	−	−
	k_{16}	6	−	+	−	−	−	−	−	−	+	−
	k_{17}	6	−	+	−	−	−	−	−	−	+	+
	k_{18}	10	−	−	+	−	−	−	−	−	−	−
	k_{19}	6	+	−	−	−	−	−	−	−	+	−
o_4	k_{20}	4	+	−	−	−	−	−	+	−	−	−
	k_{21}	10	−	+	−	−	−	−	−	−	−	+
	k_{22}	10	−	−	+	−	−	−	+	−	−	−
o_5	k_{23}	6	+	−	−	−	−	−	+	−	−	−
	k_{24}	6	+	−	−	−	−	−	+	−	−	−
	k_{25}	6	−	−	+	−	−	−	−	−	+	−

+ the task requires a certain feature; − the task does not require a certain feature.

Table 4. Features of individual resources

Resource	Features									
	e_1	e_2	e_3	e_4	e_5	e_6	e_7	e_8	e_9	e_{10}
i_1	1	−1	1	−1	−1	0	0	0	1	0
i_2	−1	1	−1	1	0	0	0	1	0	1
i_3	1	−1	1	0	1	1	1	0	0	0
i_4	1	1	−1	0	1	0	1	1	0	0
i_5	1	−1	1	0	0	0	1	0	0	0
i_6	1	−1	−1	0	0	1	1	0	0	0
i_7	1	−1	−1	0	0	0	1	0	1	0
i_8	1	1	−1	0	1	0	0	1	0	0
i_9	−1	0	1	1	0	0	0	0	1	0
i_{10}	−1	1	−1	1	0	0	0	0	0	1

The analysis of this and other similar illustrative examples showed that manual or semi-automatic/e.g. using tools such as spreadsheets /, finding answers to questions Q1..Q4 is very difficult, if not impossible. These findings became the motivation to undertake research on the development of a model to support decisions in the field of the configuration and allocation of resources with specific characteristics to tasks. An additional area of this research involved ways of implementing the model that would enable quick answers to the questions posed.

3 Decision Support Model for the Configuration of Multidimensional Resources

As a result of the problem analysis and the results of illustrative examples, work was undertaken to work out the decision support model for the configuration of multimodal dimensions. Figure 3 shows the general concept of building the model. The model is based on two basic sets, a set of constraints (Table 5) and a set of questions (Table 2). Model parameters are data on resources, their features and schedules. The model was formulated as a constraint satisfaction problem (CSP) [10]. Depending on the question included in the model, the model may take the form of binary integer programming (BIP). The description of the constraints (1).. (14) of the model is presented in Table 5, while the description of decision variables, indexes and parameters is presented in Table 6.

$$\sum_{i \in I} X_{u,i,k} + Y_{u,k} = 1 \ \forall \ k \in K, u \in U \tag{1}$$

$$X_{u,i,k} \leq g_{i,k} \ \forall \ i \in I, k \in K, u \in U \tag{2}$$

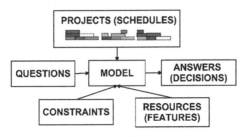

Fig. 3. Model building concept

Table 5. Description and meaning of model constraints

Constraint	Description
(1)	Every task must be done
(2)	If the resource carries out a task, it must have the necessary features to perform it
(3)	In a given state of resource unavailability, tasks are performed only with the use of available resources
(4)	Defines how many unavailability states will fail to complete tasks
(5)	The number of states in which tasks are not completed does not exceed the set value
(6)	Determination of the coefficient $es_{i,k,e}$
(7,8)	Determination of the coefficient $g_{i,k}$
(9)	The resource cannot perform two tasks at the same time
(10)	Resource can be obtained only by permitted features
(11)	The cost of acquiring by resources the features necessary to perform the tasks (Cost1)
(12)	Determining which orders will not be executed
(13)	Penalty for failure to complete orders (Cost2)
(14)	Binary and integrity

$$X_{u,i,k} \leq f_{u,i} \ \forall \ i \in I, k \in K, u \in U \tag{3}$$

$$\sum_{k \in K} Y_{u,k} \leq St \cdot Wx_u \forall \ u \in U \tag{4}$$

$$\sum_{u \in U} Wx_u \leq L \tag{5}$$

$$es_{i,k,e} = (ew_{i,e} + Ex_{i,e}) \cdot ej_{k,e} \forall i \in I, k \in K, e \in E \tag{6}$$

$$(1 - g_{i,k}) \leq \sum_{e \in E} ej_{k,e} - \sum_{e \in E} es_{i,k,e} \forall \ i \in I, k \in K \tag{7}$$

Table 6. Decision variables, indexes and parameters

Symbol	Description
Indexes	
I	Set of resources
O	Set of orders
K	Set of tasks
U	Set of resource unavailability
E	Set of features
i	Resource index ($i \in I$)
o	Order index ($o \in O$)
k	Task index ($k \in K$)
u	The resource unavailability status index ($u \in U$)
e	Resource feature index $e \in E$
Parameters	
$h_{k1,k2}$	If tasks k_1 and k_2 are performed at the same time $h_{k1,k2} = 1$ otherwise $h_{k1,k2} = 0$
$ew_{i,e}$	If resource i has the feature e $ew_{i,e} = 1$ otherwise $ew_{i,e} = 0$
$ep_{i,e}$	If the resource i can get the resource feature e $ep_{i,e} = 1$ otherwise $ep_{i,e} = 0$
$b_{o,k}$	If task k is part of order o $b_{o,k} = 1$ otherwise $b_{o,k} = 0$
r_o	Penalty for failure to complete the order o
$ek_{i,e}$	The cost of obtaining the resource feature e for the resource i
$ej_{k,e}$	If resource feature e is required to perform task k than $ej_{k,e} = 1$ otherwise $ej_{k,e} = 0$
$f_{u,i}$	If resource i is available for unavailable state u than $f_{u,i} = 1$ otherwise $f_{u,i} = 0$
St	Very large constant
Decision variables	
$X_{u,i,k}$	If the resource i performs the task k during the unavailable state ($u \in U$) than $X_{u,i,k} = 1$ otherwise $X_{u,i,k} = 0$
Wx_u	If all tasks k are completed during the unavailable state ($u \in U$) $Wx_u = 1$ otherwise $Wx_u = 0$
$Y_{u,k}$	If task k is not executed during unavailable state ($u \in U$) $Y_{u,k} = 1$ otherwise $Y_{u,k} = 0$
Z_o	If the order o has not been executed $Z_0 = 1$ otherwise $Z_0 = 0$
$Ex_{i,e}$	If the resource i is required to obtain the feature e to perform the tasks $Ex_{i,e} = 1$, otherwise $Ex_{i,e} = 0$
Determined value	
$g_{i,k}$	If the resource i has the required functionality to perform the task k $g_{i,k} = 1$ otherwise $g_{i,k} = 0$

(*continued*)

Table 6. (*continued*)

Symbol	Description
$es_{i,k,e}$	If the resource i has or has acquired the feature e needed to complete the task k $es_{i,k,e} = 1$ otherwise $es_{i,k,e} = 0$
Cost1	The cost of acquiring by resources the features necessary to perform the tasks
Cost2	Penalty for failure to complete orders
Control parameter	
L	In how many cases of unavailability states u, tasks will not be completed (0: in all; 1: in one state of absenteeism, tasks will not be completed; 2: in two states of absenteeism, tasks will not be completed, etc.)

$$ST \cdot (1 - g_{i,k}) \leq \sum_{e \in E} ej_{k,e} - \sum_{e \in E} es_{i,k,e} \forall\, i \in I, k \in K \tag{8}$$

$$X_{u,i,k1} + X_{i,i,k2} \leq 1 \forall i \in I, k1 \in K, k2 \in K \wedge h_{k1,k2} = 1 \tag{9}$$

$$Ex_{i,e} \leq ep_{i,e} \forall i \in I, e \in E \tag{10}$$

$$Cost1 = \sum_{i \in i} \sum_{e \in E} (ek_{i,e} \cdot Ex_{i,e}) \tag{12}$$

$$\sum_{u \in U} \sum_{k \in K} (Y_{u,k} \cdot b_{o,k}) \leq St \cdot Z_o \forall o \in O \tag{12}$$

$$Cost2 = \sum_{o \in O} (Z_o \cdot r_o) \tag{13}$$

$$Z_o, Wx_u, Y_{u,k}, Ex_{i,e}, X_{u,i,k} \in \{0, 1\} \forall i \in I, k \in K, u \in U, e \in E, o \in O \tag{14}$$

A significant aspect of the analyzed problem of resource configuration is the fact that the i ($i \in I$) resources may be unavailable due to various causes (e.g. breakdown, scheduled inspection, etc.). Assume that, u_j denotes the case of unavailability of selected resources (e.g. $u_1 = \{i_3, i_7\}$ means that we are analyzing a case where the i_3, i_7 resources are unavailable, whereas if $u_2 = \{i_3\}$ it denotes a case where the i_3 resource is unavailable, where $i_3, i_7 \in I$, etc.). U denotes a set of all such analyzed (interesting to us) cases of employee unavailability $u_j \in U$. It is easy to calculate that if we have 5 resources and if we examine all possible single unavailability of resources, the U set will comprise 5 elements. On the other hand, if we want to account for all possible unavailability of two resources, the U set will comprise 10 or 15 elements if we also take single unavailability into account, etc. In operating practice, a situation where the U set has to be taken into account with elements specifying unavailability of random two, three, four, etc. resources happens very rarely.

4   Computational Experiments

The model was implemented using the universal modeling language AMPL (Appendix A) language and the mathematical programming/constraint programming environment GUROBI [11]. Subsequently, numerous computational experiments were carried out, divided into two stages. In the first stage, all the questions for the illustrative example *exam_01* were answered. The answer to question Q1A was NO, the answer to questions Q1B and Q1C – in order to realize the set of projects, three resources, i_2, i_4, i_8, should acquire feature e_9, and resource i_8 additionally feature e_{10}. Figure 4 shows the appropriate allocation of resources to tasks. In this allocation, resources i_2, i_4, i_8 have new features as per the answer to question Q1C. The next questions are about resources with altered characteristics according to Q1C.

The answer to question Q2 is related to the emergence of new o_6 and o_7 designs. Assume all data are as in illustrative example *exam_01* (including modified resources i_2, i_4, i_8). There will be new projects with a task implementation schedule as in Fig. 5 with the requirements as to the characteristics of resources as in Table 7. The answer to question Q2 is as follows. In order to implement a set of projects together with new projects without changing the already planned assignments of resources to tasks (Fig. 4), resource i_1 should acquire the e_8 feature, resource i_3 should acquire the e_9 feature, and resource i_9 should acquire the e_5 feature. The new method of allocating resources to tasks consistent with the answer to question Q2 is presented in Fig. 6.

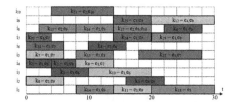

Fig. 4. Allocation of resources for the implementation of tasks

Fig. 5. Schedules for the implementation of additional projects with the required features for the tasks

Question Q3A was formulated as follows: Will the lack of the i_5 resource from $t = 8$ enable the execution of the order set $o_1..o_5$? The answer to this question is unthinkable. Therefore, question Q3B was asked in the form: *How should the configuration and resource allocation be changed?* Answer: The method of assigning resources to tasks should be changed as shown in Fig. 7.

Table 7. Resource features needed to carry out specific tasks of additional projects

Project	Task	Time	Features									
			e_1	e_2	e_3	e_4	e_5	e_6	e_7	e_8	e_9	e_{10}
o_6	k_{26}	4	+	−	−	−	−	−	−	+	−	−
	k_{27}	4	−	−	+	−	−	−	−	−	+	−
	k_{28}	4	+	−	−	−	−	−	−	−	−	−
o_7	k_{29}	4	+	−	−	−	−	−	−	−	−	−
	k_{30}	4	−	−	−	−	+	−	−	−	+	−

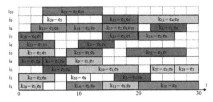

Fig. 6. Allocation of resources for the implementation of tasks, taking into account new projects

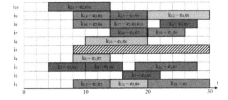

Fig. 7. Allocation of resources for the implementation of tasks (resource unavailability i5 from time t = 8)

The last question, Q4, seems to be the most difficult as it is proactive and requires a lot of checks. They were formulated in the form: *How should resources be configured to be able to implement a set of $o_1..o_5$ projects (according to the schedule in Fig. 2 for resources with characteristics from Table 4) in the event of the unavailability of any resource?* In practice, depending on the resource, the unavailability may result from breakdowns, renovation and inspection, absence, etc. For question Q4 formulated in this way, the obtained answer defines an additional configuration of resources in the form: resource i_3 should acquire feature e_9, resource i_4 should acquire feature e_4, resource i_5 should acquire the e_6 feature and resource i_9 should acquire the e_2 feature. Figure 8 shows two exemplary (there are ten of them all) allocations of resources to tasks in the event of unavailability i_1 and i_4.

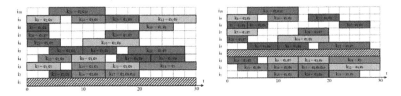

Fig. 8. The allocation of resources to tasks using the resource unavailability i_1 or i_4

The second stage of the computational experiments was to assess the effectiveness of the model implementation method. The experiments were carried out for ten different instances of In1..In10 data (instance In3 is illustrative example examp_01). Individual data instances differed in the number of projects (N_o), the number of tasks (N_k), the number of resources (N_z) and the number of features (N_e). This translates into the size of the solved examples, i.e. the number of decision variables (V) and constraints (C), and, consequently, the computation time (T). Questions Q1A (the question required the least effort, simple general question) and question Q4 (the question required the greatest effort of calculations, due to the need to check the unavailability of each of the $i_1..i_{10}$ resources) were selected for the experiments of this phase. The computation times for all data instances for both questions are presented in Table 8.

It turned out that the calculations lasted from 4 to 471 s, which was an acceptable timeframe and confirmed the correctness of the implementation method (AMPL and GUROBI). For data instances of much larger sizes, it is planned to use the proprietary hybrid approach [12] and selected metaheuristics for the implementation of the model.

Table 8. Results of the second phase of computational experiments

In	N_o	N_k	N_z	N_e	Q1A			Q4B		
					V	C	T(s)	V	C	T(s)
In1	3	15	10	5	1127(216)	1469	4	2471(1560)	4763	12
In2	4	20	10	5	1452(271)	1574	7	3271(2060)	5663	24
In3	5	25	10	10	3147(376)	3739	9	5381(2610)	9462	39
In4	7	35	10	10	4357(455)	5269	11	7481(3610)	13963	49
In5	9	45	15	10	5317(571)	9545	13	17736(10290)	32115	67
In6	10	50	15	10	9322(951)	10524	15	19656(11415)	34215	94
In7	10	60	15	15	13674(1156)	17359	17	25171(13740)	43993	189
In8	10	70	15	15	15177(1345)	20069	19	32521(15990)	47943	194
In9	15	80	20	15	27612(1981)	30344	34	57951(32320)	64232	345
In10	15	90	20	15	31022(2191)	32954	43	65151(36322)	91923	471

N_o – number of projects, N_k – number of tasks, N_z – number of resources, N_e – number of features, V – number of decision variables (non-zero), C – number of constraints, T (s) – calculation time in seconds.

5   Conclusions

The model proposed in the paper can be the basis for the design of decision support systems in the scope of the allocation and configuration of resources in multi-project management. Taking into account many features of resources (so-called multidimensions resources) in the model significantly increases the possibility of their configuration and increases the flexibility of assignment to tasks. On the other hand, the proposed model assumes the invariability of project schedules, which significantly simplifies its computational complexity and eliminates the need to additionally solve the problem of task scheduling. One of the advantages of the model is that it can be used in both proactive and reactive modes. Questions Q3B and Q4B are typically proactive in nature, question Q2 can be both proactive and reactive, while the rest of the questions are reactive in nature. All this translates into a wide range of decision support, especially in the area of resource allocation and configuration. In practice, the decision-maker, using this model, can make decisions such as: Is it possible to accept a set of projects for implementation or not? *How can you configure your resources so that the project set can be implemented? How can you configure your resource set so that in the event of the unavailability of any one, the set of projects can be implemented? etc.* Future works will cover the development of the model in terms of: (a) introducing additional questions, (b) the possibility of assigning several resources to the task, (c) adding logical constraints, (d) introducing the costs of resource configuration, and (e) implement the model using a hybrid approach integrating MP, CLP and GA [12, 13]. It is planned to use the proposed model to support decisions, including in the problems of production scheduling [14], vehicle routing problems [15], project management [16], and configuration of employee competences [17].

Appendix A Implementation of the Decision Model in AMPL

```
set Wr; set Jo; set Or; set Co; set Un;
param pa{Wr}; param pb{Wr}; param pk{Jo}; param r{Or};
param wr{Co}; param wc{Co}; param z{Wr,Jo}; param h{Jo,Jo};
param ew{Wr,Co}; param ep{Wr,Co}; param ek{Wr,Co};
param ej{Jo,Co}; param f{Un,Wr}; param b{Or,Jo}; param St;
param L;
var g{Wr,Jo} >=0; var es{Wr,Jo,Co} >=0;
var X{Un,Wr,Jo} >=0, binary; var Y{Un,Jo} >=0, binary;
var Wx{Un} >=0, binary; var Ex{Wr,Co} >=0; var Z{Or} >=0, binary;
var Cost1; var Cost2;
subject to C1 {u in Un, k in Jo}:sum{i in Wr}X[u,i,k]+Y[u,k]= 1;
subject to C2 {u in Un, i in Wr, k in Jo}: X[u,i,k] <= g[i,k];
subject to C3 {u in Un, i in Wr, k in Jo: f[u,i]=0}:
X[u,i,k]<=g[i,k];
subject to C4 {u in Un}:sum{k in Jo} Y[u,k] <= St*Wx[u];
subject to C5 :sum{u in Un} Wx[u] <= L;
subject to C6 {i in Wr, k in Jo, e in Co}:
es[i,k,e]=(ew[i,e]+Ex[i,e])*ej[k,e];
subject to C7a {i in Wr, k in Jo}:
(1-g[i,k])<=(sum{e in Co} ej[k,e]) - (sum{e in Co} es[i,k,e]);
subject to C7b {i in Wr, k in Jo}:
St*(1-g[i,k])>=(sum{e in Co} ej[k,e]) - (sum{e in Co} es[i,k,e]);
subject to C8 {u in Un,i in Wr, k1 in Jo, k2 in Jo:h[k1,k2]=1}:
X[u,i,k1]+X[u,i,k2]<=1;
subject to C9 {i in Wr, e in Co}: Ex[i,e] <= ep[i,e];
subject to C10: Cost1 = sum{i in Wr, e in Co} Ex[i,e]*ek[i,e];
subject to C11 {o in Or}:
sum{u in Un, k in Jo} Y[u,k]*b[o,k] <=St*Z[o];
subject to C15 :Cost2 = sum{o in Or} Z[o]*r[o];
```

References

1. Schwindt, C., Zimmermann, J. (eds.): Handbook on Project Management and Scheduling Vol. 2. IHIS, Springer, Cham (2015). https://doi.org/10.1007/978-3-319-05915-0
2. Walter, M.: Multi-Project Management with a Multi-Skilled Workforce. Springer, Fachmedien, Wiesbaden (2015). https://doi.org/10.1007/978-3-658-08036-5
3. Tonchia, S.: Industrial Project Management, International Standards and Best Practices for Engineering and Construction Contracting, Springer-Verlag GmbH Germany, part of Springer Nature (2018) https://doi.org/10.1007/978-3-662-56328-1
4. Best Project Management Tools & Software for 2021: https://www.proofhub.com/articles/top-project-management-tools-list. Accessed 5 May 2021
5. Sutton, I.: Process Risk and Reliability, Management Operational Integrity Management. Copyright © 2015 Elsevier Inc. https://doi.org/10.1016/C2014-0-01362-7
6. Kane, H., Tissier, A.: A resources allocation model for multi-project management. In: 9th International Conference on Modeling, Optimization & SIMulation, June 2012, Bordeaux, France. hal-00728599f
7. Home-AMPL: https://ampl.com/. Accessed 5 May 2021
8. Kerzner, H.R.: Project Management. John Wiley & Sons. ISBN: 9781119165354 (2017)
9. Maenhout, B., Vanhoucke, M.: A resource type analysis of the integrated project scheduling and personnel staffing problem. Ann. Oper. Res. **252**(2), 407–433 (2015). https://doi.org/10.1007/s10479-015-2033-z
10. Apt, K.: Constraint Logic Programming Using ECLiPSe. Cambridge University Press (2009). https://doi.org/10.1017/CBO9780511607400
11. Gurobi: http://www.gurobi.com/. Accessed 5 May 2021
12. Sitek, P., Wikarek, J.: A multi-level approach to ubiquitous modeling and solving constraints in combinatorial optimization problems in production and distribution. Appl. Intell. **48**(5), 1344–1367 (2017). https://doi.org/10.1007/s10489-017-1107-9
13. Sitek, P., Wikarek, J., Rutczyńska-Wdowiak, K., Bocewicz, G., Banaszak, Z.: Optimization of capacitated vehicle routing problem with alternative delivery, pick-up and time windows: A modified hybrid approach. Neurocomputing **423**, 670–678 (2021). https://doi.org/10.1016/j.neucom.2020.02.126
14. Nielsen, I., Dang, Q.-V., Nielsen, P., Pawlewski, P.: Scheduling of mobile robots with preemptive tasks. Adv. Intell. Syst. Comput. **290**, 19–27 (2014)
15. Schermer, D., Moeini, M., Wendt, O.: Algorithms for Solving the Vehicle Routing Problem with Drones. In: Nguyen, N.T., Hoang, D.H., Hong, T.-P., Pham, H., Trawiński, B. (eds.) ACIIDS 2018. LNCS (LNAI), vol. 10751, pp. 352–361. Springer, Cham (2018). https://doi.org/10.1007/978-3-319-75417-8_33
16. Relich, M.: Portfolio selection of new product projects: a product reliability perspective. Eksploatacja i Niezawodnosc – Maintenan. Reliabil. **18**(4), 613–620 (2016). https://doi.org/10.17531/ein.2016.4.17
17. Szwarc, E., Bocewicz, G., Bach-Dąbrowska, I., Banaszak, Z.: Declarative Model of Competences Assessment Robust to Personnel Absence. In: Damaševičius, R., Vasiljevienė, G. (eds.) ICIST 2019. CCIS, vol. 1078, pp. 12–23. Springer, Cham (2019). https://doi.org/10.1007/978-3-030-30275-7_2

New Extensions of Reproduction Operators In solving LABS Problem Using EMAS Meta-Heuristic

Sylwia Biełaszek$^{(\boxtimes)}$ ⓘ, Kamil Piętak ⓘ, and Marek Kisiel-Dorohinicki ⓘ

Faculty of Computer Science, Electronics and Telecommunications, Institute of
Computer Science, AGH University of Science and Technology, Kraków, Poland
{bielsyl,kpietak,doroh}@agh.edu.pl
https://www.agh.edu.pl/

Abstract. Agent-based evolutionary, computational systems have been
proven to be an efficient concept for solving complex computational problems. In this paper, we propose and evaluate new variants of reproduction
operators together with new heuristics for generation of initial population, dedicated to LABS – a hard discrete optimisation problem. The
paper illustrates how to design and implement particular parts of the
algorithm and discusses required conditions for evolutionary parameters
and operators.

Keywords: Agent-based evolutionary systems · LABS · Low
autocorrelation binary sequences · Crossover operators

1 Introduction

This paper concentrates on improving agent-based evolutionary computational
systems for solving the low autocorrelation binary sequence problem. It introduces new variants of reproduction operators for LABS together with new heuristics for generation of initial population. LABS, one of the hard discrete problems
despite wide research, remains an open optimisation problem for long sequences.
It belongs to CSPLIB [22] library, which consists problems that "pose a significant challenge to local search methods". It has also a wide range of applications
including communication engineering [23,24], statistical mechanics [2,17] and
mathematics [12,13].

LABS [10] consists of finding a binary sequence $S = \{s_0, s_1, ..., s_{L-1}\}$ with
length L, where $s_i \in \{-1, 1\}$, which minimises energy function $E(S)$:

$$C_k(S) = \sum_{i=0}^{L-k-1} s_i s_{i+k}$$

$$E(S) = \sum_{k=1}^{L-1} C_k^2(S)$$

(1)

© Springer Nature Switzerland AG 2021
N. T. Nguyen et al. (Eds.): ICCCI 2021, LNAI 12876, pp. 304–316, 2021.
https://doi.org/10.1007/978-3-030-88081-1_23

MJ Golay also defined a so-called *merit factor* [11], which binds the LABS energy level to the length of a given sequence:

$$F(S) = \frac{L^2}{2E(S)} \tag{2}$$

The search space for the problem with length L has the size 2^L [18] and the energy and merit factor of a sequence can be computed in time $O(L^2)$. The LABS problem has no constraints, so S can be represented naturally as an array of binary values. One of the reasons for high complexity of the problem is, that in LABS, all sequence elements are correlated. One change that improves some $C_i(S)$, has also an impact on many other $C_j(S)$ and can lead to significant changes of solutions energy.

There is a lot of various techniques that try to solve the problem. The simplest method of solving LABS is exhaustive enumeration that provides the best results, but can be applied only to small values of L. There are also a lot of various heuristic algorithms that use some plausible rules to locate good sequences more quickly. A well-known method for such techniques is *steepest descend local search* (SDLS) [1] or tabu search [9]. In recent years, a few modern solvers based on the self-avoiding walk concept have been proposed. The most promising solvers are *lssOrel* [3] and *xLostavka* [4], which are successfully used for finding skew-symmetric sequences of lengths between 301 and 401 [5]. These techniques can be also parallelized utilizing GPGPU architectures what was show in [19,25].

A promising direction of research is also using agent-based biologically-inspired computational systems. One of such meta-heuristics is the concept of an evolutionary multi-agent system (EMAS) proposed by K. Cetnarowicz [7] and successfully applied for solving complex problems. EMAS has already been used to optimise some complex continues and discrete problems such as LABS [15,19,25].

The goal of this contribution is propose and verify various crossover operators dedicated to LABS problem, as well as introduce a new operators of initial population generation and mutation, based on existing local search techniques that already proved to be successful for LABS problem.

The paper is organised as follows. In the next section the the evolutionary multi-agent system which forms the basis of the new solution proposal is described. In the third section new operators are presented in details, and then the experimental results together with conclusions are drawn in the following section. The paper is summarised in the last section where also future work is indicated.

2   Evolutionary Multi-agent Systems for Discrete Optimisation Problems

In a basic EMAS, the system is comprised of individual agents living in a population. The main concepts of evolution are realised with reproduction and death operations. In optimisation problems, the individuals contain a solution decoded in the shape of genotype. The genotype is inherited from the parents using variation operators (i.e. mutation and recombination). As there is no global knowledge, in contrast to classic evolutionary algorithms, the selection is based on energy resource, belonging to each individual. The level of energy is related to its quality and causes various behaviours of an individual: a high level of energy allows it to reproduce, an average level leads to energy transfer between individuals ("fight" operation) and a low level causes the agent's death. Each new-born individual is evaluated by a fitness function which rates it's genotype in the context of a given problem.

In the memetic variant of EMAS, the evaluation can be further improved by utilising various local optimisation techniques such as the steepest descent local search, the tabu search, the self-avoiding walk and others.

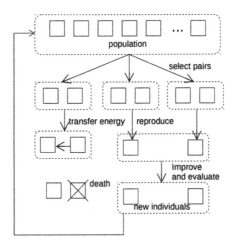

Fig. 1. Single step of the memetic EMAS.

Figure 1 illustrates a single step of the memetic EMAS – squares represent individuals gathered in a population and arrows depict the flow of the algorithm. The number of individuals in a population can vary from step to step as shown in Fig. 1 – there are two new individuals and only one is death (removed from the population). The global size of population is managed by energy resource that is constant for the whole population.

A formal description of the memetic EMAS is presented in Algorithm 1. The *processPopulation* function contains a single "step" that is called sequentially until a stop condition is reached. Within each step, individual agents try to meet other agents in a population and in this way a new set of pairs is formulated. During the "meeting", agents in a pair can reproduce or fight, depending on the level of agents' energy. If a selected pair is "good enough", then a new individual is "born" from the selected parents. Otherwise, individuals from the pair fight

Algorithm 1. A simplified algorithm of population processing in memetic EMAS

```
1: function PROCESSPOPULATION(population)
2:     pairs := selectPairs(population)
3:     newBorns := Array[]
4:     for pair in pairs do
5:         if canReproduce(pair) then
6:             newBorns+ = reproduce(pair)
7:         else
8:             fight(pair)
9:     newBorns := evaluate(newBorn)
10:    newBorns := improve(newBorn)
11:    population+ = newBorns
12:    for ind in population do
13:        if shouldDie(ind) then
14:            remove(population, ind)
       return population
```

with each other, and in consequence a portion of life energy is transferred between them. Next, all new born individuals are then evaluated and improved using local optimisation techniques. Finally, at the end of the step, all weak individuals are removed from the population (death operation).

To use the EMAS for a problem optimisation, a few elements dedicated for the problem are required to be delivered. First of all, a representation of a problem's solutions has to be declared. Based on that, adequate evolutionary operators such as mutation and crossover, as well as memetic and evaluation operators are needed. All of them have to be compliant [21] and should be further adjusted by specifying proper values of their parameters.

The representation of the LABS problem is an array of binary values. At the beginning of a computation individuals are usually generated randomly.

Evolutionary operators such as mutation and recombination are defined accordingly for this representation. We distinguish three versions of the crossing operators: one point, two point and uniform. A child is formed from two parent individuals, by combining some of the bits of each of them. In one point and two point recombination we determine one or two the division points of the parent genotype, respectively, and the offspring receives alternately fragments of the parents' genotypes. In uniform recombination child receives alternately beats of both parents.

The mutation operator consists in the negation of the sequence bits with a certain probability specified in the parameters.

The fitness function for LABS is the energy 1 or merit factor 2 for a given sequence used to determine the quality of an individual in comparisons with other individuals in the population.

There is also a lot of local search heuristics that explore a neighbourhood of an individual to find better solution. One of them, used in this paper, is steepest descent local search (SDLS) technique, which is an algorithm belonging to the class of gradient methods. It, in an iterative manner, explores the neighbourhood of a given sequence until the local optimum is reached. A found neighbor with a better energy becomes the examined element. The process is ended when it will not be possible to make such a modification of a single bit that will improve the evaluation. The formal definition is presented in Algorithm 2. The SDLS algorithm is also illustrated with sample sequence in Fig. 2.

Algorithm 2. *Steepest Descent Local Search* for LABS problem. Based on [8]. Symbols: S – an input sequence; L – length of the sequence; F – sequence evaluation(*merit factor*); S_i/F_i – the best sequence and its evaluation in a single iteration

---

1: **function** SDLS(S)
2:     $S_{best} = S$
3:     $F_{best} = \text{EVALUATE}(S_{best})$
4:     *improvement = true*
5:     **while** *improvement* **do**
6:         $F_i = -\infty$
7:         **for** $j = 0$ to $L - 1$ **do**
8:             $S_{tmp} = S_{best}$
9:             $S_{tmp}[j] = -1 * S_{tmp}[j]$
10:            $F_{tmp} = \text{EVALUATE}(S_{tmp})$
11:            **if** $F_{tmp} > F_{cand}$ **then**
12:                $S_i = S_{tmp}$
13:                $F_i = F_{tmp}$
14:        **if** $F_i > F_{best}$ **then**
15:            $S_{best} = S_i$
16:            $F_{best} = F_i$
17:            *improvement = true*
18:        **else**
19:            *improvement = false*
20:    **return** S_{best}

---

3   Extended Recombination Operators for LABS Problem

In this section we present new extensions of reproduction operators dedicated to LABS problem, that introduce additional modifications to the newly created solutions. Moreover, there are introduced improvements in initial population generation.

In EMAS, similarly to other population algorithms, the initial population is usually generated randomly. However, in case of LABS problem, starting computation from locally improved individuals seems to speed-up the whole process. Therefore, instead of a randomly generated individuals, we put into a new population random solutions, each improved by SDLS algorithm. This algorithm,

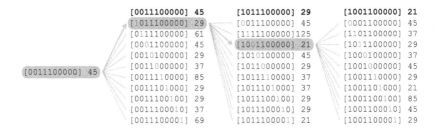

Fig. 2. An illustration of SDLS on sample input sequences

among other local search techniques for LABS, is a compromise between effectiveness and efficiency.

In EMAS, as well as other evolutionary algorithms, the mutation introduces with some low probability random changes to the genotype. The aim of this process is to introduce diversity to the population, i.e. to prevent premature convergence. However, as the new crossover operators introduce additional randomness to the newly created solution, there is no need to apply standard mutation methods.

3.1 New Variants of Recombination Operators

The purpose of the recombination phase is to increase the probability that the offspring of the two parents will inherit their best genotype fragments. The choice of a specific recombination algorithm depends on the chromosome coding method and the specificity of the problem. In the previous research we used uniform and two-point recombination.

The proposed operators derive from uniform and two-point operators and introduce additional modifications to part of newly created sequence based on crossover results. We introduced four improvements that have been applied to bot uniform and two-point recombination methods. All of the described operators are presented in Fig. 3.

The INV extension assumes that the bit order of the entire sequence is reversed in the case of uniform recombination (Fig. 3(c)), and the bit order of the middle segment defined by the parental split points is reversed in the case of two-point recombination (Fig. 3(d)).

The second extension called SHIFT, involves a cyclic shift of a specific bit length. We divide the result of the uniform recombination into two equal segments (if the result has an even length) or segments differing by 1 bit (if the result has an odd length), and then we swap them with each other (Fig. 3(e)). In the case of two-point recombination, the division and replacement of sections are performed in the middle section defined by the dividing points of the parent individuals (Fig. 3(f)).

The negHB extension in the case of a two-point recombination is the negation of a randomly selected half of the bits of the longest segment from among the segments determined by the dividing points of the parent individuals (Fig. 3(h)). In the case of uniform recombination, we negate a randomly selected half of the bits of the entire sequence (Fig. 3(g)).

The last extension, negEv2, is defined only for two-point recombination. It negates every second bit of the middle segment defined by the dividing points of the parent individuals (Fig. 3(i)).

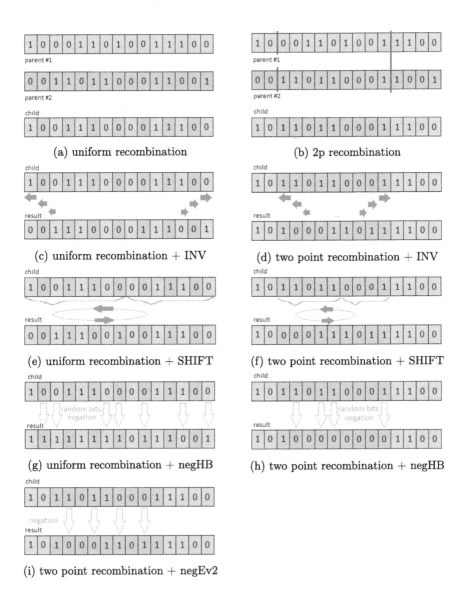

(a) uniform recombination

(b) 2p recombination

(c) uniform recombination + INV

(d) two point recombination + INV

(e) uniform recombination + SHIFT

(f) two point recombination + SHIFT

(g) uniform recombination + negHB

(h) two point recombination + negHB

(i) two point recombination + negEv2

Fig. 3. The illustration of the proposed recombination extensions

4   Experimental Study

All computations performed in this paper, has been implemented on AgE platform[1] – a Java-based solution developed as an open-source project by the Intelligent Information Systems Group of AGH-UST. AgE provides a platform for the development and execution of agent-based applications in mainly simulation and computational tasks [6,21]. The modular architecture of AgE allows to use components to assembly and run agent-based computations [20] for various problems such as black-box complex discrete problems (e.g. LABS, OGR, Job-shop) [14,16] or continuous optimisation problems.

All computations were performed at a PC workstation with Windows 7 Intel Core i5-2520M 2.50 GHz, 8 GB RAM memory and using Intel HD Graphics 3000 graphic card. The tests which constituted the reference material were also repeated on this configuration.

Table 1. Configurations of EMAS for LABS problem compared in this paper

Name	Generation of initial population	Recombination	Mutation	Local optimization
2p	random	2p	random bits change	SDLS
U	random	U	random bits change	SDLS
2p-rndS-mutS	random+SDLS	2p	random bits change	SDLS
U-rndS-mutS	random+SDLS	U	random bits change	SDLS
2p-negEv2	random+SDLS	2p+negEv2	–	SDLS
2p-INV	random+SDLS	2p+INV	–	SDLS
2p-SHIFT	random+SDLS	2p+SHIFT	–	SDLS
2p-negHB	random+SDLS	2p+negHB	–	SDLS
U-negHB	random+SDLS	U+negHB	–	SDLS
U-INV	random+SDLS	U+INV	–	SDLS
U-SHIFT	random+SDLS	U+SHIFT	–	SDLS

The goal of the conducted experiments was to verify how the proposed methodology of computing influence the effectiveness of the memetic EMAS.

In comparison to the previous works [15], we used different energy settings of individuals, resulting from the previous series of experiments. The different energy values, different types of improvements and different population sizes were tested. The starting energy of an individual in our research was set to 5, the reproductive energy was set to 7 and the energy transfer between fighting individuals was set to 1.

In our research sequences of length 201 were tested, we used the construction properties of skew-symmetric sequences in the calculations. An initial population size was set to 50. Each configuration has been run for 600 s and repeated 10

---

[1] Project homepage: https://gitlab.com/age-agh/age3.

times. Values showed in the presented charts are the arithmetic mean of this repetitions. The exact settings of our tests are presented in Table 1.

4.1 Results

New variants of crossover operators as well as utilising SDLS to improve initial population, described in the previous section, affect the results for LABS problem.

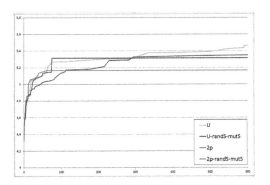

Fig. 4. Comparison of modifications in initial population generation. In all figures the X axis presents time and the Y axis depicts the merit factor of the best solutions found so far.

Figure 4 presents how local optimisation of initial population with SDLS algorithm (series with randS-mutS postfix) impacts the effectiveness of EMAS system. According to our assumptions, the modifications don't improve the whole results but significantly increase the convergence of the algorithm at the beginning what is a good starting point for further improvements.

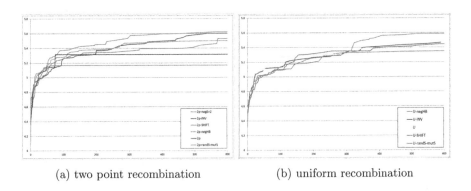

(a) two point recombination   (b) uniform recombination

Fig. 5. Results of three types of new mechanisms for algorithms using different two types of recombinations.

Figure 5 presents the influence of new operators, described in the article, on the effectiveness of EMAS for LABS problem. We can see that effectiveness improved when we included new variant of recombination. It can be seen that the results of the trials with the new modifications improved higher for two point recombination than for uniform recombination.

Best result was achieved for 2p-negEv2 on level 5,62. It is slightly above the best result in uniform recombination attempts. Other trials using two point recombination (2p-INV, 2p-SHIFT, 2p-negHB) also significantly improved the results, see Fig. 5(a).

In case of uniform recombination, shown on Fig. 5(b), best result was achieved for U-negHB on level of 5.59. U-INV also had a better average result compared to the original algorithm, only U-SHIFT had slightly worse result.

Comparing the effect of our improvements on both types of recombination, it can be seen that in both cases the improvements we made increased the result. In two point recombination to a higher value than in uniform recombination, and the increase in two-point recombination was higher compared to the base configuration than the analogous increase in uniform recombination.

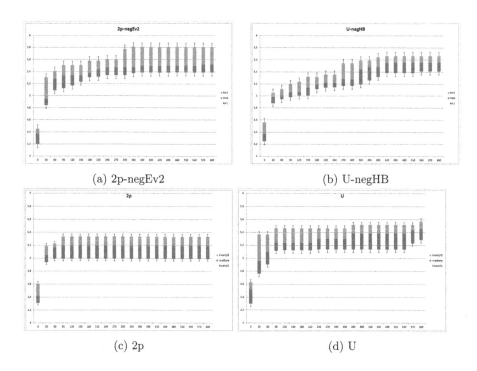

(a) 2p-negEv2   (b) U-negHB

(c) 2p   (d) U

Fig. 6. Statistical distribution of the series of results.

The statistical distribution of individuals in a population (Fig. 6) shows that 2p-negEv2 variant introduce big diversity in the population, especially comparing to U-negHB variant. This is interesting conclusions as both of them gives the best and comparable results.

4.2   Summary of the Experimental Results

The main concern of the paper was to describe the impact of introduced changes on the effectiveness of solving LABS problems using the EMAS system. From the research that has been conducted, it is possible to conclude that the introduced operations improved the results.

Best result in whole tested group was achieved when we test new mechanisms of two point recombination with negEv2 (2p-negEv2) extension. In this case mean result achieved 5,62. We have compared it with our research to date [15]. The effect looks promising. In [15], where EMAS and its memetic version using local RMHC and SDLS optimization, was used to solve the LABS problem, the average results reached the level of 4.23, 4.66, 4.87 respectively, while the maximum was 4.57, 4.96, 4.81. Therefore our average results were higher by 0,75 than [15].

The changes described in this article have had an effect on the efficiency of the algorithm. The reason is that they caused a change in ratio of exploration to exploitation. In the case of pure EMAS, we search the solution space according to random population points.

5   Conclusions and Future Work

In this article, we introduced extensions to crossover operators dedicated to LABS problem in EMAS systems. This extensions leads to better results comparing to the previous results of the basic version of the EMAS.

The results of presented experiments prove that the proposed concept speeds up computations and allows to get better solutions than the same version realised using standard EMAS operators.

The further work will be conducted to verify how the proposed variants of recombination operators work with other local optimization methods such as TABU and SAWS. The important direction will be also adjusting and verification of new extensions with use of super computers where a lot of CPUs and GPGPUs are available at the same time.

Future work includes also the application of the techniques described above to a large population located on many islands in the EMAS memetic model.

Acknowledgement. The research presented in this paper was realized thanks to funds of Polish Ministry of Science and Higher Education assigned to AGH University of Science and Technology.

References

1. Bartholomew-Biggs, M.: The Steepest Descent Method, pp. 1–8. Springer, Boston (2008). https://doi.org/10.1007/978-0-387-78723-7_7

2. Bernasconi, J.: Low autocorrelation binary sequences: statistical mechanics and configuration space analysis. J. de Physique **48**, 559–567 (1987)
3. Bošković, B., Brglez, F., Brest, J.: Low-autocorrelation binary sequences: on improved merit factors and runtime predictions to achieve them. arXiv e-prints arXiv:1406.5301 (2014)
4. Brest, J., Bošković, B.: A heuristic algorithm for a low autocorrelation binary sequence problem with odd length and high merit factor. IEEE Access **6**, 4127–4134 (2018). https://doi.org/10.1109/ACCESS.2018.2789916
5. Brest, J., Bošković, B.: In searching of long skew-symmetric binary sequences with high merit factors (2020)
6. Byrski, A., Kisiel-Dorohinicki, M.: Agent-based model and computing environment facilitating the development of distributed computational intelligence systems. In: Allen, G., Nabrzyski, J., Seidel, E., van Albada, G.D., Dongarra, J., Sloot, P.M.A. (eds.) ICCS 2009. LNCS, vol. 5545, pp. 865–874. Springer, Heidelberg (2009). https://doi.org/10.1007/978-3-642-01973-9_96
7. Cetnarowicz, K., Kisiel-Dorohinicki, M., Nawarecki, E.: The application of evolution process in multi-agent world (MAW) to the prediction system. In: Proceedings of 2nd International Conference on Multi-Agent Systems (ICMAS 1996). AAAI Press (1996)
8. Gallardo, J.E., Cotta, C., Fernandez, A.J.: A memetic algorithm for the low autocorrelation binary sequence problem. In: Proceedings of the 9th Annual Conference on Genetic and Evolutionary Computation, GECCO 2007 pp. 1226–1233. ACM, New York (2007)
9. Gallardo, J.E., Cotta, C., Fernández, A.J.: Finding low autocorrelation binary sequences with memetic algorithms. Appl. Soft Comput. **9**(4), 1252–1262 (2009)
10. Golay, M.: Sieves for low autocorrelation binary sequences. IEEE Trans. Inf. Theory **23**(1), 43–51 (1977)
11. Golay, M.: The merit factor of long low autocorrelation binary sequences (corresp.). IEEE Trans. Inf. Theory **28**(3), 543–549 (1982)
12. Günther, C., Schmidt, K.U.: Merit factors of polynomials derived from difference sets (2016)
13. Jedwab, J., Katz, D.J., Schmidt, K.U.: Advances in the merit factor problem for binary sequences. J. Comb. Theory Ser. A **120**(4), 882–906 (2013)
14. Kolybacz, M., Kowol, M., Lesniak, L., Byrski, A., Kisiel-Dorohinicki, M.: Efficiency of memetic and evolutionary computing in combinatorial optimisation. In: Rekdalsbakken, W., Bye, R.T., Zhang, H. (eds.) ECMS, pp. 525–531. European Council for Modeling and Simulation (2013)
15. Kowol, M., et al.: Agent-based evolutionary and memetic black-box discrete optimization. Procedia Comput. Sci. **108**, 907–916 (2017)
16. Kowol, M., Byrski, A., Kisiel-Dorohinicki, M.: Agent-based evolutionary computing for difficult discrete problems. Procedia Comput. Sci. **29**, 1039–1047 (2014)
17. Leukhin, A.N., Potekhin, E.N.: A bernasconi model for constructing ground-state spin systems and optimal binary sequences. J. Phys. Conf. Ser. **613**, 01200 (2015)
18. Militzer, B., Zamparelli, M., Beule, D.: Evolutionary search for low autocorrelated binary sequences. IEEE Trans. Evol. Comput **2**(1), 34–39 (1998)
19. Pietak, K., Zurek, D., Pietron, M., Dymara, A., Kisiel-Dorohinicki, M.: Striving for performance of discrete optimisation via memetic agent-based systems in a hybrid cpu/gpu environment. J. Comput. Sci. **31**, 151–162 (2019)

20. Piętak, K., Kisiel-Dorohinicki, M.: Agent-based framework facilitating component-based implementation of distributed computational intelligence systems. In: Nguyen, N.-T., Kołodziej, J., Burczyński, T., Biba, M. (eds.) Transactions on Computational Collective Intelligence X. LNCS, vol. 7776, pp. 31–44. Springer, Heidelberg (2013). https://doi.org/10.1007/978-3-642-38496-7_3

21. Piętak, K., Woś, A., Byrski, A., Kisiel-Dorohinicki, M.: Functional integrity of multi-agent computational system supported by component-based implementation. In: Mařík, V., Strasser, T., Zoitl, A. (eds.) HoloMAS 2009. LNCS (LNAI), vol. 5696, pp. 82–91. Springer, Heidelberg (2009). https://doi.org/10.1007/978-3-642-03668-2_8

22. Walsh, T.: CSPLib problem 005: Low autocorrelation binary sequences. http://www.csplib.org/Problems/prob005, Accessed 31 Jan 2017

23. Zeng, F., He, X., Zhang, Z., Xuan, G., Peng, Y., Yan, L.: Optimal and z-optimal type-ii odd-length binary z-complementary pairs. IEEE Commun. Lett. **24**(6), 1163–1167 (2020)

24. Zhao, L., Song, J., Babu, P., Palomar, D.P.: A unified framework for low autocorrelation sequence design via majorization–minimization. IEEE Trans. Signal Process. **65**(2), 438–453 (2017)

25. Żurek, D., Piętak, K., Pietroń, M., Kisiel-Dorohinicki, M.: Toward hybrid platform for evolutionary computations of hard discrete problems. Procedia Comput. Sci. **108**, 877–886 (2017)

Adam Smith's Invisible Hand as a New, Powerful and Robust Control Paradigm for Collective AI Robotics

Tadeusz Szuba$^{(\boxtimes)}$ ⓘ and Michał Drożdż ⓘ

Faculty of Social Sciences, UPJP2 University, Cracow, Poland
{tadeusz.szuba,michal.drozdz}@upjp2.edu.pl

Abstract. The market launch of Tesla electric cars with an intelligent autopilot capable of dealing with the chaos of street traffic, shows how dramatic the need to develop a theory of building control systems for autonomous intelligent robots is, where there is no central control or it only exists locally. However, a suitable theory exists in the area of economics, for free (quasi free) markets, called "Adam Smith's Invisible Hand" (ASIH). The general assumption of this theory is *"that there is no control system, which will do better for the welfare of the free market, than spontaneous, unconscious, distributed, self-control/optimization that (ASIH) is able to perform"*. In general, this theory is the front line of a harsh dispute between advocates of interventionism and advocates of liberalism. This paper presents how the ASIH theory could be distilled to obtain a general control theory for systems of autonomous, mobile, quasi-intelligent robots, for unmanned building sites, deep mines, etc. such that collective self-control is inborn into the nature of robots and no centralized control is necessary. The first theoretical results indicate that self-control and optimization systems based on such a theory should be much more intelligent in terms of problem solving than centralized systems could be and incomparably more resistant, e.g. when parts of a robot group are destroyed. The reason for this is, that such systems better exploit the potential of individual intelligences of agents.

Keywords: Adam Smith's Invisible Hand (ASIH) · Collective Intelligence · Social structures · Computational model · Collective AI robotics · New control paradigm · Emergent behavior

1 Understanding the Invisible Hand

While "power/control" in the classical sense has been the tradition for thousands of years, "power/control" on the economic platform begun to show its paradoxical behaviour (the phenomenon of the Invisible Hand) only in Adam Smith's era [1]. At that time, a relatively democratic Britain was the complete opposite of the many totalitarian European systems built by such outstanding personalities as Frederick the Great of Prussia (1712–1786), Tsarina Catherine the Great

© Springer Nature Switzerland AG 2021
N. T. Nguyen et al. (Eds.): ICCCI 2021, LNAI 12876, pp. 317–329, 2021.
https://doi.org/10.1007/978-3-030-88081-1_24

(1729–1796) and finally Napoleon Bonaparte (1769–1821). At that time, British operations were based on trade[1] in huge areas extending as far as India (implying a delay in providing information) and based on the rapid development of the metallurgical and textile industries (with the associated unpredictability of technical progress and the 1st Industrial Revolution[2]). The economy, and trade related to such conditions, were completely unsuitable for "centralistic and totalitarian management". Only a company (manufacturer, trading company) and stock market investors could be the decision-making unit. Therefore, self-steering of social and economic structures had to be spontaneously implemented. Adam Smith noticed[3] this phenomenon in 1759. Despite the apparent chaos[4] resulting from the functioning of such a system, Britain was quickly becoming a powerful economic/commercial and military superpower. The Napoleonic wars ultimately showed the strength of Britain's system.

However, the Invisible Hand ruling social structures can be also found on the level of social insects, e.g. ants (named as Elementary Invisible Hand [4]).

Ants emerged in the Cretaceous period (145 to 66 million years ago) and diversified after the rise of flowering plants. A single ant with 250,000 neurons only, is mentally too primitive to act (even as a group) as a ruler in the anthill. The ant queen is only a stud. Despite this, the anthill displays an astonishing amount of Collective Intelligence, even creativeness, when adopting to new environments of human cities. Evolution provided ants with an Elementary Invisible Hand ruling the anthill so efficiently.

Observing ants, there is no next step in a single ant neural network development. There are no super-ants with super-brains like in some sci-fi movies.

It seems that the next case of the Invisible Hand was possible on the basis of *Homo habilis*[5] as an agent - a future component of social structure. However, it took almost 2 million years of evolution of intelligence (until 9,000–8,000 B.C.E.) when the first animals (dogs, sheep, goats) were domesticated by human social

---

[1] Presumably the ancient Phoenician Republic of Cartagena, and then the Renaissance Venetian Republic were too small to make this phenomenon visible.

[2] First Industrial Revolution: 1760 to 1820 and 1840 https://en.wikipedia.org/wiki/Industrial_Revolution.

[3] Some researchers question whether Adam Smith was aware of what he said, because the phrase "Invisible Hand" was used by him only three times [2] and there are no studies that would indicate that he actually worked on this issue. However, from the point of view of T. Szuba's work on the chaotic processes of Collective Intelligence [5], this is completely irrelevant. It is important that as a prominent and respected thinker, philosopher and economist, he created this concept, it was not forgotten and other economists around 1925 began to work intensively on it [3]. Christopher Columbus also was not aware that he discovered America.

[4] Chaos it is not the same as indeterminism. Behind Chaos can be hidden e.g. equations. See https://plato.stanford.edu/entries/chaos/#BriHisCha.

[5] Homo habilis: https://en.wikipedia.org/wiki/Homo_habilis.

structures. Around 10,000 B.C.E. man began deliberately cultivating land[6]. This contributed to a change in lifestyle to sedentary. The first settlements began to emerge, and approx. 8,000 B.C.E. - the first cities - which we can compare to an anthill in terms of architecture and size of settled social structure[7]. Here, a more sophisticated version of the Invisible Hand as a control system was possible.

Despite ants looking like a more favorable platform to discussing an Invisible Hand inspired frame of control system for future AI collective robotics (external exoskeleton and simple brain), much more conclusions can be derived from the Invisible Hand functioning on the platform of human social structures/markets.

What is especially important, is computational processes behind Invisible Hand function - they are better visible in the case of humans than ants. However, better visible does not necessarily mean easy to grasp.

The evidence for this difficulty is the fact that prominent scientists are divided on the existence and nature of the ASIH. For example, Economics Nobelist Joseph E. Stiglitz and Noam Chomsky (American linguist, philosopher, cognitive scientist, historian, logician, social critic, and political activist) are counted among the critics of this paradigm. John Keynes was generally against it. Just before his death in 1946, Keynes said: *"I find myself more and more relying for a solution of our problems on the Invisible Hand which I tried to eject from economic thinking twenty years ago."*

However, there are also supporters who consider ASIH not as a myth, but as a serious hypothesis with hard arguments supporting it e.g. pointing to Economic Calculation Problem.

Economic Nobelist Friedrich Hayek was an ultimate advocate of ASIH and interpreted it as a spontaneous order. He claimed, that the so called "Economic Calculation Problem[8]" is *non-computable* by any authority, government, dictator (even using computers), thus it can be said that the problem is *not-computable*[9], but it is *solvable* by a *market price mechanism*. The Invisible Hand can solve this problem providing a social structure/market with a quasi-optimal solution and immediate/automatic implementation.

---

[6] Similarly like in human civilization, in ants' social structures there is primitive agriculture (mushroom breeding) and animal breeding (ants like aphids because of the honeydew they emit, which is their delicacy. They even protect them, for example, against ladybugs that eat aphids). Probably for human style farming, much higher intelligence is required.

[7] Jericho had 2,000–3,000 inhabitants.

[8] Economic Calculation Problem referred to, is that of how to distribute resources rationally in an economy. The free market solution is the price mechanism, wherein people individually have the ability to decide how a good or service should be distributed based on their willingness to give money for it. The price conveys embedded information about the abundance of resources as well as their desirability which in turn allows, on the basis of individual consensual decisions, corrections that prevent shortages and surpluses.

[9] Computational complexity of this problem is not constant, is growing since free market components (agents, companies) are using more and more powerful computers for market prediction.

This is very important piece of puzzle to build picture of control theory based on ASIH, for AI collective robotics. Simply put, this is a strong recommendation that central calculating and assigning tasks to AI robots should be not applied. Instead AI robots should be programmed to follow the example of an ideal human worker, i.e. individual robots should be looking (individually as well as collectively) for what could be done at a given moment, in a given situation[10].

Another example of Economic Nobelist, who was an advocate of the Invisible Hand, was H. Simon [6], who was a specialist in *Organizational Economics*.

His contribution to the Invisible Hand Engineering is very important and is utilized in this paper. In 1959 cooperating with J. C. Shaw, and Allen Newell (IT specialists) they built the General Problem Solver - a milestone in AI development[11]. They have used the Means-Ends-Analysis[12] (MEA) as the main strategy, which has been again adopted for ASIH (see next section).

Below are A. Smith's, and F. Hayek's key quotations, which are fundamental for the narration of the Invisible Hand Theory.

F. Hayek in his works recommends thinking about market processes in terms of information processing. He stated this in 1945, when computer science was newborn. Thus he can be considered a pioneer who recommended considering that computational processes are behind ASIH. For F. Hayek money was a carrier of information.

Quote 1 (F. Hayek): We must look at the price system as such a mechanism for communicating information if we want to understand its real function ... [7].

A. Smith's quotation is important from a molecular model of computations point of view, because it explains how in abstract computational space (CS) of spontaneous and unconscious computations, matching information molecules (IM) mutually attract and repel to provide or exclude computations/inferences.

Quote 2 (A. Smith): It is not from the benevolence of the butcher, the brewer, or the baker, that we expect our dinner, but from their regard to their own interest. We address ourselves, not to their humanity but to their self-love, and never talk to them of our necessities but of their advantages. [1]

This quotation underlines importance of egoism as an important component of behavior (balanced by willingness to cooperate) for general theory of ASIH. It is key for defining of "egoistic personality" of AI robot which can feel pain, can

---

[10] The spontaneous construction of a bridge by the inhabitants of a remote high mountain village, without a plan and without an engineer/construction manager, using the available materials could be an example.

[11] For this they became ACM A.M. Turing Award laureates - equivalent of Nobel Award in IT.

[12] AI version of Means-Ends-Analysis: https://computersciencewiki.org/index.php/Means-Ends_Analysis
Means-Ends-Analysis in general: https://en.wikipedia.org/wiki/Means%E2%80%93ends_analysis.

be tired or even can assume that other AI robots are so close to the problem, that they should take given duty.

Two consecutive A. Smith's and F. Hayek's quotes should be considered together, because they complement one another.

Quote 3 (F. Hayek): The knowledge necessary for the solution of the economic problem is never concentrated in a single mind, and part of the problem is how to utilize knowledge which is scattered among many individuals. Much of the knowledge needed is not scientific knowledge but "knowledge of the particular circumstances of time and place [8].

Here Hayek clearly states that algorithms constituting ASIH must be distributed among members of a market/social structure. Part of the algorithm located in the brain of a specific member must be capable of autonomous work on the basis of data acquired locally and in a restricted period of time. ASIH must be organized in such a way, that such autonomous sub-algorithms must be properly integrated on higher level of collective mind.

Quote 4 (A. Smith): By pursuing his own interest he frequently promotes that of the society more effectually than when he really intends to promote it. I have never known much good done by those who affected to trade for the public good. [1]

Adam Smith proposes the hypothesis, that ASIH organized on the basis of "own interest", also in case of future, particular AI robot, should provide better workplace/social structure control, than any program performing functions of authority can provide.

It should be noted that works of the American philosopher R. Nozick (1938–2002) have provided further progress to the understanding of the Invisible Hand phenomena [9]. He managed to abstract from economic issues and provide foundations of ASIH based on "philosophical morality". This way ASIH can be considered a universal phenomenon, not related to market economy.

The Invisible Hand is commonly associated with a free market in which it can operate. This freedom of market agents is a fundamental component of the structure to host it. F. A. Hayek fought to convince the political and economic world that this freedom is fundamental [10] for ASIH - e.g. mobility of an agent. Thus, the autonomy of AI robots who are collectively controlled, should be bigger than is widely assumed.

Meanwhile, without realizing it, Humanity has created an almost exemplary environment for the Invisible Hand, which is the Internet. This can be considered as the first step in the field of Invisible Hand Engineering.

Let's look at what the research assumptions were when considerations on Internet in the early 1960s started.

What happened, were military-inspired studies of how to build a robust communication network, that could survive an attack by the USSR and Warsaw Pact - notably a strike-first nuclear attack.

The research answer was to decentralize everything, including addressing and routing, to not have any essential Head Quarters, and also to have redundant paths in terms of communicating.

Major US academic research centers (including military research bases with links to academia) took this idea on in the late 1960s and built the ARPANET network that eventually evolved into the Internet we know today. It was full of scientists and university academics from the start. It is well known that universities are the nursery of liberal thinking, but the army surely is not liberal in its nature. Thus today the liberal impact of Internet on our civilization is a great example of unintended consequences of military initiative, but designed by the academic environment. Unintended consequences and emergent behavior are among basic elements of the Invisible Hand phenomenon, referring mainly to fact that it is difficult to identify and to describe.

The success of the Internet is an important argument for our efforts to building future self-controlled systems for collective AI robotics, inspired by ASIH.

2   The Invisible Hand as an Unconscious, Chaotic, Non-deterministic Computational Process on the Platform of Beings/Robots in Natural/Artificial Social Structure

It seems that for understanding and modeling (for needs of future Invisible Hand Engineering) of unconscious, chaotic, non-deterministic computational processes on platform of beings/robots, which are behind Invisible Hand, two models of computations must be integrated:

1. A model able to simulate Natural (or Artificial) Neural Networks. This computational layer is to provide determinism for the existence of single being/robot as well as the ability for its deep learning[13]. Recent progress in processor development confirms this, since top processors started to be equipped with Neural Engines. For example the Apple M1 processor has: an 8-core CPU, an 8-core GPU, but also a 16-core Neural Engine for machine learning tasks[14];
2. The molecular model is used to reflect chaos brought to social structure by the surrounding environment. The similarity to Brownian Movement is astonishing, since the existence and behavior of a single being/robot undergoes constant bombardment coming from surrounding world of difficulties and opportunities. Thus the behavior of a single agent/robot, despite it trying to be deterministic, from the point of view of all social structure, appears as partially chaotic. This is especially well-visible on all construction sites.

Below is a demonstration that it is most probably a sole solution to the problem of defining computational platform for ASIH derived control systems.

---

[13] Deep Learning: https://en.wikipedia.org/wiki/Deep_learning.

[14] M1 Apple processor: https://www.tomshardware.com/news/Apple-M1-Chip-Everything-We-Know.

2.1 Social Structure of Agents/Robots as Computational Platform for Invisible Hand Acting as Control System

When analyzing how Evolution develops Biological Neural Networks (brains of species) at least two symptoms of incredible lack of continuity can be found [4].

As mentioned before, ants emerged in the Cretaceous period (145 to 66 million years ago) and diversified after the rise of flowering plants.

Despite these favorable circumstances, there is no next step (progress) in a single ant neural network development. Instead of this, Evolution decided to build social structures of quasi autonomous ants, thus providing an upper level where a different model of computations is used: a molecular, much more nondeterministic (comparing to neural network) model of computations. Evolution has found that this model is more suitable to dealing with more complicated problems. In 1994 L. Adleman [11] managed to build such a computer and to use to solve a simple case of "Traveling Salesman Problem". He used DNA molecules as agents. Despite highly optimistic expectations, progress in the field of molecular computing has been very slow. Technical difficulties with DNA digital data storage (even if companies like Microsoft are engaged) justifies this[15].

The same Evolution was responsible for the development of humans.

Evolution led to the emergence of man (Homo habilis) as an agent capable of making technological discoveries, but on the level of Neanderthals took a step back.

The brain size (volume) of Neanderthals exceeded that of modern Homo Sapiens. It is understandable if we consider that the Neanderthals died out (about 40,000 years ago) before agriculture (11,500 years ago) and animal breeding (10,000 years ago) emerged as a collective effort.

Neanderthal economy was based on gathering and hunting and group size is thought to have averaged 10 to 30 individuals (similar to modern hunter-gatherers). Such activity required high individual intelligence and physical individual fitness, higher than was needed in for collective agriculture and animal breeding, where division of labor is used to reduce the universality of the individual.

It can even be speculated that in this case Evolution took a step back – it has decided that it is worth sacrificing physical prowess and a slightly higher level of intelligence for the characteristics of the human species that enable the creation of larger social structures on the basis of agriculture unified with animal breeding. The ability to make discoveries has been preserved, however discoveries are made by individuals, but the improvement process following the discovery, then implementation and dissemination, is a task for a social structure - not an individual.

Summarizing this section, for the Invisible Hand a computational process run on platform of social structure, not a single being is fundamental. A single being is only a processor, however with high computational power, very high

---

[15] DNA digital data storage: https://www.microsoft.com/en-us/research/project/dna-storage/.

reprogramming ability in case of a human (to perform different roles without biological change) and ability to be a generator (even to make discoveries).

The side effect of such reduced role of being, is emerging in case of some individuals the mental arrogance (ignoring his mental limitations). Such individuals believe that they can mentally grasp complex economic and social processes and predict necessary control actions, what leads to harmful totalitarianism - if such being managed to grasp a control over social structure.

3 Overall Architecture of Control System Derived from Invisible Hand Paradigm, for Autonomous Team of AI Robots

Artificial Neural Networks (ANN) simulate the electrical aspect of activity of Biological Neural Networks (BNN). They do this well, which is proven by Neural Engines in Tesla Autopilot[16] and M1 Apple processors, etc. However, a real biological neuron is also a biological cell, thus in terms of the afore mentioned Adleman DNA computer [11] (Sect. 2.1), "cell of a neuron" can be also molecular computer. Scientists have spotted this, claiming that a cell is a root of a plant's intelligence [12].

It is important to realize this, because it can be hypothesized that computational power of a single biological neuron is very underestimated and 250,000 of neurons in an ant's brain are a much more powerful computer than we can estimate, thinking in terms of ANN only.

On the basis that a future ANN will be as powerful, as BNNs are, it can be assumed that both Tesla Autopilot[17]) and an inference engine of an agent/robot, can be combined together.

For this to happen, it is necessary to shift AI from (traditional) mathematical logic [13] into Shape Grammars [14] and inference systems based on this formalism. Example Shape Grammar inferences are given in Fig. 1.

Other researchers have also spotted this however, without such far reaching conclusions. The paper [15] presents behavior of a 3D computer graphics simulated humanoid in an environment/maze of obstacles, displaying almost human-like behavior. Phase-Functioned Neural Network has been used for this.

This direction is confirmed by Microsoft research, however without mentioning what hardware platform such Shape Grammar inferring system will be settled on. Probably for this purpose, platform independent terminology "Spatial mapping" [16] and "Spatial Understanding" [17] is used.

Switching to Shape Grammars inferences, immediately allows to adopt general idea of famous General Problem Solver[18] (G.P.S) designed in 1959 by Herbert A. Simon, J. C. Shaw, and Allen Newell. For this they have used Means-End-Analysis (MEA) [6] and predicate calculus.

[16] Tesla Autopilot: https://www.tesla.com/en_EU/autopilotAI.
[17] Tesla car Autopilot vision system: https://heartbeat.fritz.ai/computer-vision-at-tesla-cd5e88074376.
[18] General Problem Solver: https://en.wikipedia.org/wiki/General_Problem_Solver.

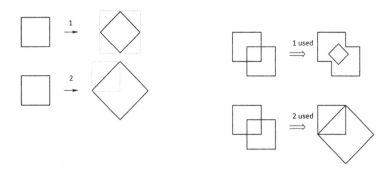

Fig. 1. On the left are given two shape grammar inference rules, on right side, are given two alternative conclusions (1-step derivatives) from the same initial shape.

Figure 2 displays how a 2D abstract ant, infers what to do now, using Shape Grammar inference (not logic) and Means-End-Analysis.

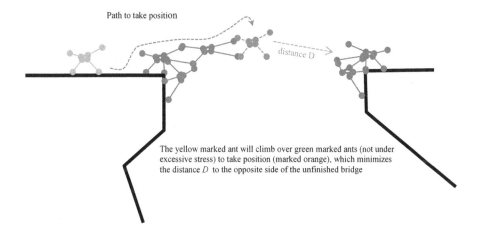

Fig. 2. Minimizing difference distance to opposite end of the bridge.

This assembly of the Invisible Hand strategy to define self-control of AI robots (at level of social structure/team), with Shape Grammar inference (convenient for neural networks) and MEA as local strategy (on individuals level) results in clear and easy overall system design.

We should remember that A. Simon has received the Nobel Prize in economy for his works on Organizational Economics. As mentioned before he was a supporter of the Invisible Hand idea[19].

---

[19] H. Simon in his last lecture in 2000 [18] was saying "... *Adam Smith's Invisible Hand is often highly visible....*"
(Authors comment) Perhaps such genius economist (Nobel Award, Turing Award for contribution in AI development) was able to see Invisible Hand often and precisely.

Please note that in such a control system design, parallel computations are not a problem - they are simply inborn into the structure of the system. However, here parallelism is not the result of central planning of how possibilities will be distributed over computational resources, but are the result of individual agents'/robots' decisions to consider a given case/possibility from a local/temporary circumstances point of view. Moreover, this parallelism is not deterministic, because some possibilities will not be taken into account by any agent/robot and some computations will be duplicated.

It is astonishing, that the above proposed assembly of components to build a paradigm of global strategy for self-control of teams of AI robots, allows to easily incorporate (abstract for AI robots) components like: *robot's liberty, robot's egoism*, etc. into the strategy.

4 Shaping Single Agents/robots

In Sect. 2.1 it has been hypothesized, that Evolution is shaping agents in terms of mental abilities and physical abilities to provide for given Invisible Hand (controlling this social structure/market), agents optimized for its needs. Let's discuss this issue.

1. Design of agents/robots - member of team designed to work under Invisible Hand supervision
   Such agent/robot, should be awarded with the following properties:
   (a) Liberty of the agent (in terms of F. A. Hayek [10]). This liberty could have several forms, e.g. liberty of displacing, liberty of inference process, liberty of self-assigning task. This means in practice, that there is no authority in the social structure. The Invisible Hand does not exclude "authority of a specialist" owning specific knowledge. This can be easily incorporated into the behavior of agents/robots when problem solving (relying on specialist, instead of struggling with the problem yourself). At most, an agent/robot can inform other agents/robots of the problem, ask for help, indicate a task waiting to be done etc.
   (b) Egoism of the agent/robot, which can be implemented in several ways, in case of an AI robot. Input data for such egoism could be: e.g. the equivalent of pain, which can be implemented via feeling mechanical overload, overheating of the device, etc. This way, engineering "Factor of Safety" can be simply implemented e.g. when a feeling of abstract pain is generated, whereas the load is only at 30% of maximal/destructive load. Another case: an abstract feeling of fatigue is generated by exceeding the standard operating hours of the device. Another case of egoism: minimizing the effort of an agent/robot, e.g. choosing the shortest path, looking for another agent/robot that can carry out the given task at a lower cost, is a specialist, etc. Output data is simply rejection to act or expressing personal reluctance.

(c) Egoism must be balanced by willingness to:
  - Participate in a collective effort. This can have the form of internal imperative[20] to look for what to do now, in case the agent is feeling rested. This can be easily implemented by MEA;
  - Immediate reaction to symptoms of overload of another, neighbor agent/robot in a situation when something goes wrong for some reason (e.g. a landslide);

2. Social structure ruled by Artificial Invisible Hand

(a) Making a detailed plan in advance (instead of only network of general tasks) is in general rejected in case of hereby proposed collective AI robotics. It requires meta-knowledge and prediction of unpredictable events. Even in case of humans, a successful plan requires a team of extraordinary specialists to make it and almost 99% of such plans require real time updates. A reliable plan requires global knowledge, whereas F. Hayek rejects the idea of "global knowledge" [7]. If we want the Invisible Hand to control a team of robots, humans cannot be engaged in making plans for robots. This can directly cause an organizational catastrophe if robots do not understand what humans have planned and why. This phenomenon is widely visible on building sites where one team of humans plans and another team has to implement it without proper communication. Thus, the behavior of a team of AI robots must be "event driven" which is kernel of Means-Ends-Analysis proposed by H. Simon;

(b) A single AI robot successfully acting under the control of the Invisible Hand, should infer and act only in a range it can mentally grasp (e.g. in visibility range). F. A. Hayek used to say: *Much of the knowledge needed is not scientific but "knowledge of the particular circumstances of time and place* [8].

Thus, the proposed control system philosophy allows budget vision systems for AI robots, members of teams. The reason is, that collective perception of the environment can be implemented on the area exceeding perception of a single agent. This perception should incorporate perception of only neighboring agents - not whole social structure. This method is used, for example, by a herd of deer grazing in a meadow, collectively observing the surroundings in order to prevent an attack by predators.

5 Conclusion

The phenomenon of Adam Smith's Invisible Hand and works of supporters of this idea like F. A. Hayek, R. Nozick and H. Simon have provided us with a clear set of axioms on how to build a team of AI robots able to spontaneously act, to fulfill a human defined task, e.g. building a bridge.

---

[20] This can be implemented with equivalent of dopamine hormone, also known as the "feel-good" hormone, satisfaction with the task performed.

It is well-known that the efficiency of a centralized system declines if the number of agents/robots and size of the problem (what implies planning problem) grows.

Whereas a system based on the Invisible Hand is expected to demonstrate its efficiency and reliability just when - if many agents are involved, they operate over a large area, carrying out for example, an extensive construction works unpredictable in detail.

Simply, self-control ensures better use of mental resources available on site of activity of the social structure and thus better coping with situations not planned and optimized if it were central control.

The case and overwhelming success of the Internet, which is based on the Invisible Hand idea (unexpected consequences), clearly demonstrates that the proposed control philosophy for collective AI robotics should provide robust control and resistance to unexpected events, e.g. a construction disaster.

Moreover, planning before starting a project may be limited only to defining a basic grid of tasks to be performed. This is a known effect when the team that will finally implement the project is experienced and very intelligent.

More on problems presented in this paper can be found in my coming monograph: Szuba T. (2022) Adam Smith's Invisible Hand as a Social Structure's self-control mechanism - Theory and Applications. Springer Nature. 400 pages [19].

References

1. Smith A.: An Inquiry into the nature and causes of the wealth of nations., W. Strahan and T. Cadell, London (1776). http://www2.hn.psu.edu/faculty/jmanis/adam-smith/wealth-nations.pdf
2. Berry, C., Paganelli, M., Smith, C.: The Oxford Handbook of Adam Smith. Oxford Handbooks. OUP Oxford (2013)
3. Kennedy G.: The myth of the Invisible Hand – view from the trenches, Social Science Research Network (SSRN), September 2012. SSRN: http://ssrn.com/abstract=2143277 or https://doi.org/10.2139/ssrn.2143277
4. Szuba, T., Sztuba, D.: Can Adam Smith's invisible hand phenomenon be used for the analysis of fourth estate's impact and behavior? In: IEEE International Joint Conference on Neural Networks, Glasgow (2020)
5. Szuba T.: Computational Collective Intelligence. Wiley Series on Parallel and Distributed Computing (2001). Monograph, 410 pages
6. Newell, A., Simon, H.: Human problem solving. Reprint from 1972. Echo Point Books and Media (2019)
7. Hayek, F.: The Use of Knowledge in Society. The American Economic Review. Also available in Hayek F.: Individualism and Economic Order 1948 (1945)
8. Hayek, F.: Individualism and Economic Order. University of Chicago Press, Routledge (1948). books.google.com
9. Nozick, R.: Invisible-hand explanations. Am. Econ. Rev. **84**, 314–318 (1991)
10. Hayek, F.A.: The Constitution of Liberty. (reprint, first published in 1960) University of Chicago Press (1978). ISBN 0226320847, 9780226320847, 567 pages. https://iea.org.uk/sites/default/files/publications/files/Hayek%27s%20Constitution%20of%20Liberty.pdf there is available concise (188 pages) version by E. F. Miller from The Institute of Economic Affairs, London

11. Adleman, L.: Molecular computation of solutions to combinatorial problems. Science **266**, 1021–1024 (1994)

12. Trewavas, A.J.: Plant behaviour and intelligence. Oxford University Press (2014). 320 pages. ISBN 10:0199539545 ISBN 13:9780199539543

13. Minker, J. (ed.) Logic-Based Artificial Intelligence. The Springer International Series in Engineering and Computer Science. Springer, New York (2000). https://doi.org/10.1007/978-1-4615-1567-8. 606 pages. ISBN 978-1-4615-1567-8

14. Stiny, G., Gips, J.: Shape grammars and the generative specification of painting and sculpture. In: Freiman, C.V. (ed.) Information Processing 71, pp. 1460–1465. North Holland, Amsterdam (1972)

15. Holden, D., Komura, T., Saito, J.: Phase-functioned neural networks for character control. ACM Trans. Graph. (2017). https://doi.org/10.1145/3072959.3073663

16. Microsoft© (2021) Spatial mapping. https://msdn.microsoft.com/en-us/magazine/mt745096.aspx

17. Microsoft© 2021 Spatial understanding. https://docs.microsoft.com/en-us/windows/mixed-reality/case-study-expanding-the-spatial-mapping-capabilities-of-hololens

18. Simon, H.A.: Public administration in today's world of organizations and markets. PS Polit. Sci. Polit. **33**(4), 749–756 (2000)

19. Szuba, T.: Adam Smith's Invisible Hand as a Social Structure's self-control mechanism - Theory and Applications. Springer (2022). 400 pages. To appear at the end of 2022

Polynomial Algorithms for Synthesizing Specific Classes of Optimal Block-Structured Processes

Costin Bădică[1](✉) ⓘ and Alexandru Popa[2,3] ⓘ

[1] Department of Computers and Information Technology, University of Craiova, Craiova, Romania
cbadica@software.ucv.ro
[2] Department of Computer Science, University of Bucharest, Bucharest, Romania
alexandru.popa@fmi.unibuc.ro
[3] National Institute for Research and Development in Informatics, Bucharest, Romania

Abstract. Synthesis of optimal business processes has practical applications in: manufacturing, scheduling, process mining, agent planning, and parallel computing. Block-structured models, in particular process trees, have certain advantages compared with other approaches regarding correctness and robustness. In this work we propose algorithms for the automated synthesis of optimal block-structured processes and then we perform a sound analysis of their correctness and complexity.

Keywords: Block structured processes · Combinatorial optimisation · Algorithms

1 Introduction

In process-centered applications (e.g. business and manufacturing, parallel computing, planning and scheduling) a natural goal is to perform the activities related to the business as quickly as possible. Based on domain-specific semantics, one can impose ordering constraints of the activities of a process. For example, if two activities are independent and there are enough resources to be allocated to each of them, then those activities can be scheduled for parallel execution. However, if an activity depends on the output produced by another activity, then the first activity can be scheduled for execution only after the completion of the second activity, i.e. their execution order is sequentially constrained.

There is a rich literature on process modeling in theoretical and applied computer science [13, 18]. Here we focus on block-structured models, in particular process trees, that are claimed to have certain advantages compared with other approaches [21].

A block-structured process is defined, informally, as a parallel or sequential composition of activities or other processes (we give a formal definition in Sect. 2). Each activity has an estimated duration of execution. The duration of two processes P and Q composed sequentially is $d(P) + d(Q)$, where $d(P)$ and $d(Q)$ is the duration of the process P and respectively, Q. Then, the duration of two processes P and Q composed in parallel is $max\{d(P), d(Q)\}$, where $d(P)$ and $d(Q)$ is the duration of the process P and

© Springer Nature Switzerland AG 2021
N. T. Nguyen et al. (Eds.): ICCCI 2021, LNAI 12876, pp. 330–343, 2021.
https://doi.org/10.1007/978-3-030-88081-1_25

respectively, Q. In this paper, we study the following problem: given a directed acyclic graph that specifies the ordering constraints on the activities, find a block structured process of minimum duration that satisfies the ordering constraints.

Motivation. The results of our work can be used in the area of business process management (BPM) with application in project scheduling [12]. BPM is a broad and well-established subject [7]. In this paper we focus on the specific problem of optimizing block structured processes that capture flexible project schedules satisfying a given set of activity precedence constraints [20].

In manufacturing there is interest for automated (i.e. using an algorithmic rather than manual) synthesis of correct process models, according to process-specific criteria like well-formedness, soundness and its variants (relaxed, weak and easy) [11]. Such correctness criteria can be ensured by synthesizing block-structured processes.

A possible approach uses standard project scheduling [12] and then synthesizes a block structured process from the schedule. However, this approach has drawbacks, as it can lead to unstructured and overly constrained processes. Moreover, as shown in [19], there are schedules that cannot be captured with a block structured process.

On the other hand, the block structured representation is a sort of template that satisfies problem constraints independently of activity durations, while a particular unstructured schedule does not always work if durations of activities unexpectedly change. Actually this can happen in realistic scenarios. For example, poorly performed work can increase duration of some activities. Moreover, activity durations are actually random variables, so in many applications, like those involving manual work, the exact value of the actual performance time depends on human performance and cannot be estimated exactly. This shows that block structured processes have obvious advantages over ordinary schedules. Therefore straightforward synthesis of block structured models is preferred and it can be based on ordering constraints [19,20] or on process mining [2,3,15].

Our work is also relevant for multiprocessor scheduling in parallel computing. For example, a new approach for parallel computing based on Series-Parallel Contention modeling was proposed by the early work of [25]. According to this approach, the parallel algorithm and the underlying machine are described as a series-parallel structured computation, similarly to a block-structured process.

Last but not least, block-structured processes are useful for developing sound intelligent distributed applications (e.g. scientific workflows) using multi-agent systems and concurrent plans, as proposed by Jason agent-oriented programming language [26].

Previous Work. Scheduling with ordering and resource constraints attracted computer science researches in the areas of multiprocessor and project scheduling. According to the early result of [24], scheduling with precedence constraints is NP-complete. Moreover, the problems of scheduling with precedence and resource constraints are included into the standard catalogue [8] of NP-complete problems (problems SS9 and SS10).

While planning and scheduling are classical problems, synthesis of block-structured processes from declarative specifications is a rather new problem that was only recently approached using heuristic algorithms [19,20]. These graphs, originally called ordering relation graphs, were first proposed and used to synthesize block-structured models in the works by Polyvyanyy et al. [22,23].

The SHAMASH knowledge-based approach for business process modeling and re-engineering was proposed in [1]. SHAMASH is claimed to be useful for process simulation and optimization (second goal is similar to ours). However, no evidence is provided, the work being focused on tool presentation, rather than its algorithmic foundation.

The problem of using automated planning in BPM, in particular for the automated design of template-based process models, was recently addressed by [16,17]. Although this declarative approach guarantees correctness (understood as sound concurrency) and reusability (focusing on process templates), process optimization is not addressed by this approach. Nevertheless we claim that this is essential for business performance.

A considerable research effort was spent during the last decade for the synthesis of business process models from event logs [3]. A special attention was given to assuring the process correctness by focusing the Split Miner synthesis tool on producing block-structured or deadlock-free processes [2]. While not explicitly focused on the synthesis of optimal processes, experimental results revealed that the processes produced by Split Miner achieved considerably faster execution times than state of-the-art methods.

A Greedy approach based on top down decomposition of the activity ordering graph was proposed in [4]. The approach was experimentally evaluated using two heuristics: hierarchical decomposition and critical path. An important result of [4] is that the hierarchical decomposition process (the basis for evaluating the hierarchical decomposition heuristic) satisfies the ordering constraints and it can be determined in polynomial time.

An exact solution based on declarative modeling using constraint logic programming was proposed in [5,6]. However, the experimental evaluation revealed that this approach is feasible in practice only for small-size problems.

Our Results. We give a thorough study of block-structured process synthesis with activity ordering constraints.

First, since there is no known polynomial time exact algorithm for this problem, we study several variants in which the input graph is more restricted than an arbitrary directed acyclic graph. More precisely, we introduce a polynomial time algorithm that provides the optimum process (i.e. the one with the minimum duration) when the input graph is a tree (Sect. 3), a tree plus one edge (Sect. 4) and when the graph is bipartite (Sect. 5). The study of these particular cases is interesting from both practical and theoretical perspective. These particular classes were considered in the scheduling with precedence constraints setting by [14] (trees) and [10] (bipartite graphs) and, thus, these classes of graphs are relevant. In Sect. 6 we present a dynamic programming algorithm for solving the problem for general DAGs.

Beside the exact algorithms, we give polynomial time approximation algorithms for the problem. Due to space restrictions some of the proofs are omitted. However, the proofs, as well as some of our results are presented in the appendix (not included in the 13 pages version of the paper).

2 Preliminaries and Problem Definition

Let us consider a finite nonempty set Σ of activities. We focus on block structured process models that are defined as algebraic terms formed using sequential ($\rightarrow$) and parallel

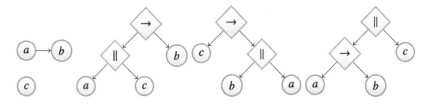

Fig. 1. From left to right: ordering graph $\mathcal{G}$, process P_1, process P_2, and process P_3

($\parallel$) operators. The semantics of a process is defined as the set of admissible traces that contain exactly one instance of each activity. Sequential composition is interpreted as trace concatenation, while parallel composition is interpreted as trace interleaving.

Let $supp(P)$ be the support set of process P, representing the activities occurring in P. We denote activities of Σ with $a, b, c, \ldots$ and process terms with $P, Q, R, \ldots$.

Block structured processes are represented as tree structured terms (or process trees) defined as follows:

- If $a \in \Sigma$ then a is a process such that $supp(a) = \{a\}$.
- If P and Q are processes such that $supp(P) \cap supp(Q) = \emptyset$ then $P \rightarrow Q$ and $P \parallel Q$ are processes with $supp(P \rightarrow Q) = supp(P \parallel Q) = supp(P) \cup supp(Q)$.

The semantics of process P is given by its set of traces (language) $\mathcal{L}(P)$ as follows:

- $\mathcal{L}(a) = \{a\}$
- $\mathcal{L}(P \rightarrow Q) = \mathcal{L}(P) \rightarrow \mathcal{L}(Q)$
- $\mathcal{L}(P \parallel Q) = \mathcal{L}(P) \parallel \mathcal{L}(Q)$

Observe that if P is a well-formed block-structured process then all its traces $t \in \mathcal{L}(P)$ have the same length $|supp(P)|$.

We can impose ordering constraints of the activities of a process, based on domain-specific semantics. These constraints are specified using an *activity ordering graph* $\mathcal{G} = \langle \Sigma, E \rangle$ [20] such that:

- Σ is the set of nodes representing activities.
- $E \subseteq \Sigma \times \Sigma$ is the set of edges. Each edge represents an ordering constraint. If $(u, v) \in E$ then in each acceptable schedule activity u must precede v.

Observe that for an activity ordering graph $\mathcal{G} = \langle \Sigma, E \rangle$, set E defines a partial ordering relation on Σ, i.e. it is transitive and antisymmetric, so it cannot define cycles. In standard project scheduling terminology, graph $\mathcal{G}$ is known as activity-on-node network [12] and it is a directed acyclic graph (DAG hereafter).

Let $\mathcal{G} = \langle \Sigma, E \rangle$ be an ordering graph and let t be a trace containing all the activities of Σ with no repetition. Then t *satisfies* $\mathcal{G}$, written as $t \models \mathcal{G}$, if and only if trace t does not contain activities ordered differently than $\mathcal{G}$ specifies.

The language $\mathcal{L}(\mathcal{G})$ of an ordering graph $\mathcal{G}$ is the set of all traces that satisfy $\mathcal{G}$, i.e. $\mathcal{L}(\mathcal{G}) = \{t \mid t \models \mathcal{G}\}$.

Let P be a process and let $\mathcal{G} = \langle \Sigma, E \rangle$ be an ordering graph. P *satisfies* $\mathcal{G}$ written as $P \models \mathcal{G}$, if and only if:

- $\mathcal{L}(P) \subseteq \mathcal{L}(\mathcal{G})$, i.e. each trace of P satisfies $\mathcal{G}$, and
- $supp(P) = \Sigma$, i.e. all the activities of Σ occur in P.

Example 1. Figure 1 shows an ordering graph $\mathcal{G}$, and three processes P_1, P_2 and P_3. The total number of possible traces for the set of activities $\Sigma = \{a, b, c\}$ is 3! = 6. Moreover, $\mathcal{L}(\mathcal{G}) = \{abc, acb, cab\}$. Observe also that $\mathcal{L}(P_1) = \{acb, cab\}$ and $\mathcal{L}(P_3) = \{cab, acb, abc\}$ showing that $P_1 \models \mathcal{G}$ and $P_3 \models \mathcal{G}$. However, as $\mathcal{L}(P_2) = \{cba, cab\}$, observe that $\mathcal{L}(P_2) \nsubseteq \mathcal{L}(\mathcal{G})$, so $P_2 \nvDash \mathcal{G}$.

The set of processes P such that $P \models \mathcal{G}$ is nonempty, as it contains at least one sequential process defined by the topological sorting of $\mathcal{G}$.

Each activity has an estimated duration of execution represented using function $d : \Sigma \to \mathbb{R}^+$. The duration of execution $d(P)$ of a process P is defined as follows:

- If $P = a$ then $d(P) = d(a)$.
- $d(P \to Q) = d(P) + d(Q)$.
- $d(P \parallel Q) = \max\{d(P), d(Q)\}$.

The *minimum duration of execution* of a process that satisfies an ordering graph $\mathcal{G}$, denoted with $d_{OPT}(\mathcal{G})$, is: $d_{OPT}(\mathcal{G}) = \min_{P \models \mathcal{G}}\{d(P)\}$

An *optimal scheduling process* that satisfies a given ordering graph $\mathcal{G}$ is a process OPT with a minimum duration of execution, i.e.: $OPT \models \mathcal{G}$, and $d(OPT) = d_{OPT}(\mathcal{G})$.

There is a finite and nonempty set of processes that satisfy an ordering graph $\mathcal{G}$, so an optimal process trivially exists. Moreover, as there is an exponential number of candidate processes satisfying $\mathcal{G}$, we postulate that the computation of the optimal process is generally an intractable problem.

Problem 1. For an activity ordering graph $\mathcal{G} = (\Sigma, E)$, find a process of minimum duration of execution satisfying $\mathcal{G}$.

In Subsect. 2.1 we define the *hierarchical decomposition process*, based on the hierarchical decomposition of the precedence DAG, initially introduced by [4]. We show that this process satisfies the problem constraints. The cost d_{HD} of this process can be computed in polynomial time. In Subsect. 2.2 we show a lower bound for the optimal solution of Problem 1.

2.1 Hierarchical Decomposition Process

Let $\mathcal{G} = \langle \Sigma, E \rangle$ be a precedence DAG.

- For each node $v \in \Sigma$ we define the set $I(v)$ of *input neighbors* of v as follows: $I(v) = \{u \in \Sigma \mid (u, v) \in E\}$.
- For each node $v \in \Sigma$ we define the *level* $l(v)$ of v as a function $l : v \to \mathbb{N}$ recursively constructed as follows:
  - If $I(v) = \emptyset$ then $l(v) = 1$.
  - If $I(v) \neq \emptyset$ then $l(v) = 1 + \max_{u \in I(v)}\{l(u)\}$.
- The *height* $l(\mathcal{G})$ of graph $\mathcal{G}$ is defined as: $l(\mathcal{G}) = \max_{v \in V}\{l(v)\}$

- If $l = l(\mathcal{G}) \geq 1$ then the family of l sets $\{\Sigma_1, \Sigma_2, \ldots, \Sigma_l\}$ defined as $\Sigma_i = \{v \mid l(v) = i\}$ for all $1 \leq i \leq l$ is a partition of Σ. If $\mathcal{G}_i$ is the subgraph of $\mathcal{G}$ induced by Σ_i then the family of graphs $\{\mathcal{G}_1, \mathcal{G}_2, \ldots, \mathcal{G}_l\}$ is known as the *hierarchical decomposition* of $\mathcal{G}$.

Proposition 1. *(Hierarchical Decomposition Process) Let $\mathcal{G} = \langle \Sigma, E \rangle$ be an ordering graph. The* hierarchical decomposition process $HD(\mathcal{G})$ *associated to $\mathcal{G}$ is defined as:*

- $P_i = \|_{v \in \Sigma_i} v$ *for all $1 \leq i \leq l$.*
- $HD(\mathcal{G}) = P_1 \rightarrow P_2 \rightarrow \cdots \rightarrow P_l$.

Then $HD(\mathcal{G}) \models \mathcal{G}$.

Proof. Let t be a trace of process $HD(\mathcal{G})$. This means that for all activities u and v of t if u is before v in t then $l(u) < l(v)$. So there is a path from u to v in $\mathcal{G}$. It follows that $t \models \mathcal{G}$, i.e. $t \in \mathcal{L}(\mathcal{G})$. We conclude that $\mathcal{L}(HD(\mathcal{G})) \subseteq \mathcal{L}(\mathcal{G})$ that completes the proof. $\square$

Observe that the duration of execution $d_{HD}(\mathcal{G})$ of $HD(\mathcal{G})$ represents a non-trivial upper bound of the duration of execution of the optimal scheduling process $d_{OPT}(\mathcal{G})$, i.e. $d_{HD}(\mathcal{G}) \geq d_{OPT}(\mathcal{G})$.

2.2 Critical Path

Observe that an activity u cannot start unless all the neighboring activities from the input set $I(u)$ are finished. This time point is denoted with $start(u)$. Activity u that started at $start(u)$ will finish at time $finish(u) = start(u) + d(u)$. The values $start(u)$ and $finish(u)$ for each activity $u \in V$ can be computed using the *critical path method* [9]:

- If $I(u) = \emptyset$ then $start(u) = 0$ and $finish(u) = d(u)$.
- If $I(u) \neq \emptyset$ then $start(u) = \max\limits_{v \in I(u)} \{finish(v)\}$ and $finish(u) = start(u) + d(u)$.

The maximum value of the finishing time of each activity, known as *critical path length*, is a lower bound for the duration of execution of the optimal scheduling process.

Proposition 2. *(Critical Path) Let $\mathcal{G} = \langle \Sigma, E \rangle$ be an ordering graph and let $d_{CP}(\mathcal{G})$ be its critical path length. Then $d_{CP}(\mathcal{G})$ is a lower bound of the duration of execution of the optimal scheduling process $d_{OPT}(\mathcal{G})$, i.e. $d_{OPT}(\mathcal{G}) \geq d_{CP}(\mathcal{G})$.*

Proof. This result follows from the definition of the critical path. From $OPT(\mathcal{G}) \models \mathcal{G}$ it follows that $OPT(\mathcal{G})$ executes sequentially the activities on the critical path so $d_{OPT}(\mathcal{G}) \geq d_{CP}(\mathcal{G})$. $\square$

3 An Exact Algorithm for Trees

In this section we show an exact algorithm for Problem 1, in the case when the activity graph is a *directed tree*. We define a directed tree to be a directed graph, where the root has indegree 0 and all the other nodes have indegree precisely 1. The algorithm presented in this section works also if we define a tree as a directed graph where the root has *outdegree 0* and all other nodes have outdegree precisely 1.

The duration of the process returned by this algorithm is the longest path in the tree, thus matching the lower bound for the optimum. The algorithm is recursive and is presented in Algorithm 1.

ALG(*Tree T*)
Let r be the root of T and $T_1, \dots, T_k$ be the subtrees of r.
if $k = 0$ **then**
   | return r;
else
   | return $r \to (ALG(T_1) \parallel \cdots \parallel ALG(T_k))$;
end

Algorithm 1: Exact algorithm for a directed tree

Theorem 1. *ALG(T) returns the optimal solution for Problem 1 if T is a tree.*

Proof. The duration of the process returned by the algorithm is the duration of the longest path starting from the root. This is also a lower bound for the optimal solution as presented in the previous sections. Thus, the theorem follows.   □

4   An Exact Algorithm for a Tree Augmented with an Edge

In this section we present an exact algorithm for Problem 1 in case when the activity graph is a tree plus an extra edge.

Let r be the root of the tree. Let $y \in \Sigma$, be the *only* node that has indegree 2. Since the activity graph G consists of a tree plus one edge, then we know that y is unique. Then, let x_1 and x_2 be the two nodes such that (x_1, y) and $(x_2, y) \in E$. In order to process the subtree rooted at y we have to process the activities x_1 and x_2.

We first explain a naive (and suboptimal) approach in order to gain intuition about our final algorithm. First, remove from G the subtrees rooted at x_1 and x_2, run the exact Algorithm 1 for trees and then compose in parallel the subtrees rooted at x_1 and x_2. The aforementioned approach may not produce the optimal process since, for example, the path from the root of G to x_1 may have longer duration than the path to x_2. Thus, before processing x_2, we may also process some part of the subtree of x_1 which is not a subtree of y. In turn, this subtree of x_1 may reduce the duration of the last step, when we process the subtrees of x_1 and x_2 in parallel.

We now present informally our algorithm (the formal definition is given by Algorithm 2). We first remove from the input graph the subgraph rooted at y. Then, let D_1 be the duration of path from the root to x_1 and D_2 the duration of the path from the root to x_2. We select the largest subtree (with respect to the number of nodes) that generates a process with the duration less than $max(D_1, D_2)$. This process is composed sequentially with the parallel composition of the remaining subtrees, including y (each of the remaining subtrees are processed according to Sect. 3).

In order to prove the correctness of Algorithm 3, we show the following lemma.

Lemma 1. *Consider an activity tree (i.e., an activity graph that is also a tree). Assume that we have a fixed budget B and the goal is to process as many activities as possible such that the duration of the process is at most B, and the constraints given by the activity graphs are preserved. The maximum set of nodes that can be processed given the budget B is unique and is obtained using Algorithm 3.*

Input: A graph G that consists of a tree T rooted at r plus one directed edge between two nodes.

1. Let y the *only* node with indegree 2. Let T_y be the subtree rooted at y. Create the tree T' from the input graph G, by removing the subtree T_y from G.
2. Let x_1 and x_2 be the two nodes such that (x_1, y) and $(x_2, y) \in E$.
3. Let D_1 be the length of the path from the root to x_1 and D_2 the length of the path from the root to x_2.
4. Run Algorithm 3 on the tree T' and budget $max(D_1, D_2)$. Let P_{budget} be the process returned by this algorithm.
5. Let $T'_1, T'_2, \ldots, T'_k$, be the subtrees of T' that are *not yet processed* after the run of Algorithm 3. Let $P(A)$ be the process returned by the exact algorithm on trees from Section 3 on an input tree A.
6. The process returned by the algorithm is

$$P_{budget} \to (P(T'_1) \parallel P(T'_2) \parallel \ldots \parallel P(T'_k) \parallel P(T_y))$$

Algorithm 2: Exact algorithm for a tree and an edge

Process(*root r, budget B*)
if $d(r) > B$ **then**
| return **nil** ;
else
| Let $r_1, \ldots, r_k$, be the roots of the subtrees of r for which Process($r_i, B - d(r)$) $\neq nil$;
| return $r \to ($ Process($r_1, B - d(r)$) $\parallel \ldots \parallel$ Process($r_k, B - d(r)$) $)$;
end

Algorithm 3: Returns a process with maximum number of nodes in a tree given a fixed budget

Theorem 2. *Algorithm 2 returns the optimal process when the input graph is a tree plus one edge.*

Proof. In order to be able to process the activity y, and, therefore, the subtree of y, any process needs a duration of at least $max(D_1, D_2)$. Thus, we aim to create a process with duration $max(D_1, D_2)$ that uses as many nodes from the input graph G as possible (except, of course, the node y and nodes from its subtree). We create such a process using Algorithm 3 that takes as an input a budget and a tree and returns a process containing the maximum numbers of the activities from the tree that can be processed with the given budget. As we show in Lemma 1, there exists a unique set of nodes of maximum size that can be processed in a tree with a given budget. Moreover, this set of nodes, contains x_1 and x_2 and thus, we can process the rest of the subtrees. □

5 An Exact Algorithm for Bipartite Graphs

We now introduce an exact algorithm for Problem 1 on bipartite graphs. We first present a recursive definition of the optimal process and we prove its correctness. Then we show

how this definition can be efficiently implemented by a top-down polynomial recursive algorithm using memoization.

Let U denote leftmost nodes and V denote rightmost nodes such that (U, V) is a partition of Σ. We sort nodes of U in non-decreasing order of their activity durations $u_1, u_2, \ldots u_n$. We denote with $U_i = \{u_1 \ldots u_i\}$.

The idea is to consider two cases. If the undirected version of G is not connected then the optimal process is a parallel composition of processes generated by the connected components (the proof, not shown here, is not difficult). Otherwise, if the undirected version of G is connected then the optimal process is defined as the best process among a series of n processes P_i, $1 \le i \le n$ defined as:

$$P_i = (\|_{j=1}^{i} u_j) \to OPT(\Sigma \setminus U_i)$$
$$d(P_i) = d(u_i) + d_{OPT}(\Sigma \setminus U_i)$$
(1)

With this observation, the recursive definition of an optimal process is:

$$OPT(\Sigma) = \begin{cases} a & \text{if } \Sigma = \{a\} \\ \|_{i=1}^{k} OPT(C_i) & \text{if } C_1, \ldots, C_k, k \ge 2 \text{ are} \\ & \text{connected components of } G \\ \arg\min_{P_i} d(P_i) \ P_i \text{ defined by (1), otherwise} \end{cases}$$
(2)

The duration of the optimal process can be defined as:

$$d_{OPT}(\Sigma) = \begin{cases} d(a) & \text{if } \Sigma = \{a\} \\ \max_{i=1}^{k} d_{OPT}(C_i) & \text{if } C_1, \ldots, C_k, k \ge 2 \text{ are} \\ & \text{connected components of } G \\ \min_{i=1}^{n} d(P_i) & P_i \text{ defined by (1), otherwise} \end{cases}$$
(3)

Theorem 3. *The process defined by recursive Eqs. (2) and (3) is the optimal process on bipartite graphs.*

In order to obtain a polynomial algorithm based on Eqs. (2) and (3), first observe that this recursive process always generates a polynomial number of subsets of Σ. This result is stated by the following lemma.

Lemma 2. *Let us consider the recursive computational process determined by Eqs. (2) and (3). This process always generates $|U| + |V|$ subsets of Σ representing connected components.*

Proof. Observe that generated subsets representing connected components can be captured as a collection of trees with nodes labelled with subsets as follows. If G is connected then there is a single tree with root Σ. Otherwise there is a collection of trees with roots labelled with connected components of G. At each step we select for expansion one leaf of a tree labelled with set C that contains at least one element of U and we label it with $u_i \in U$ of minimum i. The children of C are connected components of graph with nodes $C \setminus \{u_i\}$. The process ends when no such set C can be selected. If a leaf node cannot be further expanded then it represents a singleton subset $\{v\} \subseteq V$ so we label it with v.

Finally we obtain a collection of trees such that each internal node is labelled with $u \in U$, each external node is labelled with $v \in V$ and each tree node has a unique label. So the number of nodes representing the subsets generated by the process is $|U| + |V|$.   □

OPT ($dag \; \mathcal{G} = \langle \Sigma = U \cup V, E \rangle$, durations d)
if $\Sigma = \{a\}$ then
$\quad$| return $(a, d[a])$;
else if $\mathcal{G}$ has connected components $C_1, \ldots, C_k$ s.t. $k \geq 2$ then
$\quad$| for each $i = 1, k$ do
$\qquad$| $Opt_i \longleftarrow Completed(C_i)$;
$\qquad$| if $Opt_i = nil$ then
$\qquad\quad$| $Opt_i \longleftarrow OPT(C_i, d)$;
$\qquad\quad$| $Completed(C_i) \longleftarrow Opt_i$;

$\quad$| end
$\quad$| return $(\|_{i=1}^{k} \; Opt_i.P, \max_{i=1}^{k} Opt_i.dP)$;
else
$\quad$| $dP \longleftarrow +\infty$;
$\quad$| for each $i = 1, |U|$ do
$\qquad$| $(Q, dQ) \longleftarrow OPT(\Sigma \setminus U_i, d)$;
$\qquad$| $dQ \longleftarrow dQ + d[u_i]$;
$\qquad$| if $dQ < dP$ then
$\qquad\quad$| $P \longleftarrow \|_{u \in U_i} u \to Q$;
$\qquad\quad$| $dP \longleftarrow dQ$
$\qquad$| end
$\quad$| end
$\quad$| return (P, dP) ;
end

Algorithm 4: Recursive algorithm with memoization to compute the optimal process for a bipartite graph

We are using approach i), resulting in Algorithm 4. The algorithm is using a collection *Completed* for saving the subsets $S \subseteq \Sigma$ representing connected components generated by Eqs. (2) and (3) for which the optimal process P and its cost dP have been computed as pairs (P, dP). If *Completed*$(S) = nil$ then the computation for S has not been done yet. Otherwise *Completed*$(S) = (P, dP)$.

Theorem 4. *Algorithm 4 runs in $O(|U| \cdot (|U| + |V|)^2)$.*

Proof. When *OPT* is invoked the first time for each connected component, the call generates at most $|U|$ calls on the third **if** branch. Each such call goes through connected components determination in the second **if** branch, thus taking at most $|U| + |V|$ steps. As there are $|U| + |V|$ connected components it follows that the running time of Algorithm 4 is $O(|U| \cdot (|U| + |V|)^2)$. $\quad\square$

6   An Exact Dynamic Programming Algorithm for Arbitrary DAG

Let $\mathcal{G} = \langle \Sigma, E \rangle$ be an ordering graph. If $S \subseteq \Sigma$ is a nonempty set then $\mathcal{G}_S$ is the sub-graph of $\mathcal{G}$ induced by S. The space of sub-problems is represented by all optimal sub-processes defined by nonempty subsets of Σ. A sub-process is optimal if it is either a singleton activity or it is composed of two sub-optimal processes.

We introduce arrays *Cost* and *Proc* indexed with nonempty subsets of Σ such that:

- *Cost*[S] is the duration of the optimal sub-process with activities $S \subseteq \Sigma$
- *Proc*[S] is the root of the optimal sub-process with activities $S \subseteq \Sigma$.

If S is a singleton then *Cost*[S] and *Proc*[S] are defined by Eq. 4.

$$\begin{aligned} Cost[\{a\}] &= d(a) \\ Proc[\{a\}] &= a \end{aligned} \tag{4}$$

If $|S| \geq 2$ then *Cost*[S] and *Proc*[S] are defined by Eq. 5.

$$\begin{aligned}
C(S, \|) &= \min_{(X,Y) \models_{\|} \mathcal{G}_S} \max(Cost[X], Cost[Y]) \\
(X_{\|}, Y_{\|}) &= \arg\min_{(X,Y) \models_{\|} \mathcal{G}_S} \max(Cost[X], Cost[Y]) \\
C(S, \rightarrow) &= \min_{(X,Y) \models_{\rightarrow} \mathcal{G}_S} Cost[X] + Cost[Y] \\
(X_{\rightarrow}, Y_{\rightarrow}) &= \arg\min_{(X,Y) \models_{\rightarrow} \mathcal{G}_S} Cost[X] + Cost[Y] \\
Proc[S] &= (X_{\|}, Y_{\|}, \|) \text{ if } C(S, \|) \leq C(S, \rightarrow) \\
Cost[S] &= C(S, \|) \text{ if } C(S, \|) \leq C(S, \rightarrow) \\
Proc[S] &= (X_{\rightarrow}, Y_{\rightarrow}, \rightarrow) \text{ if } C(S, \rightarrow) < C(S, \|) \\
Cost[S] &= C(S, \rightarrow) \text{ if } C(S, \rightarrow) < C(S, \|)
\end{aligned} \tag{5}$$

A dynamic programming algorithm takes the ordering graph $\mathcal{G}$ and the array of activity durations d and computes matrices *Cost* and *Proc* following Eqs. 4 and 5. The optimal process can then be builtusing the information saved in array *Proc*.

Proposition 3. *If $(\Sigma_L, \Sigma_R) \models_{\|} \mathcal{G}$ then the undirected version of $\mathcal{G}$ is not connected, so it can be partitioned into two or more connected components. So in this case if $\Sigma_1, \ldots, \Sigma_k$ are its connected components with $k \geq 2$ then $P = P_1 \| \cdots \| P_k$.*

According to the result of Proposition 3, the proposed dynamic programming algorithm works as follows. We first compute the connected components of the undirected version of $\mathcal{G}$. If there are $k \geq 2$ connected components then we will only consider the case when the optimal process is a parallel composition. Otherwise we will only consider the case when the optimal process is a sequential composition.

Let us now assume in what follows that the undirected version of $\mathcal{G}$ is connected so in this case our optimal process is a sequential composition $L \rightarrow R$. We are interested to characterize sets Σ_L and $\Sigma_R = \Sigma \setminus \Sigma_L$ representing the alphabets of L and R.

Proposition 4. *Let us assume that the undirected version of $\mathcal{G}$ is connected and let $P = L \rightarrow R$ a process. Let $\mathcal{H}$ be the graph defined as the complement of the undirected version of $\mathcal{G}$, i.e. $\mathcal{H} = \overline{\mathcal{G}}$. For each $v \in \Sigma$ let us define $Lower(v) = \{u | (u, v) \in E \text{ or } u = v\}$. Then $P \models \mathcal{G}$ if and only if there exists a clique C of $\mathcal{H}$ such that $\Sigma_L = \cup_{x \in C} Lower(x)$.*

Note that Proposition 4 can be used to make explicit the step of exploring the pairs of subsets (X, Y) such that $(X, Y) \models_{\rightarrow} \mathcal{G}_S$.

Now, using decomposition results stated by Propositions 3 and 4, our proposed dynamic programming approach is detailed by Algorithm 5.

```
RefOptProc(dag 𝒢, durations d, matrix Cost, matrix Proc)
for a ∈ Σ do
    Cost[{a}] ⟵ d[a] ;
    Proc[{a}] ⟵ a ;
end
for i ⟵ 2,|Σ| do
    for each S ⊆ Σ s.t. |S| = i do
        Let S₁,…,Sₖ be connected components of 𝒢̄_S if k ≥ 2 then
            Cost[S] ⟵ maxᵏᵢ₌₁ Cost[Sᵢ] ;
            Proc[S] ⟵ (S₁,…,Sₖ,‖);
        else
            C→ ⟵ +∞ ;
            for each clique C of 𝒢̄_S do
                X ⟵ ∪_{x∈C}Lower(x);
                Y ⟵ S \ X ;
                if Cost[X] + Cost[Y] < C→ then
                    C→ ⟵ Cost[X] + Cost[Y] ;
                    P→ ⟵ (X, Y, →) ;
                end
            end
            Cost[S] ⟵ C→ ;
            Proc[S] ⟵ P→;
        end
    end
end
```

Algorithm 5: Refined dynamic programming algorithm to compute the optimal process and its cost

7 Conclusions and Future Works

In this paper we provided several algorithms for the block-structured activity ordering problem. A natural open problem is to investigate the existence and design a polynomial time exact algorithm for the problem on arbitrary graphs or to show that the problem is NP-hard. We conjecture that the latter is true.

References

1. Aler, R., Borrajo, D., Camacho, D., Sierra-Alonso, A.: A knowledge-based approach for business process reengineering, shamash. Knowl.-Based Syst. **15**(8), 473–483 (2002)
2. Augusto, A., Conforti, R., Dumas, M., La Rosa, M., Bruno, G.: Automated discovery of structured process models from event logs: The discover-and-structure approach. Data Knowl. Eng. **117**, 373–392 (2018)
3. Augusto, A., et al.: Automated discovery of process models from event logs: review and benchmark. IEEE Trans. Knowl. Data Eng. **31**(4), 686–705 (2019)
4. Bădică, A., Bădică, C., Dănciulescu, D., Logofătu, D.: Greedy heuristics for automatic synthesis of efficient block-structured scheduling processes from declarative specifications. In: Iliadis, L., Maglogiannis, I., Plagianakos, V. (eds.) AIAI 2018. IAICT, vol. 519, pp. 183–195. Springer, Cham (2018). https://doi.org/10.1007/978-3-319-92007-8_16

5. Bădică, A., Bădică, C., Ivanović, M., Logofătu, D.: Exploring the space of block struc- tured scheduling processes using constraint logic programming. In: Kotenko, I., Badica, C., Desnitsky, V., El Baz, D., Ivanovic, M. (eds.) IDC 2019. SCI, vol. 868, pp. 149–159. Springer, Cham (2020). https://doi.org/10.1007/978-3-030-32258-8_17

6. Bădică, A., Bădică, C., Ivanović, M.: Block structured scheduling using constraint logic programming. AI Commun. 33(1), 41–57 (2020)

7. Dumas, M., La Rosa, M., Mendling, J., Reijers, H.A.: Fundamentals of Business Pro- cess Management (2nd ed.). Springer, New York (2018) https://doi.org/10.1007/978-3-662- 56509-4

8. Garey, M.R., Johnson, D.S.: Computers and Intractability: A Guide to the Theory of NP- Completeness. W. H. Freeman and Company, New York (1979)

9. Kelley, J.E.: Critical-path planning and scheduling: mathematical basis. Math. Oper. Res. 9(3), 296–320 (1961)

10. Kinne, J., Manuch, J., Rafiey, A., Rafiey, A.: Ordering with precedence constraints and bud- get minimization. CoRR, abs/1507.04885 (2015)

11. Klai, K., Desel, J.: Checking soundness of business processes compositionally using sym- bolic observation graphs. In: Giese, H., Rosu, G. (eds.) FMOODS/FORTE -2012. LNCS, vol. 7273, pp. 67–83. Springer, Heidelberg (2012). https://doi.org/10.1007/978-3-642-30793-5_5

12. Kolisch, R., Sprecher, A.: Psplib - a project scheduling library. Eur. J. Oper. Res. 96(1), 205–216 (1997)

13. Kopp, O., Martin, D., Wutke, D., Leymann, F.: The difference between graph-based and block-structured business process modelling languages. Enterp. Model. Inf. Syst. Architect. 4(1), 3–13 (2009)

14. Kumar, V.S.A., Marathe, M.V., Parthasarathy, S., Srinivasan, A.: Scheduling on unrelated machines under tree-like precedence constraints. Algorithmica 55(1), 205–226 (2009)

15. Leemans, S.J.J., Fahland, D., van der Aalst, W.M.P.: Discovering block-structured process models from event logs - a constructive approach. In: Colom, J.-M., Desel, J. (eds.) PETRI NETS 2013. LNCS, vol. 7927, pp. 311–329. Springer, Heidelberg (2013). https://doi.org/10. 1007/978-3-642-38697-8_17

16. Marrella, A.: Automated planning for business process management. J. Data Sem. 8(2), 79– 98 (2019)

17. Marrella, A., Lespérance, Y.: A planning approach to the automated synthesis of template- based process models. SOCA 11(4), 367–392 (2017)

18. Mili, H., Tremblay, G., Jaoude, G.B., Lefebvre, E., Elabed, L., El-Boussaidi, G.: Business process modeling languages: sorting through the alphabet soup. ACM Comput. Surv. 43(1), 4:1–4:56 (2010)

19. Mrasek, R., Mülle, J., Böhm, K.: Automatic generation of optimized process models from declarative specifications. In: Zdravkovic, J., Kirikova, M., Johannesson, P. (eds.) CAiSE 2015. LNCS, vol. 9097, pp. 382–397. Springer, Cham (2015). https://doi.org/10.1007/978- 3-319-19069-3_24

20. Mrasek, R., Mülle, J., Böhm, K.: Process synthesis with sequential and parallel constraints. In: Debruyne, C., et al. (eds.) OTM 2016. LNCS, vol. 10033, pp. 43–60. Springer, Cham (2016). https://doi.org/10.1007/978-3-319-48472-3_3

21. Pesic, M., van der Aalst, W.M.P.: A declarative approach for flexible business processes management. In: Eder, J., Dustdar, S. (eds.) BPM 2006. LNCS, vol. 4103, pp. 169–180. Springer, Heidelberg (2006). https://doi.org/10.1007/11837862_18

22. A. Polyvyanyy. Structuring process models. PhD thesis, University of Potsdam (2012)

23. Polyvyanyy, A., García-Bañuelos, L., Dumas, M.: Structuring acyclic process models. In: Hull, R., Mendling, J., Tai, S. (eds.) BPM 2010. LNCS, vol. 6336, pp. 276–293. Springer, Heidelberg (2010). https://doi.org/10.1007/978-3-642-15618-2_20

24. Ullman, J.D.: NP-complete scheduling problems. J. Comput. Syst. Sci. **10**(3), 384–393 (1975)
25. Gemund, A.J.C.: SPC: a model of parallel computation. In: Bougé, L., Fraigniaud, P., Mignotte, A., Robert, Y. (eds.) Euro-Par 1996. LNCS, vol. 1124, pp. 397–400. Springer, Heidelberg (1996). https://doi.org/10.1007/BFb0024728
26. Zatelli, M., Hübner, J.F., Bordini, R.H.: Concurrency in Jason. http://jason.sourceforge.net/doc/tech/concurrency.html (2016)

Cooperative Strategies for Decision Making and Optimization

A Population-Based Framework for Solving the Job Shop Scheduling Problem

Piotr Jedrzejowicz⬭, Ewa Ratajczak-Ropel⬭, and Izabela Wierzbowska^(✉)⬭

Gdynia Maritime University, Gdynia, Poland
p.jedrzejowicz@umg.edu.pl,
{e.ratajczak-ropel,i.wierzbowska}@wznj.umg.edu.pl

Abstract. The paper proposes the framework named MPF, extending the Mushroom Picking Metaheuristics and originally proposed earlier by the authors. The framework can be used for solving combinatorial optimization problems. In the current study, the framework has been used for solving instances of the Job Shop Scheduling Problem (JSSP). The framework allows defining several solutions improving agents. Agents work in parallel trying to improve solutions. Solutions are maintained on two levels – common memory and sub-populations for each thread. The framework provides functionality allowing the implementation of a strategy for maintenance of threads and the common memory, including the information exchange between them. For the JSSP implementation, we propose 5 types of autonomous agents. The computational experiment carried out using benchmark datasets has confirmed the good performance of the proposed approach in terms of solutions quality and computation times.

Keywords: Metaheuristics · Population-based algorithms · Job Shop Scheduling · Parallel computation

1 Introduction

Population-based approaches have, by now, grown to become a standard approach for solving computationally difficult problems (see for example [1,5]). They belong to a wider class of metaheuristics that produce approximate solutions to optimization problems. According to [5], the advantages of the population– based algorithms can be attributed to several factors. Most important include the ability to review in a reasonable time a huge number of possible solutions from the search space, the ability to direct search processes towards more promising areas of the search space, ability to reduce computational efforts through implicit or explicit co-operation between population members, and ability to perform a search for the optimum solution in parallel or a distributed environment.

Population-based algorithms including swarm intelligence and evolutionary systems have already proven successful in tackling Job shop Scheduling Problem (JSSP) known as an important but computationally hard optimization problem

© Springer Nature Switzerland AG 2021
N. T. Nguyen et al. (Eds.): ICCCI 2021, LNAI 12876, pp. 347–359, 2021.
https://doi.org/10.1007/978-3-030-88081-1_26

considered in this study. The major barrier facing researchers looking for effective solutions to JSSP is the need to finding a proper balance between the quality of approximate solutions produced by an algorithm and the computation time needed to execute it. To deal with the JSSP instances we propose a framework extending the Mushroom Picking Metaheuristics originally proposed in [6]. The proposed framework named Mushroom Picking Framework (MPF) takes advantage of the parallel processing power and has been implemented using Scala and the Apache Spark environment. To perform most of the framework functionalities we are using autonomous and independent agents performing specialized actions.

The paper is organized as follows. In Sect. 2 the Job Shop Scheduling Problem is formally defined. The next section offers a brief review of the related work. In Sect. 4 we describe the main features of the proposed framework. Section 5 gives details of the MPF implementation for solving JSSP instances. Section 6 presents computational experiment results and comparisons with some other state-of-the-art approaches. Final Section contains conclusions and proposed directions for future research.

2   Job Shop Scheduling Problem

We describe the job shop scheduling problem following the Takeshi Yamada thesis [21]. The $n \times m$ minimum-makespan Job Shop Scheduling problem (JSSP) can be described by a set of n jobs $\{J_i\}_{1 \leq i \leq n}$ to be processed on a set of m machines $\{M_r\}_{1 \leq r \leq m}$. The problem is characterized as follows:

- Each job consist of so called operations, each operation $O_{jr}, 1 \leq j \leq n, 1 \leq r \leq m$ of job j is processed on machine r.
- The operations of each job must be processed on machines in the predefined order (technological sequence of machines). The order can be different for each job.
- Each machine can process only one job at a time.
- Operation O_{jr} requires the exclusive use of M_r for an uninterrupted duration p_{jr}, the preemption is not allowed. p_{jr} is the processing time of O_{jr}.
- Each operation O_{jr} has its starting time and completion time. A *schedule* is a set of all completion times $\{c_{jr}\}_{1 \leq j \leq n, 1 \leq r \leq m}$ that satisfies all above constraints.
- *Makespan* is the time required to process all the jobs: $\max\limits_{1 \leq j \leq n, 1 \leq r \leq m} c_{jr}$.

The objective of optimizing the problem corresponds to finding a schedule that minimizes the makespan.

In [10] the problem was proven to be NP-hard.

3   Related Work

Job Shop Scheduling Problem together with its several variants remains in the center of interest for numerous researchers. The challenge is to find algorithms offering high-quality stable solutions in a reasonably short time. Among a variety of approaches the most successful, so far, seem population-based algorithms. A state-of-the-art review on techniques for solving the JSSP as of 2013 can be found in [17]. In [4] the local search mechanism of the particle swarm optimization (PSO) and a large-span search principle of the cuckoo search algorithm are combined into an improved cuckoo search algorithm for solving JSSP. A hybrid algorithm integrating PSO and neural networks was proposed in [23]. Whale optimization algorithm using quantum computing paradigm was proposed by [24]. An improved GA for JSSP [2] offers some rules for increasing the effectiveness of the genetic algorithm while solving JSSP instances. Another well-performing GA for solving JSSP instances was proposed in [8]. GA combined with the local search was proposed in [18]. The approach extends the mutation operator by adding a local search strategy. Additionally, a new multi-crossover operator is proposed. A novel two-level metaheuristic algorithm was suggested in [13]. A discrete wolf pack algorithm (DWPA) for job shop scheduling problems was proposed in [20]. In [19] a novel biomimicry hybrid bacterial foraging optimization algorithm was developed.

As in the case of many other computationally difficult optimization problems, novel technologies supporting the development of parallel and distributed algorithms for JSSP have been investigated in recent years. The algorithm, called MapReduce coral reef (MRCR) for JSSP was proposed in [16]. The basic idea of the proposed algorithm is to apply the MapReduce platform and the Spark Apache environment to implement the coral reef optimization algorithm to speed up computations. More recently, a large-scale flexible JSSP optimization by a distributed evolutionary algorithm implemented on Apache Spark was proposed in [15]. In [3] the authors proposed a parallel multi-start Tabu Search algorithm for solving JSSP with blocking. The algorithm was implemented using cluster-based architecture.

4   MPF Framework

The Mushroom Picking Framework (MPF) has been designed to allow for a parallel search for the optimum solution to combinatorial optimization problems. The framework is based on the Mushroom Picking Algorithm, originally proposed in [6]. The algorithm's metaphor refers to many mushroom pickers, exploring in parallel the woods, trying to collect mushrooms with the use of different strategies. Besides applying individual strategies the mushroom pickers also cooperate directly or indirectly. They may intensify search at places where others found good crops. On the other hand, they may also choose to explore areas of woods where no other mushroom pickers have been recently present.

MPF framework requires defining some classes specifically for the task at hand (task, solution) and some algorithms that correspond to the different strategies that are used in the process of local search. There may be any number of applied strategies and any complexity, although some choices may negatively influence the overall running time needed to reach the result.

The framework works as follows:

1. The initial population of solutions is prepared in the common memory. The solutions in the population are generated with random sequences of jobs, however, the process of assigning the sequences is done later, in parallel threads.
2. Solutions from the common memory are divided into several subpopulations of equal size.
3. Each subpopulation is processed in a separate thread. Processing is understood as applying some specific solution improving strategies. Threads run in parallel for a predefined number of iterations.
4. Solutions produced in threads are stored in the common memory.
5. If the stopping criterion has not been met, solutions in the common memory are randomly shuffled and another cycle starts at step 2.
6. Else, the best solution from the common memory is taken as the final solution.

The stopping criterion of the whole process is defined as a lack of improvement in the fitness of the best solution for the predefined number of cycles.

As it has been mentioned earlier, in the first cycle solutions in each subpopulation are initialized with random sequences of jobs, which assures that the initialization is carried out in parallel too.

In all cycles, the subpopulations are processed by agents from identical sets of agents. An agent receives a specific number of solutions (one or two) as arguments and executes its internal algorithm attempting to produce an improved solution. In each cycle some predefined number of attempts takes place.

Agents of different kinds have different internal algorithms, and these may be for example some kind of local search algorithms. If a single argument agent produces a new solution that is better than the solution drawn from the subpopulation as the argument, the new solution replaces the old one in the subpopulation. If a two-argument agent produces a new solution, it is checked against the worst of the two arguments, to replace it in case of improvement.

To avoid the situation in which solutions in a subpopulation are close to the same local optimum, every time two solutions drawn as arguments for a two-argument agent are too similar to each other (the difference in fitness equals less than 2), one of these solutions, possibly the one with worse fitness, is replaced in the subpopulation with a random solution.

5   The MPF Framework Implementation for Solving JSSP Instances

In [7] similar model has been used to solve JSSP and FSSP (Flow Shop Scheduling) problems. The model proposed in this paper differs by introducing a specific algorithm for calculating the makespan. The algorithm may improve a solution by changing the order in which operations in each job are carried out. The proposed makespan calculation algorithm is an additional solution improvement procedure.

A single solution may be represented as an ordered list of the numbers of jobs. The length of the list is $n \times m$. There are m occurrences of each job in such list. When examining the list from the left to the right, the ith occurrence of the job j refers to the ith operation of this job.

Although we are using such a list as defined above, the makespan is calculated by applying the so-called left-shifting operation. The approach is inspired by the Rameshkumar idea [14] in which the function calculating the makespan partially works as a dispatching algorithm where the order in which jobs are processed is not necessarily described by the list that represents a solution. Every time the algorithm reads from the list which job is to be processed next, it checks whether processing the appropriate operation of this job leaves a gap (idle time) on the relevant machine. If this is the case, the algorithm checks whether it is possible to instead process another job on that machine to minimize or eliminate the identified gap. The algorithm is shown in pseudo-code as Algorithm 1.

Algorithm 1: Makespan calculation

$n \leftarrow$ the number of jobs
$m \leftarrow$ the number of machines
$s = (s_1, \ldots, s_{n \times m})$ - list representing a solution
while $s.size > 0$ **do**
> $job \leftarrow s.head$
> $operation \leftarrow$ the current operation of job
> $machine \leftarrow$ machine on which $operation$ should be scheduled
>   **if** scheduling $operation$ on $machine$ creates a gap **then**
>   >   **for** $otherJob \leftarrow 1 \ldots n, otherJob \neq job$ **do**
>   >   > $otherOperation \leftarrow$ the current operation of $otherJob$
>   >   >   **if** $otherOperation$ should be scheduled on $machine$ and scheduling $otherOperation$ creates a minor gap on $machine$
>   >   >   **then**
>   >   >   > $job \leftarrow otherJob$
>   >   >   > $operation \leftarrow otherOperation$
>
>   remove the first occurrence of the job from s
>   schedule $operation$

return makespan of operations scheduled as above

For improving solutions in subpopulations the following set of agents is used:

- RandomReverse – takes a random slice of the list of jobs and reverses the order of its elements.
- RandomMove – takes one random job from the list of jobs and moves it to another, random position.
- RandomSwap – replaces jobs on two random positions in the list of jobs.
- Crossover – requires two solutions. A slice from the first solution is extended with the missing jobs in the order as in the second solution.
- Makespan calculation – performs operations as defined in Algorithm 1 on a single solution.

In each thread, agents are drawn at random from the above set (except for the Makespan calculation agent) for a predefined number of iterations. One iteration is understood as drawing and running a single agent immediately followed by the Makespan calculation agent operations. Another exception is that the Crossover agent is run twice less often than each of the one-argument agents (in each parallel thread there is only one such agent, while the other agents come in pairs), which is another measure to assure the required diversification of the solutions (besides of the occasional drawing random solutions as described in Sect. 4).

A general scheme of the MPF implementation is shown as Algorithm 2 [7].

Algorithm 2: MPA

$n \leftarrow$ the number of parallel threads
$solutions \leftarrow$ a set of solutions with empty sequence of jobs
while *!stoppingCriterion* **do**

$\quad populations \leftarrow$ solutions randomly split into n subsets of equal size
$\quad populationsRDD \leftarrow populations$ parallelized in ApacheSpark
$\quad populationsRDD \leftarrow populationsRDD.map(p =>$
$\quad p.applyOptimizations)$
$\quad solutions = populationsRDD.flatMap(identity).collect()$
$\qquad\qquad\qquad\qquad$ // thanks to $flatMap$, $collect$ returns list
$\qquad\qquad\qquad\qquad$ // of solutions, not list of populations
$\quad bestSolution \leftarrow$ a solution from $solutions$ with the best fitness

return $bestSolution$

In Algorithm 2, $applyOptimization$ is responsible for improving solutions in each subpopulation in all threads. In the first cycle, $applyOptimization$ also fills solutions with randomly generated sequences of jobs.

6   Computational Experiment Results

To validate the proposed approach, we have carried out several computational experiments. Experiments were based on the well-known benchmark dataset: the Lawrence dataset for JSSP [Lawrence, 1984]. The dataset contains instances with known optimal solutions for the minimum makespan criterion. All computations have been run on Spark cluster with 8 nodes, each with 32 virtual central processing units, at the Academic Computer Center in Gdansk. Performance measures included errors calculated as a percentage deviation from the optimal solution value and computation time in seconds. The results have been averaged over 30 runs for each problem instance.

For solving the JSSP instances by the MPF, 200 subpopulations, each consisting of three solutions, have been used. Other parameter settings are as follows:

– for instances from la01 to la15 - 3000 iterations in each cycle and stopping criterion as no change in the best solution for two consecutive cycles;

– for instances from la16 to la40 - 6000 iterations in each cycle, and stopping criterion as no change in the best solution for five consecutive cycles.

The results have been compared to results obtained in [7], which were run in the same environment (Spark cluster in Academic Computer Center in Gdansk), the comparison results are shown in Table 1.

The parameters for smaller instances (la01 to la16) are the same as used in [7], and results are slightly worse, the average error for these tasks is 0,34% when left-shifting is used in function counting the makespan and 0,03% in [7]. Also, the average time for these tasks increased from 1.6 s to 2.7 s.

However, in the case of bigger instances adding left-shifting in how the makespan is calculated brought significant improvement - the average result of 1.37% from [7] changed to 1.18% and was obtained in a shorter time (change from 68.3 s to 61.8 s).

Table 2 contains a comparison of the MPF performance with results from recently published papers. In several of the compared papers, the authors did not show their results for all instances from the Lawrence dataset, presenting instead results for some subsets taken from the original benchmark dataset. In such cases, to make the comparison possible, we show in the last row of the table average results produced by the MPF for the same subset of instances as in the case of the respective article.

Instead of activating the makespan calculation agent immediately after another solution improvement agent has completed its operations one may use an alternative implementation. It assumes that the single argument left-shifting agent is added to the set of agents that are used to improve solutions in the subpopulations. The agent changes the order of operations in similar way as it is done in Algorithm 1. In this case the makespan calculation does not change the order of operations, it simply calculates the makespan for the solution as it is.

The first implementation is called Original and the second one – Alternative. The comparison of results for selected more difficult instances from the Lawrence dataset for both implementations is shown in Fig. 1.

Figure 2 shows the comparison of the average computation times for both implementation variants and selected instances from the Lawrence dataset.

It may be noted, that in most cases the Alternative implementation has been able to find the best result faster, with the average time (calculated for all instances included in both Fig. 1 and Fig. 2) of 87.9 s against 125,1 s in the Original implementation. Obtaining shorter computation times has resulted, however, in increasing the average error. The average error for the Alternative implementation calculated over the same instances was 2.24%, which is worse than 1.74% in the case of the error produced by the Original implementation.

Table 1. Comparison of results for the JSSP problem

Dataset	Opt. makespan	Avg. makespan	MPF		MPA [7]	
			Error %	Time s	Error %	Time s
la01	666	666.0	0.00%	2	0.00%	1
la02	655	665.0	1.53%	1	0.00%	1
la03	597	597.0	0.00%	3	0.41%	2
la04	590	611.0	3.56%	2	0.00%	1
la05	593	593.0	0.00%	1	0.00%	1
la06	926	926.0	0.00%	2	0.00%	1
la07	890	890.0	0.00%	2	0.00%	1
la08	863	863.0	0.00%	3	0.00%	1
la09	951	951.0	0.00%	2	0.00%	1
la10	958	958.0	0.00%	3	0.00%	1
la11	1222	1222.0	0.00%	4	0.00%	2
la12	1039	1039.0	0.00%	4	0.00%	2
la13	1150	1150.0	0.00%	3	0.00%	2
la14	1292	1292.0	0.00%	4	0.00%	2
la15	1207	1207.0	0.00%	4	0.00%	3
la16	945	946.0	0.11%	17	0.07%	21
la17	784	785.6	0.20%	19	0.01%	17
la18	848	849.0	0.12%	13	0.00%	21
la19	842	852.0	1.19%	18	0.20%	26
la20	902	907.0	0.55%	13	0.57%	16
la21	1046	1055.4	0.90%	62	1.55%	64
la22	927	934.7	0.83%	51	1.23%	63
la23	1032	1032.0	0.00%	23	0.00%	26
la24	935	961.5	2.83%	59	1.68%	57
la25	977	989.6	1.28%	57	1.60%	67
la26	1218	1218.0	0.00%	52	0.13%	88
la27	1235	1266.0	2.51%	92	3.21%	85
la28	1216	1240.6	2.02%	54	1.90%	117
la29	1152	1196.2	3.84%	119	5.69%	114
la30	1355	1355.0	0.00%	46	0.01%	68
la31	1784	1784.0	0.00%	72	0.00%	64
la32	1850	1850.0	0.00%	71	0.00%	76
la33	1719	1719.0	0.00%	71	0.00%	60
la34	1721	1721.0	0.00%	72	0.00%	88
la35	1888	1888.0	0.00%	75	0.00%	71
la36	1268	1295.9	2.20%	94	3.23%	87
la37	1397	1418.6	1.54%	107	3.84%	87
la38	1196	1261.8	5.50%	104	4.27%	116
la39	1233	1253.1	1.63%	92	2.39%	108
la40	1222	1247.9	2.12%	94	2.61%	102

Table 2. Comparison of results for the JSSP problem

Dataset	MPF this paper Avg. err %	Time s	DWPA [20] Avg. err %	Time s	HHSA [12] Best err %	NGPSO [22] Avg. err%	WOA LFDE [11] Avg. err %	NAGA NAGA [2] Avg. err %	GA-CPG-GT[9] Avg. err %
la01	0.00%	2	0.00%	1	0.00%	0.00%	0.00%	0.32%	0.00%
la02	1.53%	1	0.00%	2	0.00%	0.00%	1.07%	2.20%	0.00%
la03	0.00%	3	2.85%	2	0.00%	0.00%	1.21%	4.88%	0.00%
la04	3.56%	2	1.36%	1	0.00%	0.00%	2.66%	0.00%	0.00%
la05	0.00%	1	0.00%	1	0.00%	0.00%	0.00%	0.00%	0.00%
la06	0.00%	2	0.00%	2	0.00%	0.00%	0.00%	0.00%	0.00%
la07	0.00%	2	0.00%	3	0.00%	0.00%	0.00%	0.43%	0.00%
la08	0.00%	3	0.00%	2	0.00%	0.00%	0.00%	0.00%	0.00%
la09	0.00%	2	0.00%	2	0.00%	0.00%	0.00%	0.00%	0.00%
la10	0.00%	3	0.00%	2	0.00%	0.00%	0.00%	0.00%	0.00%
la11	0.00%	3	0.00%	4	0.00%	0.00%	0.00%	0.00%	0.00%
la12	0.00%	4	0.00%	2	0.00%	0.00%	0.00%	0.00%	0.00%
la13	0.00%	3	0.00%	2	0.00%	0.00%	0.00%	0.00%	0.00%
la14	0.00%	4	0.00%	4	0.00%	0.00%	0.00%	0.00%	0.00%
la15	0.00%	4	5.47%	3	0.00%	0.00%	0.00%	0.00%	0.00%
la16	0.11%	17	5.08%	3	0.21%	0.00%	0.66%	0.00%	0.11%
la17	0.20%	19	1.15%	2	0.38%	0.00%	0.78%	0.00%	0.00%
la18	0.12%	13	1.53%	2	0.83%	0.00%	0.59%	0.00%	0.00%
la19	1.19%	18	5.46%	3	0.95%	0.00%	2.04%	0.00%	0.00%
la20	0.55%	12	3.55%	2	0.55%	0.00%	1.82%	0.00%	0.55%
la21	0.90%	62	5.64%	7	1.43%	0.00%	0.00%	2.06%	4.21%
la22	0.83%	51	6.69%	6	1.73%	0.00%	0.00%	0.00%	2.91%
la23	0.00%	23	1.84%	6	0.00%	0.00%	0.00%	0.00%	0.00%
la24	2.83%	59	5.67%	6	2.25%	0.00%	0.00%	0.00%	4.17%
la25	1.28%	56	6.35%	5	2.05%	0.00%	0.00%	0.00%	2.25%
la26	0.00%	52	6.98%	8	0.00%	0.00%	0.00%	1.53%	1.56%
la27	2.51%	91	8.99%	9	0.00%	0.00%	0.00%	0.00%	6.32%
la28	2.02%	54	6.17%	11	0.00%	0.00%	0.00%	0.00%	5.26%
la29	3.84%	119	10.68%	12	0.00%	0.00%	0.00%	0.00%	8.25%
la30	0.00%	46	2.51%	9	0.00%	0.00%	0.00%	0.00%	0.89%
la31	0.00%	72	0.00%	17	0.00%	10.54%	0.00%	12.24%	0.00%
la32	0.00%	71	0.00%	19	0.00%	7.41%	0.00%	0.00%	0.00%
la33	0.00%	71	0.00%	15	0.00%	10.18%	0.00%	0.00%	0.00%
la34	0.00%	72	3.89%	15	0.00%	12.67%	0.00%	0.00%	0.23%
la35	0.00%	75	3.13%	17	0.00%	5.19%	0.00%	0.00%	0.00%
la36	2.20%	94	9.46%	10	0.00%	20.11%	0.00%	0.00%	3.15%
la37	1.54%	107	6.37%	18	0.00%	11.67%	0.00%	0.00%	6.59%
la38	5.50%	104	11.96%	12	0.00%	16.05%	0.00%	0.00%	6.61%
la39	1.63%	92	8.19%	17	0.00%	37.96%	0.00%	0.00%	4.62%
la40	2.12%	94	10.23%	10	0.00%	15.63%	0.00%	0.00%	2.45%
Avg	0.86%		3.53%		0.42%	14.74%	0.54%	2.37%	1.50%
					MPF	MPF	MPF	MPF	MPF
					0.52%	1.30%	0.36%	0.24%	0.86%

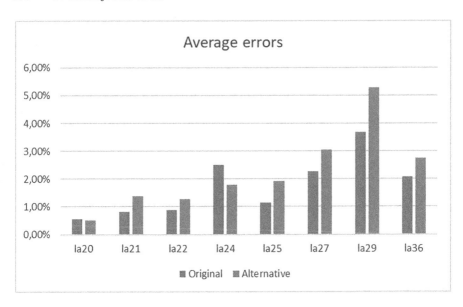

Fig. 1. Average errors for the Original and Alternative implementations

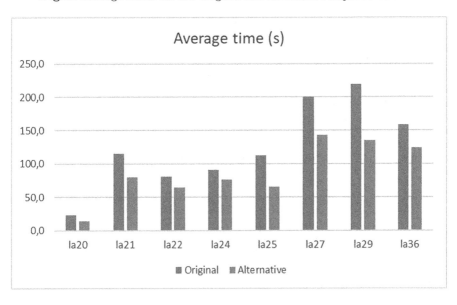

Fig. 2. Average computation times for the Original and Alternative implementations.

7   Conclusions

The main contribution of the paper is proposing the framework allowing for parallel implementation of the mushroom picking metaheuristic for solving difficult combinatorial optimization problems. In the study we have focused on the Job

Shop Scheduling Problem which has numerous practical applications, and, at the same time belongs to the most computationally difficult ones. The proposed implementation of the Mushroom Picking Framework assures, in the case of the JSSP, good quality of approximate solutions and reasonably short computation times as compared with the state-of-the-art algorithms. Such a performance can be attributed to the following factors:

- Use of the parallel computations paradigm allowing for performing several time-consuming operations over the solution space simultaneously.
- Use of the agent-based computations paradigm allowing simple autonomous agents to perform independently local search moves.
- Use of effective mechanism for detecting and avoiding being trapped in a local optimum.
- Use of effective mechanisms controlling transitions between exploration and intensification phases.
- Use of advanced computational resources.

We plan to focus the future research on extending the MPF by introducing more advanced mechanisms based, for example, on reinforcement learning techniques, for more effective selection strategy and memory management. Another direction of research could lead to proposing some adaptive mechanisms for selecting agents from the pool of available ones during computations.

References

1. Boussaïd, I., Lepagnot, J., Siarry, P.: A survey on optimization metaheuristics. Inf. Sci. **237**, 82–117 (2013). https://doi.org/10.1016/j.ins.2013.02.041
2. Chen, X., Zhang, B., Gao, D.: Algorithm based on improved genetic algorithm for job shop scheduling problem, pp. 951–956 (2019). https://doi.org/10.1109/ICMA. 2019.8816334
3. Dabah, A., Bendjoudi, A., AitZai, A., Nouali-Taboudjemat, N.: Efficient parallel tabu search for the blocking job shop scheduling problem. Soft Comput. **23** (2019). https://doi.org/10.1007/s00500-019-03871-1
4. Hu, H., Lei, W., Gao, X., Zhang, Y.: Job-shop scheduling problem based on improved cuckoo search algorithm. Int. J. Simul. Model. **17**, 337–346 (2018). https://doi.org/10.2507/IJSIMM17(2)CO8
5. Jedrzejowicz, P.: Current trends in the population-based optimization. In: Nguyen, N.T., Chbeir, R., Exposito, E., Aniorté, P., Trawiński, B. (eds.) ICCCI 2019. LNCS (LNAI), vol. 11683, pp. 523–534. Springer, Cham (2019). https://doi.org/10.1007/978-3-030-28377-3_43
6. Jedrzejowicz, P., Wierzbowska, I.: Parallelized swarm intelligence approach for solving TSP and JSSP problems. Algorithms **13**(6), 142 (2020). https://doi.org/10.3390/a13060142
7. Jedrzejowicz, P., Wierzbowska, I.: The power of a collective: team of agents solving instances of the flow shop and job shop problems. In: Paszynski, M., Kranzlmüller, D., Krzhizhanovskaya, V.V., Dongarra, J.J., Sloot, P.M.A. (eds.) ICCS 2021. LNCS, vol. 12744, pp. 406–419. Springer, Cham (2021). https://doi.org/10.1007/978-3-030-77967-2_34

8. Kalshetty, Y., Adamuthe, A., Kumar, S.: Genetic algorithms with feasible operators for solving job shop scheduling problem. J. Sci. Res. **64**, 310–321 (2020). https://doi.org/10.37398/JSR.2020.640157

9. Kurdi, M.: An effective genetic algorithm with a critical-path-guided giffler and thompson crossover operator for job shop scheduling problem. Int. J. Intell. Syst. Appl. Eng. **7**(1), 13–18 (2019). https://doi.org/10.18201/ijisae.2019751247, https://www.ijisae.org/IJISAE/article/view/790

10. Lenstra, J., Rinnooy Kan, A., Brucker, P.: Complexity of machine scheduling problems. Ann. Discrete Math. **1**, 343–362 (1977). https://doi.org/10.1016/S0167-5060(08)70743-X

11. Liu, M., Yao, X., Li, Y.: Hybrid whale optimization algorithm enhanced with lévy flight and differential evolution for job shop scheduling problems. Appl. Soft Comput. **87**, 105954 (2020)

12. Piroozfard, H., Wong, K., Derakhshanasl, A.: A hybrid harmony search algorithm for the job shop scheduling problems, pp. 48–52 (2015). https://doi.org/10.1109/ASEA.2015.23

13. Pongchairerks, P.: An enhanced two-level metaheuristic algorithm with adaptive hybrid neighborhood structures for the job-shop scheduling problem. Complexity **2020**, 1–15 (2020). https://doi.org/10.1155/2020/3489209

14. Rameshkumar, K., Rajendran, C.: A novel discrete PSO algorithm for solving job shop scheduling problem to minimize makespan. In: IOP Conference Series: Materials Science and Engineering, vol. 310, p. 012143 (2018). https://doi.org/10.1088/1757-899x/310/1/012143

15. Sun, L., Lin, L., Li, H., Gen, M.: Large scale flexible scheduling optimization by a distributed evolutionary algorithm. Comput. Ind. Eng. **128**, 894–904 (2019). https://doi.org/10.1016/j.cie.2018.09.025

16. Tsai, C.W., Chang, H.C., Hu, K.C., Chiang, M.C.: Parallel coral reef algorithm for solving jsp on spark. In: 2016 IEEE International Conference on Systems, Man, and Cybernetics, SMC 2016, Budapest, Hungary, 9–12 October 2016, pp. 1872–1877. IEEE (2016). https://doi.org/10.1109/SMC.2016.7844511

17. Çaliş Uslu, B., Bulkan, S.: A research survey: review of ai solution strategies of job shop scheduling problem. J. Intell. Manuf. **26** (2013). https://doi.org/10.1007/s10845-013-0837-8

18. Viana, M.S., Morandin Junior, O., Contreras, R.C.: A modified genetic algorithm with local search strategies and multi-crossover operator for job shop scheduling problem. Sensors **20**(18), 5440 (2020). https://doi.org/10.3390/s20185440

19. Vital-Soto, A., Azab, A., Baki, M.F.: Mathematical modeling and a hybridized bacterial foraging optimization algorithm for the flexible job-shop scheduling problem with sequencing flexibility. J. Manuf. Syst. **54**, 74–93 (2020). https://doi.org/10.1016/j.jmsy.2019.11.010

20. Wang, F., Tian, Y., Wang, X.: A discrete wolf pack algorithm for job shop scheduling problem. In: Proceedings of the 2019 5th International Conference on Control, Automation and Robotics (ICCAR), Beijing, China, pp. 19–22 (2019)

21. Yamada, T.: Studies on metaheuristics for jobshop and flowshop scheduling problems (2003)

22. Yu, H., Gao, Y., Wang, L., Meng, J.: A hybrid particle swarm optimization algorithm enhanced with nonlinear inertial weight and gaussian mutation for job shop scheduling problems. Mathematics **8**(8) (2020). https://doi.org/10.3390/math8081355, https://www.mdpi.com/2227-7390/8/8/1355

23. Zhang, Z., Guan, Z., Zhang, J., Xie, X.: A novel job-shop scheduling strategy based on particle swarm optimization and neural network. Int. J. Simul. Model. **18**, 699–707 (2019). https://doi.org/10.2507/IJSIMM18(4)CO18

24. Zhu, J., Shao, Z., Chen, C.: An improved whale optimization algorithm for job-shop scheduling based on quantum computing. Int. J. Simul. Model. **18**, 521–530 (2019). https://doi.org/10.2507/IJSIMM18(3)CO13

Imbalanced Data Mining Using Oversampling and Cellular GEP Ensemble

Joanna Jędrzejowicz[1]([✉]) and Piotr Jędrzejowicz[2]

[1] Institute of Informatics, Faculty of Mathematics, Physics and Informatics, University of Gdańsk, 80-308, Gdańsk, Poland
joanna.jedrzejowicz@ug.edu.pl
[2] Department of Information Systems, Gdynia Maritime University, Morska 83, 81-225 Gdynia, Poland
p.jedrzejowicz@umg.edu.pl

Abstract. The paper proposes a novel classifier for mining imbalanced datasets. The approach integrates three techniques – oversampling, cellular Gene Expression Programming, and dynamic selection of classifiers. The oversampling algorithm is based on the Local Distribution-Based Adaptive Minority Oversampling technique. Cellular GEP is an extension of cellular genetic algorithms. In the first step of the approach minority and majority datasets are balanced by replicating or synthesizing minority class examples. Next, cellular GEP is used to produce a set of base classifiers in the form of expression trees. Finally, a dynamic selection of classifiers is used during testing. To validate the approach an extensive computational experiment has been carried out. Its results show that the proposed classifier outperforms classic learners used for mining imbalanced datasets and is comparable with the state-of-the-art ensemble classifiers.

Keywords: Imbalanced datasets · Cellular gene expression programming · Classification

1 Introduction

Imbalanced data mining deals with the situation where considered datasets are characterized by an unequal distribution of classes. Mining imbalanced datasets is a challenging task since most of the machine learning algorithms assumes by default that in the training set there is a fairly equal number of examples for each class. If this is not the case, then traditional models lose their predictive power especially with respect to predicting the minority class instances. On the other hand, mining imbalanced data is an important practical task. There are numerous problems like for example fault diagnosis, fault detection, medical diagnosis, fraud detection or spam detection, where class imbalance is a typical feature. Prediction errors with respect to the minority class instances are as a

© Springer Nature Switzerland AG 2021
N. T. Nguyen et al. (Eds.): ICCCI 2021, LNAI 12876, pp. 360–372, 2021.
https://doi.org/10.1007/978-3-030-88081-1_27

rule more sensitive, sometimes even disastrous, than in the case of majority class. Hence, in the case of mining imbalanced datasets, dedicated algorithms assuring the required level of performance are needed.

During recent years numerous approaches for mining imbalanced datasets have been proposed (see for example reviews [6,9,14]). The existing solutions provide a satisfactory performance. Yet, there is still a room for improvements and the search for high quality learners able to deal with imbalanced data is still going on.

In this paper we tackle the problem of imbalanced data mining for 2 classes problems integrating three approaches - the cellular Gene Expression Programming (cGEP), the oversampling technique and dynamic selection of classifiers. Gene Expression Programming was proposed in [7]. GEP is an automatic programming algorithm where computer programs are represented as linear character strings of fixed-length called chromosomes which, in the subsequent fitness evaluation, can be transformed into expression trees of different sizes and shapes. It has been successfully used to construct numerous kinds of classifiers [12]. Cellular GEP is an extension of cellular genetic algorithms studied in [2]. The main feature of cellular genetic algorithms is a specific structure of the population of individuals. This structure is defined as a connected graph in which each vertex is an individual communicating with his nearest neighbors only. Cellular GEP for classification problems was proposed in [11]. Oversampling allows for balancing or reducing the imbalance ratio in the case of imbalanced datasets by replicating or synthesizing minority class examples. Finally, dynamic selection of classifiers ([13]) is used during testing. Once an ensemble of classifiers is learned, instead of choosing one classifier for all testing data, specific classifier from the ensemble is selected, for each testing instance separately.

The remaining part of the paper is organized as follows. In Sect. 2 we briefly review several approaches to mining imbalanced datasets. Section 3 provides description of the proposed approach where at the pre-processing stage one of the oversampling algorithms is used to balance the considered dataset, and next, the cGEP is used to mine it. Section 4 presents results of the computational experiment carried out to validate the approach. Final Section includes conclusions and suggestions for future research.

2 Related Work

In this section we briefly review learners used for comparison purposes in section presenting the results of the computational experiment. Techniques for mining the imbalanced datasets can be broadly divided into data-level, algorithm-level, and hybrid methods. Data-level methods can be further divided into oversampling and undersampling. A simple approach to balancing imbalanced datasets includes the random undersampling (RUS) and random oversampling (ROS). RUS works through random elimination of instances from majority class, and ROS through random replication of minority class instances. Unfortunately, RUS tends to eliminate important informative examples and ROS is known to cause over-fitting.

One of the most often used approaches for mining imbalanced datasets is the Synthetic Minority Oversampling Technique (SMOTE) proposed in [4]. SMOTE loops through the existing, real minority instance. At each loop iteration, one of the closest minority class neighbors is chosen and a new minority instance is synthesized somewhere between the minority instance and that neighbor. A popular extension of SMOTE is the ADASYN method [10]. The idea of ADASYN is to use a weighted distribution for different minority class examples according to their level of difficulty in learning. ADASYN creates more examples in the vicinity of the boundary between the two classes than in the interior of the minority class. Further, numerous, extensions and modifications of SMOTE are reviewed in [6].

Among undersampling techniques popular ones include the Edited Nearest Neighbors (ENN) algorithm based on Wilson's rules [22] and its extension known as the Repeated Edited Nearest Neighbors (RENN). ENN removes from the training set examples from different class than, at least, half of its k neighbors. RENN repeats ENN several times. Another well-known undersampling approach are Tomek's Links (TL) [19]. Tomek's links are pairs of instances of opposite classes who are their own nearest neighbors. The algorithm looks for such pairs and removes the majority instance of the pair. TL is also used by the One Side Selection (OSS) algorithm [15]. The Neighboring Cleaning Rule (NCR) [16] is similar to OSS except that instead of TL, the ENN is used to identify noisy data. The clustering-based undersampling strategy (CBU) selects centroids neighbors as the majority class representation [17]. Recently, an effective approach based on undersampling for learning Naive Bayes classifier was proposed in [3].

It has been recently shown that combining several base-learners into ensembles of classifiers may improve the performance of learners designed for mining imbalanced datasets [8]. One of the first ensemble oversampling classifiers was SMOTEBoost, proposed in [5]. A similar level of performance can be obtained by RUSBoost [18] the boosting is applied to the random undersampling method. One of the more recent undersampling approaches, named CBIS, is based on integrating clustering, example selection and ensemble learning [20]. In CBIS, the clustering part produces clusters of the majority class instances, while the selecting part removes the outliers. Instance selection is carried out using the IB3 approach [1].

3   GEP Ensemble with Oversampling and Dynamic Selection of Classifiers

General idea of the classification algorithm applied is as follows:

- perform oversampling to generate expanded minority class and balance the training dataset,
- use cellular gene expression programming on training data to create an ensemble of classifiers,
- perform dynamic selection on the ensemble of classifiers to select a specific classifier for each test example.

3.1   Oversampling to Extend Minority Set

The oversampling algorithm is based on LAMO (Local distribution-based Adaptive Minority Oversampling) introduced in [21]. It works in two steps. In the first step so called borderline instances are chosen from the minority class as seeds for generating synthetic instances. In the second step synthetic instances are generated using linear interpolation, similarly as in SMOTE and ADASYN.

Two parameters k_1 and k_2 are used in the first step which starts with extracting those instances from the majority class which are in k_1 neighborhood of minority instances. Then those minority instances which are k_2 neighbors of the extracted data are candidates for the borderline ones. Finally, some minority instances which might be noisy or redundant are removed from the border line candidates.

To formalize the approach assume that the training set TR contains both majority and minority instances, $TR = majC \cup minC$. For $x \in TR$, let $N(x)$ stand for the set of neighbors of x. Extracted majority instances are defined as:

$$S_{maj}^{bor} = \{q : q \in majC \,\&\, q \in N(x) \,\&\, x \in minC\} \tag{1}$$

For $q \in S_{maj}^{bor}$ the set of neighbors may contain instances from both $minC$ and $majC$. Those from the minority set are defined as:

$$S_{min}^{bor} = \{x \in minC : x \in N(q) \,\&\, q \in S_{maj}^{bor}\} \tag{2}$$

Instances from S_{min}^{bor} are still examined. For $x \in S_{min}^{bor}$ let z_{min}^x, z_{maj}^x stand for the nearest instances from the minority and majority sets, respectively.

$$DIS_{min}(x) = ||x - z_{min}^x||$$

$$DIS_{maj}(x) = ||x - z_{maj}^x||$$

$$DIFF(x) = |DIS_{maj}(x) - DIS_{min}(x)|$$

For the sequence $\{DIFF(x) : x \in S_{min}^{bor}\}$ mean value $\mu(DIFF)$ and standard deviation $\sigma(DIFF)$ are calculated. For border line the instances x satisfying

$$DIFF(x) < \mu(DIFF) + 3 \cdot \sigma(DIFF)$$

are chosen. Further they are seeds to generate synthetic instances with linear interpolation. For a seed w random rd_w one from k_1 neighbors is drawn and new synthetic instance is

$$\bar{w} = w + (w - rd_w) \cdot \lambda$$

where λ is a parameter. The details are shown in Algorithm 1.

Algorithm 1: Generating synthetic minority instances using LAMO method

---
Input: training data $TR = majC \cup minC$, numbers of neighbours k_1, k_2,
        parameter for interpolation λ
Output: expanded minority set EMC
1 from $majC$ distinguish S_{maj}^{bor} using (1)
2 from $minC$ distinguish S_{min}^{bor} using (2)
3 **for** $x \in S_{min}^{bor}$ **do**
4 $\quad\big|\quad$ identify closest majority instance z_{maj}^x and calculate $DIS_{maj}(x)$
5 $\quad\big|\quad$ identify closest minority instance z_{min}^x and calculate $DIS_{min}(x)$
6 $\quad\big|\quad$ calculate $DIFF(x)$
7 calculate mean $\mu(DIFF)$ and standard deviation $\sigma(DIFF)$
8 define $S^{bor} = \{x \in S_{min}^{bor} \,|DIFF(x) < \mu(DIFF) + 3 \cdot \sigma(DIFF)\}$
9 use S^{bor} and generate synthetic instances STH
10 $EMC \longleftarrow minC \cup STH$
11 **return** EMC

3.2 Learning an Ensemble of Classifiers

At the learning stage, using cellular GEP, an ensemble of classifiers EN is generated. The algorithm works on a population of genes which is random at first, with the individuals arranged on torus-like $xmax \times ymax$ grid. Thus each individual has a neighborhood of nearby individuals and genetic operations (mutation, root insertion, insertion, 1-point recombination, 2-point recombination) may take place only in a small neighborhood of each individual. In the experiments the L5, or NEWS neighborhood - 4 nearest neighbors in a given axial (north, east, west, south) direction was applied. The details of the algorithm are shown in Algorithm 2 and more information on cellular GEP can be found in [11].

3.3 Dynamic Selection of Classifiers

In order to test the generated ensemble of classifiers EN dynamic selection of classifiers is applied. For each instance in the testing dataset a classifier is selected from EN using the following criteria. First all the classifiers from EN are applied to the instance. If they all agree on the label, then this common label is the result of classification. Otherwise, the k-neighbors in training set are found. Each classifier is examined on this set of neighbors. The one which has the highest number of correct guesses is the winner and its decision on the label is the result. The process is summarized as Algorithm 3.

4 Computational Experiment

To validate the proposed approach an extensive computational experiment has been carried out. The experiment involved all two classes imbalanced datasets

---

Algorithm 2: Applying cGEP to learn one gene

Input: training data TR, number of iterations noI, $xmax \times ymax$ dimension of the grid, probabilites pm, $pris$, is, $pr1$, $pr2$ of mutation, root insertion, insertion, 1-point recombination, 2-point recombination

Output: expanded minority set EMC.

1 create the grid of size $xmax \times ymax$ with a random population Pop
2 **for** $i \leftarrow 1$ **to** noI **do**
3   express genes as expression trees,
4   calculate fitness of each gene,
5   keep best gene
6   **for** $g \in Pop$ **do**
7   nghbrs←CalculateNeighourhood(g)
8   offspring1←One-pointRecomb(g, nghbrs)
9   offspring2←Two-pointRecomb(g, nghbrs)
10         $gNew \leftarrow$ the better fitted of two offsprings
11   mutation($gNew$)
12   IStransposition($gNew$)
13   RIStransposition($gNew$)
14   Replacement($position(g)$, $AuxiliaryPop$, $gNew$)
15     $Pop \leftarrow AuxiliaryPop$
16 **return** g - best fitted gene from Pop

Algorithm 3: Testing ensemble of classifiers using dynamic selection

---

Input: training data TR, testing data TS, $EN = \{g_1, \cdots, g_n\}$ ensemble of classifiers, number of neighbours K

Output: measures of classification quality.

1 **for** $(x, y) \in TS$ **do**
2   **for** $i \leftarrow 1$ **to** n **do**
3   calculate $g_i(x) = v_i$
4   **if** $allEqual\{v_i \ i = 1, \ldots n\}$ **then**
5          $class \leftarrow v_1$
6   **else**
7          $N(x) = \{x' \in TR \ \& \ x' \text{ is K-neighbor of } x\}$
8   **for** $i \leftarrow 1$ **to** n **do**
9   calculate the number of correct classifications n_i of g_i on $N(x)$
10         $j \leftarrow argmax_{1 \leq i \leq n} n_i$
11         $class \leftarrow g_j(x)$
12   compare $class$ with y and modify TP, TN, FP, FN
13 calculate quality measures from TP, TN, FP, FN
14 **return** $quality\ measures$

---

from the Keel repository. For the experiment the 5 cross validation scheme has been used. All average values have been calculated over 6 repetitions of 5-CV scheme for each dataset. Performance measures included F1 score, geometric mean (G), area under roc curve (AUC) and balanced accuracy (BACC). These measures are commonly used for evaluating learners designed for mining imbalanced datasets. In Table 1, settings used for the experiment are shown.

Table 1. Computational experiment settings.

Parameter	Value
Number of neighbors for minority instances (k_1)	5
Number of neighbors for majority instances (k_2)	20
λ	0.25
$xmax$	10
$ymax$	10
Number of genes in the ensemble	5
Number of iterations in GEP	100
pm	0.5
$pris$, pis, $pr1$, $pr2$	0.2

In Tables 2 and 3 we show results for the datasets with imbalanced ratio (IR) higher than 9, part 2 from the Keel repository. Because of space constraints we show only a sample of the obtained results. Table 2 contains dataset characteristic and Table 3 the results, additionally with values of the standard deviation for geometric mean.

Data in Table 3 show that there is a high degree of correlation between different performance measure. It can also be observed that relatively low values of the standard deviation in the case of geometric means point to the fact that the obtained results are fairly stable.

To enable better evaluation of the proposed approach we show in Tables 4 and 5 comparisons with other approaches. In all cases the geometric mean is used as the performance measure.

Table 2. Dataset Characteristics (R – real, I – integer, N – Nominal)

Dataset	#Attribute	R/I/N	#Examples	IR
yeast-2 _vs _4	8	8/0/0	514	9,080
yeast-0-5-6-7-9 _vs _4	8	8/0/0	528	9,350
vowel0	13	10/3/0	988	9,980
glass-0-1-6 _vs _2	9	9/0/0	192	10,290
glass2	9	9/0/0	214	11,590
shuttle-c0-vs-c4	9	0/9/0	1829	13,870
yeast-1 _vs _7	7	7/0/0	459	14,300
glass4	9	9/0/0	214	15,470
ecoli4	7	7/0/0	336	15,800
page-blocks-1-3 _vs _4	10	4/6/0	472	15,860
abalone9-18	8	7/0/1	731	16,400
glass-0-1-6 _vs _5	9	9/0/1	184	19,440
shuttle-c2-vs-c4	9	0/9/0	129	20,050
yeast-1-4-5-8 _vs _7	8	8/0/0	693	22,100
glass5	9	9/0/0	214	22,780
yeast-2 _vs _8	8	8/0/0	482	23,100
yeast4	8	8/0/0	1484	28,100
yeast-1-2-8-9 _vs _7	8	8/0/0	947	30,750
yeast5	8	8/0/0	1484	32,730
ecoli-0-1-3-7 _vs _2-6	7	7/0/0	381	39,140
yeast6	8	8/0/0	1484	41,400
abalone19	8	7/0/1	4174	129,440

Source: https://sci2s.ugr.es/keel/imbalanced.php?order=featR#sub20

From Table 4 it appears that the proposed cellular Gene Expression Programming learner outperforms all other classic approach for mining imbalanced datasets. To determine whether there are any significant differences among results from Table 4, produced by different classifiers we used the Friedman ANOVA by ranks test. The null hypothesis state that there are no such differences. With Friedman statistics equal to $86,716$ and p-value equal to $0,00000$ the null hypothesis should be rejected at the significance level of $0,05$. However, the Kendall concordance coefficient expressing the simultaneous association (relatedness) between the considered samples, with the value of $0,246$ tells that there is some degree of relatedness between the considered samples.

Table 3. Computational experiment results for the example datasets

Dataset	F1	BACC	AUC	G	St.d. G
yeast-2 _vs _4	0,965	0,949	0,966	0,966	0,0109
yeast-0-5-6-7-9 _vs _4	0,917	0,885	0,894	0,892	0,0282
vowel0	0,977	0,966	0,972	0,971	0,0136
glass-0-1-6 _vs _2	0,847	0,792	0,870	0,857	0,0692
glass2	0,809	0,747	0,797	0,785	0,0781
shuttle-c0-vs-c4	1,000	1,000	1,000	1,000	0,0000
yeast-1 _vs _7	0,880	0,838	0,813	0,811	0,0777
glass4	0,989	0,983	0,989	0,989	0,0131
ecoli4	0,988	0,983	0,981	0,981	0,0290
page-blocks-1-3 _vs _4	0,995	0,993	0,996	0,996	0,0064
abalone9-18	0,888	0,847	0,849	0,847	0,0437
glass-0-1-6 _vs _5	0,973	0,962	0,975	0,974	0,0242
shuttle-c2-vs-c4	1,000	1,000	1,000	1,000	0,0000
yeast-1-4-5-8 _vs _7	0,806	0,754	0,758	0,747	0,0631
glass5	0,989	0,984	0,989	0,989	0,0115
yeast-2 _vs _8	0,934	0,909	0,896	0,893	0,0646
yeast4	0,920	0,888	0,880	0,878	0,0235
yeast-1-2-8-9 _vs _7	0,877	0,843	0,846	0,841	0,0521
yeast5	0,973	0,961	0,974	0,974	0,0062
ecoli-0-1-3-7 _vs _2-6	0,966	0,950	0,967	0,966	0,0118
yeast6	0,947	0,924	0,920	0,920	0,0319
abalone19	0,739	0,664	0,749	0,728	0,0434

Again, to determine whether there are any significant differences among results from Table 5, produced by different ensemble classifiers we used the Friedman ANOVA by ranks test. The null hypothesis state that there are no such differences. With Friedman statistics equal to $13,193$ and p-value equal to $0,00424$ the null hypothesis should be rejected at the significance level of 0.05. To compare more closely results produced by CBIS with AP+IB3 and bagging and results produced by cGEP we used signed test. With Z value at 0.385 and p-value at $0,7003$ the null hypothesis that there are no consistent differences between results produced by CBIS with AP+IB3 and bagging versus results produced by cGEP cannot be rejected.

Table 4. Performance of the cGEP versus other well-known classifiers

Dataset	NBU	ENN	NCR	OSS	RENN	RUS	SMOTE	TL	CGEP
abalone19	0,659	0,695	0,695	0,695	0,695	0,708	0,679	0,694	**0,728**
dermatology6	0,988	0,966	0,966	0,966	0,879	0,966	0,975	0,966	**0,999**
ecoli-0-1-4-6-vs-5	0,880	0,858	0,858	0,853	0,858	0,861	0,862	0,858	**0,945**
ecoli-0-1-4-7-vs-2-3-5-6	**0,960**	0,922	0,924	0,926	0,915	0,908	0,927	0,925	0,889
ecoli-0-1-4-7-vs-5-6	**0,958**	0,948	0,948	0,945	0,948	0,826	0,943	0,949	0,933
ecoli-0-2-3-4-vs-5	0,900	0,856	0,858	0,869	0,856	0,816	0,874	0,863	**0,935**
ecoli-0-3-4-6-vs-5	0,922	0,849	0,850	0,853	0,849	0,766	0,854	0,849	**0,958**
ecoli-0-3-4-7-vs-5-6	**0,941**	0,925	0,925	0,919	0,925	0,928	0,906	0,925	0,915
ecoli-0-3-4-vs-5	**0,894**	0,835	0,844	0,860	0,835	0,750	0,860	0,844	0,781
ecoli-0-4-6-vs-5	0,872	0,846	0,846	0,853	0,846	0,848	0,857	0,846	**0,952**
ecoli-0-6-7-vs-5	0,915	0,874	0,879	0,871	0,874	0,838	0,883	0,883	**0,948**
ecoli1	0,885	0,850	0,852	0,839	0,853	0,872	0,842	0,848	**0,941**
ecoli2	0,941	0,928	0,929	0,928	0,927	0,921	0,942	0,928	**0,961**
ecoli3	0,894	0,890	0,892	0,920	0,873	0,923	0,908	0,907	**0,943**
ecoli4	0,950	0,916	0,916	0,920	0,916	0,916	0,934	0,917	**0,981**
glass-0-1-4-6-vs-2	0,720	0,685	0,690	0,680	0,699	0,618	0,703	0,696	**0,841**
glass0	0,826	0,771	0,800	0,810	0,755	0,800	0,793	0,804	**0,866**
glass1	0,660	0,663	0,662	0,669	0,702	0,702	0,637	0,656	**0,789**
glass4	0,830	0,723	0,726	0,714	0,723	0,760	0,752	0,728	**0,989**
glass6	0,864	0,854	0,854	0,825	0,888	0,855	0,827	0,856	**0,981**
haberman	0,656	0,670	0,676	0,658	0,671	0,611	0,645	0,657	**00,724**
iris0	**1,000**	**1,000**	**1,000**	**1,000**	**1,000**	**1,000**	**1,000**	**1,000**	1,000
new-throid1	**1,000**	**1,000**	**1,000**	**1,000**	**1,000**	**1,000**	**1,000**	**1,000**	0,989
new-thyroid2	**1,000**	**1,000**	**1,000**	**1,000**	**1,000**	**1,000**	**1,000**	**1,000**	0,992
page-blocks-1-3-vs-4	**0,992**	0,902	0,908	0,908	0,902	0,902	0,909	0,909	0,996
page-blocks0	0,954	0,936	0,935	0,928	0,937	0,935	0,932	0,932	**0,984**
pima	**0,815**	0,799	0,809	**0,815**	0,789	0,814	0,815	0,813	0,764
poker-8-vs-6	0,531	0,437	0,439	0,427	0,437	0,456	0,500	0,437	**0,810**
segment0	0,987	0,982	0,982	0,982	0,982	0,982	0,980	0,982	**0,993**
vehicle0	0,904	0,806	0,805	0,823	0,801	0,809	0,820	0,811	**0,849**
vehicle1	**0,740**	0,709	0,713	0,717	0,708	0,719	0,717	0,713	0,727
vehicle2	**0,920**	0,861	0,859	0,850	0,857	0,834	0,849	0,857	0,914
vehicle3	**0,762**	0,701	0,700	0,698	0,700	0,697	0,699	0,698	0,728
winequality-red-4	**0,694**	0,659	0,653	0,651	0,660	0,626	0,653	0,650	0,663
winequality-red-8-vs-6-7	0,695	0,713	0,717	0,669	0,721	0,674	0,651	0,713	**0,792**
wisconsin	0,978	0,975	0,977	**0,993**	0,974	0,983	0,983	0,982	0,973
yeast-0-2-5-6-vs-3-7-8-9	0,816	0,761	0,762	0,762	0,764	0,742	0,755	0,760	**0,825**
yeast-0-2-5-7-9-vs-3-6-8	0,932	0,916	0,916	0,888	0,916	0,907	0,816	0,915	**0,936**
yeast-0-3-5-9-vs-7-8	0,721	0,695	0,690	0,712	0,680	0,713	0,731	0,698	**0,769**
yeast-1-vs-7	0,801	0,802	0,800	0,800	0,805	0,792	0,776	0,800	**0,811**
yeast-2-vs-4	0,864	0,833	0,835	0,833	0,831	0,822	0,834	0,835	**0,966**
yeast-2-vs-8	0,838	0,835	0,836	0,828	0,835	0,850	0,793	0,836	**0,893**
yeast5	**0,989**	0,987	0,986	0,986	0,987	0,976	0,982	0,986	0,974
Average	0,862	0,833	0,835	0,834	0,832	0,824	0,832	0,835	**0,892**

Source: [3] for NBU, ENN, NCR, OSS, RENN, RUS, SMOTE and TL

Table 5. Performance of the cGEP versus other ensemble classifiers

Dataset	CBU	CBIS		cGEP
		AP+IB3 (boosting)	AP+IB3 (bagging)	
Abalone9-18	0,831	0,849	**0,894**	0,847
Abalone19	**0,728**	0,624	0,617	**0,728**
Ecoli-0-vs-1	0,982	0,975	0,982	**0,996**
Ecoli-0-1-3-7-vs-2-6	0,804	0,877	0,879	**0,966**
Ecoli1	0,927	**0,958**	0,957	0,941
Glass0	0,873	**0,888**	0,885	0,866
Glass-0-1-2-3-vs-4-5-6	0,970	**0,980**	0,966	0,976
Glass-0-1-6-vs-2	0,790	0,775	0,713	**0,857**
Glass-0-1-6-vs-5	0,964	0,894	**0,987**	0,974
Glass1	0,824	0,812	**0,847**	0,789
Glass2	0,760	0,741	0,766	**0,785**
Glass4	0,853	0,944	0,971	**0,989**
Glass5	0,949	**0,994**	**0,994**	0,989
Glass6	0,905	0,951	0,934	**0,981**
Haberman	0,603	0,646	0,648	**0,724**
Iris0	0,990	0,990	0,990	**1,000**
New-thyroid1	0,973	0,979	**0,997**	0,989
New-thyroid2	0,924	0,976	**0,994**	0,992
Page-blocks0	0,986	**0,987**	**0,987**	0,984
Page-blocks-1-3-vs-4	0,992	**0,998**	0,997	0,996
Pima	0,758	0,771	**0,805**	0,764
Segment0	0,996	**0,999**	0,993	0,993
Shuttle-0-vs-4	**1,000**	**1,000**	**1,000**	**1,000**
Shuttle-2-vs-4	0,988	**1,000**	**1,000**	**1,000**
Yeast-1-2-8-9-vs7	0,692	0,818	0,775	**0,841**
Yeast-1-4-5-8-vs7	0,627	**0,777**	0,605	0,747
Yeast4	0,874	0,857	**0,914**	0,878
Yeast5	**0,987**	0,967	0,970	0,974
Yeast6	0,909	0,881	0,884	**0,920**
Average	0,878	0,893	0,895	**0,913**

Source: [17] for CBU, [20] for CBIS

5   Conlusions

The paper contributes by proposing a novel classifier for mining imbalanced datasets. The approach integrates three techniques – oversampling, cellular Gene

Expression Programming, and dynamic selection of classifiers. The LAMO technique used for oversampling allows to select the borderline examples from minority class and to synthesize minority examples using linear interpolation. The procedure provides informative synthetic minority set examples. At the learning stage, using cellular GEP, an ensemble of base classifiers is generated. Finally, a dynamic selection of classifiers is used to arrive at the final prediction. An extended computational experiment carried out has confirmed that the proposed learner offers very good performance as compared with classic approaches. Its performance is also comparable with that of the available ensemble classifiers used for mining imbalanced datasets. The very good performance of the proposed approach can be attributed to the synergistic effect coming from integrating high-quality oversampling technique, the power of cellular GEP which is an implementation of the distributed evolutionary computation paradigm, and the procedure for dynamic selection of attributes.

Future research should focus on the possible diversification of base classifiers by extending the range of learners for producing base classifiers. Another potential direction of research is searching for more advanced oversampling techniques.

References

1. Aha, D.W., Kibler, D.F., Albert, M.K.: Instance-based learning algorithms. Mach. Learn. **6**, 37–66 (1991)
2. Alba, E., Dorronsoro, B.: Cellular Genetic Algorithms. Springer, Boston (2008). https://doi.org/10.1007/978-0-387-77610-1
3. Aridas, C.K., Karlos, S., Kanas, V.G., Fazakis, N., Kotsiantis, S.B.: Uncertainty based under-sampling for learning naive bayes classifiers under imbalanced data sets. IEEE Access **8**, 2122–2133 (2020)
4. Chawla, N.V., Bowyer, K.W., Hall, L.O., Kegelmeyer, W.P.: SMOTE: synthetic minority over-sampling technique. J. Artif. Intell. Res. **16**, 321–357 (2002)
5. Chawla, N.V., Lazarevic, A., Hall, L.O., Bowyer, K.W.: SMOTEBoost: improving prediction of the minority class in boosting. In: Lavrač, N., Gamberger, D., Todorovski, L., Blockeel, H. (eds.) PKDD 2003. LNCS (LNAI), vol. 2838, pp. 107–119. Springer, Heidelberg (2003). https://doi.org/10.1007/978-3-540-39804-2_12
6. Fernández, A., García, S., Galar, M., Prati, R.C., Krawczyk, B., Herrera, F.: Learning from Imbalanced Data Sets. Springer, Cham (2018). https://doi.org/10.1007/978-3-319-98074-4
7. Cândida Ferreira. Gene expression programming: a new adaptive algorithm for solving problems. Complex Syst. **13**(2), 87–129 (2001)
8. Galar, M., Fernandez, A., Barrenechea, E., Bustince, H., Herrera, F.: A review on ensembles for the class imbalance problem: Bagging-, boosting-, and hybrid-based approaches. IEEE Trans. Syst. Man Cybern. Part C **42**(4), 463–484 (2012)
9. Guo, H., Li, Y., Jennifer Shang, G., Mingyun, H.Y., Bing, G.: Learning from class-imbalanced data: review of methods and applications. Expert Syst. Appl. **73**, 220–239 (2017)
10. He, H., Bai, Y., Garcia, E.A., Li, S.: Adasyn: adaptive synthetic sampling approach for imbalanced learning. In: IEEE International Joint Conference on Neural Networks, IJCNN, vol. 2008, pp. 1322–1328 (2008)

11. Jędrzejowicz, J., Jędrzejowicz, P.: Cellular GEP-induced classifiers. In: Pan, J.-S., Chen, S.-M., Nguyen, N.T. (eds.) ICCCI 2010. LNCS (LNAI), vol. 6421, pp. 343–352. Springer, Heidelberg (2010). https://doi.org/10.1007/978-3-642-16693-8_36

12. Jedrzejowicz, J., Jedrzejowicz, P.: Gene expression programming as a data classification tool. Rev. J. Intell. Fuzzy Syst. **36**(1), 91–100 (2019)

13. Britto, A.S., Jr., Sabourin, R., Oliveira, L.E.: Dynamic selection of classifiers - a comprehensive review. Pattern Recogn. **47**(11), 3665–3680 (2014)

14. Krawczyk, B.: Learning from imbalanced data: open challenges and future directions. Prog. Artif. Intell. **5**(4), 221–232 (2016). https://doi.org/10.1007/s13748-016-0094-0

15. Kubat, M., Matwin, S.: Addressing the curse of imbalanced training sets: one-sided selection. In: Douglas, H.F. (eds.), Proceedings of the Fourteenth International Conference on Machine Learning (ICML 1997), Nashville, Tennessee, USA, July 8–12, 1997, pp. 179–186. Morgan Kaufmann (1997)

16. Laurikkala, J.: Improving identification of difficult small classes by balancing class distribution. In: Quaglini, S., Barahona, P., Andreassen, S. (eds.) AIME 2001. LNCS (LNAI), vol. 2101, pp. 63–66. Springer, Heidelberg (2001). https://doi.org/10.1007/3-540-48229-6_9

17. Lin, W.-C., Tsai, C.-F., Ya-Han, H., Jhang, J.-S.: Clustering-based undersampling in class-imbalanced data. Inf. Sci. **409**, 17–26 (2016)

18. Seiffert, C., Khoshgoftaar, T.M., Van Hulse, J., Napolitano, A.: Rusboost: a hybrid approach to alleviating class imbalance. IEEE Trans. Syst. Man Cybern. Part A **40**(1), 185–197 (2010)

19. Ivan T.: Two modifications of CNN. IEEE Trans. Syst. Man Cybern. SMC **6**(11), 769–772 (1976)

20. Tsai, C.-F., Lin, W.-C., Ya-Han, H., Yao, G.-T.: Under-sampling class imbalanced datasets by combining clustering analysis and instance selection. Inf. Sci. **477**, 47–54 (2019)

21. Wang, X., Jian, X., Zeng, T., Jing, L.: Local distribution-based adaptive minority oversampling for imbalanced data classification. Neurocomputing **422**, 200–213 (2021)

22. Wilson, D.L.: Asymptotic properties of nearest neighbor rules using edited data. IEEE Trans. Syst. Man Cybern. **2**, 408–421 (1972)

Learning from Imbalanced Data Using Over-Sampling and the Firefly Algorithm

Ireneusz Czarnowski[(✉)] (iD)

Department of Information Systems, Gdynia Maritime University,
Morska 83, 81-225 Gdynia, Poland
i.czarnowski@umg.edu.pl

Abstract. In this paper, we consider the problem of learning from imbalanced data. This is one of the main challenges faced by machine learning and classification algorithms. An over-sampling approach is proposed to eliminate the negative influence of a lack of balanced class distribution within a dataset. Synthetic instances are produced within a subset of instances belonging to a minority class, and are generated using so-called neighbours, the selection of which is carried out using the firefly algorithm. The main contribution of the paper is to present an implementation of the firefly algorithm for the production of synthetic instances. The proposed approach is validated using selected benchmark datasets. The results of computational experiments are presented and discussed, and it is shown that the problem of neighbour selection is important with respect to the production quality of synthetic instances, and that the quality can be guaranteed using a dedicated implementation of a metaheuristic approach, i.e. the firefly algorithm. Another contribution of this paper is applying the firefly algorithm to solve a discrete optimisation problem.

Keywords: Classification · Learning from imbalanced data · Over-sampling · Firefly algorithm

1 Introduction

Machine learning algorithms form an important component of a wide range of intelligent systems, including industrial, medical, military applications, and those whose functionality is a result of advanced processing of the data. Machine learning algorithms were developed to process data, and are able to act autonomously. Moreover, the data processing step itself is also autonomous in this approaches. This intelligent behaviour arises as a result of extracting knowledge from the data, meaning that the data are crucial for machine learning.

The data processing step mentioned above involves learning from data (also known as learning from examples or learning from instances), and the data used in this process are called training data [1]. Depending on the structure of these data, machine learning methods can be classified into supervised and unsupervised learning models.

In general, the traditional machine learning paradigm is based on processing instances as multidimensional vectors of attributes. Each attribute has a domain that

© Springer Nature Switzerland AG 2021
N. T. Nguyen et al. (Eds.): ICCCI 2021, LNAI 12876, pp. 373–386, 2021.
https://doi.org/10.1007/978-3-030-88081-1_28

is determined by the type of attribute, and can be either symbolic or numerical. In the case of supervised learning, a particular attribute contains a value that represents the class label of the instance [1], and indicates how the instance has been identified. In supervised learning, this set of instances is used to develop a model that describes and distinguishes between data classes [1]. This type of model is called a classifier, and the process of classifier induction is a learning classifier from data [2]. Classifiers are sometimes referred to as mathematical functions that map input data to categories. Finally, classifiers may be used to solve a classification task, where their role is to assign data into predefined classes. In unsupervised learning the values representing the class labels of the instances are unavailable, and another kind of machine learning task must be carried out.

In real implementations of machine learning, one of the problems relates to class imbalance. Class imbalance arises when the available dataset consists of instances labelled by class, and the numbers of instances in these classes are not equally distributed. Most practical implementations are affected by this problem, meaning that machine learning algorithms must take this problem into consideration and that classifiers must be able to correctly predict instances of the minority class. In other words, the classification of minority classes is critical for many real-world problems.

There are currently four types of approaches for learning from imbalanced data. The first three are data-level, algorithm-level and cost-sensitive methods, and the last is based on a combination of these approaches [3].

In general, data-level methods process data in such a way as to eliminate the imbalance between the majority and minority classes. This balanced dataset is then processed using standard machine learning methods.

Two main data-level approaches have been developed to eliminate this imbalance by changing the distribution of instances in each class towards a more balanced ratio. These approaches are called under-sampling and over-sampling. The former changes the distribution by removing instances from the majority classes, whereas the latter adds instances to the minority class [4]. Of course, hybrid approaches can also be applied, in which the processing of imbalanced data is carried out in parallel using both over- and under-sampling [5].

In this paper, we address the imbalanced learning problem through the use of a data-level approach with over-sampling. In general, over-sampling reduces the negative effects of imbalanced data by creating synthetic instances for the minority class. A simple approach to over-sampling involves the random generation of instances for the minority class until the balance between the minority and majority class instances is restored to the same level; however, although this is a very practical approach, it has numerous weaknesses. Another approach involves creating synthetic instances based on similarities within the feature space. The main weakness of both of these approaches arises from a lack of information about which instances should be duplicated and from which region the instances should be generated. This means that an important direction for research is to search for a more effective way of duplicating minority class instances while at the same time avoiding problems with random duplication.

The most popular algorithm based on over-sampling is SMOTE (Synthetic Minority Over-Sampling Technique) [6], a very simple method that replicates minority class instances. SMOTE has several weaknesses, one of which is that each instance of the minority class can be chosen for over-sampling, and duplication may include instances that do not provide any useful information for the identification of boundaries between classes. Several additional versions of SMOTE have therefore been proposed [7–10]. A discussion of SMOTE and other approaches to over-sampling is provided in [11].

The aim of this paper is to extend the over-sampling mechanism proposed in [11]. The novel contribution of this work is the application of a metaheuristic to optimise the number of neighbours selected when determining the space from which synthetic instances will be generated. It is also important to decide what is the reference for designating these neighbours.

In this approach, the problem of neighbour selection is considered as a combinatorial optimisation problem, and is solved using the firefly algorithm (FA). The FA is one of a family of nature-inspired metaheuristics, and belongs to a set of stochastic optimisation algorithms. It was developed by Xin-She Yang as a tool for solving continuous optimisation tasks [13].

The main research questions relate to the possibility of setting an appropriate number of neighbours via an optimising process and evaluating the influence of the number of neighbours on the quality of the synthetic instances created by an over-sampling mechanism. A further important research question also concerns the possibility of applying the FA to optimise the number of neighbours in this problem. It should be highlighted that the implementation of the FA discussed here is an example in which this algorithm has been used to solve a discrete optimisation problem. The answers on performance questions of the proposed approach has been formulated based on the computational experiment results.

The paper is organised as follows. In Sect. 2, we introduce the problem of learning from imbalanced data. In Sect. 3, we describe our proposed approach and include a discussion of the details of the proposed FA. Section 4 presents the results of a computational experiment and a discussion. The final section contains our conclusions and suggestions for future research.

2 Learning from Imbalanced Data

Let D be a multiclass dataset in which $D = D_1 \cup D_2 ... \cup D_d$, where d is the number of different classes and $D_{i:i = 1,...,d}$ consists of instances from the i-th class. The dataset can be also defined as a set of pairs $\left[x_{ij}, d\left(x_j\right) \right] : i = 1, \ldots, n; j = 1, \ldots, N$, where n is the number of attributes, N is the number of instances and each instance x is associated with a class label. In this case, $d(x)$ represents the value of the class label for instance x.

The aim of learning from data is to find a hypothesis $h \in \mathrm{H}$ using a dataset D, where h optimises a given performance criterion F that can be based on a number of different measures, such as the complexity of the hypothesis or the cost of classification. The most popular performance criterion is the accuracy of classification.

In general, the aim of learning from data is to select from the space of all possible hypotheses the one that optimises a given performance criterion. In other words, the learning algorithm must select the best possible hypothesis. This hypothesis is also called a classifier, and its role is to predict the class labels for new instances that are input to the decision system without labels.

In case of learning from imbalanced data, the cardinality of the subsets $D_{i:i=1,...,d}$ is not equal, and there is at least one subset of D for which the cardinality is smaller than that of each of the remaining subsets of D, which represent the remaining classes. Let $D_{minority}$ be the subset of D that contains the minority class dataset, and let all remaining subsets contain the majority class instances, i.e. $\forall_{i\in\{1,...,d\}\setminus\{minority\}}|D_i| \gg |D_{minority}|$.

In an over-sampling approach, the number of instances in the minority class is increased by generating synthetic instances or by replicating some instances from this subset in order to increase its cardinality. We denote by $S_{minority}$ the set of instances produced in the over-sampling procedure, meaning that after the over-sampling procedure we have $\forall_{i\in\{1,...,d\}\setminus\{minority\}}|D_i| \cong |D_{minority} \cup S_{minority}|$. In this way, over-sampling eliminates the lack of a balanced class distribution within the training data.

Let D^* be a multiclass dataset modified by over-sampling, i.e. $D^* \supset D$, where $\exists_{i\in\{1,...,d\}}|D_i^*| = |D_i \cup S_i|$ and also $\exists_{i\in\{1,...,d\}}|D_i^*| = |D_i|$. This means that the process of increasing the cardinality of instances in the minority class is carried out at the data level. The aim of learning from data is to find a hypothesis $h \in H$ using the dataset D^*, and this process is carried out in a systematic way, as the input data are preprocessed to eliminate the problem of imbalanced data.

3   An Approach to Learning from Imbalanced Data

3.1   General Concept of the Proposed Approach

The general concept underlying the proposed approach is to create an extension of the framework presented in [11]. In the case of data imbalance, the process of over-sampling is applied to the minority subset. This process consists of the following steps:

- Dividing instances from the majority class into clusters using a dedicated clustering procedure,
- For each pair of closest clusters in sense of the Euclidean distance, finding the nearest neighbours from among the instances in the minority class,
- Generating synthetic instances for the minority class from among these neighbours,
- Adding synthetic instances to the training data as instances of the minority class.

The above steps are carried out for each subset of data with a minority class. This means that the process can be repeated several times to ensure the same level of cardinality for instances from each decision class in the dataset. Thus, each class in the data is considered independently and its cardinality is raised to a given level. This level can be set by the user or determined based on the size of the subset of instances from the majority class. This approach allows for the generation of artificial instances that are as close as possible to the decision boundary with all other instances belonging to the other classes. Of course, in the general case with two decision classes, this process is carried out only for the minority class.

An important aspect of the over-sampling process discussed above is clustering. In [11], clustering was carried out using the similarity-based clustering algorithm (SCA) proposed in [14]. The SCA calculates the values of the similarity coefficients for each instance, and then creates clusters of instances with identical similarity coefficients. The

SCA run independently of the parameter settings, as the number of clusters is determined by the values of the similarity coefficients. This means that SCA-based clusters are initialised automatically.

One important problem with the procedure described above is the need to decide on the number of nearest neighbours. These neighbours must be selected from instances belonging to the minority class (i.e. they are nearest minority neighbours) when the neighbourhoods are calculated for the clusters from the majority classes. The number of neighbours may of course be set by the user, but this approach may not guarantee that synthetic instances are generated in a suitable location in the data space.

A second problem concerns the reference clusters used to designate these neighbours. As mentioned above, the neighbours are selected with reference to pairs of the closest clusters of instances from the majority class. However, the question arises as to how the neighbourhood is determined. In [11], the neighbourhood was determined with respect to reference instances, which were selected from clusters of instances from the majority class. However, the authors of [11] also considered another problem with instance selection in the core of the proposed algorithm. In [12], the neighbourhood was determined with respect to reference instances, which were taken as the centres of clusters produced using the k-means algorithm. In this paper, we do not take this approach, and the production of synthetic instances we consider with respect to all data (instances) but from another class. The problems of determining the number of nearest neighbours and the neighbourhood itself can be crucial for the generation of synthetic instances. The aim is to generate synthetic instances that are relatively close to the decision boundary. We assume that addressing the two problems described above simultaneously can ensure promising results and result in effective learning of decision boundaries by the classifier. This also means that the quality of the synthetic instances is determined by the over-sampling algorithm, and thus the over-sampling algorithm has an impact on the quality of the learning from imbalanced data [18].

The problem of selecting the nearest minority neighbours and the reference instances in the clusters can be considered as a combinatorial optimisation problem. Selection can be carried out using an evolutionary search based on metaheuristics. An example of the selection of the nearest minority neighbours using a genetic algorithm was presented in [15]. Another population-based approach was reported in [16], where a crossover operator was proposed for continuous synthesis of new data samples. A genetic algorithm has been also used to learn a probability distribution from the available data and then to generate instances for the minority class [17]. Other examples of using population-based algorithms to improve the performance of imbalanced data classification were discussed in [19–21]. In the next subsection, we present details of the FA implemented in our approach for synthetic instance generation. Algorithm 1 gives pseudo-code for the general over-sampling procedure described above.

Algorithm 1. Over-sampling procedure for a minority set of instances

Input: D - training set, where $D = D_1 \cup D_2 \ldots \cup D_d$,; d - number of classes;
Output: D - updated dataset created by adding synthetic instances and eliminating unbalanced data.

Begin
    Set *majority* = majority class number.
    For $i \in \{1, \ldots, (d-1)\} \backslash \{majority\}$ **do**
    While $|D_i| \ncong |D_{majority}|$ **do**
      $D' = \bigcup_{j:j=1,\ldots,d \backslash \{i\}} D_j$;
      Run the SCA procedure and map instances from D' into clusters $D'_1, \ldots, D'_k$, where k is the number of clusters produced;
      For $\forall_{D'_j:j\in\{1,\ldots,k\}}$ **do**
        Find the cluster that is closest to it and run the procedure for finding reference instances within these closest clusters and the nearest minority neighbours from instances belonging to class i, using the FA. Randomly generate a synthetic instance x_a located between instances belonging to the nearest minority neighbours;
        Add x_a to D_i;
      End for
    End while;
    Return D;
End

3.2 Proposed Firefly Algorithm

The FA is an example of a nature-inspired metaheuristic that was developed to solve difficult optimisation problems [13]. This population-based algorithm was inspired by a natural communication mechanism used by fireflies, based on their luminescence. When applied to the process of searching for solutions, the FA involves evaluating the quality of the solutions using the so-called "glows" of the firefly. These fireflies cooperate with each other, and the candidates for cooperation are selected based on their brightness. These behaviours of the fireflies ensure efficient exploration of the search space.

When we look at the FA, we can also see an analogy to a multi-agent algorithm, in which agents communicate, improve the solutions, and finally select the best solution from the population.

In the case of the FA, the solution search process is based on a simulation of the behavioural characteristics of flashing fireflies. In this search environment, each firefly can be attractive to others, where the attractiveness of a firefly is proportional to its brightness. However, the attractiveness of fireflies to one other depends on the distance between them. This means that the effect decreases as the distance between fireflies increases. It also means that during the optimisation process and the search for a solution, fireflies change their locations and move in the direction of more attractive fireflies. It is also assumed that fireflies have some freedom, since this movement has a somewhat random character.

Let $s_i : i = 1, \ldots, S$ be the solution to the considered problem, where S is the number of solutions included in the population (i.e. S is the size of the population), and let $I(s_i)$ be the brightness of a firefly. The brightness is also related to the fitness value $f(s_i)$ calculated for solution s_i, i.e. $I(s_i) \propto f(s_i)$. Each firefly has also a certain attractiveness β, which characterises it with regard to its attractiveness to other fireflies. As described above, the attractiveness β_{ij} depends on the distance r_{ij} between firefly i and firefly j, and this distance can be calculated based on a selected metric.

In this paper, each solution (individual) is represented as a string consisting of integers. The string representing of the solution consists of three kinds of numbers, i.e. from three parts. The first type of number represents the reference instances for clusters, while the second type represents the nearest minority neighbours and the third represents a vector of feature values for a synthetic instance located between instances determined by the nearest neighbours. Having defined the solutions, the tasks of the FA are to select the most appropriate instances to represent the clusters, to determine a suitable number of nearest neighbours, to select these nearest neighbours and to determine the synthetic instances. However, the last of these is the most important.

In the first step of the FA, an initial population of potential solutions is generated. The population is generated with respect to the conditions that concern possible instances for representing reference instances and instances for nearest minority neighbours. The conditions are formulated based on the results of clustering, which was carried out previously. The process of searching for a solution is then began, based on the movement of the fireflies within the solution space.

In the proposed algorithm, the movement of the fireflies is represented in three ways:

- by replacing one instance number with another from the same cluster, within the part of the solution representing reference instances,
- by replacing instances, or adding or removing a number of instances to represent the nearest minority neighbours, within the part of the solution that represents the nearest neighbours. The proposed algorithm is also based on the assumption that the number of nearest neighbours is no smaller than two and no greater than 10. However, the upper bound may be an algorithm parameter, and is denoted as k' in this paper.
- by modifying the values for variables in the part of the solution that represents the synthetic instance.

The movement procedures described above also depend on the nearest firefly, whose position is considered when the movement procedures are carried out. The attractiveness of each firefly in the algorithm is calculated as follows:

$$\beta = \beta_0 e^{-\gamma r_m^2} + \alpha \cdot random(), \tag{1}$$

where r_m is the distance between the moving firefly and the firefly towards which it is moving. γ is the absorption coefficient, and β_0 is a maximum value of attractiveness, calculated when the distance is zero. α is a factor that determines the random movement. The $random()$ function is used to generate numbers in the range zero to one, with a Gaussian distribution.

In our approach, the distance r_m is calculated based on the values of the variables included in the improved solution and the nearest solution which is located in the space at a distance no greater than β, where the distance is calculated using the Euclidean metric.

The value of $I(s_i)$ is calculated by estimating the accuracy of the classifier, taking into account the whole dataset including the synthetic instances.

Pseudo-code for the FA is given in Algorithm 2, and for the movement procedure in Algorithm 3.

Algorithm 2. Firefly-based over-sampling algorithm

Input: D – original dataset; $D_{minority}$ – subset of D containing instances belonging to the minority class; D'_1, D'_2– two clusters consisting of instances; S – number of fireflies; α, γ, k' – input parameters;
Output: x_a – synthetic instance;

  Begin
    Generate initial population P of fireflies $s_{i:i=1,...,N}$ randomly;
    For $i \in \{1,...,S\}$ do
      Calculate the brightness $I(s_i)$ of each firefly by decoding s_i and induce a classifier using the original dataset of instances and the synthetic instances represented by s_i;
    End for
  Repeat
    For $i \in \{1,...,S\}$ do
      For $j \in \{1,...,S\}\backslash\{i\}$ do
        Calculate the attractiveness of the j-th firefly in relation to s_i using Eq. (1);
      End for j
      Repeat
        Find the solution s_j for which $I(s_j) > I(s_i)$ and the distance to solution s_i is no greater than β, using Eq. (1);
        Set r_m as the Euclidean distance between s_i and s_j;
        Run the movement procedure algorithm using the parameter vector $[D'_1, D'_2, D, s_i, s_j, k']$ and return s'_i as a improved solution;
        Calculate $I(s'_i)$;
        Set r_k as the Euclidean distance between s'_i and s_j;
        If $I(s'_i) > I(s_i)$ or $r_k < r_m$; then
          $s_i \leftarrow s'_i$;
        End if
      Until $I(s'_i) > I(s_i)$ or *stop condition for improvement is true*
    End for i
  Until *stop condition is true*
  $\varsigma :=$ get the best solution from P;
  $x_a =$ get the synthetic instance from the third part of the solution ς;
  Return x_a
  End

Algorithm 3. Movement procedure

Input: s_i – firefly that will be moved towards firefly s_j; $D_{minority}$ – subset of D containing instances belonging to the minority class; D'_1, D'_2 – clusters produced by the SCA procedure; k' – upper bound for nearest neighbours;
Output: s'_i – synthetic instance;

Begin
Set z = random(2); // a randomly selected number from the set {0, 1, 2};
Set *flag* = false;
Switch (z)
  Case 0:
    Set L_1= list of instances included in D'_1;
    Set L_2= list of instances included in D'_2;
    Replace number of instances within s_i representing the centres of D'_1, D'_2 by others numbers selected from L_1 and L_2 that are located closer in dimension space to the reference instances included in s_j;
    Set *flag* = true;
    Goto case 1;
  Case 1:
    Set L_3= list of instances included in $D_{minority}$;
    If *flag* = true **then**
      Update the list of instances within s_i representing nearest minority neighbours using the number of instance in L_3;
    Else
      Set t = random(1); // a randomly selected number from set {0,1}
      Set l = number of instances selected to represent nearest neighbours;
      If t = 1 **and** l > 2 **then**
        Randomly remove from s_i one instance representing **a** nearest neighbour;
      End if
      If t = 0 **and** l < k' **then**
        Add a new instance number to s_i to represent an additional nearest neighbour in relation to the centres of D'_1, D'_2;
      End if
    End if
    Goto case 2;
  Case 2:
    Randomly generate a new synthetic instance x_a located between the instances from s_i that represent the nearest neighbours, and update s_i;
End Switch
$s'_i \leftarrow s_i$;
Return s'_i
End

4 Computational Experiment

This section presents the results of a computational experiment and a discussion. The aim of the experiment was to validate the proposed approach, which is referred to in the following as FOA (Firefly-based Over-sampling Algorithm). The proposed method was compared with the SMOTE algorithm [6], a borderline version of SMOTE [7] and a traditional approach to learning from data (i.e. without eliminating the imbalanced data problem). We decided to use the SMOTE algorithm because it is a basic approach for producing synthetic instances very often used as a reference approach. In all cases, the C4.5 algorithm was applied to train the classifier. C4.5 was also used to evaluate the solutions produced by FOA and to train the final classifier based on the datasets produced by FOA, SMOTE and Borderline SMOTE. All of the algorithms were implemented in Java, and some packages were imported from the WEKA environment.

Table 1 shows the parameter settings used in the computational experiment. The values of the parameters were set arbitrarily using a trial-and-error process.

Table 1. Parameter settings

Parameter	
k' – maximal number of nearest neighbours for FOA	10
Number of neighbours for SMOTE	5
Number of neighbours for borderline SMOTE	5
γ – absorption coefficient	0.1
β_0 – maximum attractiveness	0.5
α – factor determining the random movement	0.1
Population size	40
Number of iterations for FA	500
Number of iterations for improvement	100

The computational experiments were carried out on datasets from the KEEL repository [22], and these are summarised in Table 2. The last column of the table (entitled IR) shows the ratio of the number of instances in the majority class to the number of instances in the minority class.

Table 2. Summary of datasets used in the experiment

Dataset	Number of instances	Number of attributes	Number of classes	IR
abalone19	4174	8	2	129.44
shuttle-c0-vs-c4	1829	9	2	13.87
vowel0	988	13	2	9.98
yeast5	1484	8	2	32.73
glass2	214	9	2	11.59
ecoli-0-1-4-6_vs_5	280	6	2	13
glass0	214	9	2	2.06
yeast2	514	8	2	9.08
vehicle2	846	18	2	2.88

We used a 10-cross-validation scheme in the experiment. The validation process was repeated 30 times for each benchmarking problem, and the resulting values were averaged over all runs. The overall results are presented in Table 3 and Table 4. The performance of each classifier trained on the updated dataset (i.e. including synthetic instances) is shown in terms of the classification accuracy (ACC) and the area under the ROC curve (AUC).

The results in Table 3 and Table 4 show that the FAO approach can be considered a useful and competitive tool for improving the quality of data and eliminating the problem of imbalanced data. The classification accuracy obtained for C4.5 using the dataset produced by FAO was better than for SMOTE and Borderline SMOTE in most cases. The results of FAO also overfit the results obtained by C4.5 using an original dataset. The good performance of FAO can be seen from the ACC and AUC results.

Table 3. Results of the computational experiment: ACC

Dataset	ACC (in %)			
	FAO + C4.5	SMOTE + C4.5	Borderline SMOTE + C4.5	C4.5
abalone19	**93.45**	91.3*	92.63*	82.02
shuttle-c0-vs-c4	97.24	95.47	**98.01**	97.17
vowel0	94.82	93.45	**95.87**	94.94
yeast5	**88.56**	87.81	88.92	87.5
glass2	84.61	83.15*	**91.57***	60.08
ecoli-0-1-4-6_vs_5	82.03	91.26*	**92.12***	81.36
glass0	**79.47**	78.5	79.47	78.13
yeast2	**80.56**	77.32	78.91	62.82
vehicle2	**95.82**	95.02	95.48	94.85

Source: *[16]

Table 4 also shows the average number of nearest minority neighbours used to produce the synthetic instances (the column #NN). Of course, it is difficult to formulate an answer regarding the optimal number of nearest minority neighbours, but we can observe that the number was different for each dataset. We can therefore assume that this value was set by FAO in the best possible way. We can also draw the conclusion that the number of nearest minority neighbours influences the performance in terms of classification accuracy, meaning that it influences the quality of the synthetic instances in the over-sampling mechanism.

Although the results presented here generally seem to be very promising, they were obtained using only one classification algorithm, and to draw more general conclusions. validation using other learning algorithms will be required. The performance of our algorithm may also be influenced by its operating parameters, and it should therefore be validated with the aim of establishing more effective values. The algorithm also needs to be optimised with regard to the time complexity.

Table 4. Results of the computational experiment: AUC

Dataset	AUC				#NN
	FAO + C4.5	SMOTE + C4.5	Borderline SMOTE + C4.5	C4.5	
abalone19	0.762	0.756*	0.7485*	0.713	4
shuttle-c0-vs-c4	0.951	0.941	0.962	0.958	6
vowel0	0.962	0.952	0.957	0.952	10
yeast5	0.843	0.852	0.8572	0.824	6
glass2	0.697	0.687*	0.7019*	0.652	5
ecoli-0-1-4-6_vs_5	0.875	0.912*	0.8437*	0.804	3
glass0	0.758	0.721	0.754	0.705	8
yeast2	0.894	0.876	0.882	0.742	10
vehicle2	0.943	0.936*	0.9434*	0.922	6

Source: *[16]

5   Conclusions

The main contribution of this paper is to propose a firefly-based over-sampling algorithm to work with imbalanced data. Our algorithm is based on an evolutionary search of the synthetic instances, which are added to the dataset to eliminate the problem of imbalance between classes. The process of searching for synthetic instances is carried out by simulating cooperation between fireflies. The results of this firefly-based approach to searching indicate that it is possible to find an appropriate number of nearest minority neighbours to produce synthetic instances and thus reduce the negative influence of imbalanced data in the original dataset.

This study extends a body of research work in which the FA has been applied. In this paper, we have applied the FA to solve a discrete optimisation problem. The results of the computational experiment show that the proposed FA is a competitive alternative to the more well-known SMOTE and Borderline SMOTE algorithms.

In future research, we will aim to investigate the influence of different parameters on the quality of the results. We will also use different learning algorithms and form more general conclusions with respect to the elimination of imbalanced data and learning from imbalanced data using an over-sampling approach. A deeper analysis of the results will be also carried out using statistical tools.

References

1. Mitchell, T.: Machine Learning. McGraw-Hill, New York (1997)
2. Han, J., Kamber, M.: Data Mining. Concepts and Techniques. Academic Press, San Diego (2001)

3. Kuncheva, L.I., Arnaiz-González, Á., Díez-Pastor, J.-F., Gunn, I.A.D.: Instance selection improves geometric mean accuracy: a study on imbalanced data classification. Progr. Artif. Intell. **8**(2), 215–228 (2019). https://doi.org/10.1007/s13748-019-00172-4

4. Tsai, C.-F., Lin, W.-C., Hu, Y.-H., Ya, G.-T.: Under-sampling class imbalanced datasets by combining clustering analysis and instance selection. Inf. Sci. **477**, 47–54 (2019). https://doi.org/10.1016/j.ins.2018.10.029

5. Lin, W.-C., Tsai, C.-F., Ya-Han, H., Jhang, J.-S.: Clustering-based undersampling in class-imbalanced data. Inf. Sci. **409–410**, 17–26 (2017). https://doi.org/10.1016/j.ins.2017.05.008

6. Chawla, N.V., Bowyer, K.W., Hall, L.O., Kegelmeyer, W.P.: SMOTE: synthetic minority over-sampling technique. J. Artif. Intell. Res.. **16**(16), 321–357 (2002)

7. Han, H., Wang, W.-Y., Mao, B.-H.: Borderline-SMOTE: a new over-sampling method in imbalanced data sets learning. Adv. Intell. Comput. **17**(12), 878–887 (2005)

8. Cieslak, D.A., Chawla, N.V., Striegel, A.: Combating imbalance in network intrusion datasets. In: Proceedings of the 2006 IEEE International Conference on Granular Computing, pp. 732–737. IEEE (2006)

9. Ma, L., Fan, S.: Cure-smote algorithm and hybrid algorithm for feature selection and parameter optimization based on random forests. BMC Bioinformatics **18**(1), 169 (2017)

10. Bunkhumpornpat, C., Sinapiromsaran, K., Lursinsap, C.: Safe-Level-SMOTE: safe-level-synthetic minority over-sampling technique for handling the class imbalanced problem. In: Theeramunkong, T., Kijsirikul, B., Cercone, N., Ho, T.-B. (eds.) PAKDD 2009. LNCS (LNAI), vol. 5476, pp. 475–482. Springer, Heidelberg (2009). https://doi.org/10.1007/978-3-642-01307-2_43

11. Czarnowski, I., Jędrzejowicz, P.: An approach to imbalanced data classification based on instance selection and over-sampling. In: Nguyen, N.T., Chbeir, R., Exposito, E., Aniorté, P., Trawiński, B. (eds.) ICCCI 2019. LNCS (LNAI), vol. 11683, pp. 601–610. Springer, Cham (2019). https://doi.org/10.1007/978-3-030-28377-3_50

12. Czarnowski, I.: Learning from imbalanced data streams based on over-sampling and instance selection. In: Paszynski, M., Kranzlmüller, D., Krzhizhanovskaya, V.V., Dongarra, J.J., Sloot, P.M.A. (eds.) ICCS 2021. LNCS, vol. 12744, pp. 378–391. Springer, Cham (2021). https://doi.org/10.1007/978-3-030-77967-2_32

13. Yang, X-S.: Nature-inspired Metaheuristic Algorithms, Second edition. Luniver Press (2010)

14. Czarnowski, I., Jędrzejowicz, P.: A new cluster-based instance selection algorithm. In: O'Shea, J., Nguyen, N.T., Crockett, K., Howlett, R.J., Jain, L.C. (eds.) KES-AMSTA 2011. LNCS (LNAI), vol. 6682, pp. 436–445. Springer, Heidelberg (2011). https://doi.org/10.1007/978-3-642-22000-5_45

15. Vishwa, V., Zhang, W., Naeim, A., Ramezani, R.: GenSample: a genetic algorithm for oversampling in imbalanced datasets. arXiv preprint arXiv:1910.10806 (2019)

16. Zhang, Y., Zuo, T., Fang, L., Li, J., Xing, Z.: An improved MAHAKIL oversampling method for imbalanced dataset classification. IEEE Access **9**, 16030–16040 (2021). https://doi.org/10.1109/ACCESS.2020.3047741

17. Saladi, P.S.M., Dash, T.: Genetic algorithm-based oversampling technique to learn from imbalanced data. In: Bansal, J.C., Das, K.N., Nagar, A., Deep, K., Ojha, A.K. (eds.) Soft Computing for Problem Solving. AISC, vol. 816, pp. 387–397. Springer, Singapore (2019). https://doi.org/10.1007/978-981-13-1592-3_30

18. Han, Z., Qiao, X., Zhan, S.: ROGA: random over-sampling based on genetic algorithm. In: Proceedings of the International Conference on Learning Representations (CLR 2021), 25–29 April (2021)

19. Qiong, G., Xian-Ming, W., Zhao, W., Bing, N., Chun-Sheng, X.: An improved SMOTE algorithm based on genetic algorithm for imbalanced data classification. Digital Inf. Manage. **142**, 92–103 (2016)

20. Jiang, K., Lu, J., Xia, K.: A novel algorithm for imbalance data classification based on genetic algorithm improved SMOTE. Arab. J. Sci. Eng. **41**(8), 3255–3266 (2016). https://doi.org/10.1007/s13369-016-2179-2

21. Kaya, E., Korkmaz, S., Sahman, M.-A., Cinar, A.-C.: DEBOHID: a differential evolution based oversampling approach for highly imbalanced datasets. Expert Syst. Appl. **169**, 114482 (2021). https://doi.org/10.1016/j.eswa.2020.114482

22. Alcalá-Fdez, J., et al.: KEEL data-mining software tool: data set repository integration of algorithms and experimental analysis framework. J. Multiple-Valued Logic Soft Comput. **17**(2–3), 255–287 (2011) (last accessed to the repository 2021/05/14)

Adaptive Goal Function of Ant Colony Optimization in Fake News Detection

Barbara Probierz$^{(\boxtimes)}$ ⓘ, Jan Kozak ⓘ, Piotr Stefański,
and Przemysław Juszczuk ⓘ

Department of Machine Learning, University of Economics in Katowice, 1 Maja,
40-287 Katowice, Poland
{barbara.probierz,jan.kozak,piotr.stefanski,
przemyslaw.juszczuk}@ue.katowice.pl

Abstract. Currently, there is a very rapid growth of information published on the Internet, both on social media and news sites. However, a serious problem is a disinformation in the form of fake news. Due to the rapid spread of information on the Internet, it is very important to be able to quickly identify true and fake news. The solution to this problem can be an initial analysis of news by its title and quick selection of true or fake news. Additionally, the possibility of balancing precision and recall as the quality of classification measures could allow for better news selection. In this paper, we propose the use of the adaptive goal function of ant colony optimization algorithms in fake news detection. The goal of this solution is to increase recall or precision of the selected class – in this case fake or true news. We use natural language processing (NLP) to describe the title of the news. In addition, a constrained term matrix is used. The choice of titles alone and the restriction of the words analyzed are related to speeding up the initial classification. Eventually, we present an analysis of a real dataset and classification results (detailing recall and precision) of news using the adaptive goal function of the ACDT algorithm.

Keywords: Fake news · Ant colony optimization · ACDT algorithm · Natural language processing

1 Introduction

Information technology now accompanies us in every area of life - from learning and work to entertainment and leisure. The speed at which information spreads and the ability to reach a huge audience means that fake news is primarily found on social media or news sites. There are a lot of fake news, fake likes, impressions, and duplicate accounts, which is admitted by large social networks such as Facebook and Twitter. Most of the information appearing on social media is questionable and should be detected as soon as possible to avoid negative impacts on the public. For this reason, many companies, in collaboration with

© Springer Nature Switzerland AG 2021
N. T. Nguyen et al. (Eds.): ICCCI 2021, LNAI 12876, pp. 387–400, 2021.
https://doi.org/10.1007/978-3-030-88081-1_29

researchers, conduct studies related to evaluating the veracity of the information provided and classifying it as true or fake news.

The purpose of this paper is to improve the selected measure (recall/precision) in classifying all news into true or fake news at the initial stage of analysis. Based on the title alone, we want to improve the classification of true or fake news – measured by recall and precision, which allow us to assess with what confidence we can assume that an object from a given class will be correctly classified into one selected class. However, the accuracy of classification only determines how many objects have been correctly classified into all classes. Additionally, we propose an analysis with a limited number of words resulting from natural language processing (NLP). Our hypothesis is that the use of algorithms that allow changing the objective function in the initial analysis of true and fake news allows for better classification than classical algorithms.

To achieve the goal and verify the hypothesis, we propose three approaches for preparing learning sets derived from word weighting measures used in natural language processing (NLP). In each case, we constrain the term matrix based on the news title to the 20 most frequent words. On the other hand, the learning is performed by the ACDT algorithm with an adaptive goal function. Depending on the target set, a classifier focused on either recall or precision for fake or true news is built.

The remainder of this paper is organized as follows. Section 1 comprises an introduction to the subject of this article. Section 2 provides an overview of related works on the definition and detection of fake news and we present natural language processing methods (NLP). Section 3 describes classification methods and ensemble methods. Section 4 we present ant colony optimization and adaptive goal function of ACDT algorithm. In Sect. 5, we explain our methodology for fake news detection and we present and discuss experimental results. Finally, in Sect. 6 we conclude with general remarks on this work, and a few directions for future research are pointed out.

2   Fake News Detection and Natural Language Processing

Fake news is false information usually created to mislead the reader. The subjects related to fake news are related to many different areas of life but are primarily political, financial, or ideological [12]. The main purpose of spreading fake news is to gain publicity or to harm opponents [20].

Due to the vast subject matter based on many different scientific fields, there are three main types of fake news [29]. The first type of fake news is information that is completely false, where no part of it is true. The second group consists of news in which true information can be found, but it is inaccurately described or taken out of context, by their truthfulness evaluation value decreases significantly. The last type of fake news is content that is satirical in nature, being a parody or joke [13]. For this reason, fake news often goes by different names and can be defined differently. Sometimes the word "disinformation" is used interchangeably instead of the name "fake news", and some experts use terms i.e. "false news" or "junk news" [14].

Research on fake news detection is a relatively new field. The sizes of fake news datasets are growing rapidly, so in order to get better fake news detection results with less computation time and less complexity, the size of the data needs to be reduced [36]. One of the best techniques to reduce the data size is to use the feature selection method. The purpose of this technique is to select a subset of features from the original set to improve classification performance.

Through the work V. Perez-Rosas et al. [25] a mechanism has been developed to automatically identify fake news in online information. The classification model is based on a combination of lexical, syntactic, and semantic information, as well as features representing text readability properties. Another way to quickly disseminate fake news placement of catchy headlines so-called clickbait [26]. Research related to satirical data detection has also been conducted. In the study [30], the content analysis of the information that was described by one of five features i.e. absurdity, humor, grammar, negative affect, and punctuation was done. Moreover, in order to find the linguistic features of unbelievable content, the language of real news was compared with the language of satire [27].

Natural Language Processing
Natural language processing (NLP) methods aim to enable created computer systems to understand text or speech. The fundamentals of natural language processing include not only exact science-related fields but also linguistics or psychology. For this reason, teams working on NLP-based systems should have extensive competence and knowledge [9].

Properly preprocessing the data, which will be used for analysis is usually the longest process compared to the work involved in the machine learning model [15]. Similarly, in our work, techniques related to natural language processing (NLP) have been applied to normalize the text under analysis.

First, the process of tokenization [35] was carried out by dividing the text into individual terms for identifying and analyzing features used in natural language modeling and processing [34]. Then, words not influencing the information content were filtered out, which constitute the so-called Stop Word list [16].

The next data processing step associated with NLP methods was to perform term normalization. For this purpose, two normalization methods were used. The first is lemmatization, which is the reduction of a word to its basic form [33], while the second method is stemming, which is used to extract the subject and ending from words and then replace similar words with one of the same in basic form [3].

When performing content analysis, a vector space model is used to represent documents as vectors of terms. In such a model, each term corresponds to a specific component of the vector. The values of the vector coordinates can be treated as term weights. The basic representation in the described model is a binary representation, where each value is taken from the set $\{0,1\}$, which determines whether a term occurs in the document or not [4]. As other representations, measures of word relevance evaluation are used, namely Term Frequency (TF) and Term Frequency-Inverted Document Frequency (TF-IDF).

Term Frequency (TF) counts the number of words appearing in documents to determine the degree of similarity between documents [21]. Term Frequency is calculated using the formula:

$$tf_{i,j} = \frac{n_{i,j}}{\sum_k n_{k,j}}, \tag{1}$$

where $n_{i,j}$ is the raw count of a term t_i in the document d_j and the denominator is the sum of the raw count of all $n_{k,j}$ terms in the document d_j.

The Inverse Document Frequency (IDF) in the text is the ratio of the number of processed documents n_d to the number of documents containing at least one occurrence of the term $\{d : t_i \in d\}$ and is expressed by the formula:

$$idf_i = \log \frac{n_d}{\{d:t_i \in d\}}, \tag{2}$$

The TF-IDF measure, on the other hand, determines the frequency of term occurrences along with an appropriate balance between the local term's importance and its importance in the context of the full document collection [21] and is computed as the product of the term frequency $tf_{i,j}$ with the inverse frequency in the text idf_i.

3 Classification Methods

Important tools in machine learning and data mining are classification methods. A popular classification method used to analyze continuous data is the Support Vector Machine (SVM) algorithm, which was first presented by Vladimir Vapnik in his work [11]. It relies on the identification of patterns to indicate to which of two classes the input dataset should be assigned.

Another method of data classification is decision tree, and one of the popular decision tree learning algorithms is Classification and Regression Trees (CART). This algorithm was first proposed by Breiman et al. in 1984 [7]. The partitioning of the data at each node is done based on the partitioning criterion, which for the CART algorithm the two partitioning criteria are: Ginie and Twoing. The Twoing criterion is included in the heuristic function of the ACDT [18] algorithm described in Sect. 4.

The classification process can also be performed using ensemble methods (EM), which are individual classifiers combined together. The most popular ensemble methods include AdaBoost, bagging, and random forest algorithms.

The boosting approach was first proposed by Schapire in 1990 [31]. It involves forming a group of classifiers to obtain a model with better characteristics. This approach involves creating a good learning set based on weak learning subsets.

The bagging approach was first developed by Breiman in 1996 [6]. It is a method based on bootstrap aggregation to improve classification and regression models in terms of stability and accuracy by lowering the variance. The final decision is made by a majority vote of individual classifiers.

Another ensemble method is random forest developed by Breiman [8] as an improvement of the bagging. It is a group of classifiers consisting of individual decision trees. Unlike standard tree construction methods, in random forests, during test selection for each node (separately), there is a random draw of attributes that will be taken into account when making the split. Therefore, each split is made on the basis of a different set of attributes.

4   Adaptive Goal Function of ACDT Algorithm

Ant colony optimization (ACO) is an approach used to solve different optimization problems. The main idea of the ACO is based on the communication process between ants living in the ant colonies. The concept of the ACO was described by Marco Dorigo [10] by making an attempt to develop an artificial ant system. Such an approach was further used to find the shortest path between two nodes in the graph.

ACO algorithm is a population-based approach, which means, that in successive iterations, agents-ants are striving to find good quality solutions. In every iteration, agent-ants are directed by the pheromone trail left by agent-ants from preceding iterations. Thanks to such mechanism, search space fragments including discovered earlier good quality solutions explored to find improved solutions.

Machine learning is one of the fields in which the ACO algorithm is present [22]. Often experiments related to ACO are focused on the classification problem, while the presented results are compared with other canonical classification methods [32], which examples are described in Sect. 3. ACO algorithm is mostly used to building the decision trees instead of generating the set of rules [5]. This algorithm is often extended (for example Ant-Miner [23,24]).

The ant colony decision trees algorithm (ACDT) is based on using ant colony optimization in the process of building the decision trees. The elements of the algorithm include the selection of division for every node on the basis of two criteria. The first one is the maximal value connected with the Twoing criterion, while the second one is the additional information included in the pheromone trail [18]. Eventually, derived decision trees are evaluated and successive iterations of the algorithm are conducted.

The most common factors impacting the evaluation of the quality of decision trees are – accuracy of the classification and the size of the decision tree. According to the rule of minimal description, the size of the decision tree should be minimized, while the accuracy of the classification – maximized. The quality of the decision tree in further consideration of the article will be understood according to the following equation:

$$Q(T) = \phi \cdot w(T) + \psi \cdot a(T, S), \tag{3}$$

where $w(T)$ is the size of the decision tree T; $a(T, S)$, is the accuracy of the classification of objects in the test set S by the decision tree T; while ϕ and ψ, are constant values specyfing the relative importance of values $w(T)$ and $a(T, S)$. The parameters ϕ and ψ were established in accordance with the results obtained in [19].

B. Probierz et al.

4.1 Quality of Classification

Evaluating the quality of classification is one of the crucial problems of machine learning. It has an important meaning in terms of the quality of the classifier. Below we present binary classification measures (for sets with two decision classes), used to derive the confusion matrix (Table 1). With the help of the matrix, it is possible to better evaluate the quality of classification. This can be done by using the information about the actual decision class of the object as well as the class, to which this object was assigned during the classification process [28]. Such information can be used to estimate accuracy, recall, and precision.

Table 1. Confusion matrix

	Predicted positive	Predicted negative
Positive examples (P)	True positive (TP)	False negative (FN)
Negative examples (N)	False positive (FP)	True negative (TN)

It should be mentioned, that the accuracy of the classification is the measure used only to estimate, what is the number of objects properly classified. While in the case of precision it is possible to evaluate the trust level related to the fact, that the object from a given decision class will be properly classified. It is especially important in the case, where we focus on the proper classification of objects belonging to a single decision class.

Accuracy rate (Eq. (4)) is one of the most popular measures of quality of classification. However, it should be noted, that it is not sufficient to measure in the case of the datasets with large differences in the cardinality of objects in decision classes (this fact was pointed out, for example, in [17].

$$ev_{acc}(T, S) = \frac{(TP + TN)}{(TP + TN + FP + FN)}. \tag{4}$$

Recall (Eq. (5)), is the measure evaluation of the classifier on the basis of objects wrongly classified from the N class to the P class. In this case, it is better to omit some objects from class P, than wrongly assign them into the set of objects in class N.

$$ev_{rec}(T, S) = \frac{TP}{(TP + FN)}. \tag{5}$$

Precision (Eq. (6)) is measured on the basis of a number of correctly classified objects to class P (relative to all objects actually belonging to class P). It can be said, that in the case of precision it is better to wrongly assign an object from class N to class P, than wrongly assign the object from class P.

$$ev_{prec}(T, S) = \frac{TP}{(TP + FP)}. \tag{6}$$

4.2   Goal Function

The goal-oriented ACDT approach is based on changing the goal function on the basis of modification of the decision tree evaluation function (Eq. (3)). By using such an approach, solutions improving the selected measure will be rewarded during the algorithm run. Thus Eq. (3) was modified to Eq. (7).

$$Q(T) = \phi \cdot w(T) + \psi \cdot ev(T, S), \tag{7}$$

where $ev(T, S)$ means the selected method of decision tree T evaluation built on the basis of dataset S. Value $ev(T, S)$ is calculated depending on the selected measure in following way: Eq. (4), (5) or (6).

5   Computational Experiments

The goal of experiments was to evaluate if the adaptive ACDT algorithm can effectively allow initial selection improvement of fake or true news to a better degree than in the case of classical algorithms. The conducted research is based on the 5 classical algorithms: CART (decision tree), Support Vector Machines (SVM), random forest, AdaBoost and bagging. These are methods often used in the case of the NLP. While ACDT algorithm was selected for 5 different goal functions: accuracy (classical version), recall for true news, precision for true news, recall for fake news, and precision for fake news. As a dataset, we selected the real-world data "ISOT Fake News Dataset" shared by the University of Victoria, Canada [1,2].

5.1   Experiment Design

The proposed solution is based on the initial recognition of fake or true news only on the basis of the limited-term matrix built on the basis of news titles. Thus the real-world data [1,2] was preprocessed. From the whole dataset; 21417 real news cases and 23481 fake news cases described by the attributes: title, text, subject, and date; the title attribute was the only one selected.

We analyzed three different approaches for building the term matrix on the basis of word weightnewsing measures: TF-IDF, TF, and binary. However, in this case, we adjusted some limitations. The developed matrix includes only 20 most frequently occurring words. Text tokenization is performed, including the removal of 326 stop words, such as 'well', 'whereas', 'yet', 'every', 'as', 'of', 'is' etc.

One should know, that in such a case – in which the term matrix is limited to 20 most frequently occurring words – titles consisting of less popular words could occur. In such a situation, there is no possibility of performing the task. Thus such eventual examples were omitted on the stage of initial preprocessing.

The developed learning set consists of 12352 real news cases and 18784 fake news cases described by 20 attributes. In the case of TF-IDF, there are real values; TF are the integer values; while binary is only two values (true – word is present, false – word is absent).

In case of all experiments, a classical approach train and test for 75% in the train test and 25% cases in the test set was used. In every experiment, we used exactly the same data division.

5.2 Results of Experiments

Conducted experiments included two aspects:

- limiting the number of terms to improve the speed of classification – in this issue, three selection methods as word weightnewsing measures to build a decision table were analyzed;
- use of the goal-oriented ACDT algorithm, to fit the classification into the selected measure of the quality of classification.

All results are presented in Table 2 (selection method: inverse term frequency (TF-IDF)), Table 3 (selection method: namely term frequency (TF)) and Table 4 (selection method: binary), where values for every analyzed measure of the quality of classification for every tested algorithm are given. The best values are boldface, while by the underlined we indicate the values slightly worse (by 0.25%).

Word Weightnewsing Measures
In the first phase, the impact of the selected method of learning set deriving (with limitation to 20 most popular words) on general classification results should be evaluated. Assuming the accuracy rate, differences between the analyzed algorithms are not large – in the case of every method, it is less than 1.5% between the algorithm with the best and the worst value of accuracy. However, it can be observed, that data derived on the basis of TF (Table 3) and binary (Table 4) shows up better classification than TF-IDF (Table 2). In case of TF-IDF, the best of algorithms (random forest) achieved an accuracy equal to 78.16%, while in case of TF and binary the worst results are respectively 78.21% and 78.02%. The best results are 79.58% (SVM) and 79.35% (ACDT with accuracy as a goal). Moreover, the observed algorithm runtime is visibly improved. The running times of the ACDT algorithm are as follows: Binary about 5 s, TF about 5.5 s, and TF-IDF about 76 s per execution. There are slight differences in the run times, which depend on which quality score one is aiming for. It follows, that the decision tables built for TF-IDF have attributes with real number values. Whle in case of the TF these values are only integer values (in case of binary – only 0 or 1 values). On this basis, it seems more reasonable in further investigations focusing on the decision tables presented with the use of selection methods: TF and binary.

Measures of Quality of Classification

Adaptation of the algorithm to selected measures of quality of classification allows for better adjustment of the algorithm to solving the presented problem. In case, where the main goal will be the detection of the highest number of fake news among all fake news available, thus the crucial measure will be the recall for the FN class (fake news). In this case, some of the true news will be wrongly classified as false. However, such a situation won't have a negative impact on the recall FN. As it can be observed, the aim to recall FN at the same time allows improving the precision for TN (true news), because the smaller number of fake news is wrongly classified as true news. It can be assumed, that the recall FN also improves the precision TN (and opposite), while the recall TN improves the precision FN (and opposite). This dependency is confirmed by the numerical experiments.

In every analyzed approach (TF-IDF, TF, and binary) the improvement of the quality of measure, which was selected as a goal of the adaptive ACDT algorithm was observed. Definite improvement is observed in the case of recall TN and precision FN, which leads to a few percent better results than in the case of classical algorithms. A smaller improvement is observed in the case of recall FN and precision TN. This means, that the improvement of precision of fake news (while at the same time the detection of actual true news – recall TN) is possible by using the goal-oriented ACDT algorithms.

What is more important, the improvement of these measures does not affect significantly on decreasing the accuracy rate. The highest improvement of recall FN can be observed in the case of using the table generated with the binary approach (approach including only the binary values of attributes. See Table 4). In this case, using the goal-oriented ACDT with the recall function TN or precision FN, recall TN measure is improved over 6% (in comparison to the classical algorithms) and 4% (in comparison to classical ACDT accuracy oriented approach). At the same time, it leads to improving the precision FN over 4% (in comparison to classical algorithms) and 3% (in comparison to the classical ACDT approach). Moreover, it leads to a decrease in the accuracy of classification by the value around 0.4–1%. These dependencies are additionally presented in Fig. 1. As it can be seen, there is a significant improvement in the case of recall TN and precision FN. However, it should be noted, that it also leads to decreasing the results for the recall FN and precision TN – which is the opposite situation.

Improvement of recall TN and recall TF is observed also in the case of setting these measures as a goal in the adaptive ACDT algorithm. In this case, the improvement often does not exceed 1%. However, it should be noted, that in contrast to the situation described earlier, in this case, the accuracy mostly is not decreased. In the case of the decision tables derived with the use of the TF-IDF (Table 2) and TF (Table 3) similar dependencies were also noted, however, the obtained differences were slightly smaller.

Table 2. Results of performed experiments for word weighting measures: TF-IDF (the best results in boldface).

	Accuracy rate	Recall true news	Precison true news	Recall false news	Precison false news
ACDT goal: accuracy	0.7801	0.8909	0.6651	0.7080	0.9088
ACDT goal: recall FN	0.7790	0.8804	0.6662	0.7129	0.9016
ACDT goal: precision FN	0.7723	0.9360	0.6457	0.6657	0.9411
ACDT goal: recall TN	0.7723	**0.9373**	0.6455	0.6650	**0.9421**
ACDT goal: precision TN	0.7790	0.8776	**0.6670**	**0.7149**	0.8997
CART	0.7812	0.8972	0.6649	0.7057	0.9134
SVM	0.7764	0.8975	0.6588	0.6975	0.9127
Random forest	**0.7816**	0.8922	0.6666	0.7096	0.9100
AdaBoost	0.7790	0.8959	0.6624	0.7029	0.9121
Bagging	0.7807	0.8879	0.6665	0.7108	0.9069

Table 3. Results of performed experiments for word weighting measures: TF (the best results in boldface).

	Accuracy rate	Recall true news	Precison true news	Recall false news	Precison false news
ACDT goal: accuracy	0.7934	0.9029	0.6669	0.7272	0.9253
ACDT goal: recall FN	0.7934	0.8900	0.6701	**0.7349**	0.9170
ACDT goal: precision FN	0.7821	**0.9332**	0.6461	0.6907	**0.9447**
ACDT goal: recall TN	0.7870	0.9290	0.6528	0.7011	0.9422
ACDT goal: precision TN	0.7936	0.8912	0.6700	0.7345	0.9177
CART	0.7914	0.8967	0.6657	0.7276	0.9209
SVM	**0.7958**	0.8998	**0.6708**	0.7328	0.9236
Random forest	0.7914	0.8916	0.6670	0.7307	0.9176
AdaBoost	0.7854	0.9152	0.6538	0.7069	0.9324
Bagging	0.7907	0.8919	0.6661	0.7295	0.9177

Table 4. Results of performed experiments for word weighting measures: binary (the best results in boldface).

	Accuracy rate	Recall true news	Precison true news	Recall false news	Precison false news
ACDT goal: accuracy	**0.7935**	0.9045	0.6746	0.7230	0.9226
ACDT goal: recall FN	0.7897	0.8651	**0.6802**	**0.7417**	0.8965
ACDT goal: precision FN	0.7802	**0.9458**	0.6490	0.6751	**0.9515**
ACDT goal: recall TN	0.7812	<u>0.9449</u>	0.6502	0.6772	<u>0.9509</u>
ACDT goal: precision TN	0.7907	0.8717	<u>0.6799</u>	<u>0.7393</u>	0.9007
CART	0.7898	0.8853	0.6749	0.7292	0.9092
SVM	<u>0.7930</u>	0.8826	<u>0.6798</u>	0.7360	0.9080
Random forest	0.7904	0.8833	0.6762	0.7314	0.9080
AdaBoost	0.7840	0.8853	0.6673	0.7196	0.9081
Bagging	0.7904	0.8819	0.6765	0.7322	0.9071

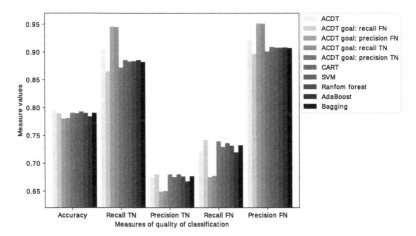

Fig. 1. Chart presenting the values of analyzed measures depending on the selected algorithm – example for word weighting: binary.

6 Conclusions

The goal in this paper was to develop a new model for initial news analysis and rapid discovery of fake news based on the news title alone without having to analyze the entire article content. Additionally, the ability to balance precision and recall as the quality of classification measures was created, which allowed for better news selection. NLP techniques were used to analyze the text and then, the Adaptive goal function of ant colony optimization algorithms was used to discover fake news.

The hypothesis of this paper indicated that using the goal-oriented ACDT algorithm and a constrained term matrix allows for better classification than classical algorithms. The conducted experiments confirmed that it is possible to perform a preliminary analysis of fake and true news based on a restricted term matrix. In this case, the use of only 20 most popular words allowed to obtain 80% classification accuracy (depending on the chosen method of word enumeration and the algorithm used). Additionally, using goal-oriented ACDT allows for a definite improvement in recall true news and precision fake news. There is also the possibility of minor improvements in recall false news and precision true news.

The best results both in terms of running time of the proposed algorithms and classification quality (measured by popular metrics) are obtained for decision tables created with the binary approach, i.e., containing only information about whether a given word is in the news title.

At the same time, the correlations between the pursuit of recall of one class and the precision of the other class were experimentally confirmed, so in the future, the target can be truncated to recall TN/precision FN and recall FN/precision TN. The effect of the number of words in the decision table on the results obtained and classification coverage should also be carefully studied. After a thorough analysis, it is worthwhile in the future to develop a two-stage verification – first based on a limited number of words from the news title, then based on the entire content, but only for news that could not be previously classified. The approach presented here can be used to flag fake news after the titles news, that appear on social media or websites.

References

1. https://www.uvic.ca/engineering/ece/isot/datasets/index.php
2. Ahmed, H., Traore, I., Saad, S.: Detecting opinion spams and fake news using text classification. Secur. Priv. **1**(1), e9 (2018)
3. Amirhosseini, M.H., Kazemian, H.: Automating the process of identifying the preferred representational system in neuro linguistic programming using natural language processing. Cogn. Process. **20**(2), 175–193 (2019)
4. Bedekar, P.P., Bhide, S.R.: Optimum coordination of directional overcurrent relays using the hybrid ga-nlp approach. IEEE Trans. Power Delivery **26**(1), 109–119 (2010)
5. Boryczka, U., Kozak, J.: Ant colony decision trees – a new method for constructing decision trees based on ant colony optimization. In: Pan, J.-S., Chen, S.-M., Nguyen, N.T. (eds.) ICCCI 2010. LNCS (LNAI), vol. 6421, pp. 373–382. Springer, Heidelberg (2010). https://doi.org/10.1007/978-3-642-16693-8_39
6. Breiman, L.: Bagging predictors. Mach. Learn. **24**(2), 123–140 (1996)
7. Breiman, L., Friedman, J.H., Olshen, R.A., Stone, C.J.: Classification and Regression Trees. Chapman & Hall, New York (1984)
8. Breiman, L.: Random forests. Mach. Learn. **45**, 5–32 (2001)

9. Chowdhary, K.: Fundamentals of Artificial Intelligence. Springer, New Delhi (2020). https://doi.org/10.1007/978-81-322-3972-7
10. Colorni, A., Dorigo, M., Maniezzo, V., et al.: Distributed optimization by ant colonies. In: Proceedings of the First European Conference on Artificial life, vol. 142, pp. 134–142. Paris, France (1991)
11. Cortes, C., Vapnik, V.: Support-vector networks. Mach. Learn. **20**, 273–297 (1995). https://doi.org/10.1007/BF00994018
12. Gelfert, A.: Fake news: a definition. Informal Logic **38**(1), 84–117 (2018)
13. Golbeck, J., et al.: Fake news vs satire: a dataset and analysis. In: Proceedings of the 10th ACM Conference on Web Science, pp. 17–21 (2018)
14. Howard, P.N., Bolsover, G., Kollanyi, B., Bradshaw, S., Neudert, L.M.: Junk news and bots during the us election: What were michigan voters sharing over twitter. CompProp, OII, Data Memo (2017)
15. Kannan, S., Gurusamy, V., Vijayarani, S., Ilamathi, J., Nithya, M.: Preprocessing techniques for text mining. Int. J. Comput. Sci. Commun. Netw. **5**(1), 7–16 (2014)
16. Kao, A., Poteet, S.R.: Natural Language Processing and Text Mining. Springer, London (2007). https://doi.org/10.1007/978-1-84628-754-1
17. Kozak, J., Boryczka, U.: Dynamic version of the acdt/acdf algorithm for h-bond data set analysis. In: ICCCI, pp. 701–710 (2013)
18. Kozak, J.: Decision Tree and Ensemble Learning Based on Ant Colony Optimization. SCI, vol. 781. Springer, Cham (2019). https://doi.org/10.1007/978-3-319-93752-6
19. Kozak, J., Boryczka, U.: Goal-oriented requirements for acdt algorithms. In: Hwang, D., Jung, J.J., Nguyen, N.-T. (eds.) ICCCI 2014. LNCS (LNAI), vol. 8733, pp. 593–602. Springer, Cham (2014). https://doi.org/10.1007/978-3-319-11289-3_60
20. Lazer, D.M., et al.: The science of fake news. Science **359**(6380), 1094–1096 (2018)
21. Luhn, H.P.: A statistical approach to mechanized encoding and searching of literary information. IBM J. Res. Dev. **1**(4), 309–317 (1957)
22. Martens, D., De Backer, M., Haesen, R., Vanthienen, J., Snoeck, M., Baesens, B.: Classification with ant colony optimization. IEEE Trans. Evol. Comput. **11**(5), 651–665 (2007). https://doi.org/10.1109/TEVC.2006.890229
23. Parpinelli, R.S., Lopes, H.S., Freitas, A.A.: An ant colony algorithm for classification rule discovery. In: Data Mining: a Heuristic Approach, pp. 191–208. Idea Group Publishing, London (2002)
24. Parpinelli, R.S., Lopes, H.S., Freitas, A.A.: Data mining with an ant colony optimization algorithm. IEEE Trans. Evol. Comput. Spec. Issue Ant Colony Algorithms **6**, 321–332 (2004)
25. Pérez-Rosas, V., Kleinberg, B., Lefevre, A., Mihalcea, R.: Automatic detection of fake news. arXiv preprint arXiv:1708.07104 (2017)
26. Potthast, M., Köpsel, S., Stein, B., Hagen, M.: Clickbait detection. In: Ferro, N., et al. (eds.) ECIR 2016. LNCS, vol. 9626, pp. 810–817. Springer, Cham (2016). https://doi.org/10.1007/978-3-319-30671-1_72
27. Rashkin, H., Choi, E., Jang, J.Y., Volkova, S., Choi, Y.: Truth of varying shades: Analyzing language in fake news and political fact-checking. In: Proceedings of the 2017 Conference on Empirical Methods in Natural Language Processing, pp. 2931–2937 (2017)
28. Rokach, L., Maimon, O.: Data Mining With Decision Trees: Theory And Applications. World Scientific Publishing, Singapore (2008)

29. Rubin, V.L., Chen, Y., Conroy, N.K.: Deception detection for news: three types of fakes. In: Proceedings of the Association for Information Science and Technology, vol. 52, no. 1, pp. 1–4 (2015)
30. Rubin, V.L., Conroy, N., Chen, Y., Cornwell, S.: Fake news or truth? using satirical cues to detect potentially misleading news. In: Proceedings of the Second Workshop on Computational Approaches to Deception Detection, pp. 7–17 (2016)
31. Schapire, R.E.: The strength of weak learnability. Mach. Learn. 5, 197–227 (1990)
32. Sowmiya, C., Sumitra, P.: A hybrid approach for mortality prediction for heart patients using ACO-HKNN. J. Ambient Intell. Humanized Comput. 12(5), 5405–5412 (2020). https://doi.org/10.1007/s12652-020-02027-6
33. Straková, J., Straka, M., Hajic, J.: Open-source tools for morphology, lemmatization, pos tagging and named entity recognition. In: Proceedings of 52nd Annual Meeting of the Association for Computational Linguistics: System Demonstrations, pp. 13–18 (2014)
34. Wang, K., Thrasher, C., Viegas, E., Li, X., Hsu, B.J.P.: An overview of microsoft web n-gram corpus and applications. In: Proceedings of the NAACL HLT 2010 Demonstration Session, pp. 45–48 (2010)
35. Webster, J.J., Kit, C.: Tokenization as the initial phase in nlp. In: COLING 1992 Volume 4: The 15th International Conference on Computational Linguistics (1992)
36. Yazdi, K.M., Yazdi, A.M., Khodayi, S., Hou, J., Zhou, W., Saedy, S.: Improving fake news detection using k-means and support vector machine approaches. Int. J. Electron. Commun. Eng. 14(2), 38–42 (2020)

Data Mining and Machine Learning

Feature (Gene) Clustering with Collinearity Models

Leon Bobrowski[1,2]([⊠]) [iD] and Paweł Zabielski[1] [iD]

[1] Faculty of Computer Science, Białystok University of Technology, Białystok, Poland
l.bobrowski@pb.edu.pl
[2] Institute of Biocybernetics and Biomedical Engineering, PAS, Warsaw, Poland

Abstract. Feature clustering techniques can be useful primarily for datasets composed of a relatively small number of multidimensional feature vectors. Genetic datasets typically have this property of "long" feature vectors.

The approach to clustering features can be based on minimizing the collinearity criterion function. The collinearity criterion function belongs to the family of the convex and piecewise linear (CPL) functions.

The minimization of the collinearity criterion function aims to discover linear relations in data sets. Multivariate linear relationships detected in genetic datasets could be useful, among other things, in better understanding and modeling the role of interactions between genes in various diseases.

Keywords: Data mining · Long feature vectors · *CPL* criterion functions · Colliner relationships · Gene interactions

1 Introduction

Data sets consisting of a small number of multidimensional feature vectors are often encountered in practice [1]. Such a property is shared by, inter alia, genetic data sets [2]. Clustering algorithms help to find interesting regularities in this type of data.

Cluster analysis involves many different methods of pattern extraction from data sets. In this context, we will consider collinear clustering [3]. The purpose of the collinear clustering procedures is to extract linear dependencies from the examined dataset. Feature clustering makes it possible to reduce the number of features included in the next stages of data exploration. This is particularly important for long data sets consisting of a small number of multivariate feature vectors.

Collinear patterns can be extracted from large data sets by minimizing the collinear criterion function which belongs to the family of convex and piecewise linear (*CPL*) functions [4]. Basis exchange algorithms are used to minimize the *CPL* criterion functions [5]. High efficiency and precision of basis exchange algorithms allow the use of *CPL* criterion functions defined on large, multidimensional data sets.

This article examines the collinear clustering algorithms targeting wide data sets, if a given dataset consists of a small number of multidimensional feature vectors. Collinear clustering of genes allows the extraction of multi-linear interaction models from genetic

© Springer Nature Switzerland AG 2021
N. T. Nguyen et al. (Eds.): ICCCI 2021, LNAI 12876, pp. 403–415, 2021.
https://doi.org/10.1007/978-3-030-88081-1_30

datasets [6]. The extracted linear relationships may help us to better understand the role of interactions between various factors and genes in systems as complex as living organisms [2].

2   Dual Planes and Vertices in the Parameter Space

Let us assume that each of m objects O_j from a given database is represented by the n-dimensional feature vector $\mathbf{x}_j = [x_{j,1},...,x_{j,n}]^T$ belonging to the feature space $F[n]$ ($\mathbf{x}_j \in F[n]$). The data set C is constituted by m feature vectors $\mathbf{x}_j$:

$$C = \{\mathbf{x}_j\}, \quad where \quad j = 1, ..., m \tag{1}$$

The components $x_{j,i}$ of the feature vector $\mathbf{x}_j$ can be treated as the numerical results of n standardized examinations of the j-th object O_j, where $x_{j,i} \in R$ or $x_{j,i} \in \{0, 1\}$.

Feature vectors $\mathbf{x}_j$ from the data set C (1) allow to define the following dual hyperplanes h_j^1 in the parameter space R^n:

$$(\forall \mathbf{x}_j \in C) \qquad h_j^1 = \{\mathbf{w}: \mathbf{x}_j^T \mathbf{w} = 1\} \tag{2}$$

where $\mathbf{w} = [w_1,...,w_n]^T$ is the parameter (*weight*) vector ($\mathbf{w} \in R^n$).

Each of n unit vectors $\mathbf{e}_i$ defines the following hyperplane h_i^0 in the n-dimensional parameter space R^n:

$$(\forall i \in \{1, \ldots, n\}) \qquad h_i^0 = \{\mathbf{w}: \mathbf{e}_i^T \mathbf{w} = 0\} = \{\mathbf{w}: w_i = 0\} \tag{3}$$

Let us consider the set S_k of r_k linearly independent feature vectors $\mathbf{x}_j$ ($j \in J_k$) and $n - r_k$ unit vectors $\mathbf{e}_i$ ($i \in I_k$).

$$S_k = \{\mathbf{x}_j : j \in J_k\} \cup \{\mathbf{e}_j : i \in I_k\} \tag{4}$$

The k-th *vertex* $\mathbf{w}_k$ can be described as the intersection point of k hyperplanes h_j^1 ($j \in J_k$) (2) and $n - k$ hyperplanes h_i^0 ($i \in I_k$) (3). The hyperplanes h_j^1 (2) and h_i^0 (3) are determined in the parameter space R^n by the feature vectors $\mathbf{x}_j$ ($j \in J_k$) and by the unit vectors $\mathbf{e}_i$ ($i \in I_k$) from the set S_k (4). The vertex $\mathbf{w}_k$ can be defined by the following set of linear equations:

$$(\forall j \in J_k) \qquad \mathbf{w}_k^T \mathbf{x}_j = 1 \tag{5}$$

$$and \quad (\forall i \in I_k) \quad \mathbf{w}_k^T \mathbf{e}_i = 0 \tag{6}$$

Equations (5) and (6) can be represented in the below matrix form:

$$B_k \mathbf{w}_k = \mathbf{1}_k \tag{7}$$

where $\mathbf{1}_k = [1,...,1, 0,...,0]^T$ is a vector with the first k components equal to one and the remaining $n - k$ components are equal to zero.

The square matrix $\mathbf{B}_k$ in Eq. (7) has the following structure [3]:

$$\mathbf{B}_k = \left[\mathbf{x}_1, ..., \mathbf{x}_k, \mathbf{e}_{i(k+1)}, ..., \mathbf{e}_{i(n)}\right]^T \tag{8}$$

where the symbol $\mathbf{e}_{i(n)}$ denotes such unit vector, which is the n-th row of the matrix $\mathbf{B}_k$.

The non-singular matrix $\mathbf{B}_k$ (8) is the *basis* of the feature space $F[n]$ related to the vertex $\mathbf{w}_k = [w_{k,1}, ..., w_{k,n}]^T$:

$$\mathbf{w}_k = \mathbf{B}_k^{-1}\mathbf{1}_k = \mathbf{r}_1 + ... + \mathbf{r}_k \tag{9}$$

where $\mathbf{B}_k^{-1}$ is the inverse matrix:

$$B_k^{-1} = \left[\mathbf{r}_1, ..., \mathbf{r}_k, \mathbf{r}_{k+1}, ..., \mathbf{r}_n\right] \tag{10}$$

According to Eq. (9), the vertex $\mathbf{w}_k$ is the sum of the first k columns $\mathbf{r}_i$ of the inverse matrix $\mathbf{B}_k^{-1}$ (10).

Remark 1: The n - k components $w_{k,i}$ of the vector $\mathbf{w}_k = [w_{k,1}, ..., w_{k,n}]^T$ (10) linked to the zero components of the vector $\mathbf{1}_k = [1, ..., 1, 0, ..., 0, 1]^T$ (7) are equal to zero:

$$(\forall i \in \{k+1, ..., n\})\ w_{k,i} = 0 \tag{11}$$

The conditions $w_{k,i} = 0$ (11) result from the equations $\mathbf{w}_k^T \mathbf{e}_i = 0$ (6) at the vertex $\mathbf{w}_k$.

3 Vertexical Planes in Feature Space

Consider the following hyperplane $H(\mathbf{w})$ in the n-dimensional feature space $F[n]$ [3]:

$$H(\mathbf{w}) = \{\mathbf{x} : \mathbf{w}^T\mathbf{x} = 1\} \tag{12}$$

where $\mathbf{w} = [w_1, ..., w_n]^T$ is the *weight vector* ($\mathbf{w} \in R^n$).

The hyperplane $H(\mathbf{w})$ (12) in the feature space $F[n]$ has the dimension $n - 1$. The *vertexical plane* $P_k(\mathbf{x}_1, ..., \mathbf{x}_k)$ linked to the vertex $\mathbf{w}_k$ (9) is defined in the feature space $F[n]$ as a normalized linear combination of k vectors $\mathbf{x}_j$ ($j \in J_k$) (4) constituting the basis $\mathbf{B}_k$ (8) [4]:

$$P_k(\mathbf{x}_1, ..., \mathbf{x}_k) = \{\mathbf{x} \in F[n] : \mathbf{x} = \alpha_1\mathbf{x}_1 + ... + \alpha_k\mathbf{x}_k\} \tag{13}$$

where the parameters $\alpha_i (\alpha_i \in R^1)$ meet the normalizing condition [4]:

$$\alpha_1 + ... + \alpha_k = 1 \tag{14}$$

The vertexical plane $P_k(\mathbf{x}_1, ..., \mathbf{x}_k)$ (13) has the dimension $k - 1$.

Example 1: Two linearly independent vectors $\mathbf{x}_{j(1)}$ and $\mathbf{x}_{j(2)}$ from the set C (1) span the below line $l(\mathbf{x}_{j(1)}, \mathbf{x}_{j(2)})$ in the feature space $F[n]$ ($\mathbf{x} \in F[n]$):

$$
\begin{aligned}
l\big(\mathbf{x}_{j(1)}, \mathbf{x}_{j(2)}\big) &= \{\mathbf{x} \in F[n] : \mathbf{x} = \mathbf{x}_{j(1)} + \alpha\big(\mathbf{x}_{j(2)} - \mathbf{x}_{j(1)}\big)\} \\
&= \{\mathbf{x} \in F[n] : \mathbf{x} = (1 - \alpha)\mathbf{x}_{j(1)} + \alpha\mathbf{x}_{j(2)}\}
\end{aligned}
\tag{15}
$$

where $\alpha \in R^1$.

The line $l(\mathbf{x}_{j(1)}, \mathbf{x}_{j(2)})$ (15) is the *vertexical plane* $P_k(\mathbf{x}_{j(1)}, \mathbf{x}_{j(2)})$ (13) spanned by two supporting vectors $\mathbf{x}_{j(1)}$ and $\mathbf{x}_{j(2)}$ with $\alpha_1 = 1 - \alpha$ and $\alpha_2 = \alpha$. In this case the basis $\mathbf{B}_k$ (8) contains only two feature vectors $\mathbf{x}_{j(1)}$ and $\mathbf{x}_{j(2)}$ ($r_k = 2$) and the vertex $\mathbf{w}_k = [w_{k,1},...,w_{k,n}]^T$ (9) contains only two nonzero components $w_{k,i}$ ($w_{k,i} \neq 0$). □

Lemma 1: The vertexical plane $P_k(\mathbf{x}_1,..., \mathbf{x}_k)$ (13) with $k > 1$ is equal to the hyperplane $H(\mathbf{w}_k)$ (12) defined in the n - dimensional feature space $F[n]$ by the vertex $\mathbf{w}_k$ (9) represented by the basis $\mathbf{B}_k$ (8).

Proof: Let us assume that the feature vector $\mathbf{x}$ is located on the vertexical plane $P_k(\mathbf{x}_1,..., \mathbf{x}_k)$ (13). Then

$$
\mathbf{w}_k^T\mathbf{x} = \alpha_1 \mathbf{w}_k^T\mathbf{x}_{j(1)} + ... + \alpha_k\mathbf{w}_k^T\mathbf{x}_{j(k)} = \alpha_1 + ... + \alpha_k = 1
\tag{16}
$$

This means that the vector $\mathbf{x}$ is located on the hyperplane $H(\mathbf{w}_k)$ (12).

Theorem 1: The vector $\mathbf{x}_j$ is situated on the vertexical plane $P_k(\mathbf{x}_1,..., \mathbf{x}_k)$ (13) if and only if the dual hyperplane h_j (2) passes through the vertex $\mathbf{w}_k$ (9).

The proof of this theorem can be found in [4].

4   Vertexical Feature Subspaces

The vertexical feature subspace $F_k[k]$ ($F_k[k] \subset F[n]$) is based on the k-th vertex $\mathbf{w}_k$ (9). Let us assume that the vertex $\mathbf{w}_k$ is represented by the basis $\mathbf{B}_k$ (8) composed of k feature vectors $\mathbf{x}_j$ ($j \in J_k$) (5) and $n - k$ unit vectors $\mathbf{e}_i$ ($i \in I_k$) (6). The components $w_{k,i}$ of the vertex $\mathbf{w}_k = [w_{k,1},..., w_{k,n}]^T$ (10) connected to unit vectors $\mathbf{e}_i$ ($i \in I_k$) (6) in the basis $\mathbf{B}_k$ (8) are equal to zero ($w_{k,i} = 0$) (11). Such zero components $w_{k,i}$ can be omitted because they do not affect the values of the inner products $\mathbf{w}_k^T\mathbf{x}_j$ (11) [7]. Omitting the zero component $w_{k,i}$ also causes the exclusion of a certain feature X_i and the i-th component $x_{j,i}$ from feature vectors $\mathbf{x}_j = [x_{j,1},..., x_{j,n}]^T$.

The k-th vertexical feature subspace $F_k[k]$ is obtained as a result of the reduction of the feature set $\mathcal{F}(n) = \{X_1,..., X_n\}$ on the basis of the matrix $\mathbf{B}_k$ (8) [7]:

($\forall i \in I_k$ (6)) X_i is excluded from

$$
\text{the feature set } \mathcal{F}(n) = \{X_1,..., X_n\}
\tag{17}
$$

and

($\forall i \in I_k$ (6)) component $x_{j,i}$ is excluded from

$$
\text{each feature vector } \mathbf{x}_j = [x_{j,1,...,}x_{j,n}]^T
\tag{18}
$$

The k-th vertexical feature subset $\mathcal{F}_k(k)$ consists of k features X_i that are not connected to the unit vectors $\mathbf{e}_i$ in the basis $\mathbf{B}_k$ (8).

$$\mathcal{F}_k(k) = \{X_i: i \notin I_k \, (6)\} \tag{19}$$

The reduced feature vectors $\mathbf{x}_j(k)$ belonging to the k-th *vertexical feature subspace* $F_k[k]$ $(\mathbf{x}_j(k) \in F_k[r_k])$ are obtained from the feature vectors $\mathbf{x}_j = [x_{j,1},...,x_{j,n}]^T$ (13) $(\mathbf{x}_j \in F[n])$ by neglecting $n - k$ components $x_{j,i}$ in accordance with the rule (18).

5 Collinearity Criterion Functions

Feature vectors $\mathbf{x}_j$ from the data set C (1) allow to define the following collinear penalty functions $\varphi_j(\mathbf{w})$ related to dual hyperplanes h_j (2) [3]:

$$(\forall \mathbf{x}_j \in C(1)) \quad \varphi_j(\mathbf{w}) = \left| 1 - \mathbf{x}_j^T \mathbf{w} \right| \tag{20}$$

Each of n unit vectors $\mathbf{e}_i$ allows to define the i-th cost function $\varphi_i^0(\mathbf{w})$ in the n-dimensional parameter space R^n, where $\mathbf{w} = [w_1,...,w_n]$ $(\mathbf{w} \in R^n)$:

$$(\forall i \in \{1, \dots, n\}) \quad \varphi_i^0(\mathbf{w}) = \left| \mathbf{e}_i^T \mathbf{w} \right| = |w_i| \tag{21}$$

The cost functions $\varphi_i^0(\mathbf{w})$ (21) are related to the hyperplanes h_i^0 (3). The cost functions $\varphi_i^0(\mathbf{w})$ (21), like the collinearity functions $\varphi_j(\mathbf{w})$ (20), are convex and piecewise linear (*CPL*) [3].

The collinearity criterion function $\Phi(\mathbf{w})$ is here defined as the sum of the penalty functions $\varphi_j(\mathbf{w}[n])$ (23) determined by m feature vectors $\mathbf{x}_j$ $(\mathbf{x}_j \in C$ (1)):

$$\Phi(\mathbf{w}) = \sum_{j=1,...,m} \varphi_j(\mathbf{w}) \tag{22}$$

It can be proved that, the minimum value Φ_k^* of the convex and piecewise linear (*CPL*) criterion function $\Phi(\mathbf{w})$ (22) can be found in one of the vertices $\mathbf{w}_k$ (9) [8]:

$$(\exists \, \mathbf{w}_k^*(9))(\forall \mathbf{w})\Phi(\mathbf{w}) \geq \Phi(\mathbf{w}_k^*) \tag{23}$$

The basis exchange algorithm allow to find efficiently and precisely the optimal vertex $\mathbf{w}_k^*$ (9) constituting the minimal value $\Phi(\mathbf{w}_k^*)$ of the collinearity criterion functions $\Phi(\mathbf{w})$ (22) even in the case of large, multidimensional data set C (1) [3]. Basis exchange algorithms use the Gauss-Jordan transformation and are therefore similar to the *Simplex* algorithm used in linear programming [8].

Theorem 2: The minimal value $\Phi(\mathbf{w}_k^*)$ (23) of the collinearity criterion function $\Phi(\mathbf{w})$ (22) defined on m elements $\mathbf{x}_j$ of data set C (1) is equal to zero $(\Phi(\mathbf{w}_k^*) = 0)$, if and only if all the feature vectors $\mathbf{x}_j$ from this set are situated on the hyperplane $H(\mathbf{w}_k^*)$ (12) defined by the optimal vertex $\mathbf{w}_k^*$.

The proof of a similar theorem can be found in [3]. From the definition of the collinearity criterion function $\Phi(\mathbf{w})$ (22) it follows that the minimal value $\Phi(\mathbf{w}_k^*)$ (23)

is equal to zero ($\Phi(\mathbf{w}_k^*) = 0$), if and only if each of the m dual hyperplanes h_j (2) passes through the optimal vertex $\mathbf{w}_k^*$.

The regularized criterion function $\Psi(\mathbf{w})$ is defined as the sum of the collinearity criterion function $\Phi(\mathbf{w})$ (22) and the weig hted sum of the cost functions $\varphi_i^0(\mathbf{w})$ (21) [3]:

$$\Psi(\mathbf{w}) = \Phi(\mathbf{w}) + \lambda \sum_{i \in \{1,\ldots,n\}} \gamma_i |w_i| \qquad (24)$$

where γ_i ($\gamma_i > 0$) are the *costs* of individual features X_i, and $\lambda \geq 0$ is the *cost level*. The standard values of the cost parameters γ_i are equal to one ($\gamma_i = 1$).

Like the collinearity criterion function $\Phi(\mathbf{w})$ (22), the regularized function $\Psi(\mathbf{w})$ (24) is convex and piecewise linear (*CPL*).

6 Minimization of Collinearity Criterion Functions

Let us assume that the training set C (1) is formed by a relatively small number m of feature vectors $\mathbf{x}_j$ ($j = 1, \ldots, m$) with a large dimension n ($m << n$). In this case, it can be expected that feature vectors $\mathbf{x}_j$ are linearly independent [3]. Feature vectors $\mathbf{x}_j$ (1) are linearly dependent in there is such a vector $\mathbf{x}_{j'}$ (1) which is a linear combination of l ($l < n$) other feature vectors $\mathbf{x}_j$ ($j \neq j'$):

$$\mathbf{x}_{j'} = \alpha_1 \mathbf{x}_{j(1)} + \ldots + \alpha_l \mathbf{x}_{j(l)} \qquad (25)$$

where ($\forall i \in \{1, \ldots, l\}$) $\alpha_i \neq 0$.

We can see that the increase of dimensionality n by incorporating a new feature X_i (17) can easily destroy the existing linear relationship (25) between m feature vectors $\mathbf{x}_j$ in the feature space $F[n]$ ($\mathbf{x}_j \in F[n]$).

The minimum value $\Phi(\mathbf{w}_k^*)$ (23) of the collinearity criterion function $\Phi(\mathbf{w})$ (22) is equal to zero if and only if the following linear equations are fulfilled in the optimal vertex $\mathbf{w}_k^* = [w_{k,1}^*, \ldots, w_{k,n}^*]^T$ (23):

$$(\forall \mathbf{x}_j \in C(1)) \mathbf{x}_j^T \mathbf{w}_k^* = 1 \qquad (26)$$

The optimal vertex $\mathbf{w}_k^*$ (23) can be found by solving the following equation [3]:

$$B_m \mathbf{w} = \mathbf{1}_m \qquad (27)$$

where the matrix B_m (27) has the structure given by the formula (8) ($m << n$):

$$B_m = [\mathbf{x}_1, \ldots, \mathbf{x}_m, \mathbf{e}_{i(m+1)}, \ldots, \mathbf{e}_{i(n)}]^T \qquad (28)$$

The matrix B_m (28) consists of m feature vectors $\mathbf{x}_j$ and $n - m$ unit vectors $\mathbf{e}_i$ ($i \in I_k$) (6). The first m components of the vector $\mathbf{1}_k = [1, \ldots, 1, 0, \ldots, 0]^T$ (27) are equal to one, the next $n - m$ components are equal to zero.

Theorem 2: If m feature vectors $\mathbf{x}_j$ are linearly independent then the matrix $\boldsymbol{B}_m$ (28) is invertible (not-singular) and can form the *basis* of the feature space $\boldsymbol{F}[n]$ ($\mathbf{x}_j \in \boldsymbol{F}[n]$).

If m feature vectors $\mathbf{x}_j$ are linearly independent, then the inverse matrix $\boldsymbol{B}_m{}^{-1}$ exists:

$$\boldsymbol{B}_m{}^{-1} = [\mathbf{r}_1, \ldots, \mathbf{r}_m, \mathbf{r}_{m+1}, \ldots, \mathbf{r}_n] \qquad (29)$$

The optimal vertex $\mathbf{w}_m{}^* = [w_{m,1}{}^*, \ldots, w_{m,n}{}^*]^T$ (23) can be determined as the sum (9) of m columns $\mathbf{r}_i$ of the inverse matrix $\boldsymbol{B}_m{}^{-1}$:

$$\mathbf{w}_m{}^* = \boldsymbol{B}_m{}^{-1} \mathbf{1}_m = \mathbf{r}_1 + \ldots + \mathbf{r}_m \qquad (30)$$

where $\mathbf{w}_m{}^* = [w_{m,1}{}^*, \ldots, w_{m,m}{}^*, 0, \ldots, 0]^T$ (11).

The zero components $w_{m,i}{}^*$ ($w_{m,i}{}^* = 0$) of the optimal vertex $\mathbf{w}_m{}^*$ (30) result from the existence of $n - m$ unit vectors $\mathbf{e}_i$ ($i \in I_m$) in the basis $\boldsymbol{B}_m$ (28).

The calculation of the optimal vertex $\mathbf{w}_m{}^*$ (23) in accordance with the Eq. (27) is linked to the inversion of the matrix $\boldsymbol{B}_m$ (28) which can have a large dimension $n \times n$. The inversion of the non-singular matrix $\boldsymbol{B}_m$ (28) can be performed in m steps k ($k = 1, \ldots, m$) using the basis exchange algorithm [6].

The reversible matrix $\mathbf{B}_k = [\mathbf{x}_1, \ldots, \mathbf{x}_k, \mathbf{e}_{i(k+1)}, \ldots, \mathbf{e}_{i(n)}]^T$ (8) determines the vertex $\mathbf{w}_k$ (9) and the value $\Phi(\mathbf{w}_k)$ of the criterion function $\Phi(\mathbf{w})$ (22) in the k-th step. In the step ($k + 1$), one of the unit vectors $\mathbf{e}_{i(l)}$ in the matrix $\mathbf{B}_k$ (8) is replaced by the feature vector $\mathbf{x}_{k+1}$ and the matrix $\mathbf{B}_{k+1} = = [\mathbf{x}_1, \ldots, \mathbf{x}_k, \mathbf{x}_{k+1}, \mathbf{e}_{i(k+2)}, \ldots, \mathbf{e}_{i(n)}]^T$ appears. The unit vector $\mathbf{e}_{i(l)}$ that leaves the matrix $\mathbf{B}_k$ (8) is indicated by an *exit criterion* based on the collinearity criterion function $\Phi(\mathbf{w})$ (22). The exit criterion allows us to determine the edge $\mathbf{r}_l$ (29) of the greatest descent of the criterion function $\Phi(\mathbf{w})$ (22). After a finite number of steps k ($k \leq m$), the collinearity function $\Phi(\mathbf{w})$ (22) becomes zero at the vertex $\mathbf{w}_k{}^*$ (9):

$$(\exists k : k \leq m) \quad \Phi(\mathbf{w}_k{}^*) = 0 \qquad (31)$$

The basis exchange algorithm based on the collinearity criterion function $\Phi(\mathbf{w})$ (20) is stopped at the k-th vertex $\mathbf{w}_k{}^*$ (9) where the condition $\Phi(\mathbf{w}_k{}^*) = 0$ is satisfied.

The optimal vertex $\mathbf{w}_k{}^*$ (23) satisfying the condition $\Phi(\mathbf{w}_k{}^*) = 0$ (31) is determined by the linear Eqs. (27) with k feature vectors $\mathbf{x}_j$ and by the linear Eqs. (6) with selected $n - k$ unit vectors $\mathbf{e}_i$ ($i \in I_k$).

$$(\forall j \in J_k) \ \mathbf{x}_i{}^T \mathbf{w}_k{}^* = 1 \ \text{and} \ (\forall i \in I_k) \, \mathbf{e}_i{}^T \mathbf{w}_k{}^* = 0 \qquad (32)$$

The location of the optimal vertex $\mathbf{w}_k{}^*$ (31) in the parameter space R^n depends on which unit vectors $\mathbf{e}_i$ ($i \in I_k$) are included in the basis $\mathbf{B}_k$ (8). The number l of different vertices $\mathbf{w}_k{}^*$ (32) can be large when $m << n$:

$$l \leq n! \, / \, m! \, (n - m)! \qquad (33)$$

The choice between different vertices $\mathbf{w}_k{}^*$ (31) may be based on minimizing the regularized criterion function $\Psi(\mathbf{w})$ (24). The regularized function $\Psi(\mathbf{w})$ (24) is the sum of the collinearity function $\Phi(\mathbf{w})$ (22) and the weighted sum of the cost functions $\varphi_i{}^0(\mathbf{w})$

(21). Since the collinearity function $\Phi(\mathbf{w})$ (22) is equal to zero at each considered vertex $\mathbf{w}_k^* = [w_{k,1},\ldots, w_{k,n}]^T$ (32), the problem of minimizing the regularized function $\Psi(\mathbf{w})$ (24) can be formulated in the following way:

$$min_{k} \{\Psi(\mathbf{w}_k): \Phi(\mathbf{w}_k) = 0\} = min_{k} \{ \sum_{i \in \{1,\ldots,n\}} \gamma_i | w_{k,i} |: \Phi(\mathbf{w}_k) = 0\} \qquad (34)$$

According to the above formulation, the search for the minimum of the regularized criterion function $\Psi(\mathbf{w})$ (24) is performed on all such vertices $\mathbf{w}_k$ (32), where the collinearity function $\Phi(\mathbf{w}_k)$ (22) is equal to zero. The regularized criterion function $\Psi(\mathbf{w})$ (24) is defined in the following manner on such vertices $\mathbf{w}_k$, where $\Phi(\mathbf{w}_k) = 0$:

$$(\forall \mathbf{w}_k: \Phi(\mathbf{w}_k) = 0) \quad \Psi_k'(\mathbf{w}_k) = \sum_{i \in \{1,\ldots,n\}} \gamma_i | w_{k,i} | \qquad (35)$$

The constrained minimization (34) of the *CPL* regularization function $\Psi_k'(\mathbf{w}_k)$ (35) can also be performed using the basis exchange algorithm [5]. In the subsequent steps l of the algorithm, one unit vector $\mathbf{e}_{i((l)}$ ($\mathbf{e}_{i((l)} \in B_k$) is removed from the basis B_k (28) and replaced in this basis by the vector $\mathbf{e}_{i((k)}$ ($\mathbf{e}_{i((k)} \notin B_k$). The *exit criterion* which is based on the function $\Psi_k'(\mathbf{w}_k)$ (36) determines the vector $\mathbf{e}_{i((l)}$ leaving the base B_k (28), and the the *entry criterion* sets out the vector $\mathbf{e}_{i((k)}$ entering the base [3].

Replacing the vector $\mathbf{e}_{i((l)}$ by the vector $\mathbf{e}_{i((k)}$ in the basis B_k (28) changes the columns $\mathbf{r}_i(k)$ of the inverse matrix $B_k^{-1} = [\mathbf{r}_1(k),\ldots, \mathbf{r}_n(k)]$ (29). The new columns $\mathbf{r}_i(k + 1)$ are defined by the Gauss-Jordan transformation [3]:

$$\mathbf{r}_l(k + 1) = (1/\mathbf{r}_l(k)^T \mathbf{e}_{i(k)})\mathbf{r}_l(k), \ and$$
$$(\forall i \neq l)\mathbf{r}_i(k + 1) = \mathbf{r}_i(k) - (\mathbf{r}_i(k)^T \mathbf{e}_{i(k)}/\mathbf{r}_l(k)^T \mathbf{e}_{i(k)})\mathbf{r}_l(k) \qquad (36)$$

Replacing the unit vectors $\mathbf{e}_i$ in the basis B_k (28) by other unit vectors according to the exit criterion and the entry criterion reults in a decrease of the criterion function $\Psi_k'(\mathbf{w}_k)$ (35). The procedure stops after a finite number of steps l, when a further reduction of the criterion function $\Psi_k'(\mathbf{w}_k)$ (35) becomes impossible.

7 Feature (Gene) Clustering

A multi-step procedure for feature (gene) X_i clustering is based on the minimization of the collinearity criterion function $\Phi(\mathbf{w})$ (22) and the regularized function $\Psi(\mathbf{w})$ (24). During the first step l ($l = 1$), the feature cluster $F_1[k_1]$ with k_1 ($k_1 << n$) features X_i is selected from the initial set $F[n]$ of n features X_i:

$$F_1[k_1] = \{X_{i(1)}, \ldots, X_{i(k1)}\} \subset F[n] = \{X_1, \ldots, X_n\} \qquad (37)$$

During the second step l ($l = 2$), the feature cluster $F_2[k_2]$ built from k_2 features X_i is selected from the reduced set $F[n] / F_1[k_1]$ of $n - k_1$ features X_i:

$$F_2[k_2] = \{X_{i(k1 + 1)}, \ldots, X_{i(k1 + k2)}\} \subset F[n]/F_1[k_1] \qquad (38)$$

During the l-th step, the feature cluster $F_l[k_l]$ built from k_l features X_i is selected from the reduced set $F[n] / (F_1[k_1] \cup \ldots \cup F_{l-1}[k_{l-1}])$ of $n - (k_1 + \ldots + k_{l-1})$ features X_i:

$$F_l[k_l] \subset F[n]/(F_1[k_1] \cup \ldots \cup F_{l-1}[k_{l-1}]) \tag{39}$$

In this approach, successive feature clusters $F_l[k_l]$ are disjoint subsets of features X_i:

$$(\forall l \in \{1, \ldots, L-1\}\ F_l[k_l] \cap F_{l+1}[k_{l+1}] = \emptyset \tag{40}$$

During the l-th step, the feature cluster $F_l[k_l]$ is formed as a result of the minimization (23) of the collinearity criterion function $\Phi_l(\mathbf{w})$ (22), followed by the minimization with constraints (35) of the regularization function $\Psi_l'(\mathbf{w})$ (36). The collinearity criterion function $\Phi_l(\mathbf{w})$ (22) and the function $\Psi_l'(\mathbf{w})$ (36) are defined on the features X_i belonging to the reduced feature subset $F[n] / (F_1[k_1] \cup \ldots \cup F_{l-1}[k_{l-1}])$ (40).

Suppose that the optimal vertex $\mathbf{w}_l^*$ (9) gives a zero value for the minimum value $\Phi_l(\mathbf{w}_l^*)$ (23) of the collinearity criterion functions $\Phi_l(\mathbf{w})$ (22) ($\Phi_l(\mathbf{w}_l^*) = 0$).

The rationale for this assumption is a large dimensionality n of the feature vectors $\mathbf{x}_j$ (1) ($m << n$). The minimization (23) of the collinearity criterion function $\Phi_l(\mathbf{w})$ (22) allows to find the optimal vertex $\mathbf{w}_{l,1}$. The optimal vertex $\mathbf{w}_{l,1} = [w_{l,1}, \ldots, w_{l,n}]^T$, (9) satisfying the condition $\Phi_l(\mathbf{w}_{l,1}) = 0$ can be related to the basis $\mathbf{B}_{l,1} = [\mathbf{x}_{j(1)}, \ldots, \mathbf{x}_{j(k)}, \mathbf{e}_{i(k+1)}, \ldots, \mathbf{e}_{i(n)}]^T$ (8) that contains at least $n - m$ unit vectors $\mathbf{e}_i$ ($I \in I_{l,1}$ (6)).

The constrained minimization (34) of the *CPL* regularization function $\Psi_k'(\mathbf{w}_l)$ (35) with the constraint $\Phi(\mathbf{w}_l) = 0$ may allow, inter alia, to further reduce the number k of feature vectors $\mathbf{x}_j$ ($j \in J_k$) contained in the basis $\mathbf{B}_l$ (8). As a result, the optimal vertex $\mathbf{w}_l^* = [w_{l,1}, \ldots, w_{l,n}]^T$ (9) satisfying the condition $\Phi(\mathbf{w}_l^*) = 0$ can be achieved:

$$(\forall \mathbf{w}_l(9):\ \Phi(\mathbf{w}_l) = 0)\ \Psi_{k'}(\mathbf{w}_l) \geq \Psi_{k'}(\mathbf{w}_l^*) > 0 \tag{41}$$

The quality of the optimal vertex $\mathbf{w}_l^*$ (41) can be determined on the basis of the minimum value $\Psi_k'(\mathbf{w}_l^*)$ of the regularization function $\Psi_k'(\mathbf{w}_l)$ (35).

If the parameters γ_i (24) are equal to one, then the constrained minimization (34) of the criterion function $\Psi_k'(\mathbf{w}_l)$ (35) leads to such a vertex $\mathbf{w}_l^* = [w_{l,1}, \ldots, w_{l,n}]^T$, which has the smallest L_1 norm (length) $\| \mathbf{w}_l^* \|_{L1} = |w_{l,1}| + \ldots + |w_{l,n}|$ among all vertices $\mathbf{w}_l$ (9) satisfying the condition $\Phi(\mathbf{w}_l) = 0$.

The vertex $\mathbf{w}_l^* = [w_{l,1}, \ldots, w_{l,n}]^T$ with the smallest L_1 length $\| \mathbf{w}_l^* \|_{L1}$ defines the linear classification (separation) rule with the largest margin $\delta_{L1}(\mathbf{w}_l^*)$ of the L_1 norm [3]:

$$\delta_{L1}(\mathbf{w}_l^*) = 2/\|\mathbf{w}_l^*\|_{L1} = 2(|w_{l,1}| + \ldots + |w_{l,n}|) \tag{42}$$

Support Vector Machines (*SVM*) is the most frequently used method of designing linear classifiers or prognostic models with margins [9]. In accordance with the *SVM* approach, the optimal linear classifier or the prognostic model should have the maximal margin $\delta_{L2}(\mathbf{w}_l^*)$ based on the Euclidean (L_2) norm:

$$\delta_{L2}(\mathbf{w}_l^*) = 2/\|\mathbf{w}_l^*\|_{L2} = 2/((\mathbf{w}_l^*)^T\mathbf{w}_l^*)^{1/2} \tag{43}$$

The basis exchange algorithm allows for the efficient and precise designing of linear classifiers or prognostic models with the largest L_1 margins $\delta_{L1}(\mathbf{w}_l{}^*)$ (42). Determining the costs γ_i (35) of individual features X_i other than unity opens the way to finding optimal vertices $\mathbf{w}_l{}^*$ (41) with other interesting properties in a similar manner.

According to the above procedure, each cluster $F_l[k_l]$ (39) of features (genes) X_i is represented by the optimal vertex $\mathbf{w}_l{}^*$ (41), where $l = 1, \ldots, L$. The number L of feature clusters $F_l[k_l]$ (39) can be large. For these reasons, it may be profitable to introduce an additional level of clustering. Namely, the optimal vertices $\mathbf{w}_l{}^*$ (41) can be grouped using, for example, K-means clustering with the L_1 norm.

8   Local Models of Linear Interactions

The optimal vertex $\mathbf{w}_l{}^* = [w_{l,1}, \ldots, w_{l,n}]^T$ (41) is the point of intersection (32) of some dual hyperplanes $h_j{}^1$ (2) in the parameter space $\mathbf{R}^n$:

$$(\forall j \in J_l) \, \mathbf{x}_j{}^T \mathbf{w}_l{}^* = 1 \tag{44}$$

$$\text{or} \quad (\forall j \in J_l) w_{l,l(1)} X_{j,l(1)} + \ldots + w_{l,l(m)} X_{j,l(m)} = 1 \tag{45}$$

where $w_{l,l(i)}$ are different from zero components of the weight vector $\mathbf{w}_l{}^* = [w_{l,1}, \ldots, w_{l,n}]^T$ (41) and $x_{j,l(m)}$ are the respective components of feature vectors $\mathbf{x}_j$:

$$(\forall l(i) \cdot \in J_l) \cdot \alpha_i = w_{l,l(i)} \neq 0 \tag{46}$$

The linear dependence (44) between selected components $x_{j,l(i)}$ of feature vectors $\mathbf{x}_j$ may reflect a similar dependence between selected features $X_{l(i)}$ $(l(i) \in J_l)$ [7]:

$$\alpha_1 X_{l(1)} + \ldots + \alpha_m X_{l(m)} = 1 \tag{47}$$

The relationship of the linear dependence (45) between selected components $x_{j,l(i)}$ of feature vectors $\mathbf{x}_j = [x_{j,1}, \ldots, x_{j,n}]^T$ and the linear dependence (47) between selected features X_i is the stronger the more dual hyperplanes $h_j{}^1$ (2) pass through given vertex $\mathbf{w}_l{}^*$ (41). This relationship should be strong for highly degenerate vertices $\mathbf{w}_l{}^*$ (41) [7].

Equation (47) can be treated as a *local model of multiple linear interactions* between the selected genes $X_{i(l)}$ $(i(l) \in J_l$ (44)) [7]. The model (47) is *local* because the linear relationship (45) between components $x_{j,l(i)}$ is satisfied exactly only for feature vectors $\mathbf{x}_j$ with dual hyperplanes h_j (2) passing through the optimal vertex $\mathbf{w}_l{}^*$ (41).

The local models (47) of linear interactions are linked to the optimal vertices $\mathbf{w}_l{}^*$ (41) representing individual clusters $F_l[k_l]$ (39) of the genes X_i. If the number L of the optimal vertices $\mathbf{w}_l{}^*$ (41) is large, additional clustering of these vertices can be recommended. In this case, the grouping of the optimal vertices $\mathbf{w}_l{}^*$ (41), means combining interaction models (47). Individual clusters $F_l[k_l]$ (39) grouped on the basis of optimal vertices $\mathbf{w}_l{}^*$ (42) contain different subsets $F_l[k_l]$ (39) of genes X_i having similar models of linear interactions (47).

9 Experimental Results

The *Colon* cancer dataset [10] was used in the experiment. The dataset contains 62 samples taken from colon adenocarcinomas patients. Among them, 40 cancer biopsies are from tumors and 22 normal biopsies are from healthy parts of the colon of the same patients. Based on confidence in the measured expression levels the heights of the minimal expressions, the dataset creators selected 2 000 genes X_i. Additionally, the features (gene expressions) X_i were normalized so that each feature value have a mean of 0 and a standard deviation of 1.

The computational procedure for genes X_i clustering was implemented in the C^{++} programming language environment. The experiment was performed using a dataset consisting of feature vectors $\mathbf{x}_j$ (1) representing 10 patients randomly selected from the colon cancer dataset [10]. Each patient was described by 2000 genes X_i.

The gene cluster $F_l[k_l]$ (39) was formed during the l-th step as a result of the minimization (23) of the collinearity criterion function $\Phi_l(\mathbf{w})$ (22), followed by the minimization of the regularization function $\Psi_l'(\mathbf{w})$ (35) with the constraints (34). The collinearity criterion function $\Phi_l(\mathbf{w})$ (22) and the function $\Psi_l'(\mathbf{w})$ (35) during the l-th step were defined on the features X_i belonging to the feature subset $F[n]/(F_1[k_1] \cup \ldots \cup F_{l-1}[k_{l-1}])$ (40) reduced during the previous l - 1 steps.

Subsequent minimization of the criterion functions $\Phi_l(\mathbf{w})$ (22) and $\Psi_l'(\mathbf{w})$ (35) followed by the gene cluster $F_l[k_l]$ (39) extraction were repeated several times ($L = 10$). In each step l, the margin $\delta_{L1}(\mathbf{w}_l)$ (42) linked to the gene cluster $F_l[k_l]$ (39) was also calculated. Table 1 presents the genes X_i selected in the subsequent steps l of the procedure together with their weights w_i ($w_i \neq 0$) and the values of the margin $\delta_{L1}(\mathbf{w}_l)$ (42).

In Table 1, we can see that, in accordance with the previous theoretical considerations, the value of the margin $\delta_{L1}(\mathbf{w}_l)$ (42) decreases with each subsequent step l.

Table 1. Cluster $F_l[k_l]$ (39) of genes X_i with their weights w_i and the margins $\delta_{L1}(\mathbf{w}_l)$ (42) obtained in subsequent steps l of the gene clustering procedure.

Step l	Selected genes X_i (weights w_i)	Margin $\delta_{L1}(\mathbf{w}_l)$ (42)
1	T61446 (0.297), R70535 (0.170), M76378 (0.120), X06614 (0.098), R59583 (-0.050), H90764 (0.042), X66975 (-0.022), M55265 (-0.017), R23907 (-0.014), R44895 (-0.013)	2.354
2	H05966 (0.241), X83535 (0.178), X01060 (-0.126), H11125 (0.102), T95318 (0.095), R34698 (-0.089), H65823 (-0.031), D21261 (-0.030), X58521 (-0.0179), R60168 (-0.003)	2.176
3	H46136 (0.377), T53549 (-0.141), M80461 (0.124), D31883 (-0.121), T65740 (-0.063), R35665 (0.061), X85786 (-0.057), X72018 (-0.032), X06614 (0.009), J04102 (-0.006)	2.004
4	X04500 (0.411), R62425 (-0.162), H40705 (0.115), T61661 (0.101), R73660 (-0.091), T40454 (-0.047), H71150 (0.041), H10925 (-0.029), T67897 (0.026), X75208 (-0.021)	1.904

(continued)

Table 1. (*continued*)

Step l	Selected genes X_i (weights w_i)	Margin $\delta_{L1}(\mathbf{w}_l)$ (42)
5	M82919 (0.393), H19272 (0.169), T40568 (-0.112), D59253 (-0.089), D14043 (0.070), R49416 (-0.065), M31516 (-0.059), M58297 (0.045), H02630 (0.040), H01346 (-0.029)	1.858
6	U20659 (0.236), M28650 (0.167), U24077 (0.154), M76378 (0.150), R60195 (-0.144), X82456 (0.096), H06877 (0.062), T57882 (0.054), L11706 (-0.025), D26067 (-0.001)	1.828
7	M55683 (0.249), T64878 (0.208), R55778 (0.141), U02081 (-0.135), R01157 (-0.082), H16991 (-0.076), M76378 (0.074), H17923 (-0.061), D16227 (-0.052), X54101 (-0.031)	1.792
8	T89649 (0.322), U04343 (0.310), X57351 (-0.164), T47213 (-0.082), X60708 (0.074), M31516 (-0.046), H27277 (-0.042), T90774 (0.040), D26018 (-0.039), M21984 (0.023)	1.742
9	R72164 (0.358), R39209 (0.340), T49838 (-0.139), M64098 (-0.104), M28650 (0.102), M21186 (-0.084), R43914 (-0.038), R10620 (-0.009), T51613 (-0.008)	1.682
10	R39209 (0.344), J00277 (0.259), U10324 (-0.190), R62945 (-0.134), L41067 (-0.065), R74066 (-0.063), X64037 (-0.051), M92287 (0.050), M19045 (-0.037), U25265 (-0.020)	1.640

10 Concluding Remarks

The considered model of multiple linear interactions is a linear combination (47) of selected features (genes) X_i which form the cluster $F_l[k_l]$ (39). The cluster $F_l[k_l]$ (39) of selected features (genes) X_i and coefficients α_i of the affine relatioons (47) are obtained from the data set C (1) consisting of a small number m of feature vectors $\mathbf{x}_j$ with a large dimension n ($m \ll n$).

The proposed procedure for designing an interaction model (47) includes two stages. The minimization (23) of the collinearity criterion function $\Phi(\mathbf{w})$ (22) is performed in the first stage. During the second stage, the constrained minimization (34) of the regularized criterion function $\Psi(\mathbf{w})$ (24) takes place. Basis exchange algorithms are used at both stages [5].

Linear interaction models (47) are designed on the basis of small samples of multidimensional feature vectors $\mathbf{x}_j$ (1). In order to better generalize the obtained interaction models, a new scheme of averaging the results is proposed. Namely, averaging over a small number of feature vectors $\mathbf{x}_j$ (1) can be replaced by averaging over functionally similar subsets $F_l[k_l]$ (39) of genes X_i. The gene clusters $F_l[k_l]$ (39) grouped on the basis of optimal vertices $\mathbf{w}_l^*$ (41) differ in the contained genes X_i. but they have similar models of linear interactions (47). This approach could create a new kind of experimental research in medicine or neuroscience.

Acknowledgments. The presented study was supported by the grant WZ/WI-IIT/3/2020 from the Bialystok University of Technology and funded from the resources for research by the Polish Ministry of Science and Higher Education.

References

1. Duda, O.R., Hart, P.E., Stork, D.G.: Pattern classification. J. Wiley, New York (2001)
2. Pevsner, J.: Bioinformatics and Functional Genomics, 3rd Edition, J. Wiley (2015)
3. Bobrowski, L.: Data Exploration and Linear Separability, pp. 1 – 172, Lambert Academic Publishing (2019)
4. Bobrowski, L.: Discovering main vertexical planes in a multivariate data space by using *CPL* functions. In: Perner, P. (ed.) Advances in Data Mining: Applications and Theoretical Aspects, pp. 200 – 213, Springer Verlag, Berlin (2014)
5. Bobrowski, L.: Design of piecewise linear classifiers from formal neurons by some basis exchange technique. Pattern Recogn. **24**(9), 863–870 (1991)
6. Bobrowski, L.: Large matrices inversion using the basis exchange algorithm. British J. Math. Comput. Sci. **21**(1), 1–11 (2017). http://www.sciencedomain.org/abstract/18203
7. Bobrowski, L. Zabielski, P.: Models of multiple interactions from collinear patterns. In: Rojas, I., Guzman, F. (eds.) Bioinformatics and Biomedical Engineering (IWBBIO 2018), pp. 153–165, LNCS 10208, Springer Verlag (2018)
8. Simonnard, M.: Linear Programming, Prentice - Hall, New York, Englewood Cliffs (1966)
9. Boser, B.E., Guyon, I., Vapnik, V.N.:A training algorithm for optimal margin classifiers. In: Proceedings of the Fifth Annual Workshop of Computational Learning Theory, vol. 5, pp. 144–152. Pittsburgh, ACM (1992)
10. Alon, U., et al.: Broad patterns of gene expression revealed by clustering analysis of tumor and normal colon tissues probed by oligonucleotide arrays. In: Proceedings National Academy of Sciences USA, vol. 96, pp. 6745–6750 (1999)

A Reinforcement Learning Framework for Multi-source Adaptive Streaming

Nghia T. Nguyen[1,2], Phuong L. Vo[1,2(✉)] , Thi Thanh Sang Nguyen[1,2] ,
Quan M. Le[1,2], Cuong T. Do[3], and Ngoc-Thanh Nguyen[4]

[1] International University, Ho Chi Minh City, Vietnam
[2] Vietnam National University, Ho Chi Minh City, Vietnam
{ntnghia,vtlphuong,nttsang}@hcmiu.edu.vn,
ITITIU16005@student.hcmiu.edu.vn
[3] Kyung Hee University, Yongin, Korea
dtcuong@khu.ac.kr
[4] Wroclaw University of Science and Technology, Wrocław, Poland
ngoc-thanh.Nguyen@pwr.edu.pl

Abstract. Dynamic adaptive streaming over HTTP (DASH) is widely
used in video streaming recently. With DASH, a video is stored in
multiple equal-playing-time chunks with different quality levels. Video
chunks are in-order delivered from a single source over a path in traditional DASH. The adaptation function in video player chooses a suitable
quality level to request depending on current network status for each
video chunk. In modern networks such as content delivery networks,
edge caching, content-centric networks, *etc.*, popular video contents are
replicated at multiple cache nodes. Utilizing multiple sources for video
streaming is investigated in this paper. We propose a reinforcement learning based algorithm, called RAMS, for rate adaptation in multi-source
video streaming. The proposed algorithm outperforms the other notable
adaptation methods.

Keywords: Multi-source streaming · Reinforcement learning · Deep
Q-learning · Dynamic adaptation streaming over HTTP

1 Introduction

In recent years, the world has witnessed the rapid growth of global internet
traffic, in which a large share is video streaming [1]. Today, dynamic adaptive
streaming over HTTP (DASH) is a major technique to stream a video from a
server to a client. A video content is chunked into equal-playback-time chunks in
DASH. Furthermore, a video is encoded in multiple quality levels with different
bitrates and resolutions. Due to the instability of the network connection between
media server and video player, traditional DASH uses a client-based adaptation

This research is funded by Vietnam National University HoChiMinh City (VNU-HCM)
under grant number DS2020-28-01.

function to choose appropriate quality level to download chunks from a media server [2–5].

Adaptation algorithm at video player plays an essential role in providing high quality-of-experience (QoE) for user. Rate adaptation algorithms can be designed based on estimated throughput for throughput-based methods, or buffer level for buffer-based methods, or a combination of these two features for hybrid approaches [6,11].

On the other hand, several networks today such as content delivery networks, edge caching networks, content-centric networks, *etc.* replicate popular videos at the intermediate nodes to reduce network congestion and delay. Utilizing multiple sources to stream a video content to a client is studied in this paper. We propose a reinforcement learning (RL) framework for rate adaptation of video streaming from multiple sources.

Few previous works have studied adaptive streaming from multiple sources, *e.g.*, [12,13,15]. The work [15] proposed MSPlayer, which is a multi-source video streaming player. However, [15] only considers video with fixed-quality-level chunks and chunk playback time is varied. The authors focus on chunk scheduling problem: estimating the network path condition to determine the chunk index and chunk time requested on the path. In work [12], MP-H2 protocol is designed on top of HTTP/2. MP-H2 splits the video into multiple chunks and client requests chunks over multiple paths, such as wi-fi and cellular. Chunk sizes are calculated based on bandwidth and round-trip-time of paths. A scheduling algorithm is then used to download the chunks over multiple paths. No adaptation method is proposed in [12]. The work [13] proposed a bitrate adaptation algorithm, called DQ-DASH. DQ-DASH can download multiple video chunks from multiple servers in parallel to enhance QoE. Distributed queueing theory is applied to address the situation when multiple clients send the requests to more than one server simultaneously. A scheduling which is quite similar to greedy scheduling in this paper is applied to customize QUETRA [14], a single-source adaptation method, to a multi-source one.

Different from [12,15], our proposed framework jointly considered rate adaptation and chunk scheduling. An action includes an index and a quality level for next download chunk. To the best of our knowledge, our work is the first study applying RL to multi-source adaptive streaming. Several previous works have applied RL to single-source adaptive streaming [7,8,10]. The work [7] applied a Q-learning method for DASH. The discrete state space includes buffer filling and bandwidth. The study [8] applied an actor-critic RL algorithm called Pensieve for rate adaptation. The work [10] has proposed a RL-based adaptation called D-DASH. The paper explores two different network architectures, *i.e.*, multilayer perceptron, and long-short term memory networks. There are some challenges when applying above RL models to multi-source streaming as mentioned in next subsection.

Challenges and Contribution: Compared to the works applying reinforcement learning to single-source adaptive streaming [8,10], there are several challenges in the research of reinforcement learning based rate adaptation for multi-source video streaming as follows.

Firstly, there are some key differences between our proposed RL model and the previous RL models applied to single-source adaptive streaming. In our proposed RL model, the state space and action space are different. In multi-source streaming, chunk scheduling is important. The paths have different network conditions; hence, which chunks should be downloaded on the paths will have an essential impact on the quality-of-experience (QoE) of users. For example, a video player is downloading a content from two sources over two network paths. With bad scheduling, the player is downloading chunk 2 on second path while chunks 1, 3, and 4 have already downloaded on the first path which has a higher throughput. Assuming that video buffer can store up to three chunks. In this situation, buffer is full, however, video freeze still happens since player waits for chunk 2. Our proposed RL integrates scheduling into the RL model by redesigning the action space and state space.

Secondly, in single-source streaming, when agent downloads a new chunk, the reward associated with that chunk which includes freezing time, quality level, and quality level switching is calculated directly. However, that reward calculation cannot be applied to multi-source streaming environment. In our proposal, the reward is estimated when player plays video chunks between two consecutive download events.

Thirdly, training in real network is impossible since RL algorithm must run thousands of episodes to train the network. As far as we know, there is not any simulation environment in the literature for multi-source streaming currently. An event-driven simulation environment for multi-source video streaming is built to train the model in this work. A 240-second video is run in less than one second in the simulation. This work is the first study applying RL to adaptive streaming from multiple sources.

The outline of the paper is as follows. Section 1 has presented the motivation and related works, Sect. 2 describes RL model applied in rate adaptation of video streaming from multiple sources. Simulation environment and results are presented in Sect. 3 and Sect. 4 concludes the work.

2   Reinforcement Learning Model

The following section presents RL model including definitions of state space, action space, reward function and RL algorithm.

2.1   Reward Function

In this work, we apply Structural Similarity Index metric (SSIM) to measure QoE, which is reward function in RL model as in [8,10]. Reward function associated with a chunk i is a function of quality level of chunk i, quality difference between chunk i and $i - 1$, and rebuffering time.

In single-source adaptive streaming, reward function when downloading chunk index i is given by

$$r_i = q_i - \beta\|q_i - q_{i-1}\| - \gamma\phi_i - \delta[\max(0, B_{thr} - B_{i+1})]^2,$$

in which

- q_i: utility associated with video quality level of chunk i,
- $\|q_i - q_{i-1}\|$: penalty for the difference in quality levels between two consecutive chunks,
- ϕ_i: rebuffering time (in seconds) associated with chunk i,
- $[\max(0, B_{thr}^l - B_{i+1})]^2$: an optional penalty for below-threshold buffer; this term helps to reduce the risk of rebuffering.

In single-source adaptive streaming, we calculate the rebuffering time ϕ_i associated with chunk i directly at the time downloading i by the following formula

$$\phi_i = \max(0, d_i - B_i), \tag{1}$$

where B_i is the buffer at the time downloading chunk i and d_i is the download time of chunk i. However, this calculation can not be applied in multi-source streaming scenarios since the chunks may be out-of-order delivered and the buffer may store non-consecutive chunk indices. E.g., the buffer may currently store chunk indices $3, 5, 6, 7$ while chunk 4 is still downloading on the lower-throughput path.

In a multi-source environment, reward can be estimated only when the chunk is played. Hence, the reward r_t when agent take action a_t is given by

$$r_t = \sum_i \left(q_i - \beta\|q_i - q_{i-1}\| - \delta[\max(0, B_{thr}^l - B_i)]^2\right) - \gamma\phi_t,$$

where i is the chunk played during two consecutive steps t and $t + 1$, ϕ_t is rebuffering time in the period from steps t and $t + 1$, and B_i is the buffer size when playing chunk i.

2.2 State Space

A state s of our reinforcement learning model includes the following components:

- vector of estimated network throughputs of past h video chunks on path i, $i = 1, \ldots, p$;
- vector of chunk sizes of L quality levels of next f chunks from the chunk playing;
- vector of quality levels of next f chunks from the playing chunk. Not-yet-downloaded chunks have level 0;
- current buffer size (in seconds);
- remaining time that have not yet played;
- quality level of the chunk playing;
- playing download times of past h video chunks on path i, $i = 1, \ldots, p$.

2.3   Action Space

Since chunk scheduling is integrated into the framework, action space $\mathcal{A}$ includes next f chunks from the playing chunk and their quality levels. For example, if quality levels for each chunk include *low*, *medium*, and *high* ($L = 3$), current playing chunk is #4, and next $f = 4$ chunks are feasible to request for next action, then $\mathcal{A}$ is the set of all quality levels of four chunks from #5 to #8, i.e., {#5-*low*, #5-*medium*, ..., #8-*low*, #8-*medium*, #8-*high*}. The size of $\mathcal{A}$ is $3 \times 4 = 12$. Assume that at step t, agent takes action $a_t = 8$. It means that the agent will download chunk index $\lceil a_t/L \rceil + 4 = \lceil 8/3 \rceil + 4 = 7$ with quality level $a_t \bmod L = 8 \bmod 3 = 2$, which is *medium* quality level (see Fig. 1). Note that with this action space, we allow the possibility of re-request a chunk index to improve the reward.

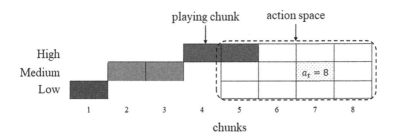

Fig. 1. A example of action space with $L = 3$ and $f = 4$.

2.4   RL-Based Adaptation for Multi-source Video Streaming (RAMS)

Deep Q-learning (DQN) is an algorithm in RL that is widely applied in many applications [9]. In DQN, action-value function is approximated to function $\hat{q}(s_t, a_t; w)$ by using a training network with weights w. Differ from standard Q-learning, DQN uses an additional target network with parameters w_{tar} fixing the target in C steps to improve stability of training. Moreover, a fixed-size experience replay memory $\mathcal{D}$ storing past (s, a, r, s') transitions is maintained to increase data efficiency. Stochastic gradient descent update is performed each step over a mini-batch taken randomly from $\mathcal{D}$.

The loss function is defined as follows

$$J(w) = \mathbb{E}[(y_t - \hat{q}(s_t, a_t; w))], \tag{2}$$

where $y_t = r_t + \gamma \max_{a'} \hat{q}(s_{t+1}, a'; w_{tar})$. Parameter γ is *discount factor*. Target y_t is generated by target network.

Algorithm 1 describes RL based algorithm called RAMS for adaptation in multi-source video streaming. At step t, agent takes an action a_t which explores with probability ϵ and exploits with probability $1 - \epsilon$ (Algorithm 1, line 6). Value

ϵ decays after each step by a *decay factor* until a minimum value is reached. After taking action a_t, agent receives reward r_t and environment has new state s_{t+1}. Agent then appends the transition to (s_t, a_t, r_t, s_{t+1}) to experience replay $\mathcal{D}$. Experience replay $\mathcal{D}$ has a fixed size and stores D newest transitions. Every C steps, target network synchronizes its weights with training network (Algorithm 1, line 12).

Algorithm 1. Reinforcement learning based adaptation for multisource streaming (RAMS)

1: Initialize replay memory $\mathcal{D}$ with fixed capacity
2: Initialize Q-network with random weights w
3: Initialize target network with weights $w_{tar} = w$
4: **for** episode $m = 1, \ldots, M$ **do**
5:    **while** not end of episode **do**
6:       $t = t + 1$
7:       Select action $a_t = \begin{cases} \text{random action,} & \text{with probability } \epsilon \\ \arg\max_{a'} \hat{q}(s_t, a'; w), & \text{otherwise} \end{cases}$
8:       Take action a_t and observe reward r_t and new state s_{t+1}
9:       Append transition (s_t, a_t, r_t, s_{t+1}) to $\mathcal{D}$
10:      Sample uniformly a random mini-batch of N transitions (s_j, a_j, r_j, s_{j+1}) from $\mathcal{D}$
11:      Set $y_j = \begin{cases} r_j, \text{if } j \text{ is the index of last download chunk} \\ r_j + \gamma \max_{a'} \hat{q}(s_{j+1}, a'; w_{tar}), \text{otherwise} \end{cases}$
12:      Perform a stochastic gradient descent step w.r.t. loss function $J(w) = \frac{1}{N} \sum_{j=1}^{N} \left(y_j - \hat{q}(s_j, a_j; w) \right)^2$
13:      Every fixed C steps, update target network $w_{\text{tar}} = w$
14:    **end while**
15: **end for**

---

3 Simulation

3.1 Event-Driven Simulation

We build an event-driven simulation that allows a video player to download video chunks from multiple sources. In simulation, downloaded chunks are buffered in the client memory before being played. Buffer is measured by the total playing time of the wait-to-be-played chunks. When a new chunk is successfully downloaded, the buffer increases by the chunk length and when a chunk is played, the buffer is decreased by the chunk length. In DASH, video player requires an initial buffer level B_{thr}^l before starting to play. The buffer also has an upper threshold level, B_{thr}^u. If the buffer exceeds B_{thr}^u, agent will stop downloading a new chunk, wait for the buffer level decreasing below B_{thr}^u and then resumes downloading. The client *re-buffers* when client's buffer size is under a defined threshold. Video player stops playing and waits for downloading the chunk until the buffer size is over an initial threshold. Re-buffering causes video freezes and reduces the QoE of the users.

Four main events includes *download, pause, play, rebuffer*. During playing a video, the events is added to the time axis. Some additional parameters can be associated with each event such as chunk index, quality level, path index, *etc.* When finishing *download* chunk n on path i, video player will *pause* downloading a new chunk if buffer exceeds the upper buffer threshold B_{thr}^u. Otherwise, player will *download* a new chunk on path i. Next chunk index and quality level are decided by RL agent.

Player plays the chunks in order. After finish *play*-ing chunk n, player *play*-s chunk $n + 1$ if this chunk is available in the buffer. Otherwise, player will enter *rebuffer*-ing period until chunk $n + 1$ is downloaded completely. The player only plays a chunk when the chunk is completely received.

Table 1. Simulation parameters

Parameter	Notation	Value
Number of sources/paths	p	2
Maximum buffer size	B_{thr}^u	30 s
Reward:		
utility function	q_i	$\log(q_i/q_1)$
switching penalty weight	β	1
rebuffering penalty weight	γ	2.8
low-buffer penalty weight	δ	0
RL model:		
size of hidden layers		256, 128, 128
activation function		ReLu
learning rate	α	10^{-5}
random batch size	N	200
target network update period	C	25
Epsilon:	ϵ	
for training phase:		
initial value		1
minimum value		0.1
decay factor		0.9999
for testing phase		0
Number of quality levels	L	7
Number of chunks in action space	f	8
Number of previous chunks used in state space	h	6

In the simulation environment for traditional single-source streaming, the reward is calculated directly when environment takes the download action.

However, this calculation cannot be applied to multi-source streaming in which the chunks may not downloaded in order. In the proposed environment for multi-source streaming, the reward is calculated when video player plays chunks in the period between two consecutive download events. Table 1 lists hyper-parameters used in the simulations and training.

3.2   Results

Training Phase: The preprocessed real-trace bandwidth dataset from [8] is used for both training phase and testing phase. Video used in the simulation is Big Bug Bunny with 7 quality levels 300, 700, 1200, 1500, 3000, 4000, and 5000 Kbps [4]. Figure 2 shows the convergence rates of the training process. Note that with different values of decay factors the RL converges at different speeds. A larger decay value means that the agent emphasizes on exploration, hence, it yields a slower convergence, however, the average reward is higher.

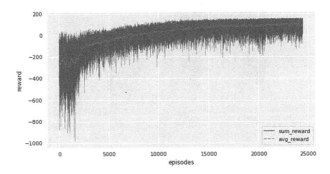

Fig. 2. Convergence of training phase.

Testing Phase: Some typical adaptation algorithms, *i.e.*, throughput-based and BOLA algorithm [11], are customized to run in a multi-source environment for the comparison. These rate adaptations are originally designed for single-source video streaming, hence, we apply *greedy scheduling*, in which chunks are in-order requested, for multi-source streaming. When the player needs to download a new chunk on a path, it will download the smallest chunk index which have not been sent the request. With throughput-based adaptation, the quality level is the maximum bitrate which does not exceed harmonic mean of experienced throughputs of past three chunks downloaded on the considered path. BOLA algorithm chooses quality level by optimizing a Lyapunov function [11]. BOLA-U version is implemented for the comparison.

We evaluate the efficiency of RAMS and compare it to throughput-based and BOLA methods in reward, utility, switching penalty and rebuffering penalty measurements. Each method is run in 100 episodes with random initial point of bandwidth trace. RAMS yields a higher reward than throughput-based and

BOLA algorithm. Figure 3 shows average reward utility, switch and rebuffering penalties of adaptation algorithms. The average utility of RAMS is around 162 whereas the one of BOLA is 141 and of throughput-based is 117. RAMS has a smaller number of switches than the other adaptations. RAMS experiences a small amount rebuffering time, which is less than 0.1 s per episode in average. We can reduce rebuffering of RAMS by increasing rebuffering penalty and low-buffer penalty weights β and δ, respectively.

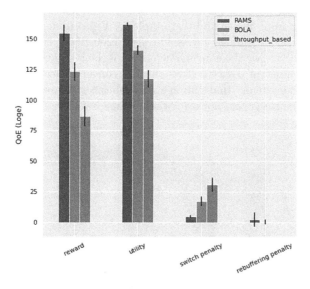

Fig. 3. Comparing RL with existing Smooth Throughput and BOLA-U by analyzing their performance on the individual components in the general QoE definition

Figure 4 shows playing quality level and buffer size of one sample episode with three adaptation methods. Although throughput-based method yields a stable buffer level, RAMS plays video at a higher quality level and lesser number of switches than BOLA and throughput-based methods.

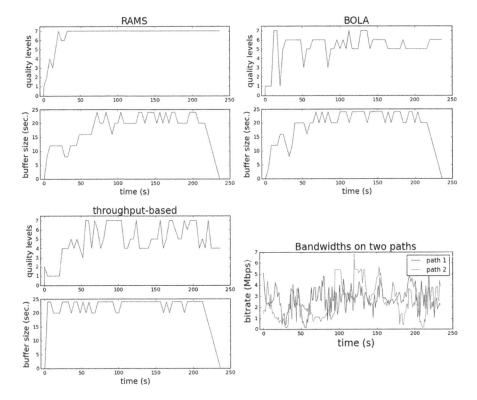

Fig. 4. Video quality level and buffer size of a sample episode with different adaptation methods.

4 Conclusions

We have proposed RAMS, a novel deep reinforcement learning-based algorithm for rate adaptation in multi-source video streaming. Chunk scheduling is integrated into the proposed framework. An event-driven simulation environment has been built to train the network and evaluate the performance of RAMS. The simulations have shown that RAMS outperforms some notable adaptation algorithms.

References

1. Cisco: Cisco Visual Networking Index: Forecast and Methodology, 2016–2021
2. Stockhammer, T.: Dynamic adaptive streaming over HTTP- standards and design principles. In: Proceedings of the Second Annual ACM Conference on Multimedia Systems, pp. 133–144 (2011)
3. Sodagar, I.: The mpeg-dash standard for multimedia streaming over the internet. IEEE Multimed. **18**(4), 62–67 (2011)

4. Lederer, S., Müller, C., & Timmerer, C.: Dynamic adaptive streaming over HTTP dataset. In: Proceedings of the 3rd Multimedia Systems Conference, pp. 89–94 (2012)
5. ISO Standard: Dynamic adaptive streaming over HTTP (DASH)-Part 1: Media presentation description and segment formats. ISO/IEC, 23009–1. (2014)
6. DASH Reference Client. https://reference.dashif.org/dash.js/. Accessed 22 June 2021
7. Claeys, M., Latré, S., Famaey, J., Wu, T., Van Leekwijck, W., De Turck, F.: Design and optimisation of a (FA) Q-learning-based HTTP adaptive streaming client. Connect. Sci. **26**(1), 25–43 (2014)
8. Mao, H., Netravali, R., Alizadeh, M.: Neural adaptive video streaming with Pensieve. In: Proceedings of the Conference of the ACM Special Interest Group on Data Communication, pp. 197–210 (2017)
9. Mnih, V., et al.: Human-level control through deep reinforcement learning. Nature **518**(7540), 529–533 (2015)
10. Gadaleta, M., Chiariotti, F., Rossi, M., Zanella, A.: D-DASH: a deep Q-learning framework for DASH video streaming. IEEE Trans. Cognitive Commun. Networking **3**(4), 703–718 (2017)
11. Spiteri, K., Urgaonkar, R., Sitaraman, R.K.: BOLA: near-optimal bitrate adaptation for online videos. IEEE/ACM Trans. Networking **28**(4), 1698–1711 (2020)
12. Nikravesh, A., Guo, Y., Zhu, X., Qian, F., Mao, Z.M.: MP-H2: a Client-only Multipath Solution for HTTP/2. In: The 25th Annual International Conference on Mobile Computing and Networking, pp. 1–16 (2019)
13. Bentaleb, A., Yadav, P.K., Ooi, W.T., Zimmermann, R.: DQ-DASH: a queuing theory approach to distributed adaptive video streaming. ACM Trans. Multimed. Comput. Commun. Appl. (TOMM) **16**(1), 1–24 (2020)
14. Yadav, P.K., Shafiei, A., Ooi, W.T.: Quetra: a queuing theory approach to dash rate adaptation. In: Proceedings of the 25th ACM International Conference on Multimedia, pp. 1130–1138 (2017)
15. Chen, Y.C., Towsley, D., Khalili, R.: MSPlayer: multi-source and multi-path video streaming. IEEE J. Sel. Areas Commun. **34**(8), 2198–2206 (2016)

Hybrid Computational Intelligence Modeling of Coseismic Landslides' Severity

Anastasios Panagiotis Psathas[1]([envelope]) [ID], Antonios Papaleonidas[1] [ID],
George Papathanassiou[1], Lazaros Iliadis[1] [ID], and Sotirios Valkaniotis[2]

[1] Department of Civil Engineering, Democritus University of Thrace, 67100 Xanthi, Greece
{anpsatha,papaleon,gpapatha,liliadis}@civil.duth.gr
[2] Koronidos str 9, 42131 Trikala, Greece

Abstract. Coseismic Landslides (COLA) are one of the most widespread and destructive hazards to result from earthquakes in mountainous environments. They are always associated with almost instantaneous slope collapse and spreading, posing significant hazards to human lives and lifeline facilities worldwide. Current methods to identify COLA immediately after an earthquake using optical imagery are too slow to effectively inform emergency response activities. Their realistic prediction is crucial for the design of key infrastructure and to protect human lives in seismically active regions. Forecasting their severity could be extremely beneficial for the effective treatment of disastrous consequences. The goal of this research is to propose a hybrid model that takes into consideration only three of the most affordable factors to acquire, the *Slope* of the active areas, the *Aspect* and the *Geological Form*. Determination of their correlation could predict the severity of COLA phenomena. The dataset used in this research, comprises of 421 records for year 2003 and 767 for 2015 from the Greek island of Lefkada. The introduced hybrid model employs *Fuzzy c-Means, Ensemble Adaptive Boosting and Ensemble Subspace k-Nearest Neighbor* algorithms. The model managed to successfully classify the *Coseismic Landslides* according to their severity. The performance was high especially for the classes of major severity.

Keywords: Forecasting landslides · Fuzzy c-Means · T-norms ·
k-Nearest-Neighbors · Ensemble Subspace k-NN · Adaptive Boosting ·
Ensemble AdaBoost

1 Introduction

Landslides occur in a variety of environments, characterized by either steep or gentle slope gradients, from mountain ranges to coastal cliffs or even underwater. Gravity is the primary driving force for a landslide to occur, but there are other factors affecting slope stability that produce specific conditions, which make a slope prone to failure. In many cases, the landslide is triggered by a specific event, such as a heavy rainfall, an earthquake, a slope cut to build a road and many others. Earthquake-induced landslides are one of the most catastrophic effects of earthquakes, as evidenced by many historic events over the past decades, especially in countries with high seismicity [1]. As a few examples,

© Springer Nature Switzerland AG 2021
N. T. Nguyen et al. (Eds.): ICCCI 2021, LNAI 12876, pp. 427–442, 2021.
https://doi.org/10.1007/978-3-030-88081-1_32

the 1994 Northridge earthquake triggered more than 11,000 landslides. In the 2008 Wenchuan earthquake in China, the Tangjiashan landslide with over 20.37 million m^3 mass movement, blocked the main river channel and formed a landslide dam, putting millions of people downstream at risk. According to Jibson et al. [18], there are cases that the consequences of landslides, triggered by an earthquake, have a massive impact in human lives and facilities. The correlation of the pattern of COLA with geological and topographical variables i.e. *lithology, slope angle* and *slope aspect* with the *volume of landslides* has been investigated by several researchers. The density of the mapped landslide concentration is normally associated with the seismic shaking magnitude. In particular, it was shown that landslide frequencies are higher in areas of highest *Peak Ground Acceleration* (PGA) and that landslide density decays with the epicentral or fault distance [2, 20, 25].

The pinpoint of the areas that are most vulnerable in Coseismic Landslides is vital in order to take actions in time and reduce the risk in those areas. Realistic prediction of COLA is crucial for the design of key infrastructure and to protect human lives in seismically active regions. Among many existing methods for landslide assessment, the Newmark sliding mass model has been extensively utilized to estimate earthquake-induced displacements in slopes, earth dams and landfills since the 1960s. As technology develops, new methods and techniques were proposed for assessing the degree of danger within an area. Such, instruments are satellite imagery and Geographic Information System technology (GIS), especially using statistical analyses of geo-environmental and seismologic factors into GIS software [29]. In particular, the characteristics of the land sliding area is statistically related to control factors such as topographic, geologic and seismic parameters e.g. *slope angle, slope aspect, curvature, lithology, PGA, seismic intensity distribution* and *distance from the seismic fault or epicenter* [27]. These correlations can provide crucial information that can be used for seismic landslide hazard analysis and planning mitigation measures for prone earthquake-induced landslides regions [6, 7, 18]. Coupling effect between topography and soil amplification, leads to complex wave propagation patterns due to scattering and diffracting of waves within the low velocity near surface layers. These ground motion effects have significant impact on COLA assessment, but only limited efforts have considered them in empirical models. There is a clear need to develop innovative numerical schemes to address the above challenges.

In existing literature, there is a lack of models that can predict the severity of Coseismic Landslides using only the slope angle, slope aspect and the geological form of a specific area. This work represents an extended version of the previous research of the authors [31]. It is very common, to use more features for the forecasting, which derive from the use of expensive equipment. Thus, it is essential for the deployment of a model, that it is not based on large financial funds and be equally effective. Being able to predict the severity of an upcoming landslide after an earthquake, it could be extremely beneficial for the effective treatment of disastrous consequences. The development of such a model, could assist risk management organizations, public agencies and stakeholders, or even governments, to apply a better distribution of the staff and financial resources to each area, for the confrontation of potential corollaries, or even develop appropriate mitigation plans, increasing the resilience of the community.

The statistical analysis of geo-environmental and seismologic factors is performed by bivariate and multivariate approaches. The purpose of this study is the recommendation of a hybrid algorithm, which could find the association of three main factors of COLA, (*slope, aspect* and *geological form*), with their severity. The proposed hybrid model uses *Fuzzy c-Means* clustering [3, 12], *Ensemble Adaptive Boosting* (ENAB) and *Ensemble Subspace k-Nearest Neighbor* (ES_k-NN) classifiers [10, 15]. The existing literature, like [23, 32] does not exploit the combination of the above algorithms. Current methods identify COLA after an earthquake, consider optical imagery. They are too slow to effectively inform emergency response activities. There is a need for a fast and flexible model to consider more affordable factors. All current approaches are using crisp values for the determination of involved features. This could lead to misclassification of COLA for values close to the borderline.

2 Area of Research

Lefkada, is a Greek island in the Ionian Sea on the west coast of Greece, connected to the mainland by a long causeway and floating bridge. Lefkada measures 35 km from north to south, and 15 km from east to west. The area of the island is about 302 km^2, the area of the municipality (including the islands Kalamos, Kastos and several smaller islets) is 333.58 km^2. The basic geological forms for the island are: a) A carbonate sequence of the Ionian zone. b) Limestone of Paxos (Apulia) zone restricted in the SW peninsula of the island. c) Few outcrops of ionian flysch (turbidites) and Miocene marls-sandstones mainly in the northern part of the island [9]. The geological Zones of "Ioanian" and "Paxos" are separated by a bountary which is located in the NW-SE direction of the region and projects onshore Southcentral Lefkada, near "Hortata" Village, in the form of a buried thrust fault by scree and late Quaternary deposits [28]. Pleistocene and especially Holocene coastal deposits are sprawling in the Nothern edge of Lefkada, where its capital is located, in the valley of "Vassiliki" and in the Coast "Nydri". Due to its location in the Ioanian sea and to its complex crustal deformation resulting from the subduction of the African Plate towards NE and to the Apulian platform continental collision further to the Northwest, Lefkada is one of the most tectonically active areas in the European continent [14, 16]. The principal active tectonic structure is 140 km long dextral strike-slip Cephalonia-Lefkada transform fault CTF [24]. It has a GPS slip-rate bracketed between 10 and 25 mm/yr. Most of the slope failure cases have been reported on the western part of the island, which owes its deep morphology to this offshore CTF and its onshore sub-parallel fault; the "Athani-Dragano" fault [9]. The latter is a NNE-SSW striking fault, forming a narrow elongated continental basin, precicely depicted in the region's morphology and indicated on satellite images and aerial photos.

There is thorough and detailed record about at least 23 events, with crucial impact on the ground of Lefkada [26]. A first conclusion drawn by the events is that earthquakes occur in pairs (twin ore cluster events) with time period of occurrence ranging between 2 months and 5 years e.g. 1612–1613 (16 months); 1625–1630 (5 years); 1722–1723 (10 months); 1767–1769 (2 years); 1783–1783 (2 months, possible aftershock); 1867–1869 (2 years); 1914–1915 (2 months); 1948–1948 (2 months). Therefore, it is of great importance to pinpoint the location of Coseismic Landslides since it will be useful in order to reduce the hazards and increase the resilience at the island.

2.1   Coseismic Landslides at the Island of Lefkada

The most recent and well examined earthquakes are those of 2003 and 2015. The penultimate earthquake caused massive slope failures at the western part of the island. The amount of the debris material that arose was remarkably larger than the one of 2015. Numerous landslides occurred on the whole island and especially in the northwestern and central area, on both natural and cut slopes, as well as, on downstream road embankment slopes. Among the most indicative rock falls with diameters up to 4m, were observed along the 6 km long road of "Tsoukalades-Agios Nikitas" which is within the epicentral area, and are accompanied by gravel, small rock and soil slides [26]. The frequent occurrence of this failures led to the closure of the road network which lasted for more than two years. The reported rock falls followed the trace of a 300 m high morphological scarp, and especially a 10–40 m high artificial slope [26].

Regarding the 2015 earthquake, the dominant geological effects were related to slope failures i.e. rock falls and slides, and shallow and deep seated landslides on both natural and cut slopes [28]. These failures were documented on the western part of the island, while the most densely concentration of these phenomena was reported on the coastal zone from "Porto Katsiki" to "Egremnoi-Gialos" beach and along the 6 km long coastal road of "Tsoukalades-Agios Nikitas" [28]. Shallow landslides and rock slides were mainly generated in areas where the clastic material covered the bedrock, and particularly in places where the rock mass was heavily jointed. Deep seated landslides were mainly documented at the area of "Egremnoi" [29]. At this area, deep seated landslides were reported, and large amount of debris material moved downslope inducing severe damages to the road network and to residential houses. The debris consists of coarse-grained size material with large diameter gravels and few boulders.

In order to investigate the earthquake-induced landslide density, event-based inventories were developed by taking into account aerial and satellite imagery in Google Earth in order to enrich and update existing landslide datasets, previously compiled for the two earthquakes [27]. Google Earth imagery of June 12, 2003 and December 19, 2005 was used for mapping 2003 earthquake landslides, and November 15, 2013 and April 15, 2016 for 2015 earthquake. Landslide activity along the western part of Lefkada is considered as minimal between major earthquakes, as observed on multi-date satellite imagery and confirmed by local residents. The short period between each satellite imagery pair (2–3 years) is believed to include only the COLA, with very few if any at all landslides triggered by other factors. In total, 301 and 596 coseismic landslides were mapped for the 2003 and 2015 earthquakes. For the extraction of morphological and terrain parameters of the compiled landslide datasets, a detailed Digital Elevation Model (DEM) with spatial resolution of 5 m was used. The 5 m DEM was obtained from Hellenic Cadastre and it was extracted from aerial imagery stereo-pairs, having a vertical accuracy of 4 m [29].

Having completed the polygon-based inventories, a statistical analysis of landslide distribution took place. In total, 596 and 301 landslides were identified covering (planar area) 1.29 km^2 and 1.6 km^2 for the 2015 and 2003 events. These planar-oriented areas are obtained as projected measurements. The minimum and maximum landslide areas were 40.4 m^2 and 42,940 m^2 for the 2015 earthquake, while for the penultimate event the relevant values were 129.8 m^2 and 98,300 m^2 [29]. The minimum and maximum landslide areas for 2015 in an area of 1.78 km², were 51.30 m² and 58.330 m². They were found by considering the DEM for the delineation of the landslide area. The values for the 2003 earthquake were 140.9 m² and 148.469 m² in an area of 2.28 km² [29].

3 Dataset Pre-processing

Five features were related to COLA, 4 of which were numeric (*Planar Area, Average Slope, Area, Average Aspect, Id*) and 1 was nominal (*Geologic Form*). Given the fact that there are several landslides with 2 or more geological forms, the Coseismic Landslides were reassigned. This resulted in 421 instances for 2003 and 767 for 2015. For both years, the features are the same. Thus, the same data preprocessing was applied for both datasets. Nonetheless, in the 2003 COLA, two additional geological forms were observed, compared to ones of 2015. The data preprocessing for these two years was done independently. This resulted in an overall evaluation of the proposed algorithm, that proves its consistency and efficiency regardless the year. For data handling, 3 steps were followed. The 1st was related to the manual processing of the *Average Slope, Average Aspect* and *Geological Forms*. The 2nd and 3rd steps were performed by developing novel code in *Matlab R2019a*.

It was observed during the experiments that there are some variations in landslides that have the same severity but appear to have quite different slopes. For this reason, the natural logarithm function *ln(x)* was applied on the values of the slopes in order to smooth out any spikes. Regarding the *average aspect*, the initial elaboration was to transform it from nominal to numeric in a scale from 1 to 8, according to Fig. 1.

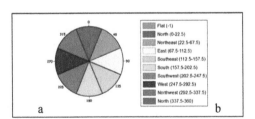

Fig. 1. Aspect and corresponding degrees

Nonetheless, it was considered more efficient to separate the landslides that have aspect 10° from the ones that have 350° (Fig. 1b). For this purpose, for each landslide the actual aspect in degrees was used.

3.1 Labeling Geological Forms

The Geological form feature was transformed to numeric, in a scale from 1 to 20 for 2003, from 1 to 18 for 2015. Table 1 presents the numeric labels for each Form.

Table 1. Geological form types for 2003 and 2015

Geological Form	al	C	Ci	Cs	Csd	E	J1	J1d	Jar	Jc
Form Label 2003	1	2	3	4	5	6	7	8	9	10
Geological Form	Jm	Js	M	Mb	Pc	Qc	Qp	Qt	Tc	Tg
Form Label 2003	11	12	13	14	15	16	17	18	19	20
Geological Form 2015	al	C	Ci	Cs	E	J1	J1d	Jar	Jc	
Form Label 2015	1	2	3	4	5	6	7	8	9	
Geological Form 2015	Jm	Js	M	Mb	Pc	Qc	Qp	Qt	Tg	
Form Label 2015	10	11	12	13	14	15	16	17	18	

al: alluvial; C, Jm, Jc, Jar, J1: limestones of Ionian; Ci, Cs: limestones of Paxos; Csd limestones; E: limestones Eocene; Js: limestone of Paxos; J1d: dolomites; M, Mb: Miocene sandstones; Pc: Pliocene conglomerate; Qc, Qp, Qt: Quaternary sediments; Tc: limestones and dolomites of Triassic; Tg:evaporites.

3.2 Fuzzy C-Means Clustering of Landslides

After applying a statistical analysis of the datasets, it was pinpointed that some values of the *area* and the *planar area*, had high standard deviation and a non-representative mean value. FCM is the fuzzy equivalent of the "hard" clustering algorithm. It has been employed, due to the fact that it allows an individual to be partially classified into more than one cluster, with different degrees of membership. It was performed on the features *Area* and P*lanar Area*, to provide the labels required for the development of the hybrid machine learning model [3, 4, 12]. The process of fuzzy partitioning is performed through a repetitive optimization of the objective function 1 with the update of membership u_{ij} and the cluster centers c_j (function 2):

$$J_m = \sum_{i=1}^{N}\sum_{j=1}^{C} u_{ij}^m \left\| x_i - c_j \right\|^2, 1 \le m < \infty \tag{1}$$

$$u_{ij} = \frac{1}{\sum_{k=1}^{C}\left(\frac{\|x_i - c_j\|}{\|x_i - c_k\|}\right)^{\frac{2}{m-1}}}, \quad c_j = \frac{\sum_{i=1}^{N} u_{ij}^m \cdot x_i}{\sum_{i=1}^{N} u_{ij}^m} \tag{2}$$

where m is the fuzzifier (determining the level of cluster fuzziness), u_{ij} is the degree of membership of x_i in the cluster j, x_i is the ith of d-dimensional measured data, c_j is the d-dimension center of the cluster, $\|*\|$ is any norm expressing the similarity between any measured data and the center. The final condition for stopping the iterations is when $\max_{ij}\left\{\left|u_{ij}^{(k+1)} - u_{ij}^k\right|\right\} < \varepsilon$, where ε is a termination criterion between 0 and 1, and k indicates the iteration steps [21, 22].

This paragraph presents the hyperparameters and their values. The corresponding membership degrees u_{ij} for large m values are small, which implies clusters with smaller bounties. The *maxIterations* (assigned the default value 100) is the maximum number of optimization iterations and *minImprovement* (assigned the default value 0.00001) is the minimum improvement in the Objective function (OBJ) per iteration. The value of m was chosen (after trial and error) to be equal to 2.

The developed *FCM.m script* in Maltab, transfers the content of the data files into Matlab Tables for further processing and applies the FCM. The FCM.m script creates the clusters of the COLA according to their severity and assigns the labels. The number of clusters was chosen to be 6. The *Linguistic* of the respective clusters is a combination of the 3 potential states (*Low Medium, High*) of the Planar area and Area (Tables 2 and 3).

Table 2. Clusters with their corresponding labels (*planar area, area*)

Cluster#	1	2	3	4	5	6
Linguistic	Low, Low	Low, Medium	Medium, Medium	Medium, High	High, High	Extreme, Extreme

Table 3. Respective landslides for each cluster for 2003 and 2015

Clusters	1	2	3	4	5	6	Total Instances
2015	448	183	74	35	22	5	767
2003	238	100	44	27	7	5	421

The *FCM.m* script is presented in the form of natural language, in Algorithm 1.

Algorithm 1. *The FCM.m Matlab script*

Inputs: *421 incidents of 2003 and 767 incidents of 2015 exported from *.xlsx files.*
Step 1: *Read and convert each *.xlsx file to a Matlab table.*
Step 2: *For each Table the column Id was used to retrieve distinct Landslides.2 new tables constructed*
Step 3: *For each new table Planar Area and Area column is chosen*
Step 4: *FCM algorithm is applied. Centers of clusters and MEVs of each observation are calculated.*
Step 5: *Each instance is classified in the cluster on which the MEV is the highest.*
Step 6: *Clusters pass to the original data. Clusters are plotted in Figss 2a and 2b*

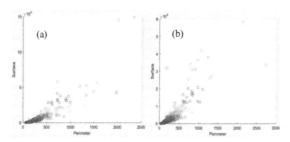

Fig. 2. Clusters for original data for 2003 (2a) and 2015 (2b) respectively.

3.3   Fuzzy Clustering with FCM Algorithm and T-Norm

Some instances had similar membership values (MEV) for two clusters, thus the need to create new clusters has proved imperative. Landslides with MEV (to their dominant class) below a certain threshold, were re-sorted. Thus, each factor was assigned a weight [5, 33] based on Eq. (3) that implements a fuzzy conjunction $f(\mu_i, w_i)$ between many fuzzy sets. Each MEV μ_i is assigned a weight w_i.

$$\mu_S(x_i) = Agg(f(\mu_A(x_i), w_1), f(\mu_A(x_i), w_2), \ldots, f(\mu_A(x_i), w_n)) \qquad (3)$$

$i = 1, 2, \ldots, k$. Function f is defined as follows: $f(a, w) = a^{\frac{1}{w}}$, a is the MEV [13, 33]. The *Hamacher T-N*orm was used as an Aggregation function.

$$A \cap B = \frac{\mu_A(x) + \mu_B(x) - 2\mu_A(x)\mu_B(x)}{[1 - \mu_A(x) + \mu_B(x)]} \qquad (4)$$

The script T-*Norm_Clustering.m* was deployed in Matlab, to apply the FCM with the Hammacher fuzzy conjunction. It is presented in natural language form in Algorithm 2.

Algorithm 2. The T-Norm_Clustering.m Matlab Script

Inputs: *All membership degrees of each observation for 2003 and 2015.*
Part 1: Step 1: *Threshold is defined at 0.7*
Step 2: *Weights definition. The weight of the highest MEV is 4, for the 2nd highest is 2, and 0 for the rest*
Part 2: Step 1: *If a MEV to a cluster is higher than 0.7 the incident belongs to this cluster.*
Step 2: *If a MEV is under 0.7 the incident belongs to a new cluster for which the MEV is calculated by Eq. (3), (4) and (5).*

The *T-Norm_Clustering.m* script developed new clusters between the already existing ones, for both 2003 and 2015. Four new clusters were created for 2003 and 5 for 2015. If a cluster was created between clusters 4 and 5, then its name would be 4.5. The result of clustering with FCM and *Hammacher* is presented in Fig. 3a and b. The T-Norm optimized the classification of each instance according to its severity. Table 4, presents the exact number of instances that correspond to each cluster.

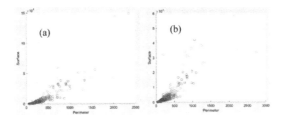

Fig. 3. Clusters for original data for 2003 (3a) and 2015 (3b) after applying T-Norm

Table 4. Total landslides of each cluster for 2003 and 2015 after T-Norm

Clusters	1	1.5	2	2.5	3	3.5	4	4.5	5	5.5	6	Total Instances
2015	417	52	145	27	56	25	18	7	15	2	3	767
2003	222	27	84	9	37	5	22	4	6	0	5	421

4 Classification Methodology

Following the clustering of *Coseismic Landslides* using the features *"planar area" and "area"*, a classification based on 3 factors was performed. The three independent variables used for the classification are *Average Slope, Average Aspect* and *Geological Form* of landslides, which was labeled as indicated in Table 1. The cluster obtained by the FCM with *Hammacher Aggregation*, is the target variable.

A total of 25 classification algorithms were employed: *Fine Tree, Medium Tree, Coarse Tree, Linear Discriminant, Quadratic Discriminant, Linear SVM, Quadratic SVM, Cubic SVM, Fine Gaussian SVM, Medium Gaussian SVM, Coarse Gaussian SVM, Cosine KNN, Coarse KNN, Cubic KNN, Weighted KNN, Fine KNN, Medium KNN, Gaussian Naive Bayes, Kernel Naïve Bayes, Boosted Trees, Bagged Trees, Subspace Discriminant, Subspace KNN, RUSBoost Trees, Ensemble Adaptive Boosting*. The one with the highest performance was the *Ensemble Adaptive Boosting Algorithm (AdaBoost)*. AdaBoost, has proved to be very efficient for all classes except the first three (clusters 1, 1.5, and 2). Thus, if an observation was classified in the first 3 clusters, another algorithm was applied in order to classify it more accurately. The best algorithm for this approach, was the *Ensemble Subspace k-NN* (Fig. 4).

4.1 Ensemble AdaBoost

It makes predictions based on a number of different models. By combining individual models, it tends to be less biased and less data sensitive. *Ensemble AdaBoost* works especially well with decision trees. It is the most popular boosting technique, developed for classification. It learns from previous mistakes, e.g. misclassification data points, by increasing their weights. The learner with higher weight has more influence on the final decision.

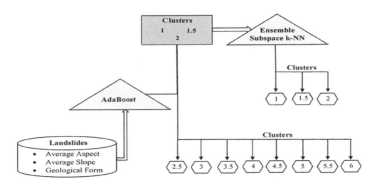

Fig. 4. The hybrid classification model

4.2 Ensemble Subspace k- Nearest-Neighbors (Ensemble Subspace k-NN)

The k-nearest neighbors (k-NN) is a lazy and non-parametric Learning algorithm [8].

It is a traditional classification rule, which assigns the label of a test sample with the majority label of its k nearest neighbors, from the training set. Given a set X of n points and a distance function, k-NN search finds the k closest points to a query point or a set of them [17]. Dunami [11] first introduced a weighted voting method, called the *distance-weighted (DW) k-nearest neighbor rule* (Wk-NN). In this approach, the closer one neighbor is, the greater the weight that corresponds to it, using the DW function.

The neighbor farthest from all the others corresponds to a weight of 0, while the one closest to the observation corresponds to a weight of 1. All neighbors in the middle area get corresponding values between 0 and 1. The most common and most consistent ensemble method for k-NN is the *Ensemble Subspace k-NN* and related works using this algorithm can be found in [10, 15, 17]. Tuning of the hyperparameters was done based on a combination of *10-fold Cross Validation* and *Grid Search*. According to the literature, this combination is one of the most widely strategies used in machine learning.

This was a multiclass classification case, so the *"One Versus All"* Strategy [19, 30] was used for the evaluation. Table 5 shows the 5 performance indices that were used.

Table 5. Indices used for the evaluation of the multi-class classification

Index	Abbreviation	Calculation
Sensitivity (also known as true positive rate or recall)	SNS	$SNS = TP/(TP + FN)$
Specificity, (also known as true negative rate)	SPC	$SPC = TN/(TN + FP)$
Accuracy	ACC	$ACC = (TP + TN)/(TP + FP + FN + TN)$
F1 score	F1	$F1 = 2*TP/(2*TP + FP + FN)$

5 Experimental Results

The experiments were performed in Matlab R2019a. The initial range of the AdaBoost hyperparameters is the following: *Maximum number of splits* (MNS) takes values in the interval [10, 500], whereas the range interval of the parameter *Number of learners* (NLE) is [1,800] and the respective one for the *Learning Rate* (LR) is [0.001, 1]. The optimal hyperparameters values found were 175, 88, 1, 10, for the MNS, NLE and LR and the *number of Grid Divisions* respectively. The *Learner Type* was a *"Decision Tree"* and the Optimizer employed was *Grid Search*. The *Ensemble AdaBoost* achieved an accuracy of 64% and 68% for 2003 and 2015. The following Tables 6 and 7 are the confusion matrices of the above optimal algorithm for 2015 and 2003, whereas Fig. 5a and b are the ROC curves for the respective years. Tables 8 and 9 present the values of all the performance indices for AdaBoost.

It is obvious that AdaBoost successfully classifies all the landslides that belong to $Cl_{2.5}$ and above. This this significant, as the algorithm can indicate with high accuracy, COLA that would be the most disastrous. Prediction of the first 3 clusters, requires more attention.

Table 6. Confusion Matrix for the Ensemble AdaBoost for 2015

	Class	Cl_1	$Cl_{1.5}$	Cl_2	$Cl_{2.5}$	Cl_3	$Cl_{3.5}$	Cl_4	$Cl_{4.5}$	Cl_5	$Cl_{5.5}$	Cl_6
					Predicted Class							
	Cl_1	300	42	75	0	0	0	0	0	0	0	0
	$Cl_{1.5}$	21	20	10	0	0	1	0	0	0	0	0
	Cl_2	51	9	72	2	9	0	0	0	2	0	0
True Class	$Cl_{2.5}$	1	1	6	18	1	0	0	0	0	0	0
	Cl_3	1	0	8	0	45	1	1	0	0	0	0
	$Cl_{3.5}$	1	0	1	0	0	22	0	0	0	0	0
	Cl_4	0	0	0	0	0	0	18	0	0	0	0
	$Cl_{4.5}$	0	0	0	0	0	0	0	7	0	0	0
	Cl_5	0	0	0	0	0	0	0	0	15	0	0
	$Cl_{5.5}$	0	0	0	0	0	0	0	0	0	2	0
	Cl_6	0	0	0	0	0	0	0	0	0	0	3

The *Ensemble k-NN* was employed. Tuning of hyperparameters was applied with the combination of *10-fold cross validation* and *grid search*. The initial range for the hyperparameters of the Ensemble k-NN are: *Maximum number of splits* takes values in [10, 500], the parameter *Number of learners* in [1,800] the *Learning Rate* in [0.001, 1] and *Subspace Dimension* takes values in [2, 10]. The optimal hyperparameters values found were 20, 30, 0.1, 3, 10, for the MNS, NLE, LR, *Subspace Dimension* and the *number of Grid Divisions* respectively. The *Distance Metric* was a *"Euclidean"* and the Optimizer employed was *Grid Search*. The Ensemble Subspace k-NN achieved an accuracy equal to 70.07% and 72.88% for 2003 and 2015. The Confusion Matrix for each year is presented in Tables 10 and 11 and the corresponding ROC Curves in Fig. 6a and b.

Table 7. Confusion matrix for the Ensemble AdaBoost for 2003

	Predicted Class									
Class	**Cl₁**	**Cl₁.₅**	**Cl₂**	**Cl₂.₅**	**Cl₃**	**Cl₃.₅**	**Cl₄**	**Cl₄.₅**	**Cl₅**	**Cl₆**
Cl₁	151	40	27	4	1	0	0	0	0	0
Cl₁.₅	10	7	7	1	1	1	0	0	0	0
Cl₂	32	11	28	7	2	3	0	0	0	0
Cl₂.₅	0	1	1	7	0	0	0	0	0	0
Cl₃	0	1	0	0	32	0	2	1	1	0
Cl₃.₅	0	0	0	0	0	5	0	0	0	0
Cl₄	0	0	0	0	0	0	22	0	0	0
Cl₄.₅	0	0	0	0	0	0	0	4	0	0
Cl₅	0	0	0	0	0	0	0	0	6	0
Cl₆	0	0	0	0	0	0	0	0	0	5

(True Class is indicated along the left side of the table.)

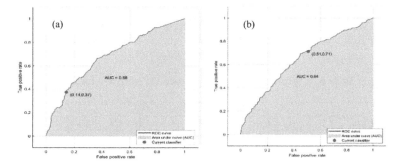

Fig. 5. ROC Curves for 2015 (5a) and 2003 (5b)

Table 8. Classification performance indices for the Ensemble AdaBoost (2015)

Index	Cl₁	Cl₁.₅	Cl₂	Cl₂.₅	Cl₃	Cl₃.₅	Cl₄	Cl₄.₅	Cl₅	Cl₆	Cl₆
SNS	0.71	0.38	0.49	0.66	0.80	0.91	1	1	1	1	1
SPC	0.74	0.90	0.81	0.99	0.97	0.99	0.99	1	0.99	1	1
ACC	0.73	0.86	0.75	0.97	0.96	0.99	0.99	1	0.99	1	1
PREC	0.80	0.27	0.41	0.90	0.81	0.91	0.94	1	0.88	1	1
F1	0.75	0.32	0.45	0.76	0.81	0.91	0.97	1	0.93	1	1

Table 9. Classification performance indices for the Ensemble AdaBoost (2003)

Index	Cl₁	Cl₁.₅	Cl₂	Cl₂.₅	Cl₃	Cl₃.₅	Cl₄	Cl₄.₅	Cl₅	Cl₆
SNS	0.67	0.25	0.33	0.77	0.86	1	1	1	1	1
SPC	0.73	0.83	0.87	0.95	0.98	0.98	0.99	0.99	0.99	1
ACC	0.70	0.78	0.74	0.95	0.96	0.98	0.99	0.99	0.99	1
PREC	0.789	0.11	0.44	0.36	0.88	0.55	0.91	0.80	0.85	1
F1	0.72	0.16	0.38	0.50	0.87	0.71	0.95	0.88	0.92	1

Table 10. Confusion matrix for ensemble subspace k-NN algorithm for 2015

	Predicted Class											
True Class	Class	Cl_{1}	$Cl_{1.5}$	Cl_{2}	$Cl_{2.5}$	Cl_{3}	$Cl_{3.5}$	Cl_{4}	$Cl_{4.5}$	Cl_{5}	$Cl_{5.5}$	Cl_{6}
	Cl_{1}	326	26	65	0	0	0	0	0	0	0	0
	$Cl_{1.5}$	21	21	9	0	0	1	0	0	0	0	0
	Cl_{2}	46	4	82	2	9	0	0	0	2	0	0
	$Cl_{2.5}$	1	1	6	18	1	0	0	0	0	0	0
	Cl_{3}	1	0	8	0	45	1	1	0	0	0	0
	$Cl_{3.5}$	1	0	1	0	0	22	0	0	0	0	0
	Cl_{4}	0	0	0	0	0	0	18	0	0	0	0
	$Cl_{4.5}$	0	0	0	0	0	0	0	7	0	0	0
	Cl_{5}	0	0	0	0	0	0	0	0	15	0	0
	$Cl_{5.5}$	0	0	0	0	0	0	0	0	0	2	0
	Cl_{6}	0	0	0	0	0	0	0	0	0	0	3

Table 11. Confusion matrix for ensemble subspace k-NN algorithm for 2003

	Predicted Class										
True Class	Class	Cl_{1}	$Cl_{1.5}$	Cl_{2}	$Cl_{2.5}$	Cl_{3}	$Cl_{3.5}$	Cl_{4}	$Cl_{4.5}$	Cl_{5}	Cl_{6}
	Cl_{1}	161	36	21	4	1	0	0	0	0	0
	$Cl_{1.5}$	7	12	5	1	1	1	0	0	0	0
	Cl_{2}	28	6	38	7	2	3	0	0	0	0
	$Cl_{2.5}$	0	1	1	7	0	0	0	0	0	0
	Cl_{3}	0	1	0	0	32	0	2	1	1	0
	$Cl_{3.5}$	0	0	0	0	0	5	0	0	0	0
	Cl_{4}	0	0	0	0	0	0	22	0	0	0
	$Cl_{4.5}$	0	0	0	0	0	0	0	4	0	0
	Cl_{5}	0	0	0	0	0	0	0	0	6	0
	Cl_{6}	0	0	0	0	0	0	0	0	0	5

Tables 12 and 13, present the values of the performance indices for the above optimal algorithm. After applying and the Ensemble k-NN algorithm, a significant increase of overall accuracy and indexes was observed. The accuracy was 70% and 72% for 2003 and 2015 respectively.

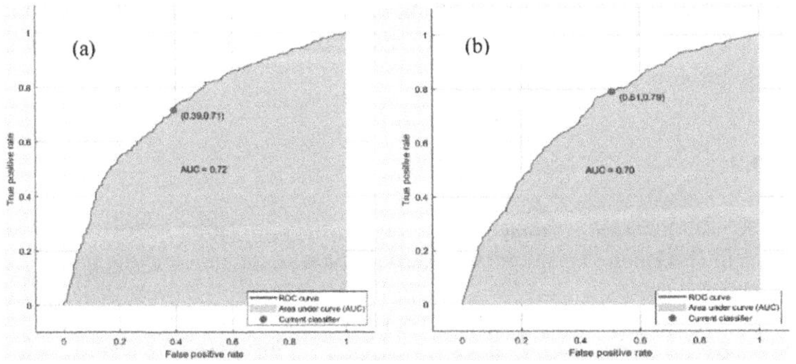

Fig. 6. ROC curve for ensemble subspace k-NN for 2015 (6a) and for 2003 (6b)

Table 12. Classification performance indices of ensemble subspace k-NN (2015)

Index	Cl_1	$Cl_{1.5}$	Cl_2	$Cl_{2.5}$	Cl_3	$Cl_{3.5}$	Cl_4	$Cl_{4.5}$	Cl_5	Cl_6	Cl_6
SNS	0.78	0.40	0.56	0.66	0.80	0.91	1	1	1	1	1
SPC	0.76	0.94	0.84	0.99	0.98	0.99	0.99	1	0.99	1	1
ACC	0.77	0.90	0.78	0.98	0.96	0.99	0.99	1	0.99	1	1
PREC	0.82	0.40	0.47	0.90	0.81	0.91	0.94	1	0.88	1	1
F1	0.80	0.40	0.51	0.76	0.81	0.91	0.97	1	0.93	1	1

Table 13. Classification performance indices of Ensemble Subspace k-NN (2003)

Index	Cl_1	$Cl_{1.5}$	Cl_2	$Cl_{2.5}$	Cl_3	$Cl_{3.5}$	Cl_4	$Cl_{4.5}$	Cl_5	Cl_6
SNS	0.724	0.44	0.45	0.77	0.86	1	1	1	1	1
SPC	0.78	0.86	0.90	0.95	0.98	0.98	0.99	0.99	0.99	1
ACC	0.75	0.83	0.80	0.95	0.97	0.98	0.99	0.99	0.99	1
PREC	0.821	0.21	0.58	0.36	0.88	0.55	0.91	0.80	0.85	1
F1	0.763	0.28	0.51	0.50	0.87	0.71	0.95	0.88	0.92	1

6   Discussion and Conclusion

At first glance, the efficiency of the model is high but not optimal. We must consider that this modeling effort has achieved to effectively classify the severity of the complicated *Coseismic Landslides* phenomenon, using only 3 independent variables. From this point of view, the performance is reliable, and it has a certain level of novelty, as to the best of our knowledge, there does not exist another approach with similar accuracy in the literature. It is a pioneer research, employing state of the art Hybrid Machine Learning algorithms in Geomechanics. Indices, especially the accuracy and F1 score, indicate a very flexible model that can predict the most severe landslides and can handle the landslides that are not so dangerous. The results of 2003 and 2015 are similar, which means that the algorithm is consistent and that it can generalize (not case dependent). The performance of the algorithm for 2015 is better, because of the more contemporary equipment used for the extraction of features. This research addresses one of the most crucial natural hazards. It is of essential importance to urban planning and to the functioning of societies. Future research will focus on predicting the timeframe and the area of a landslide after an earthquake.

References

1. Ayalew, L., Kasahara, M., Yamagishi, H.: The spatial correlation between earthquakes and landslides in Hokkaido (Japan), a GIS-based analysis of the past and the future. Landslides **8**, 443–448 (2011)
2. Barlow, J., Barisin, I., Rosser, N., Petley, D., Densmore, A., Wrigth, T.: Seismically-induced mass movements and volumetric fluxes resulting from the 2010 Mw=7.2 earthquake in the Sierra Cucapah, Mexico. Geomorphology **230**, 138–145 (2015)

3. Bezdek, J.C.: Pattern Recognition with Fuzzy Objective Function Algorithms. Springer Science & Business Media (2013)
4. Bora, D.J., Gupta, D., Kumar, A.: A comparative study between fuzzy clustering algorithm and hard clustering algorithm. arXiv preprint arXiv:1404.6059 (2014)
5. Calvo, T., Mayor, G., Mesiar, R. (eds.): Aggregation Operators: New Trends and Applications, vol. 97. Physica (2012)
6. Chang, K.T., Chiang, S.H., Hsu, M.L.: Modeling typhoon- and earthquake induced landslides in a mountainous watershed using logistic regression. Geomorphology **89**(3–4), 335–347 (2006)
7. Collins, B.D., Kayen, R., Tanaka, Y.: Spatial distribution of landslides triggered from the 2007 Niigata Chuetsu-Oki Japan Earthquake. Eng. Geol. **127**, 14–26 (2012)
8. Cover, T., Hart, P.: Nearest neighbor pattern classification. IEEE Trans. Inf. Theory **13**(1), 21–27 (1967)
9. Cushing, M.: Evoluation structurale de la marge nord-ouest hellenique dans l'ile de Lefkada et ses environs (Greece nord-occidentale). Ph.D. Thesis. Univ. de Paris-Sud (XI). Centre d'Orsay, France (1985)
10. Domeniconi, C., Yan, B.: Nearest neighbor ensemble. In: Proceedings of the 17th International Conference on Pattern Recognition, 2004. ICPR 2004, vol. 1, pp. 228–231. IEEE (August 2004)
11. Dudani, S.A.: The distance-weighted k-nearest neighbor rule. IEEE Trans. Syst. Man Cybern. **8**(4), 311–313 (1978)
12. Dunn, J.C.: A fuzzy relative of the ISODATA process and its use in detecting compact well-separated clusters. J. Cybern. **3**(3), 32–57 (1973). https://doi.org/10.1080/0196972730 8546046
13. Fan, Z.P., Ma, J., Zhang, Q.: An approach to multiple attribute decision making based on fuzzy preference information on alternatives. Fuzzy Sets Syst. **131**(1), 101–106 (2002)
14. Ath, G., et al.: GPS-derived estimates of crustal deformation in the central and north Ionian Sea, Greece: 3-yr results from NOANET continuous network data. J. Geod. **6**, 62–71 (2013)
15. Grabowski, S.: Voting over multiple k-nn classifiers. In: Modern Problems of Radio Engineering, Telecommunications and Computer Science (IEEE Cat. No. 02EX542), pp. 223–225. IEEE (February 2002)
16. Hatzfeld, D., et al.: Microseismicity and strain pattern in northwestern Greece. Tectonics **14**(4), 773–785 (1995)
17. Hechenbichler, K., Schliep, K.: Weighted k-nearest-neighbor techniques and ordinal classification (2004)
18. Jibson, R.W., Harp, E.L., Michael, J.A.: A method for producing digital probabilistic seismic landslide hazard maps. Eng. Geol. **58**, 271–289 (2000)
19. Joutsijoki, H., Juhola, M.: Comparing the one-vs-one and one-vs-all methods in benthic macroinvertebrate image classification. In: Perner, P. (ed.) Machine Learning and Data Mining in Pattern Recognition, pp. 399–413. Springer Berlin Heidelberg, Berlin, Heidelberg (2011). https://doi.org/10.1007/978-3-642-23199-5_30
20. Keefer, D.K.: Landslides caused by earthquakes. Geol. Soc. Am. Bull. **95**(4), 406–421 (1984)
21. Khalilia, M.A., Bezdek, J., Popescu, M., Keller, J.M.: Improvements to the relational fuzzy c-means clustering algorithm. Pattern Recogn. **47**(12), 3920–3930 (2014)
22. Khalilia, M., Popescu, M.: Fuzzy relational self-organizing maps. In: 2012 IEEE International Conference on Fuzzy Systems, pp. 1–6. IEEE (June 2012)
23. Kritikos, T., Robinson, T.R., Davies, T.R.: Regional coseismic landslide hazard assessment without historical landslide inventories: A new approach. J. Geophys. Res. Earth Surf. **120**(4), 711–729 (2015)
24. Louvari, E, Kiratzi, AA, Papazachos, B.C.: The CTF and its extension to western Lefkada Island. Tectonophysics **308**, 223–236 (1999)

25. Meunier, P., Hovius, N., Haines, A.J.: Regional patterns of earthquake-triggered landslides and their relation to ground motion. Geophys. Res. Lett. **34**(20), L20408 (2007)
26. Papathanassiou, G., Pavlides, S., Ganas, A.: The 2003 Lefkada earthquake: field observation and preliminary microzonation map based on liquefaction potential index for the town of Lefkada. Eng. Geol. **82**, 12–31 (2005)
27. Papathanassiou, G., Valkaniotis, S., Ganas, A., Pavlides, S.: GIS-based statistical analysis of the spatial distribution of earthquake-induced landslides in the island of Lefkada, Ionian Islands, Greece. Landslides **10**(6), 771–783 (2012). https://doi.org/10.1007/s10346-012-0357-1
28. Papathanassiou, G., Valkaniotis, S., Ath, G., Grendas, N., El, K.: The November 17th, 2015 Lefkada (Greece) strike-slip earthquake: field mapping of generated failures and assessment of macroseismic intensity ESI-07. Eng. Geol. **220**, 13–30 (2017)
29. Papathanassiou, G., Valkaniotis, S., Ganas, A.: Spatial patterns, controlling factors and characteristics of landslides triggered by strike-slip faulting earthquakes; case study of Lefkada island, Greece. Bull. Eng. Geol. Environ., submitted (2020)
30. Psathas, A., Papaleonidas, A., Iliadis, L.: Machine Learning Modeling of Human Activity Using PPG Signals. In: Nguyen, N.T., Hoang, B.H., Huynh, C.P., Hwang, D., Trawiński, B., Vossen, G. (eds.) Computational Collective Intelligence: 12th International Conference, ICCCI 2020, Da Nang, Vietnam, November 30 – December 3, 2020, Proceedings, pp. 543–557. Springer International Publishing, Cham (2020). https://doi.org/10.1007/978-3-030-63007-2_42
31. Psathas, A., Papaleonidas, A., Papathanassiou, G., Valkaniotis, S., Iliadis, L.: Classification of Coseismic Landslides Using Fuzzy and Machine Learning Techniques. In: Iliadis, L., Angelov, P.P., Jayne, C., Pimenidis, E. (eds.) Proceedings of the 21st EANN (Engineering Applications of Neural Networks) 2020 Conference: Proceedings of the EANN 2020, pp. 15–31. Springer International Publishing, Cham (2020). https://doi.org/10.1007/978-3-030-48791-1_2
32. Robinson, T.R., et al.: Rapid post-earthquake modelling of coseismic landslide magnitude and distribution for emergency response decision support. Nat. Hazards Earth Syst. Sci. Discuss. **17**, 1521–1540 (2017)
33. Wei, G., Lu, M.A.O.: Dual hesitant Pythagorean fuzzy Hamacher aggregation operators in multiple attribute decision making. Arch. Control Sci. **27**(3), 365–395 (2017)

Developing a Prescription Recognition System Based on CRAFT and Tesseract

Trong-Triet Nguyen[1,2]([⊠]) [ID], Dat-Vu Vuong Nguyen[1,2] [ID], and Thanh Le[1,2] [ID]

[1] Faculty of Information Technology, University of Science,
Ho Chi Minh City, Vietnam
lnthanh@fit.hcmus.edu.vn
[2] Vietnam National University, Ho Chi Minh City, Vietnam

Abstract. Optical Character Recognition (OCR) plays an essential role in nowadays life, which contributes to solving problems in terms of timing and accuracy of documents. The use of OCR in the health sector can help solve problems of drug handling or inventorying in drug banks to prevent unnecessary risks. However, if you apply existing OCR methods such as Tesseract or EasyOCR, it will be challenging to find out the name of the medicine or the medicine ingredient in a prescription. In this paper, we propose a system to help find the medicine names from the prescription image. We then provide users with information on the identified medicine names. Methods are built by combining and transforming many existing identity models. In addition, we have successfully developed an application running on the Android platform to get feedback on improving the system and want to help them get more information about the drugs they are using. Experimental results show that the model recognizes drug names quite well on a given database, even with medium resolution photos.

Keywords: OCR · Medicine · Prescription recognition.

1 Introduction

A prescription is a document that prescribes a doctor's medication to a patient. As the legal basis for medicine use indications, medicine sales, and prescription medicine dispensing. Works about prescription are critical, especially in obtaining drug information. The patient often carries the prescription, the doctor has printed out medicine store to buy medicine or is the seller looking for details of the drug through the prescription. The processes of checking medicine names by computer are not widespread, and this is still done manually by pharmacists entering the names of drugs on the system to fit. If the number of prescriptions is large, it will take a lot of time to manually import each medicine or more human resources to speed up the progress. In addition, when checking medications manually can lead to high errors and there is a risk that the wrong name of the medicine can be dangerous to the patient.

© Springer Nature Switzerland AG 2021
N. T. Nguyen et al. (Eds.): ICCCI 2021, LNAI 12876, pp. 443–455, 2021.
https://doi.org/10.1007/978-3-030-88081-1_33

Another essential meaning is that if the user does not have medical knowledge when looking at the prescription, he or she will not know the name of the medicine, what is the ingredient. Because many medicines have the same ingredients, but their names may not overlap and have different effects depending on the human disease. From these needs, we decided to research a solution for retrieving medicine information through ordinary prescription pictures. After that, the medicine name can be extracted and then compared with the drug bank of the health department to give the most accurate medicine name. This work can help patients learn the medicines they use and help pharmacists get medical information and check with the system in the store.

The rest of the paper is organized as follows. Part 2 will talk about the architecture of the prescription recognition system. We also list some of the current identification methods, outline their strengths and weaknesses, and find a solution to solve the problem's prescription identification system. The following section delves into the foundations of the main algorithms used in our identity system. In part 4, we will talk about the drug name dictionary we use to improve the accuracy of identified medicine names. Next is the empirical proof of our research. The final section summarizes the key points of the paper and our approach to the future.

2   Related Work

Currently, there are not many studies on the identification of medicine in prescriptions. So our team will turn the prescription recognition problem into a fundamental OCR problem and then research and develop the basic OCR system into a drug name recognition system. Currently, any OCR systems follow these steps Fig. 1.

Fig. 1. Standard OCR systems

Image processing is a method to manipulate an image to get an enhanced image or extract some useful information from that image. This method is processed through the following steps:

1. Removes noise from images
2. Remove complex backgrounds from images
3. Handling different conditions in the image

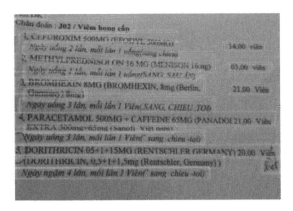

Fig. 2. Text detection using Connectionist Text Proposal Network

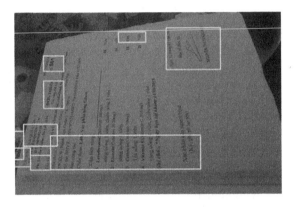

Fig. 3. CTPN on a rotated image

Text detection is the process of detecting the text contained in the image, returning results surrounding it with bounding boxes. Once we have discovered bounding boxes with text, the next step is to recognize the text. The recognition process is to scan for the symbols encountered and break them down into basic characters. In image processing, the operation of an optical character recognition model consists of two main parts: text detection and text recognition. For each part, we need to select a good model for the highest recognition process (Fig. 3).

2.1 Text Detection

Connectionist Text Proposal Network (CTPN) [6] detects a line of text in a string of text suggestions in the features map. Sequence proposals are naturally connected by a cyclic neural network, which is seamlessly incorporated into a complex network, resulting in a trainable model from start to finish. This allows CTPN [6] to discover an image's rich contextual information, making it robust

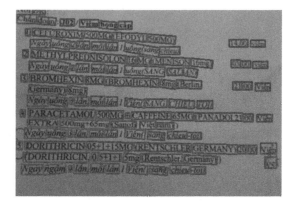

Fig. 4. Text detection using CRAFT

for detecting extremely ambiguous text. CTPN [6] works reliably on multilanguage and scaled documents without the need for extra post-processing, starting with multi-step bottom-up methods. Figure 2 shows the advantage of CTPN [6] which is it can find an entire row of text, helping the recognized text not lose its alignment. The Bounding box of CTPN [6] is quite large, facilitating the detection of Vietnamese words because Vietnamese includes diacritics.

But CTPN [7] has a big downside: with images that are not facing or tilted, CTPN does not work well.

Character-Region Awareness For Text detection(CRAFT) [5] effectively detects text areas by exploring individual character regions and relationships between characters. The limit text box is obtained by simply finding the minimum bound rectangles on the binary map after the character area threshold and preference score.

Figure 4 shows the advantage of CRAFT [5] which is its incredible accuracy, which can detect most words in text up to 98%. It has the great advantage of being invariant with rotations. For images like Fig. 5 that are not straight or skewed, this model still works very well. The common weakness of CRAFT [5] is that because it is a complex model, the detection speed is slow, bounding boxes will surround the word instead of being a row. Also, in some cases, this approach will not detect numbers.

2.2 Text Recognition

Tesseract [1] is a multi-language character recognition application that extracts text content from scans and images developed by Google. This application gives highly accurate results when recognizing black text on a white background. The prescription image is converted into a black and white image with two color channels by image processing algorithms. Then introduce the Tesseract model for identification. This model can give accurate results with pictures taken at the right angle, with good image quality. But not identifiable with tilted or reverse

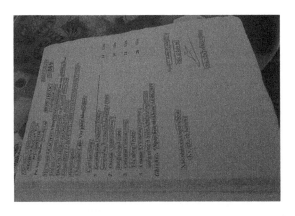

Fig. 5. CRAFT on a rotated image

images. At the same time, this approach can only extract the entire content, all the text in the image.

EasyOCR [8] is a Python package that allows computer vision developers to perform optical character recognition efficiently. The package supports more than 80 languages, including Chinese, Japanese, Korean and Thai. EasyOCR [8] was created by Jaided AI, a company specializing in optical character recognition services. This approach supports the GPU version and has good performance. With images with relative noise, It can still recognize. If the image contains languages outside of the supported languages, EasyOCR [8] does not work well.

2.3 Choosen Model

For the detection part, we will use the CRAFT [5] detection model to detect textual containers. Compared with the remaining detection algorithms, CRAFT [5] gives higher accuracy, and this model remains invariant with rotation Fig. 5. It helps to solve problems without image processing. The words on the prescription are fully and accurately discovered, so there is no need for retraining in this section to speed up producing results for the identification process. In terms of recognition, after experimenting with some cases, we used Tesseract OCR [1] recognition model to identify, and the results of Tesseract are excellent with over 90% accuracy.

3 Base Models

This section will present the architecture of the two models, CRAFT [5] and Tesseract OCR [1] , respectively, two detection and character recognition sections that we have combined with applying to the basic recognition model of the system.

3.1   Character Area Perception Model for Text Detection

Character Area Perception Model for Text Detection (CRAFT) [5] applies the architecture of a fully integrated network based on the VGG16 network as its basic framework. VGG16 is a feature extraction architecture used to encode input into a feature that represents the network. The decoding segment of a CRAFT [5] network is similar to a UNet. This model may ignore links that are supposed to be low-level aggregators of features.

CRAFT [5] predicts two types of scores for each character: 1. Region score: indicates the area of the character on the picture and will zone that character. 2. Affinity score: Relational score is a measure that indicates the association between one character and another. This number consolidates characters into a single word. From there, we will define it as separate words.

3.2   Tesseract OCR Model

The first step in Tesseract OCR [1] is the adaptive threshold, which converts the image into a binary image. The next step is to analyze the connected component, which is used to extract the character outline. This method is helpful as it performs OCR of the image with white text and black background.

The Tesseract was the first program to provide this type of handling. Then the outlines are converted to blobs. Blobs are organized into lines of text, lines, and regions parsed for some fixed area or equivalent text size. The text is divided into words using defined spaces and blurred spaces. The text recognition is then started as a double process, as shown in the figure.

On the first move, the tesseract tries to recognize each word in the text. Each qualified word is passed to the appropriate classifier as training data. The adaptive classifier tries to identify text more accurately. Since the adaptive classifier has already received some training data, what has it learned new? The final stage is used to solve various problems and extract text from images. The first thing in the prescribing institute is to detect the character container.

With the input image of a prescription, the system will start searching the information area containing characters. After being included in the CRAFT model, it will be returned with multiple bounding boxes with the prescription image. For each bounding box is one character. To identify the characters on a row that make up a string, we handled it by specifying the coordinates of the bounding box contained in the prescription. For bounding boxes of the same coordinate, we merge those bounding boxes into a row and model the Tesseract identity.

Next in the processing step is to incorporate the frames found by CRAFT into the Tesseract identity model. Perform the RGB color channel (3 channels) to GRAY (1 channel) to avoid color diversity affecting the recognition process.

4   Prescription Recognition System

With the results returned by the Tesseract, we will not know where the medicine name is and what the ingredient is because there are many

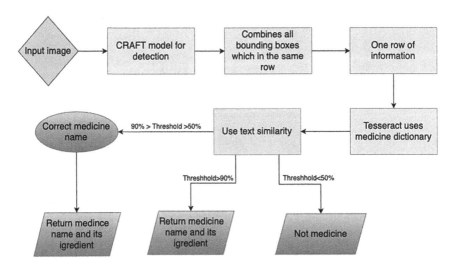

Fig. 6. Prescription recognition system

ingredients in the prescription (medicine, patient's name, dosage, etc.). There-fore, to improve the recognition model, we will use Levenshtein distance [11]. The Levenshtein distance will help our model find out the medicine names and ingredients in the prescription.

Levenshtein distance [13] between two character a, b having length a and b is calculated in $lev_{a,b}(a, b)$ with the formula:

$$lev_{a,b}(i,j) = \begin{cases} \max(i,j), & \text{if } \min(i,j) = 0 \\ \min \begin{cases} lev_{a,b}(i-1,j)+1 \\ lev_{a,b}(i,j-1)+1, \\ lev_{a,b}(i-1,j-1)+1 \end{cases} & \text{otherwise} \end{cases} \qquad (1)$$

To calculate the Levenshtein distance [11], we use a dynamic planning algo-rithm, compute on a 2-dimensional array $(n+1) * (m+1)$ where n, m is the length of the string to be calculated. two string of characters needing distance calculation and m and n are lengths corresponding to 2 strings s, t. d[m, n] is the final result showing the difference between s and t.

Figure 6 is an overview of the processing structure of the model that we propose, our model includes three main parts:

1. Defines the container that contains the string from the input image.
2. Identifies characters in the information area and extracts it as information.
3. Compare the extracted information with the drug name dictionary to find the name and ingredient of the drug.

Thanks to the Levenshtein distance [10], the strings returned by the Tesseract [1] are compared with the medicine database built by us, so the model will know the drug name and which is the ingredient of the medicine. Next is the

BỆNH VIỆN TRƯNG VƯƠNG
266 Lý Thường Kiệt, P14, Q10
ĐT: (028)54484949-38656744
Website: bvtrungvuong.vn
Đăng ký khám bệnh: 1900757555

MS : 17D/BV-01
Số TN: 200703-01594
Số Phòng Khám : 03

ĐƠN THUỐC

ĐV ĐK BHYT:
Chẩn đoán: (K21 - K29) - K21 - Bệnh trào ngược dạ dày - thực quản/ K29 - Viêm dạ dày và tá tràng

1 Evaldez 50mg (546) Levosulpirid — 14 Viên
Ngày Uống 1 lần — Mỗi lần 1 Viên — (chiều)

2 Rablet B 20mg (rabeprazol) — 14 viên
Ngày Uống 1 lần — Mỗi lần 1 Viên — (Sáng trước ăn 30 phút)

3 Onsmix (Oxethazain,dried aluminium hydroxid hydroxid gel, ma — 42 gói
Ngày Uống 3 lần — Mỗi lần 1 Gói — (Sáng, trưa, chiều TRƯỚC ĂN 5 PHÚT)

Cộng khoản : 3 — Ngày 3 tháng 7 năm 2020
BÁC SĨ KHÁM BỆNH

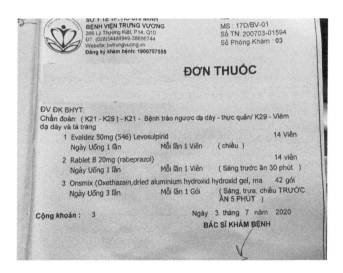

Fig. 7. An example of presciption has medicine name before ingredient

Thuốc điều trị:
1. Candesartan (SAVI CANDESARTAN 4) - 4mg — 30 Viên
Uống, 30 ngày, Sáng 1
2. Amlodipin (CARDILOPIN) - 5mg — 30 Viên
Uống, 30 ngày, Chiều 1
3. Bisoprolol (BISOSTAD 2,5) - 2,5mg — 30 Viên
Uống, 30 ngày, Trưa 1
4. Atorvastatin (ATORVASTATIN 10) - 10mg — 30 Viên
Uống, 30 ngày, Chiều 1
5. Pantoprazol (MEYERPANZOL) - 40mg — 30 Viên
Uống, 15 ngày, Sáng 1, Tối 1
6. Dextromethorphan (DEXTROMETHORPHAN 15MG) - 15mg — 30 Viên
Uống, 15 ngày, Sáng 1, Chiều 1

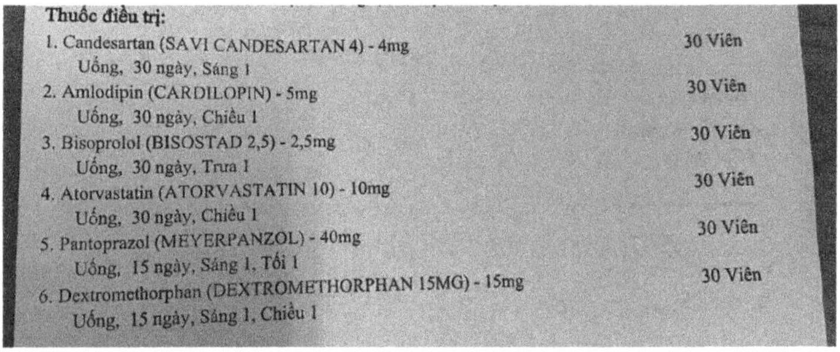

Fig. 8. An example of presciption has ingredient before medicine name

matching process to find the medicine name in the identified image. All results returned by the Tesseract [1] will be compared with the drug name dictionary. The comparison takes place using the Levenshtein space to match the character between the information produced by the Tesseract and the drug name in the dictionary. Finally, after finding the medicine, the system will return the user the name of the medicine with its ingredients, pieces of information, and instructions for use.

The primary data used in the model is DrugBank [14] data. The group uses only drug names and active ingredients in the data to classify drug names. Data on DrugBank after downloading includes more than 2300 medicines. After filtering and removing the same drug names, the data remained 1570 medicine names. In some cases, there are drugs with the same name, but different ingredients will still be kept. We should only discard medicines that have the same name and ingredient. In addition, they also collect additional data on drug names in actual prescriptions to supplement the model. Because the composition of the drug name in prescriptions will not be the same, each clinic or hospital will use a different format. For example, the drug name in Fig. 7 precedes and the ingredients of the drug after or in parentheses: "Rablet B 20mg" is the name of the drug on the market and "rabeprazole" is its medicinal ingredient.

The ingredient name of the drug in Fig. 8 comes before and the drug name is after or in parentheses: "SAVI CANDESARTAN 4" is the name of the drug in brackets and "Candesartan" is the medicinal ingredient of the drug. After collecting data from DrugBank [14] and more actual data, we have built a separate dictionary of drug names.

5 Experiments and Results

5.1 Datasets

We use datasets Synth Text, IC13, IC17 to train CRAFT detection. At the same time, we collected 15707 lines of data (after processing) from drugbank.vn (Drug Bank of Vietnam). Each data line includes name, drug formulation, and drug quantity. We collect 1000 more lines of drug name data, ingredients, functions from actual prescriptions through the app released on google play. The app also continuously collects prescription photos from users, currently has more than 500 photos.

5.2 Metrics

We used Levenshtein distance [10] and average to test the model's performance. We compare the outputs from our systems and labels to calculate accuracy. Then, we compute the average of the results to calculate our performance.

5.3 Parameters

Table 1. Parameter setting for prescription recognition system

Parameter	Description	Value
l	Config recognition language for tesseract	Eng
Oem	Specify OCR Engine mode for tesseract	1[a]
Psm	Specify page segmentation mode	7[b]
Fuzzy_param	Scoring method for Fuzzywuzzy	Token_set_ratio
Is_medicine_threshold	Threshold for classification	50
Is_exist_in_dic	Threshold for sure it exist in our dictionary	90

[a]Neural nets LSTM engine only.
[b]Treat the image as a single text line.

We set the parameters to run the training model as shown in Table 1. We experiment with many different values for each epoch to evaluate the model's effectiveness when increasing the training time.

5.4   Process

Table 2. Select threshold 90%, when the classifier's reliability reaches over 90%, the system will correct errors according to the sentence (drug names combine with the drug's ingredients in the dictionary to improve accuracy.)

Result after classification	Confident	Correction
Drotaverin clohydrat 40 mg nospa	100	Drotaverin clohydrat 40 mg NoSpa
Hemo mom	94	HemoQ Mom
Mydocalm 150 mg uong	100	Mydocalm 150 mg
Spstcefy 200 cefpodoxime	92	Spetcefy 200 mg cefpodoxime
Salbutamol sulfat 2 mg sml atisalbu	97	Salbutamol sulfat 2 mg/5 ml (Atisalbu)

We use the CRAFT pre-train model, which is used for common text recognition cases. Use the groupTextBox function to merge textboxes that are supposed to be in the same row. Help group-related information into the same box. The Tesseract uses the custom dictionary. We change the default dictionary of tesseract with drugbank's drug dictionaries. Use a drug bank dictionary and a similarity calculation algorithm as a binary classifier, with output: drug, not drug. With the words found in the drug bank dictionary, they will be weighted positively. The words not found will have a negative weight. From there, decide which word is medicine. Words classified by the positive classifier will be matched against the second dictionary (including 1000 real common drug names).

Matching result >= 90%, the name of the drug is accepted in this case. Full results will include drug name, drug ingredients, effects. For drugs with matching results >= 50% *and* < 90, errors will be corrected according to the detected words and warnings about reliability. In this case, the result is only the name of the drug/drug ingredient. Solve the problem of drug names by checking the similarity of the results just found. The possible cases are Duplicate drug name (delete duplicate name), one line of the drug name, and 1 line is drug ingredient of the above name (interpolate to combine two lines). Table 2, Table 3, and Table 4 show the detail results.

5.5   Result

Model performance increases when using CRAFT instead of the default tesseract detection. This method is beneficial for images with high contrast, rich in details. In addition, the use of specialized dictionaries for drugs is the same for the tesseract to identify more accurate words. And finally, the drug name dictionary is like correcting the mistakes of ourselves, the wrong characters in the recognition process (Table 5).

Table 3. Select threshold 50%, when the classifier's reliability reaches above 50%, the system will correct the error word by word. At the same time, we will warn about the accuracy of the identity information system.

Result after classification	Confident	Correction
Amoxcillin	57	Amoxicillin
Amuylase	50	Amylase
yrorease	67	protease

Table 4. Remove duplicate drugs by interpolating drug names and drug ingredients, We merged 3 row to only one medicine name: Brufen Suspension 100mg/50ml (Ibuprofen)

Result after classification	Confident	Interpolation
Brufen	100	Brufen Suspension 100 mg/50 ml (Ibuprofen)
Suspension	100	Brufen Suspension 100 mg/50 ml (Ibuprofen)
Ibuprofen	100	Brufen Suspension 100 mg/50 ml (Ibuprofen)

5.6 Application Software

We build mobile applications with Flutter[1]. The application helps users quickly lookup drug names, drug effects or store drug names automatically. By taking pictures of prescriptions, pill covers by phone. The system will pay the corresponding information to the user. The app is currently available on google play. You can find detailed information about the application in Google Play Store[2]. The app currently has nearly 200 downloads, with relatively good reviews from users. We can also collect more actual prescriptions through the system, from which more data to develop a better system in the future.

We received a lot of positive feedback from users. Most of them comment on the application to help them understand more about drugs, look up drugs automatically, etc. Besides, there are still some limitations, such as long processing

Table 5. Model performance

	CRAFT	Tesseract
Detection	98%	85%
Classification	95%	–
Correction	80%	–

[1] Flutter is a free and open-source mobile UI framework created by Google and released in May 2017. In a few words, it allows you to create a native mobile application with only one codebase. This means that you can use one programming language and one codebase to create two different apps (for iOS and Android).

[2] https://play.google.com/store/apps/details?id=com.devplanet.flutter_camera_app.

Fig. 9. Prescription recognition application on iOS device

time or not being identified correctly by uncommon medications. Through those valuable comments, we will continuously improve and update our system (Fig. 9).

6   Conclusion

This paper has proposed a system and advanced solutions to help identify drug names in prescriptions. By combining the CRAFT and Tesseract OCR model and additional modifications such as Levenshtein distance-based filter, the drug name dictionary has enabled the system to be applied to help identify drugs with better performance. Since then, it has supported users and pharmacists to look up drug names and find helpful information quickly. In the future, we will further improve the model in the similarity assessment step through some deep learning models to increase the accuracy and improve the response time.

Acknowledgement. This research is funded by Advanced Program in Computer Science, the Faculty of Information Technology, University of Science, VNU-HCM, Vietnam.

References

1. Patel, C., Patel, A., Patel, D.: Optical character recognition by open source OCR tool tesseract: a case study. Int. J. Comput. Appl. **55**(10), 50–56 (2012)

2. Balažević, I., Allen, C., Hospedales, T.M.: Hypernetwork knowledge graph embeddings. In: Tetko, I.V., Kůrková, V., Karpov, P., Theis, F. (eds.) ICANN 2019. LNCS, vol. 11731, pp. 553–565. Springer, Cham (2019). https://doi.org/10.1007/978-3-030-30493-5_52

3. Smith, R.: An overview of the tesseract OCR engine. In: Ninth international conference on document analysis and recognition (ICDAR 2007), vol. 2, pp. 629–633. IEEE (2007)

4. Zacharias, E., Teuchler, M. and Bernier, B.: Image Processing Based Scene-Text Detection and Recognition with Tesseract. arXiv preprint arXiv:2004.08079, (2020)

5. Baek, Y., Lee, B., Han, D., Yun, S., Lee, H.: Character region awareness for text detection. In: Proceedings of the IEEE/CVF Conference on Computer Vision and Pattern Recognition, pp. 9365–9374 (2019)

6. Huang, M., Lan, C., Huang, W., Tao, Y.: Natural scene text detection based on multiscale connectionist text proposal network. J. Eng. **2020**(13), 326–329 (2020)

7. Huang, C., Xu, J.: An anchor-free oriented text detector with connectionist text proposal network. In: Asian Conference on Machine Learning, pp. 631–645. PMLR (October 2019)

8. Shen, Z., Zhang, R., Dell, M., Lee, B.C.G., Carlson, J., Li, W.: LayoutParser: A Unified Toolkit for Deep Learning Based Document Image Analysis. arXiv preprint arXiv:2103.15348 (2021)

9. Zhang, S., Hu, Y., Bian, G.: Research on string similarity algorithm based on levenshtein distance. In: 2017 IEEE 2nd Advanced Information Technology, Electronic and Automation Control Conference (IAEAC), pp. 2247–2251 (2017)

10. Lhoussain, A.S., Hicham, G.U.E.D.D.A.H., Abdellah, Y.O.U.S.F.I.: Adaptating the levenshtein distance to contextual spelling correction. Int. J. Comput. Sci. Appl. **12**(1), 127–133 (2015)

11. Hicham, G.: Introduction of the weight edition errors in the Levenshtein distance. arXiv preprint arXiv:1208.4503 (2012)

12. Baek, Y., Lee, B., Han, D., Yun, S., Lee, H.: Character region awareness for text detection. In: Proceedings of the IEEE/CVF Conference on Computer Vision and Pattern Recognition, pp. 9365–9374 (2019)

13. Levenshtein Distance. https://en.wikipedia.org/wiki/Levenshtein_distance. Accessed 15 Apr 2021

14. Vietnam Drug Bank. https://drugbank.vn/danh-sach-thuoc. Accessed 15 Apr 2021

15. FuzzyWuzzy. https://openlibrary-repo.ecampusontario.ca/jspui/bitstream/14567 89. Accessed 15 Apr 2021

16. Flutter. https://flutter.dev. Accessed 15 Apr 2021

17. EasyOCR. https://github.com/JaidedAI/EasyOCR. Accessed 15 Apr 2021

18. Tesseract documentation. https://tesseract-ocr.github.io/tessdoc/Improve Quality. Accessed 15 Apr 2021

19. Tesseract code. https://github.com/tesseract-ocr/tesseract. Accessed 15 Apr 2021

20. Tesseract OCR with Python. https://artificialintelligence.oodles.io/blogs/tesseract-ocr-with-python/. Accessed 15 Apr 2021

Concept of Parkinson Leading to Understanding Mechanisms of the Disease

Andrzej W. Przybyszewski[1,2]([✉]) [iD], Jerzy P. Nowacki[1] [iD], Aldona Drabik[1] [iD],
Stanisław Szlufik[3] [iD], and Dariusz M. Koziorowski[3] [iD]

[1] Polish-Japanese Academy of Information Technology, 02-008 Warszawa, Poland
{przy,jerzy.nowacki,adrabik}@pjwstk.edu.pl
[2] Department of Neurology UMass Medical School, Worcester, MA 01655, USA
[3] Department of Neurology, Faculty of Health Science Medical, University of Warsaw, Warszawa, Poland
{stanislaw.szlufik,dkoziorowski}@wum.edu.pl

Abstract. The challenge of **neurodegenerative diseases** (ND) is an **aging population.** The second after Alzheimer's most common ND Parkinson's disease (PD) is characterized mainly by motor but also by cognitive disorders. In the longitudinal study, we have measured PD symptoms progression by UPDRS (Unified Parkinson's Disease Rating Scale) as a decision attribute, eye movements (EM), and cognitive tests, such as MMSE (Mini-Mental State Exam), FAS (verbal fluency), CVLT (California Verbal Learning Test) as condition attributes.

By means of ML PD development in time during our longitudinal study, we have introduced the complex granule (c-granule) approach with properties of granules that are evolving with disease progression. Basal ganglia influence not only movement execution but also learning and memory. The strongest correlated attributes with decision classes were CVLT slop of learning and CVLT delay words recognition. Both are related to short- and long-term memories. L-Dopa medication compensate motor symptoms of patients but with disease progressions, values of UPDRS are increasing. Cognitive symptoms of most PD patients are not strongly recognized like in Alzheimer's disease, but we have demonstrated that their changes are sufficient to predict with help of c-granular computing, motor decays. We propose to combine concepts of Parkinson's disease with the principle of complex object recognition. We can easily classify complex objects by comparing them with the 'Model' objects stored in our memory. Similarly, we can classify PD development based on the 'Model' – more advanced PD patients' symptoms.

Keywords: Granular computing · Cognition · Learning · Rough set theory

1 Introduction

The purpose of our study is to describe neurodegenerative processes related to Parkinson's disease and to find their common mechanisms for individual patients (personalized medicine).

© Springer Nature Switzerland AG 2021
N. T. Nguyen et al. (Eds.): ICCCI 2021, LNAI 12876, pp. 456–466, 2021.
https://doi.org/10.1007/978-3-030-88081-1_34

In our previous communication [1] we have proposed to use complex granules (c-granules) [2] to model symptoms progressions of Parkinson's disease (PD) by using interactive granular computing methods [3–5]. Schematics below demonstrate the continuation but also detailed extension of our previous model. Following [2] and [5] we have divided c-granules into the hard, link, and soft suits.

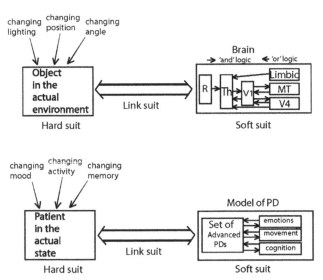

Fig. 1. A comparison of c-granule for object recognition to the estimation of PD stage. There are three parts of the c-granule: hard suit, link suit and soft suit. In the upper schematic, there is an object (hard suit), which is observed (link suit) by the visual brain (soft suit). Object's light related changes are processed by retina (R), thalamus (Th), primary visual cortex (V1) and higher cortical areas (V4) where the shape of the object is classified [6, 7]. Movements of the object are classified in area MT. There are two different logics of classifications: in afferent pathways all information is processed ('and' logic), whereas efferent pathways are selecting only expected (by their learned models) object's properties ('or' logic). This multistage mechanism is the basis for the fast and precise object classification. This classification might be also influenced by the limbic system. Notice that in the normal, natural conditions there are many factors like light, position or rotation changing that might influence this process, so the image of the object on the retina is fuzzy but brain mechanisms help in the object's recognition. We would like to use similar mechanisms to classify stage of the PD based on more advanced patients.

As you can notice in Fig. 1, there are countless similarities between object classification in the visual system (upper part of Fig. 1) and classification of the disease actual stage in Parkinson's patient (lower part of Fig. 1). In both cases there are many factors influencing the actual image of the object as well as actual stage of the patient. In order to find significant invariants, one needs the first approximation: Model [6] of the object as well as assumed stage (Model) of the disease. Both models are obtained by supervised learning: experiences from childhood with different environments with adults help, and experience and training of neurology doctors with many patients that is codded into AI expert system. As there are many factors influencing hard suits: object image, and patient's actual stage, in the brain, and in our system (soft suits) both Models must have mechanisms that extract dominating factors and put them back into the Model. In the visual brain, there are different areas extracting object's details, its movement, and emotional content (in the danger even new pathways might be activated). In the Model of Parkinson's disease, the movement symptoms are dominating, but also accompanied by cognitive and emotional disturbances. In order to find the actual patient's stage, one needs to combine these factors together. In this work, we will be mainly looking how various cognitive changes are related to the disease progression and which one is the most significant in the Parkinson's disease.

As in this work, we propose to use mainly cognitive related attributes to predict motor dominating disease progression, it is a continuation of the Theory of Mind direction in the Parkinson's and in others neurodegenerative diseases [8–10].

2   Methods

Our data mining analysis is based on granular computing implemented in RST (rough set theory proposed by Zdzislaw Pawlak [3] and by extending RST indiscernibility with concepts of the tolerance Zadeh [4].

Our data is converted to the decision table where rows were related to different measurements and columns represent different attributes. An information system [3] a pair $S = (U, A)$, where U, A are nonempty finite sets called the universe of objects U and the set of attributes A. If $a \in A$ and $u \in U$, the value a(u) is a unique element of V (where V is a value set).

We define as in [3] for RST the indiscernibility relation of any subset B of A or $IND(B)$ as: $(x, y) \in IND (B)$ or $xI(B)y$ iff $a(x) = a(y)$ for every $a \in B$ where the value of $a(x) \in V$. It is an equivalence crisp relation $[u]_B$ that we understand as a B-elementary granule. The family of $[u]_B$ gives the partition U/B containing u will be denoted by $B(u)$. The set $B \subset A$ of information system S is a reduct $IND (B) = IND (A)$ and no proper subset of B has this property [3]. In most cases, we are only interested in such reducts that are leading to expected rules (classifications). Based on the reduct we have generated rules using four different ML methods (RSES 2.2) [11]: exhaustive algorithm, genetic algorithm, covering algorithm, or LEM2 algorithm [12].

A *lower approximation* of set $X \subseteq U$ in relation to an attribute B is defined as all elements have B attribute:

$$\underline{B}X = \{u \in U : [u]_B \subseteq X\}$$

The *upper approximation* of X is defined as some elements have B attribute:

$$\overline{B}X = \{u \in U : [u]_B \cap X \neq \phi\}$$

The difference of $\overline{B}X$ and $\underline{B}X$ is the boundary region of X that we denote as BNB (X). If $BNB (X)$ is empty, then set than X is exact with respect to B; otherwise, if BNB (X) is not empty and X is rough with respect to B.

A decision table (training sample in ML) for S is the triplet: $S = (U, C, D)$ where: C, D are condition and decision attributes [3]. Each row of the decision table gives a particular rule that connects condition and decision attributes for a single measurement, RST generalizes these particular rules into universal hypotheses (object or disease classification.

We have used RST algorithms [13, 14] implemented as the RSES 2.2 (logic.mimuw. edu.pl/~rses/get.html).

2.1 Measured Attributes

We have tested two groups of PD patients: the first group (PDG1) of 23 patients was measured three times every half of the year (visits were numbered as w1, w2, w3), and the second group (PDG2) had more advanced 24 patients and were a reference model of disease progression in the first group. Both groups of patients were only on medication. The major medication in this group was L-Dopa that increases concentration of the transmitter dopamine in the specific parts of the brain as it that is lacking in Parkinson's patients. In the majority of PD patients, the neurodegeneration starts within substantia nigra part of basal ganglia that is responsible for the release of the dopamine. In the consequence so-called GO pathways became less active in contrast to NoGO pathways that lead to slowness of movements bradykinesia (see Discussion section for details).

All patients were measured in two sessions: without L-Dopa normal dose (session S# = 1 without – medication) and with patient's normal dosage of L-Dopa medication (session S# = 2 patients on medications). In addition all patients have the following procedures: neuropsychological tests: FAS (verbal fluency), cognitive tests, such as MMSE (Mini-Mental State Exam), CVLT (California Verbal Learning Test), neurological tests: eye movements and standard PD test: UPDRS (Unified Parkinson's Disease Rating Scale).

All tests were performed in Brodno Hospital, department of Neurology, Faculty of Health Science, Medical University Warsaw, Poland. In the present work, we have tested and measured fast eye movements: reflexive saccades (RS) as described in our previous publications [15]. In summary, every subject was sitting in a stable position without head movements and watching a computer screen before him/her. At the beginning he/she has to fixate in the center of the screen, and to keep on moving light spot. This spot was jumping randomly, ten degrees to the right or ten degrees to the left. Patient has to follow movements of the light spot and following parameters were measured: latency (RSLat) – time difference between beginning of spot and eyes movements, saccade duration (RSDur); saccade amplitude (RSAmp) and saccade velocity (RSVel).

3 Results

For the first group of PD patients we have performed three tests, every half-year, whereas the second group of more advanced PD we have measured only one time. The mean age of the first group (PDG1) was 57.8 ± 13 (SD) years with disease duration 7.1 ± 3.5 years; UPDRS MedOff/On was 48.3 ± 17.9 and 23.6 ± 10.3 for the first visit (w1); 57.3 ± 16.8 and 27.8 ± 10.8 for the second visit (w2), 62.2 ± 18.2 and 25 ± 11.6 for the third visit (w3). The second group (G2) of patients was more advanced with mean age 53.7 ± 9.3 years, and disease duration 10.25 ± 3.9 years; UPDRS MedOff/On was 62.1 ± 16.1

and 29.9 ± 13.3 measured one time only. Data were placed in four information tables: PDG1w1, PDG1w2, PDG1w3, and PDG2 (only one visit).

Table 1. Part of the decision table for four PDG2 patients

P#	Ses	dur	FAS	MMSE	RSLat	RSDur	CVLTdel	CVLTlslop	UPDRS
45	2	13	45	28	284	47	9	1.5	42
45	1	13	45	28	212	46	9	1.5	76
46	2	7	35	30	386	49	4	3	18
46	1	7	35	30	202	55	4	3	53
47	2	9	28	28	206	50	4	1.7	33
47	1	9	28	28	360	60	4	1.7	70
49	2	8.4	39	29	212	48	5	1.5	24
49	1	8.4	39	29	209	58	5	1.5	51

Table 1 is a part of the decision for 24 patients (with 48 rows) measured in two sessions each. Condition attributes patient number P#, S# session number, dur – disease duration, cognitive tests results: FAS, MMSE (as described above), RS parameters (there are saccades latency and duration in the table), and CVLT (see above) del -delay memory test and CVLTlslope – learning slope (how fast patient learns). In the last column is the decision attribute UPDRS that indicates the disease progression.

3.1 Rough Set Approach

In the following step, Table 1 was discretized by means of RST (RSES 2.2) and not significant attributes were removed as described in the Methods section. As we have 6 cognitive attributes, we have performed six cross-validation tests to find which attribute(s) give(s) the best predictions of the decision attribute UPDRS.

At first, we have used FAS, RSLat, and RSDur as condition attributes and UPDRS as decision attribute for PDG2 patients. After discretization, UPDRS was optimally divided by RSES into 4 ranges: "(−Inf; 43.0)", "(43.0; 47.5)", "(47.5, 63.0)", "(63.0; Inf)". We have obtained 25 rules that were bases for classification of other groups. We have obtained: for PDG1w1patients – global accuracy 0.72, global coverage 0.39; for PDG1w2 patients – global accuracy 0.79, global coverage 0.41; for PDG1w3 patients – global accuracy 0.74, global coverage 0.5. There was good accuracy in estimation of UPDRS on basis of FAS, but mean coverage was about 0.4. Another cognitive parameter MMSE is the standard in estimation of the general cognitive stage of patients not only in PD but also Alzheimer's disease. We have obtained: for PDG1w1patients – global accuracy 0.79, global coverage 0.3; for PDG1w2 patients – global accuracy 0.88, global coverage 0.37; for PDG1w3 patients – global accuracy 0.78, global coverage 0.39. The mean accuracy was very good above 0.8, but coverage was even lower than for FAS, it was about 0.35. Therefore, we have well predicted UPDRS but only for about one third of the population.

As FAS and MMSE are very common we do not get into their details. We were more interested in CVLT (California Verbal Learning Test) as we would like to know how learning is changing during disease development and if it can predict motor symptoms development. We have tested four different cases: CVLT Delay – delay learning test, CVLT 20 min delay – how learning was effective after 20 min time span, CVLT recall – how patient remembered if words were used in the tests to other words, and in the dynamics of learning: what was the rate of memorizing or what was the slope of learning and learning reliability – how many words after 5 repeating did each patient remember?

After discretization, UPDRS was optimally divided by RSES into 4 ranges (different than above): "(−Inf; 43.0)", "(43.0; 45.5)", "(45.5, 63.0)", "(63.0; Inf)". We have rules that were bases for classification of other groups.

Taking into account CVLT Delay test we have obtained large number of decision rules that were filtered based on the right-hand support into 8 rules e.g. 4 of them:

$$(Ses = 2)\&(RSDur = ``(-Inf, 48.5)'') => (UPDRS = ``(-Inf, 43.0)''[9]) \tag{1}$$

$$\begin{aligned}(Ses = 2)\&(RSLat = ``(210.5, Inf)'')\&(CVLTDelay = ``(9.5, Inf)'')\\ => (UPDRS = ``(-Inf, 43.0)''[6])\end{aligned} \tag{2}$$

$$\begin{aligned}(Ses = 1)\&(RSLat = ``(-Inf, 210.5)'')\&(RSDur = ``(48.5, Inf)'')\&(CVLTDelay = ``(-Inf, 9.5)'')\\ => (UPDRS = ``(45.5, 63.0)''[3])\end{aligned} \tag{3}$$

$$\begin{aligned}(Ses = 1)\&(RSLat = ``(210.5, Inf)'')\&(RSDur = ``(48.5, Inf)'')\&(CVLTDelay = ``(-Inf, 9.5)'')\\ => (UPDRS = ``(63.0, Inf)''[3])\end{aligned} \tag{4}$$

The first rule is for the *session* = 2 (Patient on medication) and when duration of saccades (*RSDur*) was smaller than 48.5 ms then UPDRS was smaller than 43 in 9 cases. All other rules have CVLT delay that strongly influence UPDRS – if it is larger than 9.5 UPDRS is small (patient movements are good) Eq. (2), when it is small then UPDRS is larger eqs. (3,4).

On the basis of above rules from PDG2 group we have predicted UPDRS in PDG1 patient in their three visits: w1, w2, w3:

Table 2. Confusion matrix for UPDRS of PDG1w1 patients by rules obtained from PDG2 patients with CVLT Delay

Actual	Predicted				
	"(−Inf, 43.0)"	"(45.5, 63.0)"	"(63.0, Inf)"	"(43.0, 45.5)"	ACC
"(−Inf, 43.0)"	12.0	0.0	2.0	1.0	0.8
"(45.5, 63.0)"	0.0	0.0	2.0	2.0	0.0
"(63.0, Inf)"	0.0	0.0	2.0	0.0	1.0
"(43.0, 45.5)"	0.0	0.0	1.0	1.0	0.5
TPR	1.0	0.0	0.3	0.25	

TPR: True positive rates for decision classes; ACC: Accuracy for decision classes: the global accuracy was 0.652 and global coverage was 0.5

Table 3. Confusion matrix for UPDRS of PDG1w2 patients by rules obtained from PDG2 patients with CVLT Delay

Actual	Predicted				
	"(−Inf, 43.0)"	"(45.5, 63.0)"	"(63.0, Inf)"	"(43.0, 45.5)"	ACC
"(−Inf, 43.0)"	13.0	0.0	1.0	0.0	0.93
"(45.5, 63.0)"	0.0	2.0	1.0	2.0	0.4
"(63.0, Inf)"	0.0	0.0	4.0	1.0	0.8
"(43.0, 45.5)"	0.0	0.0	1.0	1.0	0.5
TPR	1.0	1.0	0.6	0.25	

TPR: True positive rates for decision classes; ACC: Accuracy for decision classes: the global accuracy was 0.77 and global coverage was 0.57

Table 4. Confusion matrix for UPDRS of PDG1w3 patients by rules obtained from PDG2 patients with CVLT delay

Actual	Predicted				
	"(−Inf, 43.0)"	"(45.5, 63.0)"	"(63.0, Inf)"	"(43.0, 45.5)"	ACC
"(−Inf, 43.0)"	13.0	0.0	0.0	0.0	1.0
"(45.5, 63.0)"	1.0	2.0	1.0	3.0	0.29
"(63.0, Inf)"	0.0	1.0	1.0	1.0	0.33
"(43.0, 45.5)"	0.0	0.0	0.0	0.0	0.0
TPR	0.93	0.67	0.5	0.0	

TPR: True positive rates for decision classes; ACC: Accuracy for decision classes: the global accuracy was 0.70 and global coverage was 0.5

Confusion Tables 2, 3 and 4 show that accuracies are similar to FAS tests, but with better global coverage: 50–57% of populations were covered.

In other testes we have used two CVLT test results: recall (recognition of words) and slope of learning that are more specific for PD learning and memory problems.

After discretization, UPDRS was optimally divided by RSES into 4 ranges (different than above): "(−Inf; 39.5)", "(39.5; 50.0)", "(50.0, 56.5)", "(56.5; Inf)". We have obtained rules that were bases for classification of other groups (Tables 4, 5 and 6).

Below, example of several from obtained 28 filtered rules:

$$(CVLTrec = ``(10.0, 13.5)''))\&(Ses = 2)\&(RSLat = ``(-Inf, 206.5)'') => (UPDRS = ``(-Inf, 39.5)''[3])$$
(5)

$$(Ses = 2)\&(RSLat = ``(-Inf, 206.5)'')\&(CVLTslop = ``(-Inf, 1.75)'') => (UPDRS = ``(-Inf, 39.5)''[3])$$
(6)

$$(CVLTrec = ``(14.5, Inf)'')\&(Ses = 2)\&(CVLTslop = ``(-Inf, 1.75)'') => (UPDRS = ``(-Inf, 39.5)''[3])$$
(7)

$$(CVLTrec = ``(10.0, 13.5)'')\&(Ses = 1)\&(RSLat = ``(229.5, 286.5)'') => (UPDRS = ``(56.5, Inf)''[2])$$
(8)

We read above rules as Eq. (5) when CVLT recall *(CVLTrec)* was between 10 and 13.5 words, patient was on medication *(Ses = 2)* and saccade latency *(RSLat)* were below 206.5 ms then UPDRS was below 39.5 in 3 cases. The following rule Eq. (6) is like Eq. (5) with an exception that instead CVLT recall *(CVLTrec)* is CVLT slop *(CVLTslop* – learning rate), and it is also fulfilled in 3 cases.

In the next equation Eq. (7) CVLT recall *(CVLTrec)* and slope *(CVLTslop)* were combined for patient on medication that resulted UPDRS below 39.5 in 3 cases.

The last Eq. (8) was for patient without medication *(Ses = 1)* where *CVLTrec* was between 10 and 13.5 words, and saccade latency *(RSLat)* was between 229.5 and 286.5 ms then UPDRS was above 56.5.

All 28 rules were basis for classification of other of patients: during PDG1w1, PDG1w2, and PDG1w3 visits as states in Tables 5, 6 and 7 below:

Table 5. Confusion matrix for UPDRS of PDG1w1 patients by rules obtained from PDG2 patients with CVLT recall and learning slope

Actual	Predicted				
	"(39.5, 50.0)"	"(−Inf, 39.5)"	"(56.5, Inf)"	"(50.0, 56.5)"	ACC
"(39.5, 50.0)"	0.0	3.0	1.0	0.0	0.0
"(−Inf, 39.5)"	0.0	17.0	2.0	0.0	0.895
"(56.5, Inf)"	0.0	2.0	2.0	0.0	0.5
"(50.0, 56.5)"	0.0	0.0	0.0	0.0	0.0
TPR	0.0	0.77	0.4	0.0	

TPR: True positive rates for decision classes; ACC: Accuracy for decision classes: the global accuracy was 0.704 and global coverage was 0.5

Table 6. Confusion matrix for UPDRS of PDG1w2 patients by rules obtained from PDG2 patients with CVLT recall and learning slope

Actual	Predicted				
	"(39.5, 50.0)"	"(−Inf, 39.5)"	"(56.5, Inf)"	"(50.0, 56.5)"	ACC
"(39.5, 50.0)"	0.0	2.0	0.0	0.0	0.0
"(−Inf, 39.5)"	0.0	17.0	2.0	0.0	0.9
"(56.5, Inf)"	0.0	1.0	5.0	0.0	0.83
"(50.0, 56.5)"	0.0	1.0	2.0	0.0	0.0
TPR	0.0	0.81	0.56	0.0	

TPR: True positive rates for decision classes; ACC: Accuracy for decision classes: the global accuracy was 0.733 and global coverage was 0.65.

Confusion Tables 5, 6 and 7 based on mentioned above 28 rules gave comparable accuracies to Tables 2 and 3, but with the global coverage about 60% of all cases. However, by using of all 214 decision rules that were originally obtained by the exhaustive

Table 7. Confusion matrix for UPDRS of PDG1w3 patients by rules obtained from PDG2 patients with CVLT recall and learning slope

Actual	Predicted				
	"(39.5, 50.0)"	"(−Inf, 39.5)"	"(56.5, Inf)"	"(50.0, 56.5)"	ACC
"(39.5, 50.0)"	0.0	4.0	1.0	0.0	0.0
"(−Inf, 39.5)"	0.0	13.0	0.0	0.0	1.0
"(56.5, Inf)"	0.0	4.0	4.0	0.0	0.5
"(50.0, 56.5)"	0.0	1.0	0.0	0.0	0.0
TPR	0.0	0.6	0.8	0.0	

TPR: True positive rates for decision classes; ACC: Accuracy for decision classes: the global accuracy was 0.63 and global coverage was 0.59.

algorithm [13] before filtered based on the right-hand support to above mentioned 28 rules, gave the following results: PDG1w1 accuracy 0.525, coverage 0.87; PDG1w2 accuracy 0.568, coverage 0.96; PDG1w3 accuracy 0.568, coverage 0.96. In other words, the accuracy and the coverage are complementary in our granular computing method. Filtering of the rules make them more precise, but for the coverage price.

4 Discussion

In this report we have used c-granular computing (c-GrC) to estimate progression of Parkinson's disease in time (longitudinal study) of two groups of patients. The first group was less advances and tested three times every 6 months, whereas the second group more advanced PD patient was tested only ones with a purpose as being the 'Model' for the first group of patients as it was explained in Fig. 1. The recognition of PD patient's stage of the disease is as complex as classification of the unknown object (Fig. 1). We have proposed rules based on cognitive tests and applied them to predict similarity between patients in different stages of the disease to more the advanced Parkinson's disease group of patients.

These similarities were defined as accuracies: how good rules obtained from the advanced group of patients can predict disease of less advanced group of PDs. However, there are many different cognitive tests and our study showed that they gave various results. The highest accuracies gave MMSE (Mini-Mental State Exam) tests (about 0.8) but their coverage was below 0.4. Other tests like CVLT (California Verbal Learning Test) delay gave accuracies about 0.7, but their coverage was round 50% (Tables 2, 3 and 4). Other pair of CVLT tests related to the recall and learning had accuracy about 0.7 with the global coverage about 60% that is relatively good characterization of the population.

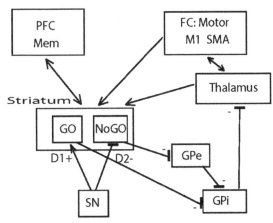

Fig. 2. Simplified schematic of motor and memory impairments in PD. In Parkinson's disease as effect of primary SN (substantia nigra) cells death amount of the DA (dopamine) is decreased that causes smaller excitation of GO striatum (by D1 receptor) and also smaller inhibition of NoGO part of striatum (through D2 receptor). In the consequence GPi (globous pallidus interior) is less inhibited directly (Go pathway) and indirectly (NoGO pathway through stronger GPe (globous pallidus exterior) stronger inhibition). It means that GPi inhibition on the thalamus is stronger, feedback frontal motor cortex (FC: Motor – primary (M1), and supplementary (SMA)) is weaker that generally slows movements. It is also related deficits in the memory (striatum – prefrontal cortex connections). Medication (L-Dopa precursor of dopamine) is given to such patients that generally reverse these mechanisms and helps patients' motor symptoms and memory [16]. However, with disease progression, patients' motor symptoms are getting worse again. Our question was if there are also related memory problems that might correlate with motor decays?

However, the most important is to find mechanisms of such predictions. There are explained in Fig. 2 above. Striatum integrates regulation of the movement executions (PD major symptoms) and memory recall (PD minor symptom). Lack of the dopamine as in PD or excess of the dopamine like in medication have opposite effects on motor and memory symptoms [16] that should be take into consideration for the optimize, personal medicine.

In Summary: We have predicted disease development in Parkinson's disease patient based on their cognitive changes. It seems unexpected as it is well known that PD is mainly related to the motor: movements disorders symptoms. However, lack of the dopamine affects not only movements' control, but also is related to the memory and cognition (prefrontal cortex – Fig. 2).

References

1. Przybyszewski, A.W.: Parkinson's Disease Development Prediction by C-Granule Computing. In: Nguyen, N.T., Chbeir, R., Exposito, E., Aniorté, P., Trawiński, B. (eds.) ICCCI 2019. LNCS (LNAI), vol. 11683, pp. 296–306. Springer, Cham (2019). https://doi.org/10.1007/978-3-030-28377-3_24

2. Skowron, A., Dutta, S.: Rough sets: past, present, and future. Nat. Comput. **17**(4), 855–876 (2018). https://doi.org/10.1007/s11047-018-9700-3

3. Pawlak, Z.: Rough Sets – Theoretical Aspects of Reasoning about Data. Kluwer Academic Pub (1991)

4. Zadeh, L.A.: From computing with numbers to computing with words – from manipulation of measurements to manipulation of perceptions. Int. J. Appl. Math. Comp. Sci. **12**, 307–324 (2002)

5. Jankowski, A.: Interactive Granular Computations in Networks and Systems Engineering: A Practical Perspective. Springer, Lecture Notes in Networks and Systems, 17, (2017)

6. Przybyszewski, A.W.: The neurophysiological bases of cognitive computation using rough set theory. In: Peters, J.F., Skowron, A., Rybiński, H. (eds.) Transactions on Rough Sets IX. LNCS, vol. 5390, pp. 287–317. Springer, Heidelberg (2008). https://doi.org/10.1007/978-3-540-89876-4_16

7. Przybyszewski, A.W.: SI: SCA Measures – Fuzzy rough set features of cognitive computations in the visual system. J. Intell. Fuzzy Syst. **36**, 3155–3167 (2019). https://doi.org/10.3233/JIFS-18401

8. Przybyszewski, A.W.: Theory of Mind Helps to Predict Neurodegenerative Processes in Parkinson's Disease. In: Paszynski, M., Kranzlmüller, D., Krzhizhanovskaya, V.V., Dongarra, J.J., Sloot, P.M.A. (eds.) ICCS 2021. LNCS, vol. 12744, pp. 542–555. Springer, Cham (2021). https://doi.org/10.1007/978-3-030-77967-2_45

9. Nobis, L., et al.: Theory of mind performance in Parkinson's disease is associated with motor and cognitive functions, but not with symptom lateralization. J. Neural Transm. **124**(9), 1067–1072 (2017). https://doi.org/10.1007/s00702-017-1739-2

10. Poletti, M., Enrici, I., Bonuccelli, U., Adenzato, M.: Theory of mind in Parkinson's disease. Behav. Brain Res. **219**, 342–350 (2011)

11. Bazan, J., Nguyen, H.S., Nguyen, S.H., Synak, P., Wróblewski, J.: Rough set algorithms in classification problem. In: Polkowski, L., Tsumoto, S., Lin, T. (eds.) Rough Set Methods and Applications, pp. 49–88. Physica-Verlag, Heidelberg New York (2000)

12. Grzymała-Busse, J.: A new version of the rule induction system LERS. Fund. Inform. **31**(1), 27–39 (1997)

13. Bazan, J.G., Szczuka, M.: The Rough Set Exploration System. In: Peters, J.F., Skowron, A. (eds.) Transactions on Rough Sets III. LNCS, vol. 3400, pp. 37–56. Springer, Heidelberg (2005). https://doi.org/10.1007/11427834_2

14. Bazan, J.G., Szczuka, M.: RSES and RSESlib - A Collection of Tools for Rough Set Computations. In: Ziarko, W., Yao, Y. (eds.) RSCTC 2000. LNCS (LNAI), vol. 2005, pp. 106–113. Springer, Heidelberg (2001). https://doi.org/10.1007/3-540-45554-X_12

15. Przybyszewski, A.W., Kon, M., Szlufik, S., Szymanski, A., Koziorowski, D.M.: Multimodal learning and intelligent prediction of symptom development in individual Parkinson's patients. Sensors **16**(9), 1498 (2016). https://doi.org/10.3390/s16091498

16. Moustafa, A.A., Sherman, S.J., Frank, M.J.: A dopaminergic basis for working memory, learning and attentional shifting in Parkinsonism. Neuropsychologia **46**(13), 3144–3156 (2008)

Cross-Level High-Utility Itemset Mining Using Multi-core Processing

N. T. Tung[1] (ID), Loan T. T. Nguyen[2,3](✉) (ID), Trinh D. D. Nguyen[4] (ID),
and Adrianna Kozierkiewicz[5] (ID)

[1] Faculty of Information Technology, Ho Chi Minh City University of Technology (HUTECH),
Ho Chi Minh City, Vietnam
nt.tung@hutech.edu.vn

[2] School of Computer Science and Engineering, International University,
Ho Chi Minh City, Vietnam
nttloan@hcmiu.edu.vn

[3] Vietnam National University, Ho Chi Minh City, Vietnam

[4] Faculty of Information Technology, Industrial University of
Ho Chi Minh City, Ho Chi Minh City, Vietnam
20126291.trinh@student.iuh.edu.vn

[5] Faculty of Computer Science and Management, Wroclaw University of Science
and Technology, Wroclaw, Poland
Adrianna.kozierkiewicz@pwr.edu.pl

Abstract. Among the useful tools for the retail stores to analyze their customer behaviors is through the task of mining high-utility itemset (HUIM), which is to reveal the combinations of items which offer high. However, most of them different abstraction levels of items. The CLH-Miner algorithm was presented to solve this problem. It adopts categorization of items with the HUIM to discover interesting itemsets not contained in traditional HUIM approaches. Whereas CLH-Miner discovers itemsets from different levels of abstraction efficiently, the algorithm is sequential. It cannot, therefore, use powerful, easily available, multi-core processors. This work tackles this drawback through the use of a parallel method called the pCLH-Miner algorithm to significantly reduce mining times. The algorithm proposes a way to split the search space into separate parts and assign them to each different core. The pCLH-miner is shown to high efficiency compared CLH-Miner by experiments on real-world databases.

Keywords: Hierarchical database · Cross-level high-utility itemset · High-utility itemset · Data mining · Multi-core algorithm

1 Introduction

Pattern mining is one of several primary topics in the area of information processes. It focuses on finding items that fit any particular one kind of interest. The results returned from this mining task acts as feedback for subsequent information discovery activities.

© Springer Nature Switzerland AG 2021
N. T. Nguyen et al. (Eds.): ICCCI 2021, LNAI 12876, pp. 467–479, 2021.
https://doi.org/10.1007/978-3-030-88081-1_35

Agrawal et al. introduced the Frequent Itemset Mining (FIM) task in 1993 [1]. In FIM, consumer habits in retail stores are analyzed from sales databases. It reveals the items that are frequently purchased together, called Frequent Itemsets (FIs). The efficiency of FIM depends mainly on search space reduction to avoid the exhaustive search. To achieve this goal, the downward closure property (DCP) on the itemset occurrence frequency (or support) is heavily utilized. As FIM considers only the occurrence frequency of the itemsets, the returned results often low in benefit. It is due to FIM ignores other important factors (such as weight or profits gained from the itemsets), thus leaving out many unpopular itemsets with high profitability.

High-utility itemset mining (HUIM) was proposed to effectively address this drawback of FIM [23]. Each item in the transaction is now has a positive integer that represents its quantity in that transaction. In addition, they also have a unique interpretation also known as its unit benefit. The utility or benefit gained by an item in a transaction is determined by taking the product of these two values. Considering an example of a transaction database given in Table 1, denoted as D, with 8 transactions. A unique identifier called TID is assigned to a transaction. The content of every transaction is simply a series of tuples in the form of *item, quantity*. Compared to FIM, HUIM is a more challenging topic since it is an even more generalized mining task. Furthermore, the utility measure is not downward-closure satisfied. Thus, HUIM cannot adopt the efficient pruning methods that were extensively used in FIM.

Table 1. A quantitative transaction database

TID	Transactions
T_1	$(a, 1), (c, 1), (d, 1)$
T_2	$(a, 2), (c, 6), (e, 1)$
T_3	$(a, 1), (b, 5), (c, 1), (d, 3), (e, 1)$
T_4	$(b, 4), (d, 3), (e, 1)$
T_5	$(a, 1), (b, 1), (c, 1)$
T_6	$(d, 2), (e, 4)$

Table 2. Unit profit of all items

Item	a	b	c	d	e
Unit profit	5	3	1	2	3

Focusing deeper into this mining task, previously introduced HUIM approaches all bypass the concept of item categorization or taxonomy of items. Figure 1 presents a taxonomy of the transaction database in Table 1, specialized items "a" and "b" can be generalized into "Y"; "d" and "e" in turn can be categorized into "Z". Then, the generalized "Y" and the specialized item "c" can be represented by an item at a higher level of abstraction, as "X". The interestingness and also the challenging point of this mining task comes from the fact that many specialized items might be not a part of any found HUIs but their generalized items might.

Previously introduced FIM approaches methods had taken the item categorizations into account [10, 20, 22]. As said, the downward-closure property does not hold for the utility measure at the level of specialized items, now it is extended to the level of generalized items. Recently, only two algorithms are already developed to solve this problem. ML-HUI Miner algorithm, introduced by Cagliero et al. in 2017 [3]. It extracts HUIs where the items can appear independently at various levels of abstraction. CLH-Miner is then proposed by Fournier-Viger et al. in 2020 [8]. It extends the problems to mine HUI in multiple levels of abstractions to mine cross-level items. The two algorithms were designed to operate as sequential, which are not effective in the era of multi-core processors. They require only one processing unit to execute even if it is executed on a processor with multiple cores, leaving the rest unoccupied. This leads to the algorithm's lengthy running time. The main contributions of this paper can be summarized as follows:

- Proposing an algorithm that uses the maximum capacity of the available processors, in order to minimize the exploration time.
- Adopting a load balancing strategy to increase the performance of the cross-level high utility itemset mining algorithm.
- Assessments on real-world databases show that the parallel algorithm's speed-up factor multiple times higher than its sequential algorithm in terms of execution time.

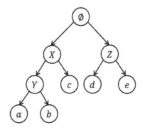

Fig. 1. An example of a taxonomy of the database D.

The remaining content of this paper is organized as follows. Section 2 carries out the literature review. Section 3 presents preliminaries and important definitions used in cross-level HUIs mining. The pCLH-Miner algorithm is presented in Sect. 4. Evaluation studies to evaluate the performance of our approach are discussed in Sect. 5. Finally, Sect. 6 draws out conclusions and discusses future works.

2 Related Works

With the proposing of FIM, several algorithms have been developed to find out the FIs effectively [1, 6, 9]. They adopted the downward closure property on item occurrence frequency to eliminate unpromising candidates. However, the major disadvantage of FIM is that it ignores the profit gained by the items. Hence, the discovered frequent patterns are often low in benefit. This problem was then addressed by HUIM to find products with high-utility. HUIM associated each item with two values [23], which are the internal and external utility. Several effective methods were introduced to reveal HUIs from databases, such as Two-Phase [12], HUI-Miner [11], FHM [7], EFIM [25], iMEFIM [13].

When it comes to the generalization of items in the database, none of those previously mentioned HUIM algorithms take into account the taxonomy of items in the transactional databases, although it was early adopted in several FIM approaches. Some notable algorithms are Cumulated [20], Prutax [10], MMS GIT-tree [22]. However, only two algorithms in the field of HUIM to our knowledge: ML-HUI Mine [3] and the CLH-Miner [8]. The idea of taxonomy-based HUIM was proposed by Cagliero et al. The author extended the HUI-Miner to discover multi-level HUIs (MLHUIs) by scanning each level of the taxonomy independently. The relationships between different abstraction levels are not considered to further reduce the search space. The second algorithm, which was introduced recently by Fournier-Viger et al., is named CLH-Miner. The authors defined a more generalized task of mining cross-level HUIs (CLHUIs). A variant of CLH-Miner was proposed to discover top-k cross-level HUI [18]. While CLH-Miner extends FHM and introduced a novel GWU (generalized-weighted utilization) upper bound, it still suffers from long runtimes and high memory usage.

All the algorithms listed above are designed to operate sequentially, thus they have a long execution time. Parallel computing is seen as one prominent method for improving the efficiency of the mining process. As the popularity of multi-core processor systems increases, allowing concurrent execution of tasks, several FIM approaches were introduced such as Par-ClosP [24], Par-CSP [5], and pSPADE [2]; For HUIM, some can be named are pEFIM [16], PHUI-Miner [4], P-FHM+ [19], MCH-Miner [21] and MCML-Miner [17]. Nguyen also introduced several approaches to dispute resolution in distributed systems [14, 15].

The purpose of this research would be to expand the algorithm CLH-Miner using multi-core processing to harness the full computing power of current processor generations to reduce the running time required to mine CLHUI.

3 Preliminaries

This section provides some main concepts and formulates the problem of mining cross-level HUIs from transaction databases enriched with taxonomy information.

Let I be the set of items in a database, $I = \{i_1, i_2, ..., i_m\}$. A transaction database D is a set of transactions $D = \{T_1, T_2, ..., T_n\}$. Each transaction T_c in D is a set of items ($T_c \subseteq I$). Every T_c has its transaction identifier (TID) of c ($1 \leq c \leq |D| = n$). Each $v \in I$ has a positive integer called its external utility, and denoted as $p(v)$ (Table 2). For each item $v \in T_c$, another positive integer is defined as the internal utility of v in T_c, represented as $q(v, T_c)$. The utility yielded by v in T_c, is defined as $u(v, T_c) = p(v) \times q(v, T_c)$. The utility of an itemset X, ($X \subseteq I$) in T_c, is defined as $u(X, T_c) = \sum_{v \in X} u(v, T_c)$. The utility of X in the whole database D is obtained as $u(X) = \sum_{T_v \in \mathcal{T}(X)} u(X, T_c)$, in which $\mathcal{T}(X)$ denotes the list of all transactions where X appears.

To model the items generalization mechanism in the database D, the concept of taxonomy τ is defined. It is an abstract tree structure constructed from the items generalization in the database D (Fig. 1), as follows: (a) Leaf nodes are all the specialized items, $\forall i \in I$. (b) The inner-node aggregates all its descendant nodes or descendant categories into an abstract category at an increased level of abstraction.

Let GI be the set containing all generalized items in τ, assuming each specialized item $i \in I$ can be generalized into one and only one specific generalized item $g \in GI$, then the set containing both generalized and leaf items are denoted as AI, thus $AI = GI \cup I$. Let LR be a relation between a generalized item g in taxonomy τ and a leaf item, GR be a relation between items in AI. The set $Desc(d) = \{f | (d, f) \in GR\}$ contains all descendant items of a (generalized) item d. The number of edges from the root node to reach d in τ is denoted as $level(d)$. An itemset $X (X \subseteq AI)$ is a set of items, such that and $\nexists v, w \in X | v \in Desc(w, \tau)$. X is a generalized itemset if $\exists g \in X$ where $g \in GI$. The set $Leaf(g, \tau) = \{v | (g, v) \in LR\}$ contains all the leaf nodes v of a generalized item g in τ. The utility of g in transaction T_q, denoted as $u(g, T_q)$, is defined as the sum utility of all its descendant nodes, $u(g, T_q) = \sum_{i \in Desc(g, \tau)} ue(i) \times ui(i, T_q)$. Extending from here, the utility of a generalized itemset GX in T_q, it is as follows: $u(GX, T_q) = \sum_{i \in GX} u(i, T_q)$; The utility of GX in D is as follows: $u(GX) = \sum_{T_q \in G(GX)} u(GX, T_q)$, whereas $G(GX) = \{T_q \in \mathcal{D} | \exists X \subset T_q \wedge X \text{ is a descendant of } GX\}$.

Let D be a transaction database enriched with taxonomy information from τ and a given minimum utility threshold μ. A (generalized) itemset X is called a cross-level HUI (CLHUI) if and only if $\mu \leq u(X)$. The goal of CLHUIM is to reveal the set of all CLHUIs and HUIs.

4   Proposed Algorithm

This section introduces the pCLH-Miner algorithm, which is designed to efficiently enumerate all CLHUIs in a transaction database D using taxonomy τ and a μ threshold. It is assumed that a total order $\prec$ is defined on $I \cup GI$ as follows: for two items $a, b \in AI$, if $level(a) < level(b)$ or $level(a) = level(b) \wedge GTWU(a) > GTWU(b)$, then $a \prec b$. This is to make sure that generalized items are always considered before their descendant items, which is important as it enables itemset pruning in the search space This ordering is defined based on the GTWU measure as follows.

Definition 1 (Generalized Transaction weighted utilization – GTWU). [3] A transaction T_c has its transaction utility calculated as $TU(T_c) = \sum_{x \in T_c} u(x, T_c)$. For an itemset $X \subseteq I$, the $GTWU$ is computed as: $GTWU(X) = \sum_{T_c \in g(X)} TU(T_c)$. In the case of $X \subseteq GI$, the $GTWU$ is obtained as: $GTWU(GX) = \sum_{T_c \in g(i \in Leaf(GX, \tau))} TU(T_c)$

For any itemset X, it can be seen that $GTWU(X) \geq u(Y), \forall Y \supseteq X$ (the $GTWU$ of X is a utility-based upper bound on X and all its supersets). To eliminate unpromising patterns from the search space, the following GTWU-based property is used.

Property 1 (GTWU-based pruning). For any itemset X, if $GTWU(X) < \mu$ then X and all of its supersets can be safely pruned [8].

Definition 2 (Extension). [8] For any itemset X, the join-based extensions – $JBE(X)$ of X are the itemsets received by appending an item y to X such that: $JBE(X) = \{v \in AI, v \succ i, \forall i \in X, v \notin Desc(i, \tau)\}$. The tax-based extensions – $TBE(X)$ of X are the itemsets obtained by substituting the last item y of X with a descendant of y

For instance, if $Z \succ X$, the itemset $\{X, d\}$ has its $TBE(\{X, Z\}) = \{\{X, d\}, \{X, e\}$ and $JBE(\{X\}) = \{Z\}$.

Definition 3 (Remaining utility of an itemset). [9] Considering an itemset X appearing in transaction T_c, its remaining utility in T_c is as follows: $re(X, T_c) = \sum_{v \in T_c \wedge v \succ x, \forall x \in X} u(v, T_c)$

Definition 4 (Remaining utility as upper-bound). [9] The upper-bound based on the remaining utility of an itemset X is defined as follows: $reu(X) = u(X) + re(X)$.

Property 2 (Remaining utility upper-bound pruning). Itemset X and all of its extensions are low-utility itemsets $reu(X) < \mu$ and can be safely pruned. This upper bound value can be quickly determined by scanning through the Tax-utility-list of X by adding all *iutil* and *rutil* values, which is defined in Definition 5.

Definition 5 (Tax-Utility-list-TUL). [8] A tax-utility-list of an itemset X, $TUL(X)$, is a set of tuples such that for each transaction T_c in D where X appears, there exists a tuple $(c, iutil, rutil)$, where $iutil = u(X, T_c)$ and $rutil = re(X, T_c)$. The tax-utility-list contains a collection of objects referred to the TUL of the children of X in the taxonomy.

CLH-Miner first scans the database to construct the TUL of every single item. Next, it generates the TUL of the extensions by joining TUL of smaller itemsets, this is based on a modified version of the utility-list construction from HUI-Miner. The major difference between the two utility-list construction methods is that child is updated in the CLH-Miner version. A variation form $TUL(X)$ is to quickly identify the utility of X without scanning the database, as $u(X) = \sum_{e \in TUL(X)} e.iutil$.

The proposed algorithm is known as pCLH-Miner (parallel Cross-Level high-utility itemset Miner). It has all the properties from the original algorithm, CLH-Miner [8]. Moreover, pCLH-Miner is extended to capable of working in parallel, exploiting the power of the multi-core processors to efficiently discover all CLHUIs. The proposed algorithm has the following characteristics: (a) It is a taxonomy-based algorithm to mine CLHUIs from the transaction database. (b) It is a one-phase algorithm. (c) The returned itemsets containing items at the cross-abstraction level. (d) The algorithm explores the search space in parallel to reduce the runtime.

It is not efficient when the original algorithm CLH-Miner scans the database multiple times when handling each item at level 1. Parallel processing is highly recommended to relieve the algorithm from this bottleneck. Almost the currently available processors contain multiple physical cores or logical cores to efficiently handle multi-tasking. With that in focus to reduce the mining time, multi-core parallel processing is adopted into this stage of the algorithm. Task Parallelism is used as our default load-balancing strategy. The search space of the problem is partitioned into sub-spaces. Each sub-space is then

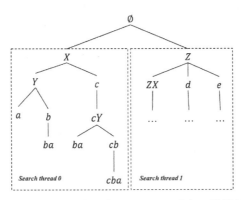

Fig. 2. An example of the partitioned search space of the pCLH-Miner algorithm

assigned a processor core to be explored in parallel recursively to discover itemsets extended from the item at level 1 (Fig. 2).

Algorithm 1. Pseudo-code of the pCLH-Miner algorithm

Input: transaction database D; taxonomy τ; the threshold μ;
Output: the set of all discovered *CLHUIs*
 1: Constructs the set I and GI from D and taxonomy τ;
 2: Scan D and τ to identify the $GTWU$ of each item $i \in I$
    and each generalized item $g \in GI$;
 3: $I^* \leftarrow \{i | i \in I \land GTWU(i) \geq \mu \land \forall g \in GI\}$ such that
    $Desc(g,\tau) \ni i, GTWU(g) \geq \mu\}$;
 4: $GI^* \leftarrow \{g | g \in GI \land GTWU(g) \geq \mu\}$;
 5: Determine the total order $\prec$ on $I^* \cup GI^*$;
 6: $itemL1 \leftarrow \{g | g \in \{GI^* \cup I^*\} \land level(g) = 1\}$;
 7: **FOREACH** $g \in itemL1$ **DO PARALLEL**
 8:    Scan D and τ to construct the TUL of each item g
       and $x \in I^* \cup GI^*$ such that $x \succ g$ in total order.
 9:    $newTULs \leftarrow \{TUL(x) | x \in itemL1 \land x \succ g\}$
10:    $newTULs \leftarrow \{TUL(y) | y \in Desc(x) \land level(y) = 2 \land x \in itemL1 \land x \prec g\}$
11:    **Explore** $(newTULs, NULL, \mu)$;

Alg. 1 presents the pseudo-code of our proposed approach. Line #1 initializes the algorithm constructing the set of I and GI using the taxonomy τ and database D. $GTWU$ of every single item in I and GI are then computed at line #2. At lines #3, #4, with the $GTWU$s obtained, the set I^* and GI^* are then formed by removing all items that do not meet the μ threshold, respectively. Line #5 sorts the set $I^* \cup GI^*$ using the total order $\prec$ of levels and the $GTWU$. Our contributions starting from line #6. It constructs the set *itemL1* to store all generalized items at level 1. Line #7 allocates and assigns a working thread to every item g in *itemL1*. Load balancing is also achieved at this step via the use of a thread-pool. Based on the $\prec$ order, line #8 builds TULs for g and items found in $I^* \cup GI^*$ and after g. Then at line #9, a new list named *newTUL* is defined to stores all items after item g in $itemL1$. Line #10 extends $itemL1$ using all items y have $level(y) = 2$ and are also descendants of the item before g. The thread-pool is then concurrently executing the Explore function for each submitted thread to traverse it assigned sub-space. The pseudo-code of this function is given in Alg. 2. This is done by combining items $i \in I$ with the generalized items $g \in GI$ which satisfy the μ threshold to form valid cross-level itemsets.

Algorithm 2. Pseudo-code of the Explore function

Input: extensions of itemset P: $TULs$, TUL of itemset P: P,
        threshold: μ;
Output: the $CLHUIs$ that are transitive extensions of P
 1: **FOREACH** $X \in TULs$ **DO**
 2:     **IF** $SUM(X.TUL.iutils) > \mu$ **THEN RETURN** X;
 3:     $ExtensionOfX \leftarrow \emptyset$
 4:     **FOREACH** itemset $Y \in TULs$ such that $X \prec Y$ **DO**
 5:         $JoinExtension.TUL \leftarrow Construct(P,X,Y)$;
 6:         **IF** $GTWU(JoinExtension) \geq \mu$ **THEN**
 7:             $ExtensionsOfX \leftarrow ExtensionsOfX \cup \{JoinExtension\}$;
 8:     **END FOR**
 9:     **IF** $SUM(X.TUL.iutils) + SUM(X.TUL.rutils) \geq \mu$ **THEN**
10:         **FOREACH** itemset $T \in X.childs$ **DO**
11:             $TaxExtensions.TUL \leftarrow Construct(P,X,T)$;
12:             **IF** $GTWU(TaxExtensions) \geq \mu$ **THEN**
13:                 $ExtensionsOfX \leftarrow ExtensionsOfX \cup \{TaxExtensions\}$;
14:         **END FOR**
15:     **END FOR**
16:     Explore($ExtensionsOfX, X, \mu$)
18: **END FOR**

Search space partitioning is one of the main contributions of this paper. Items at level 1 are divided among the available processor cores before database scans are performed to build the TUL of the according to the $\prec$ order. Each sub-search is non-overlapped and disjointed, thus the pCLH-Miner algorithm can safely assign each of them to a separate processor. The TUL of single items must be constructed and updated locally since they are different at each sub-space. Furthermore, these TULs must also contain 2nd level items which are descendants of those preceding the 1st level item currently under investigation. Otherwise, the Explore function would bypass the descendants of the items preceding g, missing out on the several itemsets that are extended based on the taxonomy of these items.

5   Experimental Evaluation

To assess the performance of pCLH-Miner algorithm, experiments were conducted on a system equipped with an AMD Ryzen™ 5 3600 (6 cores/12 threads) processor, 3.6 GHz, 24 GB DDR4 of RAM, and using Windows 10 Pro Workstation. Running time and peak memory usage factors are measured. pCLH-Miner is evaluated against the original CLH-Miner, using 2, 4, 8, and 12 processors (denoted as pCLH-Miner(2), pCLH-Miner(4), and so on) to discover CLHUIs. The algorithms were implemented in Java, thus Java API is used to measure the compared factors. The two algorithms are applied to the following databases: real database with built-in taxonomy Fruithut, Foodmart, and Liquor; Chainstore is a large database with a synthetic taxonomy. Table 3 presents their basic characteristics. Whereas, the database size is denoted as $|\mathcal{D}|$, $|I|$ denotes the number of specialized items, the number of generalized items is denoted as $|GI|$, d represents taxonomy's depth, the average length of all transactions is denoted as $Trans_{AVG}$, $ItemL1$ is the number level 1 generalized items. The size of the thread-pool is determined by selecting the minimum value between $|ItemL1|$ and the number of processor cores.

Table 3. Database details

Database	$|\mathcal{D}|$	$|\mathcal{I}|$	$|GI|$	d	$ItemL1$	$Trans_{AVG}$
Fruithut	181,970	1,265	43	4	13	3.58
Foodmart	53,537	1,560	102	5	3	4.6
Liquor	90,	2,626	77	7	4	10.2
Chainstore	1,112,949	46,086	9,674	9	3	7.2

The parameter μ was varied to evaluate its impact on the performance of pCLH-Miner. The runtime is measure starting from line #6 of the Alg. 1 until the algorithm finish. This is a block of code containing the differences between pCLH-Miner and CLH-Miner. The obtained runtimes of both algorithms are shown in Fig. 4. It's clearly visible throughout the charts that pCLH-Miner has a much lower runtime compared to its sequential version, the CLH-Miner. On all test databases, as we decreased the value of μ, the runtime raised. Using all maximum allowed threads, pCLH-Miner(12) has the highest speed-up by up to 4 times, compared to the CLH-Miner on the tested μ. Figure 3 illustrates the speed gained by using parallel processing compared to sequential as the baseline. For example, the Fruithut database at $\mu = 10K$, CLH-Miner required 2,450 s to finish, while the pCLH-Miner(12) required only 610 s to return all set of CLHUIs, that is 4 times faster. Due to the large search space of the cross-level HUI mining, with all 12 cores were put into use, the performance boost is only up to 4 times. On the Foodmart and Chainstore database, the average pCLH-Miner's speed-up factor is up to 2 times when using all 12 cores and 1.6 times for the Liquor database. This is due to the small size of the set $ItemL1$ and that the items in $ItemL1$ appearing in more transactions than other generalized items. It is also showed that pCLH-Miner has higher performance on databases where the number of items in $ItemL1$ is large.

We also compare the maximum memory used by the algorithms on each database. The results are shown in Fig. 4. It is observed that the memory usage of the pCLH-Miner algorithm is always higher than that of the CLH-Miner algorithm. The more threads were allocated, the more memory is required to store all its local data. Besides, as we lowered the μ thresholds, the memory usages are also increased but at a sustainable

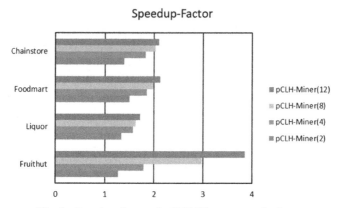

Fig. 3. Speed-up factor of pCLH-Miner on test databases

amount. pCLH-Miner(12) has the highest memory usage on the Chainstore database, which is peaked at almost 5.0 GB, while CLH-Miner is approximately 3.5 GB. The memory consumption of the pCLH-Miner in all tests is all under 8.0 GB limit of modern computers.

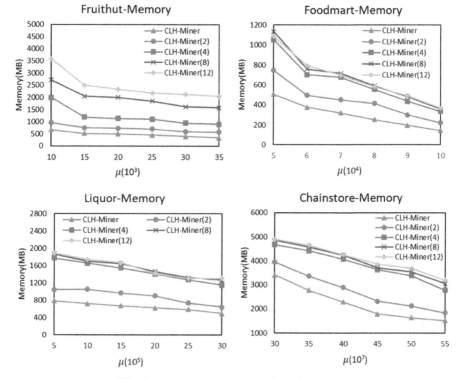

Fig. 4. Memory comparison on the test database

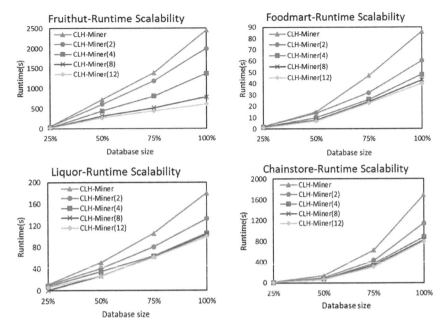

Fig. 5. Scalability comparison on the test databases

To analyze the impact of the database size on the runtime of the proposed algorithm, scalability tests were also carried out using the test databases. In these tests, we fixed the μ threshold at the lowest value used in previous tests. The number of transactions in each database is varied at the following ratio: 25%, 50%, 75% and 100%. The obtained results are shown in Fig. 5. It can be seen that the performance of pCLH-Miner is getting better than CLH-Miner as the size of the databases grows. It can be explained that as the database size is increased, the discovery time is also raised. Yet the CLH-Miner algorithm sequentially mines the itemsets, leading to a much-increased in runtime compared to pCLH-Miner. And as in the execution time evaluations, the best performance gained over database size occurred in the Fruithut database.

6   Conclusion and Future Works

With the widely available multi-core processors, utilizing them to enhance the performance of the tasks is practical. In this work, we have introduced a competitive approach to mine cross-level HUIs from the transaction database. The proposed algorithm is named pCLH-Miner, which is extended the original CLH-Miner algorithm into a parallelized algorithm. The algorithm partitions the search space into disjoint sub-spaces and assigns them to different processor cores, which is also solved the load balancing task. As seen in the experiments, the proposed algorithm has the best performance when applying on databases with a large number of generalized items at the first level of the taxonomy, which is the starting point of parallelism. However, the drawback of this approach is the high memory usages when more threads were allocated to concurrently explore the search space. Experiments on real-world and synthetic databases have demonstrated that pCLH-Miner algorithm has higher performance than CLH-Miner algorithm and has better scalability. In the future, we will continue to improve the algorithm to reduce the memory usage and the running time of the algorithm. We will enhance further the algorithm on distributed computing platforms, such as Hadoop or Apache Spark, to work with large scale databases.

References

1. Agrawal, R., et al.: Mining association rules between sets of items in large databases. ACM SIGMOD Rec. **22**(2), 207–216 (1993)
2. Alias, S., Norwawi, N.M.: pSPADE: mining sequential pattern using personalized support threshold value. In: Proceedings of the International Symposium on Information Technology 2008, ITSim, pp. 1–8 (2008)
3. Cagliero, L., et al.: Discovering high-utility itemsets at multiple abstraction levels. In: Kirikova, M., et al. (eds.) European Conference on Advances in Databases and Information Systems, pp. 224–234. Springer International Publishing, Cham (2017)
4. Chen, Y., An, A.: Approximate parallel high utility itemset mining. Big Data Res. **6**, 26–42 (2016)
5. Cong, S., et al.: Parallel mining of closed sequential patterns. In: Proceedings of the ACM SIGKDD International Conference on Knowledge Discovery and Data Mining, pp. 562–567 (2005)
6. Fournier-Viger, P., et al.: A survey of itemset mining. Wiley Interdiscip. Rev.: Data Min. Knowl. Disc. **7**(4), e1207 (2017)
7. Fournier-Viger, P., Wu, C.-W., Zida, S., Tseng, V.S.: FHM: Faster high-utility itemset mining using estimated utility co-occurrence pruning. In: Andreasen, T., Christiansen, H., Cubero, J.-C., Raś, Z.W. (eds.) ISMIS 2014. LNCS (LNAI), vol. 8502, pp. 83–92. Springer, Cham (2014). https://doi.org/10.1007/978-3-319-08326-1_9
8. Fournier-Viger, P., Wang, Y., Lin, J.-W., Luna, J.M., Ventura, S.: Mining Cross-Level High Utility Itemsets. In: Fujita, H., Fournier-Viger, P., Ali, M., Sasaki, J. (eds.) IEA/AIE 2020. LNCS (LNAI), vol. 12144, pp. 858–871. Springer, Cham (2020). https://doi.org/10.1007/978-3-030-55789-8_73
9. Han, J., et al.: Mining frequent patterns without candidate generation: a frequent-pattern tree approach. Data Min. Knowl. Disc. **8**(1), 53–87 (2004)
10. Hipp, J., Myka, A., Wirth, R., Güntzer, U.: A new algorithm for faster mining of generalized association rules. In: Żytkow, J.M., Quafafou, M. (eds.) PKDD 1998. LNCS, vol. 1510, pp. 74–82. Springer, Heidelberg (1998). https://doi.org/10.1007/BFb0094807
11. Liu, M., Qu, J.: Mining high utility itemsets without candidate generation categories and subject descriptors. In: Proceedings of the 21st ACM International Conference on Information and Knowledge Management (2012)
12. Liu, Y., Liao, W., Choudhary, A.: A twohase algorithm for fast discovery of high utility itemsets. In: Ho, T.B., Cheung, D., Liu, H. (eds.) Advances in Knowledge Discovery and Data Mining, pp. 689–695. Springer Berlin Heidelberg, Berlin, Heidelberg (2005). https://doi.org/10.1007/11430919_79
13. Nguyen, L.T.T., et al.: Mining high-utility itemsets in dynamic profit databases. Knowl.-Based Syst. **175**, 130–144 (2019)
14. Nguyen, N.T.: Consensus system for solving conflicts in distributed systems. Inf. Sci. **147**(1), 91–122 (2002)

15. Nguyen, N.T.: Using consensus methods for solving conflicts of data in distributed systems. In: Hlaváč, V., Jeffery, K.G., Wiedermann, J. (eds.) SOFSEM 2000. LNCS, vol. 1963, pp. 411–419. Springer, Heidelberg (2000). https://doi.org/10.1007/3-540-44411-4_30

16. Nguyen, T.D.D., Nguyen, L.T.T., Vo, B.: A parallel algorithm for mining high utility itemsets. In: Świątek, J., Borzemski, L., Wilimowska, Z. (eds.) ISAT 2018. AISC, vol. 853, pp. 286–295. Springer, Cham (2019). https://doi.org/10.1007/978-3-319-99996-8_26

17. Nguyen, T.D.D., Nguyen, L.T.T., Kozierkiewicz, A., Pham, T., Vo, B.: An efficient approach for mining high-utility itemsets from multiple abstraction levels. In: Nguyen, N.T., Chittayasothorn, S., Niyato, D., Trawiński, B. (eds.) ACIIDS 2021. LNCS (LNAI), vol. 12672, pp. 92–103. Springer, Cham (2021). https://doi.org/10.1007/978-3-030-73280-6_8

18. Nouioua, M., et al.: TKC: mining top-K cross-level high utility itemsets. In: 2020 International Conference on Data Mining Workshops (ICDMW), pp. 673–682 (2020)

19. Sethi, K.K., Ramesh, D., Edla, D.R.: P-FHM+: parallel high utility itemset mining algorithm for big data processing. Procedia Comput. Sci. **132**, 918–927 (2018)

20. Srikant, R., Agrawal, R.: Mining generalized association rules. Futur. Gener. Comput. Syst. **13**(2–3), 161–180 (1997)

21. Vo, B., et al.: A multi-core approach to efficiently mining high-utility itemsets in dynamic profit databases. IEEE Access. **8**, 85890–85899 (2020)

22. Vo, B., Le, B.: Fast algorithm for mining generalized association rules. Int. J. Datab. Theor. Appl. **2**(3), 19–21 (2009)

23. Yao, H., et al.: A foundational approach to mining itemset utilities from databases. In: SIAM International Conference on Data Mining, pp. 482–486 (2004)

24. Zhu, T., Bai, S.: A parallel mining algorithm for closed sequential patterns. In: Proceedings of the 21st International Conference on Advanced Information Networking and Applications Workshops/Symposia, AINAW 2007, pp. 392–395 (2007)

25. Zida, S., Fournier-Viger, P., Lin, J.-W., Wu, C.-W., Tseng, V.S.: EFIM: a fast and memory efficient algorithm for high-utility itemset mining. Knowl. Inf. Syst. **51**(2), 595–625 (2016)

Decision Combination in Classifier Committee Built on Deep Embedding Features

Jacek Treliński and Bogdan Kwolek(✉)

AGH University of Science and Technology, 30 Mickiewicza, 30-059 Krakow, Poland
{tjacek,bkw}@agh.edu.pl

Abstract. In this paper we leverage voting rules as an aggregation technique in classifier combination. We propose a voting rules-based algorithm to improve the recognition performance of human action recognition on raw depth maps. The recognition is performed by a classifier committee that is built on deep embedding features. It consists of softmax logistic regression classifiers delivering well calibrated outputs. They have been trained as one-vs-all on the concatenated class-specific features and features common for all classes. Various ranked voting rules as the aggregation technique have been investigated in decision making. The results achieved by such algorithms were compared with results achieved in optimized weighted voting. Differential evolution and sequential least squares programming have been selected for optimized weighted voting. We demonstrate experimentally that both optimized weighted voting and voting rules improve results achieved by soft voting. The best results have been achieved using voting rules determined by Coombs algorithm. We demonstrate experimentally that on SYSU 3DHOI dataset the proposed algorithm outperforms by a large margin all recent algorithms.

Keywords: Classifier committee · Decision combination · Voting rules

1 Introduction

Classifier combination approaches have been proved to be a valuable approach to boost the performance of classifiers. The rationale for this could be that the training data may not provide sufficient information for selecting a single best classifier. Moreover, the weakness of individual classifiers can be compensated by other committee members, and consequently, the multiple classifier systems exhibit better performance than a single model [1]. In general, multiple classifier systems yield better results when there is a vast diversity among the models [2].

The combination of classifiers can be done at three different levels, i.e. at sensor data level, at the feature level, or at the decision level. In [3] several combination techniques including voting, Bayesian, and Dempster-Shafer theory are discussed. A theoretical study and comparison of classifier combination strategies has been done in [4]. Fumera and Roli [5] demonstrated that the performance

© Springer Nature Switzerland AG 2021
N. T. Nguyen et al. (Eds.): ICCCI 2021, LNAI 12876, pp. 480–493, 2021.
https://doi.org/10.1007/978-3-030-88081-1_36

of linear combiners hinges on the accuracy of the individual classifier from the committee and the correlation between their outcomes. In voting-based multiple classifier systems the decision is made upon a voting of the system members. In a technique called majority voting every individual classifier votes for a class, and the majority wins. The soft voting techniques predict the class label upon the argmax of the sums of the predicted probabilities of the individual estimators that make up the multiple classifier system. In [6] the impact of ensemble size with majority voting and optimal weighted voting aggregation rules has been discussed. Ranked voting approaches are recommended for classifier combination if and when the classifiers can rank the order of the classes [1]. Borda counts is a rank-based combination technique in which each classifier ranks the classes according to their potentiality to be the correct class [7]. It is considered to be one of the simplest scoring rules.

Human-object interaction occupies the most of daily human activities. Daily human activities are complex, ambiguous and differ in realization by individuals. Due to such factors, current algorithms have poor performance in comparison to human ability to recognize human motions and actions [8,9]. There are many potential applications of human action recognition including video surveillance, health care [10], and human-computer interaction. 3D-based approaches to human action recognition provide higher accuracy than 2D-based ones. Most of current approaches to action recognition on depth maps are based on the skeleton [11]. The number of depth map-based approaches, particularly using deep learning is very limited [9]. Conventional approaches to activity recognition on depth maps are built upon handcrafted features [12–14]. In a recent work [14], depth motion images (DMI) and Laplacian pyramids as structured multi-scale feature maps have been employed to classify human actions on depth maps. As opposed to handcrafted representation-based algorithms, in which engineered features describe actions, deep learning methods are capable of discovering the most discriminative and informative features directly from raw data [15]. Recently, in [16] deep embedding features for action recognition on raw depth maps have been proposed. In this work a classifier committee that is built on features mentioned above is enhanced by the ranked voting.

This paper is devoted to leveraging voting rules as the aggregation technique in classifier combination with aim of improving the classification performance. We propose a voting rules-based algorithm to increase the recognition performance of human action recognition on raw depth maps. The recognition is carried out by a classifier committee that is built on deep embedding features. The multiple classifier system comprises softmax logistic regression classifiers delivering well calibrated outputs. They have been trained as one-vs-all upon the concatenated class-specific features and common features for all classes. Various voting rules as the aggregation technique have been investigated in decision making. The results achieved by multiple classifier systems with soft voting as well as ranked voting were compared with results achieved in optimized weighted voting. Differential Evolution (DE) and Sequential Least SQuares Programming (SLSQP) have been selected for optimized weighted voting. We demonstrate experimentally that both optimized weighted voting and voting rules improve results achieved by the soft voting. The best results have been achieved using voting rules determined by the Coombs algorithm. We demonstrate experimentally that on the challenging SYSU 3D Human-Object Interaction Set the proposed algorithm outperforms by a large margin all recent algorithms.

2 Combining Class Labels

2.1 Majority Voting

Multiple classifier systems collect the results of multiple simple models and then combine them into a single aggregated output. The aggregation techniques are also known as combining rules or voting rules. In Multiple Classifier Systems (MCS) such rules play a central role in shaping their performance. In classification tasks, typically, aggregation is done using majority voting. It is the most straightforward combination strategy for labeled output. In majority voting every classifier has one vote that can be cast for any one candidate class. The candidate class, which collected the majority, i.e. more than half of the votes, is used as the decision [7]. When combining categorical outputs the majority voting usually permits improving results. Hard voting is the simplest approach to majority voting. In this approach, the class label $\hat{y}$ is predicted via majority voting of m classifiers h_j:

$$\hat{y} = mode\{h_1(x), h_2(x), \ldots, h_m(x)\} \tag{1}$$

Here, each classifier votes for a particular class, and the class with the most votes is selected as the classifier committee output. In a more sophisticated approach the contribution of each committee member can be weighted by a factor that indicates the trust or expected performance of the model. Given votes from classifiers $h_1, h_2, \ldots, h_m$, the weighted majority voting can be expressed as follows:

$$\hat{y} = \arg\max_i \sum_{j=1}^{m} w_j I(h_j(x) = i) \tag{2}$$

where $w_1, w_2, \ldots, w_m$ are weights that sum to 1 and $I(\cdot)$ is an indicator function $[h_j(x) = i \in A]$, where A is the set of unique class labels.

The simplest, but exhaustive approach to seek weights for the committee members is to use the grid search, i.e. Cartesian product. In a more sophisticated approach the predictions can be averaged using weights which are optimized using a nonlinear optimization. The searching for weight values can also be performed using a stochastic global optimization algorithm, for instance a variant of differential evolution (DE) [17].

2.2 Optimized Weighted Voting

To aim of nonlinear optimization is minimization of some objective function $f(x)$, where $f : \mathbb{R}^d \to \mathbb{R}$, $x \in \mathbb{R}^d$, and the solution is subject to some constraints.

Box constraints enforce a lower or upper bound on each of d parameters. They are usually defined as $lb = (lb_1, \ldots, lb_d)$ and $ub = (ub_1, \ldots, ub_d)$ such that $lb_j \leq x_j \leq ub_j$ for $j = 1, \ldots, d$. Another constraints are inequality constraints $f_{c_k}(x) \leq 0$, where $k = 1, \ldots, k$, and $f_{c_k}(x)$ are constraint functions. Some optimizers support also nonlinear equality constraints of the form: $f_h(x) = 0$. The objective function can be mean square error (MSE), and the optimization problem can be formulated as a nonlinear convex optimization problem:

$$\min \frac{1}{n} \sum_{i=1}^{n} (y_i - \sum_{j=1}^{m} w_j \hat{y}_{ij})^2$$

$$\text{s.t.}$$
$$\sum_{j=1}^{m} w_j = 1 \qquad\qquad (3)$$
$$w_j \geq 0, \forall j = 1, \ldots, m$$

where w_j is the weight corresponding to classifier j, $j = 1, \ldots, m$, and n denotes the total number of instances, y_i is the true value of observation i, and $\hat{y}_{ij}$ is the prediction of observation i by the classifier j. In the optimized weighted voting the true labels are used to determine the weights in the optimization process.

2.3 Soft Voting

In soft voting the class label is predicted upon the probabilities p of the classifiers. The voting combiner calculates weighted average predicted probability of class membership that can be expressed as follows:

$$\hat{y} = \arg\max_{i} \sum_{j=1}^{m} w_j p_{ij} \qquad\qquad (4)$$

where w_j denotes the weight that can be assigned to the j-th classifier, whereas p_{ij} stands for the probability assigned to i-th category by the j-th classifier. The discussed kind of voting is recommended if the classifiers are well calibrated.

2.4 Ranked Voting

In ranked voting methods the ranking preferences of the classifiers are taken into account. In Borda count-based methods [7] a complete preference ranking from all classifiers over all candidate classifiers is determined. Then, the mean rank of each candidate class over all classifiers is computed. Finally, candidate classes are reranked by their mean rank and the top ranked class is the output. This method does not require the training. It is considered to be one of the simplest scoring rules. A scoring rule is any method that calculates a score based on weights assigned to candidates according to where they fall in the voters' rankings. In a method called Bucklin [18] we utilize rankings of the candidates as the input. At the beginning we count first place votes. If the candidate has more than 50% votes then algorithm stops. If there is no candidate with a strict majority then second place votes are added to the first place votes. If there is still no candidate with majority, lower rankings are added as needed. Coombs method [19] utilizes candidate elimination and redistribution of votes cast for that candidate until one candidate achieved a majority of the votes. At the beginning, as previously, we count first place votes and if the candidate has more than 50% votes then the algorithm stops. If there is no candidate with a strict majority, the candidate that receive the most last-place votes is repeatedly deleted, and remaining votes are recounted. If there is still no candidate with majority we repeat the previous step. If all candidates with last-place votes were deleted then the candidate with the most second last-place votes is deleted, and so on.

3   The Algorithm

Due to limited number of depth map sequences in most frequently used benchmark datasets for human action recognition we use a multiple classifier system. In the proposed approach to classify human actions on raw depth maps, various features are learned in different domains, like single depth map, time-series of embedded features, time-series warped by DTW (dynamic time warping), and final decision is taken using voting rules as the aggregation technique in classifier combination. The multi-stream features are processed to extract action features in sequences of depth maps. Action features are extracted using DTW, TimeDistributed and LSTM layers (TD-LSTM), and convolutional autoencoder followed by a multi-channel, temporal CNN (1D-CNN) [16]. The TD-LSTM features that are extracted by independently trained networks are class-specific, whereas 1D-CNN and DTW features are common for all classes. In order to cope with variability in the observations as well as limited amount of training data, particularly in order to improve model uncertainty the final decision is made on the basis of several models that are simpler but more robust to the specifics of noisy data sequences. The multiple classifier system comprises softmax logistic regression classifiers. They are learned as one-vs-all on the concatenated class-specific features and common features for all classes. The final decision is made by a classifier committee as a result of the ranked voting. Alternatively, the final decision can be taken on the basis of soft voting or optimized weighted voting.

In Subsect. 3.1 we briefly outline features describing the person's shape in single depth maps. Afterwards, in Subsection 3.2 we overview features representing multivariate time-series. Then, in Subsect. 3.3 we concisely outline embedding human actions using a neural network with TimeDistributed and LSTM layers. In Subsect. 3.4 we overview multi-class classifiers to construct a classifier committee. Finally, in Subsect. 3.5 we describe the classifier committee as well as explain how voting rules as the aggregation technique in classifier combination are used to achieve improvements in classification performance.

3.1   Embedding Action Features Using CAE and Multi-channel, Temporal CNN

Embedding Frame-Features. Having on regard that present benchmark datasets for depth-based action recognition encompass not enough number of sequences to learn deep models with acceptable generalization capabilities, we employ a convolutional autoencoder (CAE) operating on single depth maps to determine frame-features. Given time-series of such features representing actions in frame sequences we employ a multi-channel, temporal CNN that is responsible for extracting the embedded features.

In order to extract frame-features we implemented a convolutional autoencoder. After training the CAE, the decoding layers were excluded from the autoencoder. The network trained in such a way has been utilized to extract low dimensional frame-features. The input depth maps were projected two 2D orthogonal Cartesian planes to represent top as well as side view of the maps. The convolutional autoencoder has been trained on depth maps of size $3\times64\times64$. The size of depth map embedding is equal to 100. On the training subsets we learned a single CAE for all classes.

Embedding Action Features Using Multi-channel, Temporal CNN. The CAE-based feature extractor operating on depth map sequences representing human actions produces multivariate time-series. Having on regard that depth map sequences differ in the length, such variable length time-series have been interpolated to a common length, set to 64. In multi-channel, temporal CNNs the 1D convolutions are executed in the temporal domain. The time-series of frame-features that were extracted by the CAE-based feature extractor have been employed to train a multi-channel 1D CNN. The number of channels at the input of the neural network is equal to 100, i.e. the size of depth map embedding. After training the discussed neural network the output of its dense layer has been used to embed the features, which are referred to as 1D-CNN features. The size 1D-CNN feature vector is equal to 100.

3.2   DTW-Based Action Features

Frame-Feature Vector. In order to compactly represent the person's shape we calculate also statistical features in single depth maps. This is because the statistical properties can help reducing the effects of outliers such motion-less sub-actions occurring at an early temporal stage. As in case of learned frame-features, which were shortly outlined in Subsect. 3.1, the input depth maps are projected onto three orthogonal Cartesian views in order to capture the 3D shape and 3D motion information. The frame-feature are calculated only on the foreground pixels representing the extracted person in depth maps. The following features representing person's shape in single depth maps have been calculated: (1) correlation (xy, xz and zy axes), (2) $x-$coordinate for which the corresponding depth value represents the closest pixel to the camera, $y-$coordinate

486   J. Treliński and B. Kwolek

for which the corresponding depth value represents the closest pixel to the camera. It follows that in each depth map the person's shape is described by five features. A human action represented by a number of depth maps is described by a multivariate time-series of length equal to number of frames in the sequence and dimension equal to five.

DTW-based Features. Dynamic time warping (DTW) is an effective algorithm for measuring similarity between two temporal sequences, which may vary in speed and length. It calculates an optimal match between two given sequences, e.g. time series [20]. In time-series classification one of the most effective algorithms is 1-NN-DTW, which is a special k-nearest neighbor classifier with $k = 1$ and a dynamic time warping for distance measurement. In DTW the sequences are warped non-linearly in time dimension to determine the best match between two samples such that when the same pattern exists in both sequences, the distance is smaller.

The feature vector contains the DTW distances to all time-series from the training subset. This means that the resulting feature vector has size equal to $n_t \times 2$, where n_t denotes the number of training depth map sequences, and second dimension stands for the number of features sets. At the training stage, for each depth maps sequence from the training subset we calculate the DTW distances to all depth maps sequences in the training subset. This means that every feature vector contains a single DTW distance between the same multivariate time-series. At the testing stage, for each depth maps sequence from the testing subset we calculate the DTW distances to all depth maps sequences in the training subset. The DTW distances between multivariate time-series have been determined for the mentioned above frame-features. They have been calculated using implementation of DTW from library [21].

3.3 Embedding Actions Using Neural Network Consisting of TimeDistributed and LSTM Layers

The neural network consisting of TimeDistributed and LSTM layers operates on depth map sequences, where each sample is of size 64×64, across 30 time-steps. The frame batches have size equal to 30 and they have been constructed by sampling with replacement. Similarly as in [16] in first three layers we utilize TimeDistributed wrapper in order to apply the same Conv2D layer to each of the 30 time-steps, independently. In the last layer we employ 64 LSTMs and then 64 global average pooling filters. The means that the discussed neural network delivers feature vectors of size 64. The discussed models have been trained as one-vs-all and the resulting features are called TD-LSTM.

3.4 Multi-class Classifiers to Construct Classifier Committee

The features described in Subsects. 3.1–3.3 have been employed to train multi-class, logistic regression classifiers with softmax encoding, see Fig. 1. Having on regard that for each class an action-specific classifier has been trained, the number of such classifiers is equal to the number of actions to be recognized. The convolutional autoencoder operating on sequences of depth maps delivers time-series of CAE-based frame-features, on which we determine 1D-CNN features (Subsect. 3.1). Similarly to features mentioned above, the DTW-based features (Subsect. 3.2) are also common features for all classes. The base networks of TimeDistributed-LSTM network (Subsect. 3.3) operating on sequences of depth maps deliver class-specific action features. The discussed TD-LSTM features are then concatenated with action features mentioned above, see also Fig. 1. The multi-class classifiers delivering at the outputs the softmax-encoded class probability distributions are finally used in a classifier committee responsible for classification of human actions.

3.5   Classifier Committee

Figure 1 depicts the classifier committee for action classification. The final decision is calculated on the basis of classifier rankings and voting. In essence, the final decision is taken using a committee of individual models. One advantage of this approach is its interpretability. Because each class is expressed by one classifier only, it is possible to gain knowledge about the discriminative power of individual classifiers. As we can see, for each class the action features that are common for all actions are concatenated with class-specific features, and then used to train multi-class classifiers.

At the beginning we implemented a basic classifier committee. In discussed implementation all classifiers that have been trained in advance attended in the hard voting. After implementing end evaluating the soft voting, it turned out that classifier committee built on it permits to achieve better results in comparison to results achieved by the basic classifier committee. Next, we implemented a classifier committee based on differential evolution, which was responsible for determining the weights for the voting. The objective function has been calculated as: 1 - classification accuracy. The bounds were set as a D-dimensional hypercube with values between 0.0 and 1.0, where D stands for the number of actions. The optimization has been performed using differential_evolution() method from SciPy[1]. Afterwards, in a weighted voting the weights were determined in a constrained nonlinear optimization using the Sequential Least SQuares Programming (SLSQP) algorithm. The log loss has been utilized in the objective function, among others to penalize predicted probabilities far away from their expected value. Assuming that the true labels for a set of observations are encoded such $y_{i,k} = 1$ if observation i has label k from a set of K labels, the log loss of the whole set can be expressed in the following manner:

$$L_{log} = -\frac{1}{N} \sum_{i=0}^{N-1} \sum_{k=0}^{K-1} y_{i,k} \log p_{i,k} \tag{5}$$

---

[1] https://github.com/scipy/scipy/blob/master/scipy/optimize/_differentialevolution.py.

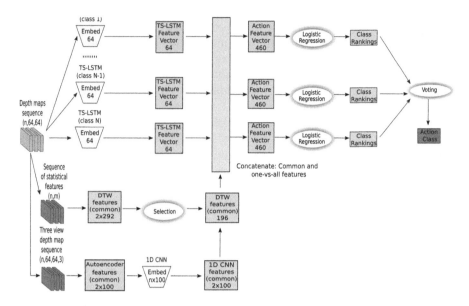

Fig. 1. Decision combination in classifier committee that is built on: features extracted by DTW, features embedded by CAE and 1D-CNN, which are then concatenated with class-specific features that are embedded by TimeDistributed and LSTM neural networks.

Finally, we implemented and evaluated the ranked voting methods, which have been discussed in Sect. 2. We investigated Borda counts [7], Bucklin [18] and Coombs [19].

4   Experimental Results

The proposed algorithm has been evaluated on publicly available SYSU 3D Human-Object Interaction Set (SYSU 3DHOI) [22]. The SYSU 3D Human-Object Interaction (3DHOI) dataset was recorded by the Kinect v1 sensor and comprises 480 RGB-D sequences with 12 action classes. The activities include calling with cell phone, playing with a cell phone, pouring, drinking, wearing backpack, packing a backpack, sitting on a chair, moving a chair, taking something from a wallet, taking out a wallet, mopping and sweeping. Actions were performed by 40 subjects. Each activity is a kind of human-object interaction. Some motion actions are fairly similar at the beginning since the subjects operate or interact with the same objects, or actions start with the same sub-action, such as standing still, or have the same motion of picking up a phone, i.e. actions of "playing phone" and "calling phone". The above mentioned issues make this dataset challenging. The algorithm has been evaluated in setting-1 and setting-2 [23]. In setting-1 we selected half of the samples for training and the rest for testing, whereas in the second cross-subject setting the depth map sequences with actions of half of the subjects have been used to learn model parameters and the rest for the testing. Since in the SYSU 3DHOI dataset the performers are not extracted from depth maps, the subjects have been extracted by our software. For each depth map we determined a window surrounding the person, which has then been scaled to the required input shape.

Table 1 contains experimental results that were achieved on the 3DHOI dataset in setting-1. As we can see the best results have been achieved by the Coombs algorithm.

Table 1. Recognition performance on SYSU 3DHOI dataset in setting-1.

Voting	Accuracy	Precision	Recall	F1-score
soft voting	0.8792	0.8828	0.8792	0.8798
Borda counts	0.8792	0.8829	0.8792	0.8798
Bucklin [18]	0.8792	0.8819	0.8792	0.8792
Coombs [19]	**0.8875**	**0.8907**	**0.8875**	**0.8880**

Table 2 illustrates results that have been achieved in setting-2. First row contains results that have been achieved by the committee consisting of classifiers operating on one-vs-all features (LSTM-based) concatenated with features embedded by CAE and 1D-CNN, and concatenated with DTW features. The discussed results were achieved by the logistic regression classifiers. Soft voting using all classifiers gives better results, cf. results in second row. The results achieved by soft voting with weights determined by differential evolution are slightly worse than results achieved by the soft voting. As we can observe, the algorithm based on the SLSQP optimization was unable to improve results obtained by DE. The results achieved by soft voting, differential evolution and the SLSQP optimizer are better in comparison to results achieved by the base algorithm. In SLSQP-based classifier committee we considered the two-fold and five-fold evaluation on the test subset. The difference between the results in discussed settings were not statistically significant. As we can see, Borda counts permits to achieve better results in comparison to results mentioned above. The best results have been obtained by the Coombs algorithm. Figure 2 illustrates the confusion matrixes that has been achieved by this algorithm. It can be seen that the proposed algorithm distinguishes well all twelve actions of the dataset, which demonstrates that it can effectively represent the interaction between human and the object.

Table 3 presents results achieved by recent algorithms on 3DHOI dataset in comparison to results achieved by our algorithm. As we can observe, our algorithm achieves superior results on this challenging dataset. The results are better in comparison to results achieved in our previous work [16] in which we

Table 2. Recognition performance on SYSU 3DHOI dataset (cross-subject setting).

Voting	Accuracy	Precision	Recall	F1-score
–	0.8947	0.8953	0.8947	0.8941
soft voting	0.9167	0.9187	0.9167	0.9163
diff. evol.	0.9123	0.9159	0.9123	0.9121
SLSQP	0.9079	0.9106	0.9079	0.9073
Borda counts	0.9211	0.9244	0.9211	0.9209
Bucklin [18]	0.9211	0.9257	0.9211	0.9207
Coombs [19]	**0.9298**	**0.9332**	**0.9298**	**0.9296**

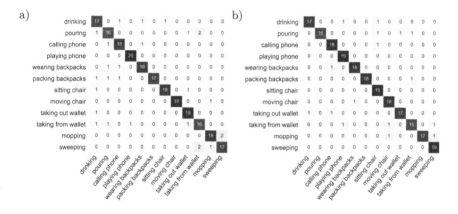

Fig. 2. Confusion matrix on 3DHOI dataset, setting-1 a), setting-2 b).

performed evaluations according to setting-2. It is worth noting that method [24] relies on depth and skeleton modalities, whereas [23] additionally utilizes RGB images jointly with the skeleton data. As far as we know, a recently published SGN algorithm [25] achieves the best classification accuracies among skeleton-based algorithms. The proposed algorithm outperforms it by a large margin in terms of classification accuracy.

We demonstrated experimentally that on challenging SYSU 3DHOI dataset the proposed algorithm attains promising results and outperforms recent state-of-the-art depth-based algorithms [23,24]. It is worth noting that our algorithm outperforms most recent skeleton-based methods that usually achieve better results in comparison to methods based on depth maps only. The algorithm has been implemented in Python language using Keras library. The source code, including scripts for learning preferences is freely available at the following URL: https://github.com/tjacek/ICCCI.

Table 3. Comparative recognition performance of the proposed method with recent algorithms on 3DHOI dataset.

Method	Modality	setting	Acc. [%]
LGN [26]	skel	II	83.33
SGN [25]	skel	II	86.90
MSRNN [23]	depth+RGB+skel	II	79.58
LAFF [27]	depth+RGB	II	80.00
PTS [24]	depth+skeleton	II	87.92
bidirect. rank pooling [28]	depth	I	76.25
bidirect. rank pooling [28]	depth	II	75.83
emb. feat. [16]	depth	II	90.35
Proposed method	depth	I	**88.75**
Proposed method	depth	II	**92.98**

5   Conclusions

In this paper we proposed an approach to human action recognition on raw depth maps using voting rules as the aggregation technique in classifier combination. The action recognition is achieved by a multiple classifier system that is built on logistic regression-based classifiers. The novelty of the proposed method lies in leveraging voting rules as the aggregation technique in classifier combination for effective human action recognition on depth map sequences. We demonstrated experimentally that the proposed voting strategies in the classifier committee permit improving the classification performance. Comparing results achieved by classifier committee using Borda counts, or Bucklin or Coombs algorithm the best results were achieved by the last one algorithm, which achieves more than 1% gain of the recognition performance in comparison to performance achieved by the soft voting. Owing to using multiple classifiers the algorithm achieves promising results in scenarios in which the amount of training data is small. It achieves superior results in comparison to recent algorithms on challenging 3D Human-Object Interaction Set (SYSU 3DHOI).

Acknowledgment. This work was supported by Polish National Science Center (NCN) under a research grant 2017/27/B/ST6/01743.

References

1. Polikar, R.: Ensemble based systems in decision making. IEEE Circuits Syst. Mag. **6**(3), 21–45 (2006)
2. Kuncheva, L.I., Whitaker, C.J.: Measures of diversity in classifier ensembles and their relationship with the ensemble accuracy. Mach. Learn. **51**(2), 181–207 (2003)
3. Xu, L., Krzyzak, A., Suen, C.: Methods of combining multiple classifiers and their applications to handwriting recognition. IEEE Trans. SMC **22**(3), 418–435 (1992)
4. Kuncheva, L.I.: A theoretical study on six classifier fusion strategies. IEEE Trans. Pattern Anal. Mach. Intell. **24**(2), 281–286 (2002)

5. Fumera, G., Roli, F.: A theoretical and experimental analysis of linear combiners for multiple classifier systems. IEEE Trans. PAMI **27**(6), 942–956 (2005)
6. Bonab, H., Can, F.: Less is more: A comprehensive framework for the number of components of ensemble classifiers. IEEE Trans. on Neural Networks and Learning Systems 30(9) (2019) 2735–2745
7. van Erp, M., Vuurpijl, L., Schomaker, L.: An overview and comparison of voting methods for pattern recognition. In: Proceedings of Eighth International Workshop on Frontiers in Handwriting Recognition, pp. 195–200 (2002)
8. Liang, B., Zheng, L.: A survey on human action recognition using depth sensors. In: Int. Conf. on Digital Image Comp.: Techn. and Appl., pp. 1–8 (2015)
9. Wang, L., Huynh, D.Q., Koniusz, P.: A comparative review of recent Kinect-based action recognition algorithms. IEEE Trans. Image Process. **29**, 15–28 (2020)
10. Haque, A., Milstein, A., Fei-Fei, L.: Illuminating the dark spaces of healthcare with ambient intelligence. Nature **585**(7824), 193–202 (2020)
11. Ren, B., Liu, M., Ding, R., Liu, H.: A survey on 3D skeleton-based action recognition using learning method. arXiv, 2002.05907 (2020)
12. Yang, X., Zhang, C., Tian, Y.L.: Recognizing actions using depth motion maps-based histograms of oriented gradients. In: Proceedings of the 20th ACM International Conference on Multimedia, pp. 1057–1060. ACM (2012)
13. Xia, L., Aggarwal, J.: Spatio-temporal depth cuboid similarity feature for activity recognition using depth camera. In: CVPR, pp. 2834–2841 (2013)
14. Li, C., Huang, Q., Li, X., Wu, Q.: A multi-scale human action recognition method based on Laplacian pyramid depth motion images. In: Proceedings the 2nd ACM International Conference on Multimedia in Asia. ACM (2021)
15. Majumder, S., Kehtarnavaz, N.: Vision and inertial sensing fusion for human action recognition: a review. IEEE Sensors J. **21**(3), 2454–2467 (2021)
16. Trelinski, J., Kwolek, B.: Deep embedding features for action recognition on raw depth maps. In: Paszynski, M., Kranzlmüller, D., Krzhizhanovskaya, V.V., Dongarra, J.J., Sloot, P.M.A. (eds.) ICCS 2021. LNCS, vol. 12744, pp. 95–108. Springer, Cham (2021). https://doi.org/10.1007/978-3-030-77967-2_9
17. Hassan, S., Hemeida, A.M., Alkhalaf, S., Mohamed, A.A., Senjyu, T.: Multi-variant differential evolution algorithm for feature selection. Scientific Reports 10(1), October 2020
18. Erdélyi, G., Fellows, M.R., Rothe, J., Schend, L.: Control complexity in Bucklin and fallback voting: a theoretical analysis. J. Comput. Syst. Sci. **81**(4), 632–660 (2015)
19. Pacuit, E.: Voting methods. Stanford Encyclopedia of Philosophy (Fall 2017 Ed.), Edward N. Zalta (ed.) (2017)
20. Paliwal, K., Agarwal, A., Sinha, S.: A modification over Sakoe and Chiba's dynamic time warping algorithm for isolated word recognition. Signal Proc. **4**(4), 329–333 (1982)
21. Meert, W., Hendrickx, K., Craenendonck, T.V.: DTAIdistance, ver. 2.0 (2021). https://zenodo.org/record/3981067
22. Hu, J., Zheng, W., Lai, J., Zhang, J.: Jointly learning heterogeneous features for RGB-D activity recognition. In: CVPR, pp. 5344–5352 (2015)
23. Hu, J., Zheng, W., Ma, L., Wang, G., Lai, J., Zhang, J.: Early action prediction by soft regression. IEEE Trans. PAMI **41**(11), 2568–2583 (2019)
24. Wang, X., Hu, J.F., Lai, J.H., Zhang, J., Zheng, W.S.: Progressive teacher-student learning for early action prediction. In: CVPR, pp. 3551–3560 (2019)

25. Zhang, P., Lan, C., Zeng, W., Xing, J., Xue, J., Zheng, N.: Semantics-guided neural networks for efficient skeleton-based human action recognition. In: IEEE/CVF Conference on Computer Vision and Pattern Recognition, pp. 1109–1118. IEEE

26. Ke, Q., Bennamoun, M., Rahmani, H., An, S., Sohel, F., Boussaid, F.: Learning latent global network for skeleton-based action prediction. IEEE Trans. Img. Proc. **29**, 959–970 (2020)

27. Hu, J.F., Zheng, W.S., Ma, L., Wang, G., Lai, J.: Real-time RGB-D activity prediction by soft regression. In: European Conf. on Comp. Vision, pp. 280–296. Springer (2016)

28. Ren, Z., Zhang, Q., Gao, X., Hao, P., Cheng, J.: Multi-modality learning for human action recognition. Multimed. Tools Appl. **80**(11), 16185–16203 (2020). https://doi.org/10.1007/s11042-019-08576-z

Deep Learning with Optimization Techniques for the Classification of Spoken English Digit

Jane Oruh⬤ and Serestina Viriri$^{(\boxtimes)}$⬤

School of Mathematics, Statistics and Computer Science,
University of KwaZulu-Natal, Durban, South Africa
viriris@ukzn.ac.za

Abstract. Multiclass classification is a fundamental problem for many speech recognition systems. A typical example of multiclass classification in speech recognition is spoken digit classification. This type of classification is generally a challenging task since the signals last for a short period and often some digits are acoustically very similar to each other. To resolve this challenge, an intelligent based system is proposed using an enhanced deep feedforward network technique for the spoken digit classification. In the proposed method, Short Time Fourier Transform (STFT) features were first extracted from audio data and one hot encoding was performed on the audio data to generate the target audio class label. This was then used as input into the deep learning model. The model performance was evaluated using hyper-parameter optimization techniques such as Adam optimization algorithm and Stochastic Gradient Descent (SGD) optimization algorithm to reduce losses and to provide the most accurate results possible. The experimental results show that the system when used with Adam optimization algorithm outperformed the classical SGD optimization algorithm on the well-established public benchmark spoken English digit dataset, PCM and achieved an overall accuracy of 99.65%. The results show that the choice of a good hyper-parameter optimizer like Adam optimization algorithm can achieve optimal accuracy.

Keywords: Automatic speech recognition · Deep learning optimization · Short Time Fourier Transform (STFT) · One hot encoding · Speech classification

1 Introduction

1.1 Background

Speech consists of a sequence of uttered sounds (phonemes), at an average rate of approximately 12 phonemes per second. The conversion of a speech signal into a useful message (its corresponding text) is called automatic speech recognition (ASR) [17]. Classification of speech is one of the highest crucial issue in speech

© Springer Nature Switzerland AG 2021
N. T. Nguyen et al. (Eds.): ICCCI 2021, LNAI 12876, pp. 494–507, 2021.
https://doi.org/10.1007/978-3-030-88081-1_37

processing [18]. Although studies have been conducted on the classification of speech, the outcome of researches in this area are still restricted.

The recognition of short and isolated words is a difficult problem even for nowadays commercial ASR systems. This, as of today, is still an open issue, and a serious barrier to overcome due to the limitations of ASR systems. This challenge was evident in [5], where the recognition of isolated words was practically difficult for Google ASR system. The authors observed in the research that pairs of words for example "were/where" may be wrongly though normally reduced to the same pronunciation. Their proposed model based on minimal-pairs setting therefore, integrates an educational gesture that could be further developed.

Several works on spoken digit recognition have adopted multiple abductive network classifier strategy to improve the reliability of the classification process [10]. Multiclass classification is a fundamental problem for most speech recognition systems [12]. The problem in multiclass classification could be identified as: (1) the Spoken digits are of short acoustic duration, typically a few seconds of speech; (2) Some digits are acoustically very similar to each other (for example, 'one' and 'nine') [22].

To address this challenge, the model proposes an enhanced deep supervised feedforward network that will make use of a mathematical function to map some set of input values to output values on spoken English digits dataset. Short Term Fourier Transform (STFT) features were extracted from the audio data, while one hot encoding was used to generate the target audio class label as input for the proposed model. The choice of a deep feedforward network is based on the fact that its goal is to approximate some function $f*$. For instance, for a classifier, $y = f(x)$ maps an input x to a category y. "A feedforward network defines a mapping $y = f(x; \theta)$ and learns the value of the parameters θ that result in the best function approximation". Hence they are the typical deep learning models [6].

Furthermore, the model's performance was evaluated through the use of hyper-parameter optimization techniques such as Adam optimization algorithm and Stochastic Gradient Descent (SGD) optimization algorithm. Adam optimization algorithm outperformed the classical SGD procedure in the course of the model's training. Optimization tends to provide the foremost achievement with the least investments [2]. "The goal of optimization techniques for test cases is to minimize the number of test cases without affecting the fault coverage of the testing process [24]". Optimization algorithms or strategies are responsible for reducing the losses and to provide the most accurate results possible [3]. This is the main objective of deep learning optimization algorithms as demonstrated in this work.

The contributions of this research can be summarized as follows;

1. The research performs the investigation of the use of a deep feedforward network with deep learning optimization algorithms for the classification of English spoken digit.

2. An enhanced deep learning method is modeled for spoken digit classification to resolve the classification challenge with the signals that last for a short period and some digits that are acoustically very similar to each other.

The rest of this work is organized as follows. Section 2 reviews the related work in the field of speech classification. Section 3 describe deep feedforward network architecture and the experimental setup. Section 4 discusses the findings and presents a comparative analysis. Finally, Sect. 5 presents the conclusion.

2   Related Work

Several authors in recent times have carried out research on speech classification, but still there is a gap in determining the best methodology in order to achieve optimum accuracy.

A novel approach towards classifying Bengali spoken digits with Convolutional Neural Network (CNN) was proposed in [21]. The model classifies the digits, that were spoken by ten different people with different gender, dialects, and of different age-groups. An accuracy of 98.37% was achieved, which shows the usefulness of the proposed method. The approach shows result for only Bengali spoken digits.

Levenberg Marquardt Algorithm, and the Restricted Boltzmann Machine algorithm techniques were adopted for the classification of voice signals of patients, who have a draw back inside the vocal cords to differentiate the voice signal as normal or pathological [16]. Accuracy measure was used to analyze both algorithms to determine the best algorithm among them. It was observed that using the Restricted Boltzmann Machine algorithm an accuracy of 98% was achieved, which is preferable to Levenberg Marquardt Algorithm which gives 92% accuracy in predicting the voice pathology. Using a deep learning optimization algorithm would yield a better accuracy still than Restricted Boltzmann Machine Algorithm.

The model here combines a lexicon-based and a machine learning techniques to predict hate speech in a text, using sentiment analysis [14]. The emotional information contained in the text helped in improving the accuracy of hate speech detection from 41.00% in the original research to 80.64% in their tests result. The accuracy on the hate speech can further be improved through experimentation on deep learning optimization approaches.

This work shows a step by step representation of a real-time speech emotion recognition implementation using Alex-Net image classification network [11]. Results showed that the standard method when used on the Berlin Emotional Speech (EMO-DB) data with seven categorical emotions, achieved an accuracy of 82.00%. The transfer learning approach which was adapted to improve the pre-trained image classification network (AlexNet), did not result to an optimal accuracy in the model.

The model has proposed a novel multi-modal deep learning structure that spontaneously extracts features from textual-acoustic data for sentence-level speech classification [7]. Two independent convolutional neural network structures, were first used to extract textual and acoustic features from the data, and later fed into a decision softmax layer. The proposed model was tested in a real medical environment, using speech recording, and it's transcribed record. The model achieved 83.10% average accuracy in detecting 6 different intentions. The model achieved a low accuracy of 83.10%.

The paper examined a number of speech preprocessing and classification algorithms problems [13]. From the analysis of the experimental results, a multilayer perceptron of 93.00% accuracy for scaling using the Robust scaler method was proposed, and hence the speech signal was being classified using the multilayer perceptron. The proposed accuracy could possibly be achieved only when multilayer perceptron is scaled by Robust Scaler method. But, the model in this work used a multilayer perceptron with optimization algorithms to achieve 99.65% accuracy.

An isolated Pashto digit recognition system using MFCC for feature extraction and KNN classifier for actual classification achieved an accuracy of 84.17% for testing which show 7.32% improved performance compared to related works [25]. The work carried out here is only bounded into Pashto isolated digit recognition.

Multiclass classification was performed on Spoken English Digit dataset using Support Vector Machine (SVM) and K-Nearest-Neighbour (KNN) and Random Forest (RF) [12]. The RF method outperformed the SVM and KNN at a different number of frames. The RF method achieved the highest accuracy of 97.50% by taking 10% testing data. Other deep learning methods used on the same dataset could possibly yield better accuracy, as demonstrated in this work.

3 Methods and Techniques

This section introduces a step by step approach that was deployed in developing the proposed model. A flowchart diagram for the proposed Experimental Procedure is as shown in Fig. 1.

3.1 Pre-processing the Dataset

STFT features are extracted from the spoken English digit audio data [19]. The basic concept for the STFT is to break up the signal in time domain to a number of signals of shorter duration, then transform each signal to frequency domain. STFT is an algorithm that breaks the recording into small windows and computes the Discrete Fourier Transform (DFT) for each window. This shows the different frequencies in different parts of the voice recording. The standard mathematical definition of the STFT is as proposed in [1], given by

$$X_m(\omega) = \sum_{m-\infty}^{\infty} x(n)w(n - mR)e^{-j\omega n} \qquad (1)$$

$$= DTFT_\omega(x.SHIFTmR(w)) \qquad (2)$$

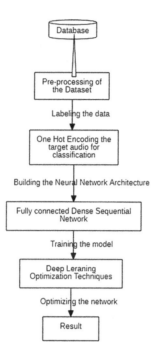

Fig. 1. Flowchart of the proposed experimental procedure.

where $x(n)$ = input signal at time n
$w(n)$ = length M window function (e.g. Hamming)
$X_m(\omega)$ = DTFT of window centered about time mR
R = hop sizes, in samples, between successive DTFTs.

The output of STFT features extraction is as shown in Fig. 2.

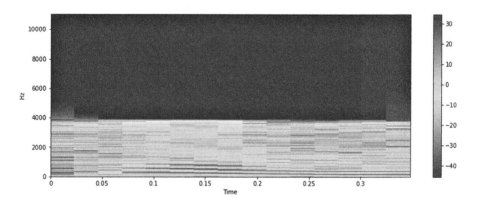

Fig. 2. STFT representation of audio data.

3.2   One Hot Encoding Technique

The proposed method also utilized One Hot Encoding technique for representing categorical variables as binary vectors. This requires mapping the categorical variables to integer values. The conversion in this form is necessary because integer values obtained from the STFT frequency feature representation of the audio data cannot be fed directly into the neural network. The technique transforms categorical features of the STFT features into a format that works better with the classification algorithms. This generates the target audio label. This technique addresses the problem with modeling challenge in speech recognition.

3.3   Adam Optimization Algorithm

Adam is a powerful method for stochastic optimization that requires only first-order gradients with small-scale memory requirement [9]. The name Adam being obtained from adaptive moment estimation, evaluates the individual adaptive learning rates for different parameters from estimates of first and second moments of the gradients. Adam has shown advantage over the SGD by merging the advantages of two other extensions of stochastic gradient descent, specifically Adaptive Gradient Algorithm (AdaGrad) [4], that works excellently with sparse gradients while the network learns, and the Root Mean Square Propagation (RMSProp) [23] that performs pretty good in on-line and non-stationary environment.

"Let $f(x)$ be a noisy objective function: a stochastic scalar function that is differentiable w.r.t. parameters x. The interest is in minimizing the expected value of this function, $E[f(x)]$ w.r.t. its parameters x. With $f_1(x)$, ..., , $f_T(x)$ we denote the realisations of the stochastic function at subsequent time steps 1, ..., T. The stochasticity might come from the evaluation at random subsamples (minibatches) of datapoints, or arise from inherent function noise. With $g_t = \nabla_x f_t(x)$ we denote the gradient, i.e. the vector of partial derivatives of f_t, w.r.t x evaluated at time step t" [9].

Adam also keeps an exponentially decaying average of past gradients $M(t)$. $M(t)$ and $V(t)$ are values of the first moment which is the Mean and the second moment which is the uncentered variance of the gradients respectively.

$$\hat{m}_t = \frac{m_t}{1 - \beta_1^2} \tag{3}$$

First order of momentum.

$$\hat{v}_t = \frac{v_t}{1 - \beta_2^2} \tag{4}$$

Second order of momentum.

Here, we are taking mean of $M(t)$ and $V(t)$ so that $E[m(t)]$ can be equal to $E[g(t)]$ where, $E[f(x)]$ is an expected value of $f(x)$. To update the parameter:

$$\theta_t + 1 = \theta_t - \frac{\eta}{\sqrt{v_t} + \epsilon} \hat{m}_t$$

The values for $\beta_1 = 0.9$, $\beta_2 = 0.999$, θ_t is the parameter vector at a given time t, η is the learning rate for each parameter and at every time step 't' and 'ϵ' $= 10^{-8}$.

The Adaptive Moment Estimation (Adam) optimizer used in this work, allows the network to attain a high accuracy through an adaptive moment gradient change, i.e. by adjusting the weights in the network in order to reduce the losses and achieve better accuracy. In addition Adam has functioned well in case of noisy objectives. Hence Adam works well in such cases of stochastic objectives with high-dimensional parameter spaces.

3.4   The Proposed Network Architecture

Deep neural networks have become an integral part of state-of-the-art ASR systems [8].

The proposed network architecture makes use of dense sequential fully connected layers consisting of three hidden layers with 256, 128 and 128 dimensions respectively. The input and output layers for the system are 1025 and 10 dimensions respectively. In the first layer, the input layer is of 1025 dimension while the input for the second dense layer is output of the first layer which is of 256 dimensions. The third layer is similar, the model automatically consider the input dimension to be same as the output of the last layer which is 256 since the model is sequential.

In the last layer which is the output layer, the output dimension is 10 which also represent 10 classes. The output layer takes different activation function and for the case of multiclass classification, it is softmax. The proposed system applied hyperbolic tangent (tanh) activation function at each level of the network except for the output layer which made use of softmax activation function. The choice of tanh activation function is due to its nonlinerality to stack layers. It is bound to the range $(-1, 1)$. The angle is more grounded for tanh than sigmoid (subordinates are more extreme). A number of nonlinear activation function are present, such as the hyperbolic tangent (tanh) or Sigmiod for the neural network, and often give a well optimization during training of DNN [25].

The top layer of the DNN consists of nodes employing the softmax function. This function enables the DNN to output class probabilities for each node which sum to 1.

$$P(Y = i|x, W, b) = softmax_i(W_x + b) \tag{5}$$

$$= \frac{e^{W_i x + bi}}{\sum_j e^{W_j x + b_j}}$$

where the target mixtures are expressed as Y, and the weight matrix and bias vector by W and b respectively. Cross-entropy minimization is employed as the objective loss function, which maximizes target mixture membership probabilities for training data.

$$\ell(\theta = W, b, D) = -\sum_{i=0}^{|D|} log(P(Y = y_i | x_i, W, b)) \; [21].$$ (6)

The model has used cross entropy loss, and in particular categorical_crossentropy which specifies multiple classes. Adam and SGD were the optimization algorithm for reducing the losses during network training and their performances were evaluated and compared. The architecture diagram for the proposed deep feedforward network model is illustrated in Fig. 3.

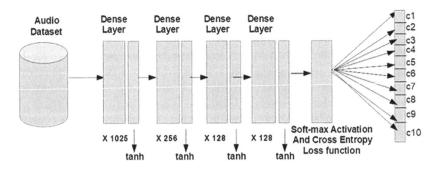

Fig. 3. Architectural Diagram for the proposed method.

3.5   Experiments

Dataset. A well-established publicly available dataset under Pannous, a collaboration working on improving Speech Recognition [20], used in the evaluation of the proposed method is from the Librosa Library [15] and described below. The dataset contains spoken numbers file which is a composition of an isolated spoken digit that was used as the benchmark dataset for this work. This file contains 15 different speakers (male and female), with 10 different phrases, and each phrase sampled at 16 different frequencies. Each speaker utters a digit 16 times which leads to $15 * 16 = 240$ instances for each digit. The phrases contain numbers: 0–9, while the sample rates are from 100–400 in 20 [unit] increments. This gives us a total of 2400 different audio files with wav format for training the system.

The proposed model is evaluated on the core speech condition of spoken numbers audio dataset which is an isolated spoken English digit dataset. The dataset was then split into training and testing sets (75% training and 25% testing). The dataset uses STFT audio features as input and audio class as target label. The model was first trained for 20 epochs using Adam optimization algorithm, and later it was increased to 30, 50 and 100 epochs. The same was repeated for SGD optimization algorithm. All the networks were trained with binary cross-entropy loss using softmax activation function, on a multi-core CPU.

Now, the training step output will also contain validation accuracy since the validation data was included in the model fit function while training. The model accuracy for Adam optimization algorithm for the different epoch sizes were compared with that of the SGD optimization algorithm. The best accuracy was obtained when 100 epochs were used in both Adam and SGD optimizations respectively. Adam showed an accuracy of 99.65% over 98.42% for SGD as represented in Table 1.

3.6   Algorithm for the Proposed Model

Algorithm for the proposed Model is as shown in Algorithm 1. The proposed classification algorithm initiates a procedure known as classification with variable X and Y which represents STFT features of each audio sample and target audio class label respectively. A library known as "librosa" was used to read the audio dataset. STFT features was Extracted from the audio, before performing One Hot Encoding on the dataset. By this process, the categorical variables are being represented as binary vectors. Then, the training of the model takes place through a deep feedforward network model of densed sequential layers consisting of an input layer, three hidden layers and an output layer.

Algorithm 1. The Proposed Classification Model

1: **procedure** CLASSIFICATION(X, Y)   ▷ X contains the STFT features of each audio sample, while Y contain the target audio class label
2:     Reading the dataset using the library "librosa"
3:     Extract STFT features from the audio.STFT (Short Term Fourier Transform)
4:     One Hot Encoding on the audio data to generate the target audio class label.
5:     Split the dataset into training and testing set with STFT audio features as input, audio class as target label
6:     Start Neural Network model
7:     Epoch = N; audio=first audio
8:     **for** $i = 1$: N **do**
9:         First_Layer = Dense(first audio, input dim = 1025, output dim =256)
10:        Second_Layer = Dense(input dim =256, output dim =128)
11:        Third_Layer = Dense(Input dim =128, output dim = 128)
12:        Fourth_Layer =Dense(input dim=128, output dim = 128)
13:        Output_Layer=Dense(input dim=128, output dim = 10)
14:        **if** Output_Layer == the target_Layer **then**
15:            audio=next audio
16:        **end if**
17:     **end for**
18: **end procedure**

---

4   Results and Discussion

This area of research is still an open issue and a serious barrier due to the limitations of ASR systems. It is practically a bottleneck in the recognition of isolated words/digits that needs to be overcome. The model here, has proposed a deep feedforward network with deep learning optimization algorithms for the classification of the spoken English digit data.

The proposed model was trained and validated on audio datasets containing 1800 training samples and 600 validation samples respectively. The model was first trained with Adam optimization algorithm and then retrained with the SGD optimization algorithm. The performance of the model with each algorithm was evaluated and compared.

Figure 4 shows the accuracy and loss curve diagram of the model performance when trained with Adam optimization algorithm for 100 epochs. The result shows that the model achieves a validation accuracy of 99.65% and a minimal validation loss of 0.25%. Figure 5 shows the accuracy and loss curve diagram of the model's performance when trained with SGD optimization algorithm for 100 epochs. The result shows that the model achieves a validation accuracy of 98.42% and a validation loss value of 0.54%.

The result shows that the choice of a good optimizer like the Adam optimization algorithm can help achieve optimal accuracy as demonstrated in the model's training output. Adam optimization method is too fast and converges rapidly and rectifies vanishing learning rate and high variance. Also, from the result of the model network training, it is imperative to state that Adam optimization algorithm is computationally powerful, and well suited for problems that are large in terms of data and/or parameters. The method is also appropriate for non-stationary objectives and problems with very noisy and/or sparse gradients [9].

Table 1 shows a summary of the result of the model training at different epochs with corresponding accuracy. This shows the effects of the optimization algorithm on the model performance. The performance of the model was compared with some traditional classifier [12] such as; Support Vector Machines (SVM), K-Nearest Neighbor (KNN) and Random Forest (RF) when used together for the same dataset. The model achieved the highest accuracy of 99.65% when compared with the existing method as shown in Table 2. This is to say, that the model proposed in this work has proven to be the optimum methodology for speech classification.

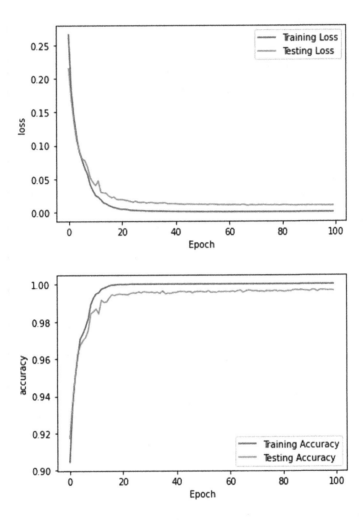

Fig. 4. Model's accuracy curve diagram with ADAM optimization algorithm.

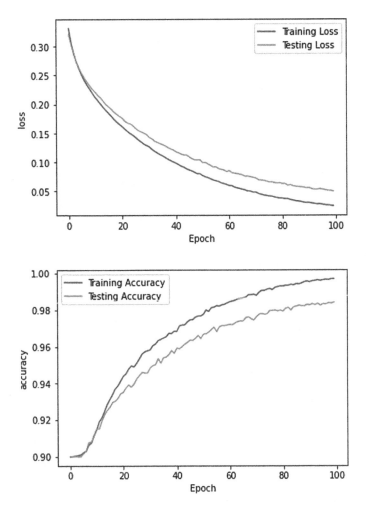

Fig. 5. Model's accuracy curve diagram with SGD optimization algorithm.

Table 1. Summary of results for the model's training at different epochs with corresponding accuracy

Adam epoch	Loss	Accuracy	SGD Epoch	Loss	Accuracy
20	0.1777	0.9373	20	0.1700	0.9383
30	0.0150	0.9953	30	0.1412	0.9492
50	0.0111	0.9957	50	0.0960	0.9670
100	0.0097	0.9965	100	0.0496	0.9842

Table 2. Summary of the performance parameters.

Technique	Dataset	Features	Classifier	Accuracy
Supervised Learning	Spoken English digit	MFCC	SVM + KNN+ RF	97.50%
Proposed Model	Spoken English digit	STFT	One Hot Encoding	**99.65%**

5   Conclusion

In this research, an enhanced deep learning method that used a deep supervised feedforward network with optimization algorithms for the classification of spoken English digit has been implemented. STFT features were extracted from the audio data, and one hot encoding was performed on the audio data to generate the target audio class label, which was used as input into the deep learning model. The proposed model performance was evaluated using hyperparameter optimization techniques such as Adam Optimization algorithm and SGD optimization algorithm to reduce losses. The model when used with Adam optimization algorithm outperforms the classical SGD optimization technique. Hence, the use of Adam optimization algorithm has shown optimal performance for speech classification.

References

1. Allen, J.B., Rabiner, L.R.: A unified approach to short-time Fourier analysis and synthesis. Proc. IEEE **65**(11), 1558–1564 (1977)
2. Chen, J., Mahfouf, M.: Artificial immune systems as a bio-inspired optimization technique and its engineering applications. In: Handbook of Research on Artificial Immune Systems and Natural Computing: Applying Complex Adaptive Technologies, pp. 22–48. IGI Global (2009)
3. Doshi, S.: Various Optimization Algorithms For Training Neural Network, January 2019. https://towardsdatascience.com/optimizers-for-training-neural-network-59450d71caf6. Accessed 14 Nov 2020
4. Duchi, J., Hazan, E., Singer, Y.: Adaptive subgradient methods for online learning and stochastic optimization. J. Mach. Learn. Res. **12**(7), 2121–2159 (2011)
5. Escudero Mancebo, D., Cámara Arenas, E., Tejedor García, C., González Ferreras, C., Cardeñoso Payo, V., et al.: Implementation and test of a serious game based on minimal pairs for pronunciation training. International Speech Communication Association Archive (2015)
6. Goodfellow, I., Bengio, Y., Courville, A., Bengio, Y.: Deep Learning, vol. 1. MIT press Cambridge (2016)
7. Gu, Y., Li, X., Chen, S., Zhang, J., Marsic, I.: Speech intention classification with multimodal deep learning. In: Mouhoub, M., Langlais, P. (eds.) AI 2017. LNCS (LNAI), vol. 10233, pp. 260–271. Springer, Cham (2017). https://doi.org/10.1007/978-3-319-57351-9_30
8. Hinton, G., et al.: Deep neural networks for acoustic modeling in speech recognition: the shared views of four research groups. IEEE Signal Process. Mag. **29**(6), 82–97 (2012)

9. Kingma, D.P., Ba, J.: Adam: A method for stochastic optimization. arXiv preprint arXiv:1412.6980 (2014)
10. Lawal, I.A.: Spoken character classification using abductive network. Int. J. Speech Technol. **20**(4), 881–890 (2017). https://doi.org/10.1007/s10772-017-9460-y
11. Lech, M., Stolar, M., Best, C., Bolia, R.: Real-time speech emotion recognition using a pre-trained image classification network: effects of bandwidth reduction and companding. Frontiers Comput. Sci. **2**, 14 (2020)
12. Maddimsetti Srinivas, K.M., Ashok, G.L.P.: Spoken English digit classification using supervised learning. Int. J. Res. Signal Process. Comput. Commun. Syst. Design **5**(1), 49–53 (2019)
13. Mamyrbayev, O., Mekebayev, N., Turdalyuly, M., Oshanova, N., Medeni, T.I., Yessentay, A.: Voice identification using classification algorithms. In: Intelligent System and Computing. IntechOpen (2019)
14. Martins, R., Gomes, M., Almeida, J.J., Novais, P., Henriques, P.: Hate speech classification in social media using emotional analysis. In: 2018 7th Brazilian Conference on Intelligent Systems (BRACIS), pp. 61–66. IEEE (2018)
15. McFee, B., McVicar, M., Raffel, C., Oriol Nieto, D.L., Moore, J., Ellis, D., et al.: Librosa: v0.4.0.Zenodo, 2015. In: Proceedings of the 14th Python in Science Conference (SCIPY 2015) (2015)
16. Megala, D.S.S., Padmapriya, D.R., B.Jayanthi, D., M.Suganya, D.: Detection and classification of speech pathology using deep learning. Int. J. Sci. Technol. Res. **8**(12), 3045–3051 (2019)
17. Nasreen, P.N., Kumar, A.C., Nabeel, P.A.: Speech analysis for automatic speech recognition. In: Proceedings of International Conference on Computing, Communication and Science (2016)
18. Nguyen, Q.T., Bui, T.D.: Speech classification using SIFT features on spectrogram images. Vietnam J. Comput. Sci. **3**(4), 247–257 (2016). https://doi.org/10.1007/s40595-016-0071-3
19. Oruh, J., Viriri, S.: Spectral analysis for automatic speech recognition and enhancement. In: Renault, É., Boumerdassi, S., Mühlethaler, P. (eds.) MLN 2020. LNCS, vol. 12629, pp. 245–254. Springer, Cham (2021). https://doi.org/10.1007/978-3-030-70866-5_16
20. Pannous.Github: Pannous/tensorflow-speech-recognition, December 2014. http://github.com/pannous/tensorflow-speech-recognition. Accessed 3 May 2020
21. Sharmin, R., Rahut, S.K., Huq, M.R.: Bengali Spoken Digit Classification: A Deep Learning Approach Using Convolutional Neural Network. Procedia Computer Science **171**, 1381–1388 (2020)
22. Silva, D.F., de Souza, V.M.A., Batista, G.E.A.P.A.: A comparative study between MFCC and LSF coefficients in automatic recognition of isolated digits pronounced in Portuguese and English. Acta Scientiarum. Technology **35**(4), 621–628 (2013)
23. Tieleman, T., Hinton, G.: Lecture 6.5-rmsprop, coursera: Neural networks for machine learning. University of Toronto, Technical Report (2012)
24. Tyagi, K., Tyagi, K.: A comparative analysis of optimization techniques. Int. J. Comput. Appl. **131**(10), 6–12 (2015)
25. Zada, B., Ullah, R.: Pashto isolated digits recognition using deep convolutional neural network. Heliyon **6**(2), e03372 (2020)

An Implementation of Formal Framework for Collective Systems in Air Pollution Prediction System

Rafał Palak[1,2] , Krystian Wojtkiewicz[1(✉)] , and Mercedes G. Merayo[2]

[1] Faculty of Computer Science and Management, Wrocław University of Science and Technology, Wybrzeże Stanisława Wyspiańskiego 27, 50-370 Wrocław, Poland
{rafal.palak,krystian.wojtkiewicz}@pwr.edu.pl
[2] Complutense University of Madrid, Facultad de Informática, C Prof. José García Santesmases 9, 28040 Madrid, Spain

Abstract. Greater attention to the quality of life forces increased activity in the field of air quality monitoring. Many cities official perceive air pollution as an increasing issue worth investigating and managing. Thus, research focuses on delivering reliable real-time information on pollutants across the city area. The main focus of this article is the presentation of a collective framework to predict air pollution implementation. This solution allows informing about air pollution in places where no meters are available. The experimental results showed that the collective framework emerges the collective members' knowledge and delivers prediction better than any algorithm used for agent predictions. It proves that collectives achieve better results than their members.

Keywords: Collective intelligence · Crowd wisdom · Multiagents · Air pollution · Reasoning stop condition

1 Introduction

Air pollution has become a huge problem for rapidly developing modern cities. Thus it has drawn worldwide attention. Many studies showed the bad impact of air pollution on people's health. Time-series analyses conducted in large cities in the United States found relations between variations in daily deaths and air pollution levels in days prior (immediate mortality) [3,9,34]. Since air may contain different pollutants with different properties and consequently different impacts on health, the air pollution issue is very complex. Commonly we use indicators to track pollutants levels, e.g., particulate matter ($PM_{2.5}$ and PM_{10}), carbon monoxide (CO) and sulphur dioxide (SO_2). Research showed that PM2.5 could cause negative health effects, such as excessive morbidity and mortality from cardiovascular and respiratory diseases. Prolonged critical levels of any pollutant are hazardous for human health.

Many cities try to fight with all possible means. Cities invest in infrastructure to measure pollution and inform citizens about pollution in different areas of the

© Springer Nature Switzerland AG 2021
N. T. Nguyen et al. (Eds.): ICCCI 2021, LNAI 12876, pp. 508–520, 2021.
https://doi.org/10.1007/978-3-030-88081-1_38

city. This approach has some drawbacks: the air pollution meters measure only air pollution at one point. Often, it is too costly in terms of time, finance, and human resources to collect air pollution samples over significant areas. Another problem is the fact that sometimes meters can break and show inaccurate values of pollution. Besides that, the collection of data is a challenging task to do. The problems may arise due to unskilled data collectors, inappropriate methods of collecting data, meters malfunctions, and others. It is vital since many cities restrict car communications based on air pollution meters showing pollution above the given value. This article describes a multiagent system that validates air pollution meters and predicts air pollution. The presented method assumes irregular distribution of meters in the city. Thus we can estimate values of air pollution at random fields based on values from known locations.

The remaining paper comprises the background section that presents state of the art in air pollution models and collective intelligence. The following section introduces the formal definition of the collective structure and the framework for collective systems. Then details on the framework implementation are discussed. Following, the authors present the results of an experiment and discussion. The last section is the conclusions.

2   Related Works

The paper addresses the field of computational intelligence and air pollution models. Thus, we will discuss those two areas below, starting from the collective approach toward prediction computation.

Many authors have proven that approaches based on collectives are an effective method for forming accurate judgments in an uncertain environment [2,14,35]. However, it is hard to find a straightforward answer to the question, *why does collective intelligence work?*. One of the most popular is the Surowiecki explanation [42]. In his work, he proposed the following properties of a wise crowd [42]:

- **diversity** - each agent should have some private information, even if it is just an eccentric interpretation of the known facts,
- **independence** - the opinions of those around them do not determine the agent's opinions,
- **decentralization of opinion** - an agent can specialize on and draw on local knowledge,
- **aggregation** - some mechanism exists for turning private judgements into a collective decision.

Due to Surowiecki's background as a journalist in his work, he mainly focused on human crowds. Nevertheless, collective intelligence has proven its effectiveness for various types of agents, even artificial ones [19]. Therefore it is used in many disciplines, e.g., in deep learning, where it is called ensembling [45]. The use of collectives allows us to achieve much more accurate results with the help of simple solutions.

For the sake of uniformity, in [30] authors proposed the universal definition of collective. It is suitable for the identification of its features regardless of the implementation area. They assumed the collective to be a graph defined as a tuple:

$$C = (M, E, t) \tag{1}$$

where

- M is a set of collective members,
- E is a set of edges,
- t is collective *target*, that can be understood as either a pursued value or quality.

There exist other approaches to the definition of collectives such as, e.g., [17,20,43]. However, they lack the flexibility of the model mentioned above. Based on the model in [30] authors in [37] introduced framework for collective systems. This paper's main emphasis is on establishing the theoretical framework that combines various reasoning methods into a collective system. The system's formal abstraction uses the graph theory and provides a discussion on possible aggregation function definition. One of the key elements is the stop condition for collectives reasoning. It is crucial in situations when collective members take each other decisions as input for their own decision. Such a situation may cause infinite iteration. The followings conditions to solve the stop problem authors proposed:

- stop iteration when the biggest change in collective member output is lower than predefined threshold q
- stop iteration when the number of iteration with the same outcome is higher than the given value m

Work described in [37] is purely theoretical. Therefore in our work, we implement this framework and check how its conditions work in practice.

The most popular method to predict pollution in different areas is Land Use Regression Model (LUR). LUR modeling gained popularity for estimating NO2 and NOx because of the availability of relevant land data and the ease with which empirical data for NO2 and NOx could be collected from multiple locations using passive samplers [15]. It has been used to estimate pollutant concentrations in various geographic settings ranging from very local scales, including a previous study on 50 km^2 area of Sydney, Australia [39], to intra-city scales in Canada [16, 26,28] the US [21,29], Europe [7], the UK [8], and Asian cities [10,11,25]. LUR models allow us to predict and analyze within-city variations of air pollutants. Therefore, Land Use Regression Model is usefull for high-density areas, where such prediction and analysis is critical [7]. The main idea of LUR models is based on predictable pollution patterns. Therefore, LUR models require information about the environmental characteristics of the area, especially characteristics that influence pollutant emission intensity and dispersion efficiency. The issue with LUR could be proper model selection. Some publications solve this problem with defined procedures [7]. It makes model development a little bit easier, but the whole process is still very complex. Another problem with LUR models is that they require a lot of sampling data and a huge amount of additional information such as land use data, elevation data, resident population data, number of dwellings, traffic data, etc.

An alternative approach to the problem of pollution estimation at unobserved points is Kriging. Kriging, firstly introduced by Krige in [32], is the basic statistical methodology for predicting values at unsampled locations based on the indices sampled spatially surrounding the unsampled one. In other words, Kriging is a geostatistical technique to estimate the values of random fields at unobserved points from the observation of values at known locations [41]. Kriging Indicator, a variation on Kriging, is usually used to approximate the conditional cumulative distribution function at each point of a grid, based on the correlation structure of indicator-transformed datapoints [31]. Classical Kriging estimator is a linear predictor based on the spatial observations directly. Kriging often requires fuzzy mathematics in process [24,44] to analyze spatially distributed imprecise data [4,5,18,33,36]. The version of Kriging based on fuzzy logic inevitably involves complicated mathematical operations on fuzzy sets, fuzzy statistical estimation, and hypothesis testing. Thus, it is difficult to implement in geographic information systems (GIS). Therefore, some authors try to simplify the approach i.e. [23] proposed a fuzzy membership grade Krigin methodology. The idea is very straightforward. [44] generalized the 0, 1-two-valued indicator function which characterizes a crisp set into a [0, 1]- infinite-valued membership function which defines a fuzzy set. Author in [23] generalized [31] threshold indicator coding, indicator variogram, and indicator Kriging into fuzzy membership grade, fuzzy membership grade variogram, and fuzzy membership grade Kriging. Following such a simple route, the author uses membership to transform fuzzy data into membership grades. Therefore, the analysis is converted into Kriging on spatially distributed membership grades (which are numbers from [0, 1]) [24]. But, even with improvements, the process of Kriging is complicated and could be challenging.

Another approach to pollution estimation in unobserved points is atmospheric dispersion modeling, and chemical transport models (CTMs) [6]. Atmospheric dispersion modeling is the mathematical simulation of how air pollutants disperse in the ambient atmosphere. Such simulation usually is performed by computer applications that use algorithms to solve the mathematical equations that govern the pollutant dispersion [22,27]. Atmospheric dispersion models are used to estimate:

– the downwind ambient concentration of air pollutants,
– toxins emitted from sources such as industrial plants, vehicular traffic, or accidental chemical releases.

Models can also predict future concentrations under specific scenarios (i.e., changes in emission sources). Therefore, they are the dominant type of model used in air quality policymaking. They are most useful for pollutants that are dispersed over large distances, and that may react in the atmosphere [27]. Dispersion modeling utilizes data from emissions inventories, meteorological data, knowledge of air chemistry, and relatively complex mathematical modeling. This characteristic creates a relatively high entry threshold, and as a result, it could be a problem in the further use of this method.

Another known approach similar to Kriging is Bayesian Maximum Entropy (BME) developed by Christakos [12]. BME is interpolation method that assign a series of weights to observed monitoring station data to compute interpolated values of pollutants at unmonitored sites [1,13,38,40]. BME analysis uses the following inputs:

- general knowledge describing generalizable characteristics,
- the site-specific knowledge that includes hard data (corresponding to measurements) and soft data (having uncertainty characterized by a probability density function which can be non-Gaussian).

Bayesian Maximum Entropy has the following advantages:

- simulating spatial/temporal variances,
- accounting for missing data using a nonlinear formulation of the probability density function at each spatiotemporal point.

The main difference between BME and CTM is that it relies on a geostatistical method. As such, it does not require emission inventory or meteorological data. However, BME, similarly to previous approaches, requires a lot of data.

3 System Overview

In [37] authors proposed a formal framework for collective intelligence. Based on that framework, we implemented the system described in this article. The system is built on multiple agents that use some part of the known data to predict air pollution in a given place. We should begin the description of our system with proof that it is, in fact, a collective. In [37] authors define collective as a set of agents that share the common target, as defined in Eq. 2 and 3. Authors understand target as either the pursued value or quality of any sort.

$$target : M \rightarrow t \qquad (2)$$

$$\forall i \in \{1, 2, \ldots, n\} \ (target(m_i) = t) \qquad (3)$$

where

M is a set of collective members, in our case it is agents that based on individual algorithms predict the air pollution value

m_i is a subsequent collective member,

t is a target, in our case it is prediction of air pollution in given place

i is a collective member number, in our case it is one agent

n is a number of collective members in our case it is number of algorithms

The next step for the implementation of the framework was the definition of attributes for each collective member. Below, the characteristics of collective members as in the original model are presented.

Each collective member has a type assigned, which is defined in 4 as a tuple $\sigma(M)$.

$$\sigma(M) = (a_1, a_2, \ldots, a_{man}) \tag{4}$$

$$a = (name, type) \tag{5}$$

$$MA = \{a_1, a_2, \ldots, a_{man}\} \tag{6}$$

where

a is an attribute characterised by *name* and *type*,
i is an index of an attribute,
man   is number of attributes,
MA is a set of all attributes.

Each collective member $m \in M$ can be thus understood as a tuple of values v defined in 7. Each value $v \in V$ of collective member $m \in M$ corresponds to appropriate attribute $a \in MA$ of $\sigma(M)$.

$$m = (v_1, v_2, \ldots, v_{man}) \tag{7}$$

$$MemberValue : M \times MA \to V \tag{8}$$

In [37] authors distinguished the following attributes as sufficient for description:

- set of input values *input*,
- output value *output*,
- confidence factor CF.

In this paper, we use the following model specific attributes:

- number of station readings taken into account,
- average distance from stations taken into account and target prediction,
- number of used algorithms,
- weights for other collective members predictions,
- weight for own prediction.

In our implementation, the agents accept inputs from either meters data or other algorithms' output. The weights for both inputs are fully parameterized. Therefore, it is possible to build an algorithm that works on meters data, other agents' predictions or mix those inputs. In our implementation, weights for agents are randomly chosen for each simulation according to the following rules:

- weight for agent's prediction is taken from range [0.5, 1],

– sum of weights for other agents predictions is equal to:

$$sum = 1 - own_weight \tag{9}$$

other agents predictions are taken into account if the weight for agent prediction is $agent_weight > 0$, the $agent_weight$ is calculated for each collective member individually

We have implemented two orthogonal stop conditions, as was described in the previous section:

– minimal value change was set to 0.001
– minimal number of the same value for each agent was set to 2 (if the state would repeat two times the simulation stops)

Such configuration guarantees that prediction won't stack in an infinite loop, and the computational cost of the system running is acceptable.

The last step in a model definition is to set aggregate predictions from collective members. We implemented three aggregation functions to choose from:

– weighed average aggregation function:

$$J = \sum_{i=1}^{n} w_i x_i \tag{10}$$

where
x_i is the decision of a i-th member,
n is the number of all members,
w_i is the weight for i-th deductive system.
– median aggregation function
– minimum aggregation function

4   Experiment

In our work, we used pollution data set from Opole city in Poland. The following parameters characterize the data set:

– 47 monitoring stations
– 30473 PM2.5 and PM10 measurements dating from 12-th November 2017 01:00 to 4-th May 2021 17:00 (each measurement contains at least reading from one station)

Since only reading from one station is available in some cases, some records have to be omitted. As a result, the final prediction was made 577 938 times based on readings from 47 stations.

The goal of the performed simulation was to predict the value of pollution in a given place. To achieve that in our implementation, agents use a variety of methods to make their predictions:

- average from minimum and maximum value of nearby stations readings (AvgMinAndMaxAlgorithm)
- average of nearby stations readings (AvgAlgorithm)
- average without minimum and maximum value of nearby stations readings (AvgWithoutMinAndMaxAlgorithm)
- minimum value of nearby stations readings (MinValueAlgorithm)
- maximum value of nearby stations readings (MaxValueAlgorithm)
- value of the nearest station (NearestStationAlgorithm)
- random value between 0 and maximum reading (RandomValueAlgorithm)
- weighted an average of nearby stations (WeightAvgAlgorithm)

In proposed implementation, we used narrow diversity of methods. It was primarily caused by a lack of additional pollution data, weather, and other information that could be useful in a used dataset. Algorithms used by agents could be changed to more sophisticated ones anytime without additional changes in the whole system. It is worth to mention that each agent could use one or more algorithms to make its predictions. Such approach allows to create higher number of different agents, and all this comes with a cost of diversity. Moreover, we used random algorithms. With this choice we show the stability of the proposed solution. It might cause slightly worse results, but stability of results is an important aspect to research, and for the proposed framework in particular.

The first step of the experiment was to compute the individual prediction for each algorithm. Each of them is deterministic, but as stated before, we will choose them randomly. Table 1 and 2 presents obtained results. Based on those results it isn't possible to determine which algorithm is the best one. However, there is a visible tendency for the solution based on average to have smaller error, in particular for PM2.5.

Table 1. Results of individual prediction of PM_{10} for selection of algorithms

No.	Algorithm	PM_{10} MSE	PM_{10} % error
1	MinValueAlgorithm	351.7241	3.3494
2	AvgMinAndMaxAlgorithm	358.9014	3.6914
3	AvgAlgorithm	143.9999	2.0164
4	AvgWithoutMinAndMaxAlgorithm	143.0342	1.9277
5	MaxValueAlgorithm	1685.0325	8.8478
6	MinValueAlgorithm	351.7241	3.3494
7	NearestStationAlgorithm	250.1362	2.5405
8	RandomValueAlgorithm	791.0661	5.7868
9	WeightAvgAlgorithm	141.5202	1.9520

Table 2. Results of individual prediction of $PM_{2.5}$ for selection of algorithms

No.	Algorithm	$PM_{2.5}$ MSE	$PM_{2.5}$ % error
1	MinValueAlgorithm	154.2515	3.5149
2	AvgMinAndMaxAlgorithm	148.0618	3.8228
3	AvgAlgorithm	61.3437	2.1041
4	AvgWithoutMinAndMaxAlgorithm	60.9507	2.0136
5	MaxValueAlgorithm	696.8667	9.1246
6	MinValueAlgorithm	154.2515	3.5149
7	NearestStationAlgorithm	100.7876	2.5593
8	RandomValueAlgorithm	345.1671	6.1746
9	WeightAvgAlgorithm	59.4382	1.9996

In the next step, we iterate over each station prediction and based on readings from other stations; agents try to predict pollution value in this station. Table 3 presents the achieved results. Due to the fact that weights for predictions and

Table 3. Results of best 10 simulation for AVG and MAX aggregation functions conducted for PM_{10} and $PM_{2.5}$

No.	Aggregation	PM_{10} MSE	$PM_{2.5}$ MSE	PM_{10} % error	$PM_{2.5}$ % error
1	AVERAGE	6.4044	73.4007	2.0145	2.1111
2	AVERAGE	6.4474	64.6958	2.1004	2.1844
3	AVERAGE	7.8067	82.0978	2.6136	2.7068
4	AVERAGE	6.5880	66.7180	2.1471	2.2279
5	AVERAGE	6.8633	68.4333	2.2663	2.3475
6	AVERAGE	7.0308	70.6270	2.3292	2.4177
7	AVERAGE	6.5616	65.5451	2.1469	2.2220
8	AVERAGE	7.1691	73.4649	2.3725	2.4574
9	AVERAGE	6.5179	66.5779	2.1180	2.2085
10	AVERAGE	6.6413	66.9204	2.1725	2.2584
11	MAXIMUM	15.6693	299.5982	5.3860	5.5406
12	MAXIMUM	21.8437	516.1834	7.5253	7.7469
13	MAXIMUM	25.4489	692.7744	8.7677	9.0309
14	MAXIMUM	22.7825	559.7780	7.8521	8.0867
15	MAXIMUM	25.4489	692.7744	8.7677	9.0309
16	MAXIMUM	25.4489	692.7738	8.7677	9.0309
17	MAXIMUM	20.2211	464.6848	6.9730	7.1586
18	MAXIMUM	22.1058	526.9063	7.6132	7.8372
19	MAXIMUM	17.9955	353.3619	6.1982	6.3823
20	MAXIMUM	20.6510	474.8776	7.1157	7.3128

algorithms used for each collective member are selected randomly, each type of simulation has to run several times. Each simulation is conducted on a collective size of 50, and each collective member used a maximum of 4 algorithms at the same time. The number of used algorithms was randomly chosen for each agent.

A short analysis of the results shows that average-based aggregation provides better results based on the mean square error (MSE) and percentage mean square error (% error). The latter is a normalized value based on the maximum value returned by any meter.

The experiment proved that collectives return much more reliable results compared to individual predictions. If we consider individual algorithms, they are unpredictable in case of reliability. However, if we randomly use them, as in the experiment, and aggregate the output, the overall quality of the prediction will rise. An important aspect of each simulation was the fact the results were mostly stable. The stability of results shown in the Table 3 was obtained even when the maximum values and distribution of the predictions differed significantly from one simulation to another. It confirms assumptions made in [37] about the considerable role of aggregations function in collective prediction.

Apart from the confirmation of collective effectiveness, the experiment provided some insights into the investigated problem. The results of predictions for PM_{10} and $PM_{2.5}$ turned out to be independent. It is a clear signal to distinguish these two pollutants in future simulations and search for their different configurations.

It needs to be noted that the experiment used elementary algorithms both for agent operation and for aggregation function. Nevertheless, the results are promising, and the Authors will carry out further work in pollution prediction. However, the authors believe that better configuration of the framework will be needed as well as the introduction of more sophisticated methods.

5   Conclusions

This paper introduces the implementation of a multi-agent prediction system for air pollution prediction. The idea was to experimentally prove the assumption that collective predictions are more reliable than those made by a single algorithm. On the other hand, the experiment is an early phase of an approach toward a complex prediction system capable of validating station readings. The obtained results are promising since the average MSE oscillated around 2%. As such, the proposed solution can be considered a proof of concept. The authors believe the results can be significantly improved using more sophisticated methods. It is possible since the authors created the proposed approach based on the framework introduced in [37] and [30]. The adopted model is flexible and expendable. What is worth noting, the authors strive to use deterministic solutions and improve the quality of predictions based on enriching the model with more data.

Acknowledgement. This work has been supported by the Region of Madrid (grant number FORTE-CM, S2018/TCS-4314) and the Spanish MCIU-FEDER (grant number FAME, RTI2018-093608-B-C31).
This work has been carried out on data provided by courtesy of the city of Opole.

References

1. Akita, Y., Chen, J.C., Serre, M.L.: The moving-window Bayesian maximum entropy framework: estimation of PM 2.5 yearly average concentration across the contiguous united states. J. Exposure Sci. Environ. Epidemiol. **22**(5), 496–501 (2012)
2. Armstrong, J.S.: Combining forecasts: the end of the beginning or the beginning of the end? Int. J. Forecast. **5**(4), 585 (1989)
3. Atkinson, R.W., et al.: Acute effects of particulate air pollution on respiratory admissions: results from APHEA 2 project. Am. J. Respir. Crit. Care Med. **164**(10), 1860–1866 (2001)
4. Bandemer, H., Gebhardt, A.: Bayesian fuzzy kriging. Fuzzy Sets Syst. **112**(3), 405–418 (2000)
5. Bardossy, A., Bogardi, I., Kelly, W.: Kriging with imprecise (fuzzy) variograms. I: theory. Math. Geol. **22**(1), 63–79 (1990). https://doi.org/10.1007/BF00890297
6. Baxter, L.K., et al.: Exposure prediction approaches used in air pollution epidemiology studies: key findings and future recommendations. J. Exposure Sci. Environ. Epidemiol. **23**(6), 654–659 (2013)
7. Beelen, R., et al.: Development of NO2 and NOx land use regression models for estimating air pollution exposure in 36 study areas in Europe-the escape project. Atmos. Environ. **72**, 10–23 (2013)
8. Briggs, D.J., et al.: A regression-based method for mapping traffic-related air pollution: application and testing in four contrasting urban environments. Sci. Total Environ. **253**(1–3), 151–167 (2000)
9. Brunekreef, B., Holgate, S.T.: Air pollution and health. Lancet **360**(9341), 1233–1242 (2002)
10. Chen, L., et al.: A land use regression for predicting NO2 and PM10 concentrations in different seasons in Tianjin region, China. J. Environ. Sci. **22**(9), 1364–1373 (2010)
11. Choi, G., Bell, M.L., Lee, J.T.: A study on modeling nitrogen dioxide concentrations using land-use regression and conventionally used exposure assessment methods. Environ. Res. Lett. **12**(4), 044003 (2017)
12. Christakos, G.: A Bayesian/maximum-entropy view to the spatial estimation problem. Math. Geol. **22**(7), 763–777 (1990). https://doi.org/10.1007/BF00890661
13. Christakos, G., Serre, M.L.: BME analysis of spatiotemporal particulate matter distributions in North Carolina. Atmos. Environ. **34**(20), 3393–3406 (2000)
14. Clemen, R.T.: Combining forecasts: a review and annotated bibliography. Int. J. Forecast. **5**(4), 559–583 (1989)
15. Cowie, C.T., et al.: Comparison of model estimates from an intra-city land use regression model with a national satellite-LUR and a regional Bayesian Maximum Entropy model, in estimating NO2 for a birth cohort in Sydney, Australia. Environ. Res. **174**, 24–34 (2019)
16. Crouse, D.L., Goldberg, M.S., Ross, N.A.: A prediction-based approach to modelling temporal and spatial variability of traffic-related air pollution in Montreal, Canada. Atmos. Environ. **43**(32), 5075–5084 (2009)

17. DeGroot, M.H.: Reaching a consensus. J. Am. Stat. Assoc. **69**(345), 118–121 (1974)
18. Diamond, P.: Fuzzy kriging. Fuzzy Sets Syst. **33**(3), 315–332 (1989)
19. Ferber, J., Weiss, G.: Multi-agent Systems: An Introduction to Distributed Artificial Intelligence, vol. 1. Addison-Wesley, Reading (1999)
20. Golub, B., Jackson, M.O.: Naive learning in social networks and the wisdom of crowds. Am. Econ. J. Microeconomics **2**(1), 112–49 (2010)
21. Gonzales, M., et al.: Evaluation of land use regression models for NO2 in El Paso, Texas, USA. Sci. Total Environ. **432**, 135–142 (2012)
22. Grigoras, G., Cuculeanu, V., Ene, G., Mocioaca, G., Deneanu, A.: Air pollution dispersion modeling in a polluted industrial area of complex terrain from Romania. Romanian Rep. Phys. **64**(1), 173–186 (2012)
23. Guo, D., Guo, R., Thiart, C.: Integrating GIS with fuzzy logic and geostatistics: predicting air pollutant pm10 for California, using fuzzy kriging. Doctoral dissertation, MSc. thesis (2003)
24. Guo, D., Guo, R., Thiart, C.: Predicting air pollution using fuzzy membership grade kriging. Comput. Environ. Urban Syst. **31**(1), 33–51 (2007)
25. Gurung, A., Levy, J.I., Bell, M.L.: Modeling the intraurban variation in nitrogen dioxide in urban areas in Kathmandu Valley, Nepal. Environ. Res. **155**, 42–48 (2017)
26. Henderson, S.B., Beckerman, B., Jerrett, M., Brauer, M.: Application of land use regression to estimate long-term concentrations of traffic-related nitrogen oxides and fine particulate matter. Environ. Sci. Technol. **41**(7), 2422–2428 (2007)
27. Hurley, P.: The air pollution model (TAPM) version 2. Part 1: technical description. CSIRO Atmos. Res. Tech. Pap. **55**, 1–49 (2002)
28. Jerrett, M., et al.: Modeling the intraurban variability of ambient traffic pollution in Toronto, Canada. J. Toxicol. Environ. Health A **70**(3–4), 200–212 (2007)
29. Jerrett, M., et al.: Spatial analysis of air pollution and mortality in Los Angeles. Epidemiology **16**, 727–736 (2005)
30. Jodłowiec, M., Krótkiewicz, M., Palak, R., Wojtkiewicz, K.: Graph-based crowd definition for assessing wise crowd measures. In: Nguyen, N.T., Chbeir, R., Exposito, E., Aniorté, P., Trawiński, B. (eds.) ICCCI 2019. LNCS (LNAI), vol. 11683, pp. 66–78. Springer, Cham (2019). https://doi.org/10.1007/978-3-030-28377-3_6
31. Journel, A.G.: Nonparametric estimation of spatial distributions. J. Int. Assoc. Math. Geol. **15**(3), 445–468 (1983)
32. Krige, D.G.: A statistical approach to some basic mine valuation problems on the Witwatersrand. J. South Afr. Inst. Min. Metall. **52**(6), 119–139 (1951)
33. Lee, E.S.: Neuro-fuzzy estimation in spatial statistics. J. Math. Anal. Appl. **249**(1), 221–231 (2000)
34. Makri, A., Stilianakis, N.I.: Vulnerability to air pollution health effects. Int. J. Hyg. Environ. Health **211**(3–4), 326–336 (2008)
35. Nielsen, M.: Reinventing Discovery: The New Era of Networked Science, vol. 70. Princeton University Press, Princeton (2011)
36. Omre, H.: Bayesian kriging–merging observations and qualified guesses in kriging. Math. Geol. **19**(1), 25–39 (1987)
37. Palak, R., Wojtkiewicz, K.: The formal framework for collective systems. Axioms **10**(2), 91 (2021)
38. Reyes, J.M., Serre, M.L.: An LUR/BME framework to estimate PM2.5 explained by on road mobile and stationary sources. Environ. Sci. Technol. **48**(3), 1736–1744 (2014)

39. Rose, N., Cowie, C., Gillett, R., Marks, G.B.: Validation of a spatiotemporal land use regression model incorporating fixed site monitors. Environ. Sci. Technol. **45**(1), 294–299 (2011)

40. Serre, M.L., Christakos, G.: Modern geostatistics: computational BME analysis in the light of uncertain physical knowledge-the Equus Beds study. Stoch. Env. Res. Risk Assess. **13**(1), 1–26 (1999). https://doi.org/10.1007/s004770050029

41. Shad, R., Mesgari, M.S., Shad, A., et al.: Predicting air pollution using fuzzy genetic linear membership kriging in GIS. Comput. Environ. Urban Syst. **33**(6), 472–481 (2009)

42. Surowiecki, J.: The wisdom of crowds. Anchor (2005)

43. Wagner, C.: Consensus through respect: a model of rational group decision-making. Philos. Stud. **34**(4), 335–349 (1978)

44. Zadeh, L.A.: Fuzzy sets. In: Fuzzy Sets, Fuzzy Logic, and Fuzzy Systems: Selected Papers by Lotfi A Zadeh, pp. 394–432. World Scientific (1996)

45. Zhou, Z.H., Wu, J., Tang, W.: Ensembling neural networks: many could be better than all. Artif. Intell. **137**(1–2), 239–263 (2002)

Computer Vision Techniques

Ensembles of Deep Convolutional Neural Networks for Detecting Melanoma in Dermoscopy Images

Melina Tziomaka$^{(\boxtimes)}$ ⓘ and Ilias Maglogiannis ⓘ

Department of Digital Systems, University of Piraeus, Pireas, Greece
{tziomakamel,imaglo}@unipi.gr

Abstract. Malignant melanoma is the deadliest form of skin cancer and is one of the most rapidly increasing cancers in the world. In this paper, a methodology for the SIIM-ISIC Melanoma Classification Challenge, where the goal is to detect melanoma from dermoscopic images, is described. The EfficientNet family of convolutional neural networks is utilized and extended for identifying malignant melanoma on a dataset of 58,457 dermoscopic images of pigmented skin lesions. This binary classification problem comes with a severe class imbalance, which is tackled using a loss balancing approach. Furthermore, the dataset contains images with different resolution sizes. This property is addressed by considering different model input resolutions. Lastly, an ensembling strategy of models, trained with different activation functions is applied to increase the diversity of the ensembler and to further improve individual results.

Keywords: Deep learning · Convolutional neural networks · Dermoscopy · Melanoma classification · EfficientNet · Ensemble models

1 Introduction

Skin cancer is one of the most common cancers around the world, with the most harmful form of it being melanoma. Melanoma has been ranked at the ninth position among the most common types of cancer [1] and it's estimated that the number of new cases diagnosed in 2021 will increase by 5.8%. Approximately 207,390 cases of melanoma will be diagnosed in the U.S. only. Of those, 106.110 cases will be noninvasive, restricted to the epidermis and 101.280 cases will be invasive, penetrating the epidermis into the skin's second layer. The number of new invasive melanoma cases diagnosed annually has increased by 44% in the past decade. Stage I melanoma patients treated within 30 to 59 days after diagnosis and stage I melanoma patients treated more than 119 days after diagnosis have 5% and 41% respectively higher risk of dying compared to those treated within 30 days [2]. This indicates the importance of early detection and treatment so as to increase the survival rate of patients with melanoma [3]. One of the dermatologist's most popular imaging techniques is dermoscopy. The structure of the skin lesion becomes more visible for examination by magnifying the affected area. This technique is used by

© Springer Nature Switzerland AG 2021
N. T. Nguyen et al. (Eds.): ICCCI 2021, LNAI 12876, pp. 523–535, 2021.
https://doi.org/10.1007/978-3-030-88081-1_39

trained physicians and is based on the practitioner's experience [4]. With dermoscopy an expert dermatologist can achieve an average accuracy of 65%–75% [5]. Accuracies can be further improved by capturing dermoscopic images with a high-resolution camera and a magnifying lens to improve visibility of the skin area affected. With this technological support the accuracy of a skin cancer diagnosis can be improved by an estimated 50% [6]. To automate the process of melanoma detection and change the unsettling situation of skin cancer mortality rate for the better, many efforts have been made for the development of computer aided diagnosis platforms, aiming to assist doctors in their day-to-day clinical routine, by allowing economical and quick access to life-saving diagnoses.

Proper diagnosis of melanoma at an earlier stage is crucial for a high rate of complete cure. Both patient and physician awareness regarding the signs and symptoms of early melanoma remains paramount. Hence, a reliable automatic melanoma screening system would provide a great help for clinicians to detect the malignant skin lesions as early as possible. In the last years, the efficiency of deep learning-based methods increased dramatically, and their performances seem to outperform conventional image processing methods in classification tasks. The International Skin Imaging Collaboration (ISIC) [7] has played a significant role in the adoption of new techniques in the field. With the purpose to spread awareness regarding skin cancer and to drive the research in automated skin lesion classification ahead, the community has been providing dermoscopic image datasets with expert annotations, and organizing yearly challenges since 2016, where participants are asked to develop computer vision algorithms for the segmentation and classification of digital skin lesion images.

In this paper, we describe our approach for the SIIM-ISIC Melanoma Classification Challenge. We utilize established methods for skin lesion classification including loss balancing, data augmentation, pretrained state-of-the-art Convolutional Neural Networks (CNNs) and ensembling. Furthermore, we extend the architecture of the pretrained CNN's to an architecture, which incorporates the metadata of the images and uses a different activation function from the one, which was pretrained. The finetuned models are aggregated with an ensembling strategy and the predictions on example images are visualized. The rest of the paper is structured as follows: Sect. 2 presents related research works, while Sect. 3 describes the proposed methodology. Section 4 describes the performed experiments and the corresponding results. Section 5 presents the interpretability method and example visualizations. Finally, Sect. 6 discusses and concludes the paper.

2   Related Work

Due to the astounding advancement of skin image capturing devices over the years, the data is quite large and image quality has been improved, attracting the interest of image analysts in the classification of dermoscopic images. The first approaches were based mostly on feature extraction methods and followed three primary steps: i) preprocessing and skin lesion segmentation, ii) feature extraction and selection, and iii) classification. Fundamentally, the first step involves preprocessing of the image data, such as image resizing, contrast enhancement, noise reduction and hair removal [8]. After preprocessing, segmentation of skin lesions, i.e. regions of interest (ROIs) is performed, in order to exclude the lesional area from normal surrounding skin, by drawing an accurate border around it. The lesion segmentation literature covers a lot of different methods that can be implemented to tackle the problem, either individually or by combining multiple techniques, to achieve the best results. Some of these researched methods include: probabilistic modelling, active contours, clustering, histogram thresholding, edge detection and graph theory [9]. During the feature extraction process, a set of specific dermoscopic characteristics, such as border irregularity [10, 11], asymmetry [12], color [13–15] and texture [16–18] is computed from the segmented skin lesion to describe it. Finally, the extracted features from the skin lesion are used as inputs to a feature classification module to classify each skin lesion. Among the most used classifiers for the task are the support vector machines [9, 19], Bayesian classifiers [20], decision trees [21] and k-nearest neighbors [20, 21]. These systems use traditional machine learning techniques, therefore the chosen representation for the image and the quality of the extracted features can heavily affect their performance. Hence, a certain level of expertise is required for the feature extraction of the skin lesions. Deep learning has proven to outperform these methods. In the recent years, deep learning started to be utilized and is becoming the gold standard in melanoma detection and skin lesion classification, employing methods such as deep CNNs and transfer learning to achieve state-of-the-art results [22]. The feature extraction process becomes completely automated and depends on the algorithm to find the more descriptive features of the dataset and train the model properly [23–25].

The first breakthrough on skin cancer classification came from Esteva et al. [26], who utilized a pre-trained GoogleNet Inception v3 CNN model on a dataset of 129,450 clinical skin cancer images including 3,374 dermoscopic images. They conducted two validation experiments for checking the performance of the classification rate of their network. The first test consisted of three prediction classes of benign lesions, malignant lesions and non-neoplastic lesions and the second validation test involved nine different classes of skin lesions. The results they observed of the two validation tests were 72.1% $\pm$ 0.9% and 55.4% respectively and were compared against certified dermatologists performing the same tasks under the same conditions, who received a peak accuracy of 66% and 55%. The work of Kawahara et al. [27] explored the idea of using a pretrained CNN as a feature extractor rather than training a CNN from scratch. Furthermore, the paper demonstrates that the use of filters from a CNN pretrained on natural images can be generalized into classifying 10 classes of non-dermoscopic skin images. Liao's [28] work attempted to construct a universal skin disease classification by applying transfer learning on a deep CNN and fine-tuned its weights by continuing the backpropagation. Y. Li and L. Shen [29] conducted their research utilizing deep learning for the detection of melanomas on a testing set, containing a total of 2000 images of dermoscopic images of different resolutions. Three tasks were performed: Lesion segmentation, feature extraction and classification, achieving accuracies of 92.2%, 91.4% and 85.2% respectively. They used a straight-forward CNN for the feature extraction task, whereas the other two tasks (lesion segmentation and classification) were handled by two fully convolutional residual networks, that made up a deep learning framework. In 2018 A. Rezvantalab et al. [30] developed an algorithm using Support Vector Machines combined with a deep CNN for multiclass classification of clinical skin cancer images and Codella et al. [31] reported new state-of-the-art results by utilizing an ensemble of deep CNNs to classify the clinical images of 12 skin diseases.

3   Materials and Methods

3.1   The ISIC Archive

Annually, ISIC makes publicly available new annotated images that add up to the datasets of the previous years, as a result the total number of the ISIC archive has grown significantly, making it the largest publicly available collection of quality controlled dermoscopic images of skin lesions. Thus, for the application of the proposed method for melanoma classification, the datasets that were deployed are: the ISIC2019 Challenge Dataset: 'Skin Lesion Analysis Towards Melanoma Detection' [32–34] and the ISIC 2020 Challenge Dataset: 'Skin Lesion Analysis Towards Melanoma Detection' [35]. The ISIC2019 dataset is composed of 25,331 labeled dermoscopy images, and their metadata, which include the site of the skin lesion, and the age and gender of the patient. The labels of the ISIC2019 dermoscopy images are among eight different diagnostic categories. Specifically, the diagnoses present in the dataset are: melanoma, melanocytic nevus, basal cell carcinoma, actinic keratosis, benign keratosis, dermatofibroma, vascular lesion and squamous cell carcinoma. The ISIC2020 dataset consists of 32,542 benign and 584 malignant skin lesions from over 2,000 patients. The metadata of each image is also provided and include information about: the diagnosis and site of the lesion, the approximate age and gender of the patient, and an anonymized patient identification number, which allows lesions from the same patient to be mapped together. The goal of the ISIC2020 Challenge is to classify benign and malignant lesions, with the ranking's evaluation metric being the Area Under the Curve (AUC) score. The benign images of the dataset are among 8 types (nevus, seborrheic keratosis, lichenoid keratosis, solar lentigo, lentigo NOS, cafe-au-lait macule, atypical melanocytic proliferation and unknown) and all malignant images are the melanoma type of diagnosis. Notably, no basal cell and squamous cell carcinoma cases are present in the dataset, as a result, this makes it a melanoma detection problem only. For evaluation purposes, a dataset composed of 10,982 unlabeled images along with their metadata, except from the diagnosis feature, is also available from ISIC. The evaluation of algorithms on the unlabeled images is completely automated by ISIC and provides the ROC-AUC score metric for every submission. The aforementioned datasets have no common instances, since the ISIC2019 dataset contains images from all the previous year challenges and ISIC2020 contains only the images that were generated by ISIC for the year 2020. As a result, the total number of instances from both datasets is 58,457, with 5,106 melanoma instances and 53,351 non-melanoma instances. Figure 1 shows sample images from the ISIC archive.

3.2   Methodology

Metadata Preparation. The metadata of the ISIC2019 dataset had to be modified so as to be merged with ISIC2020's metadata. The categories, present in the 'anatomy site general' feature, were mapped accordingly to this year's categories and the feature of 'patient identification number' was added with the value of 'unknown' for all instances. After merging the metadata, a feature, containing information about the size of each image in bytes was added and the categorical variables of 'biological sex' and 'anatomy

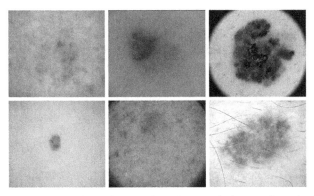

Fig. 1. Melanoma (top) and non-melanoma (bottom) sample images from the ISIC2019 and ISIC2020 datasets.

site general' were converted to binary vectors. Additionally, the feature 'patient id' was modified to contain the information about the number of all images from that patient of both the dataset and the unlabeled 10,982 images. These transformations were also applied to the unlabeled dataset's metadata, which were considered for the normalization of the numerical features: age, number of images and image size. The final metadata features that resulted after these transformations are: age, biological sex, site head/neck, site lower extremity, site oral/genital, site palms/soles, site torso, site upper extremity, site none, number of images and image size.

CNN Architectures. The EfficientNet [36] family of CNNs has state-of-the-art models of high performance and low computational cost, thus it was a natural choice. This model family contains eight different networks that are structurally similar and follow the compound scaling rule for adjustment to larger image sizes. EfficientNet's baseline model, EfficientNet-B0, was developed using multi-object neural architecture search on the ImageNet dataset to optimize accuracy and FLOPS, and its main component is known as the Mobile Inverted Bottleneck Conv (MBconv) Block with the depth-wise separable convolution. The activation function used in EfficientNet models is a function, which was proposed as a better alternative to the successful and widely used ReLU (Rectified Linear Unit), the Swish activation function [36]:

$$f(x) = x \cdot \sigma(x) \tag{1}$$

where $\sigma(x) = (1 + \exp(-x))^{-1}$ is the sigmoid function. The models that were utilized and explored with the proposed method for melanoma detection are the architectures of the EfficientNet-B3 – B6 and each of the models was deployed with two approaches. In the first approach, the only modification to the network architectures was the replacement of the final softmax-layer, which is specific for the ImageNet classification task (i.e. 1000-dim), by a two-neuron softmax layer to obtain probabilistic output for the melanoma and non-melanoma classes. In the second approach, the models were deployed to a modified architecture, which takes into consideration the metadata and has a different activation function. The proposed model uses the Mish [37] activation function and has 3 additional layers. The first layer takes as input both the metadata and the output of the default EfficientNet model, while the second layer, along with a final 2-neuron softmax layer for the output, perform the final classification task. The techniques of batch normalization (BN) and dropout with a 30% chance were also utilized for the two lower additional layers. The approach is illustrated in Fig. 2.

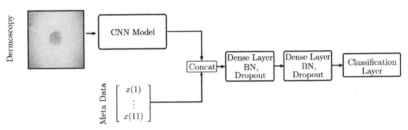

Fig. 2. The modified architecture, which incorporates the metadata and uses the Mish activation function.

Mish is a recent activation function, that was introduced in the paper "Mish: A Self Regularized Non-Monotonic Neural Activation Function" and has outperformed Swish and ReLU in numerous tasks. The Mish activation function is defined as:

$$f(x) = x \cdot \tanh(\varsigma(x)) \tag{2}$$

where, $\varsigma(x) = \ln(1 + e^x)$ is the softplus activation function. It presents similarities to Swish and ReLU as it is a smooth non-monotonic function, that is both bounded below and unbounded above. In fact, the graph of Mish is almost identical to Swish. However, the differences of the two functions are more prominent to their derivative graphs. Figure 3 shows the graph of Mish and the graphs of the first and second derivatives of Swish and Mish.

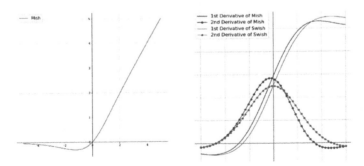

Fig. 3. The Mish activation function (left) and the comparison between first- and second-derivative of Mish and Swish (right).

Image Preprocessing and Data Augmentation. Several preprocessing techniques may be applied to dermoscopic images for noise removal and image enhancement, such as hair removal, lesion segmentation or contrast enhancement. The aim of this work is to evaluate the efficiency of ensembling CNNs for tackling the specific task of melanoma detection. Considering this, such measures were not implemented. The only pre-processing techniques that were used, in order to prepare the images before passing them through the network, are resizing and normalization. As mentioned previously, the images of the dataset have been acquired from various sources. This presents inherent changes to the color constancy and resolution size of the skin lesion images, due to illumination and acquisition methods. Such variations in color can slow down and even disrupt the training process. To ensure that input parameters, i.e. pixels, have a similar data distribution, all images were normalized by subtracting the mean and dividing by the standard deviation RGB values of the ImageNet dataset, that were used to pretrain the EfficientNet models. The images were also resized so as to have a common dimension before training each network. Due to the fact that each EfficientNet model has been built to perform optimally on images of a specific size, e.g. EfficientNet-B3 on 300×300 and EfficientNet-B4 on 380×380 sized inputs, all images were resized according to each model's default input size.

In order to avoid overfitting and increment the diversity and quantity of the dataset without actually aggregating new data, the technique of data augmentation was used. After experimenting with several different augmentation scenarios, the following augmentation pipeline was applied for the entire dataset during training: horizontal flip, vertical flip, color jitter and random erasing. Figure 4 is an illustration of the images before and after the proposed augmentation scheme.

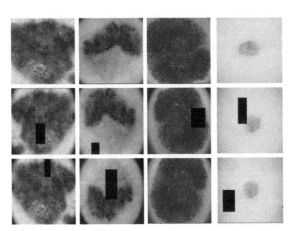

Fig. 4. Training augmentation of the original images. First row: original images; second and third row: augmented images.

Training. To accelerate and enhance the learning process, the method of transfer learning was employed as an initialization theme, with weights pretrained on ImageNet. The same method was applied to both approaches, where the additional layers of the second approach were initialized with the uniform LeCun method. To address the class imbalance problem, a weighted cross-entropy loss function [38] was used, where the class weights were computed by normalizing the inverse class frequencies from the training set. All the layers, including lower convolutional layers, were fine-tuned using the Adam optimizer. For each model the starting learning rate was selected according to Leslie Smith's 2017 paper "Cyclical Learning Rates for Training Neural Networks" [39] and a decay of 0.97 ratio was applied on each epoch. All training codes are based on Pytorch framework and were carried on a Nvidia Titan RTX 24GB GPU card.

Ensembling. To improve performance and robustness the predictions from the individual models are combined. The strategy utilized to combine predictions is the average ensembling method. The three combinations analyzed are the ensemble method of i) the models from the first approach, ii) the models from the second approach and iii) the optimal subset of models from both approaches, in terms of the ROC-AUC score.

4   Experiments and Results

For validation purposes, the dataset was partitioned into 3 subsets, with 80% of the original data going to the training set, 10% to the validation set and 10% to the test set. During the training of each model, observations were made over a sufficient number of

Table 1. All model's ROC-AUC scores on the test set and on the 10,982 unlabeled images from ISIC's automatic evaluation system. Ensemble EN B3–B6 refers to the ensemble modeling of the models from the first approach, while EN B3–B6 Mish Meta refers to the models from the second approach, which use the Mish activation function and Metadata. Ensemble optimal refers to the optimal subset of models from both approaches in terms of the ROC-AUC score on the validation set.

Model	Test set AUC	SIIM-ISIC leaderboards
EN B3 300 × 300	0.9582	0.8920
EN B3 300 × 300 Mish Meta	0.9593	0.9121
EN B4 380 × 380	0.9567	0.9039
EN B4 380 × 380 Mish Meta	0.9582	0.9087
EN B5 456 × 456	0.9576	0.9101
EN B5 456 × 456 Mish Meta	0.9580	0.9111
EN B6 528 × 528	0.9600	0.8820
EN B6 528 × 528 Mish Meta	0.9643	0.9006
Ensemble EN B3–B6	0.9737	0.9340
Ensemble EN B3–B6 Mish Meta	0.9755	0.9355
Ensemble Optimal	**0.9810**	**0.9404**

epochs to visualize overfitting and the best performing models are subsequently chosen as those that maximize the ROC-AUC score on the validation set (Table 1).

Notably, the deeper and more complex networks with larger input resolutions don't provide that much greater results. However, the models with the Mish activation function, that take into consideration the metadata provide slightly improved AUC scores. Furthermore, all ensemble models achieved superior metrics from individual networks, with the best model being the optimal ensemble (which consist of the EfficientNet-B4–B5 and EfficientNet-B3–B6, with the Mish activation function and metadata) with a 0.904 AUC score on the automatic evaluation system for the dataset of the 10,982 unlabeled images.

5 Visualizations and Explainability

The integrated gradients method [40] was utilized to calculate feature attributions for the EfficientNet-B3–B6. The integrated gradients method computes the importance scores φ_i^{IG} by accumulating gradients interpolated between a baseline x_i' input (intended to represent the absence of data, in this case this is a black image) and the current input x_i.

$$\varphi_i^{IG} = \left(x_i - x_i'\right) \times \int_{\alpha=0}^{1} \frac{\theta F\left(x' + \alpha \times \left(x - x'\right)\right)}{\theta x_i} d\alpha \tag{3}$$

The CNN model is represented as F in Eq. 3. Figures 5 and 6 illustrate examples of melanoma and non-melanoma images and the corresponding integrated gradient attributions for the networks. It can be observed that the models tend to focus primarily on the edges of the skin lesions. This aligns with expectation, since uneven or notched

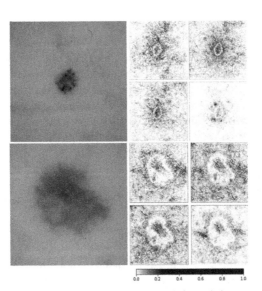

Fig. 5. Examples 1–2: Non-melanoma test set images (left) and the corresponding integrated gradient attributions for EfficientNet-B3 – B6 (right).

edges are common in melanoma. Secondary to the edges, there is some importance to the lesion itself and surrounding skin.

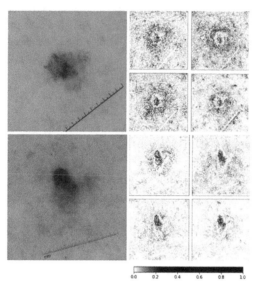

Fig. 6. Examples 3–4: Melanoma test set images (left) and the corresponding integrated gradient attributions for EfficientNet-B3 – B6 (right).

6   Discussion and Conclusion

In this paper, it is demonstrated that an ensemble method of varying scale deep neural networks, trained with different activation functions, can achieve competitive classification performance in detecting melanoma from dermoscopic images, with the best model achieving a 0.9404% ROC-AUC score in public leaderboards, which is among the top-5% performances. The typical problem of severe class imbalance was addressed with a loss balancing approach and a heavy augmentation pipeline was applied to the images during training to avoid overfitting. To deal with multiple image resolutions, the multi-resolution EfficientNets were employed and to further diversify the ensemble method, the models were utilized again in an architecture with a different activation function that incorporates the metadata.

In previous challenges, the utilization of EfficientNets with the technique of transfer learning has shown to provide better results compared to other CNN architectures. Also, data augmentation and ensembling strategies were key factors for high-performing methods. This prior knowledge is incorporated in this work and in order to diversify even further the ensembler, the models are also trained with a different activation function. In general, ensembles are known to perform better than single models and diversity has been identified as an important factor in explaining their success. An assumption as to the nature of the diversity present in the proposed ensemble methodology, can foremost be based on the fact that the EfficientNets have different scales and input resolutions. Thus, each pretrained network has learned, to a certain degree at least, different representations of the categories of the ImageNet dataset. Considering this with the fact that each network has then been finetuned on resized dermoscopic images, that illustrate lesions from different scales and angles, each resulting model considers also to a certain degree different features from an image to detect melanoma. As a result, some networks can be a better candidate for determining the outcome for images with certain attributes, while not being the most suitable for images with other attributes. Hence, an ensemble method, which considers the confidence levels of these varying models, generalizes better to the unseen data. Additionally, the optimal ensembler, includes networks trained with different activation functions, which diversify their architecture even further, by taking into consideration also the metadata. Activation functions play a crucial role in deep learning as they define the output of every node of a network. Therefore, by changing the activation function of a CNN architecture, the performance and the training dynamics of the network change as well. Taking this into account, and in order to make a more robust ensembler that can generalize more to the unseen data, the models were utilized again in an architecture, which takes into consideration the metadata and uses also a different activation function. Thus, the performance of the optimal ensemble method improves even more than the ensemble of just varying scale networks.

Acknowledgment. This research has been co-financed by the EU and Greek national funds through the Operational Program Competitiveness, Entrepreneurship and Innovation, under the call RESEARCH – CREATE – INNOVATE (project code: Transition - T1EDK-01385).

References

1. N. C. Institute. https://www.cancer.gov/types/common-cancers. Accessed 14 May 2021
2. Skin Cancer Foundation. https://www.skincancer.org/skin-cancer-information/skin-cancer-facts. Accessed 14 May 2021
3. Maglogiannis, I., Doukas, C.: Overview of advanced computer vision systems for skin lesions characterization. IEEE Trans. Inf. Technol. Biomed. **13**(5), 721–733 (2009)
4. Siegel, R., Miller, K., Jemal, A.: Cancer statistics, 2018. CA Cancer J. Clin. **68**(1), 7–30 (2018)
5. Nami, N., Giannini, E., Burroni, M., Fimiani, M., Rubegni, P.: Teledermatology: state-of-the-art and future perspectives. Expert. Rev. Dermatol. **7**, 1–3 (2012)
6. Haenssle, H., Fink, C., Uhlmann, L.: Reply to the letter to the Editor "Reply to 'Man against machine: diagnostic performance of a deep learning convolutional neural network for dermoscopic melanoma recognition in comparison to 58 dermatologists' by H. A. Haenssle et al." by L. Oakden-Rayner. Ann. Oncol. **30**(5), 854–857 (2019)
7. ISIC Archive. https://www.isic-archive.com. Accessed 14 May 2021
8. Mahajan, P., Vyavahare, A.: Artefact removal and contrast enhancement for dermoscopic images using image processing techniques. Int. J. Innov. Res. Electric. Electron. Instrum. Control Eng. **1**, 418–421 (2013)
9. Bakheet, S.: An SVM framework for malignant melanoma detection based on optimized HOG features. Computation **5**, 4 (2017)
10. Maragoudakis, M., Maglogiannis, I.: A medical ontology for intelligent web-based skin lesions image retrieval. Health Inform. J. **17**(2), 140–157 (2011)

11. Abbas, Q., Emre Celebi, M., Fondón, I.: Computer-aided pattern classification system for dermoscopy images. Skin Res. Technol. **18**(3), 278–289 (2011)
12. Stoecker, W., Li, W., Moss, R.: Automatic detection of asymmetry in skin tumors. Comput. Med. Imaging Graph. **16**(3), 191–197 (1992)
13. Celebi, M., Zornberg, A.: Automated quantification of clinically significant colors in dermoscopy images and its application to skin lesion classification. IEEE Syst. J. **8**(3), 980–984 (2014)
14. Stanley, R., Stoecker, W., Moss, R.: A relative color approach to color discrimination for malignant melanoma detection in dermoscopy images. Skin Res. Technol. **13**(1), 62–72 (2007)
15. Doukas, C., Stagkopoulos, P., Maglogiannis, I.: Skin lesions image analysis utilizing smartphones and cloud platforms. Methods Mol. Biol. **1256**, 435–458 (2015)
16. Delibasis, K., Kotari, K., Maglogiannis, I.: Automated detection of streaks in dermoscopy images. IFIP Adv. Inf. Commun. Technol. **458**, 45–60 (2015)
17. Iyatomi, H., et al.: Computer-based classification of dermoscopy images of melanocytic lesions on acral volar skin. J. Invest. Dermatol. **128**(8), 2049–2054 (2008)
18. Maglogiannis, I., Delibasis, K.: Enhancing classification accuracy utilizing globules and dots features in digital dermoscopy. Comput. Methods Programs Biomed. **118**(2), 124–133 (2015)
19. Maglogiannis, I., Kosmopoulos, D.: Computational vision systems for the detection of malignant melanoma. Oncol. Rep. **15**(4), 1027–1032 (2006)
20. Li, L., et al.: Automatic diagnosis of melanoma using machine learning methods on a spectroscopic system. BMC Med. Imaging **14**, 36 (2014)
21. Victor, A., Ghalib, M.: Automatic detection and classification of skin cancer. Int. J. Intell. Eng. Syst. **10**(3), 444–451 (2017)
22. Kontogianni, G., Maglogiannis, I.: A review on state-of-the-art computer-based approaches for the early recognition of malignant melanoma. Stud. Comput. Intell. **891**, 81–101 (2020)
23. Georgakopoulos, S.V., Kottari, K., Delibasis, K., Plagianakos, V.P., Maglogiannis, I.: Detection of malignant melanomas in dermoscopic images using convolutional neural network with transfer learning. In: Boracchi, G., Iliadis, L., Jayne, C., Likas, A. (eds.) EANN 2017. CCIS, vol. 744, pp. 404–414. Springer, Cham (2017). https://doi.org/10.1007/978-3-319-65172-9_34
24. Georgakopoulos, S.V., Kottari, K., Delibasis, K., Plagianakos, V.P., Maglogiannis, I.: Improving the performance of convolutional neural network for skin image classification using the response of image analysis filters. Neural Comput. Appl. **31**(6), 1805–1822 (2018). https://doi.org/10.1007/s00521-018-3711-y
25. Gessert, N., et al.: Skin lesion classification using ensembles of multi-resolution EfficientNets with meta data. MethodsX **7**(7), 100864 (2020)
26. Esteva, A., et al.: Dermatologist-level classification of skin cancer with deep neural networks. Nature **542**(7639), 115–118 (2017)
27. Kawahara, J., BenTaieb, A., Hamarneh, G.: Deep features to classify skin lesions. In: 2016 IEEE 13th International Symposium on Biomedical Imaging (ISBI), pp. 1397–1400 (2016)
28. Liao, H.: A Deep Learning Approach to Universal Skin Disease Classification (2015)
29. Li, Y., Shen, L.: Skin lesion analysis towards melanoma detection using deep learning network. Sensors **18**(2), 556 (2018)
30. Rezvantalab, A., Safigholi, H., Karimijeshni, S.: Dermatologist Level Dermoscopy Skin Cancer Classification Using Different Deep Learning Convolutional Neural Networks Algorithms. arXiv:1810.10348 (2018)
31. Codella, N.C.F., et al.: Deep learning ensembles for melanoma recognition in dermoscopy images. IBM J. Res. Dev. **61**(4–5), 1–15 (2017)
32. Tschandl, P., Rosendahl, C., Kittler, H.: The HAM10000 dataset, a large collection of multi-source dermatoscopic images of common pigmented skin lesions. Sci. Data **5** (2018)

33. Codella, N.C.F., et al.: Skin lesion analysis toward melanoma detection: a challenge at the 2017 International symposium on biomedical imaging (ISBI), Hosted by the International Skin Imaging Collaboration (ISIC). arXiv:1710.05006 (2018)
34. Combalia, M., et al.: BCN20000: Dermoscopic Lesions in the Wild. arXiv:1908.02288 (2019)
35. Rotemberg, V., et al.: A patient-centric dataset of images and metadata for identifying melanomas using clinical context. Sci. Data **8**(1), 34 (2021)
36. Tan, M., Le, Q.V.: EfficientNet: Rethinking Model Scaling for Convolutional Neural Networks. arXiv:1905.11946 (2019)
37. Misra, D.: Mish: A Self Regularized Non-Monotonic Activation Function. arXiv:1908.08681 (2020)
38. Ho, Y., Wookey, S.: The real-world-weight cross-entropy loss function: modeling the costs of mislabeling. IEEE Access **8**, 4806–4813 (2020)
39. Smith, L.N.: Cyclical learning rates for training neural networks. In: 2017 IEEE Winter Conference on Applications of Computer Vision (WACV), pp. 464–472 (2017)
40. Sundararajan, M., Taly, A., Yan, Q.: Axiomatic attribution for deep networks. In: Proceedings of the 34th International Conference on Machine Learning, pp. 3319–3328 (2017)

Deep Learning Models for Architectural Façade Detection in Spherical Images

Marcin Kutrzyński⬤, Bartosz Żak, Zbigniew Telec⬤, and Bogdan Trawiński$^{(\boxtimes)}$⬤

Department of Applied Informatics, Wrocław University of Science and Technology, Wrocław, Poland
{marcin.kutrzynski,zbigniew.telec,bogdan.trawinski}@pwr.edu.pl

Abstract. Maintaining a public register by extracting urban objects from photos taken in the city is one of the most important tasks for municipal services. It is of great importance in the field of protection and shaping of the cultural landscape, protection of monuments, and registration of the urban tissue development. The current state of the art shows that deep learning models (DL models) can cope with the problem of extracting urban objects with the same or better performance than non-DL models, and can process video and photos automatically. This paper compares the three main DL models for facade instance detection and facade segmentation: Mask R-CNN, YOLACT, and Mask-Scoring R-CNN. The training and validation datasets used for transfer learning were created on the basis of spherical photos taken in an artificially generated virtual city. The test dataset, on the other hand, included spherical façade photos taken in a real city. The comparative analysis of the DL models was performed using parametric and nonparametric statistical tests for pairwise and multiple comparisons.

Keywords: Deep learning · Façade segmentation · Object detection · Spherical images · Region-based convolutional neural networks

1 Introduction

An important task of municipal services is maintaining records of urban tissue. It is of great importance for the valuation of real estate, the protection of monuments, the development of habitats that take into account natural human needs, as well as the implementation of the smart city concept ensuring sustainable economic development and a high quality of life. The automation of this process allows for faster and cheaper registration of changes taking place in the city and enables municipal services to manage the registers more efficiently. This contributes to an increase in the quality of life.

The recently developed deep learning models (DL models) from the family of Region-based Convolutional Neural Networks (R-CNNs) [8] enable fully automated registration of urban objects. As shown in [13], the deep learning

© Springer Nature Switzerland AG 2021
N. T. Nguyen et al. (Eds.): ICCCI 2021, LNAI 12876, pp. 536–548, 2021.
https://doi.org/10.1007/978-3-030-88081-1_40

methods not only allow the registration of urban objects from photos with a quality comparable to classic methods, but also do not require a long and complicated process of preparing photos before the analysis. In classic methods, such as gradient accumulation [11], region growing [18], or repetitive patterns [19], obtaining information about urban objects requires reducing the perspective, rectifying photos, or taking photographs in a very specific way. The deep learning methods have no such limitations. Preparing a working deep learning model is laborious, but later such models can work automatically.

The purpose of this study is to compare different deep learning models to each other and to find out in which area individual solutions are best. The first of these areas is the quantitative approach, where we compare how many objects are recorded by a given method. The second area concerns the quality of creating the mask of the discovered object. Such a mask allows the separation of an appropriate area from the photo and enables other works related to urban registration. The research presented in this paper is the continuation of our recent work on automatic detection of architectural façades in spherical images published in [13].

Three different modern deep learning model subjects are compared: Mask R-CNN, Mask Scoring R-CNN, and YOLACT. Mask R-CNN [9] follows the success of Faster R-CNN [17] in branch classification and bounding box regression, however, Mask R-CNN has an additional branch for predicting segmentation mask. It is based on ResNet 50 [10] architecture and consists of two parts: RPN (region proposal network) finds object bounding boxes, whereas BMC (binary mask classifier) builds a mask for each RoI. Mask R-CNN is unique in that class prediction and bounding box are done in parallel and are separated. Therefore, the classification does not depend on the mask prediction.

YOLACT [6] is based on a similar concept to Mask R-CNN, but YOLACT performs the instance segmentation in a different way. While Mask R-CNN extends Faster R-CNN, YOLACT extends YOLO [16] to real-time operation and runs two parallel tasks: generating mask prototypes and predicting a set of linear combination coefficients for each instance. Finally, each instance is combined with both the predicted coefficient and the corresponding prototype. Since YOLACT computes the whole image simultaneously (Mask R-CNN uses a sliding window) it is much faster.

The last tested deep neural network is the Mask Scoring R-CNN [11], which includes an additional block scoring the quality of the predicted instance masks and enabling the calibration of mask quality and mask score misalignment. Furthermore, this step improves performance by focusing on more accurate mask prediction.

We applied statistical methods to compare the models together. Calculating the statistical significance of the obtained data cause high reliability of the result. Thanks to this, we prove that our result does not depend on the data set used in the tests and is objective.

2   Method for Constructing Deep Learning Models

To obtain reliable deep learning models, you need to prepare large datasets for training or transfer learning. The idea proposed in [13] is used to create a training and validation dataset from spherical photos made in an artificial city. It allows stratification of training façades in terms of architectural style, population density, visual obstacles, and weather conditions. Unlike training and validation data, the test subset consists of real spherical photos taken in a real city. In this way, the deep learning procedure is simplified and allows high-quality detection/separation of façades to be obtained. The block diagram presented in Fig. 1 summarizes the idea.

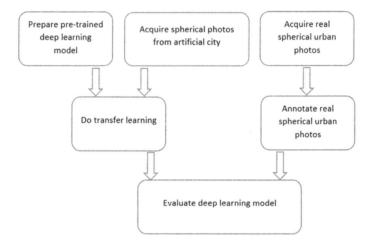

Fig. 1. Flowchart of developing and evaluating deep learning models.

All artificial training and validation data sets were prepared using ESRI CityEngine®, ESRI CityEngine Procedural Runtime® and the PyPRT library [2] in conjunction with the py360convert library [5] . The 3D model for collecting spherical images was built based on the principles described in [13]. Spherical data obtained from the virtual city is represented by three images:

- realistic view of a virtual city with buildings and obstacles in Fig. 2(a),
- façades, distinguished by a color mask, on which the façade textures were later applied in Fig. 2(b),
- mask of all obstacles in view in Fig. 2(c).

Real world spherical images for the test set were collected with an omnidirectional camera. Each photo was manually annotated in the VIA VGG Image Annotator [4], excluding obstacles such as lamps, cars, trees or pedestrians from the façade area as illustrated in Fig. 3. As a result, we tagged 50 images that contained 267 annotated façade instances. For comparative analysis, two test sets

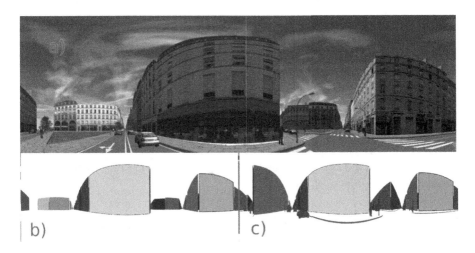

Fig. 2. Instance mask labeling of training data. **(a)** Fully textured view **(b)** Marked façade instances in different shades of green **(c)** Obstacles mask in blue (Color figure online)

were employed. The first one was the whole set of 267 façade instances. The second one contained 127 façade instances that had an area of at least 10,000 pixels. This means that smaller façades were discarded, the area of which in the spherical image was less than 2% of the façade area in the actual non-spherical image. The results for this dataset were denoted in this paper by adding "GT>10000 px" after the model name.

Fig. 3. Annotation of spherical photos.

Mask R-CNN [8] model was pre-trained on the COCO dataset [14] with Caffe model zoo [1]. ResNet50 backbone was used as a model in conjunction with SGD optimizer. The training was carried out using mini-batches with samples resized to 512 × 1024 and parameters: learning rate 0.002, step policy 8, 11, momentum

0.9, and weight decay 0.0001. The parameters for the linear warm-up were: size 1000 iterations with a ratio of 0.0005. Additionally, three different ratios (0.5, 1, 2.0) were used with the anchor sizes (32, 64, 128, 256, 512) to account for different sizes of objects of interest. The Mask Scoring R-CNN [12] model was also pre-trained on the COCO dataset [14] using the Caffe model zoo [1]. It had the same hyperparameters as the Mask R-CNN model described above.

YOLACT construction was based on ResNet50 backbone and SGD optimizer [6]. The learning parameters were set as follows: rate to 0.003 with step policy (steps: 20, 42, 49, 52), momentum to 0.9, and weight decay to 0.0005. Four different ratios (0.5, 1, 2, 4) and anchor sizes (16, 32, 64, 128, 256) were used for different sizes of objects of interest.

3   Measures to Evaluate Deep Learning Models

We applied two approaches to the comparison, adopting the measures proposed in [18]. In this study, we named them: Façade Instance and Façade Segmentation. The first: Façade Instance is the quantitative approach based on counting façade instances, in which the number of detected façades is compared with the number of façades in the real image (Ground Truth - GT). When detecting the façades, the Intersection over Union (IoU) coefficient is calculated according to Eq. 1. IoU not less than 0.5 is considered True Positive (TP). False positives (FP) are detections that do not match any of the GT façades or whose IoU is less than 0.5. GT façades that have no matching detection are classified as False Negative (FN). Then, the obtained values are used in *Precision* (Eq. 2), *Recall* (Eq. 3) and *F1* (Eq. 4) for overall accuracy.

$$IoU = \frac{TP}{TP + FP + FN} \tag{1}$$

$$Precision = \frac{TP}{TP + FP} \tag{2}$$

$$Recall = \frac{TP}{TP + FN} \tag{3}$$

$$F1 = \frac{2 * Precision * Recall}{Precision * Recall} \tag{4}$$

The second: Façade Segmentation is based on segmentation of façades, in which the quality of the masks of detected façades is determined as shown in Fig. 4. The calculated masks (marked in pink in Fig. 4) are compared with their real GT counterparts (marked in green in Fig. 4) to classify the pixels as True Positive (TP), False Positive (FP), and False Negative (FN).

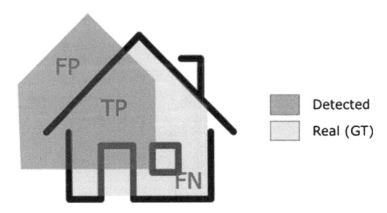

Fig. 4. The idea of comparing the quality of façade segmentation (Color figure online)

Finally, three measures are computed to compare DL models. To measure the object detection performance, the Percentage of Façade Detection (FDP) is calculated using Eq. 5, which describes how much of the GT façade has been detected. The Branching Factor (BF), calculated by Eq. 6, measures over-segmentation. It is equal to 0 if all detected pixels relate to the GT mask area. Finally, Quality Percentage (QP) evaluates the absolute quality of the separated façades. A value of 100% QP represents a perfect segmentation of façades with respect to the corresponding GT data. QP is defined by Eq. 7.

$$FDP = \frac{100 * TP}{TP + FN} \tag{5}$$

$$BF = \frac{FP}{TP} \tag{6}$$

$$QP = \frac{100 * TP}{TP + FP + FN} \tag{7}$$

The obtained DL models were compared in terms of the above-defined measures in the context of the Façade Instance and Façade Segmentation using statistical tests selected depending on the data characteristics. Table 1 describes the statistical tests and the conditions for their application. All tests were performed using the Stats module of the SciPy [15] library and the scikit-posthocs [3] library in the Python language environment.

4   The Analysis of Façade Instance Detection Results

For Façade Instance analysis, we applied two test datasets prepared from spherical images collected in a real city: the whole set containing all 267 annotated

Table 1. Statistical tests depending on data characteristics

	Data with normal distribution	Data with non-normal distribution
Two paired samples	Paired t-test	Wilcoxon test
Two unpaired samples	Unpaired t-test	Mann-Whitney test
Three or more matched samples	One-way repeated-measures ANOVA	Friedman test
Three or more unmatched samples	One-way ANOVA	Kruskal-Wallis test

façade instances, and a subset containing 127 façade instances at least 10,000 pixels in size. Using these test sets, the values of the *Precision, Recall* and *F1* measures were calculated for the Mask RCNN, Mask Scoring R-CNN and YOLAC models.

The calculated *p-values* of Shapiro-Wilk normality test are presented in Table 2. The null hypothesis (H0) assumes that the data is normally distributed. The H0 is rejected if the *p-value* is lower than 0.05. If H0 is rejected, we assume that the dataset has non-normal distribution. The normally distributed measures are marked in bold in Table 2.

Table 2. *p-value* for Shapiro-Wilk Normality test of façade instance detection metrics

Metric	Mask R-CNN	Mask scoring R-CNN	YOLACT	Mask R-CNN GT >10000px	Mask scoring R-CNN GT >10000px	YOLACT GT >10000px
Precision	0.000	0.000	0.000	0.000	0.000	0.000
Recall	**0.098**	**0.131**	0.000	0.000	0.000	0.000
F1	**0.152**	**0.056**	**0.119**	0.000	0.000	0.000

The results of Wilcoxon test for pairwise comparison of models for the whole set of façade instances with models for the subset where GT >10000px are presented in Table 3. The null hypothesis (H0) for this test is that there is no significant difference between the values of the metrics. The rejected H0 hypotheses

Table 3. *p-value* calculated with Wilcoxon's test to compare the results for the whole set of façade instances with the subset where GT >10000px

Metric	Mask R-CNN	Mask R-CNN GT >10000px	Mask scoring R-CNN	Mask scoring R-CNN GT >10000px	YOLACT	YOLACT GT >10000px
Precision	0.329		0.263		0.971	
Recall	**0.000**		**0.000**		**0.000**	
F1	**0.012**		0.267		**0.001**	

are marked in bold in Table 3. When analyzing Table 3, it cannot be concluded that there is a significant difference in *Precision* for any pair of models. Considering that the *FP* value remains the same in both cases, this means that most of all façades found by the detectors exceed the assumed threshold of 10,000 pixels. Unlike *Precision*, there are significant differences in *Recall* for each pair of models. This can be explained by the fact of throwing out FNs associated with smaller façades. This means that if our goal is to only find façades larger than 10,000 pixels, our detectors find more relevant objects. This fact is also confirmed by the results presented in Table 7.

Table 4. *p-value* for one-way repeated measures ANOVA and Friedman tests for multiple comparison of façade instance detection metrics.

Metric	Mask R-CNN	Mask scoring R-CNN	YOLACT	Mask R-CNN GT >10000px	Mask scoring R-CNN GT >10000px	YOLACT GT >10000px
Precision	0.520			0.616		
Recall	0.000			0.001		
F1	0.000[a]			0.789		

[a]Calculated with One-Way Repeated Measures ANOVA

Table 5. *p-value* for post-hoc pairwise t-test and Nemenyi's test for *F1* and *Recall* for the whole set of façade instances.

	Pairwise T-test - *F1*			Nemenyi's Test - *Recall*		
	Mask R-CNN	Mask scoring R-CNN	YOLACT	Mask R-CNN	Mask scoring R-CNN	YOLACT
Mask R-CNN		0.819	0.002		0.857	0.001
Mask scoring R-CNN	0.819		0.003	0.857		0.001
YOLACT	0.002	0.003		0.001	0.001	

Additional checking of the equality of variance with Levene's test was carried out due to the fact that the hypothesis about data from the normal distribution was not rejected only for the group of *F1* values for the whole set of façade instances. The H0 hypothesis assumes that populations can have equal variances. In our case, the calculated *p-value* was 0.893, so we had no evidence to reject H0. In consequence, in the next step, we used for *F1* the ANOVA One-Way Repeated Measures test for the whole set of façade instances and the Friedman test for other metrics.

The results in Table 4 show that there are no significant differences between the tested groups for *Precision* for both the whole set of façade instances and the subset where GT >10000px and for *F1* for the subset where GT >10000px. In turn, for the *F1* and *Recall* groups in which the H0 hypotheses were rejected in the Friedman and One-Way Repeated Measures ANOVA tests, the post-hoc tests were performed. Test results for the whole set of façade instances are presented in Table 5 and for the subset where GT >10000px in Table 6.

Table 6. *p-value* value for post-hoc Nemenyi's test for *Recall* for the subset of façade instances where GT >10000px.

	Nemenyi's test - recall		
	Mask R-CNN (GT >10000px)	Mask scoring R-CNN (GT >10000px)	YOLACT (GT >10000px)
Mask R-CNN (GT >10000px)		0.819	**0.002**
Mask scoring R-CNN (GT >10000px)	0.819		**0.003**
YOLACT (GT >10000px)	**0.002**	**0.003**	

Based on the test results, it can be concluded that there is a significant statistical difference between YOLACT and the R-CNN family models for the whole set of façade instances. This observation is supported by the average instance detection results shown in Table 7. YOLACT finds on average about one instance less per image than the Mask R- CNN and Mask Scoring R-CNN. Considering only the subset of façade instances where GT >10000px, YOLACT finds 0.4 instances per image less than the models from the R-CNN family. Taking into account the values in Table 7, we can state that Mask R-CNN outperforms the other methods.

Table 7. The average values of façade instance detection metrics.

Method	Avg TP (n)	Avg FN (n)	Avg FP (n)	Avg GT (n)	Avg precision	Avg recall	Avg F1
Mask R-CNN	2.40	2.90	0.98	5.30	0.713	0.490	0.550
Mask scoring R-CNN	2.32	2.98	1.06	5.30	0.698	0.485	0.541
YOLACT	1.34	3.96	0.62	5.30	0.708	0.303	0.395
Mask R-CNN (GT >10000px)	1.74	0.74	0.98	2.48	0.659	0.708	0.652
Mask scoring R-CNN (GT >10000px)	1.74	0.74	1.06	2.48	0.648	0.715	0.646
YOLACT (GT >10000px)	1.34	1.14	0.62	2.48	0.708	0.571	0.610

5   The Analysis of Façade Segmentation Results

To determine which model best performs façade mask extraction, we compare the models with each other based on the results obtained on correctly detected façades. In this case, the number of correctly detected façades was 120 for Mask R-CNN, 116 for Mask Scoring R-CNN, and 67 for YOLACT. To compare the results of all models, we select the same set of correctly detected images, so we only consider the façades that have been correctly detected by each of our models. Thus, we obtained 57 matching façades.

Table 8. *p-value* for Shapiro-Wilk normality test for façade segmentation metrics.

Metric	Mask R-CNN	Mask scoring R-CNN	YOLACT
FDP	0.000	0.000	0.002
BF	0.000	0.000	0.000
QP	0.001	0.001	0.016

The calculated *p-values* of Shapiro-Wilk normality test are presented in Table 8. The null hypothesis (H0) assumes that the data is normally distributed. The H0 is rejected if the *p-value* is lower than 0.05. It is clearly seen in Table 8 that no metrics is normally distributed. Thus, consequently to the path described in Table 1, for data with nonnormal distribution and more than 2 matched groups, the Friedman's test is used. Calculated *p-values* are shown in Table 9. The H0 of Friedman's test is rejected if the *p-value* is lower than 0.05. For such cases, we assume that there are significant differences in the results, so we can apply a post-hoc test. H0 was rejected for the *FDP* and *QP* metrics marked in bold in Table 9. So we used the Nemenyi's post-hoc test for *FDP* and *QP*. The results are presented in Table 10. The obtained results indicate that Mask R-CNN differs significantly from the other models. Taking into account the values in Table 11, we can conclude that this model surpasses Mask Scoring R-CNN and YOLACT in terms of *FDP* and *QP*.

Table 9. *p-value* for Friedman test for multiple comparison of façade segmentation metrics.

Metric	Mask R-CNN	Mask scoring R-CNN	YOLACT
FDP	**0.000**		
BF	0.805		
QP	**0.000**		

Table 10. *p-value* for post-hoc Nemenyi's test for the *FDP* and *QP* façade segmentation metrics.

	FDP			QP		
	Mask R-CNN	Mask scoring R-CNN	YOLACT	Mask R-CNN	Mask scoring R-CNN	YOLACT
Mask R-CNN		0.001	0.001		0.014	0.001
Mask scoring R-CNN	0.001		0.339	0.014		0.221
YOLACT	0.001	0.339		0.001	0.221	

Table 11. The average values of façade segmentation metrics.

Method	Avg *FDP* (%)	Avg *BF*	Avg *QP* (%)
Mask R-CNN	84.645	0.079	79.670
Mask scoring R-CNN	82.062	0.092	76.603
YOLACT	80.647	0.077	76.139
Mask R-CNN (GT >10000px)	85.168	0.070	80.597
Mask scoring R-CNN (GT >10000px)	81.769	0.094	76.203
YOLACT (GT >10000px)	80.647	0.077	76.139

6   Conclusion

A comparison of three deep learning models for façade instance detection and façade instance segmentation was performed. The models compared were Mask R-CNN, Mask Scoring R-CNN, and YOLACT. All three models were built on the same ResNet50 backbone and transfer learned on data generated from a 3D artificial city. The city model was parametric and consisted of buildings of varied architecture: from the 19th century Haussmann style to contemporary postmodernism. The learned models were tested on real photos taken in one of Polish cities.

The Mask R-CNN model achieved the best results for both the detection of the façade instances and the segmentation of the façade instances. Considering that all DL models tested are based on the same ResNet50 architecture, the results of the more modern YOLACT and Mask Scoring R-CNN networks were disappointing. However, it should be taken into account that YOLACT was designed as a real-time solution and the speed of this deep neural network is noticeably faster, while maintaining performance not much inferior to Mask R-CNN.

Further work will focus on greater automation of the process of obtaining information about the urban structure from spherical images, e.g. by adding the possibility of automatic rectification of the mask from spherical space to a plane. We plan also to examine the usefulness of new solutions, such as TensorMask [7] or YOLAC+ [6].

References

1. Caffe2 model zoo. https://caffe2.ai/docs/zoo.html. Accessed 6 Aug 2021
2. Pyprt - python bindings for cityengine sdk. https://github.com/Esri/pyprt. Accessed 6 Aug 2021
3. scikit-posthocs. https://scikit-posthocs.readthedocs.io/. Accessed 6 Aug 2021
4. Vgg image annotator (via). https://www.robots.ox.ac.uk/~vgg/software/via/via.html. Accessed 6 Aug 2021
5. py360convert. https://github.com/sunset1995/py360convert (2020). [Online; Accessed 15 Jan 2021
6. Bolya, D., Zhou, C., Xiao, F., Lee, Y.J.: YOLACT: real-time instance segmentation. In: Proceedings of the IEEE/CVF International Conference on Computer Vision, pp. 9157–9166 (2019)
7. Chen, X., Girshick, R., He, K., Dollár, P.: TensorMask: a foundation for dense object segmentation. In: Proceedings of the IEEE/CVF International Conference on Computer Vision, pp. 2061–2069 (2019)
8. Girshick, R.: Fast r-cnn. CoRR abs/1504.08083 (2015). http://www.cv-foundation.org/openaccess/content_iccv_2015/papers/Girshick_Fast_R-CNN_ICCV_2015_paper.pdf
9. He, K., Gkioxari, G., Dollár, P., Girshick, R.: Mask R-CNN. In: 2017 IEEE International Conference on Computer Vision (ICCV), pp. 2980–2988 (2017). https://doi.org/10.1109/ICCV.2017.322
10. He, K., Zhang, X., Ren, S., Sun, J.: Deep residual learning for image recognition. In: 2016 IEEE Conference on Computer Vision and Pattern Recognition (CVPR), pp. 770–778 (2016). https://doi.org/10.1109/CVPR.2016.90
11. Hernández, J., Marcotegui, B.: Morphological segmentation of building façade images. In: 2009 16th IEEE International Conference on Image Processing (ICIP), pp. 4029–4032 (2009). https://doi.org/10.1109/ICIP.2009.5413756
12. Huang, Z., Huang, L., Gong, Y., Huang, C., Wang, X.: Mask scoring R-CNN. In: Proceedings of the IEEE/CVF Conference on Computer Vision and Pattern Recognition, pp. 6409–6418 (2019)
13. Kutrzyński, M., Żak, B., Telec, Z., Trawiński, B.: An approach to automatic detection of architectural façades in spherical images. In: Intelligent Information and Database Systems: 13th Asian Conference, ACIIDS 2021, Phuket, Thailand, 7–10 April 2021, Proceedings 13, pp. 494–504. Springer (2021). https://doi.org/10.1007/978-3-030-73280-6_39
14. Lin, T.Y., et al.: Microsoft COCO: common objects in context. In: Fleet, D., Pajdla, T., Schiele, B., Tuytelaars, T. (eds.) ECCV 2014. LNCS, vol. 8693, pp. 740–755. Springer, Cham (2014). https://doi.org/10.1007/978-3-319-10602-1_48
15. Pedregosa, F., et al.: Scikit-learn: machine learning in python. J. Mach. Learn. Res. 12(Oct), 2825–2830 (2011)
16. Redmon, J., Farhadi, A.: YOLOv3: an incremental improvement. arXiv preprint arXiv:1804.02767 (2018)
17. Ren, S., He, K., Girshick, R., Sun, J.: Faster R-CNN: towards real-time object detection with region proposal networks. IEEE Trans. Pattern Anal. Mach. Intell. 39(6), 1137–1149 (2016)

18. Sümer, E., Türker, M.: An automatic region growing based approach to extract facade textures from single ground-level building images. J. Geodesy Geoinf. **2**(1), 9–17 (2013)
19. Wendel, A., Donoser, M., Bischof, H.: Unsupervised facade segmentation using repetitive patterns, vol. 6376, pp. 51–60 (2010). https://doi.org/10.1007/978-3-642-15986-2_6

Ensemble of Convolution Neural Networks for Automatic Tuberculosis Classification

Mustapha Oloko-Oba(ID) and Serestina Viriri$^{(\boxtimes)}$(ID)

School of Mathematics, Statistics and Computer Science,
University of KwaZulu-Natal, Durban, South Africa
viriris@ukzn.ac.za

Abstract. Tuberculosis (TB) is curable, and millions of deaths could be averted if diagnosed early. One of the sources of screening TB is through a chest X-ray. Still, its success depends on the interpretation of skilled and experienced radiologists, mostly lacking in high TB burden regions. However, with the intervention of a computer-aided detection system, TB can be automatically detected from chest X-rays. This paper presents an Ensemble model based on multiple pre-trained models to detect TB from chest X-rays automatically. The models were trained on the Shenzhen dataset and validated on the Montgomery dataset to achieve good generalization on a new (unseen) dataset. Improved classification accuracy was however achieved through the Ensemble model compared to the individual models. The proposed model indicates the strength of combining multiple models to improve model accuracy.

Keywords: Ensemble · Tuberculosis · Convolutional Neural Network · Chest X-Ray · Pre-processing

1 Introduction

Over the years, Tuberculosis (TB) has ranked among the highest causes of mortality. In 2019, about 10 million persons fell sick globally from TB [23]. TB disease is most widespread in developing regions. According to the world health organization (WHO), TB is a disease of economic distress, poverty and vulnerability, which is evident in the geographical incident of TB cases where South-East Asia and Africa accounted for about 69% of the total cases [24] as shown in Table 1.

TB is certainly preventable and curable but needs to be diagnosed early [24]. Early diagnosis is fundamental in effectively tackling TB, and significantly reducing the mortality rate in line with the WHO "End TB Strategy". This strategy has been hampered by the advent of COVID-19 pandemic, which exhibits similar symptoms with TB and could increase the mortality rate by about 0.2–0.4 million [24].

For early diagnosis of TB, proper diagnostic procedures are essential. Various test procedures have been employed to detect TB, but chest X-ray (CXR)

© Springer Nature Switzerland AG 2021
N. T. Nguyen et al. (Eds.): ICCCI 2021, LNAI 12876, pp. 549–559, 2021.
https://doi.org/10.1007/978-3-030-88081-1_41

Table 1. Geographical tuberculosis incidence

Region	South-East Asia	Africa	Western Pacific	Eastern Mediterranean	The Americas	Europe
Cases (%)	44	25	18	8.2	2.5	2.9

is more prominent and recommended due to high sensitivity in screening lung abnormalities [22,26]. Regardless of the CXR suitability in screening abnormalities, accurately interpreting CXR images requires a skilled and expert radiologist mostly due to different manifestations of TB on CXR images as well as in co-infection cases where other pulmonary diseases have similar symptoms with TB, such as lung cancer and COVID-19 [6].

Unfortunately, in TB epidemic regions, lack of skilled radiologist to adequately interpret CXR and other factors like outdated screening equipment, electricity, and lack of awareness have been among the reasons for the delay in diagnosing leading to a widespread of TB [19,33]. These challenges gave rise to the development of Computer-aided detection (CAD) system using Convolutional Neural Network (CNN), for screening CXR to detect pulmonary abnormalities. Various CAD has been developed to automatically detect TB, thereby resulting in many patients' early diagnosis and reducing the burden of an expert radiologist in the TB prevalent areas [11,18]. DL models (CNN) application to medical imaging has shown tremendous performance, especially in lung abnormalities screening, to detect/classify CXR images [12]. CNN architectures often require large data samples to learn distinctive features useful for predictions and attain high performance [30]. The first CNN model trained on CXR for TB classification was the ALexNet [12]. AlexNet [15] was initially introduced on the ImageNet dataset in 2012 and then fine-tuned to train CXR datasets. This process is called "Transfer Learning" and is very useful compared to training a model from scratch with small data samples [25] as evident from literature. Therefore, some of the CAD systems that employed CNN models are reviewed to highlight the strength and challenges that form the basis for this study.

The study presented in [28] modified the VggNet [31] and AlexNet architectures for screening and classifying CXR images as healthy and unhealthy. The architectures were independently trained on the Montgomery and Shenzhen dataset to evaluate the model. VggNet performed slightly above the AlexNet, achieving classification accuracy of 81.6% and 80.4% respectively. The study showed that having large data samples will increase the model accuracy as distinctive features are learned from different data samples. Three pre-trained CNN models were customized and employed in [14] to classify TB abnormalities in CXR. Image pre-processing such as "Data Augmentation" was applied to artificially increase the dataset size before training the models. Thereafter, the model's performance was evaluated to determine accuracy, specificity, and sensitivity where CapsNet [29] outperformed the other models concerning affine image prediction. The use of pre-trained CNN models to extract features from images has been an effective approach, especially in the medical field where annotated CXR are limited. This is evident in [20]. The study employed "Vgg16" to extract distinctive features from CXR then train a classifier on the extracted features to identify the infected CXR from the healthy ones. Contrast limited adaptive histogram equalization and data augmentation were applied to boost the quality of the CXR to obtain a reasonable accuracy. The study further highlights that having a large dataset of annotated CXR could result in building a deeper and more robust CAD from scratch.

A CNN architecture consisting of five convolutional, pooling and Softmax layers is presented in [27] to screen for TB abnormalities in CXR. This model also incorporates a visualization procedure to assist radiologist with visual diagnosis while minimizing computational complexity to achieve a faster and efficient model. In [4], GoogLeNet [32] model was applied to diagnose different manifestation of TB. CXR was classified either as healthy or unhealthy with one or more of pleural effusion, consolidation, pneumothorax, cardiomegaly, and edema. The CXR were pre-processed where the images with shorter and larger dimensions were padded and normalized respectively before training. AUC, specificity and sensitivity were used to evaluate the model performance and then compared with the result of 2 board-certified radiologists. An approach proposed in [8] fine-tuned CNN to detect TB automatically. The CXR was collected alongside the patient's demographic details such as height, weight, gender, and age. Two experiments were conducted to compare the performance of CXR with demographic details and CXR without demographic details. The former shows higher performance in terms of AUC and sensitivity over the latter. The study in [1] employed Vgg16 to train CXR images for the detection of TB. Two experiments performed where data augmentation was applied to the CXR in one case and not applied in the other. The experiment with the augmented CXR performed slightly higher than the non-augmented experiment.

While different CNN models, either pre-trained or trained from scratch, have been used to predict objects, there have also been cases where multiple models are employed to improve/attain better and accurate predictions than any individual model; this phenomenal is called "Ensemble Learning". An Ensemble of ResNet [7], VggNet, and GoogLeNet was introduced in [17] along with "Bag of features and Simple feature extractor". Experiments were performed for each method where the input CXR were down-sampled to conform with different CNNs except for Bag of features where CXR images were not resized. Downsampling may result in loss of vital detail, which will affect the performance of the model. The Ensemble model achieved better performance than the other two models. The study shows that class imbalance, down-sampling and dataset size can affect performance. In [2], deep CNN models were integrated with the hand-craft technique through Ensemble learning to extract features from CXR images. The extracted features were then employed as inputs to train a classifier for identifying infected CXRs. In all the experiments, the Ensemble model performed better compared to the individual model.

Similarly, the study proposed in [10] employed Ensemble technique where features were extracted from raw CXR images and edge detected images. The approach begins with image pre-processing followed by classifier development before classification using different combinations to represent the Ensemble. The CNN architectures were applied to both image type using accuracy, sensitivity, and specificity as the evaluation metrics. The Ensemble model achieved the highest accuracy and sensitivity. An Ensemble classifier was proposed in [9] for classifying TB abnormalities in CXR. Individual CNN models are firstly employed for training using different hyper-parameters after which an Ensemble of these models is created and used for training. These models are then compared and the Ensemble attain an improved accuracy. Although the Ensemble model performed better in this study, but another single model [21] has achieved better accuracy.

In summary, efforts have been invested in developing CAD systems to detect TB abnormalities automatically. Evidently, from literature, deep learning models trained from scratch are computationally expensive and are hugely dependent on large dataset size which is limited in the medical field. However, studies have found Transfer Learning using pre-trained models as a useful approach to compliment limited datasets. Accurately diagnosing TB is a sensitive and challenging task due to its different manifestations and high risk to life, hence the need to develop an effective CAD that can efficiently detect different TB manifestation.

This paper proposed an Ensemble technique that takes advantage of the strength of different pre-trained CNN models with the expectation that a misclassified image from model "A" can be correctly classified by model "B" or "C". Therefore, fusing several classifiers can increase the rate of detection compared to any stand-alone classifier. The contributions of this study are as follows:

- Development of Ensemble model that leverage on different pre-trained models' strength to increase the TB detection rate.
- Models trained with one dataset (Shenzhen) and validated on a different dataset (Montgomery). The tradition has been using the same datasets for training and validation
- Data augmentation and contrast adaptive histogram equalization techniques to improve the quality of the datasets

The next section presents the proposed methodology, followed by the result section where the experimental outcome is presented before the Discussion section and finally, Conclusion.

2   Proposed Methodology

The proposed model is made up of Image pre-processing techniques, the generation of individual CNN classifiers, and combination of multiple models to build an Ensemble classifier for TB classification. The Ensemble implemented in this paper is the "Bagging" method because of its strength to achieve low variance, thereby controlling model overfitting. Bagging yield stability and achieve better performance by combining multiple models. In other words, it employs two

or more models to learn distinctive features independently of the other participating models; the output of each participating model is then combined and
averaged to obtain a final prediction.

The flow diagram of the proposed model is shown in Fig. 1.

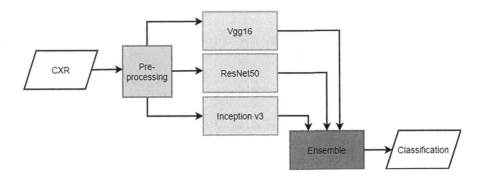

Fig. 1. Process diagram of the proposed model

2.1 Image Pre-processing

The pre-processing techniques applied to the CXR images in this study include
Contrast Limited Adaptive Histogram Equalization [16], to improve the quality
of the images in terms of clarity, then Data Augmentation [3], was applied to
adequately increase the diversity of training samples by way of flipping, and
padding. Finally, since we are training multiple models, the CXR images were
resized to conform to the individual model's original input size. The input size
for Inception v3 is $229 \times 229 \times 3$ while Vgg19 and ResNet50 have similar input
size of $224 \times 224 \times 3$.

2.2 Building Ensemble of CNN

In constructing the proposed Ensemble model, we consider three powerful pre-
trained CNN models, "Vgg16, ResNet50, and Inception v3," initially trained on
the ImageNet [5], dataset. These models were trained to identify about 1000
classes of objects, hence adopting it to CXR dataset; their final layer (classifier)
is substituted with a binary classifier. Each of the CNN models is trained independently using different hyper-parameters that perform best in terms of the
optimizer, learning rate, and activation function. The models were trained each
for 80 iterations (epochs) with a batch size of 32 to obtain the probability of
each CXR samples belonging to either a positive or negative class representing
TB and non-TB classes. The output from the individual model is then combined
to obtain the final prediction through the Ensemble classifier. The performance

of the proposed model is measured in terms of the popular evaluation metrics defined as follows:

Accuracy: is the rate of correctly predicted samples from the overall samples examined and is defines as:

$$Accuracy = \frac{TP + TN}{TP + FP + TN + FN} \tag{1}$$

Sensitivity: refers to the measure of confirmed positive samples that are correctly identified as positives.

$$Sensitivity = \frac{TP}{TP + FN} \tag{2}$$

Specificity: is the rate of confirmed negative samples that are correctly identified as negatives.

$$Specificity = \frac{TN}{TN + FP} \tag{3}$$

where:
TP = True Positive, FP = False Positive, TN = True Negative, and FN = False Negative respectively.

3   Results

The proposed model was trained on the Shenzhen dataset and validated on the Montgomery dataset [13]. These datasets contain TB specific CXR images provided by the National Library of Medicine (NLM) and publicly made available for research purposes. The Shenzhen dataset is made up of 336 infected CXR samples and 326 healthy CXR samples. All the samples are 3000 × 3000 pixels in resolution. Meanwhile, the Montgomery dataset contains 58 infected CXR samples and 80 healthy samples having a size of either 4892 × 4020 pixels or 4020 × 4892 pixels. Both datasets are accompanied by clinical readings that provide demographic details about each of the CXR samples with respect to diagnosis, sex, and age of the patients. The diagnostic information given for each CXR sample serves as a standard ground truth to validate the proposed model's output. These datasets are accessible from the NIH website[1]. Figure 2 shows sample CXR from both datasets.

Several experiments were performed aimed at minimizing false negative and positives as much as possible. In this regard, Vgg16, ResNet50, and Inception v3 trained and evaluated for detection of TB abnormalities. Different outcomes are expected since different models exhibit diverse characteristics in terms of depth, parameters, and overall configurations. In the first experiment where the above models are individually employed to classify CXR, the best performance was obtained with the Inception v3 model at 93.50% followed by a 92.10% performance with the Vgg16 and the lowest accuracy of 89.51% with the ResNet50

---

[1] https://lhncbc.nlm.nih.gov/publication/pub9931.

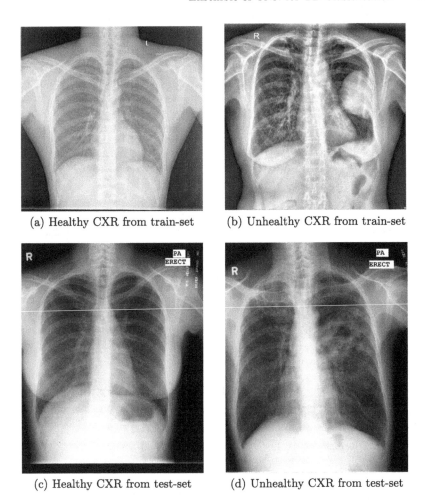

(a) Healthy CXR from train-set   (b) Unhealthy CXR from train-set

(c) Healthy CXR from test-set   (d) Unhealthy CXR from test-set

Fig. 2. Sample of CXR images from both datasets

model. Meanwhile, ResNet50 surpass the other models in terms of sensitivity. The next experiment is the Ensemble of all models from the previous experiment. The performance of the individual models is combined/averaged to build an Ensemble classifier for Tb detection. The Ensemble model output surpasses all the individual models to boost the overall classification accuracy. The detail experimental results are shown in Table 2 and Fig. 3 respectively.

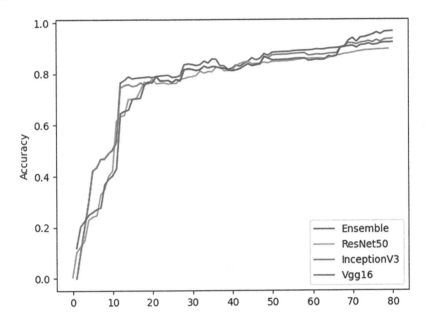

Fig. 3. Models accuracy performance

Table 2. Experimental results

	Ensemble	ResNet50	Vgg16	Inception v3
Accuracy (%)	96.14	89.51	92.10	93.50
Sensitivity (%)	90.03	89.09	88.25	79.31
Specificity (%)	92.41	90.08	91.00	83.36

4   Discussion

It is evident from Table 2, the performance of individual models shows the Inception V3 model with the best accuracy, Although the overall best performance is achieved through the Ensemble model. One of the obstacles that affect CNN model is overfitting which is common when a model is run on a new dataset. It is essential to control overfitting to achieve better generalization of the model on new datasets. In this study, we employed techniques such as "data augmentation, normalization, dropout, and least absolute deviations (LAD), also known as L1, to control overfitting. As a result of various manifestations of TB, depending on a single model might not be too effective. Hence Ensemble of multiple models employed in this study makes the CAD system more robust with an improved detection rate because with Ensemble, different models could compliment themselves such that where a model misclassifies an image, one or more of the other models can accurately classify the image. The proposed model generalized well despite having the training, validation and test set from different datasets. The model performed well when compared with recent Ensemble CAD systems as shown in Table 3.

Table 3. Proposed model compared with related work. The performances are measured in terms of Accuracy (ACC) and Area Under Curve (AUC)

Authors ref	Models combined	Performance (%)
Hijazi et al. [10]	2	89.77
Hernandez et al. [9]	3	86.40
Ayaz et al. [2]	6	0.99
Proposed	3	96.14

Hijazi et al. [10], Hernandez et al. [9], and the **Proposed** model are evaluated using the accuracy, while Ayaz et al. [2] is measured using area under the curve.

5 Conclusion

An Ensemble model comprising of multiple pre-trained models is presented in this study to aid early and accurate TB diagnosis from CXR. The proposed model is trained on one dataset and tested on an alternative dataset, resulting in a good generalization. Due to limited datasets in medical fields, the dataset were augmented along with other techniques to control overfitting. However, the individual CNN classifier achieved good results and was improved through the Ensemble classifier. The proposed model can also be deployed to detect other pulmonary abnormalities. Future work will focus on developing a robust CAD system that could accurately identify foreign objects that may be seen on CXR. Objects such as "pieces of bones, coins, rings, or button found in the chest can be likened to one of many TB manifestations which will result in misclassification.

References

1. Ahsan, M., Gomes, R., Denton, A.: Application of a convolutional neural network using transfer learning for tuberculosis detection. In: 2019 IEEE International Conference on Electro Information Technology (EIT), pp. 427–433. IEEE (2019)
2. Ayaz, M., Shaukat, F., Raja, G.: Ensemble learning based automatic detection of tuberculosis in chest x-ray images using hybrid feature descriptors. Phys. Eng. Sci. Med. **44**, 1–12 (2021)
3. Bloice, M.D., Stocker, C., Holzinger, A.: Augmentor: an image augmentation library for machine learning. arXiv preprint arXiv:1708.04680 (2017)
4. Cicero, M., et al.: Training and validating a deep convolutional neural network for computer-aided detection and classification of abnormalities on frontal chest radiographs. Invest. Radiol. **52**(5), 281–287 (2017)

5. Deng, J., Dong, W., Socher, R., Li, L.J., Li, K., Fei-Fei, L.: Imagenet: a large-scale hierarchical image database. In: 2009 IEEE Conference on Computer Vision and Pattern Recognition, pp. 248–255. IEEE (2009)
6. Hammen, I.: Tuberculosis mimicking lung cancer. Respir. Med. Case Rep. **16**, 45–47 (2015)
7. He, K., Zhang, X., Ren, S., Sun, J.: Deep residual learning for image recognition. In: Proceedings of the IEEE Conference on Computer Vision and Pattern Recognition, pp. 770–778 (2016)
8. Heo, S.J., et al.: Deep learning algorithms with demographic information help to detect tuberculosis in chest radiographs in annual workers' health examination data. Int. J. Environ. Res. Public Health **16**(2), 250 (2019)
9. Hernández, A., Panizo, Á., Camacho, D.: An ensemble algorithm based on deep learning for tuberculosis classification. In: Yin, H., Camacho, D., Tino, P., Tallón-Ballesteros, A.J., Menezes, R., Allmendinger, R. (eds.) IDEAL 2019. LNCS, vol. 11871, pp. 145–154. Springer, Cham (2019). https://doi.org/10.1007/978-3-030-33607-3_17
10. Hijazi, M.H.A., Hwa, S.K.T., Bade, A., Yaakob, R., Jeffree, M.S.: Ensemble deep learning for tuberculosis detection using chest x-ray and canny edge detected images. IAES Int. J. Artif. Intell. **8**(4), 429 (2019)
11. Hooda, R., Mittal, A., Sofat, S.: Tuberculosis detection from chest radiographs: a comprehensive survey on computer-aided diagnosis techniques. Curr. Med. Imaging **14**(4), 506–520 (2018)
12. Hwang, S., Kim, H.E., Jeong, J., Kim, H.J.: A novel approach for tuberculosis screening based on deep convolutional neural networks. In: Medical imaging 2016: Computer-Aided Diagnosis, vol. 9785, p. 97852W. International Society for Optics and Photonics (2016)
13. Jaeger, S., Candemir, S., Antani, S., Wáng, Y.X.J., Lu, P.X., Thoma, G.: Two public chest x-ray datasets for computer-aided screening of pulmonary diseases. Quant. Imaging Med. Surg, **4**(6), 475 (2014)
14. Karnkawinpong, T., Limpiyakorn, Y.: Chest x-ray analysis of tuberculosis by convolutional neural networks with affine transforms. In: Proceedings of the 2018 2nd International Conference on Computer Science and Artificial Intelligence, pp. 90–93 (2018)
15. Krizhevsky, A., Sutskever, I., Hinton, G.E.: Imagenet classification with deep convolutional neural networks. Adv. Neural Inf. Process. Syst. **25**, 1097–1105 (2012)
16. Kurt, B., Nabiyev, V.V., Turhan, K.: Medical images enhancement by using anisotropic filter and clahe. In: 2012 International Symposium on Innovations in Intelligent Systems and Applications, pp. 1–4. IEEE (2012)
17. Lopes, U., Valiati, J.F.: Pre-trained convolutional neural networks as feature extractors for tuberculosis detection. Comput. Biol. Med. **89**, 135–143 (2017)
18. Meraj, S.S., Yaakob, R., Azman, A., Rum, S.N.M., Nazri, A.: Artificial intelligence in diagnosing tuberculosis: a review. Int. J. Adv. Sci. Eng. Inf. Technol. **9**(1), 81–91 (2019)
19. Oloko-Oba, M., Viriri, S.: Diagnosing tuberculosis using deep convolutional neural network. In: El Moataz, A., Mammass, D., Mansouri, A., Nouboud, F. (eds.) ICISP 2020. LNCS, vol. 12119, pp. 151–161. Springer, Cham (2020). https://doi.org/10.1007/978-3-030-51935-3_16
20. Oloko-Oba, M., Viriri, S.: Pre-trained convolutional neural network for the diagnosis of tuberculosis. In: Bebis, G., et al. (eds.) ISVC 2020. LNCS, vol. 12510, pp. 558–569. Springer, Cham (2020). https://doi.org/10.1007/978-3-030-64559-5_44

21. Oloko-Oba, M., Viriri, S.: Tuberculosis abnormality detection in chest x-rays: a deep learning approach. In: Chmielewski, L.J., Kozera, R., Orłowski, A. (eds.) ICCVG 2020. LNCS, vol. 12334, pp. 121–132. Springer, Cham (2020). https://doi.org/10.1007/978-3-030-59006-2_11

22. Organization, W.H., et al.: Chest radiography in tuberculosis detection: summary of current who recommendations and guidance on programmatic approaches. World Health Organization, Technical report (2016)

23. Organization, W.H., et al.: Global tuberculosis report 2019: executive summary (2019)

24. Organization, W.H., et al.: Global tuberculosis report 2020: executive summary (2020)

25. Pan, S.J., Yang, Q.: A survey on transfer learning. IEEE Trans. Knowl. Data Eng. **22**(10), 1345–1359 (2010)

26. Parsons, L.M., et al.: Laboratory diagnosis of tuberculosis in resource-poor countries: challenges and opportunities. Clin. Microbiol. Rev. **24**(2), 314–350 (2011)

27. Pasa, F., Golkov, V., Pfeiffer, F., Cremers, D., Pfeiffer, D.: Efficient deep network architectures for fast chest x-ray tuberculosis screening and visualization. Sci. Rep. **9**(1), 1–9 (2019)

28. Rohilla, A., Hooda, R., Mittal, A.: Tb detection in chest radiograph using deep learning architecture. In: ICETETSM-17, pp. 136–147 (2017)

29. Sabour, S., Frosst, N., Hinton, G.E.: Dynamic routing between capsules. arXiv preprint arXiv:1710.09829 (2017)

30. Shorten, C., Khoshgoftaar, T.M.: A survey on image data augmentation for deep learning. J. Big Data **6**(1), 1–48 (2019)

31. Simonyan, K., Zisserman, A.: Very deep convolutional networks for large-scale image recognition. arXiv preprint arXiv:1409.1556 (2014)

32. Szegedy, C., et al.: Going deeper with convolutions. In: Proceedings of the IEEE Conference on Computer Vision and Pattern Recognition, pp. 1–9 (2015)

33. Van't Hoog, A., et al.: High sensitivity of chest radiograph reading by clinical officers in a tuberculosis prevalence survey. Int. J. Tuberculosis Lung Dis. **15**(10), 1308–1314 (2011)

An Improved Forecasting Model from Satellite Imagery Based on Optimum Wavelet Bases and Adam Optimized LSTM Methods

Manel Rhif[1]([✉]) [iD], Ali Ben Abbes[1] [iD], Beatriz Martinez[2] [iD],
and Imed Riadh Farah[1] [iD]

[1] RIADI Laboratory, National School of Computer Sciences La Manouba,
Manouba, Tunisia
`manel.rhif@ensi-uma.tn`
[2] Departament de Física de la Terra i Termodinàmica, Universitat de València,
Valencia, Spain

Abstract. This paper proposes a new hybrid approach I-WT-LSTM (i.e., Improved Wavelet Long Short-Term Memory (LSTM) Model) for forecasting non-stationary time series (TS) from satellite imagery. The proposed approach consists of two steps: The first step aims at decomposing TS using Multi-Resolution Analysis wavelet (MRA-WT) into inter- and intra-annual components using 18 different mother wavelets (MW). Then, the energy to Shannon entropy ratio criterion is calculated to select the best MW. The second step is based on the LSTM model using Adam optimizer to predict the future. The proposed approach is tested using TS derived from Moderate Resolution Imaging Spectroradiometer (MODIS) images from 2001 to 2017. The results were compared with the predictions of the LSTM models using different optimizers. Additionally, the importance of selecting the optimal MW is analysed. The obtained results prove that the I-WT-LSTM approach outperforms all other methods.

Keywords: Image processing · Time series forecasting · Satellite imagery · Wavelet · LSTM

1 Introduction

The forecasting of time series (TS) derived from satellite imagery is an important mathematical problem with many applications (e.g. Land use and land cover, vegetation monitoring) to make a better development and decision-making. TS is defined as a sequential set of data points over successive times: TS_i^t where i is the pixel number in the image and t is the temporal resolution for $\{1,2,..,N\}$ (N is number of satellite images). The main propose of TS modelling is to extract the main features obtained from the past observations in order to forecast future values (TS_i^{t+1}). Recently, the application of artificial intelligence and deep learning

© Springer Nature Switzerland AG 2021
N. T. Nguyen et al. (Eds.): ICCCI 2021, LNAI 12876, pp. 560–571, 2021.
https://doi.org/10.1007/978-3-030-88081-1_42

(DL) models (e.g., long short term memory (LSTM), Bidirectional LSTM (BiL-STM)) has been developing rapidly and has brought about miraculous results for TS forecasting. For DL, optimization methods play a particularly important role in learning backward propagation and to update weights in the network. Several optimization methods were developed such as Adam, stochastic gradient descent (SGD), AdaGrad and RMSProp. In fact, optimizers hel to speed up DL algorithms which will save time and improve the performance of hardware computation [1].

Despite the flexibility and usefulness of DL methods for forecasting TS, some drawbacks appear when dealing with highly non-stationary responses due to the lack of input/output data pre/post processing [2]. In fact, real-world systems exhibit mostly non-stationary behaviours. Mathematically, TS (TS_i^t) is stationary if, for all t [3]: $E(TS_i^t) = E[(TS_i^{t-1})] = \mu$, $Var(TS_i^t) = \gamma_0 < \infty$ and $Cov(TS_i^t, TS_i^{t-k}) = TS_i^t$, where $E(.)$ is the expected value defined as the ensemble average of the quantity, and $Var(.)$ and $Cov(.)$ are the variance and the covariance functions, respectively. This makes several challenges and significantly complicate the acquisition of an effective predictive model. To solve this problem, hybrid approaches are proposed in the literature in several fields which combine method to decompose the original TS_i^t into inter- and intra-annual components (i.e., multi resolution wavelet transform (MRA-WT) with DL model [2,4–6]). For MRA-WT, the choice of an adequate mother wavelet (MW) has been studied in several fields to improve the performance of non-stationary TS analysis [7].

To the best of our knowledge, the mix of the wavelet decomposition and the LSTM has some significant novelty for time series prediction in remote sensing field. As well as the choice of best optimizers have not been explored in the application of NDVI TS forecasting. Therefore, the aim of this paper is to propose a novel forecasting approach called I-WT-LSTM (improved wavelet transform LSTM) by combining the feature extraction obtained from MRA-WT and learning ability of LSTM. Additionally, the proposed approach analyzed the selection of some parameters, such as MW and Adam optimizer of both MRA-WT and LSTM, respectively, in order to improve forecasting quality. In this study, the normalized difference vegetation index (NDVI) derived from satelite images are used. This index is proposed by Rouse et al. [8] and considered as the most popular index [9,10]. It is calculated as the difference between the infrared (NIR) and red reflectance (R) divided by their sum $(NDVI = (NIR-R)/(NIR+R))$. NDVI TS are generally non-stationary due to the presence of different information such as trend, seasonal and abrupt change [11–13].

The contributions of this paper are as follows: (i) Propose a new approach I-WT-LSTM based on WT using the best MW and Adam optimized LSTM for non-stationary SITS forecasting, (ii) analyze the significance of selecting the best parameters for MRA-WT and LSTM (i.e., the optimal MW and optimizer) and (iii) propose a I-WT-LSTM approach using NDVI TS extracted from real satellite images, which achieves a smaller prediction error than other current methods.

To this end, the proposed I-WT-LSTM is first introduced followed by the study area and the data used; finally, the results of the proposed approach are discussed.

2   Related Works

We mainly focused on two issues in this paper: non-stationary NDVI time series analysis and NDVI time series forecasting. In the literature, several methods are developed for non-stationary TS analysis such as Fourier transform, wavelet transform, Break for Additive Season and Trend (BFAST), Seasonal Trend Loess (STL), Detecting Breakpoints and Estimating Segments in Trend (DBEST), etc. The wavelet transform has proved its effectiveness in several fields for non-stationary time series analysis [7]. According to [12], the MRA-WT is more informative due to the multi-level decomposition and the hierarchical extraction strategy of multiple frequency dynamics within the NDVI time series. Additionally, the wavelet transform has been investigated to analyse the change in Spain [11] by decomposing the TS into different temporal resolutions. Recently, the analysis of non-stationary and unequally spaced NDVI TS is studied based on the Least-Squares Wavelet (LSWAVE) software [14].

The choice of an adequate mother wavelet (MW) has been studied in several fields to improve the performance of wavelet transform for non-stationary time series analysis [7]. Recently, the energy to entropy ratio proved its effectiveness in different Fields (i.e.,mechanical engineering [15] and medicine) for best MW selection. This criterion is more efficient as it gives the result more quickly than other techniques (e.g., variance method and correlation method) and can be applied to any type of application [15]. For this reason, we have adapted this criterion to select the optimal mother wavelet for NDVI time series forecasting.

In the other hand, deep learning (DL) has proved its effectiveness for forecasting TS in different fields. Several methods are recently used such as Deep Belief Neural network (DBN), Bidirectional LSTM (BiLSTM) and Conventional-LSTM (CNN-LSTM) network, Long Short-Term Memory (LSTM) model, etc. For satellite imagery time series (SITS) forecasting, principally, LSTM and BiL-STM model were used [13, 16]. Both models have a good performance for forecasting SITS. More specifically, LSTM gives better performance to detect changes [13].

Before model training, the selection of the hyperparameters is important. The optimizer is one of the most important parameters that influences forecasting accuracy. In fact, the role of the optimizer is to update the weight and learning rate in each step to reduce the losses function. Several optimization methods were developed in the literature such as Adam, stochastic gradient descent (SGD), AdaGrad and RMSProp. Kingma et al. [17] proved that Adam shows a better performance for time series prediction.

Recently, hybrid approaches based on wavelet transfrom and DL models proved their effectiveness in different fields for non-stationary time series forecasting . For examples, an hybrid model wavelet LSTM was applicated for stock market time series prediction [6]. In this paper, several MW are studied. Rafiei et al. [18] introduced an improved Wavelet Neural Network Trained by a generalized extreme learning machine for a probabilistic electricity load forecasting application. In fact, combining wavelet analysis with artificial intelligence machine learning have advantages in both methods. Wavelet is used to decrease the non-stationary of the original time series and to provide more sub-layers to be used for the DL prediction. It improves the performance of DL to forecast non-stationary time series.

3   Improved Wavelet Long-Short Term Memory Approach (I-WT-LSTM)

The proposed approach is shown in Fig. 1. The I-WT-LSTM model is mainly composed of two parts: MRA-WT for SITS decomposition based on the optimal MW and LSTM model using Adam algorithm. In the satellite imagery, each pixel (x_i, y_i) is considered, where i is the index of the pixel in the image. With the time step (t), the TS data are finally formed. We use TS_i^t to represent the TS which contains all the values for the same pixel (x_i, y_i) for a specific time t (x_i^t, y_i^t). Then, the obtained TS_i^t are decomposed using optimal MRA-WT. More details are introduced in Sect. 3.1. Finally, the Adam LSTM is investigated to obtain the forecasted TS at $t+1$ (TS_i^{t+1}). A detailed description of LSTM and Adam optimizer are introduced in Sect. 3.3.

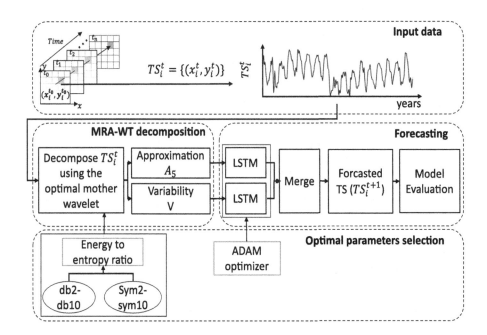

Fig. 1. The scheme of the proposed I-WT-LSTM approach .

3.1 Multi-resolution Analysis Wavelet Transform (MRA-WT)

The MRA-WT is defined as a hierarchical representation of DWT [19,20]. It is based on decomposing the original signal into an m level by successively translating and convolving the MW using low-pass (LP) and high-pass (HP) filters [7]. A detailed description is presented in [7,11,21]. The approximation (A) components are calculated using the LP filters whereas, the detail (D) components are obtained from HP filter [22]. For a particular level of decomposition m, D_m and A_m are defined as:

$$A_j(k) = \sum_{m=0}^{L-1} A_{j-1}(2k - m)LP(m) \tag{1}$$

$$D_j(k) = \sum_{m=0}^{L-1} A_{j-1}(2k - m)HP(m) \tag{2}$$

where k is the kth A and D at level j; in this step $j = 1$ and $k = 1$. The last approximation component A_m presents the inter-annual variation. However, the first detail component D_1 is considered as a noise component. The sum of all the detail components presents the intra-annual variation (V), calculated as $V = \sum_{i=2}^{m} D_i$.

3.2 Selection Optimal MW:

The choice of the best MW is one of the most challenges of MRA-WT that affects the obtained results. In this paper, 18 MWs (i.e. Daubechies (db2-db10) and Symlet (sym2-sym10)) are used. The orthogonality properties is considered as a first criteria to select these MW. This property is necessary to extract high- and low-frequency details from the TS_i^t without losing information. The next step consists on calculating the energy to Shannon entropy criterion ($R(S)$). It is mathematically defined as follows [15]:

$$R(S) = \frac{E_{energy(S)}}{E_{entropy}} = \frac{\sum_{i=1}^{n} |wt(s,i)|^2}{-\sum_{i=1}^{n} p_i.log_2(p_i)} \tag{3}$$

where $wt(s,i)$ are the wavelet coefficients, n presents the number of wavelet coefficient at each scale and p_i is the energy probability distribution of the wavelet coefficients ($p_i = \frac{|wt(s,i)|^2}{E_{energy}(S)}$). In the first step, the energy is calculated and the highest value is considered as the dominant wavelet coefficients. Then, the obtained coefficients were used to calculate the Shannon entropy for each MW. Finally, the MW with the highest $R(S)$ value presents the optimal MW.

3.3 Long-Short Term Memory Model (LSTM)

LSTM is introduced by Hochreiter and Schmidhuber in [23]. There are three types of gates in LSTM model: input, forget and output gate. All gates functions are based on the previous LSTM layer and current input. In fact, the input gates (i) control the flow of input activation into the memory cell. It is presented as: $i = \sigma(TS_i^t w_i + U_i h_{t-1} + b_i)$.

The first step in our LSTM is to decide which new information has to be removed from the cell state. This decision is made by a *sigmoid* layer called the forget gate layer. The forget gate (f) was added to the memory block. It is defined as : $f = \sigma(TS_i^t w_f + U_f h_{t-1} + b_f)$. However, the output gate (o) controls the output flow of cell activation into the rest of the network. It's defined as: $o = \sigma(TS_i^t w_o + U_o h_{t-1} + b_o)$.

The next step is to decide which new information has to be store in the cell state. This has two parts. First, a *sigmoid* layer called the "input gate layer" decides which values will be updated. Next, a *tanh* layer creates a vector of new candidate values. Then, the two layers are combined to update the output in LSTM model. The cell state vector is calculated as follows: $c_t = f_t \circ c_{t_1} + i_t \circ tanh(W_c TS_i^t + U_c h_{t_1} + b_c)$, where TS_i^t refers to the input vector, U_i and w_i are the learned parameter, σ is the activation function and $h_t = o_t \circ tanh(c_t)$.

Adam Optimizer: Adam is an algorithm for first-order gradient-based optimization of stochastic objective functions [17]. It is based on an adaptative estimation of lower order moments. Indeed, Adam optimizer has several advantages such as little memory requirement, easy implementation and appropriateness for non-stationary TS. It has combined the advantages of two known optimizer: AdaGrad which used the sparse gradient and RMSProp, which has a better performance with non-line and non-stationary TS.

The Adam algorithm is fully defined through the parameters set ($f(\theta)$, θ_0, α, β_1, β_2, ϵ), where $f(\theta)$ presents the stochastic objective function with parameters θ with θ_0 as the initial parameter vector. The learning rate or step size is noted as α . It presents the proportion that weights are updated (e.g., 0.001). β_1, β_2 are the exponential decay rate for the first moment estimates (e.g., 0.9) and second-moment estimates (e.g., 0.999), respectively. ϵ is referred to a very small number to prevent any division by zero in the implementation (e.g., 10^{-8}).

Then the parameters vector were initialized to 0 (i.e. the first moment vector (m_0), the second moment vector (v_0) and the timestep (t). Finally, an iterative loop is used to update the various parameters until the θ converges. This step contains the following five functions:

i) Update the timestep $t = t + 1$

ii) Obtain the gradient g_t from the stochastic objective function at timestep t: $g_t = \nabla_\theta f_t(\theta_{t-1})$

iii) Update both the first (m_t) and second moment (v_t) estimate: $m_t = \beta_1 m_{t-1} + (1 - \beta_1) g_t$ and $v_t = \beta_2 v_{t-1} + (1 - \beta_2) g_t^2$ where g_t^2 indicates the elementwise square $g_t \odot g_t$.

iv) Create unbiased estimate for first and second moment $mb_t = m_t/(1 - \beta_{1t})$ and $vb_t = v_t/(1 - \beta_{2t})$.

v) Update the objective function parameters $\theta_t = \theta_{t-1} - \alpha mb_t/(vb_t + \epsilon)$.

4 Experimental Results

4.1 Study Area and Dataset

Our proposed methodologyI-WT-LSTM is used for forecasting NDVI TS in the north-west of Tunisia (Fig. 2). The north part of the study area is basically compound of croplands, shrublands and forests. However, the south part contains roches and bare soil. The climate in the northwest of Tunisia is Mediterranean with mild, rainy winters and hot, dry summers and no marked intervening seasons. To forecast the change in the northwest of Tunisia, the 16-day composites of Moderate Resolution Imaging Spectro-radiometer (MODIS) product (MOD13Q1 collection 6) at 250 m spatial resolution are used to extract the NDVI TS. The data were provided to cover the 2001–2017 analysed period with 23 images per year. As presented in Fig. 2, two pixels were selected. The NDVI1 and NDVI2 describe an olive tree area and forest fire in North Forest of Mellègue, respectively .

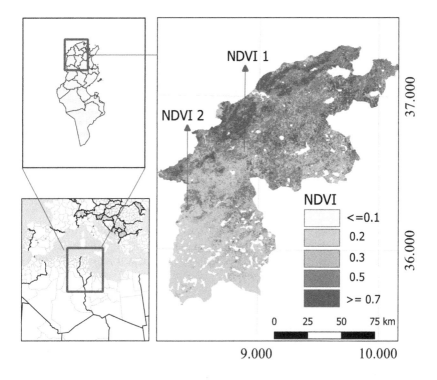

Fig. 2. Geographical location of northwest of Tunisia.

4.2   Results and Discussion

The NDVI TS was decomposed for the two selected pixels using the MRA-WT. Figure 3 illustrates an example of NDVI TS decomposition. In this paper, level 5 is considered as the best level that accounts for the inter-annual vegetation variations. Then, the choice of the optimal MW was obtained by calculating $R(S)$, described in Sect. 3.2. Therefore, the optimal MW are sym4 with $R(S) =$ 3.81 and db9 with $R(S) = 1.49$ for NDVI1 and NDVI2, respectively. However, sym10 is the worst MW with $R(S) = 2.01$ and $R(S) = 1.02$ for NDVI1 and NDVI2 respectively. Additionally, for a better understanding of the importance of the MW selection, a spatial analysis based on $R(S)$ in all the study area is illustrated in Fig. 4. The obtained results in Fig. 4 confirm that sym4 and db9 are dominated for all the study area. Additionally, it is clearly that the Symlet MW shows a better performance for shrub and cropland, whereas the Daubechies MW family may yield better results for forest area.

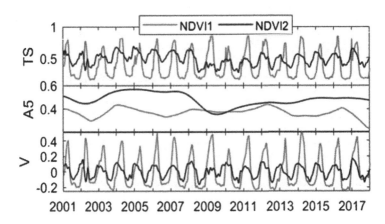

Fig. 3. Decomposition of NDVI TS using the MRA-WT for the two selected sites. The A_5 components presents the inter-annual change; however, the V is the intra-annual variability.

The LSTM model is applicated for both A_5 and V components. Each TS is categorized into training and testing data. In this paper, we have used 14 years (322 observations) data for train and 3 years (69 observations) for test. Also, all LSTM layers are 128 dimensional in size and the nonlinear ReLU (rectifying linear element) is used as an activation function. Table 1 shows prediction errors between predicted and real changes for each period.The evaluation of the proposed method is performed by using the root mean squared error (RMSE) and mean absolute error (MAE).

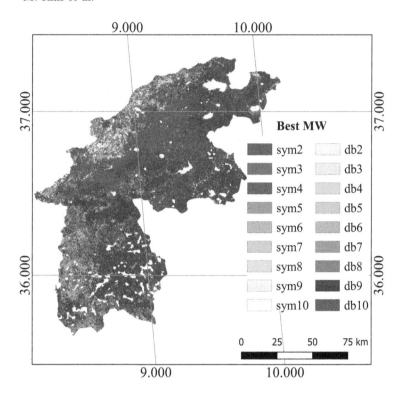

Fig. 4. Optimal MW pixel-wise selection based on the energy to entropy ratio criterion for the study area.

Table 1. NDVI TS forecating: RMSE, MAE using ADAM-LSTM, SGD-LSTM, AdaGrad-LSTM, RMSProp-LSTM, WT-Adam-LSTM and I-WT-LSTM

		Adam-LSTM	SGD-LSTM	AdaGrad-LSTM	RMSProp-LSTM	WT- Adam-LSTM	I-WT-LSTM
NDVI1	RMSE	0.108	0.213	0.189	0.201	0.050	**0.038**
	MAE	0.100	0.196	0.174	0.185	0.039	**0.028**
NDVI 2	RMSE	0.052	0.082	0.054	0.062	0.051	**0.036**
	MAE	0.045	0.070	0.046	0.053	0.050	**0.035**

Based on Table 1, we note that the I-WT-LSTM produces better results than other methods, followed by WT-Adam LSTM (using worst MW) and Adam-LSTM. We can conclude that the hybrid method between WT and LSTM improve the forecasting quality, specifically when the optimal MW is used. Also, the Adam optimizer has shown the best performance. The forecasting results for I-WT-LSTM, WT-adam-LSTM and Adam LSTM are illustrated in Fig. 5.

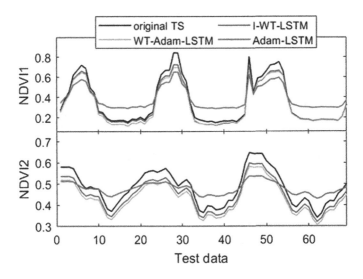

Fig. 5. Original and predicted NDVI time series using ADAM-LSTM, WT-Adam-LSTM and I-WT-LSTM for the different time series (NDVI1 and NDVI2)

5   Conclusion

This work proposed the I-WT-LSTM model by taking advantage for of the optimal MW in the MRA-WT and Adam optimizer in the LSTM. The WT extracts both inter- and intra-annual components to reduce non-stationarity from TS, and the energy to entropy ratio was investigated to select the best MW. However, the LSTM model with Adam optimizer were used to forecast change. The evaluation based on NDVI TS derived from satellite images results show that our proposed model achieves better prediction results compared to other existing models.

References

1. Phan, D.H., Huynh, L.D.: Evaluation of the cleft-overstep algorithm for linear regression analysis. In: Nguyen, N.T., Hoang, B.H., Huynh, C.P., Hwang, D., Trawiński, B., Vossen, G. (eds.) ICCCI 2020. LNCS (LNAI), vol. 12496, pp. 400–411. Springer, Cham (2020). https://doi.org/10.1007/978-3-030-63007-2_31
2. Rhif, M., Ben Abbes, A., Martinez, B., Farah, I.R.: A deep learning approach for forecasting non-stationary big remote sensing time series. Arab. J. Geosci. **13**(22), 1–11 (2020). https://doi.org/10.1007/s12517-020-06140-w
3. Huang, N., Shen, Z., Steven, L., et al.: The empirical mode decomposition and the Hilbert spectrum for nonlinear and non-stationary time series analysis. In: Proceedings of the Royal Society of London. Series A: Mathematical, Physical and Engineering Sciences **454**(1971), 903–995 (1998). https://doi.org/10.1098/rspa.1998.0193

4. Chang, Z., Zhang, Y., Chen, W.: Electricity price prediction based on hybrid model of adam optimized LSTM neural network and wavelet transform. Energy **187**, 115804 (2019)

5. Zhang, Q., Li, F., Long, F., Ling, Q.: Vehicle emission forecasting based on wavelet transform and long short-term memory network. IEEE Access **6**, 56984–56994 (2018)

6. Li, Z., Tam, V.: Combining the real-time wavelet denoising and long-short-term-memory neural network for predicting stock indexes. In: 2017 IEEE Symposium Series on Computational Intelligence (SSCI), pp. 1–8. IEEE (2017)

7. Rhif, M., Abbes, A.B., Farah, I., Martinez, B., Sang, Y.: Wavelet transform application for/in non-stationary time-series analysis: a review. Appl. Sci. **9**(7), 1345 (2019). https://doi.org/10.3390/app9071345

8. Rouse Jr, J., Haas, R., Schell, J., Deering, D.: Monitoring vegetation systems in the great plains with ERTS. In: Third Earth Resources Technology Satellite–1 Syposium 1, pp. 309–317 (1974)

9. Xue, J., Su, B.: Significant remote sensing vegetation indices: a review of developments and applications. J. Sens. **2017** (2017)

10. Abbes, A.B., Farah, M., Farah, I., Barra, V.: A non-stationary NDVI time series modelling using triplet Markov chain. Int. J. Inf. Dec. Sci. **11**(2), 163–179 (2019)

11. Martínez, B., Gilabert, M.: Vegetation dynamics from NDVI time series analysis using the wavelet transform. Remote Sens. Environ. **113**(9), 1823–1842 (2009). https://doi.org/10.1016/j.rse.2009.04.016

12. Abbes, A.B., Bounouh, O., Farah, I., de Jong, R., Martínez, B.: Comparative study of three satellite image time-series decomposition methods for vegetation change detection. Eur. J. Remote Sens. **51**(1), 607–615 (2018). https://doi.org/10.1080/22797254.2018.1465360

13. Rhif, M., Ben Abbes, A., Martínez, B., Farah, I.: Deep learning models performance for NDVI time series prediction: a case study on north west Tunisia. In: 2020 Mediterranean and Middle-East Geoscience and Remote Sensing Symposium (M2GARSS), pp. 9–12. IEEE (2020)

14. Ghaderpour, E., Ben Abbes, A., Rhif, M., Pagiatakis, S.D., Farah, I.R.: Non-stationary and unequally spaced NDVI time series analyses by the lSWAVE software. Int. J. Remote Sens. **41**(6), 2374–2390 (2020)

15. Rodrigues, A., Daazmello, G., et al.: Selection of mother wavelet for wavelet analysis of vibration signals in machining. J. Mech. Eng. Autom. **6**(5A), 81–85 (2016)

16. Reddy, D., Prasad, P.: Prediction of vegetation dynamics using NDVI time series data and LSTM. Model. Earth Syst. Environ. **4**(1), 409–419 (2018)

17. Kingma, D., Ba, J.: Adam: a method for stochastic optimization. arXiv preprint arXiv:1412.6980 (2014)

18. Rafiei, M., Niknam, T., Aghaei, J., Shafie-Khah, M., Catalão, J.P.: Probabilistic load forecasting using an improved wavelet neural network trained by generalized extreme learning machine. IEEE Trans. Smart Grid **9**(6), 6961–6971 (2018)

19. Mallat, S.: A theory for multiresolution signal decomposition: the wavelet representation. IEEE Trans. Pattern Anal. Mach. Intell. **11**(7), 674–693 (1989). https://doi.org/10.1109/34.192463

20. Jawerth, B., Sweldens, W.: An overview of wavelet based multiresolution analyses. SIAM Rev. **36**(3), 377–412 (1994)

21. Percival, D.B., Wang, M., Overland, J.E.: An introduction to wavelet analysis with applications to vegetation time series. Community Ecol. **5**(1), 19–30 (2004). https://doi.org/10.1556/ComEc.5.2004.1.3

22. Su, W., Qu, Y., Deng, C., Wang, Y., Zheng, F., Chen, Z.: Enhance generative adversarial networks by wavelet transform to denoise low-dose CT images. In: 2020 IEEE International Conference on Image Processing (ICIP), pp. 350–354. IEEE (2020)
23. Hochreiter, S., Schmidhuber, J.: Long short-term memory. Neural Comput. **9**(8), 1735–1780 (1997)

Fast Imaging Sensor Identification

Jarosław Bernacki(ID) and Rafał Scherer(✉)(ID)

Department of Intelligent Computer Systems, Częstochowa University of Technology,
al. Armii Krajowej 36, 42-200 Częstochowa, Poland
{jaroslaw.bernacki,rafal.scherer}@pcz.pl

Abstract. We consider identification of imaging devices by analysing images they produce. The problem is studied in the literature, yet the existing solutions are rather computationally demanding. We propose a high-speed algorithm for identification of imaging devices. The aim is to provide additional security by identification of legitimate imaging devices or an identification for forensics. The experimental evaluation confirms efficient identification of devices models and brands by the proposed algorithm, compared with the state-of-the-art method. Moreover, our algorithm is approximately two orders of magnitude faster, which is very important in resource-constrained IoT ecosystems or very large databases.

Keywords: Security · Image processing · Imaging sensor identification · Camera identification · Digital forensics

1 Introduction

Distinguishing the model of sensor that was used to generate a digital image is one of the tasks of digital forensics. In many cases, it is important to determine the source of a digital image, for example, for criminal or forensic investigation. Usually, the goal is to identify a digital camera or flatbed scanner. Digital camera identification is understood as identification of the sensor that produced an image. Similarly, recognition of the flatbed scanner relies on identification of the scanner sensor that captures scanned materials [21]. The aim to provide additional security can be understood in the context of an authentication protocol. For example, the user wants to log to a certain system using a dedicated smartphone to take a photo of her or his iris. Then the system checks the iris and camera's fingerprint in the base. If both things match, the user is considered legitimate, and the system grants access; otherwise, user login fails. For such purpose, there is a need for a fast and accurate camera identification algorithm that checks the imaging device origin in real-time. Due to its highly connected nature, Internet of Things technology is vulnerable to many threats and breaches.

The project financed under the program of the Polish Minister of Science and Higher Education under the name "Regional Initiative of Excellence" in the years 2019–2022 project number 020/RID/2018/19, the amount of financing 12,000,000.00 PLN.

Adequate security measures are crucial to ensuring computer network safety as IoT devices can be used to penetrate or attack their host computer networks. As the IoT idea is relatively new, and the market is very dynamic; thus, many devices are out without serious security protection or with gaps. Moreover, many devices are low-end ones not allowing to implement enough security. Similarly, legacy devices were sometimes not designed to work online and can be insecure. IoT security breaches and attacks can hurt any industry or even smart homes. An example of a fragile ecosystem can be healthcare. In the paper, we propose a method of securing imaging devices by extracting features responsible for the manufacturer and type of the imaging system. The method can be used to detect external, not authorized imaging devices in the IoT network.

Recently, many algorithms for sensor identification have been proposed. A state-of-the-art algorithm for digital camera identification was proposed by Lukas et al. in [25]. An analogous algorithm for scanner identification is described in [21]. Both approaches are based on searching for the so-called sensor pattern noise by denoising source material with a wavelet-based denoising filter. The main assumption is that source materials are represented according to the RGB model by three data arrays that define red, green and blue colour components (channels) for each individual pixel. It is usually suggested to denoise all the channels. Algorithms based on wavelet denoising are efficient in classification tasks; however, very time-consuming. Typical time for processing an image of 6000×4000 pixel resolution by algorithms presented in [21,25] takes at average 2–3 min (http://dde.binghamton.edu/download/). According to [25], the optimal number of processed images for representative calculation of the fingerprint is 45. It is then clearly visible that such algorithms are inefficient in terms of processing time, which makes them impractical for dense traffic in IoT network or large datasets. Therefore, these facts motivated us to propose faster solutions.

In this paper, we propose a very fast imaging device identification method for resource-constrained IoT devices and high network traffic. We apply the denoising filter only to one colour channel of a RGB image. Moreover, we process only fragments of images of size 512×512 pixels instead of the whole image. As a result, a significant increase in the speed of source materials processing time is observed.

The rest of the paper is organized as follows. The next section describes related works and recalls a state-of-the-art algorithm. In Sect. 3 the proposed method is described. Section 4 shows experimental results of evaluation. The final section concludes this work.

2   Related Work

One of the most common algorithm in camera forensics is Lukás et al.'s approach, presented in [25]. This algorithm is used often for digital camera identification, and even to distinguish different copies of the same camera. It gives precise classification results but can be time-consuming, especially for high-resolution images. Note also that the considered algorithm assumes that images should not be processed as fragments, but in their full resolution, which also may have a negative impact on the performance. We will recall this algorithm in detail in the next section. The idea of this algorithm has been further investigated and extended in many works, for example in [16,17]. There have been considered other approaches for camera identification, like entropy and image quality measures [1], analysis of camera's white balance algorithm [6], JPEG compression [14], clustering techniques [3,30] or compact representation of the camera's fingerprint [24,33]. Recently very popular are approaches based on deep learning (DL) and convolutional neural networks (CNN). A convolutional neural network with fully connected layers was described in [31]. The convolutional layers are responsible for feature representation, and the fully connected layers were used for classification. The layer of feature representation collects the noise pattern $\mathbf{N}$ which is extracted from images from the well-known formula $\mathbf{N} = \mathbf{I} - F(\mathbf{I})$ [9–11,17,25], where $\mathbf{I}$ denote the input image and F is the denoising filter. Noise patterns are treated with 64 kernels of size 3×3, and the size of produced feature maps is 126×126. The second layer produces feature maps of size 64×64. The third layer applies convolutions with 32 kernels of size 3×3. The Rectified Linear Unit (ReLU) is applied to the output of every convolutional layer as an activation function. Nvidia GeForce Titan X (12 GB) GPU is used as the hardware. Despite that classification accuracy achieves 98%, time for learning the network takes 5 h and a half only for 12 camera models. Another CNN-based approach was discussed in [29], where the DenseNet convolutional network was used for camera identification. The classification accuracy reached 98%. In [32] a machine learning classifier was trained on the concatenation of the co-occurrences of colour band noise residuals with features computed with a Markovian model in discrete cosine transform (DCT) domain. The usage of deep models is also considered in [4,5,8,34,35]. However, such approaches are time-consuming, and the classification accuracy is comparable to the previous algorithms.

To the best of our knowledge, the most popular algorithm for flatbed scanner identification is proposed by Khanna et al. in [21]. Further improvements were described by the authors in [18,19,22]. This approach shows that flatbed scanner identification can be realized in the same spirit as the state-of-the-art algorithm for digital camera identification proposed by Lukás et al. [25]. Another approach for recognizing scanners is presented in [18] (and its journal extension [22]). The core of the algorithm is similar to [25]. The image $\mathbf{I}$ and its denoised version $F(\mathbf{I})$ is took and the *residual* $\mathbf{R}$ is calculated in the following way: $\mathbf{R} = \mathbf{I} - F(\mathbf{I})$. The experimental evaluation proved that for any scanner, matrix $\mathbf{R}$ is unique for any scanner and therefore can serve as the scanner fingerprint. These approaches use the wavelet denoising filter for image processing. A somewhat similar approach is presented in [15]. In [19,21] there are showed different experiments for comparing scanner and camera identification by images. In [26] there is proposed a technique for differentiating between computer-generated and photographic images. The base is the usage of wavelet statistics. Work [20] presents a method for classification of images based on their sources. An SVM classifier is trained by the appropriate features of the sensor pattern noise. Distinguishing if the image was taken by a camera or scanned is performed with the accuracy of 95%. In [12], a method for digital camera identification based on spatial noise is applied to flatbed scanner identification. Since scanners and digital cameras use similar technologies, the application of camera-related forensics methods for scanner identification can be successful. Work [7] presents an approach based on the presence of dust and physical scratches over the scanner platen.

3 Imaging Sensor Identification

In this subsection we recall algorithms for digital imaging sensor identification and propose our MSE-DSI method.

3.1 State-of-the-Art Algorithms

Lukás/Khanna et al.'s Algorithm. The most popular algorithm for digital imaging sensor identification, especially used for digital camera identification, seems to be proposed by Lukás et al. in [25]. Although recently deep learning (DL) approach including convolutional neural networks (CNN) is very popular, this algorithm is still widely used for digital forensics purposes. Moreover, many modern approaches using DL like [31] are also based on this approach. This algorithm extracts a specific pattern called the Photo-Response Nonuniformity Noise (PRNU), which serves as a unique identification fingerprint. The idea of the algorithm is to extract the noise from the input image $\mathbf{I}$ by using a denoising filter F. Using a wavelet-based denoising filter has been proposed [13,16,17]. After denoising, the camera fingerprint is calculated as $\mathbf{N} = \mathbf{I} - F(\mathbf{I})$ following the summary below.

Input: Image $\mathbf{I}$ in RGB of size $M \times N$;
Output: Matrix $\mathbf{N}$ of noise residual, size $M \times N$.

1. Calculate $\mathbf{K} = \frac{\mathbf{I_R} + \mathbf{I_G} + \mathbf{I_B}}{3}$;
2. Denoise all colour channels of the input image $\mathbf{I_R}, \mathbf{I_G}, \mathbf{I_B}$ with filter F;
3. Calculate mean $\mathbf{D} = \frac{F(\mathbf{I_R}) + F(\mathbf{I_G}) + F(\mathbf{I_B})}{3}$;
4. Calculate the matrix of noise residual: $\mathbf{N} = \mathbf{K} - \mathbf{D}$.

where $\mathbf{I_R}, \mathbf{I_G}$ and $\mathbf{I_B}$ are matrices of each component of the RGB model of the input $\mathbf{I}$; F is the denoising filter. Matrix $\mathbf{I}$ comes from a single image of a particular camera. PRNU for each camera is calculated from at least 45 images and then $\mathbf{N} = \frac{\mathbf{N_1} + \cdots + \mathbf{N_{45}}}{45}$. Afterwards, a correlation coefficient between the new image $\mathbf{N_x}$ and $\mathbf{N}$ is calculated. If the correlation coefficient exceeds some threshold, it is assumed that $\mathbf{N_x}$ comes from the same camera as $\mathbf{N}$. The efficiency of recognizing the sensor in this approach is very high (True Positive Rate greater than 90%). The algorithm also identifies different cameras of the same model with similar probability.

Khanna et al. in [21] showed that flatbed scanner identification can be realized in the same spirit as Lukás et al.'s algorithm for camera identification. It also calculates the PRNU of each flatbed scanner based on scans it produced and the classification of a new scan is realized similarly as in Lukás et al.'s algorithm.

Wavelet based denoising filters are often used for digital forensics. The most common filters used for calculation of the PRNU is sigma [25] and Mihcak filters [2,28]. Here, we recall the formula for Mihcak denoising. This filter uses spatially adaptive statistical modelling of wavelet coefficients. The noisy coefficients $\mathbf{G}(i)$ are considered as the addition of the noise-free image $\mathbf{I}(i)$ and the noise component $\mathbf{N}(i)$. The noise component $\mathbf{N}(i)$ is the white Gaussian noise with known variance σ_n^2. The goal is to retrieve the original image coefficients as well as possible from the noisy observation by using a local Wiener filter described in Eq. 1.

$$\mathbf{I}'(i) = \frac{\sigma_X^2(i)}{\sigma_X^2(i) + \sigma_n^2}\mathbf{G}(i) \tag{1}$$

Convolutional Neural Network-Based Methods. Recently camera identification is mostly realized with the use of convolutional neural networks (CNN). We consider two methods: one proposed by Mandelli et al.'s [27] and the other by Kirchner & Johnson [23].

Mandelli et al.'s CNN architecture can be described as follows:

1. The first convolutional layer of kernel 3×3, producing feature maps of size 16×16 pixels with Leaky ReLU as an activation method and max-pooling of 3×3;
2. The second convolutional layer of kernel 5×5, producing feature maps of size 64×64 pixels with Leaky ReLU as an activation method and max-pooling of 3×3;
3. The third convolutional layer of kernel 5×5 producing feature maps of size 64×64 pixels with Leaky ReLU as an activation method and max-pooling of 3×3;
4. A pairwise correlation pooling layer;
5. Fully connected layers.

Kirchner & Johnson proposed a CNN with the following structure:

1. 17 layers implementing 64 convolutional filters with 3×3 kernels;
2. ReLU as an activation method after each layer;
3. No pooling layers.

Both Mandelli and Kirchner & Johnson' networks can be trained with the PRNU $\mathbf{N}$ calculated in the same manner as in Lukás et al.'s algorithm: $\mathbf{N} = \mathbf{I} - F(\mathbf{I})$, where $\mathbf{I}$ is the input image, and F is the denoising filter.

3.2 Proposed Approach

The Mean Square Error (MSE) is a quality metric that can be used for assessing the quality of images or videos. We propose the Mean Square Error-Digital Sensor Identification (MSE-DSI) algorithm which uses this metric for a scanner identification. To the best of our knowledge, it is the first attempt to use such an algorithm for scanner identification purposes. Calculating MSE-DSI is defined as in Eq. 2.

$$\text{MSE-DSI} = \frac{1}{MN} \sum_{i=1}^{M} \sum_{j=1}^{N} [\mathbf{R}(i,j) - \mathbf{D}(i,j)]^2 , \tag{2}$$

where: M, N – image resolution (in pixels); $\mathbf{R}$ – pixel intensities of red color channel of the original image $\mathbf{I}$; $\mathbf{D} = \text{F}(\mathbf{I})$ – denoised red color channel of image $\mathbf{I}$, and F is the denoising filter. A wavelet-based denoising filter is commonly used filter for forensics purposes [19,20,25], therefore we chose this filter as it was the most common choice in the literature [9–11] and our initial experiments confirmed the best suitability of this filter. It turned out to be the most discriminative of all denoising filters. We have observed that this MSE value seems to be unique for different scanners; thus, we consider it as a unique scanner fingerprint. The core of the algorithm is to calculate the MSE value on the difference of pixel intensities of only one colour channel of image $\mathbf{I}$ and its filtered version $\mathbf{D}$. Unlike in the Khanna et al.'s algorithm, we propose to process only one colour channel instead of all colour channels, which has a positive impact on the time of image processing. We also propose to process only small parts of scanned images, for example, of size 512×512 pixels instead of the full resolution. This also speeds up the process of flatbed scanner identification. The MSE-DSI algorithm is repeated for each image from a particular scanner, and then the average value of MSE-DSIs is calculated and serves as the scanner fingerprint.

4 Experimental Evaluation

4.1 MSE-DSI Algorithm for Digital Camera Identification

We have used a set of 45 modern digital single-lens reflex (DSLR) and mirror-less (DSLM) cameras, compact cameras and smartphones with built-in multiple sensors. This set includes the following models: Apple iPhone 8, Apple iPhone Xr, Canon 1D X Mark II, Canon 5D Mark IV, Canon 90D, Canon G9X Mark II, Canon M6 Mark II, Canon M10, Canon M100, Canon R, Canon RP, Huawei P9 Plus, Huawei P20 Pro, Nikon D3X, Nikon D5, Nikon D500, Nikon D610, Nikon D750, Nikon D810, Nikon D850, Nikon D7200, Nikon D7500, Nikon Z6, Nikon Z7, Panasonic Lumix GX800, Panasonic Lumix S1, Samsung S9 Plus, Samsung S10 Plus, Sony A7R III, Sony A7S, Sony A7S II, Sony A9, Sony A6500, Sony RX100 II, Sony Xperia 1, Sony Xperia XZ1, Xiaomi Mi 9. The number of all images is 1919, what means that at least 30 images were used per device. The experiments were performed on a MSI notebook with Intel Core i5-7300HQ@2.5 GHz CPU with 24 GB of RAM and nVidia GTX 1050 GPU with 4 GB of video memory.

Device Identification. As evaluation, we use standard *accuracy* (ACC), *true positive rate* (TPR) and *false positive rate* (FPR) measures, defined as:

$$\text{ACC} = \frac{\text{TP} + \text{TN}}{\text{TP} + \text{TN} + \text{FP} + \text{FN}} , \quad \text{TPR} = \frac{\text{TP}}{\text{TP} + \text{FN}} , \quad \text{FPR} = \frac{\text{FP}}{\text{FP} + \text{TN}}$$

where TP/TN denotes "true positive/true negative"; FP/FN stands for "false positive/false negative". TP denotes cases correctly classified to a specific class; TN are instances that are correctly rejected. FP denotes cases incorrectly classified to the specific class; FN are examples incorrectly rejected. For graphic visualization, we have used the ROC curves (receiver operating characteristic) with the AUC (area under curve) measure. ROC curves show the relation between true positive rate (TPR) against the false positive rate (FPR). Results of classification are described in Fig. 1.

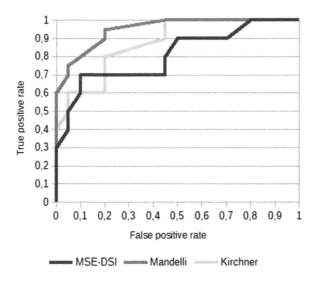

Fig. 1. ROC curve of camera model recognition of MSE-DSI vs. CNNs proposed by Mandelli et al.'s and Kirchner & Johnson.

The AUC for MSE-DSI equals 0.81; Mandelli and Kirchner & Johnson obtained 0.95 and 0.88, respectively. This means that identification performed by CNN-based methods is slightly more accurate than the proposed MSE-DSI algorithm but much slower.

The state-of-the-art algorithms are better in classification because they process all image colour channels as well as the full image size. Therefore, more pixels are processed and the CNNs are more precisely trained. The proposed algorithm processes only one colour channel and a fragment of this channel instead of the whole matrix. That is why it is less accurate.

Time Performance. The experiments showed that the CNN-based methods process images much longer than the proposed MSE-DSI algorithm. At average, one image of MSE-DSI algorithm is processed in about 6 s. The time for learning one epoch with considered CNNs is about 1.5 of min. Therefore, calculating the MSE values of all tested 1919 images took about 3.5 h, while CNNs needed 50 h.

Graphical interpretation of time performance comparison is presented in Fig. 2.

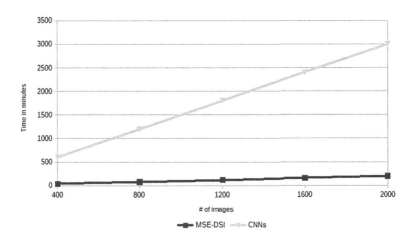

Fig. 2. Time performance comparison of Khanna et al. and the MSE-DSI algorithm.

The main reason for the long processing of the images is the usage of a denoising filter on all three colour channels of the image, which is computationally inefficient. In our method, we propose processing only a fragment of an image of size 512×512 pixels instead of the whole image what is faster, and we also apply it to only one colour channel of the image instead of all three colour channels.

4.2   MSE-DSI Algorithm for Flatbed Scanner Identification

In this section we present the results of scanner identification by the MSE-DSI algorithm and compare them with state-of-the-art Khanna et al.'s algorithm [21]. The following ten scanners were used: Brother MFC 9970CDW, Canon C2020i, HP Deskjet F4180, HP Laser Jet M1005 MFP, HP ScanJet 3670, HP ScanJet PLS 2800, OKI MC562w, PLUSTEK, Ricoh SP 112SU and Samsung SCX-3205. Scanner classification was performed with a set of 290 JPEG photographs (29 images per device). Sample images can be seen in Fig. 3. Scripts for the proposed method and Khanna et al.'s algorithm were implemented in MATLAB (http://dde. binghamton.edu/download/). All the tested scanners were connected to computers with installed Microsoft Windows 8.1 or 10 operating systems. We used the Fax & Scan application in Windows OS to manage the scanners. All the scanners were set to their default settings, and all the images were scanned at 300 dpi resolution.

Fig. 3. Sample images used in the experiments.

Device Identification. Classification was performed with the k-nearest neighbors algorithm (k-NN) with experimentally picked $k = 5$ as the best value.

First, the MSE-DSI values for each device (based on 29 images) are calculated. A new image is acquired with a particular device and its MSE-DSI value is calculated. Then, the device is classified by a plurality vote, i.e. to the class most common among its k nearest MSE-DSI values. All the experiments were performed with 10-fold cross-validation. The results of device classification by the proposed methods are presented in Fig. 4.

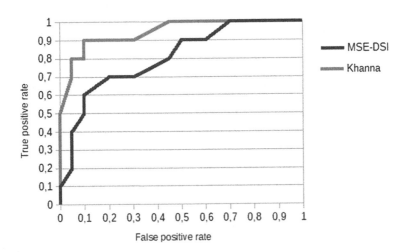

Fig. 4. ROC curve of scanner model recognition of MSE-DSI vs. Khanna et al.'s algorithm.

The results of classification presented in the confusion matrices point that the proposed method is less accurate in scanner classification compared with the state-of-the-art algorithm. The Khanna et al.'s algorithm obtained the AUC = 0.94. The proposed MSE-DSI algorithm gives the AUC = 0.81 accuracy for model recognition.

The proposed algorithm may even work as preprocessing, e.g. for pre-selection of photos according to the device model before subjecting these photos to further analysis by a more sophisticated or accurate algorithm. The advantage of the proposed algorithm is processing a small amount of data that makes the algorithm fast. However, at the same time, this is a potential weakness because the smaller amount of data make the algorithm slightly less accurate.

Time Performance. The experiments showed that Khanna et al.'s algorithm processes images much longer than the proposed MSE-DSI algorithm. On average, one image in the MSE-DSI algorithm is processed in about 2 s. Therefore, calculating the MSE values of all tested 290 images took nearly 10 min. The Khanna et al.'s algorithm processes one image on average in 120 s, resulting in total time for processing 290 images at nearly 10 h. Graphical interpretation of time performance comparison is presented in Fig. 5. We have also performed the statistical analysis of obtained results, but due to paper size limitations, we skip them.

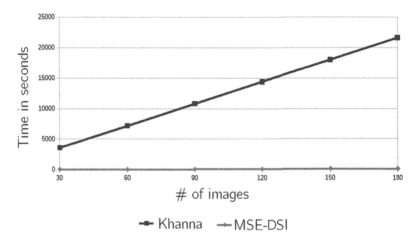

Fig. 5. Time performance comparison of Khanna et al. and the MSE-DSI algorithm.

5   Conclusions and Future Work

We proposed the MSE-DSI algorithm for image device identification and compared it with the state-of-the-art algorithms for flatbed scanner and digital camera identification. It can be used, for example, in IoT network security by detecting imaging device compromise or in forensics. Experimental results showed a slightly better classification performance of the proposed method. Moreover, the MSE-DSI algorithm is more efficient than the state-of-the-art algorithms in terms of the processing time (about two orders of magnitude). The Khanna et al.'s algorithm and CNNs proposed by Mandelli et al.'s and Kirchner & Johnson calculate the image device fingerprint by denoising all colour channels of the scanned images at their full resolution. We proposed to process only one colour channel, which significantly speeds up the process of image processing. Furthermore, we process only a fragment of the scanned image of size 512×512 pixels. Calculating device fingerprints for 290 images by the proposed method takes about 10 min, while the Khanna/CNNs need almost 10 h. The processing speed is crucial in IoT networks, where we usually deal with energy-efficient devices, low computational requirements, and rather dense traffic. Future work will concern further analysis of the proposed MSE-DSI algorithm in order to increase its classification accuracy. We are going to extend the experiments in order to check if our method works for several flatbed scanners of the same model.

References

1. Agarwal, A., Singh, R., Vatsa, M.: Fingerprint sensor classification via mélange of handcrafted features. In: 23rd International Conference on Pattern Recognition, ICPR 2016, Cancún, Mexico, 4–8 December 2016, pp. 3001–3006 (2016)
2. Amerini, I., Caldelli, R., Cappellini, V., Picchioni, F., Piva, A.: Analysis of denoising filters for photo response non uniformity noise extraction in source camera identification. In: 2009 16th International Conference on Digital Signal Processing, pp. 1–7, July 2009
3. Baar, T., van Houten, W., Geradts, Z.J.M.H.: Camera identification by grouping images from database, based on shared noise patterns. CoRR abs/1207.2641 (2012). http://arxiv.org/abs/1207.2641
4. Bondi, L., Baroffio, L., Guera, D., Bestagini, P., Delp, E.J., Tubaro, S.: First steps toward camera model identification with convolutional neural networks. IEEE Signal Process. Lett. **24**(3), 259–263 (2017). https://doi.org/10.1109/LSP.2016.2641006
5. Chen, Y., Huang, Y., Ding, X.: Camera model identification with residual neural network. In: 2017 IEEE International Conference on Image Processing, ICIP 2017, 17–20 September 2017, Beijing, China, pp. 4337–4341 (2017)
6. Deng, Z., Gijsenij, A., Zhang, J.: Source camera identification using auto-white balance approximation. In: IEEE International Conference on Computer Vision, ICCV 2011, 6–13 November 2011, Barcelona, Spain, pp. 57–64 (2011)
7. Dirik, A.E., Sencar, H.T., Memon, N.D.: Flatbed scanner identification based on dust and scratches over scanner platen. In: Proceedings of the IEEE International Conference on Acoustics, Speech, and Signal Processing, ICASSP 2009, 19–24 April 2009, Taipei, Taiwan, pp. 1385–1388 (2009), https://doi.org/10.1109/ICASSP.2009.4959851
8. Freire-Obregón, D., Narducci, F., Barra, S., Santana, M.C.: Deep learning for source camera identification on mobile devices. CoRR abs/1710.01257 (2017). http://arxiv.org/abs/1710.01257
9. Fridrich, J.J., Goljan, M.: Determining approximate age of digital images using sensor defects. In: Media Forensics and Security III, San Francisco Airport, 24–26 January 2011, CA, USA, Proceedings, p. 788006 (2011), https://doi.org/10.1117/12.872198

10. Galdi, C., Nappi, M., Dugelay, J.-L.: Combining hardwaremetry and biometry for human authentication via smartphones. In: Murino, V., Puppo, E. (eds.) ICIAP 2015. LNCS, vol. 9280, pp. 406–416. Springer, Cham (2015). https://doi.org/10.1007/978-3-319-23234-8_38

11. Galdi, C., Nappi, M., Dugelay, J.: Multimodal authentication on smartphones: combining iris and sensor recognition for a double check of user identity. Patt. Recogn. Lett. **82**, 144–153 (2016). https://doi.org/10.1016/j.patrec.2015.09.009

12. Gloe, T., Franz, E., Winkler, A.: Forensics for flatbed scanners. In: Security, Steganography, and Watermarking of Multimedia Contents IX, 28 January 2007, San Jose, CA, USA, p. 65051I (2007)

13. Goljan, M.: Digital camera identification from images - estimating false acceptance probability. In: Digital Watermarking, 7th International Workshop, IWDW 2008, 10–12 November 2008, Busan, Korea. Selected Papers, pp. 454–468 (2008)

14. Goljan, M., Chen, M., Comesaña, P., Fridrich, J.J.: Effect of compression on sensor-fingerprint based camera identification. In: Media Watermarking, Security, and Forensics 2016, 14–18 February 2016, San Francisco, California, USA, pp. 1–10 (2016)

15. Gou, H., Swaminathan, A., Wu, M.: Robust scanner identification based on noise features. In: Security, Steganography, and Watermarking of Multimedia Contents IX, 28 January 2007, San Jose, CA, USA, p. 65050S (2007)

16. Jiang, X., Wei, S., Zhao, R., Zhao, Y., Wu, X.: Camera fingerprint: a new perspective for identifying user's identity. CoRR abs/1610.07728 (2016), http://arxiv.org/abs/1610.07728

17. Kang, X., Li, Y., Qu, Z., Huang, J.: Enhancing source camera identification performance with a camera reference phase sensor pattern noise. IEEE Trans. Inf. Forensics Secur. **7**(2), 393–402 (2012). http://dx.doi.org/10.1109/TIFS.2011.2168214

18. Khanna, N., Chiu, G.T., Allebach, J.P., Delp, E.J.: Forensic techniques for classifying scanner, computer generated and digital camera images. In: Proceedings of the IEEE International Conference on Acoustics, Speech, and Signal Processing, ICASSP 2008, 30 March–4 April 2008, Caesars Palace, Las Vegas, Nevada, USA, pp. 1653–1656 (2008). https://doi.org/10.1109/ICASSP.2008.4517944

19. Khanna, N., Chiu, G.T., Allebach, J.P., Delp, E.J.: Scanner identification with extension to forgery detection. In: Security, Forensics, Steganography, and Watermarking of Multimedia Contents X, 27 January 2008, San Jose, CA, USA, p. 68190G (2008). https://doi.org/10.1117/12.772048

20. Khanna, N., Mikkilineni, A.K., Chiu, G.T., Allebach, J.P., Delp, E.J.: Forensic classification of imaging sensor types. In: Security, Steganography, and Watermarking of Multimedia Contents IX, 28 January 2007, San Jose, CA, USA, p. 65050U (2007). https://doi.org/10.1117/12.705849

21. Khanna, N., Mikkilineni, A.K., Chiu, G.T., Allebach, J.P., Delp, E.J.: Scanner identification using sensor pattern noise. In: Security, Steganography, and Watermarking of Multimedia Contents IX, 28 January 2007, San Jose, CA, USA, p. 65051K (2007)

22. Khanna, N., Mikkilineni, A.K., Delp, E.J.: Scanner identification using feature-based processing and analysis. IEEE Trans. Inf. Forensics Secur. **4**(1), 123–139 (2009). https://doi.org/10.1109/TIFS.2008.2009604

23. Kirchner, M., Johnson, C.: SPN-CNN: boosting sensor-based source camera attribution with deep learning. CoRR abs/2002.02927 (2020). https://arxiv.org/abs/2002.02927

24. Li, R., Li, C., Guan, Y.: Inference of a compact representation of sensor fingerprint for source camera identification. Patt. Recogn. **74**, 556–567 (2018). https://doi.org/10.1016/j.patcog.2017.09.027
25. Lukás, J., Fridrich, J.J., Goljan, M.: Digital camera identification from sensor pattern noise. IEEE Trans. Inf. Forensics Secur. **1**(2), 205–214 (2006). https://doi.org/10.1109/TIFS.2006.873602
26. Lyu, S., Farid, H.: How realistic is photorealistic? IEEE Trans. Signal Process. **53**(2–2), 845–850 (2005). https://doi.org/10.1109/TSP.2004.839896(410)53
27. Mandelli, S., Cozzolino, D., Bestagini, P., Verdoliva, L., Tubaro, S.: CNN-based fast source device identification. IEEE Signal Process. Lett. **27**, 1285–1289 (2020). https://doi.org/10.1109/LSP.2020.3008855
28. Mihçak, M.K., Kozintsev, I., Ramchandran, K.: Spatially adaptive statistical modeling of wavelet image coefficients and its application to denoising. In: Proceedings of the 1999 IEEE International Conference on Acoustics, Speech, and Signal Processing, ICASSP 1999, 15–19 March 1999, Phoenix, Arizona, USA, pp. 3253–3256 (1999). https://doi.org/10.1109/ICASSP.1999.757535
29. Rafi, A.M., et al.: Application of DenseNet in camera model identification and post-processing detection. In: IEEE Conference on Computer Vision and Pattern Recognition Workshops, CVPR Workshops 2019, 16–20 June 2019, Long Beach, CA, USA, pp. 19–28 (2019)
30. Tomioka, Y., Kitazawa, H.: Digital camera identification based on the clustered pattern noise of image sensors. In: Proceedings of the 2011 IEEE International Conference on Multimedia and Expo, ICME 2011, 11–15 July 2011, Barcelona, Catalonia, Spain, pp. 1–4 (2011). https://doi.org/10.1109/ICME.2011.6012060
31. Tuama, A., Comby, F., Chaumont, M.: Camera model identification with the use of deep convolutional neural networks. In: 2016 IEEE International Workshop on Information Forensics and Security (WIFS), pp. 1–6 (2016)
32. Tuama, A., Comby, F., Chaumont, M.: Camera model identification based machine learning approach with high order statistics features. In: 24th European Signal Processing Conference, EUSIPCO 2016, 29 August–2 September 2016, Budapest, Hungary, pp. 1183–1187 (2016)
33. Valsesia, D., Coluccia, G., Bianchi, T., Magli, E.: Compressed fingerprint matching and camera identification via random projections. IEEE Trans. Inf. Forensics Secur. **10**(7), 1472–1485 (2015)
34. Yang, P., Ni, R., Zhao, Y., Zhao, W.: Source camera identification based on content-adaptive fusion residual networks. Patt. Recogn. Lett. **119**, 195–204 (2019). https://doi.org/10.1016/j.patrec.2017.10.016
35. Yao, H., Qiao, T., Xu, M., Zheng, N.: Robust multi-classifier for camera model identification based on convolution neural network. IEEE Access **6**, 24973–24982 (2018). https://doi.org/10.1109/ACCESS.2018.2832066

Semantic Segmentation of Small Region of Interest for Agricultural Research Applications

Dan Popescu$^{(\boxtimes)}$ ⓘ, Loretta Ichim ⓘ, and Octavian Andrei Sava ⓘ

Faculty of Automatic Control and Computers, University Politehnica of Bucharest, Bucharest, Romania
{dan.popescu,loretta.ichim}@upb.ro

Abstract. The artificial intelligence and, in particular, the artificial neural networks proved to be useful tools in the field of computer vision, with promising results of applications in various domains, such as: industry, agriculture, medicine, transport, and environment. Detecting and locating crops using images received from aerial robots can make a positive contribution to assessing possible damage, reducing losses and minimizing analysis time. The paper proposed different implementation of the conditional generative adversarial network to better accomplish the task of semantic segmentation the agricultural region of interest. To this end the images were acquired by unmanned aerial vehicles. The network consists of a generator built using the U-Net architecture model and a discriminator that provides a probability matrix for each prediction, the elements of the matrix corresponding to portions of the input image. The resulting model, implemented with GPU processors provided by Google, performs a binary segmentation of images to determine the areas containing crops. The results of five experiments obtained, in the best configuration of hyper-parameters tested, an average accuracy of 97.93% in relation to reference (manual) segmentation.

Keywords: Aerial images · Unmanned aerial vehicle · Agricultural crops · Machine learning · Semantic segmentation · Generative adversarial networks

1 Introduction

The efficient segmentation of regions of interest in images can be considered as a complex cognitive and intelligent process. Thus, various researches have been conducted to study the behaviour of neural networks in this area.

An image can be divided into several parts, called segments. Applications that detect objects in the images frame objects into boxes without concrete information about the edges of the object. Image segmentation means that pixels having similar attributes are grouped into corresponding classes, providing important location, size or shape information [1]. Two types of image segmentation can be distinguished:

© Springer Nature Switzerland AG 2021
N. T. Nguyen et al. (Eds.): ICCCI 2021, LNAI 12876, pp. 585–598, 2021.
https://doi.org/10.1007/978-3-030-88081-1_44

- Semantic segmentation that links each pixel of an image to a corresponding class, performing a pixel level classification. All objects corresponding to a class are represented in the same colour;
- Segmentation of the instances which link each pixel of an image to a corresponding class, but objects corresponding to a class are coloured differently, making a difference also at the object level.

Image classification is one of the areas that have made progress in recent years. The main purpose of this task is to specify a label to each image, from a set of well-defined categories. Despite the fact that it may seem trivial, the problem is becoming more complex due to the large number of information that can be contained in an image. The evolution of this domain started in 2012, when a network called AlexNet [2] achieved the best performance by then, and this side of automatic learning has progresses steadily, in some cases outperforming the human brain in image classification tasks [3]. In [4] the authors have implemented methods that use convolutional neuronal networks to achieve semantic segmentation. This technique achieved an Intersection over Union – IoU result of more than 73% on the Pascal VOC benchmark level [5, 6]. The IoU is a scale used to measure the accuracy of a pattern of detection or segmentation of objects on a particular data set. Although segmentation methods based on convolutional neuronal networks have achieved promising results, they can still be improved on the main problem, pixel-level prediction, which can guarantee high accuracy but at the same time lead to discontinuous cross-class segmentation, resulting in deformations of these observed in the generated image. This has led to the development of post-processing methods, for ex-ample Fully Connected Conditional Random Fields – CRFs [7] or Markov Random Fields – MRFs [8], necessary to improve the segmentation results. These methods linked the input image to feature maps generated by convolutional network models to improve prediction, both in terms of colour information and pixel position [9].

In [10] the authors proposed a method for semantic segmentation using Fully Convolutional Networks (FCNs) to achieve the pixel classification. They pointed out that this network, with convolutional layers and deconvolution layers used to produce a map to mark each class, had good results without using other architectures, creating a pixel-level classification network with encoder-decoder architecture [9]. The model from [11] is an adversarial one trained to achieve semantic segmentation, the segmentation network and the adversarial network being alternately trained to generate semantic maps that are hard to distinguish from real maps. The authors in [12] presented the SEGAN model for the segmentation of medical images, which consists of a segmentation network and an analytical network with a loss function, minimized and maximized alternately to train the two networks. SEGAN achieved higher segmentation performance than the GANs in the original work [9].

With the advancement of technology, the quality of aerospace images is growing rapidly. As a result, their automatic and precise semantic labelling has an important significance, receiving wide attention nowadays. The challenge of semantic segmentation is the great variety of classes and also the small differences between them. The use of aerial vehicles with or without a pilot in the creation of overviews, combined with machine learning techniques, facilitates the analysis and autonomous inspection of areas of interest in the images.

The main objective of this paper is to create a model, using machine learning techniques, to perform the semantic segmentation of images received from UAVs, assigning each pixel to a corresponding class. The results will be evaluated from the perspective of the accuracy of the semantic segmentation of the input image, compared to manual segmentation. For better accuracy and to reduce the training and testing time the input images of 2944 × 2944 pixel are partitioned in patches of 32 × 32 pixel on which the proposed model is applied. The solution proposed for the semantic segmentation task is based on the architecture of generative adversarial networks (GANs) [13]. To get better results, depending on input and specific requirements, the process of conditioning the output depending on the input was added. These conditional models have also been used in the generation of photographs with certain characteristics [14] or the generation of images starting from various annotations [15].

2   Materials and Methods

The method used the U-Net architecture [16] and a Markovian convolutional classifier discriminator, with image patch differentiation efficiently for a wider range of discrimination problems. Such a network has also been used to differentiate texture from images [17]. On the other hand, the GAN is complex system of generating models using an adversarial process in which two networks are involved at the same time: a generator that has the role of generating new images, plausible according to the purpose of segmentation and a discriminator that has the role of classifying images as real or false. The two models are simultaneously driven in an adversary mode, the generator having the role of maximizing the probability that the discriminator will notice wrong images, while the discriminator tries to identify the false images as correct as possible [13]. GAN models are trained to generate an image, starting from a random noise [17]. Figure 1 shows the schematic diagram of a GAN network [18].

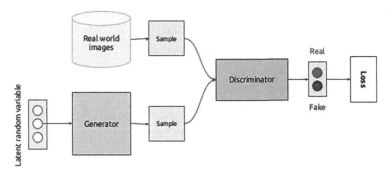

Fig. 1. GAN conceptual architecture [18].

As can be seen in Fig. 1, the architecture proposed in this paper is composed of two parts: the segmentation part (generator) and the adversarial part (discriminator). The segmentation network (the generator) is based on the U-Net architecture [16].

To avoid overfitting, a batch normalization technique was used. This method minimizes the effect of the phenomenon generated by changes in input distributions as the parameters of the previous convolutional layer change during training, also increasing the stability of the networks. To avoid over-learning, the dropout method was added, which consists in setting a percentage of network neurons to 0, forcing them to no longer participate in the dissemination of information from current iteration and also not to be involved in the backpropagation process. Thus, each neuron in the network is forced to learn new features, being constantly in conjunction with another subset of neurons compared to the previous iteration [19].

The dataset used consists of images taken using an OSMO + FC350Z device attached to a UAV. The images are taken at an altitude of 30 m in the Fundulea area (Romania), the total area flown by UAV being 40,000 m². These images include a variety of characterstics of agricultural crops, but also of land, dry land or dry culture. The images are of 4000 × 3000 pixels, and the total number of images in the dataset is 400. The training set is formed by augmenting the cropped images from an otophotoplan obtained by original images acquired by UAV. The images were rotated by 90°, 180°, and 270°, thus forming three new images, respectively three new masks [20].

In order to evaluate the performances of the semantic segmentation of small agricultural crops it is necessary to introduce the following coefficients for evaluating the results compared with manual segmentation: accuracy [21] – *ACC* (1), intersection over union [22] – *IoU* (2), and Dice similarity coefficient [22] – *DSC* (3). To this end, four representative values (*TP*, *TN*, *FP*, and *FN*) about the relationship between the model-generated and the actual (target) image must be calculated for each pixel in the images. These values are represented in the confusion matrix (Table 1).

Table 1. Pixel link matrix between the generated image and the target image

		Target image	
		Crop	Other class
Generated image	Crop	True positive (TP)	False positive (FP)
	Other class	False negative (FN)	True negative (TN)

$$ACC = \frac{TP + TN}{TP + TN + FP + FN} \quad (1)$$

$$IoU = \frac{TP}{FP + TP + FN} \quad (2)$$

$$DSC = 2 * \frac{TP}{(TP + FP) + (TP + FN)} \quad (3)$$

The implementation of artificial intelligence architectures can require a lot of time, a well-structured work environment being mandatory in this field which is based on a large number of experiments. Python includes a large set of libraries to help in machine learning processes that contain common operations already implemented. One of the most used in this field is the PyTorch library [23] used to create machine learning models. Also, an important factor that makes this library the right choice is the concept of parallelization, making it possible to distribute processes across multiple CPU or GPU processors. PyTorch is also integrated with libraries used to make applications in image preprocessing, post-processing, visualization or evaluation of data such as NumPy [24], scikit-image [25], matplotlib [26].

To achieve the semantic segmentation of the images in the dataset, the following operations were made: a) dividing the orthophotoplan into 2944 × 2944 pixel images, b) dividing each image into 32 × 32 pixel patches, c) patch classification, and d) image segmentation.

The purpose of the generator is to generate plausible images according to the segmentation requirement. Modifying the original U-Net architecture [16], to achieve the task of semantic segmentation, a new architecture was designed, adapted to the structure from [17], the scheme being described in Fig. 2.

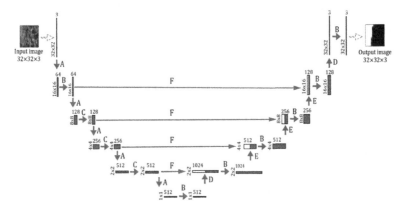

Fig. 2. Generator architecture.

Each box corresponds to a pixel map. The number of channels is represented at the top of each box. A represents the 2-D convolution with 4 × 4 size filters, sliding step $s = 2$, padding $p = 1$, B represents the activation operation (ReLU/LeakyReLU/Tanh), C represents the batch normalization operation + activation function LeakyReLU applied in the encoder, D represents the 2-D transposed convolution with 4 × 4 size filters, sliding step $s = 2$, padding $p = 1$, E represents the 2-D transposed convolution with 4 × 4 size filters, sliding step $s = 2$, padding $p = 1$ to which is added the batch normalization operation applied in the decoder and F is the concatenation operation. A block of patches of 32 × 32 × 3 size (R, G, and B channels) are used as generator input in the training part. The number of filters initially applied is 64, at the input in each convolutional block of the encoder they double. There are four convolutional blocks in both the encoder part and the decoder part, and the image size at the lowest level of the segmentation network (bottleneck) is 1 × 1 × 512. The size of each convolutional filter is 4 × 4, and the sliding step is $s = 2$ for each 2-D convolution. The activation function used in the construction of the encoder is LeakyReLU, which, compared to the activation function used in the original work, ReLU, where $f(y) = 0$ for $y < 0$ and $f(y) = y$ for $y \geq 0$ increases the range by adding a constant α, so that $f(y) = \alpha y$ for $y < 0$ [27].

Applying these parameters, the image size after applying the operations in a convolutional block must be reduced by half in the contracting part. Except for the first convolutional block in the encoder and the last one in the decoder, for the data regularization was introduced, compared to the original U-Net architecture [16], the batch normalization technique, the rate at which the parameters are updated (momentum) being 0.1. The proposed structure for the generator encoder is described in Table 2.

Table 2. Proposed structure for the encoder

Layer	Details	Input dimension	Output dimension
Input	–	$32 \times 32 \times 3$	$32 \times 32 \times 3$
Conv2D	64 filters	$32 \times 32 \times 3$	$16 \times 16 \times 64$
Activation	LeakyReLU, $\alpha = 0.2$	$16 \times 16 \times 64$	$16 \times 16 \times 64$
Conv2D	128 filters	$16 \times 16 \times 64$	$8 \times 8 \times 128$
BatchNorm	momentum $= 0.1$	$8 \times 8 \times 128$	$8 \times 8 \times 128$
Activation	LeakyReLU, $\alpha = 0.2$	$8 \times 8 \times 128$	$8 \times 8 \times 128$
Conv2D	256 filters	$8 \times 8 \times 128$	$4 \times 4 \times 256$
BatchNorm	momentum $= 0.1$	$4 \times 4 \times 256$	$4 \times 4 \times 256$
Activation	LeakyReLU, $\alpha = 0.2$	$4 \times 4 \times 256$	$4 \times 4 \times 256$
Conv2D	512 filters	$4 \times 4 \times 256$	$2 \times 2 \times 512$
BatchNorm	momentum $= 0.1$	$2 \times 2 \times 512$	$2 \times 2 \times 512$
Activation	LeakyReLU, $\alpha = 0.2$	$2 \times 2 \times 512$	$2 \times 2 \times 512$

The structure of the decoder in the generator is shown in Table 3. The last convolutional block of the expansion part of the segmentation network consists of a transposed convolution, applying 3 filters of size 4×4, with sliding pitch $s = 2$, and padding $p = 1$, and a Tanh activation function [28], used in networks that perform the classification between two classes. The segmentation network applies the model to images extracted from the original image and generates an image measuring $32 \times 32 \times 3$, representing the prediction of that segment from the initial image. This is concatenated at the color channels with the corresponding segment in the target image and the result is used as input to the opposing network, with the architecture described in Fig. 3, where each box corresponds to a pixel map and the number of channels is represented in top of each box. A represents the generator, B represents the concatenation operation at channel level, C represents the convolution, activation or normalization operations, described in Table 4.

The output of the adversarial network is a 16×16 size matrix. This is equivalent to the fact that each element in the 16×16 output matrix generated by the adversarial network corresponds to a 16×16 size portion of the input matrix. This type of discriminator does not generate a scalar output that classifies the input image as real or false, the generated matrix being composed of patch probabilities, the size of the receptive field, as real or false. The activation function that is applied in the last layer (sigmoid) is the right choice to generate probability predictions because it provides values between 0 and 1 [27].

Table 3. Proposed structure for decoder

Layer	Details	Input dimension	Output dimension
Concatenation	–	$2 \times 2 \times 512$ $2 \times 2 \times 512$	$2 \times 2 \times 1024$
Activation	ReLU	$2 \times 2 \times 1024$	$2 \times 2 \times 1024$
Conv Transpose2d	256 filters	$2 \times 2 \times 1024$	$4 \times 4 \times 256$
BatchNorm	mom = 0.1	$4 \times 4 \times 256$	$4 \times 4 \times 256$
Concatenation	–	$4 \times 4 \times 256$ $4 \times 4 \times 256$	$4 \times 4 \times 512$
Activation	ReLU	$4 \times 4 \times 512$	$4 \times 4 \times 512$
Conv Transpose2d	128 filters	$4 \times 4 \times 512$	$8 \times 8 \times 128$
BatchNorm	mom = 0.1	$8 \times 8 \times 128$	$8 \times 8 \times 128$
Concatenation	–	$8 \times 8 \times 128$ $8 \times 8 \times 128$	$8 \times 8 \times 256$
Activation	ReLU	$8 \times 8 \times 256$	$8 \times 8 \times 256$
Conv Transpose2d	64 filters	$8 \times 8 \times 256$	$16 \times 16 \times 64$
BatchNorm	mom = 0.1	$16 \times 16 \times 64$	$16 \times 16 \times 64$
Concatenation	–	$16 \times 16 \times 64$ $16 \times 16 \times 64$	$16 \times 16 \times 128$
Activation	ReLU	$16 \times 16 \times 128$	$16 \times 16 \times 128$
Conv Transpose2d	3 filters	$16 \times 16 \times 128$	$32 \times 32 \times 3$
Activation	Tanh	$32 \times 32 \times 3$	$32 \times 32 \times 3$

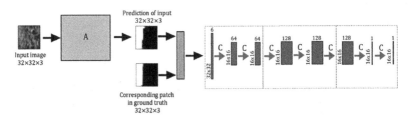

Fig. 3. Discriminator architecture.

After establishing the architecture of the neural network, with the dataset processed especially for the learning phase, follows the process of training the model. The network will learn to generate new images, segmenting agricultural crops and marking this with black, the rest of the existing classes in the test image (soil, dry land, dry crop, water, building roofs etc.) being marked in white. In order to arrive at the right model, it is necessary to find the appropriate values for certain hyper-parameters. The loss function makes a correspondence between the values of the network parameters and a scalar value that indicates how well these parameters perform the task of the neural network, being used to optimize them. Two of the most used loss functions are the mean square error (MSE) and the binary co-entropy (BCE).

In order to train the network effectively, a platform was needed to achieve learning, because ordinary computers are an inefficient alternative, especially in terms of training time. Due to the resources, the Google Colab platform [29] was used for the learning phase, which offers free access to Graphics Processing Unit – GPU processors, but also Tensor Processing Unit – TPU. In terms of hardware, the model described in this paper was trained by a system that has as its main features the NVIDIA GPU 16GB graphics processing unit. The training dataset was uploaded to Google Drive [30], and the training methods were uploaded to GitHub [31]. The Google Colab platform facilitates a connection between the graphics processors it offers, the dataset uploaded to Google Drive and the code available on GitHub. This approach was used for both training and testing phase.

Table 4. Proposed structure for discriminator

Layer	Details	Input dimension	Output dimension
Input1	Generator prediction	$32 \times 32 \times 3$	$32 \times 32 \times 3$
Input2	Patch in target image	$32 \times 32 \times 3$	$32 \times 32 \times 3$
Concatenation	[Input1], [Input2]	$32 \times 32 \times 3$ $32 \times 32 \times 3$	$32 \times 32 \times 6$
Conv2D	64 filters	$32 \times 32 \times 6$	$16 \times 16 \times 64$
Activation	LeakyReLU, $\alpha = 0.2$	$16 \times 16 \times 64$	$16 \times 16 \times 64$
Conv2D	128 filters	$16 \times 16 \times 64$	$16 \times 16 \times 128$
BatchNorm	mom $= 0.1$	$16 \times 16 \times 128$	$16 \times 16 \times 128$
Activation	LeakyReLU, $\alpha = 0.2$	$16 \times 16 \times 128$	$16 \times 16 \times 128$
Conv2D	1 filter p $= 1$	$16 \times 16 \times 128$	$16 \times 16 \times 1$
Activation	Sigmoid	$16 \times 16 \times 1$	$16 \times 16 \times 1$

The discriminator is not involved in the testing strategy, it being necessary only in the training phase. Also, the generator used in the testing phase is identical, in terms of structure, with the generator on which the training was performed, but without the dropout technique, all the neurons of the network being involved in the testing phase.

3 Experimental Results

In this section, a series of hyper-parameters were varied and the performances of the created CGAN models were evaluated. For learning or testing image, the first step was to resize it (2944 × 2944) and create 32 × 32 patches. Examples of augmented images for learning and images for testing are given in Figs. 4 and 5, respectively. Four experiments were performed (Table 5). Each experiment was tested on the images in the test dataset. The testing was integrated on the Google Colab platform, the necessary methods being uploaded on the GitHub platform and the results saved on the Google Drive platform. An improvement of the test time was observed about 18 times by using Google Colab, compared to the ordinary computer. Details for the experiments are given in Tables 6, 7, 8 and 9. Even if the results are close, the analysis the evaluation indices shows that the model resulting from experiment 4 has the best results in terms of test image. But, evaluating both the average ACC calculated on the whole dataset used for testing, as well as IoU and DCS indices, respectively, calculated in relation to manual segmentation, the best performances are obtained from experiment 3, as it can be observed in Table 9, where Average percent includes also the test image used in experiment results.

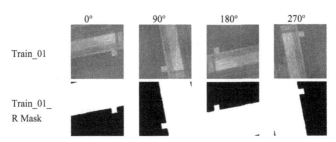

Fig. 4. Examples of augmented images used for training.

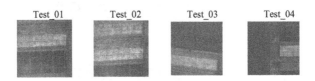

Fig. 5. Images used for testing.

As can be seen in the experiments, some hyper-parameters of machine learning networks can positively or negatively influence the results of the segmentation task. The training time (Table 7) is calculated up to the time when the best models were generated in each experiment. The test time (Table 7) is calculated for the 8464 32 × 32 patches that make up the test image. As can be seen, the architecture created to perform the task of semantic segmentation of images received from UAVs successfully solves the problem of training datasets in this field, providing even better results on set 1, which has a smaller size than the set 2. Also, the evaluation indices is good, even if the model has

Table 5. Experiments performed: characteristics

Experiment	Characteristics
1	The epoch number was 10, meaning 296960 iterations. The internal parameters are updated after each iteration, the resulting model provided good results from the first epochs, but the training time was longer. The loss function was BCE
2	The number of epochs was 10. The model generated good results since from the first epochs, but the training time was long. The loss function was changed (MSE)
3	The loss function was changed (BCE). The results were superior to the previous models even from epoch 4, followed by a decreasing trend
4	The training time was reduced by increasing the size of the data packs after which the internal parameters of the model were updated. The results were observed after a larger number of epochs than in previous cases, but after a shorter total time. The set for the batch size was 16. The best results are obtained in epoch 11

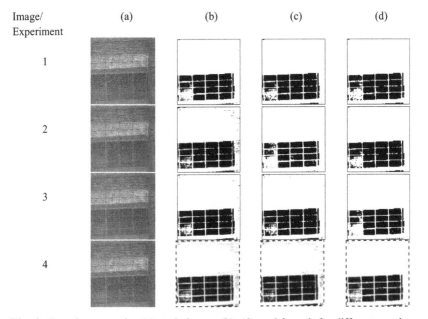

Fig. 6. Experiment results: (a) study image; (b)–(d) model result for different epochs.

been trained for fewer epochs. These properties of the created model are due to the generative adversarial network with which the training was performed, but also to the way of processing the data from the training sets. Even if the results are close, the analysis of the values of the evaluation indices, represented in Table 9, shows that the model resulting from experiment 3 has the best results in terms of test images, evaluating the average accuracy calculated on the whole set as well as IoU and DCS indices (Fig. 6) .

Table 6. Experiments: hyper-parameters

Experiment	Dataset	Iterations	Batch size	Loss function	Dropout
1	Set 2	296960	1	BCE	True
2	Set 2	296960	1	MSE	True
3	Set 1	165760	1	BCE	True
4	Set 1	165760	16	BCE	True

Table 7. Experiments: time performances

Performances	Exp. 1	Exp. 2	Exp. 3	Exp. 4
Total training time	2.0 h	1.7 h	1.0 h	11.60 min
Training time/epoch	12.0 min	10.2 min	3.0 min	34.80 s
Total testing time	39.03 s	38.80 s	37.58 s	38.23 s

Table 8. Experiments: indices for statistical performances. The bold represent the best results

Experiment	Coefficient	Epoch 1	Epoch 4	Epoch 10
1	ACC	95.26%	**96.34%**	95.45%
	IoU	89.05%	**91.58%**	89.54%
	DCS	94.14%	**95.57%**	94.42%
		Epoch 1	Epoch 4	Epoch 10
2	ACC	**96.25%**	92.93%	95.79%
	IoU	**91.56%**	83.68%	90.40%
	DCS	**95.56%**	90.95%	94.91%
		Epoch 4	Epoch 10	Epoch 20
3	ACC	**97.26%**	94.68%	95.17%
	IoU	**93.69%**	87.68%	88.88%
	DCS	**96.72%**	93.35%	94.05%
		Epoch 1	Epoch 11	Epoch 20
4	ACC	94.75%	**97.83%**	96.47%
	IoU	88.38%	**95.01%**	91.78%
	DCS	93.77%	**97.43%**	95.68%

Table 9. Results of the evaluation indices for experiments 1–4 on images

	Indices	Test_02	Test_03	Test_04	Average
Experiment 1	ACC	97.12%	99.04%	98.46%	97.74%
	IoU	90.20%	98.09%	96.91%	94.19%
	DCS	94.72%	99.03%	98.43%	96.93%
Experiment 2	ACC	96.18%	98.92%	96.72%	97.01%
	IoU	87.77%	97.86%	93.46%	92.66%
	DCS	93.31%	98.92%	96.62%	96.10%
Experiment 3	ACC	96.75%	99.07%	98.64%	**97.93%**
	IoU	89.38%	98.15%	97.26%	**94.62%**
	DCS	94.26%	99.07%	98.61%	**97.16%**
Experiment 4	ACC	95.44%	98.81%	97.65%	97.43%
	IoU	86.12%	97.64%	95.31%	93.52%
	DCS	92.32%	98.87%	97.60%	96.53%
	DCS	92.85%	98.74%	96.05%	96.13%

4   Conclusion

CGANs were used to perform the task of segmenting small agricultural crops from images received from UAVs. The proposed network was tested in five variants of hyper-parameters, and the model with the best results for the test dataset obtained an average accuracy of 97.93%, compared to the manual segmentation, for the test set. This indicates that the proposed method is viable and suitable for the task of semantic segmentation of agricultural crops. Moreover, it can be used in many areas, without the need for structural changes to the architecture, the only necessary configurations being the datasets for training and testing. The data preprocessing process, which includes resizing to a size favorable for splitting into 32×32 patches without losing information, being used in the testing phase, provides some independence from the size of the input image in the mechanism, successfully solving the problem of very large images. The experiments show that better results are obtained on the set training with a smaller number of data. Performance was positively influenced by using of GPU graphics processors made available through the Google Colab platform, obtaining the best results after 12 min of training.

Even if the results obtained are highly accurate in relation to manual segmentation, they can be improved in terms of inter-class boundaries by applying edge detection techniques, such as the one presented in the paper [32], which are based on convolutional neuronal networks. The second direction of network development is to configure the architecture so that semantic segmentation of agricultural crops takes place in more than two classes. The necessary changes are both in the training dataset and in the network structure, the presence of several features generating the need to add more convolutional layers to achieve correct segmentation.

Acknowledgements. This work was supported by a grant of the Ministry of Research, Innovation and Digitization, CNCS/CCCDI – UEFISCDI, project number 202/2020, within PNCDI III.

References

1. Sharma, P.: Computer Vision Tutorial: A Step-by-Step Introduction to Image Segmentation Techniques (Part 1). https://www.analyticsvidhya.com/blog/2019/04/introduction-image-seg mentation-techniques-python (2019). Accessed June 2020
2. Krizhevsky, A., Sutskever, I., Hinton, G.E.: ImageNet classification with deep convolutional neural networks. Commun. ACM **60**, 84–90 (2017)
3. Lazo, J.F.: Detection of archaeological sites from aerial imagery using deep learning, FYTM03 20182 (2019)
4. Papandreou, G., Chen, L., Murphy, K., Yuille, A.L.: Weakly- and semi-supervised learning of a deep convolutional network for semantic image segmentation. arXiv:1502.02734v3 (2015)
5. Everingham, M., Eslami, S.M.A., Van Gool, L.: The PASCAL visual object classes challenge: a retrospective. Int. J. Comput. Vis. 98–136 (2015)
6. Mwiti, D.: A 2019 Guide to Semantic Segmentation. https://heartbeat.fritz.ai/a-2019-guide-to-semantic-segmentation-ca8242f5a7fc (2019). Accessed May 2020
7. Koltun, V., Krahenbuhl, P.: Efficient inference in fully connected CRFs with gaussian edge potentials. arXiv:1210.5644v1 (2012)
8. Li, C., Wand, M.: Precomputed real-time texture synthesis with markovian generative adversarial networks. In: Leibe, B., Matas, J., Sebe, N., Welling, M. (eds.) ECCV 2016. LNCS, vol. 9907, pp. 702–716. Springer, Cham (2016). https://doi.org/10.1007/978-3-319-46487-9_43
9. Pan, X., et al.: Building extraction from high-resolution aerial imagery using a generative adversarial network with spatial and channel attention mechanisms. Remote Sens. **11**, 917 (2019)
10. Long, J., Shelhamer, E., Darrell, T.: Fully convolutional networks for semantic segmentation. arXiv:1411.4038v2 (2015)
11. Luc, P., Couprie, C., Chintala, S.: Semantic segmentation using adversarial networks. arXiv: 1611.08408v1 (2016)
12. Xue, Y., Xu, T., Zhang, H., Long, L.R., Huang, X.: SegAN: adversarial network with multi-scale L_1 loss for medical image segmentation. arXiv:1706.01805v2 (2017)
13. Goodfellow, I., et al.: Generative adversarial nets. In: 27th International Conference on Neural Information Processing Systems (NIPS), vol. 2, pp. 2672–2680. Montreal, QC, Canada (2014)
14. Yoo, D., Kim, N., Park, S., Paek, A.S., Kweon, I.S.: Pixel-level domain transfer. In: Leibe, B., Matas, J., Sebe, N., Welling, M. (eds.) ECCV 2016. LNCS, vol. 9912, pp. 517–532. Springer, Cham (2016). https://doi.org/10.1007/978-3-319-46484-8_31
15. Karacan, L., Akata, Z., Erdem, A., Erdem, E.: Learning to generate images of outdoor scenes from attributes and semantic layouts, arXiv:1612.00215v1 (2016)
16. Ronneberger, O., Fischer, P., Brox, T.: U-Net: convolutional networks for biomedical image segmentation. In: Navab, N., Hornegger, J., Wells, W.M., Frangi, A.F. (eds.) MICCAI 2015. LNCS, vol. 9351, pp. 234–241. Springer, Cham (2015). https://doi.org/10.1007/978-3-319-24574-4_28
17. Isola, P., Zhu, J.Y., Zhou, T.H., Efros, A.A.: Image-to-image translation with conditional adversarial networks. In: IEEE Conference on Computer Vision and Pattern Recognition, pp. 5967–5976. Honolulu, Hawaii, July 22–25 (2017)
18. Damien, A.: Generative Adversarial Network Example. https://wizardforcel.gitbooks.io/ten sorflow-examples-aymericdamien/3.11_gan.html. Accessed June 2020

19. Vrejoiu, M.H.: Convolutional neural networks, big data and deep learning in automatic image analysis (Reţele neuronale convoluţionale, Big Data şi Deep Learning în analiza automată de imagini). Roman. J. Inf. Technol. Automat. Control **29**, 91–114 (2019)

20. Popescu, D., Ichim, L., Stoican, F.: Flooded area segmentation from UAV images based on generative adversarial networks. In: 15th International Conference on Control, Automation, Robotics and Vision (ICARCV 2018), pp. 1361–1366. Singapore, November 18–21 (2018)

21. Vemuri, P.V.N.: Image Segmentation with Python. https://kite.com/blog/python/image-seg mentation-tutorial (2019). Accessed June 2020

22. Tiu, E.: Metrics to Evaluate your Semantic Segmentation Model. https://towardsdatas cience.com/metrics-to-evaluate-your-semantic-segmentation-model-6bcb99639aa2 (2019). Accessed June 2020

23. Python. https://www.python.org. Accessed June 2020

24. NumPy. https://numpy.org. Accessed May 2020

25. Scikit-image. https://scikit-image.org. Accessed May 2020

26. Matplotlib. https://matplotlib.org. Accessed May 2020

27. Sharma, H.: Activation Functions: Sigmoid, ReLU, Leaky ReLU and Softmax Basics for Neural Networks and Deep Learning. https://medium.com/@himanshuxd/activation-fun ctions-sigmoid-relu-leaky-relu-and-softmax-basics-for-neural-networks-and-deep-8d9c70 eed91e (2019). Accessed June 2020

28. Tanh. http://pytorch.org/docs/master/generated/torch.nn.Tanh.html. Accessed June 2020

29. Google Colab. https://colab.research.google.com. Accessed June 2020

30. Google Drive. https://drive.google.com. Accessed June 2020

31. GitHub. https://github.com. Accessed June 2020

32. Soria, X., Riba, E., Sappa, A.: Dense Extreme Inception Network: Towards a Robust CNN Model for Edge Detection. arXiv:1909.01955v2 (2020)

Severity Assessment of Facial Acne

Anh Nguyen[1,2]([✉]) [ID], Huong Thai[1,2] [ID], and Thanh Le[1,2] [ID]

[1] Faculty of Information Technology, University of Science,
Ho Chi Minh City, Vietnam
{ntmanh,tmhuong}@apcs.vn, lnthanh@fit.hcmus.edu.vn
[2] Vietnam National University, Ho Chi Minh City, Vietnam

Abstract. Nowadays, facial acne is a popular skin disease. Acne is distributed in different regions on the face, and the severity of acne varies from patient to patient. Therefore, it is necessary to have an exact and objective diagnosis for each patient's case before treatment. The problem of assessing severity of acne on human face is highly applicable in practice, as acne severity is essential for dermatologists to make a precise and standardized treatment decision. We perform surveys of automatic acne detection and classification systems. Our work follows the implementation by Xiaoping Wu et al. that grades and counts acne via label distribution learning applying on ACNE04 dataset, and the method of transfer learning regression model using image rolling data augmentation from Microsoft and Nestlé collaboration. We give discussion and conclusion about the two approaches from different experiments' result.

Keywords: Acne severity · Deep learning · Label distribution learning

1 Introduction

Computer Vision extracts information from digital images, high dimensional data in the real world; aims to come up with computational models and build autonomous systems that can perform tasks of the human visual system [3]. Along with the dramatic development of Artificial Intelligence, Computer Vision gradually proofs its important and essential role among all the fields in life. Its implications suggest host of benefits to the healthcare industry. As the medical field requires as much accurate results as possible, it embraces more innovations and cutting-edge technologies and direct its gaze to Computer Vision.

In recent years, because of air pollution, clogging of sebaceous glands in the skin along with the hair shafts in addition to the bacterial infection, people have been facing numerous severe health's problems, and facial acne is one of them. According to recent study, acne vulgaris is known as one of the most common skin diseases, which is estimated to affect 9.4% of the global population, making it the eighth most prevalent disease worldwide [5]. It affects up to 80% of the adolescent population which witness a prevalence peaks among those from 28 to 33 years old and persists in approximately 3% of middle-aged adults [6].

© Springer Nature Switzerland AG 2021
N. T. Nguyen et al. (Eds.): ICCCI 2021, LNAI 12876, pp. 599–612, 2021.
https://doi.org/10.1007/978-3-030-88081-1_45

The traditional diagnosis methods for acne assessment such as manual observation or using ordinary flash photography are usually considered to be labor-intensive, time-consuming, and subjective to the experience and knowledge of expert and dermatologists [4]. Since then, a computerized imaging method is very necessary. Through non-contact inspections, doctors and patients do not need to be in face to face but still can analyze patient's facial skin conditions and defect detection for consultation before cosmetology is possible [7]. Works carried out on the automatic diagnosis for facial acne with image processing techniques and machine learning theories [8] take less time, gain more accurate and proper results, and thus easier for the acne treatment.

There are still challenges for the acne severity assessment at the present time. First, although the problem has been researched recent years, its available data for training is extremely hard to be found online, since most of the authors does not public them. Besides that, because assessing the severity of acne problem requires a large amount of precise dataset that has been consulted by dermatologists to achieve the most accurate result. Therefore, having more data labeled by the expert will be more helpful in addressing the facial acne analysis problem.

We research the acne severity assessment problem for the face and the face's skin patches. Face approach consists of two branches, one for global acne severity grading and the other for lesion counting. It tends to output the grading and counting result as diagnostic evidence at the same time, and carries out steps such as label distribution generation and multi-task learning strategy through a deep convolutional neural network. The skin patches approach detects and extracts skin patches on faces, then applies an innovative image augmentation method for better generalization. The framework applies transfer learning methodologies, which uses pre-trained model as feature extractor and trains a full-connected neural network on the feature set targeting severity level.

2   Background and Related Works

2.1   Object Detection

Object detection is now becoming one of the most core and important parts of computer vision, which has been applied in face detection, pose estimation, vehicle detection, surveillance etc. and even in facial treatment such as detecting lesions or counting acne in human face. The algorithms helps us draw bounding boxes around the locations of object within the image. It has been proposed generally by machine learning-based approaches, in which we first define hand-crafted feature extraction, then classifying them using technique such as support vector machine (SVM); and by deep learning-based approaches which can do an end-to-end object detection system, such as Faster R-CNN [9], YOLO (You Only Look Once) [11], RefineDet [10].

2.2   Hand-Crafted Feature Learning

Existing image features can be divided into two categories: the hand-crafted and the learned ones. Hand-crafted features (HCF) are extracted from separate images according to a certain manually predefined algorithm based on the expert knowledge. LBP [14] (Local Binary Pattern), HOG [15] (Histogram of Oriented Gradient), SIFT [16] (Scale Invariant Feature Transform) are commonly known image descriptors for HCF [13]. The learned features are derived from an image dataset by a training procedure to fulfill a certain task. HCF works relatively well in specific domain with small number of data and has much lower time complexity, while deep features are capable of learning from heterogeneous and unfamiliar datasets, though CNN needs many labeled training instances [13].

2.3 Deep Feature Learning

Recently, convolutional networks are at the core of so many state-of-the-art computer vision solutions for a wide variety of tasks, especially image classification. A common approach which brings a lot of success is Deep Neural Network (DNN) basing on the CNNs which uses several layers, and these models try to extract feature from input image, following with Inception [12], VGGNet [17], ResNet (Residual Neural Network) [18]. In addressing the facial acne analysis problem, many studies and application applying deep feature learning technique based on well-known CNNs have been carried out such as using deep CNN for classifying different types of acne [4] or assessing the severity of facial acne [1].

2.4 Label Distribution Learning

Label Distribution Learning (LDL) [19] is a general learning framework suitable for many label ambiguity problems. It aims at learning the relative importance of each label involved in the description of an instance rather than a single label or multiple labels. LDL methods can be generalized into three main strategies: problem transformation (PT-Bayes, PT-SVM), algorithm adaptation (AA-kNN K-nearest neighbors, AA-BP Back-propagation), and specialized algorithm design (SA-IIS Improved Iterative Scaling, SA-BFGS Broyden-Fletcher-Goldfarb-Shanno, SA-CPNN Conditional Probability Neural Network) with their own state of the art approaches. Recently, a CNN-based LDL method, Deep Label Distribution Learning [21] (DLDL), has been introduced, and we also apply it in the severity assessing framework [1] where label distributions of lesion number and acne severity are matched using professional medical criterion [20].

3 Methods

We evaluate facial acne severity base on two approaches, one that calculate the severity one whole face and one that assesses on different skin patches. For face's acne severity assessment, we build a unified deep framework for joint acne image grading and counting, optimized by the multi-task learning loss. Two acne label distributions were generated considering the relationship between the similar number of lesions and severity of acne [1]. With the skin patches approach, we access the problem of acne image analysis via CNN transfer learning regression models with image rolling data augmentation [2].

For face's acne severity, because acne images belonging to the same severity level may have a greatly varied number of lesions, professional medical criterion is considered to generate distribution. The Hayashi criterion [20], which combines the outcome measures of lesion counting and global assessment, is a standard criterion used by dermatologists for grading acne severity. Acne can be graded into four levels of severity according to the number of lesions, with best divisions as follow: 0–5 for mild (level 0), 6–20 for moderate (level 1), 21–50 for severe (level 2) and more than 50 for very severe (level 3) in the half faces.

3.1   Face's Acne Severity Assessment Approach

After input image going through CNN backbone, the framework is divided into two branches. The grading branch estimates the severity of acne globally. The counting branch predicts the label distribution of acne lesion count based on Gaussian distribution, then it is converted into the label distribution of acne severity based on Hayashi criterion [20]. Finally, prediction results from the global severity grading and the mapped one from local counting models are merged, oriented by the medical criterion, and optimized by the multi-task learning loss. Figure 1 is the pipeline of this approach.

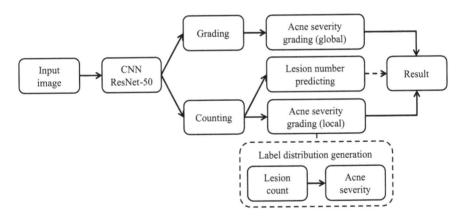

Fig. 1. Face's acne severity assessment pipeline

First, input image is resized and normalized, then passed through the CNN model (ResNet-50) and the outputs are used in the acne counting and grading task. We have N input training images with corresponding single labels of acne severity and ground-truths of lesion counts $\{(x_1, y_1, z_1), \ldots, (x_N, y_N, z_N)\}$, where $y_i \in [0, \ldots, Y]$ with Y denotes the class number of acne severity and $z_i \in [1, \ldots, Z]$ with Z stands for max number of lesion counts. In the system, Y is equal to 3, which is the highest severity of acne.

Label Distribution Generation in Counting Task

Lesion Number Predicting in Counting Task: By applying Gaussian function, label distribution for acne counting task of input image x_i can be generated. The description degree $d_{x_i}^{c_j}$ of a particular count label c_j can be defined as follow:

$$d_{x_i}^{c_j} = \frac{1}{\sqrt{2\pi}\sigma M} \exp\left(-\frac{(c_j - z_i)^2}{2\sigma^2}\right), \tag{1}$$

where $j \in [1, \ldots, Z]$. σ is a standard deviation of the distribution, which is set as 3 in this system. The normalization factor M is defined as:

$$M = \frac{1}{\sqrt{2\pi}\sigma} \sum_{j=1}^{Z} \exp\left(-\frac{(c_i - z_i)^2}{2\sigma^2}\right). \tag{2}$$

Then, label distribution of x_i in **lesion number predicting** is represented as a vector $d_{x_i}^c = \left[d_{x_i}^{c_i}, \ldots, d_{x_i}^{c_z}\right]$, which requires $d_{x_i}^{c_j} \in [0, 1]$ and $\sum_{j=1}^{Z} d_{x_i}^{c_j} = 1$, and the ground-truth label of lesion count represents the highest degree $d_{x_i}^{z_i} \geq d_{x_i}^{c_j}$.

Acne Severity Grading in Counting Task: After being predicted in counting task, label distribution for lesions is used in **local acne severity grading**, by being mapped to a specific class of acne severity according to Hayashi criterion. The description degree $d_{x_i}^{s_k}$ of acne severity label of image x_i is then calculated by summing all the description degrees of all lesion count labels belonging to the corresponding mapping interval $\phi(k)$ according to the medical criterion:

$$d_{x_i}^{s_k} = \sum_{j \in \phi(k)} d_{x_i}^{c_j}, \tag{3}$$

where $k \in [0, \ldots, Y]$. The label distribution $d_{x_i}^s = \left[d_{x_i}^{s_0}, \ldots, d_{x_i}^{s_Y}\right]$ of local grading task also satisfies the two constraints similar to the counting task.

Lesion Counting and Acne Severity Grading

Simultaneously Grades Acne Severity and Predicts Lesion Number in Counting Task: Given input x_i with label distribution y, we assume $x = \phi(x_i; \theta)$ is the activation of last fully connected layer in a deep CNN. A softmax function is used to turn x into probability distribution, where the predicted probability belonging to each lesion number class $j \in [1, \ldots, Z]$ is calculated as below:

$$p_i^{(j)} = \frac{\exp(\theta_j)}{\sum_{m=1}^{Z} \exp(\theta_m)}, \tag{4}$$

where θ_j is predicted score for the jth class outputted from the last fully connected layer. After that, the KL loss is applied to reduce the deviation between the predicted label distribution $p_i^c = \left[p_i^{(1)}, \ldots, p_i^{(Z)}\right]$ and the ground-truth label distribution $d_{x_i}^c$ in the counting branch, which is defined as:

$$L_{cnt}(x_i, z_i) = -\sum_{j=1}^{z} \left(d_{x_i}^{c_j} \ln p_i^{(j)} \right). \tag{5}$$

For further acne classification, predicted counting result $p_i^{(c)}$ is converted into grading result $\hat{p}_i^s = \left[\sum_{j \in \phi(1)} p_i^{(j)}, \ldots, \sum_{j \in \phi(Y)} p_i^{(j)} \right]$ with the loss calculated as:

$$L_{cnt2cls}(x_i, y_i) = -\sum_{k=1}^{Y} \left(d_{x_i}^{s_k} \ln \sum_{j \in \phi(k)} p_i^{(j)} \right). \tag{6}$$

Global Acne Severity Grading: Given input instance x_i with label distribution y, we assume $x = \phi(x_i; \theta)$ is the activation of last fully connected layer in a deep CNN. A softmax function is used to turn x into probability distribution, where the predicted probability belonging to each acne severity class $k \in \{0, \ldots, Y\}$ of instance x_i is calculated as:

$$p_i^{(k)} = \frac{\exp(\delta_k)}{\sum_{n=0}^{Y} \exp(\delta_n)}, \tag{7}$$

δ_k is the predicted score for the kth class, outputted from the last fully connected layer. After that, the KL loss is applied to reduce the deviation between the predicted label distribution $p_i^s = \left[p_i^{(0)}, \ldots, p_i^{(Y)} \right]$ and the ground-truth label distribution $d_{x_i}^s$ in the global grading branch, which is defined as:

$$L_{cls}(x_i, y_i) = -\sum_{j=0}^{Y} \left(d_{x_i}^{s_k} \ln p_i^{(k)} \right). \tag{8}$$

Multi-task Learning Model

A unified multi-task learning model is proposed to lead the model to learn more detail and accurate description of features and classifier. At the training phase, the multi-task learning loss is:

$$L_i(x_i, y_i, z_i) = (1 - \lambda)L_{cnt}(x_i, z_i) + \frac{\lambda}{2} \left(L_{cts}(x_i, y_i) + L_{cnt2cls}(x_i, y_i) \right), \tag{9}$$

where λ is the parameter which is the trade-off between acne grading and lesion counting tasks and a larger λ will make the model focus more on the counting task. The model was experimented to gain the best performances on accuracy and MAE metrics when $\lambda = 0.6$, so $\lambda = 0.6$ is applied in the proposed model. Meanwhile at the testing phase, the model combines results of acne severity classification from counting branch $\hat{p}_i^y$ and grading branch p_i^y by taking the average of them $\frac{1}{2}(\hat{p}_i^y + p_i^y)$. Therefore, the model can achieve an end-to-end procedure of simultaneously providing diagnostic evidence of acne number counts and grading the acne severity. Besides, the model also combines the acne counting task and global estimation both in training and testing phases.

3.2   Skin Patches' Acne Severity Assessment Approach

Beside grading the face's acne severity, our system can give scores of the skin patches from dominant areas of acne (forehead, cheeks, and chin). Two image processing steps are extracting skin patches (by facial landmark detection model and One Eye model) and rolling skin patches to augment the set. The model is developed by transfer learning idea, that uses a pretrained model (ResNet-152 in CNTK) to extract features from the lower layers then trains a fully connected neural network (FCNN) regression model to solve the problem. Figure 2 shows the pipeline for skin patches' acne severity assessment approach.

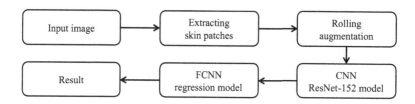

Fig. 2. Skin patches' acne severity assessment pipeline

Image Processing

Extracted Skin Patches from Facial Skins: Skin patches from different sectors of the face are extracted to minimize irrelevant background. A coupling method for skin patch extraction is proposed. The facial landmark model (frontal face) is the first step, and if there was only one eye clearly visible in the image (side view), the One Eye model is employed to detect the location of the single eye, then the regions of forehead, cheek side, and chin skin patches will be inferred. The same overall acne severity level of entire face assigned by the dermatologists is labeled to all skin patches from the same image.

Rolling Skin Patches: The CNN model cannot recognize the acne lesion well when the acne lesion on the testing image appears on new locations that the model had never registered before. To address the spatial sensitivity of CNN models on small sample training data, an image rolling augmentation technique for facial images is introduced. Each skin patch is rolled for a certain number of pixels to mitigate this problem and help the trained model generalize better. Forehead image patches are rolled from right to left, while cheeks and chin image patches are rolled bottom up. The rolling step size is determined by rolling dimension size X (pixels) and the number of rolling times N:

$$roll\_size = int\left(\frac{X}{N+1}\right) \tag{10}$$

The class with most image patches is rolled twice to increase the coverage of acne lesion locations. Then with the aim to make the skin patch images after rolling among all 4 severity classes as nearly balanced as possible, we calculate to the ratio between the numbers of images in dominating class and minor classes to choose a suitable parameter N. Forehead, cheeks, and chin skin patches after being rolled can be seen in Fig. 3.

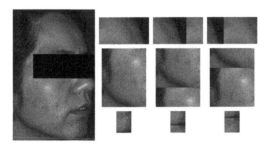

Fig. 3. Skin patches rolling

Model Development

Classification to Regression Problem: The original authors [2] have their testing dataset being labeled by many different dermatologists to create a golden set, then use an average score from the panel as ground truth, thus due to noisy image labels a regression model is built instead of classification. With that idea in mind, though our current dataset is only labeled once, we think that a regression model can still work when having many dermatologists label the images in further development, so we adapt and adjust the work to reach our desired goal.

Transfer Learning Model: Transfer learning method utilizes the knowledge from one area to solve the problems in another area. A pre-trained model ResNet-152 by CNTK is used to extract features in training image skin patches from the lower layers. Then a customized 3-layer FCNN regression model (with 1024, 512, and 256 neurons) is trained on these features to make the entire deep learning model specific to the acne severity domain. The framework gives individually score of all the skin patches extracted, also the final score of entire face can be calculated as the average of all predicted skin patch labels.

4   Experiments and Results

4.1   Dataset and Evaluation Metrics

ACNE04 dataset was built by Xiaoping Wu et al. [1]., which provides the annotations of global acne severity and lesion numbers of each image for evaluation and annotated by professional dermatologists. Images are taken at an approximately 70-degree angle from the front of acne patients with no constraints on background; the relationship between acne lesions in an image and the class of acne severity is represented by medical criterion [20]. The ACNE04 contains a total of 1,457 images with 18,983 lesions, divided into 4 severity levels of acne. For evaluating, the dataset is split into 80% training set and 20% testing set, containing 1,165 and 292 images, respectively. On top of that, 5-fold cross-validation is applied for robust evaluation.

Different evaluation metrics are selected for the tasks of classification and object counting, respectively. To evaluate the classification performance, the commonly utilized accuracy and precision are applied. Considering that the work of the acne severity grading is related to medical image processing, several important metrics from the medical field are additionally chosen, including sensitivity, specificity, and Youden Index. Mean absolute error (MAE) and root mean squared error (RMSE) are adopted to evaluate the counting performance.

4.2   Experimental Setup

Implementation Details for the Face Approach: ResNet-50 with parameters pre-trained on the ImageNet dataset is adopted as the architecture's backbone. The algorithm is based on the PyTorch framework and runs on system using GeForce RTX 2080 GPU with 8 GB RAM. The model is trained for 120 epochs with Stochastic Gradient Descent optimizer and the mini batch of 32. The momentum is set to 0.9 and weight decay is set to $5e-4$. The learning rate starts at 0.001 and decays by 0.5 every 30 epochs. The input images are resized into $224 \times 224 \times 3$ pixels and normalized to the range of $[0, 1]$ in RGB channels.

Experimental Environment for the Skin Patches Approach: The dataset for training and testing model is uploaded on Google Drive, and the implementation are conducted on Google Colaboratory for the easier installation cntk library.

4.3   Two Approaches' Results

Face's Acne Severity Assessment Approach Results

After having been trained and tested in 5-fold and the training set with the shuffled training set activated in each training session, the model gains results as shown in Table 1. Figure 4 is the visualizations of accuracy and multi-task loss for 5 cross validations.

It can be seen from Table 1 that the model trained in the cross-validation index 3 gained the highest accuracy amongst 5 folds (85.27%). Therefore, we use the model saved after the end of this cross-validation as our final model to carry out further tests in real images. Also, Fig. 4 illustrates that fold 3 has the most significant growth of accuracy among other folds.

Skin Patches' Acne Severity Assessment Approach Results

All skin patches extracted from test images are individually scored by RMSE. The face score is their average, rounded to nearest integer to be final predicted score. After having been trained and tested in 5 folds, the model gains result as shown in Table 2, with fold 2 having the smallest RSME (0.5818).

Table 1. Face's acne severity grading results based on various evaluation metrics

Cross val index	MAE	RMSE	Precision	Specificity	Sensitivity	Youden Index	Accuracy
0	3.048	5.791	0.8346	0.9369	0.8118	0.7355	0.8253
1	**2.729**	**4.669**	**0.8723**	0.9394	**0.8398**	**0.7771**	0.8493
2	2.955	4.977	0.8227	0.9362	0.8148	0.7464	0.8322
3	2.832	5.023	0.8478	**0.9436**	0.8317	0.7753	**0.8527**
4	3.253	6.734	0.8299	0.9345	0.8039	0.7332	0.8322
Average	**2.9634**	**5.4388**	**0.8415**	**0.9381**	**0.8204**	**0.7535**	**0.8383**
	±0.20	±0.83	±0.02	±0.00	±0.01	±0.02	±0.01

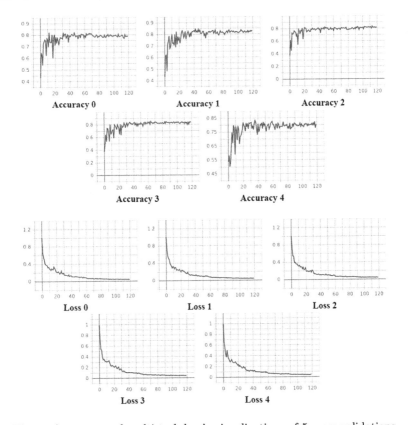

Fig. 4. Accuracy and multi-task loss's visualizations of 5 cross validations

Table 2. Skin patches' acne severity result based on RMSE

Fold 0	Fold 1	Fold 2	Fold 3	Fold 4	Average
0.6551	0.6117	**0.5818**	0.6186	0.6109	**0.6156**

4.4   Further Experimental Results

Comparison Between the Two Approaches

For a clearer comparison between the face's severity assessment approach (1st approach) and skin patches' severity assessment approach (2nd approach), we calculated the accuracy of both methods on face and each skin patch. We choose the fold that brings the best result of each model for the measurement. Then we have the final comparison in Table 3.

Table 3. Accuracy comparison between two approaches

	Face accuracy	Skin patch accuracy
1st approach	0.8527	0.5277
2nd approach	0.5856	0.5561

The 1st approach takes in half face to learn and it has a conversion from total acne lesions on the face to severity by Hayashi criterion [20], so asking it to grade skin patches would give a low performance. On the other hand, the 2nd approach assigns entire face label to each skin patches and learns, though this step introduces additional noise as the severity of acne lesion on different skin patches are different [2]. Therefore, the 2nd system could predict skin patch's severity slightly better than the 1st, but its outcomes are less standout in overall.

Above is our explanation for the results. From thinking about the essence of two methods and how they approach the assessing acne severity problem, and execute then compare them, we will use the method of jointing grading and counting acne images via LDL in our final demonstration application.

Results in Real Images Test

The model getting the highest accuracy amongst 5 folds (85.27%) is used to test several images collected from the internet, that they do not appear in the dataset for training and testing sessions. The console windows will show the predicted acne severity and acne number of real images test as in Fig. 5.

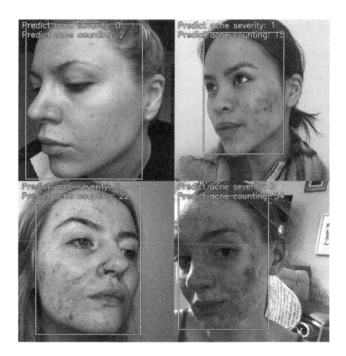

Fig. 5. Real images test result for facial acne assessment

5   Conclusion

5.1   Results

The acne severity assessing system basing on ResNet-50 network shows significant result when training and testing on ACNE04 dataset. The framework applies LDL for CNN model, combines counting and grading tasks for more precise and robust outcome. More specifically, the system achieves the average accuracy at 83.83%. We also approach the problem with ResNet-152 - FCNN model that augment skin patch images and evaluate their severity, which could not reach our result's expectations but still helps us to understand this problem more and gain a further vision of a bigger picture generally.

5.2   Future Works

We think that low-level and hand-crafted features approaches can also be applied together in detection process of the implemented system using LDL with deep framework to give a promising efficiency. We also would like to develop the dataset with more adequate quantity and balanced distribution between the severity classes. We can execute the ACNE04 dataset to the range of middle-age group, since it covers primarily on adolescent age group currently.

Acknowledgment. This research is funded by Advanced Program in Computer Science, the Faculty of Information Technology, University of Science, VNU-HCM, Vietnam.

References

1. Wu, X., et al.: Joint acne image grading and counting via label distribution learning. In: 2019 IEEE/CVF International Conference on Computer Vision (ICCV) (2019)
2. Zhao, T., Zhang, H., Spoelstra, J.: A computer vision application for assessing facial acne severity from selfie images (2019)
3. Huang, T.S.: Computer vision: evolution and promise. In: 19th CERN School of Computing (1996)
4. Junayed, M.S., et al.: AcneNet - a deep CNN based classification, approach for acne classes. In: 12th International Conference on Information and Communication Technology and System (ICTS) (2019)
5. Tan, J.K.L., Bhate, K.: A global perspective on the epidemiology of acne. Br. J. Dermatol. **172**, 3–12 (2015)
6. Taylor, M., Gonzalez, M., Porter, R.: Pathways to inflammation: acne pathophysiology (2011)
7. Chang, C.-Y., Liao, H.-Y.: Automatic facial skin defects detection and recognition system. In: Fifth International Conference on Genetic and Evolutionary Computing (2011)
8. Shen, X., Zhang, J., Yan, C., Zhou, H.: An automatic diagnosis method of facial acne vulgaris based on convolutional neural network (2017)
9. Ren, S., He, K., Girshick, R., Sun, J.: Faster R-CNN: towards real-time object detection with region proposal networks. IEEE Trans. Pattern Anal. Mach. Intell. **39**, 1137–1149 (2016)
10. Zhang, S., Wen, L., Bian, X., Lei, Z., Li, S.Z.: Single-shot refinement neural network for object detection. In: IEEE Conference on Computer Vision and Pattern Recognition (CVPR) (2018)
11. Redmon, J., Divvala, S., Girshick, R., Farhadi, A.: You only look once: unified, real-time object detection. In: IEEE Conference on Computer Vision and Pattern Recognition (CVPR) (2016)
12. Szegedy, C., et al.: Going deeper with convolutions. In: 2015 IEEE Conference on Computer Vision and Pattern Recognition (CVPR) (2015)
13. Antipov, G. Berrani, S.-A. Ruchaud, N., Dugelay, J.-L.: Learned vs. hand-crafted features for pedestrian gender recognition. In: ACM Multimedia Conference (2015)
14. Ojala, T., Pietikäinen, M., Mäenpää, T.: Multiresolution gray scale and rotation invariant texture classification with local binary patterns. IEEE Trans. Pattern Anal. Mach. Intell. **24**, 971–987 (2002)
15. Dalal, N., Triggs, B.: Histograms of oriented gradients for human detection. In: 2005 IEEE Computer Society Conference on Computer Vision and Pattern Recognition (2005)
16. Lowe, D.G.: Distinctive image features from scale-invariant keypoints. Int. J. Comput. Vision **60**, 91–110 (2004)
17. Simonyan, K., Zisserman, A.: Very deep convolutional networks for large-scale image recognition. In: International Conference on Learning Representations (ICLR) (2015)

18. He, K., Zhang, X., Ren, S., Sun, J.: Deep residual learning for image recognition. In: IEEE Conference on Computer Vision and Pattern Recognition (CVPR) (2015)
19. Geng, X.: Label distribution learning. IEEE Trans. Knowl. Data Eng. **28**, 1734–1748 (2016)
20. Hayashi, N., Akamatsu, H., Kawashima, M.: Establishment of grading criteria for acne severity. J. Dermatol. **35**, 55–260 (2018)
21. Gao, B.-B., Xing, C., Xie, C.-W., Wu, J., Geng, X.: Deep label distribution learning with label ambiguity. IEEE Trans. Image Process. **26**, 2825–2838 (2017)

Processing and Visualizing the 3D Models in Digital Heritage

Minh Khai Tran[1], Sinh Van Nguyen[1(✉)], Nghia Tuan To[1],
and Marcin Maleszka[2]

[1] School of Computer Science and Engineering, International University,
Vietnam National University, Ho Chi Minh City, Vietnam
nvsinh@hcmiu.edu.vn
[2] Department of Applied Informatics, Wroclaw University of Science and Technology,
Wrocław, Poland

Abstract. In recent years, the information technology has been greatly
developed and widely applied to many fields. Its application can be used
in product design, education and training, military, aerospace and entertainment fields. Currently, Virtual Reality (VR) and Augmented Reality (AR) are research trends, that can be used in the fields of simulation, game industry, medical training, virtual tourism or digital heritages,
etc. In this research project, we combine several techniques in computer
graphics, geometric modeling and image processing to build an application of both VR-based and AR-based. Our final product of this research is
an application of virtual museum simulation. The research work includes
exploring techniques for VR and AR software development as well as creating a sample product based on the studied framework. Specifically, we
construct a virtual museum that allows user to visualize and interact
with the statues in the museum. Using the Unity 3D is considered as
a powerful tool to build VR-applications. We also enhance it with AR
processing capabilities with android studio. The application provides an
interesting simulation of the Museum of Cham Sculpture (in Danang,
Vietnam). It is also compared with other existing applications.

Keywords: 3D objects reconstruction · 3D objects visualization ·
Digital heritage · Virtual reality (VR) · Augmented reality (AR)

1 Introduction

Cultural heritage is a common wealth of humanity. It tells us about the mankind
history, scientific development and evolution of our planet. How to protect the
cultural heritages is not only the duty of scientists but also the task and responsibility of every person. Recently, because of several reasons such as time, wars
and natural disasters, many cultural heritages were destroyed. For these reasons,

This research activity is funded by Vietnam National University in Ho Chi Minh City
(VNU-HCM) under the grant number C2021-28-08.

© Springer Nature Switzerland AG 2021
N. T. Nguyen et al. (Eds.): ICCCI 2021, LNAI 12876, pp. 613–625, 2021.
https://doi.org/10.1007/978-3-030-88081-1_46

they can be disappeared very fast out of the human life. In order to restore the cultural heritages for conserving, researching, digital heritage (DH) is one of the essential solution. As mentioned in [1], DH is well-known as a product made up of computer-based materials that can be kept and used for future generations. Using techniques in the fields of computer graphics and image processing, we can create and visualize the 3D model of DH products. Because of the several conditions like geographical distance, finance and even the Covid pandemic as in present, we cannot go to see the natural heritages directly. This is one of the reasons why more and more applications of VR and AR are currently being developed and became research trends in many scientific projects or game industry [2]. Instead of visiting in practice, we can touch and interact directly with the artifacts in a VR or AR application, by using a device of VR Headsets with its controllers or a smart phone. The 3D models of DH are built in the virtual environment [3]. They are controlled based on the graphical transformation steps of the 3D objects. Many applications are built to reconstruct (restore) the DH objects such as monuments, temples, cultural and historical relics. In Vietnam, many DH applications are buit such as cultural heritages, smart museums, 3D simulations, ets., [4]. They have been shown some limited features: show 2D images, 3D images and videos at specific museums. Due to this, our motivation is to create an interesting application, a virtual environment where we can be immersed in this world and interact directly with objects, instead of watching a picture on the monitor. Our contribution in this research paper is focused on processing 3D objects and building an application using VR and AR based on the Unity 3D [8]. The input data are 3D point cloud objects obtained from the Museum of Cham Sculpture in Danang, Vietnam. They are processed and simulated on a virtual environment for seeing and interacting based on the VR Headset (Oculus Quest). A mobile-app for AR on smart phone has also been created to provide additional information of the real sculptures for visitors. Comparing to the existing solutions in Vietnam [4], our application have shown more convenient and usable.

The remainder of the paper is structured as follows. Section 2 presents several researches, tools and techniques for building and visualizing VR and AR apps. Section 3 describes in detail our method for both AR and VR simulations. We present the implementation and obtained results in Sect. 4. Section 5 includes discussion and evaluation. The last section is our conclusion and future work.

2   Related Works

In this section, we review the existing researches and application of AR and VR. They are not only mentioned in the game industry but also in education application. The immersive nature of VR has been identified as a tool that facilitate the learning process [6]. The retailer Walmart is using virtual reality to train its employees [7], they are set in a virtual environment where they can prepare for a situation like dealing with rush crowds or cleaning up a mess made by a customer. Google has opened a VR expedition, the tool that allows a teacher to virtually bring his/her students to different places like Antarctica or even a space station. There is also its AR counterpart, where they can bring virtual elements to the classroom like a 3D version of the Earth. In the field of entertainment, many game applications and their online tutorials [5] often in Unity 3D [8] have been introduced. They can help users in exploring how to self-develop a game based on VR & AR and in studying how to share experiences between the game development community. In learning, there are fewer examples, though there is some promising work that explores how a virtual museum could emulate the social experience of visiting a physical museum by allowing learners to interact with virtual artefacts with VR or AR together [9]. In this research, Li et al. has shown an interesting point that learners can interact with artifacts that are moving in the virtual environment. The cooperation in this environment was not intentioned when handling objects on AR (e.g. rotate a model) while the VR application could not handle such tasks and they had to work together to share information. In the field of tourism, VR is used as a strong marketing tool. It can provide a full picture, an opportunity to attract more potential customers by offering a more compelling image of the destination, giving them a taste of what it is like to be there [6], especially to the types of exploration travel. In those cases, a VR application can present an exact simulation of these places. Therefore, it can help the tourists decide about where they want to travel and even enable them to consider destinations they never thought about. In AR, a mobile application associated with IKEA [10] allow you virtually place the IKEA products in your space [10]. The application allows user to setup environment, determine a location of the furniture such as sofas, armchairs, footstools or coffee tables in the room by using a smart phone. With the 3D and true-to-scale models, users can know how to choose a suitable one for their room and imagine how does it looks in the real room. The latest version of this application can directly scan the floor for determining a position of the furniture instead of using a maker as before. The research and development of virtual museums has been started two decades ago [11,12]. Initially, the virtual museum could only provide a simple hyper-link text with graphics which contained the basic information about the museum. However, as they begun to realize the potential of new technologies, they developed various contents and services to their visitors such as advanced using the multimedia, clips, animations, 3D collections and audio files. The application in [13] is an example for both viewing and interacting the virtual 3D objects. Missing information about data objects or noisy data in the obtained 3D objects (resulting during the use of acquisition techniques) always bring us problems in reconstructing step of the 3D objects. The holes on the surface of a 3D object is a case in this often occurring situations. The problem of hole filling and restoring the 3D shapes of real data objects have been solved by many researchers, e.g. a proposed method in [14]. Different solutions have been presented in [15] (for both determining the hole and recovering the missing data) that can be roughly classified according to the way in which the input data are given as a point cloud or a mesh. For another example, the method in [16] for filling the hole required a previous knowledge of the input model and focused on the hole filling problem of the CAD model. For this reason, the disadvantage of this algorithm is difficult to apply in data consisting of mesh models. To summarize, the benefits of context-based approaches is that they learn the characteristics of the given surface making them able to restore lost geometrical features without affecting the data consisting of mesh far from the hole. However, the drawbacks of these approaches are their deficiency of robustness in the case of noisy inputs and difficulty in preventing geometric overlaps. Also if they are not similar geometric patches in the meshes, the repaired surface is likely to be unreasonable.

2.1 Selected VR Framework

The selected framework for the application is the Unity 3D game engine [17]. It is developed based on the Unity SDK. CryEngine does not support mobile VR and Unreal Engine [18] only supports GearVR and Daydream. Unity also offers better ways to implement 360 footage. Unity has an active community and a thorough documentation that we can use (see Table 1)

Table 1. Comparison of the several frameworks

Game engine	Unreal (free)	Unity (free)
CPU	Quad-core Intel 2.5 GHz or faster	1 GHz or faster
RAM	8 GB (16 GB)	2 GB
Video card	Nvidia GeForce 470	GTX Basic

2.2 Selected Headset

In order to implement our application for VR, we use the Oculus Quest as a hardware device to perform the application because of its characteristics comparing to other devices (see Table 2):

Table 2. Comparison of VR headsets. All of them support the hand-controller

Headset	HTC vive	Oculus Rift S	Oculus quest
Storage	PC dependent	PC dependent	64 GB – 128 GB
Portability	No	No	Yes
RAM	PC dependent	PC dependent	4 GB
Resolution per eye	1440 × 1600	1280 × 1440	1440 × 1600
Refresh rate	90 Hz	80 Hz	72 Hz
Platform	SteamVR	SteamVR, Oculus	SteamVR, Oculus
Connectivity	1 HDMI + 2 USB 3.0	1 USB 3.0	Wi-Fi
Price	15.999.000 VND	14.999.000 VND	16.999.000 VND
PC requirements	- Graphic Card: NVIDIA GTX 970 - CPU: Intel i5-4590 - RAM: 8 GB - 2 USB 3.0	- Graphics Card: NVIDIA GTX 1060 - CPU: Intel i5-4590 - RAM: 8GB - 1 USB 3.0	

2.3   Selected AR SDK

Vuforia is the most popular SDK for developing AR-applications on a wide selection of devices [19]. The main features of Vuforia's Unity version include tracking, image recognition, object recognition, text recognition, video playback. The table below (see Table 3) shows the comparison with other AR SDKs:

Table 3. Comparison of AR SDKs [20]. They are supported by the unity.

	Kudan	AR toolkit	Apple ARKit	Vuforia
License	Free (W-Mark), Commercial	Free Open Source	Free	Free (W-Mark), Commercial
Supported platforms	Android, iOS	Android, iOS, Linux	iOS	Android, iOS, UWP
Cloud recognition	No	No	Yes	Yes (1,000 recos/month)
3D recognition	Yes	Yes	No	Yes

3   Our Proposed Method

3.1   Overview

The main idea of our proposed method is presented as follows: we use the techniques in computer graphic and image processing to construct a virtual museum for the VR application. An AR application is built to serve for user interacting with the real objects in the museum. The application is built using Unity 3D with the real data collected from the Museum of Cham Sculpture in Danang, Vietnam. The method is described in the following steps: (1) We collect data by using a digital camera to capture and scan the real statues in the museum (the output are images with and video frame sets). (2) The obtained data is then processed and convert into the 3D data objects with the format of .PLY files. (3) We design and construct a virtual museum based on the programming environment of Unity 3D (for both VR and AR applications). (4) The last step is performing functions to handle the 3D objects. Adding more functions that allow user interacting with digital heritages in virtual environment (e.g. show additional information, process color and manipulate the objects directly).

3.2   Workflow for VR

According to the system flow, interior design of a virtual room is first needed to model the virtual environment. In this study, a museum is chosen. The intended idea for the layouts of the showroom is sketched before creating a 3D model. After that, assets for the showroom, which include textures, images, 3D models, that are found as suitable for the showroom are imported. For example: in each room, we put each kind of digital heritages to represent each dynasty (Rome,

Cham, Asia). The following steps are added into the algorithm (Algorithm 1) of data processing.

Algorithm 1. Pseudocode for data processing
1: **Input**
2:    List of images (*.JPG, *.PNG...)
3: **Process:**
4:    Load images into software and Align photos
5:    Build dense point cloud
6:    Clean up point cloud files
7:    Build mesh (3D polygonal model)
8:    Generate texture and Export results
9: **Output:**
10:    Point cloud files (*.PLY)

The next algorithm (Algorithm 2) contains steps for building a virtual environment for our VR application. We use the API of Unity 3D to write many controlled functions to handle the statues.

Algorithm 2. Pseudocode for building VR
1: **Input**
2:    Point cloud or Mesh files (*.PLY)
3: **Process:**
4:    Create museum 3D model
5:    Create avatar & camera
6:    Add 3D models as furniture
7:    Add lighting, texture, light mapping & baking
8:    Add scripting to handle (select, rotate, change color)
9: **Output:**
10:    Virtual museum application

3.3 Workflow for AR

AR is the second application that we aim to implement in this research work. It is developed to make enhanced interactions of the digital heritage objects. We use Vuforia (an existing SDK for working and creating AR apps) to develop our AR application. It offers excellent tools for real-time marker tracking, which we take advantage of to handle the 3D objects based on the real context as follows. When a user comes to a museum and looks at the heritage objects which are missing some parts (e.g. the statues without leg, arm or head, etc.,), user can use our AR application to check by moving the smart phone over the statues. At that time, it will provide additional information about the heritages and load the missing part (leg, arm or head) to match them together for a full picture of the statues. We can also adjust directly the 3D object in the application. The next algorithm (Algorithm 3) details the process of building our AR application.

Algorithm 3. Pseudocode for building AR

1: **Input**
2:    Point cloud or Mesh files (*.PLY)
3: **Process:**
4:    Add target from image of real object
5:    Upload result to "Target Manager" on Vuforia
6:    Download these targets & add to Unity 3D
7:    Add functions to adjust (select, rotate, change color)
8: **Output:**
9:    AR application

---

4 Implementation and Results

4.1 Data Acquisition and Processing

In order to process input data of a set of images, we use the VisualSFM [21] (a free tool for academic that allows to take a series of images and create a 3D point cloud as output data) to handle the processing based on the following steps:

- Add photos: to add photos, we use the "Add Photos" option in the Workflow menu and select the ones chosen for processing.
- Align photos: At this stage VisualSFM estimates the camera position for each photo and builds the sparse point cloud. We use the Align Photos command in the Workflow menu. After finishing photo alignment, we refine bounding box position and orientation to fit the desired volume for reconstructing step. This step is optional since VisualSFM calculates bounding box dimensions, orientation and location automatically, but it is recommended to check if any correction is needed, because further reconstruction steps only deal with the data inside of the volume. Bounding box can be re-sized, moved and rotated with the support of Resize Region, Move Region and Rotate Region tools.
- Build dense cloud: based on the estimated camera positions the program calculates depth information for each camera to be combined into a single dense point cloud. We use the Build Dense Cloud command in the Workflow menu.
- Build mesh: after dense point cloud has been reconstructed, it is possible to generate polygonal mesh model based on the dense cloud data or depth maps data. The second approach supports GPU-acceleration and mostly provides a better results for the same depth maps quality of objects and scenes with big number of minor details. We use Build Mesh command in the work-flow menu.
- Build texture: we use the Build Texture command in the Workflow menu. To export model, we use the Export Model command in the File menu and in the Export Model in the dialog box, select options to export the 3D model.

4.2   Building a VR Application

This application is developed based on Unity 3D and Oculus Quest SDK that support some functions: position tracking, hand tracking, hand controllers. After loading application, user can enter at main entrance, and then they can go through 3 rooms connected together: Ancient Greece and Rome, Ancient Egypt and Ancient Asia. In each room, they can see many cultural heritages (pictures, statues) put along the walls. They can use hand controllers or walk directly along the wall. Pointing a laser from controller to each part on the statues will allow them to see additional information that are displayed after clicking, while holding the button allows to rotate the statue.

A museum 3D model: at the beginning, we design and draw layout for a museum with three rooms with different heritages inside. After drawing the layout, we create a museum 3D model by using a Sweet Home 3D. This is a free interior design software application that allows planning and developing the floor plans; as well as the ability to arrange furniture inside for viewing in 3D space.

Create the Virtual Environment: starting Unity 3D and creating a new 3D project. We use all files (3D model, textures, etc.) that were created in the previous step. We add the 3D model to the hierarchy. We also add the OVR PlayerController to the hierarchy. Finally, we set the original location of the FPS GameObject in the 3D museum.

- Adding furniture: we create more furniture for a room such as: doors, columns, items, symbols
- Point lights: the model is not imported to Unity with any kind of light. Without any light the scene will look dark and dull. Adding lights is required for convincing and realistic feeling.
- Spot lights: as a point light, a spot light has a specified location and range over which the light falls off. However, the spot light is constrained to an angle, resulting in a cone-shaped region of illumination. The center of the cone points in the z direction of the light object. Light also diminishes at the edges of the spot light's cone. Extending the angle, increasing the width of the cone and the size of this fade are known as the 'penumbra'.
- Lightmapping: using Unity's Light-mapping system instead on relying on real-time lights, especially for the interior part of the building where you need multiple lights to fully enlighten the rooms. Light-mapping is a technique where the lightening is calculated in advance and captured in additional layer of textures that are mixed with the regular material.
- Wallwashers: the distance from the wall (for wallwashers) is one third of the room height to achieve a uniform light distribution on the wall. The luminaire spacing is the same as the wall offset. For a balanced illumination of the room and the exhibition, uniform wallwashing for a bright impression of the room is combined with accent lighting for a good model of sculptures in the room.
- Raycast: we used raycast to display laser from handcontroller that is pointing to an object.

– Tooltip/dialog: the important thing to create tooltip/dialog for each object in museum is the scale border of window, which allows us to force the resolution, but not scale all the parts of our image. This helps maintain the original appearance of the image.

Interaction with digital heritages (Fig. 1): when everything in the virtual showroom has been set, the next step is to create interactivity in the showroom. To create the interactivity in the virtual scene, we write functions based on C# source codes (Change color (Fig. 1b); Show tooltip/dialog of all/part of model (Fig. 1a) and Rotation of model). The final VR application is presented as in Fig. 3.

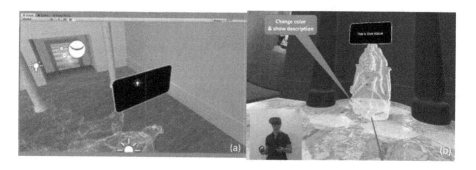

Fig. 1. (a) Using the Sprite Editor to define the window dialog; (b) Raycast & Change color & Show dialog of Siva statue

4.3 Building an AR Application

Object recognition: the target image and object should already be uploaded to Vuforia's developer portal before continuing with the project. Next part required is the target object. To make this object pop out in the image target is very simple in Unity, just drag the object from resource folder and drop it to the Image Target which makes object its child object. According to the size and position required, the object can later be configured from its properties. The next step for the developer is to select the image target. There needs to be at least one Database and one Image target. Developers can also twist different behaviors of objects through the properties menu. (see Fig. 2)

Adding Scripts: in order to add more functions on the applications, the scrips in the Unity 3D allows the user to add programmed source codes to create more interaction or make the scenes with the objects more realistic to the objects. This helps to trigger the game objects, modify component's properties over time and respond to user input. The scripts are compiled based on Visual Studio IDE, an external code editor. The source codes are written in C# programming language. Adding script to the object is easy, which can be set by selecting the target object which needs to be programmed and from the inspector view, use the add component option to add a New Script with a custom name. The only part needed to be programmed here is the GameObject which must move according to the MobileJoyStick and the animations according to the movement. In Unity 3D, to move a GameObject, the easiest method is to get the Vector of the object and transform it by adding velocity to its movement.

Fig. 2. The obtained result of our AR application: (a) a picture without head of the statue (as a maker); (b) moving the smart phone over the maker, the head of statue will appear; (c) showing the head at the right position.

5   Discussion and Evaluation

5.1   Data Acquisition by Photogrammetry

The photogrammetry application is not really new, it is a popular technique in the 3D printer community. Unlike the other methods, this tool provides information within an image that is used to create a model. There is no limitation on the quality or number of images but the hardware is the limiting factor required as an important condition. Some objects we tested that showed good results: natural stone, trees, ground (streets, paths, etc.), fruit (apples), buildings on a larger scale (complete building and not just single walls), car interior (depending on the surface, polished surfaces are hard to capture, but the normal plastic surfaces with a bit of roughness work well). On the other hand, there are some difficult objects to scan: car exterior (little to no texture, shiny surfaces, glass, reflections, etc.), rooms (large areas like walls without texture).

5.2   Disadvantages of Unity 3D

The Unity 3D is a very useful environment for game building or creating a VR application. However, there are many disadvantages such as the user not being able to access the source code directly. Lighting settings are not convenient as in other game engines (e.g. Unreal Engine). Another weak point of the Unity 3D is designing the open world games. Editing terrain and object placements are not strong point when compared to other engines. Users can use the engine for free in research or education but for better quality settings, there is a paid license.

Fig. 3. Our VR application: (a) entering the room; (b) controlling the statues

5.3   Disadvantage of Vuforia SDK

The license fee is one of the main drawbacks of Vuforia SDK (e.g. the license cost is about \$499 for each application). The next disadvantage is requiring a printed marker to kickstart the augmentation. Although the marker recognition for 3D tracking has several benefits, the use of 2D images for augmentation can become slightly restricted when you present a model application remotely, or outside setting. The printed marker also limits the size of the AR visualization to the confines of paper size. Therefore, it prevents the user from having seamless walkthrough demonstrations without large-scale industrial printouts (Table 4).

5.4   Comparing to Other 3D Museums

Table 4. Comparing to other 3D museums

	Smart museums	Virtual museum 3D	VR3D	VR and AR museum App
Device	Smart phone	Website	Website	VR: 3D VR headset, AR: Smartphone
Viewscreen	3D artifacts	3D artifacts, videos, panorama pictures,	3D artifacts	Virtual space, 3D artifacts
Interaction	Zoom, Rotate	Zoom, Rotate, Voice, Video	Zoom, Rotate	Change color, Zoom, Rotate, show description
Support data				Point Cloud

6   Conclusion and Future Work

In this research project, we have researched and built the VR and AR apps which applied the following processes: scanning, processing and transferring the data into the VR and AR apps. In the scanning phase, it is important to collect enough data such that it covers as much of the shape of the real object as possible. Multiple scans should be used to cover blind spots of the scanner. The quality of scanning makes the most considerable difference in the final model. The goal of the processing phase is to reduce the amount of noisy data and obtain the last model that is as accurate as possible. The next process is to create a VR application for user visualization and interaction. A game engine and toolkits are used to make the process effortless. The final product is an application that can be transferred and executed anywhere with suitable VR equipment and software. Additionally, we have researched and implemented an AR application as a mobile app. First, we have analyzed and compared each approach that can be taken while making a mobile AR application. In the next step, we have studied and proposed a solution after reviewing necessary tools to develop it. With knowledge gained in this research, we have successfully designed an AR app and run fine on the Android-based smart phone.

In general, the two proposed application in this research bring us the motivation for future work. It will open a new research in the trends of using new techniques in VR and AR applications. Combining knowledge in different fields in IT to produce a new application that not only supports researchers in research activities but also help us to improve technical skills. We will improve and finish the application that focuses on reconstruction of the real heritage objects in practice. One of necessary improvements in the VR area would be investment in the hand controller. This function will create more attractive interaction for the users. Further research plans involve processing the voice recognition, adding music and introduction to support users visiting the museum. We might also attempt to submit this application to Unity VR service. If successful, it could be considered as our free contribution to the research communities.

Acknowledgment. This research activity is funded by Vietnam National University in Ho Chi Minh City (VNU-HCM) under the grant number C2021-28-08. We would like to thank for the funding and support from the International University, HCMIU.

References

1. Wang, X., et al.: Digital heritage. In: Guo, H., Goodchild, M.F., Annoni, A. (eds.) Manual of Digital Earth, pp. 565–591. Springer, Singapore (2020). https://doi.org/10.1007/978-981-32-9915-3_17
2. Scurati, G.W., Bertoni, M., Graziosi, S., Ferrise, F.: Exploring the use of virtual reality to support environmentally sustainable behavior: a framework to design experiences. J. Sustain. **13**(2), (2021). ISSN: 2071–1050, https://doi.org/10.3390/su13020943
3. Shehade, M., Stylianou-Lambert, T.: Virtual reality in museums: exploring the experiences of museum professionals. J. Appl. Sci. **10**, 4031 (2020) https://doi.org/10.3390/app10114031

4. 3D cultural heritages in Vietnam (VR3D). https://vr3d.vn/en/cultural-heritage-3d. Accessed Mar 2021
5. AR&VR in online training. www.evolvear.io. Accessed Mar 2021
6. Tussyadiah, I.P., Wang, D., Jia, C.H.: Virtual reality and attitudes toward tourism destinations. In: Schegg, R., Stangl, B. (eds.) Information and Communication Technologies in Tourism 2017, pp. 229–239. Springer, Cham (2017). https://doi.org/10.1007/978-3-319-51168-9_17
7. Walmart is using virtual reality to train its employees. www.businessinsider.com/walmart-using-virtual-reality-employee-training-2017-6. Accessed Mar 2021
8. AR&VR Game Homepage. unity.com/solutions/ar-and-vr-games. Accessed Mar 2021
9. Li, Y., Ch'ng, E., Cai, S., See, S.: Multiuser interaction with hybrid VR and AR for cultural heritage objects. In: 2018 3rd Digital Heritage International Congress (DigitalHERITAGE) held Jointly with 2018 24th International Conference on Virtual Systems & Multimedia (VSMM 2018), pp. 1–8. IEEE, San Francisco, CA, USA (2018). https://doi.org/10.1109/DigitalHeritage.2018.8810126
10. Ozturkcan, S.: Service innovation: using augmented reality in the IKEA place app. J. Inf. Technol. Teach. Cases (2020). https://doi.org/10.1177/2043886920947110
11. Wojciechowski, R., Walczak, K., White, M., Cellary, W.: Building virtual and augmented reality museum exhibitions. In: Web3D Symposium Proceedings, pp. 135–144 (2004). https://doi.org/10.1145/985040.985060
12. Mata Rivera, M., Claramunt, C., Juarez, A.: An experimental virtual museum based on augmented reality and navigation, pp. 497–500 (2011). https://doi.org/10.1145/2093973.2094058
13. Lepouras, G., Charitos, D., Vassilakis, C., Charissi, A., Halatsi, L.: Building a VR-museum in a museum, 8 (2001)
14. Van Nguyen, S., Tran, H.M., Maleszka, M.: Geometric modeling: background for processing the 3d objects. Appl. Intell. **51**(8), 6182–6201 (2021). https://doi.org/10.1007/s10489-020-02022-6
15. Guo, X., Xiao, J., Wang, Y.: A survey on algorithms of hole filling in 3D surface reconstruction. Vis. Comput. **34**(1), 93–103 (2016). https://doi.org/10.1007/s00371-016-1316-y
16. Quinsat, Y., lartigue, C.: Filling holes in digitized point cloud using a morphing-based approach to preserve volume characteristics. Int. J. Adv. Manuf. Technol. **1**, 411–421 (2015). https://doi.org/10.1007/s00170-015-7185-0
17. Takoordyal K.: Introduction to Unity. In: Beginning Unity Android Game Development. Apress, Berkeley, CA (2020). https://doi.org/10.1007/978-1-4842-6002-9_2
18. Pv S.: Introduction to Unreal Engine 4. Beginning unreal engine 4 blueprints visual scripting. Apress, Berkeley, CA (2021). https://doi.org/10.1007/978-1-4842-6396-9_1
19. Sarosa, M., Chalim, A., Suhari, S., Sari, Z., Hakim, H.: Developing augmented reality based application for character education using unity with Vuforia SDK. J. Phys. Conf. Ser. **1375**, 012035 (2019). https://doi.org/10.1088/1742-6596/1375/1/012035
20. Nowacki, P., Woda, M.: Capabilities of ARCore and ARKit Platforms for AR/VR Applications. Presented at the 01/2020. https://doi.org/10.1007/978-3-030-19501-4_36
21. Wu, C.: VisualSFM: A Visual Structure from Motion System. http://ccwu.me/vsfm. Accessed Mar 2021

Natural Language Processing

Morphology Model and Segmentation for Old Turkic Language

Dinara Zhanabergenova$^{(\boxtimes)}$ ⓘ and Ualsher Tukeyev ⓘ

Al-Farabi Kazakh National University, Almaty, Kazakhstan

Abstract. Old Turkic language is the basis of all modern Turkic languages. Its study is very important for Turkic peoples who possess modern Turkic languages. This is important both from a historical point of view and for the study of modern issues of neural machine translation, issues of the linguistic distance of modern Turkic languages from their progenitor. This paper proposes the development of a computational model of the morphology of Old Turkic language based on the CSE (Complete Set of Endings) – model of morphology and a study on this basis of the issue of morphological segmentation of the texts of Old Turkic language, which will subsequently be used for neural machine translation of Old Turkic language into modern Turkic languages. Since most of the modern Turkic languages, except for the Turkish language, belong to low-resource languages, the issues of developing computational models of morphology, developing models, algorithms and software for processing Turkic languages are relevant.

Keywords: Old Turkic language · Turkic languages · Morphological segmentation · Stemming · Complete set of endings

1 Introduction

Turkic languages belong to one of the biggest language families, which includes 35 officially documented languages. It is spoken natively by more than 200 million people in Turkey, Azerbaijan, Kazakhstan, Kyrgyzstan, Uzbekistan, Tajikistan, Turkmenistan and as a second language in some areas of Russia, China and the Caucasus. Turkic language family includes the languages as Turkish (80 million), Azerbaijani (23 million), Kazakh (13 million), Uzbek (24 million), Kyrgyz (4.5 million) and many others.

The motivation for the ongoing research on the ancient Turkic language is the significant interest of the peoples of the Turkic languages in the study of the PraTurkic language, in the knowledge of historical materials written in Old Turkic language. For this purpose, this work proposes the construction of a computational model of morphology of Old Turkic language based on the CSE (Complete Set of Endings)-model [1], which allows using universal programs of stemming, morphological segmentation, morphological analysis [2], to perform neural machine translation Old Turkic language into modern Turkic languages.

A novel contribution of this work is the construction of computational CSE-model of Old Turkic language, the study of stemming of words and morphological segmentation

© Springer Nature Switzerland AG 2021
N. T. Nguyen et al. (Eds.): ICCCI 2021, LNAI 12876, pp. 629–642, 2021.
https://doi.org/10.1007/978-3-030-88081-1_47

of texts of Old Turkic language. The obtained experimental results of morphological segmentation of texts of Old Turkic language using the constructed computational CSE-model show, on average, 94% accuracy.

2 Related Works

The morphological segmentation task was presented in work [3]. Most of the study has introduced the surface segmentation task, involving unsupervised methods as LINGUISTICA [4] and Morfessor [5, 6] played a significant role. The Morfessor method was lately expanded to a semi-supervised version [7]. Rule-based methods were used often for morphological segmentation with low resources, since they do not require huge amounts of data. They have been created, for example, using tools such as the finite state transducer (FST) like FOMA [8] or HFST [9].

Efforts to build unsupervised, morphologically aware segmentations mostly originate from the Morfessor family of morphological segmentation tools. Besides the extensions of Morfessor, as Cognate Morfessor, in [10] and [11] are presented the LMVR (Linguistically Motivated Vocabulary Reduction) model, which was originated from Morfessor FlatCat, and used it to NMT tasks on Arabic, Czech, German, Italian, Turkish and English, linking that LMVR surpasses a BPE (Byte-Pair Encoding) in BLEU (Bilingual Evaluation Understudy) and CHRF3 (character n-gram F-score, where the recall has three times more weight). However, contrary to their results, [12] found that applying LMVR gave mixed results: when performing the task of NMT from Kazakh to English, the authors noted slight improvements in BLEU compared to BPE, while for English-Kazakh, the authors observed that LMVR is slightly worse than BPE in terms of CHRF3.

In addition to above, there were conducted studies on combining linguistically motivated approaches with BPE. For example, [13] suggested merging BPE with different linguistic heuristics as suffix, prefix and compound splitting. The authors have done experiments with English-German and German-English pairs and noticed a performance advancement of about 0.5 BLEU compared to the baseline for BPE only. As another case, [14] merged BPE with a complete morphological analysis on the source and target sides of an English-German NMT task, and observed performance changes surpassing one BLEU point over a BPE-only approach.

Some systems concentrate on revealing morphologically related word pairs, as (stop, stopped), and then convert the output into morpheme segmentations so that they are consistent with the available segmentation-based estimation. Such works include [15, 16]. These systems have the benefit of finding morphologically related word sets, which is identical to finding roots for complex words.

At last, in spite of the fact that [17] initially applied the NMT training set for training their morphological segmentation model; others have lately found advantage in including monolingual data to the method. In specific, [18] applied both Morfessor and SentencePiece as segmentation models on an Upper Sorbian–German NMT and found a monotonic increment in BLEU when the segmentation model has been trained with extra information, whereas at the same time keeping the NMT training information consistent.

3 General Characteristics of Old Turkic Language

As with every worldwide nation and language, Turkic nations have their own history of development and formation. An article [19] divides the general stages of development of the Turkic languages into six stages:

1. Altai era.
2. Hun era (III century BC – V century BC).
3. Old Turkic era (V-X centuries).
4. Middle Ages (X-XV centuries).
5. New era (XV-XX centuries).
6. Late era.

The vital influence on the grammatical structure of modern Turkic languages was made in the Old Turkic era. Old Turkic language is the language of the peoples, which are the basis of modern Turkic peoples. The main data are preserved in ancient Turkic inscriptions (5th-8th centuries). The period of writing of the Orkhon-Yenisei inscriptions corresponds to the "Old Turkic period". The main types of old Turkic inscriptions are preserved in the form of carved inscriptions, especially on the tombstones of the Turkic kagans as Bilge kagan, Kultegin, Tonykok (V-VIII centuries) are used expressive inscriptions. It is considered as a book written on stone, which is the initial official source for Turkic languages [20].

Grammatical structure, exactly the morphology and syntax of old Turkic inscriptions is similar to all of the modern Turkic languages. Depending on the composition of the words in the monuments are divided into five groups: base(root) words, derivatives, double words, compound words and complex words. The words in the written versions are divided into the following word groups called part-of-speeches in terms of meaning, personality and function: nouns, adjectives, pronouns, numerals, verbs, adverbs, conjunctions, interdependencies.

Nouns in the inscription have the forms of the number, case, personal and possessiveness. They do not have the form of gender and person.

There is no difference between the adjectives in the Orkhon-Yenisey inscriptions and the adjectives in modern Turkic languages. In Old Turkic language there are three levels of adjectives: simple (sary – yellow), comparative (ten'riteg – deeper), and superlative(en'ilki – the biggest). Adjectives in monuments serve as attributes [21].

Numerals occur often in the monuments because there are several descriptions of days, years and military. Based on the structure, numerals in Orkhon-Yenisey the monuments are classified into individuals (uch – three) and complex (ieti iuz – seven hundred). Numerals in Old Turkic inscriptions are divided according to their meaning as follows: Cardinal numerals (bes, otuz – five, thirty), Ordinal numbers (uchinch – third), Fractional numbers, collective (uchegu – three of them), mixed (uch otuz – twenty-three), predictive numerals (uchdey – probably three).

Pronouns by the meaning are classified into personal (men, sen – I, you), reference (bul – this), query pronoun (kim – who), indefinite pronoun (keibir – some), negative pronoun (eshkim – no one).

Verbs are considered the most difficult part of speech by its lexical meaning and the morphological structure. By structure, verbs are divided into base (ait – say) and derivative (sana – count). Verbs have the forms of negative, tense, mood, voice, participle, adverbials.

Adverbs are divided into base (uze – beyond) and derivative (beriye – to the right) by the morphological structure. By their meaning, adverbs are classified as follows: time (kiche – late), local (sheg – far), quantitative (azcha – little bit), descriptive (egere – around).

In the Orkhon-Yenisei inscriptive monuments, different types of sentences occur. Firstly, by the meaning and expressional features sentences are divided into narrative, exclamatory, interrogative. All words in sentences have a fixed position in the sentence; each word has its serve. For example, a verb, which serves as a predicate, occurs at the end of a sentence. Subject is the main member of sentences; it can be expressed through noun, pronoun, and participles and mostly occurs in the beginning of the sentence. Attributes define the subject, expressed through mostly adjectives, numerals and participles and positioned behind the subject. Adverbial describes the feature of action, mostly describes the predicate and expressed through the adverbs and adverbials. In addition, there is object, which gives the additional information in the sentences. All the syntax features from Old Turkic language are observed in the modern Turkic languages.

4   Development of CSE-model of Old Turkic Language

In this section the morphological structure of Old Turkic language from the Orkhon-Yenisei monument is analyzed, which makes it possible to build the CSE-model. The CSE-model of Turkic languages, the approach that proposed in [1] is applied.

The endings in Old Turkic language, as in all modern languages in Turkic group, are classified to nominal endings and verbal endings. Nominal based endings involve nouns, numerals, adjectives and adverbs [22]. Verb based endings involve verbs, tenses, participles, voices, mood. In this work, in order to obtain endings, a combinatorial approach is applied, counting the law of harmony of sounds and semantically possible.

In Old Turkic language, the nominal endings system includes three types of affixes: Plural affixes (denoted by K), Possessive affixes (denoted by T), Case affixes (denoted by C), Personal affixes (denoted by J). These affixes can appear in combination with others. The quantity of several placements of these affixes is calculated by the next formula:

$$A_{nk} = n!/(n-k)!; \qquad (1)$$

$$A_{41} = 4!/(4-1)! = 4, \quad A_{42} = 4!/(4-2)! = 12, \quad A_{43} = 4!/(4-3)! = 24, \quad A_{43} = 4!/(4-4)! = 24 \qquad (2)$$

The number of all possible combinations is 64. However, not all of the possible sequences of affixes can be semantically valid. Each ending with only one type of affix (K, T, C, J) is semantically right by definition. The number of one-type affixes is presented in Table 1.

The semantically valid two-affix combinations are six from 12 possible ending placements: KT, KC, KJ, TC, TJ, and CJ.

The semantically valid three-affix combination is four from 12 possible ending placements: KTC, KTJ, KCJ, and TCJ.

The semantically valid four-affix combination is one from 12 possible ending placements: KTCJ. Thereby, the complete number of nominal-based endings is 15(4 + 6 + 4 + 1). Below in Tables 2, 3, 4 and 5 are presented examples of the inferring of endings for some kinds of placements of affix types.

Table 1. One-type nominal based suffixes

Suffix type	Ending in old Turkic	Number
K	-lar	2
	-ler	
T	-ym, im, um, úm, m	22
	-ymyz,imiz, myz, miz	
	-yń,iń,uń,úń, ń	
	-yńyz, ińiz, ńyz, ńiz	
	-y, i, sy,si	
C	-yń, iń, ń	34
	-qa, ke, ġaru, geru, a, e, ra, re, ia, ie	
	-yġ, ig, g, ġ, ni, ny	
	-da, de, ta, te, nda, nde, nta, nte	
	-dan, den, tan, ten	
	-yn, in, n	
J	-myń, syń, syz,	12
	myz,syńlar,syzlar;	
	-miń,siń,siz, miz,sińler,sizder;	

Examples: apa-m-yń; apa-m-a; apa-m-ny; ana-m-da; ana-m-dan; ana-m-yn.

Thus, the total number of nominal-based endings – 1192. Without the one type placements-1122.

The set of verb-based endings in Old Turkic language involves the following types: set of verb endings, set of participle endings, set of verb adverbial endings, set of moods endings, and set of voices endings.

The verb endings system consists the next types:

- Tense type suffixes (8 types):
- Person with number type suffixes (4 types): 1 person, 2 person, 2 person (formal), 3 person.
- Negation type suffixes (two types): ma, me.

Table 2. Examples for sequences of nominal endings in old Turkic

Type	Examples	Number
KT	Budun+lar+ym	16
	Beg+ler+i	
KC	Budun+lar+qa	12
	Beg+ler+iń	
TC	Budun+y+da	144
	Beg+ler+in	
KTC	Budun+lar+y+dan	96
	Beg+ler+i+de	

Table 3. Inferring of endings for 2-type placement TC (possessive-case)

Examples	Suffix type T				Suffix type C		Number of endings
	Last sound (Sońǵy dybys)						
	Juan (solid)	Jiniśke (soft)	Juan (deaf)	Jiniśke (voiced)	Case name	Case suffixes	
	T1)-m, myz; T2)-ń, ńyz; T3)-ńyz; T4)-sy	-m, miz; -ń,ńyz; -ńiz -si	-ym, um, ymyz; -yń, uń, yńyz; -yńyz; -y	-im, ún, imiz; -iń, ún, ińiz; -ińiz; -i	1. nom 2. gen 3. dat 4. acc 5. loc 6. abl 7.instr	- -yń, iń, ń; -a, e, qa, ke, ia, ie; -n, ny, ni, yǵ, ig, g, ǵ; -da, de, nda, nde; -dan, den; -n, in, yn;	24 * 6 = 144
ana-	-m-				2,3,5,6,7-	-yń, a, ny, da, dan, yn;	6
kisi-		-m-			2,3,4,5,6,7	-iń, e, ni, de, den, in;	6
budun-			-ym-		2,3,4,5,6,7	-yń, a, ny, da, dan, yn;	6
kúlúk-				-im-	2,3,4,5,6,7	- iń, e, ni, de, den, in;	6

Table 4. Inferring of endings for type placement KTC (plural-possessive-case)

Suffix type K	Suffix type T	Suffix type C		Number of endings
-lar	T1- ym, im; um, úm; ymyz, imiz;	1. nom	-	K-T1-C: 2 * 3 * 6 = 36
-ler	T2- yń, iń; uń, úń; yńyz, ińiz;	2. gen	-yń, iń, ń;	K-T2-C: 2 * 3 * 6 = 36 K-T3-C: 2 * 2 * 6 = 24
	T3- y, I; sy, si;	3. dat	-a, e, qa, ke, ia, ie;	
		4. acc	-ny, ni, yg, ig, g, ġ;	
		5. loc	-da, de, nda, nde;	Total: 96
		6. abl	-dan, den;	
		7. inst	-n, yn, in	

Table 5. Inferring of endings for type placement KTCJ (plural-possessive-case-personal)

Examples	Suffix type K	Suffix type T		Suffix type C	Suffix type J		Number of endings
		Dauyssyz (consonants)			Singular	Plural	
		Juan (deaf)	Jiniśke (voiced)				
	K1-lar; K2-ler;	T1 -ym; T2 -yń; T3 -yńyz; T4 -y	-im; -iń; -ińiz; -i	3) barys (dat) -qa, ke, na, ne 5) jatys (loc)- da, de, nda,nde; 6) śygys (abl)-dan,den; 7)komektes (inst) - yn, in, n	J1)- myn, min J2)- syń, siń; J3)-syz, siz;	-myz, miz; -syńlar, sińler; -syzlar, sizler	Links: K1-T-C-J: 4 * 4 * 6 = 96 K2-T-C-J: 4 * 4 * 6 = 96 Total: 96 * 2 = 192
ana-	-lar	-ym, yń, yńyz, y-		-3,5,6,7-	- J1,J2,J3	- J1, J2, J3	4 * 4 * 6 = 96
ini-	-ler		-im, iń, ińiz, i-	-3,5,6,7-	- J1,J2,J3	- J1, J2, J3	4 * 4 * 6 = 96

There is a certain set of suffixes for each of these types. A combinatorial approach is used to describe the various variants of the combinations (placements) of the types

Table 6. Inferring of endings for voices

Type of voice	Examples	Suffixes of voice	Suffixes (jedel ótken śaq)	1 person	2 person	2 person (polit)	3 person	Number of endings
Reflexive (Ózdik)	ju- kı- tara-	-yn- -in- -n-	-dy,di-	-m; myz -m; miz -m; myz	-ń; ńlar, -ń; ńler; -ń; ńlar	-ńyz; ńyzlar -ńiz; ńizler -ńyz; ńyzler	– – –	3 * 7 = 21
Passive (Yryqsyz)	ju- kı- tara-	-yl- -il- -l-	-dy,di;	-m; myz -m; miz -m; myz	-ń; ńlar, -ń; ńler; -ń; ńlar	-ńyz; ńyzlar -ńiz; ńizler -ńyz; ńyzler	– – –	3 * 7 = 21
Joint (Ortaq)	jaz- kór- qara-	-ys- -is- -s-	-ty,ti;	-m; myz -m; miz -m; myz	-ń; ńlar, -ń; ńler; -ń; ńlar	-ńyz; ńyzlar -ńiz; ńizler -ńyz; ńyzler	– – –	3 * 7 = 21
Compulsory (Ózgelik)	jaz- kı- aıt- juyn- kıin- śap- sep- qara-	-ǵyz,giz; -qyz,kiz; -dyr,dir; -tyr,tir;	-dy,di- -ty,ti-	-m; myz -m; miz	-ń; ńlar, -ń; ńler;	-ńyz; ńyzlar -ńiz; ńizler	– –	9 * 7 = 63

of the suffix, considering the sequences of types, the harmonizing laws of the set of the sounds of types.

The combinatorial approach is applied for the system of participle endings as for the nominal-based endings. The system of participle endings consists of: base participle affixes (denoted as R); possessive affixes (T); plural affixes (K); case affixes (C), personal affixes (J). Then, considering potential variants of placements of affixes types (base participle affixes are the same for all variants) on semantic validity. There is defines next sequence of placements: for sequence of valid one-type affixes; RT, RK, RC, RJ – for sequence of valid two-type affixes; RKT, RKC, RTC, RKJ, RCJ – for sequence of valid three-type affixes; RKTC, RKCJ – for sequence of valid four-type affixes. Therefore, the number of valid placements of participle endings is 11.

Table 7. Total number of verb-based endings

Type of verbal ending	Number
Verb	218
Participle	1680
Adverbial verb	12
Mood	24
Voice	126
Total	2060

The same combinatorial approach is used for the set of endings of verbs, verbal adverbs, moods, and voices to define different options for combining affixes, taking into account sequences of types, suffixes of person, harmonizing law of sequences, sounds of types.

The same combinatorial approach is used for the set of endings of verbs, verbal adverbs, moods, and voices to define different options for combining affixes, taking into account sequences of types, suffixes of person, harmony law of sequences, sounds of types (Table 6).

Total number of verb-based endings is 2060 (Table 7). Complete set of word endings – 3252 (1192 + 2060).

5 Stemming and Morphological Segmentation of Old Turkic Language

In order to use the morphological segmentation on the base of CSE-model it is necessary to collect linguistic resources. The CSE-model based morphological segmentation consists of two stages: 1) splitting words into stems and endings, and 2) segmentation

Table 8. Segment of relational decision table of Old Turkic endings segmentation

Word ending	Suffix components
ġanlarymyzdan	ġan@@lar@@ymyz@@dan
ġanlarymyzyń	ġan@@lar@@ymyz@@yń
laryńyzqa	lar@@yńyz@@qa
larymda	lar@@ym@@da
ynda	y@@nda
ym	ym
sy	sy
i	i

Table 9. Example for morphological segmentation of Old Turkic language with CSE-model

Iteration	Word splitting into stem and ending on each iteration	Explanation
1	bu-dunymyzdan	There is no match for "dunymyzdan" from first column of the table with endings list
2	bud-unymyzdan	There is no match for "unymyzdan" from first column of the table with endings list
3	budu-nymyzdan	There is no match for "nymyzdan" from first column of the table with endings list
4	budun-ymyzdan	There is a match for "ymyzdan" and the word is split with this ending and stem
Result: Returning segmented sequence of suffixes from the second column of table with old Turk endings		budun@@ymyz@@dan

endings to component suffixes. Both stages work with the help of a complete set of endings. In first stage, in stemming of words is used the constructed list of complete set of endings of Old Turkic language. In the second stage is used relational decision table of segmentation of endings of Old Turkic language on affixes, separated by characters @@ (Table 8).

In the first stage, the considered word is processed with the stemming universal program [2].

For the second stage is used universal segmentation program based on the relational decision table of segmentation of endings of Old Turkic language [2].

The segmenting algorithm, which divides word's ending into component suffixes, includes two steps: searching the ending of analyzed words in the complete table of endings of Old Turkic language and returning segmented sequence of suffixes of matched ending. Table 9 demonstrates the example of steps and results of morphological segmentation of Old Turkic language based on its CSE-model.

In order to execute the morphological segmentation, it is recommended to use a dictionary of stop words, which cannot be segmented as the suffixes. Because, there might be the possibility that the word as the base might have the symbols as some suffixes and algorithms can segment this word incorrectly. For example, there is a word "buyn", result of segmentation the word is split as 'bu@y@n' (TC). However, in the context, the word "buyn" is considered as a whole stem. Thus, the CSE-model based segmentation requires the list of stop words as well as a table of complete endings.

Stop words, in terms of morphological analysis and segmentation, are types of words that cannot be divided into components. The word base, adverbials, conjunctions are considered as stop words (Table 10). The stop words of Old Turkic language have been collected in a separate file. This file includes the stop words of adverbials (10 words), participle (25 words), conjunctions (13 words), and complex verb derivatives (4 words).

Table 10. Possible stop words in Old Turkic language

Part of speech		Example
Adverbials		teg, ók, óń, arqa, qody,ioqary,úze,kúndiz,ebrú, iany
Participles		ben, men, sin, sen, siz, ol, biz, olar, kach, ne, neke, anteg, bu, sol, óz,
		neń, bary, úkúl, qai, qandai, neshe, anau, sonau, kim, ár
Complex	Verb	túr, iúr,iatyr, olur
Derivatives		
Conjunctions		tegi, úchún, ótrú, kisre, saiyn, iane,da, de, ta, te, siyaqty, soń, búryn
Total		52

6 Experiments and Results

In the experimental part, the morphological segmentation on the base of CSE-model of Old Turkic language were tested. For testing, 100 sentences of Old Turkic language (overall words number-1635) were received, and checking was executed with incorrect segmentation of the words (Table 11). The texts have been collected mainly from the books [23] and [24] and typed manually, because there is no available electronic version of the book. The typed text was composed into five texts in order to better control.

There are two options for calculating the accuracy of segmented text. First option is to take the segmented file, which was made by the result of the segmentation program, and count the incorrect segmented words by hand. Second option is writing a special program for counting accuracy automatically, which defines the difference between two files. There was chosen the second option, which counts the accuracy, by the written

Table 11. Description of texts for segmentation

Resource[a]	Count of total words		Correct segmentation	Accuracy
Text-1	227		219	96,5%
Text-2	436		400	91,7%
Text-3	380		354	93,2%
Text-4	378		348	92%
Text-5	214		208	97,2%

[a] https://github.com/dinaraZh/OldTurkicSegmentation/.

formula. All of the accuracy percentages of each segmented file are stored and added in one file. Based on every percentage, the average of accuracy is calculated. In order to execute this method, a file is requested, which is tagged manually and is the correct version of segmentation. Let this file be called a "check file". The segmented file by the segmentation program is then compared with the "check file" and the difference between two files is counted. This difference count is considered as incorrect samples.

The content of check file, which consists the correct version of segmentation, is as below:

"Suret@@ler@@de   sal@@yn@@g'an
bol@@dy@@myz. Budun@@lar@@dan al@@dy@@m. Ata@@myz@@yn
kel@@di@@miz. Sog'ys@@lar@@qa qatys@@g'an@@lar@@ymyz tugil
syilyq@@lar tapsyr@@dy."

Here is the content of file, which was segmented by the program based on the seg-mentation algorithm:

"Suret@@ler@@de   sal@@yn@@g'an   bol@@dy@@myz.
Budun@@lar@@dan al@@dy@@m. Ata@@myz@@yn kel@@di@@miz.
Sog'ys@@lar@@qa qat@@ys@@g'an@@lar@@ymyz tugil syilyq@@lar tap-
syr@@dy".

In addition, the difference between the two files is the word "qatysg'anlarymyz" and the correct samples are 11 out of 12. Thus, by the formula, the accuracy of this fragment text is 92%.

The output was 94% of average accuracy. The accuracy of different texts ranges from 91.7% to 97.2%. Incorrect segmentation occurred because of word ambiguity as some endings; mostly one-type endings might be attached to the words as base. For instance, the word "bolar" has to be segmented as "bol-ar", instead algorithm segments as "bo-lar", because there is a "-lar" ending in the table. This problem can be avoided by using version of stemming program with stems dictionary, which improves the quality of the segmentation results.

7 Conclusion and Future Works

In this paper, there was developed morphological segmentation method based on CSE-model of Old Turkic language. The work presents the language resource split by suffixes of the Old Turkic language endings, essential for solving the task of segmentation of source Turkic texts for neural machine translation. In order to execute morphological segmentation, the complete set of endings was conducted, and the possible valid types of nominal-based and verb-based word endings were received by the combinatorial approach based on the semantical accordance and the harmony of syllables. The proposed segmentation based on CSE-model can be applicable to other languages in the Turkic language group.

In the future works, it is planned to collect corpora in Old Turkic language and use neural machine translation into Kazakh language. Also based on the CSE-model of modern languages in use like Kazakh, Turkish, Uzbek, etc. in Turkic group, we can compare the above languages with Old Turkic endings and define language distance problems. Furthermore, based on the CSE-model morphological analysis of Old Turkic language can be investigated.

References

1. Tukeyev, U.: Automaton models of the morphology analysis and the completeness of the endings of the Kazakh language. In: Proceedings of the International Conference "Turkic Languages Processing" TURKLANG 2015, Kazan, Tatarstan, Russia, pp. 91–100, 17–19 Sep 2015
2. NLP-KazNU. https://github.com/NLP-KazNU?tab=repositories. Accessed 16 Apr 2021
3. Harris Z.: Methods in Structural Linguistics. Chicago University Press (1951)
4. Goldsmith, S.: Unsupervised learning of the morphology of a natural language. Comput. Linguist. **27**(2), 153–198 (2001)
5. Creutz, M., Lagus, K.: Unsupervised discovery of morphemes. In: Proceedings of the ACL 2002 Workshop on Morphological and Phonological Learning, vol. 6, pp. 21–30 (2002)
6. Poon, H., Cherry, C., Toutanova, K.: Unsupervised morphological segmentation with log-linear models. In: NAACL-HLT, pp. 209–217. Association for Computational Linguistics (2009)
7. Gronroos, S., Virpioja, S., Smit, P., Kurimo, M.: Morfessor flatcat: an HMM-based method for unsupervised and semi-supervised learning of morphology. In: COLING, pp. 1177–1185 (2014)
8. Hulden M.: Foma: a finite-state compiler and library. In: Proceedings of the 12th Conference of the European Chapter of the Association for Computational Linguistics: Demonstrations Session, pp. 29–32. Association for Computational Linguistics (2009)
9. Lindén, K., Axelson, E., Hardwick, S., Pirinen, T.A., Silfverberg, M.: HFST—framework for compiling and applying morphologies. In: Mahlow, C., Piotrowski, M. (eds.) SFCM 2011. CCIS, vol. 100, pp. 67–85. Springer, Heidelberg (2011). https://doi.org/10.1007/978-3-642-23138-4_5
10. Ataman, D., Negri, M., Turchi, M., Federico, M.: Linguistically motivated vocabulary reduction for neural machine translation from Turkish to English. Prague Bull. Math. Linguist. **108**(1), 331–342 (2017)
11. Ataman, D., Federico, M.: An evaluation of two vocabulary reduction methods for neural machine translation. In: Proceedings of the 13th Conference of the Association for Machine Translation in the Americas, vol. 1, pp. 97–110 (2018)
12. Toral, A., Edman, L., Yeshmagambetova, G., Spenader, J.: Neural machine translation for English-Kazakh with morphological segmentation and synthetic data. In: Proceedings of the Fourth on Machine Translation (Volume 2: Shared Task Papers, Day 1), pp. 386–392. Association for Computational Linguistics, Florence, Italy (2019)
13. Huck, M., Riess, S., Fraser, A.: Target-side word segmentation strategies for neural machine translation. In: Proceedings of the Second Conference on Machine Translation, pp. 56–67. Association for Computational Linguistics, Copenhagen, Denmark (2017)
14. Weller-Di, M., Fraser, A.: Modeling word formation in English–German neural ma-chine translation. In: Proceedings of the 58th Annual Meeting of the Association for Computational Linguistics, pp. 4227–4232, Online. Association for Computational Linguistics (2020)
15. Schone, P., Jurafsky, D.: Is knowledge-free induction of multiword unit dictionary headwords a solved problem? In: Proceedings of the 2001 Conference on Empirical Methods in Natural Language Processing, pp. 100–108 (2001)

16. Wu, Y., Zhao, H.: Finding better subword segmentation for neural machine translation. In: Sun, M., Liu, T., Wang, X., Liu, Z., Liu, Y. (eds.) CCL/NLP-NABD-2018. LNCS (LNAI), vol. 11221, pp. 53–64. Springer, Cham (2018). https://doi.org/10.1007/978-3-030-01716-3_5

17. Sennrich, R., Haddow, B., Birch, A.: Neural machine translation of rare words with subword units. In: Proceedings of the 54th Annual Meeting of the Association for Computational Linguistics, vol. 1, pp. 1715–1725 (2016)

18. Scherrer, Y., Gronroos, S., Virpioja, S.: The University of Helsinki and Aalto university submissions to the WMT 2020 news and low-resource translation tasks. In: Proceedings of the Fifth Conference on Machine Translation, pp. 1129–1138. Online Association for Computational Linguistics (2020)

19. Baskakov, A., Xasanov, B.: Languages of interethnic communication in Kazakhstan. In: Wurm, S.A., Mühlhäusler, P., Tryon, D.T. (eds.) Atlas of Languages of Intercultural Communication in the Pacific, Asia and the Americas, vol. 2, pp. 933–936. de Gruyter, Berlin (1996)

20. Kondratiev, V.: The Grammatical Structure of the Language of the Ancient Turkic Manuscripts of the VIII–XI Centuries, pp. 191–200. Publ. House of Leningrad University, Leningrad (1981)

21. Erdal, M.: A Grammar of Old Turkic. Brill, Leiden and Boston (2004)

22. Aydarov, G., Kuryshzhanov, A., Tomanov, M.: A Language of Ancient Turkic Written Monuments. Mektep, Almaty (1971)

23. Aydarov, G., Kuryshzhanov, A., Tomanov, M.: A Language of Ancient Turkic Written Monuments, pp. 111–123. Almaty, Mektep (1971)

24. Malov, S.: Monuments of the Ancient Turkic Writing of Mongolia and Kyrgyzstan, pp. 48–50. Leningrad, Moscow (2005)

Universal Programs for Stemming, Segmentation, Morphological Analysis of Turkic Words

Ualsher Tukeyev⑩, Aidana Karibayeva(✉)⑩, Aliya Turganbayeva⑩, and Dina Amirova⑩

Al-Farabi Kazakh National University, Almaty, Kazakhstan

Abstract. In this paper are proposed universal programs for Turkic languages stemming, segmentation, and morphological analysis based on the "complete set of endings" (CSE) model of Turkic morphologies. The CSE-model is based on four types of endings: plural, case, personal, and possessive. For all Turkic languages, these four types of endings are similar. For each of considered NLP tasks is created a special relational data model – decision table. Relational data models – decision tables, algorithms and programs for stemming, segmentation, morphological parsing is shown for the examples of the Kazakh language.

Keywords: Turkic languages · Universal program · Stemming · Segmentation · Morphological analysis

1 Introduction

The total number of speakers of Turkic languages is over 200 million. The Turkic language family is part of the Altai macro-family. All Turkic languages belong to agglutinative languages.

All Turkic languages, excepting Turkish, are low resources languages. Developing NLP tools is a laborious process for each language. Especially important and relevant for the NLP language are basic tasks such as stemming, segmentation, and morphological analysis, which are used for other NLP tasks. Therefore, the problem is to reduce the expenses of developing them for each new language. Of course, the best option would be to create a universal tool for solving stemming, segmentation, and morphological analysis for any language.

This article proposes an approach based on the universalization of NLP tools for agglutinative languages based on complete set of endings (CSE) morphology model [1], and thus reduce the labor costs of creating NLP tools for new languages.

For implementation of the proposed approach of universalization of NLP tools, a class of agglutinative languages considered, namely, the Turkic languages. The universalization of NLP tools for Turkic languages on the CSE-model morphology based on the construction of a complete set of endings for a new language. In addition, for each task of stemming, segmentation, and morphological analysis of new languages, relational (tabular) data structures need build, which work as decision tables.

© Springer Nature Switzerland AG 2021
N. T. Nguyen et al. (Eds.): ICCCI 2021, LNAI 12876, pp. 643–654, 2021.
https://doi.org/10.1007/978-3-030-88081-1_48

The novelty of this work lies in the proposed approach for universalizing NLP tools, which consists in developing a special relational data structure for each type of NLP tools based on the CSE morphology model for each new language and developing a universal program for each type of NLP tasks.

The rest of this paper organized as follows. Section 2 provides an overview of the previous works conducted in the field of the stemming, segmentation, and morphological analysis of natural languages. Section 3 describes the CSE-model on the example of Kazakh. Section 4 describes the stemming with a stem-words dictionary and stop-word dictionary. Section 5 describes the universal algorithm and program for morphological segmentation on an example of Kazakh. Section 6 describes the universal algorithm and program for morphological analysis on an example of Kazakh. Section 7 describes experimental results and its analysis. Finally, Sect. 8 presents the conclusions and suggests for future work.

2   Related Works

Stemming is one of the most important tasks in natural language processing. This task is a one main part of linguistic studies in morphology and information retrieval and extraction.

The development algorithms of stemming were presented in quite a lot of work. An efficient stemming algorithm for Russian language with Porter's stemmer in [2, 3] is proposed. Porter's stemmer applies a series of rules to chop the endings, regardless of the basis of the word.

The advantage and disadvantage of Porter's stemmer described in [4]. It is important to note that the word base and vocabulary are not used in this stemmer. Although, it gives an erroneous selection of the basis of the word in some cases.

The English lemmatizer is used to improve Malay-English statistical machine translation (SMT) system [5]. English stemmers are used to lemmatize the word in the training and testing sets to English stem and its suffix. The division of an English word into a lemma and its suffix made it possible to translate English words with the same lemma if there was in the training data. In the Malay language, some words translated in the same way into English; with at least one possible basis, can get a translation into the target language. Stanford, Porter, Snowball, Lancaster, and Lovins stemmers were used to stemming English words. Stanford's stemmer gave the best quality result.

In addition, for low-resource languages a rule-based stemmer has been proposed in works [6, 7]. Urdu language is complex and morphologically rich. The proposed Urdu rule-based stemmer gave accuracy of 86.5%, whereas Sundanese stemmer recognized 68.87% of the Sundanese affix types and showed 96.79% of the correctly affixed words.

The majority of works on segmentation used the BPE method as de-facto standard to segmentation. In 2019, English-Kazakh and Kazakh-English language pairs were added as a new translation task in WMT. Majority of researchers WMT 2019 proposed technology of transfer learning and mostly the BPE method was used for the segmentation for source data.

In [8] it was compared to different configurations of Byte-Pair Encoding (BPE) and Soft Decoupled Encoding (SDE). The text with Romanization and without Romanization (text in Cyrillic) was preprocessed. The former improved quality metric BLEU to 0.20, whereas the latter had improvement in 1.24 metric.

The complexity of the morphology of the Kazakh and Russian languages is considered in [9]. The 10K comparative BPE operations also used BPE for each language in NMT. The results were too low in NMT with 2.32 BLEU metric. The translation systems with Russian language taken as pivot language in [10, 11].

The rule-based morphological analyzer technology for morphological segmentation was applied in [12]. Apertium's rule-based morphological analyzer segmented words of source data. The morphological analyzer provides a many possible analyses made of a lemma and morphological information. If a word has no valid analysis, it generates many segmentation variants as known suffixes match the word. The BPE is used after morphological segmentation too.

In the article [13] described the creation of lemmas consisting ~60.000 lemmas which correspond to ~710.000 different word forms for Modern Greek language. They divide to 9 fields the morphological entries as lemma, stem, suffix, part of speech, number, case, tense, translation and other fields. These fields describe each specific word form for morphological entries. Generation of word forms based on morphological categories which contained in the morphological categories database. These categories involve describing instructions of generating the various word forms from the word lemma and association of it with morphological feature values. These approaches of generation were available for nouns and adjectives, but it is not work for other parts of speech, like verbs, articles, etc.

The technology based on the electronic version of Zaliznjak's dictionary for lemmatization and tagging the Russian language was developed in [14]. They present a hierarchical lexical database that is used in DATR (declarative language for representing lexical knowledge) by mapping the basic Zaliznjak data. In the article, special attention is paid to morphological polysemy of nouns and adjective names, and comparative analysis of the most frequent grammatical categories is also considered. Zaliznjak defined a special notation for types in the form of numeric values, and corresponding patterns in the alphabetical designation that were used to define the morphological types. These notations were used to find the corresponding morphological word form from the hierarchically arranged table used in DATR.

In [15] were presented a morphological lexicon for the Persian language. Taking into account the characteristics of the Persian language was developed the complete description of Persian morphology. The description of the morphology is presented in the form of a table that includes tables of 27 verbs and 5 nouns. The lexical entries were obtained by three stages: constructing, cleaning and expanding. By using 35,914 lemma-level entries, it generated 524,700 word form entries.

Cross-lingual morphological tagging using tags projected across Bitext was proposed in [16]. The training data of low-resource language was at target side, whereas high-resource English language considered at source side. The proposed method shows best morphological tagger projecting between related language pairs.

Morphological features, the division into morphemes, as well as the synthesis of word forms was considered in [17]. Herein, the corpora for low-resources languages were presented too. The work is considered in low-resource languages of Russia, namely, Evenki, Karelian, Selkup, and Veps.

In [18] authors predict syntactic properties on the source-side using the learned sentence encoding vectors by logistic regression. They receive 92.8% accuracy in predicting voices in English-French NMT. The global and local syntactic information of the source side is covered with the encoder of 'sequence to sequence' model.

Having considered the three NLP problems, namely morphological segmentation, analysis, and stemming, mentioned, in this article will propose the universal approach for creating its programs based on the CSE-model of morphology.

3   CSE-Model on Example of the Kazakh Language

Morphology of Turkic languages are very similar, it is agglutinative and suffixing. Morphology is regular and each used suffix in word express one grammatical notion. The creation of CSE-model of morphology shows below on example of Kazakh [19].

Words in the Kazakh language have a nominal and verbal basis. The former has four types of base affixes: Plural affixes (denoted by K); Possessive affixes (denoted by T); Case affixes (denoted by C); Personal affixes (denoted by J). The latter has following tense, person, negative form,

It is important to consider that in the Kazakh language there are rules, which an ending are glued to the stem depending on softness/solidness of the stem (harmony law).

The number of different placements of affixes types is determined by the formula:

$$A_{nk} = n!/(n - k)!, \tag{1}$$

where n – is the number of affixes types (equal 4), k – is the number of types is taken for placements. So, $A_{41} = 4$, $A_{42} = 12$, $A_{43} = 24$, $A_{44} = 24$.

The first step is checking the semantical validity of each placement of base types of Kazakh affixes. The endings placements of one type (K, T, C, J) are semantically valid.

The semantically valid placements for the two types are six from 12 possible affixes type placements: KT, TC, CJ, KC, TJ, and KJ.

The semantically valid placements of the three types are four from 24 possible affixes type placements: KTC, KTJ, TCJ, and KCJ.

The semantically valid placements of the four types are 1 from possible 24 possible affixes type placements: KTCJ [1].

Then, using a combinatorial approach, we enumerate the possible endings for each type of placements. The enumeration of possible endings for other types of parts of speech with verb stems is carried out in a similar way. Inferring of endings for Kazakh is described in the article [19]. The total number of all possible endings is 4679.

4   Stemming Algorithm with Stop-Words Lexicon and Stems-Lexicon on the CSE-Model

The Lexicon-free stemming algorithm from [20] is improved by using stop-words lexicon and stems-lexicon for increasing the quality of stemming.

The steps of the stemming algorithm with stop-words lexicon and stems-lexicon are as follows:

1. Search word w on matching in the list of stop-words of language. If it matches, then go to 9;
2. Calculation L(w).
3. Calculation the maximum length of an ending of the analyzed word: $L[e(w)] = L(w) - 2$, where 2 is the minimum length of the word stem.
4. Selection of the ending e(w) of the length L[e(w)] for analyzed word w.
5. Search e(w) on matching in the list of endings. If it matches, then the stem of the word is selected: $st(w) = w - e(w)$.
6. Search stem st(w) on matching in the list of stems of language. If it matches, then go to 9;
7. Otherwise, the calculated length of the ending of the analyzed word is decreased by one: $L[e(w)] = L[e(w)] - 1$.
8. If $L[e(w)] < 1$, then word w is without the ending. Go to step 9. Otherwise, go to step 4.
9. End.

In Table 1 is presented an example of the stemming Kazakh word 'balalarymyzdan', which translates to English as 'from our children'. In the first step the current word is checked in stop words. It is not in the stop words list. In the second step is calculated the length of the current word, it is 14. In the third step, from the current word two characters were subtracted as stem and word's ending length is 12. The received ending is checked in the endings list. In the endings list does not consist of 'lalarymyzdan', so current word's ending is reduced to one unit. Herein, in the endings list does not consist of 'alarymyzdan'. The reduction on one unit performed again, then the ending's length equal to 10. The received ending found in endings list. The stem is deter-mined by subtracting from the given word the matched ending.

Table 1. Example of stemming on the CSE-model.

Steps of algorithm	Example in realization
W	balalarymyzdan
L(w)	14 (balalarymyzdan)
$L[e(w)]max = L(w) - 2$	12 (ba + lalarymyzdan)
$L[e(w)]1 = L[e(w)] - 1$	11 (bal + alarymyzdan)
$L[e(w)]2 = L[e(w)]1 - 1$	10 (bala + larymyzdan)
e(w)	larymyzdan
w − e (w)	14 (balalarymyzdan) − 10 (larymyzdan)
St(w)	bala

5 Universal Algorithm and Program for Morphological Segmentation on the Example of Kazakh

The volume of a dictionary is an important parameter in learning NMT. A big dictionary can lead to a memory error. Adding all word forms to the dictionary increases a required volume of memory. The use of the complete set of Kazakh ending has also been considered for the morphological segmentation problem for low-resources languages [21].

The use of the CSE-model makes it possible to represent the solution to the word segmentation problem as a decision table, one column of which contains endings, and the second column contains segmented endings into affixes. Thus, if the word is divided into stem and ending, then using the endings segmentation table, a solution for segmenting the endings of the word can be obtained in one-step. A segment of the relational data model – decision table for segmentation task based on CSE-model is presented in Table 2.

Table 2. The segment of relational data model – decision table for segmentation task

Endings	Inner segmentation
Darynyzdanbyz	dar@ @ ynyz@ @ dan@ @ byz
Lerimizden	ler@ @ imiz@ @ den
Ymnan	ym@ @ nan
Dan	dan

The universal algorithm for segmentation of words on the CSE-model of morphology. This algorithm includes two stages:

1) the splitting of given word on a stem and an ending.
2) the segmentation of a word ending into component affixes.

The first stage of the algorithm, the stemming of words, is described in Sect. 4.

The second stage: the segmentation of words ending into affixes is realized using the single state's transducer, presented as the decision table of segmented affixes for given ending. Each suffix is segmented by @ @ symbols. Table 3 presents the examples of morphological segmentation of endings in the Kazakh language.

Universal program for morphological segmentation for Turkic languages on the base of CSE-model morphology as an open-source resource is on the site [22].

Table 3. Example of morphological segmentation of endings in the Kazakh language.

Examples	Whole endings	Inner segmentation of endings
Dostarymyzbenmin	tarymyzbenmin	tar@@ ymyz@@ ben@@ min
Studentteriñizden	teriñizden	ter@@ iñiz@@ den
Tatusyzdar	syzdar	syz@@ dar
Dápterleriń	leriń	ler@@ iń
Dosymnan	ymnan	ym@@ nan
Kitapxanadan	dan	dan

6 Universal Algorithm and Program for Morphological Analysis on Example of Kazakh Words

The use of the CSE-model makes it possible to represent the solution to the word morphological analysis problem as a decision table, one column of which contains endings, and the second column contains the word morphological analysis. The morphological analysis decision table based on the CSE-model is shown in Table 4.

Table 4. The segment of relational data model – decision table for morphological analysis task.

Endings	Morphological analysis	Comments
taryñyzdan	*tar<pl>*yñyz<pos><p2><frm>*dan<abl>	<pl> – plural; <p2> – 2nd person; <frm> – formality <abl> – ablative case
syzdar	*syzdar<p2><frm><pl>	<p2> – 2nd person <frm> – formality <pl> – plural
ymnan	*ym<pos><sg><p1>*nan<abl>	<pos> – possessive <sg> – singular <p1> – 1st person

Examples of endings and its morphological analysis are given in Table 5.
Universal program for morphological analysis for Turkic languages on the base of CSE-model morphology as an open-source resource is on the site [22].

Table 5. Results of comparative analysis messages.

Example	Morphological analysis of given word	Comments
dostaryńyzdan	dos+<NB>*tar<pl>yńyz<pos> <frm><p2>dan<abl>	<pl> – plural; <p2> – 2nd person; <frm> – formality <abl> – ablative case
dossyzda	dos+<NB>*syzdar<p2> <frm><pl>	<p2> – 2nd person <frm> – formality <pl> – plural
dosymnan	dos+<NB>*ym<pos> <sg><p1>*nan<abl>	<pos> – possessive <sg> – singular <p1> – 1st person

7 Experimental Results and Analysis

The purpose of the experiments is to substantiate the hypothesis of the possibility of using the CSE-model of the morphology of Turkic languages for various NLP tasks, the possibility of constructing special relational data structures for each NLP problem of the considered class of natural languages and use the proposed universal programs for considered NLP tasks. It is assumed that the use of the CSE model will make it possible to apply it to all Turkic languages in the tasks of natural language processing, namely stemming, morphological segmentation, morphological analysis.

In this section, results for each task mentioned in this article are shown. In Table 6 examples of sentences with stemming, CSE-based morphological segmentation and CSE-based morphological analysis are given. In addition, in Table 7, the results are shown for stemming and morphological segmentation and morphological analysis for sentences with different type of part of speech of words. The experiments were done on a corpus with a volume of 1000 sentences. The corpus covers a variety of topics.

Analysis of experimental results. The main reasons of mistakes in stemming with lexicon are:

- one word can contain several stems. For example, for the word 'келісімнің' stem is 'келісім', but the program returns stem 'келіс'. Since the search for an affix starts from the longest possible, in this case this affix 'імнің' is found and stem 'келіс' is returned.
- the stem dictionary should cover all possible stems in the language, however, there are situations when a stem of a word is not found in the dictionary.
- the result of stemming directly affects the results of morphological segmentation and analysis. The obtained results of stemming, divided into stem and endings are further used for morphological segmentation and morphological analysis. Therefore, from Table 7 the ratio for the 3 mentioned tasks of finding correctness are the same.

The universal programs based on the CSE-model morphology gives an accurate finding of word stems, right segmentation, and morphological analysis and will also be useful to other Turkic group languages.

Table 6. Examples of sentences with stemming, morphological segmentation and morphological analysis.

Example of sentences in Kazakh	Translation of examples	Stemming	CSE-based morphological segmentation	CSE-based morphological analysis
Баланың ұйықтайтын уақыты болды және балалардың мектепке баруы қажет	It was time for the child to go to bed and children had to go to school.	Бала ның ұйықта йтын уақыт ы бол ды және бала лардың мектеп ке бару ы қажет .	Бала@@ ның ұйықта@@ йтын уақыт@@ ы бол@@ ды және бала@@ лар@@дың мектеп@@ ке бару@@ ы қажет	Бала+ <NB>*ның<gen> ұйықта+ <VB>*йтын<prpt> уақыт+<NB>*ы<pos> <sg><p3> бол+<VB>*ды<pt><sg><p3> және бала+<NB>*лар<pl>* дың<gen> мектеп+<NB>*ке<dat> бару<VB>*ы<pos><sg><p3> қажет
Тамыз да тұрғын үйді сатып алу-сатудың тіркелген мәмілелер саны 24 919 құрады	In August, the number of registered transactions for the purchase and sale of housing amounted to 24,919	Тамыз да тұрғын үй ді сат ып ал у-сату дың тіркел ген мәміле лер сан ы 24 919 құр ады	Тамыз@@ да тұрғын үй@@ ді сат@@ ып ал@@ у-сат@@ у@@ дың тіркел@@ ген мәміле@@ лер сан@@ ы 24 919 құр@@ а@@ ды	Тамыз+<NB>*да<loc> тұрғын үй+<NB>*ді<acc> сат+<VB>*ып<vadv> ал+<VB>*у<inf>-сат+<VB>*у<inf>*дың<gen> тіркел+<VB>*ген<ppt> мәміле+<NB>*лер<pl> сан+<NB>*ы<pos><sg><p3> 24 919 құр+<VB>*а<ttv>*ды<sg><p3>
Қабылданған заңдар : " цифрлық қазақстан " кешенді бағдарламасы қабылда нды .	Adopted laws: a comprehensive program "Digital Kazakhstan" was adopted.	Қабылда нған заң дар : " цифрлық қазақстан " кешенді бағдарлама сы қабылда нды .	Қабылда@@ н@@@ған заң@@ дар : " цифрлық қазақстан " кешенді бағдарлама@@ сы қабылда@@ н@@ ды .	Қабылда+<VB>*н<rfv>*ған<ppt> заң+<NB>*дар<pl> : " цифрлық қазақстан " кешенді бағдарлама+<NB>*с ы<pos><sg><p3> қабылда+<VB>*н<rfv>*ды<sg><p3> .

(*continued*)

Table 6. (*continued*)

Сабақтан шыққан соң үйге аман жетсең екен.	I hope you get home safely after school.	Сабақ тан шық қан соң үй ге аман жет сең е кен.	Сабақ@@ тан шық@@ қан соң үй@@ ге аман жет@@ се@@ ң е@@ кен.	Сабақтан+<NB>*тан<abl> шық+<VB>*қан<ppt> соң үй+<NB>*ге<dat> аман жет+<VB>*се<cmv> *ң<sg><p2>
Студенттер келесі жылы Америкаға оқуға барғалы жатыр.	The students are going to study in America next year.	Студент тер келес і жыл ы Америка ға оқ уға бар ғалы жатыр.	Студент@@ тер келес@@ і жыл@@ ы Америка@@ ға оқ@@ у@@ ға бар@@ ғалы жатыр.	Студент+<NB>*тер<pl> келес+<NB>*i<pos><sg><p3> жыл+<NB>*ы<pos><sg><p3> Америка+<NB>*ға<dat> оқ+<NB>*у<inf>*ға<dat> бар+<VB>*мақ<ftt>*шы<pl><p3>
Демалысқа шығып, Бурабайға баруға болады.	Having gone on vacation, we can go to Burabay.	Демалыс қа шы ғып, Бурабай ға бар уға бол ады.	Демалыс@@ қа шы@@ ғып, Бурабай@@ ға бар@@ у@@ ға бол@@ а@@ды.	Демалыс+<NB>*қа<dat> шығ+<VB>*ып<vadv>, Бурабай+<NB>*ға<dat> бар+<VB>*у<inf>*ға<dat> бол+<VB>*а<ttv>*ды<sg><p3>.

Table 7. Results of estimation of the experiments.

File – the volume of the corpus in words	Number of non-repeating words	Number of words with wrong stem cut	The ratio of the correct cut off the stem in% value	File – the volume of the corpus in words
Lexicon-free stemming, morphological segmentation, morphological analysis				
exp1000.kk – 1000 sentences	5106	1337	74%	exp1000.kk – 1000 sentences
Stemming with lexicon, morphological segmentation, morphological analysis				
exp1000.kk – 1000 sentences	5106	136	97%	exp1000.kk – 1000 sentences

8 Conclusion and Future Works

In this paper were considered the common tasks of NLP as segmentation, lemmatization, and morphological analysis. Herein, it was a proposed universal approach for creating universal programs of some NLP tasks for agglutinative Turkic languages.

Experiments show an improvement in results due to the use of the CSE-model for the mentioned tasks. In a morphological segmentation task, the CSE-model has been shown to be effective in reducing the volume of vocabulary, which is important for training the neural translation system, as well as for rare word tasks. In the stemming problem, the proposed model showed fairly good results in reduction to the stems of a word when are used stop-words lexicon and stems-lexicon.

In order to improve the results of the proposed technology, the dictionary of stems will be expanded. In future, is planned to apply this approach based on CSE-model morphology to other languages of the Turkic language group.

References

1. Tukeyev, U.: Automaton models of the morphology analysis and the completeness of the endings of the Kazakh language. In: Proceedings of the International Conference "Turkic languages processing" TURKLANG-2015, pp. 91–100. Kazan, Tatarstan, Russia, 17–19 Sep 2015 (in Russian)
2. Porter Stemming for Russian language. https://eigenein.xyz/snowball/Russian_stemming_a lgorithm (2015)
3. Segalovich, I.: A fast morphological algorithm with unknown word guessing induced by a dictionary for a web search. In: Proceedings of the International Conference on Machine Learning; Models, Technologies and Applications, MLMTA 2003, pp. 273–280. Las Vegas, Nevada, USA (2003)
4. Willett, P.: The Porter stemming algorithm: then and now. Program Electron. Library Inf. Syst. B **40**(3), 219–223 (2006)
5. Yeong, Y., Tan, T., Mohammad, S.: Using dictionary and lemmatizer to improve low resource English-Malay statistical machine translation system. Procedia Comput. Sci. **81**, 243–249 (2016)
6. Gupta, V., Joshi, N., Mathur, I.: Rule based stemmer in Urdu. In: Proceedings of 4th International Conference on Computer and Communication Technology (ICCCT), pp. 129–132 (2013)
7. Suryani, A.A., Widyantoro D.H., Purwarianti A., Sudaryat Y.: The rule-based Sundanese stemmer. ACM Trans. Asian Low Resour. Lang. Inf. Process. **17**(4) Article No. 27 (2018). https://doi.org/10.1145/3195634
8. Briakou, E., Carpuat, M.: The University of Maryland's Kazakh–English neural machine translation system at WMT19. In: Proceedings of the Fourth Conference on Machine Translation, pp. 134–140. Florence, Italy (2019)
9. Casas N., Fonollosa, J.A.R., Escolano, C., Basta, C., Costa-jussà, M.R.: The TALP-UPC machine translation systems for WMT19 news translation task: pivoting techniques for low resource MT. In: Proceedings of the Fourth Conference on Machine Translation (WMT19), pp. 155–162. Florence, Italy (2019)
10. Littell, P., Lo, C., Larkin, S., Stewart, D.: Multi-source transformer for Kazakh-Russian-English neural machine translation. In: Proceedings of the Fourth Conference on Machine Translation (WMT19), pp. 267–274. Florence, Italy (2019)

11. Kocmi, T., Bojar, O.: CUNI submission for low-resource languages in WMT news 2019. In: Proceedings of the Fourth Conference on Machine Translation (WMT19), pp. 234–240. Florence, Italy (2019)

12. Sánchez-Cartagena, V., Pérez-Ortiz, J.A, Sánchez-Martínez, F.: The Universitat d'Alacant submissions to the English-to-Kazakh news translation task at WMT 2019. In: Proceedings of the Fourth Conference on Machine Translation (WMT19). Florence, Italy (2019)

13. Petasis, G., Karkaletsis, V., Farmakiotou, D., Androutsopoulos, I., Spyropoulo, C.D.: A Greek morphological lexicon and its exploitation by natural language processing applications. In: Manolopoulos, Y., Evripidou, S., Kakas, A.C. (eds.) PCI 2001. LNCS, vol. 2563, pp. 401–419. Springer, Heidelberg (2003). https://doi.org/10.1007/3-540-38076-0_26

14. Brown, D.P., Evans, N., Tiberius, C., Corbett, G.G.: A large-scale inheritance based morphological lexicon for Russian. In: Erjavec, T., Vitas, D. (eds) Proceedings of the Workshop on Morphological Processing of Slavic Languages, 10th Conference of the European Chapter of the Association for Computational Linguistics. Budapest (2003)

15. Sagot, B., Walther, G.: A morphological lexicon for the Persian language. In: Proceedings of the 7th Language Resources and Evaluation Conference (LREC 2010). La Valette, Malta (2010)

16. Buys, J., Botha, J.: Cross-lingual morphological tagging for low-resource languages. In: Proceedings of the 54th Annual Meeting of the Association for Computational Linguistics, vol. 1, pp. 1954–1964 (2016)

17. Klyachko, E., Sorokin A., Krizhanovsky, N., Krizhanovsky, A., Ryazanskaya, G.: LowResourceEval-2019: a shared task on morphological analysis for low-resource languages. Dialog 2019, Issue 18, Supplementary volume, pp. 45–62 (2020)

18. Shi, X., Padhi, I., Knight, K.: Does string-based neural MT learn source syntax? In: Proceedings of the 2016 Conference on Empirical Methods in Natural Language Processing, pp. 1526–1534. Austin, Texas (2016)

19. Tukeyev, U., Karibayeva, A.: Inferring the complete set of Kazakh endings as a language resource. In: Hernes, M., Wojtkiewicz, K., Szczerbicki, E. (eds.) ICCCI 2020. CCIS, vol. 1287, pp. 741–751. Springer, Cham (2020). https://doi.org/10.1007/978-3-030-63119-2_60

20. Tukeyev, U., Turganbayeva, A., Abduali, B., Rakhimova, D., Amirova, D., Karibayeva, A.: Lexicon-free stemming for Kazakh language information retrieval. In: Proceeding of 12th International Conference on Application of Information and Communication Technologies (AICT), pp. 95–98. Almaty (2018)

21. Tukeyev, U., Karibayeva, A., Zhumanov, Z.: Morphological segmentation method for turkic language neural machine translation. Cogent Eng. 7(1), 1856500 (2020). https://doi.org/10.1080/23311916.2020.1856500

22. NLP-KazNU. http://github.com/NLP-KAZNU

Establishing the Informational Requirements for Modelling Open Domain Dialogue and Prototyping a Retrieval Open Domain Dialogue System

Trent Meier and Elias Pimenidis(✉)

Department of Computer Science and Creative Technologies, University of the West of England, Bristol, UK
Elias.Pimenidis@uwe.ac.uk

Abstract. Open domain dialogue systems aim to coherently respond to users over long conversations through multiple conversational turns. Modelling open domain dialogue is challenging as both the syntactic and semantic features of language play a role in response formation. As similarity to human dialogue has been considered the goal of open domain dialogue systems, this paper takes the view that human linguistic reasoning research can be informative to the requirement engineering process of modelling open domain dialogue. Through a review of linguistic reasoning research and modern approaches in open domain dialogue systems, the authors present informational hypotheses impacting the modelling of open domain dialogue systems. Furthermore, this paper discusses the design and testing of an open domain dialogue system presenting response BLEU-1 scores of 35.41% based on the DailyDialogue Dataset.

Keywords: Natural language processing (NLP) · Open domain dialogue modelling · DailyDialogue dataset

1 Introduction

Dialogue systems are a field of natural language processing (NLP) that seeks to produce conversational responses to user inputs. With dialogue systems finding application in diverse use cases ranging from chatbots to personal assistants and video game NPCs, advancements in deep learning techniques have led to significant improvements in system capabilities. Dialogue systems can largely be categorized between task-based dialogue systems and open domain dialogue systems. Task-based dialogue systems typically have fixed objectives while open domain dialogue systems attempt to conduct open conversation with users [25]. Open domain dialogue is challenging to NLP through the role of syntactics and semantics in forming conversational responses, compounded by the variety of topical domains found in open dialogue.

This paper presents a literature review of linguistic reasoning, comparing the findings with a review of related work in modern open domain dialogue techniques. The authors

© Springer Nature Switzerland AG 2021
N. T. Nguyen et al. (Eds.): ICCCI 2021, LNAI 12876, pp. 655–667, 2021.
https://doi.org/10.1007/978-3-030-88081-1_49

then propose informational hypotheses informed by the findings of the literature reviews which influence the requirements engineering for the paper's open domain dialogue system. Finally, this paper will discuss the dialogue system's design considerations, methodology and the results of testing.

2 Linguistic Reasoning

Linguistic reasoning describes the process of natural language understanding, reasoning, and response formation. While the cognitive processes of human linguistic reasoning are an open area of research, the authors compare literature regarding language and grammar with the findings of research discussing linguistic reasoning, cognitive sciences, and analogical reasoning. This review aims to identify the informational elements of language used in linguistic reasoning to inform the evaluation of open domain dialogue systems and to establish the informational requirements for language modelling in dialogue systems.

2.1 Language and Grammar

Literature widely acknowledges that language consists of elements that capture temporal, spatial, and objective information about the experienced environment [5]. Language encodes this information in structures that communicate these experiences to others or for self-reference. The shared nature of informational exchange has led Chomskain linguists to suggest that language has a common underlying structure leading to the suggestion that language models and formal grammar symbolize the cognitive processes that underlie them. It has been the focus of many language researchers to demonstrate the universality of grammar, with work including evaluating subject-verb sentence structures, reflexive bindings of pronouns, semantic dependency identification, and syntactic hierarchies [20]. The study of Universal Grammar (UG), while initially focusing on the English language, has been expanded to consider comparisons of other languages including multi-lingual translation. Findings from this cross-comparison have resulted in the criticism of UG with researchers suggesting that variations between languages invalidate the suggestion of UG [9]. While no definitive language structures have emerged as an answer to the suggestion of UG, consensus is growing that universality would occur at a higher abstraction of language than the commonly held grammar structures.

2.2 Linguistic Reasoning and Cognitive Science

Attempts to improve understanding of linguistic reasoning have used cognitive science research to identify key informational and structural attributes of human language processing [20]. The study of analogical reasoning includes disciplines ranging from linguistic reasoning to visuospatial and numeric reasoning including memory theories. Advancements in the field have resulted from analogical reasoning experimentation combined with eye tracking, brain imaging, and developmental studies [24]. It is beyond the aims of this review to discuss the physical processes of analogical reasoning, but the informational processing of natural language in linguistic reasoning is relevant to the aims of identifying the informational requirements for open domain dialogue modelling.

Analogical reasoning comprises the processes of knowledge acquisition, storage, and memory reuse as part of a problem-solving paradigm. It has been used to explain human problem solving, creativity, and has even been suggested to underlie human cognition [5]. Analogical reasoning matches environmental stimuli with similar experiences through a mapping process that impacts the outcome of memory retrieval. Once retrieved, the memories of experience inform the outcomes of analogical reasoning through a process of further mapping and executive function [24].

Developmental studies of analogical reasoning show that children's objective focus leads to inferior analogical reasoning, while adult attenuation to relational information leads to more successful analogical reasoning [23]. Christie, Gao, and Ma [5] suggest that language plays a key role in conveying both objective information and relational information suggesting that these informational elements demonstrate that analogical reasoning rather than UG is common across linguistic differences. Temporal information conveyed through language forms another important element of linguistic reasoning and can be conveyed through language directly or as sequential information captured as experience through the consumption of language [2]. The preponderance of analogical reasoning research places emphasis on the importance of relational and temporal information in higher abstraction analogical mapping, memory retrieval, and reasoning.

2.3 Informational Attributes of Language

The following presents key informational components of language, each of which holds importance to linguistic reasoning outcomes.

Syntactic Information. The syntactic component of language describes linguistic elements including commonly experienced information (nouns) and named entities. Other syntactic information includes relational, temporal, and spatial information explicitly described by language [19].

Semantic Information. The semantic component of language describes implicit language meaning that captures relational, temporal, and spatial information conveyed through the consumption of languages. Christie, Gao, and Ma [5] emphasize the importance of relational information and temporal information in discourse processing, highlighting the importance of semantic information in modelling open domain dialogue systems.

Some authors note that even the linguistic elements widely accepted as syntactic are semantically influenced through the process of language learning [11]. This work acknowledges these findings but adopts the common definitions of syntax and semantics for the precision afforded to discussion by differentiating the explicit and implicit information in language.

3 Related Work in Open Domain Dialogue Modelling

Conversational dialogue systems have seen recent advances resulting from improvements in Deep Neural Network (DNN) architectures in modern approaches. An emphasis of research in open domain dialogue has focused on modelling the semantic information contained in multi-turn dialogue with the goal of more accurately forming natural language responses.

3.1 Dialogue Representation

DNN approaches to open domain dialogue require numeric language representations that encode the informational elements of language for processing. Embedding methods have emerged as the most successful methodology of representing dialogue in DNN techniques but vary in the embedding methodologies, informational capture, and intended application. This review of language encodings will evaluate the suitability of embedding methodologies for open domain dialogue systems informed by the findings of the review of linguistic reasoning.

One-hot encoding uses vector representations of a predefined set of vocabulary using the count of the occurrence of each word to represent the feature value in an embedding vector. Kim, Hong, and Cha [14] note that One-Hot encoding ignores the relational and temporal features of language, and as a result demonstrates lesser performance and increased memory requirements compared to alternative approaches. Due to the loss of relational and temporal language features, One-Hot encoded vector representations can be described as unsuitable for language encoding in open domain dialogue systems.

Skip-Gram encoding methods represent words as multi-dimensional vectors derived from the occurrence words adjacent to the word of the embedding. Skip-Gram language representation captures important informational elements of language but lacks direct representational capture of dialogues temporal or sequential information which forms an important element of linguistic reasoning.

Sequence-to-Sequence encoders describe the encoding element of encoder-decoder networks which form the basis for many modern approaches in open domain dialogue systems. Yang, Rong, and Xiong [25] state that Sequence-to-Sequence encoders have been demonstrated with Recurrent Neural Networks, Long-Term Short-Term Memory Networks, and Gated Recurrent Unit Networks, capturing improved semantics through high dimensional hidden state vectors. Through the capture of natural language semantics Sequence-to-Sequence based encoders demonstrate better suitability for open domain dialogue generation than other language encoding methodologies.

Zhou et al., [26] describe attention-based sequence embedding techniques as a key element in the advancement of dialogue representation in modern state-of-the-art language models. Attention-based Sequence-to-Sequence encoders use attention mechanisms to achieve embeddings by evaluating words in a sequence preserving the objective information, relational information, and temporal information at varying levels of abstraction [7]. This encoding scheme combined with transformer encoder-decoder networks has demonstrated state-of-the-art performance in open domain dialogue [1, 22]. Despite these advances, deep semantic feature embeddings remain an open area of research due to the computational complexity of training such language models. More work is needed to integrate the deeper level relational and temporal informational encoding necessary for higher abstraction semantic reasoning. Other important areas of research correlate the incorporation of extra-lexical information, such as environmental information, with improved performance of dialogue systems [10].

3.2 Dialogue Response Formation

Modern open domain dialogue systems are generally classified by the manner conversational responses are generated as either retrieval dialogue systems or generative dialogue systems. Retrieval dialogue systems leverage an available corpus of dialogue using matching mechanisms to retrieve similar conversational responses to an input. Modern approaches have demonstrated neural network-based representation and matching methodologies to perform dialogue retrieval for conversational systems [18]. While retrieval based open domain dialogue systems have used a variety of language encoding methodologies, attention-based encoding methodologies such as BERT models have been demonstrated to produce state-of-the-art retrieval-based dialogue performance [12].

Generative dialogue systems differ from retrieval-based dialogue systems through the mechanism of response formation. Huang and Zhou [12] describe generative dialogue systems as forming responses by predicting each word of the response for each word of the input sequence. Sequence-to-sequence models have seen wide application in generative dialogue systems following an encoder-decoder network model. Other frameworks include Generative Adversarial Networks and Conditional Variational Autoencoders [13]. During the Convai2 challenge, Sequence-to-Sequence generative dialogue systems outperformed response-based approaches with the winning proposals all utilizing BERT based architectures [8].

The relative advantages of both dialogue system methodologies have led to hybridization of architectures that combine generative approaches with retrieval-based approaches. Facebook's Blender open domain dialogue model which claims state-of-the-art performance in response formation, uses a hybridized poly-encoder retrieval methodology with a response ranking and blending module based on decoder networks [22]. Other hybrid solutions demonstrate improvements through the incorporation of increasingly complex semantic representations of language supporting the findings of the literature review of linguistic reasoning which identified semantic information as a key element of linguistic reasoning [6].

4   Hypotheses Development

The review of linguistic reasoning and related work in open domain dialogue systems identified the need for multi-turn semantic processing for language comprehension but drew no direct correlation between their findings. Drawing on the findings of this research, the authors propose the following informational hypotheses.

4.1 Preservation of Informational Atomicity

Training embedded representations of a dialogue corpus necessarily generalize corpus variations to an approximated fit of the distribution. Preservation of informational atomicity predicts that any informational generalization beyond its least subdivisible component holds the potential to obscure informational elements that may differentiate a conversational response. This hypothesis recognizes the necessity of generalization as subject to processing requirements, cost, and complexity, and notes that human linguistic reasoning similarly generalizes environmental experience. Despite this, the hypothesis suggests that lower informational atomicity in informational representation will result in improved open domain dialogue response formation.

4.2 Modelling Dialogue as Semantics, not Ontologies

Modelling language as semantics rather than ontology suggests that open domain language models should represent language as semantics, or discreet experiences of the environment and dialogue, rather than as universal types. This hypothesis is supported by the findings of the literature review that highlights the role of linguistic reasoning as a communication medium for experience rather than UG or ontological structures [10]. This hypothesis further suggests that natural language itself is the least atomic form of linguistic reasoning which is founded in the diverse experience of environmental stimuli and uses a process of mapping language to experiences rather than reasoning based solely on the information conveyed in language. This hypothesis predicts that systems that only model communicated language will be unable to match the distribution of user-generated dialogue. This hypothesis suggests that any environmental information that can be perceived by the users of natural language or that has an influence on response formation, has the potential to improve modelling of language for open domain dialogue.

4.3 The Role of Distant Semantic Features

The role of distant semantic features hypothesizes that distant or multi-sequence semantic features are impactful to response formation and linguistic reasoning outcomes. This hypothesis is supported by the growing evidence demonstrating the importance of distant semantic features to response formation both from linguistic reasoning and related work in open domain dialogue [1, 19]. While this hypothesis acknowledges that application environments often limit a deployed language models' ability to capture temporal semantics, it suggests that modelling of distant semantic features combined with preservation of the temporal continuum and preservation of informational atomicity will improve open domain dialogue response formation.

5   Methodology

The paper's dialogue system implementation followed a methodology that used the proposed informational hypotheses to inform the selection of technologies and dialogue modelling architectures. The authors' hypotheses informed the requirements engineering of the system's implementation, but it was beyond the scope of the paper's work to control for all the hypotheses implications.

5.1 Dialogue Representation

Attention-based Sequence-to-Sequence encoding methodologies demonstrate state-of-the-art performance for generating language representations and can capture the objective and semantic features of language [1]. Another benefit of using attention-based encoders for language encoding is the availability of pre-trained and open-sourced language models for use in transfer learning. A disadvantage of using embedded language models, however, is the violation of the hypothesized preservation of informational atomicity which suggests that language encoding necessarily generalizes corpus variation. Another disadvantage of transfer learning is the lack of availability of models that incorporate other environmental information in addition to language. This makes pre-trained language models unsuitable for testing the hypothesized modelling of language as semantics rather than ontology. The drawbacks of Sequence-to-Sequence DNN approaches led the paper's implementation to develop two alternative dialogue representation and response formation architectures.

The first dialogue representation tested used directed graph-based language representation that stored dialogue as values in the nodes of a directed graph with conversational turns indicated using turn tokens. In this representation, a dialogue corpus was loaded into a graph database for corpus storage. A graph-based language representation was selected as it enables the preservation of atomic conversational features and implicitly preserves sequential semantics (Fig. 1).

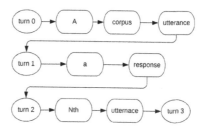

Fig. 1. Directed conversation graph

The second dialogue representation tested used feature vector-based language representation using the established approach demonstrated by Sequence-to-Sequence language encoding methodologies. This selection was justified by the findings of the review of related work suggesting that attention-based Sequence-to-Sequence encoding methodologies preserve semantic information better than alternatives. It was beyond the scope of the paper's work to train language encoding models, so two pre-trained dialogue encoding models were selected for evaluation through transfer learning. The first of these models, the Universal Sentence Encoder was trained on a variety of natural language including dialogue and is provided by Cer et al., [4]. The second, Sentence-BERT was trained for dialogue-based response generation and is provided by Reimers et al., [21]. In the vector-based representation, a dialogue corpus was encoded as feature vectors and stored in a vector database for corpus storage. A conceptual visualization of the language representation using feature vectors is given in Fig. 2.

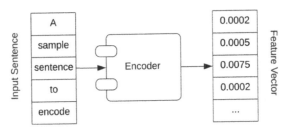

Fig. 2. DNN encoding

5.2 Response Formation

Comparing architectures between generative and retrieval architectures demonstrates advantages and disadvantages between both approaches. Modern generative approaches demonstrate state-of-the-art performance compared to retrieval architectures but have trade-offs such as expensive computational requirements, reduced fluency, and decreased syntactic correctness compared to retrieval-based systems [12]. Lan et al., [15] note that hybrid architectures minimize some of these downsides but are comparatively more computationally expensive. Due to the prohibitive computational requirements of generative and hybrid architectures and paper's prototype selected a retrieval architecture for both the graph-based approach and the embedding-based approach.

Retrieval in the graph-based representations used graph transversal-based query matching combined with keyword feature extraction to match similar results from an input conversational graph returning a result set of similar corpus responses. In the graph-based approach, system responses were selected from the next conversational turn in the dialogue graph enabling corpus responses to be reused in the current conversational context.

The embedding-based approach used cosine similarity-based matching between embeddings of the current conversational input with the embeddings of the dialogue corpus in a vector database. System responses were selected by matching a key value stored in both the embedding and a paired natural language response stored in a NoSQL database. As with the graph-based approach, corpus responses were reused in the current conversational context.

5.3 Response Evaluation

Evaluating open dialogue systems presents unique challenges as many possible responses could be considered valid in a dialogue's context. While evaluation of open domain dialogue is an important area of ongoing research, current evaluation methodologies are divided between the retrieval-based and generation-based system architectures. Huang et al. [12], note that both BLEU and ROUGE, statistical metrics commonly used in dialogue evaluation, rely heavily on system responses lexical similarity with a target response and not with a human's judgement of coherence. Lan et al. [15] suggest that the most reliable means of evaluating open domain dialogue is human annotation but adds that it is not reproducible and is further time-consuming.

While literature notes the limitations of using BLEU and ROUGE in scoring open domain dialogue, they remain popular accuracy measures for response formation. Campillos-llanos et al. [3] suggest that F-Measure scoring correlates more closely to human evaluation than BLUE or ROUGE and has the added benefit of correcting for false positives. Motivated by the widespread use of these measures, this paper's evaluation of the prototype open domain dialogue system used a combination of BLEU, ROUGE, and F1 to enable comparison and provide an objective measure of system accuracy.

6 Results

Proof-of-concept testing during the paper's implementation of the graph-based feature extraction and response formation architecture demonstrated unanticipated limitations. To verify the preliminary test results, a systematic review of query matching approaches was conducted. The result of this testing is presented below with reliability indicating the frequency of returned results-sets and semantic cohesion measured by subjective user evaluation (Table 1).

Table 1. Proof of concept testing graph-based representation

Query match type	Reliability	Semantic cohesion
Exact node values with wildcard pattern	Very low	Low
Exact node values with exact path pattern	Very low	Low
Node value set with wildcard pattern	Medium	Very low
Node value set with exact pattern	Low	Very low
Limited node sets with wildcard pattern	Medium	Very low

The methodical testing presented results indicating the limitation of the implementation. Further testing was conducted into alternative matching approaches such as Jaccardian Similarity, KNN similarity, ANN similarity, and Overlap Similarity. Testing of these matching methodologies produced similar results leading the authors to conclude that a graph-based representation would have to be more thoroughly explored in future work.

Testing was undertaken to evaluate the embedding-based dialogue representation using the encoding models Universal Sentence Encoder [4] and Sentence-BERT [21]. Testing was conducted using varying conversational context over dialogue turns from the DailyDialogue corpus. The result of this testing is presented in Table 2.

Table 2. Performance testing embedding-based representation

Model	Turns	BLEU -1	ROUGE	F-measure (0.5)
Universal sentence encoder	1	34.812%	34.633%	33.565%
Universal sentence encoder	2	34.758%	34.499%	33.491%
Universal sentence encoder	4	22.355%	21.934%	20.928%
Sentence-BERT	1	33.188%	32.880%	31.930%
Sentence-BERT	2	35.409%	32.145%	31.347%
Sentence-BERT	4	19.821%	19.653%	19.574%

7   Discussion of Performance

The prototypes testing aimed to evaluate the suitability of the systems response formation of the course of open domain dialogue. While appropriate metrics for testing semantic cohesion remain an outstanding research question, BLEU, ROUGE, and F-Measure were identified as commonly implemented metrics and were used in testing the accuracy of the system's responses. To further evaluate the success of the system's response formation, the performance test results are compared with the results of other open domain dialogue systems using the DailyDialogue dataset [16]. These results are presented in Table 3.

Table 3. Comparison of performance of vector-based representation

Author	Network type	BLEU-1	ROUGE	F (0.5)
Li et al. [16]	Sequence-to-sequence (retrieval)	35.1%	–	–
	Attn-sequence-to-sequence (retrieval)	33.5%	–	
	Hierarchical encoder-decoder (generative)	**39.6%**	–	–
Luo et al. [17]	Sequence-to-sequence (generative)	12.43%	–	–
	Auto-encoder-matching (generative)	13.55%	–	–
	Attn-sequence-to-sequence (generative)	13.63%	–	–
	Auto-encoder-matching (generative)	14.17%	–	–
This paper	Universal-sentence-encoder (retrieval)	34.81%	34.63%	33.57%
	Sentence-BERT (retrieval)	**35.41%**	32.14%	31.35%

The testing demonstrated that the paper's implementation of open domain response formation compared competitively to the results of both paper's in BLEU scoring. Of the test results, the Sentence-BERT encoder implementation performed best with a BLEU score of 35.41% exceeding all but the Hierarchical Encoder-Decoder implemented by Li et al., [16]. The best accuracy was achieved using a conversational context of two turns in the systems's corpus encoding and matching process.

While the hypothesised improvements resulting from the preservation of informational atomicity were not controlled for in the testing of the open domain dialogue system, the results indicated outcomes supporting the hypothesis. The higher-performing Sentence-BERT encoder represents its embeddings with larger feature vector lengths of 1024 compared to the Universal Sentence Encoder's vector length of 512. While the finding does not control for encoder architecture or training data, the higher degree of informational atomicity enabled by the larger encoding provides limited supporting evidence for the hypothesis.

The hypothesised role of distant semantic features in improving response formation was tested in the system's accuracy testing. The authors of both encoding models suggest that near semantic features are preferred in the pre-trained encodings models training data [4, 21]. This suggestion was confirmed by the results of the systems testings. Despite this, a semantic depth of two conversational turns resulted in the most successful response formation using the Sentence-BERT encoder. The results indicate that distant semantic features play a role in response formation, but limitations of the pre-trained encoding scheme prevented testing of more distant feature extraction.

7.1 Future Work

The paper's open domain dialogue system was able to demonstrate response formation using the syntactic and semantic features of language in an architecture enabling continuous learning through the preservation of experience. The hypotheses identified during the literature review played an important role in informing requirements analysis, design decisions, and implementation. Although the use of a transfer-learning model prevented controlled experimentation for the paper's hypotheses, future work could more directly test each of the hypothesised informational elements of language to establish their veracity.

Future work could test the hypothesised role of informational atomicity by measuring differences in the statistical distributions or long-range dependencies between a language models responses and the distribution of a dataset. Results of such work could measure the role that informational atomicity plays in a models accuracy. Testing the hypothesis suggesting that language be modelled as semantics rather than ontology could take different approaches, but integrating environmental sensor data in modelling open domain dialogue could correlate environmental data to response outcomes. Such testing would require the availability of high-quality datasets incorporating environmental information.

Finally, future work could directly test the role of distant semantic features by varying the training regimes of open domain dialogue systems and comparing the semantic cohesion of the resulting responses. Analogical reasoning literature suggests that multi-sequence long-range semantic dependencies are integrated into linguistic reasoning through a mapping process from shorter sequences of inputs [24]. Modelling short-to-long sequence mapping could produce more efficient feature extraction and improved outcomes in open domain dialogue modelling.

8   Conclusion

The paper's view of linguistic reasoning provided informational hypotheses that corre-lated findings between the fields of Linguistics, Cognitive Sciences, and related work in Open Domain Dialogue modelling. While the informational hypotheses proposed by the paper were not directly tested in the paper's open domain dialogue system the hypotheses informed the requirement engineering and technology selection of the sys-tem's implementation. Following the implementation and testing the system responded with a BLEU-1 accuracy of 35.41% using the DailyDialogue Dataset using the vector embedding based language representation tested. Further work could build on the infor-mational hypotheses proposed by the paper having the potential to impact open domain dialogue modelling and improving response formation.

References

1. Adiwardana, D., et al.: Towards a human-like open-domain chatbot. arXiv:2001.09977 (2020)
2. van den Broek, P., Helder, A.: Cognitive processes in discourse comprehension: passive processes, reader-initiated processes, and evolving mental representations. Discourse Process. **54**(5–6), 360–372 (2017). https://doi.org/10.1080/0163853X.2017.1306677
3. Campillos-Llanos, L., et al.: Designing a virtual patient dialogue system based on terminology-rich resources: challenges and evaluation. Nat. Lang. Eng. **26**(2), 183–220 (2020). https://doi.org/10.1017/S1351324919000329
4. Cer, D., et al.: Universal sentence encoder. arXiv:1803.11175 (2018)
5. Christie, S., et al.: Development of analogical reasoning: a novel perspective from cross-cultural studies. Child Dev. Perspect. **14**(3), 164–170 (2020). https://doi.org/10.1111/cdep.12380
6. Cui, C., et al.: User attention-guided multimodal dialog systems. In: Proceedings of the 42nd International ACM SIGIR Conference on Research and Development in Information Retrieval, pp. 445–454. Association for Computing Machinery, New York, NY, USA (2019). https://doi.org/10.1145/3331184.3331226.
7. Devlin, J., et al.: BERT: Pre-training of deep bidirectional transformers for language understanding. arXiv:1810.04805 (2019)
8. Dinan, E., et al.: The second conversational intelligence challenge (ConvAI2). arXiv:1902.00098 (2019)
9. Evans, N., Levinson, S.C.: With diversity in mind: freeing the language sciences from universal grammar. Behav. Brain Sci. **32**(5), 472–492 (2009). https://doi.org/10.1017/S0140525X09990525
10. Hammer, R., et al.: Individual differences in analogical reasoning revealed by multivariate task-based functional brain imaging. Neuroimage **184**, 993–1004 (2019). https://doi.org/10.1016/j.neuroimage.2018.09.011
11. Horvath, S., et al.: Acquisition of verb meaning from syntactic distribution in preschoolers with autism spectrum disorder. Language Speech Hearing Serv. Schools **49**(3S), 668–680 (2018). https://doi.org/10.1044/2018_LSHSS-STLT1-17-0126
12. Huang, M., et al.: Challenges in building intelligent open-domain dialog systems. ACM Trans. Inform. Syst. **38**(3), 1–32 (2020). https://doi.org/10.1145/3383123
13. Ke, P., et al.: Generating informative responses with controlled sentence function. In: Pro-ceedings of the 56th Annual Meeting of the Association for Computational Linguistics (vol. 1: Long Papers), pp. 1499–1508. Association for Computational Linguistics, Melbourne, Australia (2018). https://doi.org/10.18653/v1/P18-1139.

14. Kim, H.J., et al.: seq2vec: analyzing sequential data using multi-rank embedding vectors. Electron. Commer. Res. Appl. **43**, 101003 (2020). https://doi.org/10.1016/j.elerap.2020.101003

15. Lan, T., et al.: Self-attention comparison module for boosting performance on retrieval-based open-domain dialog systems. arXiv:2012.11357 (2020)

16. Li, Y., et al.: DailyDialog: a manually labelled multi-turn dialogue dataset. arXiv:1710.03957 (2017)

17. Luo, L., et al.: An auto-encoder matching model for learning utterance-level semantic dependency in dialogue generation. arXiv:1808.08795 (2018)

18. Mehndiratta, A., Asawa, K.: Non-goal oriented dialogue agents: state of the art, dataset, and evaluation. Artif. Intell. Rev. **54**(1), 329–357 (2020). https://doi.org/10.1007/s10462-020-09848-z

19. Nahatame, S.: Revisiting second language readers' memory for narrative texts: the role of causal and semantic text relations. Read. Psychol. **41**(8), 753–777 (2020). https://doi.org/10.1080/02702711.2020.1768986

20. Progovac, L., et al.: Diversity of grammars and their diverging evolutionary and processing paths: evidence from functional MRI study of Serbian. Frontiers Psychol. **9** (2018). https://doi.org/10.3389/fpsyg.2018.00278.

21. Reimers, N., Gurevych, I.: Sentence-BERT: sentence embeddings using Siamese BERT-networks. arXiv:1908.10084 (2019)

22. Roller, S., et al.: Recipes for building an open-domain chatbot. arXiv:2004.13637 (2020)

23. Simms, N.K., et al.: Working memory predicts children's analogical reasoning. J. Exp. Child Psychol. **166**, 160–177 (2018). https://doi.org/10.1016/j.jecp.2017.08.005

24. Westphal, A.J., et al.: Shared and distinct contributions of rostrolateral prefrontal cortex to analogical reasoning and episodic memory retrieval. Hum. Brain Mapp. **37**(3), 896–912 (2016). https://doi.org/10.1002/hbm.23074

25. Yang, H., et al.: Open-domain dialogue generation: presence, limitation and future directions. In: Proceedings of the 2019 7th International Conference on Information Technology: IoT and Smart City, pp. 5–12. Association for Computing Machinery, New York, NY, USA (2019). https://doi.org/10.1145/3377170.3377248.

26. Zhou, M., et al.: Progress in Neural NLP: modeling, learning, and reasoning. Engineering **6**(3), 275–290 (2020). https://doi.org/10.1016/j.eng.2019.12.014

Estimating Semantics Distance of Texts Based on Used Terms Analysis

Krystian Wojtkiewicz[1]([envelope])([ORCID]) and Michał Kawa[2]

[1] Faculty of Computer Science and Management, Wrocław University of Science and Technology, Wrocław, Poland
krystian.wojtkiewicz@pwr.edu.pl
[2] Knowledge and Information Engineering Group, Guimaraes, Portugal

Abstract. Every day we are facing countless texts on various topics. With a growing number of resources, it is getting harder to find valuable content. There is a need for automated tools to evaluate texts and propose new reads based on their similarity to the original one. The paper aims at introducing a method for calculating the semantic distance between two texts. We use well-known morphological tools to disambiguate the meaning and function of each word in the text. Next, we create the similarity matrixes utilizing the weight of WordNet synset relations. Each term can be part of one of three sets, which visualize three levels of semantic distance. While calculating the distance between texts, we consider statistical characteristics that partly use the identification of terms. However, the primary stress is put on the meaning each word brings to the utterance.

Keywords: Semantic similarity · Text similarity · Semantics analysis

1 Introduction

Natural Language Processing (NLP) covers a wide range of topics joining two research areas, i.e., computer analysis and linguistics. It is presumably one of the most extensively explored too. Hundreds of languages are used nowadays and even more that we consider dead. These languages differ in terms of grammar, morphology, lexicon, and phonology. The latter is mainly a concern of voice recognition and won't be a subject of further consideration in this article. All other properties mentioned above make it impossible to switch NLP algorithms between languages smoothly. Families of languages share similar grammar, morphology, and lexicon characteristics, e.g., Roman or Slavic languages. Thus, it makes it easier to adjust or reuse the algorithms between them. The ultimate goal of any NLP technology is to provide computer understanding of natural languages. That, in turn, implies working with semantics, i.e., the meaning of an utterance in natural language. In this paper, we will focus on the aspect of similarity of texts. The similarity between texts can be measured in many ways and focused on various factors. However, in most cases, it is focused on the similarity

© Springer Nature Switzerland AG 2021
N. T. Nguyen et al. (Eds.): ICCCI 2021, LNAI 12876, pp. 668–681, 2021.
https://doi.org/10.1007/978-3-030-88081-1_50

of strings, i.e., calculating the number of words occurring in the same order in two texts. The application of it is evident, i.e., the plagiarism check [5]. This approach doesn't take into account semantics, just pure statistics. The authors believe that there is space for another method to evaluate the similarity of texts based on their meaning [4].

This paper aims to introduce a method for calculating the semantic distance between two texts. We assume that those texts might use a different style, their length is different, and even the authors have no idea about each other work. To present the method in the following section, we will go through the related work in NLP. The third section of the paper is dedicated to the description of the technique itself. The last section concludes the paper.

2   Related Works

There are various techniques in the NLP area that researchers explored in recent years. This paper will focus on grammar, morphology, and lexicon as the primary source of information on text semantics. Since we aim at the implementation to run on Polish text, below, we will focus on NLP tools and techniques related to this natural language. . Polish is one of the Slavic languages characterized by complex words' morphology, exhaustive lexicon, and complicated grammar. Over the years, several research groups developed more sophisticated tools to discover meaning either at the level of words or whole sentences. Below, we will characterize a choice of tools useful for us in developing the semantic similarity distance.

Morfeusz

The main goal of this tool is to provide a morphological analysis of sentences in Polish [12,13]. It is critical since, unlike languages like English, simple tokenization does not work well. On the other hand, once identified, every word gives a lot of information on its usage. Morfeusz works on lexemes which are considered abstract grammatical units that aggregate word forms having similar relation to reality. For each word and punctuation, the tool returns the list of suitable lexemes. Each of them is provided with detailed characteristics, including:

Segment identifies the word in the sentence,
Orthographic form the actual word from the sentence,
Lemma one of possible interpretation of meaning associated with a given the word based on its form,
Tag List of tags associated with Lemma. The tags are positional, where the first position defines the part of speech. The following ones stand for the values of grammatical categories of each class.

Polish WordNet - plWordNet

It is based on the original Princeton WordNet project [8]. The work on the Polish version started in 2005 and is continued nowadays. At this stage, the project is running in its fourth revision and is much more advanced than the original one [3,7,9]. plWordNet uses synsets as its primary unit. Synsets are lists of words ordered with descending strength of the relation. The essential association in WordNet is synonymy, which was used to create the very name of Synset. Nowadays, 27 other are defined, e.g., meronymy, hypernymy, hyponymy, instance, and type. The WordNet approach supplements the morphological one to show the word's meaning based on its relations with other words.

Jasnopis

This project provides means to compute the readability of texts [1,2]. The output is a value from the 1–7 range. The highest number on the scale refers to complicated text, e.g., doctoral thesis, while the lowest indicates elementary text understandable by children. For those, who require more details, the system provides a vector of values statistically characterizing the text. Apart from simple indicators, some more sophisticated ones are based on the type of word identified in the text. Nevertheless, the whole approach is purely statistical and doesn't focus on semantics at all.

MorphoDiTa

It is an open-source tool designed for the morphological analysis of natural language texts. According to its authors, it performs morphological analysis, morphological generation, tagging, and tokenization [10]. It was adopted for the Polish language by the CLARIN infrastructure with the use of the NKJP tagset [11]. MorphoDiTa uses machine learning techniques based on artificial neural networks. The project initially developed for the Czech language can also be used for the English language.

3   The Description of Semantic Distance Calculation

The primary assumption underlying the developed method was to define the semantic similarity of two texts, understood as the distance between the topics of these texts. The authors normalized the target range of the obtained values to $[0, 1]$. Full thematic compatibility of the two texts, i.e., they are identical, is marked as 0. On the other hand, the value 1 refers to a situation in which two texts are maximally distant, i.e., their semantic distance is maximum; thus, the similarity is the smallest. The method consists of three main steps. The first of them is the identification of text properties and metrics (S1). Next, we compute the measures for each texts' properties and metrics (S2). We could use those measures for the simple characterization of text. Instead, the third part of the method uses it as an input to the formula that computes the similarity factor for two chosen texts (S3). Below, we will describe in detail each step.

3.1   S1 - The Identification of Text Properties and Metrics

The method presented in this paper doesn't put any limitation on the length of text. However, for clarity, we have decided to work with four levels of complexity, namely, letters, words, sentences, and paragraphs. The first group of measures is simple statistics:

1. number of paragraphs
2. number of sentences
3. number of words
4. number of letters
5. number of words having a given number of letters - this is simply the distribution of words according to their length
6. number of simple sentences in the whole text
7. number of complex sentences in the whole text
8. number of sentence equivalents in the whole text.

Based on the set above, the authors defined more complex measures.

9. the average number of words in the sentence
10. the average number of sentences in the paragraph
11. the average number of words in paragraph
12. the average length of words
13. the average number of simple sentences in the paragraph
14. the average number of complex sentences in the paragraph
15. the minimum length of the sentence in the whole text
16. the maximum length of the sentence in the whole text
17. the minimum number of words in the paragraph
18. the maximum number of words in the paragraph
19. the minimum number of sentences in paragraphs
20. the maximum number of sentences in paragraphs.

Another set of measures is based on the morphological properties of the identified sentence elements. With morphological analysis, we can assign both parts of speech and parts of a sentence to each word. For the sake of simplicity, we have narrowed the set of sentence parts to:

– subject
– predicate
– sub-subject
– meaningful words.

We can also determine whether a sentence is simple or complex or even a sentence fragment. Having this information, we supplement measures with the following:

21. the number of words of each part of words
22. the number of unique words of each part of words
23. the number of words of each sentence part

24. the number of unique words of each sentence part
25. the average number of verbs in the sentence
26. the verbs to nouns ratio
27. the average number of nouns in the sentence
28. the subjects to predicates ratio.

Moreover, the authors build sets of words for each text:

– *SUBJECTS*,
– *SUBSUBJECTS*,
– *IMPORTANTS*.

While the two first sets are self-explanatory, the third one consists of all other words in the utterance, except for interpunctuation, conjunctions, prepositions, abbreviations, pronouns, and personal pronouns. In the process of set creation, the authors used the morphological analyzers from the Sect. 2.

Once we identified the sets, the last element that needed to be defined in this stage was the similarity index for relations between words. The method will use the binary relations between sets' elements from two texts. Thus, for each relation, the weight from $[0, 1]$ was defined. The weights' index is presented in Table 1. The majority of weights have been taken from [6] and were marked in blue and italic. The authors of this paper defined the remaining weights and kept them green.

3.2   S2 - Calculation of Text Properties and Metrics

The second step of the method focuses on computing the values of metrics for texts. An important aspect is that once calculated, those values won't change in time. We will have several statistical characteristics and a few complex structures for each text in the database. Each word will have its morphological features as well as pointers to WordNet synsets. It is the most technical step. Therefore, its further description doesn't contain any vital information for the recreation of the method.

3.3   S2 - Calculation of Semantic Distance

It is the last part of the method. It is assumed that we compute the semantic distance between two texts that are presumably different. Since we are calculating the distance, we expect it to fulfill the basic concept such as:

$$D_{(T_1, T_2)} = D_{(T_2, T_1)} \tag{1}$$

where

D is the semantic distance calculated for two texts,
T_i is a subsequent text.

Nevertheless, at first, we will obtain two one-sided similarity indexes that will be later normalized.

Table 1. Weights for individual synset relations.

plWordNet id	Relation name (+subtype)		Weight
–	Synonymy		1,0
10	Hyponymy		0,7
11	Hypernymy		0,49
14	Meronymy	–	0,42
20		part of	0,42
21		portion of	0,42
22		place of	0,42
23		collection element of	0,42
24		meterial of	0,42
25		part (reflexive relationship to rel. 20)	0,42
26		portion (reflexive relationship to 21)	0,42
27		place (reflexive relationship to 22)	0,42
28		collection element (reflexive relationship to 23)	0,42
29		material (reflexive relationship to 24)	0,42
86	processivity		0,38
80	causation		0,45
106	type		0,49
107	instance		0,7
108	fuzzynymy		0,55
–	other		0,2

Similarity matrix

A similarity matrix is a primary tool used in the method. It is calculated for two texts and identifies the similarity of set elements across two sets of words. Having two word sets S_1 and S_2, we assume that rows represent elements of S_1, while columns represent elements of S_2. The values at the intersection of the row and column represent a similarity measure of two words. This measure is a similarity computed for the synsets of each word with the use of the Table 1. However, if we cannot find the synset for a word, e.g., name, we check if the words are equal in terms of the text strings, and if that is true, we assign 1.

Let's consider an example, where we have two sets of words

$$S_1 = \{wybory, wynik, obywatel, prezydent, Warszawa\} \qquad (2)$$

$$S_2 = \begin{Bmatrix} policja, wynik, kraj, sukces, glosowanie, \\ urna, komisja, Warszawa, lista \end{Bmatrix} \qquad (3)$$

The similarity matrix for those two sets is presented in the Table 2.

Similarity Measures

Using the similarity matrix mentioned above, the authors propose eight potential measures that the authors might later use to compute the similarity of texts.

Table 2. The similarity matrix for set S_1 and S_2

	policja	wynik	kraj	sukces	głosowanie	urna	komisja	Warszawa	lista
wybory	0	0	0	0	0,7	0	0	0	0
wynik	0	1	0	0,49	0	0	0	0	0
obywatel	0	0	0,42	0	0	0	0	0	0
prezydent	0	0	0	0	0	0	0	0	0
Warszawa	0	0	0	0	0	0	0	1	0

Below, we will provide a short description, along with an equation for each of the measures. It is assumed that some proposed measures might be neglected at later stages, and only the chosen ones will be helpful.

COVERAGE_UNIQUE

The *COVERAGE_UNIQUE* measure is depicted by M_{CU} symbol. It is the quotient of the number of words with at least one relation and the number of all words in the given set.

$$M_{CU} = \frac{\sum\limits_{i=0}^{n} o_i}{n}, \tag{4}$$

where,

o_i has value 1, if *i-th* word synset has at least one relation with a synset identified by a word in the second set; otherwise it takes value of 0,

n is a number of unique words in a set.

COVERAGE_ALL

The *COVERAGE_ALL* measure is depicted by M_{CU} symbol. It is a generalization of the abovementioned measure since it takes into account all words. If the synset for a given word has a relationship with any of the words in the opposing set, we evaluate the number of this word occurrences in the text (not a set).

$$M_{CA} = \frac{\sum\limits_{i=0}^{n} k_i}{|Z|}, \tag{5}$$

where,

k_i is the cardinality of *i-th* word whose synset has at least one relation with the synsets of the second set words,

$|Z|$ is the number of all words in a given set (with repetitions),

n is a number of unique words in a set.

MAX_ALL

Another similarity measure, denoted by M_{MA}, takes into account the values of the synset similarity measures of the given words. For each word (synset), we identify all possible similarity types according to Table 1 to a word (synset) from the opposing set. Next, we choose the maximum of those. It is later used as a weight to the number of words.

$$M_{MA} = \frac{\sum_{i=0}^{n} (m_i \times k_i)}{|Z|} \tag{6}$$

where,

m_i is the maximum similarity index value for a i-th word,
k_i is the cardinality of i-th word whose synset has at least one relation with the synsets of the second set words,
$|Z|$ is the number of all words in a given set (with repetitions),
n is a number of unique words in a set.

MAX_UNIQUE

In this measure, like the previous one, we focus on the maximum similarity index. However, we only compute this for words with at least one similar counterpart in the opposing set.

$$M_{MU} = \frac{\sum_{i=0}^{n} (m_i \times k_i)}{\sum_{i=0}^{n} l_i} \tag{7}$$

where,

m_i is the maximum similarity index value for a i-th word,
k_i is the cardinality of i-th word whose synset has at least one relation with the synsets of the second set words,
l_i is the number of all words in a given set that have at least one similarity index greater than 0,
n is a number of unique words in a set.

AVG_ALL

The following measure, denoted as M_{AA}, consists in calculating the weighted mean of mean similarity measures of words. The primary value is the average similarity measure of a word, while the weights are the number of words.

$$M_{AA} = \frac{\sum_{i=0}^{n} (a_i \times k_i)}{|Z|} \tag{8}$$

where,

a_i is the mean similarity index value for a i-th word,
k_i is the cardinality of i-th word whose synset has at least one relation with the
  synsets of the second set words,
$|Z|$ is the number of all words in a given set (with repetitions),
n is a number of unique words in a set.

AVG_UNIQUE

In the case of the measure marked as M_{AU}, similarly to the previous one, we
will calculate the weighted average of the mean similarity measure. However, in
this case, we will use only the words for which the mean similarity measure was
greater than zero (the term was significant in the semantic relation).

$$M_{AU} = \frac{\sum_{i=0}^{n} (a_i \times k_i)}{\sum_{i=0}^{n} l_i} \tag{9}$$

where,

a_i is the mean similarity index value for a i-th word,
k_i is the cardinality of i-th word whose synset has at least one relation with the
  synsets of the second set words,
l_i is the number of all words in a given set that have at least one similarity index
  greater than 0,
n is a number of unique words in a set.

AVG_MAX

The seventh proposed similarity measure is the average of the maximum similarity measures. We take the maximum value for each word from the set, sum
them up, and divide by the number of significant words (whose maximum value
of similarity is greater than 0).

$$M_{AM} = \frac{\sum_{i=0}^{n} m_i}{w} \tag{10}$$

where,

m_i is the maximum similarity index value for a i-th word,
w is the sum of words whose maximum similarity measure is greater than 0,
n is a number of unique words in a set.

AVG_COV_SEC

The last measure depends on the word similarity measure and the number of similar word occurrences in the other set. For each significant word (for which there is a measure of similarity with another word greater than zero) in the set, we calculate the weighted average of the word's similarity measure and the cardinality of the word in the second set.

$$M_{ACS} = \frac{\sum_{i=0}^{n} (v_i \times g_i)}{\sum_{i=0}^{n} g_i} \tag{11}$$

where,

v_i is the maximum similarity index value for a i-th word,
g_i is the number of similar words in an opposing set,
n is a number of unique words in a set.

Selection of the Measure

Table 3. Average values for individual measures of similarity within the same category

		COVERAGE _UNIQUE	COVERAGE_ALL	MAX_ALL	MAX_UNIQUE	AVG_MAX
K1	SUBJECTS	0,212275	0,228019	0,217033	0,692191	0,688864
	SUBSUBJECTS	0,334451	0,363937	0,323568	0,861917	0,839555
	IMPORTANTS	0,372115	0,446457	0,405612	0,890660	0.841684
K2	SUBJECTS	0,199653	0,210266	0,210266	0,440000	0,440000
	SUBSUBJECTS	0,296149	0,307689	0,277674	0,841277	0,832228
	IMPORTANTS	0,319153	0,354939	0,312788	0,829387	0,813210
K3	SUBJECTS	0,251909	0,292846	0,282726	0,850912	0,840000
	SUBSUBJECTS	0,341044	0,371925	0,339387	0,884040	0,869252
	IMPORTANTS	0,391062	0,497967	0,460757	0,916002	0,869512
K4	SUBJECTS	0,240631	0,247351	0,236135	0,817502	0,815934
	SUBSUBJECTS	0,368611	0,395506	0,354490	0,868722	0,854054
	IMPORTANTS	0,386375	0,435745	0,385158	0,859114	0,819352
K5	SUBJECTS	0,372824	0,460658	0,431805	0,922466	0,902153
	SUBSUBJECTS	0,399191	0,456618	0,421322	0,906507	0,887889
	IMPORTANTS	0,475922	0,589722	0,544919	0,916135	0,869440

The authors tested a set of fifty texts to select measures that best reflect semantic similarity. The analysis of the obtained values allowed us to determine which measure gives the most promising results. We selected ten texts in 5 categories. 7500 values were calculated (50 texts × 50 texts × 3 set types). Note that it still treats *K1_T04* to *K1_T10* and *K1_T10* to *K1_T04* as separate relationships. Values for the same measure were collected in three 50 by 50 tables (separately for SUBJECTS, SUBSUBJECTS, and IMPORTANTS). Then the authors analyzed the obtained values.

First, the measures AVG_ALL, AVG_UNIQUE, and AVG_COV_SEC were rejected due to the facts, they lack the potential to score full similarity (value 1) for two identical texts. If such a possibility was allowed, there could be a case where the resulting value for two identical texts would be less than 1. By definition, the text is semantically similar to itself, so it should obtain 1. For $COVERAGE\_UNIQUE$, $COVERAGE\_ALL$, MAX_ALL, MAX_UNIQUE, and AVG_MAX the authors prepared the Table 3 where the mean values of similarity within the same category for individual sets of texts and individual measures were put.

When analyzing the data in the table, one can observe some interesting properties. Most often, the greatest similarity measures are for the set of IMPORTANTS and the smallest for SUBJECTS. The values for individual measures arrange in ascending order as follows: $COVERAGE\_UNIQUE$, $COVERAGE\_ALL$, MAX_ALL, AVG_MAX, MAX_UNIQUE. Further, one can find that the five measures can be divided into two groups with similar values. The first group is $COVERAGE\_UNIQUE$, $COVERAGE\_ALL$, MAX_ALL and the second is AVG_MAX, MAX_UNIQUE. Based on this breakdown, we can discard the first group since its mean values are abnormally low, almost always below 0.5. In this case, only the measures MAX_UNIQUE and AVG_MAX should be further analyzed.

The average values in the second group are very close to each other. The authors checked the average values of measures from different categories to choose the measure that best reflects the text similarity. Due to the limited length of this paper, details regarding this analysis will be omitted. The differences observed during the research showed that those two measures differ by approximately 1–5%. However, looking at the components from which these measures are calculated, AVG_MAX is more promising as a measure that better estimates semantic similarity. For both measures, the final score is influenced by the maximum word similarity index. However, in the case of MAX_UNIQUE, amplifying the final value by the occurrence of terms can lead to an overestimation of similarity in some cases.

Final Measure Normalization

After selecting the appropriate measure of similarity, the next step is to normalize the value of similarity. Until now, when we considered the distance between texts, we broke it down into three sets: SUBJECTS, SUBSUBJECTS, and IMPORTANTS. Now we will reduce this value to the only one that determines the similarity of one text to another (one-sided relationship).

The easiest way would be to calculate the arithmetic mean of the similarity values obtained for each set. However, the authors believe that the similarity of each set type should have a different effect. SUBJECTS are the least numerous set, yet they hold more meaning than the most numerous set of IMPORTANTS.

Therefore, the authors propose to use the weight mean, with weights calculated based on the text features described in Sect. 3.1.

To determine the weights for SUBJECTS and SUBSUBJECTS, we use the quotient of all elements and the number of unique elements of a given set. IMPORTANTS includes SUBJECTS and SUBSUBJECTS. Therefore, while calculating the intermediate mean for IMPORTANTS, we put the power of the IMPORTANTS set in the numerator minus the power of SUBJECTS and SUBSUBJECTS sets. We normalize the weights at the end. For example, if SUBJECTS consists of 9 elements (7 unique), SUBSUBJECTS of 43 elements (37 unique), and IMPORTANTS of 105 words (88 unique) words, then the intermediate weights are as follows:

$$\text{SUBJECT intermediate mean} = \frac{9}{7} \approx 1,2857,$$

$$\text{SUBSUBJECT intermediate mean} = \frac{43}{37} \approx 1,1622,$$

$$\text{IMPORTANTS intermediate mean} = \frac{105 - 9 - 43}{88} \approx 0,6023,$$

Then we normalize them:

$$\text{normalized SUBJECTS weight} = \frac{1,2857}{1,2857 + 1,1622 + 0,6023} \approx 0,42,$$

$$\text{normalized SUBSUBJECTS weight} = \frac{1,1622}{1,2857 + 1,1622 + 0,6023} \approx 0,38,$$

$$\text{normalized IMPORTANTS weight} = \frac{0,6023}{1,2857 + 1,1622 + 0,6023} \approx 0,20.$$

Such normalized weights are used to compute the one-way similarity measure of the entire text (on all three levels) to another text ($S_{T1 \ xrightarrow T2}$). Thus, we can write a formula that normalizes these values in the form:

$$S_{T1 \to T2} = M_{AMp} \times w_{podm} + M_{AMsp} \times w_{sp} + M_{AMiz} \times w_{iz}, \qquad (12)$$

where,

w weights computed for the text T_1,

M_{AM} is the value of the similarity measure (p - SUBJECTS, sp - SUBSUBJECTS, and iz - IMPORTANTS).

For the data given above, the similarity is computed as:

$$S_{K4\_T01 \to K4\_T02} = 1,0 \times 0,42 + 0,8842 \times 0,38 + 0,8537 \times 0,20 \approx 0,9267.$$

At this stage, we can compute one-sided semantic similarity. The last step is to introduce normalization, which will turn two one-sided values into one. The authors decided to adopt the formula based on the number of words in each text. It is intuitive and will allow balancing the values of one-sided similarities properly. Thus, the symmetric $S_{T1,T2}$ similarity measure of two texts has the following formula:

$$S_{T1,T2} = S_{T1 \to T2} \times w_1 + S_{T2 \to T1} \times w_2, \tag{13}$$

$$w_i = \frac{\text{number of words in } T_i}{\text{sum of words in } T_1 \text{ and } T_2}, \tag{14}$$

where,

$S_{T1 \to T2}$ one-sided similarity measure of T_1 and T_2,
$w_1 \text{ and } w_2$ are the weights computed with the use of Eq. 14.

It is obvious that $S_{T1,T2} = S_{T2,T1}$.

Semantic Distance Between two Texts

Until now, this chapter uses the term *text similarity*. However, this paper aims to propose a way to compute the semantic distance of texts. For identical texts, the distance should be 0, while it should take the maximum value for entirely different ones. We stated that the text similarity value is in the range of $[0, 1]$, where 0 means no similarity, and 1 the maximum similarity. To achieve the expected result, the authors decided to transform the similarity value into a semantic distance value by complementing it to 1. Thus, the formula to compute the semantic distance of two texts is defined as follows:

$$D_{T1,T2} = 1 - S_{T1,T2}, \tag{15}$$

4   Conclusions

The paper introduces the novel method for calculating the semantic distance of texts. It was designed using NLP tools for the Polish language. However, the majority of the steps can be easily replicated or any other natural language. The method works with semantics since it focuses on the terms' function in the sentence and their meaning. The method has been checked against 50 selected texts, 10 in each of five categories. The detailed description of the experimentally obtained results, and comments, unfortunately, exceeds the page limit of this paper and will be presented in a separate article.

The future work of the authors includes the development of a universal library for similarity matrix computation. The universality refers to the number of natural languages and the ability to use multiple WordNets. We will also focus on building the framework for the semantic similarity computation that would allow the storage of texts and their characteristics.

References

1. Broda, B., Niton, B., Gruszczynski, W., Ogrodniczuk, M.: Measuring readability of polish texts: baseline experiments. In: LREC, vol. 24, pp. 573–580 (2014)
2. Debowski, Ł., Broda, B., Nitoń, B., Charzyńska, E.: Jasnopis-a program to compute readability of texts in polish based on psycholinguistic research. In: Natural Language Processing and Cognitive Science, p. 51 (2015)
3. Dziob, A., Piasecki, M., Rudnicka, E.: plwordnet 4.1-a linguistically motivated, corpus-based bilingual resource. In: Fellbaum, C., Vossen, P., Rudnicka, E., Maziarz, M., Piasecki, M. (eds.) Proceedings of the 10th Global WordNet Conference, Wroclaw, Poland, 23–27 July 2019, pp. 353–362. Oficyna Wydawnicza Politechniki Wrocławskiej, Wrocław (2019)
4. Krótkiewicz, M., Wojtkiewicz, K.: Introduction to semantic knowledge base: Linguistic module. In: 2013 6th International Conference on Human System Interactions (HSI), pp. 356–362. IEEE (2013)
5. Krótkiewicz, Wojtkiewicz: Features for text comparison. In: Pietka, E., Kawa, J. (eds.) Information Technologies in Biomedicine, pp. 468–475. Springer, Heidelberg (2008). https://doi.org/10.1007/978-3-540-68168-7_52
6. Kedzia, P., Piasecki, M., Orlińska, M.: Word sense disambiguation based on large scale polish CLARIN heterogeneous lexical resources. Cogn. Stud. Cogn. **15**, 269–292 (2015)
7. Maziarz, M., Piasecki, M., Rudnicka, E., Szpakowicz, S., Kedzia, P.: PlWordNet 3.0 - a comprehensive lexical-semantic resource. In: Calzolari, N., Matsumoto, Y., Prasad, R. (eds.) Proceedings of the 26th International Conference on Computational Linguistics: Technical Papers, COLING 2016, Osaka, Japan, 11–16 December 2016, pp. 2259–2268. ACL (2016). http://www.aclweb.org/anthology/C16-1213
8. Miller, G.A.: WordNet: An Electronic Lexical Database. MIT press (1998)
9. Piasecki, M., Szpakowicz, S., Broda, B.: A WordNet from the ground up. Oficyna Wydawnicza Politechniki Wroclawskiej, Wroclaw (2009). http://www.dbc.wroc.pl/Content/4220/_Wordnet.pdf
10. Straková, J., Straka, M., Hajič, J.: Open-source tools for morphology, lemmatization, POS tagging and named entity recognition. In: Proceedings of 52nd Annual Meeting of the Association for Computational Linguistics: System Demonstrations, Baltimore, Maryland, pp. 13–18. Association for Computational Linguistics (June 2014). http://www.aclweb.org/anthology/P/P14/P14-5003.pdf
11. Walentynowicz, W.: MorphoDiTa-based tagger for polish language (2017). CLARIN-PL digital repository. http://hdl.handle.net/11321/425
12. Woliński, M.: Morfeusz – a practical tool for the morphological analysis of Polish. In: Kłopotek, M.A., Wierzchoń, S.T., Trojanowski, K. (eds.) Intelligent Information Processing and Web Mining. Advances in Soft Computing, pp. 503–512. Springer, Heidelberg (2006). https://doi.org/10.1007/3-540-33521-8_55
13. Woliński, M.: Morfeusz reloaded. In: Calzolari, N., et al. (eds.) Proceedings of the 9th International Conference on Language Resources and Evaluation, LREC 2014, Reykjavík, Iceland, pp. 1106–1111. European Language Resources Association (ELRA) (2014). http://www.lrec-conf.org/proceedings/lrec2014/index.html

Internet of Things: Technologies and Applications

AI Threat Detection and Response on Smart Networks

Konstantinos Dermetzis[1,2(✉)] [iD] and Lazaros Iliadis[2] [iD]

[1] School of Civil Engineering, Democritus University of Thrace, Xanthi, Greece
kdemertz@fmenr.duth.gr
[2] Department of Physics, International Hellenic University, Kavala, Greece
liliadis@civil.duth.gr

Abstract. The main goal of smart cities is to dynamically optimize the quality of life, through the application of information and communication technologies (ICT). The involved networks, require a continuous increase in data exchange, in order to intelligently control services and in particular, mechanisms that activate a higher degree of automation in the city. As many critical services are interconnected, the need for cyber security is increasing, in order to ensure data exchange protection, privacy, and better health and safety services for all citizens. The security and evolution of smart cities is based on the security of their smart networks which are activated by specific automation mechanisms, such as the SCADA networks and the pre-eminent automation systems. This paper presents the *AnomaTS*, an advanced *Machine Learning* system, for anomaly detection in sensors of SCADA networks, taking into account the temporal state of their mechanisms.

Keywords: Smart city · AI · Anomaly detection · Cyber threat · Computational intelligence · SCADA

1 Introduction

Attacks against SCADA [1] networks and in particular against the *Industrial Control Systems* (ICS) aim to undertake the mechanical control, the dynamic rearrangement of the centrifuge or the reprogramming in complex devices. The aim of such attacks is to speed up or slow down their operation, leading to the destruction or to the cause of permanent damage of all industrial equipment [2]. One of the most common attacks against SCADA industrial infrastructure is related to the case where the attacker, having first installed himself as *Man-In-The-Middle* in an *Ethernet ring* using the *Device-Level-Ring* protocol, carries out a *Stealthy Sensor* attack [3]. This is achieved by taking advantage of fieldbus communication in the industrial *EtherNet/IP* protocol.

Specifically, the *Fieldbus* protocol is used for distributed real-time control, allowing daisy-chain, star, ring, branch, and tree network topologies. The analog sensor control signals are coded using 4–20 mA measurements, while the I/O settings use messages that do not follow specific formats and sizes, as they are specified by the designer of the

© Springer Nature Switzerland AG 2021
N. T. Nguyen et al. (Eds.): ICCCI 2021, LNAI 12876, pp. 685–695, 2021.
https://doi.org/10.1007/978-3-030-88081-1_51

control system [4]. Communication between sensors and control devices is performed via multicast EtherNet/IP connection over UDP. As IP Multicast is organized the data is transferred to UDP datagrams, using Class D address space network and the communication is done without ensuring the accurate transmission of the data to the information receivers. It should be specified that the opposite happens for the datagrams of the address spaces related to Classes A–C [1].

As each address in the Class D address space, represents the group of those who wish to receive the data, a host participates in the group for as long as it wishes by simply sending a JOIN Internet Group Message Protocol (IGMP) message. Due to the fact that there is no group owner, it is not necessary to be a member of the group in order to send data or to monitor the transmitted information. Obviously, it is generally very easy to install an intruder as *Man-In-The-Middle*. After establishing Man-In-The-Middle, the attacker launches a Stealthy Sensor attack. This attack configures the settings of sensors and actuators, in order to change the operation of specific mechanisms. However, this cannot be figured by the received measurements and it cannot be perceived by the offered displays of the overall system. More sophisticated forms of attack are applied against the sensors used in the control loops to collect measurements on SCADA infrastructure [3]. The sensors, which are active devices of the infrastructure network, are PLCs which are properly connected to each other, in order to allow remote monitoring and control of processes with high response speed.

This is the case even when the devices are distributed between different remote points. Communication (sending and receiving data) is achieved with the widely used SCADA MODBUS messaging protocol, which was originally published by *Modicon* (now Schneider Electric) for use with its programmable logic controllers (PLCs) [5]. It must be clarified that this is part of the *application layer protocol*, located at level 7 of the *OSI model*. Modbus Masters devices request information about the transfer of discrete/analog I/O and data logging from slave Modbus by performing a simple request-response format. A serious vulnerability of MODBUS lies in the inability of the protocol to recognize a forged slave/master IP address in the SCADA network. An attacker who performs a *Man-In-The-Middle* attack, can exploit this vulnerability and collect network MSU/MTU information from the returned messages, by sending queries containing invalid addresses [6].

Initially, the attacker selects network MSU/MTU information from the returned messages, and then he triggers a DoS (denial of service)/DDoS (distributed denial of service) attack, by sending request or response parameters, which contain malicious values related to the selection of the data field [7]. A very common attack scenario is related to the protocols and algorithmic ways of strategic control, which are used by control centers for smooth operation, cost minimization and security of power systems.

Power system safety is usually defined by a set of lower and upper limits for various system parameters, such as power of transmission line, and the allowed minimum/maximum operating frequency [8]. The control strategy is essentially a set of control commands which are sent to sensors and actuators, such as power generator adjustment points, error margins that have no effect on system's security, and various on/off commands. Possible removal of alerts when the system is out of range, as well as the replacement of the cost function parameters, can create the conditions for an enemy attack on the control strategy, with completely disastrous results.

2   Anomaly Detection

Various anomaly detection techniques have been proposed in the literature [9], aiming to resolve severe cases of industrial equipment behavior deviation [10]. They can perform even when the nature of the attack is new and therefore unknown [11]. They are based on a tactic of comparing the current situation, with a model or more generally with a set of parameters that are considered to describe the normal operation of the system. To achieve these results, behavioral analysis related to key network parameters such as operating specifications, average power per time window is widely used.

Detection of abnormalities is related to other technical or heuristic forms of analysis, in order to identify patterns that help detect, identify and predict their occurrence, without leading to false alarms [9, 12]. The implementation of a powerful anomaly detection system requires [9, 13, 14]:

1. Minimization of false positives: False positives lead to reduced categorization performance and to potential loss of events in the future. In order to avoid the problems in question, it is necessary to implement a sensitive system, capable of carrying out warnings only for the most serious anomalies. Accordingly, it should be possible to draw up customized warning rules if additional sensitivity is needed.
2. Alerting: When an incident occurs, there should be real-time or near-real-time alerts to minimize the impact.
3. Scaling: Anomaly detection systems should be able to perform hundreds of checks on data flows over time, automatically scaling forecast methods to deal with increased demand events.
4. Robustness: When an anomaly occurs, the algorithm should not integrate these data points in order to estimate normal system behavior, but it should be able to avoid the anomaly, using large windows of historical data.
5. Handle missing data: Missing measurements may create a decomposing coherence structure that weakens the ability to predict. This should be adequately addressed by anomaly detection algorithms.
6. Filtering: Some anomalies are much more important than others, so it should be possible to filter them and take respective action.

The proposed *AnomaTS* anomaly detection system, seeks to understand the interactions between the mechanisms of intelligent networks and their automation processes, aiming to identify cyber-attacks. More specifically, the proposed approach creates a model that correlates the status of a system and its evolution over time, using modern Machine Learning (ML) techniques. Its target is to detect specialized cyber-attack patterns.

3   The Proposed Anomaly Detection Methodology

The proposed anomaly detection methodology is implemented as a system of iterative tasks that is applied on dataflows. Basically, there are three types of performed processes:

1. Data ingestion. They collect input source data in a buffer and they process them.
2. Anomaly detection. They receive measurement data from the buffer and apply anomaly detection methodologies.
3. The anomaly detection algorithm makes a real-time prediction, based on a trained model that has been trained in dead time.
4. It can maintain abnormal points and predictions in the buffer and it can display them centrally, through a centralized anomaly control panel.
5. Alerting. It takes the abnormal points from the buffer and it filters them with the configured rules, which are synthesized as concentrations of diametric measurements and they are compared to predefined boundaries
6. If these rules are followed, notifications are sent and actions are imposed.

The system is assisted by a database that enhances the anomaly detection workflow by storing the following:

1. Metrics metadata: They include measurement aliases, measurement levels and measurement relationships
2. Ingestion configuration: It determines data retention windows, data source types and endpoints.
3. Anomaly detection rules: They are defining anomaly retention time windows, model references and limits.
4. Configurations: They are related to configurations of notification rules, and anomaly visualization.

The actual anomaly detection problem, can be considered as a problem of analysis – prediction of time series [6, 13]. The aim is to find the mathematical relation that can model historical data in relation to time. The general modeling method, uses non-parametric techniques offering significant advantages over conventional methods. It gives an opportunity to overcome the statistical problems associated with the normality and linearity assumptions that are necessary in conventional or linear regression methods. The hypothesis of the underlying technique [15], suggests that the predictors have a cumulative structure, which allows their easy interpretation and modeling. At the same time, a detailed search of the transformation of each variable is not required. More specifically, the estimation of the dependent variable Y in this case, for a single independent variable X, can be given by the following Eq. 1:

$$\Upsilon = s(X) + error \tag{1}$$

Where $s(X)$ is an unspecified smoothing function, whereas *error* is the error which usually has zero mean value and constant dispersion. The smoothing function can be determined, for example, by the *current mean* or by the *current median,* or by the local *least-squares*, the *Kernel*, the *Loess* or the *spline* method. The term "*current*" means the serial calculation of a statistic, which is applied to overlapping intervals of values of the independent variable, such as *running mean*. In modeling, the *classical linear hypothesis* is extended to include any error probability distribution (*Poisson, Gamma, Gaussian, Binomial* και *Inverse Gaussian*).

3.1 Description of the Dataset

The *Factry.io* data collection platform, combined with the *InfluxDB* were employed to create an ideal simulation scenario [16]. The aim was the collection of industrial environment data, based on the *OPC-UA* open-source collector protocol. It is a collection of sensor data in the form of time series.

Sensor data is collected from construction equipment, via programmable PLC controllers and SCADA systems in order to be stored in InfluxDB. The storage database is optimized for timestamp or time series. Time series data is obtained by measurements or by events that are monitored and collected over time. Such events can be server metrics, application performance monitoring and transactions. Potential sources can be sensors, or various types of analytics.

In this case, one-year data were collected from hourly measurable values of three sensors, in the context of a machine condition that operates 24/7. The attack configures the sensor settings, in order to change the operation of specific mechanisms, but this is not perceived by the meters and displays of the overall system.

Specifically, there is a storage tank for raw water. This includes a water level sensor, a valve that opens when the sensor shows a level lower or equal to 0.5 m and closes when the level is higher than 0.8 m. It also contains a pump, whose action depends on a process according to which the pressure levels lead in separation through a semipermeable membrane. If the water level in the tank is below 0.25 m, the pump is immediately switched off, which is interpreted as a safety mechanism. The attacker's goal is to exaggerate the water without being detected by a standard detection mechanism based on the detection of anomalies. This is achieved by modifying the sensor and actuator information, by constructing appropriate packets, which are adapted so that the fieldbus communication can change the functionality of the devices.

A graphical representation of the anomalies contained in the time series under consideration is shown in Figs. 1 and 2 below.

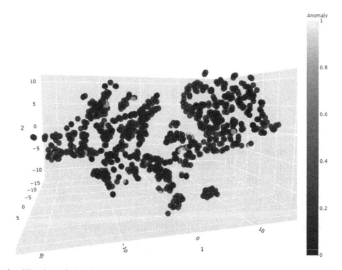

Fig. 1. 3D plot of the time-series anomalies in the IoT (internet of things) dataset

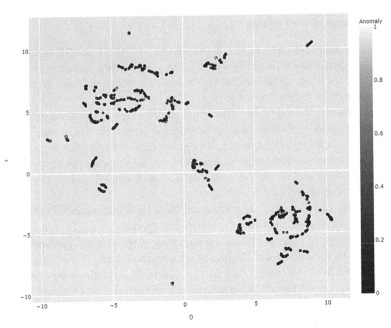

Fig. 2. 2D plot of the time-series anomalies in the IoT dataset

4 The Proposed Intelligent AnomaTS Algorithm

Considering the enormous difficulty of the attack scenario, the algorithm additionally receives the pressure drop measurements in a water filter present in the tank. The difference in the measurements of water pressure collected at the input from the ones collected at the output, in combination with the indications of other sensors, can give a clear sign of an anomaly related to a cyber-attack.

To solve the given scenario, the intelligent *AnomaTS* algorithm is proposed, which adapts as components, many linear and non-linear time functions, where in their simplest form three basic elements are used: trend, seasonality, and events, which are combined in the following Eq. 2 [17]:

$$y(t) = g(t) + s(t) + ev(t) + e(t) \tag{2}$$

where:

$g(t)$, trend models *non-periodic* changes (i.e. growth over time)
$s(t)$, seasonality presents *periodic* changes (i.e. weekly, monthly, yearly)
$ev(t)$, ties in effects of events (on potentially irregular schedules ≥ 1 day(s))
$e(t)$, covers idiosyncratic changes not accommodated by the model

A more general form of the above equation can be as follows:

$$y(t) = piecewise\_trend(t) + seasonality(t) + events\_effects(t) + noise(t)$$

In a more thorough analysis, the test variables can be deconstructed as follows:

1. *Trend*. The process includes two possible trend models for g(t), namely a Saturating Growth Model and a Piecewise Linear Model as follows:

   a. Saturating Growth Model. If the data suggests promise of saturation:

$$g(t) = \frac{C}{1 + exp(-k(t - m))} \tag{3}$$

   where C is the carrying capacity, k is the growth rate and m is an offset parameter.

   The integration of trend changes in the model is explicitly defined by the S change points S_j, $j = 1, \ldots, S$ where the change in growth rate is located. This defines a change of settings vector δ_j respective to time s_j with $\delta \in R^S$. For every moment t the rate k can be expressed as $k + \sum_{j:t>S_j} \delta_j$. If in this relation we estimate the vector $\alpha(t) \in \{0, 1\}^S$ such as:

$$a_j(t) = \begin{cases} 1, & \text{if } t \geq S_j \\ 0, & \text{otherwise} \end{cases} \tag{4}$$

   The rhythm at the moment t is $k + a(t)^T \delta$. When the rythm k is set, the offset parameter m must also be adapted to connect the endpoints of the sections. The correct setting at the point of change j is estimated as follows:

$$y_j = \left(S_j - m - \sum_{i<j} y_t \right) \left(1 - \frac{k + \sum_{i<j} \delta_t}{k + \sum_{i\leq j} \delta_t} \right) \tag{5}$$

   The final function is completed as follows:

$$g(t) = \frac{C(t)}{1 + exp\left(-\left(k + a(t)^T\delta\right)\left(t - \left(m + a(t)^Ty\right)\right)\right)} \tag{6}$$

   b. *Linear Trend with Changepoints*. It is a Piecewise Linear Model with stable development rate, estimated as follows:

$$g(t) = \left(k + a(t)^T\delta\right)t + \left(m + a(t)^Ty\right) \tag{7}$$

   where k is the growth rate, δ has the rate adjustments, m is the offset parameter and, to make the function continuous, y_j is set to $-S_j\delta_j$.

   c. *Automatic Changepoint Selection* is used to estimate the changepoints as follows:

$$\delta_j \sim Laplace(0, \tau) \tag{8}$$

   where τ directly controls the flexibility of the model in altering its rate. It should be noted that a sparse earlier adjustment δ has no effect on the primary growth rate k, such as τ evolves to 0 and the adjustment reduces the typical (no piecewise) logistic or linear growth.

d. *Trend Forecast Uncertainty.* When the model deviates beyond background to make a prediction, the trend $g(t)$ will have a stable rythm. Uncertainty in the forecast trend is estimated by extending the production model forward, where there are S change points over a history of points T, each of which has a change of pace $\delta_j \sim Laplace(0, \tau)$. The simulation of future rhythm changes (imitating those of the past) is achieved by replacing τ t with a variance derived from the data. This is achieved by estimating the maximum probability of the rate scale parameter as follows:

$$\lambda = \frac{1}{S} \sum\nolimits_{j=1}^{S} |\delta_j| \tag{9}$$

Future sample change points are randomized in such a way that the average frequency of the change points matches the corresponding historical points as follows:

$$\forall_j > T, \begin{cases} \delta_j = 0 \, w.p. \frac{T-S}{T} \\ \delta_j \sim Laplace(0, \lambda) \, w.p. \frac{S}{T} \end{cases} \tag{10}$$

2. *Seasonality.* Seasonal variable $s(t)$ offers adaptivity to the model, allowing changes based on everyday, weekly and annual seasonality. Approximate smooth seasonal snapshots are connected to a standard *Fourier series* in order to produce a flexible model of periodic modeling.

$$s(t) = \sum_{n=1}^{N} \left(a_n \cos\left(\frac{2\pi nt}{P}\right) + b_n \sin\left(\frac{2\pi nt}{P}\right) \right) \tag{11}$$

3. *Events.* The $ev(t)$ element reflects predictable events, including those on irregular schedules, which may create serious bias in the model. Assuming that the results of the events are independent, seasonality is calculated by the model creating a regression matrix:

$$Z(t) = [1(t \in D_1), \ldots, 1(t \in D_L)] \tag{12}$$

$$h(t) = Z(t)k \tag{13}$$

5 Running and Testing the AnomaTS Algorithm

Utilizing the procedure described above, the model was trained to detect the abnormalities that occur during the operation of the SCADA automations that control the water tank of the scenario under consideration. The class separation threshold, plays the most important and critical factor in the success or failure of the anomaly recognition method. To determine an optimal threshold, this paper proposes a reliable heuristic method of selection, based solely on evaluation criteria. In particular, the proposed algorithm assumes that a distance function is defined in the training phase, which measures the distance d between the objects and the respective target category. The threshold

θ, is used for the binary class separation (*normal* or *abnormal*) [11, 18]. The samples (outliers) for which the anomaly score deviates from the normal operation by more than 25% are characterized as *abnormals*. This percentage emerged after a thorough analysis following a trial and error approach. Finally, the threshold θ was set at *Anomaly score* > 0.6 in order to strengthen the classifier and isolate any divergent actions (Fig. 3).

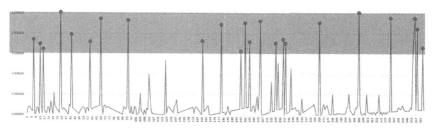

Fig. 3. Outliers with *Anomaly score* > 0.6

The following Figs. 4 and 5 show the results of the tests performed to select the proper threshold, that could offer the best performance.

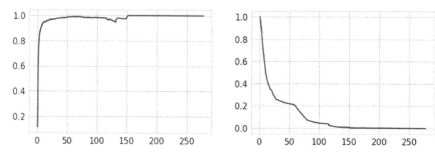

Fig. 4. Precision for different threshold values   **Fig. 5.** Recall for different threshold values

The following Table 1, is the Confusion Matrix of the Binary Classification performed following the proposed *AnomaTS* method. Table 2 presents the values of the classification accuracy for five different Machine Learning algorithms.

Table 1. Confusion matrix

	Normal	Abnormal	
TP	**80**	7	**FN**
FP	5	**273**	**TN**

In conclusion, based on the obtained values of the performance indices and taking into account the objective difficulties raised in this research, the proposed model has been proven very efficient, able to cope with complex situations and to recognize anomalies.

Table 2. Classification accuracy and performance metrics

Classifier	Accuracy	RMSE	Precision	Recall	F-score	AUC
AnomaTS	96.72%	0.0841	0.967	0.967	0.967	0.9823
One class SVM	94.18%	0.0942	0.942	0.942	0.942	0.9790
Isolation forest	93.57%	0.0936	0.935	0.935	0.936	0.9712
k-NN	92.29%	0.1009	0.991	0.930	0.930	0.9697
Clustering	88.57%	0.1128	0.886	0.886	0.886	0.9464

6 Conclusions

An extremely innovative, reliable, low-demand and highly efficient anomaly recognition system, based on advanced computational intelligence methods, was presented in this paper. The proposed framework, utilizes advanced techniques in order to detect malfunctions or deviations from the normal operation mode of industrial equipment, which in most of the cases is due to cyber-attacks. The proposed digital security system was tested on a complex data set, which responds to specialized operating scenarios of normal and malicious behavior.

Proposals for the development and future improvements of this system, should focus on the automated optimization of the appropriate pre-training parameters, so as to achieve an even more efficient, accurate and faster classification process. It would also be important to study the expansion of this system by implementing more complex architectures with the implementation of multidimensional chronological data. Finally, an additional element that could be studied in the direction of future expansion, is the development and application of self-improvement techniques, capable of redefining its parameters automatically, so that it can fully automate the process of anomalies detection.

References

1. Ghosh, S., Sampalli, S.: A survey of security in SCADA networks: current issues and future challenges. IEEE Access **7**, 135812–135831 (2019). https://doi.org/10.1109/ACCESS.2019.2926441
2. Irmak, E., Erkek, İ.: An overview of cyber-attack vectors on SCADA systems. In: 2018 6th International Symposium on Digital Forensic and Security (ISDFS), pp. 1–5 (March 2018). https://doi.org/10.1109/ISDFS.2018.8355379
3. Irmak, E., Erkek, İ.: An overview of cyber-attack vectors on SCADA systems. In: 2018 6th International Symposium on Digital Forensic and Security (ISDFS), Antalya, pp. 1–5 (March 2018). https://doi.org/10.1109/ISDFS.2018.8355379
4. Kang, D., Kim, B., Na, J.: Cyber threats and defence approaches in SCADA systems. In: 16th International Conference on Advanced Communication Technology, pp. 324–327 (Feb. 2014). https://doi.org/10.1109/ICACT.2014.6778974

5. Deng, L., Peng, Y., Liu, C., Xin, X., Xie, Y.: Intrusion detection method based on support vector machine access of Modbus TCP protocol. In: 2016 IEEE International Conference on Internet of Things (iThings) and IEEE Green Computing and Communications (GreenCom) and IEEE Cyber, Physical and Social Computing (CPSCom) and IEEE Smart Data (SmartData), pp. 380–383 (Dec. 2016). https://doi.org/10.1109/iThings-GreenCom-CPSCom-SmartData.2016.90

6. Aminuddin, M.A.I.M., Zaaba, Z.F., Samsudin, A., Juma'at, N.B.A., Sukardi, S.: Analysis of the paradigm on tor attack studies. In: 2020 8th International Conference on Information Technology and Multimedia (ICIMU), pp. 126–131 (Aug. 2020). https://doi.org/10.1109/ICIMU49871.2020.9243607

7. Al-Hawawreh, M., Sitnikova, E.: Leveraging deep learning models for ransomware detection in the industrial internet of things environment. In: 2019 Military Communications and Information Systems Conference (MilCIS), Canberra, Australia, pp. 1–6 (Nov. 2019). https://doi.org/10.1109/MilCIS.2019.8930732

8. Al-Hawawreh, M., den Hartog, F., Sitnikova, E.: Targeted ransomware: a new cyber threat to edge system of brownfield industrial internet of things. IEEE Internet Things J. **6**(4), 7137–7151 (2019). https://doi.org/10.1109/JIOT.2019.2914390

9. Deorankar, A.V., Thakare, S.S.: Survey on Anomaly detection of (IoT)-internet of things cyberattacks using machine learning. In: 2020 Fourth International Conference on Computing Methodologies and Communication (ICCMC), pp. 115–117 (Mar. 2020). https://doi.org/10.1109/ICCMC48092.2020.ICCMC-00023

10. Demertzis, K., Iliadis, L.: A Hybrid Network Anomaly and Intrusion Detection Approach Based on Evolving Spiking Neural Network Classification. In: Sideridis, A.B., Kardasiadou, Z., Yialouris, C.P., Zorkadis, V. (eds.) E-Democracy 2013. CCIS, vol. 441, pp. 11–23. Springer, Cham (2014). https://doi.org/10.1007/978-3-319-11710-2_2

11. Demertzis, K., Iliadis, L., Tziritas, N., Kikiras, P.: Anomaly detection via blockchained deep learning smart contracts in industry 4.0. Neural Comput. Appl. **32**(23), 17361–17378 (2020). https://doi.org/10.1007/s00521-020-05189-8

12. Gaddam, A., Wilkin, T., Angelova, M.: Anomaly detection models for detecting sensor faults and outliers in the IoT – a survey. In: 2019 13th International Conference on Sensing Technology (ICST), Sydney, Australia, pp. 1–6 (Dec. 2019). https://doi.org/10.1109/ICST46873.2019.9047684

13. Cook, A.A., Misirli, G., Fan, Z.: Anomaly detection for IoT time-series data: a survey. IEEE Internet Things J. **7**(7), 6481–6494 (2020). https://doi.org/10.1109/JIOT.2019.2958185

14. Demertzis, K., Iliadis, L., Bougoudis, I.: Gryphon: a semi-supervised anomaly detection system based on one-class evolving spiking neural network. Neural Comput. Appl. **32**(9), 4303–4314 (2019). https://doi.org/10.1007/s00521-019-04363-x

15. Anezakis, V.-D., Demertzis, K., Iliadis, L., Spartalis, S.: A Hybrid Soft Computing Approach Producing Robust Forest Fire Risk Indices. In: Iliadis, L., Maglogiannis, I. (eds.) AIAI 2016. IAICT, vol. 475, pp. 191–203. Springer, Cham (2016). https://doi.org/10.1007/978-3-319-44944-9_17

16. InfluxDB OSS 2.0 Documentation: https://docs.influxdata.com/influxdb/v2.0/. Accessed 19 July 2021

17. Žunić, E., Korjenić, K., Hodžić, K., Đonko, D.: Application of Facebook's prophet algorithm for successful sales forecasting based on real-world data. Int. J. Comput. Sci. Inf. Technol. **12**(2), 23–36 (2020). https://doi.org/10.5121/ijcsit.2020.12203

18. Demertzis, K., Iliadis, L., Anezakis, V.: MOLESTRA: a multi-task learning approach for real-time big data analytics. In: 2018 Innovations in Intelligent Systems and Applications (INISTA), pp. 1–8 (July 2018). https://doi.org/10.1109/INISTA.2018.8466306

A Resource-Aware Method for Parallel D2D Data Streaming

Stanisław Saganowski$^{(\boxtimes)}$ and Przemysław Kazienko

Department of Artificial Intelligence, Faculty of Information and Communication
Technology, Wrocław University of Science and Technology, Wrocław, Poland
stanislaw.saganowski@pwr.edu.pl

Abstract. Smartphones have become an integral part of our lives. One of their crucial functionalities is sharing data. We analyze the communication modules in Android devices (WiFi, Bluetooth, NFC) in terms of parallel data streaming capabilities. We find that increasing the number of concurrent threads reduces the broadcast time, but also consumes a lot of other resources, e.g. RAM. Furthermore, the linear increase in the number of threads created does not guarantee the linear decrease in transfer time. We also find that the Bluetooth 5.0 has, in fact, slower transmission rate than its predecessors.

Keywords: D2D · Data transfer · Parallel streaming · WiFi Direct

1 Introduction

Nowadays, media content plays a crucial role in our life. We share photos and movies, which quality (and file size) grows proportionally to our demands of rapid content transfer. Hence, data transfer technologies are continually being developed. The second-generation 2G cellular networks were commercially launched in 1991, 3G in 1998, and 4G in 2008. Currently, we are desperately waiting for the implementation of the fifth-generation 5G networks, and the requirements stated by the Next Generation Mobile Networks Alliance are tremendous.

A key factor in developing 5G networks is device-to-device (D2D) communication. It allows user devices (UEs) to exchange data directly, without engaging the cellular infrastructure. Researchers and engineers believe that D2D might offload cellular networks, improve spectrum utilization and energy efficiency. Therefore, D2D communication is currently investigated at an unprecedented scale. Every year few surveys are being conducted presenting up-to-date state-of-the-art: [1–12]. Most recently, research is focused on device discovery [13–15],

This work was partially supported by the National Science Centre, Poland, projects no. 2020/37/B/ST6/03806 and 2016/21/B/ST6/01463; by the statutory funds of the Department of Computational Intelligence, Wroclaw University of Science and Technology; by the European Regional Development Fund as a part of the 2014–2020 Smart Growth Operational Programme, CLARIN - Common Language Resources and Technology Infrastructure, project no. POIR.04.02.00-00C002/19.

© Springer Nature Switzerland AG 2021
N. T. Nguyen et al. (Eds.): ICCCI 2021, LNAI 12876, pp. 696–707, 2021.
https://doi.org/10.1007/978-3-030-88081-1_52

security and privacy [7,8,16], mobility management [17–19], interference management [20–22], and power control [23–25].

All these aspects are fundamental, however, we have to remember that in most cases end users are interested in the highest possible transfer rate with smartphones they already possess and with already deployed technologies. For that reason, we analyze the data transfer modules in nowadays Android devices, namely WiFi, Bluetooth (BT), and Near Field Communication (NFC), in terms of data streaming to many devices at the same time. We investigate whether the attributes such as device system version, BT standard version, the size of the transferred file, and the number of devices to which the file is transferred, influence the transfer time. Based on our analysis, we propose a dynamic parallel broadcast solution that is tailored to the sender resources (the number of CPU cores, available RAM, and overall device efficiency). We validate our solution in a real-world scenario.

The proposed solution will be helpful in many everyday activities like sharing media content, multi-player games, group multi-casting, and local voice services.

2   Related Work

Among existing D2D technologies, the ubiquity makes BT, NFC, and WiFi Direct (WFD) especially attractive. Hence, their critical aspects, such as security and power consumption, are being improved continuously. Recently, Shen et al. [26] introduced a short authentication-string-based key agreement protocol, which guarantees secure WFD connection at the cost of exchanging short password over an out-of-band channel. They successfully integrated the protocol into the existing WFD protocol, and also implemented the solution for Android smartphones. Saleh and Dong [16] proposed secure routing protocols for the vehicular ad hoc networks. Xiao and Li [27] mixed current WFD power saving modes to decrease battery consumption. Usman et al. [28], in turn, achieved savings in power consumption in multi-hop D2D network by controlling the WFD group size and transmit power of the devices.

With the Dynamic Adaptive Streaming over HTTP (DASH) technique, which allows dividing large video files (e.g. live stream) into small chunks, it is possible to utilize D2D collaboration to improve video streaming. In recent years several solutions have been proposed that make use of the cellular D2D and WFD D2D to enhance video streaming [29–34]. We discuss only the most relevant to our problem.

Gong et al. [29] proposed a cooperative video streaming system in which a group of WFD connected devices exchange chunks of videos between each other. A group of client devices is managed by the group owner (GO), who allocates downloading tasks of clients and broadcasts video chunks among them. Once the client downloads a video chunk through the cellular network, it passes the chunk to the GO, who then sends the chunk to other clients, thus minimizing the number of exchanged packets. The authors validated the system in a real environment and found that a system consisting of three devices is sufficient to ensure smooth video streaming with bitrate more than 10 Mbps.

Le et al. proposed MicroCast [30], a very interesting solution that takes advantage of signal overhearing. The system allows downloading videos over cellular network faster if done in collaboration of devices connected in WiFi Ad-hoc network. At first, the tasks (chunks) are distributed among all participating devices, which then download designated parts. When a single device downloads a chunk it transfers the chunk over a WiFi or BT connection to the device acting as an access point (AP). Other devices in the network obtain the chunk by overhearing; therefore, there is no need to broadcast the chunk by the AP device. To this day, this is the most efficient and the fastest way to share a file with a group of devices, because the chunk is transmitted only once. Unfortunately, the overhearing is not possible on the standard smartphone, unless its operating system (OS) has been modified. For example, to enable overhearing on the Android devices, one has to root the device and install a custom version of the OS. Developing custom OS is not a trivial task, even for an experienced developer. Such a system requires, among others, that only relevant packets from all packets overheard are processed and passed to the application layer. Additionally, rooting smartphones voids their warranty, and the overhearing is highly insecure communication technique.

Jahed et al. [31] presented a scalable cooperative system for multimedia streaming, which is robust against device mobility, allows seamless neighbour discovery and link quality estimation, as well as intelligent clustering and channel allocation algorithms. The system identifies master devices which will function as APs and share content with slave devices. Unfortunately, the system requires a management server that performs optimized group formation, content management, and APs management (channel allocation and power management). The system will not work without the management server, which, due to the complexity of operations, cannot be a smartphone device.

There is also a number of works aiming at reducing: transmission slots, retransmission energy consumption, and the number of retransmission packets in cooperative WFD D2D networks. Proposed solutions utilize the global network topology [35], optimize scheduling decisions [36], and applies integer linear programming and graph partitioning [37–40].

Although the solutions mentioned above are exciting, they do not fulfil our needs - sharing content with multiple devices simultaneously using explicitly standard (not modified) smartphones. Additionally, most of the proposed solutions are validated on models (e.g. created with MATLAB), in which environmental factors or device imperfections are not considered. In real conditions, a regular TV or fridge can cause a signal disturbance and affect communication. Therefore, our solution has been deployed to standard Android devices and validated in a real-world scenario. Mtibaa et al. [41], have recently performed a study in real conditions, but they focused only on one-to-one communication and the distance between the devices. They arranged three set-ups: (1) indoor line-of-sight, (2) indoor with obstacles (offices), and (3) outdoor line-of-sight, and they considered three connection types: (1) Bluetooth, (2) WiFi ad-hoc, and (3) WiFi Direct. Their findings confirm the intuition that the transfer parameters (e.g.

signal strength and the effective throughput) decrease as the distance between devices increases. Interestingly, in the case of line-of-sight indoor set-up, some parameters were preserving high values even with a great distance. The authors explain this as a result of the signal reflections, e.g. in corridors.

To the best of our knowledge, a dynamic parallel broadcast solution proposed in this work is the first one that works with standard devices, do not require any additional devices such as routers or servers, and has been validated in a real-world scenario.

3   Modules for Data Streaming

Most of the nowadays devices are equipped with BT, NFC, and WiFi modules. BT technology is the oldest among them, first presented in 1994 by Ericsson company. It was designed to connect devices located close to each other wirelessly, the main application idea was to connect phones with wireless headphones or hands-free sets. BT utilizes 2402–2480 MHz frequency range and since its debut uses frequency-hopping spread spectrum (FHSS). BT protocol implements master-slave architecture, thus allowing the master for up to 7 connections with slave devices. Most Android devices on the market have BT version 4.0, 4.1 or 4.2, which, according to manufacturers, performs with the maximum data rate of 24 Mbps and its maximum range is 100 m. In 2016 the BT version 5.0 was introduced, advertised with a boost of the data rate to 48 Mbps, and a more excellent range of up to 400 m. In 2018 the first smartphones with BT 5.0 were released. Since 2010 BT Low Energy is also available, a version featuring much less energy consumption and maintaining similar communication parameters. However, since it favours low power consumption over the file transfer speed, it is not considered in this study.

Not long after BT release the IEEE 802.11 (WiFi) was standardized and deployed as well. WiFi was designed to allow wireless communication at high speed from the very beginning, starting at 2 Mbps in 1997 to 9608 Mbps available with the most recent, 6th generation WiFi. The most common WiFi standards implemented in nowadays smartphones are 802.11 a, b, g, n, and ac, which allows communicating at 2.4 and 5 GHz radio frequencies. The WiFi communication at 5 GHz band allows using more channels, which results in better transfer rate. Additionally, the number of devices supporting 5 GHz band is significantly lower. Thus the interference is not as bad as among 2.4 GHz band devices. The only downside of the 5 GHz band is that it covers a much shorter range.

Two WiFi modes are particularly interesting for our study: (1) WiFi Direct, and (2) WiFi ad-hoc. Devices operating in WiFi ad-hoc mode can communicate directly with each other, without the need to talk to an AP. Each device is required to route traffic, hence creating a decentralized network properly. Unfortunately, the ad-hoc mode is not available on standard Android devices. Therefore it is not considered in this study. On the contrary, all devices running Android version 4.0 or higher can use WiFi Direct (WFD). In this mode, one of the devices acts as an AP and routes all the traffic. However, no additional router or access point is necessary. The standard does not specify the maximum number of devices that can join the WFD network. However, the unmodified Android implementation assumes 254 IP addresses to be assigned to clients (besides the AP address). This would result in up to 255 devices connected to the network, but phone manufacturers usually limit this number to 8–12 devices, besides the device acting as an AP.

As the name states, Near Field Communication (NFC) technology, transmits the data within the short-range only, up to 20 cm. It operates at 13.56 MHz radiofrequency and data rate of up to 424 kbps. The NFC technology, available on Android device, can work in three modes: (1) to read from and write to NFC tags, that do not require power (the slight current generated by the inductive coupling allows to exchange the information), (2) to respond to the card terminal, thus acting as an intelligent card, and (3) peer-to-peer mode allows to transfer data between two devices. Our use-case assumes the communication among multiple devices, which NFC cannot provide (at least not in parallel). Therefore, the NFC technology will be used only as a reference and possible way of communication when there are only two devices.

Let us emphasize that all technologies mentioned above, namely Bluetooth, WiFi Direct, and NFC, are available on standard Android devices since system version 2.0, 4.0, and 2.3 respectively (for comparison the most recent Android version is 10.0). Hence BT, WFD and NFC technologies are available on 99.9% of devices present in the market.

4   Resource-Aware Parallel Data Streaming Method

The most straightforward approach to transfer data to multiple devices is the serial transfer. It means sending data to the first recipient, waiting for confirmation of receipt, and then the analogous data transfer to other recipients. However, if the data is static and does not need to be updated, we may attempt transferring data in parallel. To achieve this task on the Android platform, we have used Java multi-threading, which requires extending the Thread class and implementing the Runnable interface.

The method assumes that the sender and recipients are already configured (paired and connected). At first, resources (the number of CPU cores and RAM) available on the sender device are identified. The sender device is responsible for maintaining all the connections with recipients (clients). Next, depending on the number of recipients and available resources, concurrent threads are dynamically created. If the resources are sufficient enough, a separate thread is created for each client. If this is not possible, recipients not assigned to the thread are waiting in the queue until a thread is available. Finally, the data is transferred in parallel in all threads until the recipient pool is exhausted.

In the case when there is only one recipient, the transfer is handled in the main thread of the application (no additional threads are created), because of the overhead cost of creating the thread (more details on this topic are provided in the experimental section). The code of the application (and method) is publicly available at [42].

5   Experimental Setup

The experiments were conducted using nine commonly available smartphones, see Table 1. The devices were selected in such a way to cover various market segments. We have used both, top models (e.g. Samsung Galaxy S9+), as well as less expensive models (e.g. LG G2 mini). This very well reflects the diversity of devices on the market, and also allows us to analyze various parameters, e.g. the BT version, the number of CPU cores, and other. For all devices, the latest operating system versions and updates were installed.

All the experiments were performed using the Android application, which code is publicly available at [42]. The application allows to set-up a connection between sender and recipients using four considered technologies (BT, WiFi, NFC, Amazon Web Services - AWS). Furthermore, the application allows to transfer prepared files and measure the time of data transfer. Our research is focused on the time required to transfer data from the sender device to the receiver devices. We consider from one, up to eight concurrent recipients (clients). The time measured in the study is related to the file transfer phase only, i.e. we assume that the devices are already paired and connected. The timer embedded into the application starts counting the time when the transfer to the first recipient begins and ends when the last recipient notifies about the successful file transmission. Each experiment (file streaming) is repeated 30 times, and the data transfer time is averaged.

We are considering four data transfer technologies: BT, WiFi, NFC, and, for reference purposes, Amazon Web Services (AWS) cloud transfer. When analyzing the data transfer time, we use various file sizes: 10 kb (the size of short text message with emoticons), 100 kb, 300 kb (the size of a compressed photos sent through Messenger), 500 kb, 1 Mb, 2 Mb (the size of a compressed short movies sent through Messenger), 5 Mb, 10 Mb (the size of a RAW photo or a short video sent through WhatsApp). We do not analyze device discovery, pairing, nor connecting time, as it usually takes a fraction of the data transfer time, and is performed once per session (connecting devices) or once per lifetime (pairing devices). Furthermore, ping and the packet loss ratio was close to zero due to the short distance, and are not considered as well.

6   Experimental Results

At first, we have compared the time of file transmission to a single recipient using four considered technologies (BT, WiFi, NFC, and AWS), see Fig. 1A. The results support the intuition that the transfer time is correlated linearly with the file size. By far the fastest technology is WiFi - on average it took only 17 ms for a 10 kb file transfer, and about 3 s for a 10 Mb transmission. At the same time, NFC required about 8 s for 10 kb, and 80 s for 10 Mb, while BT needed 131 ms for 10 kb and 135 s for a 10 Mb file. The streaming via the AWS cloud was the slowest and required 540 ms for 10 kb and 150 s for a 10 Mb transfer. Interestingly, NFC technology is slower than BT and AWS for files up to 1 Mb,

Table 1. The specification of devices used in the experiment.

Device name	Full name	Version	Release date	CPU [cores]		RAM [GB]	WiFi [GHz]	BT version	OS version
Mate20	Huawei Mate 20 Pro		2018, Nov	8	2 × 2,6 2 × 1,92 4 × 1,8	6	5, 2.4 a/b/g/n/ac	5.0	9.0
S9	Samsung Galaxy S9+	G965F	2018, Mar	8	4 × 22,7 4 × 21,8	6	5, 2.4 a/b/g/n/ac	5.0	8.0
Mate9	Huawei Mate 9		2016, Dec	8	4 × 22,4 4 × 21,8	4	5, 2.4 a/b/g/n/ac	4.2	8.0
S6	Samsung Galaxy S6 edge+	G928F	2015, Aug	8	4 × 22,1 4 × 21,5	4	5, 2.4 a/b/g/n/ac	4.2	7.0
Note4	Samsung Galaxy Note 4	N910F	2014, Oct	4	4 × 22,7	3	5, 2.4 a/b/g/n/ac	4.1	6.0.1
Note4	Samsung Galaxy Note 4	N910F	2014, Oct	4	4 × 22,7	3	5, 2.4 a/b/g/n/ac	4.1	6.0.1
G3	LG G3	D855	2014, Jun	4	4 × 22.5	2	5, 2.4 a/b/g/n/ac	4.0	6.0
G2	LG G2 mini		2014, Apr	4	4 × 21,2	1	2.4 b/g/n	4.0	5.0.2
Note2	Samsung Galaxy Note II	N7100	2012, Sep	4	4 × 21,6	2	2.4 a/b/g/n	4.0	4.4.2

but faster for data larger than 1 Mb. Perhaps the overhead of initializing the NFC communication is more substantial than for BT. For BT, WiFi, and AWS, we have also checked the transfer time in the parallel mode (dashed lines in Fig. 1A) - of course, only one thread was used, as the file has been transferred to a single device. For all considered technologies, one can observe the time overhead for creating a separate thread for file transmission.

The advantage of parallel streaming quickly becomes apparent when we share data with more than one device. See Fig. 1B for the comparison of BT, WiFi, and AWS when transferring a file to four devices. For each technology, the parallel transfer is much faster than serial transfer. For WiFi, the time saving is as much as 33%, for BT 27% and AWS 14%. The advantage of parallel streaming over serial streaming is even more obvious in Fig. 1C, where we analyze file transmission using WiFi serial and WiFi parallel methods to different numbers of devices. In this case, the number of parallel threads is equal to the number of recipients. For better readability, only the results of 1 Mb and 10 Mb transfers are presented. For two recipients, the parallel transfer is faster than serial transfer by about 20%. When sharing data with eight recipients, the parallel transfer is two times faster than serial streaming.

At this point, the obvious question is why parallel data transfer to eight devices is only twice as fast as the serial transfer. We would expect to reduce the time by almost eight times, as we use eight parallel threads. It turns out that increasing the number of threads leads to much faster consumption of other resources, i.e. RAM. When the RAM is running out, it needs to be released. Because Android uses the Java run time environment, releasing RAM is done

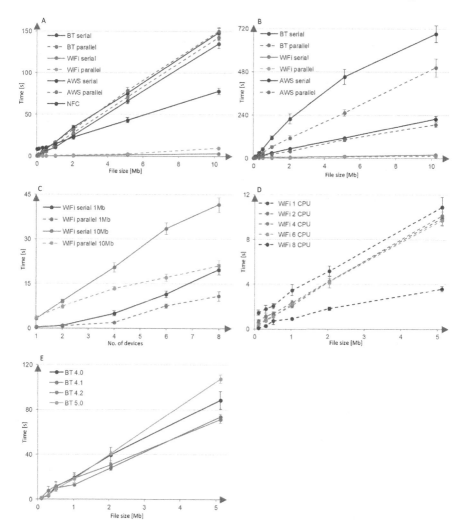

Fig. 1. (**A**) Data transfer time to a single device. (**B**) Data transfer time to four devices. (**C**) Comparison of WiFi serial and parallel transfers. (**D**) Influence of the number of threads used in the data transfer. (**E**) Data transfer time for various Bluetooth versions.

automatically through the Garbage Collector (GC) process. GC can even pause all working threads to perform some critical work, e.g. moving variables. This situation occurs much more often during the transmission of large amounts of data and when using multiple threads. Furthermore, data transfer technology also has an impact on resource consumption. For example, WiFi typically consumes over 40% of CPU resources, while BT consumes at maximum 15% of CPU.

To validate whether the time profit of the parallel transfer is impacted by time overhead caused by overfilled RAM, we have conducted another experiment. The data has been transmitted to eight devices several times, and each time the number of working threads has been reduced (from eight threads to a single thread), see Fig. 1D. It turns out that despite a much higher number of GC interventions, the parallel transfer with as many threads as recipients is the most time-effective. In this case, the transfer time using two, four, and six threads do not differ significantly. However, the transfer using eight threads is almost three times faster than the transmission on a single thread.

The next parameter tested was the BT protocol version. We have compared versions 4.0, 4.1, 4.2, and 5.0 see Fig. 1E. Surprisingly, BT 5.0 performed the worst out of all considered BT versions. Let us remind that BT 5.0 is supposed to offer twice the speed than BT 4.2. Therefore, we have repeated the experiment twice to make sure that nothing random disturbed the transfer, e.g. system updates or application synchronization running in the background. Both experiments (each consisting of 30 repetitions) gave the same result. Our only assumption is that one of the manufacturers incorrectly implemented the standard, hence the result worse than BT 4.2. To validate that experiments will be repeated with devices of different manufacturers. Other results are in line with expectations. BT versions 4.1 and 4.2 were better than version 4.0; however, it may as well be related to the device's parameters other than the BT version. Devices with a higher BT version are newer and have more RAM and CPU power.

7 Conclusion and Future Work

We have analyzed the data transfer time between multiple devices using technologies embedded in the standard smartphones, namely WiFi, Bluetooth (BT), and Near Field Communication (NFC). Let us emphasize that we have used standard, non-modified, smartphones, thus our research applies to 99.9% of devices on the market. The experiments conducted in a real-world scenario suggest that sharing content with more than one device should be performed using parallel WiFi connection. Furthermore, the sender device should use as many threads as recipients awaiting the data, if such resources are available. However, the linear increase in the number of threads created does not guarantee the linear decrease in transfer time, unless the RAM resources are increased as well. The Garbage Collector process responsible for releasing the RAM resources has a significant impact on the file transmission time. When transmitting the data to a single device, it is better to use the main thread of the application, since the separate thread would create the overhead. The experiments also confirmed that the transfer time is correlated linearly with the file size being transmitted and with the number of recipients. Last but not least, BT 5.0 performed much worse than expected, transferring files slower than its predecessors (BT 4.2, BT 4.1, and even BT 4.0).

The next possible research direction is reducing the number of GC calls (e.g. by sharing memory between threads), which would further increase the parallel transfer advantage over the serial file transfer. Nevertheless, another parameter interesting to analyze is the WiFi band, i.e. 2.4 GHz vs 5 GHz.

References

1. Camps-Mur, D., Garcia-Saavedra, A., Serrano, P.: Device-to-device communications with Wi-Fi Direct: overview and experimentation. IEEE Wirel. Commun. **20**(3), 96–104 (2013)
2. Asadi, A., Wang, Q., Mancuso, V.: A survey on device-to-device communication in cellular networks. IEEE Commun. Surv. Tutor. **16**(4), 1801–1819 (2014)
3. Feng, D., Lu, L., et al.: Device-to-device communications in cellular networks. IEEE Comm. Mag. **52**(4), 49–55 (2014)
4. Liu, J., Kato, N., et al.: Device-to-device communication in LTE-advanced networks: a survey. IEEE Commun. Surv. Tutor. **17**(4), 1923–1940 (2015)
5. Noura, M., Nordin, R.: A survey on interference management for device-to-device (D2D) communication and its challenges in 5G networks. J. Netw. Comput. Appl. **71**, 130–150 (2016)
6. Gandotra, P., Jha, R.K.: Device-to-device communication in cellular networks: a survey. J. Netw. Comput. Appl. **71**, 99–117 (2016)
7. Haus, M., Waqas, M., et al.: Security and privacy in device-to-device (D2D) communication: a review. IEEE Commun. Surv. Tutor. **19**(2), 1054–1079 (2017)
8. Hamoud, O.N., Kenaza, T., Challal, Y.: Security in device-to-device communications: a survey. IET Netw. **7**(1), 14–22 (2017)
9. Wang, M., Yan, Z.: A survey on security in D2D communications. Mob. Netw. Appl. **22**(2), 195–208 (2017)
10. Fomichev, M., Álvarez, F., et al.: Survey and systematization of secure device pairing. IEEE Commun. Surv. Tutor. **20**(1), 517–550 (2017)
11. Jameel, F., Hamid, Z., et al.: A survey of device-to-device communications: research issues and challenges. IEEE Commun. Surv. Tutor. **20**, 2133–2168 (2018)
12. Shaikh, F.S., Wismüller, R.: Routing in multi-hop cellular device-to-device (D2D) networks: a survey. IEEE Commun. Surv. Tutor. **20**, 2622–2657 (2018)
13. Li, H.-B., Miura, R., Kojima, F.: Channel access proposal for enabling quick discovery for D2D wireless networks. In: International Conference on Computing, Networking and Communications (ICNC), pp. 1012–1016. IEEE (2017)
14. Xu, C., Gao, C., et al.: Social network-based content delivery in device-to-device underlay cellular networks using matching theory. IEEE Access **5**, 924–937 (2017)
15. Kushalad, K., Sarkar, M., Patel, P.: Asynchronous device discovery and rendezvous protocol for D2D communication. In: Conference on Computer Communications Workshops, pp. 199–200. IEEE (2016)
16. Saleh, M., Dong, L.: Secure location-aided routing protocols with Wi-Fi Direct for vehicular ad hoc networks. arXiv preprint arXiv:1707.00654 (2017)
17. Wang, Z., Sun, L., Zhang, M., Pang, H., Tian, E., Zhu, W.: Propagation-and mobility-aware D2D social content replication. IEEE Trans. Mob. Comput. **16**(4), 1107–1120 (2017)
18. Wang, R., Zhang, J., Song, S., Letaief, K.B.: Mobility-aware caching in D2D networks. IEEE Trans. Wirel. Commun. **16**(8), 5001–5015 (2017)
19. Krishnan, S., Dhillon, H.S.: Effect of user mobility on the performance of device-to-device networks with distributed caching. IEEE Wirel. Commun. Lett. **6**(2), 194–197 (2017)

20. Yang, T., Cheng, X., Shen, X., Chen, S., Yang, L.: QoS-aware interference management for vehicular D2D relay networks. J. Commun. Inf. Netw. **2**(2), 75–90 (2017)

21. Celik, A., Radaydeh, R.M.M., Al-Qahtani, F.S., Alouini, M.-S.: Resource allocation and interference management for D2D-enabled DL/UL decoupled het-nets. IEEE Access **5**, 22735–22749 (2017)

22. Sun, W., Yuan, D., et al.: Cluster-based radio resource management for D2D-supported safety-critical V2X communications. IEEE Trans. Wirel. Commun. **15**(4), 2756–2769 (2016)

23. Xu, H., Huang, N., Yang, Z., Shi, J., Wu, B., Chen, M.: Pilot allocation and power control in D2D underlay massive MIMO systems. IEEE Commun. Lett. **21**(1), 112–115 (2017)

24. Yang, C., Li, J., et al.: Distributed interference and energy-aware power control for ultra-dense D2D networks: a mean field game. IEEE Trans. Wirel. Commun. **16**(2), 1205–1217 (2017)

25. Zhai, D., Sheng, M., et al.: Energy-saving resource management for D2D and cellular coexisting networks enhanced by hybrid multiple access technologies. IEEE Trans. Wirel. Commun. **16**(4), 2678–2692 (2017)

26. Shen, W., Yin, B., et al.: Secure device-to-device communications over WiFi direct. IEEE Netw. **30**(5), 4–9 (2016)

27. Xiao, S., Li, W.: Mixed power saving mode for D2D communications with Wi-Fi Direct. In: Qiao, F., Patnaik, S., Wang, J. (eds.) ICMIR 2017. AISC, vol. 691, pp. 234–240. Springer, Cham (2018). https://doi.org/10.1007/978-3-319-70990-1_35

28. Usman, M., Asghar, M.R., et al.: Towards energy efficient multi-hop D2D networks using WiFi Direct. In: IEEE Global Communications Conference, pp. 1–7. IEEE (2017)

29. Gong, Q., Guo, Y., Chen, Y., Liu, Y., Xie, F.: Design and evaluation of a WiFi-Direct based LTE cooperative video streaming system. In: Global Communications Conference (GLOBECOM), pp. 1–6. IEEE (2016)

30. Le, A., Keller, L., et al.: MicroCast: cooperative video streaming using cellular and local connections. IEEE/ACM Trans. Netw. **24**(5), 2983–2999 (2016)

31. Jahed, K., Sharafeddine, S., et al.: Scalable multimedia streaming in wireless networks with device-to-device cooperation. In: Proceedings of the 2016 ACM on Multimedia Conference, pp. 762–764. ACM (2016)

32. Wainer, G., Fernandes, S., et al.: Improving video streaming over cellular networks with dash-based device-to-device streaming. In: Symposium on Performance Evaluation of Computer and Telecommunication Systems (SPECTS), pp. 1–8. IEEE (2017)

33. Fernandes, S., Wainer, G., et al.: Dash-based peer-to-peer video streaming in cellular networks. In: International Symposium on Performance Evaluation of Computer and Telecommunication Systems (SPECTS), pp. 1–8. IEEE (2016)

34. Siris, V.A., Dimopoulos, D.: Multi-source mobile video streaming with proactive caching and D2D communication. In: IEEE 16th International Symposium on World of Wireless, Mobile and Multimedia Networks (WoWMoM), pp. 1–6. IEEE (2015)

35. Chen, Y.-J., Wang, L.-C., Wang, K., Ho, W.-L.: Topology-aware network coding for wireless multicast. IEEE Syst. J. **12**, 3683–3692 (2018)

36. Zhan, C., Wen, Z.: Efficient video transmission in D2D assisted mobile cloud networks. China Commun. **13**(8), 74–83 (2016)

37. Zhan, C., Wen, Z., Wang, X., Zhu, L.: Device-to-device assisted wireless video delivery with network coding. Ad Hoc Netw. **69**, 76–85 (2018)

38. Chi, K., Yu, Z., Li, Y., Zhu, Y.-H.: Energy-efficient D2D communication based retransmission scheme for reliable multicast in wireless cellular network. IEEE Access **6**, 31469–31480 (2018)
39. Xia, Z., Yan, J., Liu, Y.: Cooperative content delivery in multicast multihop device-to-device networks. IEEE Access **5**, 6314–6324 (2017)
40. Militano, L., Condoluci, M., et al.: Single frequency-based device-to-device-enhanced video delivery for evolved multimedia broadcast and multicast services. IEEE Trans. Broadcast. **61**(2), 263–278 (2015)
41. Mtibaa, A., Emam, A., et al.: On practical device-to-device wireless communication: a measurement driven study. In: Wireless Communications and Mobile Computing Conference, pp. 409–414. IEEE (2017)
42. Szóstak, W.: Implementation of a resource-aware method for parallel D2D data streaming. https://bitbucket.org/multiishare/wifi-direct. Accessed 10 Feb 2021

Impact of Radio Map on the Performance of Fingerprinting Algorithms

Juraj Machaj[1]([✉]) [iD], Peter Brida[1] [iD], and Ivana Bridova[2] [iD]

[1] Faculty of Electrical Engineering and Information Technology, University of Zilina, Univerzitna 1, 010 26 Zilina, Slovakia
{juraj.machaj,peter.brida}@feit.uniza.sk
[2] Research Centre, University of Zilina, Univerzitna 1, 010 26 Zilina, Slovakia
ivana.bridova@fri.uniza.sk

Abstract. The paper is focused on the investigation of localization accuracy of NN and RBF fingerprinting algorithms under different conditions related to radio map. The radio map is crucial for the implementation of fingerprinting localization system, however, the process of creating the radio map can be time-consuming. Moreover, conditions under which the radio map is created can affect the localization accuracy, due to changes in the radio channel during the localization phase, caused for example by a large number of users, that were not present during the calibration measurements. The problems in real-world implementations can also be caused by the use of different devices. Different devices can have various hardware and software equipment, thus RSS measurements provided by devices under the same conditions can vary. The density of the radio map, which is also related to the cost of system deployment can also play a significant role in the performance of the localization system.

Keywords: Localization · Fingerprinting · Positioning · RBF · Particle filter · Dynamic radiomap

1 Introduction

Indoor positioning attracted a lot of attention recently as service providers seek new ways to provide location-based services in the indoor environment [1]. The basic requirement for providing location-based service is knowledge of the position of a mobile user [2]. This can be achieved by utilization of Global Navigation Satellite Systems (GNSS) in the outdoor environment [3]. However, GNSS require an unobstructed Line of Sight (LoS) between the transmitter, i.e. satellite on space orbit, and receiver, i.e. localized device. Due to this limitation GNSS can only provide accurate position estimates in the outdoor environment with a clear view of the sky [4]. This condition may not always be met in a dense urban environment.

Moreover, the situation is even worse in the indoor environment, where LoS is blocked by the ceilings of the building. Therefore, the GNSS receivers in the indoor environments are able to receive mainly signals reflected from other buildings, resulting in higher localization error.

© Springer Nature Switzerland AG 2021
N. T. Nguyen et al. (Eds.): ICCCI 2021, LNAI 12876, pp. 708–720, 2021.
https://doi.org/10.1007/978-3-030-88081-1_53

Since GNSS signals are not a viable option for indoor positioning, the development of alternative localization systems has attracted a lot of attention from the research community. In recent years, a vast number of localization systems and algorithms has been proposed, utilizing various sources of data required to estimate the position of mobile devices. Indoor localization systems can utilize signals from Inertial Measurement Units (IMU) implemented in the smart devices [5], various radio signals [6–8], magnetic signatures [9], data from cameras [10], sound waves [11] etc. However, each of these has its advantages as well as drawbacks.

When IMUs are used to estimate the position of the mobile devices, there is a need for an initial position estimate from some other source [12], as IMU data are used by a dead reckoning algorithm. Moreover, data from IMU are affected by noise as well as bias, this leads to localization error increased over time due to the integration of errors [13].

Indoor localization based on magnetic signal is not affected by multipath propagation [14]. However, the installation of magnetic signal emitters is not a viable option in all indoor environments, as it can affect the function of other devices in the area. The other option is to utilize magnetic signatures of the buildings to estimate the position of mobile users. However, this solution has drawbacks related to the sampling rate and movement speed of the user which represent a challenge for the alignment of data from calibration and localization measurements [15].

Systems based on sound can achieve high accuracy, however, there is a need for new infrastructure that will allow transmission of the signals [16]. Moreover, sound signals have to be pre-processed to be inaudible for the users. The other way how to tackle this problem is to use inaudible ultrasound signals, however, not all mobile devices may be able to process ultrasound signals with built-in microphones.

Systems based on image processing from cameras can be used for positioning purposes as well. There are two ways how to implement a localization system based on computer vision. One way is to build the infrastructure of cameras covering the whole area, however, in this case, positioning and tracking of individual users can be done only with the implementation of face recognition algorithms [17]. This can be considered to be a legal problem since a user may be identified and tracked without his permission.

The other approach is to utilize cameras in mobile devices. This approach can achieve relatively high accuracy [10]. However, a lot of tests was done with mobile devices fixed to the body of a user, which may not be a realistic scenario. In a realistic scenario, the user is holding his device in hand while moving around the building. In such a pose, cameras are usually facing downwards and upwards. Therefore, most of the environment features that could be used for position estimation, e.g. doors, signs, pillars, etc., are not in the field of view of cameras.

Most of the attention was given to the localization systems and algorithms based on wireless networks. This might be because these networks can be considered to be ubiquitous, and some of the wireless technologies shown huge potential in positioning applications. Wireless network-based localization can utilize signals from various technologies, the most popular include Ultra-Wide Band (UWB) [8, 18], Radio Frequency Identification (RFID) [19], Bluetooth [20], Wi-Fi [21–24] and GSM [7]. However, other wireless technologies can be used for positioning purposes as well.

The localization systems based on UWB can provide high localization accuracy, however, their implementation requires investment in both infrastructure as well as mobile equipment [8]. This is because UWB transceivers are not yet implemented in commercially available smart devices. Thus, it is needed to develop and use specialized devices only for position estimation.

Similarly, RFID positioning requires investments in both devices and infrastructure. For RFID localization a dense network of RFID tags is required since position accuracy is dependent on the density of reference tags.

Some degree of investments into infrastructure is required also for Bluetooth technology since fixed Bluetooth tags are not widely deployed. On the other hand, the devices supporting Bluetooth technology are widely available. Bluetooth based positioning can provide room-level accuracy, however, the cost of deployment and maintenance of Bluetooth tags which usually are battery-powered can be a drawback if the system should provide positioning service in large areas [25].

Wi-Fi has attracted the most attention in the research of localization systems. This can be caused by the availability of the mobile device as well as the good adaption of Wi-Fi technology in indoor environments. Wi-Fi signals can be considered to be ubiquitous and there is a large number of signals from Wi-Fi access points available in all indoor spaces. Thus, the cost of localization system infrastructure can be kept at a minimum. Moreover, all modern smart devices are equipped with Wi-Fi transceiver, making the Wi-Fi based localization service available for all smartphone users.

In this paper, we will focus on the performance of the localization system based on Wi-Fi fingerprinting [26] when different approaches are taken for the radio map construction. The radio map construction represents a main drawback of the fingerprinting-based positioning since it represents a time-consuming process. The goal is to evaluate the impact of a dynamic radio map on the performance of localization algorithms.

The rest of the paper is organized as follows, Sect. 2 will describe previous work in the area of fingerprinting localization, the process of dynamic radio map construction will be described in Sect. 3, test scenario as well as achieved results will be presented in Sect. 4 and Sect. 5 will conclude the paper.

2 Fingerprinting Localization

The most widely used positioning technique in Wi-Fi networks is fingerprinting. Fingerprinting is based on an assumption that position can be estimated based on a comparison of received signals (i.e. fingerprint) with received signals measured in the area during the offline, also called calibration, phase.

As mentioned above, the fingerprinting positioning system requires calibration measurements, stored in a database called a radio map. The process of radio map collection can be time-consuming because measurements have to be performed on a large number of reference points. The larger number of reference points in the area will result in a higher density of radio map and higher localization accuracy. However, performing calibration measurements on a large number of reference points leads to an increase in labour cost and time required to set up the localization system.

Therefore, alternative solutions based on data from IMU can be used to automatically create a dynamic radio map from data collected from user walking around the area. The solution used to create a dynamic radio map is described in Sect. 3.

The algorithms used in the fingerprinting framework can be divided into two large groups, probabilistic and deterministic algorithms.

The statistical algorithms are modelling the position of a mobile device as a random vector, taking into account the distribution of the signal in the area. Therefore, the location estimate can be calculated based on posterior probability using Bayes' theorem, as follows:

$$P(\gamma_i|S) = \frac{P(S|\gamma_i)P(\gamma_i)}{P(S)}, \tag{1}$$

where posterior probability $P(\gamma_i|S)$ is a function of likelihood $P(S|\gamma_i)$, prior probability $P(\gamma_i)$ and $P(S)$, which stands for observed evidence and can be expressed as:

$$P(S) = \sum_i P(S|\gamma_i)P(\gamma_i), \tag{2}$$

where the vector S consists of RSS samples measured by the mobile device in the online stage and γ_i represents the position of the i-th reference point. Examples of other likelihood functions that can be used for position estimation can be found in [26].

On contrary, deterministic localization algorithms are based on assumption that the RSS values depend on the position of the mobile device. Thus, the position of the mobile device can be estimated based on a comparison of RSS values. In this paper, we used deterministic algorithms to estimate the position of the mobile device. Therefore, NN and RBF algorithms used in the experiments will be described in the following subsections.

2.1 Deterministic NN Fingerprinting Algorithms

The deterministic algorithms from the NN family seem to be the most widely used for the comparison of localization performance. These algorithms are based on a comparison of RSS samples stored in the radio map database. The position of a mobile device can be estimated using the estimator:

$$\hat{x} = \frac{\sum_{i=1}^{M} \omega_i \cdot \gamma_i}{\sum_{i=1}^{M} \omega_i}. \tag{3}$$

In the equation, $\hat{x}$ is the final position estimate and ω_i stands for the weight assigned to the i-th reference point from the radio map database. The weights are most widely estimated as the inverse value of Euclidean distance:

$$d_E = \sqrt{\sum_{k=1}^{N} (a_k - b_k)^2}, \tag{4}$$

Where N is the number of unique APs detected in the localization phase or stored in the radio map database, a_k and b_k represent RSS measurements from the localized device and reference point from the radio map database, respectively. The distance is given by the difference in RSS values measured from the same AP in localization and calibration phases. In case that RSS values are missing for some APs it is possible to assign them a value of -100, which represents the sensitivity threshold of the Wi-Fi receiver.

The estimator (3) that takes into account only the reference point with the highest weight and sets other weights to 0 is referred to as NN (Nearest Neighbour) [27]. When k highest weights are set to 1 and others are set to 0, the estimator becomes KNN (K Nearest Neighbours) and position is given as a centre of gravity of reference points with weights set to 1 [26]. The last modification of the estimator keeps the k highest weights and sets others to 0 and is named WKNN (Weighted K Nearest Neighbours) [6].

KNN and WKNN algorithms usually achieve better localization accuracy than the NN algorithm, since the NN algorithm can estimate position only on reference points [26]. However, differences in performance depend on the density of reference points in the radio map.

2.2 Rank Based Fingerprinting

The Rank Based Fingerprinting (RBF) algorithm was proposed in order to reduce the impact of heterogeneous devices on the accuracy of position estimates [28]. The algorithm is based on the assumption, that rank of APs assigned based on RSS values is more stable than RSS values. This assumption holds not only stands with the use of different devices, where reported values are affected by different software and hardware setup. However, it seems to provide more stable results even when RSS values are affected by changes in the environment.

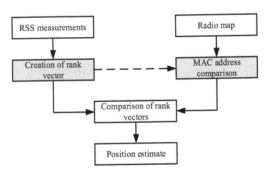

Fig. 1. Block diagram of the RBF algorithm

The RBF algorithm, shown in Fig. 1, is a modification of the WKNN algorithm and the same estimator is used to calculate the position estimate. The differences between WKNN and RBF are in additional data processing required to create rank vectors, represented by grey blocks in the figure, as well as in the calculation of the weights. The measured RSS values in the localization phase are sorted and ranks are assigned to the individual APs based on their position in the sorted RSS vector.

The sorting is also done for the data stored in the radio map, however, rank vectors are created based on comparison od MAC addresses of APs. Therefore, the rank vector created from the radio map does have the same rank values assigned based on MAC address comparison and not based on position in the vector.

In the RBF algorithm, weights in the estimator (3) have to be estimated as differences between ranks. Metrics used for rank vectors as well as their impact on localization performance of the RBF can be found in [28].

In the experiments, we have used the Canberra distance to estimate the difference between rank vectors from the localization phase and radio map. The Canberra distance is a weighted version of the Spearman distance and is given by:

$$D_C = \sum_{k=1}^{N} \frac{|x_k - y_k|}{|x_k| + |y_k|} \cdot \omega_k, \tag{5}$$

where x_k is the rank of k-th element in vector X, y_k is the rank of k-th element in vector Y and n is the number of elements in vectors X and Y. Weights ω_k were from interval 1 to 0 with a decreasing trend. Moreover, only the first 12 elements have assigned weight higher than 0. This will help to reduce the impact of APs with very low RSS values that are more affected by signal fluctuations and thus can have a negative impact on localization accuracy [29].

3 Dynamic Radio Map

The dynamic radio map is based on the implementation of the Pedestrian Dead Reckoning (PDR) algorithm with Particle Filter (PF) presented in [30]. The PF-PDR algorithm was used to process data measured on a mobile device while walking around the area. The advantage of the PF algorithm, in comparison with other data fusion algorithms, is that it helps to achieve much higher accuracy in indoor environments with a relatively large number of obstacles i.e. walls, which represent constraints for assigning weights to the generated particles used for prediction of the position of the user.

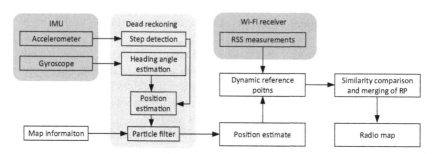

Fig. 2. Block diagram of dynamic map creation

The implemented solution for dynamic map creation (Fig. 2) was described in [31] and consists of three stages. In the first stage, the user walks around the area carrying his mobile device and collecting data from both IMU and Wi-Fi receiver.

In the second stage, the data are processed with the PF-PDR algorithm and the track of the user is reconstructed. Since Wi-Fi measurements are performed periodically it is possible to link the measurements to position estimates from the PF-PDR algorithm.

The third stage of the dynamic map creation is responsible for the fusion of reference points in the radio map that are either too similar or are very close to each other. Since PF-PDR can provide position estimates with an accuracy below 2 m for the majority of the time, reference points with positions less than 2 m these reference points are merged.

This step is required since some spaces could end up with a very high density of reference points. For example, users are usually moving along the corridors, while movement around offices or lecture rooms is more limited. Without the fusion of reference points, the radio map would have extremely different properties.

4 Experiments and Achieved Results

The experiments were focused on the impact of the dynamic radio map on the performance of the RBF localization algorithm as well as traditional KNN algorithms. The experiments were performed at the Department of Multimedia and Information-Communication Technology of the University of Zilina.

Implemented algorithms were tested under four different scenarios with the following conditions:

- static radio map and localization under same conditions,
- static radio map and localization under different conditions,
- static radio map and localization under same conditions and different devices
- dynamic radio map.

In the first scenario, the radio map as well as positioning phase were performed during the evening time, without moving users presented in the area. Therefore, Wi-Fi signals can be considered to be more stable. On the other hand, the positioning phase in the second scenario was performed during the time when a large number of moving people was present in the area, therefore, the signal from APs was less stable and there were much more fluctuations of the signal caused by shadowing as well as multipath propagation.

The third scenario is using the same radio map as the previous two scenarios, however, positioning was performed in evening hours with a different device. This represents another interesting localization scenario since different devices usually report different RSS values. This is due to differences in hardware and software implementation, which results in different gain characteristics of a Wi-Fi receiver.

The fourth scenario is using a dynamic radio map to estimate the position. In this case measurements in both the online and offline stage were performed during the working hours with a large number of moving people in the area. The reason to create a dynamic radio map under such harsh conditions was motivated by further use of the dynamic map construction in crowdsourcing where a large number of moving people in the area is expected.

The achieved mean localization error and standard deviation of localization error achieved in all four scenarios are presented in Table 1 and Table 2, respectively.

From the results presented in the tables above it is clear that the RBF algorithm achieved the highest localization accuracy in the first 3 scenarios, while in the last

Table 1. Mean localization error [m] achieved in all scenarios.

	NN	KNN	WKNN	RBF
Scenario 1	2.86	2.18	2.58	2.03
Scenario 2	3.04	2.79	2.61	2.15
Scenario 3	6.12	4.15	4.17	3.37
Scenario 4	3.97	4.33	4.77	4.44

Table 2. Standard deviation of localization error [m] achieved in all scenarios.

	NN	KNN	WKNN	RBF
Scenario 1	2.98	1.14	1.19	1.97
Scenario 2	2.59	1.56	1.81	1.69
Scenario 3	4.91	3.47	3.66	2.32
Scenario 4	1.24	2.79	2.18	2.17

Scenario the lowest error was achieved by the NN algorithm. This is caused by the fact that in Scenario 4 the density of reference points in the radio map was much smaller, therefore using multiple reference points in the position estimation process resulted in the higher localization error.

However, it can be seen that among KNN, WKNN and RBF algorithms the achieved performance in Scenario 4 was almost the same with differences in achieved mean localization error below 0.5 m, however, the standard deviation of the error was favourable for the RBF algorithm.

For further analysis boxplot of achieved localization errors for all algorithms in all scenarios is presented in Fig. 3.

In the figure, the central mark indicates the median localization error, while the bottom and top edges of the box indicate the 25th and 75th percentiles of localization error, respectively. The whiskers in the figure show distribution up to the most extreme data points, not considering outliers which are depicted individually using the + symbol.

From the results, it can be seen that when more people were present in the environment the localization accuracy was not affected significantly. However, when a different device was used in the localization phase, the impact on the performance of the NN based algorithm was significant, causing increased localization error.

From the results achieved for Scenario 4, it can be seen that the best performance was achieved for the NN algorithm, which was expected due to the sparse radio map. The second best results were achieved by the RBF algorithm, proving that it can be used successfully even with a dynamic radio map.

Since the RBF algorithm is using K nearest neighbours to estimate position, similarly to the WKNN algorithm, further comparison of these algorithms is presented. The CDF

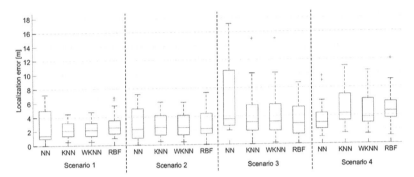

Fig. 3. Localization errors of individual algorithms under different scenarios.

functions of localization errors achieved in all scenarios for RBF and WKNN algorithms are presented in Fig. 4 and Fig. 5, respectively.

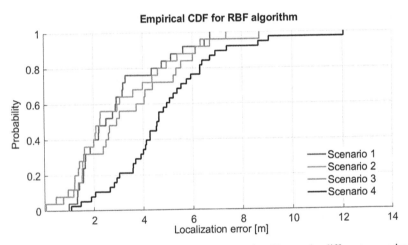

Fig. 4. CDF of localization error achieved with RBF algorithm under different scenarios.

From the figure above it can be seen that the RBF algorithm provided very stable position estimates in the first 3 scenarios, when the density of the radio map was relatively high, even though RSS values were affected by changes in both environments and used device. However, the performance was significantly lower with a dynamic map, due to the low density of reference points.

From the results presented for the WKNN algorithm, it is clear that the algorithm performed reasonably well in the first two scenarios when RSS values were affected by a changed number of people in the area. However, its performance dropped significantly when a different device was used in the localization stage in scenario 3. The performance in scenario 4 with the dynamic radio map was lower due to the low density of reference points. It is important to note that the performance of the WKNN algorithm was very

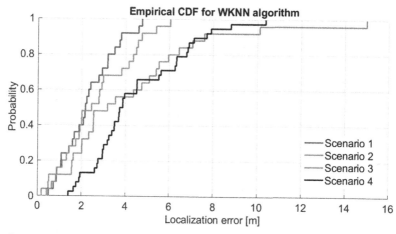

Fig. 5. CDF of localization error achieved with WKNN algorithm under different scenarios.

similar in scenarios 3 and 4, therefore we can expect that the performance would drop even more if a different device was used in combination with a dynamic radio map.

This disadvantage of the WKNN algorithm may represent a problem in further implementation. Since a dynamic radio map can be created by different users and thus use of different devices is expected with a dynamic radio map.

5 Conclusion

In the paper, both NN and RBF algorithms were tested under different scenarios. The scenarios presented in the paper were used to test the performance of the algorithms under different conditions, including different approaches to create a radio map, the impact of different conditions in the radio channel as well as the impact of different devices on localization performance.

From the achieved results it can be seen that with the traditional approach to create a radio map the RBF algorithm provided the best localization accuracy. However, it was outperformed in the case when a dynamic radio map was used. This was caused by a low density of reference points in the radio map. Therefore, the best performance was achieved by the NN algorithm.

From the comparison of RBF and WKNN algorithms, it is clear that the performance of the WKNN algorithm was negatively affected by both use of different devices and the density of the radio map. However, the performance of RBF suffered only in the case of low radio map density.

It is important to note that the density of the dynamic radio map can be increased as a dynamic collection of data allows implementing of a crowdsourcing approach to the radio map creation process. Therefore, the use of different devices has to be considered, making RBF a better candidate for localization in combination with a dynamic radio map.

Acknowledgement. This work has been partially supported by the Slovak VEGA grant agency, Project No. 1/0626/19 "Research of mobile objects localization in IoT environment", the European Union's Horizon 2020 research and innovation programme under the Marie Skłodowska-Curie grant agreement No 734331 and Operational Programme Integrated Infrastructure: Independent research and development of technological kits based on wearable electronics products, as tools for raising hygienic standards in a society exposed to the virus causing the COVID-19 disease, ITMS code 313011ASK8, co-funded by European Regional Development Fund.

References

1. Basiri, A., et al.: Indoor location based services challenges, requirements and usability of current solutions. Comput. Sci. Rev. **24**, 1–12 (2017). https://doi.org/10.1016/j.cosrev.2017.03.002
2. Adesipo, A., et al.: Smart and climate-smart agricultural trends as core aspects of smart village functions. Sensors **20**, 5977 (2020). https://doi.org/10.3390/s20215977
3. Mikusova, M., Zukowska, J., Torok, A.: Community Road Safety Strategies in the Context of Sustainable Mobility. In: Mikulski, J. (ed.) TST 2018. CCIS, vol. 897, pp. 115–128. Springer, Cham (2018). https://doi.org/10.1007/978-3-319-97955-7_8
4. Update: GNSS Accuracy: Lies, Damn Lies, and Statistics – GPS World : GPS World, https://www.gpsworld.com/gpsgnss-accuracy-lies-damn-lies-and-statistics-1134/. Last accessed 29 Sept 2020
5. Khedr, M.E., El-Sheimy, N.: SBAUPT: Azimuth SBUPT for frequent full attitude correction of smartphone-based PDR. IEEE Sens. J. 1 (2020). https://doi.org/10.1109/JSEN.2020.3047990
6. Li, B., Salter, J., Dempster, A.G., Rizos, C.: Indoor positioning techniques based on wireless LAN. In: Lan, First IEEE International Conference on Wireless Broadband and Ultra Wideband Communications, pp. 13–16
7. Gorak, R., Luckner, M., Okulewicz, M., Porter-Sobieraj, J., Wawrzyniak, P.: Indoor localisation based on GSM signals: multistorey building study. Mob. Inform. Syst. **2016**, 2719576 (2016). https://doi.org/10.1155/2016/2719576
8. Pala, S., Jayan, S., Kurup, D.G.: An accurate UWB based localization system using modified leading edge detection algorithm. Ad Hoc Netw. **97**, 102017 (2020). https://doi.org/10.1016/j.adhoc.2019.102017
9. Ashraf, I., Kang, M., Hur, S., Park, Y.: MINLOC: magnetic field patterns-based indoor localization using convolutional neural networks. IEEE Access **8**, 66213–66227 (2020). https://doi.org/10.1109/ACCESS.2020.2985384
10. Werner, M., Kessel, M., Marouane, C.: Indoor positioning using smartphone camera. In: 2011 International Conference on Indoor Positioning and Indoor Navigation, pp. 1–6 (2011). https://doi.org/10.1109/IPIN.2011.6071954
11. Hammoud, A., Deriaz, M., Konstantas, D.: Robust ultrasound-based room-level localization system using COTS components. In: 2016 Fourth International Conference on Ubiquitous Positioning, Indoor Navigation and Location Based Services (UPINLBS), pp. 11–19 (2016). https://doi.org/10.1109/UPINLBS.2016.7809975
12. Ma, L., Fan, Y., Xu, Y., Cui, Y.: Pedestrian dead reckoning trajectory matching method for radio map crowdsourcing building in WiFi indoor positioning system. In: 2017 IEEE International Conference on Communications (ICC), pp. 1–6 (2017). https://doi.org/10.1109/ICC.2017.7996457

13. Jimenez, A.R., Seco, F., Prieto, C., Guevara, J.: A comparison of pedestrian dead-reckoning algorithms using a low-cost MEMS IMU. In: 2009 IEEE International Symposium on Intelligent Signal Processing, pp. 37–42 (2009). https://doi.org/10.1109/WISP.2009.5286542

14. Montoliu, R., Torres-Sospedra, J., Belmonte, O.: Magnetic field based Indoor positioning using the Bag of Words paradigm. In: 2016 International Conference on Indoor Positioning and Indoor Navigation (IPIN), pp. 1–7 (2016). https://doi.org/10.1109/IPIN.2016.7743596

15. Liu, G.-X., Shi, L.-F., Chen, S., Wu, Z.-G.: Focusing matching localization method based on indoor magnetic map. IEEE Sens. J. **20**, 10012–10020 (2020). https://doi.org/10.1109/JSEN.2020.2991087

16. Chen, J., Tao, Z., Jianhong, S.: Convolutional neural network based indoor microphone array sound source localization. Laser Optoelectron. Prog. **57**, 081021 (2020). https://doi.org/10.3788/LOP57.081021

17. Sattler, T., Leibe, B., Kobbelt, L.: Efficient effective prioritized matching for large-scale image-based localization. IEEE Trans. Pattern Anal. Mach. Intell. **39**, 1744–1756 (2017). https://doi.org/10.1109/TPAMI.2016.2611662

18. Mayer, P., Magno, M., Schnetzler, C., Benini, L.: EmbedUWB: low power embedded high-precision and low latency UWB localization. In: 2019 IEEE 5th World Forum on Internet of Things (WF-IoT), pp. 519–523 (2019). https://doi.org/10.1109/WF-IoT.2019.8767241

19. Wang, J., Dhanapal, R.K., Ramakrishnan, P., Balasingam, B., Souza, T., Maev, R.: Active RFID Based Indoor Localization. IEEE, New York (2019)

20. Spachos, P., Plataniotis, K.N.: BLE beacons for indoor positioning at an interactive IoT-based smart museum. IEEE Syst. J. **14**, 3483–3493 (2020). https://doi.org/10.1109/JSYST.2020.2969088

21. Chen, Z., Zou, H., Yang, J., Jiang, H., Xie, L.: WiFi fingerprinting indoor localization using local feature-based deep LSTM. IEEE Syst. J. **14**, 3001–3010 (2020). https://doi.org/10.1109/JSYST.2019.2918678

22. Deng, Z.-A., Qu, Z., Hou, C., Si, W., Zhang, C.: WiFi positioning based on user orientation estimation and smartphone carrying position recognition. Wirel. Commun. Mob. Comput. **2018**, 1–11 (2018). https://doi.org/10.1155/2018/5243893

23. Liu, F., et al.: Survey on WiFi-based indoor positioning techniques. IET Commun. **14**, 1372–1383 (2020). https://doi.org/10.1049/iet-com.2019.1059

24. Zhang, Z., He, S., Shu, Y., Shi, Z.: A self-evolving WiFi-based indoor navigation system using smartphones. IEEE Trans. Mob. Comput. **19**, 1760–1774 (2020). https://doi.org/10.1109/TMC.2019.2915221

25. Pelant, J., et al.: BLE device indoor localization based on RSS fingerprinting mapped by propagation modes. In: 2017 27th International Conference Radioelektronika (RADIOELEKTRONIKA), pp. 1–5 (2017). https://doi.org/10.1109/RADIOELEK.2017.7937584

26. Honkavirta, V., Perala, T., Ali-Loytty, S., Piche, R.: A comparative survey of WLAN location fingerprinting methods. In: Navigation and Communication 2009 6th Workshop on Positioning, pp. 243–251 (2009). https://doi.org/10.1109/WPNC.2009.4907834

27. Bahl, P., Padmanabhan, V.N.: RADAR: an in-building RF-based user location and tracking system. In: Proceedings IEEE INFOCOM 2000. Conference on Computer Communications. Nineteenth Annual Joint Conference of the IEEE Computer and Communications Societies (Cat. No. 00CH37064), vol. 2, pp. 775–784 (2000). https://doi.org/10.1109/INFCOM.2000.832252

28. Machaj, J., Brida, P., Piché, R.: Rank based fingerprinting algorithm for indoor positioning. In: 2011 International Conference on Indoor Positioning and Indoor Navigation, pp. 1–6 (2011). https://doi.org/10.1109/IPIN.2011.6071929

29. Machaj, J., Brida, P.: Performance investigation of the RBF localization algorithm. Adv. Electr. Electron. Eng. **11**(2), 100–107 (2013). https://doi.org/10.15598/aeee.v11i2.761

30. Racko, J., Brida, P., Perttula, A., Parviainen, J., Collin, J.: Pedestrian dead reckoning with particle filter for handheld smartphone. In: 2016 International Conference on Indoor Positioning and Indoor Navigation (IPIN), pp. 1–7 (2016). https://doi.org/10.1109/IPIN.2016.7743608
31. Brida, P., Machaj, J., Racko, J., Krejcar, O.: Algorithm for dynamic fingerprinting radio map creation using IMU measurements. Sensors **21**, 2283 (2021). https://doi.org/10.3390/s21072283

The Adaptive Calibration Method for Single-Beam Distance Sensors

Piotr Biernacki[(✉)], Adam Ziębiński, and Damian Grzechca

Institute of Informatics, Silesian University of Technology, Gliwice, Poland
{piotr.biernacki,adam.ziebinski,damian.grzechca}@polsl.pl

Abstract. The agility process used in Industry 4.0 increasingly influences on the location changes of the used production resources. Ensuring safety in a production environment is critical, especially when objects are moving or change their location e.g. transport trolleys, Autonomous Guided Vehicles or mobile robots. One of the methods of moving object discovery by other objects, e.g. AGV is application of distance sensors. Different sensors enable various measurement quality. In order to improve their accuracy, diverse calibration and filtration methods are often used. The article presents adaptive curve fitting method to increase accuracy of measurements for single-beam distance sensors. The research results of calibration were presented based on example of low cost ultrasounds and LiDARs sensors. Proposed adaptive curve fitting method enables to improve measurement accuracy even by 97%.

Keywords: Curve fitting · Sensors calibration · Single-beam distance sensors

1 Introduction

A smart production systems require multi-process support, manufacturing support techniques, internal logistics solutions, intelligent monitoring, and autonomous decision-making. They are often implemented in the Industry 4.0 [1] environment which consists of several Internet of Things (IoT) [2] solutions, Cyber-Physical Production Systems (CPPS) [3], and internal transport systems (ITS) [4]. Nowadays in ITS, Autonomous Guided Vehicles (AGV) [5] are often used to cooperate with production staff and automatic production loading station which can be equipped with robot [6] or collaborative robot [7]. The logistics tasks for AGV must be monitored [8] and performed in a dynamic, autonomous and safety manner [9]. The high precision movements of AGVs and mobile robots in an industrial environment [10] are very important factor for safety assurance in production plant. Precisely determining the position [11] of an AGV enables the navigation system [12] to give orders correctly and increases the accuracy of the movement of an AGV.

AGVs are equipped with different sensors [13] to ensure control of their movements, e.g. encoders, hall sensors [14], ultrasounds, LiDARs, cameras, energy measurement [15, 16], etc. Encoders and hall sensors [17] enable to determine the direction of the rotation and speed of wheels. In effect, they can be used by the AGV to calculate the

© Springer Nature Switzerland AG 2021
N. T. Nguyen et al. (Eds.): ICCCI 2021, LNAI 12876, pp. 721–732, 2021.
https://doi.org/10.1007/978-3-030-88081-1_54

speed, distance and direction of movement. Ultrasounds, LiDARs and cameras enable to determine the distance to the obstacle [18]. They enable on safe driving of the AGVs by detecting obstacles [19] and bypassing them [20]. Additionally, they can be used to recognize obstacle [21] and localise them [22].

Ensuring safe and accurate driving near production lines is a prerequisite for use AGV systems in industry [23]. High precision measurements [24] are required especially in the implementation of the docking function [25] and cooperation with a production staff [26]. For this reason, it is important to obtain accurate measurements from the sensors used by AGV. However, the sensors have different properties as well as the range of measurement and accuracy [27]. The use of calibration [28], filter [29] and data fusion methods [30] enable to obtain the high degree of accuracy, what will determine the range of motion and ensure a more accurate moving of an AGV.

The aim of the article is to present the possibilities of increasing overall measurements accuracy of low cost distance sensors.

The purpose of the research was to develop a method of calibrating measurements for single-beam distance sensor based on adaptive curve fitting.

The paper is organized as follows: the second section presents a single-beam distance sensors solutions, including ultrasonic and LiDAR sensors. The third section describes the proposed adaptive calibration methods. The fourth section presents the results of calibration for chosen ultrasounds and LiDARs sensors. The conclusions are presented in the fifth section.

2   A Single-Beam Distance Sensors

There are many types of sensors that uses a single-beam [31, 32] in various areas of distance measuring (e.g. LiDARs, ultrasounds). Each of them enables to understand the surrounding environment using different features, methods and properties of environment (e.g. light, reflection, sound).

LiDARs enables to perform precise distance measurement with high frequency. There are two main methods of distance measurement using laser sensor – triangulation and Time of Flight (ToF). Triangulation method uses the laser light source and sensing matrix pointing in the same direction with known yaw angle to each other. Laser light reflects off the obstacle and falls on the matrix. The location of detected light on matrix is closely related to the angle from which it fell, which depends on the distance that laser light has to travel [33, 34]. ToF method enables to measure the distance using the time of flight of the laser light with a known speed. But it also divides in two methods, the direct and the indirect ToF. Direct ToF based on generating short pulses of light and measuring the time until each pulse returns to the sensor to measure distance to obstacle [28]. Indirect ToF generate a continuous wave of modulated light and the change in phase of reflected light is used to measure the distance to the obstacle [35].

Ultrasonic sensors also enable to measure distance. In comparison with LiDARs they have lower frequency of measurements, however they don't suffer for presence of ambient light or the dark obstacle colours. They emit sound wave which reflects from the obstacle and then it is detected by the sensor. The time spend by that wave in the air until it was received by the sensor is then multiplied by the speed of sound in the air (343 m/s) and divided by 2, the result is the distance travelled by the wave.

Each of sensors has various features (Table 1), so for a specific task right sensors should be selected. Some of them are very sensitive to color of the surface or ambient light. They have a different operating range, measuring resolution and accuracy or fields of view (FOV) across the operating range. Leica D510 could be used as reference measurement device because it has got a certificate (ISO 16331-1) which confirms the accuracy of the measurements up to 1 mm. Additionally the measurements can be performed manually or via Bluetooth communication and can be stored on a computer.

Table 1. The comparison of selected LiDAR and ultrasonic sensors

Type	Model	Range	Resolution	Measurement error	FOV
LiDAR 1D	DFRobot TF Mini	0.3–12 m	5 mm	max 60 mm @ 0.3–6 m 1% @ >6 m	2.3°
LiDAR 1D	DFRobot TF Mini-S	0.1–12 m	5 mm	max 60 mm @ 0.1–6 m 1% @ >6 m	2°
LiDAR 1D	Leica D510	0.05–200 m	0.1 mm	1 mm @ 0.05–10 m, 0.1 mm/m @ 10–30 m, 0.2 mm/m @ 30–100 m, 0.3 mm/m @ >100 m	0.034°
LiDAR 1.5D	Continental SRL-01	1–10 m	1 mm	100 mm	27°
LiDAR 1D	ST VL53L1X	0.04–1.35 m	1 mm	25 mm	27°
Ultrasound	HC-SR04	0.02–4 m	0.17 mm	1%	15°
Ultrasound	URM37 v5	0.02–8 m	10 mm	1%	30°

Distance measurements quality verification was performed for 4 sensors (DFRobot TF Mini/-S, HC-SR04, URM37 v5) from Table 1 within range of 0.05–2.25 m (vary according to operational range of individual sensor). Leica D510 acted as reference sensor because of precise measurement capabilities. Figure 1 shows results of distance measurements of all the sensors. On the top side of the figure there are distance measurements of not calibrated sensors and the reference one. On the bottom side of the figure there are differences between distance measurements of not calibrated sensors and the reference one.

Table 2 provides additional information about the distance measurements quality of individual sensor. Standard deviation describes sensor's precision and the residuals values represents overall sensor's accuracy. Standard deviation values were first calculated across given measurement series and then minimum, maximum and average values of standard deviation was chosen from whole measurement range of given sensor. Difference between max. and min. of standard deviation shows the spread of measurements across whole measurement range. Minimum, maximum and average values of residuals were also calculated and chosen from whole measurement range of given sensor. The most precise sensor according to the data from Table 2, with smallest avg. (0.0011 m) std. deviation and spread (0.0018 m) is TF Mini LiDAR. On the other hand, TF Mini has the biggest RMSE (0.056 m), so has the worst accuracy. The smallest precision has the HC-SR04 ultrasound sensor with the biggest std. deviation avg. (0.0042 m) and spread (0.0098 m). Best overall capabilities have the TF Mini-S with fairly low std. deviation

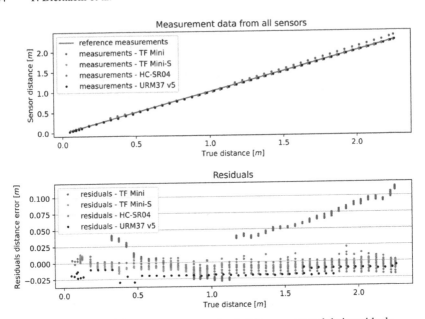

Fig. 1. Results of distance measurements of all the sensors and their residuals.

avg. (0.0014 m) and spread (0.0023 m) values and the lowest RMSE (0.0072 m). Poor precision can be fixed using filtration algorithms. Low accuracy also is not the problem because of calibration possibilities.

Table 2. The comparison of sensors' standard deviations and residuals values.

Sensors	Std. deviation [m] in range 0.05–2.25 m				Residuals [m]			
	Min	Avg	Max	Max - Min	Min	Avg	Max	RMSE
TF Mini	0.0002	0.0011	0.0020	0.0018	−0.0290	0.0383	0.1140	0.0560
TF Mini-S	0.0003	0.0014	0.0026	0.0023	−0.0190	−0.0055	0.0130	0.0072
HC-SR04	0.0001	0.0042	0.0099	0.0098	−0.0203	−0.0062	0.0219	0.0100
URM37 v5	0	0.0004	0.0045	0.0045	−0.0300	−0.0168	−0.0060	0.0177

3   Calibration Methods

In order to increase sensors measurements accuracy [27], there is need to perform their calibration [28]. Calibration is a process of comparison of the measurements and their adjustment to the true values. Distance sensors for calibration process need other sensor as the reference one or space with series of obstacles with known distances to them.

The calibration of distance sensors should start with a precise aligning the sensors with each other and with the object they will point on. Then a series of measurements for different distances should be made. Having data from distance measurements, the next step of calibration can be made – determination of regression line (curve fitting) to obtained distance measurements.

Curve fitting is an iterative process of linear, nonlinear approximation. The result of curve fitting is a function and the parameters which describes trend in the data. Before starting the curve fitting there is need to choose which model (e.g. polynomial, exponential, power series) will fit to the data the best.

For curve fitting procedure, least square method can be used. There are also alternatives, like robust regression method which can help to eliminate the influence on estimated function parameters by the outliers (big errors in measurements). After curve fitting to given data there is need to check the goodness of fitting and for this purpose root mean square error (RMSE) was calculated.

To perform precise sensor calibration, precise measurements are needed, that is why it is very important to perform a series of distance measurements at equal distance sections within the desired range by the sensors under calibration and the reference one. Distance measurements calibration using curve fitting can be performed on whole data set or on the data set divided in sections.

One of the commonly used single-beam distance sensor calibration method, which treats whole sensor dataset as a single section, consists of following steps:

1. Reference sensor measurements curve fitting,
2. Assessment goodness of curve fitting to reference sensor measurements,
3. Curve fitting of not calibrated sensor measurements,
4. Assessment goodness of curve fitting to not calibrated sensor measurements,
5. Measurement of differences between reference regression line and the curve of not calibrated sensor (residuals),
6. Curve fitting of differences determined in step 5,
7. Assessment goodness of the final fitting.

Above steps allows to perform curve fitting to the whole data range at once and the final result will be single calibration function. But final precision will depend on the quality of the data given by the not calibrated sensor. For smooth transitions between the data points this method can give satisfactory results but if the measurement data has rapid, spiky changes in the measurement characteristic it may be better to divide the data into the sections and apply adaptive calibration method.

Adaptive sensor calibration method consists of following steps:

1. Reference sensor measurements curve fitting,
2. Assessment goodness of curve fitting to reference sensor measurements,
3. Averaging of all measurement series of not calibrated sensor,
4. Measurement of differences between reference regression line and the mean points of not calibrated sensor,
5. Finding a minima and maxima points of differences from step 4 and determination of descending and ascending sections,

6. Performing single section calibration for every section determined in step 5

If the RMSE of curve fitting in any of the goodness assessment steps is not satisfying, there is need to increase degree of fitted regression line or change the model of that line and repeat the curve fitting step.

The goal of calibration process is to correlate the distance measurement error of given sensor with the distance it perceives. That way it is possible to determine correction function or set of correction functions that describes measurements characteristic of the sensor and correct the measurements given by the sensor in many measurement segments.

After calibration the correct distance measurement can be obtained by passing measurement from the sensor to the correction function and subtracting the result of that function from the passed measurement.

4 Experiment

For experiment, single-beam distance sensors were chosen which were described in Sect. 2. In order to perform the test of sensors' distance measurements characteristics custom research station was built.

It consisted of two aluminium angular profiles which were the rails for the transport trolley on which white Styrofoam (1 m × 0.5 m) was mounted vertically. Sensors was mounted on one side of the rails, perpendicular to the transport trolley movement direction. The transport trolley acted as the mobile obstacle. LiDAR sensors were spaced apart from each other by 0.5 m to prevent from disruption. Ultrasound sensors was tested separately because of their wide FOV and possible mutual arousing. All the sensors were facing the trolley with obstacle and were mounted that way to align their measuring starting positions.

To acquire distance measurements from the sensors, they were connected to the STM32F429ZI that was streaming periodically (10 ms) via Ethernet all the data gathered from the sensors. STM32 was connected to the computer that was saving the distance measurements data. The LiDARs and URM37v5 was connected to the STM32 using UART interface and the HCSR04 was connected via two signal lines (trigger and echo).

After that everything was mounted and all necessary programs were enabled, the mobile obstacle was placed at the starting position - 0.05 m away from the sensors. Then the program responsible of saving the data was triggered by the keyboard key to start saving 40 measurements where each measurement from all connected sensors was saved in equal time interval (500 ms). After that all measurements from single series were saved, the mobile obstacle was shifted on the rails away and next distance measurements saving process started, and so on. Full test was performed in range of 0.05–2.25 m where from 0.05 m to 0.13 m mobile obstacle was shifted by 0.02 m and within range 0.13–2.25 m by 0.05 m.

Having the distance measurements gathered, there is possibility to perform sensor calibration. Figure 2 presents results of curve fitting using the single section calibration method described in Sect. 3, where whole measurement range was treated as single section. On the top side of the Fig. 2 there are distance measurements gathered from the

TF Mini-S LiDAR sensor together with the reference measurements and the regression line. There is also result of curve fitting - TF Mini-S's polynomial regression line of 7th degree. On the bottom side of the Fig. 2 there are differences between the TF Mini-S and the reference regression lines. These points represent the correlation between the residual value and the distance measurement given by the TF Mini-S sensor. There are also polynomial regression lines of specific degree fitted to the residuals. For both distance measurements and the residuals there were fitted polynomial regression lines from 1st to 7th degree.

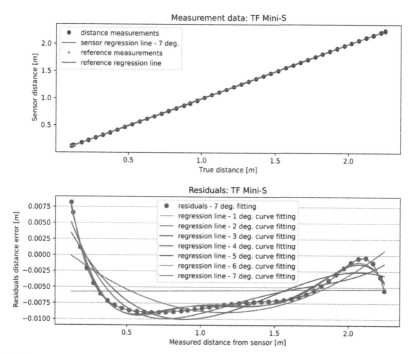

Fig. 2. Results of single section curve fitting calibration method – 7th degree polynomial.

The accuracy of sensor measured by the RMSE depends on the quality of fitting to the distance measurements and then quality of fitting to the residuals. The better fitting to the data, the better reflection of sensor's measurement characteristics and lower error. For single curve fitting to distance measurements, there were performed 7 curve fittings to the residuals. Figure 3 shows the goodness assessment results of the curve fitting presented in Fig. 2. Each line represents the sum of RMSEs of curve fitting to the residuals given by the regression line of specific degree fitted to the distance measurements and the RMSE of curve fitting to the distance measurements. The best curve fitting results for TF Mini-S with the smallest sum of RMSEs (0.0025 m) gave 7th degree polynomial fitted to the distance measurements and the 7th degree polynomial fitted to the residuals. It is an improvement of 65% compared to the accuracy before the calibration (0.007 m). Results of single section curve fitting for other sensors are gathered in Table 3.

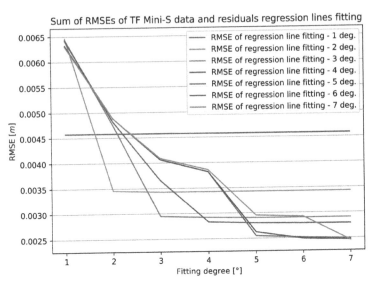

Fig. 3. Fitting assessment results after single section curve fitting calibration method.

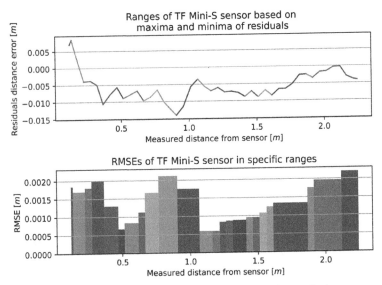

Fig. 4. Results of adaptive curve fitting calibration method.

Figure 4 shows results of adaptive curve fitting method. Top side of the Fig. 4 presents the sections of residuals which were divided based on the minima and maxima points of residuals' means of measurements series. After dividing the residuals to sections, they were separately curve fitted as described in Sect. 3. Each section was fitted with polynomial regression lines from 1st to 4th degree and that one with the best fitting RMSE were chosen. Goodness of each fitting is presented on the bottom of Fig. 4 in form of RMSE bars. What's worth mentioning not for all sections high degree was chosen. Some of them are fitted with the 1st degree polynomial regression line because it gave the best fitting result. Overall accuracy after adaptive curve fitting calibration raised to 0.0016 m which compared to the value before the calibration (0.007 m) is an improvement of 77.78%. Results of adaptive curve fitting for other sensors are presented in Table 3.

Table 3 presents results of calibration methods for all of the sensors used in this article. RMSE values were rounded to the 4th decimal place after percentage improvement calculation. What can be observed is that both used calibration methods improved measurements accuracy. The biggest improvements can be observed for sensors with the largest RMSE before the calibration. After single section curve fitting the best accuracy has TF Mini-S sensor (0.0025 m) and the worst HC-SR04 sensor (0.0054 m). What is worth of noticing, after adaptive curve fitting almost all sensors improved their measurement accuracy to the same level except HC-SR04. The best measurement accuracies after adaptive curve fitting are presented by TF Mini and URM37 v5 sensor. HC-SR04 sensor stopped the accuracy improvement on the 0.005 m level because of his low precision - high std. deviation which equals 0.0042 m (average). Better results for HC-SR04 would be obtained after measurements filtration. Adaptive curve fitting method has better improvement results than single section curve because of ability to fit precisely to every measurements characteristics.

Table 3. Summary of curve fitting calibration methods results.

Sensors	Single section curve fitting			Adaptive curve fitting		Improvement between calib. methods [m]	Improvement between calib. methods [%]
	RMSE [m]		Percentage of improvement [%]	RMSE [m]	Percentage of improvement [%]		
	Before calibration	After calibration		After calibration			
TF Mini	0.0560	0.0103	81.58	0.0014	97.48	−0.0089	15.90
TF Mini-S	0.0072	0.0025	65.83	0.0016	78.31	−0.0009	12.48
HC-SR04	0.0100	0.0054	46.28	0.0050	49.69	−0.0004	3.41
URM37 v5	0.0177	0.0035	80.38	0.0014	92.30	−0.0021	11.92

5 Conclusions

The calibration method for single-beam distance sensors based on adaptive curve fitting was prepared. The proposed method enables to divide the measuring range for a given sensor into sections based on the determination of the minima and maxima points of difference between measurements taken by not calibrated sensor and the reference one.

For each designated section, the lowest RMSE value for 1–4 degree polynomials are searched.

This approach enables to obtain the smallest possible measurement error for a given measuring section. As a result, it is possible to obtain the greater measurement accuracy for a given sensor in different parts of the measuring range. The developed method enables to obtain greater accuracy than in the case of determining the polynomial for the entire measuring range (even with higher degrees of polynomials) or its division into 2 or 3 segments resulting from the characteristics for a given sensor.

Sensors from different production batch may have slight differences in measurement results. The proposed solution enables the calibration of a given batch of sensors or a single sensor. Due to the requirement to use a large number of polynomials to perform calculations, it is advisable to tabulate the calibration results. This approach will further enable measurement correction to work quickly, especially in systems that do not possess high computing power. Additionally, it enables the use of low-cost sensors in IoT, AGV and commonly used CPS solutions requiring good quality of measurements.

Further research will be related to the use of filtration and statistical methods that allow to exclude outliers or too wide range of measurement results for a given distance from the measurement data. This problem especially occurs for sensors with a wide FOV, e.g. an ultrasound detecting reflection from other objects than in the search area of the system.

Acknowledgements. The research leading to these results received funding from the Norway Grants 2014–2021, which is operated by the National Centre for Research and Development under the project "Automated Guided Vehicles integrated with Collaborative Robots for Smart Industry Perspective" (Project Contract no.: NOR/POLNOR/CoBotAGV/0027/2019 -00) and partially by the Statutory Research funds of the Department of Applied Informatics, Silesian University of Technology, Gliwice, Poland (grant No no BK-281/RAU8/2020).

References

1. Wang, S., Wan, J., Li, D., Zhang, C.: Implementing smart factory of Industrie 4.0: an outlook. Int. J. Distrib. Sens. Netw. **12**, 3159805 (2016) https://doi.org/10.1155/2016/3159805.
2. Botta, A., de Donato, W., Persico, V., Pescapé, A.: Integration of Cloud computing and Internet of Things: a survey. Futur. Gener. Comput. Syst. **56**, 684–700 (2016). https://doi.org/10.1016/j.future.2015.09.021
3. Shafiq, S.I., Sanin, C., Szczerbicki, E., Toro, C.: Virtual engineering object / virtual engineering process: a specialized form of cyber physical system for Industrie 4.0. Procedia Comput. Sci. **60**, 1146–1155 (2015). https://doi.org/10.1016/j.procs.2015.08.166.
4. Andresen, S.H., Evensen, K.: Standardisation and trends – why is standardisation of ITS needed? In: Intelligent Transport Systems. p. 161 (2003)
5. Shi, D., Mi, H., Collins, E.G., Wu, J.: An indoor low-cost and high-accuracy localization approach for AGVs. IEEE Access. **8**, 50085–50090 (2020). https://doi.org/10.1109/ACCESS.2020.2980364
6. Kyrkjebø, E.: Inertial human motion estimation for physical human-robot interaction using an interaction velocity update to reduce drift. In: Companion of the 2018 ACM/IEEE International Conference on Human-Robot Interaction. ACM, Chicago IL USA, pp. 163–164 (2018). https://doi.org/10.1145/3173386.3176955.

7. Realyvásquez-Vargas, A., et al.: Introduction and configuration of a collaborative robot in an assembly task as a means to decrease occupational risks and increase efficiency in a manufacturing company. Robot. Comput.-Integr. Manuf. **57**, 315–328 (2019). https://doi.org/10.1016/j.rcim.2018.12.015

8. Flak, J., Gaj, P., Tokarz, K., Wideł, S., Ziębiński, A.: Remote monitoring of geological activity of inclined regions – the concept. In: Kwiecień, A., Gaj, P., Stera, P. (eds.) CN 2009. CCIS, vol. 39, pp. 292–301. Springer, Heidelberg (2009). https://doi.org/10.1007/978-3-642-02671-3_34

9. Moleda, M., Momot, A., Mrozek, D.: Predictive maintenance of boiler feed water pumps using SCADA data. Sensors **20**, 571 (2020). https://doi.org/10.3390/s20020571

10. Schuh, G., Potente, T., Varandani, R., Hausberg, C., Fränken, B.: Collaboration moves productivity to the next level. Procedia CIRP **17**, 3–8 (2014). https://doi.org/10.1016/j.procir.2014.02.037

11. Grzechca, D., Paszek, K.: Short-term positioning accuracy based on mems sensors for smart city solutions. (2019). https://doi.org/10.24425/MMS.2019.126325.

12. Tokarz, K., Czekalski, P., Sieczkowski, W.: Integration of ultrasonic and inertial methods in indoor navigation system. Theor. Appl. Inform. **26**, 107–117 (2015)

13. Fleming, W.J.: Overview of automotive sensors. IEEE Sens. J. **1**, 296–308 (2001). https://doi.org/10.1109/7361.983469

14. el Popovic, R., Randjelovic, Z., Manic, D.: Integrated Hall-effect magnetic sensors. Sens. Actuators A: Phys **91**, 46–50 (2001)

15. Paryanto, Brossog, M., Bornschlegl, M., Franke, J.: Reducing the energy consumption of industrial robots in manufacturing systems. Int. J. Adv. Manuf. Technol. **78**, 1315–1328 (2015). https://doi.org/10.1007/s00170-014-6737-z

16. Grzechca, D., Ziębiński, A., Rybka, P.: Enhanced reliability of ADAS sensors based on the observation of the power supply current and neural network application. In: Nguyen, N.T., Papadopoulos, G.A., Jędrzejowicz, P., Trawiński, B., Vossen, G. (eds.) ICCCI 2017. LNCS (LNAI), vol. 10449, pp. 215–226. Springer, Cham (2017). https://doi.org/10.1007/978-3-319-67077-5_21

17. Ziebinski, A., Bregulla, M., Fojcik, M., Kłak, S.: Monitoring and controlling speed for an autonomous mobile platform based on the hall sensor. In: Nguyen, N.T., Papadopoulos, G.A., Jędrzejowicz, P., Trawiński, B., Vossen, G. (eds.) ICCCI 2017. LNCS (LNAI), vol. 10449, pp. 249–259. Springer, Cham (2017). https://doi.org/10.1007/978-3-319-67077-5_24

18. Wen, S., Othman, K., Rad, A., Zhang, Y., Zhao, Y.: Indoor SLAM using laser and camera with closed-loop controller for NAO humanoid robot. Abstr. Appl. Anal. **2014**, 1–8 (2014). https://doi.org/10.1155/2014/513175

19. Jia, X., Hu, Z., Guan, H.: A new multi-sensor platform for adaptive driving assistance system (ADAS). In: 2011 9th World Congress on Intelligent Control and Automation, pp. 1224–1230 (2011). https://doi.org/10.1109/WCICA.2011.5970711

20. Ziebinski, A., Cupek, R., Nalepa, M.: Obstacle avoidance by a mobile platform using an ultrasound sensor. In: Nguyen, N.T., Papadopoulos, G.A., Jędrzejowicz, P., Trawiński, B., Vossen, G. (eds.) ICCCI 2017. LNCS (LNAI), vol. 10449, pp. 238–248. Springer, Cham (2017). https://doi.org/10.1007/978-3-319-67077-5_23

21. Bertozzi, M., Broggi, A.: GOLD: a parallel real-time stereo vision system for generic obstacle and lane detection. IEEE Trans. Image Process. **7**, 62–81 (1998). https://doi.org/10.1109/83.650851

22. Grzechca, D.E., Pelczar, P., Chruszczyk, L.: Analysis of object location accuracy for iBeacon technology based on the RSSI path loss model and fingerprint map. Int. J. Electron. Telecommun. **62**, (2016). https://doi.org/10.1515/eletel-2016-0051

23. Cupek, R., et al.: Autonomous guided vehicles for smart industries – the state-of-the-art and research challenges. In: Krzhizhanovskaya, V.V., et al. (eds.) ICCS 2020. LNCS, vol. 12141, pp. 330–343. Springer, Cham (2020). https://doi.org/10.1007/978-3-030-50426-7_25

24. Karger, D.W., Bayha, F.H.: Engineered Work Measurement: The Principles, Techniques, and Data of Methods-Time Measurement Background and Foundations of Work Measurement and Methods-Time Measurement, Plus Other Related Material. Industrial Press Inc. (1987)

25. Roth, H., Schilling, K.: Navigation and docking manoeuvres of mobile robots in industrial environments. In: 24th Annual Conference of the IEEE Industrial Electronics Society, Germany, pp. 2458–2462 IEEE (1998). https://doi.org/10.1109/IECON.1998.724112

26. Mörtl, A., Lawitzky, M., Kucukyilmaz, A., Sezgin, M., Basdogan, C., Hirche, S.: The role of roles: Physical cooperation between humans and robots. Int. J. Robot. Res. **31**, 1656–1674 (2012). https://doi.org/10.1177/0278364912455366

27. Grzechca, D., et al: Accuracy analysis for object positioning on a circular trajectory based on the UWB location system. In: 14th International Conference on Advanced Trends in Radioelectronics, Telecommunications and Computer Engineering, pp. 69–74. IEEE (2018). https://doi.org/10.1109/TCSET.2018.8336158

28. Lindner, M., Schiller, I., Kolb, A., Koch, R.: Time-of-flight sensor calibration for accurate range sensing. Comput. Vis. Image Underst. **114**, 1318–1328 (2010). https://doi.org/10.1016/j.cviu.2009.11.002

29. Guan, H., Li, L., Jia, X.: Multi-sensor fusion vehicle positioning based on Kalman Filter. Presented at the Information Science and Technology (ICIST). In: 2013 International Conference on (2013)

30. Sidek, O., Quadri, S.A.: A review of data fusion models and systems. Int. J. Image Data Fus. **3**, 3–21 (2012). https://doi.org/10.1080/19479832.2011.645888

31. Sheik-Bahae, M., Said, A.A., Wei, T.-H., Hagan, D.J., Van Stryland, E.W.: Sensitive measurement of optical nonlinearities using a single beam. IEEE J. Quantum Electron. **26**, 760–769 (1990). https://doi.org/10.1109/3.53394

32. Bhardwaj, B., et al.: Tracking of localized sensor node using single-beam echo sounder. In: International Conference on Communication and Signal Processing, India, pp. 0858–0861. IEEE (2020). https://doi.org/10.1109/ICCSP48568.2020.9182124

33. Dorsch, R.G., Häusler, G., Herrmann, J.M.: Laser triangulation: fundamental uncertainty in distance measurement. Appl. Opt. **33**, 1306 (1994). https://doi.org/10.1364/AO.33.001306

34. Genta, G., Minetola, P., Barbato, G.: Calibration procedure for a laser triangulation scanner with uncertainty evaluation. Opt. Lasers Eng. **86**, 11–19 (2016). https://doi.org/10.1016/j.optlaseng.2016.05.005

35. Bhandari, A., all: Super-resolved time-of-flight sensing via FRI sampling theory. In: IEEE International Conference on Acoustics, Speech and Signal Processing, Shanghai, pp. 4009–4013. IEEE (2016). https://doi.org/10.1109/ICASSP.2016.7472430

Internet of Things and Computational Technologies for Collective Intelligence

Application of Traditional Machine Learning Models to Detect Abnormal Traffic in the Internet of Things Networks

Evgeniya Istratova$^{(\boxtimes)}$, Mikhail Grif , and Dmitry Dostovalov

Novosibirsk State Technical University, Novosibirsk, Russia

Abstract. The relevance of solving the problem of choosing machine learning models for detecting anomalies in network traffic of the Internet of Things is associated with the need to analyze a large number of security events to identify abnormal behavior of smart devices. The aim of the research was to investigate machine learning models for detecting anomalies in IoT network traffic. A comparative analysis of machine learning models was carried out and recommendations for their use for detecting anomalies in the Internet of Things network traffic were provided. Naive Bayes, Support Vector Machine, Logistic Regression, K-nearest neighbors, Boosting and Random Forest were considered as basic machine learning models. Anomaly detection efficiency indicators were the following metrics: accuracy, precision, recall and F score, as well as the time spent on training the model. As a result of the study, it was found that the preparation of traditional machine learning models takes a little time, since it does not require more resources and computing power. The machine learning models built during the experiment demonstrated high accuracy rates for detecting anomalies in large heterogeneous traffic typical of the Internet of Things. The distinctive features of the research were both conducting an experiment on a single software and hardware and using the same data-set and taking into account the estimate of the time spent on training the model, in addition to the accuracy, precision, recall and F score of anomaly detection efficiency. Practical significance is that the results obtained in the research can be used to build systems for detecting network anomalies in the Internet of Things.

Keywords: Internet of Things · Intrusion detection · Machine learning · Abnormal traffic · Network

1 Introduction

The development of technologies for wireless high-speed telecommunications, sensor network technologies, as well as technologies for building next generation networks have led to the emergence and development of the Internet of things. Currently, this concept is an integral part of the concept of intelligent all-pervading networks [1].

There is a rather heterogeneous traffic in networks built in accordance with the concept of the Internet of Things [2]. For example, multimedia traffic of voice and video,

N. T. Nguyen et al. (Eds.): ICCCI 2021, LNAI 12876, pp. 735–744, 2021.
https://doi.org/10.1007/978-3-030-88081-1_55

which is very sensitive to delays, traffic of monitoring of various objects, traffic of command-signaling information, traffic of messages and e-mail, etc. At the same time, it must be met the specified requirements for the quality of the services and services provided. According to this concept, IoT networks can be classified as multiservice networks. Thus, the complexity of the logical and physical architectures of the Internet of Things networks causes objective difficulties in building network management subsystems and protecting network and subscriber information. One of the key tasks of managing IoT networks is promptly detecting the state of the network. So the key tasks of identifying the network state is the task of promptly detecting abnormal behavior of network traffic. This way the urgent tasks are prompt anomalous behavior detection with unacceptable parameters of traffic in IoT networks and prompt decision-making to eliminate or block destructive influences on these networks.

There are various approaches to detecting abnormal traffic on the network nowadays. Known approaches that use the history of changes in network traffic [3], time series from the control database [4], nonparametric cumulative sums [5], the estimate of the maximum entropy [6] and other methods. There are also solutions based on intrusion detection systems (IDS) which include proactive approaches to prevent and remediate vulnerabilities in the system. However, these approaches must adapt and evolve towards new technologies and communication networks such as the IoT. One of the approaches to solving this problem can be the use of machine learning to analyze the passing traffic and detect anomalies in it.

2 Problem Definition

The peculiarities of IoT networks are their highly segmented topology and the presence of several interface points with other networks. The overall system traffic can no longer be monitored from one point on the network. This circumstance necessitates the use of intelligent agent technology for solving such problems [7, 8]. Agents develop and implement themselves part of the management decisions for detecting traffic anomalies. This way it is advisable to use a centralized-decentralized network management system for the Internet of Things. This concept can increase the efficiency of decision-making to counteract any destructive effects on the network and reduce the management traffic.

To security threats respond are needed tools for analysis a large number of events in IoT networks. Such tools should collect network traffic, logs and other data, the volume of which might be sometimes very large. In addition, the heterogeneity of sources and information stores leads to high heterogeneity of the analyzed data. Machine learning is currently a powerful technology for analyzing security events, detecting attacks and abnormal behavior of smart devices [9]. As a rule, it is generally difficult to compare different machine learning models with each other. This is because researchers use different data-sets or differing subsets of a particular data-set to evaluate the effectiveness of models.

Thus the main research purpose is the comparative analysis of machine learning models based on assessing the efficiency of detecting anomalies in the Internet of Things network traffic using a single software and hardware and the same subsets of the training and testing data-set.

3 Related Works

Most researchers in the field of IoT security consider machine learning methods as part of approaches to detecting attacks and anomalous device behavior [10, 11]. The main advantages of traditional machine learning methods are: high performance and scalability for growing volumes of data, as well as the ability to automatically select informative features from raw data.

The article [8] compares the developed model with classifiers based on traditional machine learning methods: Support Vector Machine (SVM), Naive Bayes, Random Forest, Adaptive Boosting (AdaBoost) and the K-nearest neighbors algorithm (kNN). The analysis demonstrates that the deep learning approach provides the best possible outcome.

The article [5] contents a description about distributed cloud-based machine learning environment for detecting and preventing phishing and botnet attacks on smart devices. The developed model is compared with the models developed by other researchers. The main disadvantage of the comparative analysis in this work is that the models under consideration are not evaluated on the same data-sets.

The authors of the article [12] analyze several learning models for detecting DdoS attacks. For analysis they use the following machine learning models: Support Vector Machines, Naive Bayes and Random Forest.

The article [13] describes the role of artificial intelligence methods in the process of ensuring cybersecurity of IoT networks, which presents the main methods of attacks on IoT devices and machine learning models used to protect them. The following were considered as such models: Decision Trees, K-nearest neighbor models, Support Vector Models, Artificial Neural Networks.

The article [14] provides an overview of modern intrusion detection systems developed for the Internet of Things model. The authors present an analysis of the vulnerabilities of the architecture of the Internet of Things with an emphasis on the corresponding methods, functions and mechanisms and their relationship with the all architecture layers.

The authors [15] propose to use functional clusters in terms of flow, message queue telemetry transmission and transmission control protocol to detect and remove malicious packets from the Internet of Things network using functions in the UNSW-NB15 data-set. The authors used such supervised machine learning algorithms as: Random Forest, Support Vector Model and Artificial Neural Networks on clusters. The research showed that the proposed feature clusters provide higher accuracy and less training time compared to other modern supervised machine learning approaches.

The analysis of these relevant works was carried out according to the following indexes (Table 1): accuracy (A), precision (P), recall (R), F score (F) and time (T) which the data-set used for training on analyzed models.

Thus, the main research features to compare with the relevant works are:

1) conducting an experiment on a single data-set and using the same software and hardware;
2) expanding the comparative sample of traditional machine learning models;
3) estimation of the time spent on training the model, in addition to such indicators of the efficiency of detecting anomalies as accuracy, precision, recall and F score.

Table 1. Results of relevant works analysis.

Article	Index					Data-set	Models	Precision, %
	A	P	R	F	T			
[8]	+	−	−	−	−	VirusTotal	Naive Bayes	90
							kNN	94
							SVM	82
							AdaBoost	93
							Random Forest	92
[5]	+	+	+	+	−	CSIC 2010	SVM	99
[12]	+	+	+	−	−	CICIDS 2017	Naive Bayes	95
							SVM	95
							Random Forest	94
[15]	+	+	+	−	−	UNSW-NB15	Random Forest	96

4   Modeling of the Architecture for Detecting Abnormal Traffic

It is usually used to traffic analysis a model, which could reflect its intended features. Typically, a model has three components:

1. Trend - the general behavior of the series in terms of increasing or decreasing values.
2. Seasonality - periodic fluctuations in values associated, for example, with the day of the week or month.
3. Random value - the result left after exclusion from a number of other components. This is where should be searched anomalies.

First of all, after choosing a model, it is needed to start decomposing it into components. Then select the trend by smoothing the original data (sliding window, exponential smoothing, regression). To determine the seasonal component, the trend should be subtracted from the source data or divided by it, depending on the type of model selected. In turn, the average season is determined by dividing the result obtained by a specific period, for example, a week or a month, then, by removing the trend and the seasonal factor from the original series. Removing the trend and the seasonal factor from the original series, it could get the desired random component. Examples of anomalies include outlier, shift, change in the nature (distribution) of values, deviation from "everyday" and joint anomalies.

There is an overview of how machine learning can improve the analysis of abnormal traffic. The result of the architecture of this approach is shown in Fig. 1.

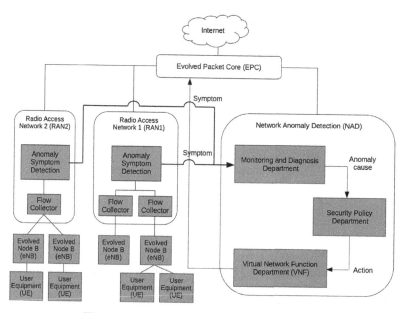

Fig. 1. Architecture for detecting abnormal traffic.

This architecture consists of two main virtualized components: Anomaly Symptom Detection (ASD) and Network Anomaly Detection (NAD). The first is located in the Radio Access Network (RAN) infrastructure and it is focused on quickly finding an anomaly symptom, that is, any trace or sign of an anomaly in the network traffic generated by User Equipment (UE) connected to the RAN. On the other hand, NAD collects timestamps and symptoms, and then a central process analyzes this data and tries to identify patterns that can be attributed to abnormal (malicious) traffic. As soon as an anomaly is detected, an incident message is immediately sent to the monitoring and diagnostics module.

This approach is very flexible, because it allows you to dynamically deploy new virtualized resources to detect anomaly symptoms in a specific RAN as network traffic increases. Also it is extensible as symptom detection, which is the most expensive analysis process, is shared across RANs, while anomaly detection is centralized on a core network known as the Evolved Packet Core (EPC), which only needs symptoms as input.

In the considerate architecture anomaly detection is organized on two levels. At the lower level the flow collector receives all the different flows for a given period of time, calculates a vector of features that the ASD module classifies as abnormal or normal. This initial classification should be done as quickly as possible, even it needed to sacrifice accuracy for lower response times. When an anomaly is suspected, a symptom package consisting of a feature vector, a timestamp, and the type of anomaly detected is sent to the next level, the NAD module. NAD receives multiple symptom streams from all ASDs, sorts them into time stamps and collects a temporal sequence of symptoms.

According to this concept, each RAN must support a huge amount of traffic, which is why it is extremely important to be able to handle a sufficient number of streams per second, even if the detection is not as accurate as it might be. Considering all of the above, it is necessary that the selected machine learning model meets the following requirements [16]:

- it must be suitable for efficient execution on the GPU;
- it must be calculated in a finite number of steps for a given size of the feature vector;
- it must have the same memory requirements regardless of the number of samples used in training;
- it should achieve good accuracy in classification, but at the same time its accuracy should not deteriorate sharply when working with real traffic.

5 Results

Evaluating the performance of any IoT anomaly detection system requires raw data that includes a set of network features such as features based on source and destination port numbers, payload-based, behavior based and flow based.

To analyze the machine learning models in the problems of detecting network anomalies in the Internet of Things was chosen an open data-set UNSW-NB15 as experimental data-set [17, 18]. It contains 2,540,044 records which include vectors of signs of TCP/IP network connections and their corresponding class labels. In this data-set network packets include both information about the real normal network activity and nine types of attacks: Fuzzers, Analyzers, Backdoors, Denial of Service (DoS), Exploits, Generalized (Generic, Reconnaissance, Shellcode and Worms). UNSW-NB15 data for training and testing of intrusion detection systems contains 47 features such as IP addresses, port numbers, transaction bytes, etc. [19], and two class labels such as the attack category and the connection anomaly label. The first 35 features are integrated information from data packets, and the rest are defined for connection scenarios.

Anomaly detection is the process of identifying deviations from the normal profile of the system. Thus, a binary classification is used to detect anomalies in the UNSW-NB15 network traffic, and the link anomaly criterion is used as the class label, where 0 corresponds to a normal profile and 1 is an anomaly. The analysis of machine learning models for the problems of detecting network anomalies in the Internet of Things consists of the steps described below.

Data preprocessing is a transforming process from the input data-set that includes 47 features of network connections and a class label to a form fed to the input of the analyzed models. The one-hot encoding method and the method of representing categorical variables in the form of binary vectors are applied to features of the nominal type, such as IP-addresses, the name of the protocol and data transfer service. Next the values of all attributes are normalized to the range [0...1].

Data normalization is needed to carry out, because an imbalance between feature values can cause instability of the model, worsen training results and slow down the modeling process. Thus, 80% of the original data-set (1,547,081 records) was selected as data for training models, and 20% (386,771 records) - for model testing. An important feature of this research stage is the lack of a high balance between the normal and anomalous class of network connections, which is closest to real conditions when anomalies in network traffic occur. So, in this case, the ratio of abnormal data to normal data is 1:4. The training and test samples were homogeneous.

Models are trained on the same training data-set, and anomaly detection is performed on the same test data-set. For training and validation of machine learning models the following hyperparameters were used: batch size - 64, optimization algorithm - adam, loss function - binary cross-entropy.

The traditional machine learning models developed were implemented using Python 3.6, Tensorflow 2.1, Scikit-learn 0.23.2, Numpy 1.19.2, Pandas 1.1.3 and Scipy 1.5.2. All experiments were conducted on an Acer Swift SF315-52G with an Intel Core i5 1.8 GHz processor, 8 GB RAM and Windows 10 operating system.

Anomaly detection efficiency assessment consists in calculating the following metrics: accuracy (A), precision (P), recall (R), F score (F), and training time (T).

Accuracy characterizes the proportion of instances of network connections for which the model made the correct decision about belonging to a normal or anomalous class.

Precision measures the proportion of correctly classified instances of network connections relative to all instances of network traffic.

Recall characterizes the proportion of network connection instances found by the model that belong to a normal or anomalous class relative to all network traffic instances.

The F score is the harmonic average between precision and recall.

As a result, the following traditional machine learning models were analyzed: Naive Bayes, Support Vector Machine, Logistic Regression, K-nearest neighbors, AdaBoost and Random Forest.

The results of experiments on the machine learning models analysis are presented in Table 2. The results of comparison on the accuracy of the considered models and the training time for detecting anomalies is shown in Fig. 2.

Table 2. Results of machine learning models research.

Machine learning models	Values				
	A, %	P, %	R, %	F, %	T, c
Naive Bayes	90,22	94,32	90,22	91,28	130,46
SVM	97,66	97,68	97,68	97,68	9786,77
Logistic Regression	96,83	96,87	96,83	96,84	131,26
kNN	97,17	97,17	97,17	97,17	11074,83
AdaBoost	98,30	98,30	98,30	98,30	940,27
Random Forest	98,97	98,95	98,95	98,55	468,05

Finally, it was shown the foundational machine learning models for detecting anomalies in IoT network traffic in the research. They can operate in one of the following three modes:

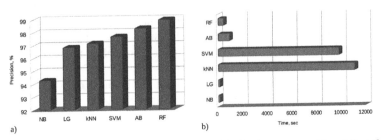

Fig. 2. Results of training machine learning models for the accuracy (a) and time (b).

1. Supervised discovery: a training set is available with traffic flagged as normal or abnormal.
2. Partially supervised detection: the training set contains only normal traffic and anything that is not related to this type of traffic is considered anomalous;
3. Unsupervised detection: no need for a labeled training set [20].

In supervised discovery the main question is how to build a truly complete training set with all abnormal traffic properly tagged. This can be difficult to achieve and more difficult to maintain. In this case, each piece of traffic belonging to one of the defined categories will be correctly classified, but if a new type of traffic anomaly appears, it will be classified incorrectly.

With partially controlled detection, the entire algorithm is not tied to specific types of anomalous traffic and can itself determine anomalies of a new type, but has a lower accuracy on a known sample compared to detection with a teacher. On the other hand, unsupervised detection has poorer accuracy than previous approaches, but does not require a training sample.

6   Discussion and Conclusion

The results of the carried out experiments allow to conclude that most machine learning models have a high accuracy of detecting anomalies in large heterogeneous traffic for their application in practice. The best results among traditional machine learning models in accuracy were shown by ensembles of classifiers such as AdaBoost (98.3%) and Random Forest (98.95%).

When comparing the basic machine learning models of different classes among themselves, it can be established that the difference in the accuracy of detecting anomalies is not very significant - no more than 1.5%, with the exception of Naive Bayes.

The network training time is a more variable characteristic. It is worth noting that the preparation of traditional machine learning models takes little time for the most part, with the exception of Support Vector Models and K-nearest neighbors. This is due to the fact that the application of these training models requires more computing power.

For systems operating in real time and frequently updated, simulation speed is a significant characteristic and should be minimized. While for some systems that are trained offline, the simulation time can be increased for more detailed tuning and increased efficiency.

This research presents an analysis of basic machine learning models for the problems of detecting anomalies in network traffic of the Internet of Things. Experimental evaluation of machine learning models was carried out using the same software and hardware and the same subsets of the UNSW-NB 15 data-set for training and testing.

The following machine learning models were considered as basic in the research:

- Naive Bayes;
- Support Vector Machine;
- Logistic Regression;
- K-nearest neighbors method;
- AdaBoost;
- Random Forest.

The constructed machine learning models demonstrated high accuracy rates of anomaly detection - from 98.8%. In conclusion, the large increase in the number of devices connected to the Internet, as well as the high requirements for network bandwidth, lead to new information security problems that can be solved by improving intrusion detection tools through the use of machine learning models.

References

1. Marrocco, G.: Pervasive electromagnetics: sensing paradigms by passive RFID technology. IEEE Wirel. Commun. 17(6), 10–17 (2010)
2. Goldstein, B.S., Kucheryavy, A.E.: Post-NGN communication networks. Inf. Control Syst. 6(4), 160–172 (2013)
3. Brutlag, J.D.: Aberrant behavior detection in time series for network monitoring. In: Proceeding of the 14th Systems Administration Conference, pp. 139–146 (2000)
4. Thottan, M., Chuanyi, J.: Anomaly detection in IP networks. IEEE Trans. Sig. Proc. 8(51), 2191–2204 (2003)
5. Wang, H., Zhang, D., Shin, K.G.: Detecting SYN flooding attacks. Proc. IEEE INFOCOM. 6(23), 1530–1539 (2002)
6. Staniford, S., Hoagland, J., MCalerney, J.M.: Practical automated detection of stealthy portscans. Proc. IDS Workshop 2(4), 197–216 (2000)
7. Ageev, S.A., Saenko, I.B.: Method of intellectual multi-agent information security risk management in protected multiservice special-purposed networks. T-Commun. 1, 5–10 (2015)
8. Gorodetsky, V., Kotenko, I., Karsayev, O.: Multi-agent technologies for computer network security: attack simulation, intrusion detection and intrusion detection learning. Int. J. Comput. Syst. Sci. Eng. 4(18), 191–200 (2003)
9. Branitskiy, A.A., Kotenko, I.V.: Network attack detection based on combination of neural, immune and neuro-fuzzy classifiers. Inf. Control Syst. 4, 69–77 (2015)
10. Al-Garadi, M.A., Mohamed, A., Al-Ali, A., Du, X., Guizani, M.: A survey of machine and deep learning methods for Internet of Things (IoT) security. IEEE Commun. Surv. Tutorials 3(22), 1646–1685 (2020)
11. Levshun, D., Gaifulina, D., Chechulin, A., Kotenko, I.: Problematic issues of information security of cyber-physical systems. Inf. Autom. 5(19), 1050–1088 (2020)
12. Roopak, M., Tian, G.Y., Chambers, J.: Deep learning models for cyber security in IoT networks. In: IEEE Annual Computing and Communication Workshop and Conference (CCWC), Las Vegas, USA, pp. 0452–0457 (2019)

13. Kuzlu, M., Fair, C., Guler, O.: Role of artificial intelligence in the Internet of Things (IoT) cybersecurity. Discov. Internet Things 1(1), 1–14 (2021). https://doi.org/10.1007/s43926-020-00001-4

14. Elrawy, M.F., Awad, A.I., Hamed, H.F.A.: Intrusion detection systems for IoT-based smart environments: a survey. J. Cloud Comput. 7(1), 1–20 (2018). https://doi.org/10.1186/s13677-018-0123-6

15. Ahmad, M., Riaz, Q., Zeeshan, M., Tahir, H., Haider, S.A., Khan, M.S.: Intrusion detection in internet of things using supervised machine learning based on application and transport layer features using UNSW-NB15 data-set. J. Wirel. Commun. Netw. **2021**(1), 1–23 (2021). https://doi.org/10.1186/s13638-021-01893-8

16. Maimó, L.F., et al.: On the performance of a deep learning-based anomaly detection system for 5G networks. In: IEEE SmartWorld, Ubiquitous Intelligence & Computing, Advanced & Trusted Computed, pp. 1–8 (2017)

17. UNSW-NB15 Dataset (2021). https://www.unsw.adfa.edu.au/unsw-canberra-cyber/cybersecurity/ADFA-NB15-Datasets/. Accessed 06 Mar 2021

18. Moustafa, N., Slay, J.: UNSW-NB15: a comprehensive data set for network intrusion detection systems (UNSW-NB15 network data set). In: Military Communications and Information Systems Conference (MilCIS), Canberra, ACT, pp. 1–6 (2015). https://doi.org/10.1109/MilCIS.2015.7348942

19. Moustafa, N., Turnbull, B., Choo, K.R.: An ensemble intrusion detection technique based on proposed statistical flow features for protecting network traffic of internet of things. IEEE Internet Things J. **3**(6), 4815–4830 (2019). https://doi.org/10.1109/JIOT.2018.2871719

20. Deshevih, E.A., Ushakov, I.A., Kotenko, I.V.: Overview of big data tools and platforms for information security monitoring. In: Information Security of Russian Regions (IBRR-2015), pp. 67–87 (2019)

Algorithmic Approach to Building a Route for the Removal of Household Waste with Associated Additional Loads in the "Smart Clean City" Project

Olga Dolinina[1]([✉]) [ID], Vitaly Pechenkin[2]([✉]) [ID], Madina Mansurova[3]([✉]) [ID],
Dana Tolek[3] [ID], and Serik Ixsanov[3] [ID]

[1] Ulyanovsk State Technical University, Ulyanovsk, Russia
[2] Institute of Information Systems and Technology, Yuri Gagarin State Technical University of Saratov, SSTU, Saratov, Russia
[3] Al-Farabi Kazakh National University, Almaty, Kazakhstan

Abstract. Growing population in urban areas has led to the necessity of solving the problem of targeted municipal garbage collection. In the smart city Optimization problem for complex smart city dynamic systems is one of the most important elements for garbage collection analysis. The paper contributes with a mathematical model for solving optimization problems and transport scheduling for the targeted garbage collection is suggested, which is a part of a wide range of "Smart City" concepts. The model is based on the apparatus of network optimization algorithms. The possibility of additional loading of the garbage truck during waste collection is the basis for optimizing the parameters of the entire process. As optimization criteria, the cost of the services rendered, the weight of the removed waste, and the reduction in idle run can be considered.

Keywords: Smart city · Optimal route · Simulation modeling · Targeted garbage collection

1 Introduction

The task of effective garbage collection is a part of the overall problem of creating an environmentally friendly environment in the urban space, usually associated with the natural habitat, protecting the city's ecology from pollution [1]. "Smart Environment" can be considered as a part of the "Smart City" concept, the core of which is using the mobile communication technologies (Internet of Things). It is obvious that the targeted garbage collection on time saves expenditures, fuel, reduces exhaust gas emissions.

When considering the essence of the "Smart City" concept it is important to identify a set of factors that are necessary for understanding the projects implemented within its framework. These factors can be divided into internal and external ones, which have an impact on the various stages of development, implementation and operation of solutions within the framework of the urban space intellectualization initiative. The project

© Springer Nature Switzerland AG 2021
N. T. Nguyen et al. (Eds.): ICCCI 2021, LNAI 12876, pp. 745–755, 2021.
https://doi.org/10.1007/978-3-030-88081-1_56

initiatives for the smart city should be focused on the creation of urban space infrastructure and organizational systems based on modern technologies that respond to emerging problems. Among the considered factors one must mention the following [2]:

- management and organization;
- technologies;
- policy;
- social communities;
- the economy;
- infrastructure;
- natural environment.

Typical task for the most of the projects implemented within the framework of the "Smart City" concept is the targeted managing of the removal process of solid industrial and domestic garbage. This task is directly related to the all characteristics of a typical project, given in the definition of "Smart City" [3]. As a rule, in the solution methods there are components responsible for the use of mobile technologies, information systems based on the intellectual intelligence approach using the knowledge bases. This approach involves information, communication (based on mobile communication) and Web 2.0 technologies, which make it possible to accelerate decision-making processes, apply innovative methods of city management, and improve the urban space environmental safety [4]. Similar tasks are relevant and at the present time methodological fundamentals and applied methods of their practical solution are being actively developed [5–7]. Various studies have addressed the problem of management of the garbage collection by using different intelligent techniques. One of the priority areas for the analysis of the problem is the development of mathematical models that allow to determine the formal criteria for the effectiveness of the functioning of systems for the collection and disposal of household waste [8, 9]. Among the new approaches BAT algorithm based on the hunting behavior of bats where the prey of bats is the solution, and bats move to find the best prey [10] is considered to be rather perspective.

A separate topic of research is the use of modern communication technologies in the organization of household waste treatment within the framework of the "Smart City" concept" [11, 12].

2 Project "Smart Clean City" for Development of Applications

To optimize garbage collection a special system called "Smart Clean City" (SCC) was developed to manage process. The system allows to carry out following tasks:

- specialized truck performs garbage collection only if the containers are filled;
- each container generates the message on filling;
- rational distribution of containers according to the areas of the city.

SCC allows to solve the following city problems:

- increasing the economic efficiency (fuel, funds for maintenance of equipment, optimization employment staff, resources and time for garbage collection) of the company responsible for the garbage collection;
- maintaining the proper urban sanitary and epidemiological situation.

The functioning of the SCC system is schematically shown in the Fig. 1. The system consists of two parts: software and special signaling equipment. The technical part is represented by:

- equipment installed on each garbage site with containers (GS);
- equipment installed on garbage trucks (GT).

Each GS is equipped with two types of equipment: transmitter unit of the sensor area and the filled containers with a transmitter. Each garbage site is equipped with two types of equipment: two-way receiver-transmitter unit for the garbage site and fullness sensors of each container on this site with a transmitter.

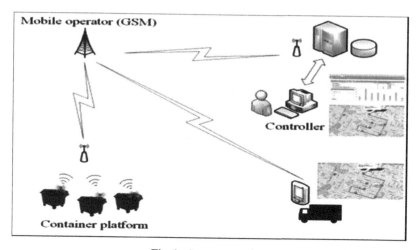

Fig. 1. System overview

The general structure of the system "Smart Clean City" and optimization schedules algorithms for garbage collection trucks are described in [12, 13] where the system model is presented in the form of a dynamic graph, which weight functions depend on time and are determined by the current state of the area for garbage containers (GC) and current road traffic. The structure of the platform for application development within the project "Smart clean city" is presented in the Fig. 2.

The platform unites several subsystems, which allow to solve various problems of analysis and management of the system for collecting and exporting of the solid waste. These subsystems are combined by means of special adapters that allow you

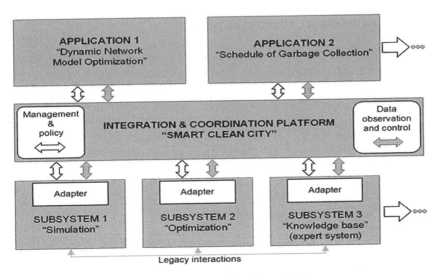

Fig. 2. SCC operation diagram [13]

to synchronize data, manage various parts of the entire system. At an early stage of development such interaction was carried out directly between subsystems with the help of inherited interactions between them. Developed applications have a unified interface and allow to manage the data integrity model in various subsystems.

The subsystems are server applications that allow to model the system of collection and removal of waste (SUB_1), apply optimization algorithms for the schedule of trucks on several parameters (SUB_2), use in the decision-making system a knowledge base built on the experience of the enterprise organization of waste disposal (SUB_3), special expert knowledge of the traffic situations in the city. Developed applications are located both on the server part of the system, and in client applications using mobile platforms.

The structural hardware-software implementation of the solution is shown in Fig. 3. When managing the removal of household waste, information on the degree of filling of containers with an indication of the type of waste in (1) is recorded online in the database of the system. This makes it possible to automatically determine the possibility of its joint transportation with other wastes. These requests, taking into account the economic parameters of the operation, the required processing time and possible optimal routes to visit the sites with containers, are checked for the possibility of additional loading for the transport units (GT) on the route.

It is assumed that before running the algorithm, a predetermined primary route for collection and removal of household waste is known.

The software and hardware complex allows to store and process information about transport units, the current state of containers for household waste, and waste disposal processes in general. The algorithm for constructing the GT route automatically monitors the received requests from GS and selects the options for passing additional loading. The mobile component of the entire complex, placed on the GT, is a system for automatically transmitting information about the geolocation and the state of the GT.

It consists of a mobile device (7) with a mobile application installed, a GPS/GLONAS module (8) connected to the vehicle's electric engine control system (9). The module (8) is a hardware complex that includes everything necessary for the operation of the mobile part of the system as part of the entire system.

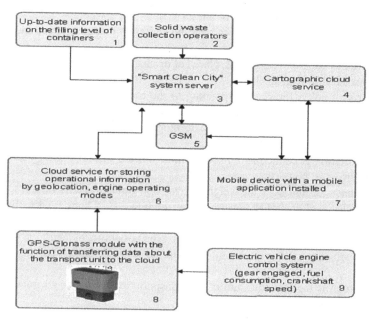

Fig. 3. The structural hardware-software implementation

In the next section, there is described the algorithm for optimizing the routes of the garbage trucks, which is used for developing of the garbage collection system model and for analyzing of its effectiveness.

3 Formal Statement of the Route Optimization Problem

The task of the optimal routing modelling for the logistic systems of transport [14, 15] in the situation of global networks has been formulated. Operation methods and procedures of multicriterial decision making in risky conditions have been developed. Procedures of evaluation for formalized goals models are developed: for transportation schedules. The practical evaluation of the efficiency of the SCC system and constructing optimal routes for the collection of household waste is to calculate dynamic optimal routes for garbage trucks. Often, companies operating in the field of household waste collection receive requests for the removal of household waste that are not regular and are not included in the general schedule of garbage trucks.

More specific to optimize the solution of such a problem based on changing the route of movement and the ccollection of additional volumes of associated garbage is proposed. To solve the problem, a mathematical model of the transportation system in the form of a weighted network is determined as follows:

$$G = (V, E, f, g, w). \tag{1}$$

V – the set of nodes (vertices) of the model network.

There is the following partition of the set $V = V_1 \cup V_2$, where

V_1 – nodes corresponding to locations and addresses that are sources and points of delivery of garbage;

V_2 – nodes corresponding to the places of discharge of garbage having geographic coordinates as additional attributes;

E – set of edges (arcs) corresponding to the road network (taking into account one-way and two-way traffic), which connects the above sets of nodes of different types.

The structure and functionality of the developed SCC system are described in more detail in [17, 18].

Transportation is defined as a list of S tuples of the form $<v, u, w, volume, cost, type>$, where

$w, volume$ – accordingly, the weight of available garbage and its volume;

$cost$ – declared cost of the operation for the removal of household garbage from node v;

$type$ – type of household waste, determining the possibility of their joint utilization.

For an arbitrary route $p = v_1, v_2, ...,v_n$ in the network model, we determine the function $f : p \times T \to R$,

which returns the cost (the sum of the transportations cost) for all transportations included in route p at time t:

$$f(p, T) = \sum_{i=1}^{n-1} cost(v_i, v_{i+1}) | \exists s \in S, s =< v_i, v_{i+1}, ... > \tag{2}$$

$g : p \times T \to R$ – function for determining the distance passing along the route p at time t. The function g is defined as the sum of the shortest distances between pairs of vertices in G.

$w : p \times T \to R$ – function for determining the travel time of the route p, determined taking into account the distances and average speed provided by the map services.

The dynamics of the network change is associated with a change in the travel time of the sections of the route, in accordance with the current traffic situation, vehicle load.

Formally, the problem can be formulated as follows: for a given list of requests for the household garbage collect S, allowable distance for increasing route length L and permissible increase in the value D of the travel time along the route, the primary transportation route with the initial vertex v_1 and final vertex v_n, find such a route $p = v_1, v_2, ...,v_n$ in the network G, that for a given time t

$$f(p, t) \to max \tag{3}$$

under the condition

$$|g(p, t) - g(v_1, v_n)| \le L \tag{4}$$

$$|w(p, t) - w(v_1, v_n)| \le D \tag{5}$$

Formula 5 represents the optimality condition for the objective function f, Formulas 4, 5 represent the constraints under which the extremum of the objective function is sought. With this formalization, we have a single objective function and functional limitations on the proposed solution.

In the proposed formulation, the formulation of the multicriteria optimization problem is also possible, when the requirements for finding extrema for functions will be superimposed simultaneously on one or more functions from the list f, g, w.

4 Dynamic Algorithm for Finding Ways with Additional Loading of Passing Cargo

When developing the algorithm, it is initially assumed that there is a certain initial route (primary route) for the removal of household waste, starting from which ways to increase its economic return are calculated.

This route is initially selected by the logistics organization of the freight carrier based on a request received on an irregular basis. The associated waste search algorithm is based on the several principles:

– the logistics of the carrier organization determines the restrictions on deviations from the primary route (by distance, by time, by the timing of the delivery checkpoints), additional incidental requests for the removal of waste are determined based on these restrictions;
– each garbage collection operation is supplied with attributes that determine the admissibility (inadmissibility) of additional loading, if additional loading is prohibited, optimization is carried out only by constructing the shortest route in the framework of optimization algorithms of the SCC system;
– associated additional loads should be compatible with the type of household waste of the primary route from the point of view of their joint utilization, as the associated cargo is added, it is necessary to control the general parameters of the tonnage and volumetric characteristics of garbage.

Main algorithm calls the PGR and COMP procedures. PRG procedure build a ranked list of all requests for removal of waste that can be considered "passing" for the primary route. The result of the algorithm is a list of all requests that are concurrent in the sense described above. It is important to note that concurrent requests can be mutually exclusive in terms of their possible addition to the primary route.

Different types of household garbage can be combined in one trip only if it is possible to jointly dispose of all waste along the route. If it is permissible to additional load the vehicle, it is necessary to take into account not only the "passing" and restrictions on the timing, distance, but also on the parameters of the garbage involved in the joint transportation.

It is assumed that each type of garbage is associated with types permitted for joint disposal. This is required not only by the rules of possible sharing, but also by restricting the use of certain vehicles having special equipment for carrying out transportation. It is also necessary to take into account the general weight parameters of jointly trans-ported goods and restrictions on the dimensions of transportation. It is clear that the sequence of rebooting the car can lead to exceeding the permissible weight of the cargo, incompatible with general restrictions. COMP procedure checks the compatibility of associated requests for garbage collection. This check is carried out only if the primary route implies the permissibility of additional loading. A detailed description of the PGR and COMP procedures is presented in [15].

The Block diagram of the algorithm for constructing a ranked list of routes (RList) with possible additional loadings shown in Fig. 4.

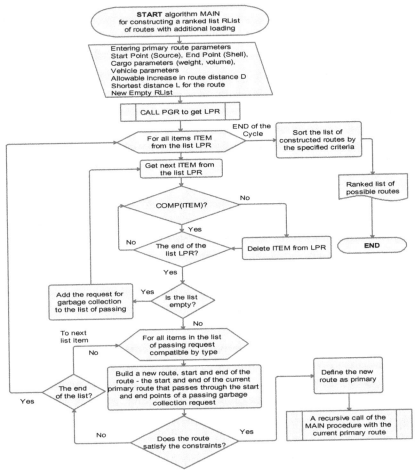

Fig. 4. Block diagram of the MAIN algorithm for constructing a ranked list of routes with on-the-way loadings

The algorithm is recursive and at each step completes the current route by adding requests for garbage collection compatible with the current route parameters that are allowed by restrictions.

The algorithm performs exhaustive search and implements the branch and bound method. At each step, the algorithm makes an attempt to "embed" a waste removal request into the current primary path.

At the initial stage of the algorithm, a list of all associated routes for a given initial one is constructed, at the second, all routes that are incompatible in type, weight characteristics and dimensions with the load of the reference route are deleted from it. Next, the algorithm makes an attempt to add a passing request to the primary route. In reality, there is a complete enumeration of all options for constructing a new route. The complexity of the algorithm and the time of its operation are also affected by restrictions on the size of the permissible deviation from the reference route.

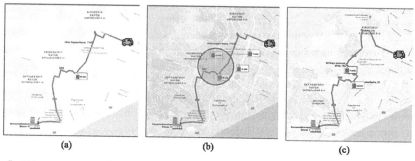

(a)   (b)   (c)

Fig. 5. Primary route on the cartographic service (a), primary route with an additional waste disposal request included (b), new route includes an additional waste disposal site (c).

Figure 5 shows the software interface with the marked primary waste collection route (a), additional waste disposal requests available in the system that can be used to build the final route (b), a route that is built on a primary basis and includes an additional waste disposal site. The route is built taking into account data on the current state of traffic.

5   Discussions and Conclusions

To increase the effectiveness of waste collection, it is necessary to develop a dynamically managed targeted waste collecting system. The proposed algorithm allows to solve the problem of constructing a waste collection route operatively, taking into account actual data on the fullness of waste containers. The solution obtained by the algorithm can be used to update the waste collection procedure within a predetermined schedule. It can also be used to build a route in case of an unscheduled request for waste collection. The results of the algorithm application are the reduction of the empty run of the garbage truck, the reduction of time for waste collection, and the increase in the efficiency of the whole process.

The separate solutions, which are currently implemented in conglomerations, should be prepared for integration into the intellectual urban infrastructure. Tasks that arise in real life require a quick response to requests that arise outside the regular schedule.

The described system "Smart Clean City" can be considered as a targeted waste management system, it has been tested in Saratov (Russia), city with a population of approximately 1 million people. Pilot implementation of the system in the period from September 2015 to the present time shows 21% decrease in the processing time of containers compared to traditional manual planning, without taking into account the dynamic parameters of the system described above. The trucks company, which uses the system as a tool for preparing timetables for the GCTs, has 24 trucks in its composition.

The described algorithm is used to reduce costs when responding to garbage collection requests that are not in the regular schedule of garbage trucks. They cannot be predicted with a reasonable degree of certainty. The proposed approach allows to reduce the empty run of garbage trucks, to increase the weight and volume of garbage taken out.

Comparative analysis has been carried out using real data and simulation results. The area of the city for which the model has been developed has about 250 containers at 56 sites. Two landfills for the removal of solid household waste are used. Each container has a capacity of 100 kg. The carrying capacity of the truck is estimated at 5000 kg (the actual capacity depends on the degree of compressibility of the waste).

As for the discussion which requires further analysis, it is necessary to note the necessity to develop ways of taking into account the effect on the performance indicators of the processes of the subsystems listed in Fig. 1 in the proposed model. Of particular interest is the modeling of optimization based on the current traffic in the city, the inclusion of expert knowledge in the decision-making system, use of an automatic alarm system on the filling of containers. Such an analysis makes it possible to estimate the contribution of the optimization subsystems to the improvement of the whole model parameters.

References

1. Global Innovators: International Case Studies on Smart Cities. Research paper number 135, Oct 2013. https://www.gov.uk/government/publications/smart-cities-international-case-studies-global-innovators
2. Chourabi, H., et al.: Understanding Smart Cities: An Integrative Framework. In: Proceedings of the 2012 45th Hawaii International Conference on System Sciences, IEEE Computer Society, pp. 2289–2296 (2012)
3. IEEE Smart City definition. http://smartcities.ieee.org/about
4. Toppeta, D.: The smart city vision: how innovation and ICT can build smart, "livable", sustainable cities. The Innovation Knowledge Foundation. https://inta-aivn.org/ (2010)
5. Hemidat, S., Oelgemöller, D., Nassour, A., Nelles, M.: Evaluation of key indicators of waste collection using GIS techniques as a planning and control tool for route optimization. Waste Biomass Valor 8, 1533–1554 (2017). https://doi.org/10.1007/s12649-017-9938-5
6. Haddoun, N., Khomsi, D.: Design of a computer tool for the optimization of solid waste collection circuits. In: E3S Web of Conferences, pp. EDE7–2019 (2019). https://doi.org/10.1051/e3sconf/202015.002016

7. Ahmad, S., Jamil, F., Iqbal, N., Kim, D.: Optimal route recommendation for waste carrier vehicles for efficient waste collection: a step forward towards sustainable cities. IEEE Access **8**, Digital Object Identifier https://doi.org/10.1109/ACCESS.2020.2988173
8. Maiti, S., Vaishnav, M., Ingale, L., Suryawanshi, P., Kumar, S.: Optimization of garbage collector tracking and monitoring system analysis. CSIT **4**(2–4), 187–192 (2016). https://doi.org/10.1007/s40012-016-0103-2
9. Nurprihatina, F., Lestarib, A.: Waste collection vehicle routing problem model with multiple trips, time windows, split delivery, heterogeneous fleet and intermediate facility. Eng. J. **24**(5). https://engj.org/https://doi.org/10.4186/ej.2020.24.5.55 (2020)
10. Yang, X.-S.: A new metaheuristic bat-inspired algorithm. In: González, J.R., Pelta, D.A., Cruz, C., Terrazas, G., Krasnogor, N. (eds.) Nature Inspired Cooperative Strategies for Optimization (NICSO 2010). Studies in Computational Intelligence, vol 284. Springer, Heidelberg. https://doi.org/10.1007/978-3-642-12538-6_6
11. Mishra, A., Ray, A.K.: IoT cloud-based cyber-physical system for efficient solid waste management in smart cities. IET Cyber-Phys. Syst. Theor. Appl. **5**(4), 330–341 (2020)
12. Bányai, T., Tamás, P., Illés, B., Stankevicˇiute, Z., Bányai, A.: Optimization of municipal waste collection routing: impact of industry 4.0 technologies on environmental awareness and sustainability. Int. J. Environ. Res. Public Health **16**, 634. https://doi.org/10.3390/ijerph16040634
13. Borozdukhin, A., Dolinina, O., Pechenkin, V.: Approach to the garbage collection in the "Smart Clean City" project. CIST 2016, pp. 918–922. (IEEE CIST 2016). https://doi.org/10.1109/CIST.2016.7805019
14. Brovko, A., Dolinina, O., Pechenkin, V.: Method of the management of the garbage collection in the "smart clean city". Commun. Comput. Inf. Sci. **718**, 432–443. CN 2017 (2017). https://doi.org/10.1007/978-3-319-59767-6_34
15. Dolinina, O., Pechenkin, V., Gubin, N., Aizups, J., Kuzmin, A.: Development of semi-adaptive waste collection vehicle routing algorithm for agglomeration and urban settlements. In: Proceedings of the 7th IEEE Workshop on Advances in Information, Electronic and Electrical Engineering AIEEE'2019, pp. 1–6 (2019). https://doi.org/10.1109/AIEEE48629.2019.8976918

Autonomic Nervous System Assessment Based on HRV Analysis During Virtual Reality Serious Games

Mariana Jacob Rodrigues[1,2(✉)] ⓘ, Octavian Postolache[1,2] ⓘ,
and Francisco Cercas[1,2] ⓘ

[1] Iscte–Instituto Universitário de Lisboa, Av. das Forças Armadas, 1649-026 Lisbon, Portugal
mariana_jacob@iscte-iul.pt
[2] Instituto de Telecomunicações, Av. Rovisco Pais, 1, 1049-001 Lisbon, Portugal
opostolache@lx.it.pt

Abstract. The virtual reality serious game in the field of physical rehabilitation are mentioned as complementary tools to assure highly motivated training for patients that are following a physical rehabilitation plan. Different virtual reality (VR) serious game framework is reported and different interface that provide information dynamic and kinematic parameters associated with the user body motion during training are reported in literature. Physical training affect not only the patient motor condition but is also reflected on the level of cardiac and respiratory activity. Taking into account the necessity to monitor the health status of patient during the training, reflected on the level of autonomous nervous system, the paper provides information about relevant works presented in the literature that sought to explore the effects of virtual reality exergaming on autonomic nervous responses based on wearable sensor data. The contributions of serious exergames on physical performance, and on rehabilitation processes has also been addressed. Particular contributions focus on heart rate variability (HRV) changes in younger adults while experiencing VR serious gaming of different time durations and exercise intensity. Moreover, the application of artificial intelligence algorithms to classify the VR serious game intensity levels is also presented.

Keywords: Wearable sensors · Virtual reality serious game · Heart rate variability · Artificial intelligence

1 Introduction

The acquisition of vital signs throughout the practice of physical exercise has served as an important measure that follows the subject's physical performance avoiding accidents related to high level of exercise intensity. The measurement of physiological parameters, such as heart rate (HR), body temperature, respiratory rate, and oxygen saturation (SpO2), also become common in the implementation of smart assistive environments. The deployment of such environments has been greatly facilitated with the inclusion of wearable biomedical sensors that can monitor physiological signals in real-time. Usually, such sensors are part of a wireless sensor network (WSN), more precisely a Body

N. T. Nguyen et al. (Eds.): ICCCI 2021, LNAI 12876, pp. 756–768, 2021.
https://doi.org/10.1007/978-3-030-88081-1_57

Sensor Network (BSN), in case they are placed directly on a person's body. Such WSNs are used to connect these sensors to a smart gateway and send information to cloud services, allowing healthcare entities to remotely monitor the patient's health status in real-time.

Other than the casual monitoring of common physiological signals, the assessment of the autonomic nervous system (ANS) through heart rate variability analysis (HRV) has been gaining significance, since it allows the evaluation of sympathetic and para-sympathetic branches of the ANS - a direct measure of the patient's health conditions. The three different methods of evaluating HRV comprise time-domain, frequency-domain, and non-linear analysis.

Since it is possible to have a robust assessment of a patient's health status using wearable sensors, its use during physical exercising has been extensively studied. In the current context, and due to COVID-19 pandemic and the corresponding containment measures adopted, the practice of physical exercise at home has been especially valued. Moreover, physical therapy sessions have been suspended in clinics due to coronavirus lockdown, so the patients requiring physical training (e.g. limb strength, resistance, body balance) should practice rehabilitation exercises at-home. In this context, exergaming – a system that combines physical exercise with digital gaming – has shown to bring positive benefits to a patient's physical and cognitive conditions, and help individuals maintain the recommended levels of physical activity. In addition, virtual reality (VR) serious exergames that are focused on physical rehabilitation may constitute a complementary tool of physiotherapy sessions. Their highly engaging and immersive scenarios help patients to stay motivated while executing rehabilitation exercises imposed by the game.

This paper aims to address relevant works presented in the literature exploring virtual reality exergaming and its influence on autonomic nervous responses and on physical performance, based on the analysis of wearable sensor data.

Additionally, a contribution was made regarding the study of HRV changes in younger adults while experiencing VR serious gaming of different time duration and exercise intensity. Moreover, the application of artificial intelligence algorithms to classify the VR serious game intensity levels is also presented.

This paper is organized as follows: Section 2 presents a literature review on the evaluation of physiological signs during exergaming sessions; Section 3 addresses the materials and methods used for this experiment; Section 4 presents and discusses the obtained results and, finally, Section 5 summarizes the conclusions.

2 Physiological Signals Assessment During Exergaming

In this section, we discuss works carried out in the scope of obtaining physiological signals during the practice of physical exercise through exergaming and explore their potential benefits on physical activity in different age groups.

Munoz et al. [1] focused on finding how physiological parameters were regulated in elderly users during exergaming sessions of different difficulties and audio-visual stimuli. This study is based on the analysis of physiological data obtained through wearable sensors that acquired electrocardiograms and electrodermal activity signals. HR and HRV parameters were extracted, as well as maximum oxygen uptake (VO_2max),

Energy Expenditure (EE), Metabolic Equivelents (METs) and Galvanic Skin Response (GSR). The exergame, which was an adaptation of the famous two-dimensional Pong game, mostly relied on lower limbs movements, as the player needed to move horizontally to control a virtual paddle projected on the floor. The experimental procedure was based in a control and exergaming group, and the obtained results suggest that parasympathetic activity based on HRV analysis is significantly different between the control and exergaming group rather than between different difficulty levels (easy, medium and hard).

The way how physical activity based on engaging exergames influences executive functions of a younger population was investigated by Benzing et al. [2]. The levels of physical exercise demanded by a chosen exergame were higher than those used for rehabilitation purposes, as the main purpose was to elucidate the impact of cognitive engagement of adolescents during physical activity practiced with active exergames. One of the objective measures used was HRV based on the analysis of the root mean square of successive differences between heartbeats (RMSSD). Such measurement was assessed before the physical activity (5 min), during activity (15 min) and after the activity ended (5 min). The three different experimental conditions involved exergaming experiences of high engagement levels, low engagement levels, and a control condition based on watching a video. The physical activity based on a high cognitive engaging exergame resulted in significant better performance levels compared with the other two conditions. Exergaming as a tool to maintain weekly doses of physical exercising was also validated by studies from Polechoński et al. [3]. HR data of healthy young participants was monitored for 15 min during moderate and high level of difficulty fitness Kinect game. The criterion to assess such physical activity intensity was based on the calculation of average percentage of maximum heart rate (%HRmax) and heart rate reserve (%HRR) during the game.

Under the scope of virtual reality (VR) games, other contributions were made regarding the influence of VR exergaming in terms of engagement levels and rehabilitation performance [4, 5]. For instance, Charoensook et al. [6] compared player engagement between VR videogames (e.g. Beat Saber, Space Pirate, Gorn and Final Approach) and traditional games through average HR analysis and breath rate variability (BRV). This study, which considered a younger population, shows a clear difference in HR levels between the playing of VR and traditional games. Changes in BRV, however, were not statistically significant between the two gaming environments.

Besides revealing their importance in ambient assisted living deployments and under free-living conditions, wearable biomedical sensors have allowed to study the contributions of physiotherapy sessions and evaluate physical and cognitive outcomes during the rehabilitation process. Moreover, it allows the study of VR serious games direct contributions on the rehabilitation process and health conditions of the patient.

In this context, exergaming has been showing promising results regarding player performance and engagement when practicing physical activity. Kafri et al. [7] showed that energy expenditure (EE) and exercise intensity from post-stroke participants after playing upper-limb and mobility Kinect and Wii-based exergames was considered of moderate intensity, regarding inherent clinical implications, according to the three levels of exercise intensity considered: low, moderate and vigorous. Besides EE, the percentage of predicted maximal HR rate of perceived exertion (RPE) and respiratory exchange ratio (RER) were used to characterize different games.

VR training has also shown significant improvements in strength and balance in elderly adults [8–13], which has been evidenced by objective measurements of postural components [14]. A recent study also showed the ability of immersive VR environments to improve postural stability of the elderly as well as increasing their levels of engagement during motor rehabilitation exercising [15].

With the increasing occupancy rate in intensive care due to COVID-19 outbreak, VR exergaming become a physical therapy solution that has been strongly validated by their promising results shown. Such rehabilitation systems can become practical solutions for physiotherapy treatment of patients in the ICU or in remote physiotherapy home-based sessions, where the progress and performance of patients can still be monitored by a physiotherapist. Gomes et al. [16] conducted an experimental study for evaluating rehabilitation procedures and physical exercising based on VR exergaming for patients in intensive care units. As an objective measure of physical activity, acceleration data was collected by tri-axial accelerometers placed on the wrist and ankle, while a subjective measure relied on the use of a modified Borg scale score and a satisfaction questionnaire. The conducted physical therapy sessions showed that almost all patients were willing to play a VR exergame in future sessions. Also, VR exergaming for physical rehabilitation was able to induce light to moderate levels of physical activity intensity, which is an important factor to consider when aiming to prevent immobility syndrome after intensive care or encourage the participation in rehabilitative processes.

The effectiveness of applying an exercise routine based on exergaming in the elderly population has been proven by several studies, with similar or even superior effects of exergames on cognitive functions, when compared to traditional types of exercises [17]. Common physiological measures used in these studies for monitoring physical performance and exercise intensity include the monitoring of heart rate, assessment of the rating of perceived exertion (RPE), heart rate reserve (%HRR) and average percentage of maximum heart rate (%HRmax).

With the aim of exploring how the HRV indices and the ANS response are modelled and improved through exergaming, Eggenberger et al. [18] conducted a 6-month training session composed of traditional cognitive-motor exercises and exergames for healthy older adults. The authors not only discovered a substantial correlation between HRV indices and cognitive executive functions, but also found great improvements in global and parasympathetic autonomic nervous system responses in the elderly when physical training was associated with exergaming.

3   Materials and Methods

3.1   Procedures and Participants

The present study sought to investigate: (1) the variance in HRV indices during a VR rehabilitation serious game considering different intensity levels; (2) the variance of HR levels characterized by a more complex gameplay session of different time durations; (3) how artificial intelligence methods can be used to estimate the different intensity levels of the game based on wearable sensor data and subjective measures.

3.2 Virtual Reality Rehabilitation Serious Game

A VR serious game specifically tailored for upper limb rehabilitation was used for this investigation. This system has been developed and reported by Postolache et al. [19]. It was developed using the Unity3D game engine and relies on a Microsoft Kinect platform for real time detection of the upper limbs' joint angles, thus allowing the user to interact with the VR scenario. The Kinect platform has shown to be a highly reliable rehabilitation platform, as it can accurately measure upper and lower limbs' joint angles during rehabilitation exercises [21–23]. The virtual scenario of this game is expressed by a virtual farm. The main objective of this game is to pick-up fruits placed randomly at different heights from surrounding trees and shrubs, which assures different ranges for the upper limb motion. The objects can be reached by left hand, right hand, or both, depending on the chosen game settings for the training session. The upper limb movements executed by the player are detected by the Kinect platform and reproduced in the game's avatar. The game has two different gameplay modes: a) high-angles (90°–180°), with apples being placed on trees and 2) low-angles (0°–90°), with raspberries being placed on shrubs. Different difficulty levels, namely higher or lower intensity, can be implemented based on the gameplay mode, the movement speed of the avatar and the amount of fruits to be harvested. Different audio-visual stimuli are available during gameplay to motivate players, including different immersion levels, such as farm sounds, animals, and other elements, and performance feedback, like a positive sound when a fruit is picked.

3.3 Participants

The participants of this study were 6 healthy young adults, 3 males and 3 females aged 24.6 ± 1.9 years old, weighting 64 ± 16 kg, with heights around 176 ± 9 cm and body mass indexes (BMI) 20.3 ± 3 kg/m^2. All participants enrolled in the gaming sessions after informed consent. 4 volunteers were already familiar with the game mechanics and the Kinect platform. Details regarding the purpose and procedures involved in this study, as well as an explanation of the game's instructions and objectives were given before the gameplay session. A Borg rating of perceived exertion (RPE) scale was used as a subjective measure to assess exercise intensity during each game session, along with a Subjective Units of Distress Scale (SUDS) with a scale of 0–100 for measuring the level of distress and anxiety felt during each game session.

3.4 Experimental Procedure

The participants enrolled in two sessions of this serious exergame. Each session presented different difficulty/intensity levels. The first was based on a higher intensity level, in which game configurations were set for the high angles mode, increased number of fruits to pick up, large number of stimuli and the need to stay in a standing position during all gameplay. The second session was based on a less intense level, in which game settings were set to a lower angles mode, slow-paced avatar, less stimuli and finally, participants were seated during gameplay. Physiological measurements were collected for different experimental conditions (Fig. 1). Prior to the first game session, all participants sat in a relaxed upright position under spontaneous breathing for 5 min. In order to investigate the effects that a gameplay of different time durations has on HR levels, participants consecutively played the higher intensity game mode 3 times: the first one during 1 min, the second for 2 min and the third during 4 min. These 3 conditions were only applied for the first session, once that this is the session intended to induce higher exertion levels and fatigue. After the 4 min gameplay, participants were asked to seat and stay calm and silent for 5 min, so that physiological signals could return to a resting-state. The second session took place 5 min after the first one, and all participants were invited to sit and play the low-angles game mode during 4 min. While they were seated, 5 min of physiological data was acquired after the game was ended. HRV analysis was performed during periods of 5 min, according to the standard of short-term recordings [20].

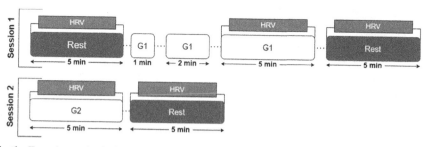

Fig. 1. Experimental schedule for Session 1 (higher intensity level) and Session 2 (lower intensity level), and the respective HRV recording periods.

3.5 Experimental Setup

Physiological data was collected using an electrocardiogram (ECG) sensing module. A wearable Shimmer 3 ECG sensor was used for this experiment [21]. This compact and small module facilitates its usage as a wearable module without compromising the comfort and movements of an individual, and has been widely used for biomedical research [22]. Its baseboard is composed by a MSP420 ultra-low power microcontroller, from Texas Instruments™, and its communication module relies on a Chipcon CC2420 radio transceiver, compliant with IEEE 802.15.4, and a RN42Class 2 Bluetooth module. A wider variety of functionalities are available in Shimmer 3 thanks to the incorporation of kinematic sensors, in addition to the physiological sensing modules already present. This particular Shimmer model includes ECG and Electromyography (EMG) functionalities, as well as 10 Degrees of Freedom (DoF) inertial sensing capabilities. For this experiment, only its ECG feature was used. A five-lead ECG monitoring was considered, which allows feasible readings since the electrodes are placed on the torso and are less susceptible to motion artifacts caused by limb movements. The ECG signals were recorded at 512 Hz and sent in real-time to a personal computer through Bluetooth. LabView software was used to configure the Shimmer module and collect the ECG data, which was then saved in a local file for later processing. Figure 2 shows the VR serious game setup (high-angles gameplay mode), as well as the placement of the AgCl electrodes (RA, RL, LA, LL and V1).

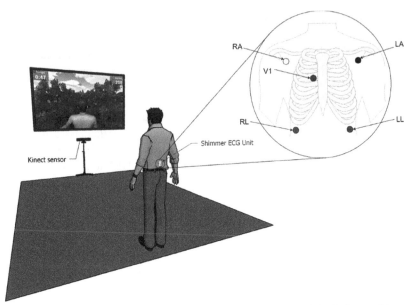

Fig. 2. VR serious game setup including a Kinect sensor and a physiological wearable sensor (Shimmer ECG unit), and positioning of the electrodes for a 5-lead ECG measurement.

3.6 Data Analysis

ECG signal pre-processing was made offline on a personal computer using an open-source Python library [23]. Filtering methods based on the implementation of a band-stop filter with cut-off frequency of 0.05 Hz were necessary for removing baseline wander of the ECG signal. A peak detection algorithm was used to extract the temporal position of R peaks from the QRS wave complex and get the time-series of the R-R interval. The R-R intervals were obtained for the specified periods of resting and gameplay conditions depicted in Fig. 1, and thus, they were used to extract HRV measures. Data analysis based on HRV was performed with the Kubios HRV Software (ver. 3.3) [24]. Time-domain and frequency-domain parameters were considered in this study, as well as the quantification of the Stress Index. The time-domain variables included were: mean R-R interval; mean HR; standard deviation of successive NN intervals (SDNN) and root mean square of successive NN interval differences (RMSSD). For the frequency-domain analysis, low frequency (LF, 0.04–0.15 Hz) and high frequency (HF, 0.15–0.40 Hz) components were selected. The Baevsky's stress index (SI), a geometric measure of HRV, was also assessed using Kubios.

4 Results and Discussion

4.1 Variance in HRV Indices During Different Intensity Levels

The obtained HRV values for the different experimental sessions are presented in Table 1. A one-way analysis of the variance (ANOVA) was separately performed to compare the means and to identify significant changes in HRV measures between different conditions: the higher difficulty gameplay versus easier level gameplay; between resting-period after the gameplay or both difficulty levels, as presented in Table 1; and between rest-period (Control) and the gameplay period of each session. A p-value of ≤ 0.05 was considered statistically significant.

These tests revealed that the gameplay of higher difficulty and intensity (Session 1) induced significant alterations on the average HR levels ($p = 0.004$) and maximum HR ($p = 0.001$) when compared with rest-period (Control) measures. Low and high frequencies did not show any statistically significant changes (LF: $p = 0.06$, HF: $p = 0.07$). The HR response during the exercise of higher difficulty showed an increase of approximately 17 bpm for all volunteers when compared with the Control group. Moreover, the ratio between low and high frequencies (LF/HF) increased twice the value measured in the control group, which indicates sympathetic activation during the exergaming experience.

Regarding the gameplay session of easier difficulty levels (Session 2) and the Control group measures, there were no significant alterations on HRV parameters. This was expected as the volunteers remained in a relaxed sitting position throughout the whole session. Additionally, the game was physically less demanding since it did not present the same levels of complexity, stimuli, and the need of a faster-reaction time as in the higher difficulty mode. However, although not significantly, LF/HF ratio seemed to be higher during gameplay of Session 2 than on Session 1. This may be explained by the protocol followed, as presented in Fig. 2. The gameplay of Session 2 occurred right after a resting-period, whereas on Session 1 the HRV analysis during gameplay (4 min) was performed right after volunteers played the 1 min and 2 min gameplay sessions. Being accustomed with the game's mechanics of that specific difficulty level may also have helped to reduce stress in participants and decrease the sympathetic tone.

One-way ANOVA on the difference between the gameplay of different difficulty levels from both sessions revealed significant main effects on the average HR ($p = 0.04$), maximum HR ($p = 0.02$) and HF power ($p = 0.04$). HF components were much higher during the easier difficulty game level (HF = 597 ± 750 ms^2) than on the higher intensity one (HF = 251 ± 214 ms^2). Thus, parasympathetic stimulation decreased the cardiac output. Moreover, the stress index remained lower and almost at the same level as that obtained for resting periods. No significant interaction of different game complexities on RMSSD ($p = 0.72$) and SDNN ($p = 0.86$) and LF ($p = 0.34$) parameters was found.

During the recovery phase of the lower difficulty/intensity gameplay characterized by a reduced limb motion range, which lasted for 5 min, the majority of HRV parameters – HR, SDNN, LF/HF - regained almost the same values registered on pre-exercise/resting periods. On the other hand, the higher intensity gameplay revealed lower parasympathetic recovery after the exercise.

Table 1. Mean and standard deviation (SD) of HRV parameters for each game session and one-way ANOVA results

HRV parameters		Control (Pre-Game)	Session 1 (Higher Intensity)	Session 2 (Lower Intensity)	P-value
Time – domain analysis					
Mean HR (bpm)	*during*	82 ± 5	99 ± 9	86 ± 9	≤ 0.05
	post		86 ± 10	83 ± 6	0.59
Max HR (bpm)	*during*	93 ± 6	112 ± 8	97 ± 9	≤ 0.05
	post		101 ± 11	97 ± 7	0.53
Mean RR (ms)	*during*	737 ± 44	613 ± 51	709 ± 67	≤ 0.05
	post		706 ± 79	726 ± 47	0.65
SDNN (ms)	*during*	52 ± 14	42 ± 28	47 ± 12	0.86
	post		46 ± 13	51 ± 20	0.55
RMSSD (ms)	*during*	49 ± 30	45 ± 51	36 ± 19	0.72
	post		37 ± 20	46 ± 34	0.62
Frequency - domain analysis					
LF/HF	*during*	2.6 ± 1.7	4.8 ± 3	5.4 ± 4	0.78
	post		2.9 ± 2	2.7 ± 1.4	0.92
Stress Index	*during*	8.9 ± 2	11.5 ± 4	8.2 ± 3	0.22
	post		9.4 ± 4	8.3 ± 3	0.62

As a complement to the obtained physiological measures, subjective measures were also obtained from volunteers to assess exercise intensity and distress/anxiety levels felt during each gameplay session. Exercise intensity, as assessed by a Borg rating of perceived exertion (RPE) scale, was considered very low for both rehabilitation games (Session 1: 9.8 ± 2; Session 2: 9 ± 3). The volunteer's impression on distress and anxiety assessed by a Subjective Units of Distress Scale (SUDS) was higher for Session 1 (Mean = 28.3) when compared with Session 2 (Mean = 20), which is in accordance to the obtained stress index levels values and LF/HF ratio variation among the different sessions.

4.2 Variance of HR Levels During a More Complex Gameplay with Different Time Durations

The variance of HR parameter during the more complex gameplay from Session 1 (high-angles gameplay mode) was compared for three different time intervals of 1 min, 2 min and 4 min. This study allowed to verify if gameplays of different time periods induce changes on cardiovascular activity and if a longer game duration requires higher levels of effort from the subject. For a HRV analysis of equal time segments, the last 1 min of each gameplay duration was considered. Only time-domain parameters were examined in this study phase: mean HR, RMSSD and SDNN. As a directly correlated measure of HF power, the RMSSD parameter gives insights of parasympathetic activity during these shorter-term recordings [20].

A one-way ANOVA revealed no significant changes on HRV parameters between 1 min and 2 min gameplay. The same was also verified between the 1 min and 4 min gameplay duration. Heart rate levels remained constant between the three gameplay sessions (Mean = 94 bpm). RMSSD levels got slightly higher as the gameplay duration increased (Mean = 21 ms for 1 mn; Mean = 24 ms for 4 mn). As a parameter that is correlated with HF power and parasympathetic activity, these values of RMSSD corroborate the explanation given in Sect. 4.1, regarding the measurement of a lower LF/HF ratio in Session 1 when compared to session 2.

4.3 Artificial Intelligence Algorithms for Game Intensity Levels Classification

Various classification algorithms were investigated for predicting the game complexity/intensity levels. Considering remote physiotherapy sessions based on this VR serious exergame, this classification can help the physiotherapist keep track of the participant's performance and assess which type of upper limb rehabilitation exercises, low angles or high angles, are being executed, to check whether a patient is following the imposed training plan or not. Moreover, if a certain game intensity level is misclassified, e.g. a lower intensity game is classified has a high intensity one, it may reveal that HRV levels selected are not at the most appropriate level. Thus, the imposed rehabilitation exercise may not be recommended for a particular patient and the physiotherapist should re-adjust the rehabilitation plan. A set of physiological data from 6 subjects containing HRV measures during a 4-min gameplay of two different intensity levels was created. The dataset comprises 8 features (HR, maximum HR, mean RR, SDNN, RMSSD, LF, HF and Stress Index) and a target which is game intensity. For binary classification purposes, three different machine learning algorithms were considered in this study: Support Vector Machines (SVM), k-nearest neighbours (k-NN) and Decision Trees. All classifiers were implemented using the Python programming language and Scikit-learn machine learning library. Pre-processing steps included label encoding of the prediction target, therefore converting categorical values that defined the game intensity into "0" (lower) and "1" (higher). A local outlier factor was (LOF) applied for identifying and removing outliers in the dataset. Considering the limited data samples, a cross-validation technique based on k-fold cross-validation was applied for estimating the performance of our model, since the common train/test split method could exclude data points with useful information during the training phase. A 4-fold cross validation was considered regarding the total number of samples present in the dataset and the achievement of better classification results when compared with other values of k. The obtained performance metrics for our model are presented in Table 2. From the three classification models, k-NN provided the highest classification accuracy of 81% for the predicting game intensity level, and 0.789 for the best F1-score when compared with the other models.

Table 2. Accuracy, precision, F1-score and recall values obtained for the three classification algorithms in a 4-fold cross validation

Evaluation metrics	SVM	k-NN	Decision tree
Accuracy	72%	81%	77%
F1-score	0.714	0.789	0.639
Recall	0.729	0.812	0.667
Precision	0.792	0.792	0.575

5 Conclusions

This paper aimed to explore how virtual reality exergaming experiences can be related with autonomic nervous system responses, as a highly promising and effective engaging alternative to common physical activity exercises. Firstly, the main results from relevant works that attempted to investigate such influences based on physiological data analysis collected by wearable devices were presented. As a complementary tool for physical rehabilitation exercises, the impact of VR serious games on physical and cognitive performance, as well as on the rehabilitation process were also addressed. More contributions were made in this sense, as this present study sought to evaluate how a VR serious game for rehabilitation modulates physiological responses of younger adults. Two different game complexities were experienced by the subjects, and physiological data collected by biomedical wearable sensors evidenced significant changes in HRV parameters between each game difficulty levels.

Stimulation of the parasympathetic branch of the ANS was mostly notable during easier difficulty game levels. On the other hand, it was verified that a higher intensity gameplay induced lower parasympathetic recovery during post-exercise/resting periods.

Gameplays of longer time durations did not reveal a significant impact on physiological responses of younger adults, when compared with shorter ones.

Finally, this contribution involved the implementation of machine learning algorithms to estimate the different serious game difficulty levels based on HRV measures, and it was verified that the k-NN algorithm achieved the best results amongst other classifiers.

References

1. Munoz Cardona, J.E., Cameirao, M.S., Paulino, T., Bermudez i Badia, S., Rubio, E.: Modulation of physiological responses and activity levels during exergame experiences. In: 2016 8th International Conference on Games and Virtual Worlds for Serious Applications (VS-GAMES), pp. 1–8, Barcelona, Spain, September 2016. https://doi.org/10.1109/VS-GAMES.2016.7590353
2. Benzing, V., Heinks, T., Eggenberger, N., Schmidt, M.: Acute cognitively engaging exergame-based physical activity enhances executive functions in adolescents. PLoS ONE 11(12), e0167501 (2016). https://doi.org/10.1371/journal.pone.0167501

3. Polechoński, J., Dębska, M., Dębski, P.G.: Exergaming can be a health-related aerobic physical activity. Biomed. Res. Int. **2019**, 1–7 (2019). https://doi.org/10.1155/2019/1890527

4. Wittmann, F., et al.: Self-directed arm therapy at home after stroke with a sensor-based virtual reality training system. J. NeuroEng. Rehabil. **13**(1), 75 (2016). https://doi.org/10.1186/s12984-016-0182-1

5. Standen, P., et al.: A low cost virtual reality system for home based rehabilitation of the arm following stroke: a randomised controlled feasibility trial. Clin. Rehabil. **31**(3), 340–350 (2017). https://doi.org/10.1177/0269215516640320

6. Charoensook, T., Barlow, M., Lakshika, E.: Heart rate and breathing variability for virtual reality game Play. In: 2019 IEEE 7th International Conference on Serious Games and Applications for Health (SeGAH), pp. 1–7, Kyoto, Japan, August 2019. https://doi.org/10.1109/SeGAH.2019.8882434

7. Kafri, M., Myslinski, M.J., Gade, V.K., Deutsch, J.E.: Energy expenditure and exercise intensity of interactive video gaming in individuals poststroke. Neurorehabil. Neural Repair **28**(1), 56–65 (2014). https://doi.org/10.1177/1545968313497100

8. Cho, G.H., Hwangbo, G., Shin, H.S.: The effects of virtual reality-based balance training on balance of the elderly. J. Phys. Ther. Sci. **26**(4), 615–617 (2014). https://doi.org/10.1589/jpts.26.615

9. Donath, L., Rössler, R., Faude, O.: Effects of virtual reality training (exergaming) compared to alternative exercise training and passive control on standing balance and functional mobility in healthy community-dwelling seniors: a meta-analytical review. Sports Med. **46**(9), 1293–1309 (2016). https://doi.org/10.1007/s40279-016-0485-1

10. de Amorim, J.S.C., Leite, R.C., Brizola, R., Yonamine, C.Y.: Virtual reality therapy for rehabilitation of balance in the elderly: a systematic review and META-analysis. Adv. Rheumatol. **58**(1), 18 (2018). https://doi.org/10.1186/s42358-018-0013-0

11. Lei, C., et al.: Effects of virtual reality rehabilitation training on gait and balance in patients with Parkinson's disease: a systematic review. PLoS ONE **14**(11), e0224819 (2019). https://doi.org/10.1371/journal.pone.0224819

12. Fang, Q., et al.: Effects of exergaming on balance of healthy older adults: a systematic review and meta-analysis of randomized controlled trials. Games Health J. **9**(1), 11–23 (2020). https://doi.org/10.1089/g4h.2019.0016

13. Wiley, E., Khattab, S., Tang, A.: Examining the effect of virtual reality therapy on cognition post-stroke: a systematic review and meta-analysis. Disabil. Rehabil.: Assistive Technol., 1–11, (2020). https://doi.org/10.1080/17483107.2020.1755376

14. Brachman, A., et al.: The effects of exergaming training on balance in healthy elderly women—a pilot study. IJERPH **18**(4), 1412 (2021). https://doi.org/10.3390/ijerph18041412

15. Bourrelier, J., Ryard, J., Dion, M., Merienne, F., Manckoundia, P., Mourey, F.: Use of a virtual environment to engage motor and postural abilities in elderly subjects with and without mild cognitive impairment (MAAMI Project). IRBM **37**(2), 75–80 (2016). https://doi.org/10.1016/j.irbm.2016.02.007

16. Gomes, T.T., Schujmann, D.S., Fu, C.: Rehabilitation through virtual reality: physical activity of patients admitted to the intensive care unit. Revista Brasileira de Terapia Intensiva **31**(4) (2019). https://doi.org/10.5935/0103-507X.20190078

17. Stojan, R., Voelcker-Rehage, C.: A Systematic review on the cognitive benefits and neurophysiological correlates of exergaming in healthy older adults. JCM **8**(5), 734 (2019). https://doi.org/10.3390/jcm8050734

18. Eggenberger, P., Annaheim, S., Kündig, K.A., Rossi, R.M., Münzer, T., de Bruin, E.D.: Heart rate variability mainly relates to cognitive executive functions and improves through exergame training in older adults: a secondary analysis of a 6-month randomized controlled trial. Front. Aging Neurosci. **12**, 197 (2020). https://doi.org/10.3389/fnagi.2020.00197

19. Postolache, O. et al.: Tailored virtual reality for smart physiotherapy. In: 2019 11th International Symposium on Advanced Topics in Electrical Engineering (ATEE), pp. 1–6, Bucharest, Romania, March 2019. https://doi.org/10.1109/ATEE.2019.8724903

20. Malik, M.: Heart rate variability: standards of measurement, physiological interpretation, and clinical use: task force of the European society of cardiology and the North American society for pacing and electrophysiology. Ann. Noninv. Electrocard. 1(2), 151–181 (1996). https://doi.org/10.1111/j.1542-474X.1996.tb00275.x

21. Shimmer: Shimmer3 ECG. https://www.shimmersensing.com/shimmer3-ecg/

22. Burns, A., et al.: SHIMMER^{TM} – a wireless sensor platform for noninvasive biomedical research. IEEE Sensors J. 10(9), 1527–1534 (2010). https://doi.org/10.1109/JSEN.2010.2045498

23. van Gent, P., Farah, H., van Nes, N., van Arem, B.: HeartPy: a novel heart rate algorithm for the analysis of noisy signals. Transport. Res. F: Traffic Psychol. Behav. 66, 368–378 (2019). https://doi.org/10.1016/j.trf.2019.09.015

24. Tarvainen, M.P., Niskanen, J.-P., Lipponen, J.A., Ranta-aho, P.O., Karjalainen, P.A.: Kubios HRV – heart rate variability analysis software. Comput. Methods Programs Biomed. 113(1), 210–220 (2014). https://doi.org/10.1016/j.cmpb.2013.07.024

Computational Intelligence
for Multimedia Understanding

Anomaly Detection on ADS-B Flight Data Using Machine Learning Techniques

Osman Taşdelen[1]([⊠]) (ID), Levent Çarkacioglu[1] (ID), and Behçet Uğur Töreyin[2] (ID)

[1] Aselsan Inc., 06200 Ankara, Turkey
{otasdelen,lcarkacioglu}@aselsan.com.tr
[2] Istanbul Technical University, Informatics Institute, 34469 Istanbul, Turkey
toreyin@itu.edu.tr

Abstract. With the rapid increase in the number of flights all over the world, the management and control of flight operations has become difficult in recent years. Moreover, the expectations for the aviation sector indicate that this increase will continue in the upcoming years. Therefore, safer and systematic monitoring systems by eliminating the requirement of human-dependent tracking during the air travel of an aircraft and automating the detection of abnormal situations has become a major problem in aviation sector. With the recent advances in artificial intelligence, a safer and systematic tracking system for controlling the airspace by eliminating the need for human-dependent tracking during the flight of aircraft in the air has become possible.

In this study, we aimed to create a system that detects and predicts movements to indicate abnormal, dangerous situations in the airspace by monitoring radar flight data using machine learning and deep learning techniques. We applied two different methods, i.e., Proximity Based kNN and Auto Encoder We used real-life historical radar flight data set which consists of Flight Radar 24 data were converted from ADS-B messages for learning. We created simulation data and used this data for testing and validation for our trained model. Within the scope of this project, we also developed a system to monitor air traffic through radar tracks with our model and present the abnormal situations to the user through a visual interface for decision support. In this visualization, we present the abnormal situations if one of the algorithms labeled as anomaly. Results for both methods have shown that our findings were similar to the real-life predictions.

Keywords: Anomaly detection · Deep learning · Machine learning · Proximity based kNN · Auto encoder · Flight control · ADS-B · Air traffic management

1 Introduction

The aviation sector has been developing rapidly all over the world in recent years. Moreover, the expectations for the aviation industry indicate that the air

© Springer Nature Switzerland AG 2021
N. T. Nguyen et al. (Eds.): ICCCI 2021, LNAI 12876, pp. 771–783, 2021.
https://doi.org/10.1007/978-3-030-88081-1_58

traffic density will continue to increase in the coming years [1]. With the increase in the number of aircrafts, the aircraft traffic in circulation increases. Moreover, because the air traffic density increases, the management and control of flight operations has become difficult. In order for the flight operations to be carried out safely, efficiently and quickly, the air travel must be well controlled and managed. Therefore, by taking advantage of the artificial intelligence technology, it was aimed to reveal a safer and systematic tracking system for controlling the airspace by eliminating the need for human-dependent tracking during the flight of aircraft in the air.

The system was aimed to detect situations that are thought to indicate an unusual dangerous situation in the airspace. In this study, what is meant by extraordinary situations is deviation from course, speed, altitude, abnormal change in position values and sudden change of direction, and it was evaluated that artificial intelligence technology can be used to detect the extraordinary situations mentioned. Research has been done on different machine learning and deep learning methods and the studies which were carried out previously have been examined. Researches were done to obtain the data set used within the scope of this study and the information obtained was examined in detail.

In this study, we encountered the following challenges:

- Flight radar parameters may vary depending on flight dynamics. When a flight parameter changes, it is likely that other parameters will be affected. Determination of the parameters of decision support algorithms in this study was one of the most difficult challenges. The relationship between the parameters involved in the flight and the variability relationships between parameters made this challenge more difficult.
- There are different flight stages and different variations within the data set, which makes it difficult to extract a pattern from the data. Due to the lack of prior knowledge of patterns in flight data, it was a challenge to select the best machine learning method that needs to be capable of processing patterns in different variations.
- Identifying unusual situations in the airspace was another challenge. It is required to define abnormal situations and create test data based on this definition so that the success of algorithms can be tested. Identification of abnormal situations with limited expert support was also one of the challenges in the study.
- The last challenge in this study was the outlier detection problem. An outlier can be deviation from course, speed, altitude, abnormal change in position values and sudden change of direction. Since prior assumptions are needed to solve this problem, many researchers consider this problem as one of the most challenging problems of anomaly distribution [2].

As a summary, by using the mentioned technological methods, we made it easier to detect unusual behaviors that airspace control operators have difficulty in detecting. To the best of our knowledge, this is the first study on air flight data with real-life tracking data using machine learning techniques and visualizing the results.

The rest of this paper is organized as follows: Sect. 2 overviews the related work. Section 3 outlines methods used in this study. Data set and implementation details are discussed in Sect. 4. Results are discussed in Sect. 5. Finally, Sect. 6 finalizes the paper with future work.

2   Related Work

There are various approach related to the detection of irregularities on aircraft and flight routes. The evaluations of these studies in general terms are given in this section. Most of the studies on the detection of irregularities in flight data are directly related to the anomaly detection techniques. Charu C. Aggarwal, has included bases for anomaly detection in his book [29]. Researchers studied many different methods for anomaly detection [32]. Anomaly Detection methods are divided into different categories as shown in Fig. 1. We will give a brief overview of these methods in the following subsections.

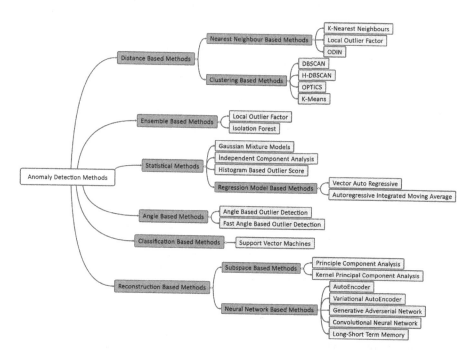

Fig. 1. Anomaly detection methods are divided in 6 main categories, which are further subdivided into 24 subcategories.

2.1   Distance Based Methods

Distance-based algorithms for anomaly detection utilization is a common approach. This category which was defined by Pimentel et al. [2] includes not only the nearest neighbor-based but also clustering-based anomaly detection perspective which were described as two fundamental categories in the characterized by Chandola et al. [3].

In Nearest Neighbor Based Methods, the distance of a data point to its k-nearest neighbors is used to define proximity. Most of these methods usually work well while the data is highly clustered, and outliers can be distinguished from dense regions of data. In clustering based methods, the outlier detection problem turns into clustering point as either clusters or outliers. The most well-known density-based clustering algorithms are DBSCAN [4], HDBSCAN [5], OPTICS [6] and K-Means [7].

2.2   Ensemble Based Methods

A wide analysis of the ensemble-based algorithms for outlier detection was offered by Aggarwal [8]. In the category of ensemble-based methods, Aggarwal involves traditional models for anomaly detection like Local Outlier Factor (LOF) when they are used with many sets of hyper parameters in order to bring together the outcomes [9]. Another ensemble-based algorithm is Isolation Forest (IF) [10]. This algorithm is especially designed to detect anomalies with performance challenges sometimes the ones which are more advanced and modern neural network approaches. Zhang et al. presented a methodology called isolation-based abnormal route (Isolation-based Abnormal Trajectory - IBAT) and used this methodology to detect abnormal routes in taxis using GPS data [11]. As a continuation of this study, Chen et al. introduced the version of the Isolation-Based Online Anomalous Trajectory (IBOAT) to the literature that taxis do not follow the correct route to the point in real time [12].

2.3   Statistical Methods

Among the fundamental categories described by Chandola et al. statistical methods [3]. Anomaly detection methods which are in the mentioned categories are rely on the estimation of the probability intensities of the data [33]. They are also based on the supposition that, normal data will take part in high probability regions where anomalies take part in low probability ones [33]. The most well-known statistical based algorithms are Hidden Markov Model (HMM) Gaussian Mixture Model (GMM) [13,14].

2.4   Angle Based Methods

In Angle based methods, decision of an anomaly is based on the measurement of the angle formed by a set of three points in the data space [15]. The variation in the magnitude of the angular enclosure comes out to be different for outliers and others become the metric to cluster normal and outlier points in different clusters. Angle Based Outlier Detection (ABOD) and Fast Angle Based Outlier Detection (Fast ABOD) algorithms are used for anomaly detection [15]. ABOD and Fast ABOD relate data to high-dimensional spaces by using the variance in the angles between a data point to the other points as anomaly score.

2.5 Classification Based Methods

In Classification based methods, a boundary or domain is defined in order that normal data from anomalies according to the training data can be separated [16]. The Support Vector Machines (SVM) [17] is the most commonly implemented technique in this category. It is the only one cover and more accurately the variant known as one-class SVM (OC-SVM) [18]. Piciarelli and Foresti presented a study in which they detected the irregularities in routes using SVM [19]. Two-dimensional route data were kept at a fixed length and used and classified as a feature in the training phase. Thus, outliers resulting from the classifications were determined as anomalies. The Multiple Kernel Anomaly Detection (MKAD) algorithm is designed to detect anomalies over a set of files which was developed by NASA. This algorithm takes places among the first methods which could successfully detect the anomalies in heterogeneous flight data [20]. It brings together multiple kernels into a single optimization function using OC-SVM.

2.6 Reconstruction Based Methods

Chandola et al. identified reconstruction based methods as spectral-based anomaly detection where it is presumed that data which is located in a lower dimension assists to separate normal instances from abnormal ones [3]. Within subspace based methods, a great number of the anomaly detection methods utilize from Principal Component Analysis (PCA) [21]. A number of variants are available to address the various constraints of the primary PCA technique, i.e., Kernel PCA introduce certain kernels for nonlinear projections [22]. High computational complexity of these models makes them inappropriate to be trained on very large datasets. Neural Network techniques can also be implemented for anomaly detection. AutoEncoder(AE) is a powerful nonlinear dimensionality reduction tools widely utilized to detect anomalies. There are also known variants of AE such as Deep Auto Encoder (DAE) or Variational Auto Encoder (VAE) used in anomaly detection. DAE is a hybrid AE, which uses Recurrent Neural Network(RNN) or Convolutional Neural Network(CNN) cells in the encoding and decoding parts of the neural networks [24]. VAE is an unsupervised and generative AE model that forces the distribution of vectors in hidden space according to normal distribution [25]. Generative Adversarial Networks (GAN) is another popular approach to generative modeling using deep learning methods [26]. It involves automatically discovering regularities in such a way that the model can be used to generate new examples. This network type, consists of two or more neural networks which work as opposed to each other. CNN are specific type of neural networks, which are generally used for image processing.

It has been seen that the use of the sliding window approach on time series is quite common in CNN. It is observed that CNN is skilled at learning complex, hidden features. Long-Short Term Memory(LSTM) is a type of RNN that can learn long-term dependencies. LSTM are structures that contain RNNs in their architecture and are generally used in sequential or time series. They are skilled in extracting both long- and short-term features from historical data.

3 Methods

Statistical and clustering methods based on Gaussian Distribution and DBSCAN algorithms were generally examined in the previous studies for anomaly detection [14,27]. According to literature searches, Proximity Based kNN and AE algorithms generate better in terms of performance and the ease of development and they are predicted to have potential, as in the case of anomaly detection applications [28,29]. Therefore, we decided to use these algorithms in our study. A brief overview of these algorithms are given in the following subsections.

3.1 Proximity Based kNN Algorithm

It is a modified version of kth nearest neighbor (kNN) algorithm. kNN is among the basic distance based algorithms that stores all current states and classifies novel states based on a similarity measure. Basically, it works by checking the nearest k neighbors of the data to be classified by giving the k (i.e., number of neighbors) parameter to the cluster. Proximity Based kNN rests on the distance of a point from its kth nearest neighbor. Every point is ranked on the basis of its distance to its kth nearest neighbor and top n points in this ranking are labeled as anomalies. Then, a threshold is used to determine if a data point is abnormal or not. This algorithm creates a tree structure to quickly find the nearest k data thus improving search performance. It uses KD Tree algorithm [30] to create this tree structure. For a new point; the Euclidean distance between the nearest neighbor and the farthest neighbor in the tree is computed. This distance is compared with a threshold value in order to classify it as normal or abnormal. All the radar tracks in the data set obtained for the detection of anomalies in the airspace contain a single class with only normal data. Therefore, Proximity Based kNN is generally preferred algorithm in anomaly detection [28].

3.2 AutoEncoder

Auto Encoder (AE) is a generative unsupervised deep learning algorithm which is used to reconstruct high-dimensional input data by using a neural network [23]. A simple AE, as shown in Fig. 2, has three layers, namely input, hidden and output layers. AE compresses multidimensional data into hidden layers first and then rebuilds the data in compressed hidden layers. The area between the input layer and the hidden layer is called encoder whereas the area between the hidden layer and the output layer is called decoder. Encoder provides reduction of a high dimensional data and compress it to a less size for the hidden layer. Decoder tries to rebuild the input by increasing the size of the compressed hidden layer. AE tries to minimize the reconstruction error. We applied AE on radar track data for training. In this study, we provide selected features of radar track data as input to AE. It reduces to hidden layers with random weights and output nodes are created by expanding the values in hidden layers with random weights. The number of back propagation epoch in increased until a small reconstruction error is reached. We detect the anomalies by checking the magnitude of the reconstruction error. At the end of the training process, if the reconstruction error in the encoded data is higher than the determined threshold value, this data is classified as abnormal.

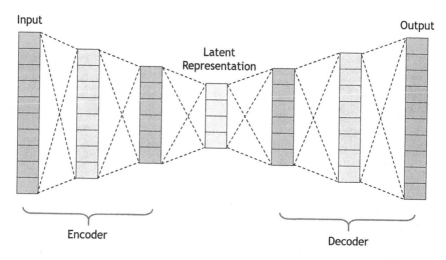

Fig. 2. Architecture of an encoder and decoder in Auto Encoder.

4   Implementation Details

In the following subsections, we first give brief information about our data set. Then, we will explain the implementation details.

4.1   Data Set

Literature reviews have confirmed the importance of data for anomaly detection. After a careful literature search, we decided to work on radar track dataset which consists of FlightRadar24 data converted from ADS-B (ASTERIX CAT21) messages. ASTERIX (All-purpose structured EUROCONTROL surveillance information exchange), is an air traffic control messaging format developed by EUROCONTROL [31] to transfer information between any surveillance and automation system. It defines the structure of the data over a communication medium, from the coding of each bit of information to the arrangement of the data in the data block, without any loss of information throughout the entire data. Our dataset includes civilian flights for one day around Turkey. There are approximately two million radar tracks that consists of all the tracks in geo-localized points in our data set. One-day flight data consists of normal flight data sets. In order to create normal flight data sets, flights with uncertain destination and departure points were excluded from the data set. A visualization of civilian flights data for one day in and around Turkey can be seen in Fig. 3. The original data set contains register address, latitude, longitude, heading, altitude, speed, squawk code, aircraft type, tail number, departure, arrival, flight number, call sign information. In this study, we removed attributes related with aircraft identification and used attributes latitude, longitude, heading, altitude and speed data.

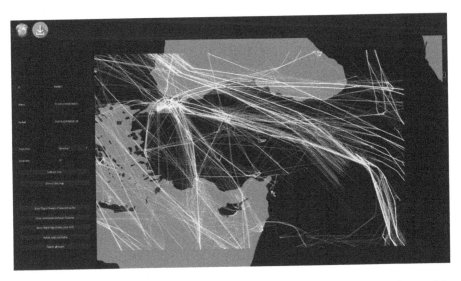

Fig. 3. Visualization of civilian flight data over a period of one-day in Turkey and its environs.

4.2 Parameters and Values

We studied two different methods on one day historical real life radar flight data around Turkey for training. First, we applied Proximity Based kNN algorithm. The parameters and values used in this algorithm are given in Table 1.

Table 1. Parameters for the proximity based kNN algorithm.

Parameter	Value	Explanation
n_neighbors	5	the number of nearest neighbors for voting
outlier score method	largest	largest: the largest distance to the kth neighbor mean: the average of all k neighbors median:the median of the distance to k neighbors
nearest neighbors algorithm	kd_tree	'ball_tree' as BallTree algorithm 'kd_tree' as KDTree algorithm 'brute' as brute-force search algorithm
leaf_size	30	affects the speed of the construction and query
metric	euclidean	metric for distance computation

Table 2. Parameters for the AE algorithm.

Parameter	Value	Explanation
hidden_neurons	[5,128,64,2,64,128,5]	the number of neurons per hidden layers
hidden_activation	ReLU	activation function for hidden layers
output_activation	ReLU	activation function for output layer
loss	mean squared error	method of evaluating how well a certain algorithm models the given data
optimizer	adamax	used to alter the attributes of a given neural network so as to decrease the losses
epochs	40	number of epochs to train the model
batch_size	64	number of training examples utilized in one iteration
dropout_rate	0.1	the dropout to be used across all layers
l2_regularizer	0.000001	the regularization strength of activity regularizer applied on each layer
validation_size	0.2	the percentage of data to be used for validation

Second, we applied AE algorithm. We used the Keras open source library in implementation. We select the EarlyStopping method of this library to determine the most suitable epoch number of the AE algorithm. The parameters and values used in this algorithm are given in Table 2.

5   Results

We created 100 different simulation data and tested the algorithms with them. The abnormal radar flight data within these simulated data was created with the support of experts in airspace management. We used Precision, Recall, F1 Score and Accuracy metrics to compare the performance of the algorithms. Definitions of these metrics are given in following equations. We applied two different algorithms on these simulation data to detect abnormal flights in the airspace. The results are shown in Table 3. It has been observed that Proximity Based kNN outperforms AE in all metrics.

True Positives (TP) : Number of correct normal labeled tracking data.
True Negatives (TN) : Number of correct abnormal labeled tracking data.
False Positives (FP) : Number of incorrect normal labeled tracking data.
False Negatives (FN) : Number of incorrect abnormal labeled tracking data.

$$Precision = \frac{TP}{TP + FP} \tag{1}$$

$$Recall = \frac{TP}{TP + FN} \tag{2}$$

$$F1 - Score = 2 * \frac{precision * recall}{precision + recall} \tag{3}$$

$$Accuracy = \frac{TP + TN}{TP + FP + TN + FN} \tag{4}$$

Table 3. Results for the algorithms used in this study.

Algorithm	Precision	Recall	F1-Score	Accuracy
Proximity based kNN	0.91	0.82	0.86	**0.87**
AutoEncoder	0.76	0.84	0.75	**0.81**

We developed a user interface for visualization of abnormal situations on real-life tracking with real-life Flight Radar 24 tracking data. If any of our models label radar track as anomaly we visualize it as abnormal situations. In Fig. 4, visualization of an anomaly detected by AE algorithm is shown as an example. This anomaly is detected according to aircrafts speed, location and irregularity parameters. It is further validated with expert judgement.

Fig. 4. Visualized speed anomaly in radar flight data. In this figure, the red coloured aircraft represents the anomaly found by one of our algorithms and the yellow coloured aircraft represents the normal flights. Detailed information about this anomaly is located at the upper right of the figure. Red dots represent past radar traces of that aircraft. Also, a warning message appears at the bottom right of the screen to inform users. (Color figure online)

6   Conclusion

In this study, we applied two different algorithms, namely Proximity Based kNN and Auto Encoder algorithms, to detect and predict movements to indicate abnormal, dangerous situations in the airspace. We further developed a visual interface to monitor air traffic through real-life radar tracks and present the abnormal situations labeled using these models. Results for both methods have shown that our findings were similar to the real-life predictions.

For future study, the following works can be studied. The flight data set can be divided into flight phases and the model can be trained according to these phases. Other well-known algorithms for anomaly detection, like Generative Adversarial Networks (GAN), Long-Short Term Memory(LSTM) and Convolutional Neural Networks(CNN) can be studied as a future work. Extending the study by adding intension to the detected anomalies would also be challenging future work.

In scope of this project, we also studied adaptation of our system to detect anomalies on other real-life data sets i.e., NASA Flight Data Recorder(FDR) data set and Automatic Identification System (AIS). However, the attributes in this dataset are not compatible with our model. Another study, to detect anomalies using this data set can be studied as future work.

Acknowledgements. Osman Taşdelen extends his gratitude to Aselsan for their support and his colleagues for their cooperation and fruitful discussions. It was always helpful to exchange ideas about his research with his team mates.

References

1. Akça, M., Pınar, R.İ.: Air traffic controller performance: a field study. Empirical Econ. Soc. Sci. **1**, 68–82 (2019)
2. Pimentel, T., Monteiro, M., Viana, J., Veloso, V., Ziviani, N.: A Generalized active learning approach for unsupervised anomaly detection, Section 3 (2018)
3. Chandola, V., Banerjee, A., Kumar, V.: Anomaly detection: a survey. ACM Comput. Surv. **41**, 1–58 (2009)
4. Ester, M.; Kriegel, H.P.; Sander, J.; Xu, X.: A Density-based algorithm for discovering clusters in large spatial databases with noise, pp. 226–231 (1996)
5. Campello, R.J.G.B., Moulavi, D., Sander, J.: Density-based clustering based on hierarchical density estimates. In: Pei, J., Tseng, V.S., Cao, L., Motoda, H., Xu, G. (eds.) PAKDD 2013. LNCS (LNAI), vol. 7819, pp. 160–172. Springer, Heidelberg (2013). https://doi.org/10.1007/978-3-642-37456-2_14
6. Ankerst, M., Breunig, M.M., Kriegel, H.P., Sander, J.: OPTICS: ordering points to identify the clustering structure. ACM Sigmod. Record **28**, 49–60 (1999)
7. Hartigan, J.A.; Wong, M.A.: Algorithm AS 136: a k-means clustering algorithm. J. R. Stat. Soc. Ser. C (Appl. Stat.) **28**, 100–108 (1979)
8. Aggarwal, C.C.: Outlier ensembles: position paper. ACM SIGKDD Explor. Newslett. **14**, 49 (2013). https://doi.org/10.1145/2481244.2481252
9. Breunig, M.M., Kriegel, H.P., Ng, R.T., Sander, J.: LOF: identifying density-based local outliers. ACM SIGKDD Explor. Newslett. **29**, 93–104 (2000)
10. Liu, F.T.; Ting, K.M.; Zhou, Z.H.: Isolation forest. In Proceedings of the 2008 Eighth IEEE International Conference on Data Mining, pp. 413–422. IEEE, Pisa, Italy (2016) . https://doi.org/10.1109/ICDM.2008.17
11. Zhang, D., Li, N., Zhou, Z., Chen, C., Sun, L., Li, S.,: iBAT: detecting anomalous taxi trajectories from gps traces. In: Proceedings of the 13th international conference on Ubiquitous computing, pp. 99–108. ACM (2011)
12. Chen, C., et al.: iBOAT:Isolation-based online anomalous trajectory detection. IEEE Trans. Intell. Transp. Syst. **14**(2), 806–818 (2013)
13. Wang, L., Mehrabi, M.G., Kannatey-Asibu, E., Jr.: Hidden markov model-based tool wear monitoring in turning. J. Manuf. Sci. Eng. **124**, 651–658 (2002)
14. Biernacki, C., Celeux, G., Govaert, G.: Assessing a mixture model for clustering with the integrated completed likelihood. IEEE Trans. Pattern Anal. Mach. Intell. **22**, 719–725 (2000)
15. Kriegel, H., Schubert, M., Zimek, A.: Angle-based outlier detection in high-dimensional data. In: Proceedings of the 14th International Conference on Knowledge Discovery and Data Mining, pp. 444–452 (2008)
16. Pimentel, M.A., Clifton, D.A., Clifton, L., Tarassenko L.: A review of novelty detection, signal Process **99**, 215–249 (2014). https://doi.org/10.1016/j.sigpro.2013.12.026

17. Vapnik, V.: The Nature of Statistical Learning Theory. Springer, New York (2013). https://doi.org/10.1007/978-1-4757-2440-0

18. Schölkopf, B., Williamson, R.C., Smola, A.J., Shawe-Taylor, J.; Platt, J.C.: Support vector method for novelty detection. In: Advances in Neural Information Processing Systems, MIT Press, pp. 582–588 (2000)

19. Piciarelli, C. and Foresti, G.L.: Anomalous trajectory detection using support vector machines. In 2007 IEEE Conference on Advanced Video and Signal Based Surveillance, pp. 153–158. IEEE (2007)

20. Das, S., Matthews, B.L., Srivastava, A.N., Oza, N.C.: Multiple kernel learning for heterogeneous anomaly detection: algorithm and aviation safety case study. In: Proceedings of the 16th ACM SIGKDD International Conference On Knowledge Discovery and Data Mining, pp. 47–56. ACM (2010)

21. Jolliffe, I.T: Principal Component Analysis, Springer Series in Statistics, Springer, New York (1986). https://doi.org/10.1007/978-1-4757-1904-8

22. Günter, S.; Schraudolph, N.N.; Vishwanathan, S.V.N.: Fast iterative kernel principal component analysis. J. Mach. Learn. Res. **8**, 1893–1918 (2007)

23. Kramer, M.: Nonlinear principal component analysis using autoassociative neural networks. AIChE J. **37**(2), 233–243 (1991)

24. Reddy, K.K., Sarkar, S., Venugopalan, V., Giering, M.: Anomaly detection and fault disambiguation in large flight data: a multi-modal deep auto-encoder approach, In: Proceedings of the Annual Conference of the Prognostics and Health Management Society, Denver, CO, USA (2016)

25. Kingma, D.P., Welling, M.: Auto-Encoding Variational Bayes, arXiv (2013). arXiv:1312.6114

26. Goodfellow, I., et al.: Generative adversarial nets. In: Advances in neural information processing systems, pp. 2672–2680 (2014)

27. Li, L., Hansman, R.J.: Anomaly Detection in Airline Routine Operations using Flight Data Recorder Data. MIT ICAT, Cambridge (2013)

28. Ramaswamy, S., Rastogi, R., Shim, K.: Efficient algorithms for mining outliers from large data sets. ACM Sigmod Rec. **29**(2), 427–438 (2000)

29. Aggarwal, C.C.: Outlier analysis. In Data mining, pp. 237–263. Springer, Cham (2015)

30. Bentley, J.L.: Multidimensional binary search trees used for associative searching. ACM (1975). https://doi.org/10.1145/361002.361007

31. EUROCONTROL   Page.   https://www.eurocontrol.int/publication/cat021-eurocontrol-specification-surveillance-data-exchange-asterix-part-12-category-0

32. Taha, A., Hadi, A.: Anomaly detection methods for categorical data: a review. ACM Comput. Surv. **52**, 1–35 (2019). https://doi.org/10.1145/3312739

33. Dave, D., Varma, T.: A review of various statistical methods for outlier detection. IJCSET **5**(2), 137–140 (2014)

Detection of Monolayer Graphene

Sankari Balasubramaniyan[1]([⊠]), François Parmentier[2], Preden Roulleau[2],
Mathieu Thevenin[2], Alexis Brenes[3], and Maria Trocan[3]

[1] School of Electronics Engineering, Vellore Institute of Technology, Vellore, India
[2] Service de Physique de l'Etat Condensé, IRAMIS/DSM (CNRS UMR 3680), CEA Saclay,
91191 Gif-sur-Yvette, France
[3] Institut Supérieur d'Electronique de Paris, Paris, France

Abstract. In the domain of condensed matter physics the monolayer graphene material is of interest. Researchers have started to develop new quantum circuit models that rely on this material properties. Unfortunately, the process to obtain pieces of monolayer graphene useable for nanocomponent design produces a lot of undesired other structures on the same substrate. In this paper, we have developed an approach to target and detect monolayer graphene from alternating layers of graphene and other particles (corrugated crystals and tape residues). We describe a region of interest-based image segmentation process to extract 2D atomic crystals; however, some unwanted particles remain in the segmented region. An intensity-based discrimination of monolayer graphene from other particles is applied and it is observed that the red color space of the monolayer graphene differs 1.8–6%, green 2.5–8% and blue differ 2.5% to 3% from the surrounding background pixel.

Keywords: Monolayer graphene recognition · Intensity based detection · 2D material · Heterostructures

1 Introduction

Graphite is a Van der Waal heterostructure, comprising graphene which is a 2D lattice of carbon atoms and are known to possess unprecedented properties [1]. The family of exfoliated and functional 2D crystals are only a few atoms thin and are known to be stable under ambient conditions [2, 3], exhibits high crystal quality, and various electronic properties such as semiconductors [4] and super conductors [5]. Since the advent of these crystals, a key time has arrived to leverage its properties in development of novel nanocomponents and heterostructure devices [6]. These graphene materials enable to have high technical potential that is not even merely achieved by any other conventional semiconductor heterostructures. Thus, introducing new routes for identifying the graphene layer is highly advantageous. However, the basic process of graphene flakes recognition on SiO_2/Si substrate has highly relied on human intervention and manual operators, subsequently automation in image visualization and analysis can eliminate the same.

Deep learning methods are rapidly growing in recent years and opening up new avenues, solving many image recognition and classification programs [7]. Some technological components concerning two-dimensional (2D) materials have been proposed

© Springer Nature Switzerland AG 2021
N. T. Nguyen et al. (Eds.): ICCCI 2021, LNAI 12876, pp. 784–791, 2021.
https://doi.org/10.1007/978-3-030-88081-1_59

such as image analysis algorithm to segment graphene flakes [9] and classification of n-layered graphene using unsupervised data-driven machine learning algorithm [10]. In 2018, a group of 8 members held a research on graphene flakes and introduced Robotic automation which enabled autonomous search for 2D crystals and assembly of the same into Van der Waals lattices [8]. This paper was the first to present the state-of-the-art research on differentiating alternating layers of graphene. They developed a system that could autonomously detect 400 monolayer graphene an hour with very less false detection rate and enabled fabrication of superlattice containing different layers of graphene and hexagonal boron nitride. Here, the optical microscopic images were analyzed using a computer vision algorithm and once the desired 2D crystals were detected, their shape and positions were recorded and finally the robotic arm directed by the algorithm assembles the crystal to form Van der Waals superlattices.

In this study, optical exfoliated graphene images are obtained and an image analysis algorithm is applied for segmenting graphene flakes on SiO_2/Si to get the region of interest. The main goal is to find the pixel intensity difference between the monolayer graphene and the background using a 3×3 kernel and ultimately use that to recognize monolayer graphene.

The Sect. 2 of this paper details the methodology followed that led to the design of a novel image analysis algorithm for the discrimination of monolayer graphene obtained from optical microscopic images. The Sect. 3 presents the results obtained on 160 images. Finally, the last section concludes the paper and draws further work directions.

The contributions of this paper are: a) a new image segmentation algorithm for detection of graphene in optical picture; b) developed a new approach for the discrimination between monolayer graphene on SiO_2 substrate and other types of graphene or spurious elements; c) the proposition of a novel indicator based on calorimetry; this indicator is used for image segmentation.

2 Methodology and Proposed Algorithm

This section depicts the methodology developed for the design of image analysis algorithm presented in this paper.

2.1 Dataset

Microfabrication of graphene devices are possible due to the fact that graphene crystallites can be visualized using optical microscope if it is exfoliated on the top of SiO_2 wafers. Centimeter sized SiO_2/Si substrate were cleaned [11] and graphite was mechanically exfoliated onto the substrate using scotch tape mechanism [2]. SiO_2/Si chips were then tiled on top of chip trays and scanned using an optical microscope with objective lens. The graphene flakes of various shapes and thicknesses were randomly distributed over the substrate. The dataset is composed of images with resolution size 1536×1024 pixels, 1920×1200 pixels and 3072×2048 pixels and a total of 160 optical images of graphene were used for the purpose of this study (Fig. 1).

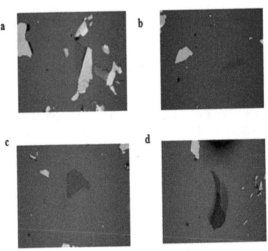

Fig. 1. Optical microscopic images. (**a**) Monolayer Graphene. (**b**) Bilayer Graphene. (**c**) Trilayer Graphene. (**d**) Multizone image containing 1-, 2-, 3- layer graphene flakes.

2.2 Optical Image Segmentation Pipeline

We present here an image segmentation pipeline to distinguish 2D crystals and obtain the region of interest. Initially the algorithm was applied to grayscale images, but since the graphene particles are almost translucent and similar to the shade of its surrounding background pixels, more bands of information about graphene and background proved useful. Each image has to undergo this image segmentation method before being fed into detection model.

The pipeline was composed of double -thresholding process based on color contrast of the images. Above 3 layers, the samples are not considered to have the properties of graphene anymore, so that no image processing is exerted. Color thresholding is applied, using the function f_{thresh} (Eq. 1) on the acquired image $I^{r,g,b}$ where, $I_{BG}^{r,g,b}$ is the background image and **min** and **max** are the thresholding parameters adjusted to get the desired output.

$$f_{thresh} = \begin{cases} 1, & \min \leq I^{r,g,b} - I_{BG}^{r,g,b} \leq \max \\ 0, & otherwise \end{cases} \tag{1}$$

Based on the segmentation, the images are cropped maintaining the region of interest and consequently reducing the unwanted information from the image. This procedure recognizes and extracts the targeted thin 2D crystals, along with some unwanted particles. At the end, the images are resized to 256×256 resolution. The Fig. 2 presents an original monolayer graphene image and the output of the segmentate (Fig. 3).

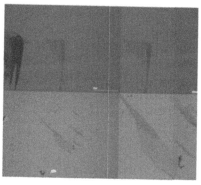

Fig. 2. Input (left) and output (right) of the segmentation pipeline.

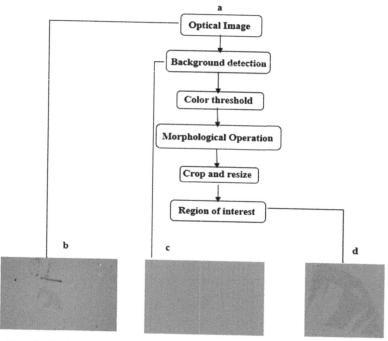

Fig. 3. The pipeline and the result of the image segmentation algorithm. (**a**) Schematic of segmentation algorithm to deduce the region of interest. (**b**) Optical image of monolayer graphene. (**c**) Background of the given image. (**d**) Result of the proposed algorithm.

2.3 Intensity Based Detection

The image segmentation process successfully extracted the maximum portion of region of graphene flakes, the next step is to introduce an algorithm to automatically detect the monolayer graphene in the given region of interest. To model the optical values of monolayer recognition, utilization of pixel intensity difference between the region and the background is salient. The application of this model is appropriate because the color contrast of graphene changes less discretely from its background and also works for different lighting conditions. The percentage of pixel intensity difference between the region and the background are ascertained in the RGB color space, using a 3 × 3 kernel with a stride value equals to 3. To qualitatively evaluate the extreme percentage parameters, we manually inspected the monolayer optical images that exhibit a value of pixel intensity difference for the defined graphene region, for each RGB color space.

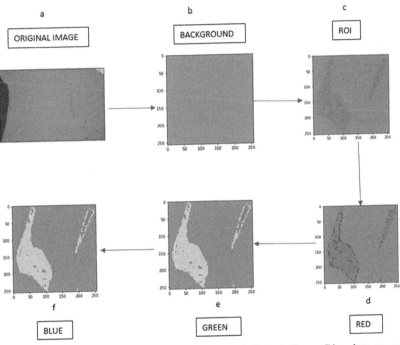

Fig. 4. Representative images generated in each step. (**d–f**) Red, Green, Blue dots are present in the regions which differs from its background within the mentioned percentage. (Color figure online)

Here,

1. For the Fig. 4, percentage of intensity difference between the background and the targeted region were

o Red > 5.5% and Red < 6%
o Green > 6% and Green < 8%
o Blue > 2.8% and Blue < 3%

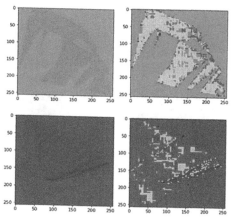

Fig. 5. Output of the model. (Color figure online)

For the Fig. 5, the parameters were

o   Red > 2% and Red < 6%
o   Green > 2.5% and Green < 4%
o   Blue > 2.5% and Blue < 3%

3   Result and Discussion

Ever since the advent of 1-, 2-, 3-layer graphene, the detection of monolayer relied on the interference color of the substrate and the color contrast of 2D flakes are subtle towards the substrate thickness. However, the presented method provides a solution in determining whether the monolayer graphene is present or not, in an image containing n-layers of graphene material and other unwanted particles. The obscuring effects of pixel intensities for various graphene flakes is due to the difference in the thickness of the SiO_2/Si [12]. After examining about 40 samples of images containing monolayer graphene, an optimal solution for detection of the same is obtained, where the red color space of the monolayer graphene differs 1.8–6%, green 2.5–8% and blue differ 2.5% to 3% from the surrounding background pixel. An intersection of these constraints helps spot regions containing monolayer graphene. The constraints are chosen corresponding to the background pixels surrounded by it, adhering to the translucent nature of mono-layer graphene. The output of the model discerns if the input image has monolayer or not, and if so, indicates the regions containing the same. The representative output of the model is presented in Fig. 6.

The system analyzed about 160 images and was able discern whether it has monolayer graphene present in them or not, with error rate of 18.125%. In contrast to the landmark publication [8] containing entropy and color threshold algorithm in image segmentation pipeline resulted in false detection <7%, generates a comparability of different computer vision algorithms. The regions of the monolayer graphene are successfully partitioned from 2-layer and 3-layer graphene and ignored the contaminating objects. Subsequently,

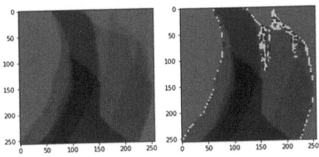

Fig. 6. Before (left) and after (right) applying monolayer calorimetric indicator on multizone image. (Color figure online)

most of the false detections are due to wrong background pixel value, which can be avoided by extracting the medians of the optical intensities of plain SiO_2/Si substrates before exfoliation of graphene. In order to compensate for the unequal illumination of the field, and avoid static impulse noise across the entire region (*i.e.*, when the original image is subtracted from its background), the spray-paint ring like feature [9] is removed in mono layer graphene images by cropping it out finding the largest contour of the image. This helped in finding the region of interest of monolayer graphene much precisely.

4 Conclusion

In this paper, the optical microscopic images were analyzed by computer-vision algorithm and a model is developed which discerns whether the given multizone image of graphene has monolayer graphene present it in or not. It is observed that the region of monolayer graphene varies from its background (about 2–8%) less discretely compared to 2-, 3- layer graphene. The future perspective is to integrate the optical microscope with the algorithm to discern the presence of monolayer graphene in real time, with this one can develop a fully automated identification system of graphene flakes and expand it to detection of other exfoliated 2D crystals, owing to similar crystal structures developing a universal classification algorithm with very less human intervention. The false detection of monolayer can be decreased by recording the background pixel value before starting segmentation pipeline. Considering the rapid growth of machine learning and neural networks, one can expect better results in classification of altering layers graphene.

References

1. Zhang, Y., Tan, Y.-W., Stormer, H.L., Kim, P.: Experimental observation of the quantum Hall effect and Berry's phase in graphene. Nature **438**, 201–204 (2005)
2. Novoselov, K.S., et al.: Electric field effect in atomically thin carbon films. Science **306**, 666–669 (2004)
3. Novoselov, K.S., et al.: Two-dimensional atomic crystals. Proc. Natl. Acad. Sci. USA **102**, 10451–10453 (2005)

4. Xu, X., Yao, W., Xiao, D., Heinz, T.F.: Spin and pseudospins in layered transition metal dichalcogenides. Nat. Phys. **10**, 343–350 (2014)

5. Xi, X., et al.: Ising pairing in superconducting NbSe2 atomic layers. Nat. Phys. **12**, 139–143 (2015)

6. Novoselov, K.S., Mishchenko, A., Carvalho, A., Castro Neto, A.H.: 2D materials and van der Waals heterostructures. Science **353**, aac9439 (2016)

7. Szeliski, R.: Computer Vision: Algorithms and Applications. Springer-Verlag, New York (2010)

8. Masubuchi, S., et al.: Autonomous robotic searching and assembly of two-dimensional crystals to build van der Waals superlattices. Nat. Commun. **9**, 1413 (2018)

9. Nolen, C.M., Denina, G., Teweldebrhan, D., Bhanu, B., Balandin, A.A.: High-throughput large-area automated identification and quality control of graphene and few-layer graphene films. ACS Nano **5**, 914–922 (2011)

10. Masubuchi, S., Machida, T.: Classifying optical microscope images of exfoliated graphene flakes by data-driven machine learning. Nature (2019)

11. Garcia, A.G.F., et al.: Effective cleaning of hexagonal boron nitride for graphene devices. Nano Lett. **12**, 4449–4454 (2012)

12. Blake, P., et al.: Making graphene visible. Appl. Phys. Lett. **91**, 63124 (2007)

Scale Input Adapted Attention for Image Denoising Using a Densely Connected U-Net: SADE-Net

Vedat Acar[1]([✉])(iD) and Ender M. Eksioglu[2](iD)

[1] Graduate School, Istanbul Technical University, Istanbul, Turkey
acarv19@itu.edu.tr
[2] Electronics and Communication Engineering Department, Istanbul Technical
University, Istanbul, Turkey
eksioglue@itu.edu.tr

Abstract. In this work, we address the problem of image denoising using deep neural networks. Recent developments in convolutional neural networks provide a very potent alternative for image restoration applications and in particular for image denoising. A particularly popular deep network structure for image processing are the auto-encoders which include the U-Net as an important example. U-Nets contract and expand feature maps repeatedly, which leads to extraction of multi scale information as well as an increase in the effective receptive field when compared to conventional convolutional nets. In this paper, we propose the integration of a multi scale channel attention module through a U-Net structure as a novelty for the image denoising problem. The introduced network structure also utilizes multi scale inputs in the various substages of the encoder module in a novel manner. Simulation results demonstrate competitive and mostly superior performance when compared to some state of the art deep learning based image denoising methodologies. Qualitative results also indicate that the developed deep network framework has powerful detail preserving capability.

Keywords: Deep learning · Convolutional Neural Networks · Image denoising

1 Introduction

Image denoising is one of the fundamental, low level tasks of computer vision. Noise is a commonly encountered distortion in digital images. There are several types of possible noise distributions encountered for vision data including additive white Gaussian noise (AWGN), Poisson noise, shot noise etc. A noisy digital image can be formulated as $y = x + v$, and the aim of the denoising process is to recover x from y. For this work, v is assumed to be AWGN.

This work is supported by TUBITAK (The Scientific and Technological Research Council of Turkey) under project no. 119E248.

High-level computer vision tasks such as image classification, object detection, and segmentation have made significant advances with the introduction of deep Convolutional Neural Networks (CNNs). CNNs have attracted quite an interest due to their strong representation ability and wide applicability, leading to much improved results compared to conventional methods. The training of deep networks is a challenging issue due to the rise of the vanishing gradient problem with increasing depth. One structure which handles this issue is the ResNet which proposes residual connections to provide a better information flow [6]. Another example is the DenseNet which restrengthens connections through every layer [8]. Although these algorithms aid the vanishing gradient problem, there are more powerful modules to provide low loss feature transference. Channel attention is one of the popular such blocks, and it acts as an effective plug-and-play module. Another very recent approach is the use of smaller versions of the input which are named as scale inputs. These scale inputs can be used in the lower scales of the encoder to add more features to the encoder-decoder network. In this paper, we propose a U-Net architecture with attention layers, and the architecture also benefits from scale inputs in a novel manner. We will call this new structure as Scale input Attentive Network with Dense connections, namely SADE-Net.

2   Prior Art

2.1   Image Denoising

Image denoising is a fundamental task in image restoration, and its main aim is to preserve details while suppressing noise. There have been various methods tackling this problem. These have included transform domain methods and non local methods [2]. One particular algorithm which utilizes non-local similarities and transform methods together is the BM3D [4]. BM3D searches similar patterns in the image patches to process them together in a 3D transform. DnCNN was the earliest algorithm which combined denoising with CNNs [21]. DnCNN utilized a residual learning strategy to obtain better information flow and batch normalization to accelerate the training. The FFDNet algorithm on the other hand uses both the noise map and noisy image's subsamples [22] . Hence, FFD-Net feeds both the noise map and noisy image's subsamples to the network to handle the problem of working in global noise level environment.

Recent deep network frameworks incorporate new structures and modules such as channel attention [1], non local blocks [19] or memory blocks [17]. Several state-of-the-art networks have benefited from the use of such novel blocks in the image denoising setting. We will give a short list of some of the well performing examples. MemNet structure proposed a memory network which incorporates short term and long term memory to cope with the long range dependency problem [17]. MWCNN adopted a wavelet transform strategy to upscale and downscale feature maps in a modified U-Net [11]. This structure demonstrated the efficiency of wavelet transform which avoids the detrimental gridding effects. RIDNet proposed a blind real image denoising network which utilized a residual-in-residual structure [1]. This network implemented feature attention inside Enhanced Attention Mechanism (EAM) blocks. PANET network on the other hand proposed pyramid attention blocks to better obtain long range correspondences of features and adopted a multi scale self-similarity prior [13].

2.2 Channel Attention

Attention mechanisms have become a quite popular ingredient which deep networks utilize for computer vision. Attention modules can model dependencies over longer distances, and their origins are motivated from human perception characteristics [3]. Treating all of the extracted feature maps in the same manner seems to hamper the discriminative power and the representation ability of the networks. An attention mechanism causes the deep neural network to focus its learning effort on more informative components of the input data by putting differing emphasis on different feature maps.

Attention modules are also rather lightweight, because they often utilize only two 1×1 convolutions. In this work, we have incorporated channel attention modules into a U-Net structure devised for gray level image denoising. Inspired by [14] and [9], we place the attention mechanism right next to the downsampling blocks, and the attention module outputs are transferred to the upsampling side by skip connections. We used the squeeze and excitation mechanism [7], which first applies global average pooling and extracts global spatial information. Afterwards, this mechanism uses two convolutions to capture the feature channel dependencies. Lastly, the input feature maps are rescaled by multiplying them with the obtained coefficients.

The mathematical description of the employed channel attention module is as follows. Let us consider f_c which carries features created by a convolutional layer having c feature maps of size $h \times w$. We first obtain global statistics of the feature maps.

$$g_p = \frac{1}{h \times w} \sum_{i=1}^{h} \sum_{j=1}^{w} f_c(i,j) \tag{1}$$

Here, $f_c(i,j)$ is the value of feature map at position (i,j). We implement an additional gating process to better exploit the channel dependencies.

$$s_g = \alpha(C_1(\delta(C_2(g_p)))) \tag{2}$$

C_1 and C_2 are the kernels to expand and contract the channels. δ is the ReLu operation, and α denotes the sigmoid function. Lastly, we rescale input f_c with s_g to obtain the final statistics.

$$\hat{f} = f_c \times s_g \tag{3}$$

The graphical description of the described channel attention structure is given in Fig. 1.

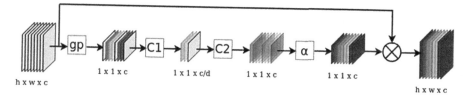

Fig. 1. Channel attention mechanism.

2.3 Scale Input for U-Nets

Traditional U-Net type networks only consider the overall input image, but not the subbands or scaled versions of this input. When one considers pyramid networks such as PANET [13], these networks also consider multi scale versions of the original input. These additional inputs give the network extra information and supervision to work from. These additional inputs do not burden the computational complexity of the network, while in general boosting the performance. In the new network here, we employ the rather recently introduced scale input approach [16]. In our strategy, the downsampled outputs at the encoder side get concatenated with subscaled versions of the noisy input image.

3   A Novel Network for Image Denoising: SADE-Net

In this section we detail the building blocks for the novel image denoising architecture as introduced here, namely "Scale input Attentive Network with Dense connections" (SADE-Net). Figure 2 depicts the complete architecture of the novel SADE-Net framework for image denoising. As can be seen from Fig. 2, after the noisy image enters the network, a 1×1 convolutional layer followed by a parametric rectified linear unit (PReLu) extracts the initial features from the image. Then, two Densely Connected Residual (DCR) blocks transmit the information further. After the DCR blocks, the feature maps are downsampled by a ratio of two by using max pooling. The number of feature maps are also doubled at this stage. This operation is repeated three times for the encoder stage, leading to four distinct resolution levels. Every resolution scale has two DCR blocks both at the encoder and the decoder side.

At each resolution level of the encoder stage, downsampled versions of the noisy input image (scale inputs) get concatenated with the outputs of the downsampling stage. The scale inputs include the same number of maps as the outputs of downsampling. They are produced via a convolution kernel with 1×1 size and unit stride. After the concatenation of scale input and downsampled output, again a 1×1 convolution is used to halve the number of feature maps. In the decoder side, we utilized pixel shuffling to upsample the features by a ratio of two. We also transferred the input of the downsampling block to the encoder side via skip connections for all resolution levels. The channel attention block is applied inside this skip connections linking the encoder and decoder sides.

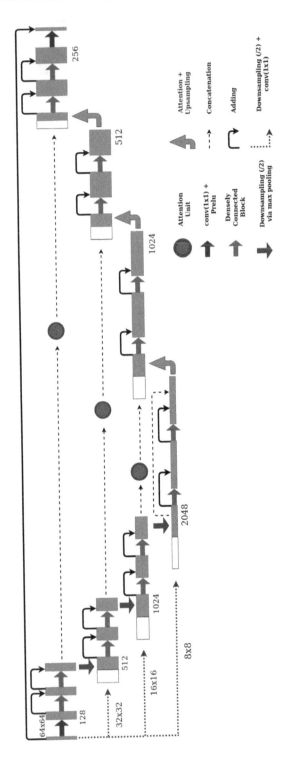

Fig. 2. Overall architecture of the proposed network.

The overall structure of the employed channel attention block is again given in Fig. 1. The further stages at the decoder side reverse the actions of the decoder side. Finally, a global residual connection provides the final denoised output by adding the residual output of the network to the input noisy image as shown in the final stage of Fig. 2.

Table 1. Quantitative denoising results for BSD68 [12] dataset.

Method	Noisy	BM3D	DnCNN	FFDNet	IRCNN	DHDN	SADE-Net
Noise level	PSNR(dB)						
$\sigma = 10$	28.26	33.32	_33.88_	33.76	33.74	33.42	**33.89**
$\sigma = 30$	18.97	27.75	28.36	28.39	28.26	**28.55**	_28.50_
$\sigma = 50$	14.92	25.60	26.23	26.29	26.19	**26.44**	_26.41_
Noise level	SSIM						
$\sigma = 10$	0.7094	0.9158	_0.9270_	0.9266	0.9262	0.9213	**0.9300**
$\sigma = 30$	0.3348	0.7731	0.7999	0.8032	0.7989	**0.8110**	_0.8090_
$\sigma = 50$	0.1984	0.6838	0.7189	0.7245	0.7171	_0.7296_	**0.7308**

Table 2. Quantitative denoising results for Kodak24 [5] dataset.

Method	Noisy	BM3D	DnCNN	FFDNet	IRCNN	DHDN	SADE-Net
Noise level	PSNR(dB)						
$\sigma = 10$	28.22	34.39	_34.90_	34.81	34.76	34.43	**35.01**
$\sigma = 30$	18.87	29.12	29.62	29.69	29.52	**29.93**	_29.91_
$\sigma = 50$	14.78	26.98	27.49	27.62	27.45	**27.88**	_27.84_
Noise level	SSIM						
$\sigma = 10$	0.6573	0.9127	0.9223	_0.9226_	0.9215	0.9153	**0.9273**
$\sigma = 30$	0.2729	0.7877	0.8071	0.8123	0.8056	**0.8211**	_0.8207_
$\sigma = 50$	0.1998	0.7140	0.7368	0.7437	0.7342	_0.7528_	**0.7545**

4 Experimental Results

4.1 Implementation Details

The DIV2K dataset [18] includes a large number of high quality images, and currently it is a commonly used dataset in image denoising applications [1,15]. We employ the DIV2K validation and training datasets for training the introduced denoising network. The training set constitutes 800 images with 1920 × 1080 resolution. Validation set has 100 images with the same resolution. For the testing, we use BSD68 [12] and Kodak24 [5] datasets which are also highly popular for image denoising [15,20] . Kodak24 has 24 images at 768 × 512, and BSD68 consists of 68 images at 321 × 481 resolution.

We firstly extract patches of size 64×64 from the training images, and we randomly flip these patches to augment the training data. One training batch has 16 randomly selected patches from the generated training data. We train the novel SADE-Net for grayscale image denoising with unknown noise level. We consider noise standard deviation levels which are between 5 and 55. For each training batch, we randomly sample the noise level σ from a uniform distribution defined on [5, 55]. Then, Gaussian noise realizations with the randomly chosen standard deviations are added to the images (patches) in the overall training batch.

For optimization, we utilize Adam optimizer [10] with $\beta_1 = 0.9$ and $\beta_2 = 0.999$. For the other hyperparameters of Adam, the default settings are used. For the competing methods, the hyperparameters were in general chosen as in their original papers, such as [15]. The initial learning rate is $1e^{-4}$, and it gets halved every three epochs. We use ℓ_1 mean absolute error as the loss function. All the training and testing procedures for the various deep networks experiments were conducted on two Nvidia RTX 2080 Ti GPUs. The training and testing of the deep networks are realized using CUDA version 10.2 in a PyTorch environment.

4.2   Performance Comparison

We compare the proposed network with several state of the art image denoising algorithms, including some recent and powerful image denoising networks. The competing methods are BM3D [4], DnCNN [21], FFDNet [22], IRCNN [23] and DHDN [15]. We used publicly available pretrained version of these networks for comparison purposes.

As quantitative performance metrics, we employed the peak-signal-to-noise-ratio (PSNR) and the structural similarity index (SSIM). Average PSNR and SSIM results for the image denoising experiments using the BSD68 test dataset are given in Table 1. The results for the the Kodak24 test dataset are listed in Table 2. In both tables, the highest result is marked with bold, and the second best result is marked with italics. As can be inferred from Table 1 and Table 2, the proposed network performs better than the competing methods for a multitude of testing conditions. For all the simulated testing settings for both test datasets, the developed SADE-Net performed either best or second best in PSNR and SSIM among the realized approaches. To give an idea for the qualitative comparison of the various denoising results, we picked one sample test image from both BSD68 and Kodak24 datasets. We provide the denoised image results for our novel SADE-Net in addition to some high performance image denoising networks including DHDN [15], DnCNN [21] and FFDNet [22]. Figure 3 gives the denoised image results for a particular sample image from the BSD68 dataset, whereas Fig. 4 includes the results for the sample image from the Kodak24 dataset. The denoised image results and the corresponding zoomed sections indicate that the introduced network is able to preserve details and texture while suppressing noise. The details in the zoomed sections showcase the improved detail preserving ability of the SADE-Net when compered with the competing deep networks.

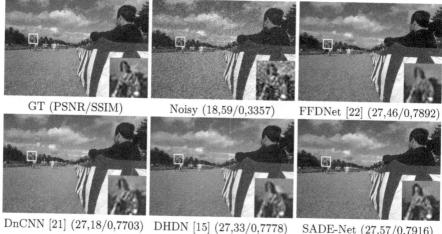

Fig. 3. Qualitative denoising results of our proposed network and other recent deep networks for the 'test019'image from BSD68 dataset, $\sigma = 10$.

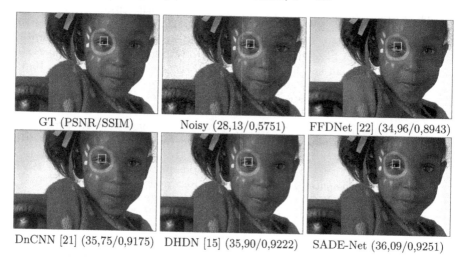

Fig. 4. Qualitative denoising results of our proposed network and other recent deep networks for the 'kodim15' image from Kodak24 dataset, $\sigma = 10$.

5   Conclusion

In this paper, we propose a new image denoising deep network starting from a U-Net structure. In the novel network, we utilized a novel combination of channel attention blocks and the recently developed scale input idea. Another important feat is the use of densely connected DCR blocks to reduce the vanishing gradients problem and to facilitate robust transmission of information. The performance of the developed network is tested by using some of the most widely used test and training image dataset from the literature. The novel combination of scale inputs and channel attention blocks at the different resolution stages leads to improved denoising performance when compared to recent and effective deep methodologies for image denoising. The PSNR and SSIM results showcase the quantitative performance improvement. The proposed network is flexible and gives satisfactory denoising results for a wide range of noise levels. Denoised image samples on the other hand exhibit the qualitative performance enhancement in the preservation of details.

Acknowledgment. This work is supported by TUBITAK (The Scientific and Technological Research Council of Turkey) under project no. 119E248.

References

1. Anwar, S., Barnes, N.: Real image denoising with feature attention. In: 2019 IEEE/CVF International Conference on Computer Vision (ICCV), pp. 3155–3164 (2019)
2. Colak, O., Eksioglu, E.M.: Image denoising using patch ordering and 3D transformation of patches. IET Image Process. **13**(13), 2636–2646 (2019)
3. Corbetta, M., Shulman, G.: Control of goal-directed and stimulus-driven attention in the brain. Nat. Rev. Neurosci. **3**, 201–15 (2002). https://doi.org/10.1038/nrn755
4. Dabov, K., Foi, A., Katkovnik, V., Egiazarian, K.: Image denoising by sparse 3-D transform-domain collaborative filtering. IEEE Trans. Image Process. **16**(8), 2080–2095 (2007). https://doi.org/10.1109/TIP.2007.901238
5. Franzén., R.: Kodak lossless true color image suite, vol. 4 (1999). http://r0k.us/graphics/kodak.
6. He, K., Zhang, X., Ren, S., Sun, J.: Deep residual learning for image recognition. In: 2016 IEEE Conference on Computer Vision and Pattern Recognition (CVPR), pp. 770–778 (2016)
7. Hu, J., Shen, L., Sun, G.: Squeeze-and-excitation networks. In: 2018 IEEE/CVF Conference on Computer Vision and Pattern Recognition, pp. 7132–7141 (2018)
8. Huang, G., Liu, Z., Weinberger, K.Q.: Densely connected convolutional networks. In: 2017 IEEE Conference on Computer Vision and Pattern Recognition (CVPR), pp. 2261–2269 (2017)
9. Huang, Q., Yang, D., Wu, P., Qu, H., Yi, J., Metaxas, D.: MRI reconstruction via cascaded channel-wise attention network. In: 2019 IEEE 16th International Symposium on Biomedical Imaging (ISBI 2019), pp. 1622–1626 (2019). https://doi.org/10.1109/ISBI.2019.8759423
10. Kingma, D.P., Ba, J.: Adam: a method for stochastic optimization. CoRR abs/1412.6980 (2015)
11. Liu, P., Zhang, H., Zhang, K., Lin, L., Zuo, W.: Multi-level Wavelet-CNN for Image Restoration, pp. 886–88609 (2018)
12. Martin, D., Fowlkes, C., Tal, D., Malik, J.: A database of human segmented natural images and its application to evaluating segmentation algorithms and measuring ecological statistics. In: Proceedings Eighth IEEE International Conference on Computer Vision, ICCV 2001, vol. 2, pp. 416–423 (2001). https://doi.org/10.1109/ICCV.2001.937655
13. Mei, Y., et al.: Pyramid attention networks for image restoration. ArXiv abs/2004.13824 (2020)

14. Oktay, O., et al.: Attention U-Net: Learning where to look for the pancreas. ArXiv abs/1804.03999 (2018)

15. Park, B., Yu, S., Jeong, J.: Densely connected hierarchical network for image denoising. In: 2019 IEEE/CVF Conference on Computer Vision and Pattern Recognition Workshops (CVPRW), pp. 2104–2113 (2019)

16. Peng, Y., Cao, Y., Liu, S., Yang, J., Zuo, W.: Progressive training of multi-level wavelet residual networks for image denoising. ArXiv abs/2010.12422 (2020)

17. Tai, Y., Yang, J., Liu, X., Xu, C.: MemNet: a persistent memory network for image restoration (2017)

18. Timofte, R., et al.: NTIRE 2017 challenge on single image super-resolution: methods and results. In: 2017 IEEE Conference on Computer Vision and Pattern Recognition Workshops (CVPRW), pp. 1110–1121 (2017). https://doi.org/10.1109/CVPRW.2017.149

19. Wang, X., Girshick, R.B., Gupta, A., He, K.: Non-local neural networks. In: 2018 IEEE/CVF Conference on Computer Vision and Pattern Recognition, pp. 7794–7803 (2018)

20. Yu, S., Park, B., Jeong, J.: Deep iterative down-up cnn for image denoising. In: Proceedings of the IEEE/CVF Conference on Computer Vision and Pattern Recognition (CVPR) Workshops (2019)

21. Zhang, K., Zuo, W., Chen, Y., Meng, D., Zhang, L.: Beyond a Gaussian denoiser: residual learning of deep CNN for image denoising. IEEE Trans. Image Process. **26**, 3142–3155 (2017)

22. Zhang, K., Zuo, W., Zhang, L.: FFDNet: toward a fast and flexible solution for CNN-based image denoising. IEEE Trans. Image Process. **27**(9), 4608–4622 (2018)

23. Zhang, K., Zuo, W., Gu, S., Zhang, L.: Learning deep CNN denoiser prior for image restoration. 2017 IEEE Conference on Computer Vision and Pattern Recognition (CVPR), pp. 2808–2817 (2017)

Author Index

Printed in the United States
by Baker & Taylor Publisher Services